Bes

Above : Vaux-Andigny © Otsi Laon / Claude Jacquot
Cover photo : Saint-Tropez © Iconotec.com
Azay-le-Rideau © J.-L. Péchinot

Come on a trip

From place to place

Contents

Come on a trip

Louvre museum

The People and the Place

FRENCH GEOGRAPHY

Metropolitan surface area: 543,965sqkm, plus the surface area of its overseas dominions (Guadeloupe, Martinique, Réunion and Guyane)totalling 88,876sqkm, and a few square km for its territories. France is the world's 47th biggest country.

Position: in the middle of the Northern hemisphere, equidistant from the Equator and the North Pole. Climate, plants and wildlife are varied. The Greenwich Meridian (longtitude 0) crosses France, but the country is not in the centre of universal time (MT+1). Like other European countries, summer and winter times are adopted (+ or - an hour).

Coasts & borders: 5,500km of coastline on the Channel, Atlantic Ocean and Mediterranean, and three sides forming inland borders with Belgium, Luxembourg and Germany to the north-east; Germany, Switzerland and Italy to the south-east and Spain in the south. This gives France a hexagonal shape. The coastal and continental regions are quite different.

Geology: France is an old country, with stable sedimentary land formation. In the north and west, there are plains and plateaux (lowest point Moeres (Nord) 2m below sea level.) In the south and east, the Pyrenees and Alps are the continent's highest mountains (Mont Blanc, 4,808m). Between mountains and coast are the Massif Central (volcanic) Parisian basin, Languedoc and Provence, the Saône-Rhône corridor and the Jura, Vosges and Alsace plateaux. Average altitude: 342m.

To summarise, France boasts a complex and varied topography, with different types of arable land.

Rivers

The waterway network is extensive, and played an important part in the country's economic development.

Main rivers: Loire (1,020km) Rhône (800km) Seine (775km) Garonne (575km) and Rhine (184km in France though 1,325m in all). The Rhône and Rhine are powerful rivers, rapid and constant; the Loire, Garonne and Seine are capricious and slower-running. They have shaped the landscape as well as the economy, are poles of local life and considerable tourist attractions. Generally speaking, they flow east-west, but after the Massif Central, they turn southwards or northwards according to the slope of their basin. France has the longest European navigable waterway network (8,500km), with canals that are useful as well as attractive: the Canals du Midi, Centre and Bourgogne are almost monuments.

Mountains

Two major ranges (Alps, Pyrenees: 3,000m) and other lesser massifs (Massif Central, Vosges, Jura: approx. 2,000m). Both Pyrenees and Alps were formed 40 million years ago. In the first case, continental land movements left a space filled with sediment by the ocean; this sediment rose into relief as if caught in a vice. In the second case, Iberian and Italian land movements at the same period compressed the sedimentary massif, forcing it upwards into high peaks. These continue to rise even today, still squeezed by the continental land plates. Summer and winter mountain sports and leisure activities play a large part in French tourism.

Forests

The first men sheltered in them, and the first dwellings were made with their wood. Later, this was used in the framework of castles and cathedrals, and to make ships, furniture and paper. There are 15 million hectares of woodland in France (28% of its territory) two-thirds leafy (birch, chestnut, maple, oak, ash,

beech, poplar), one-third coniferous (fir,spruce and pine). Forestry and its associated industries in the public and private sector are encouraged, to reduce the import of wood and and its derivatives. Sadly, French forests were badly hit by the December 1999 hurricane, and also suffer each summer from fires.

Famous forests to visit: Tronçais, with its ancient oaks, Paimpont (Brocéliande of Arthurian legend) and Fontainebleau.

OFFICE NATIONAL DES FORETS 2, ave. de Saint Mande - PARIS (12e) ✆ 01 40 19 58 00

Climate

France has a temperate climate, with warm summers and fairly mild winters. Each region has its own weather: rain from the Atlantic along the ocean seaboard (which accounts for the green landscapes and damp air in Brittany); cold air falling quickly and turning to rain in the North; continental extremes in the Centre and East (hot summers and hard winters make up the Alpine climate) and Mediterranean warmth in the South.

Gulf Stream

This blue channel off the Brittany and Vendée coast is 600km wide and 300km deep. It brings equatorial heat to latitudes that ought to be cold, and is responsible for France's good weather.

Winds: There are four main regional ones, though on a local level every parish has its own!

Vent d'antan: Blows from the southeast in mid-Garonne, Quercy and Rouergue. The white version is continental (cold in winter, warm in summer). The antan noir, or black wind, is less frequent, and is warm, bringing short-term rain.

Bise: Blows north-northeast, all over France. This cold, moderately strong wind bites the nose and ears in winter and spring.

Mistral: Blows from the Rhône Valley between Alps and Massif Central over most of the Mediterranean Coast. Cold, dry and violent, it comes in gusts.

Tramontane: Blows from the northwest in Languedoc and Roussillon, often violent, cold and dry, though it may also bring rain.

METEO FRANCE ✆ 08 92 68 08 08 (0.34 /min) www.meteo.fr

METEO by department ✆ 08 92 68 02 ** (dept. no.) (0.34 /min)

Natural disasters

France being a temperate country, there is little risk of natural disaster. Even the 2003 heatwave (40°C in Paris and 42 in the shade in the South) did not reach the record levels of 1911 and 1976 (with its drought), despite its 15,000 victims. Mouthe (Jura) is the coldest point. The country's most recent disaster was the 1999 hurricane, which destroyed a quarter of French forests. Floods regularly threaten both north (Baie de Somme) and south (Vaucluse and Gard) but popular fears of serious earthquakes in the Alps-Côte d'Azur or volcanic eruptions in the Massif Central are pretty well groundless.

FLORA AND FAUNA

Fauna

With its many forests and marshy areas, the environment provides a natural habitat for a variety of temperate zone wildlife.

Mammals: 5,000 stags and 40,000 roebuck live in the Ile-de-France alone! Like other hoofed animals (chamois, moufflons, ibex) they are hunted, and the first French nature reserve (Vanoise Park) was set up to protect endangered ibex rather than mountains or plants.

Other mammals to look out for: foxes, rabbits and hares, badgers, boars, ermine and marmots.

There are conservation projects afoot to reintroduce rare species into their original habitat: bears in the Pyrenees, wolves in the Southern Alps and lynx in the eastern massifs. In 1937, there were well over 150 bears in the Pyrenees, but their number had fallen to 5 in 1996, and it was decided to import them to the Ariège from Central Europe. This initiative is now opposed, and the 10 or so bears threatened with capture. Wolves had completely disappeared in the 20thc., hunted to extinction by ignorant villagers. Yet these animals do not even approach human dwellings, let alone human beings. They came back into France via Italy in the 1990s and about ten of them live in the Mercantour massif.

OFFICE NATIONAL DE LA CHASSE ET DE LA FAUNE SAUVAGE 85bis Ave. de Wagram PARIS (17e)

Birds: Some live here all year, others pass through during migration. On the whole, 1,500 species of bird are found in France, due to the diversity of ecosystems: marshy zones from Dombes to the Marais Poitevin; great stretches of water like the Baie de Somme and Camargue; Alpine cliffs (eagles) and Alsace rooftops (storks).

Sunflower

The biggest wild birds found in France are the swan and the crane; the widest is the bearded vulture with its 3m wingspan.

LIGUE DE PROTECTION DES OISEAUX La Corderie Royale - ROCHEFORT ✆ 05 46 82 12 34

Shooting sports

With its 1,450,000 sportsmen, France ranks first in Europe for shooting. The sport is strictly regulated (law passed 26 July 2000) with a test for the licence and fixed seasonal opening and closing dates. Animals hunted are hares (Auvergne, Languedoc-Roussillon, Limousin, Poitou-Charentes), woodpigeons (subject of great controversy in the southwest, but chiefly hunted in the Jura), wild boar, pheasants (North, Parisian basin, Massif Central) partridges, mallards and rabbits. Stags are found in the South of France and roebuck in Normandy, Alsace and Limousin.

FEDERATION NATIONALE DES CHASSEURS DE FRANCE 48, rue d'Alésia - PARIS (14e) ✆ 01 43 27 85 76

Fishing

20% of the population has been fishing at some time in France's impressive waterway network. You have to join an association and get your card - there are six different ones, according to fishing methods and catch. The complete card gives you access to all techniques in 1st and 2nd category rivers (54-80). Meanwhile, carp, roach, gudgeon, tench, trout and salmon wait for you to throw the line.

The plain rivers are slow-running; the mountain streams more rapid, and you adapt your methods to suit, but fly- and rod and reel-fishing are effective in any current. A wide variety of fish is also found in canals and ponds (bream, carp, tench, pike, perch).

UNION NATIONALE POUR LA PECHE EN FRANCE ET LA PROTECTION DU MILIEU AQUATIQUE 17, Rue Bergère - PARIS (9e) ✆ 01 48 24 96 00

Flora

About 4,900 indigenous plant species are found in France, plus 1,000 'naturalised' varieties; only 200 of the 6,000 are endemic (do not exist elsewhere). There are 4 major types of vegetation corresponding to the geographic zones.

Atlantic: Scots and maritime pines, juniper, oak, birch, beech, hornbeam, gorse, broom and heather. Northern Continental: moors, pastures and lichen forests.

Lower mountain regions. Ardennes: oaks, beech, birch, alder, sorbs. Lorraine and Vosges: fir, spruce, hornbeam, myrtle.

Mountain: trees tend to disappear above 2,000m, giving way to pastures and rare plants (edelweiss). Alpine vegetation(Mediterranean and Corsica) consists of laricio pines, asters, chestnuts and the maquis.

French Mediterranean: cork-oaks and holm oaks, Alep and umbrella pines, Atlas cedars (imported) bay-tree, almond and fig trees and blackberry bushes, olive trees (from imported varieties) plane, palm, orange and lemon trees.

HUMAN GEOGRAPHY

Who are the French?

France has a low population density: 59,900,268 inhabitants (metropolitan figures on 1 January 2004) in all. Both Germany and the United Kingdom have more inhabitants per square km. The industrial areas (North, Rhône-Alpes, Ile-de-France) and main communication axes (Seine, Garonne and Rhône Valleys) have an average density of 80 inhabitants per sq.km. which can fall to 20 in mountain and forest areas. The drift from the land began in the 19thc. and accelerated after 1946. Today, 75% of people live in towns and only 4.6% work in agriculture. The typical Frenchwoman lives to the age of 83, is 1.63m tall and weighs 61kg; her male partner lives to 75.5, is 1.75m tall and weighs 74.8kg. They live in town and have their first baby at 30, after a long course of university study. The population is ageing and the birth rate falling (even if the average is 2 children per woman): only 25% of French people are under 20 whereas 20 % are over 70. If life expectancy is on the rise, so is the amount of time the French devote to leisure pursuits.

Source: *Francoscopie* (G. Mermet, Larousse 2003).

Administration

France is an indivisible, secular, democratic and social Republic; its motto is 'Liberté, Egalité, Fraternité'. Every 5 years, the President of the

Republic is re-elected (Jacques Chirac since 1995) and names a government headed by a Prime Minister. Executive power is shared between President and Prime Minister, while Parliament has legislative power. The Assemblée Nationale and Sénat are the lower and upper chambers that discuss and vote laws. Apart from the President, the French elect their M.P.s, European M.P.s , regional councillors, general councillors and mayor. Administrative power is centralised on Paris, despite decentralisation attempts and even legislation. The administrative divisions are complicated, with communes, cantons, departments and regions, tending to weaken local political power in favour of central government. The public service sector covers hospitals, education, the post-office and social insurance, but also culture and ecology. It manages public transport (SNCF, RATP and Air France), energy (EDF-GDF) and communication (France Télévision, Radio France) and its standards are high. The role of the State in daily life is thus quite important, guaranteeing a certain standard of living and well-being to all citizens as defined by the Fifth Republic (de Gaulle 1958).

Consult www.service-public.fr or www.vie-publique.fr.

LANGUAGE AND TRADITIONS

From Latin to French

French is a Romance language, like Italian or Spanish, with its roots in Latin, but unlike these two languages, it has been modified by Germanic influence. The fall of the Roman Empire (which had enforced the use of Latin) gave people the freedom to speak in local dialects (lorrain, bourguignon, angevin, etc.): until the Middle Ages, the provinces had difficulty understanding each other! The Romance language resisted the invasion of Germanic tongues, called francique (though francique dialects still exist in Northern France, notably Lorraine) and like in the rest of Europe, the scholarly written language was Latin throughout the Middle Ages and into the Renaissance, for the nobility and churchmen. The first official Act written in francien was the Serments de Strasbourg in 842, really the first piece of written French. As the language developed, it had no difficulty being recognized on an international scale, but within its own borders, it had to struggle against regional tongues and dialects (patois). Basque, Breton and Catalan, Alsacien, Flamand and Provençal: in the 15thc. 99% of the population still didn't speak French! Later, François I signed the Edict of Villers-Cotterêts, estblishing French as the official language, confirmed by the spread of printed texts. Until 1919, French was the only international language. It is still the official diplomatic language, and is used by the UNO.

Regional languages

In the 18thc., regional dialects were still dominant: less than a quarter of the population could understand or speak French. Trade and business contacts spread the national language through the provinces; schools (which taught Latin) were not yet compulsory. The French Revolution forbade the written use of regional dialect in 1794, and although many writers championed local tongues ("All words have equal rights" said Victor Hugo) French gradually became universal, and patois disappeared (in 1863, less than 20% of people couldn't speak French). Compulsory school attendance finally killed off dialect, notably in Brittany, last bastion of its defence.

Today, the trend is reversed, and France has signed the European Charter of Regional and Minority Languages. Bilingual teaching exists in Corsica and Brittany. Breton, Catalan, Corsican, Occitan, Basque, Alsacien and Flamand are recognised languages (as are Melanesian and Polynesian in the overseas territories). Basque (Euskara) is the oldest language spoken in Europe, and Breton (Brezhoneg) spoken west of a line from Paimpol to Vannes is used more and more by the media (Breizh TV). Corsican is spoken everywhere except Bonifacio, where they use a Genoan dialect. Though it has never been culturally imposed, intellectuals and communication professionals are now developing a unified 'official' form of Corsican. In the southern Pyrenees and Roussillon, over 6 million people speak Catalan. From the 19thc. Renaixença came a sophisticated tongue, adapted for official and scientific use. It is the co-official language in Catalunya (Spain).

Regional traditions

French administrative divisions respect cultural identity. Brittany and Provence have strong historical roots, and Corsica even has an individual administrative status. The media take this into account (the public regional channel's lunchtime news is the most-watched news programme). Public interest in popular traditions dates back to the 18thc., and regional beliefs, oral tradition, costumes, festivals, folklore and gastronomy have become increasingly fashionable ever since. Lorient Inter-Celtic Festival draws the crowds seeking their Celtic roots. In Alsace, the Christmas Markets and Saint Nicolas recall Germanic tradition; the Basque Country has its pelota, typical crafts and berets, and Provence, the crèche with its santons, and its own poetic language.

MUSEE NATIONAL DES ARTS ET TRADITIONS POPULAIRES 6, ave. du Mahatma Gandhi – PARIS (16e) ✆ 01 44 17 60 00.

Chenonceau castle

© Iconotec.com / Pierre Delaguerard

History and Heritage

FROM HOMO ERECTUS TO ZIDANE

Human history in France begins 2 million years ago...

Prehistory

1,800,000 B.C. Homo Erectus arrives in the South of France from Africa. Over the next million years, he will develop his hunting techniques and tools. He shelters from the cold and wild animals in caves, and leaves traces (Tautavel).

400,000 B.C. Homo Erectus discovers fire (Terra Amata near Nice).

100,000 B.C. Neanderthal Man stands out from other primates.

50,000 B.C. Neanderthal Man hews stone and buries his dead (La Chapelle-aux-Saints in Corrèze).

35,000 B.C. Cro-Magnon Man develops painting and sculpture, the first art forms.

15,000 B.C. His descendants cover their cave walls with designs and animal paintings (cave walls at Lascaux in Dordogne).

10,000 B.C. The earth warms up, the glaciers disappear, along with the mammoth. Man can now master his surroundings, tame animals and plant crops..

Antiquity

4,000 B.C. The Neolithic Age. The first crops are planted in the Vaucluse; cows and sheep are bred in southeast France. In the west, the megalithic civilization puts up dolmens as burial mounds. 3,000 menhirs are lined up at Carnac.

1,000. Northern Celts settle in France. They have mastered iron working.

620. Marseille founded by the Phoceans (Greece). The Celts (ou Gauls) and Greeks begin to trade intensively.

390. The Gauls pillage Rome. Arvernes et Eduens fight for control of Gaul.

58. Caesar returns to Gaul.

52. Victory over Caesar's troops at Gergovie Battle of Alésia; Vercingétorix defeated. End of the Gaul Wars.

43. The Romans found Lyon, capital of the Three Gauls.

177 A.D. Blandine is the first Christian Martyr (Lyon)

400. Gaul is invaded by barbarians from the East (Burgonds, Alamans, Francs, Visigoths)

Middle Ages

481. Clovis proclaimed king of the Northern Francs.

496. Clovis marries a Burgond and wins a decisive battle aginst the Alamans. He receives Christian baptism from Bishop Rémi at Reims on Christmas Day 496.

511. Clovis dies in his capital, Paris. His Merovingian sons divide the kingdom, and end up killing each other.

613. The kingdom is reunified under Clotaire II., followed by Good King Dagobert .

732. Charles Martel holds back the Arab invasion at Poitiers

800. Barbarian king Charlemagne (son of Carolingian Pépin le Bref) is crowned Roman Emperor in Rome. He extends the borders of the Empire, stabilises the institutions and opens monastic schools to teach children to read and write.

840. The Vikings sail upriver and invade the kingdom, now governed by Charles the Bald.

843. The Treaty of Verdun divides Charlemagne's

Empire into two countries: the future France and Germany, with Lotharingie (Lorraine) in the middle. The two fight over it for centuries

987. Hugues Capet's reign begins the Capetian dynasty.

1096. First crusades against the Turks who are persecuting Christians in Jerusalem.

1208. Philipe Auguste's troops go violently to war against the Cathars.

1244. The last Cathars are burnt alive at Montségur with Saint Louis consent.

1259. The Treaty of Paris ends the fight against England.

1302. The States General are summoned by Philippe le Bel.

1314. Suppression of the Knights Templars Order, guardians of the royal treasure.

1337. The Hundred Years' War begins, between Philippe VI and Edward III of England.

1346. French army defeated by the English at Crécy.

1347. The Black Death ravages Europe.

1370. Du Guesclin and his mercenaries drive back the English to the coast

1415. French army beaten by Henry V's troops at Agincourt

1429. Joan of Arc frees Orléans from the English siege.

1431. Joan of Arc burnt alive on the Place du Vieux-Marché in Rouen.

1453. The Hundred Years' War comes to an end, the English having lost all their French territories except Calais.

1491. Having defeated Charles the Bold, Duke of Burgundy (then a vast realm including the Low Countries and north-eastern France) Charles VIII establishes a new kind of monarchy, reinforcing the king's power before his nobles.

1494. Charles VIII campaigns against Italy where the French discover the Renaissance.

1512. The Pope and his Holy League alliance of France's enemies attack Louis XII's army, which surrenders.

1515. Newly-crowned François I takes up the war against Italy and is victorious at Marignan.

1525. François I gives up Italy after the Pavia disaster.

1562. The Duc de Guise massacres Protestants worshipping in a barn, thus violating their right to religious freedom. The Wars of Religion begin.

1572. Saint-Barthélemy Massacre. 3,000 Protestants trapped in Paris and 25,000 in the provinces are massacred by Charles IX's troops.

1584. Protestant King Henri of Navarre fights the Holy Catholic League led by the Guise family.

1588. Duke de Guise assassinated at Blois.

1589. Henri III assassinated. Henri IV becomes king by first becoming a Catholic ('Paris is worth a Mass')

1598. The Edict of Nantes grants freedom of worship to Protestants.

1610. Henri IV assassinated by Ravaillac.

1624. After Marie de Médicis' regency, Cardinal Richelieu becomes Louis XIII's adviser.

1661. Death of Cardinal Mazarin. Louis XIV decides to rule alone as an absolute monarch. .

1685. The Edict of Nantes is revoked. 200,000 Protestants flee the kingdom.

1674. Louis XIV settles the court at Versailles.

1715. Louis XIV dies unpopular, leaving huge debts incurred by war and expensive living (Versailles).

1751. Diderot and d'Alembert's Encyclopedia is published.

Alba castle

1768. France buys Corsica from the Genoese Republic.

1778. The French, led by La Fayette, support the Americans against the English in the War of Independence.

The Revolution

1789. French Revolution. The Declaration of Human Rights proclaims the new principles of Liberty, Equality, Fraternity and national sovereignty.

1791. Louis XVI flees the capital, and is arrested at Varennes.

1793. Victory over the Prussians at Valmy Louis XVI is judged, condemned and guillotined. Robespierre's Reign of Terror against the Girondins begins.

1794. Danton demands an end to the Terror and is guillotined.

1795. General Bonaparte puts down a Royalist revolt in Paris.

1797. Bonaparte wins brilliant victories in Italy and France makes peace with its neighbours.

1799. 18 Brumaire Coup d'Etat. Three consuls, including Bonaparte, take power. End of the Revolution.

19th century

1800. Bonaparte becomes First Consul, centralises state administration and names préfets. Creation of the Banque de France.

1804. Napoleon establishes the Code civil and is crowned Emperor in Notre Dame.

1805. Napoléon loses to Nelson at Trafalgar, but wins brilliant victories over the Austro-Russians and founds a great empire.

1812. The Russian campaign begins. The Grande Armee is wiped out, partly by the Russian winter.

1814. Napoleon exiled to Elba. Louis XVIII becomes King of France.

1815. Napoleon comes back to France via the Alps and takes power (the Hundred Days). He is defeated at Waterloo and dies in exile on Saint Helena in 1821.

1824. Death of Louis XVIII. Charles X succeeds him.

1830. Three days of riots in July send absolute monarch Charles X into exile. Louis-Philippe d'Orléans (Philippe Egalité) becomes the new 'People's King'

1848. More demonstrations in Paris. Louis-Philippe abdicates and the II Republic is proclaimed. Louis Napoléon Bonaparte is the first democratically-elected Head of State (but cannot be re-elected after 4 ans).

1852. Coup d'Etat. End of the II Republic. Napoleon III announces the Second Empire.

1870. Parliamentary government introduced. Franco-Prussian War breaks out. Napoléon III imprisoned. Gambetta proclaims the III Republic.

1871. Paris besieged by the Prussians. The Parisians rebel against the Government and set up the Commune. This working-class movement is put down by the loyalist Versaillais, who execute the last Communards. Thiers negotiates peace with Germany, and France loses Alsace and Lorraine.

1882. Jules Ferry reorganises the school system, making primary education secular and compulsory.

1894. Sadi Carnot assassinated. The working class increasingly rejects bourgeois authority.

1898. The Dreyfus Affair. Emile Zola publishes «J'accuse» in defence of a Jewish army officer accused of spying for Germany.

20th century

1905. Separation of Church and State.

1908. Clemenceau is Employment Minister, and represses strike action.

1914. Germany declares war on France. Jean Jaurès (pacifist politician and founder of L'Humanité) assassinated. The United Front goes to war. General Joffre forces the Germans back to the Marne. Trench warfare begins along a 800km front.

1916. Petain defends Verdun against a German offensive. The battle costs a million lives.

1917. The Americans enter the war. Russian Revolution. The United Front is broken, but Clemenceau continues the war effort.

1918. The Allies sign an armistice with Germany on 11 November. End of the Great War.

1919. The Versailles Treaty forces Germany to give back Alsace-Lorraine, compensate France and disarm.

1920. Strikes and social unrest. The left-wing SFIO splits into two new parties: communists and socialists

1931. Worldwide economic depression hits Poincaré's stable Republic and strong franc.

1933. Confrontation between Fascist and Communist leagues in the Stavisky Affair. Hitler rises to power in Germany. Fascism is Europe's new enemy.

1936. The Front Populaire is elected in France. Léon Blum signs the Matignon Agreement with industrial bosses, granting trade union rights and paid holiday.

1938. Daladier signs the Munich Agreement: France recognises Nazi Germany's annexing of Czechoslovakia.

1939. Germany invades France's ally Poland. The Second World War breaks out.

1940. German troops invade. France falls to Hitler: Pétain imposes the armistice. The country is split in two: the occupied zone in the north and 'free zone' in the south. From London, General de Gaulle calls on France to rally and resist.

1941. The Vichy Government. Pétain meets Hitler and agrees to collaborate. Jewish status established.

1942. French Resistance becomes organised. The police begin systematic Jewish arrests. The Allies land in North Africa: the Germans move into the free zone.

1944. Allied troops land in Normandy. The Germans continue to hunt down resistants.

1945. Germany surrenders. End of World War II. Women vote for the first time to elect the new Assembly. De Gaulle's government is the unanimous choice.

1946. De Gaulle disagrees with the Assembly's constitutional projects and resigns. Vincent Auriol is the IV Republic's first President.

1951. France, Benelux, Italy and the German Federal Republic sign a treaty in Paris, creating the European Coal and Steel Community.

1954. End of French occupation in Indochina . Pierre Mendès France elected President.

1956. France grants independence to former colonies Morocco and Tunisia

1957. The Treaty of Rome lays the basis for the European Economic Community. In Algeria, war breaks out against the independentist FLN.

1958. Coup d'Etat by the Algerian Generals; de Gaulle re-elected President to avoid civil war in France. Creation of the V Republic, strengthening Presidential power.

1962. Referendum on Algerian self-determination, followed by another coup d'etat by the Algerian Generals against this decision. De Gaulle signs the Evian Agreement with the FLN. Algeria is independent, and a million 'pieds noirs' (French colonial settlers) are repatriated to France.

1968. In May, student and trade union unrest shake the established order. Though the Government triumphs at the next elections, progressive social ideas now take hold: 'Soixante-Huit' is a milestone in French social and cultural terms.

1969. De Gaulle resigns after a massive 'no' to his referendum on regionalisation. Georges Pompidou is elected President.

1973. First oil crisis. The French economy goes into recession.

1974. Death of Georges Pompidou, Valéry Giscard d'Estaing elected President. The official adult age limit is lowered to 18. Simone Veil has her pregnancy termination Bill passed by the Assembly.

1981. François Mitterrand is elected president. Abolition of the death penalty.

1986. The Gaullists win the general election: cohabitation between a right-wing government and a Socialist President.

1988. François Mitterrand re-elected against Jacques Chirac.

1993. Heavy defeat of the left in the elections: new cohabitation. The Maastricht referendum creates the European Union and plans a single currency.

1995. Jacques Chirac elected President.

1997. Chirac dissolves the Assembly. A Socialist victory in the resulting election forces the Gaullists to cohabit. End of National Service: the army goes professional.

1998. France wins the football World Cup on home territory.

1999. Creation of the single currency (euro). In December, France is shaken by a severe hurricane; forests are destroyed and many lives lost.

21st century

2001. Massive popular reaction against far-right nationalist Jean-Marie Le Pen in the Presidential Elections: Jacques Chirac is re-elected with 82% of votes. France supports the United States after the 11 September bombings.

2002. 1 January: arrival of the euro. The franc retires (in service since 1795).

2003. France refuses to take part in the American-led intervention force against Saddam Hussein's Iraq, and falls out with its old American ally. The heatwave (apparently) causes 15,000 deaths.

2004. Europe goes on growing (25 countries) and France continues to stand firm against the war in Iraq. The Olympic Games return to Athens, and the Tour de France celebrates its centenary.

A BRIEF HISTORY OF ART

France is world-famous for its artists: you find art everywhere, in galleries, museums, universities and the streets.

Cave paintings

Our Cro-Magnon ancestors sheltered in caves near their hunting grounds around 50,000 B.C. (Chauvet in Ardèche; Lascaux in Périgord).

Their wall paintings and drawings, and sculptures, give us an idea of their daily lives (and the animals they hunted).

Outdoors

Crop-growing replaced the glaciers: Neolithic man made pots to store his food in, and decorated them with bronze. The Celts carved stone steles (later statues) and used iron. Their artwork became increasingly sophisticated.

The cultural melting pot

Around 500 B.C. Greeks and Romans brought their architectural and engineering skill (Nîmes, Vienne, Orange, Pont du Gard) and decorative talents (mosaic-covered villas). These works were mostly destroyed in the Barbarian invasions, and the Merovingians had difficulty building on the ruins, their monasteries and churches being rudimentary in comparison.

Romanesque Art

Charlemagne revolutionized religious building: stone vaults replaced wood and walls were monumental and vertical, resulting in beautiful, luminous churches and abbeys (Vézelay). The fortress was primarily a defensive structure, but decorative refinements such as wall-paintings and tapestries were soon added behind those impressive ramparts (Angers).

The monks designed illuminated texts on parchment in the Middle Ages. The first French book is the Chanson de Roland (11thc).

Gothic Art

This was the age of majestic cathedrals, soaring into the sky. The walls were strengthened to suppport huge vaulted ceilings (Reims, Amiens, Paris) in 'Flamboyant' style. The cathedrals occupied the town centres and were places of learning; scholars discovered Greek philosophers and Arab mathematicians, and questioned the earth's recognised limits. Painting in the later Middle Ages became more lifelike; realism replaced the stylised saints. Stained glass windows reached a peak of perfection. Poetry (Francois Villon), chronicles (Jean Froissart), and polyphonic music (Burgundy), were the new art forms.

Renaissance

Charles VIII discovered the Italian Renaissance on his Naples campaign; Francois I had artists like Leonardo da Vinci brought to court, and the arts flourished, with notably the elegant and decorative Loire châteaux (Chambord) replacing the old fortified castles.

Books were printed, in French rather than Latin or Greek (Rabelais, Montaigne's Essays and the Pléiade poets).

Classicism

Louis XIV founded the Royal Academy to regulate the arts, and decide on rules and precepts to be taught in schools. 17thc. architecture prefered straight lines; right-angles and perfect symmetry were the fashion (Versailles). Realism prevails in painting, whether religious (Caravaggio) or

Traditional costumes

secular (Watteau, Chardin). Literature had its Academy too, set up by Richelieu. This was the golden age of French theatre, with Racine and Corneille's tragedies, and Moliere's comedies reflecting the values of his time.

Lumières

Artists soon wanted to go beyond Louis XIV's regulations. The development of science raised questions and brought new ideas, but the 18thc. is chiefly known for its literature. Diderot and d'Alembert popularised general knowledge with their Encyclopédie. Montesquieu thought the individual should have his place in society; Voltaire exposed human stupidity and ignorance; and Rousseau approved of his noble savage's natural innocence, in contrast to the corrupting influence of civilisation.

In the last years of the century, David painted great events with neo-classical mastery (Marat's death; Napoleon's coronation). The Lumières laid the cultural groundwork for the Revolution, and the artistic movements that followed.

Romantic art

Classical antiquity (form) was rejected in favour of emotional expression (feeling). Géricault (*Radeau de la Méduse*) and Delacroix paid attention to colour, light and detail (sometimes macabre).

French musicians followed German, Austrian and Italian trends: Berlioz's poetic Symphonie Fantastique breaks with tradition; Gounod's lyric drama Faust reflects the period's sensibility. Lamartine, Châteaubriand, Vigny and Musset followed Goethe, trying to seize and fix the same elusive Romantic melancholy in their literature.

Realism

The preoccupations of daily life replaced spleen: Courbet's *L'Origine du Monde* shocked society. The Impressionists painted everyday scenes, with close attention to facial expression and light. Manet destructured light and space, attacking the established precepts. Balzac's *Human Comedy*, Flaubert's *Madame Bovary* and Zola's Rougon-Macquart saga depict human weakness in a realistic social and material context. Poetry dominated the century's later years: Baudelaire, Mallarmé, Verlaine and Rimbaud sought for their own absolute art form, influencing the *fin de siècle* decadent and symbolist movements.

Modern art

In industrial societies, the human being replaced by machines is constantly seeking new forms of expression. After the Impressionists came the Post-Impressionist, Pointillist, Fauvist, Cubist (Picasso, Leger, Braque and Matisse) and Surrealist movements, followed by abstract and comtemporary art. Architecture developed along the same lines: Le Corbusier's functional concrete homes are listed modern art masterpieces. You love or hate the great Parisian structures (La Défense, Opéra Bastille, Grand Bibliothèque) which have already marked the landscape; controversial but here to stay. Finally, the 20thc. was the age of the cinema. France has a still-thriving film industry with great filmmakers well able to compete on an international level. Information about France's artistic and architectural heritage:

MINISTERE DE LA CULTURE Direction de l'Architecture et du Patrimoine - Hôtel de Vigny - 10, rue du Parc-Royal - PARIS (3e) ✆ 01 40 15 75 50. *www. culture.gouv.fr*

FOOD AND DRINK

General de Gaulle claimed it was impossible to govern a country with 258 cheeses! France has a huge variety of regional specialities, and a wide range of produce grown in local soil. The best-known are a combination of the right climate and agricultural conditions and human skill and know-how. To ensure and maintain quality levels, the Institut National des Appellations d'Origine created the AOC in 1935. At the time, this institute dealt with wines and spirits; today other products (such as cheese) can have an AOC. Conditions are strict; all AOC requests must be submitted to the Ministry of Agriculture, which issues a decree on approval.

Look out for the *Site remarquable du goût*, where you can be sure to taste a top-quality speciality, while discovering its history and how it is made. France has about 70 of these sites.

INSTITUT NATIONAL DES APPELLATIONS D'ORIGINE 138, av. des Champe-Elysees - PARIS (8e) *www.inao.gouv.fr*

Wines

Vines have existed in France since Antiquity, classified into different categories for the last 200 years. There are AOC, *vins délimités de qualité supérieure* (less strictly monitored than the AOC) *vins de pays* and *vins de table*. The great winegrowing regions are Bordeaux, Côtes-du-Rhône, Beaujolais, Champagne, Alsace, Loire, Bourgogne and the Mediterranean area.

Cheeses

Goat's, ewe's and cow's milk are used to make a huge variety of French cheeses: hard or soft, pressed or not, blue-veined, matured or new-made, each has its own unique appearance, texture and flavour. Top producers: Normandy (Camembert), Massif Central (fourme, Cantal), Franche-Comté (emmental, comté) Alps (tomme, reblochon) and Poitou (chabichou).

Fruits and vegetables

France is a major producer - but (as TV ads tell us) the French don't eat enough of them! They are spoilt for choice, however: Roussillon apricots, Céret and Auxerre cherries, Moissac grapes, Agen prunes, Mediterranean olives, Touraine asparagus, Woippy strawberries, Cavaillon melon. Lorraine mirabelles, Antilles bananas, Réunion pineapples...the list is long. The best place to find fresh fruit and veg is the local market; a French institution where you can chat to the market-gardener while tasting his produce.

Meat and poultry

The French have been eating less beef since the mad cow period, and more poultry. The best beef comes from Salers or Limousin (the Charolais breed is recommended) and pork from Brittany (or Saint-Yrieix Cul-Noir). Objat veal, Deux-Sevres mutton, Bresse poultry, Mans fatted chickens and Drôme guinea-hen are equally reputed.

Each region described in the guide contains a section on its specialities, called Food and Drink.

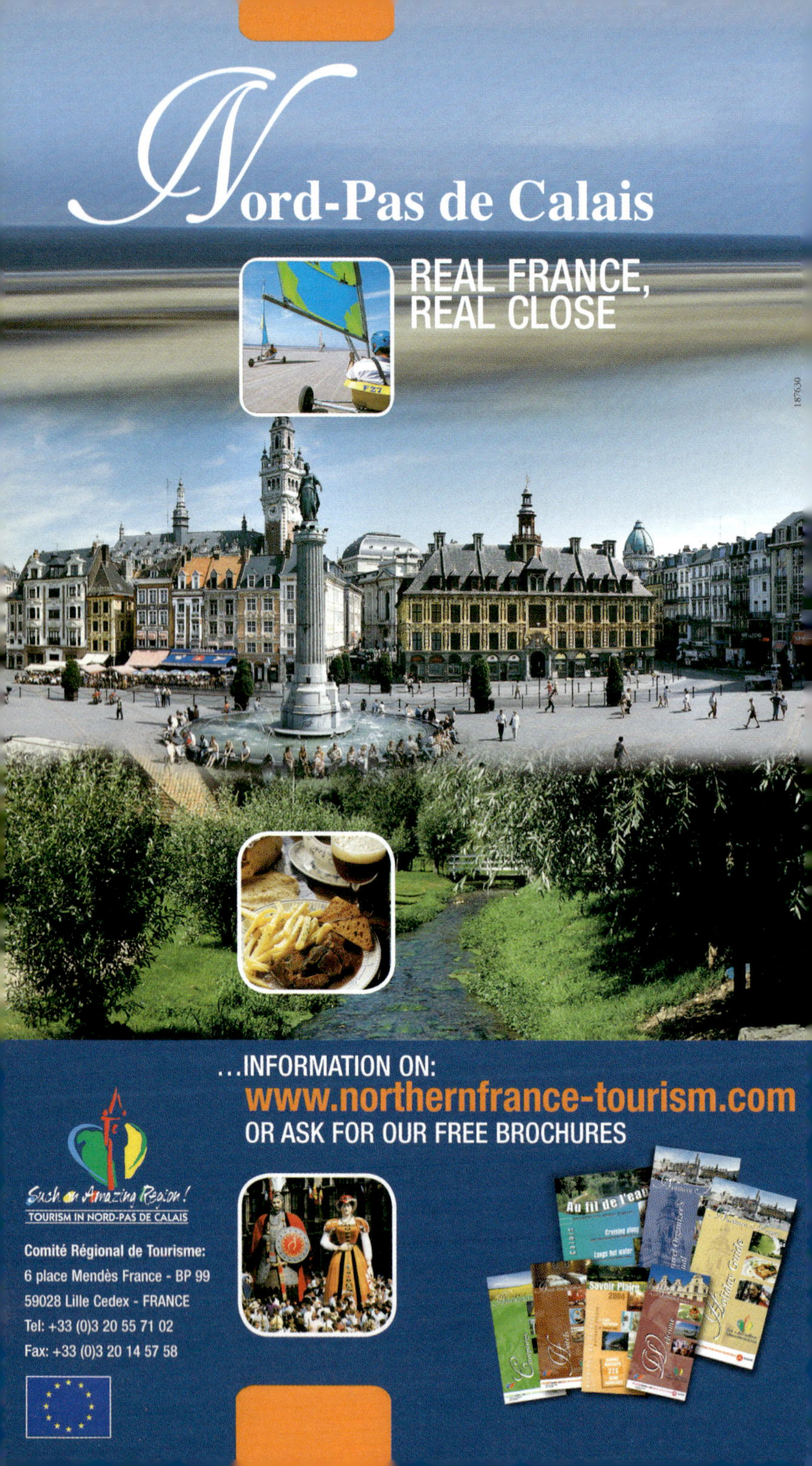
Nord-Pas de Calais
REAL FRANCE, REAL CLOSE
…INFORMATION ON:
www.northernfrance-tourism.com
OR ASK FOR OUR FREE BROCHURES
Such an Amazing Region!
TOURISM IN NORD-PAS DE CALAIS
Comité Régional de Tourisme:
6 place Mendès France - BP 99
59028 Lille Cedex - FRANCE
Tel: +33 (0)3 20 55 71 02
Fax: +33 (0)3 20 14 57 58

Events and Manifestations

Menton, festival of the lemon

The following annual events are not to be missed!

February

La Chandeleur (Candlemas) celebrates the candles that were lit to light up the long winter nights. In France today, pancakes are made.

1 April

Jokers stick paper fishes on unsuspecting backs and say 'Poisson d'avril!' (April Fool!), probably because the fishing season once opened on 1 April. In the Middle Ages it was the first day of the New Year (changed to 1 January in 1564).

1 May

The Fête du Travail. According to an old French tradition, you buy and offer lily-of-the-valley (muguet) to bring luck.

8 May

A number of official and military ceremonies commemorate the Allied victory in 1945.

6 June

Not a public holiday, but celebrated in Normandy on the Landings beaches. In 2004, the French and US Presidents came to mark the 60th commemoration since 1944.

21 June

The Fête de la Musique was created in 1982 to mark the arrival of summer. All kinds of musicians (amateur and professional) take their instruments out into the streets; there is a band on every corner, and a number of more formal organised concerts.

14 July

France's National Day celebrates the taking of the Bastille in 1789. Military marches, firecrackers and dances (including those organised by firemen) mark the occasion, which ends with a firework display. You'll see plenty of liberty and fraternity!

September

The Journee du Patrimoine (Heritage Day) is held the second weekend in September. Public institutions and monuments are open to the public free of charge: some (like the Elysee Palace) are only open at this time.

November

France remembers the 1918 Armistice on 11 November. The President places a wreath on the Unknown Soldier's tomb at the Arc du Triomphe, with the last veterans of the Great War.

The Beaujolais Nouveau has arrived! All over France (and the world) fans meet to taste this year's product, identify its flavour and often criticise, though the quality is improving. A successful marketing strategy!

25 December

Christmas is celebrated with presents under the tree, Santa Claus for the kids, oysters, turkey and a Christmas Log for dessert.

Festivals on a theme

Food

FOIRE AUX ANDOUILLES Val d'Ajol (Vosges). *3rd Monday in February*. The andouillettes eaten at this ancient festival are made in early December (Saint Nicholas), smoked and dried over a wood fire. **Information ✆ 03 29 30 66 69.**

Salon international de l'agriculture

Paris, February/March. The French provinces set up their stands and livestock; biological agriculture and farm machines are also featured. Information ✆ 01 49 09 60 94. www.salon-agriculture.com

OLIVADES de Nyons (Drôme). A Sunday in mid-July. The olive is celebrated with processions, dancing and tasting.

FÊTE DE LA MIRABELLE Metz (Moselle). *2nd fortnight in August.* A dance opens the festival, and the Mirabelle Queen is elected with her ladies in waiting. The Royal cortege passes through the streets during the next fortnight, and the festival closes with floats, international folklore exhibitions and a huge firework display. **Information ✆ 03 87 55 53 73.**

FÊTE DU CASSOULET Castelnaudary (Aude). *1st weekend in September.* 50,000 people come to taste as much cassoulet as they can eat. A local produce market and flowered corso complete the festival. **Information ✆ 04 68 23 05 73.**

FERIA DES PREMICES DU RIZ Arles (Bouches-du-Rhône). *2nd and 3rd weekends in September.* Bullfights are held in Arles ring, and floats process through the town centre, decorated with ears of wheat. The gardians' saddles carry rice stalks, and the new rice is enjoyed in a variety of recipes. **Information ✆ 04 90 96 03 70.**

FRAIRIE DES PETITS-VENTRES Limoges (Haute-Vienne). *3rd Friday in October.* Limoges celebrates its local beef in the Rue de la Boucherie with entertainment, folklore and culinary traditions: tripe and all kinds of beef dish are eaten. The festival dates back to 1861. **Information ✆ 05 55 45 18 80.**

VENTE DES VINS DES HOSPICES DE BEAUNE (Côte d'Or). *3rd Sunday in November.* The world's biggest charity sale attracts the international jet set and wine dealers. Grands and premiers crus are auctioned from the Hôtel-Dieu.

QUATRE GLORIEUSES DE BRESSE (Ain). *Mid-December.* Site remarquable du goût. Over 1,500 poultry are exhibited and sold, in four days and four places (Bourg-en-Bresse, Pont-de-Vaux, Montrevel-en-Bresse, Louhans) and with Christmas bird competitions and markets. **Information ✆ 03 85 76 04 44.**

Carnivals

CARNAVAL DE NICE. *February.* Now ranking with Venice and Rio, this carnival began in 1830, and features flower fights on the Promenade des Anglais and Place Massena. On Shrove Tuesday, a pasteboard King goes up in flames. **Information ✆ 04 92 14 48 14.**

CARNAVAL DE DUNQUERQUE *March (Ash Wednesday).* Traditional songs, giants, procession, dances and plenty of rumpus. **Information ✆ 03 38 58 10 10.**

Sport

MARATHON DE PARIS *4 April.* Tens of thousands take part every year; the Kenyans in front, the rest behind. Information ✆ 08 2000 75 75.

PARIS-ROUBAIX *April.* France's other great cycling event. Hard on the calves and the morale. **Information ✆ 03 20 65 31 90**

GRAND PRIX DE FORMULE 1 DE MONACO. *May.* Set up right in the town centre. this Grand Prix circuit attracts the rich and famous. Information **✆ 00 377 92 166 166.**

TOURNOI DE ROLAND-GARROS The world's biggest hard court tennis tournament. The national sport consists of lying back in your seat behind dark glasses instead of being at the office. **Information ✆ 01 47 43 48 00.**

24H DU MANS *June.* The world's high-powered racing cars compete for 24 hours on the Bugatti circuit. The 24-hour motorbike race takes place in April, and the French motorbike Grand Prix in May. **Information ✆ 02 43 40 24 75.**

GRAND PRIX DE FRANCE *July.* Threatened with cancellation every year, this race takes place on the Magny Cours circuit (Nièvre). **Bookings ✆ 03 86 21 80 00.**

TOUR DE FRANCE *July.* American cyclist Lance Armstrong has won 6 times, with 6 yellow jerseys. Will he do it again this year? France's most popular sporting event.

Marathon des châteaux du Medoc (Gironde)

Physical exercise and wine tasting combine in this great château-to-château marathon (Pauillac, Saint-Estèphe, etc.). Known as the world's longest marathon - since not everyone follows the straight line! - this very convivial French event takes place in September. www.marathon-medoc.com

Ferias

FERIAS DE NÎMES. *Primavera/February* - Pentecôte/June - Vendange/September. These three ferias celebrate bullfighting, and feature street music, dancing, equestrian displays and sometimes Languedoc jousting. **Festivities service ✆ 04 66 76 70 01.**

FERIA D'ARLES *April.* Apart from the tauromachie, this is a festive occasion celebrated in the cellars and bodegas. **Information ✆ 04 90 96 03 70.**

FERIA DE BEZIERS *Round 15 August.* The brick bullring (1897) is a lively place this weekend, and the festival continues in the town. You'll get a warm welcome. **Information ✆ 04 67 76 47 00**

FÊTES DE DAX. *August.* Dressed mainly in red and white, the participants sing, dance and drink for a week. The bullring seats 8,000 aficionados. **Information ✆ 04 58 56 86 86**

FÊTES DE BAYONNE August *(Wednesday before 1st Sunday).* Four days and nights of celebrations on the Basque Coast, with plenty of events and lively displays. **Information ✆ 05 59 46 01 46**

Other events

BRADERIE DE LILLE *1st weekend in September.* Don't miss the atmosphere: everyone buys and sells what he likes and eats mussels, for two days and nights. **Allo Braderie ✆ 03 20 49 54 42.**

FÊTES DES LUMIERES *8 December.* Lyon celebrates with Chinese lanterns at nightfall.

CRECHES VIVANTES *December.* The living crèche is a Provençal tradition; baby Jesus takes his place among the big santon statues with the occasional live animal for company.

MARCHE DE NOEL *December.* Alsace's towns and villages set up their Cristkindelsmarkt or Christmas Market.

Festivals

Often held in the open air, preferably in summer!

French popular music

NUITS DE CHAMPAGNE Reims (Marne). Last weekend in October. French singers pay tribute to a famous guest-star.

FRANCOFOLIES de La Rochelle (Charente-Maritime). *July.* A host of French singing stars invade the harbour. This festival began 20 years ago, and has become an internationally-recognised French language event. **Information ✆ 05 46 28 28 28**

PRINTEMPS DE BOURGES (Cher). Quality music, from electric to French popular songs, and plenty of new talent. **Information ✆ 02 48 27 40 40**

Film Festivals

FANTASTIC ARTS DE GERARDMER (Vosges). January/February. This 10-rear-old film festival has a growing reputation. Information ✆ **03 29 60 98 21**

FESTIVAL INTERNATIONAL DU FILM POLICIER DE COGNAC (Charente). Gregory Peck, Claude Chabrol and Alain Delonhave graced this film festival for thriller fans in their time. **Information ✆ 05 45 35 60 00**

FESTIVAL DU CINEMA A CANNES (Alpes-Maritimes) *May.* Meet the stars on the Croisette at the Côte d'Azur's very mediatic International Film Festival. **Information: ✆ 04 93 39 24 53**

FESTIVAL DU FILM ROMANTIQUE A CABOURG (Calvados). *June.* Four days of films for lovers.

FESTIVAL DU FILM AMERICAIN A DEAUVILLE (Calvados). *September.* The famous boardwalk is thronged with French and American stars.

FESTIVAL DES TROIS CONTINENTS A NANTES (Loire-Atlantique). *Late November.* This 25-year-old festival acts as a showcase for Asian, African and Latin American films (with debates). **Information ✆ 02 40 20 60 00**

Circus

FESTIVAL INTERNATIONAL DU CIRQUE A MONACO. *December.* The world circus elite performs in Monaco for the Royal Family and TV camaras. **Information ✆ 00 377 20 52 345.**

Classical music

CHOREGIES D'ORANGE (Vaucluse). *July.* Lyric art festival in one of the world's best-preserved antique theatres. **Information: ✆ 04 90 34 24 24.**

FESTIVAL D'ART LYRIQUE D'AIX-EN-PROVENCE (Bouches-du-Rhône). *July.* This festival has a much-deserved international reputation, playing host to some great opera singers. **Information ✆ 04 42 17 34 34**

FESTIVAL DE RADIO FRANCE ET DE MONTPELLIER (Hérault) *July.* Opera, symphonic and chamber music, with some ancient and modern world music thrown in for good measure. A must for music lovers. **Information ✆ 04 67 02 02 01.**

FESTIVAL INTERNATIONAL DE MUSIQUE BAROQUE A BEAUNE (Côte d'Or) *July & August.* The town's finest medieval buildings play host to this musical event. The theme is Baroque music, but the Middle Ages, Renaissance and Mozart also feature on the programme, along with new discoveries and re-creations. A concert in the Cour des Hospices with its glazed roofs is not to be missed. **Information ✆ 03 80 24 45 00. wwwfestivalbeaune.com.**

FESTIVAL INTERNATIONAL DE PIANO DE LA ROQUE D'ANTHERON (Bouches-du-Rhône). *July/August.* Unknown and forgotten piano music, including contemporary and jazz, in a daring and ambitious programme. **Information ✆ 04 42 50 51 15**

FESTIVAL INTERNATIONAL DE MUSIQUE - LA CHAISE-DIEU (Haute-Loire). *August.* One of France's great classical music festivals, founded in 1966. The concerts take place in Chaise-Dieu Abbey's sublime setting.

FESTIVAL INTERNATIONAL DE MUSIQUE DE BESANÇON (Doubs). *September*. Every year, prestigious orchestras, chamber music ensembles and soloists come to Besançon. **Information ✆ 03 81 25 05 80.**

PIANO AU JACOBINS Toulouse (Haute-Garonne). *September.* The only French all-piano festival, with talented performers and exciting new creations. An event to look out for. **Information ✆ 05 61 22 40 05**

Dance

BIENNALE DE LA DANSE Lyon (Rhône). *August-September.* Held every two years (even numbers: the next is in 2006). Dozens of contemporary dance companies meet in and around Lyon for a month of shows and displays.

Information ✆ 04 72 07 41 41

FESTIVAL INTERNATIONAL DE LA DANSE Nice (Alpes-Maritimes). *November.* Great artistic and technical skill and fine choreography are displayed on the Côte d'Azur. **Information ✆ 04 93 39 24 53**

Folklore

FESTIVAL INTERCELTIQUE DE LORIENT (Morbihan). *1st weekend in August.* France's biggest festival welcomes half a million visitors for this traditional Celtic music festival (all Celtic origins represented). **Information ✆ 02 97 21 24 29.**

Jazz

JAZZ IN MARCIAC (Gers). *October/May.* The Gers countryside vibrates to jazz rhythms between October and May (one concert per month). **Information ✆ 05 62 09 31 98**

JAZZ SOUS LES POMMIERS Coutances (Manche). *May.* Twenty years of jazz under the apple trees.

JAZZ A VIENNE (Isère). *1st fortnight in July.* Held in Vienne's antique theatre; an exceptional setting for jazz instrumentalists and vocalists, with various kinds of world music included in the programme. **Information ✆ 04 74 78 87 87**

FESTIVAL DE JAZZ DE JUAN-LES-PINS (Alpes-Maritimes). *July.* The world's jazz-lovers have flocked here since 1949. **Information ✆ 04 92 90 53 05**

NANCY JAZZ PULSATIONS. *October.* National and international performers have been coming to the NJP since 1973, for the official concerts and off-stage programme in the town's cafés. **Information ✆ 03 83 35 40 86.**

Books

FESTIVAL INTERNATIONAL DE LA BANDE DESSINEE Angoulême (Charente). *January.* The world's finest comic-strip designers and scriptwriters spend four days meeting their fans. **Information ✆ 05 45 97 86 50**

SALON DU LIVRE PARIS *March.* An important literary event. 1,800 French and foreign authors get to meet the general public, publishers and booksellers. In 2005, Russia is the guest country. *www.salondulivreparis.com*

ETONNANTS VOYAGEURS Saint-Malo. *Whitsun.* This book festival has welcomed a thousand guests from 60 countries over the last 15 years. Literature-lovers cannot afford to miss it. *www.etonnants-voyageurs.net*

FOIRE DU LIVRE Brives (Corrèze). *November.* Second-biggest French book fair (after Paris's Salon du Livre). Exhibits, conferences, literary café. **Information ✆ 05 55 92 39 39.**

Marionnettes

FESTIVAL MONDIAL DES THEATRES DE MARIONNETTES Charleville-Mézières (Ardennes). *Every three years*, puppeteers the world over come here to demonstrate their creations (giant African characters; Vietnamese water puppets etc). The next festival takes place in 2006. *www.marionette.com*

Rock

EUROCKEENNES DE BELFORT (Territoire de Belfort). *July.* A huge open-air concert with five stages at the water's edge. Rock, electrobeat, rap and reggae feature on the programme over 5 days. **Information ✆ 03 84 55 90 90.**

FESTIVAL DES VIEILLES CHARRUES DE CARHAIX (Finistère). *July.* Gouel an Erer Kozh is its Breton name, and it is a surprising musical meeting-place.

Informations: ✆ 02 98 99 44 75

TRANSMUSICALES DE RENNES (Ille-et-Vilaine). Late November-early December. World-wide rock and techno, including some famous musicians.

Theatre

FESTIVAL D'AVIGNON (Vaucluse) *July.* Founded in 1947 by Jean Vilar, this great French theatre festival takes place in the Palais des Papes' main courtyard (haunted by Gerard Philipe's brilliant Cid)

Bookings ✆ 04 90 14 14 14

FESTIVAL DE THEATRE DE RUE D'AURILLAC (Cantal). *August.* Profesionals and amateurs meet up for street theatre.

Information ✆ 04 71 45 47 47.

Discovering France

Pond in Lorraine

The best way to discover France is not necessarily by car. Take things slowly, and enjoy the open air.

On foot

Hiking is a great way to make contact with France's natural heritage. This beautiful country boasts thousands of kilometres of marked-out footpaths in the most varied scenery. Grande Randonnée paths are marked in red and white, for instance. Respect the environment by not leaving rubbish, lighting fires or throwing away cigarette ends - and don't forget your map. Topo-guides are available from Tourist Offices (the best are published by Didier Richard). They are often thematic, and contain tourist information as well as distances and detailed maps.

FEDERATION FRANCAISE DE LA RANDONNEE PEDESTRE 14, rue Riquet - PARIS (19e) ✆ 01 44 89 93 90 *www.ffrp.asso.fr*

ESPACE IGN 107, rue La Boétie - PARIS (8e) & 01 43 98 85 10. *www.ign.fr*

By barge

Even the Dutch come to France for barge trips! The country offers 8,500km of navigable waterways including the great rivers and canals: easy to manage by barge, with beautiful scenery (Canal du Midi). Barge hire is becoming less expensive (no licence needed), and a pleasant holiday can be had on the Nantes Canal (west) and Rivers Mayenne and Sarthe; Dordogne side canal (southwest); Canal du Midi (south); Canal du Centre and Canal de Bourgogne; and in the northeast, the Ardennes and Marne Canals and Rivers Moselle and Rhine.

VOIES NAVIGABLES DE FRANCE 175, rue Ludovic-Boutleux - BETHUNE ✆ 03 21 63 24 24. *www.vnf.fr.*

National Boat Hire

CONNOISSEUR CRUISERS Ile Sauzay - GRAY ✆ 03 84 64 95 20

CROWN BLUE LINE Le Grand Bassin CASTELNAUDARY ✆ 04 68 94 52 72

LOCABOAT PLAISANCE Quai du Port au Bois JOIGNY ✆ 03 86 91 72 72

By bicycle

Cycling is popular in France, especially on Sunday mornings along the country roads. What better way to discover a region at your own rhythm? These days, you even meet cyclists equipped with a cart, to carry their camping gear.

Fashionable mountain biking enables you to ride over rough and rocky ground (mountains, fields and rivers) and to get close to woodland wildlife (tyres are less disturbing than footsteps for animals). The downhill run is also more exciting!

FEDERATION FRANCAISE DE CYCLOTOURISME 12, rue Louis Bertrand - IVRY-SUR-SEINE ✆ 01 53 20 88 88 *www.ffct.org*

FEDERATION FRANCAISE DE CYCLISME Bâtiment Jean Monet - 5, rue de Rome - ROSNY-SOUS-BOIS ✆ 01 49 85 69 00

On horseback

French countryside boasts plenty of bridlepaths, and riding centres often organise theme holidays on horseback, in woodland or open country (Vercors, Camargue) or along the beaches (Aquitaine). These centres have their own mounts and equipment for hire.

DELEGATION NATIONALE AU TOURISME EQUESTRE 9, bd. Macdonald - PARIS (19e) ✆ 01 53 26 15 15

FEDERATION FRANCAISE D'EQUITATION 9, bd. Macdonald - PARIS (19e) ✆ 01 53 26 15 15. *www.ffe.com*

By sea

France's three coasts are dotted with coves and magnificent yachting harbours. Sailing is a booming leisure activity, mainly in Brittany with its many clubs. Once you've got your coastal or sea licence, you can sail off into Corsican creeks, round Marseille's calanques or even to the Breton or Channel Islands. If you don't have your own boat, you can hire one in a big sailing harbour (about 1,000 a week depending on boat size).

FEDERATION FRANCAISE DE VOILE 17, rue Henri Bocquillon - PARIS (15e) ✆ 01 40 60 37 00. *www.ffv.fr*

From the air

There are two ways of looking down on France's rural patchwork (apart from hiring your own private plane and pilot, of course!) Paragliding is an increasingly popular sport. You need a take-off site, and a certain amount of practice at manipulating the sail. In the summer season, French mountain areas are covered in these brightly-coloured sails, and you can join them for about 80 ago.

Equally sensational though less physical is hot-air ballooning, currently back in fashion. You can float over the Loire, Alps and Massif Central (the balloon is discreetly attached to the ground by a cord) taking time to enjoy the scenery. A new view of France!

FEDERATION FRANCAISE DE VOL LIBRE 4, rue de Suisse - NICE ✆ 04 97 03 82 82. *www.ffvl.fr*

FEDERATION FRANCAISE D'AEROSTATION 6, rue Galilée - PARIS (16e) ✆ 01 47 23 56 20. *www.ffaerostation.org*

By rail

France is proud of its TGV (high-speed train) but it also boasts a number of picturesque country (or secondary) lines and old-fashioned steam trains, diesels and railcars, still pulling a few carriages from Ambert to Dome or Puisaye to Forterre, through magnificent scenery. Take a trip on the Chemin de Fer de la Mure in Isère, Train des Pigne (Provence-Côte d'Azur) or Gentiane Express in the Massif Central and feel yourself relax as you slip back into a gentler era.

UNION NATIONALE DES EXPLOITANTS DE CHEMINS DE FER TOURISTIQUES Gare de l'Est - PARIS (10e) ✆ 01 ?0 38 41 39. *www.trains-fr.org.* **The French railway network's secondary lines can be found on this site.**

Alps
White valley, Chamonix

Alps
LAC LEMAN
Evian-les-Bains
Thonon-les-Bains
Yvoire
Gex
Abondance
Avoriaz
Morzine
GENEVE
Annemasse
BOURG-EN BRESSE
Nantua
Bonneville
Samoëns
SION
SUISSE
HAUTE-SAVOIE
Argentière
Chamonix-Mont-Blanc
Mont Blanc 4808 m.
Le Grand-Bornand
La Clusaz
ANNECY
Fier
Pérouges
AIN
Ain
Rhône
St-Gervais-les-Bains
Megève
Courmayer
AOSTE
Lac du Bourget
Lac d'Annecy
PARC DU MASSIF DES BAUGES
Belley
Albertville
Beaufort
Aix-les-Bains
Le Bourget-du-Lac
CHAMBERY
Isere
Les Arcs
SAVOIE
ITALIE
La Tour-du-Pin
La Plagne
Tignes
Val d'Isère
Valmorel
PARC DE LA VANOISE
PARC DE CHARTREUSE
Pontcharra
Méribel
Courchevel
Grande Casse 3858 m.
Bonneval-sur-Arc
Les Menuires
ISERE
St-Pierre-de Chartreuse
St-Jean-de-Maurienne
Arc
40 km
GRENOBLE
Modane

Altitude (in meters)
3000
2000
1000
Major road
Motorway
Main town
Secondary town
ITALIE
N
S
E
O
ROMANS-SUR-ISERE
Villard-de-Lans
La Chapelle-en-Vercors
PARC DU VERCORS
Clelles
Die
Drôme
Drac
Le Bourg-d'Oisans
Romanche
Les Deux-Alpes
PARC DES ECRINS
Barre des Ecrins 4102 m.
Super-Dévoluy
Orcières-Merlette
Serre-Chevallier
BRIANCON
Sestrière
Durance
PARC DU QUEYRAS
St-Véran
Guillestre
HAUTES-ALPES
Vars
GAP
Lac de Serre-Ponçon
Ubaye
DROME
Serres
Aygues
Nyons
Ouvèze
Barcelonnette
Pra-Loup
PARC DU MERCANTOUR
St-Etienne-de-Tinée
Isola 2000
ALPES DE HAUTES-PROVENCE
Sisteron
Bléone
Allos
Verdon
Valberg
Tinée
St-Martin-Vésubie
Tende
CUNEO
DIGNE-LES BAINS
CARPENTRAS
Forcalquier
Moustiers-Ste-Marie
Castellane
PARC DU VERDON
Var
Sospel
ALPES-MARITIMES
Menton
MONACO
NICE
MER MEDITERRANEE

ALBERTVILLE, BEAUFORTAIN, MAURIENNE AND TARENTAISE

Albertville, Olympic site in 1992, has become one of the world's best-known Alpine towns. It grew out of the merging of two villages: l'Hôpital-sous-Conflans and Conflans, at the Arly-Isère confuence. Albertville is also an 'Art and History Town', and can be visited with lecturing guides: in July and August, there are guided tours of Conflans at 10.30am, 2.30pm and 4.30pm. (adult 5 €, child 2.50 €).

MAISON DES JEUX OLYMPIQUES 11, rue Pargoud ✆ 04 79 37 75 71 *Open 9am-12 noon and 2pm-6pm, except Sundays and public holidays: 2pm-7pm.* In the heart of Albertville, some way from the Olympic Stadium, you can discover the history of the Winter Olympics, and of the mountains in the last century. Costumes, photos and videos from the 1992 Games are permanently on display, while plenty of space is given to temporary exhibitions.

Conflans

This medieval city perches like a belvedere 412m up a steep, rocky slope. It overlooks the whole valley, and the Arly-Isère confluence (its Latin name is Ad Conluentem). It was once a stopping-place on the Roman road from Vienne to Milan; Henri IV, Richelieu and Louis XIII all stayed here. The city was burned down by François I in the early 16thc., but the 14thc. wall remained intact. Don't miss the Grand-Place with its fountains, where markets and fairs were held, or the Porte Tarine, gateway to the Tarentaise and Italy. Before leaving, climb up to the Grande Roche terrace, with its proud 12thc. 'Saracen' tower; the view stretches right over the Savoy coomb.

Beaufortain

Arèches-Beaufort

This little village, reached from Beaufort on the D218, has a pretty church and a sundial in the square; not far off is a chalet dating back to 1666. Continue as far as the Saint-Guerin dam (150m x 70m) with its charming view of the balancing reservoir.

COOPERATIVE LAITIERE ✆ 04 79 38 33 62 *Admission free every day, group bookings in advance (Au pays de Beaufort film showing included). 8am-12 noon and 2pm-6pm;7pm in summer.* You can visit this famous dairy co-operative in season (groups all year), and watch cheese making from the milk churns to the maturing cellars. 1,000 tonnes of cheese are made, using 10 million litres of milk from Beaufortain's 150 farmers.

Roselend

The Beaufortain's main tourist attraction is at a height of 1,557m. Roselend balancing reservoir has swamped former pastures, but you tend to forget that when admiring the site's beauty. Doron de Roselend dam was built in 1960, 143m high and 804 long, with a buttressed vault. The reservoir holds 185 m^3 for a surface area of 320 ha. This is one of Savoy's finest places for hiking; park at the Cormet de Roselend and set off on well-worn paths through the high mountain pastures where you might see an acrobatic siskin. With the reservoir in the background, this is a corner of heaven.

Maurienne

The River Arc carved out this valley through 120km of the inter-alpine zone and massifs. It separates into two distinct types of country: the Maurienne Valley and the Haute-Maurienne, leading to the Vanoise National park. The Maurienne has always been the route into Italy (today via the Frejus Tunnel) mainly because of its semi-circular path, from the spring east of Bonneval to its confluent with the Isère. The Maurienne ski-resorts are not as fashionable as the ones in the neighbouring Tarentaise valley, though the scenery is just as spectacular. Haute-Maurienne has 7 villages ranked among the most beautiful French mountain sites, and provides a genuine refuge from the pressures of life.

Aussois

ESSEILLON FORTS. Aussois tourist office ✆ 04 79 20 30 80. *Guides office 04 79 20 32 48. Guided tour of the site.* The forts look out across France from the old Esseillon tollgate. They were put up by the Sardinians between 1817 and 1834, to protect Piedmont (and Europe) from French invasions, and are a practical application of the Marquis de Montalembert's theories. This defence system, unique in France, is based on the principle of perpendicular fortifications and cannon towers. The system was built in five parts, each protecting the others with crossfire, which is one of its particularities. Weakened by the invention of the shell, these cold and isolated buildings soon lost their strategic interest and were reduced to housing disciplinary battalions or prisoners, 1,500m or more above sea-level, though they did see some fighting again during World War Two. You can visit each fort and redoubt by following the 'builders' path' on foot or with racquets (careful not to slip). You begin with the Marie-Thérèse redoubt, lingering for a while in the Victor-Emmanuel fort, currently undergoing restoration work (the roof is being re-covered with lauze tiles).

Bonneval-sur-Arc

Bonneval is halfway between Val-Cenis and Val-d'Isère on the D902, at the foot of the Iseran pass (2,770m). This listed site and 'Beautiful French Village' did not suffer in World War II, and its old stone houses with their shale roofs are charming. Don't miss seeing the Ecot hamlet nearby; it's worth the trip.

Saint-Jean-de-Maurienne

Traditionally the valley's administrative, industrial and business capital, this town now promotes tourism in the many surrounding ski-resorts (summer and winter) and village resorts offering mountain leisure activities. It is also famous among cycling fans for the high Alpine passes close by. The Tour de France comes through regularly, and cycling tourists often meet at Saint-Jean-de-Maurienne.

MUSEE DES COSTUMES Place de la Cathedrale ✆ 04 79 83 51 51 *Admission free. Open in summer, Monday-Saturday: 10am-12 noon and 2pm-6pm. Other periods: Tuesday: 4pm-6pm; Wednesday: 10.30am-12 noon and 4pm-6pm.* Housed in the former Bishop's Palace, a collection of Savoie costumes, archeological findings and religious objects retrace the region's history and traditions. A Maurienne period room completes your visit.

MUSEE DE L'OPINEL Av. Henri Falcoz ✆ 04 79 64 04 78. *Open all year Monday-Saturday: 9am-12 noon and 2pm-7pm. Admission free.* Discover the famous Savoie penknife, invented at Gevoudaz, a hamlet at Albiez-le-Vieux. Visit the former workshop and see how the knives used to be made, then watch the film about modern production in the Chambery factory.

Kid contest

© E. Moy / Ot des Houches

Moutiers and Tarentaise

Moutiers

Stretching along the Isère, Moutiers is a pleasant town with a busy pedestrian centre and plenty of shops. Fans of nature (notably canoe-kayak) have plenty to do. The historical tour of the town (follow the arrows) begins at the Tourist Office: go alone or with a guide.

SAINT PIERRE CATHEDRAL. *Open 9am-7pm. Guided tours for groups.* Next to the Tourist Office, in the former Archbishop's Palace, the cathedral is a blend of Lombard Romanesque, Gothic, Classical and Neo-Classical styles. There are some remarkable 13th-18thc. statues inside.

MUSEE DES TRADITIONS POPULAIRES Place Saint Pierre ✆ 04 79 24 12 28. *Open all year, Monday-Saturday: 9am-12 noon and 2pm-6pm. Admission: adult 2.30 € , concessions 1.50 € , under-15s free. Guided tours for groups and children's activities can be arranged: contact the museum.* The history of Tarentaise rural life is exhibited in 6 rooms, on 25 themes. Ethnographical, educational and fun; the kids' activities make sure that boring glass cases are a thing of the past.

MUSEE D'HISTOIRE ET D'ARCHEOLOGIE Tourist Office Information ✆ 04 79 24 04 23. *For admission, ask at the Tourist Office. Monday-Saturday 9am-12 noon and 2pm-6pm.* Darentasia (Moutiers) local history, from protohistory to 1860, displayed in 5 rooms. Includes the ex-voto to Mantounos, god of the Salin-les-Thermes springs, and the water-raising machinery from the Royal Saltworks.

Courchevel

Savoie's Conseil General launched Courchevel as a ski resort in 1946. In time, first French, then international celebrities were attracted, hoping to find better snow above 1,800m, and put off by temporary ski-lift problems at Mégève. The name brings to mind crowned heads and showbiz stars: Courchevel at 1,850m is out of reach for ordinary folk in more ways than one! The resort boasts a new floodlit 2km-sledging track, not to mention a total of 9 stars, 4 luxury stars and two gastronomic restaurants close to the celebrity arrival-point.

Méribel

Undoubtedly one of the Alps' most pleasant resorts, in the heart of the Three Valleys. The superb setting (not a high-rise block in sight) with chalets of varying sizes and shale-covered roofs is as well fitted-out as the ski-slopes. The resort is reached in stages, beginning with Allues village at 1,100m with its charming church and museum.

TUEDA LAKE AND RESERVE Maison de la Réserve ✆ 04 79 01 04 75. The majestic Vanoise reserve is perfect for hiking. Leave your car in the huge car park, and start with the shortest but most beautiful route which leads to Tueda mountain lake in its protected natural reserve. Look out for the bearded

Val Thorens, mountains

vulture in flight above the pines. You can discover 80 species of alpine plant, fish and even eat at the water's edge (9am-8pm) in this magical place, on your way up to Meribel. Toughies find the stamina for a 6-hour climb to the Saut refuge, having booked first for the night. 06 85 66 45 76.

Val-Thorens

Perched 2,300m above sea level, this is the peak of the Three Valleys and Europe's highest ski-resort. Six glaciers surround it; the snow is perfect and skiers of all levels can find the right track, with 7 passes at over 3,000m to choose from. The resort is modern, yet you find the traditional mountain atmosphere in its pedestrian streets. The main attraction is sport, of course, and among other facilities, a 'new generation' centre offers 20 fun activities.

ANNECY AND THE LAKE

Annecy

Few French towns are as lovely or as much-visited in summer. The Haute-Savoie's prefecture draws the tourists with its original medieval architecture lapped by the River Thiou, and a host of events like the Fêtes du Lac, a spectacular fireworks display on the lake (Annecy is in fact hoping to host the 2014 Winter Olympics). This is also a gastronomic centre, with some famous tables around the lake, including Marc Veyrat's at Veyrier-du-Lac, but you'll enjoy some excellent fish at one of the simpler inns or guingettes while drinking in the splendid scenery.

CHATEAU D'ANNECY Place du Château ✆ 04 50 33 87 30. *Open 10.30am-6pm every day June-September, otherwise 10am-12 noon and 2pm-5pm (closed Tuesday). Admission: adult 4.70 € , 12-25s 1.60 € , under-12s free.* Built from the 13th-15thc, the castle houses various art, archeological and natural collections in its Logis Nemours, with alpine lakes in the Tour Perrière. An exhibition of cinema animation is held during Annecy International Festival (June-September).

PALAIS DE L'ISLE 3, passage de l'Isle ✆ 04 50 33 87 30. *Same opening hours as the castle. Admission: adult 3.20 € , 12-25s 0.90 € , under-12s free.* These former prisons (12thc.) house the town history museum, their thick stone walls plunging into the water as though on a peninsula. A much-photographed site. Annecy Lake is 32 km of banks around 1,124,500,000 m3 of water from 41m to 78.7m deep. France's second-biggest natural lake holds first place for its sports and tourist facilities, and circular network of purifying drains and pumps.

COMPAGNIE DES BATEAUX DU LAC D'ANNECY 2, place au Bois ✆ 04 50 51 08 40. *www.annecy-croisieres.com. Grand lac boat trip: adult 10.50 € , child 7.40 € , under-5s free. Trip including lunch on board: from 41.70 €; dinner-dance from 44 €.* Discover the banks and villages in a relaxing guided trip on board the Allobroge, Belle Etoile, Cygne or Savoie. The MS Libellule invites you for lunch, or a dinner-dance, with cooking done on board by chef P. Chirat in the boat's modern kitchens.

Annecy Lake is 32 km of banks around 1,124,500,000 cubic metres of water from 41m to 78.7m deep. France's second-biggest natural lake holds first place for its sports and tourist facilities, and circular network of purifying drains and pumps.

Around the Lake

La Clusaz

The village's traditional Savoie style is intact; some of the chalets are 100 years old, and not a single concrete building has spoilt the village since 1950.

Col de la Forclaz

A fantastic site to the south of the lake, largely invaded by paragliders in summer.

Grand Bornand

This alpinists' meeting place was the start of a real expedition, with guides from the Bouchet Valley, in the early years of the last century. Later came ski-ing on the Chinaillon slopes discovered by a Swiss skier. The first ski-lift appeared in 1946, and the resort has been growing ever since. It has kept its traditions, though, in building, agriculture and local produce. Authenticity is the keynote.

MAISON DU PATRIMOINE ✆ **04 50 02 79 18**. *Open every day July & August (except Monday): 10am-12 noon and 3pm-5.30pm, Sunday, 4pm-7pm. Christmas-Easter, open during school holidays Monday-Friday: 3pm-7pm, outside holidays, Tuesday and Friday: 3pm-7pm. Admission: 2 €* . Housed in a typical 1830 chalet, this centre recalls life on a 19thc. mountain farm, houses thematic exhibitions and organises guided tours of Grand-Bornand village and its typical hamlet, Chinaillon.

Menthon-Saint-Bernard

CHATEAU DE MENTHON ✆ **04 50 60 12 05**. *May, June & September, open Thursday, Saturday and Sunday: 2pm-6pm. July & August, open every day: 12 noon-6pm. Admission: adult 6 € (7 € weekends); 6-15s 3 € (4 €).* The alpinists' patron Saint Bernard de Menthon was born here. The castle overlooks Annecy Lake, its massive shape and fortress exterior hiding 19thc. comfort inside. Weekends and public holidays, you meet characters in period costume, and a son et lumière with an excellent costumed show takes place in July and August.

Saint-Jorioz

FACTORY SHOP "VARAGES FRANCE" 850, route d'Albertville ✆ **04 50 32 03 08**. *www.varages.com. Open every day from 9am-6pm.* A good place to buy your tableware and decorative pottery. Oddments, old stocks, seconds but also market quality. New articles made every day in the Varages tradition (since 1695).

Sevrier

MUSEE DE LA CLOCHE RN508 ✆ **04 50 52 47 11**. *Open every day June-August: 10am-12 noon (except Sunday morning) and 2.30pm-6.30pm. Closed on Monday and from 5.30pm the rest of the year. Admission: adult 4.70 € , 6-16s 4 €* . Local foundry Paccard is widely known in bell-manufacturing circles. Audiovisual and documentary material tells you about the foundry's work, and the development of the bell from the 17thc onwards. On-site souvenir shop.

Talloires

The clientele is upmarket on the half-mountain golf course and in the hotels and restaurants around the protected bay. Not surprising, for the place is charming with its banks, old buildings, famous 17thc. Talloires Abbey (now a luxury hotel) and 11thc. priory.

BRIANÇONNAIS

Briançon

The 'highest town in Europe' is a busy place: prefecture (Hautes-Alpes) and mountaineering base; passing-point between five Alpine valleys, on the edge of the 'Grand Serre-Chevalier' ski slopes and Ecrins National Park. As a border town between France and Italy, Briançon is famous for its fortifications, notably Vauban's (late 17thc.), which are well worth the visit. The Ville-Haute (Upper Town) has kept its typically medieval structure, which you notice in the street layout and tall houses, old buildings, fountains, and alleyways.

MAISON DU PARC Place du Medecin General Blanchard ✆ **04 92 21 42 15**. *Open all year: July & August: 10am-1pm and 2pm-7pm. Other months: call for information about opening times. Admission free.* The park's environmental and cultural heritage is presented with scale models, photos and audiovisual material. You can visit at your own pace and learn a lot more about the exhibits with an audio-guide.

The resorts

Montgenèvre

The Montgenèvre pass has existed since before Julius Caesar's time; he went through it, as did Charlemagne and Louis XIII, much later. Napoleon had a road built as far as Italy, as the obelisk on the way out of the village shows: this Imperial symbol was put up in 1804. The major attractions are the climate (300 days of sunshine a year) and rich and varied flora, and the village itself is interesting, with its Notre Dame des Sept Douleurs Chapel and 18thc. Saint Maurice Church, which has a pretty steeple. A tunnel is currently being dug to reroute traffic to Italy, thus making the resort a lot more peaceful by 2006. That year, neighbours Turin and Sestrieres are hosting the Winter Olympics, so Montgenèvre should reap the benefits!

Serre-Chevalier

The Southern Alps' biggest and liveliest modern resort offers a range of sports activities. You can choose between three main centres in the same valley: 1,200 Briançon linked by the Prorel telecabin; 1,350 Chantemerle/Saint-Chaffrey - 1,400 Villeneuve - 1,500 le Monetier-les-Bains. Local hamlets (Le Bez and its fountain) are of historical interest, as is the centre of Monetier, a thermal site whose springs date back to antiquity.

ESPACE THALASSOFORME - LE SPORTING – La Salle les Alpes ✆ 04 92 24 77 82. *www.serrechethalasso.com. Open all year, by appointment. Closed mid May-mid June. Relaxation programme 350 € , Anti-Stress 580 € , Expectant Mums 290 € , Thalassothys 320 € . Sauna, jacuzzi, relaxation 16 € . Massages 29 €* . You find this Shape Up and Relax centre in the Serre Chevalier resort, 5 minutes from Briançon. Jean François and his team create a personalised programme for you, with professional skill and talent. Beauty and relaxation treatment is on offer in a warm and friendly atmosphere, with qualified physio-masseurs and beauticians: face and body treatment, sunbeds, depilation, massages, sauna, jacuzzi, relaxation gym, and several get-fit and anti-stress methods developed by the centre. Jean François and his team create a personalised programme for you, with professional skill and talent.

GAPENÇAIS

Gap

Gap is a smallish town with fewer than 40,000 inhabitants. Highest French prefecture (735m), it was once an important crossroads on the Roman road from Turin to the Rhone Valley. This part of the Alpes du Sud, between Provence and Dauphine, has a gentle climate with 300 days of sunshine a year, and an authentic way of life unffected by the many tourists.

OFFICE DE TOURISME Cours Frédéric Mistral ✆ 04 92 52 56 56. *www.ville-gap.fr.*

COMITE DEPARTEMENTAL DU TOURISME 8bis, rue Capitaine-de-Bresson ✆ 04 92 53 62 00. *www.hautes-alpes.net.*

GAP TOWN HALL 3, rue du Colonel Roux ✆ 04 92 53 24 24

Points of interest

Now a major tourist spot, Gap's old town centre has a pedestrian shopping precinct. The medieval housefronts, repainted in pastel tones, have kept their original framework and old-world charm. Wander through the lamp-lit alleys at dusk, and admire the oldest houses in the Place aux Herbes and Place Gavotte, behind the cathedral. Gap is also a traditional stage on the Tour de France (just after the Alpine passes), witness a number of cycle shops and tourists on bikes. All you need to know about the town's history and layout, and the main sites in the vicinity can be found in the leaflet "Invitation à visiter Gap", available free from the Tourist Office.

CATHEDRAL. The 70m belltower contains three bells known as Le Bourdon, Caroline-Napoléon and Pierrette. The cathedral was built in different -coloured local stone and pink marble, from 1867-1904, in Provencal Romanesque and Gothic style, and is dedicated to Our Lady. An imposing organ (above your head as you enter) and balconies with arcades and columns can be seen inside, along with the Saint-Arnoux altar, carved wooden angels (1720) stained glass and mosaics.

MUSEE DEPARTEMENTAL 6, avenue du Maréchal Foch ✆ 04 92 51 01 58. *Open all year. 1 July-15 September, every day: 10am-12 noon and 2.30pm-6.30pm. Out of season, every day except Tuesday: 2pm-5pm. Admission: 3 € , under-12s free.* The museum is housed in the Parc de la Pepinière, in a purpose-built early 20thc. building. The archaeological collection traces the history of human life in the Alps from prehistory to the Middle Ages. The Fine-Arts section contains 14th-20thc. European paintings and local 19thc. sculptor Jean-Esprit Marcellin's academic works, along with ceramics (Moustiers, Nevers, Manises) and contemporary art. Ethnography and Natural History collections, and a model of the 16thc. town complete the exhibits.

DOMAINE DE CHARANCE ✆ **04 92 51 21 79**. *www.ville-gap.fr. Guided tours May-September. Adults 4.50 €, under-12s free.* Follow signs from the Gap exit, direction Veynes. This huge 220ha. estate boasts a lake, forest and the Pic de Charance (1,903m) with its panoramic view of the Southern Alps. Footpaths and hiking trails are laid out for the walker, and there are many different plants and shrubs to discover. Don't miss the rose-garden in season, with its 800 varieties.

MAISON DU PARC Domaine de Charance ✆ **04 92 40 20 10**. *Open all year, every day: opening hours vary (documentation centre: 2pm-4.30pm).* Housed in one of the Château de Charance's outbuildings, this is the Ecrins National Park's H.Q., specialised in the mountain environment. Free literature is available, and books, postcards, video cassettes and T-shirts are on sale. Presentation films of the park environment are shown, so you know what to expect when setting off in your mountain boots.

LE SPORTING ESPACE THALASSO FORME ✆ **04 92 24 77 82.** *Website: www.serrechethalasso.com. Open all year by appointment.Closed mid-May to mid-June. Open in autumn by appointment. All-in relaxation treatment 360 €. Anti-stress 595 €. Expectant mums 290 €. Thalassothys 330 €. Sauna, jacuzzi, relaxation 17 €.Massage 32 €.* This centre is located in the Serre-Chevalier ski resort (1,400m) in the heart of the Ecrins National Park, 5 minutes from Briancon. Your stay in the Hautes-Alpes will be nicely rounded off by a few health and beauty sessions, after the mountain hikes or ski-ing. The setting is pleasant, and the welcome warm. Trained beauticians and physiotherapists take care of your face, body, legs, back and feet, and there are solar treatments, depilation, drainage, massage, sauna and jacuzzi, and a realaxation room. Specific sessions of cryotherapy (cold and pressure treatment) pressotherapy (for heavy legs) 'sympathicotherapy' for stress management, and others, can be booked over several days.

CHAMBERY AND BOURGET LAKE

Chambéry

Savoie's capital is surrounded by mountains: the Bauges and Chartreuse massifs in the east and south, with their respective natural parks and the majestic Belledonne massif further away in the Isère. The town has grown up in the narrowest part of the valley, and despite its slow growth (owing chiefly to lack of space), has played an important historical role. The House of Savoie, one of Europe's major dynasties, chose it as capital city, and its Dukes built a fortress, now housing the Conseil General and Prefecture. The Elephants' Fountain was put up in honour of General Boigne, native of Chambery and local benefactor. In the old town, flowers decorate the recently-renovated pedestrian conservation area, a pleasant place for a stroll.

CHATEAU DES DUCS DE SAVOIE. *Guided tours with Chambery lecturers.* The Dukes of Savoy lived here until moving to Turin in 1563, and the buildings date from the Middle Ages to the 19thc. Their former splendour all but disappeared in the fires of 1532, 1743, 1798 and 1997, although seen from the Place du Château, you still get a fair idea of what it was like.

SAINT FRANÇOIS DE SALES CATHEDRAL Place Métropole. *Open Monday-Saturday: 8am (9am out of season)-11.45 am and 1.30pm-6pm (2pm-5.30pm out of season).* The cathedral treasure is open 15 May-15 September on Saturdays: 3pm-5pm. The locals call it 'Metropole'. This former 15thc. Franciscan church built on 30,000 larch piles became a cathedral when Chambery gained its Bishopric in 1779.

FONTAINE DES ELEPHANTS. Known as 'Quatre-sans-Cul' (Four-without-an-Arse), these four elephants joined at the rump form the Savoy heraldic cross and symbolise local hero General Boigne's Indian career.

MUSEE DES BEAUX-ARTS Place du Palais de Justice ✆ **04 79 33 75 03**. *Open every day except Tuesday and public holidays: 10am-12 noon and 2pm-6pm. Adult 3.10 €.* 150 paintings dating back to the Quattrocento period are on display, including works by great Florentine, Venetian and Neopolitan artists. All the diversity of the Italian school from the 14th to 17th centuries can be seen in these Renaissance, Mannerist and Baroque works. The Chambery collection is the second finest in France, after the Louvre in Paris.

Round the lake

Aix-les-Bains

Aix's old-fashioned spa town image is changing; the traditional tea-dances still take place, but the town now offers sports and leisure activities in tune with a younger and more energetic clientele. Fitness, sailing or golf - there's a weekend for everyone.

AQUARIUM - MAISON DU LAC DU BOURGET Le Petit Port ✆ 04 79 61 08 22 *www.aquarium-lacdubourget.com. Open March-September, except Tuesday: 2pm-5pm (6pm in July and August). Admission: adult 5.25 €.* Don't miss this chance to see what goes on underwater - and on it. You can learn all about Bourget Lake; past, present and even future with the Great Lake Project (work in progress).

MUSEE FAURE 10, boulevard des Côtes ✆ 04 79 61 06 57. *Open every day except Tuesday and public holidays: 10am-12 noon and 1.30pm-6pm. Admission: adult 4 €.* A rich collection of 19thc. and early 20thc. paintings and sculptures. This exhibition traces the development of painting during the 19thc. including Impressionism and the modern period. Paintings by Monticelli, Corot, Cézanne, Pissaro, Degas, Bonnard and other masters are on view. There is also a beautiful Rodin room, and a reconstruction of Lamartine's room in the Perrier boarding house.

THERMES D'AIX-LES-BAINS Place Maurice Mollard ✆ 04 79 35 38 50. *May-October: Tuesday-Saturday. October-May: Wednesdays.* The thermal baths are not to be passed over, especially the Thermes Nationaux, where the antique Roman baths can still be admired.

AQUASCIENCE INSTITUT Domaine D'Aix-Marlioz ✆ 04 79 61 78 78. *www.thalassa.com. Open every day; times vary according to season. Packages fron 55 € in high season (two treatments per day).* Getting fit and looking great are the priority, with water therapy and beauty parlour combined in an attractive setting.

ESPACE BIEN-ETRE DES THERMES CHEVALLEY Route du Revard ✆ 08 10 44 33 32. *www.thermaix.com. Open all year, every day; Monday, Friday & Saturday: 2pm-8pm; Tuesday, Wednesday and Thursday: 2pm-6pm; Sunday: 10am-8pm. Subscription for 25 sessions, 200 € (15 € session). Weekly sessions available.* Pamper yourself at these superb modern thermal baths up on the town heights, and get back into shape with some help from the water-therapy professionals.

Le Bourget-du-Lac

Once a Gallo-Roman port, this peaceful town at the southern tip of the lake boasts a marvellous natural setting (you can watch the local fauna without disturbing it from two observation posts), fascinating history and several gastronomic restaurants. The Chambery-Aix airport is located here.

Canal de Savières

Links the boisterous Rhone to the calm waters of Bourget Lake over 4km. The lake actually fills up from the River Leysse in the south, and flows out into the Rhone via the canal in the north. Popular with canoeists and motorboats alike, it is pleasant to sail along in a *bateau mouche*. Admire pretty Chanaz village as you pass, and look out for beavers and herons at the mouth of the lake.

BATEAUCANAL Chanaz ✆ 04 79 54 51 80. *Port: 06 12 50 25 48 Or 06 12 84 71 92. Email: bateaucanal73@wanadoo.fr. Every day: 1 May-last Sunday in September, grand tour leaves Chanaz at 3pm (time varies in high season). Cost: petit tour (1hr) 11 €, grand tour (2hrs 15mins) 15 €* Bateaucanal offers two itineraries on the Canal de Savières: the shorter (Petit Parcours) goes round in a loop on the Rhone or the lake; the longer (Grand Parcours) follows the whole canal. Trips are made on three boats; you can organise your meals on board the 'flagship' Savoyard .

Lac du Bourget

A vast project thought up by the local and regional authorities is currently underway, with the aim of renovating the lake's environmental and historical beauty, rather neglected over the last decades. Although a natural part of the landscape, its banks needed reorganising and the water quality left much to be desired. Tourists were voting with their feet. Yet Le Bourget is one of Natures's marvels. The 19thc. Romantic poets fell in love with it, especially in the mist (see the statue of Lamartine on the northern banks). It is also France's biggest natural lake (4,400 ha), situated at a height of 232m, and 145m deep. The waters contain over 30 varieties of fish including roach, perch, trout and charr.

COMPAGNIE DES BATEAUX DU LAC DU BOURGET ET DU HAUT-RHONE Grand Port ✆ 04 79 88 92 09. *www.gwel.com.* Set off on France's biggest lake and sail up the Savieres canal aboard the Hydraaix or the superyacht Alain Prud'homme. You'll see rare flora and fauna and sublime landscapes, all part of an exceptional heritage. Choose your own trip, with lunch or dinner on a modern boat with top of the range facilities and excellent cooking.

GRENOBLE AND CHARTREUSE

Grenoble

Prefecture of the Isère department, Grenoble used to be frequently and heavily flooded by the River Isère which flows through the town. The river was eventually diverted, a colossal undertaking lasting several centuries until the 1800s. Grenoble was thought of as a fortress-town until the 19thc., when cement and paperworks sprang up, and electricity brought an industrial boom (electricity was first transported in France between Grenoble and Vizille). The town developed quickly, with little building cohesion, noticeable when you look down at the town's various quarters from the Bastille belvedere. Today Grenoble is a university as well as an industrial town.

BASTILLE. You need stamina to climb up to the Bastille, which is why there's now a cable-car available! The panorama from the top is breathtaking. This is Grenoble's symbolic monument, and is to be completely renovated.

TELEPHERIQUE de Grenoble-Bastille Quai Stéphane-Jay ✆ 04 76 44 33 65. *www.telepherique-grenoble.com. Open every day, February-December. Annual closing January. Cost (round trip): adult 5.70 € , student 4.60 € , child 3.90 € , under-5s and over-75s free.* Put up in 1934, this was the first urban cable-car in France. 210,000 visitors use it, and 300,000 go up on foot, making it Grenoble's most popular tourist site.

MULTIPASS'GRENOBLE 14, rue de la République ✆ 04 76 42 41 41. *www.grenoble-Isère.info. This passport costs 10 €, 14.50 €/24h + 7 museums, or 23 €/48 hours, and gives you admission to one museum, a ticket for the little tourist train, a round trip on the Bastille cable-car, a guided tour in French or English from the Tourist Office, unlimited use of public transport (one day) and a car-park cheque for 2 € (museum or Place de Verdun).* Convenient!

MUSEE DE GRENOBLE 5, Place de Lavalette ✆ 04 76 63 44 44. *www.museedegrenoble.fr. Open every day, except Tuesday: 10am-6.30pm. Admission: adult 5 € , concessions 3 € , student 2 € . Free 1st Sunday of the month.* Grenoble Museum houses some impressive collections: Veronese, Canaletto, Rubens, Gauguin, Corot, Matisse, Fernand Léger, Picasso, Chagall, Miro, Van Doesburg and Kupka, to mention only the best-known. French and foreign contemporary art is also included, with newly-refitted rooms for the 20thc. paintings.

MUSEE DAUPHINOIS 30, rue Maurice-Gignoux ✆ 04 76 85 19 01. *www.musee-dauphinois.fr. Open every day, except Tuesday. Admission free. Guided tours for groups by appointment.* This ethnological museum relates the Dauphiné's history, with its local communities and the traditional Alpine way of life. There is an exhibition of skis throught the centuries, going back to prehistory.

MUSEE DE LA RESISTANCE ET DE LA DEPORTATION 14, rue Hébert ✆ 04 76 42 38 53. *Open every day except Tuesday from 9am to 12am and from 2pm to 6pm. Book up for guided tour. In July and August open from 10am to 7pm. Free entrance.* The museum is first of all dedicated to the part of French Resistance in the departement. 5 topics are evoked such as getting into resistance, underground forces, the restoration of the Republic and value of the French Resistance. Some temporary exhibitions occured from time to time.

MUSEE DES AUTOMATES 12, rue des Arts ✆ 04 76 43 33 33. *Open every day: 2pm-6.30pm.* This wonderful world of automatons and mechanical music will enchant you. Barrel organ, puppets, animated tableaux and shadowgraphs, with their history and techniques explained.

Chamrousse

Chamrousse resort is only half-an-hour from Grenoble. It hosted the Alpine events in the 1968 Olympics, and is now a snowboard paradise, snowboarders making up a quarter of its visitors.

Vizille

On 21 July 1788, Claude Périer, manufacturer, hosted the Dauphiné States in his château. The main decision reached was to request an assembly of the States General. This was duly held, and sparked off the French Revolution. The rest, as they say, is history.

MUSEE DE LA REVOLUTION FRANCAISE Place de la Liberation ✆ 04 76 68 07 35 *Open every day except Tuesday: 10am-12.30pm and 1.30pm-6pm. Admission free.* This is the only museum in France specifically dedicated to the French Revolution.

La Chartreuse

This small pre-alpine massif has no major peaks, despite its steep cliffs and deep gorges, but it offers some interesting hikes. Discover the mysterious Chartreuse liqueur which originated in the rural villages at the foot of the Voironnais mountains.

PARC REGIONAL DE CHARTREUSE Maison du Parc - Place de la Mairie - SAINT-PIERRE-DE-CHARTREUSE ✆ 04 76 88 75 20. *Fax: 04 76 88 75 30. Email: pnr.chartreuse@wanadoo.fr. Open all year except the weekend.*

Entremont-le-Vieux

MUSEE DE L'OURS DES CAVERNES EN CHARTREUSE ✆ 04 79 26 29 87. *Open all year, summer 10am-12.30pm and 2.30pm-6.30pm. Adult 4.40 €.* Plunge into the bowels of the earth and the beginnings of history on the track of the Cave Bear. In 1988, two pot-holers in the Balme cave discovered a gallery closed off for over 33,000 years. It contained paleontological treasure: the remains of over 10,000 cave bear skeletons. The bears were probably born, lived and died in that cave during a period of 100,000 years. You can visit the cave today with no fear of disturbing this impressive mammal's hibernation.

Saint-Pierre-de-Chartreuse

Genuine mountain village, 900m above sea-level, and the best-equipped of the massif's ski-resorts. You can do alpine and cross-country ski-ing, snowboarding, snowshoe-hiking and paragliding. In summer, 270km of paths are marked out for walkers.

MAISON DU PARC - Place de la Mairie ✆ 04 76 88 75 20. *Fax: 04 76 88 75 30. Email: pnr.chartreuse@wanadoo.fr*

MUSEE DE LA GRANDE-CHARTREUSE La Correrie ✆ 04 76 88 60 45. *Open Easter to November. June-September 9.30am-6.30pm. Admission: adult 3 €.* Attached to the Grande-Chartreuse Monastery (closed to the public), this museum shows you monastic life, by means of photos, scale models, audiovisual montages and recorded spoken commentaries. The building has not changed since the monks' day.

Voiron

CAVES ET DISTILLERIE DE LA CHARTREUSE 10, boulevard Kofler ✆ 04 76 05 81 77. *Open every day Easter-November: 9am-11.30am and 2pm-6.30pm. Admission and tasting free.* Display and sale of products onsite. Chartreuse liqueur is made here, from 130 plants. The recipe is known only to the monks, though it does contain balm, angelica and gentian. These are the world's biggest liqueur cellars; both visit and tasting are free. A 3-D film shows you the distillery. Products on display and on sale.

LAKE LEMAN

Lake Geneva is an inaccurate name, referring only to the western part of the lake round the French Yvoire peninsula. The Haute-Savoie (south bank) and Swiss Vaud canton (north bank) are left out, and could be offended. Let's talk about Lake Léman, then, almost an inland sea, 73km long and 14km wide; with a complex wind regime bringing both intense calm and violent storms. The Swiss-French lake has a tradition of navigational co-operation and exchange, and its tourist scenery, ports, beaches and museums, and gastronomic resources make it extremely attractive to visitors.

Evian

Known the world over for its mineral water, this international resort recalls Cannes or Miami, quiet in winter but dazzling in season. There is a luxury hotel, golf-course, modern thermal baths, exclusive pleasure-craft harbour - not to mention a Swiss-French lake offering the very best in leisure activities.

USINE D'EMBOUTEILLAGE DES EAUX MINERALES D'EVIAN Plaine d'Amphion ✆ 04 50 26 93 23. *Guided tours 16 June-12 September, from Evian. Cost: adult 1.70 €.* Enquiries in the exhibition hall, rue Nationale. At the bottling factory, you learn the history of Evian mineral water, and discover the bottling assembly line up to the final dispatching by train to the rest of France and the world.

Thonon-les-Bains

The town has plenty of interesting monuments. Some of them recall the time when the region was governed by the Dukes of Savoy, from Turin: the Hôtel-Dieu is Tuscan and the Town Hall Sardinian in style. Saint Hippolyte Church is typically Baroque, richly-decorated inside. The many fountains and washing-places are also worth looking at.

EGLISE BAROQUE SAINT-HIPPOLYTE. Enquiries at the Tourist Office ✆ 04 50 71 55 55. *(Currently undergoing restoration work).* Built in the 12thc. above a Romanesque crypt, reshaped in the 17thc. under Louis XIV, this church is remarkably decorated in Baroque style, with some exuberant frescoes. Recently some more ancient frescoe have come to light. One of the most beautiful works of Baroque architecture in Haute-Savoie and Savoie.

MUSEE DU CHABLAIS Chateau de Sonnaz ✆ 04 50 71 56 34. *Open late April-early October, Wednesday-Sunday: 2.30pm-6.30pm. July & August every day (mornings too, 10am-12 noon). Admission: 2 € , under-8s free.* Exhibition of regional traditions in a pleasant, flowery setting.

CHATEAU DE RIPAILLE ✆ 04 50 26 64 44. *Open except December and January: 10am-12 noon and 2pm-6pm. Admission: adult 6 €* Ripaille is known for the art of living and its good wines. The castle interior, gardens and arboretum are all superb and well worth the visit

Yvoire

This famous 'flowery village' adds to the lake's charm, with its long-preserved architecture. The town was fortified round the castle in the 13thc., and has kept its medieval look, especially two of the gates. The houses are mostly 18thc. All this is thanks to Paul Jacquier, restaurant-owner and mayor from 1945-1995, who spearheaded the campaign to preserve local heritage. It is best to visit Yvoire out of season, which also gives you a better choice of restaurant. Don't forget to see the charming little port.

LE LABYRINTHE - JARDIN DES CINQ SENS Rue du Lac ✆ 04 50 72 88 80. *www.jardin5sens.net. Private garden open every day mid April-mid October. In spring: 11am-6pm; summer: 10am-7pm; autumn: 1pm-5pm. Admission varies according to season: adult 8 € /9 € , under-16s 4.50 € /5.50 € , families 20.50 € /23.50 €* . Amazing gardens in the heart of the medieval city near the castle. Based on the traditional Middle-Ages garden, with a maze on the theme of the five senses where you can meditate in peace.

VIVARIUM Rue de l'Eglise ✆ 04 50 72 82 28. *Open all year except November. Easter-September, every day: 10am-12.30pm and 2pm-8pm. Out of season, every day except Monday; 2pm-5.30pm. Admission: adult 7 € , child 5 €* . 200 reptiles (60 different species) including crocodiles, turtles, iguanas and snakes can be observed in this magnificent vivarium.

THE MERCANTOUR

Mercantour National Park

Covers two departments: Alpes-de-Haute-Provence and Alpes-Maritimes. The heart of the park (68,500ha) comprises 7 valleys: Roya, Bevera, La Vesubie, Tinee, Haut-Var/Cians, Verdon and Ubaye. Despite being in the mountains, the park has a Mediterranean feel, and this double allegiance makes for very varied flora and fauna. You find both olive-trees and larches, though at different altitudes. All in all, there are over 2,000 plant species catalogued here. The fauna is as diverse: golden eagles, chamois, marmots, and controversial wolves. The park is twinned with its Italian neighbour across the border. Apart from its natural attractions, it contains one of Europe's richest sets of rupestrian carvings in the Vallée des Merveilles, a listed historical monument.

Barcelonette

This little town was founded in 1231 by Raymond Bérenger IV of Barcelona, and its influence was to go far beyond the Ubaye. In 1812, some of its citizens decided to go in search of pastures new. They chose to take their commercial and technical skills with silk and wool to Mexico. Barcelonette's historic centre is full of superb houses, mostly built between 1880 and 1930 by local boys who made good in the textile business in Mexico, and which sparked off a new type of urban development, like in the watering towns.

MUSEE DE LA VALLEE 10, avenue de la Libération - Villa la Sapinière ✆ 04 92 81 27 15. *Open all year. Admission: adult 3.30 €.* This charming museum illustrates the links between Barcelonette and Mexico, which developed after the Arnaud brothers settled there in 1804. There are some superb Fine-Arts collections (Jean and Marie Caire-Tonoir, Pierre Michel, Demoiselles Reynaud, Gilles Aillaud)

photographic exhibitions, pre-Colombian and Mexican popular art objects, the story of Emile Chabrand's round-the-world tour and temporary exhibitions (Mexican costumes, contemporary art). The uncommon history of a town and a valley that went into exile in order to bring life back to its own countryside.

Ubaye

Around Barcelonette, it feels a little like Provence and a lot like the mountains. A wide range of sports activities is on offer: mountain-bike descents, rock-climbing, ski-ing (at Pra-Loup or Super-Sauze) and hiking, as well as whitewater sports. For heritage-seekers there is Tournoux Fort, Barcelonette and the 'Mexicans' Houses', and Jausiers Church.

Tende and the Vallée des Merveilles

At the foot of Mont Bego (2,872m above sea-level) on the edge of the Mercantour Park, the valley owes its name to thousands of rupestrian carvings on stone blocks, dating back to the Bronze Age. The best way to see them is with a guide.

Enquiries at Tende Tourist Office (04 93 04 73 71) Bureau des Guides (04 93 04 67 00) Refuge des Merveilles (04 93 04 64 64) and Refuge de Fontanalbe (04 93 04 89 19).

MUSEE DES MERVEILLES Avenue du 16 Septembre 1947 ✆ 04 93 04 32 50. *Open all year, every day in July and August. Closed Tuesday out of season. Admission: adults 4,55 € . Free first Sunday of the month.* Before seeing the carvings, visit the museum. Three thematic exhibitions help you understand this valley: natural history and geology; archeology and rupestrian carvings; and the Roya Valley's popular arts and traditions. Guided tours of the valley are organised in season, and there is also a research laboratory for rupestrian art.

OISANS

Le Bourg-d'Oisans

MAISON DU PARC (Oisans sector) Rue Gambetta ✆ 04 76 80 00 51. Bourg-d'Oisans is situated on a wide plain on the edge of Ecrins National Park, where Oisans valleys and massifs meet.

MUSEE DES MINERAUX ET DE LA FAUNE DES ALPES Place de l'Eglise ✆ 04 76 80 27 54. *Closed from november 15th to december 15th. Open all days from 2 pm to 6 pm, and 1st of july to 31 august from 10 am to 6pm. Adults : 4,60.* This museum contains an extensive mineral collection, and also an exhibition of alpine fauna; you learn about extinct, rare and protected species while hearing their calls and cries around you. A third section deals with paleontology, displaying those extinct species that once inhabited the Oisans.

MAISON DES ALPAGES ✆ 04 76 80 19 09. *Open all year. July & August: 10am-12 noon and 3pm-7pm. Other months, 2pm-6pm. Closed Wednesday.* This centre deals with the past, present and future of the alpage, or mountain pasture. The realities of pastoral life, the environment and its traditions are explained; vital if you want to understand the region. Not to be missed.

Alpe-d'Huez

Some brochures would have us believe it only snows here at night! Be that as it may, Alpe-d'Huez is the Isère's top resort. Known as the Sunshine Isle, it began to develop in 1936, and now offers a complete range of sports and leisure activities, with over 2,200m of ski-ing on some slopes (Sarenne, 16km), quality accommodation facilities and efficient ski-lifts! You can also access the Sarenne Glacier via the funitel, which can transport up to 1,000 people per hour. A new floodlit sledge slope has been set up for evening sledgers, and you can try the sport with family and friends at Butte de L'Eclose (open Tuesday and Thursday evenings: 5.30pm-7.30pm), reached by chairlift (1.50 € or 5 € for 5 trips). Sledges not supplied.

The Pistes de l'Alpe d'Huez have developed a system installed on tracked vehicles, which interprets the land in 3D, assessing the quantity of snow pisted down under the caterpillar tracks and guarranteeing the driver's security by identifying danger points. Coming soon: pisted snow in real time on the Internet!

To sum up: 238 km of slopes at all levels, over 2,210m of height difference, making 3,000 skiable hectares.

A few satellite resorts and mountain villages :

Auris-en-Oisans (Tourist Office 04 76 80 13 52) : 17 lifts, 20 slopes (2 black, 7 red, 6 blue and 5 green) over 35 km. 8 km cross-country; sledging; snowshoes.

Oz-en-Oisans (Tourist Office 04 76 80 78 01) and Vaujany (Tourist Office 04 76 80 72 37) : two neighbouring villages with deux villages with 20 lifts, 35 slopes (3 black, 10 red, 13 blue et 9 green) over 63 km. Villard-Reculas (Tourist Office 04 76 80 45 69) : closest to the Alpe, with 7 lifts, 7 slopes (1 black, 2 red, 3 blue and 1 green) over 20 km.

OFFICE DE TOURISME ALPE D'HUEZ Place Paganon ✆ 04 76 11 44 44. *Open every day in season: 8.45am-7pm. Spring & autumn: 9am-12.30pm and 2.30pm-6pm. Closed weekends and public holidays. http://www.alpedhuez.com.*

MUSEE D'HUEZ ET DE L'OISANS Route de la Poste ✆ 04 76 11 21 74. *Open December-April, July & August every day: 10am-12 noon and 3pm-7pm, except Saturday. Admission: 2 €* . The museum houses the exhibition on Oisans 'From mountain village to international tourist resort', and features Brandes-en-Oisans archeological site (12th-14thc. silver mines).

MUSEE RURAL Auris-en-Oisans ✆ 04 76 80 15 25. *Open in july and august, sunday to friday from 3pm to 6 pm. Free admission* Une étable voûtée dans une vieille maison de montagne sert de cadre à ce petit musée qui expose de multiples objets de la vie d'autrefois : ustensiles agricoles, mobilier, objets du quotidien…

Deux-Alpes

It all began with some Grenoble students, who were looking for a cheap site with good sport. The local authorities came up with 'the Two Alps', a new partnership between Venosc and Mont-de-Lans villages. The resort mushroomed, haphazardly, but enough to shake up neighbouring Alpe!

MAISON DE LA MONTAGNE ET DU PATRIMOINE 20, av. de la Muzelle ✆ 04 76 79 53 15. *Open afternoons: 2pm-6pm in winter; every day: 10am-12 noon and 3pm-7pm in summer. Admission: adult 2 € , 5-8s 1 €* . This museum in a renovated traditional house contains sections on flora, fauna, and Oisans geology, but also mountain sports, with plenty of scale models and photos.

MAISON DES TRADITIONS ET DES ARTS ✆ 04 76 80 23 97. *Same opening hours as the Maison de la Montagne. Admission: adult 2 €*. Discover Oisans village history in this renovated presbytery, where a typical period interior has been reconstructed and can be visited. There is also a section devoted to the famous Oisans peddlars who left the region to sell their wares and were away for months at a time.

PUB WINDSOR 70 Avenue de la Muzelle ✆ 04 76 79 22 95. *Open all week: 8.30am-2am in season, 8.30am- 12 noon and 4pm-9pm out of season. Internet access.* This 25-year-old pub offers tapas and a huge selection of whiskies and beers as well as the usual drinks. Owner Franck chooses the music (jazz, blues, rock); relaxed and cheerful atmosphere guarranteed.

BAR THE RED FROG 1, place de l'Alpe de Venosc ✆ 04 76 79 23 28. *Open 7am-2am non stop. Open all week, including low season. Bar brasserie. www.theredfrog.net.* Run by Paddy, who speaks English and French and has personalised his bar. There is TV football (English and international) and food in the same style: English breakfasts and traditional recipes, grills, Mexican chicken, burgers and kebabs at attractive prices, with Happy Hour from 5pm to 7pm. Internet access and laptop rental (1hr=5 euros). Plasma screens for DVD concerts are planned for future relaxation.

MONT BLANC COUNTRY

This legendary country of soaring peaks is dominated by the glorious Mont Blanc, Europe's highest point (between the textbook 4,807m and the scientists' 4,810m) but has plenty of other treasures too.

Chamonix

This mythical town attracted the first great mountaineers (Balmat, Paccard and Saussure, and Englishman Whymper, among others). Today, Chamonix is still an ideal base for climbing the Mont Blanc massif, but also a tourist town of luxury hotels, stifling during the crowded summer season.

MUSEE ALPIN La Résidence - 89, av. Michel Croz ✆ 04 50 53 25 93. *Open every day: 2pm-7pm (also 10am-12 pm July & August and school holidays). Admission: adult 4 € , 12-18s 1.50 €* . Housed in the former Chamonix Palace built at the turn of the last century, the Alpine Museum retraces two centuries of the valley's life, from the first trips to the 'Savoy Glaciers' to the creation of a winter sports season. Furniture, everyday objects, mountaineering equipment, paintings, engravings, posters, cards, crystals, etc. are on display.

TELEPHERIQUE DE L'AIGUILLE DU MIDI 100, Parking de l'Aiguille-du-Midi - Vallée-Blanche ✆ 04 50 53 30 80 *(enquiries)/08 36 68 00 67 (bookings). Cost: round trip, adult 36 €, child 25.20 €. Family (2 adults, 2 children) 108 €. Open all year, depending on the weather.* The most striking site in the French Alps gives everyone the chance to climb the Aiguille du Midi slopes (2,747m) in 20 minutes. At the northern piton, take the walkway towards the central piton and a pause, where (for a fee) a lift takes you to the famous 3,842m level with its unforgettable view of Europe's giant. Then you take a new cable-car over the Vallée Blanche, flying above the glacier towards Italy.

MONTENVERS TRAIN 35, place de la Mer de Glace ✆ 04 50 53 12 54. *Open all year. Tickets: round trip, adult 14.50 €.* From Chamonix, Montenvers rack railway (running since 1908) takes you to the foot of the Mer de Glace, Europe's biggest live glacier, in 20 minutes. The Montenvers site has ice grottoes, galleries with crystals, a museum of Alpine fauna and a Grand Hôtel.

LE REFUGE PAYOT 255, rue du Docteur Paccard ✆ 04 50 53 16 86 *Website: www.refugepayot.com* Come and visit the owners of the 'refuge Payot'. You will be given advice concerning finer local specialities and delicatessen (cheese, ham, Savoy's wine, brandy sweets and cakes). Try the grelot sausage or their delicious bilberry pie. A new shop has just opened in front of Bellevue cable car.

SNELL 104/118, rue Paccard ✆ 04 50 53 02 17. *www.cham3s.com.* Mountain sports specialist for over 30 years. Experienced in alpine walking, climbing, ski-ing and snowboard, cross-country, trekking and trail running. Top of the range equipment on sale. Other addresses: COQUOZ 297/306 Rue Paccard 04 50 53 15 12 - SPORTS ALPINS 7, place de Chamonix Sud 04 50 53 13 60.

LA TRACE 123, avenue Michel-Croze ✆ 04 50 53 08 60. The ideal boutique for gift-shopping, located in Chamonix centre. On the ground floor, you find souvenirs: postcards, glass balls with 'magic' snow scenes featuring Mont Blanc and Chamonix, fun gadgets for all ages, and crockery decorated with traditional Savoy motifs. In the basement is a collection of soft toys (including stuffed marmots) and children's games in general, and on the first floor, clocks, paintings and posters to help you recall the magnificent Mont Blanc landscapes. The sales staff are friendly and keen to help you.

CHEVERNY 126, rue du Docteur Paccard ✆ 04 50 53 03 74. *www.savoie-specialite.com.* A large store on three floors, specialising in kitchenware and interior decor, typical Savoyard utensils and accessories for regional cooking, and wooden furniture.

Contamines - Montjoie

The Contamines are just how you picture mountains. A real village with its Baroque church and the Mont Blanc range behind. Heaps of snow in winter, and in summer, flowers, varying shades of green, and white peaks on top.

Combloux

One of those resorts that refused to put up concrete, preferring its traditions to property development. The result is unspoiled vistas of fir trees and mountain pastures with superb panoramic views. Combloux's chalets, farms and markets attract families and groups of friends, looking for the genuine article, but also for comfort and activity, be it ski-ing, snowshoe hiking or dancing. Saint-Nicolas Church steeple is typically Baroque; visit it with a Heritage Guide if you'd like some inside information.

TOURIST OFFICE ✆ **04 50 58 60 49.** *Fax : 04 50 93 33 55. www.combloux.com. Bookings: resa@combloux.com.* A few kilometres from Megeve, this charming mountain village (1,200m) has a marvellous panoramic view across the Mont Blanc range. Sledge rides, farm produce tasting and guided tour of granite-hewing site on offer.

MEUBLES SAVOYARDS 1199, chemin Passerands ✆ **04 50 58 65 52.** *meublessavoyards@wanadoo.fr.* Typical Savoy furniture and crafts, kitchenware and decoration.On-site hand-made personalised wooden furniture.

Les Houches

Historically known for top male competition ski-ing, thanks to its famous slope called la Verte, but which is of course very black.

MUSEE MONTAGNARD ✆ **04 50 54 54 74**. *Open all year except October. Opening times vary according to the season. Admission: adult 3 €.* The association 'Les Houches dans l'temps' has recreated a period living environment in one of the valley's oldest houses, with bedroom, kitchen, dairy etc. Thoroughly detailed and educational. There is also a bienniel exhibition, always well-researched and presented.

LES SAINT-BERNARD DU PAYS DU MONT-BLANC 223, chemin des Vorziers ✆ **04 50 47 23 60**. *Open July & August: 10am-11.30am and 2.30pm-6.30pm. Out of season: 10am-11.30am and 2pm-5.30pm. Closed Sunday morning and Monday morning.* The Saint Bernard has a place in all our hearts, but watch out! Behind this large and gentle cuddly toy is a real mountain rescuer, with his famous little barrel instead of a collar. Renee and Jean-Pierre breed short-haired Saint Bernards in a pleasant country setting, and are happy to share their love of the dog with you.

LA DIOSAZ GORGES. Enquiries ✆ 04 50 47 21 13. Listed site. These gorges in the bowels of the mountain owe their reputation to some impressive cliffs, where the Diosaz River cascades in magnificent waterfalls through the middle. The path from the village runs alongside the torrent at first, then overlooks the waterfall. Several passages have been carved in the rock and footbridges cross the water, enabling you to follow the gorges for almost 1.5 km.

Megeve

What can we say about Megeve? Its reputation as a jet-set resort is known to everyone. The town has kept its old centre, with its warm and lively partly-pedestrian streets...and their luxury shop signs.

MUSEE DU HAUT VAL D'ARLY 88, ruelle du Vieux-Marche ✆ 04 50 91 81 00. *Open every day except Sunday: 2.30pm-6.30pm. Admission: adult 3.20 € , child 2.50 €* . You might think that Megeve is rather too'genuine' to be real, unlike so many charming time-mellowed mountain villages. Yet the town started life as a simple hamlet in the Haut Val d'Arly, and has its history, pastoral traditions and authentic homes, like the old farm where you can still find an agricultural and crafts heritage deeply shaken by the discovery of 'white gold'.

AU SOLI 33, rue de la Poste ✆ 04 50 91 97 20. The shop's owner Jean-Luc Freundorfer continues the family cabinet-making tradition inspired by the Alps (Bavarian, Austrian and Savoy designs), making and restoring fine wooden furniture and adding his personal touch to the premises. Exquisite craftsmanship.

Passy

Set between green countryside and snowy slopes, Passy is chiefly interesting for its Notre-Dame-de-Toute-Grace church, which has housed a modern art museum since 1950.

NOTRE DAME DE TOUTE GRACE. Built on the Assy plateau in the 1920s for the sanatorium population, the church's stone and exposed columns put you in mind of a solid mountain chalet. Its soaring 28-m spire draws the eye to the mountains, then the sky. The works of art signed Bonnard, Braque, Chagall, Leger, Matisse and Rouault were collected by the Savoie architect Novarina are on sacred themes, proving that religious art has its modern and contemporary forms.

Saint-Gervais-les Bains

This is a reputed watering-place, but also a big ski and summer holiday resort at the foot of Mont Blanc.

TRAMWAY DU MONT-BLANC Rue de la Gare ✆ 04 50 47 51 83. *Return ticket Le Fayet-Nid d'Aigle : adults : 24 €* . In winter, the tram carries skiers to the Houches slopes, but you must take it in summer to the Nid d'Aigle (Eyrie) at the foot of Bionassay Glacier. The tram is in fact a sweet little rack train that snakes through forests and prairies to the Gouter Needle Peak. Make sure you book in advance in summer, as it's likely to be full.

THERMES DE SAINT GERVAIS Parc Thermal - LE FAYET ✆ 04 50 47 54 54. *www.thermes-st-gervais.com.* Saint-Gervais mainly treats skin and respiratory problems, but you can also get back into shape, a real pleasure in this mountain setting.

SERRE-PONÇON AND THE EMBRUNAIS

Serre-Ponçon Lake is Europe's biggest reservoir, with 80km of banks, and deep blue waters that reflect the sky. It spreads its 3,000ha. of water over the Durance and Ubaye valleys, magnificent with its wild natural scenery and surrounding mountain peaks. Apart from this exceptional setting, there are plenty of water sports on offer.

Embrun

This is the southern part of Ecrins National Park. Once unattractive black countryside gullied by erosion, Embrun's fortunes changed with the building of the Serre-Ponçon dam from 1948-1960.

Rousset

MUSEOSCOPE DU LAC Belvedere de Serre-Ponçon ✆ 04 92 54 50 00. *Open February-October, every day in July & August. Admission: adult 7.90 €.* Overlooking Serre-Ponçon dam and reservoir, the museum tells you about the dam's construction and the villages it swallowed up. Local produce is on sale in the museum shop, and you'll find works by the department's main writers in the bookshop.

Savines-le-Lac

BATEAU PROMENADE DU LAC DE SERRE-PONCON ✆ **04 92 44 26 88.** *Open 1 March-15 December. July & August: every day at 10am, 2.30pm and 4.15pm.* Extra trips in busy periods. Cost: adult 11 €. Two pretty barges, La Carline (118 seats) and Le Courlis (50 seats) take you on a guided tour of the reservoir. Peaceful and pleasant.

ECOLE FRANCAISE DE VOILE Chemin Chadenas ✆ **04 92 43 00 02**. All water sports can be tried in complete safety on Serre-Ponçon reservoir, from age 7; there is also a sailing club for the 5-6s.

VANOISE

Vanoise National Park was the very first in France. Created on 6 July 1963, so as to protect the endangered Alps ibex, it contains 28 Savoie villages on 45,000ha. Apart from ibex, there are 2,000 kinds of flower, 100 bird species (golden eagles and rock partridges) and some big mammals, like the chamois. To see those famous ibex, go to Pralognan-la-Vanoise, resort and park gate, and the ideal base for setting off on a hike.

PARC NATIONAL DE LA VANOISE 135, rue du Docteur Julliand ✆ **04 79 62 30 54.** *www.vanoise.com*

Ibex

The French Alps are home to over 20 000 ibex (there were only about 50 of them left in the early 19thc.). If you leave the beaten path, and are extremely quiet - and lucky - you can spot them on the steep rocky slopes. These bovines reach 1.10m in height; the males have pale brown fur, and the females are greyish-brown. You can recognise them by their horns which curve backwards, and continue growing, so the animal's age can be determined from their length. Male horns may reach 1m!

Champagny-en-Vanoise

This charming mountain village, reached by dizzy gullied paths rising from the Tarentaise Valley, has kept all its warmth and authenticity, despite the coming of the tourist hordes. Cows summer in the 'upper' village, where the traditional wood-and-stone houses ares steeped in an olden-days atmosphere so pleasant you won't want to leave! In winter, the resort is linked to extensive ski-slopes at La Plagne and Paradiski, while in summer, hikers find wonderful scenery and a rich variety of flora and fauna.

SAINT SIGISMOND CHURCH Champagny-en-Vanoise. *Open every day except Monday from 3pm-6pm. Guided tours available (Chemins du Baroque); enquire at the Tourist Office (04 79 55 06 55).* This superb church balances on a gypoum rock between Champagny and Champagny-le-Haut, and is interesting both as a spiritual refuge and from an artistic point of view. Its twisted columns, hosts of cherubs and gilded wooden characters are typically Baroque.

Pralognan-la-Vanoise

This is the world's end, far from the built-up concrete resorts; a natural setting where ibex come down the mountain in the spring, and traditional habits and customs prevail. Come to Pralognan-la-Vanoise before dawn, park in the Ibex car-park and wait in the cool early morning for the sun to rise over the horns of the village's monumental statue. You can ski, hike, climb, simply rest, or even follow a personal coaching programme here, to help you unwind and get your priorities right. In this charming village in the wilds, that doesn't seem impossible!

PARC NATIONAL DE LA VANOISE ✆ **04 79 62 30 54. Open in summer only.**

TELEPHERIQUE DU MONT BOCHOR ✆ **04 79 08 70 07.** ts the village eyrie, 2,000m above sea-level, overlooking Pralognan. The cable-car takes you to the ski slopes in winter and to the starting-point of your hike in summer. It also gives you an amazing view of the Vanoise glaciers and surrounding country.

Termignon-la-Vanoise

Covering a third of Vanoise Park with its 17, 834 ha., this is the third biggest French commune in terms of surface area. It contains 16 glaciers and 63 peaks over 3,000m, and has been here since the Middle Ages. The wide mountain pasture grazing favoured cheese-making; the rare bleu de Termignon is greatly appreciated by commoisseurs. The church is remarkable, thanks to some magnificent reredos ordered (with local wealth) in the 17th and 18thc.; the high altar and reredos are among the finest in the region. Admire the Visitation and Saint Andre Chapels, and the bronze 1920s statue of a 'pleureuse'. Termignon village reflects the Haute Maurienne's traditional architecture in stone, wood and shale. Part of the village built on water reveals a few exposed canals.

VERCORS

Vercors Natural Regional Park has existed since 1970; the high plateaux were listed as a natural reserve in 1985. The magnificent massif includes Royans, or Western Piedmont, which spreads its rustic wealth between the River Isère and the first Vercors slopes; its plunging cliffs at Combe-Laval and Grands-Goulets are quite spectacular. Ibex were released into the park in 2000, as part of a continuing attempt to restore wild fauna to its former habitat.

PARC REGIONAL DU VERCORS Maison du Parc - Chemin des Fusillés - LANS-EN-VERCORS ✆ 04 76 94 38 24. *www.pnr-vercors.fr.* The Vercors seems to be an impregnable fortress caught between Isère and Drome, containing some magnificent open spaces for nature-lovers. At the foot of its cliffs, the Royans and Diois scenery and local produce are equally impressive! Wherever you are, you'll be welcomed; there are no crowds, and both sites and prices are attractive for ski-ing and hiking.

Autrans

The resort for cross-country skiers, a small and charming medium-mountain town.

MAISON DU PARC DES QUATRE-MONTAGNES ✆ 04 76 95 35 01. *Open Monday-Friday: 10am-12 noon and 3pm-6pm in winter, 4pm-7pm in summer; Sunday afternoons in season.* The Maison organises exhibitions linked to the park's activities, and is also a library and information centre for the Vercors.

La-Chapelle-en-Vercors

Today, this commercial centre of the southern Vercors and Drome is a busy, friendly place, but the dark days of 1944 are not forgotten.

COUR DES FUSILLES. The atmosphere seems heavy with painful memories. 16 young men were massacred by enemy bullets against the wall near the Post Office, on 25 July 1944. Automatic audiovisual guide.

GROTTE ET PARC ANIMALIER DE LA DRAYE-BLANCHE ✆ 04 75 48 24 96. *Ouvert toute l'année, sauf du 15 novembre au 31 janvier (excepté pendant les vacances de Noël). Adultes 6,50 €.*. You learn all there is to know about the Vercors underground world from the expansive guides in this impressive cave, then visit the animals in the park outside.

Choranche

GROTTES DE CHORANCHE ✆ 04 76 36 09 88. *www. choranche.com.* In the heart of the Bourne Gorges (D531). Open every day, all year. The famous Choranche Caves are both interesting and moving. You learn about the earth's history, with the fistulous stalactites that codify the past and the protee, a cave-dwelling batrachian contemporary of the dinosaurs. The great caverns and underground lakes are magical with the son et lumière.

Die

Known for its clairette, an ancient wine that brightens any table, and also for the pleasant pastoral atmosphere in its narrow streets. A big transhumance festival takes place every year, when hundreds of sheep cross the town on their way to the summer pastures.

LA CAVE DE DIE-JAILLANCE Avenue de la Clairette ✆ 04 75 22 30 15. *www.jaillance.com. Open every day: 9am-12.30pm and 2.30pm-6.30pm. July & August: 9am-7pm. Admission: adult 3 € , under-16s free.* Three jars were lost in icy water...and today, millions of bottles wait in Jaillance's huge cellars. This visit awakens your interest and your taste buds. A unique audiovisual presentation 'When water, earth, air and fire meet,' for all the family, is followed by a trip round, to discover the soil, vinification methods and secret of Jaillance's bubbles.

Saint-Nazaire-en-Royans

Sunlit cliffs reflected in the Bourne, a great aqueduct arching over the small village and the Vercors Mountains in the background. This breathtaking landscape draws you from your car, to go down and get a better view. Saint-Nazaire-en-Royans is also worth visiting for its winding streets climbing up to an old feudal tower.

AQUEDUCT ✆ **04 75 48 49 80**. *Open in July & August every day: 10am-12 noon and 1pm-7pm. Enquire about other opening hours. Admission: adult 3.50 € , child 2 €* . You reach the aqueduct by lift for a 30-minute visit. The explanatory panels and interactive guides tell you all about the canton's 12 towns. There is also an exhibition describing the canal irrigation project and how it is carried out.

GROTTE PREHISTORIQUE DE THAIS Le Village ✆ **04 75 48 45 76**. *Open April-mid October, telephone for opening hours. Admission: adult 6.50 € , 3-13s 4.50 € . Groups of 15+ all year (bookings).* Explore the many facets of the underground world: Cro-Magnon daily life and archeology; cave formation and pot-holing; exploratory dives in the Tai underground river. For all ages. Activity days are organised (don't hesitate to enquire).

Sculpture dans la neige

Vassieux-en-Vercors

This big village is sadly best-known for the bitter and bloody fighting that took place there during World War II. It was systematically destroyed by the occupant: 174 resistants and inhabitants lost their lives. Vassieux is a Compagnon de la Liberation, a high honour only granted to four other towns: Paris, Nantes, Grenoble and the Ile de Sein.

MEMORIAL DE LA RESISTANCE Col de la Chau ✆ **04 75 48 26 00**. *Open may to september from 10 am to 6 pm (5 pm the other months). Adults : 5 €* . This building is anchored in the rock, like a symbol of undying memory. You stand before the Memorial in silence, plunged into thought and history.

Villard-de-Lans

Villard-de-Lans is the Vercors' tourist capital. Busy all year, it has managed to keep urban development to a human scale and remain unpretentious.

LA MAISON DU PATRIMOINE 1, place de la Liberation ✆ **04 76 95 17 31**. *Open all year. Admission: adult 3.50 € , 11-18s 1.55 €* . Centrally housed in the former Town Hall, the Maison contains souvenirs and descriptions of daily life in the Four Mountains, from the 19thc. to the mid-20thc. Jacques Lamoure, a Vercors-lover, collected part of these treasures in his lifetime.

TOURIST OFFICE Villard de Lans BP 54 ✆ **04 76 95 10 38.** *Fax 33 (0)4 76 95 98 39. mailto ot.info@villarddelans.com. www.villarddelans.com.* This resort is located on the edge of the impressive Bourne Gorges, with sunshine and pure mountain air all year round, and is Europe's biggest Alpine ski-ing area, with 125km of slopes for gliders. Villard (meaning village) has a long tradition of cattle-breeding, and though the fair is no longer held, you can see the cows in the meadows, and taste the famous Vercors-Sassenage blue cheese. Hiking, horse-riding , mountain-biking and pot-holing are some of the more popular summer leisure activities, with snowshoe trips and sleigh rides in winter. The Villard de Lans/Corrençon-en-Vercors Association also offers swimming (wave pool), golf and museums. Correncon, in the centre of a varied forest, offers winter sports (ski, snowboard) and superb hikes in all seasons.

RUINES DE VALCHEVRIERE. Tout d'abord camp aux maquisards puis théâtre de sévères affrontements les 22 et 23 juillet 1944, le village de Valchevrière, situé en pleine forêt, est l'un des sites les plus émouvants du Vercors. Il conclut un chemin de croix édifié depuis Villard-de-Lans. Sur le belvédère qui domine la commune, le lieutenant Chabal et ses hommes se sacrifièrent pour retarder l'avance allemande et moururent les armes à la main. Les maisons furent ensuite incendiées. Le village ruiné est resté en l'état, avec ses poutres calcinées, ses pierres à nu et noircies. Seule la petite chapelle est encore debout.

FOOD AND DRINK

Alpine gastronomy is not only about fondue, raclette and tartiflette. True, cream and cheese are big local products in this region of cows, but there are the lakes and rivers offering succulent fish like charr and trout; market-gardening on the plains and red and white wines, not forgetting that the Alps are on the spice route, and the people natural pedlars.

Traditional mountain cooking

Soups, potato-based recipes and salted meats (rare, and often only goat) were daily fare in the high valleys, with rice pudding, fritters and rissoles on special occasions. Bread was baked - in one batch for the whole year.

Tartiflette

'Tartiffle' is potato in dialect; hence the name. Some put onions in it, others brown the potatoes before they go in the oven, or cut the crust off the reblochon - each to his own recipe. Here is one for 4 people: 800g of potatoes, one whole ripe reblochon, 150g of smoked lardons, 25g butter, salt & pepper and onions if you like them.

Gratin dauphinois

The Northern Alps' gastronomic speciality - but who has the real recipe? It contains potatoes, garlic and milk; whether you add pepper, nutmeg and creme fraiche is debatable.

Cheeses

Most Savoie cheeses are made with cow's milk (beaufort, raclette and reblochon) but goat and ewe's milk are also used, especially in the Southern Alps.

Abondance

Made from unpasteurised full-fat milk, coagulated slowly at 27°C, this AOC cheese with its amber crust and creamy texture originally comes from one of the Chablais valleys between Leman and Valais. Today, not only the abondance breed of cow is used, but also tarine and montbeliarde. After moulding and pressing, the abondance is bound with a wooden circle, giving it its typical concave form. The cheese is matured for 3 months at least, whence come the ivory-yellow colour and slightly acid nutty taste.

Beaufort

This is an ancient Savoie cheese, though its name did not appear until 1865. It is made in the Beaufortin, Maurienne and Tarantaise region, and is a cooked and pressed cheese with a nutty flavour, best eaten in strips or cubes, or in the famous fondue.

Reblochon

Its name comes from la rebloche, or 'second milking', a common practice among farmers in the Middle Ages so as to pay less tax by hiding part of their milk production from their overlord, and transforming it into cheese. Today, this cheese is made in other regions, but most often in Savoy. It is cylindrical, pressed and uncooked.

Tome or tomme

The tome de Bauges (which has just got its AOC) is disc-shaped, 15cm for 1kg. Whether farm or dairy-produced, this cheese is made from unpasteurised cow's milk. The tomme de Savoie is the best-known variety, and is protected and guarranteed with the Savoie regional label. The crust is grey, covered with red or yellow mould, and the pale yellow cheese has a typical nutty flavour.

Wine

Vines were cultivated early at the foot of the Alps, often during the Roman era; Allobrogie wine was prized in 1stc. Rome. In the Middle Ages, vines were planted in the upper valleys by the monks, but they remain concentrated in areas with microclimates, on the south-facing slopes round the lakes, up to 500m. Two-thirds of the wines produced are white, with 4 AOC: Seyssel, Crépy, Roussette de Savoie and Vins de Savoie.

Clairette de Die

The Diois' claim to fame is this ancient wine, which is vinified so as to limit the transformation of sugars into alcohol. The vines are among the highest-grown, with converging Alpine and Mediterranean climates, and Clairette-de-die is an AOC. Taste it as an aperitif or with dessert; it contains little alcohol, and is pleasant to drink.

Vins de Savoie

There are plenty of good wines to go with Savoie's recipes. Chambery is the biggest wine-growing region, producing over half the whites. The chignin-bergeron, Savoie's most reputed wine, is from Chambery.

The seyssel AOC on the borders of Haute-Savoie and the Ain gives still or sparkling whites, from the altesse or roussette and molette cepages.

Crépy AOC in Haute-Savoie produces whites from green or red chasselas.

Roussette de Savoie, like frangy (Haute-Savoie) marestel, monterminod and monthoux (Savoie) is a white from the roussette and altesse cepages.

The Vins de Savoie, spread over 59 villages (17 with the name of a wine) are white or red, from a variety of cepages.

Bugey wines (Ain) from chardonnay, roussette, poulsard, gamay noir, pinot noir and mondeuse cepages, have an appellation VDQS (Vins Delimites de Qualite Superieur).

Finally, the Allobrogie vins de pays (Savoie, Haute-Savoie and Ain) are superior quality table wines outside the AOC, but with similar soils, at a lower altitude and less well-exposed to the sun.

Cheese

Hotels & Restaurants

HAUTES-ALPES

Aspres-les-Corps

HOTEL MONT-BRISON 3, avenue Général de Gaulle ✆ 04 92 21 14 55. *Open all year, except 1 November-20 December and 1 May-30 May. Double rooms 30 €-50 €. Breakfast 6 €.* Located in the heart of the new town, at the foot of the wide street leading to the Citadelle, and close to the station. The same family has been running the hotel for thirty years, and the staff are well able to advise and inform you about the region. 44 spacious and functional rooms with modern comfort: TV, bath or shower, WC and washbasin. Sheltered parking space available. A simple, inexpensive place, in good taste.

Briançon

AUBERGE DE LA PAIX 3, rue Porte-Méane Cité Vauban ✆ 04 92 21 37 43. *Fax: 04 92 20 44 45. Website: www.auberge-de-la-paix.com. Double rooms 46 €-64 €. Half-board 43.50 €-46 € per person.* This venerable stone building is located in the Cite Vauban between the two gargoyles - large and small - and must be one of the few hotels in the heart of the citadel, if not the only one. It is a pleasant setting, but you have to bring up your luggage on foot. The rooms are well-equipped with TV and phone. Car park and private garage. Several nearby restaurants offer local specialities, notably the Passe Simple close by.

Gap

LE PASTURIER 18, rue Pérolière ✆ 04 92 53 69 29. *Open every day, except Sunday, Monday and public holidays. Set menus 24.50 € and 62 €.* Having converted his father's former zinc workshop

into a restaurant, Pascal, with his Gap hotel school diploma, and his partner Djema have managed to make it one of the most reputed in this gastronomic region that isn't short of good local produce. Customers come from quite a way to sample the leg of lamb and foie gras pêle-mêle, and the regional menu with its cold lamb cuts, Champsaur *tourtons*, (stuffed pastry cushions stuffed with potato, onions, fresh cream and cheese) Valgaudemard oreilles d'ane (donkeys' ears: a dish of wild spinach au gratin in a bechamel sauce with fresh cream) local cheeses and mountain flavours. Each dish on the *dégustation* menu has a story; make sure the lady of the house tells you some of them. A sunny, tasty overnight break.

LE PRE VERT ** RN85 – Direction Marseille– – Quart. Micropolis ✆ 04 92 52 45 84. *Fax: 04 92 52 06 91. Open all year. Double rooms and breakfast from 40 € to 50 €. Large, free car park.* On Napoleon's road, in a calm, green setting only a stone's throw from the ski resorts, Serre-Poncon Lake and the Ecrins National Park, this hotel is also on the way into a town you must discover. The standards are high, with clean, spacious rooms redecorated every 2 or 3 years, and well equipped with modern comforts (TV, Canal + and satellite, WC, showers and a direct phone line). Family rooms are available. The staff provide a smiling welcome, and Petit Futé readers benefit from attractive prices. This is an ideal place for mountain sports like cycling, golf and hiking, and also for business seminars. As pleasant as its name (green meadow) suggests, the Pré Vert guarrantees you a successful stay in the Hautes-Alpes.

La Grave

LES CHALETS DE LA MEIJE 04 76 79 99 00/04 76 79 97 97 . *Fax : 04 76 79 97 98. Website: www.chalet-meije.com. Winter: double room 80 €-94 €. Chalets sleeping 6-8, 1,480 €-1,950 € per week. Apartments sleeping 2-4, 750 €-1,000 € per week.* This chalet village to let, on the way into la Grave, is an original idea, ideal for families or groups of friends. Comfortable hotel rooms are also available. The chalets are charming and convenient, decorated and furnished with good taste. If the prices seem steep at first, divide by the number of people in the group, and you'll see they are actually quite reasonable for such an idyllic setting.

HOTELS-CHALETS® de TRADITION
Logis de France
Logis de France
Logis de France
Serre-Chevalier
Col du Lautaret
2058 m
186024
Bonnabel
Lautaret
★★★★
Tel: +33 (0)4 92 24 42 21
www.hotel-bonnabel.com

Le Monêtier-les-Bains

BONNABEL DES GLACIERS **** **Col du Lautaret** ✆ **04 92 24 42 21.** *Website: www.hotel-bonnabel.com. Open 17 December - 15 September. Rooms from 165€ to 352€. Breakfast 15€.* This hotel seems to protect the Lautaret pass from its strategic position 2,058m up, overlooking the valley, 30 minutes from Briancon. It was rebuilt in 2001 and gained two new stars in the process, which makes 4 in all. The Bonnabel family has been welcoming visitors and providing creature comforts since 1871 (the great grandfather was the mountain refuge guardian). Their chalet-hotel enables you to enjoy mountain activities off the beaten track, and away from the bustle of the big resorts. Sabine and Dominique welcome you in a convivial family environment, with superb decor all in natural wood. The hotel has 15 duplex rooms, 6 standard rooms and a magnificent apartment and suite, on three floors, with wide openings giving you a view of the starry night sky. This top-of-the-range comfort extends to the restaurant, overlooking the swimming pool, which reflects blue light in the evenings.

L'AUBERGE DU CHOUCAS *** **17, rue Fruitière** ✆ **04 92 24 42 73.** *Fax: 04 92 24 51 60. Website: www.aubergeduchoucas.com. Rooms from 80€ to 205€.* Once a 17thc. farmhouse, now an inn, the Auberge du Choucas faces the Town Hall behind the church, in the heart of the old village Monetier-les-Bains, and on the edge of the Ecrins National Park. The bourgeois cuisine is confident and just inventive enough to be mentioned in the best hotel and gastronomy guides. You certainly won't be disappointed. The rooms are sophisticated, scented with mountain flowers and very quiet. They look south, and provide prestigious comforts - bath, heated towel rail, independent WC, phone and TV, mini-bar and safe - and some rooms have a terrace or balcony, or even a 'mountain corner'. The natural scenery, snowy peaks in the sunlight, is breathtaking. The restaurant with its stone walls and fine, vaulted ceilings is an ideal place to discover the region's produce, prepared with care and delicacy by the excellent chef. Relaxing, convivial but very professional welcome. Poetic, romantic, absolutely not to be missed!

Montgenèvre

NAPOLEON **Route d'Italie** ✆ **04 92 21 92 04.** *Fax: 04 92 21 95 06. Website: www.hotel-napoleon.com. Open all year. Double rooms 40€-50€. A week's stay half-board 455€-630€ per head.* The

resort's traditional hotel, facing the slopes on the village side. In summer you can play golf, and in winter, enjoy the ski-ing. The hushed atmosphere may seem a mite old-fashioned, but the rooms are cosily comfortable and well up to 3-star standard. There's a terrace for a bit of *apres-ski* relaxing, and a restaurant to build up your strength after a day's exertion.

Saint-Bonnet-en-Champsaur

LA CREMAILLERE Route de la Motte ✆ 04 92 50 00 60. *Fax: 04 92 50 01 57. Website: www.alacremaillere.com. Logis Nature et Silence. Half-board available: room, breakfast and evening meal, 60 € (double room). Menu du terroir 23.50 €.* You stop at La Cremaillère for a well-earned breather; we recommend it for those trying to give up smoking! The setting is magic; a green park with the purest of air, and the hotel is comfortable, cosy and bright. Modern decor and period objects go well together, and the rooms all have a view of the surrounding mountains. In the restaurant you find regional produce, like the delicious Champsaur *tourton* salad, Valgaudemar ravioli, and even a rabbit and chicken in jelly recipe from Northern France, *potjevslesh*, unpronounceable but delicious! You'll sleep like a baby in the peace and quiet of this overnight break, highly recommended by the Petit Futé.

Saint-Véran

HOTEL-CHALET DES VILLARDS Le Villard ✆ 04 92 45 82 08. *Website: www.leschaletsduvillard.fr. Double rooms 40 €-65 €. During winter school holidays, 346 €-422 € per person per week, 496 €-572 € half-board.* Comfortable chalet-hotel with a big garden where kids can play in fine weather. The rooms have a fantastic panoramic view of Queyras park. South-facing studio rooms equipped with full kitchenette - luxury rooms with water therapy and electric beds - are available for greater independence.

Serre-Chevalier

AUBERGE DE L'IMPOSSIBLE ** 43, avenue de Savoie ✆ 04 92 21 02 98. *Fax: 04 92 21 13 75. Website: http://auberge.impossible.free.fr Double rooms from 49 € to 56 €, with breakfast from 61 € to 68 €.* Nothing is impossible in this inn that changed hands last season. You find it on the way into Briançon, at the foot of the Serre-Chevalier slopes, run by Ludivine and Olivier. The rooms are pleasant, decorated in Provencal tones, and there is a warm and welcoming family atmosphere. The traditional cuisine is carefully prepared with talent, and recipes that vary according to the market produce available: home made foie gras, knuckle of lamb with thyme and tagliatelli, and seasonal desserts.

LA CAPONNIERE 12, rue Commandant Carlhan – Petit Gargouille ✆ 04 92 20 36 77. *Open all year, except in June and 15-26 December, every day except Wednesday. Set menus from 14 € to 25 €.* The Caponnière, in the heart of the old town, located in the upper part of the Petite Gargouille near the collegiate church, seems to have materialised out of the past. A caponnière was a small building which sheltered defenders shooting into the ditch from the ramparts. Today, they defend good taste and quality cooking. The dining room is decorated with antique objects and bottles with curious corks, the service is efficient, and the cooking includes traditional mountain fare like fondue and old-fashioned raclette, as well as Bourgogne snails and tasty fish dishes. We recommend a Hautes-Alpes wine, which goes especially well with meat. You could say the owners of this Caponnière shoot straight to the heart - or the stomach.

LES CASTORS ** Domaine de la Vachère Route de Grenoble ✆ 04 92 25 69 00. *Fax: 04 92 25 69 59. Website: www.lescastors.com. Closed in November. Double rooms from 70 € to 140 €. Set* *menus 23 € and 32 €.* On the way into Briançon, on the Grenoble road 1,326m up, this spacious hotel welcomes family ski-ing parties come for the Serre-Che slopes. You can warm up first in the fitness centre, or in summer, rest by the pool after a day's hiking, with a magnificent view of the Prorel slopes and the mountains. The single, double and family rooms are large and airy, looking south. Most have balconies, enabling you to enjoy the setting - wooded park, small garden and outdoor swimming pool. The hotel provides a free shuttle to the ski lifts, and aquagym classes in summer. In the restaurant you find traditional, seasonal home cooking: duck breast, roast pikeperch steak with a leek *fondue*, and mountain specialities.

Villar d'Arène

LE FARANCHIN RN91 – Villar d'Arène ✆ 04 76 79 90 01. *Website: www.lefaranchin.com. Open 20 December-15 April and 1 June-15 October. Double rooms 31 €-58.50 €. Half-board 37 €-51 € per head. Full board 51.20 €-66 € per head. Express menu 12 €. 'Sympa' menu 19 €. 'Terroir' menu 23 €. Gastronomic menu.* This attractive mountain residence is located 1,650m above sea-level at the foot of the Meije massif, in the beautiful village Villar-d'Arene (a *faranchin* is an inhabitant of this village). The rooms are simple but functional and comfortable, with balconies, decorated on a mountain theme, with exhibition of local animals (follow the squirrels through the hotel to your room).Local specialities have pride of place in the restaurant, including the famous tourtes with cabbage or potatoes, smoked Hautes-Alpes trout fillet, fondue, tartiflette and raclette, and a varied choice of dishes whose recipes are the chef's secrets. *A la carte* or part of a formula, they are reasonably priced and the servings generous. Reputable Logis de France site, boasting pure air and river water, and a beautiful setting.

HOTEL RESTAURANT LES AGNEAUX RN 91 ✆ 04 76 79 90 62. *Fax: 04 76 79 05 40. Website: www.les-agneaux.fr.st. Open mid-December to mid-April and 1 May-late September.Double rooms from 50 € to 80 €. Set menus from 14 € to 30 €.* You can't miss this beautiful hotel, with its pleasant family atmosphere, on the Lautaret pass road in the heart if the Ecrins National Park. You can't miss the sheep either, who wander freely in the high mountain pastures in summer. From Les Agneaux, you have a marvellous view of the serene, snow-covered Meije peaks, and the 6 suites and 20 rooms are well equipped with TV and phone, plus a sauna and sports centre. On the menu are duck breast with genepi (a digestive alcohol made from the mountain plant of the same name), Villar d'Arene rissoles, trout *meunière*, bred locally, *crozets* (small cubes of pastry) *au bleu* and desserts home made with the day's market produce.

HAUTE-SAVOIE

Annecy

LA CIBOULETTE (A) Cour du Pré-Carré - 10, rue Vaugelas 04 50 45 74 57 *Open every day, annual closing in July. Set menus 25 € (lunchtime) and from 37 € to 47 €.* Annecy is a town of secret passages revealing all kinds of treasures, and the Ciboulette is definitely one of them. Firstly, it is excellent value for money: three courses with cheese and dessert for only 47 €! The dining room is well-decorated and the service friendly, a fitting setting for Georges Paccard's menus which change daily according to what's available at the local market. Home smoked salmon pannequet (type of pancake) with green asparagus and horseradish cream, followed by a lake pike *quenelle des mères lyonnaises*, (the famous Lyon women cooks), crayfish tails and shell cream. Then you choose from the dessert trolley. This inspired cooking with top quality produce, and simple preparation, is very attractive. You might try the Savoy lake whitefish in a cereal crust, wild bear garlic butter or young Pornic grain-fed pigeon, roasted then boned with its hulled juice and spring bouquet. A talented restaurant that can compete with the best.

NOVOTEL ATRIA 1, avenue Berthollet ✆ 04 50 33 54 54. *Fax: 04 50 45 50 68. Website : www.www.accorhotels.com – email : h1357@accor-hotels.com. Open all year. 95 rooms 93 €-114 €. Breakfast 12 €. Disabled access.* Nowhere is more contemporary, more functional or closer to the TGV train station! The Novotel Atria is part of a futuristic complex - most attractive in our opinion - including the station and a congress centre with large-capacity meeting rooms for seminars (holds 150). Tourists are as welcome as businessmen however: the hotel even offers children's games (note that 2 children can sleep for free in their parents' room). The rooms are equipped with modern technology - including WiFi access - and top-of-the-range comfort. As far as the food goes, you can enjoy freshly-caught lake fish and Savoy cheese. The infrastructure may be modern, but the welcome and service remain traditional. Ideal for meetings and professional events, but also for family visits.

L'IMPERIAL PALACE ** Allée de l'Impérial ✆ 04 50 09 30 00** *Fax: 04 50 09 33 33. Website: www.hotel-imperial-palace.com. Open all year. Rooms from 225 €. Breakfast 25 €.* Impressive and sophisticated Belle Epoque architecture on the banks of Lake Annecy. This luxury hotel welcomes prestigious guests, and also serves as a casino and congress centre, hosting the International Animated Film Festival and some fascinating exhibitions. Excellent service, tastefully decorated rooms blending classical and modern styles, sumptuous suites and faultless restaurants, from the Voile to the Terasses, overlooking the lake. You can hire a car (Smart), and benefit from the fitness centre and beauty parlour. A night in such a posh hotel is not an inaccessible dream!

Annecy-le-Vieux

LE CLOS DES SENS **13 rue Jean-Mermoz** ✆ **04 50 23 07 90.** *Fax 04 50 66 56 54. Set menus from 29 € to 90 €. A la carte 60 €. Closed Sunday evening (except in July and August), Monday and Tuesday lunchtime. Closed first fortnight in January and first fortnight in September.* Everyone is talking about this Alpine restaurant, up in the heights of Annecy, near *chef au chapeau* Laurent Petit's inn. Though only 40, he is hot news, one of the most spied-on chefs in France. The simplified lines of his restaurant setting are superb, with top-level service and the cuisine now up to standard, having gone through an unnecessarily complicated phase. Not yet as good as neighbour Veyrier du Lac, but five or six times cheaper: the best idea is to try them both, if you can afford it! Laurent Petit's cooking is lively and creative, this self-styled 'culinary craftsman' is worth discovering. Rabbit, warm calamar vinaigrette, soft polenta, poached pigeon savory juice and Savoy cabbage, raw marinated bass, watermelon and leek sprouts, lobster, conserved tomatoes and garlic sorbet, passion fruit, *ile flottante* and toasted almonds. Excellent cellar for both local wines and *grands crus*, at fairly reasonable prices.

Carroz-d'Arâches

LES SERVAGES 853, route des Servages © 06 76 95 45 41. *Fax: 04 50 90 08 23. Website: www.lesservages.com. Closed in May and October-November. Apartments, sleep 8. Summer prices 450 € to 1,000 € per week. Prices 1,250 € to 2,750 € per week.* Warmly welcomed by Marie-Claire, you find yourself at a level of luxury that goes beyond the simple term 'hotel residence'. These three apartments in the magic Servages setting occupy 200 sqm on two floors, with three bedrooms (each the size of a whole Parisian flat) bathroom, lounge with fireplace, fully equipped kitchen and huge terrace. Not to mention the heated garage and panoramic lift! It's beautiful, and unique, and shared among families or a group of friends, not as expensive as all that. The slopes are nearby; you couldn't find a better setting for a dream winter holiday.

Chamonix

ATMOSPHERE 123, place Balmat © 04 50 55 97 97. *Website: www.restaurant-atmosphere.com. Open every day. Set menus from 20 € (lunch) to 28 €. A la carte 35 €.* Come snow, come shine, you absolutely must discover the unique atmosphere on the beautiful covered terrace of this restaurant in the heart of Chamonix. More like a gallery, in fact, with the River Arve murmuring below and Mont Blanc stretching up ahead. As for the menus, Savoy or traditional, you will appreciate the simple, well-composed dishes: mashed potato with fresh goat's cheese, raw, marinated salmon duo, roast cod steak, Bresse chicken with cream, pan-cooked veal loin with morels, and of course fondue and Aravis tartiflette (potato and cheese dish) with prunes. For dessert, eggs 'à la neige' or roast pineapple with a pina colada sorbet. The cellar has around 300 recommended wines, including grands crus. One of the resort's classic eating places.

RESTAURANT ALBERT 1er 38, route du Bouchet © 04 50 53 05 09. *Fax 04 50 55 95 48. www.hameaualbert.fr. Set menus from 58 € to 138 €. A la carte 120 €. Closed Tuesday lunchtime, Wednesday, Thursday and Friday lunchtimes, second fortnight in May and early November-early December.* Five minutes from central Chamonix, this hamlet contains farms and ancient chalets, with a hotel de charme, a beauty parlour, swimming pools and a gastronomic restaurant. Its reputation has grown up over the years, thanks to the Carrier family's passion and persistence. Pierre has been looking after the resort's finest eating place for 25 years now, training young chefs every day who go on to work in some of the top French restaurants. The cooking is somewhere between Italy and Savoy; only the quality of the produce used never varies. Royal Dublin Bay prawns with pine kernels, black garden radish *remoulade* with pistachio vinaigrette, pumpkin, home cured bacon, slice of bread with truffles, sole cooked on the bone, pumpkin risotto, suckling veal chop, country cepes with savory, Bosses ham, rosemary leaves and souffléd potatoes, roast partridge *en cocotte*, autumn fruit and vegetables, and for afters, rum-vanilla *bouchon*, crème caramel-bergamot tea and lemon with a glass of Martinique rum. All that doesn't come cheap, though you'd expect that in a Chamonix *Relais et Château*, and it is a great experience!

LE REFUGE PAYOT 255, rue du Docteur Paccard © 04 50 53 16 86 *Website: www.refugepayot.com* Come and visit the owners of the 'refuge Payot'. You will be given advice concerning finer local specialities and delicatessen (cheese, ham, Savoy's wine, brandy sweets and cakes). Try the grelot sausage or their delicious bilberry pie. A new shop has just opened in front of Bellevue cable car.

LA SAVOYARDE * 28, route des Moussoux © 04 50 53 00 77.** *Fax: 04 50 53 00 77. Website: www.lasavoyarde.com. Annual closing 15-30 May and 3 weeks in November-December. Double rooms from 100 € to 140 €. Set menus from 15 € to 31 €.* La Savoyarde, a little way out of the town centre, looks like a traditional mountain chalet, and serves local recipes, but can also come up with a wider and very talented repertory when you've had enough of *tartiflettes* and fondues. The cooking is seasonal: steamed lake whitefish fillet with mushrooms and lime, reblochon cheese and seasonal salad, and venison steak with bilberries. It is useful to note that the two brothers who run La Savoyard are from the Carrier family, with its long hotel and restaurant tradition, and they also manage Chamonix's luxury establishments L'Auberge du Bois Prin and the Hotel Albert I.

HOTEL LES GOURMETS ET ITALY * 96, rue du Lyret © 04 50 53 01 38.** *Fax: 04 50 53 46 74. Website: www.hotelgourmets-chamonix.com. Double rooms from 70 € to 153 €.* This hotel de charme is a stone's throw from the town centre, in a quiet little street. The warm and cosy ambiance at reception makes you feel welcome straight away, and the rooms are equipped with all mod cons, some of them including a balcony where you can breakfast with a view of Mont Blanc. The sports centre and casino are just nearby, in case you have a spare hour or so during your winter sports activities. In the evening, you will enjoy playing chess by the fireside. The River Arve flows peacefully below the garden. A delightful place.

La Chapelle d'Abondance

FER ROUGE **Les Thoules** ✆ **04 50 73 50 29** Friendly pub atmosphere, warm shades for the decor, and home-made beer. In La Chapelle, you can enjoy stout, lager, bitter or 'white' beer all brewed on the premises, while thinking you could almost be in Ireland...

Evian-les-Bains

LE CAFE ROYAL **Rive Sud du lac de Genève** ✆ **04 50 26 85 00.** *Fax 04 50 75 38 40. Website: www.royalparcevian.com. Set menus from 60 € to 130 €. Closed every lunchtime from Monday to Friday. Annual closing in January.* This magnificent hotel is completely cut off from the world. 'Majesty, exception, authenticity and charm' claims the brochure, of an establishment boasting no less than 9 restaurants! Michel Lentz has been in charge of the gastronomic restaurant for two decades, and has enjoyed being able to create a luxury *cuisine* for well-heeled customers, with such dishes as duck foie gras and red-claw crayfish *royale*, grayling and an infusion of garden herbs in foamy butter, beef fillet from the Abondance Valley and real cow parsnip root juice, then a lime and Victoria pineapple parfait with lychees and coriander. The cellar contains all the local stars - Quenard, Perrier, Grisard, Bouvet, and the best bordeaux and burgundies at fairly logical prices. High-class service in a timeless setting.

LES CYGNES ** **8, avenue Grande-Rive** ✆ **04 50 75 01 01.** *Fax: 04 50 26 67 02. Website: http://hotellescygnes.com. Double rooms, lakeside view from 67 € to 77 €. Breakfast 8.50 €. Set menus from 14 € to 22 €. Children's menu 10 €. Pets welcome.* Few hotels can boast being so close to Lac Leman: this one is part of the '*Les pieds dans l'eau*' (literally, feet in the water) chain. It dates back to 1926, but has been entirely renovated to update comfort levels in the personalised rooms, now all equipped with satellits TV. Inside, character and charm are apparent; outside, you can enjoy excellent cuisine on the terrace under the climbing vine. Perch fillets simply cooked *meunière*, with their garnish, grayling millefeuille with aubergines and spinach, pan-cooked venison with chestnuts, redcurrant sauce, and an iced souffle with marc de Savoie alcohol to finish. The wine list is very good. Later, you can chill out in the calm waters of the lake, or go on a short boat trip. You are made so welcome here that you soon feel at home.

La Chapelle-d'Abondance

LES CORNETTES ** ✆ **04 50 73 50 24.** *Fax: 04 50 73 54 16. Website: www.lescornettes.com. Double rooms from 75 € to 95 €. Breakfast 10 €. Set menus from 20 € to 60 €.* This hotel's history goes back over a century, and its reputation brings back the customers year after year. There are different types of panelled rooms; a 30 sqm apartment with balcony can acommodate the whole family. The setting is typically 'mountain' in style, with a heated indoor pool, a hammam, sauna and jacuzzi, ideal for relaxing after a day's ski-ing or hiking. The dining room has a coffered ceiling, and offers home-made Savoy specialities like charcuterie and Cornettes salad, or perch fillet pan-cooked with chanterelles.

La Clusaz

LES CHALETS DE LA SERRAZ Route du Col des Aravis ✆ 04 50 02 48 29. *Fax: 04 50 02 48 29. Website: www.laserraz.com. Annual closing May and October. 10 rooms. 5 rooms from 105 € to 160 €. 2 suites from 165 € to 195 €. 3 duplex in chalets (sleeps 4/5) from 150 € to 210 €. Breakfast buffet (for room only, without half-board) 15 €. Restaurant open every day, evenings only in winter; every day (lunchtimes only at weekends) in summer. Set menu 38 €.* On the road winding up to the Aravis pass, you may be intrigued by a small door which seems to open onto a small paradise facing the mountain pastures. Go down a few steps and you'll find yourself in a picture postcard of mountain scenery, with the main chalet and traditional mazots (miniature chalets) covered in snow in winter, and nestling in green pastures to the sound of cowbells in summer. Inside the main building, comfortable rooms with warm panelling and traditional furnishings are close to the swimming pool and solarium, but if you like wood and peace and quiet, and are rather romantic, you'll find the mazots to your taste. The hotel welcomes children too, with communicating rooms (real little apartments), a TV and games room, baby-sitting service, sledges in winter and appropriate meals: many thanks! The Serraz Chalets boast an excellent restaurant run by Jean-Christophe Pergod, with a dinner menu Col des Aravis offering duck terrine with cepes, monkfish medallions with lime, duck breasts with grapes and Rivesaltes muscat, a cheeseboard and an assortment of home made desserts. On Tuesday evening, you can enjoy a real Savoy buffet made up of local dishes. We'd like to add that the staff in this fairytale hotel always welcome you with a smile.

Le Grand-Bornand

L'HYSOPE Route du Bouchet ✆ 04 50 02 29 87. *Open every day, except Wednesday, and Thursday in low season. Menu decouverte 27 €, gourmand 36 €, degustation 65 €. Petits gourmets menu 10 €. A la carte 45 €.* Not large, but full of charm with its panelled ceiling and picture-covered walls. L'Hysope is a genuine gastronomic restaurant with a cuisine quite different from local traditions, rooted in the landscape yet integrating recipes from elsewhere, and the chef knows how to surprise you. The découverte menu includes a light pumpkin velouté with conserved chestnuts and fine herbs, pikeperch fillet pan-cooked with liquorice aroma and parsley; the gourmand menu a lobster blanquette and small winter vegetables and veal fillet mignon with morels. The wine list completes a master picture.

Les Houches

BEAU SITE * Rue de l'Eglise – Chef-Lieu ✆ 04 50 55 51 16.** *Fax: 04 50 54 53 11. Website: www.hotel-beausite.com. 18 rooms from 62 € to 95 € (double rooms). Breakfast 7 €.* This comfortable inn is opposite the Aiguille du Gouter. There are light wood furnishings, duvets, satellite TV and balcony in the spacious rooms, and a bar and sauna for the *après-ski.* The Perrin family work hard at keeping up a pleasant atmosphere in the warm panelled setting, and the inn has its own restaurant Le Pile (?) whose chef reinvents the most delicious traditional recipes, starting with home made bread.

Machilly

LE REFUGE DES GOURMETS 90, route des Framboises ✆ 04 50 43 53 87. *Website: www.refugedesgourmets.com. Set menus from 31 € to 79 €, truffle menu in season. 'Apprentice gourmet' menu 20 €.* You will be impressed by the splendid scenery between Chablais and Leman, even before arriving at Florence and Jean-Marie Chanove's magnificent residence. Skilfully renovated, the house boasts an immense glass ceiling in the Belle Epoque style, as beautiful as the mahogany panelling in the dining room. The food is seasonal, the chef cooks according to his moods, and you feel inclined to trust him. At truffle time, there is a thematic menu: foie gras and black truffle stuffing, creamed swede, quail breast dotted with truffle under the skin, reblochon cheese stuffed with truffles and even walnut and bitter chocolate meringue with a truffle sauce! Pure happiness. Of course, Machilly being the world's raspberry capital, there is also a special menu when the fruit is in season. The chef is available for comment, and willingly comes to talk cookery with his customers. He also supports equal trading initiatives towards fruit producers, especially tropical producers, such as Fruits de la Solidarite. The cellar gives pride of place to the great Rhone Valley vintages (relatively inexpensive), but doesn't forget Savoy wine. A superb place to eat; pass the word on!

Morzine

LA CLEF DES CHAMPS ** **Avenue de Joux-Plane** ✆ **04 50 79 10 13.** *Fax: 04 50 79 08 18. Website: www.clefdeschamps.com. Rooms from 50 € to 95 €, attractive prices for babies and children. Breakfast 8.50 €.* This magnificent chalet-hotel is singled out by its setting, among the pastures at the foot of the slopes, and its sophisticated appearance. The three types of room - Tradition, Prestige or Charm - are very comfortable, even luxurious: the Prestige category rooms are furnished in light wood with balconies overlooking the snow. There is a large summer swimming pool, sauna and fitness centre for relaxing, and an excellent restaurant where you find the same good taste and family atmosphere as elsewhere in the hotel. Grilled scallops and fisherman's pot-au-feu taste as good in the warmly decorated dining room as on the terrace. Delectable.

LE MAS DE LA COUTETTAZ **Chemin de la Coutettaz** ✆ **04 50 79 08 26.** *Fax: 04 50 79 18 53. Website: www.thefarmhouse.co.uk. Closed in May and partially in October and November. Half-board in winter only, with 'royal' gouter. Double rooms from 70 € to 120 €, breakfast 10 €.* This is surely Morzine's oldest and most beautiful building: a farmhouse built in 1771, but now much more than an ancient farm, since Dorrien Ricardo began sharing his roof and table - and a warm and friendly welcome - with visitors. The 8 rooms in this rustic setting are, like their owner, unique, one for each situation: the blue room, family suite and 'The Cell', particularly cosy and now famous. Lovebirds will go for the mazot; sooo romantic! The guests meet up round a big table, seated boy-girl-boy alternately, and taste specialities from all over, while the armchairs are pushed back to improvise a dance floor - the evening is just beginning. If you'd rather, you can simply have a drink in the bar beside the huge old fireplace, where a log fire crackles. It's a magic environment, and a haven of peace in the heart of the mountains. You won't ever want to go out again!

Saint-Gervais-les-Bains

LE CARLINA *** **95, rue du Rosay** ✆ **04 50 93 41 10.** *Fax: 04 50 93 56 26. Website: www.carlina-hotel.com. Double rooms half-board from 81 € to 105 € per day and 496 € to 552 € per week according to the period. Breakfast 8.50 €. Set menus 21 € and 28 €. Children's menu 11.45 €.* This is Saint-Gervais' most luxurious hotel-restaurant, and fully deserves its three stars. The relaxation area has a heated indoor pool (with counter-current swimming) in a pale panelled setting, a sports centre and sauna for chilling out after a day's ski-ing (the Bettex Mont d'Arbois lifts are really close, reachable with your skis on) or a long hike through the mountain pastures. Le Carlina is a spacious and elegant chalet, where you can spend time with friends playing billiards or in the bar, or savour the delicate regional cuisine beside an imposing fireplace. Viande de grisons (charcuterie) carpaccio, duck breast with honey and gentian root, or roast monkfish tournedos and pissaladière are served in a well-kept setting. The rooms are extremely comfortable, and in summer, the terrace offers superb views of the surrounding mountains. This place is in a category of its own, between town and mountain, and provides plenty of leisure and relaxation activities

Samoëns

LES GLACIERS *** ✆ **04 50 34 40 06.** *Fax: 04 50 34 16 75. Website: www.hotel-les-glaciers.com. Double rooms from 85 € to 110 €. Assiette savoyarde 15 €, traditionelle 18 €. Set menus 20 € and 25 €.* In every village and resort, their is a hotel which seems to date right back to the early days of tourism. This one is impressive because of its size, facilities and comfort. Built of stone and light wood, it boasts a terrace where meals are served in fine weather, both sophisticated (salmon trout fillet with almonds, lake whitefish fillet with lemon cream) and regional (plates of assorted mountain fare). The rooms offer top-of-the-range three-star comfort, and there are indoor and outdoor pools and a garden where children can play. You can even try jet ski on a private lake - amazing!

RELAIS GOURMAND CHEF-LIEU ✆ **04 50 34 42 19.** You stop off at this lovely chalet to taste regional specialities with a Savoy menu featuring a country ham salad and old comté cheese, pork fillet mignon with cream, whitefish or trout fillet, tartiflettes and fondues. Don't miss out on the amazing scallop and crayfish *fricassee* with saffron, if you feel like a change. The warm dining room has a log fire, but the terrace is very pleasant in fine weather. The best is yet to come, for the ice creams are home made, a real treat for both small and bigger *Futés*.

Sciez

CHATEAU DE COUDREE **** **Sciez-sur-Léman ✆ 04 50 72 62 33** *Fax: 04 50 72 57 28. Website: www.coudree.fr –www.coudree.com in English. Closed in November. You can reach this hotel from the Route Nationale 5 Douvaine-Thonon, or directly by boat or even helicopter. 19 rooms and apartments from 132 € to 330 €. Breakfast 18 €. Set menus from 37 €, (lunch menu du marché from Monday to Saturday, except in July and August with the buffet fraicheur) and 54 €, 68 € and 88 €.* The Francois I restaurant is closed Tuesday and Wednesday. Imagine you're sailing along the banks of Lake Leman with a charming companion. You see a private landing stage, get out onto the jetty, walk up the avenue - and there is the most romantic castle for miles around. Before going off to sleep in one of its sumptuous rooms (12thc., magnificently reshaped) you really have to take a gastronomic break in the Francois I restaurant with its medieval setting and splendid monumental fireplace. Chef Sullivan Breton suggests dishes made with the region's fresh ingredients: blue lobster tail, gaspacho with Espelette pepper, grayling cooked on lake shingle, carrots fondantes with honey, Charolais beef fillet and foie gras, steamed grenaille potatoes (with their violet flesh) and chanterelles, and a slice of bread and bone marrow with lean bacon. After that, you really must enjoy an old Armagnac in the Renaissance bar. Next day, lunch on the terrace from the buffet fraicheur, with access to the private beach or swimming pool. This dream could come true, with the gift of an Evasion Romantique - you only need to find someone to offer you an all-in stay at the Château de Coudrée!

Talloires

L'ABBAYE DE TALLOIRES **** **Chemin des Moines ✆ 04 50 60 77 33** *Fax: 04 50 60 78 81. Website: www.abbaye-talloires.com. Rooms from 130 € to 210 €. Breakfast 18 €.* What began as a modest priory put up by monks in the 17thc. is now an internationally reputed hotel with top-of-the-range facilities. Behind its massive facade it hides a setting appreciated by Cézanne when he was in these parts painting the lake. From the flower-filled cloister you reach the bedrooms via a superb oak-panelled gallery, which leads you to contemplate the past, even among the most modern of comforts: sauna, Jacuzzi, and well-being and relaxation treatments are on offer. The restaurant combines past and present too, with old-fashioned cooking and contemporary sophistication on its menus. You'll enjoy the concerto dinners, where you can savour classical music and elegant *cuisine* together.

AUBERGE DU PÈRE BISE Route du Port ✆ 04 50 60 72 01. *Fax 04 50 60 73 05. Website: www.perebise.com. Set menus from 80 € to 170 €. A la carte 100 €. Closed Tuesday, Wednesday lunchtime and Friday lunchtime (from 10 February-23 April and 4 September-5 November) and Tuesday and Friday lunchtime the rest of the year. Annual closing 7 November-10 February.* It would be unfair to relegate this mythical inn to obscurity, on the pretext that one of the world's greatest chefs is within walking distance, in another (but less charming) lakeside residence. The Père Bise has the advantage of age, and has been facing that lake Winston Churchill called "the most beautiful country in the world" for 105 years. The culinary skills have been passed down from Bise to Bise during that time, and are now in the capable hands of Sophie. She inherited them in turn from father François and grandmother Marguerite, who gave the inn its reputation. The cooking has to be good to rival the enchanting setting, and the Burgundy snails, little pork trotter *caillettes* (minced pork and spinach or Savoy cabbage meatballs), sweet garlic and parsley, steamed sole, green peas in emulsion scented with peppermint, roast pigeon breast with citronella and ginger, corn waffle, saddle and loin of Sisteron lamb, right down to the dessert trolley that whisks you back to childhood for 25 €, make the grade. The cellar is classic and thorough (but you pay for it) and the service stylised.

LA VILLA DES FLEURS *** **Route du Port ✆ 04 50 60 71 14.** *Fax: 04 50 60 74 06. Logis de France. Closed 28 November-5 February. Double rooms from 90 € to 126 €. Breakfast 12 €. Set menus from 29.50 € to 40 €.* The Villa des Fleurs is a beautiful Savoy chalet on a superb islet of greenery offering rest, leisure and gastronomic quality. The rooms have been renovated, and Sebastien Jaegler cooks local recipes served on the shady terrace under hundred-year-old trees. Home smoked salmon, marinated with dill and lime, whitefish fillet with sorrel, and pan-fried country rib steak appear on his menus, not forgetting the Terroir et Specialites menu which features excellent seasonal ingredients cooked according to perfectly mastered traditions. The Villa des Fleurs is taking part in a Talloires en Liberte initiative, and offers a green fee per person per night so you can discover golf, along with plenty of other free activities: tennis, mini-golf, kayak, windsurfing and cultural visits, and some cut-price ones: catamaran, paragliding and 'adventure forest'. An ideal place for a family stay, with its wooded park and outdoor leisure activities, or a professional seminar (fully-equipped room and catering).

Veyrier-du-Lac

LA MAISON DE MARC VEYRAT 13 vieille route de Pensières ✆ 04 50 60 24 00. *Fax 04 50 60 23 63. Website: www.marcveyrat.com. Set menus from 290 to 380 €. A la carte 250 €. Closed Sunday, Monday, Tuesday (except evenings in July and August) Wednesday, Thursday and Friday lunchtimes and from mid-November to mid-May.* Recently christened 'La maison de Marc Veyrat' (so as to tell it apart from the maestro's second restaurant, La Ferme de mon Père in Mégève), the former Auberge de l'Eridan opened in 1992 by the lakeside embodies the extraordinary work of creation that France's most mediatic chef is still improving, and structuring day by day. The 55-year-old self-made chef became famous here, and laid the basis for his 21stc. cooking, symbolised today by two amazing menus at 290 € and 380 €. Fortunately the 19.6% VAT is included! Marc Veyrat is without doubt one of modern history's greatest cooks, and his reconstituted 9am.egg yolk, syringe with nutmeg, stuffed virtual cannelloni (with neither starch nor eggs), pepper coulis, line of cepes, bass *éclaté* ('exploded'), white chocolate brush, sugar-free Madagascar citronella syrup, Breton lobster in grilled slices, sugar-free verbena sweets, loin of lamb and steamed wild thyme, light infusion, polenta cubism with beaufort cheese and souffléd mango pancakes, 'passions' and 'exploded' rice ice cream are light years ahead of the standards, and absolutely impossible to copy.

ISERE

Alpe-d'Huez

EDELWEISS Route de la Poste © 04 76 80 65 64. *Open all year. One set menu 12 € between seasons, open lunchtimes from Monday to Friday. Set menus 14 € (lunchtime) 16 €, 18 €, 21 € and 24 € in season, open lunchtime and evenings all week. Terrace.* Don't be surprised if you see a stray Tour de France cyclist, escaped from the race to enjoy a quiet moment at Edelweiss! This little chalet in the heart of the resort is prettily decorated in the mountain style, and Valerie and Jean-Luc welcome you warmly, and let you into a few of their culinary secrets. This is real home cooking with fresh ingredients, from the beef potence (cooked at your table suspended from a bracket) *flambéd* in cognac to the Pogone (chicken fillets, chorizo, onions and Comte cheese au gratin in the oven and served in the pan), not forgetting the home made cassoulet. Meat cooked on hot stones, fish - boneless trout, bream, red mullet fillets - and the local *ravioles*; there's something for everyone. Leave room for the desserts; you'll be tempted to taste them all! Cooking, reception and service are all up to the standard you look for on holiday - don't miss this place if you're staying at the Alpe d'Huez.

Corps

HOTEL BOUSTIGUE ** Route de la Salette Boustigue ✆ 04 76 30 07 07. *Website: www.hotelboustigue.com. Open mid-April to mid-October, every day. 27 rooms from 47 € (double). Set menu formule 16 €, menu du terroir 19 €, children's menu 8.40 €, menu detente 23 €.* A magnificent mountain road leads you up to this eagle's nest: a hotel-restaurant with an exceptional view of Sautet Lake. At this junction of the Dauphine and Champsaur regions, between fir trees and pasture, the cooking is original and delicious: ram's horns, pig's cheek, snail ravioles (small quenelle-shaped stuffed pasties), vacherin cheese with green Chartreuse, braised sweetbreads, and suckling pig in a civet (stew). The ingredients are local and the prices very reasonable. For 15 years, the inn has also let out 27 comfortable rooms, enabling its customers to benefit from the beautiful scenery a little longer.

HOTEL-RESTAURANT DU TILLEUL Route Napoléon ✆ 04 76 30 00 43. *Website: www.hotel-restaurant-du-tilleul.com. 18 rooms. Double room 40 €, suite with private lounge 65 €. Half-board 45 € per head, full board 57 € per head. Set menus 12.50 €-31 €, or a la carte. Brasserie formula. Children's menu 8.80 €. Logis de France 2 fireplaces. Group meals and seminars.* Sylvie and Claude have been welcoming guests in a family atmosphere for 30 years now. The rooms are comfortable, soundproofed and tastefully decorated, and the split-level suite is almost a small apartment. Claude Jourdan, chef and gardener, prepares local dishes based on seasonal produce and his own fresh vegetables (3,000 sqm of orchards and kitchen garden): *gratin dauphinois*, casseroled pork shoulder with crayfish, mountain tourte, trout with almonds, and 'donkey's ears', a local speciality (explained elsewhere in the guide). Everything is precisely timed and cooked to perfection. Leave room for dessert; the home-made ice-cream is delicious.

Corrençon-en-Vercors

HOTEL DU GOLF * Les Ritons ✆ 04 76 95 84 84.** *Website: www.planete-vercors.com/hotel-du-golf. Double rooms from 84 € to 100 €. Under-11s 35 €. Set menus from 20 € to 36 €.* This beautiful hotel is ideally situated at the start of the cross-country ski-ing slopes and the golf course, a stone's throw from the departure point of local hikes and 500m from the village slopes. In winter, you can relax in a massage bubble bath after a sauna, and in summer, lounge by the pool with the mountains to contemplate. In the restaurant, the talented chef concocts gastronomic and sophisticated regional dishes: suckling veal, foie gras, and pan-fried Dublin Bay prawn tails in a spicy sauce. A charming place, with plenty of new pleasures to discover.

Grenoble

AUBERGE NAPOLEON 7, rue Montorge ✆ 04 76 87 53 64. *Website: www.auberge-napoleon.fr. Open weekday evenings and lunchtime with advance booking. Closed Sunday. Minimum price à la carte 35 €. Set menus from 39 € to 77 €.* This inn is famous for its history - the Emperor, Stendhal and Liszt all stayed here - and for its cuisine. Anne and Frederic Caby manage their restaurant with talent, and offer sophisticated service and a delicate and surprising cuisine. The foie gras menu at 65 € alternates duck liver on poached oysters, *mi-cuit* on gingerbread with pollen, foie gras soufflé with quince juice and *crème brulée* with vin jaune and crystallised foie gras.The *dégustation* menu (77 €) concentrates on fish and shellfish, fresh roast scallops and turbot. And the bouillabaisse menu (39 €), as its name indicates, gives off a delicious smell of scorpion fish, with crab as a starter. Chef Agnes Chotin creates these marvels, and we'd like to congratulate her: no easy thing to do, as she tends to keep to that all-important place, the kitchen, watching over her sauces. Don't forget to ask for your Privilege Card.

GRAND HOTEL * 5, rue de la Rèpublique 04 76 44 49 36.** *Website: www.grand-hotel-grenoble.com. Rooms from 75 € to 108 €.* This hotel provides cheerful rooms, with flowers, in a 19thc. building in the town centre, near the Tourist Office. It boasts three conference rooms.

Les Deux-Alpes

BLUE SALMON 98, avenue de la Muzelle ✆ 04 76 79 29 56. *Set menu 16 € or 26 €. A la carte.* Karine ' the salmonette' and Vincent 'the fish' run this restaurant; these are the nicknames given them in the resort. Their little wooden chalet with its mountain decoration and Canadian cabin atmosphere is warmly welcoming, and their cooking stands out from the traditional specialities. No fondues, but a cuisine that changes with the seasons, like the excellent house soup to start with. After, why not be tempted by a salade gourmande with home made duck foie gras? Gourmets will appreciate the smoked salmon or foie gras with fresh kiwi and conserved onions, and the Vendée chef's mussels with french fries are excellent. The restaurant also serves as a cafe where friends meet up to chat, a bar and a tearoom, known for its conviviality and good humour. Don't forget to feed the birds, if you make a detour to the toilets: this is a mountain chalet habit - though you'll have to find them first!

HOTEL CHALET MOUNIER * 2, rue de la Chapelle ✆ 04 76 80 56 90.** *Website: www.chalet-mounier.com. Annual closing early May to mid-June and early September to mid-December. Prices according to type of room and period chosen.* This beautiful 3-star hotel in the Deux Alpes resort began life as a mountain refuge, then became a farm-inn in 1879. Georgia, Robert and Alban are passionate about their hotel, and proud of its development and the prestigious facilities it provides. Facing the Ecrins National Park, built entirely of wood and tastefully decorated, it has an excellent reputation in the resort for its elegant, comfortable and luminous rooms with their pretty view of the Oisans from the balcony. Breakfast is composed of regional produce. There is also a sauna, jacuzzi, two heated pools, fitness centre (Aquaflor Est Well-being workshop), hammam, suntanning centre, tennis courts and billiards. The staff are attentive and always available, smiling and friendly. As for the gastronomic restaurant, Le P'tit Polyte, it specialises in sober and interesting creations from a skilful chef with a sense of flavours, such as roast monkfish tail with *crozets* (small traditional squares of pastry) and mountain ham, and pigeon supreme with gingerbread. An excellent address to know and pass on!

LA GRANGE 11, rue des Sagnes ✆ 04 76 11 21 87. *Open all year, except between seasons. Set menus 18.50 €, 25 €, 15 € and 8 € for children. Snack menu at lunchtime.* The name of this restaurant means 'barn', and the decoration is in keeping: wooden fork on the wall, wicker baskets, cow bells exhibited, logs and mangers, all traditional mountain farm objects. The cooking follows, with very generous helpings of Savoy specialities such as *raclette, tartiflette* and fondue. Grilled meat also features on the menus, however, and the giant home made kebab is impressively composed and presented. You can order rib steak, rib of beef or lamb chop, andouillette with tournedos Rossini or Savoy *diots* (small rustic sausages), all washed down with an excellent wine list. This is traditional *cuisine*, carefully prepared and inexpensive. Owner Frédéric and his team are friendly and good humoured, which seems to rub off on the atmosphere in the spacious dining room. The bar is a pleasant place to meet people, and in fine weather you can enjoy the sunshine on the magnificent terrace. A most relaxing restaurant and a 'must' in this resort.

BAR THE RED FROG 1, place de l'Alpe de Venosc &✆ 04 76 79 23 28. *Open 7am-2am non stop. Open all week, including low season. Bar brasserie. Website: www.theredfrog.net.* Run by Paddy, who speaks English and French and has personalised his bar, and Phil. There is TV football (English and international) on plasma screens, and food in the same style: English breakfasts and traditional recipes, grills, bangers and mash, Mexican chicken, burgers and kebabs at attractive prices, with Happy Hour from 5pm to 7pm. You can enjoy a delicious cocktail while relaxing to background jazz or blues, or catch up with news and films in the private lounge. Internet access (reasonably priced) and laptop rental - there's even one with an English keyboard.

La Mure

HOTEL RESTAURANT MURTEL Coteau de Beauregard ✆ 04 76 30 96 10. *Fax: 04 76 30 91 38. Website: www.logisdefrance-isere.com. Open all year. Double rooms 54 €. Half-board 49 € per head (double room). Breakfast 6.50 €. Set menus 12.50 € lunchtime and weekday evenings, 17 €-31 €.* This beautiful, well-kept building with its outdoor pool and terrace is located in the heart of a little-known region well worth discovering. The rooms are comfortable, the welcome genuinely warm, and the chef cooks traditional regional dishes - local tourte and green salad with walnut oil, soft white cheese, rennet with herbs. A good place to stop off during your holiday, on the Route Napoleon.

Uriage-les-Bains

LE MANOIR ** 62, route de Prémol ✆ 04 76 89 10 88. *Website: www.hotel-manoir.fr. Open every day. Double rooms from 37 € to 59 €. Set menus from 15 € to 30 €.* This pretty restaurant changed hands a year ago, and is now under new management. It boasts a magnificent green setting 15 minutes from Grenoble and 20 minutes from the Chamrousse ski slopes, with a sumptuous shady terrace and private car park. The menu is varied, offering traditional dishes but also regional ones, such as Chausson de Saint Barnard from the Cochet farm on a salad of green shoots and young leaves with walnut oil, home made foie gras, seasonal fruit chutney, roast lamb in a pistachio crust, and veal grenadin with cherries and sugar snap peas. You'll certainly leave with a full stomach! The two magnificent dining rooms with exposed stones and the mezzanine can seat groups, summer and winter. Everything is home made, and only fresh ingredients are used in the cooking. The hotel has 15 rooms, and we were given a very pleasant welcome. All the charm of the countryside - near town and the ski slopes!

LES TERRASSES Place de la Déesse-Hygie ✆ **04 76 89 10 80** *Fax 04 76 89 04 62. Website: www.grand-hotel-uriage.com Set menus from 80 € to 120 €. A la carte 115 €. Closed Sunday and Monday, and Tuesday, Wednesday and Thursday lunchtimes; in January and the the second fortnight in August.* This splendid Napoleon III building built in this spa town near Grenoble in 1864, houses one of the great French restaurants that attracts least media attention. This is no doubt owing to its untouristic location, youth (it was only opened in 1990) and chef Philippe Bouissou's extreme discretion, backed up by his second Christophe Aribert, who looks set to take over very soon. What does it matter, though, since the recipes are among the region's most interesting? The aperitif has its own appetisers menu with an amazing range of dishes to help you wait for the next course. This could be crayfish, mushroom stock, rougette lettuce and wild herbs, grilled Lake Leman whitefish, lemon, bergamot, fennel and conserved leeks, 'roast-poached' pigeon, parsley root, pink Roscoff onions, pigeon juice and liver, followed by chocolate leaf, tea and cocoa mousse, cocoa sorbet. There is a modern approach to cooking, with finely worked taste and texture and a cellar full of prestigious vintages looked after by the competent Sebastien Maucarre. 40 comfortable rooms enable you to enjoy the superb setting and park without ruining yourself (110-175 €).

Venosc

LES AMIS DE LA MONTAGNE–LE COURTIL ✆ **04 76 11 10 00.** *Website: www.hotel-venosc-deux-alpes.com. Open 18 December-23 April and 15 June-10 December. 29 rooms. Summer: from 308 € per head per week half-board, from 50 € per head per day according to choice of room, and season. Winter: 6-day stay half-board in double room 336 €-462 € per head according to choice of room and season. Ski-ing supplement 101 €-149 € per week. Prices for extra adults and children. Set menus 18 €, 26 € and children's menu 7 €.* This hotel lives up to its name. Located on the way into the Veneon Valley near the Deux Alpes ski resort, 1,000m above sea-level in the old village of Venosc, it comprises several buildings. You are warmly and naturally welcomed, the staff take great care of you, and you soon feel at home. Activities and cultural events on a mountain theme are on offer: the Durdan Emane family have considerable knowledge and experience of the subject, being former guides and ski instructors. This is also a good place for cycling. The telecabin link to the Deux Alpes (6 mins) is a great advantage. The hotel provides comfortable rooms (2 categories) with TV, shower and WC; some have balconies. Relax in the hammam or sauna while the kids play baby football, or by the heated pool (28 degrees C). The restaurant has two dining-rooms where you can taste mountain specialities and traditional cooking (fondues, raclettes, tartiflettes).

Vienne

LA PYRAMIDE 14 bd Fernand-Point ✆ **04 74 53 01 96.** *Fax 04 74 85 69 73. www.lapyramide.com. Set menus from 98 € to 150 €. A la carte 120 €. Closed Tuesday Wednesday and February.* The adjective *mythic* tends to be over-used, but it has real meaning when applied to this marvellous restaurant created by the huge (in every sense of the word) Fernand Point in 1923. Fifty years after the death of this great trainer of top chefs, and 15 after the arrival of Patrick Henriroux, the myth clings on. Though the establishment no longer has quite the same aura as in the fifties, new arrivals still enter with a feeling of apprehension. The decor is rather kitsch, but so what? Patrick Henriroux's cooking is up-to-date, lively, fresh and effective: cream soufflé with oscietre caviar, raw artichokes Provence-style, steamed lobster with salt and seasoning, lime emulsion, vegetable and ginger tagine, roast veal chop with new potatoes, peas and braised rougette lettuce, genuine juice *à l'ancienne, transparence* of berries, red and blackcurrants, lemon ball and mascarpone *onctueux* (smooth, creamy dessert). Classic, indeed, but seriously treated, and in line with the Pyramide's image.

Villard-de-Lans

LE CHRISTIANA * 220, avenue Professeur-Nobécourt – LE TETRAS ✆ 04 76 95 12 51.** *Fax:04 76 95 00 75. Website: www.hotel-le-christiania.fr. Hotels et Chateaux de Tradition. Closed 15 April-20 May and late September to mid-December. Set menus from 25 € to 50 €. Children's menu 10 €.* 23 rooms from 75 € to 170 €. After a day's hiking, climbing, canyoning, riding, golf or mountain-biking, or ski-ing and snowshoeing in winter, you'll appreciate the smiling, friendly welcome. All the rooms are comfy, and tastefully and colourfully decorated to relax and envigorate you at the same time. In summer, you can end your day by the heated pool, and in winter, forget your stiff muscles in the fitness area or enjoy a hot drink by the fire. From your balcony, you have a heavenly view of the Vercors peaks with the sounds of Nature all around, while you're asking yourself if it's time to eat at the excellent Le Tetras restaurant yet.

SAVOIE

Aix-les-Bains

ADELPHIA* 215, boulevard Barrier -04 79 88 72 72.** *Fax: 04 79 88 27 77. Website: www.adelphia-hotel.com. Air-conditioned double rooms from 82 € to 136 €. Breakfast 12 €. Indoor car park. Disabled access. Pets admitted. Restaurant Delices d'Adelphia open every day. Set menus from 21 €.* This establishment a few feet from the lake, with its charming, fully renovated rooms and excellent restaurant, is more than just a top-quality hotel-restaurant. It is a genuine health and fitness complex, to get you feeling in harmony with the natural world around you. The water therapy centre (1,800 sqm) with its indoor pool overlooking the garden, fitness centre, sauna, hammam, muscle-building, aquagym, get fit classes and health and beauty treatments are available at 150 € per person per day, or for a longer stay. The hotel also offers specific treatments, like the Nirvana Anti-stress concentrating on the back, shape and leg muscle tone. The shape-up area and various treatments ensure you spend time on yourself, and relax enough to enjoy life. Gastronomy is part of the programme; light meals round the pool after exercise and total relaxation. Adelphia certainly offers a full range of hedonistic pleasures.

HOTEL AGORA* Rue de Chambéry -04 79 34 20 20.** *Website: www.hotel-agora.com. Double rooms from 69 € to 86 €. Set menus from 16 € to 25 €.* The Agora offers luxury facilities in a large modern building, yet keeps its prices down. The hotel is new and purpose-built, with a heated indoor pool, sauna, hammam, and 60 comfortable rooms well equipped with Wi-Fi access. This is the ideal place to organise your meetings and seminars, with its three convertible meeting rooms. The hotel restaurant is the Patio, where the cooking is traditional: haddock fillet with seasoning or Savoy specialities like pork mignon Savoy-style or tartiflette with mountain charcuterie.

L'HYSOPE 4, rue Albert-Ier ✆ 04 79 34 28 18. *Formulas from 15 € to 29 €.* This is Aix-les-Bains' novelty of the year. The Hysope, with its trendy decoration, has replaced the Rutabaga. Chef Pierre Koenig has not materialised out of nowhere, however: this Alsatian is the Matafan's chef, in Chamonix, and his recipes are known the world over. His Aix restaurant offers sober and elegant dishes with good local ingredients: duck leg confit in cannelloni, lovage emulsion, foie gras terrine with Sichuan pepper, fig caramel, grayling in *matelote*, and bouchot mussels with saffron, crusty bass, cod *brandade* (potato dish) with citrus fuits, pork knuckle braised in bitter, conserved shallots, guinea hen fricassée, roast ratte potatoes. Pierre Koenig suggests a simplified menu, like in the famous 'bistrots du chef', that varies with the seasons. Don't forget to try out this place during the winter; it'll be back in our guide next year!

Albertville

HOTEL MILLION* 8, place de la Liberté ✆ 04 79 32 25 15.** *Website: www.hotelmillion.com. Single rooms from 81 € to 98 €. Double rooms from 127 € to 159 €. Triple rooms from 168 € to 190 €. Set menus ville 264 or 40 €. Set menus 52 € and 70 €.* The name Million calls up a certain idea of French sophistication, good taste and good food in the town centre. In this beautiful white building, you find a hushed ambiance, impeccable service, comfortable rooms and gastronomic cuisine with new discoveries in store. On the *menu ville* are snails and gambas in stock with a polenta cake and shellfish juice, fish *panaché* (a variety), potatoes in olive oil with a seasonal *sauce vierge* (olive oil, lemon juice, tomato, basil and coriander), and a seasonal fruit minestrone with Indian flavours.This must be the best restaurant in Alfortville, complete with small delicacies like the cheeses matured by 'friend' Guillot from Notre-Dame des Millières, or the Savoy wine *granité* with grenadine, blackcurrant sorbet with a citrus fruit tuile biscuit. There's no place like Million for an overnight break in town.

Beaufort-sur-Doron

HOTEL LA ROCHE* Rue du Capitaine-Bulle ✆ 04 79 38 33 31. *Fax: 04 79 38 38 60. Formula from 10.80 €. Set menus 15 € -32.50 €.* This attractive hotel in the town centre, opposite the small wooden bridge, boasts four floors of well-kept rooms and consistent cooking 'Cote Jardin' (since the recent change of management). You can enjoy tartiflette or mussels *mariniere*, and meat or fish dishes prepared by the chef with fresh local ingredients, on the beautiful lawn terrace - followed by a nap, or a post-prandial hike.

Bourg-Saint-Maurice

L'AUTANTIC* 69, route d'Hauteville ✆ 04 79 07 01 70.** *Website: www.hotel-autantic.com. Double rooms from 40 €. Breakfast 8 €.* This 3-star hotel is open all year, and boasts 23 rooms in a superb natural setting. The building in local wood and stone is located in Bourg-Saint-Maurice, which explains the attractive prices, but with the funicular you're on the Arcs resort ski slopes in 7 minutes. The rooms are well equipped, with balconies where you can relax in the sun after a day's ski-ing or hiking. There is also a sauna, and a warm and attentive welcome.

Chambéry

L'ESSENTIEL 183 place de la Gare ✆ 04 79 96 97 27. *Fax 04 79 96 17 78. Website: www.l-essentiel.com. Set menus from 25 € to 85 €. A la carte 70 €. Closed Saturday lunchtime, Sunday, Monday lunchtime (from September to late April) and all day Monday the rest of the year. Annual closing 1-7 January and 1-8 May.* When, like Jean-Michel Bouvier, you can't offer your customers a charming environment (in the town centre, but beside the station) nor an unforgettable setting (the dining room under a glass half-pyramid is well-lit but that's about all) you have to risk everything on the cooking. The talented Alexandre Ongaro backed him up from 1997 until last June, when he left to set up his own restaurant in Perpignan. He has been replaced by Bouvier's former second, Jérôme Beauregard, who looks set to follow in his predecessor's footsteps. Grilled Landes foie gras, cider syrup with star aniseed, lentils and artichokes, scallops rolled in grilled hazlenuts, fresh herb *mousseline*, Roseval potatoes, citronella emulsion, pan-fried turbot, clear shellfish stock with citronella and little herb ravioles, coffee *crémeux* dessert, *crème anglaise* with chicory, pistachio ice cream feature on the menu. The cellar is well stocked with regional bottles, recommended by a good wine waiter.

Chambéry-le-Vieux

LE CHATEAU DE CANDIE ** Rue du Bois-de-Candie ✆ 04 79 96 63 00.** *Website: www.chateaudecandie.com. Open every day except Sunday evening and Monday. Set menus retour du marché 25 € (weekday lunchtimes only), menu confiance 65 € and two summer menus 44 € and 56 €. A la carte 60 €. Double rooms from 110 € to 220 €.* This superb 14thc. fortified house built on the ruins of a former Knights Templars building, tastefully restored, contains plenty of talent recognised recently by a famous guide. The Chateau de Candie has been thrilling romantics for 10 years already with many good things, in fact Boris Campanella got his first star at the age of 28, and has now added another to those 4 already under his belt. His royal Dublin Bay prawns *à la plancha,* Japanese horseradish, slices of fennel conserved with orange and coriander, pan-fried lake whitefish, crayfish and morels blanquette-style, crusty sweetbread *grillons*, purple artichoke fricassee and conserved tomatoes, and meat juices with balsamic vinegar are delicious proof of that talent. The desserts - chocolate tourte with a melting heart, or a dark chocolate dome - are the height of pleasure. The terrace is pleasant, as are the property's extensive grounds. From the gastronomic as well as the tourist point of view, a stay in this four-plus-one star establishment is highly recommended.

Courchevel

L'ARBE Rue Verdons ✆ 04 79 06 57 93. *Open all year. Dish of the day 12€* This is one of the rare restaurants that the Futé recommends in Courchevel, where there are plenty of gastronomic restaurants, but with nothing futé (clever) about them, and often poor value for money. At L'Arbe, you find good humour, a friendly atmosphere and good family cuisine, generously served for large appetites spending the day on the slopes. The mixed salads are well composed with a variety of ingredients, and there is hot stone cooking and several Savoy specialities.

LE CHABICHOU Rue des Chenus ✆ 04 79 08 00 55. *Fax 04 79 08 33 58.Website: www.courchevel.com/chabichou. Set menus from 80€ to 200€. A la carte 200€. Closed in June, September, October and November.* Michel Rochedy's hotel no longer heads the list of the resort's most expensive and luxurious establishments, overtaken by one or two competitors on the slopes. However, he has no difficulty keeping gastronomic supremacy in the area, thanks to four decades of constant quality. Though not necessarily in the kitchen himself every day, he has excellent backup from his second, a *Meilleur Ouvrier de France* who masters his recipes to perfection. Lobster salad, warm leek vinaigrette with truffles, large roast Dublin Bay prawns in risotto with olive oil, thick slice of sole cooked on the bone in salted butter, fillet and loin of Limousin lamb in a kadaif crust, mountain honey *croquant*, and pumpkin mousse with vanilla are examples. The plates are well filled, and only the freshest and best ingredients are used in the cooking. You can choose between the comfortable dining room and a delightful terrace opening onto the slopes. All this adds up to a certain idea of happiness, though the prices are what you'd expect for luxury services, especially the wine list, with all those bottles apparently reserved for Eastern European nouveaux riche visitors.

Le Bourget-du-Lac

AUBERGE LAMARTINE Route du Tunnel du Chat ✆ 04 79 25 01 03. *Website: www.lamartine-marin.com. Open every day, except Sunday evening, Monday and Tuesday lunchtime from December to May. Set menus from 27€ to 80€.* As you're heading towards the Tunnel du Chat (or Cat's Tunnel), the Auberge Lamartine invites you in to enjoy an exceptional view of the lake from the terrace. In this enchanting setting, Pierre Marin's gastronomic restaurant continues the family tradition, having been opened by his father Jean in 1964. The dining room is imposing, with an impressive fireplace, and remarkable service. You soon feel at home, and ready to discover cooking that gives pride of place to local produce without trying to conceal its natural flavours. Simple dishes like fine Dublin Bay prawns, bass *à la plancha*, and mushroom risotto interpret traditional know-how with a modern touch. The cellar is admirable. As the poet said, "Let us savour the rapid delights of our finest days!"

LE BATEAU IVRE RN 504 ✆ 04 79 25 00 23. *Fax 04 79 25 25 77. Website: www.hotel-ombremont.com. Set menus from 80€ to 150€. A la carte 100€. Closed Monday, Tuesday and Thursday lunchtimes and late November to early May.* Lake Bourget and its surroundings boast plenty of good restaurants, and the Château de Candie's recent rebirth has made it a fit rival (almost) for the Bateau Ivre. Run for over ten years by Jean-Pierre Jacob, who spends the rest of the year in the other Bateau Ivre at Courchevel, this proud bourgeois restaurant built in the 1930s has plenty of strong points; a marvellous view of lake and mountains, calm location in a 3 ha. park and top-of-the-range absolutely up-to-date cooking. Pan-fried duck foie gras, rhubarb and reduced caramel, pike quenelles, crayfish emulsion, Pertuis asparagus and morels, roast tuna, little new onions, braised and roast sweetbreads, vanilla fennel, juice with conserved grapefruit, strawberry millefeuille, sorbet and *jus tranché* (the juice ingredients are kept separate). The cellar is extraordinary (the prices too). Service in the great restaurant style, chic ambiance.

Montsapey

RELAIS DU LAC NOIR Hameau de Tioulévé ✆ 04 79 36 30 52. *Double rooms 58€. Independent chalet 89€. Breakfast 8€.* One of our favourite places this year. Located 1,300m above sea-level in a protected natural environment, this is a genuine postcard inn. You can go hiking, and ski-ing or exploring with snowshoes in winter. Anne and Christophe welcome you with a smile. The rooms are cosy and prettily decorated, or there is the *mazot*, a real love nest with its local charm and private terrace, and a family chalet. The cooking is regional with fresh ingredients (theme weeks are organised) and very welcome after a day's exertion. You'll love it.

Méribel

HOTEL ALBA* Rond-Point des Pistes - Route du Belvédère ✆ 04 79 08 55 55**. *Fax: 04 79 00 55 63. Website: www.meribel-hotelalba.com. Rooms half-board from 150 € to 169 € per person per day.* This magnificent wooden chalet at the foot of the slopes, in the heart of the Three Valleys, is run by Laurence and Gilles Chardonnet. You enter a cosy and comfortable universe, welcomed in the grand traditional manner. A sophisticated panelled decor and efficient professional service characterise the hotel, which has a sports shop on the premises for skiers, and a relaxation area with sauna, hammam and whirlpool bath. The greatest pleasure comes when you sit down at your table by the crackling log fire, however, to savour the gastronomic cooking.

LA CROIX JEAN-CLAUDE Méribel-les-Allues ✆ 04 79 08 61 05.** *Fax: 04 79 00 32 72. Rooms half-board from 60 € to 80 €. Set menus 20 €, 28 € and 39 €.* On the road to Meribel lies les Allues, a genuine Savoy mountain village where cars pass with difficulty in the narrow streets. After parking your car quite easily, you discover a superb building, which shares its history with the village, and the family that has been running it since 1930. You've arrived at the Croix Jean-Claude, the Three Valleys' oldest hotel, and can expect to taste cooking quite out of the ordinary, thanks to the owners' knowledge of the mountain and all the best local producers. Seated on the little terrace among the flowers in summer, or in the folksy dining room, you can savour a cake composed of rabbit in jelly, crayfish salad with truffle vinaigrette, and veal steak en cocotte before being tempted by M. Provent's cheeses and grandmother's desserts: prunes in tea or tea soup with mint. Old-fashioned cuisine with modern flavours, in fact. The rooms are a similar mixture of traditional style and modern comfort. Mark this address with a cross, or even several!

Motz

AUBERGE DE MOTZ Chef-Lieu ✆ 04 79 88 42 86. *Fax: 04 79 88 40 29. Website: www.aubergedemotz.com. Open all year. Double rooms 45 €. Breakfast 6.50 €. Gite rental. Auberge menu 12 € (weekday lunchtimes only).* Marie and Michel Jotreau welcome you warmly and will recommend things to do and places to see in the region. The natural setting is beautiful, in the heart of Motz village close to a number of hiking paths. The inn itself is a former farm, well restored and comfortable, where you can enjoy regional dishes like *ravioles* with cheese, mushrooms or fish, a fine mullet and basil tart, veal with pears and honey, Savoy specialities and fresh frogs' legs or *bouillabaisse* to order. Located on the Compostella road, the inn also offers accommodation for pilgrims. Sporty guests will be keen to try the outdoor activities run by the Espace Sport et Nature du Fier.

Moutiers

AUBERGE DE SAVOIE Square de la Liberté ✆ 04 79 24 20 15. *Website: www.aubergedesavoie.com. Double rooms from 60 € to 144 €. Breakfast 9 €. Lunchtime formula 15.90 € and 25.50 €.* This restaurant's central terrace is as pleasant as the elegant dining room, with its efficient staff, to enjoy the pizzas (pizzeria closed Saturday lunchtime, Sunday and Wednesday evening) fresh pasta (with pistou or fresh salmon) or traditional cooking; we especially recommend the fish: cod steak Provencal-style, and sole meunière. On the specialities menu, the Piedmont aubergine and tartiflette are delicious, as are the Chinese noodles with scallops and fresh bean sprouts and the Dublin Bay prawn salad with grenache grapes and fresh goat's cheese. The wine list features plenty of *grands crus*. The same freshness and sophistication can be found in the tastefully decorated rooms. A must for an overnight break in your journey.

Pralognan-la-Vanoise

HOTEL DU GRAND BEC Rue Aiguille-de-Mey 04 79 08 71 10.** *Fax: 04 79 08 72 22. Website: www.hoteldugrandbec.fr. Logis de France. Closed 10 April-1 June and 1 September-20 December. Double rooms from 52 € to 92 €. All-in formulas include hikes, relaxation, cross-country or downhill ski-ing. Breakfast 7 €. Set menus from 15 € to 28 €.* This hotel-restaurant is solidly rooted in ths magnificent Vanoise Park region and in its local soil. Rooms and facilities seem better than the usual two-star standard, if you take into account the comfort, soundproofing, balconies facing the mountains, and satellite TV (thought the best show is outside), and the heated summer pool, sauna, jacuzzi, private tennis courts and children's indoor and outdoor play areas. The cooking is all about discovering local recipes, such as pan-fried sirloin steak with reblochon cream, grayling fillet with a liquorice cream, and a tasty 'mountain pasture flavours' menu featuring foie gras terrine with genepi liqueur and petit farcement en habit vert (a dish based on stuffing 'in green clothing'). This is a restaurant to recommend, and the no-worries all-in stay formulas are excellent.

Saint-Jean-de-Maurienne

HOTEL SAINT-GEORGES 334, rue de la République ✆ 04 79 64 01 06. *Fax : 04 79 59 84 84. Website : www.hotel-saintgeorges.com. Rooms from 50 € to 54 €.* If you look beyond the rather worn facade you will discover a hotel full of character with a real history. The interior has been completely renovated, yet retains a bygone charm. The rooms are perfectly equipped with soundproofing, cable TV and Canal+, a direct phone line, shower or bath, WC and hair drier. This is a discreet place, not at all showy, but with a certain charisma, that will welcome you warmly for a stay of any length.

Valloire

GRAND HOTEL DE VALLOIRE ET DU GALIBIER* Rue des Grandes-Alpes ✆ 04 79 59 00 95**. *Fax: 04 79 59 09 41. Website: www.grand-hotel-valloire.com. Logis de France. Closed 9 April-18 June, and 10 September-17 December. 44 rooms from 60 € to 92.40 €. Breakfast from 7 € to 11 €. Set menus from 16 € to 61 €.* This large, beautiful hotel on the way into Valloire is 20m from the ski lifts, and boasts a heated swimming pool in its park, a sauna and fitness centre. The rooms are regularly renovated - in fact, no expense is spared to make sure customers enjoy their stay. This is also the legendary Galibier stage of the Tour de France, so race officials know the hotel well. There are attractive all-in prices on offer: 7 days half-board, with a via ferrata (mountaineering) pass and an entry ticket for the Parc Aventure, from 498 €. Regine and Gilles will be happy to give you more information. The restaurant dining room rotunda has a hushed atmosphere, a huge fireplace and 1950s American furniture - superb! The *terroir* menu suggests a beaufort cheese tartlet, whitefish steak cooked on the skin, pork fillet mignon with a honey and Chambery vermouth marinade, grilled polenta with country bacon and *tomme fraiche* cheese. The perfect dessert is an iced parfait with genepi liqueur and cherries: simply unforgettable.

LE PLANCHER DES VACHES Rue de Tigny 04 79 59 07 27. *Children's menu: 6 €.* The name means the cows' floor, which is presumably the mountain pastures - yet you won't find cheese or milk specialities in this crêperie. The delicious crepes and galettes served with a pleasant small green salad could be from Breton pastures, of course. You'll find it hard to choose from such a variety of excellent compositions, but that doesn't matter. This beautiful converted barn with its wooden floor and fireplace is so welcoming, you might as well stay here for as long as it takes to taste them all! On the downside, sadly, credit cards are only accepted above 20 €. Rather a steep floor, we feel.

Les Houches

Alsace

ALSACE
Motorway
Major road
Minor road
Paris
STRASBOURG
Moselle
Meurthe-et-Moselle
ALLEMAGNE
Bas-Rhin
Wissembourg
Vers Karlsruhe
Lauterbourg
Lembach
Hunspach
Seebach
Wœrth
Soultz
Seltz
Vers Sarreguemines
Niederbronn-les-Bains
Reichshoffen
D263
A35
N62
Soufflenheim
N63
Haguenau
Drusenheim
Bischwiller
N340
Vers Metz
Sarralbe
Vers Metz
Herbitzheim
Sarre-Union
Sarre
la Petite-Pierre
Ingwiller
Eschwiller
Drulingen
Bouxwiller
A4
Hochfelden
Brumath
Vers Nancy
Saverne
0
10 km
Reproduction interdite
Jean-Baptiste Nény
Marmoutier
Truchtersheim
la Wantzenau
Wasselonne
N4
STRASBOURG
Wangenbourg
Molsheim
Oberhaslach
A352
Rosheim
Obernai
Schirmeck
N420
A35
N83
Mont. Ste-Odile
Erstein
Barr
le Hohwald
Benteld
Saales
Villé
Rhinau
Haut-Kœnigsbourg (château)
Vers Epinal
N59
Sélestat
Ste-Marie-aux-Mines
N
E
S

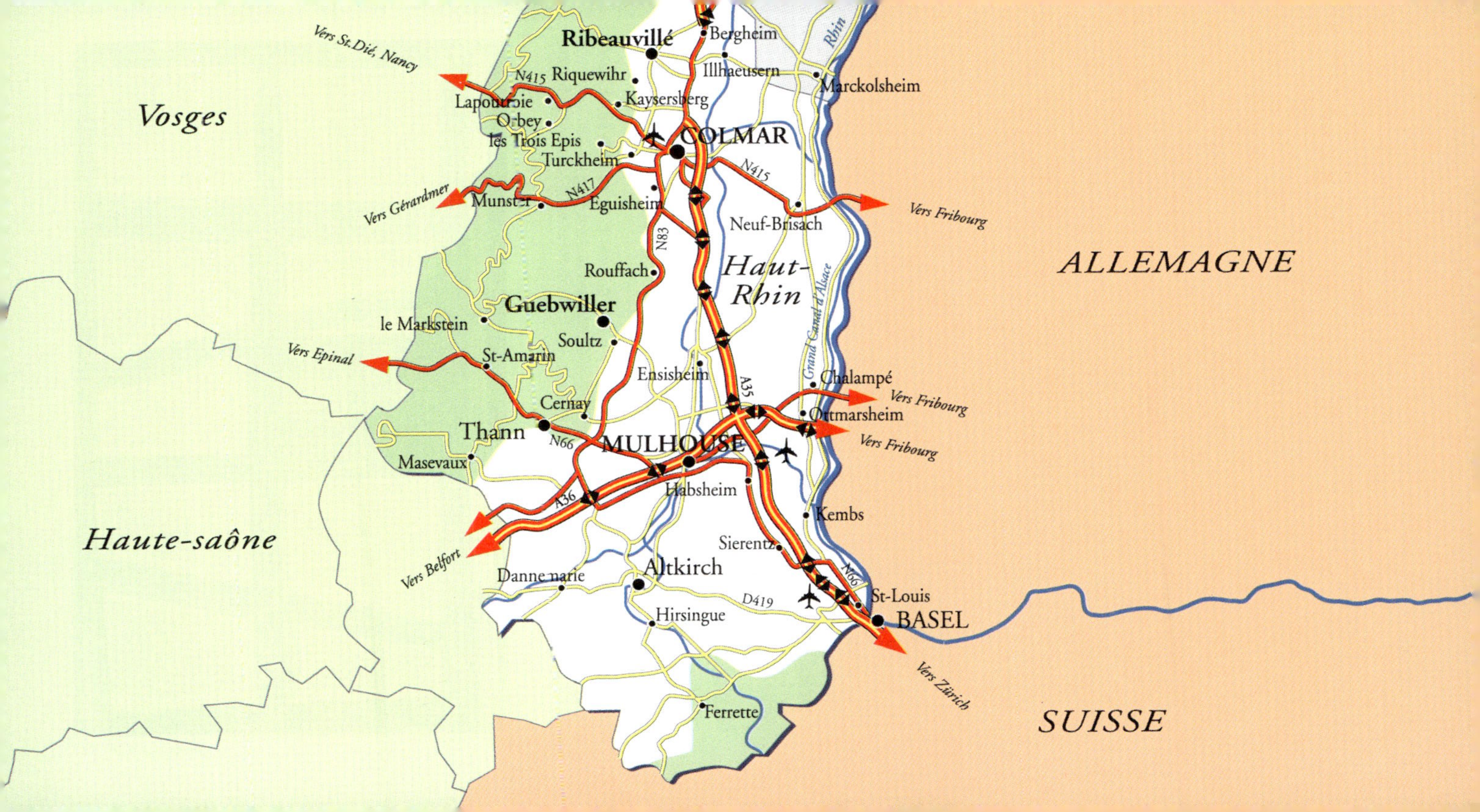

ALLEMAGNE
SUISSE
Vosges
Haute-saône
Haut-Rhin
Rhin
Grand Canal d'Alsace
Ribeauvillé
Bergheim
Illhaeusern
Marckolsheim
Riquewihr
Kaysersberg
Lapoutroie
Orbey
les Trois Epis
Turckheim
COLMAR
Munster
Eguisheim
Neuf-Brisach
Rouffach
Guebwiller
le Markstein
Soultz
St-Amarin
Ensisheim
Cernay
Thann
Masevaux
MULHOUSE
Chalampé
Ottmarsheim
Habsheim
Kembs
Sierentz
Altkirch
Dannemarie
Hirsingue
St-Louis
BASEL
Ferrette
N415
N417
N83
N66
A35
A36
D419
Vers St.Dié, Nancy
Vers Gérardmer
Vers Fribourg
Vers Epinal
Vers Belfort
Vers Zürich

BALLONS DES VOSGES

Magnificent landscapes and an environment protected by a nature reserve: this is the Ballons' idyllic setting. The Grand Ballon reaches 1,424m. Charming spa towns nestle in their valleys.

Ballon d'Alsace

This mountain resort is as popular in summer as in winter. The Ballon d'Alsace (1,241m) overlooks three regions. Crowned with grassy moors, its slopes are covered in coniferous forest, giving its blue colour to the *ligne bleue des Vosges.*

Guebwiller and Grand Ballon

At the entrance to the Florival Valley, between vineyards and hillsides, Guebwiller, on the River Lauch, has no less than three churches. Over the years, the town has managed to keep its cultural and environmental wealth.

DOMINICAN MONASTERY. *Reception, tickets and shop, open May-October, Monday-Friday: 8.30 am-12 noon and 1pm-5pm. Admission free. Bookings for the musical programme: on site or on 03 89 62 21 82/81.* The 14thc. Dominican Monastery has been entirely restored. The church and cloister are fabulous: a rood screen and 3,000 m^2. of 14th, 16th and 18thc. religious frescoes. A wide musical repertoire has been programmed regularly since the 19thc, as the building has such excellent acoustics.

SAINT LEGER CHURCH. One of Alsace's finest Romanesque churches. The west front is framed by two high 'hanging' towers, with a porch open on three sides. Like the nave, transept and side-aisles, it was built in the 12th and 13thc. Going round the church, you can't miss the former 16thc. leasing tribunal at no. 2, Rue des Blés, or the fine tithe cellar and old Town Hall, also 16thc.

NOTRE DAME CHURCH Rue de la République. The church's dimensions are striking. It was founded by the last Murbach abbot between 1760 and 1785 in Neo-Gothic style. Along the front are 8 statues of the Virtues. The chancel contains a superb Assumption sculpted by the Sporrers, who also carved the pannelling in the stalls and the organ case.

Munster

The Munster Valley is as popular as the Route des Vins. Alsace's city-dwellers like to walk in the mountains, follow the Vosgian Club paths, skim down the ski slopes or go mountain-biking. The ferme/auberge (farm-inns offering food and drink) is an ancient regional tradition; for decades, local farmers have been feeding hungry walkers.

OFFICE DE TOURISME DE LA VALLEE DE MUNSTER 1, rue du Couvent © 03 89 77 31 80. Munster's history is linked to its abbey, founded around 660 and dedicated to Saint Gregoire (the valley was named after him for many years; he now has a new cheese to his name as well). Munster has become

Typical house

an essential tourist centre, owing much to Andre Hartmann who in the 18thc. set up one of the region's first textile factories in the old abbey buildings.

BALLONS DES VOSGES REGIONAL NATURE RESERVE 1, cour de l'Abbaye ✆ 03 89 77 90 34 Admission free. Set up in 1989, the reserve is spread over three regions (Alsace, Lorraine and Franche-Comte) 300,000ha and 200 towns and villages. In Alsace, it includes the Hautes Vosges. The Maison du Parc can tell you all you want to know; this exhibition centre covers the region's natural habitats, cultural heritage, landscapes, geology and economic activities.

Route des Crêtes

This strategic route was built to make troop movement and communication easier during the 14-18 War. Over 80km long, it follows the watershed which is a natural border between Alsace and Lorraine, and provides wonderful views over the region.

JARDIN BOTANIQUE DU HAUT-CHITELET Col de la Schlucht ✆ 03 29 63 31 46. *Open June: 10am-12 noon and 2pm-6pm; July & August: 10am-6pm; September: 10am-12 noon and 2pm-5.30pm.* Lining the Route des Cretes, this garden contains high mountain flora, with 2,900 plant varieties from all over the world.

Grand Ballon and Markstein

Follow the Route des Crêtes towards the Amic Pass (825m). On your right is the ruined Chateau de Freundstein. From the pass, the road goes on to the Grand Ballon, 1,424m high. You can climb up on foot (30mins there and back) to admire the prettiest panoramic view of the Vosges; on a clear day, you can see the Jura and the Alps. In winter, this ski-resort gets plenty of snow, ensuring its popularity. The road continues along the mountain ledges to Markstein (1,146m) crossroads and winter sports centre. In 1983, it hosted the Alpine Ski-ing World Cup events. In summer, paragliders and hang-gliders take off from here.

Hohneck

The Route des Crêtes passes under Markstein ski-lift and reaches Hohneck via the Hahnenbrunnen (1,180m) Herrenberg (1,186m) and Rothenbachkopf (1,205m) Passes, with magnificent views over the Lauch, Thur and Fecht river valleys. The mountain crests are bare here, almost bald: this is Hautes Chaumes scenery. Cows graze freely in the wide pastures. Just before Blanchemer Lake is the Tourbiere de Machais Natural Reserve (a protected peat-bog). The road runs by the ski-tow arrival point at La Bresse resort, before reaching the Hohneck, at 1,362m one of the Vosges' highest peaks. What a breathtaking view! The scenery is magnificent in all directions: Vosges, Donon, Grand Ballon, Alsace Plain, Black Forest and even the Alps and Jura are marked on a viewpoint indicator. Come in fine cloudless weather, and go carefully on the paths: the slopes are very steep and dangerous.

ROUTE DES VINS

The Route des Vins, or Wine Route, is rightly famous for the quality of its wines and the beauty of its villages. From Marlenheim to Thann, the vines flow like a river between Vosges and plain, and the road is not quite straight, linking villages on either side of the vineyards.

Andlau

A village in the heart of the Route des Vins, known for its abbey

ABBEY CHURCH. This 12thc. church is famous for its superbly sculpted scenes. The Romanesque sculpture and long frieze on the portal are particularly fine. Inside, some beautiful Flamboyant Gothic decoration reveals 17thc. reshaping.

CHATEAUX. The Andlau châteaux can be reached from the Hungerplatz forest house on the road from Barr, or by taking the Kastelberg path from the village, if you've got the stamina. The first castle, Haut-Andlau, has an impressive 14th and 16thc. outline, with two huge cylindrical keeps on either side of a powerful wall. The 13th and 14thc. Spesbourg still has its square keep and the living-quarter walls.

Beblenheim

The village nestles against the famous Sonnenglanz hillside, with vineyards producing excellent quality wine.

TERROIRS ET TRADITIONS D'ALSACE Route du Vin © 03 89 47 91 33. The Fédération des Cooperatives Vinicoles d'Alsace groups together 17 cellars, where co-operative wine-growers reveal the secrets of Alsace wines. Other home-made regional products are also on sale.

Eguisheim

The town has kept its picturesque concentric alleyways and richly-decorated half-timbered houses, some with oriel windows. You can follow the ancient walkway round the ramparts; the prettiest part is the South Rampart. An octagonal wall is all that is left of the medieval castle; the existing palace and chapel were built at the turn of the century in Neo-Romanesque style. Eguisheim is the centre of one of Alsace's main cooperatives.

Kintzheim

The castle has a rectangular courtyard, keep, remains of living-quarters and a 15thc. chapel, It serves as a theatre for birds of prey displays. The other main attraction is the Monkey Mountain (easy to reach from the village). Kintzheim also gives direct access to the Chateau du Haut-Koenigsbourg.

VOLERIE DES AIGLES Château de Kintzheim © 03 88 92 84 33. *Open every afternoon. Adults 8 €.* In the shadow of the Haut-Koenigsbourg, Kintzheim castle provides a medieval atmosphere and inpressive birds of prey (eagles, condors and vultures). Different demonstrations are organised every day.

MONTAGNE DES SINGES La Wick © 03 88 92 11 09. *www.montagnedessinges.com. Open every day, 1 April-31 October. 1-11 November, Saturdays, Sundays, public and school holidays. July & August: 10am-6pm.* Experience some unforgettable moments in direct contact with 280 Magot monkeys living in the wild in a 24ha forest.

Mittelbergheim

The narrow streets have kept their medieval look, and are lined with charming Middle-Ages and Renaissance houses, with pretty courtyards inside. The number of winegrowers is striking: don't miss the chance of a tasting, especially as the village produces one of the best grand crus.

Ribeauvillé

This prosperous little town is an important stopping-point on the Route des Vins, and is known for its vineyards, Carola mineral water, fine buildings and past remains. It has some beautiful houses (like the Pfifferhuis), an 18thc. Town Hall, superbly decorated inside, the Tour des Bouchers and a 13thc. belfry with a fine clock of later date. The monastery church is Late Gothic (1473) and Saint-Gregoire Church, also Gothic, contains a fine organ and the Lords of Ribeaupierre family crypt.

NOTRE-DAME DE DUSENBACH. On leaving Ribeauvillé, follow the Stations of the Cross path on foot. Half-an-hour's walk will bring you to a famous place of pilgrimage, grouping together a monastery, Neo-Gothic church and pilgrims' shelter, as well as the magnificent Virgin Chapel clinging to the side of a steep headland overhanging the ravine. Inside, you discover Talenti wall paintings and a miraculous statue of Our Lady; a moving 15thc. pieta just above the altar.

The wines

In Alsace, the cépage gives its name to the wine, unlike in other French regions. More whites than reds are produced (20% of national production): riesling, gewurztraminer, tokay, pinot gris, sylvaner, muscat, pinot blanc and pinot noir. The riesling, dry and elegant, is the best-known Alsace wine; the gewurztraminer is fuller-bodied with a powerful bouquet, while the pinot gris is strong and heady. Very dry but delicately fruity, the sylvaner is more discreet. The Alsace muscat is drier than its Mediterranean cousins, and the pinot noir simple, but fruity. The pinot noir, Burgundian cepage par excellence, makes both reds and roses with quite unusual fruitiness. From the end of the last century, sparkling wines have been grown in Alsace, reputed only for the last twenty years. The cremants d'Alsace occasionally manage to rival their Champagne cousins. The very best of the Alsace vineyards has to be the vendanges tardives though. The grapes are picked at the very end of the season and are concentrated, powerful and aromatic, giving costly wines rather like a Sauternes. Follow the beautiful Route des Vins, just 50 years old, and discover splendid vines and wine-growing villages.

COMITE INTERPROFESSIONNEL DES VINS D'ALSACE 12, av.de la Foire-aux-Vins - COLMAR © 03 89 20 16 20. *www.vinsalsace.com*

CHATEAUX. You can reach the three Ribeaupierre châteaux on foot via a path that leaves from near the cemetery; it takes a good hour.

Riquewihr

At the bottom of a vine-covered valley, Riquewihr's 16th and 17thc. residences are magnificent, with their fine inside courtyards and galleries, old wells and fountains. The main street leads to the taverns and narrow alleyways; good wines seem to fill the atmosphere of this little town. The perfumed muscat, noble gewurztraminer, and riesling with its scented bouquet come from various sunny hillsides (the best-known are sporen and schoenenberg). There is a categoric refusal to accept inferior quality *cépages*.

MUSEE DU DOLDER Rue du General De Gaulle ✆ 03 89 49 08 40. *Open March-November; every day in July & August. Admission: adult 3 €.* The museum is housed in the Dolder Tower, built in 1291, and it narrates the history of this little town of wine-growers, from the Middle Ages. Among other things, there is a fine collection of weapons. Don't miss the view from the top.

MAISON DE HANSI 16, rue du Général De Gaulle ✆ 03 89 47 97 00. *Admission: adult 2 €, student 1 €, under-16s free. Open 1 April-30 December, every day: 10am-6pm, except Monday. February & March, open every afternoon, except Monday. January, weekends 2pm-6pm. July & August, every day: 10am-6pm, except Monday, 2pm-6pm.* You can admire 150 lithographs, etchings, watercolours and postcards signed by Hansi, famous designer of popular pictures. Downstairs in the shop, postcards, books and posters are on sale.

Typical villages

Alsace is full of villages with well-preserved 16th to 18thc. houses, simply designed inside but quite ostentatious outside, often covered with coloured roughcast and always decorative. These villages also contain municipal buildings put up to show their local power and autonomy; you have plenty of towers, Town Halls, exchanges and covered markets to admire. Bennwihr, Riquewihr and Ribeauville are concentrations of typical Alsace.

ECOMUSEUM ✆ 03 89 74 44 74. *www.ecomusee-alsace.com. Open every day: 10am-5pm (opens earlier and closes later March-September, consult timetable).* This museum is a paradox: one of Alsace's oldest villages, yet one of the most recent due to its reconstruction. 70 houses were taken down then rebuilt patiently in the museum, beam by beam. You can thus see the traditional living environment in Alsace in its reality. Since 2004, visitors have been able to discover how the potassium mines were worked with the 'Clair de mine' exhibition (open May-October). Absolutely not to be missed.

Thann

Arrival (or departure) point on the Route des Vins and the Route des Crêtes, and border between vineyards and Vosges. This wine-growing community also depends on its industries: copper, silver and lead mines; textile and chemical industries.

SAINT THIEBAUT COLLEGIATE CHURCH. Saint Thiebaut has a beautiful Gothic steeple, 76m high with a stone lace spire; and a superb portal decorated with a rich tympanum (500 characters) on the west front. The Flamboyant north portal is remarkable too. Inside are 15thc. sculpted stalls and stained-glass windows.

THE WITCH'S EYE CHATEAU D'ENGELBOURG. Enquiries ✆ 03 89 37 96 20. Pedestrian access. Admission free. Louis XIV ordered the Engelbourg (Angels'Castle) to be dismantled in 1673. Originally built by the Comtes de Ferrette, it lies in ruins today, although the site is being restored. The Witch's Eye (L'œil de la Sorcière) is that part of the keep lying on its side, looking towards the Alsace Plain with the Black Forest in the distance. The Alsatian Resistance Monument stands on the Staufen mountain top, over on the other side.

CASTLES AND FORTIFIED TOWNS

Alsace has an impressive number of castles, quite a few in ruins up above the valleys they were built to defend. Three famous and totally different examples are the Haut-Koenigsbourg, Neuf-Brisach and Obersteinbach.

Haut-Koenigsbourg

CHATEAU DU HAUT-KOENIGSBOURG - Orschwiller ✆ 03 88 82 50 60. *www.monum.fr. Open every day, except 1 January, 1 May and 25 December: 9.30am-6.30pm June, July & August, shorter hours during the other months: enquire at the castle). Admission: adult 7 €, 18-25s 4.50 € and big families, under-18s free. Free first Sunday in January, February & March, and October-December.* Perched at over 700m above sea-level, this castle was set to stay a ruin, until Wilhelm II had the architect Bodo Ebhardt restore it in 1899. He wanted to reinforce Alsace's German qualities, and integrate it into the Empire. Hundreds of builders were mobilised, and the original Hohenstaufen castle was recreated from existing documents. The pink sandstone result is the quintessence of romantic Alsace, and as an architectural success, a useful educational tool as well.

Lembach

FLECKENSTEIN ✆ 03 88 94 41 07. *Closed mid-November to mid-March. Open every day 1 May-31 October: 10am-6pm. Admisssion: adult 2.40 €.* A major fortress, built between the 12th and 17thc. The watchtower and certain inside rooms were dug out of the rock on which it stands. The castle itself was destroyed by Louis XIV's troops in 1689.

Neuf-Brisach

A masterpiece of military architecture. Vauban started a new fortification campaign between 1698 and 1709, and added a new town (Neuf Brisach) to the ancient fortified Vieux-Brisach, on a regular octagonal plan. The town's squared interior was largely destroyed in the 1870 and 39-45 wars, but the walls and two of the gates are well preserved. The huge Place des Armes in the town centre has a well at each corner, and an 18thc. garrison church. You can walk round the ramparts (half an hour for 2.4km) from the Colmar to the Belfort Gates, and admire the fortifications' attacking and defensive systems.

MUSEE VAUBAN Porte de Belfort ✆ 03 89 72 03 93. *Open every day except Tuesday: 10am-12 noon and 2pm-5pm, 1 May-31 October. Admission: adult 2.50 €, 10-18s 1.65 €, under-10s free.* Two rooms set up in the ramparts of Vauban's octagonal fortified town explain its history and military use.

Obersteinbach

You can admire 30 or so feudal fortresses in the region, put up from the 12th to 14thc., though they are often in ruins.

MAISON DES CHATEAUX FORTS 42, rue Principale ✆ 03 88 09 50 65. Housed in the former village presbytery, the Maison explains the history and architecture of local castles with scale models, maps, documents, seals, genealogy etc, retracing the turbulent lives of their lords.

CHATEAU DU PETIT ARNSBERG. Overlooking Obersteinbach from its stone perch, this 14thc. ruin had several rooms hewn out of the rock itself. It still seems to protect the town.

Storks

There were only 50 or so storks left in Alsace in the mid-70s; the birds were electrocuted on the wires while migrating, or shot by sportsmen. Efforts were made to protect the species, and now it is prospering, though no longer migratory. The stork has its place in the region's legends and traditions, and can be seen gliding over a village steeple (or even in the heart of Strasbourg) or perched gracefully on one leg to meditate. Of course we know it brings babies, but a young girl who is approached by a stork can expect to be married in the near future!

CIGOLAND Le Parc des Cigognes - KINTZHEIM ✆ 03 88 92 05 94. *www.cigoland.com. Open every day, 1 April-30 September: 10am-7pm and depending on the weather, Wednesday, Saturday and Sunday in October, November and March. Admission: adult 10 €, 3-11s 8 €.* What would Alsace be without its storks and their park!

COLMAR

Colmar is the capital of wine-growing country, and hosts the Foire aux Vins in early August every year. It is one of the most beautiful French towns, with its old quarters and superb half-timbered houses smothered in geraniums. Half-way between Strasbourg and Mulhouse, it makes a good base for a stay in Alsace.

DOMINICAN CHURCH *Place des Dominicains. Admission: adult 1.50 €, students and groups of 15+, 1 €. Open every day: 10am-1pm amd 3pm-6pm, late March-31 December.* Martin Schongauer's painting La Vierge au buisson de rose (1473) is of major interest. The surrounding panels explain the religious symbolism of the flowers.

SAINT MARTIN COLLEGIATE CHURCH. *Open every day : 8am-6pm (6.30pm Tuesday & Thursday), closed Sunday morning and during services.* This Gothic church was built in 1234 on the remains of a 9thc. basilica. The ochre Rouffach sandstone with its golden lights make it intensely luminous, best admired at dawn or dusk.

MAISON DES TETES 19, rue des Têtes ✆ 03 89 24 43 43. This magnificent bourgeois house in Rhenish Renaissance style dates back to the early 17thc. Its name comes from the 105 grotesque masks decorating the façade, but could also refer to culinary excellence, since it houses a restaurant. Another of Colmar's famous houses is the Maison Pfister. You can't miss this superb building at the corner of the Rue des Marchands and Rue Mercière. It has an oriel window on two floors and a gallery, both remarkable. The house is a perfect example of Renaissance art in the Rhine area.

LE KOIFHUS Place de l'Ancienne Douane. Finished in 1480, this building was at the centre of Colmar's business life. On the first floor, magnificent stained-glass windows are decorated with the arms of the Decapole towns.

MUSEE ANIME DU JOUET ET DES PETITS TRAINS 40, rue Vauban ✆ 03 89 41 93 10. *www.museejouet.com. Open October-June every day except Tuesday: 10am-12 noon and 2pm-6pm. July & August every day: 10am-7pm. September-December every day. Admission: adult 4 €, concessions 3 €, under-8s free, special family rates.* Cinderella's carriage, dolls, cars puppets, model boats, steam trains and a railway line are only some of the toys on display.

MUSEE BARTHOLDI 30, rue des Marchands ✆ 03 89 41 90 60. *Open every day: 10am-12 noon and 2pm-6pm, closed Tuesdays in January & February. Admission: adult 4.20 €, concessions 2.60 €, under-12s free.* The famous sculptor Auguste Bartholdi was born in this house on 2 August 1834. His widow made a donation to the town in 1907, thanks to which you can admire the biggest collection of works by the creator of the Statue of Liberty and the Belfort Lion.

MUSEE D'UNTERLINDEN 1, rue d'Unterlinden ✆ 03 89 20 15 50. *www.musee-unterlinden.com. Open May-October, every day: 9am-6pm. November-April, every day except Tuesday: 9am-12 noon and 2pm-5pm. Admission: 7 €, senior citizens and groups 6 €, 12-17s and students under 26 5 €, under-12s free. Audio-guides available.* This museum contains the Issenheim reredos. It is housed in the former Unterlinden Dominican monastery, and contains an exceptional collection of medieval and Renaissance painting and sculptures. The archeological section illustrates Colmar's past from Neolithic to Merovingian times. Urban and rural life in Alsace can be discovered in the Decorative Arts and Popular Arts and Traditions sections; Revolutionary and Empire souvenirs trace Colmar's later past. Avant-garde trends in painting from the Impressionists to the 20thc. can be found in the Modern Art section, including 1950s and 60s abstract painters.

NORTHERN VOSGES

In the north of the Bas-Rhin department on the Moselle-German border, a vast forest covers the mountains, containing fauna of all kinds. Marvellous scenery and walks are on offer.

NORTHERN VOSGES REGIONAL NATURE RESERVE ✆ 03 88 01 49 59. *www.parc-vosges-nord.fr.* Set up in 1975, between Alsace and Lorraine, it covers 122,000 ha. with over 100 towns and villages. Admire the splendid pink Vosges sandstone (used to build Strasbourg Cathedral) in the form of cliffs, strangely-shaped rocks and castles, and discover the reserve via the many paths for hikers. Enquire at the Maison du Parc or on the website.

Haguenau

North of Strasbourg, Haguenau blends into the superb forest with its potters' villages. This industrial and economic centre contains fine 18thc, buildings: houses with Louis XV fronts, a mansion (Rue Clémenceau), half-timbered farm (Rue de la Mare aux Canards), former Royal Moneylender's mansion (now a tribunal), and churches. Earlier buildings can still be seen, however: the Tour des Pecheurs on the

Moder banks and the Tour des Chevaliers (next to Place Charles de Gaulle) are the remains of the 1230 wall. The Wissembourg Gate is left from the 1300 wall.

MUSEE ALSACIEN 1, place Joseph Thierry ✆ 03 88 73 30 41. *Open Monday-Friday: 9am-12 noon and 1.30pm-5.30pm; Saturday & Sunday (and public holidays): 2pm-5pm.* Contains examples of local popular arts and traditions. Decorative objects, costumes and caps, furniture, ceramic and pottery, cake tins and holy images retrace life in Alsace over the past centuries, with period rooms (kitchen, living-room. potter's workshop) and scenes.

La Petite-Pierre

Mountainous and wooded, with streams gurgling through the valleys, this country is perfect for hiking. Afterwards, stop off in a hotel-restaurant like the local weekenders, and indulge your taste buds.

MAISON DES PAIENS. The Celts knew this site for its vibrations, the most powerful life-wave hitting exactly this spot. It is a magic and sacred place, where you can feel the enchantment.

Saverne

Gateway to 'the rest of France' in the southwest of the Northern Vosges regional nature reserve.

CHATEAU DES ROHAN ✆ MUSEUM *Open all year. 15 June-15 September: 10am-12 noon and 2pm-6pm (closed Tuesday). Admission: adult 2.70 €.* The original 12thc. fortress developed into this castle. Its museum has a section on the journalist Louise Weiss (1893-1983), a room on the history of the Château des Rohan de Saverne (formerly the Bishops of Strasbourg's residence) and a room with polychrome wooden sculptures. Archeological, Gallo-Roman and medieval collections are exhibited in the castle's vaulted cellars.

NOTRE-DAME-DE-LA-NATIVITE CHURCH. Overlooks the-castle. Though rebuilt in the 15thc., it has kept its Romanesque steeple and portal. Contains Robert de Bavière's mausoleum, a beautiful pulpit, paintings and frescoes and fine stained glass in the Holy Sacrement Chapel.

JARDIN BOTANIQUE DU COL DE SAVERNE ✆ 03 88 91 21 00. *Open 1 May-15 September, Sundays & public holidays: 2pm-6.30pm. 1 July-31 August, Saturday, Sunday and public holidays: 2pm-6.30pm.*

Saverne

Admission: adult 2.50 €, child/student 1.50 €. Pharmacist Emile Walter created this garden in 1931. 2,000 varieties of plant can be found in over 2 ha.; a real maze of peat, pools, conifers, insectivores and aquatic plants. Includes France's biggest orchid collection.

Wissembourg

Dates back to 650, when Benedictine monks founded an abbey on a small island in the Lauter. The abbey expanded, thanks to a gift from King Pepin le Bref. Stanislas Leszczynski, deposed King of Poland, lived here in exile until his daughter Marie maried Louis XV in 1725, making him Duke of Nancy. Wissembourg has some fine buildings, including the Maison des Chevaliers (1606) and the famous Maison du Sel (after the Lauter Bridge) topped by a huge and sumptuous roof with wave-shaped openings. Built in 1448, it served as hospital, salt warehouse and finally abbatoir. The Town Hall, built by Joseph Massol, former Dominican Church and Hôpital Stanislas are also worth seeing, as is the beautiful Renaissance Vogelsberger house. Bartholdi's family lived in the Maison à l'Ancienne Couronne. It is especially pleasant to walk round the rampart remains.

SAINT PIERRE ET PAUL CHURCH. Put up in the 13thc, this Gothic masterpiece was linked to the monastery. A square tower remains from the Romanesque period, and the cloister is pure Gothic, though unfinished. The stained glass is remarkable, as is the 15thc. fresco with its 11m Saint Christopher (no other character has been painted so tall in France).

MULHOUSE

There are lots of things to discover in Mulhouse, though it's rarely considered to be a tourist place. It was Alsace's industrial capital, nicknamed French Manchester in the 19thc. Most of its museums deal with technical history. Don't miss the Automobile Museum, with the world's biggest and finest collection of cars.

MUSEE NATIONAL DE L'AUTOMOBILE (Collection Schlumpf) 192, av. de Colmar ✆ 03 89 33 23 23. *www.collection-schlumpf.com. Open every day, 1 April-31 October: 10am-6pm. 1 November-31 March: 10am-5pm. Admission: 10 €, concessions 7.50 €, 7-18s 5 €, under-7s and 3rd child+ free.* The industrial magnate Fritz Schlumpf turned his passion for cars into a museum with 400 cars (100 Bugatti). Admire the Bugatti Royale, Rolls Royce, Hispano-Suiza, Panhard & Levassor, De Dion Bouton etc.

ELECTROPOLIS (MUSEE EDF) 55, rue du Paturage ✆ 03 89 32 48 60. *www.electropolis.tm.fr. Open every day: 10am-6pm. Closed Mondays, 1 January, Good Friday, 1 May, 1 & 11 November, 25 & 26 December. Admission 7.50 €.* Electricity, from its beginnings in the 17thc. to the present day. 500 objects illustrate this major industrial revolution, and its development is explained with an 80m-long model.

MUSEE DE L'IMPRESSION SUR ETOFFES 14, rue Jean-Jacques Henner ✆ 03 89 46 83 00. Open every day. 10am-12 noon and 2pm-6pm, except Monday, and Tuesday from 1 October-30 April. Admission: adult 7 €. Ticket including entry to Rixheim Wallpaper Museum, 10 €. 6 million samples and 50,000 textile objects take you on a trip through three centuries of fabrics: cottons and printed calicos, Liberty prints and paisley patterns. The contemporary section has splendid seventies kitsch on display.

MUSEE DES BEAUX ARTS 4, place Guillaume Tell ✆ 03 89 45 43 19. *Open every day: 10am-12 noon and 2pm-6pm/6.30pm July & August.* Mulhouse's Fine Arts Museum is housed in a splendid 18thc residence built by the painted canvas manufacturer Jean Vetter, then bought by Georges Steinbach in the 19thc. It is known today as the Villa Steinbach. The museum contains European paintings from different schools and periods: medieval religious paintings, works by Pieter Brueghel, Le Jeune, Courbet and Teniers. Temporary exhibitions of contemporary artists like Yann Pei Ming (last year) are held, and there is an art library, where you can borrow works of art; an original touch.

MUSEE FRANCAIS DU CHEMIN DE FER 2, rue Alfred de Glehn ✆ 03 89 42 83 33. *Open every day: 10am-6pm, 1 May-30 September; 10am-5pm, 1 October-30 April (except 25 & 26 December and 1 January).* This spectacular museum was set up along the Strasbourg-Bâle railway line: over 100 steam, electric and diesel locomotives, railcars, trucks and carriages are on view, in a reconstructed station. Admire the 'Saint Pierre' (1844 Buddicom) and the fine Bugatti railcar, not forgetting the luxury Pullman carriages and Heads of State's trains.

PARC ZOOLOGIQUE & BOTANIQUE 51, rue du Jardin-Zoologique ✆ 03 89 31 85 10. *Open all year. May-August: 9am-7pm. Admission: adult 9 €* Over 1,200 animals from 190 species, some rare or almost extinct (Siberian tiger, Persian panther, bald ibis, Prince Alfred stag) and others more common (monkeys, otters, vultures and polar bears). The park also contains an interesting botanical collection.

STRASBOURG

Alsatian city and European capital, Strasbourg has many faces. The old quarters (Petite France) are remarkably well-preserved, the winstubs continue a gastronomic tradition, and you can breathe the atmosphere of past times in the markets. You also hear the local dialect spoken everywhere. Strasbourg is a modern city too, with avant-garde architecture (Palais des Droits de l'Homme, the new addition to the European Parliament and the Modern Art Museum).

CATHEDRAL Place de la Cathedrale. Enquiries: ✆ 03 88 21 43 34. Built by Erwin von Steinbach in pink sandstone, its spire soars to 142m, adding beauty and coherence to the whole. The rose window, tympanum, astronomical clock, wonderful stained glass windows, angel pillar and pulpit can be singled out for admiration.

PETITE FRANCE. You reach the main tourist quarter by following the quays as you come down from the cathedral. Admire the banks of the Ill with its lock and little bridges, and the 16th and 17thc. Alsatian houses (Maison des Tanneurs and Rue du Bain-aux-Plantes). This was once a disreputable area; now it is neat and picturesque.

SAINT THOMAS CHURCH Place Saint Thomas. This 13th and 14thc. church is known as the 'Protestant Cathedral'. Inside, you can see Le Tombeau du Marechal de Saxe, by Pigalle.

MAISON KAMMERZEL Place de la Cathédrale. One of the town's finest houses, this Renaissance building has always been a place of business. Its wooden sculptures represent the Zodiac signs, Five Senses and heroes of classical antiquity

MUSEE ALSACIEN 23-25, quai Saint Nicolas ✆ 03 88 52 50 01. *Open every day except Tuesday: 10am-6pm (or 12 noon-6pm according to season). Admission: adults 4 €.* This Popular Arts Museum illustrates the region's past customs and folklore, tracing a path through old Strasbourg houses linked by staircases and wooden gangways. Thousands of objects, souvenirs of rural life in 18th and 19thc. Alsace, are on display. You'll love the reconstructions of typical period interiors from different parts of Alsace, and craftsmen's workshops from bygone days.

MUSEE ARCHEOLOGIQUE 2, place du Château (Palais Rohan) ✆ 03 88 52 50 00. *Open every day, except Tuesday: 10am-6pm. Admission: adult 4 €, concessions 2 €, under-18s free.* The Archeological Museum, housed in the palace basement, contains Alsace's distant past, from Paleolithic, Neolithic, Bronze and Iron Ages to Gallo-Roman civilisation and the Merovingian era.

MUSEE DES ARTS DECORATIFS 2, place du Château (Palais Rohan) ✆ 03 88 52 50 00. *Open every day except Tuesday: 10am-6pm. Admission: 4 €, concessions 1.50 €.* The Palais des Rohan's ground floor (built from Robert de Cotte's plans) houses the King's and Cardinal de Rohan's Grands Appartements (18thc.) There is a collection of Hannong china, gold plate and Strasbourg furniture in the stable wing. The Palace is worth visiting for both its architecture and its contents.

MUSEE D'ART MODERNE ET CONTEMPORAIN 1, place Hans-Arp ✆ 03 88 23 31 31. *Open every day except Monday: 11am-7pm; Thursday 12 noon- 10pm. Admission: adult 5 €, concessions 3 €.* Modern and contemporary works housed in a recent building (Fainsilber, 1998). You can see Picasso and Brauner downstairs, and Boltanski, Arman and Buren are on view on the first floor.

MUSEE DES BEAUX ARTS 2, place du Chateau (Palais Rohan) ✆ 03 90 24 04 85. *Open every day except Tuesday: 10am-6pm. Admission: adult 4 €, concessions 2.50 €. Palais des Rohan, first floor.* The museum contains a fine collection of medieval to 19thc. paintings, including works by Giotto, Canaletto and Tiepolo.

MUSEE ZOOLOGIQUE 29, bd. de la Victoire ✆ 03 90 24 04 85. *Admission: 3 €, concessions 1.50 €. Open every day: 10am-6pm, except Tuesday. School groups by appointment, bookings 03 90 24 04 83.* France's second-biggest zoological collection (after Paris) is housed in acrid-smelling rooms with creaking floorboards.

NAVISCOPE ALSACE 18, rue du General-Picquart ✆ 03 88 60 22 23. *Open Tuesdays, Wednesdays, Saturdays and Sundays: 2.30pm-5.30pm. Admission: adult 4 €, concessions 2.50 €, under-4s free. Guide: 15 €.* From machine-room to wheelhouse. the Alsace Naviscope, set up aboard the 'Strasbourg'

Christmas Markets

Christmas in Alsace begins in early December, when towns and villages set up their Cristkindelsmarkt, or Christmas Market. Stalls full of light sell baubles, *santons* and a variety of decorations, but also sweets, toffee-apples and mulled wine. The tradition is widespread throughout the region.

Strasbourg, Palais des Rohan

© Iconotec.com

moored in the Bassin des Ramparts, explains Rhine river transport; navigation, bridges, harbours and life on the Rhine. Temporary exhibitions.

BOAT TRIPS ON THE ILL 15, rue de Nantes ✆ 03 88 84 13 13. *www.strasbourg.port.fr. Cost: 6.80 €, concessions 3.40 € (evening trips slightly more expensive).* See Strasbourg from the water, from the ultramodern European Parliament buildings to Petite France's half-timbered houses. Trips leave from the Palais Rohan embarkation point every half-hour from 9.30am-9pm in April; 9.30am-10pm, May-October and 10.30am, 1pm, 2.30pm and 4pm other months. Trip lasts 1hr 10 mins.

Mont-Sainte-Odile

Odile founded the first convent in Alsace, where she lived a saint's life, and performed miracles, curing the blind. It is built on the site of Hohenbourg Castle, offered by the saint's father, which in turn once housed a Roman castrum. This is a quiet place for meditation, although it has had its ups and downs. Influential in the 12thc, burned down in 1546 but rebuilt in 1661, condemned by the Revolution, it finally became a place of pilgrimage in 1853. Today daily services, meditation and prayers are held. The building was restored in 1930. The great courtyard is beautiful, and parts of the Romanesque church were preserved in its later 17thc. structure. In the cloister, the former refectory now houses a tea-room! The 12thc. Chapelle de la Croix contains (copies of) Adalric and Bereswinde's tombs ; they were Saint Odile's parents. Sainte-Odile Chapel itself houses her sarcophagus; her relics have been authenticated. Major works of artistic marquetry from the 1930s (Charles Spindler) can be seen in the church.

PAGAN WALL. From the Mont-Saint-Odile, you go up the steps to the path along the Pagan Wall. This impressive structure dates back to Celtic times, and is 1.7m thick and 3m high, spreading its huge blocks over 10km. It takes several hours to go the whole length, but the walk is instructive; you see traces of the Druid cult, like dolmens, as well as the ruins of Dreistein and Hagelschloss medieval castles (in Strasbourg library).

BIRKENFELS LANDSBERG CHATEAUX. Near Mont Saint Odile, there is a path to Birkenfels, small 13thc. castle reinforced in the 14thc. and restored in 1976. Towards Barr, another path climbs to Landsberg Castle, with its interesting ruins (13thc. keep and oriel window in the primitive chapel) where the Abbess Herade of Landsberg was born. She played her part in the Mont's spreading influence, and designed the Hortus Deliciarum, an illuminated manuscript for instructing nuns, which sadly disappeared in the fire of 1870.

Obernai

This small, ultra-touristy capital of the Lower Rhine is also an industrial town, housing a Kronenbourg brewery production site. It really is a beautiful place, despite being such a tourist trap.

KAPELTURM. This belfry is a chapel steeple, put up in 1285 (only chancel and tower remain from the period). The belfry's gallery and Gothic spire were added in the 16thc. Beautiful sculptures.

PUITS AUX SIX SCEAUX. This superb, much-photographed Renaissance well attracts thousands of tourists.

Obernai

HISTORIC BUILDINGS. Splendid buildings, portals and inside courtyards with their secrets fill the town. First influenced by Mont Saint Odile Abbey, Obernai became independent, then was one of the Decapole's 10 cities in 1354, finally flourishing in the 16th and 17th centuries. Parts of the ramparts have been preserved: Foch, with its round tower, the Tour de Swal, Monseigneur Freppel, Joffre and Monseigneur Caspar. The River Ehn runs along the edge of the old town and under the fine Neo-Gothic Saints Pierre and Paul Church, put up in 1806.

Rosheim

A wine-growing town, with plenty of ancient buildings. Rosheim was important in the Middle Ages: a free (1303) then Imperial town (1323), and finally part of the Decapole (1354).

SAINTS PIERRE AND PAUL CHURCH. Romanesque masterpiece of 12thc. Rhenish style. Built of yellow sandstone, with a later red sandstone steeple, the church has some fine sculpted scenes on the outside, and the capitals inside are superb.

ROMANESQUE HOUSE. At the corner of Rue de l'Hôpital, this must be Alsace's oldest stone house. Built in 1170, it reminds you of a 12thc. fortress.

HISTORIC BUILDINGS. Ramparts, and three gates - the Lion, the Porte Basse and the Ecole - are signs of a former defensive wall. There are also some beautiful Renaissance houses, a sculpted well (1605), former butchers' and the clocktower.

RHINE VALLEY & ALSACE PLAIN

From Strasbourg to Basle, the Rhine is part of the landscape, and is a natural border berween France and Germany. A border marked by war, and the famous Maginot Line, but now flowing peacefully, with its wonderful glints and highlights. The Alsace Plain runs down to the Rhine Valley; this is central Alsace, with its capital Sélestat, between Lower and Upper Rhine.

The Maginot Line

In 1929, Andre Maginot became Minister for War, and the following year, he had a law voted on France's new defence organisation. A string of fortified defences were to be built along the German, Belgian and Italian borders, but the work was not finished until 1935 in the north east and 1940 in the south-east. In Alsace, there are 2,000 forts, blockhouses and shelters on the Line, making it a 200 km fortified rampart. You can visit Schoenenbourg, Hatten, Leutenheim, Lembach, Dambach-Neunhoffen and Marckolsheim.

MAGINOT LINE MEMORIAL MUSEUM Route du Rhin - MARCKOLSHEIM ✆ 03 88 92 56 98. *Closed 16 November-14 March 2006. Adults 2 €.* Blockhouse 35 of the 3rd Line saw violent fighting on 15, 16 and 17 June 1940. Thirty brave soldiers stopped the enemy advance, though the Maginot Line was outflanked. The inside has been reconstructed and contains a museum and a memorial. Headquarters, ammunition store, dormitory and various weapons are reminders that living conditions were hard. There are some rare material and period documents concerning other historic events: a Russian howitzer, 1st DFL half-track, 2nd DB Hartmannswillerkopf tank and a Division Leclerc machine-gun.

Rouffach

Fortified from the 12thc., this town has a Tour des Sorcières (Witches' Tower); a result of the Inquisition. In the reign of Henri V, the town revolted against the King, who simply had it burned down. Marechal Joseph Lefebvre, Duc de Dantzig and Madame Sans-Gêne's husband, was born here. Isenbourg Castle overlooks the town, today known chiefly for its organic market.

Rouffach has some fine buildings; the Witches' Tower, capped with a storks' nest (when there were no witches, it served as a prison); 16thc. Cornmarket and Rouffach Museum with its Roman and Romanesque remains. The Tourist Office is housed in the old Town Hall and the Maison de l'Oeuvre Notre Dame is now the Haxakessel restaurant. You must also see the Tour des Bouchers, Recollets convent (late 13thc) and Notre Dame de l'Assomption Church (fine example of transitional architecture, Romanesque to Gothic) containing a Callinet organ. Thirty metres from the office, a Stork Reserve has fifteen residents. You find some superbly picturesque sites on the plain around Rouffach, between Colmar and Soultzmatt.

Sélestat

Sélestat grew up around its historic centre which is almost a museum. There are 11th-15thc. churches and chapels, 16th and 17thc. Renaissance houses and the 17th-18thc. royal period, when many of the town's bourgeois and working-class buildings were put up. A few examples of military architecture complete your history trip.

SAINT GEORGES CHURCH. Today, this is the Parish Church. Building began in the 13thc, it has Romanesque foundations and a 1430 chevet. The 60m Flamboyant Gothic tower was completed in 1490. Inside, there is a fine Renaissance pulpit dating back to 1619. The 15thc. stained-glass is striking; the rose window goes back to 1400.

SAINTE FOY CHURCH. Built of granite and pink sandstone between 1152 and 1190. This fine Romanesque building was restored in Baroque style by the Jesuits, then again from 1875 to 1893 in Rhenish Neo-Romanesque. Notice the transept crossing's octagonal tower and the beautiful sculptures on the front and narthex. Inside, the Baroque pulpit dates back to 1733, and in the crypt you can see the Inconnue de Sélestat bust, cast from an unknown woman who died around 1100, and who could have been Hildegarde or her daughter.

FORTIFICATIONS. The Witches' Tower was built in 1216, and reshaped in 1280 and 1390. There are 38 towers surrounding the town, where women accused of witchcraft were locked up. The Tour Neuve (or Clocktower) put up during the second fortification campaign in 1280 was transformed in the 17thc. The Strasbourg Gate is a rare reminder of the Tarade wall; the ramparts were two bastions, one on the river side (Manege), the other on the mountain side (Capucins).

MAISON DU PAIN D'ALSACE Rue du Sel ✆ 03 88 58 45 90. *Open all year. Adults : 4,60 €.* This is first and foremost a touristic, cultural and economic centre. The general public can do some hands-on breadmaking in the working bakehouse, and trace the history of bread from its origins to the present day, with loaf-tasting! The products made and sold onsite are excellent.

FOOD & DRINK

Alsace's traditional cooking, like its beer, has recently become fashionable everywhere, especially on brasserie menus. Don't be fooled by the eternal choucroute; this cuisine is richer and more varied than it seems. Not so easy to digest, but so tasty that you don't mind.

Asparagus

The asparagus officinalis likes the region's soil, and is savoured in April and May. Exquisite to taste, it is also good for you, being low in calories, carbohydrates and fats, and containing iron and Vitamin C.

Baeckeofe

Traditionally, this dish, a meat and potato stew, was cooked in the village baker's bread-oven. Times have changed, but the recipe is the same: a mixture of pork, lamb and beef marinated overnight in riesling with onions, salt and pepper. The meat is then layered with potatoes in a casserole dish, and the lid sealed with a strip of pastry (often tinfoil nowadays). The dish cooks slowly at 180 degrees C for about 3 hours. Delicious!

Bretzels

The name means 'pastry in the shape of linked arms'. Bretzels are eaten with beer or an aperitif, and must be tasted fresh, for nothing is worse than an old, dry bretzel, even dipped in your pint.

La charcuterie

Very popular in Alsace: ham, sausages, frankfurters (Strasbourg-style) and saveloy fill the tables. Salade Alsacienne is often composed chiefly of grated cheese and saveloy. Not healthy, but very good. Local producers include Geismar, Kirn, Pierre Schmidt and Tempé.

Choucroute

Flagship of regional gastronomy and internationally known, the fermented cabbage accompanied by a variety of sausages and charcuterie is not for those on a diet. Pity to miss it, though.

Foie gras

Invented by Jean-Pierre Clause (a Lorrain!) chef to the Marechal de Contades, 18thc. military governor of Strasbourg, and not in the South West, as you might think. Forget the quarrels between Alsace and Périgord, though; the main thing is the taste (cooked or uncooked). As we're in Alsace, enjoy your foie gras with a gewurztraminer 'Vendanges Tardives', in one of the region's winstubs.

Munster (Munster-Gerome)

The name comes from Irish monks who settled in the Munster Valley long ago. The local cheese has much more flavour than the industrially-produced kind: after all, it is matured for 3-6 weeks. Try it with jacket potatoes, cumin, thick slices of bread and a nob of butter, washed down with an excellent beer. Munster has an AOC that turns out 9,000 tonnes a year.

Pain d'épices

Good children get a *pain d'épices* (gingerbread) on Saint Nicolas' Day, in the form of a heart, a star or a well-known character. Honey, sugar, cinnamon and other spices go into the making, and Gertwiller is its town (10 manufacturers at the turn of the century).

Horseradish

This was an aphrodisiac in ancient Greece! It is also popular in Alsace, as a condiment to go with pot-au-feu meat. Mietesheim even has a horseradish festival.

Beer

Brewing goes back to the late Middle Ages in Alsace: there are a lot of hop fields, giving top-quality beers. After World War II, economic development and competition led to the disappearance of many small breweries, and the bigger ones merged (Kronenbourg, Meteor). Today, there is a new fashion for micro-breweries, like the Brasserie de Saint-Pierre (www.lasaint-pierre.com) which produces exquisite pale, light and brown ales.

BRASSERIE DE SAVERNE 60, rue de Dettwiller ✆ 03 88 02 19 99. *www.karlsbrau.com.* The Scheickhardt family brewery, started in 1845, and later bought by the German group Karlsberg.

KRONENBOURG 68, route d'Oberhausbergen - STRASBOURG ✆ 03 88 27 42 06. *www.brasseries-kronenbourg.com.* The famous brewery dates back to 1664 (as it says on the bottle), set up in the centre of Strasbourg. It is now on the outskirts of the city, and you can visit the 17thc. mash tuns and learn about making beer: malting, brewing, fermenting and maturing.

Hotels & Restaurants

BAS-RHIN

Blaesheim

CHEZ PHILIPPE SCHADT 8, place de l'Eglise ✆ 03 88 68 86 00. *Closed Sunday evening and Monday. Set menus 35 €, 50 € and 60 €.* This little village, just about opposite the international airport, boasts a restaurant popular with artists and politicians; you'll soon realise why! Philippe Schadt's extrovert personality counts, of course, as does his warm welcome and the attention he pays to his customers. The *cuisine* is sophisticated, influenced by seasonal produce, and his specialities feature on the blackboard: foie gras in brioche, pikeperch fillet (22 €), game, frogs' legs (22 €) and mushrooms, but the undisputed leader is definitely the choucroute. Philippe also suggests his grandmother Caroline's recipes: a traditional dish served in the casserole pot for the whole table, with second helpings for everyone. An excellent idea – and a great place to eat!

La Wantzenau

LE RELAIS DE LA POSTE ** 21, rue du Général-De-Gaulle ✆ 03 88 59 24 80. *Website: www.relais-poste.com. Closed Saturday lunchtime Sunday evening and Monday. Set menus from 35 € to 95 €, surprise menu, 10 dishes. Rooms from 77 € to 244 €. Breakfast 11 €.* Jeôme Daull has a star in the Michelin Guide, which means inspired regional cooking for his customers! His cuisine is sincere, respects culinary tradition and harmonises with the seasons; it also specializes in fish. Lobster with pink grapefruit, fresh foie gras with Muscat jelly, stuffed boned quail with a morel sauce, young roast chickens grand-mère, grilled bass *flambée* with Provence herbs, and scallops with celery purée, spinach fondue and truffle juice feature on his menu.The setting is superb in the dining room and typically Alsatian rooms alike; warm, colourful, and very comfortable, with plenty of carved wood and soft rugs. You feel great here – what more could you want? Perhaps a terrace (hard to resist), a perfect welcome and service, and business lunches that are excellent value for money.

Lembach

AUBERGE DU CHEVAL BLANC 4 rue de Wissembourg ✆ 03 88 94 41 86 *Fax 03 88 94 20 74. Website : www.au-cheval-blanc.fr. Set menus from 35 € to 90 €, à la carte 80 €. Closed Monday and Tuesday lunchtimes, Friday lunchtime, 23 January-10 February and 21 August-8 September.* Like the Cygne, her sister-hotel 15km away at Gundershoffen, this White Horse embodies the best aspects of the hotel business Alsatian-style: a warm welcome at reception and in the restaurant, a well-decorated rustic setting, classic cuisine and a cellar bound to please even the most demanding wine-tasters. The Mischler family looks after the hotel, with Fernand overseeing the kitchens. The menus feature langoustines, scallops and oysters pressed in seawater, oyster and sea urchin cappucino, shallot and red wine vinegar emulsion to spread on rye bread, frog *jambonnettes* on a garlic flan with parsley juice, frog soup with frog emulsion on little bread slices, pollack fillet in a clam and cockle risotto, and their juice flavoured with star aniseed and lime, pan-fried fillet, roast duck liver escalope, steamed carrots with cumin and a conserved chicory *rouelle,* a raisin sweet with Pinot Noir jelly and rosé crémant (sparkling wine), and marc de Gewurztraminer sorbet. Service relaxed and smiling.

Obernai

LE BISTRO DES SAVEURS 35 rue de Sélestat ✆ 03 88 49 90 41 *Fax 03 88 49 90 51. Set menus 41 € to 76 € (including wine) à la carte 60 €. Closed Monday and Tuesday, 29 January-16 February, 17 July-8 August and 22 October-10 November.* In barely 3 years, Thierry Schwartz has turned this village inn (once known as Le Boeuf Rouge) upside down. The original woodwork and exposed beams are still there, but otherwise the four-hundred-year-old Alsatian house has been transformed, and given a cosy but uncluttered look. The dining room has just been completely repainted too, and now provides the right setting for Thierry's personalised regional cuisine. He is a native of Strasbourg, and won his spurs with the Ibarboure brothers, Emile Jung and Robuchon before opening his restaurant in October 2002. His "Maréchal de Contades" goose liver pâté, green Pertuis asparagus with fresh morels grilled over a log fire, *lomo ibérico* (Spanish-style chops) wild Adour salmon (home-fished) with herbs and almonds, and suckling pig in all forms from head to trotters, violet mustard and buckwheat noodles brought him instant success. The desserts are excellent, especially the strawberries, melon and rhubarb with Baux-de-Provence olive oil, and the eclectic cellar reveals an intelligent choice of wines.

Ottrott

L'AMI FRITZ * 8, rue des Châteaux ✆ 03 88 95 80 81. Fax : 03 88 95 84 85.** *Website: www.amifritz.com. Double rooms from 70 € to 100 €, breakfast 11 €. Restaurant closed on Wednesday. Set menus from 21 € to 59 €, children's menu 10 €.* This beautiful 18thc. stone residence up on the village heights is both cosy and rustic in style, with typically Alsatian woodwork inside, and a terrace planted with trees and flowers. It must be the ideal setting for tasting Patrick Fritz's light and delicate regional cooking. Warm suckling pig salad, choucroute - traditional, fish or duck – veal with morels, roast saddle of lamb with herbs, tomato conserve, artichokes and potato gnocchi are on the menu. The 22 rooms are pleasant, colourful, comfortable and perfectly equipped.

Sélestat

ABBAYE DE LA POMMERAIE * 8, avenue Foch ✆ 03 88 92 07 84.** *Website: www.pommeraie.fr. Rooms from 141 € to 246 €. Suites 291 € and 316 €. Breakfast 16 €. Winstub open every day. Gastronomic restaurant closed Sunday evening and Monday lunchtime.* This hotel, with its splendid rooms and two restaurants, is housed in a superb Renaissance–style building, and has two restaurants, Le S'Apfelstueble and Le Prieuré. The first has a *winstub* (Alsatian pub or wine-bar) ambiance, simple and convivial with a lunch menu at 26 €, a set menu at 51 € and an excellent choice *à la carte*. The second boasts a gastronomic *cuisine* highly thought-of in the area, with a set menu at 89.50 €. The setting is exquisite: thanks are due to the Funaros, for their warm welcome, and to Daniel Stein for his top-quality cooking.

Strasbourg

BUEREHIESEL 4 parc de l'Orangerie ✆ 03 88 45 56 65 *Fax 03 88 61 32 00. Website : www.buerehiesel.com. Set menus from 126 to 148 €, à la carte 130 €. Closed lunchtimes Monday-Friday, closed Sunday evening and Tuesday, 1 January-19 January and 1-28 August.* The Buerehiesel and Antoine Westermann have been inseparable for over 30 years. The young chef set up in business in the early 70s, in a 17thc. Alsatian farmhouse with a winter garden in the Orangerie Park near the European Institutions, and within 10 years, was known for one of France's finest *cuisines*. His restaurant is reputed, without being the least bit severe or intimidating, and the service is always relaxed and smiling. Steamed green and white asparagus, morels stuffed with duck liver in a reduction of natural juices, pan-fried Dublin Bay prawn tails, an assortment of raw and cooked vegetables, citronella and ginger jelly, steamed bass, oyster tartare with iodised cream reduced with Riesling, roast saddle and leg of Pyrenean lamb, braised fennel and lamb Parmentier, strawberries and rhubarb in their juice and in sorbet, and pistachio and coconut moelleux. The chef has 3 stars now, and is rising 60, so he plans to hand over to his son Eric, barely 30 and a qualified chef since 2004. The Buerehiesel can look forward to a bright future with confidence.

CHEZ YVONNE 10, rue du Sanglier ✆ 03 88 32 84 15. *Website: www.chez-yvonne.net Open every day and all year, except Christmas and New Year.* It seems only yesterday that Yvonne Haller, that legend in Alsatian gastronomy, retired, leaving her almost-mythical restaurant in capable hands. French President Chirac and the German Chancellor Helmut Kohl have dined there together; the President no doubt ordered the calf's head at 15 €. The menu is influenced by pure Alsatian tradition, such as ham knuckle with a potato salad (14 €) but there are also creative dishes like goat's cheese terrine with vegetable conserve and pistou salad (10 €). Game features in season. *Winstub* setting and atmosphere.

AU CROCODILE 10 rue de l'Outre ✆ 03 88 32 13 02 *Fax 03 88 75 72 01. Website : www.au-crocodile.com. Set menus from 58 € to 127 €, à la carte 120 €. Closed Sunday, Monday, 9-13 July and 24 December-8 January.* Almost 35 years after opening, Emile Jung and his chef Laurent Huguet go on flying the Alsatian flag in their internationally-famous restaurant, now completely recovered from its turn-of-the-century setback. This is a generous and aristocratic place; you may even spot an ambassador or high-ranking politician at the next table. The menu is attractive too: foamy lobster cream and ravioli with massala, roast pikeperch and carp roe with a mix of cabbage and choucroute and fresh coriander, whole oven-cooked sea bream, chicory braised in velvet swimming crab juice, Alsace farm-bred chicken breast in a pot-au-feu with citronella, roast figs with late raspberries and Tahiti vanilla ice cream. Up-to-date cuisine in a historic setting; a beautiful and unforgettable restaurant.

HOTEL DU DRAGON * 2, rue de l'Ecarlate ✆ 03 88 35 79 80.** *Fax : 03 88 25 78 95. Website : www.dragon.fr. Single rooms from 69 € to 103 €. Double rooms from 79 € to 112 €. Breakfast 9.90 €.* This hotel is only a stone's throw from the quays, yet it is perfectly quiet. You can enjoy a peaceful breakfast in the courtyard under the lime trees - in summer at least. The Dragon could have chosen a traditional decorative approach with Alsatian furnishings, to suit its 17thc. architecture, but prefers to go for contrast, so the huge, light rooms are decorated in sober modern style. There are works of art at reception, and some pieces of furniture signed Philippe Starck. It all adds up to zen and state-of-the-art in a historic framework - and it works!

HAUT-RHIN

Colmar

BRASSERIE L'AUBERGE – hôtel Bristol 7, place de la Gare ✆ 03 89 23 17 57. *Website : www.grand-hotel-bristol.fr Open every day. Dish of the day at lunchtime 9.85 €. Terrace.* Alsace's regional produce in all simplicity, yet so professionally cooked. That sums up this pleasant brasserie in a few words. The dining room is huge, with wide, welcoming banquettes to relax on, and the prospect of a really good meal ahead. The *salade vigneronne* (winegrower's salad) is generous at 9 €, and the choucroute (15 €) is light, whatever you may have been led to expect. You could round off the experience with a *vacherin glace à l'alsacienne* (ice cream dessert Alsace-style) at 7.50 €; it's truly delicious.

AU FER ROUGE 52, Grand'Rue ✆ 03 89 41 37 24. *Fax : 03 89 23 82 24. Website : www.au-fer-rouge.com. Set menus: 50 €, 70 € and 99 €. Closed Sunday evening and Monday. Closed all day Sunday and Monday in low season. Terrace.* You can't miss this beautiful 16thc. building as you stroll through the town, especially at Christmas, when it sparkles with a thousand lights - rather like its reputation. Chef-owner Patrick Fulgraff has been thrilling gourmet taste buds since 1977, and developing his culinary arts in all delicacy, so this is bound to be a special, and very tasty meal - but you'll be hard put to choose from so many appetising dishes. Pan-cooked pigeon breast in a port sauce, perhaps (35 €), or pike and scallop mousseline, Noilly sauce (30 €) or for dessert, a *berawecka* (typical Christmas patisserie) fruit croustillant flavoured with gingerbread liqueur (15 €). There are more complex compositions, but we aren't going to give away *all* their secrets. You'll enjoy discovering French gastronomic art for yourself.

JY'S 17 rue de la Poissonnerie ✆ 03 89 21 53 60 *Fax 03 89 21 53 65. Website: www.jean-yves-schillinger.com. Set menus from 28 € to 65 €, à la carte 55 €. Closed Sunday, Monday lunchtime and February school holidays.* JY's for Jean-Yves Schillinger, son of a chef brought to notice by the 1980s culinary guides. His restaurant is also a concept: an ultra-trendy dining room decorated by a famous interior designer, and a thematic cuisine, which can't fail to impress, Schillinger being a skilful technician who knows his products. Variations on the egg theme, for instance: boiled in its shell, spread with herring caviar and a bread finger with lemon butter to dip; scrambled with truffles and a foie gras finger to dip, and poached Japanese-style with a chickpea finger. Then roast dory fillet on fig and tomato chutney, creole black pudding and carrot juice flavoured with ginger and lime, roast sweetbreads on 'forgotten' vegetables glazed with poultry cooking juices and the roast emulsion, hazlenut clafoutis, and dates and pine kernels with a mandarin salad and sorbet, among other amazing recipes. The service seems to have been cast for a filmset. Well worth looking into.

Kaysersberg

LE CHAMBARD * 9, rue du Général-De-Gaulle 03 89 47 10 17.** *Fax : 03 89 47 35 03. Website : www.lechambard.fr. Restaurant closed all day Monday, Tuesday and Wednesday lunchtimes. Winstub open every day. Set menus from 45 € to 71 €. Rooms from 93 € to 195 €.* Chambard is stylishly traditional, as befits a great Alsatian hotel. The rooms are spacious and pleasant, especially the ones with a balcony overlooking the vines. Friendly welcome and logical prices, more attractive for single rooms. The restaurant is very well run, though you'll find the *winstub* especially good value for money. Excellent choucroute.

Mulhouse

L'ARDOISE GOURMANDE 3, rue des Tanneurs 03 89 46 66 98. *Closed Sunday and Monday, restaurant open 12 noon to 11.30pm, brasserie open 8.30am to 3.30pm. Set menu of the day 13 € (starter and main course). À la carte 12 € to 20 €.* In the first place, you feel at home in this Parisian brasserie ambiance. As the meal goes on, you realise it's much more than that. Young chef Vincent Mura gives of his best, and this can be tasted and seen, in the quality of the meat and its presentation. Offal is the house speciality, though other seasonal suggestions feature on the large slates along the walls: asparagus *feuilleté* with morels and their sauce (17 €), oysters, or a seafood salad, saddle of lamb with herbs (served with particularly good vegetables) and for dessert, fresh fruit with sorbets. There are also suggestions on the wine list; as with the food, let yourself be tempted; you won't regret it.

Stork in Hunawihr

AUBERGE DES FRANCISCAINS 46, rue des Franciscains 03 89 45 32 77. *Closed Tuesday and Sunday evenings. Set menu of the day 9.80 €.* In this picturesque Alsatian residence, located in the town's historic quarter, the customers jostle each other in the doorway for a table. The region's traditional cuisine is carefully concocted by a lively and good-humoured chef, who offers a second, seasonal menu as well as the usual one. There's something for everyone, and no-one leaves with an empty stomach. Among the specialities you find the inevitable choucroute *garni* (14.50 €), the *surlawerla,* or liver cooked in madeira, with spaetzles (14 €), liver quenelles with fried potatoes and green salad (12.90 €) and *bibbeleskas* and potatoes (8 €). Apart from the menu of the day, served every lunchtime except Sunday and holidays, there is the menu *du marché* (20 €) with its vegetable cream and charcuterie cocktail. prime beef cut with onion puree and french fries, cheese or dessert. These menus are for the daring, of course - the careful customer will settle for a flambéd tarte - or even two!

HOTEL BRISTOL * 18, avenue de Colmar – Parking in the rue d'Illzach. ✆ 03 89 42 12 31.** *Rooms from 55 €. Restaurant service for groups, banquets and* *family celebrations only. Receptions and seminars organised (4 large rooms). Car park.* Close to the town centre and Mulhouse's museums, but away from the Tram-Train roadworks, the Hotel Bristol stands proudly behind its fine1900 facade. Inside, the reception area is beautifully fitted out, in warm colours with two cosy lounges. There are 90 rooms, including 25 suites, all differently decorated. You'll appreciate the staff's kind and attentive welcome.

Ribeauvillé

HOSTEL LA PEPINIERE* - RESTAURANT AU VALET DE CŒUR 40, route de Sainte-Marie-aux-Mines © 03 89 73 64 14.** *Fax : 03 89 73 88 78. Website: www.levaletdecoeur.fr Restaurant closed Sunday evening, all day Monday and Tuesday lunchtime, except public holidays. Hotel open 7 days a week. Double rooms from 48 € to 82 €. Triple rooms available (70 € to 92 €). Apartment, sleeps 4, 92 €. Breakfast 10 €. Set menus from 33.50 €.* This hotel is outside Ribeauville, and seems to suggest rest and relaxation on first sight. Inside, however, the emphasis is on discovery. Firstly, your taste buds are invited to discover the *découvertes gustatives* menu at 62 € (often renewed, like the other menus). A pan-fried foie gras escalope with mirabelles might be matched with wild boar and fig puree, then a dessert on an apple theme. After, you can learn *sabrage*, which means opening a bottle of champagne with your sabre in a most dashing manner. You even get a diploma!

Riquewihr

LA TABLE DU GOURMET 5 rue de la 1re-Armée © 03 89 49 09 09 *Fax 03 89 49 04 56. Website: www..jlbrendel.com. Set menus from 38 € to 90 €, à la carte 100 €. Closed all day Tuesday, Wednesday and Thursday lunchtimes in low season (mid-October to late March), all day Tuesday and Wednesday, and Thursday lunchtime in season and early January to mid-February.* When you come into the dining room, the shock to the eyes is considerable. Riquewihr, splendid little pedestrian village, and this solid winegrower's house with its austere 16thc. facade will have led you to expect anything but this setting: an original and innovative combination of alternate red and black. Jean-Luc Brendel's cooking follows the trend; no ham in pastry or choucroute on his menus, but saint-georges meadow mushrooms on a jack-straws arrangement of grilled bread, rock lobster tail with angelica, green peas and their shoots, beef fillet with hot jelly and pot-au-feu herbs, charlotte potatoes *dentelle* and marrow 'kneppfle', and iced vacherin with lemon milk and sorbet made of red fruit candied in alcohol. The chef's sister Fabienne Brendel looks after the cellar, and keeps it well stocked with Alsace wines, along with a few fine Burgundies.

LE SARMENT D'OR ** 4, rue du Cerf © 03 89 86 02 86. *Closed Sunday evening and Monday. Set menus from 20 € to 48 €. Double rooms from 60 € to 80 €. Breakfast 8 €.* Away from the tourist bustle, but close to the Dolder, this hotel is sophisticated in every detail, from the rooms to the restaurant. These 9 rooms and duplex are charming, and select, there being so few of them. The cuisine is skilled and enthusiastic: pheasant tart, saddle of suckling veal with summer truffles, pan-fried foie gras escalope with apples. In autumn, you find one of the region's finest game menus.

Turckheim

AUBERGE WINSTUB DU VEILLEUR 12, place Turenne © 03 89 27 32 22. *Set menus from 20 € to 30 €. Set menu of the day 9.10 €.* You get an idea of Turckheim before even crossing the first doorstep. Exposed beams and half-timbering are fairly typical in a winstub, but the carefully presented and garnished plates are a cut above many of them. Try these potatoes with soft white cheese, two small portions of munster and raw salad vegetables, and the house speciality, calf's head with its tongue and vinaigrette sauce. You will be full up after an outlay of 11.20 €, and ready to take in details like the kelsch tablecloths (Alsatian checked fabric), Alsatian chairs and glass plate design. You can be very clever by tasting a selection of wines here, then buying them 800m down the road, at the Turckheim cellar.

Aquitaine

Biarritz, the Virgin's rock

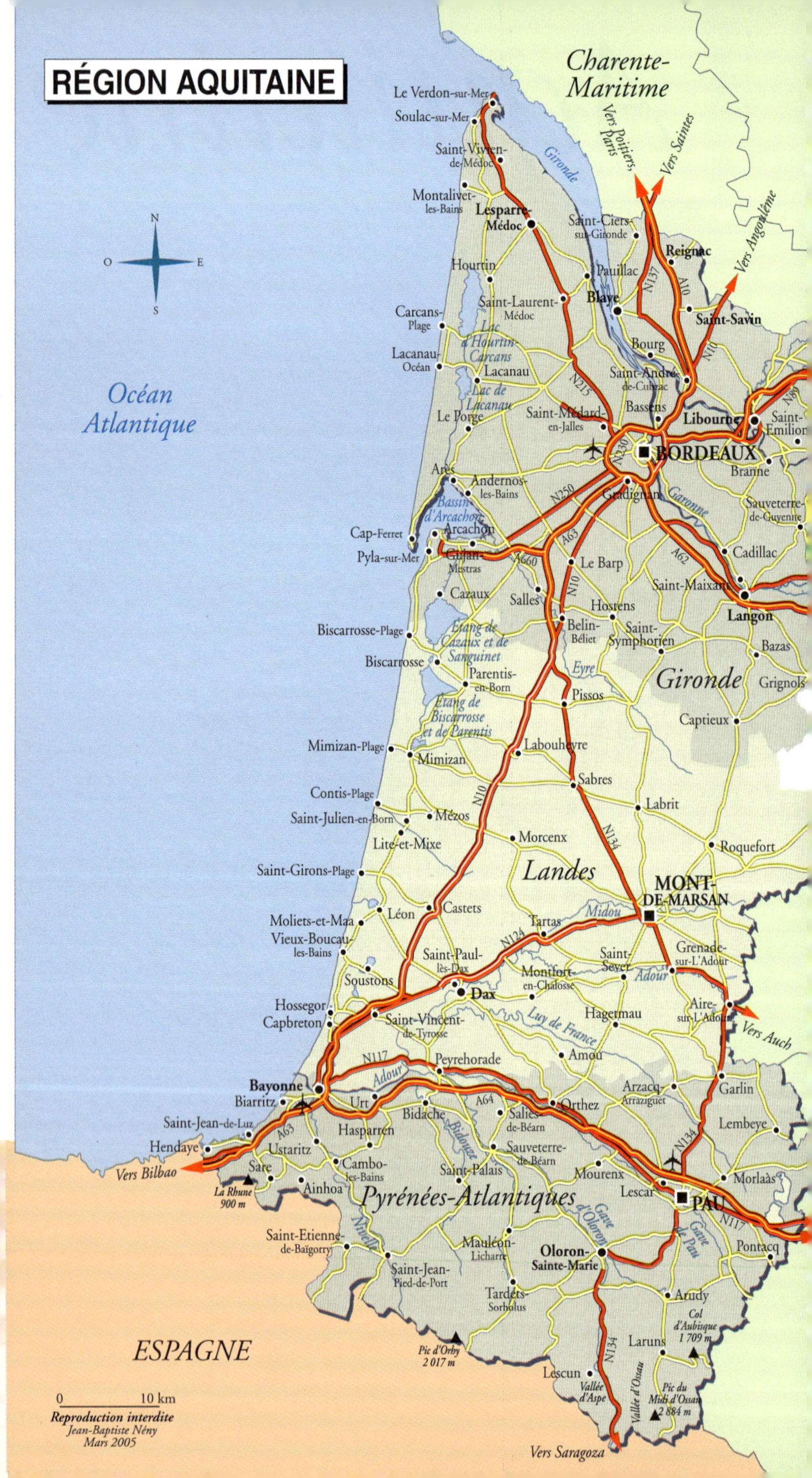
RÉGION AQUITAINE
Charente-Maritime
Vers Poitiers, Paris
Vers Saintes
Vers Angoulême
Océan Atlantique
N
O
E
S
Le Verdon-sur-Mer
Soulac-sur-Mer
Saint-Vivien-de-Médoc
Gironde
Montalivet-les-Bains
Lesparre-Médoc
Saint-Ciers-sur-Gironde
Reignac
Hourtin
Pauillac
N137
A10
Saint-Laurent-Médoc
Blaye
Saint-Savin
Carcans-Plage
Lac d'Hourtin-Carcans
Bourg
Lacanau-Océan
Lacanau
N215
Saint-André-de-Cubzac
N10
Lac de Lacanau
Bassens
N89
Le Porge
Saint-Médard-en-Jalles
Libourne
Saint-Émilion
N230
BORDEAUX
Branne
Arès
Andernos-les-Bains
Bassin d'Arcachon
N250
Gradignan
Garonne
Sauveterre-de-Guyenne
Cap-Ferret
Arcachon
A63
Pyla-sur-Mer
Gujan-Mestras
A660
Le Barp
A62
Cadillac
Cazaux
Salles
N10
Saint-Maixant
Langon
Hostens
Biscarrosse-Plage
Étang de Cazaux et de Sanguinet
Belin-Béliet
Saint-Symphorien
Bazas
Biscarrosse
Eyre
Parentis-en-Born
Gironde
Grignols
Pissos
Étang de Biscarrosse et de Parentis
Captieux
Mimizan-Plage
Mimizan
Labouheyre
Sabres
Contis-Plage
Labrit
Saint-Julien-en-Born
Mézos
N134
Morcenx
Lite-et-Mixe
Roquefort
Saint-Girons-Plage
Landes
MONT-DE-MARSAN
Léon
Castets
Midou
Moliets-et-Maa
Tartas
Vieux-Boucau-les-Bains
N124
Saint-Paul-lès-Dax
Saint-Sever
Grenade-sur-L'Adour
Soustons
Montfort-en-Chalosse
Adour
Dax
Hossegor
Capbreton
Saint-Vincent-de-Tyrosse
Hagetmau
Aire-sur-L'Adour
Luy de France
Vers Auch
N117
Amou
Peyrehorade
Adour
Bayonne
Arzacq-Arraziguet
Garlin
Biarritz
Urt
A64
Orthez
Saint-Jean-de-Luz
Bidache
Salies-de-Béarn
Lembeye
A63
Hasparren
Bidouze
N134
Hendaye
Ustaritz
Sauveterre-de-Béarn
Vers Bilbao
Sare
Cambo-les-Bains
Saint-Palais
Mourenx
Morlaàs
La Rhune 900 m
Ainhoa
Lescar
PAU
Pyrénées-Atlantiques
Gave d'Oloron
N117
Saint-Etienne-de-Baïgorry
Nivelle
Mauléon-Licharre
Oloron-Sainte-Marie
Gave de Pau
Pontacq
Saint-Jean-Pied-de-Port
Tardets-Sorholus
Arudy
Col d'Aubisque 1 709 m
ESPAGNE
Pic d'Orhy 2 017 m
Laruns
N134
Lescun
Vallée d'Aspe
Vallée d'Ossau
Pic du Midi d'Ossau 2 884 m
0 10 km
Reproduction interdite
Jean-Baptiste Nény
Mars 2005
Vers Saragoza

Charente
Haute-Vienne
Vers Limoges
Bussière-Badil
Nontron
La Coquille
Mareuil
Saint-Crépin-de-Richemont
Brantôme
Thiviers
Lanouaille
Corrèze
Verteillac
Dronne
Auvézère
Ribérac
Hautefort
PÉRIGUEUX
Saint-Aulaye
Terrasson-Lavilledieu
Vers Brive-la-Gaillarde
La Roche-Chalais
Saint-Astier
A89
N89
Thenon
Montpon-Ménestérol
Mussidan
Isle
Dordogne
Montignac
Peyzac-le-Moustier
Vergt
N21
Vézère
Salignac-Eyvigues
Les Eyzies-de-Tayac
Sarlat-la-Canéda
Castillon-la-Bataille
Vélines
Bergerac
Saint-Cyprien
Sainte-Foy-La-Grande
La Roque-Gageac
Sainte-Mondane
Belvès
Domme
Issigeac
Duras
Eymet
Villefranche-du-Périgord
Castillonnès
Lot
La Réole
Seyches
Miramont-de-Guyenne
Villeréal
Lacapelle-Biron
Marmande
Cancon
Monflanquin
Saint-Pastour
Fumel
N113
Gontaud-de-Nogaret
Villeneuve-sur-Lot
Tournon d'Agenais
Tonneins
Castelmoron-sur-Lot
Penne-d'Agenais
Casteljaloux
Lot-et-Garonne
Aiguillon
Garonne
Houeillès
Lavardac
AGEN
Nérac
A62
Tarn-et-Garonne
Laplume
Vers Montauban
Vers Toulouse
Poudenas
Gabarret
Vers Auch
Tarn
Gers
Haute-Garonne
Vers Tarbes
0
30 km
Ariège
Hautes-Pyrénées
Autoroute
Nationale
Départementale

BEARN

Pau

Its historical tradition and defensive position have always been strong, as has English influence (first continental golf-course). Pau is Aquitaine's second-biggest town, modern and 'multimedia'. Between Bordeaux and Toulouse, Atlantic and Mediterranean, it has a marvellous view of the Pyrenees.

BOULEVARD DES PYRÉNÉES. This magnificent walk, linking Henri IV's castle with the town casino, has seen crowned heads, great 19thc, poets and rich tourists go by, and was once lined with great hotels, now converted into apartments with a mountain view.

MUSEE DES BEAUX ARTS DE PAU Rue Mathieu-Lalanne ✆ 05 59 27 33 02. *Guided tours every day except Tuesday: 10am-12 noon and 2pm-6pm. Admission: adult 3 €.*

One of Aquitaine's biggest museums, dating back to 1864, and now housed in a sober 1930s building. Renovation work has given a new dimension to the exhibitions, organised thematically: traditional Spanish, Arab-influenced Spanish, Orientalists; then art deco and contemporary art. Among the artists are El Greco, Rubens, Piazetta, Fantin-Latour, Morisot, Rodin, Degas and Marquet. There is a permanent educational service for schools, and a mediatheque extension is planned.

MUSEE NATIONAL DU CHATEAU DE PAU Château d'Henri IV ✆ 05 59 82 38 00. *www.musee-chateau-pau.fr. Open every day: 9.30am-12.15pm and 1.30pm-5.45pm. Guided tours in French, Spanish and English, lasting 1 hour. Admission: 5 €, concessions 3 €, under-18s free.* The town's castle and chief monument is one of France's 33 National Museums. Henri IV was born there in 1553, but it was on his accession that it came into its own as a Crown possession, both he and Louis XIII transferring some of the Louvre's riches to Pau. In the reign of Louis-Philippe and the Second Empire, the castle was restored in Renaissance style, and after extensive work, the second floor was re-opened to the public. There are 16th and 17thc. paintings to see, and further on, Henri IV and his mother Jeanne d'Albret's bedchambers, with the legendary turtle-shell that served as a crib for the baby king.

MUSEE BERNADOTTE Rue Tran ✆ 05 59 27 48 42. *Open every day except Monday. Admission: adult 3 €.* Birthplace of the Marshal of France who founded the current Swedish dynasty. Discover his life through various objects, documents, original engravings and paintings exhibited in his 18thc. house. The museum attracts Scandinavians, especially Swedes; it is largely ignored by the French.

PAU-GELOS NATIONAL STUD-FARM (HARAS) Ave. du Général Leclerc ✆ 05 59 06 60 57. *Open from Tuesday to Sunday. Admission: adult 5 €* The stud-farm was the result of Napoleon I's visit to the Chateau de Gelos in 1808. Today it owns 100 draught, thoroughbred and racing stallions of local breeds, regularly mounted or harnessed in winter. Find out all about the site's history, horse-drawn vehicles housed in the stables, forge, tack room and three stables.

Aspe Valley

This superb natural site is often in the news, owing to the topicality of its monuments. Take the Portalet Fort: for the moment, this marvellous ruin's future is undecided. Or the abandoned Pau-Canfranc railway line, so much a part of the valley's landscape. Finally, the Somport, and the opening of the controversial tunnel which made - and still makes - feelings run high.

Accous

Former passing place for Crusaders and pilgrims (Jouers Chapel), perhaps the most important from 1385 onwards. Today this is a lively town which aims to develop the arts in the heart of the mountains.

SAINT SATURNIN DE JOUERS CHAPEL. 12thc. Romanesque. The semi-circular apse has a remarkable carved frieze, and the gabled wall-tower is topped with a square structure and recent quadrangular roof. Arras' troops burned it down in 1569; it was recovered in the late 16thc, improved in the 17thc, and totally restored from 1952-1953. Compostella pilgrims once used it as a refuge.

SAINT MARTIN D'ACCOUS CHURCH. The sanctuary dates back to the 14thc. The main body was demolished in the 18thc. and replaced by the present full-arched style.

Etsaut

Nestling at the foot of the Tour des Maures, the town's 14thc. defensive tower, Etsaut contains some old houses with ogival barn doors, and a beautiful medieval Bear's House.

MAISON DU PARC NATIONAL Le Bourg ✆ 05 59 34 88 30. *www.parc-Pyrénées.com. Open in season May-October: 9.30am-12.30pm and 2pm-6.30pm.* By appointment the rest of the year. One of six French National Parks, covering the southern part of the Aspe and Ossau Valleys in the Pyrénées-Atlantiques department, together with the Azun, Cauterets, Barèges and Aure Valleys. You will find information about the path network, refuges and rangers-instructors in this centre, plus exhibitions, projections, lectures and literature.

Le Somport

This cross-border resort has exceptional ski-ing slopes set between France and Spain, in the Pyrenees National Park.

CHEMINS DE LA NATURE. *Open Wednesdays in July & August, all year for groups. Enquiries and bookings at Bedous Tourist Office.* The Aspe Valley forests, chosen for the size and quality of their trees, were intended to provide wood for the Royal Navy's sailing ship masts in the 18thc. Christophe André, Issaux Forest warden, will be your guide and explain the grouping on three forest sites: Benou, Pacq and Issaux.

ECOMUSEE DE LA VALLEE D'ASPE Notre-Dame-de-la-Pierre ✆ 05 59 34 55 51. *Ouvert toute l'année. De juillet à septembre de 10h à 12h et de 14h à 19h. Adultes 4 €.* Marcel Amont tells the legend of stone and water in an original audio-visual production. Guided by the valley's sounds, light and scents, you identify miniature villages and rivers on a scale model, then follow the village's history from the Middle Ages to today. The whole experience takes about 1 hour 30 minutes.

TUNNEL DE SOMPORT. 275 million euros and 9 years of building work went into the Somport International Road Tunnel, now to be opened after final security checks. The tunnel measures 8,602m (2,848m in France, 5,754m in Spain) and is equipped with safety shelters every 400m, with a gallery to facilitate access for rescue teams.

Urdos

The valley's last village, 760m above sea-level. Urdos has an ancient past: traces of a Roman road and 'un Espitau de Peyrenere', surely the last halt on the road to Compostella. In the 16thc. the narrow Urdos pass was barred by a small fort,'lou Pourtalet', where a toll had to be paid. Alfred de Vigny was quartered there from 1823-1824. Between Urdos and the Somport Pass, heaps of slag and ore are all that remain of the Abel ironworks, built by a former Aydius goatherd.

FORT DU PORTALET. The Portalet Fort has left impressive ruins, reflected in the mountain stream 150m below. To get up there, you climb the 258 steps linking three covered ways. This 11thc. military fort became a 16thc. redoubt and a prison after World War II, never having seen any action. It did have some famous prisoners, though: Daladier, Blum, Reynaud, Mandel and Marshal Petain. Privately-bought in 1966, it slowly crumbled, and is a mere shadow of itself today after the ravages of time. It was listed in 1992, and in 1999, the valley village community bought it; restoration seemed at hand. Great projects are in the offing; for the present, the site is closed to the public.

Ossau Valley

One of the three main Bearn Valleys hollowing out the Pyrenees range. It is also a glacial valley: the Ossau Pic du Midi is Pau's emblem.

This is bear territory; a controversial subject that attracts plenty of media attention.

Artouste

In summer, this is a hikers' paradise with its little train. In winter, it attracts glide fans.

PETIT TRAIN D'ARTOUSTE ✆ 05 59 05 49 61. *Open June-early October. Admission: adult 17.30 €, child 13 €.* You go 690m up from Lake Fabrege (1,240m) in a cablecar to Sagette station on Europe's highest railway line. The little train covers 10km on narrow rails close to the cliff edge. The mountain scenery is breathtaking, and herds of cows, marmots, black grouse, bearded vultures and izards wander freely among the rhododendrons, sorbs, gentians and foxgloves. On arriving, climb up to Lake Artouste (1,994m) reflecting the Pic d'Ariel in its waters.

Arudy

Perched 414m above sea-level, Arudy's past is still present in its bridge, washing-place and Saint Germain Church with its Flamboyant Gothic portal, keystone and capitals.

MAISON D'OSSAU - Musee d'Arudy et du parc national ✆ **05 59 05 61 71**. *Open all year. July & August, open every day : 10am-12 noon and 3pm-6pm. Admission: adult 2.50 €.* Housed in a former 17thc. lay abbey with its carved door and 17th and 18thc. fireplaces, this Maison (a listed monument) contains Ossau's Natural History and Archeology Museum. Temporary exhibitions and video films can be viewed on the first floor. On the second, you find pastoral activities and local crafts and industries (marble quarries).

Gourette

One of the valley's biggest and busiest villages, and a meeting-place for tourists in season

MAISON DU PARC NATIONAL ✆ **05 59 05 41 59**. *www.parc-Pyrénées.com. Open in summer, every day: 9am-12 noon and 2pm-7pm. Monday-Friday in winter.* Don't forget to stop here before starting out into the valley, for environmental information (flora, fauna, vulture reserve) and advice. The exhibition is on two floors, with 15 showcases of birds, bears, izards, etc.

Tracking Bears

Environmental agents track the bear, bringing back clues (hairs, traces, faeces) to its whereabouts. From these, the Brown Bear network draws conclusions. This follow-up system has existed for 20 years, and a census is kept via itinerary cards, collections and a map, all available for scientific use, to determine the zones where dens may be found, or bears passing through. In Ossau, the bear population seems stable: there was only one native female left, the famous Cannelle (Cinnamon) shot down by a huntsman. Numbers have fallen dramatically since 1985, when 15 to 18 bears were counted in the whole of the Pyrenees.

Baretous valley

Arette

La Pierre-Saint-Martin's moonscape gives way to huge forests and some pastures below, while on the low slopes, chestnut groves, orchards and cornfields against a backdrop of hills foreshadow the Basque Country. -

ARBORETUM. *Open all year. Admission free (2-hour visit).* Your trip to the Bois de Calvaire (Calvary Woods) starts from the village. A theme path explains the ecological and historical aspects of these trees of all ages (the most ancient are over 300 years old).

CENTRE SISMOLOGIQUE ✆ **05 59 88 90 82.** *Visits by appointment.* Arette was severely shaken up on 13 August 1967 by the worst earthquake for a century. A network of 9 seismology stations was set up in 1978, from the Ossau Valley to Arbailles in the Basque Country, linked to Arette recording centre by radio, to give the alert in the event of a tremor.

CHURCH. Destroyed in the earthquake, rebuilt and inaugurated in 1973. A fine 16thc. lectern and the reredos were saved, and new stained-glass put in (made by M. Ambille, of Arette).

Iraty Forest

Perched between Larrau and Sainte-Engrâce a stone's throw from Spain, Iraty Forest spreads out its thousands of hectares of leafy trees, broken by pasture land and rocky ridges, between 1,200 and 1,500m above sea level. This is a migratory bird-watchers' paradise, and perfect for fishing, hiking and cross-country ski-ing in winter. Comfortable chalets welcome hikers in all seasons, in the heart of the massif.

La Pierre-Saint-Martin

Set up in 1961, this resort now has 22 km of hiking paths marked out. It is a unique karstic site, prized by pot-holers and cross-country walkers alike.

GORGES DE KAKUETTA ✆ **05 59 28 73 44.** *Open 15 March-15 November: 8am-dusk.* A trip to canyon country. One of Europe's wildest sites, now protected. In the heart of the mountain, you're in the Amazon basin, following the river through the rocks, between towering cliffs smothered in greenery. This picturesque place of legends and pastoral traditions was a stopping point on the Compostella Road.

Mountain streams and plain

Bellocq

BASTIDE. Little is left of this building, except a few mullioned windows and a carriage entrance holding up the ruins.

CHATEAU Les Amis du Vieux Bellocq ✆ **05 59 65 20 66**. Put up from 1250-1280, this fortress (listed in 1997) was simply-built without a keep, to shelter the villagers in the event of an attack, and must have seen plenty of action. Louis XIII had it demolished in 1621, threatened by the strength of Protestant Béarn.

CHURCH. Dates back to the late 13thc. The church was an integral part of the bastide's defences, with its tower a west-facing keep. It was successfully restored in 1969; you can admire the nave, portals and tombstones of Bellocq's noble families.

Biron

SALIGUE AUX OISEAUX ✆ **05 59 67 14 22**. The history of this reserve is rooted in the marsh, once drained, then reflooded by the Shooting Federation to bring back the birds that used to live there. Today it is open to the public. You can spot 95 different species of bird outside, and learn about them comfortably inside the museum in its old Béarn farmhouse. Identify barnacle geese, snipe, avocet, osprey and egret: climb to the top of a mirador and admire the four lakes laid out for the region's wild duck.

Navarrenx

This is the capital of salmon-fishing and a 'green' holiday resort. Old houses, a small church and a great reputation stem from its salmon-rich stream. The town began as a 13thc. bastide, and was rebuilt by the King of Navarre in 1542 on the right bank of the Oloron. Architect Fabricio Siciliano raised an Italian-style bastioned wall, revolutionary for the period, but which protected the town throughout all its sieges.

ARSENAL DE NAVARRENX. You can visit the outside during a guided tour organised by the Tourist Office on Wednesdays and Fridays. The arsenal was built on the remains of the 'Kings of Navarre's house' and finished in 1693. This imposing structure (590sqm) surrounds a rectangular courtyard (245sqm). It can house up to 500 soldiers but its real role was stocking arms, ammunitions and provisions for Navarrenx and Béarn. In the courtyard, 30,000 cannon balls or grenades, 60 gun carriages or mortars and 150,000 bullets were stored. Navarrenx commune bought the arsenal in 1992 and restored it, making it the town's cultural and tourist centre.

SAINT GERMAIN CHURCH. Built in 1562. Henri IV's mother Jeanne d'Albret took communion here for the first time as a Calvinist, establishing Protestantism in Bearn. In 1620, Louis XIII came to re-establish Catholicism. It was a failure; the Protestant faith prevailed in the community. Inside is more interesting than out, despite the chevet and cross: vaults interwoven with ivy and tiercerons, fine capitals on the pillars and a white marble altar.

Nay

BASTIDE DE NAY. The bastide (walled town) is of classic design: a central square with warehouses for merchandise and streets at the four corners, lined with houses whose overhanging first floors formed a covered gallery or emban.

SAINT VINCENT CHURCH. This typical Bearn church of striking proportions is Gothic in style, 40m high, with Arros stone walls and a tower-keep, first square then octagonal. Inside are a 16thc. stoup, historiated keystones and a 17thc. organ case.

MAISON CARREE. *Open July & August every day except Monday, May-October. Closed Monday, out of season; open Saturday. Admission: 3.05 €, exhibitions free.* This beautiful 'Square House' was a rich 16thc. merchant draper's residence. Its chief interest is its three floors of Italian-style galleries, looking onto the inside courtyard in classic Renaissance fashion.

MUSEE DU BERET Place Saint-Roch ✆ **05 59 61 91 70.** *www.museeduberet.com. Open July & August, every day: 10am-12 noon and 2pm-7pm. Other periods: call for information. Admission:*

adult 4€, under-10s free. This unique museum, housed in a Directoire building, traces the history of the 'Béret Basque' (although it actually comes from Bearn). France's most famous headgear is still fashionable even in the 21st century.

Oloron-Sainte-Marie

An age-old meeting-place, at the crossroads of three valleys, the mountains and the plain, Bearn and the Basque Country, France and Spain.

QUARTIER SAINTE-CROIX. Perched between the mountain streams, this sloping medieval quarter turns its face to the wind. At the top, the 11thc. church with its square fortified tower stands out against the Pyrénées. Going down, you find a 13thc. house (Rue Cujas), and a building with lancet arches (Rue Dalmais), then the Maison du Patrimoine and the 14thc. Tour de Grede.

SAINTE-MARIE-D'OLORON CATHEDRAL Rue Auguste-Peyre ✆ 05 59 39 04 15. *Guided tours in summer: 3pm-6.30pm every day.* Built by Gaston Fébus in 1102, the cathedral is now listed UNESCO World Heritage, and celebrated its 900th birthday in 2002 with a Medieval Day. Extensive work began the same year, to reinstall the Arbore Cross, refurbish the treasure and repair general wear and tear. Under the porch-tower, the 12thc. door displays two Atlantas chained to a pier, and Heaven and earth are on the tympanum. Chapels, chancel and ambulatory date back to the 14thc., while organ, gallery, pulpit and wooden crib figures are all 17thc. Not forgetting the 18thc. stoup! You can admire one of Murillo's paintings; Tableau de l'Assomption

Orthez

This town has a prestigious past. It was the capital of Bearn for two centuries, and pilgrims on the road to Compostella used to break their journey here. In the 16thc. it was a Protestant stronghold under Jeanne D'Albret, mother of Henri of Navarre. Today, the town is busy with sports and festivities (a feria is held in July). You can visit a number of monuments illustrating Orthez's colourful history: Moncade Château keep, the only surviving part of a once-magnificent castle overlooking the town, and Saint Pierre Church built in the late 13thc. which boasts an 18m-high nave without side-aisles. The Tourist Office can be found in the 15th and 16thc. manor known as the Maison Jeanne D'Albret, famous for its mullioned windows.

View of Orthez

CHATEAU MONCADE Rue Moncade. *May-September. Admission: adult 2€, 8-12s 1€.* A glance at this keep gives you an idea of what the castle was like . Protected by a ditch and 3 lines of ramparts, the living quarters backed onto the keep itself, which contained a prison without access at ground-floor level and the guards' room on the first floor. Gaston Fébus added 3 floors to the tower and set up his court there. A son et lumière model reconstructs medieval life in the castle.

SAINT PIERRE CHURCH. Built in the 13thc. on the site of a small church dedicated to St Thomas. Saint Pierre came out of the Wars of Religion in ruins, but the 14thc. Gothic portal (typical of Languedoc), its chancel and 18m-high nave without side-aisles are still visible.

MUSEE JEANNE-D'ALBRET - HISTOIRE DU PROTESTANTISME BEARNAIS Rue Bourg-Vieux ✆ 05 59 69 14 03. *Guided tours or individual access every day. Groups by appointment. Admission: adult 4.50€* Bearn is the only region in modern France where calvinism has been the offical religion. This was during the reign of Jeanne d'Albret (1572-1620), mother of Henri IV. The museaum located on the first floor of the Maison Jeanne d'Albret traces the history of the Reformation in the region, from the 16th right up to the 20thc. A large number of objects, engravings, scale models (galley) and religious furniture set the scene for historic figures like Henri IV, Antoine Court de Gébelin and the Reclus brothers. A unique story.

ORGUE DU TEMPLE ✆ **05 59 69 32 87**. The Reformed Church got a new German Baroque-style organ in 1996, considered to be one of the best in France, comprising choir organ, pedal-board, 25 organ stops and a painted and gilded case. Pre-Romantic compositions, Mendelssohn, Brahms and 20thc. music can be played to advantage on it.

PONT VIEUX. The 13thc. Orthez bridge was a crossing place for Compostella Pilgrims. Gaston VII Moncade built it and Gaston Fébus added the unequal arches, central tower and the town's motto (Toquey Si Gaonses). Damaged in the Wars of Religion, it managed to resist Napoleon's cannons in 1814. The town is proud of it, and has an expression, «Bieilh coum lou poum d'Orthez»: as old as Orthez Bridge.

Salies-de-Béarn

Set in a green landscape, with its narrow alleys, 16th and 17thc. houses and 18thc. church, Salies has developed its one saltwater spring into a resort for thermal therapy and getting into shape. Houses on piles line the River Saleys flowing through the town, which is known as the Venice of Bearn.

MUSEE DU SEL Rue des Puits-Salants ✆ **05 59 38 06 97.** *Open 15 May-15 October, Tuesday-Saturday: 3pm-6pm. Other periods: groups by appointment. Ticket including entry to the Museum of Bearn Traditions: 3 €.* Salies has been mining salt since the Bronze Age. The town grew up around this activity, and its story is told on the museum's 3 floors. Traditional methods of salt-making are demonstrated at local fêtes.

Bordeaux

Bordeaux and the towns around are the gateway to the Gironde region. Roman Burdigala developed into a medieval town which is still part of the modern city, contrasting with 18thc. influence round the Grand Theatre, and the contemporary Meriadeck quarter. Bordeaux is also a port, with strong maritime traditions currently being revived.

BORDEAUX MONUMENTAL 28, rue des Argentiers ✆ **05 56 48 04 24**. *Open every day. Admission free. Disabled access.* Discover Bordeaux's architectural heritage. This showcase on the ground floor of an 18thc. building in the Saint Pierre quarter leads you down the centuries from Burdigala to today's tramway, with sound effects, contemporary video clips and objects from Montesquieu's Ville des Lumières, Aliénor of Aquitaine's medieval Bordeu or Montaigne's Bourdeaux.

ESPLANADE DES QUINCONCES. The Bordelais are proud of their 12-ha. esplanade. On the eastern side stand two rostrum columns, on the western side, a monument (columns and fountain) to the Girondins (group of moderate Revolutionary MPs who protested against the Terror). Funfairs, second-hand markets and circuses are set up here every year, under the watchful stone eyes of Montaigne and Montesquieu.

PLACE DE LA BOURSE. Former Place Royale, designed by Louis XV's architect Jacques Gabriel, and inaugurated in 1755. The Three Graces fountain (1869) stands on the site of the sovereign's statue, dismantled during the Revolution. The houses along the quays offer a superb perspective of symmetrical arcades, floors and slate roofs.

PLACE DU PARLEMENT. Difficult not to admire these splendid fronts decorated with agrafes and mascarons. The square was laid out in 1760 and its fountain added in 1867, a neo-Louis XV composition with four mascarons on the base spouting trickles of water.

GRAND THEATRE Place de la Comédie ✆ **05 56 00 85 95**. *www.opera-bordeaux.com.* Bordeaux Grand Theatre is on of Europe's finest 18thc buildings. The classical peristyle is topped with 12 statues: the nine Muses and three goddesses Junon, Minerva and Venus, as the sculptor Berruer imagined them. Inside, the theatre is magnificently gilded, and was renovated in 1991.

SAINT MICHEL BASILICA Place Canteloup ✆ **05 56 94 30 50**. This Gothic church was built in the late 14thc; the inside is well worth a visit. The steeple is separate from the church, and was put up between 1472 and 1492 on the cemetery's former mass grave. It is 114m high: you have a superb view of town and river from the top.

SAINT SEURIN BASILICA ✆ ARCHEOLOGICAL CRYPT Place des Martyrs de la Resistance. *Open every day, 1 June-30 September, 3pm-7pm.* This is a truly ancient basilica: 11thc. porch and crypt; 12thc. chevet and transept. Notre Dame de la Rose Chapel dates back to the 15thc, as do the Bishop's pulpit, carved stalls and some fine alabaster. The site itself was occupied long before, however, being the town's oldest monument after the Palais Gallien.

SAINT ANDRE CATHEDRAL Place Pey-Berland ✆ 05 56 52 68 10. The world's first cathedral dedicated to Saint André. You find it on the Compostella road: the western face (and oldest part) goes back to the 11thc. The wall with its small bond is the only remains of the old church. The huge 12thc. single nave had its walls raised and its bays doubled in number in the 13thc., and the Porte Royale was opened up in 1250, a French Gothic masterpiece. The statues are striking with their realistic draperies and fine-featured faces.

MUSEE DES CHARTRONS 41, rue Borie ✆ 05 57 87 50 60. *Open Tuesday-Saturday, 10.30am-12.30pm and 2pm-5pm. Close Sundays & public holidays. Guided tours for groups on request.* This 18thc. royal wine-broker's building has the only vaulted cellars in the town open to the public. You can see how wine matures in casks, and discover a collection of 16th-19thc. wine bottles, the first series of labels lithographed, metal stencils for marking cases and cask-bottoms, and stories about wine and its travels across the world.

MUSEE DES BEAUX ARTS 20, cours d'Albret ✆ 05 56 10 20 56. *Open every day, closed Tuesday and public holidays. Open 11am-6pm; weekends 2pm-6pm. Admission; adult 4 €/5.50 €, concessions 2.50 €/3 €. First Sunday of the month: admission free.* Set up by Bonaparte in 1801, and now housed in the two garden wings of the Town Hall (Charles Burguet 1881), the museum has grown with the years. Start in the south wing, where you find 16th-18thc. European and French works (Titian, Rubens, Bruegel de Velours), and finish with the 19th and 20thc in the north wing (Delacroix, Matisse, Picasso). Discover the Bordeaux painters Andre Lhote and Albert Marquet, as well as monumental works like A chacun sa chimere by Henri Martin (6.47m long).

CROISEUR COLBERT Ancre face au cours de la Martinique ✆ 05 56 44 96 11. *Open all year. Opening times differ according to season. Closed January. Admission: adult 7.80 €. Groups of 10+ all year by appointment.* Now in retirement, the Colbert saw active service from 1959-1991. This giant naval fortress (180m for 10,600 tonnes) can be visited in under 2 hours; the operations room has been recently rehabilitated. One room is given over to the Legion d'Honneur, and there are exhibitions, photos and scale models to see.

JARDIN PUBLIC. Intendant Tourny created this 18thc. green oasis in the heart of Bordeaux. It was landscaped English-fashion in 1856, and its 11 hectares enclose a botanical garden, Museum of Natural History, lakes and playgrounds. On the Rue du Docteur-Albert-Barreau side is the ruined Palais Gallien, listed amphitheatre built in the 3rdc. A.D. by Emperor Gallien, and holding 15,000 spectators on its wooden tiers.

Médoc beaches

Lacanau

Vineyard in Blaye

At the turn of the last century, Lacanau saw the arrival of the 'holiday trains' from Bordeaux transporting townies keen to see the sea - which makes it the oldest seaside resort in the area. Today it offers dozens of cycle and hiking tracks, and wide beaches with huge waves. The Lacanau Pro international surfing competition is held here in August, with a fly-surfing contest in September, recently started. Watch out for the waves when you're swimming: they are very fierce (there are firemen in a 4X4 on the beach, ready to fly to the rescue by jet-ski).

MUSEE DE LA MEMOIRE CANAULAISE 77, ave. de la Liberation ✆ 05 56 03 53 73. *Open out of season by appointment. March & April, Thursday: 2.30pm-5.30pm. June-August, Tuesday & Thursday: 2.30pm-5.30pm. Admission free.* Housed in an 18thc. residence, this museum displays objects, tools and ancient domestic utensils recalling old-fashioned trades: joiner, saddler, wine waiter, stilt-maker, pit sawyer, collier, blacksmith, etc. A team of historians is currently preparing Lacanau's centenery, for 2006.

Soulac

Typical seaside resort. Soulac grew out of the 19thc. fashion for sea-bathing and the railway boom together. In a few decades, a thriving town with station, casino, covered market, hotels, bathing establishments and 500 or so Neo-Colonial style villas had sprung up. Today the site is listed, and very chic.

NOTRE DAME DE LA FIN DES TERRES BASILICA ✆ 05 56 09 86 61. *Open every day: 9am-6pm. Admission free.* The basilica has a marvellous 11thc. nave with four bays, a 12thc. chancel, 14thc. Gothic steeple and magnificently-worked historiated capitals.

Cordouan Lighthouse

Cordouan is the oldest lighthouse in France, and only the second French monument to be listed, in 1862, along with Notre Dame de Paris. White and majestic, it rises to 66m, 9km from the Grave headland, and has been watching over the troubled waters of the Gironde estuary for centuries. A first tower was put up in the 14thc, with a hermit on the top who kept big fires going to guide ships. In 1584, Louis de Foix was given the task of rebuilding a new lighthouse, to be a Royal Work. This was finished under Henri IV, and is today considered as one of the world's finest. Cordouan has seven storeys, with a marvellous view of the Gironde estuary, Arvert Coast, Coubre headland and Medoc Coast from the top.

Bordeaux Vineyards

This must be the world's best-known and most reputed winegrowing region: 115,200ha. of vines (112,000ha. of AOC) producing an annual average of 6.6 millions of hectolitres, which means 800 millions of bottles sold. The great vintages are exported to each continent, and even the 'little wines' can be kept and age well. There is a wide variety of Bordeaux wines to discover.

CIVB 1, cours du 30-Juillet ✆ 05 56 00 22 66. www.ecole,vins-bordeaux.fr. Open Monday-Friday: 9am-5.30pm. Opposite the Tourist Office, the Conseil Interprofessionnel du Vin de Bordeaux's school invites you to get to know, and taste, Bordeaux wines.

PLANETE BORDEAUX 1, route de Pasquina - Beychac et Caillau ✆ 05 57 97 19 35. *www.maisondesbordeaux.com. Open Monday-Friday : 9am-12 noon and 2pm-5.30pm. Summer opening hours June-October: Monday-Saturday 9am-6pm. Admission: adult 5 €.* 15km from Bordeaux, this is a fun experience. Use your senses to discover the world of Bordeaux and Bordeaux Superieur, with explanations from a professional wine-taster at the dégustation. The Cellar of 1001 Châteaux names you 1,001 winegrowers selling at château prices.

VINORAMA MUSEE DU VIN 12, cours du Medoc ✆ 05 56 39 39 20. *Open all year. July & August, open Tuesday-Saturday: 10am-12.30pm and 2.30pm-6pm, Sunday 2pm-6pm. Admission: adult 5.40 €.* This museum's storehouse traces the history of Bordeaux wine up to the 19thc. and reveals manufacturing secrets in reconstructed scenes with sound effects and 75 characters. The tasting that follows is as instructive: you taste a wine made to a Roman recipe, an 1850s wine and a contemporary one. Interesting for families of all ages.

Blaye

Blaye Citadel is a town within a town, a fortified city set up on a strategic site. It is also a port where different goods were loaded and unloaded: Bordeaux wines and produce from neighbouring Charente.

You can board the ferry 'Côtes de Blaye' for Lamarque in the Medoc region on the opposite bank, or go further afield, towards Le Verdon or Royan.

CITADEL TOURIST RECEPTION Rue du 144eme regiment d'Infanterie - La Citadelle ✆ 05 57 42 86 64. Open Sundays and public holidays April-September, 2pm-5pm. French and English fought over this medieval fortified town, of great defensive importance. Between 1686 and 1689, Vauban built the present citadel to defend the river, with Fort Pâté and Fort Médoc. It only had to resist a very short siege in 1814, and has never been taken. Compostella pilgrims had to come through Blaye until 1830, and it was a busy port.

LA MANUTENTION Citadelle - Place des Armes ✆ 05 57 42 80 96. *Open all year (opening times 05 57 42 12 09).* Built in 1677 to house the citadel and town prison, this square building was later a bakery, shop and storehouse. Today it contains exhibitions of the estuary Conservatory and Blaye Archeological Association, 7,000 years of History.

SAINT ROMAIN BASILICA ✆ 05 56 58 54 49. *By appointment, Saturday & Sunday.* The basilica's remains can be seen on the outside weathering of the citadel, and a recent dig has excavated the layout. It is difficult to imagine, though, what it was like when Roland de Roncevaux (Charlemagne's peer) was buried there in 778.

MAISON DES VINS DES PREMIERES CÔTES DE BLAYE 11, cours Vauban ✆ 05 57 42 91 19. *www.premieres-Côtes-blaye.com. Open Monday-Saturday, 8.45am-12.30pm and 2pm-6.30pm.* 250 wine references out of 450 of the AOC's producers are to be found here. Visitors are given a guide to the Côtes de Blaye, and can learn to taste wine (free sessions during July and August, Tuesday, Wednesday & Thursday: 4.45pm-5.45pm, book before 1pm on the day).

La Brède

One of southern Gironde's biggest baronies, and Montesquieu's home town. He was born here a century before the Revolution, and his grandfather Jean de Secondat's tombstone can be seen in the cemetery, among others. The church was reshaped in the 19thc.

SYNDICAT D'INITIATIVE DES GRAVES ET DE MONTESQUIEU 3, ave. du Général-de-Gaulle ✆ 05 56 78 47 72. *www.graves-montesquieu.com. Open Monday-Saturday: 9.30am-12 noon and 2.30pm-5pm.*

CHATEAU DE LA BREDE Ave. du Chateau ✆ 05 56 20 20 49. *Open Easter-30 June and 1 October-11 November, Saturdays, Sundays and public holidays, 2pm-6pm. 1 July-30 September, every day: 2pm-6pm, except Tuesday. Admission: over-7s 6,50 €.* Montesquieu was born here 1689, and often came back to the castle after going to study in Paris. The writer (L'Esprit des lois) liked to look after his land and grew wine (mostly entre-deux-mers) at Chateau Ramonet. Chateau La Brede (listed historical monument) is a fortified manor, surrounded by a moat. Parts of it go back to the 12th and 15thc., though it was transformed in the 16th and 17thc. It is still a superb building, with water flowing under its drawbridge and an 18thc. keep. Inside, you can visit the writer's library and his bedroom furnished from the period. The castle is set in a vast green park.

Cadillac and Entre-Deux-Mers

Between Dordogne and Garonne, the Entre-deux-Mers contains some marvellous architecture. Abbeys, bastides, castles and churches recall the English presence during the Middle Ages (villages to see: Rions, La Réole, Monségur and Cadillac). This is a region of vineyards: dry white Entre-deux-Mers, Bordeaux and Bordeaux Superieur reds and sweet Premières-Côtes-de-Bordeaux from Saint-Croix-du-Mont or Loupiac.

TRIPS TO PREMIERE CÔTES DE BORDEAUX AND CADILLAC. The Premier Côtes de Bordeaux and Cadillac Winegrowers' Syndicate publishes and distributes (free) a guidebook to trips in their region, where you can find the adresses of winegrowers who welcome visitors and offer tastings, walking and hiking paths and the country's most remarkable sites marked in red and gold (the colours of Bordeaux wine and Cadillac grapes). For a free guide, call 05 57 98 19 20 or get one at the Syndicat Viticole des Premières Côtes de Bordeaux et Cadillac.

CHATEAU DE CADILLAC Place de la Libération ✆ 05 56 62 69 58. *Open all year, except Monday from October to late May: 10am-1.15pm and 2pm-6pm (in season) Admission: adult 4.60 €. Admission free first Sunday of the month October-May.* Jean-Louis de Nogaret de la Valette, first Duc d'Epernon was first one of Henri III's 'mignons', later, an ambitious and important courtier under Henri IV and Louis XIII. His castle's first stone was laid in 1599, and building took 30 years. Damaged during the Revolution, it became a women's prison until the late 19thc. then a specialised education centre for young girls until the mid-20thc. Inside, the ceilings are pannelled and there are some fine tapestries and richly-decorated marble fireplaces.

TOUR DES REMPARTS. A walk round Cadillac shows you the central square with its arcades and some ancient houses, then the Tour de l'Oeuille (a gate of the same name disappeared in 1818) and the Ruet, a passage between houses and ramparts which once went right round the town. Further on, the Porte de la Mer looks towards the river with its high square tower and flood scale. Finally, you come to the second gate still intact (out of four), the 14thc. Porte de l'Horloge.

Fronsac

MAISON DES VINS DE FRONSAC 3, chemin du Tertre © 05 57 51 80 51. *Open mid June-mid September: 10.30am-7pm. Other periods: 9.30am-12.30pm and 2pm-6pm.* The fronsac AOC showcase: you should definitely call in here before discovering its chateaux. There are 1,100ha. of vines grouping together fronsac and canon-fronsac. There are over 90 wines on sale (château prices).

Lalande-de-Pomerol

A great reputation for such a tiny village! The pretty 12thc. church, recently renovated, is the region's only Knights Templars church (Saint Jean of Jerusalem order). It is rectangular, has two 18thc. chapels and a flat chevet with 5 windows. The cemetery contains a fine Gothic cross.

SYNDICAT VITICOLE AOC LALANDE DE POMEROL 2, rue du 8 Mai 1945 © 05 57 25 61 60. *www.lalande-pomerol.com. Open Monday-Friday: 2pm-6pm, Tuesday & Thursday: 9am-12 noon and 2pm-6pm.* This winegrowers' syndicate groups together 210 producers of this AOC, spread over the villages of Lalande-de-Pomerol and Neac. The 1,100 ha. of vines include merlot, cabernet franc and cabernet-sauvignon. The Lalande-de-Pomerol vineyards may be small (4ha. on average) but they produce great wines.

The Mascaret

During the Equinox period with its high tides, a tidal wave called the mascaret forms in the ocean, and rises up the Gironde, Garonne and Dordogne estuary, providing plenty of fun for surfers. The scene is most impressive in front of Vayres and Saint Pardon villages.

Libourne

An important crossroads on the Isle and Dordogne confluence, Libourne is the gateway to the great vineyards Saint-Emilion, Fronsac, Pomerol and Lalande-de-Pomerol. The town has access to the sea (the Dordogne flows into the Gironde, on its way to the Atlantic) which helped the growth of trade and established Libourne as a bourgeois town.

MUSEE DES BEAUX ARTS Place Abel Surchamp © 05 57 55 33 44. *Open Monday-Friday: 10am-12 noon and 2pm-5pm. Admission free.* This Fine Arts Museum contains a collection of 15th to 20thc. paintings, including the works of Libourne painter René Princeteau.

Listrac

CAVE DE VINIFICATION DES GRANDS VINS DE LISTRAC-MEDOC 21, ave. de Soulac © 05 56 58 03 19. *www.cave-listrac-medoc.com. Open Monday-Saturday: 8am-12 noon and 2pm-6pm, Sunday: 9am-12noon and 3pm-6pm.* Shady car park. Set up in 1935 by the commune's winegrowers for the great Listrac-Médoc wines, this vinification cellar handles the wine-making process for 50 producers, a quarter of the AOC's output. Some use a separate process.

Loupiac

Fans of sweet wines recognise the name, and the site was already known in Roman times: the remains of a 2nd and 3rd-century Gallo-Roman villa were probably the poet Ausone's residence. Loupiac's Romanesque church portal has four decorated archivolts set on six columns with carved capitals.

Margaux

This little village is world-famous. A third of listed grands crus (great vintages) come from this strip of land representing only one tenth of Médoc vines. The greatest of all is the Château Margaux, classified premier grand cru in 1855.

CHATEAU MARGAUX ✆ **05 57 88 83 83**. *www.chateau-margaux.com. Visits by appointment Monday-Friday: 10am-12noon and 2pm-4pm. Closed weekends, public holidays, August and during the grape-harvest.* This is the biggest Neo-Classical building in the Bordeaux region. Architect Louis Combes designed it in 1810, on four storeys lit by wide bay windows. The vineyards of this Margaux first classified grand cru cover 87ha. of the 262ha. estate, producing 200,000 bottles on average. You can visit storehouse and installations, but there is no tasting or sale, Château Margaux wines being handled exclusively by wine merchants.

MAISON DU VIN ET DU TOURISME DE MARGAUX 7, place de la Tremoille ✆ **05 57 88 70 82**. *Enquire about opening hours.* This centre has a fine wine cellar, as is the region's custom. It contains all the Margaux, and the AOC's grands crus classified in 1855, crus exceptionnels, crus grands bourgeois, crus bourgeois and crus artisans.

Pauillac

Half-way between Bordeaux and the Grave headland (50km on each side), 30km from the seaside resorts, this little town is divided between vineyards and river. Pauillac has 36 wine-growers' estates on the banks of the Gironde, including 18 classified crus and 3 classified premier crus, known the world over: Chateaux Lafite-Rothschild, Latour and Mouton-Rothschild.

MAISON DU TOURISME ET DU VIN DE PAUILLAC La Verrerie ✆ **05 56 59 03 08**. *www.pauillac-medoc.com. Open every day, weekends and public holidays, all year.* This tourist centre is unique, for it contains a shop stocking 300 vintages from the 8 Médoc AOCs, sold by the bottle and at château prices. You can taste some of the Médocs by the glass, and choose a souvenir or present from among a selection of corkscrews, decanters, glasses and accessories, personalised stickers, books etc.

CHATEAU LAFITE-ROTHSCHILD ✆ **05 56 73 18 18**. *Bookings by fax : 05 56 59 26 83. Guided tours in English or French for groups. Open early November to late July. Tour + tasting free.*

This 18thc. château is furnished in Napoleon III style, and set in a landscaped park. Classified premier grand cru in 1855, Lafite's 100ha. of vines surround the castle. The tour is mainly in the storehouses, where wine-production is explained beside the majestic vat with its giant tuns; the traditional first-year storehouse, and second-year storehouse designed by Catalan architect Ricardo Boffil in 1988. Its dimensions are impressive, as is its octagonal shape, massive pillars and the circular storing of 2,000 casks. This design breaks with the traditional linear organisation and is both attractive and functional.

CHATEAU MOUTON-ROTHSCHILD ✆ **05 56 73 21 29**. *Visits by appointment Monday-Thursday 9.30am-11am and 2pm-4pm (3pm on Friday). Open weekdays November-March; weekends and public holidays April-October. Admission: 5 €. Visit & tasting: 13 €.* Baron Philippe called this imposing building a 'wine theatre', with its oak casks lined up perfectly straight, and the classified premier grand cru ageing inside. Baronne Philippine de Rothschild exhibited her personal collection of works of art linked to vines and wine from Classical Antiquity to the present day just next-door. This museum of wine in art explains the entry price, but it is worth it, to see the labels designed by Picasso, Warhol and Cocteau, among others.

Pessac

Stop off at Chateau Pape Clement and Chateau Haut-Brion (15th-17thc.). These two superb properties produce pessac-leognan wines.

CHATEAU HAUT-BRION 135, ave. Jean-Jaures ✆ **05 56 00 29 30.** *www.haut-brion.com. Visits by appointment only.* In 1533, Jean de Pontac bought the noble house of Haut-Brion, and began building the castle in 1549. It changed hands over the years, growing in size and beauty. Château Haut-Brion is the oldest of the four premiers grands crus from the 1855 Bordeaux wine classification.

Pomerol

Another small village of international renown. The world's most expensive wine, Château Pétrus, is grown on Pomerol land. The village was once a Knights Templars fort (Saint-Jean-de-Jerusalem Order) and a stopping point for Compostella pilgrims. The Romanesque church was rebuilt in the 19thc., and there are some pretty houses and parks in the district.

CHATEAU HAUT-BRION 135, avenue Jean Jaurès ✆ **05 56 00 29 30**. *Visits by appointment. Visit and tasting free.* In 1533, Jean de Pontac came into the noble Haut-Brion title, and began building the castle in 1549. The estate went on growing in size and beauty over the years, and with a series of different owners. Château Haut-Brion is the oldest of the first four Bordeaux grands crus to be classified in 1855.

MAISON DES GRANDS VINS DE POMEROL **32, rue de Catusseau ✆ 05 57 74 18 18.** *www.wine-french.com. Open Monday-Friday: 10.30am-12.30pm and 2pm-7pm. Saturday, Sunday and public holidays: 10.30am-12.30pm and 3pm-6pm.* The wine merchants Jacques Soulat are specialised in Pomerol grands crus. The Pomerol AOC Châteaux Beauregard, Evangile, Gazin, La Conseillante and Trotanoy are on offer, as are some old vintages for collectors: Petrus (from 1945), Cheval Blanc, Mouton Rothschild, Latour and Yquem. Wines from the whole Bordeaux region are also on sale, at more affordable prices!

Saint-Emilion

This fortified town was built in the shape of an amphitheatre, in a limestone coomb, and its medieval architecture is exceptional, as you can see from Saint Georges Tower, overlooking town and vineyards. Walk through the streets and admire the Place du Marche, Porte de la Cadène, Jacobin monastery and houses, shops, washing-places and markets: the whole setting is perfect.

COLLEGIATE CHURCH AND CLOISTER *Enquiries from the Tourist Office: ✆ 05 57 55 28 28.* The splendid church with its 12thc. Romanesque nave and 15thc. Gothic choir boaste frescoes and a number of sculptures. The cloister is very well preserved, and is a perfect setting for cultural exhibitions, or just a quiet walk.

MUSEE SOUTERRAIN DE LA POTERIE, HOSPICES DE LA MADELEINE **21, rue André Loiseau ✆ 05 57 24 60 93**. *Open all year, every day: 10am-7pm (evenings by appointment). Admission: adult 4 €.* This museum tells the story of Gironde life throughout the centuries. A considerable amount of ancient pottery is on display (over 600 items from the 1st to the 19thc.) together with documents explaining how our Aquitaine ancestors heated and lit their homes, washed their clothes, cooked and conserved food in oil before the invention of the refrigerator, and prepared soups and gruels. The pottery museum is located on a remarkable site, probably Saint Emilion's oldest quarry: its stone was used to build the royal castle and town ramparts in the 12th and 13thc. You can also admire a fresco designed by ceramist Daniel Piron - an exact copy of 12th and 13thc. engravings - representing the Aquitains' lives under the Plantangenets.

MAISON DU VIN De SAINT-EMILION **1, place Pierre-Meyrat ✆ 05 57 55 50 55**. *www.vins-saint-emilion.com. Open March-November: 9.30am-12.30pm and 2pm-6.30pm. August: 9am-7pm. December-February: 10am-12 noon and 2pm-6pm.* No doubt the best place to get an overview of this AOC's wines. The choice is wide (château prices) and there is a photo exhibition illustrating the wine-making process to admire. Don't hesitate to ask for advice on choosing your wine. Saint-Emilion's Ecole du Vin offers introductory wine-tasting courses; ask here for more information.

Saint-Estèphe

The town nestles among the vines, overlooked by its church. You have a panoramic view of the Gironde from the old port.

MAISON DU VIN DE SAINT-ESTEPHE **Place de l'Eglise ✆ 05 56 59 30 59**. *Open Monday-Saturday: 10am-7pm July & August (ask about opening times at other periods).* The Maison du Vin groups together all the Saint Estèphe AOC wines, at château prices. The wines are sold by the bottle, can be dispatched and there are plenty of ideas for presents.

Saint-Macaire

Listed historic village, Saint-Macaire is a splendid medieval site with ramparts. Start (on foot) with the 14thc. Porte de Benauge (also known as the Horloge, Hôtel de Ville or Cadillac Gate) at the fortified village entrance, then move on to the Place du Mercadiou in the middle, with its pale stone arcades, 14th-16thc. housefronts and Renaissance posting-inn, now the Post-Office Museum.

The village contains many ancient houses, from the 13th-18thc. The finest are the Tardes, La Roque, Eyquem or Baritault, Flous and Rue Carnot houses. Saint Sauveur Priory Church is an imposing Romanesque building, reshaped in the 13th, 15th and 17thc. Wall paintings on the Apocalypse theme decorate the apse; though dating back to the 14thc. they were unfortunately restored in the 19thc.

MAISON DU PAYS DE SAINT MACAIRE **8, rue du Canton ✆ 05 56 63 32 14**. *Open all year, except Monday: 10am-1pm and 3pm-7pm in season.* Housed in a typical 16thc. merchant's house, this is the district's showcase, containing documentary information and an exhibition and sale of regional wines (Côtes-de-Bordeaux Saint-Macaire whites, sweet and dry; Bordeaux; Premières-Côtes-de-Bordeaux; Bordeaux-Superieur reds and whites; bordeaux rose; bordeaux dry whites) with winegrowers on site during July and August who'll help you taste their wines! You'll find out plenty about Saint-Macaire country, with free brochures as well.

Sauternes

10km west of Langon, the Sauternes AOC spreads out over Sauternes, Barsac, Fargues-de-Langon, Bommes and Preignac. The most prestigious is the exorbitantly-priced Chateau Yquem: you're better off with other chateaux and more down-to-earth value for money.

MAISON DES SAUTERNES 14, place de la Mairie © 05 56 76 69 83. *www.sauternes.com. Open all year: 9am-7pm (10am weekends). Mail-order, deliveries in France and abroad.* You have time to chat over the big wooden counter set on casks. The Maison is association of 80 AOC producers, and makes its own 'Duc de Sauternes' wine, representing 1% of each member's production (their contribution). You can taste the Sauternes, and some are available in half-bottles and magnums.

CHATEAU D'YQUEM © 05 57 98 07 07. *www.chateau-yquem.fr. Visits by appointment only.* Classified in 1855, this is the AOC's only premier cru superieur. The castle is based on a 15thc. fortified farm, reshaped over the years, with round towers, on of which was a dovecôte. The Sauvage family obtained this Crown property in 1593, and Leon de Sauvage bought the title in 1711. The Lur-Saluces family acquired Yquem by marriage in 1785, and Comte Alexandre de Lur-Saluces now represents the sixth generation to take charge of the property.

BASSIN D'ARCACHON

South-East Gironde has partly been made into a natural park to protect its unique heritage: pine forests (pignada), Pyla dune (highest in Europe), oyster-farming villages and various nature reserves (Teich bird sanctuary, Ares salt meadows). The architecture is no less exceptional: magnificent 19thc. villas in Arcachon's winter town, cabanes tchanquées, or huts built on piles, on the Ile d'Oiseaux and the rows of wooden huts lining the oyster ports, like Andernos.

Arcachon offers the usual seaside activities; swimming, water sports, beach, fishing, collecting shells, restaurants and festive events. It is an oyster-farming area, with countless beds and as many producers. What really interests local visitors when they come here to relax, though, is the protected natural environment.

Arcachon

Founded during the Renaissance, Arcachon took off in the 19thc. when the fashion for sea-bathing and rail travel established it as a seaside resort. Emile Pereire bought 100ha. of wooded dunes which became the winter town, and mayor Aldalbert Deganne had the château built.

NOTRE DAME DE BON PORT BASILICA © 05 56 83 30 83. *Admission free, with an explanatory video shown in July & August on Thursdays, at 4pm.* This neo-Gothic church contains a sailors' chapel (1722) with a Virgin and Child statue and ex-voto from sailors giving thanks for a safe return from terrible storms.

NOTRE DAME DES PASSES CHURCH. Built in 1864 in the town's eastern quarter (le Moulleau), to protect sailors coming from the ocean into the basin, often dangerous in bad weather. The church contains one of the three French statues of the pregnant Virgin, sculpted in the last century and brought from the Filles de Charité's mother house in Paris.

JETEE THIERS (PIER). Thiers pier was entirely rebuilt after consulting the townspeople, who chose an old-fashioned but original style. It is the place to stroll in late afternoon in summer, or to catch the winter sunshine.

MUSEE AQUARIUM 2, rue du Professeur-Jolyet & 05 56 83 33 32. *Open every day February-November. Admission: adult 4.50 €.*

One of the world's oldest aquariums, opened in 1865. You can admire various kinds of marine fauna from the comfortable vantage point of dry land: conger eels, turtles, octopus, sea-horses etc. A short, educational text gives details of each species on display.

VILLE D'AUTOMNE. Includes the fishing harbour, yachting harbour (1965) and Saint Elme college, the first to teach navigation and to set up a training boat, the Saint Elme.

VILLE D'ETE. Piers and esplanade fronting the ocean. You have direct access to the beach from Arcachon's 5km of seafront.

VILLE D'HIVER. Maritime pines could help treat tuberculosis, said Dr Jean Hameau in the 19thc. Their balsamic scent soon attracted an aristocratic clientele, and elegant villas were built, oddly-assorted in style but all fashionably luxurious.

VILLE DE PRINTEMPS. The quietest part of the town, with Pereire Park, the Abatilles spring, sports complex and Arbousiers, Moulleau and Pereire beaches. At Moulleau, on the little seafront square, a canon recalls the period of anti-English defences.

Around Arcachon

Andernos-les-Bains

A pleasant family holiday-resort, with its plane tree-lined avenues and the superb tamarisks on the pier. Discover the Villa Tijuka, Villa Magali, Villa Eureka (once lived-in by the actress Sarah Bernhardt, now holiday flats) and Villa Ignota (Maison Louis David) with its museum and painting and plastic arts exhibitions.

MAISON LOUIS DAVID 14, ave. Pasteur © 05 56 82 02 95. *Open 1 April-30 September: 10am-12 noon and 3pm-7pm. Other periods, by appointment. Admission free.* In this museum you find pottery, statues and epitaphs found during a dig at a Gallo-Roman villa in 1904, and manuscripts and plans concerning the town's origins. The museum is housed in the Villa Ignota ('unknown') which belonged to Louis-Theodore David, mayor of Andernos from 1900-1929. From April-August, there are paintings and plastic arts exhibitions. You can also enjoy the public park.

Banc d'Arguin

This sandy island brings to mind a Pacific lagoon, reshaped by wind and wave, and only accessible by boat. It is a nature reserve for sea-birds; few of them nest here, but the migrating breeds like to rest and feed in these waters rich in fish. The site houses the world's biggest caugeck tern colony.

Cap-Ferret

An oyster-farming peninsula between Arcachon and the ocean, with its coloured huts and forest all around; enchanting when the mimosa flowers in February. The village contains some typical villas like La Cigale, which belonged to the singer Marie Boyer, La Lorraine, built of stone from the former lighthouse, and the early 20thc. Villa Argentine, with its striking architecture and stained glass. In summer, beaches and countryside bring the holidaymakers, some famous. Yet Cap Ferret is jealously guarded by its locals, to prevent its being spoiled by fashionable tourism.

LE PHARE (LIGHTHOUSE) © 05 56 03 94 49. *Open all year except October. uly & August every day: 10am-7.30pm. Admission: adult 4.50 €.* Standing in a wooded park, the lighthouse is 53m high, with 258 steps. It was rebuilt in 1947, and given an optical system of four Fresnel lenses; its beam has a 50 km reach. From the top you can see the oyster beds, Pilat dune and ocean, but also the coastal forest and villages. An audiovisaul projection shows the path taken by a grain of sand from the Pyrenees to the Atlantic coast; sand dune formation; sea and wind rhythms; and the secret life of the oyster. You can learn about lighthouse history in general, and their place in the maritime environment, from the gallery of screens with their animation, cards, photos, and satellite images. Two webcams on the top of the lighthouse are linked to the Tourist Office's Internet site.

Gujan-Mestras

This village has no fewer than seven picturesque harbours, one after the other. Visit them on foot, and you may see an oyster-farmer working by his hut.

ILE AUX OISEAUX. An inhabited island, still wild despite the many visitors (tourists, sportsmen for the shooting) and oyster-farmers. You see the famous wooden houses on piles called tchanquees, after the Gascon word for stilts (tchanque), once used by shepherds.

MAISON DE L'HUITRE - MUSEE OSTREICOLE Port de Larros © 05 56 66 23 71. *www.maisondelhuitre.com. Open all year: 10am-12.30pm and 2.30pm-6pm (every day 1 June-31 August, closed Sunday other periods). Admission: adult 3 €, 6-12s 2 €.* Larros is a typical oyster harbour, a perfect site for this museum. The guided tour and documentary on oyster-farming techniques are both educational and fascinating.

Hourtin

LAGUNE DE CONTAUT Route de Contaut ✆ 05 56 09 19 00. *Free guided tour 15 June-15 September, by appointment at the Tourist Office. Admission free for individual visitors.* On the way to the beach at Hourtin Plage, Contaut laguna is one of the lakes and marshes stretching behind the sand-dunes. Take the wooden walkway round the laguna and discover a mysterious marsh with silver birch and giant ferns, where you can spot deer, squirrels, turtles, herons and dragonflies.

Pyla-sur-Mer

The resort was set up in the 1920s by a property company, and has magnificent Art Deco and contemporary villas. Villa Tethys and Villa Rothschild are the most-photographed. You can glimpse them going along the coast in a boat, or from the street, though they are hidden behind high hedges. Pyla is chiefly famous for the Pilat dune.

DUNE DU PYLA. The result of a strange and unexpected freak of nature. The present dune comes from the destruction of a huge 18thc. sandbank which spread forward of today's coastline, with sand added constantly by the wind. The dune grew from 60 to 118m in height in a century. It is 2,700m long, 500m wide and contains 60 million cubic metres of tiny grains, giving it a height of 102-105m. Perfect for hang-gliding and paragliding, it attracts over a million visitors every year, and has all the facilities: huge fee-paying car-parks (3.05 per day), souvenir shops, drinks stalls and wooden steps to climb the dune. At the top, you have a magnificent and unique view from the vast pine forest to Cap Ferret, with the Arguin bank.

Le Teich

Environmental beauty is the main attraction, with the Leyre Delta like a miniature Camargue, and unique scenery from the delta prairies to the shadowy forest. Local birdlife is also unique; you can meet it along the hiking paths and in the bird reserve with its 260 species of sedentary and migratory wild birds.

PARC ORNITHOLOGIQUE DU TEICH Rue du Port ✆ 05 56 22 80 93. *www.parc-ornithologique-du-teich.com. Open every day: 10am-6pm. Admission: adult 6.80 €. Guided tours by appointment for groups.* On the Bassin d'Arcachon's wildest bank, between the Leyre Delta and huge Gascogne Forest. The 120ha. reserve is on a major migration route, and houses migratory birds for a few hours or months according to their habits. You have 6km of paths and 20 covered observation posts (four set high up, with a view of the park).

Mont-de-Marsan

Mont-de-Marsan castlenau was founded around 1135-1140 by Pierre de Lobaner, Vicomte de Marsan. The region was linked by marriage to Foix-Bearn. Gaston Febus (1346-1391) declared his neutrality in the Hundred Years' War, and for this reason, Mont-de-Marson was never sacked, and the town has kept some medieval houses (Rue Maubec and Rue des Fosses).

In the first half of the 19thc., Mont-de-Marsan housed the prefecture, law courts, gendarmerie (police) and prison. The architect Panay designed several of these official buildings in neo-Classical style. The railway brought competition for water transport, and the port was closed down in 1903. The Industrial Revolution left no mark, but the town's economy was boosted by pine tree exploitation.

In 1912, Mont-de-Marsan airbase was opened, still a capital link in the National Air Defence chain.

ARENES DE PLUMACON (BULLRING). Built in 1889, consolidated and extended in 1933, it recalls the bullrings of Andalusia, and seats 7,000. Free visit by appointment: 05 58 75 06 09

DONJON LACATAYE Place Marguerite de Navarre. Built in the early 13thc to protect the town's south east side. The keep was part of a fortified house and observation post on the River Midou, and is a crenellated tower in conchiferous stone. It was restored in 1860 by the mayor Antoine Lacaze, and given to the town to install a garrison. Since 1962, it has housed the Despiau Wlerick Museum.

DAX AND LA CHALOSSE

Dax

Convergence point for North-South routes, Dax was already an important market in Gallo-Roman times. The fertile agricultural Chalosse meets Marensin animal breeding and forestry country at Dax, which consequently has a big market and hosts frequent fairs and shows. Above all, though, Dax is France's main spa town, for thermal treatment.

ARENES. Wooden bullrings have now to be replaced by more solid materials, and Dax has a tiled building with red shutters against white walls in Spanish Moorish style. It seats 8,200 during the August feria bullfights and the Toros y Salsa event in September.

SAINTE MARIE CATHEDRAL. The present neo-Greek Classical cathedral was built on a previous 11thc. building which collapsed in the 18thc. A remarkable portal with piers remains from the original church.

SOURCE DE LA NEHE (SPRING). The hot fountain known as Nehe's Spring (Nehe is a water goddess) was built in the early 19thc. on the site of Roman thermal baths in the heart of the city. 2,400 cubic metres per day of water leave the ground at 64 degrees C.

THERMES. These hotel apartments were designed by Jean Nouvel. The glass and wooden blinds play with light and transparency, contrasting with steel and concrete. There are plants inside and out, and the building is mirrored in the River Adour.

Around Dax

Brassempouy

Famous for its caves: Grande Grotte (prehistoric shelters), Hyenes and the Grotte du Pape, where the Brassempouy Lady was discovered by Piette and de Laporterie in 1894. This Aurignacian statuette carved in mammoth ivory is about 25,000 years old, the oldest known human figure in art.

MAISON DE LA DAME DE BRASSEMPOUY ✆ 05 58 89 02 47. *Open all year except January, February and December 2006 (except bookings). July & August: 11am-12 noon and 2pm-6pm. Admission: adult 4.50 €.* Housed in the remains of the Chateau de Poudenx, this museum contains copies of the ivory figurines discovered in the Grotte du Pape. La Poire (Pear) and L'Ebauche (Outline) found in 1892, the Brassempouy Lady, dagger handle, belted figurine, figurine in a cape, doll outline (1894) and torso (1896) are exceptional objects, displaye with reproductions of other female figures discovered in France, Italy, Central Europe, Russia and Siberia.

Capbreton and the South Coast

Capbreton has always produced sailors. It is a natural refuge harbour due to the Gouf fault, an ocean deep reaching 3,400m, which can reduce the movement of surface waves, calming the waters in this zone and making it a resting place for boats in difficulty. Capbreton is the only Landes harbour with 1,000 places for pleasure craft and fishermen.

PORT DE PLAISANCE DE CAPBRETON La Capitainerie Mole-Sud - Quai Pompidou ✆ 05 58 72 21 23. *www.port-capbreton.com*

Eugénie-les-Bains

The Empress Eugenie sponsored this town, officially established in 1861 by grouping together some existing villages. The Romans knew the virtues of water containing sulphates, calcium and sodium, but the first thermal treatments here began in the 16thc.

FERME THERMALE D'EUGENIE Le Bourg ✆ 05 58 05 06 06. *Open weekdays: 8.45am-7pm, and Sunday mornings: 8.45am-1pm.* This 18thc. Landes farm offers thermal treatment combined with plant-based therapy. The medicinal ritual of the water comes down from Classical Antiquity, and from the Celtic and Oriental cultures.. The farm treats rheumatic, metabolic, urological and gastric disorders.

Labastide d'Armagnac

One of the most attractive Landes villages, full of medieval charm. Labastide's economy is agricultural, but the production of Armagnac is its main resource. Along the road, signposts point out properties, estates and chateaux selling Armagnac.

ECOMUSEE DE L'ARMAGNAC Chateau Garreau ✆ **05 58 44 88 38**. *Open every day: 9am-12 noon and 2pm-6pm. April-November, open Sunday at 3pm. 1 November-late March: 2pm-6pm. Admission: adult 5 €*. This museum lets you discover the region's popular arts and traditions. You visit the storehouse, and the winegrower's museum in a 16thc. Gascon barn, with a lot of old-fashioned tools. Further on are the distillery and alambic collection.

Moliets-et-Maa

Moliets beach, 3km from the village, is vast, with enormous dunes and ocean view. On a clear day, you can see the Rhune, and 300km of French and Spanish Pyrénées.

HUCHET COASTAL DUNE. Fixed in the 19thc, by the planting of oyets, this dune is composed of pure, mobile sand but also of grey dune, with some humus in it.

Montfort-en-Chalosse

MUSEE DE LA CHALOSSE Domaine de Carcher ✆ **05 58 98 69 27**. *Open every day, except Monday. Temporary exhibitions, library, guided tours: 10.30am, 3pm, 4.30pm. Admission: adult 4.60 €, concessions 3.80 €*. A huge 17thc. family mansion with outbuildings and garden. The museum shows you what rural life was like for 19thc.farmers and winegrowers.

Saint-Sever

One of Charles VII's letters dated 1457 mentions bull-running in the streets of Saint-Sever on John the Baptist's feast day; it is the oldest town in France with this custom. Today, the town is a 'green' holiday resort, with plenty of interesting architecture, known for its poultry breeding. You'll enjoy its hilly countryside, leisure facilities, reputed foie gras and mischievous festivals.

SAINT SEVER ABBEY CHURCH. Saint Sever Church is Benedictine in style, with 7 parallel apses spaced out at the end of one main nave. One of Aquitaine's chief monuments.

ABBEY. The current monastery was founded at the end of the 10thc. by Comte Guillaume Sanche. Pilgrims to Compostella stopped off there.

LANDES FOREST AND BEACHES

The Landes region was once a vast unhealthy swamp, feared by Compostella pilgrims who had to cross it. From the 18thc. onwards, attempts were made to stop the sand-dune invasion, forced forward by the wind. The solution to both problems was to plant pines. Napoleon III had a law passed in 1857, recommending the Landes villages 'to drain and plant trees on the remaining commons'. in 1865, 122,000ha. were drained; the air became fresher, the death-rate dropped and the population began to increase. The forest covers 1,166,000ha. with 80% maritime pines and 10% oaks. Its three ennemies are processionary caterpillars, fire and storms (a lot of damage was done among 100-year-old pines in 1999).

Biscarrosse and the great lakes

Two great lakes meet at Bisacarrosse, which is a young and active seaside resort opening onto the ocean.

MUSEE DES TRADITIONS ET DE L'HISTOIRE 216, ave. Louis-Breguet ✆ **05 58 78 77 37.** *Open every day, except Sunday morning: 9.30am-7pm July & August (enquire about other periods)*. Discover marvellous and otherwise inaccessible flora and fauna on a boat-trip between lakes and marshes. The trip continues in the museum where you find regional archeology and Landes life in byegone days. There is a small farm with animals, for the kids.

Hossegor

Hossegor's range of beaches pleases bathers and surfers alike. There are four on the lake: Plage Blanche, Plage du Ray, Plage du Parc and the Plage des Chênes-Lièges; and four by the ocean: the southern, central and Gravière beaches, and the northern beach, which is naturist. The resort has an excellent reputation for surfing, and the French Surfing Federation is implanted here.

Mimizan

This is an important centre of industrial forestry, which began in the 1920s when local forest-owners founded the Gascony papermills. The industry diversified and developed after the great fires of 1949.

Today, forestry supports a range of activities, from preparing the earth and selecting the maritime pine species to a variety of uses for the wood (Mimizan papermill chiefly makes wrapping paper).

MUSEE DU VIEUX BOURG Rue de l'Abbaye ✆ 05 58 09 00 61. *Open 15 June-15 September, Monday-Saturday: 10.30am-7pm. Out of season, visits by appointment. Admission: adult 2 €, under-14s free.* The museum traces local history through documents, cards and things such as prehistoric tools, ceramics, bits of the Roman road etc.

Sabres

Sabres has a rich environmental heritage and also houses the Grande Lande Ecomuseum, keeping local collective memory safe.

ECOMUSEE DE LA GRANDE LANDE Route de Solferino ✆ 05 58 08 31 37. Train leaves every 40 minutes. 30 March-31 May and 16 September-2 November, open every day Monday-Saturday (afternoons only). Sunday and public holidays, all day: 10am-4.40pm. 1 June-15 September, open every day: 10am-5.20pm. Tickets (train & museum): adult 8 , child 6 , students and unemployed 7.30 . You can learn how to grow rye or millet, or breed ewes, make honey or work in forestry, depending on the season. A fascinating frieze of country activities.

LANDES DE GASCOGNE REGIONAL NATURE RESERVE 38, rue de Bayonne ✆ 05 58 08 31 37. This reserve spreads through the Leyre Valleys from the grande Lande to the Arcachon basin, grouping together 41 villages. You discover its gallery forests and the waterways running through them, used to float logs in the last century.

THE BASQUE COUNTRY

The Pyrénées-Atlantiques department stretches across two different geographical regions: Bearn with its vineyards and ski-resorts on one side, and the Basque Country and the ocean on the other.

Coast

Anglet

LA BARRE or EMBOUCHURE DE L'ADOUR. The mouth of the Adour is a traditional meeting-place for hikers and fishing fans. The waves are often spectacular, but the main attraction for local teenagers is the skating-rink, kingdom of the Hormadi Ice-Hockey Club.

BEACHES. There are 4.5km of golden sandy beaches along the coast; breakwaters and piers have been set up to break the waves. Eight beaches share the coastline between the Adour Estuary in the north and Cap Saint Martin in the south.

Bayonne

This walled town has 3 quarters: Grand-Bayonne (upper town), Petit-Bayonne (lower town) and Saint-Esprit (cut off from the others by the Adour). Its ramparts stand out between the Château Vieux (16thc.) where princely retinues were received, and the Porte d'Espagne. It is also an ancient bullfighting town.

BORDS DE NIVE . Coloured fronts mirrored in the river? You've all seen the postcard!

ARENES MUNICIPALES (BULLRING) Ave. des Fleurs ✆ 05 59 25 48 19. *Open Monday-Friday: 9am-12 noon and 1.30pm-6pm. Visits free.* The Plaza de Bayonne, with its buttresses and Moorish openings, ochre roughcast and 42m-diameter bullring. Ordonez and Domingin fought here in the 1960s.

SAINTE MARIE CATHEDRAL Place Monseigneur-Vansteenberg ✆ 05 59 59 17 82. *Open Monday-Saturday, 7.30am-12 noon and 3pm-7pm; Sundays and public holidays: 3.30pm-6.30pm.* Built on the Grande Bayonne hill, in the heart of the medieval city. This Gothic cathedral was built on the site of an earlier Romanesque church that had burnt down.

CLOISTER Place Pasteur ✆ 05 59 46 11 43. *Open October-May: 9am-12.30pm and 2pm-5pm, June-September until 6pm. Guided tours of the southern tower Easter-September.* Adjoining the cathedral's southern flank, this 13thc. High Gothic cloister is one of the most spacious in France. In August, 30 craft designers exhibit their fabric, weaving, spinning and leather.

Biarritz

Between the Middle Ages and the Belle Epoque, sea-bathing gained in interest and popularity. The town's population trebled in the late 19thc. and it became an elegant resort attracting the crowned heads of Europe. New architecture sprang up, such as the Villa Eugenie, destroyed in a fire in 1903, now the Hôtel du Palais. Tourism is still the town's strong point; don't be surprised to meet a showbiz star, this is a very chic place for a holiday.

ARCHITECTURAL DISCOVERIES. Not many seaside towns are as lucky as Biarritz! The list includes an Orthodox church, Byzantine-inspired chapel, neo-Louis XIII château, Château Gramont, medieval villa, surprising Villa Belza rising above the ocean (now restored as flats), Art Deco buildings (Town Hall, Sea Museum, Galeries Lafayette, Hôtel Plaza) and lots of Basque houses.

BEACHES. From the lighthouse to Bidart, there are fine stretches of sand and surfing spots, all within easy reach. The Grande Plage is the most prestigious (casino, the Palais), then the Port-Vieux, sheltered from the wind and the curious. The Côte des Basques is the wildest, followed by Marbella and la Milady, with its panoramic view and scenic promenade (car-park and Handi-Plage reception).

PORT DES PECHEURS. You must go for a stroll round this marvellous harbour, close to the town centre. Set up with the leftovers of an Imperial donation after work on the Port du Refuge was abandoned in 1870, it now houses fishing boats and pleasure craft. It is a picturesque and brightly-coloured place, lined with craft shops, bistrots and fashionable restaurants.

ROCHER DE LA VIERGE. Napoleon III decided to use this imposing rock to anchor the dike in his planned Port du Refuge. The rock was thus linked to the mainland by a wooden bridge (the current metallic walkway was designed by Eiffel) and a tunnel was cut through to pass the stone blocks needed to build the dike. The name comes from the statue of the Virgin put up on the top in 1865. At nightfall, surrounding spotlights show you what the famous waves can be like, with the ocean for background.

PHARE ✆ CADRAN SOLAIRE ANALEMMATIQUE Avenue de l'Imperatrice. *Lighthouse (and sundial) open 1 July-31 August every day (except Monday): 10am-12 noon and 3pm-7pm. Every weekend from 15 April. Out of season, during school holidays, Saturday & Sunday, from 3pm. Under-14s accompanied. Admission: 1.55 €.* The climb is straightforward, with a marvellous view of the Gulf of Gascogne.

MUSEE DU CHOCOLAT 14, ave. Beaurivage ✆ 05 59 41 54 64. *Open Monday-Saturday, 10am-12 noon and 2.30pm-6pm. Admission: adults 5 €, 4-12s 2.50 €, teenagers & students 4 €.* On the Beaurivage coast-road above Biarritz stands this listed building, which once housed the Henriet chocolate factory workshops. You'll learn all there is to know about chocolate in an hour. Educational and mouth-watering.

MUSEE DE LA MER Esplanade du Rocher de la Vierge ✆ 05 59 22 33 34. *www.museedelamer.com. Open every day, 9.30am-7pm, June-September (6pm other periods; midnight in July & August). Admission: 4 €-7.20 € according to age and number.* Facing the ocean and the Rocher de la Vierge, in an beautiful setting and Art Deco building. Discover the aquariums: 150 species of fish and invertebrates from the Gulf of Gascogne; seals; sharks in their grotto; and collections (cetaceans, fishing, birds). Panoramic bar and fast-food in season. A lively and original museum.

Ciboure - Socoa - Ziburu

Ciboure, village of corsairs and artists, was once a simple quarter of Urrugne, at one end of the Nivelle Bridge (the name in Basque, 'Ziburu', means bridge-head). Today, its superb half-timbered housefronts can be seen from Saint-Jean-de-Luz. Not to be missed, with its narrow streets, Maurice Ravel's birthplace overlooking the port, and Socoa Fort.

Guéthary

Guéthary's character stems from its archetypal Basque village layout, and the surprising pelota wall on its Town Hall. The old 19thc. *jeu de paume* (ancestor of tennis) above the port was moved upwards, while the Town Hall, originally housed in the presbytery, was transferred to the first floor of the Cazenave house. Then architect Ferdinand Brana built the new Town Hall next to the pelota wall. The resulting Eskualduna de Guéthary Town Hall and front wall is thus interesting in both architectural and urban development terms. There are two beaches: les Alcyons, rocky with a steep climb down, and Cenitz, a sandy beach in a wild and picturesque creek. Parlementia Beach (part of Bidart commune), follows on from Guethary harbour.

Hendaye

Whale-fishing brought prosperity to Hendaye, although the town, at the southern tip of the Basque coast, was continually at war with Irun and Fontarbie (Spain) from the 16th to 18thc., as well as quarrelling with Urrugne. Once this troubled period was over, the town took years to rebuild.

LA CORNICHE. Forget the motorway, and take the coast-road, with the ocean crashing against the cliffs. From Socoa to Hendaye, you have a marvellous view of the wild and beautiful Atlantic coast.

LE PORT Direction du Port ✆ 05 59 48 06 00. *Fax: 05 59 48 06 08. Capitainerie: 05 59 48 06 10.* Nestling between the Grande Plage and Txingudi Bay, in the new Sokoburu quarter. Its modern, top-quality facilities attract pleasure craft of up to 20m.

ILE DES FAISANS. Pheasant Island is governed by France for six months, then Spain for the next six, turn and turn about.

The GR 10

This long-distance hiker's kingdom runs from Hendaye to the Mediterranean shores through the Pyrenees, 385 km as the crow flies but 870 km on foot following the red and white markings on the path. The GR 10 is a mythical route, with its fabulous mountain passes - Aubisque, Tourmalet, Peyresourde, Aspet, Puymorens etc. - valleys and plateaux, refuges and villages. The Atlantic section crosses the Basque Country hills in 17 stages, passing close to the Pic d'Anie (2,504m) and the Aiguilles d'Ansabère, then running through the Aspe Valley, round the Ossau and meeting up with the Aubisque and the Soulor via Gourette.

Saint-Jean-de-Luz

At the gates of Spain, opening on to the ocean, Saint-Jean-de-Luz/Ciboure is the biggest French tuna-fishing port, as a result of its use of live bait. Every summer a tuna thanksgiving festival takes place here. Since the early 20thc., Saint-Jean has been a reputed seaside resort, its history and scenery attracting plenty of tourists.

PORT A charming, picturesque place, with its brightly-painted wooden boats. It was built in the 12thc, after the sanding-up of the Adour had limited Bayonne port activity. The houses along the quays are typical of the local labourdin style.

SAINT JEAN BAPTISTE CHURCH Rue Gambetta ✆ 05 59 26 08 81. *Open every day: 8.30 am-12 noon and 2pm-6.30pm. Admission free. Guided tours Monday-Friday at 5pm in summer (free).* This building was burned down several times during Spanish raids, and rebuilt step by step; the oldest part is 15thc. Louis XIV's wedding was held in its spectacular interior, with its single nave and wooden galleries on three floors.

MAISON DE L'INFANTE Rue de l'Infante ✆ 05 59 26 36 82. *Open 15 June-15 October: 11am-12.30pm and 2.30pm-6.30pm. Closed Sunday & Monday morning.* Not far from the Place Louis XIV. The Spanish Infanta Maria Teresa stayed here on her marriage to Louis XIV in 1660. The great 18thc. salon

Saint-Jean-de-Luz

has a carved and painted monumental fireplace and beams richly decorated with mysterious motifs. You have a splendid view of the Rhune and the harbour.

MUSEE GREVIN Pavillon de l'Infante - 7, rue Mazarin ✆ 05 59 51 24 88. *Open every day April-October: 10am-12 noon and 2pm-6pm (6.30pm in summer); every day of the year for groups (bookings only). Weekends and school holidays 2pm-6pm. Admission: adult 6 €, 6-13s 3 €*. The town's past is brought to life by 50 life-size waxworks in 10 tableaux.

ECOMUSEE BASQUE RN10 ✆ 05 59 51 06 06. *Open May-October, every day in July & August: 10am-6.30pm. Admission: adult 5.50 €*. Discover what it means to be Basque: traditional arts and crafts, festivals and culture, including old stills, legends, and culinary secrets.

A world-famous wave off Saint-Jean-de-Luz

Known as Bélharra, this wave is formed during a heavy swell on a high sea bed, about 1 km south of Saint-Jean-de-Luz harbour mouth. It is one of the world's biggest waves, and a sailor's nightmare: an 8 to 12 metre wall of water, against which only 5 years ago, no-one had yet managed to compete. On 10 April 2002, six local surfers dared to defy the monster, and won. 12 hours later, the photos of the exploit were on the Internet and going round the world. Bélharra had made its claim to fame.

Inland

Ascain

A typical Basque village, crossed by the Nivelle and overlooked by three peaks: Bizkarzun, Esnaur and Larrun, or La Rhune (905m). From the front wall square, you take in at a glance the delightful church with its tower-keep (1626) and streets lined with hotel-restaurants. La Rhune looms up in the background. Pierre Loti wrote Ramuntcho from the square, inspired by an Ascain pelota-player, and Churchill painted a watercolour here.

Cambo-les-Bains

This spa town and ancient river port has a perfect site; warm in summer, cool in winter, surrounded by big gardens and meadows. There are four main quarters: Haut-Cambo, Bas-Cambo, Basseboure and the Thermes, marked by many disputes over freedom of river transport. The many medical establishments are found in this quarter. There are magnificent villas to see in Haut-Cambo, as well as Saint-Laurent Church, on the left bank.

MUSEE ARNAGA ✆ 05 59 29 70 57. *Open April-October; groups all year. Guided tours.* Edmond Rostand, author of Cyrano de Bergerac, built his dream house in this leafy setting. Wandering through avenues of hydrangeas and a wooded park, you discover a Versailles-style garden with its flowerbeds, pergolas and lakes. Inside the villa, newly-restored and sumptuously decorated, an original collection of objects and works of art illustrate the lives of the famous author and his family.

Espelette

Brightly-coloured and flavoured, Ezpeleta ('planted with boxwood' in Basque) was once a fortress, part of the Kingdom of Navarre. Today it is a pretty village a step away from the ocean, with agricultural (sheep and corn) and tourist resources, and above all, the famous red peppers drying on the housefronts.

CHATEAU FORTERESSE. Built in the 11thc. the fortress has been attacked many times since. Lord Bertrand d'Ezpeleta, a vassal of the English Princes of Aquitaine, tried to rebuild it in 1414, but in 1637 it was razed to the ground by the villagers following Louis XIII's confiscation of the baronny. From the 17thc. to 1967, it was a presbytery, housing the Town Hall from the 19thc. to the present day. One round 16thc. tower stands proudly in a corner; a listed monument since 1937. Espelette has finally finished the castle's restoration, adding a Tourist Office, library and exhibition hall to the Town Hall sheltering within its walls.

SAINT ETIENNE CHURCH. This is one of the Basque Country's most beautiful churches, built close to a small Romanesque bridge and delightful shady cemetery with disc-shaped steles. Its Renaissance tower-door is especially striking. Inside, notice the nave leaning on its solid buttresses, the pannelled pulpit, gilded Baroque reredos with twisted columns and alcoves (17thc.) and the gallery on three floors.

PANORAMA. The village rises in tiers on a knoll, with Mont Urzumu in the distance (216m), then the Ereby (583m), Artzimendi (936m) Ezcondray (550m) and Mondarain (749m). In the south, on a clear day, you can see the Rhune (900m). The little stream is the Latxa; it joins the Nive at Larressore.

Saint-Jean-Pied-de-Port

Capital of the Basse-Navarre province, this prehistoric and Episcopal town is 55km from Biarritz and Bayonne and 8km from the Spanish border. Its name comes from its position at the foot of Roncesvalles 'port' or pass. Charlemagne's army came through after the Roncesvalles disaster. Tourists come to admire the Roman bridge, Gothic church, Bishops' prison and ramparts; to buy locally-spun Basque linen in the shops, or simply to taste typical dishes, since Saint-Jean is known for its gastronomy.

HOTEL DE VILLE 13, place Charles de Gaulle. The Town Hall is a fine Louis XIV-style building, with an Arradoy stone façade.

PONT DE LA NIVE. The best view to be had of the town. From this bridge you can admire the old Navarre houses with their wooden balconies, bathing in the Nive. It opens into the church tower and buttresses.

VAUBAN CITADEL. Built on the site of an earlier medieval castle, overlooking the town. A paved ramp leads to the monumental arch (Porte du Roy) and half-moon. Stop half-way to admire the view over the valley and its circle of mountains. Follow the inside walkway with its postern staircase (269 steps) if the weather is good. Notre Dame Gate still has its heavy nailed doors complete with locks, hinges and bolts.

PRISON DES EVEQUES. The Bishops' prison is in Rue de la Citadelle, and its name combines two historical facts: firstly, there were bishops here during the 14th-15thc. schism, and secondly, this building was used as a prison from the 18th-20thc. Despite being a town house, prison and security depot, its origins are enigmatic: recent work has excavated some fine arcades, latrines and ancient openings. There is a 13thc. underground room, and 16thc. disciplinary cells. Local people arrested while fleeing to the unoccupied zone were locked up here during the German Occupation.

NOTRE-DAME DU BOUT DU PONT. Just opposite the Navarre Gate, this 14thc, Gothic church has a portal with small columns and a triangular gable wall. The first foundations go back to the primitive church built in 1212. Inside is a wide nave, two side-aisles and galleries on two levels, all pink sandstone pillars and columns. On either side of the chancel are stained glass windows displaying the arms of the town and Navarre.

PORTE DE NAVARRE. The Navarre Gate is typical of 13thc. gates pierced in city walls. Go under the archway, up a small courtyard and climb the staircase to the walkway. Then come two fine corbelled residences on two floors. On the right the first house recalls the Indian apostle. The second (1796) has two stars on its front, with a Phrygian bonnet between them (symbol of the young Republic).

RUE DE LA CITADELLE. Opposite the church, the street slopes steeply upwards. It is lined with stone-fronted houses, of different colours. The overhanging roofs display intricately-worked girders, and the lintels bear inscriptions, geometric designs and religious symbols. In the middle of the street stands the Porte de France with its straight staircase leading to the walkway, which comes out in the marketplace

Sare

This village among mountain peaks 8km from the ocean is known for its festivals.

LA RHUNE. Historic, touristy, even sacred: at 900m the Rhune rises above the neighbouring peaks. It has symbolic value for the Basques, and has been the site of many a battle in the Labourd province's past.

TRAIN DE LA RHUNE Col de Saint-Ignace ✆ 08 92 39 14 25. *www.rhune.com. Open every day, mid March-late October. Trips every 35mins in summer. Admission: adult 12E round trip, child 6.50E. Disabled access.* Restaurant at the top. You travel to the top in wooden carriages (Pyrenees fir, Landes pine, Ariège chestnut and African iroko), with the windows down. The first carriages were built in 1924. From the departure station (Saint Ignace Pass) to the top (905m) the little train covers 4.2km in 30 minutes, at a speed of 8km/h. The route is steep, with a 25% change in gradient. Admire the mountain, the different tree species (10) vultures in flight and wild horse; or pottoks. From the top, you have a superb view of all seven Basque provinces, and the Landes beaches as far as San Sebastian.

GROTTES DE SARE ✆ 05 59 54 21 88. *Open all year, except January. July & August: 10am-7pm. Admission: adults 6.50 €.* 45,000 years of prehistory and 2,000 years of history in son et lumière. Discover the cave's rock formation, but also the origins of the Basque people and their mythology through the work of the Spanish-Basque anthropologist Jose Miguel de Barandiaran. The action of water on rock over millions of years will amaze you, as you go from one gallery to the next, admiring the majestic natural porch, meanders, tubulures and concretions. Don't forget the upper level, which was human territory. These caves will surprise you wit their hands-on interactive approach. After your visit, enjoy a stroll round the megalithic park and museum.

Val d'Adour

Bastide-Clairence

This walled village was founded in 1314 by the King of Navarre, so as to gain access to the Adour waterway. Craftsmen and artists abound. Go for a bucolic stroll on the small roads around the village, leading to Belloc Abbey.

Hasparren

CENTRE ARCHEOLOGIQUE HATZEN BIDEA Place du Fronton ✆ 05 59 29 10 66. *Admission : adult 4 €, 9-15s 1.60 €, groups of 15+ and students 3 €.* This archaeological open space shows you what life was like for prehistoric men; cave and environment are meticulously reconstructed. You can also see the treasures excavated from digs: some are of later date, like the ceramic found on the Bayonne Cordelier monastery site. Stage-set rather than museum, the centre introduces you to the archaeologist's work and methods. Educational and fascinating.

Saint-Martin-d'Aberoue

GROTTES PREHISTORIQUES D'ISTURITZ ET D'OXOCELHAYA Route D251 ✆ 05 59 29 64 72. *Open March-November; groups all year. Admission: adult 6.50 €.* These caves were inhabited from 50,000 B.C., witness a reindeer carving on a stalagmite pillar. They lead out of one another, with their mineral concretions, stalactites and stalagmites. A natural curiosity that will fire your imagination.

PÉRIGORD

Périgord has four types of countryside: white (blanc) purple (pourpre) black (noir) and green (vert), each with its own character.

Périgord blanc

Périgueux

Périgueux has a new image, though Middle Ages and Renaissance still coexist in this capital of the Dordogne (department) and Périgord (region). Place Saint-Louis and its famous patissier's house are symbolic of the old quarters' renewal. You can stroll through the streets at your own pace, and take in the de Nervaux, Gamenson, de Fayolle and de Méredieu mansions, to name but a few.

MUSEE GALLO-ROMAIN VESUNNA Parc de Vésone ✆ 05 53 53 00 92. *Open every day except Monday September-June: 10am-12.30pm and 2pm-5.30pm. July and August, open every day : 10am-7pm. Admission: adult 5.50 €, 6-12s 3.50 €. Groups: contact Semitour-Périgord (05 53 05 65 65).* In the heart of the Antique city, architect Jean Nouvel (native of Périgord) designed this site museum. The archeological remains exhibited are unique in Aquitaine, and are organised in two sections: 'Town and Public Life' (architecture, monuments, religion, economic exchange), and 'Houses and Private Life' (building and decoration, costume, jewellery food, heating, etc.)

MUSEE DU PERIGORD Allée de Tourny ✆ 05 53 06 40 70. *Open 1 April-30 September every day except Tuesday: 10.30am-5.30pm, Saturday & Sunday : 1pm-6pm. 1 October-31 March, open every day except Tuesday: 10am-5pm, Saturday & Sunday 1pm-6pm. Admission: 4 € and 2 €, under-18s free.* This is the department's oldest museum, founded in 1835. It originally housed African, Asian and American collections supplied by missionaries, soldiers and travellers of all kinds. Later, Perigord and Limousin arts and crafts found their place here, and over the years, different kinds of artwork - objects and paintings - have been added, bringing the grand total to more than 45 000 pieces dating from prehistoric times to the present day. The Fine Arts collection from the Renaissance period to the 20thc. includes superbly-presented masterpieces, some recently brought out from long years of storage. There are also temporary exhibitions, mainly featuring excellent local artists, Disabled access available to the large ground-floor room.

Antonne-et-Trigonant

CHATEAU DES BORIES ✆ 05 53 06 00 01. *Open July ✆ August: 3pm-6pm. Admission: adult 4.80 €, under-18s 2 €.* Easily seen from the N21, approaching from Limoges, this chateau is pure and classic Périgord. Put up in 1497 on the remains of a feudal hideout, its three floors are built on superb vaulted cellars. The oldest room is one of Périgord's finest Gothic kitchens, with two facing fireplaces and diagonal ribs spreading out in palm-tree fashion from a central support.

Chancelade

Around Chancelade, the hiking paths are well marked and cared-for. Andrivaux hamlet was a Knights Templars' command post in 1139, and bears traces of a Romanesque church crypt and an ancient dovecote.

ABBEY ✆ 05 53 04 86 87. Consecrated in 1147, the abbey played an active part in the region's intellectual life, before suffering in the Hundred Years' War, Wars of Religion and Fronde. Admire the monastery buildings on either side of a garden made for meditation. Barn, outhouses and abbot's quarters date back to the 17thc. Outside the abbey, the small Romanesque Saint Jean Chapel (former Parish Church) contains a painting of Christ by Georges De La Tour.

Grignols

Look out for the old market and half-timbered houses as you walk through the village.

CHATEAU DE GRIGNOLS. The remains of a 13thc. military fortress overlook the village. This was the home of the Comtes Talleyrand-Périgord from the 11th-15thc. and remained in the family until the late 19thc. After many sieges, the fortress was wiped out by the Prince of Condé's army during the Fronde on 20 June 1652. The remains hung on in a pitiful state until 1920, since when the owners have been restoring it. It has kept its moat carved out of the rock, ramparts, walkways, curtains, 14thc. porch, polygonal tower with staircases and two 15thc. fireplaces, keep and oubliettes, and seven rooms containing tapestries, 15th and 19thc. furniture and a weapons collection.

ECOMUSEE DES ARTS ET TRADITIONS POPULAIRES ✆ 05 53 54 25 99. *Open all year by appointment. Admission: adult 4 €, child 2 €.* This little Popular Arts and Traditions Museum contains tools and utensils used in the Périgord countryside in bygone days. How our grandparents used to live.

Neuvic-sur-l'Isle

CHATEAU ✆ 05 53 80 86 65. This 16thc. castle is made up of two main buildings at right-angles, and turrets, with Renaissance façades and high roofs. The chapel was added in the 18thc.

CHATEAU DE FRATTEAU ✆ 05 53 81 11 02. *Guided tours in July & August: 2.30pm, 4pm and 5.30pm, and all year for groups. Admission: adult 5.50 €, 8-16s 3 € (includes park).* Overlooking the plain and new prison, on the way out of Neuvic. Ruined 15th and 16thc. fireplaces have been preserved, and a 17thc. vaulted porch. Local artists make and display their pottery on site.

PARC BOTANIQUE DU CHATEAU ✆ 05 53 80 86 65. *Opening hours vary according to season. Open every day July & August: 10am-7pm. Admission: adult 3.80 €, child 2 €.* Known across Périgord for its park, laid out in 1720, with a rockery and some rare trees. Périgord Botanical Society, together with Neuvic Syndicat d'Initiative had the botanical gardens set up, with various species of oak, viburnum, dogwood, lilac and roses supplied by collector nurseries. All 1,200 plants are labelled and arranged freely in clumps and beds.

Saint-Astier

CHATEAU DE PUYFERRAT ✆ 05 53 07 86 26. *Tours July-September, Monday-Friday: 10am, 11am, 2pm, 3pm, 4pm and 5pm. Out of season, by appointment. Adult admission (park only) 2,50 €, park and castle 5 €.* A Renaissance castle built for pleasure, with decorative fortifications, including an elegant machicolated walkway. Don't miss the vaulted chamber, listed framework and chapel with its coloured contemporary frescoes inspired by the Byzantine.

CHURCH ✆ 05 53 54 13 85. The view over the church with the Isle in the foreground is striking. This 12thc. building restored in the 15thc. has a high and massive steeple tower that you can visit in summer. It looks like a real fortress, with its buttresses, arrow-slits, walkway, bartizans and machicolations, yet it also has a 16thc. porch, Romanesque carving on the front and grand siecle furniture inside: 17thc. walnut choirstalls, 19thc. reredos and 17th-18thc paintings. Don't miss the 11thc. crypt, and find time for a walk to the Bois Chapel and Saint Astier's hermitage.

Sorges

Périgord's stony ground can be tiring, but you see some beautiful buildings, discreetly situated. Sorges is the local truffle-capital, and a well-marked path traces the 'black diamond's' history through oaks and dry stone huts.

ECOMUSEE DE LA TRUFFE © **05 53 05 90 11**. *Open every day mid June-late September: 9.30am-12.30pm and 2.30pm-6.30pm. Mid November-early February, every day except Monday: 2pm-5pm. Other periods, every day except Monday: 10am-12 noon and 2pm-5pm. Tuesdays & Thursdays in July & August, tour of the museum at 2.30pm, truffle-path at 3.30pm and a goose farm at 6pm. Admission: adult 4 €, child 2 €.* The melanosporum tuber was beginning to run out when the town decided to preserve its living memory in a museum, together with the truffle-path. You can find out all about the origins and future of truffles: how to find, grow and cook them, and how to avoid confusing the Périgord Queen with its insignificant rivals.

Périgord pourpre

Bergerac

Stroll through the old streets to the Quai Salvette, with the busy Dordogne below, and enjoy the view over the ancient roofs and the old brick bridge across to the Madeleine quarter.

RECOLLETS CLOISTER Maison des Vins - Quai Salvette © **05 53 63 57 55**. *Open all year except January, from 10.30am-12.30pm and 2pm-6pm, Tuesday-Saturday. July & August, every day 10am-7pm.* An interesting place, linking Bergerac's history and its vineyards. Elegant columns support the galleries round the 17thc. cloister's inside courtyard.

MUSEE DU TABAC Place du Feu © **05 53 63 04 13.** *Open in high season Tuesday-Friday: 10am-12 noon and 2pm-6pm. Open Sunday: 2.30pm-6.30pm and in July & August, Monday: 2pm-6pm. Admission: adult 3.50 €, 10-18s 1.80 €. Students free. Guided tours, advance bookings only. Disabled access by lift.* This tobacco museum contains tobacco pouches, pipes and Joseph Dalloz's famous pipe-carving machine (there are only two in the world). It certainly makes you think about the role of tobacco in our society. There is also some beautiful 18thc. china made here in Bergerac.

Biron

The medieval village at the foot of the castle is worth seeing for its cornmarket and old houses. The war memorial was recently transformed by a German contemporary artist, in agreement with the villagers.

CHATEAU DE BIRON © **05 53 63 13 39.** *Open out of season: 10am-12.30pm and 2pm-5.30pm. In season: 10am-7pm. Admission: adult 5.30 €, child 3.30 €.* Built over 8 centuries, the main building with its Renaissance chapel, 12thc. keep and fortified terraced courtyard provides a superb view of the wild wooded countryside. The lower courtyard, States room and vaulted kitchen are striking. The powerful Gontaut-Biron family, Barons of Périgord, lived here for 8 centuries.

Cadouin

The abbey, founded in 1115 by Gerard de Salles and brought into the Cistercian Order in 1119 is now listed by UNESCO. The 11thc.Romanesque church and Flamboyant Gothic cloister (15th-16thc.) also deserve some attention.

CLOISTER & MUSEE DU PELERINAGE ✆ **05 53 63 36 28**. *Opening hours vary out of season. July & August, open every day: 10am-7pm. Admission: adult 5.20 €, 6-12s 3.20 €.* In 1117, the abbey was given what was long believed to be the Saint Suaire (shroud in which Christ's body was wrapped), and was transformed so as to be worthy of the honour. The Wars of Religion and Revolution left their scars, but the Flamboyant Gothic cloister is still superb. You can contemplate the stone characters (part-angel, part-demon) in peace, or slip inside the church through a Renaissance door, where you find architectural beauty, a spiritual atmosphere, meditation - whatever strikes you.

GROTTES DE MAXANGE Mestreguiral ✆ **05 53 23 42 80.** *Open Easter-1 November: 10am-12 noon and 2pm-6pm, 9am-7pm in high season. Admission: adult 6.50 €, 4-12s 4 €.* Group prices available on request. Discovered in August 2000 in a quarry (3,000 cubic metres of soil were removed to excavate them), these caves contain a calcite fairyland of stalactites and stalagmites subtly lit up by modern technology. Car park, bar, souvenir shop and kids' playground (open 12 noon-2pm).

Issigeac

This cosy town grew up in the Middle Ages round the Benedictine abbey, and was a bishopric by the 15thc. Recent digs have excavated Gallo-Romain and Merovingian mosaics and sarcophagi. The narrow alleys with their tall, half-timbered housesand wooden galleries are set within a surrounding wall. Stop and look at the Gothic church with its octagonal porch tower, and the Bishops' Palace with turrets on its tall corner pavillions. (17thc.) In the village, you'll enjoy the grotesque carvings on the maison des tetes. Further on is La PrevÛte, an 18thc. charterhouse and dovecote crowned with flat tiles. The town is a thriving arts and crafts centre, and holds a popular second-hand fair.

Monbazillac

World-famous for its sweet wine.

CHATEAU ✆ **05 53 63 65 00.** *Closed 1 January-31 January and Monday in winter. Opening hours vary according to season. Enquire for guided tours.* The round towers watch over the vineyards from their hilltop. Monbazillac is actually the result of 'noble rot' in the grapes. You can learn more in this 16thc. castle, half-fortress, half-residence, with its cellar for tasting (and buying) wine and museum (wine, popular arts and traditions, Périgord furniture and Protestantism). The way back to Bergerac leads through the vines .

Monpazier

One of Périgord's major sites, that you mustn't miss. The walled town is over 700 years old, and has survived the test of time intact, with its arcade-lined square, mouldings and ancient measures in the cornmarket, Saint Dominique Church and 14thc. Chapterhouse. It is a model bastide with a perfect rectangular ground-plan. The Place des Cornières is lined with medieval to 17thc. houses; 32 buildings are listed. You can see Jean Galmot's birthplace; he was a journalist, writer and Member of Parliament for French Guyana, ruined and assassinated by his political enemies at the turn of the 20thc.

Périgord noir

Beynac-et-Cazenac

You can reach the castle on foot from the village, admiring its 15th, 16th and 17th houses as you go. The view is well –earned!

CHATEAU ✆ **05 53 29 50 40**. *Open March-May: 10am-6pm. June-September: 10am-6.30pm. October ✆ November: 10am-dusk. December-February: 11am-dusk. Guided tours for groups on request. Admission: adult 7 €, child 3 €.* Set on a cliff overlooking the river, glowering across at its medieval enemy Castlenaud, Beynac is rather intimidating. It has a double wall with a barred vault in the Périgord States chamber. The oratory is decorated with naÔve Gothic frescoes. Go up the 17thc. stairs to the walkway, and don't forget the beautiful little chapel with its shale-tiled roof.

PARC ARCHEOLOGIQUE ✆ **05 53 29 51 28**. *1 July-15 September : 10am-7pm, except Saturday. Picnics allowed. Groups by appointment out of season. Admission: adult 5,50 €, 6-16s 4 €.* Discover the daily life of the first farmers and metalworkers, from Neolithic to Gothic times. One civilisation followed another on the site from 2,000 B.C., including an Iron Age village (8thc. B.C.). The archeological park has reconstructed fortifications, earth and wood huts and Gallic workshops (smith, potter, flint-cutter and gardener) and there is a museum in a 14thc. tower.

Le Bugue-sur-Vézère

Important crossroads for tourists, teeming with activities and things to see. Tuesday is market day, and the bridge is jammed; you're better off crossing it on foot to enjoy the market, with its riot of smells and colours. The Tourist Office is in a restored mill, Porte de la Vézère.

AQUARIUM DU PERIGORD NOIR ✆ 05 53 07 10 74. *www.parc-aquarium.com. Open 7 days a week: April 10am-5pm, May and September 10am-6pm, June 10am-7pm, July and August 9am-7pm. Admission: adult 8.30 €, 4-15s 5.50 €, under-4s free.* Special prices for groups. Admire over 6,000 river fish in their natural environment, along 300m of glass-fronted aquariums. A background of trees and rocks varies the perspective. A new insect section has now been installed, and you can watch a swarm of 80,000 bees in a transparent hive.

GOUFFRE DE PROUMEYSSAC ✆ 05 53 07 27 47. *www.Périgord.com/proumeyssac. Open all year except January. February, November and December: 2pm-5pm. March, April, September and October: 9.30am-12 noon and 2pm-5.30pm. May and June: 9.30am-6.30pm. July & August: 9am-7pm. Disabled access. Admission: adult 8 €, 5-15s 5.50 €. Advance booking (05 53 07 85 85) and descent by nacelle (16 € and 11 €).* Known as the Crystal Cathedral, this cave was carved out of rock by running water over 15 million years. The stalactites and stalagmites are amazing, and the triangular concretions rising from the ground, unique in the world. The natural effect is enhanced by music and lights. You can go down to the site in a nacelle, like they used to do at the turn of the 20thc.

GROTTE DE BARA-BAHAU ✆ 05 53 07 44 58. *Open all year except January. February-June: 10am-12 noon and 2pm-5.30pm. July & August: 9.30am-7pm. September-December: 10am-12 noon and 2pm-5pm. Last visit 30mins before closing. Admission: adult 5.50 €, 6-16s 3.50 €.* This huge cave-passage blocked by a mass of fallen rocks is the most westerly of the Vezere Valley caves. It contains 15 or so large animal carvings: horses, oxen, ibex, deer and bears, with some symbols of the Magdalenian era. This is one of the collective memory's oldest sites, in terms of wall paintings, and a rare example of art history listed as a historic monument.

VILLAGE DU BOURNAT ✆ 05 53 08 41 99. *www.best-of-Périgord.tm.fr. Open mid February-mid November. May-September: 10am-7pm; 10am-5pm out of season. Restaurant open 1 April-11 November. Private car-park free of charge. Admission: low season, adult 8.90 €, 4-16s 6 €. High season, adult 12 €, child 6 €.* This village reconstructs scenes from Périgord rural life in 1900, organised round the school, farming, old crafts (nut-oil mill, still, tools, horse-drawn vehicles), toys and local fîtes, as well as everyday objects. You can see the craftsmen working, bread being made in the village oven, a forge in action and a funfair of bygone days.

JARDINS D'ARBORIE ✆ 05 53 08 42 74. *Open July & August: 10am-12 noon and 2.30pm-6.30pm. May, June & September: 2.30pm-6pm. Admission: adult 5 €, child 3 €.* Discover the flora of 5 continents (groups, by appointment). The Arborie gardens take you on a trip through a varied and surprising world of plants. There is a collection of 2,000 cacti, old and genuine bonsais, and Périgord in miniature hidden round a corner.

Domme

Known as Black Périgord's Acropolis, this walled town was built in 1280 by Philippe III (the Bold), taken with the geographical situtuation and its panoramic view. From the Porte de Tours, where Knights Templars were imprisoned in the 14thc., to the 16thc. cornmarket, the old Moulin du Roy (King's mill) or the 15thc. Governor's Mansion now housing the Town Hall, this is a pleasant and athletic walk, on one of the three pedestrian routes round the town, between scented private gardens. Information from the Tourist Office 05 53 31 71 00

GROTTES Place de la Halle ✆ 05 53 31 71 00. *Open February & March and September-December: 10.15am-12 noon and 2.15pm-5.15pm. April-June -6pm. July & August: 10am-7pm. Admission: adult 6,50 €, child 3.50 €.* A panoramic lift with a wide-angle view of the valley takes you to this cave with its concretions, which inspired the painter and writed François Augieras. The lighting sets off the stalactite columns and reflecting pools. You may even see some prehistoric bones.

Les Eyzies

MUSEE NATIONAL DE LA PREHISTOIRE ✆ 05 53 06 45 45. *Open every day except Tuesday : 9.30am-12.30pm and 2.30pm-5.30pm September-June; every day in July and August: 9.30am-6.30pm. Admission: adult 4.50 €, student 3 €, under-18s free. One 3 € admission fee for all on Sunday; admission free for all the first Sunday of each month. Advance booking for guided tours.* Les Eyzies is world-famous for its prehistoric sites, and this museum, open since July 2004, does justice to that reputation, helping the visitor to place the nearby caves in their prehistoric context. It features local

park
aquarium
in Black Perigord
OVER 6000 FISHES
5 ZONES TO VISIT
Activities organised every day !
Tel. (+33) (0)5 53 07 10 74 - Le Bugue/Vézère
OPEN EVERY DAY from mid-february to mid-November
www.parc-aquarium.com
planète MINI-GOLF
CROC - O - GRILL
Dordogne

acquisitions, but also finds from other parts of France. Curator Jean-Jacques Cleyet-Merle and his colleagues have reconstituted the chronological order of events in the Paleolithic era, from the arrival of the first hunters in Aquitaine (400,000 BC) to the end of the Ice Ages (10,000 BC). The collections of tools and prehistoric art excavated in the region are arranged chronologically and geologically. There is carved silex but also plenty of European 'Venuses'; carved and sculpted blocks, primitive furniture, sepulchres and prehistoric fauna. You can visit this magnificent museum for only 3 € on Sundays, and admission is free on the first Sunday of each month, with the aim of making prehistory accessible to everyone.

ABRI PATAUD ✆ 05 53 06 92 46. *Open every day in season. Open every day in high season, closed Monday in low season. Open late January-December. Guided tour lasts about an hour. Disabled access. Admission : adult 5.50 €, child 3.50 €.* This strange building on the way out of the village (towards Perigueux) is one of France's greatest prehistoric deposits. You can see tools, jewellery, works of art, interiors, the remains of game, sepulchres and our ancestors' bones, dug up on site. Stratigraphic section contrasts the different prehistoric occupants from 33,000 B.C. to 18,000 B.C. One of the most impressive sights is an ibex sculpted in bas-relief. The exhibits and work of research scientists give us a more accurate idea of Cro-Magnon man.

GROTTE DE FONT-DE-GAUME ✆ 05 53 06 86 00. *For conservation reasons, you need to book a fortnight ahead to visit this site (open every day except Saturday). 1 April-30 September: 9am-12 noon and 2pm-6pm. 2 November-late February: 10am-12 noon and 2pm-5pm. October and March: 9.30am-12 noon and 2pm-5.30pm. Admission: adult 6.50 €, 18-25s 4.50 €, children free.* This is the last cave with polychrome paintings open to the public in Aquitaine. Over 200 animal figures have been counted in this 120m network, with 84 bison, carved and/or painted in colour. One of the world's most beautiful paleolithic sites.

GROTTE DES COMBARELLES ✆ 05 53 06 86 00. *For conservation reasons, you need to book ahead to visit this site (open every day except Saturday) and access is limited. Same opening hours and admission fees as Font-de-Gaume.* On the left bank of the Beune, this cave, discovered in 1901, is a major Magdalenian sanctuary (13,000 B.C.). It contains over 600 figurative wall carvings, with a variety of animals. There are some anthromorphic examples and a lot of symbols.

GROTTES DU GRAND-ROC LAUGERIE BASSE ✆ 05 53 06 92 70. *www.grandroc.com. Open every day, February-December : 9.30am-6pm in low season, 9.30am-7pm in high season. Admission: adult 7 €, 6-12s 3.50 €.* Set into a magnificent cliff overhanging the Vézère at Les Eyzies, the Grand-Roc cave is an active geode containing all types of underground crystallisation: stalactites and stalagmites; triangles; excentric and fistulous. In the same cliff, Laugerie Basse Prehistoric Shelter once housed Cro-Magnon Man. Both are listed UNESCO World Heritage.

SAINT-CIRQ ✆ 05 53 07 14 37. *Open every day: 10am-7pm from mid-May to mid-September, afternoons only in low season. Admission: cave and museum 4 €.* This cavity between Les Eyzies and the Bugue was discovered in 1951. It is known for the famous carving 'Le Sorcier' (the Magician), and some animals, mainly horses, from the early and mid-Magdalenian era.

Hautefort

Birthplace of Eugene Le Roy (1836-1907), author of Jacquou le Croquant. The village nestles at the foot of the castle, with its own attractions amid the scenic beauty. Don't miss a walk through the hidden streets full of flowers, and a look at the Town Hall in the covered market.

ANCIENS HOSPICES - MUSEE DE LA MEDECINE ✆ 05 53 51 62 98 / Tourist Office: 05 53 50 40 27. *Open April & May, every day: 10am-12 noon and 2pm-6pm. June & September, every day: 10am-7pm. October, Monday-Friday: 10am-12 noon and 2pm-6pm. Closed December-March. Admission: adult 4.50 €, 12-16s 2 €, concessions 3 €.* Founded by the Marquis de Hautefort in 1669, to house the poor, this building developed from a circular chapel on the same lines as the castle; a Greek cross with a lantern dome on top. There were three rooms for the sick on the ground floor and and four upstairs. Today, this is an exhibition centre for the hospice's history. You can visit a 17thc. communal room, a reconstructed dental cabinet and hospital ward and a thematic exhibition on lung ailments, with explanatory documents and objects.

CHATEAU DE HAUTEFORT ✆ 05 53 50 51 23. *Open February & March: 2pm-6pm. April, May ✆ June: 10am-12 noon and 2pm-6pm. July & August: 9.30am-7pm. September: 10am-12 noon and 2pm-6pm. October & November: 2pm-6pm. Admission: adult 8 €, 7-14s 4 €.* This medieval fortress reminds you of the Loire Valley; its lines and curves are both severe and fanciful. The present castle goes back to the 17thc., and was restored by the architect Nicolas Rambourg. On 31 August 1968, a half-stubbed-out cigarette sent it up in flames. The Baroness, who had already dragged her property out of danger once before, managed to save it again. Don't miss the view of the gardens from the terraces: everything is home-produced here.

Montigny-Lascaux

In September 1940, some youngsters chasing their dog came across the decorated Lascaux cave. Today, you visit the replica, but before rushing to it, take time to look at the charming village with its 14th, 15th and 16thc. houses scattered through the old streets or in the Place des Armes.

CHATEAU JARDINS DE LOSSE ✆ 05 53 50 80 08. *Open Easter weekend & every day 15 April-30 September. July & August: 10am-7pm. Admission: 6,50 €.* A 16thc. Renaissance ch,teau was built in the heart of the medieval fortress overlooking the Vézère. It contains period furniture, tapestries, paintings, drawings and weapons characteristic of the place.

LASCAUX II ✆ 0800 891 991 (No Vert) and 05 53 51 95 03. *www.semitour.com. Open all year : 9am-7pm. Closed January, and Monday in low season. Admission: adult 8 € (or 10 € including admission to Thot Museum) 6-12s 5 € (or 7 € including admission to Thot Museum). Guided tour lasts around 40 minutes.* The real cave was closed to the public in 1963 when the walls were attacked by moss resulting from the carbon dioxide breathed out by visitors. To prevent further damage to 'Prehistory's Sistine Chapel', a faithful replica was built in 1983, 200m from the original cave. This facsimile reconstucts the Bull Room and the Diverticule Axial. Black bulls, red bisons, stags, horses and ibex parade through polychrome paintings, just like those of 17,000 years ago. You won't leave Lascaux unmoved. On-site information centre and souvenir shop.

Peyzac-le-Moustier

GROTTE TROGLODYTIQUE LA ROQUE SAINT CHRISOPHE la Roque © 05 53 70 70 45. *www.roque-st-christophe.com. Open all year, every day: 10am-7pm July & August (10am-6pm in winter). Admission: adult 6,50 €, 12-16s 4 €, 5-11s 3 €.* A limestone wall, 1km long, in a sublime Périgord landscape has been continuously eroded, producing shelters under the rock and impressive terraces overhanging them. Humans occupied these cavities from prehistoric times until the Middle Ages, when they were made into a fortified town. Don't miss this visit.

GROTTE DE ROUFFIGNAC Rouffignac-Saint-Cernin-de-Reilhac © 05 53 05 41 71. *Open 9 April-1 November : 10am-11.30am and 2pm-5pm. July & August : 9am-11.30am and 2pm-6pm. Admission : adult 6.10 €, child 3.80 €. Special prices for groups.* The Rouffignac cave figures were discovered exactly 50 years ago, and a free exhibition has been set up at the cave entrance to mark the occasion. The first part retraces the history of these caves before 1956, and the second explains contemporary archaeology, with its use of modern techniques like onsite pigment analysis which brings the laboratory to the cave, so as to speak, and avoids destruction. In 50 years, the cave has become not only a tourist site, but also a place where archaeological research can be evaluated. The exhibition will be officially opened at the anniversary ceremony on 26 June 2006, and a seminar for professionals is to take place in October. This cave was already being visited in the 15thc. Its unusual architecture features a number of flint prominences and some naturally-formed domes. The galleries are over 10km long, which means that visitors cover 1km of the route in a small electric train – thereby saving their legs and protecting site conservation at the same time. This stage also includes an hour-long talk on our origins, from both a geological and a prehistoric viewpoint. In these particular caves, the mammoth is the dominant figure: they contain about half the existing paintings of this animal to be found in Western Europe's 300 decorated caves. 154 mammoths cover the walls and ceilings – rather a surprising choice, for prehistoric artists generally preferred to portray bisons or horses, and mammoths apparently did not fascinate them as they do us today. When you consider that mammoth bones are quite rare in south-west France, there is clearly a mystery surrounding this 'cave of a hundred mammoths'. Don't miss the magnificent black line drawings and engravings of horses and bisons from the Magdalenian era

La Roque-Gageac

One of France's most beautiful villages, with its many alleys and houses clinging to the cliff.

Saint-Léon-sur-Vézère

The streets converge on the heart of the village, where you find a superbly-restored Romanesque church (once part of a 12thc. Benedictine priory). It is interesting from all sides, with its apses and apsidioles. The square tower has arcatures on two levels, contrasting with the curves of the main shale-covered body. The inside is just as beautiful. You can also admire the Chateau de la Salle with its square, machicolated 14thc. keep, and the Ch,teau de Clerans at the water's edge.

CHATEAU DE CHABANS © 05 53 51 70 60. *www.chateaudechabans.com. Open 1 May-27 September. May, June & September: 2pm-7pm, closed Saturday. July & August, 2pm-8pm, open every day. Admission: adult 7,50 €, under-15s free. Guided tours (interior): 1h.* The Dordogne's great families have owned and lived in Chabans. This vast estate with its 14thc. round tower became one of the first Renaissance chateaux for the Calvimonts, and stayed in the family for 3 centuries. Later, it was owned for 25 years by Dulas, bosom friend of Victor Hugo. Chabans was the Dordogne Resistance headquarters in 1944, and Jacques Chaban-Delmas took its name as his Resistance alias - with a spelling mistake.

Sarlat

Black Périgord's capital nestles in those hills known as 'pechs'. The medieval city was rehabilitated in the 1970s , and the streets have recently been repaved and relit. Rather spoilt by too many tourists in summer, the town is splendid out of season, with its narrow alleyways, inside courtyards, private mansions of all periods: medieval foundations, Renaissance storeys, classical roofs. The 13th, 15th and 16thc. houses have new lustre (half-timbering, corbelling and shale roofs). Place de la Liberté is lined with 16th and 18thc. buildings and restored arcades, and you can admire the colossal 15thc. de Gisson mansion and the remains of Sainte Marie Church. In the Rue des Consuls, there is the striking Plamon mansion (Maison des Consuls) built from the 14th-17thc. The de Vassal mansion opposite goes back to the 15thc. Follow Sainte Marie Fountain to the Mirandol and Tapinois de Betou mansions; the latter has a fine 17thc. wooden staircase. Guided tours are available, but it is just as pleasant to stroll through the medieval streets at your own pace.

Puymartin castle, Sarlat

© Iconotec.com

Terrasson-la-Villedieu

JARDINS DE L'IMAGINAIRE © **05 53 50 86 82**. *Open every day except Tuesday, from early April to mid-October : 9.50am-11.20am and 1.50pm-5.20pm (last tour). Open every day in July & August : 9.50am-11.20am and 1.50pm-6.10pm (last tour). Admission: adult 6 €, 10-16s 3.50 €. Tour lasts about 1h10mins.* Experience Nature's cycles, and the symbolic and mythical aspects of human civilisation, in an hour's walk. The rose-garden containing 2,000 plants; the irises and perennials are of chief interest, but this earthly paradise also boasts a water garden and a sacred wood marked out by five fountains representing the world's major rivers.

Périgord Vert

Brantôme

The 'Venice of Périgord', built within a loop of the Dronne is one of the region's most pleasant sites.

ABBEY Bd. Charlemagne © **05 53 05 80 63**. *Open July & August: 10am-7pm every day. Enquire about other opening times. Admission: adult 6 €, child 3 €.* Former Benedictine Abbey (17th and 18thc. buildings, fine monumental staircase, boat-shaped framework). The route takes you through cave-dwellings, and ends with the Fernand Desmoulins Museum, which houses the works of this Third Republic official, painter and engraver and occasional medium; the collection boasts over a hundred 'spirit' drawings.

MUSEE FERDINAND DESMOULINS. *Same opening times as abbey. Admission: adult 6 €, over-8s 3 €.* This talented artist (1859-1914) was an engraver, illustrator and portrait-painter in the political and literary circles of his day. He specialised in etchings, and did Hugo, Zola, Poincaré, Pasteur, Maupassant and Dumas portraits. Then in 1900, he discovered the spirit world, and sketched about 100 surprising and mysterious drawings while acting as medium. The spirit signed three different names via his hand: l'instituteur (primary teacher), ton vieux maitre (your old master) and Astarte. The reconstructed artist-medium's studio, complete with animating spirits, adds to this museum's particular atmosphere.

PARCOURS TROGLODYTIQUE. Same opening hours as the Musee F. Desmoulin. This historic tour of the caves behind the abbey explains how town and abbey came into being. You walk through shelters hewn from rock at the 17thc. Medicis Fountain, pass through the surprising Last Judgement cave with its enigmatic 'Death's Triumph' bas-relief, take in Saint-Sicaire Fountain and its miraculous waters, the former abbey fish-breeding pond and the monks' dovecote. The town surroundings contain caves and holy fountains, dolmens, menhirs and hermitages. There are also Celtic and Gallo-Roman souvenirs, and standing or lying stones at Valeuil, Paussac and Condat.

Nontron

The town is organised on 'levels'; at the bottom, the quarters along the Bandiat, wher there used to be forges and tanneries, and on the cliff. The ramparts and old streets make a pleasant walk, from Place Paul-Bert (no trace left of the former castle). Half-timbered medieval houses can be spotted here and there.

LE COUTEAU DE NONTRON. A blend of the useful and the decorative, the Nontron knife has been the town's pride since the 15thc. The distinctive spots and V on its boxwood handle set it apart from all others. You can visit Nontron's cutlery works in July & August by appointment (groups all year: 05 53 56 01 55)

COUTELLERIE Place Paul-Bert. ✆ 05 53 56 01 55. Cutlery works open Monday-Friday : 9am-12 noon and 1.30pm-5.30pm. Admission free. Nontron's famous knives are made here. You can buy one to take home in the shop at 33, rue Carnot.

Ribérac

Town founded in the 11thc. Arnaud Daniel, one of Perigord's great medieval troubadours, was born in the castle: his poetic works in Occitan are typical of the courtly love period, and draw a discreet veil over the social and political realities of feudalism. Ribérac was famous for its wine until the late 19thc, when phylloxera destroyed the vineyards - the splendid old wine chateaux bear witness to this luxurious but long-gone age. The town, on the edge of the River Dronne, is a canton capital, and a commercial centre even today, the local economy consisting of agriculture (cereals, walnuts, tobacco, poultry and suckling veal) cultural tourism and sports and leisure activities. The weekly market is the department's biggest and most influential.

LA COLLEGIALE NOTRE-DAME *Open 15 June-15 September, every afternoon : 2pm-7pm. Group visits out of season organised by the Tourist Office. Wheelchair access.* Soundproofed Romanesque church (music by Rameau and Purcell) with atmospheric lighting. Ribérac collegiate church was founded after the signing of a charter in 1500, but the building was originally the chapel of a castle put up around 1000. Badly damaged by fire during the Wars of Religion, its condition deteriorated still further in the Revolutionary period. It was made a parish church in the early 19thc, but later deconsecrated in 1935. Today, Notre Dame is an arts centre for contemporary art exhibitions and concerts. It has been beautifully restored, and features a panelled ceiling decorated with 19thc paintings and Henri Guérin's modern stained glass windows incorporating blocks of glass.

Varaignes

CHATEAU ✆ 05 53 56 35 76/05 53 56 31 31. *Opening hours variable according to season. July & August, open every day except Sunday morning: 10am-12 noon and 2pm-6pm. Admission: adult 4 €, child 2.50 €.* The whole town rallied round to restore the castle when the Town Hall bought it in 1965, and won first prize for 'works of art in danger' in 1981. The blend of styles, 13th-16thc., includes one medieval façade and one Renaissance, a machicolated keep and a polygonal staircase tower.

ATELIER MUSEE DES TISSERANDS ET DE LA CHARENTAISE ✆ 05 53 56 35 76. Same opening hours and fees as the castle, which houses this working weavers' museum and a Bandiat-Tardoire Valleys Museum of local life since the 19thc. (cooking, costumes, tools). You can make your own Charentaise slippers and leave with them on!

Lot-et-Garonne

Agen

Famous for its prunes, the Lot-et-Garonne prefecture has other attractions: the Gothic Jacobin church, oldest in the South of France, Saint Caprais Cathedral (12th-14thc.) and some private mansions. The Fine Arts Museum, housed in four of these (Estrades, de Vaurs, Verges and Montluc) exhibits regional arts and history from Prehistoric times, together with a Gallo-Roman Venus (no head or arms) and the works of Goya, among other things. Other things to see: the Resistance and Deportation Museum, Walibi theme park (not far away) and Puymirol, a beautiful walled town with ramparts you can walk along. Montesquieu spent his childhood in Agen, and the learned philosopher Michel Serres was born here.

SAINT CAPRAIS CATHEDRAL. A classic 11thc. Romanesque building, that has developed over the centuries. The chapter house contains relics of Agen martyrs, and local tutelary saints are portrayed in the wall frescoes.

JACOBIN CHURCH Place des Jacobins. This Dominican church was built on the lines of a Roman 'cella' (there are two in France; the other is in Toulouse). It has Gothic trompe-l'oeil frescoes.

NOTRE DAME DU BOURG CHURCH. A beautiful but sober building in brick and stone, in the transitional Gothic style (13thc.). The porch-tower has openings for the bells.

MUSEE DES BEAUX ARTS Place du Docteur-Esquirol © 05 53 69 47 23. *Open every day except Tuesday: 10am-6pm. Admission: 3.70 €.* Housed in four superb Renaissance mansions with fine inside courtyards, this is one of the South West's richest museums. You feel you are in a wealthy collector's home, as you admire the paintings, sculptures, furniture and European earthenware from the Middle Ages to the 19thc. The museum is known for its five marvellous Goyas.

L'AGENAIS Port de Plaisance d'Agen © 05 53 87 51 95. *April, May, June, September & October: Saturdays, Sundays and public holidays: 3pm. 14 July-20 August: every day exceptMonday 2.30pm and 4.30pm. Trip to the Agen lock, 6.20 € per person. 5-13s 3.70 €. Under-5s free.* Boarding at the Villeneuve roundabout, opposite Agen University. Captain Lionel Darriet's pleasure cruiser takes you along the river, under the Canal bridge and through one of the 53 locks on the Garonne's side canal, linking Toulouse to Castets-en-Dorthe. Trip includes guide.

PONT CANAL. After leaving Agen, this famous bridge on the Garonne's side canal is a real pleasure to pass under.

Clairac

Plums and tobacco, the region's chief agricultural products, were first grown here by Benedictine monks. The town is also known for its automaton museum.

AUTOMATON ABBEY 4, place de l'Eglise © 05 53 79 34 81. *Open all year except January. Price includes 4 sites - Abbey, Train Museum, Magic Forest and Santa's Village - adults 10 €.* Snack bars on site. This extraordinary abbey contains 250 life-size animated characters, grouped into scenes showing the monks' daily life in the Middle Ages, with a sound track. Further on, you discover another world of gnomes, elves etc. in the Magic Forest.

Duras

Well worth stopping off for. The castle was built in the 14thc. on an earlier 12thc, structure. Square-shaped with six round towers, it was reshaped in the 17thc. and three wings were added to the inside courtyard. The fine double portico is of the same period. Don't miss the Parchment and Illumination Museum which explains techniques, with a demonstration of gold-leaf script.

MUSEE VIVANT DU PARCHEMIN ET DE L'ENLUMINURE © 05 53 20 75 55. *www.museeduparchemin.com. Open all year for groups. 1 April-30 September for individual visitors. Admission: adult 7 €.* The museum explains book-making in the Middle Ages. You can see how parchment is made from skin; ink and colours from stones, earth, oxides and plants, and watch the creation of illuminated manuscripts gilded with gold-leaf.

Granges-sur-Lot

This building founded in 1281 recalls a time when the English were on the banks of the Lot. Don't miss the Musée du Pruneau gourmand, a prune museum set up on a plum-growing farm.

MUSEE DU PRUNEAU GOURMAND Famille Berino-Martinet © 05 53 84 00 69. *Open all year (except 15-30 January) every day:9am-12 noon and 2pm-7pm (3pm-7pm Sunday and public holidays). Under-10s free, adults 3.30 €.* 20-minute video, maze (1h30mins) evening events (birds of prey demonstration), hores-riding, museum workshops, farm shop. The Plum and Prune Museum reconstructs an early 20thc. workshop where prunes were made, with documents and archives from the 18thc. to the present day. In summer, you can look for the 'lost plum' in the maze, and find out the legend of Lady Plum and the Prune Knight.

Mézin

PARC DE LA GARENNE. The park, with its 100-year-old oaks and fountains, is laid out along the River Baise, opposite the old castle gardens. The listed 16thc. Bains du Roy pavilion adds to the site's beauty. Cross the 16thc. bridge, and go through the old alleys on the right bank. On the Mezin road, a few kilometres from the town on the right, is Tasta, a fine medieval castle.

MUSEE DU LIEGE ET DU BOUCHON Rue du Puits-Saint-Come © 05 53 65 68 16. *Open April-October (all year for groups). July-September: 10am-12 noon and 2pm-7pm. April-June and October: 2pm-6pm. Admission: adult 3.50 €, 14-18s 2* . Mezin has specialised in corks since the 17thc. The daily life of a 19thc. cork-making family is reconstructed with a sound track.

Monflanquin

This 13thc. walled town was founded in 1256 by Alphonse de Poitiers. The streets converge on the central Place des Cornieres, busy in summer. From the walls, you have a superb view over the countryside.

LA BASTIDE. Between the 12th and 14thc., under both French and English rule, South West towns were built as bastides. These 300 new towns were organised round a square with arcades and streets arranged in an octagonal grid, inside a wall with ramparts; and played an economic, political and military role. Today, 40 bastides are left, many with period features. Around Monflanquin, are Castillones (25km), Villeréal (12km), Monpazier (27km), Villeneuve-sur-Lot (18km) and Beaumont-du-Périgord (29km).

MUSEE DES BASTIDES Place des Arcades ✆ 05 53 36 40 19. *Guided tours in French: Monday: 3pm, 5pm. Tuesday & Thursday: 5pm. Friday: 11am, 5pm. In English: Tuesday: 11am, Thursday: 3pm. Admission: adult 3 €, under-12s free.* Learn all about 13thc. bastide town planning, with scale models, sculptures and audiovisual guides to bring the subject alive.

Nérac

This Gallo-Roman and Renaissance town on the banks of the Baïse has plenty of historic and architectural attractions. Nérac is the capital of the Albret, and the first Lot-et-Garonne town to be listed in the 'four flowers' category, Its Henri IV castle-museum, old town, half-timbered houses , medieval alleys, river banks and harbour, ancient (listed) bridge and Saint Nicolas (listed) and Notre Dame churches are a pleasure to visit. You can also enjoy the Parc de la Garenne , Aquitaine's oldest listed site, on the right bank of the Baïse. It was fitted out by Henri IV's grandfather Henri d'Albret II and boasts a number of fountains and ornamental ponds, as well as some age-old trees.

CHATEAU HENRI IV Impasse Henri IV ✆ 05 53 65 21 11. *Open every day except Monday, June-September: 10am-12 noon and 2pm-6pm. October-May: 2pm-6pm. Admission: adult 4 €, concessions 3 €, under-12s free.* This magnificent Renaissance building was put up by the Albret family in the 15thc. Henri IV stayed there during his childhood, and later with his wife Marguerite de Valois from 1576-1588.

Pujols

Ancient medieval city set up by Alphonse de Poitiers in 1264, and perched 180m above the Lot Valley and Villeneuve-sur-Lot. The only way in is through the fortified gate protecting the former chapel, which became Saint-Nicolas Church in the 14th and 15thc. Half-timbered houses of the same period line the main street, and mysterious alleyways open off it. The village was recently restored.

Roquefort

The village was once known for its 13th and 14thc. fortress overlooking the Garonne plain. Today, the hordes of visitors come mainly for Walibi theme park.

WALIBI AQUITAINE Chateau de Caudouin ✆ 05 53 96 58 32. *www.sixflagseurope.com. Open April-October. Admission: adult 22.50 € (20.50 € if you buy tickets from Agen Tourist Office), 3-17s 17 €, under-3s free.* Close to Agen and the motorway exit, this theme park covers 30ha. of greenery overlooked by a superb 18thc. chateau. The rides are typically sensational; there is a sea-lion display in a Greco-Roman amphitheatre and a musical fountain attraction. In July and August, there will be a new Wild West show, 'La Legende de l'Ouest'.

Le-Temple-sur-Lot

The name comes from a 12thc. Knights Templars' command-post. The King of England had the bastide built in 1318. Botany fans will want to see the Latour-Marliac waterlily and peony gardens.

LATOUR-MARLIAC-LE JARDIN DES NENUPHARS ✆ 05 53 01 08 05. *www.latour-marliac.fr. Open every day, 15 March-30 September: 10am-6pm. Admission: adult 4,50 €, over-12s 2.50 €, under-12s free. Shop open every day 15 March-30 September: 10am-6pm.* This is the world's oldest and most prestigious water plant nursery, housing the French white water lily collection. There are some beautiful lotus-flowers, 200 species of water lily and bamboos dating back to 1860. The site inspired Claude Monet's Waterlilies.

FOOD AND DRINK

In this region, the cooking owes a lot to goose fat, and plenty of wine is drunk, yet the cholesterol levels are lower than in other parts of the country! They say it's due to the traditional combination (red wine is good for the arteries), authenticity and quality. Be that as it may, the South-West has a well-deserved international reputation for gastronomy.

Cepes

From September, the rush is on for these mushrooms. There are markets every day in August and September in the Monpazier bastide, from 3pm in the covered market; and in the Villefranche du Périgord bastide from August -October from 4pm (all day Sunday).

Foie gras

Specially famous in the Landes or Périgord, Fans argue about the superior merits of duck or goose; it's all a matter of taste. Foie gras producers are now opening their farms to tourists (product on sale). You can also visit the Foie gras Museum at Frespech (Lot et Garonne).

Arcachon oysters

The oyster now farmed in the Bassin d'Arcachon is Japanese, but its particular qualities come from the beds, placed where the ocean current is strongest. You can eat oysters any time, but the best seasons are January-February (when they begin to mature) to July (when they become clearer). From June to mid-July they are full of soft roe (laiteuses); in July-August, rather green. They are roe-filled again, without being fatty, from October onwards.

Bayonne country ham

A geographic appellation now protects the jambon de Bayonne, delicious by itself or in sandwiches. On Basque Country farms, it is fried in thicker slices, with piperade (tomatoes and peppers) and a beaten egg added at the last minute.

Discover the oberena, made by 23 associated charcutiers with their own drying and salting facilities (this is the only home-made Bayonne ham with the red quality label, or Label rouge); and the ibaiona from the Aldudes Valley and a rustic Basque pig that has almost died out. It is made from 12-month-old pigs fed on cereals, barley, wheat and corn.

COOPERATIVE ARTISANALE DES ARTISANS CHARCUTIERS BASQUES Rue du Lazaret - ANGLET ✆ 05 59 42 08 53

PIERRE OTEIZA 16, complexe Republique - PAU ✆ 05 59 82 86 18. *Maison Dionionea Ainhoa ✆ 05 59 29 30 43. Route Urepel - Aldudes ✆ 05 59 37 56 11. 10, rue Republique – Saint Jean de Luz ✆ 05 59 51 94 55. Maison Errea 31, rue Espagne – Saint Jean Pied de Port ✆ 05 59 37 23 26*

Piment d'Espelette

The strings of red peppers across the Basque housefronts probably originated in Mexico, and were adopted by most of the region's farmers in the 16thc. Used to season and preserve meat, they found their way into family cooking, and are now part of many Basque recipes.

SYNDICAT DE DEFENSE DU PIMENT D'ESPELETTE Espelette ✆ 05 59 93 88 86

Agen Prunes

Imported from the Mediterranean to Agen's sunsoaked countryside. The plums are harvested from mid-August to mid-September, washed, sorted, weighed, dried and stored, to become the soft prunes so popular with consumers. Eat them on their own, or in meat dishes (such as rabbit) and desserts.

CABAN BOUTIQUE 57, rue Molinier - AGEN ✆ 05 53 48 03 49. This famous confectioner has been selling locally-made chocolates, dried fruits, stuffed prunes and old Armagnac since 1855.

Truffles

The most prized is Périgord's black truffle. It grows underground, among roots (oak and hazlenut, but also hornbeam, lime and pine). Truffles can be found on the Sorgues, Périgueux, Excideuil, Vergt and Saint Alvère markets from January. They are walnut-sized, and can be eaten in omelettes, with eggs or in small pieces on toast with butter and salt. You can find out more the Truffle Ecomuseum in Sorgues (05 53 05 90 11) or by taking part in the annual Truffle Fair, also in Sorgues, on the third Sunday in January.

Hotels & Restaurants

DORDOGNE

Antonne-et-Trigonant

HOSTELLERIE DE L'ECLUSE *** **Route de Limoges ✆ 05 53 06 00 04** *Website: www.ecluse-perigord.com. Open every day and all year. 47 rooms from 45 €, suite from 80 €. Set menus from 20 €, lunchtime and evening, except weekends and public holidays. À la carte 35 €.* In this idyllic setting, about ten minutes from Périgueux, you find a superb building on the Isle riverbank, housing a comfortable hotel and a top-quality restaurant. Inside the decor is rustic, and the *cuisine* regional, but with an original twist; the chef only cooks with fresh local produce and respects the seasons. His foie gras is as excellent as ever, and we especially like the *mi-cuit* served with monbazillac jelly. We ordered a domaine-de-la-vitrolle to go with lunch, a very good vin de pays that has won several medals, and is reasonably priced. You can digest your meal in peace on the small adjacent beach.

LES CHANDELLES Route de Limoges ✆ 05 53 35 12 54. *Open every day in high season (closed Saturday lunchtime and Sunday evening in low season). 8 rooms from 45 €, breakfast 8 €. Satellite TV, swimming pool, tennis courts, private car park. Set menus 18 €-35 €, formula of the day 12 €.* This superb Périgord building housing a hotel-restaurant was closed for several years, before reopening under M and Mme Rousset's capable management. All the rooms are modern and comfortable, and overlook the park. The restaurant has a genuine country feel, with its exposed stonework and beams, and is decorated in warm tones. M Rousset looks after the dining room while his wife runs the show in the kitchens - and nothing is left to chance, from the lunchtime formula at 12 € to the typical regional dishes such as veal cheek. She loves cooking foie gras in all its forms, including the delicious *marbré*, but her specialities also include marbled duck thigh (prepared like ham with parsley), red fruit au gratin and monbazillac sabayon. The shady terrace facing the pool is a real pleasure in sunny weather.

CHARMILLE *** **Route de Limoges ✆ 05 53 06 00 04** *Website: www.ecluse-perigord.com. Open every day and all year. 47 rooms from 45 €, suite from 80 €. Set menus from 20 €, lunchtime and evening, except weekends and public holidays. À la carte 35 €.* In this idyllic setting, about ten minutes from Périgueux, you find a superb building on the Isle riverbank, housing a comfortable hotel and a top-quality restaurant. Inside the decor is rustic, and the *cuisine* regional, but with an original twist; the chef only cooks with fresh local produce and respects the seasons. His foie gras is as excellent as ever, and we especially like the *mi-cuit* served with monbazillac jelly. We ordered a domaine-de-la-vitrolle to go with lunch, a very good vin de pays that has won several medals, and is reasonably priced. You can digest your meal in peace on the small adjacent beach.

LE PLAT DANS L'ASSIETTE 18, rue du Mourrier ✆ 05 53 24 25 26 *Open lunchtime and evenings, Tuesday to Saturday. Service until 10pm. Formula from 10 €, set menus from 19.50 €-34.50 €.* Sylvain's Lyon-style restaurant in the heart of the pedestrian quarter of Bergerac is a must. At lunchtime, seasonal dishes of the day are chalked up on the slate: mixed salads and other recipes with traditional Lyonnais names, but also foie gras carpaccio on a bed of lentils, snails in flaky pastry cooked with *aligoté* wine, grilled Limousin rib steak, Hugon farm veal tendron and baked camembert to finish. A new dining

room on the first floor provides plenty of room for groups, and several associations of *bon vivants* - like the Bergerac Cigar Club - have settled there. Sylvain has since produced an armagnac and cognac list, and another featuring cigars.

Bergerac

BISTROT GAMBETTA 36, rue Gambetta ✆ 05 53 27 30 50. *Open every day, all year. Formulas 11 € (starter and dessert or main course and dessert) and 13.60 € lunchtime (starter and main course). Set menus from 16 € to 24 € and à la carte.* The Bistrot Gambetta is the Hotel du Commerce's restaurant, the said hotel being part of the Logis de France group. The cuisine is traditional yet original. The formulas or menu at 16 € comprising a starter (foie gras terrine), a main course (thin strips of duck breast called *aiguillettes*, in pepper sauce) and a dessert are perfect for lunchtime. If you have a little more time to appreciate good cooking, let yourself be tempted by the chef's great speciality, the *canard en folie* (mad duck) menu at 24 €. For that price, you discover 5 different ways to taste duck: in soup, in the form of hot and cold rillettes, duck salmi, foie gras pan-fried with apples and the *aiguillettes* with pepper sauce. You'll have no difficulty finding a parking space, the Bistrot being right opposite the sous-prefecture's own car park.

HOTEL DU COMMERCE* 36, place Gambetta ✆ 05 53 27 30 50.** *35 rooms from 35 € to 53 €, all equipped with Canal Satellite. Breakfast 7 €. Logis de France.* Professional welcome. Top-quality hotel with newly redecorated rooms, well located in the town centre with a large car park nearby. You can eat in the hotel at the Bistrot Gambetta, one of the town's best restaurants.

LE MODERNE 21, avenue du 108e-RI ✆ 05 53 57 19 / 62. *Open every day except Friday. Annual closing two weeks in October. Formula 15 €, set menus 17 € to 27 €.* You can't miss the modern front facing the station. The ambience is friendly, and chef Patrick's cooking an excellent blend of tradition and originality. Try the grilled entrecote with shallots, home-made dessert and coffee for 15 € at lunchtime. Gourmets will enjoy the specialities. *A la carte*: home-made foie gras, snails with garlic butter, pikeperch in champagne and grilled duck breast with monbazillac, and should make sure they leave some room for dessert. Patrick himself runs the dining room, ably helped by his charming waitresses. The service is never slow, so customers in a hurry needn't worry about missing their train.

LA TREILLE 12, quai Salvette ✆ 05 53 57 60 11. *Open every day in summer, except Wednesday. Closed Tuesday evening and Wednesday in low season. Dish of the day 10 €, set menus 13 €, 15 € and 26 €. Children's menu 8 €.* This restaurant boasts one of the finest settings in Bergerac, right opposite the River Dordogne. Inside, the decor is rustic and quite charming, with the pub-style bar downstairs, and the restaurant with its more select ambiance and balcony overlooking the Dordogne upstairs. Christian's welcome is just as warm in all seasons, and the chef communicates his passion for cooking with some local specialities, but also fish: pikeperch with monbazillac sauce, or smoked salmon carpaccio with lime and red fruit. The menu changes with the seasons. Come the summer, you'll enjoy having lunch or a drink on the terrace, in the shade of the Virginia creeper.

VEROTEL * Route d'Agen ✆ 05 53 24 89 76** *B&B rooms from 47 €. 50 rooms from 57 €. Duplex sleeping 2-5 from 77 € to 88 €. Breakfast buffet 7 €. The rooms - single, double, duplex 3-4, for the disabled - are all air-conditioned and equipped with bathroom, toilet, direct phone line, automatic alarm clock, TV Canal Satellite, lift and Wi-Fi network.* Véronique and Jean-Claude Rey's hotel is located in the heart of the Bergerac vineyards 2 minutes by car from the Chateau de Monbazillac and Bergerac town centre. They know all the best local addresses and will give you plenty of advice. There is a private car park and a coach park at residents' disposal all year round. Add two lounges, a sauna, swimming pool and terrace, and a welcome for pets, and you can see that great pains are taken to make guests feel at home.

Beynac

HOTEL-RESTAURANT DU CHATEAU Le Bourg – Beynac ✆ 05 53 29 19 20** *Website: www.hotelduchateau-dordogne.com Open all year. Closed mid-December to mid-January. 18 rooms from 40 €. Half-board from 45 € per head. Breakfast 6.80 €. Swimming pool. Lunchtime bistrot formula 12 €, set menus 18 €-28 €. A la carte. Children's menu 10 €.* This hotel at the foot of Beynac Château, just opposite the Dordogne, provides extremely comfortable rooms, and Christoph and Sarissa Kusters give you a warm welcome. The dining room and covered terrace are air-conditioned, and there is a charming river terrace too. On weekday lunchtimes, the Bistrot Rapide formula is good value for money. Chefs André and Josette Roucheyrolle also prepare local specialities like duck foie gras escalope pan-fried with tangerines, cabbage stuffed with duck foie gras and Sechuan pepper, and genuine grilled beef rib with sarladaise potatoes and vegetables. The pikeperch fillet with two peppers, sturgeon steak with onion preserve, and grilled red tuna en *habits de fleurs* should satisfy fish-lovers. Not forgetting the delicious homemade *crème brulée* for dessert, of course.

Boulazac

BUFFALO GRILL Agora Commercial Park ✆ 05 53 07 86 75 *Open every day: 11am-11pm. Car park. Games room. 'Buffalo' menu 11 €, 'Indians' menu 4.70 €.* Quick service if you're in a hurry, more leisurely if you want to take your time: the staff here know how to meet customer requirements. A wide choice of the best beef cuts (French, German, Brazilian and Argentinian breeds) are on offer, ranging from the simple steak to the rib steak carefully cut to guarantee healthy meat. You can also taste bison and ostrich, cooked to perfection. The menu caters for fish and salad-lovers too, and there is a very decent selection of desserts.

Bourdeilles

CHATEAU DE LA COTE ✆ **05 53 03 70 11** *Website: www.chateaudelacote.com. Open every evening, Sunday and public holiday lunchtimes, Christmas and New Year, and all year for groups, weddings and seminars. Annual closing 15 November-15 March. 16 rooms from 67 € to 149 €, breakfast 10 €. Swimming pool. Set menus from 27 € to 64 €. Children's menu 11 €.* This magnificent chateau is set in the middle of an extensive park, with swimming pool. It dates back to the 15thc., and is a peaceful spot 15 km from Périgueux in the direction of Brantume and Bourdeilles. You will be warmly welcomed, with no trace of the stiff formality you might expect in such a place. Each room is different, but they are all decorated with attention to authenticity and detail. In the beautiful, high-ceilinged dining-room with its warm pannelling and huge fireplace, you discover a menu devoted mainly to Perigord's own produce: pan-fried duck liver escalope, and duck leg confit caramelised in honey, with cepes, for instance. The chef doesn't neglect fish dishes however, and his salmon tournedos stuffed with cepes, chicken juices flavoured with spices is succulent. You can eat on the terrace in summer: a real pleasure.

Brantôme-en-Périgord

HOTEL CHABROL CHEZ CHARBONNEL*** **57, rue Gambetta** ✆ **05 53 05 70 15** *Open every day except Sunday evening and Monday from 1 January to1 August, except public holidays. Annual closing 15 November-28 February. Set menus, à la carte from 26 € to 63 €. 20 rooms from 45 € to 70 €.* You can't miss this great building overlooking the river, with its *hotel de charme* and excellent restaurant. The Charbonnel family hands down its experience in hotel management and the culinary arts from generation to generation. Chef Jean-Claude Charbonnel's *cuisine* is sophisticated, traditional and generous, and the setting is pleasant, whether you're in the dining room or on the terrace above the river. You might start with a delicious foie gras *mi-cuit*, then pigeon Rossini, with the hearty *assiette gourmande* (selection of desserts) to finish. If you feel it's too early to quit, then why not enjoy a *digestif* and a cigar in one of the cosy lounges?

Le Bugue

LA BRASSERIE DU PARC Route de Limeuil ✆ **05 53 04 10 00**. *Open all year; every day in high season, Monday-Friday lunchtimes and Friday, Saturday and Sunday evenings in low season. Lunchtime menu 10.50 €, set menus 17 €-28 €. A la carte.* This peaceful place on the edge of a lake is about 1km from Bugue towards Limeuil. The dining room with its bay windows offers a fine view while keeping the customers warm in winter, and can cater for group meals, weddings and banquets. In fine weather, you can eat comfortably under the spacious arbour. The lunchtime menu comprising soup, hors d'oeuvres buffet, dish of the day, dessert or coffee is excellent value for money (10.50 €) – unusual in this part of Périgord. If you're less hungry, why not try the unlimited hors d'oeuvres buffet formula or a large gizzard salad for 8.50 € (5.50 € for a smaller salad). The 20 € menu takes longer to enjoy, with a choice of snails or cepes to start with, followed by duck thigh confit stuffed with cepes, and cabecou goat's cheese. A la carte, you have duck breast or salmon carpaccio, beef rib and fish (fresh salmon steak or scallop kebab). Finally, pizza-lovers are not forgotten, with a selection of homemade pizzas available too. We suggest you walk off the calories by the lakeside, as a relaxing follow-up to your meal. This is one of the few local restaurants that open on Sunday evening all year round.

Chaleix

CHATEAU DE MAVALEIX Chaleix - Thiviers ✆ 05 53 52 82 01. *Open all year. Rooms from 65 € to 85 €, half-board 55 € to 65 €. Full board 65 € to 75 € 2 gites with 3 bedrooms, from 350 € the weekend. Breakfast 9 €. Set menus 14.50 € (lunchtime) to 45 €, children's menu 10 €.*This beautiful medieval castle is only a stone's throw from the Route Nationale 21 but has none of the drawbacks. The hotel-restaurant is well-kept, and all the rooms are prettily decorated and fully equipped. The new chef has already made an impression, with regional cooking using produce from the castle's big kitchen garden. The lunchtime menu at 14.50 € is quite adequate; customers in a hurry can be served in less than an hour.A la carte you can be sure of the warm, pan-fried foie gras Normandy-style, scallops in pastry on a bed of leeks, pan-cooked cote d'azur gambas, home-bred lamb prepared according to the mood of the moment, and beef *flambéd* with pepper. If you've time, stroll through the green park with its ancient trees, beautiful swimming pool and tennis courts. The castle can hold around a hundred guests for weddings and banquets. A word of advice: drive quickly through the village to avoid potential lurking photographers.

Chancelade

CHATEAU DES REYNATS** - L'OISON Les Reynats – Chancelade ✆ 05 53 03 53 59** *Open all year. 37 roooms including 5 suites in the chateau and 24 rooms in the orangery, from 120 € to 250 €. Breakfast 14 €. Swimming pool, tennis courts. 18-hole golf nearby. Restaurant L'Oison. Set menus from 28 € to 45 €.* This establisheclusement is rated top of the range, both for the luxury services it provides for hotel residents and its culinary quality. Chef Gilles Gourvat from Perigord offers a most inventive cuisine, which varies according to the seasons; you will be pleasantly surprised by his expertise in the mixing and matching of flavours. Foie gras lasagna with woodland mushrooms and black truffle emulsion, or farm-bred pigeon cassolette, steamed truffled vegetables and pigeon juice with vin jaune feature on his menus and will thrill your tastebuds. The wine list is exceptional, and the service reflects the general high standard.

Domme

L'ESPLANADE * Rue Pont-Carrat ✆ 05 53 28 31 41** *Open every day in high season, closed Monday and Wednesday lunchtime in low season. Annual holiday from mid-November to early March. Disabled access. 25 rooms from 77 €. Breakfast 12 €. Set menus from 30 € (lunchtime) and à la carte.* This is an excellent place to stay all year round. René Gillard and his son-in-law Pascal Bouland are active members of the *Toques du Perigord* chefs' association, and together concoct a *cuisine* which gives pride of place to the region's excellent produce, including fish and seafood. Examples are the Dublin Bay prawns and foie gras duo pan-cooked in a sweet and sour sauce with a herb salad, the truffle *croque* with Guérande salt, duck liver with truffles in a pot-au-feu or sweetbreads with morels. Some of the rooms haev a marvellous view over the Dordogne Valley, and they are all superbly equipped.

Excideuil

LA TABLE D'ESSENDIERAS Domaine d'Essendieras – Saint-Médard-d'Excideuil ✆ 05 53 55 34 34 *Open every day in high season, closed Monday and Tuesday out of season. 5 guest rooms from 69 € per night. 5 apartments in the chateau from 49 € per night, 8 individual houses each with 2-6 rooms from 375 € per week. Brasserie, with set menus from 16 €-22 €. Gastronomic restaurant, set menus 28 €-60 €.* The Domaine d'Essendieras is located on one of the region's highest hills, with a superb view over the Isle Valley. The estate stretches across 350 ha. and includes 2 châteaux, dating from the 16th and 19thc, with their outbuildings (stables, barns, steward's houses) extensive park and orangery. In the old, restored château, all the rooms have a fireplace for the long winter evenings, and the gastronomic restaurant and brasserie with its wide outdoor terrace can be found on the ground floor. On the first floor, there is a new dining room, and a superb library for professional meetings. The restaurant is open every day in high season (closed Monday and Tuesday out of season) and is run by M and Mme Chiron. Their menu includes specialities like pan-fried foie gras escalope with apples and sauce perigourdine (26 €), pikeperch escalope cooked in Bergerac verjus (15 €), cod steak with *sauce vert* (19 €), veal sweetbreads with morels (28 €) and duck breast in an elderberry sauce (22 €). Mr Bakker, the château owner, also provides a very good residents' table on weekday evenings, for an all-in price of 19 €.

Les Eyzies-de-Tayac

HOTEL RESTAURANT LE CRO MAGNON* 54, avenue de la Préhistoire - Les Eyzies-de-Tayac** ✆ **05 53 06 97 06** *Open every day in season. 15 rooms from 70 €-75 €, 2 suites at 100 €. Breakfast buffet 9 €. Set menus from 23 €. A la carte.* Valérie Besse in the dining room and husband Laurent in the kitchen are attracting more and more customers with their very professional approach. The prettily-decorated hotel rooms are well-equipped, and the restaurant spoils you for choice with a dining room, verandah and pleasant shady terrace. The menus feature those unavoidable Périgord specialities, but also langoustine and foie gras gâteau, small seasonal vegetables in a vinaigrette, rabbit *fondant* with rosemary, mustard-flower cream, and pigeon baked in a casserole with foie gras butter. The desserts are all terribly tempting: we liked the dacquoise with caramelised walnuts and dark chocolate *fondant.*

Fouleix

LE MOULIN DE SAINT-PIERRE ✆ **05 53 82 91 09.** *E-mail: jfleocata@wanadoo.fr <mailto: jfleocata@wanadoo.fr Set menus : Découverte (3 courses) 23 €, Evasion (4 courses) 32 € and Gourmand (5 courses) 48 €. A la carte. Open all year. Closed Monday. Receptions.* The Moulin de Saint-Pierre is a 4-ha estate on the Périgueux-Bergerac road via Vergt, with the gastronomic restaurant 'Le Moulin' at its heart. Marlène and Jean-François Leocata fell in love with this property at first sight, and have gone on embellishing and improving it ever since. In two years, they have gained a faithful local customer base, including a number of British expats, and have recently recruited a talented young chef - which should persuade gourmets that Fouleix is well worth the trip. Franck Sanna has worked with Michel Bras (Laguiole) and with France's youngest starred chef Yannick Delpech (l'Amphitryon, Toulouse). He has experience of the Indian Ocean countries, and uses it when concocting recipes with

Perigord produce. The result is sunshine cooking: local specialities that are a blend of exotic spices and Southern flavours. Try the duck foie gras cooked in a cloth in spiced wine and the delicious desserts *chocolat coulant* (runny chocolate!) with Combava in a crunchy samosa and Victoria pineapple soup with sweet spices. The18thc. setting is elegant, and the mill workings can still be seen in the main dining-room - you can hear the stream flowing past outside as you eat. You have a restful view of the park from the veranda, and jazz dinners are held on summer Fridays if you prefer a more up-tempo rhythm - book ahead, as they fill up quickly. The tapas formula is new this season, a welcome complement to the gastronomic menus. You can fish here all year, and take advantage of the picnic formula (a filled picnic basket for 10 € with the aperitif free) and barbecue. Next year, the owners are planning to develop these open air services, and add a swimming pool, chalets and children's play area.

Issigeac

LA BRUCELIERE Place de la Capelle ✆ 05 53 73 89 61 *Open all year. Annual closing in January, and Wednesdays. 5 rooms from 46 €. Set menu Issigeac-sur-Mer 23.50 €.* Maffe and Nicolas De Vish have set up an excellent hotel in this former 19thc. coaching inn with its rustic charm, and their cooking is original, witness the pressed rabbit terrine with duck liver and roast aubergines. Their great speciality is fish, however: warm grilled swordfish and barbet fillet salad with walnut oil and beetroot vinaigrette, halibut steak with coco beans, beef marrow and Dublin Bay prawns, monkfish medallions with chicory conserved in veal juices with Japanese horseradish and lime feature on the Issigeac-sur-Mer menu and à la carte, along with the lobster *meli-melo* and green onions with lobster juices, garlic, basil and ratte potatoes, and scallop, Dublin Bay prawn and sweetbread salad flavoured with white truffle oil. If the pear and mascarpone *bavarois*, mint soup with kiwis and mandarins traditional-style is on the dessert menu, you're in for a treat.

LE RELAIS DE L'ANCIENNE GARE Route d'Eymet – Issigeac ✆ 05 53 58 70 29 *Open every day except Monday and Tuesday evenings, and Wednesday. Set menus from 21.50 €. Lunchtime formula 12 €.* In the tastefully-decorated and air-conditioned dining rooms, Sylvie advises you on your choice of dish prepared by her husband, chef Hervé. He cooks with seasonal ingredients, and the result is a sophisticated and original cuisine: duck foie gras escalope pan-fried with grapes and gingerbread, poached eggs with mussels in curry cream with leek seeds, and beef fillet with a foie gras escalope or steamed salmon with a vegetable and parsley juice minestrone. Dessert fans will go for the cold citrus fruit and armagnac souffle. A terrace for fine-weather eating completes the buccolic setting, and there is a glass-blower's workshop next door - well worth the visit if you have time after your meal.

Le Bugue

LE CYGNE ** 2, rue Cingle ✆ 05 53 07 17 77. This hotel-restaurant in its old town house is part of the Logis de France group, and is perfectly run by Thierry and Antonella Baux. The chef changes his menu with the seasons, so as to use only fresh produce in his cooking, such as the cepe millefeuille with a walnut sauce, the young pigeon stuffed to the chef's own recipe, crayfish au gratin, ling fillet with a coconut and ginger sauce, and so on. The great house speciality is duck foie gras pan-fried with seasonal fruit, which appears on the menu all year round. There is a vegetarian menu too, at 17 €, and at lunchtime, the menu entreprise at 12 € with starter, main course and dessert. In summer, the shady garden and terrace are extremely pleasant.

Les Eyzies-de-Tayac

LE CENTENAIRE 2 rue du Cingle ✆ 05 53 06 68 68 *Fax 05 53 06 92 41. Website: www.hotelducentenaire.fr. Set menus from 70 € to 100 €, à la carte 85 €. Closed Monday, Tuesday, Wednesday and Friday lunchtimes, and from early November to early April.* Roland Mazère has spent thirty-five years running the kitchens in this celebrated hotel, almost as famous as the village itself. He could quite well rest on his laurels (he is a member of the *Chambre Syndicale de la Haute Cuisine Française*) and simply go on serving goose steaks Rossini or young pigeon with a drop of blood to coachloads of tourists already won over by his reputation. These dishes certainly feature on his menus, and rightly so, for they serve as a yardstick, but beside them you'll find much more exciting creations, which may not revolutionise French *haute cuisine*, but can hold their own against the competition. Delicate spider crab jelly and rice cream with Aquitaine caviar, steamed bass in sea water, fennel conserved with liquorice, bitter salad with ginger, sweetbread tournedos, lemon sauce with sansho pepper, broad beans and green asparagus, and fine chocolate, nougatine and soft caramel leaves with cardamom and litchi sorbet. The impressive wine cellar is run by the very available and articulate Tim Harrison.

Meyrals

L'AUBERGE DE MEYRALS ✆ **05 53 29 22 08** *Website: www.aubergedemeyrals.com Open every day, April to September and Friday to Monday in low season. Annual closing in February. Lunchtime menu on the slate 11 € with starter, main course and dessert, set menus from 26 € to 39 € and à la carte.* In this charming village between the Dordogne and Vézère Valleys 12 km from Sarlat and 5km from Les Eyzies, you find the most convivial inn this side of Black Perigord. As the cooking is excellent too, your enjoyment will be complete, once settled in the small dining room with its prettily set tables and stone fireplace. Local artists' work is hung around the walls, and more of it arrives on your plate in the form of traditional regional recipes concocted and presented with originality. Your potatoes *sarladaises* (fried in goose fat) are served in a small individual black cauldron, for instance. The pork fillet mignon medallion *flambé* in cognac, beef fillet with five sorts of peppercorn and accompanying potato cake with cepes, and duck breast with seasonal fruits, raspberry vinegar reduction with *mille-fleurs* honey feature on the set menus from 10 € to 22 €, enabling you to enjoy good food without breaking the budget. Superb wine list.

Monbazillac

LA TOUR DES VENTS Le Moulin de Malfourat ✆ **05 53 58 30 10** *Open every day in high season except Monday in July. Closed Sunday evening, Monday and Wednesday evening in low season. Set menus 23 € to 46 €. Vegetarian menu 21 €. A la carte 38 €. Children's menu 10 €.* This is the best restaurant in the Bergerac, which is just too bad for the misogynists among us, since the chef-owner's name is Marie Rougier. She puts her culinary arts to good use, with plenty of talent, backed up by Fabrice Jean. The fresh produce used in her recipes is often very local indeed; most of the herbs and vegetables come from her friend M. Salvat's garden. The duck foie gras trilogy and the sweetbread fricassee with Dublin Bay prawns and cepes are standards on her menu, among other delicacies like open lobster ravioli with parsley juice or the farm-bred chicken jigounette with Dublin Bay prawns. There is a wide choice of desserts, but we have a weakness for Marie's crèpes suzettes. Women can cook professionally just as well as men; the proof is right here. The vegetarian menu is perfectly balanced. Comfort and space are the watchwords in the dining room, and the terrace has a magnificent panoramic view of the vineyards and the Bergerac Valley. An enchanting place.

Montignac

LOU CANTOU DE COSTE Route des Eyzies ✆ **05 53 51 86 92** *Open every day in high season. Lunchtime formula 12 €, set menus 21 €-30 €.* On the way out of Montignac towards Les Eyzies, this attractive place serves traditional local fare, but also fish and seafood, less usual in a region of meat-breeders! Chef Alban has just arrived from Dunkerque, bringing his turbot, sea bass fillet and gambas and scallop suspension with two sauces. His partner Yannick runs the dining room with cheerful, friendly efficiency. The set menu of the day (12 €) comprises rib steak or confit with an assortment of vegetables, dessert and coffee. The menu at 21 € includes speciality dishes from the *carte*, like the house salad (gizzards, smoked duck breast, pine kernels) duck thigh, and warm Rocamadour goat's cheese in a walnut crust.

Périgueux

LE CLOS SAINT-FRONT 5, rue de la Vertu ✆ **05 53 46 78 58** *Open Tuesday lunchtime to Sunday lunchtime and every day in July and August. Slate of the day: starter-main course or main course-dessert 17 €, starter-main course-dessert 21 €, set menu à la carte 30 €, menu affaire (lunchtime) 23 €, menu vigneron 50 €, with wine tasting included.* You'd be wise to book in advance at this restaurant, which is often full in low season, the pretty terrace providing additional seating space in fine weather. The style is Art Deco, in a blend of wood and stone, and the motto can be conveyed in three words: passion, quality and wine. Patrick Feuga, the owner, can advise you how to get the best from his chef Philippe Barbier's excellent cooking, based entirely on fresh produce. The slate changes every day, and you can compose your menu from it, starting from 17 €. At lunchtime, the *menu affaire* (business menu) with starter and main course for 23 € lets you choose from the *carte*: duck confit nems with tarragon and seasoned juice, and as a main course, veal quasi with caramelised hazlenut juice, for example. If you have time, the *menu du vigneron* (winegrowers' menu) at 50 € is worth discovering. This menu is designed for wine lovers, who can taste an assortment of nectars served by the glass with each course; starter, main course, cheese and dessert. To finish the meal in style, cognac and armagnac lovers will be delighted with the *Soyons Fous* formula (Let's go crazy!) which enables them to taste 3 armagnacs or 3 cognacs for 16 €, accompanied by a precious cigar from Patrick's cellar if they wish.

L'EDEN 3, rue Aubergerie ✆ **05 53 06 31 08.** *Open Tuesday-Saturday. Lunchtime formulas 9 € and 12.50 €, set menus 19 € and 25 €, à la carte.* This restaurant is located in the Place Hoche, just opposite the Francois-Mitterand Cultural Centre. Inside, the setting is all stone and exposed beams. Talented chef Etienne Pagot has managed to attract a gourmet clientele in a very short time with his cuisine, a clever blend of seasonal produce and all kinds of spices. The menu changes regularly; typical dishes are the Oriental poultry confit croustade, and the braised pork in a coco-curry sauce. Leave room for dessert; it would be a pity to pass up on the fruit soup with mint and vanilla ice cream. The lunchtime formulas are excellent value for money. As for the wine, there is an excellent bergerac at 14 €. Service smiling and efficient.

L'EPICURIEN 1, rue du Conseil ✆ **05 53 09 88 04** *Open Tuesday to Sunday lunchtime. Set menus 14.50 €, 23 €, 29 € and 35 €.* Chef Jean-Luc Dalverny loves his job, and excels in the art of cooking fresh regional produce with the right blend of flavours and spices. His menu changes with the seasons, and as he also likes cooking fish and seafood, there's something for everyone. His speciality is hare à la royale; the experts all agree it is exceptional. The pan-fried duck foie gras escalope with caramelised peaches is divine, as is the pan-cooked fillet of bass with a delicious gratin dauphinois. We appreciated Jean-Luc's wife Marie-Christine's discreet and efficient service. The children's menu (9.50 €) is composed with the aim of introducing kids to culinary art and taste; it's worth calling in here just for that! In fact, the whole set-up is so attractive that you should book in advance, for even with an extra pretty dining room upstairs, the restaurant is often full.

LE FOU DU ROY 2, rue Montaigne ✆ **05 53 09 43 77** *Open Monday evening to Friday evening, and Saturday evening. Closed Saturday lunchtime, Monday lunchtime and Sunday. Main course 12 €. Main course + dessert 15 €; starter + main course 17 € ; starter, main course + dessert 19 €. Saveurs de Dordogne menu 22 €, set menus from 28 €-38 €.* This restaurant is located in one of the old town's typical alleyways, a stone's throw from the Montaigne car park. Owner Virginie Noíl and chef Olivier Magdeleine offer some of the best food in Périgueux, in a charming setting with a large and beautiful fireplace. We recommend the Saveurs de Dordogne menu if you have the whole evening before you, starting with the duck *harmonie* (fresh salad, duck foie gras shavings, duck confit and fresh walnuts) followed by a duck tournedos with Brive violet mustard or a crunchy duck *croustillant*, and closing with a truly delicious fresh fruit sabayon with Grand Marnier. The restaurant belongs to the 'Confrerie des Chevaliers de la Coquille Saint-Jacques de la baie de Saint-Brieuc,' so a Confrerie menu is on offer during the scallop fishing season (15 October-15 April), and includes a scallop trilogy with three different flavours (three dishes) and a fabulous dark chocolate *craquelin*, plus wine and coffee. Fans please note! The smaller dining room seating 15 is available for private functions or conference meals.

LE GRAIN DE SEL 7, rue des Farges ✆ **05 53 53 45 22** *Open Tuesday-Saturday. Set menus 12 € lunchtime, 19 €-32 € evenings.* In the heart of the old town, a stone's throw from the Tour-Mataguerre. Chloe Zuber runs the dining room with Fred Chabanaud in charge of the kitchen, and the inventive cooking is fresh market produce-based, with subtle harmonies of flavours and tastes and attention to the basics. Meat, poultry and fish are subtly prepared - try the fish *croustillant* with vegetables and Eastern scents, or duck breast petals in juice seasoned with Penga pepper. The simplest menu costs 12 €, so you can enjoy a meal that won't break the bank. In summer, the tables are set out in the pedestrian street during the evening.

ROCHER DE L'ARSAULT 15, rue de l'Arsault ✆ **05 53 53 54 06** *Open every day lunchtimes and evenings, even on Sunday. Set menus from 20 €. Children's menu 10 €. Disabled access.* Three generations of the Leymarie family run this beautiful restaurant, and Valérie and her daughter welcome you warmly. You can enjoy a drink in the opulent lounge before finding your table in the prettily decorated dining room. Grandma Marie in the kitchen prepares generous and tasty Périgord dishes based on fresh local ingredients: assortment of foie gras, braised veal sweetbreads *en cocotte* with cepe cream, and lobster tournedos Rossini. The menu is seasonal, but there are some things that don't change, like Marie's fabulous chocolate profiteroles, always a great success. Groups of 18 or more can book a room to themselves. Note that this is one of the few restaurants in Périgord that open on Sunday evening.

Sarlat-la-Canéda

LA COULEUVRINE** **1, place de la Bouquerie** ✆ **05 53 59 27 80** *Hotel open every day all year. Restaurant closed early January –early February. Closed Monday lunchtime. Lift. 23 rooms from 44 €-58 €. Breakfast 7 €. Set menus from 19 €. Bistrot open from Monday lunchtime to Saturday lunchtime. Wine bar in the evenings.* This hotel-restaurant is housed in a tower forming part of Sarlat's medieval ramparts, which date back to the 13thc (with 18thc.additions). The rooms are all different, and combine period furniture with modern comfort. Isabelle Lebon-Mallet has done up the dining room with excellent taste; a vast 13thc. fireplace has pride of place. The tables are spaced out for privacy, with comfortable armchairs – in short, the best possible conditions to enjoy chef Pascal Planet's cooking. Whole duck foie gras with quince jelly, scallops in *vieille prune* alcohol with a panfull of vegetables, duck breast in a fan with mango served with tagliatelli and courgettes – you'll be hard put to choose between them! Pleasant terrace in summer.

LE QUATRE SAISONS **2, cÙte de Toulouse** ✆ **05 53 29 48 59** *Open all year, every day except Wednesday and Thursday lunchtime out of season. Set menus from 18 €. A la carte. Menus at 18 € and 26 €: starter + meat course or meat course + dessert. Menus at 29 € and 33 €: starter, meat course and dessert.* The Delpech tandem of father and son, members of Eurotoques and Club Privilèges des Vins de Bordeaux run this well-kept restaurant. You eat in a pretty 14thc. setting where a spiral staircase has pride of place, leading to the dining room, an open terrace on the first floor and another (covered) at the top. Fresh market ingredients are the rule throughout the year, on all the menus, which are seasonal and original. The Périgord specialities, like foie gras cooked in a number of ways, are always excellent. A word of advice: book your table in advance during the summer, since this place is very popular with the locals.

LA MADELEINE*** **1, place de la Petite-Rigaudie** ✆ **05 53 59 10 41.** *Open mid-February to late December. Restaurant closed Monday and Tuesday lunchtime from mid-November to mid-March. Open every day in July and August. 39 rooms, from 73 € to 123 €. Breakfast 9 €. Set menus from 26 € and à la carte. Disabled access. Private garage.* This hotel, housed in a traditional hundred-year-old building, is well located on the way into the Traverse. The rooms are soundproofed and air-conditioned, and there is a lift to all three floors. The restaurant is warm and welcoming; Philippe Melot who owns the hotel is also the chef. His menu at 26 € is perhaps a little pretentious. It comprises a starter (smoked duck breast and goose gizzards in a salad) main course (salmon steak with balsamic vinegar) and a pastry. On the other hand, the menu at 32 € gives you a *tourin*, or garlic soup, a starter (goose neck stuffed with foie gras and served with a cepe *fricassée*) a main course (young rabbit in a *ballotin* with fresh pasta) cheeseboard and a dessert, and is better value for money.

LE REGENT **6, place de la Liberté** ✆ **05 53 59 03 91** *Open all year, except Sunday evening in low season. Disabled access. Lunchtime dish of the day 9.50 €, set menus 17 €-22 €. A la carte.* Located opposite the Town Hall in the magnificent Place de la Liberté. Member of the Toques du Périgord. Alexandre Arlie offers traditional Périgord dishes: in the brasserie, a duck cassoulet costs you 9.50 € and will satisfy even the biggest appetites. The Terroir menu (22 €) includes an aperitif (made with vin de noix), a starter and a main course. There is a dining room for groups, seating 40, but the terrace is everyone's favourite place to eat - even in winter, so long as the sun is shining.

Terrasson

HOSTELLERIE L'IMAGINAIRE **place du Foirail** ✆ **05 53 51 37 27** *Open Tuesday lunchtime-Sunday lunchtime, from September to late April. Closed Monday lunchtime, July-1 September. Closed Sunday evening and Monday in low season. Set menus from 20 € (lunchtime) and 39 € (evenings). Dégustation menu from 58 €. Hotel: double rooms from 76 € in low season and 105 € May-September, suite 115 €-149 €. Half-board 89 €-125 € (for the suite). Breakfast 10 €.* This attractively-restored building was a hospice in the 17thc. Today, it houses the Imaginaire hostelry, reputed for its cooking, with 6 top-quality rooms and a suite on offer. The rooms are named after Terrasson's old quarters, and there is a charming breakfast room. Delphine runs the dining room while her husband, talented chef Eric Samson, prepares some excellent dishes including farm eggs with truffles; goose foie gras, mushroom and truffle *millefeuille* with fine salt and a few drops of beetroot oil; and venison tournedos stuffed with foie gras Rossini-style. His fish gets the special treatment too: braised turbot in champagne with green asparagus and truffles. Last but far from least, baked pear with vanilla, Tonka bean and crispy salted caramel ice cream – make sure you leave some room! The place to celebrate special occasions.

ROSSIGNOL 15, rue Fénelon ✆ 05 53 31 02 30 *Open all year, closed Thursday. Disabled access. Set menus from 15 € to 48.50 €.* You don't often find a 15 € set menu as good as this in Sarlat. Perigord specialities are well prepared here, and the helpings generous, with warm and friendly service in a pleasant setting. The fresh duck foie gras terrine, truffle or cepe omelette, tournedos Rossini and stuffed quail, or fish like the pikeperch with *pieds de mouton* (woodhedgehog mushrooms) are among the chef's favourites. You can be sure to find the same quality here, all year round.

Trémolat

LE VIEUX LOGIS Le Bourg ✆ 05 53 22 80 06 *Fax 05 53 22 84 89. Website: www.vieux-logis.com. Set menus from 30 € to 75 €, à la carte 50 €. Open every day, all year.* Five years ago, Vincent Arnaud came from the Vosges (trained by Eric Jung in Strasbourg) via Provence (Chibois, Le Petit Nice, Passedat in Marseille) to run the kitchens in this splendid *Relais et Château*, under manager Bernard Giraudel who takes good care of the former agricultural property. At only 35, Vincent is a young chef with a technical bent, who understands his clientele perfectly, and is sure of his skills. He enjoys using luxury products in his menus: duck foie gras duo, one raw, marinated in salt, the other half-cooked with prunes and caramelised hazlenuts, Dublin Bay prawns served in kadaif, broad bean salad and garlic shoots, reduced juices with carrot, spring vegetables in a *cassolette*, stock flavoured with Piment d'Espelette and Oteiza ham shavings, slow-cooked sole with a fine hazlenut and Comte cheese crust, green asparagus and whipped butter, pigeon breast glazed with *vin de noix*, leg confit pan-cooked with sweet onions, and pear cooked and chilled served with a Grand Marnier cream and chocolate biscuit. The cellar could do with some redevelopment, to show an interest in the new generation.

Vergt

AUBERGE DES FONTILLES La Douze ✆ 05 53 06 71 43. *Open every day. 8 rooms with shower, washbasin and WC, 35 €-40 €. Set menus 17 €-28 €. A la carte.* The Auberge des Fontilles is located on the edge of 'Black' Périgord towards Sarlat, about 20 minutes from Périgueux. It's worth going out of your way for the marvellous foie gras (perhaps the Dordogne's best) prepared in all kinds of ways - dried duck liver, whole duck liver with truffles, whole goose liver with truffles, and so on. The homemade *apéritifs* are another speciality, concocted with bush peaches, raspberries, plums and walnuts. The food is delicious in general, whatever your choice of menu, but we especially enjoyed the rare duck breast, served by Jean-Louis. His wife Françoise runs the kitchens, and her genuine *soupe paysanne* is an excellent start to the meal, followed by what you like – though don't forget the foie gras! You can even buy a few tasty souvenirs from the shop on the way out of the restaurant.

HOTEL DU PARC 12, place Marty ✆ 05 53 54 90 50. *Open all year. 11 rooms from 40 €. Breakfast 5 €. Menu of the day 11 € ; set menus 18.50 €-32 €.* Brigitte and Patrick fell in love with Périgord on a visit from their native Anjou, and are now running this hotel-restaurant ideally located in the town centre. The day's menu is certainly not disappointing, with soup, a hors d'oeuvres trolley, dish of the day and dessert for 11 €. The chef's recipes include Périgord specialities like the foie gras terrine, foie gras *millefeuilles* with apples, and duck confit, but also a sweetbread and kidney timbale with morels. Patrick's other speciality is seafood platters (for 6 or more people) but you need to order these 48 hours before. Spacious and pleasant setting, suitable for banquets and receptions, with a superb terrace in a leafy, shady garden at the back.

GIRONDE

Arcachon

LA CABANE DU TCHANQUET 8, rue du Professeur-Jolyet ✆ 05 56 83 97 70. *Open all year. Set menu 17 €, children's menu 7.50 €. Dish of the day weekday lunchtimes 8.50 €.* This little restaurant facing the aquarium and a stone's throw from the casino offers a sincere welcome (from Marinette and Belette) and well-filled plates. You can choose oysters and mussels (including the Tchanquet mussels with cream and salmon) à la carte, also escalope in a cream sauce, grilled rib steak or beef rib, bass fillets with white butter, monkfish saute *à l'américaine* and fisherman's stewpot, 24 €. The beach is handy for a short nap afterwards.

L'ENCOCHE 37, cours Lamarque de Plaisance ✆ 05 56 83 16 10. *Open every day 1 May -30 September. Closed Monday from 1 October-30 April. Weekday lunchtime formula 24 €. One course 20 €. One course + starter or dessert 31 €. Starter, main course and dessert 39 €. Children's menu 15 €. Terrace. Disabled access.* This restaurant had hardly opened (July 2005) before its praises were being sung in the Petit Fute's receptive ears. We were down there in a flash, and were amazed. M and Madame de Saint-Germain have created a Paradise for the tastebuds, far removed from the usual

Arcachon stereotypes. Their son Olivier is the chef, a virtuoso in the culinary arts whose home-made foie gras and quince chutney, Bavaria sirloin steak à la planche and cepe macaroni, roast turbot and creamy risotto with foie gras melt in the mouth. Your welcome is warm, the service irreproachable - in short, you'll want to come back again as soon as you can!

Bordeaux

ALTON HOTEL* 107, rue de la Pelouse de Douet Bordeaux ✆ 05 56 99 55 55** *Website: www.hotel-alton.tm.fr Email : hotel.alton@wanadoo.fr Rooms from 70 € (standard) to 160 € (suite with terrace). 4 rooms for the disabled. Buffet 11 € (+2 € served in your room). Pets 5 €. Closed underground car park 6 €. Seminar rooms.* Close to the Pellegrin hospital. This is both a hotel-restaurant and a hotel-residence, and has 170 rooms and suites with bathrooms and private WC, outside phone line, satellite TV and hairdryer. Some have a kitchenette and small balcony. The best rooms overlook the interior garden, but those on the street side are double-glazed. The residents' bar is open till 2am. The Olicia restaurant has a dining room and a terrace, and serves traditional cuisine with a lunchtime formula at 14.90 € (3 courses or a la carte). The tram station is on Line A, which takes you to the Town Hall in 8 minutes.

LE BURDIGALA ** 115, rue Georges-Bonnac ✆ 05 56 90 16 16.** *Website: www.burdigala.com 68 rooms and 15 suites from 180 € to 480 €. Breakfast 18 €. Soundproofing and air-conditioning, satellite TV and Canal +. Broadband Internet socket. Lifts. Disabled access. Private underground garage 12 €. Bar and restaurant open 7 days a week. Room service 7am-midnight.* Comfort and luxury only minutes from the town centre's pedestrian streets. The bar is pleasant, and the gastronomic restaurant Jardin de Burdigala serves a traditional regional cuisine; among chef Jean-Francois Basquin's specialities are hot liver escalope, saddle of lamb and a scallop and Dublin Bay prawn fantaisie, not forgetting the delicious home-made pastries. The rooms contain an individual safe, broadband Internet access and a mini bar, and are fitted out in sophisticated wood, marble and leather.

LE CAFE DES 4 SŒURS 6 bis, cours du 30-Juillet ✆ 05 56 81 52 26. *Open every day, 7am-midnight. Lunchtime brasserie. Terrace.* This cafe was opened in 1841, and features among Europe's historic and heritage cafes, like the Procope in Paris (opened in 1686). The decor is rococo, complete with panelling, Napoleon III chandeliers, mirrors and angels, yet so much history does not seem to weigh heavy in the atmosphere thanks to Patrick Urtizverea, who took over the place in 1988, and has cultivated a convivial regional ambiance. Contemporary and local paintings blend happily in with the gilding, and customers come to lunch on a Basque speciality, or drink hot chocolate in the afternoon, without feeling they're in a museum. The boss's father was himself a chef specialised in Basque cuisine (as his name implies) in 1970s Bordeaux, and so you find calamars in their ink, Basque-style monkfish and cod, roast goose breast, confit and duck breast with honey and cepes. This is home cooking in the noble sense of the term, and M. Urtizverea's kindness is simply natural.

HOTEL ACANTHE 12-14, rue Saint-Rémi ✆ 05 56 81 66 58. *Website : www.acanthe-hotel-bordeaux.com email : info@acanthe-hotel-bordeaux.com . 20 single and double rooms 42 €-62 €. Breakfast 6 €. Lift. Disabled access. Bourse car park nearby.* Located in the old part of Bordeaux, a stone's throw from the Place de la Bourse, tram station, pedestrian streets and Garonne quays, within easy reach of restaurants and cultural monuments. There are two categories of room; standard and comfort, equipped with double glazing and Wi-Fi Internet access. The staff are energetic and the setting peaceful. This is a popular hotel, so advance bookings are recommended.

CAJOU CAFFE Place Camille Julian ✆ 05 56 52 50 50 *Open every day from 7am-2am, brasserie 11am-1am. Set menus 14.50 € to 24.50 €. Children's menu 10 €. Dish of the day 9.50 €. Terrace. WiFi point. TV.* One of this edition's 'finds', an absolute jewel of a brasserie with its high mirrors, red lampshades, parquet, banquettes, glasses lined up at the bar, newspaper on the counter and suggestions on the slate. Pleasant service, perfect dishes, clever ideas, top-quality produce and a subtle blend of the classic and the innovative are the key ingredients in a recipe for success. Home-made french fries and pumpkin, duck confit with Morello cherries, pan-cooked scallops with courgette julienne, Provencal-style gambas, golden duck breast with french-fries, ratte potatoes with saffron, and to finish up, profiteroles made with canneles (small spongy cakes that are a Bordeaux speciality). You stop in for a simple salade nicoise - and come out several hours later, full up and delighted with everything, from the salad dressing to the choice of coffee. The cordless Internet terminal has filled the terrace with students and other Internauts, all wifi-ing away; Saturday night revellers eat a generous Sunday brunch (13.50 €); kids watch cartoons while their parents enjoy a welcome digestive. Open hours, availability and a taste for doing things properly without going over the top make this a place worth patronising - even at 10am for an undercut steak with shallots!

LE CHAPON FIN 5 rue Montesquieu ✆ 05 56 79 10 10 *Fax 05 56 79 09 10. Website: www.chapon.fin.com. Set menus from 29 € to 77 €, à la carte 60 €. Closed Sunday, Monday, 23 July-20 August and a week during the February school holidays.* The Chapon Fin was among the first group of restaurants to qualify for Michelin's 3 'macaroons' in 1933!. Since then, it has been through some tricky periods. Francis Garcia, who had put the place back on its feet in 1987 was wanting a change by the year 2000, and suggested Thierry Marx should replace him. Helped out first by Franck Ferrigutti, Thierry then handed over to young Nicolas Frion, who has been in charge of the kitchens since April 2003. His impressive career (commis at Bocuse, for a year, chef de partie for 3 years with Boyer in Reims then Thierry Marx's second in the Cordeillan-Bage Chateau for 5 years) has stood him in good stead, for at barely thirty, he has made a success of his Chapon. Pressed red tuna, crunchy tubes with avocado and truffle pieces, crusty Dublin Bay prawns, thai peppers and basil, pink pepper stock, lamb stuffed with onions and tomato conserve, 'buttered' broad beans with chorizo and a crusty almond dessert with coconut cream and sorbet feature on his menu. The cellar run by Nicolas Geoffroy is compact, yet representative even of those exotic far-flung regions like Alsace or the Loire.

EL BODEGON 14, Place de la Victoire ✆ 05 56 94 74 02 / 39 *Open 7 days a week: 7am-2am. Happy hours from 6pm-8pm. Set menus from 6,5 € to 10,5 €. Dish of the day 7 €. Ambience bar and terrace. Small brasserie 5 days a week.* El Bodégon was one of the first bars to choose a Latin theme, and is now a pillar of the Place de la Victoire, popular with students and party-goers. The decoration is Spanish, with Miro's paintings on the walls, and the atmosphere resolutely festive. A variety of musical influences and menu formulas (including tapas) make it an ideal place to get into the mood and start the evening.

HOTEL DES QUATRE SŒURS * 6, cours du XXX-Juillet ✆ 05 57 81 19 20.** *Fax : 05 56 01 04 28. Website: www.4soeurs.free.fr 34 soundproofed rooms, single 65 €, double 75 €. Reception 24 hours a day. Breakfast buffet 8 €. Supplement for pets 7 €. Air-conditioning, cable TV.* This hotel, recently renovated from top to bottom, wears its third star with pride. The building dates back to the 19thc. and has historic connections, Richard Wagner having stayed there in 1850. Two superb salons with 18thc. panelling and a view of the Tourny avenues, and the wall frescos in the breakfast room recall this period. The old centre of Bordeaux and the Grand Théatre are only a walk away, and the hotel offers plenty of services: laundry pressing, lift, Internet access, car hire, and even its own special chateau-des-quatre-soeurs vintage.

LE PAVILLON DES BOULEVARDS 120 rue Croix-de-Seguey ✆ 05 56 81 51 02 *Fax 05 56 51 14 58. Set menus from 65 € to 100 €, à la carte 85 €. Closed Saturday lunchtime, Sunday, Monday lunchtime, 2-8 January and 7-27 August.* Denis Franc celebrated his 20th year as manager of this discreet restaurant in 2005. He represents that community of great but little-known chefs ignored by the media (like Jean Marie Gautier, the Villa Eugénie's chef) who seem to hide behind what really counts for them: their restaurant's success. His cooking, he says soberly, «tends to be inventive», and he certainly would not claim to be a local leader. His dishes speak for themselves, in fact: pan-cooked scallops, *frassinette* bananas in breadcrumbs with coconut and combava emulsion, sole browned in salted butter, cockle meunière with coriander, sea urchins and Chinese artichokes, sweetbreads braised in their juice, souffléd apricot and apple puree, crème brulée with chestnuts, Spanish melon marmalade and whisky milkshake. The service is efficient and discreet, with a regional cellar, recommendations made by Alexandre Céret.

PUB SAINT-AUBIN ✆ Place de la Victoire 40 *Open 7days a week : 7am - 2am. Set menus from 10 € to 20 €. Dish of the day 9,50 €.* This is a new pub in Place de la Victoire, serving British and American food like fish and chips and hamburgers, though brasserie and fresh market produce menus are also available. You find the typical pub atmosphere, in a wood and chocolate-coloured setting that aims to be traditional and trendy at the same time. The staff come from all parts and are dressed in kilts.

LA TUPINA 6-8, rue Porte-de-la-Monnaie ✆ 05 56 91 56 37. *Open every day. Service from 12 noon to 2pm and 7pm to 11pm. Weekday set menus 16 € and 32 €, menu and a la carte 50 €. Parking valet available.* Jean-Pierre Xiradakis' restaurant is entirely devoted to South West gastronomy, and has a solid reputation for it. The salted and conserved meats, vegetables and old-fashioned charcuterie spread on the wide country table in the entrance wake up your taste buds in anticipation. Vegetables in jelly, in a terrine? Or a salad of French beans and foie gras shavings? Or perhaps roast chicken with croutons and the stuffing juices, served with thick french fries cooked the old-fashioned way? There is also leg of lamb, saddle of black Pyrenean pork, or lampreys Bordeaux-style. And to finish off the feast, the desserts our grandmothers made, either singly, or sampled together in an impressive *dégustation* dish. The wine list is a notebook written in ink pen, with some judicious recommendations and careful descriptions. As for the cigars, they sum up the house philosophy: enjoy life's pleasures - and share them.

Cap-Ferret

PINASSE CAFE 2 bis, avenue de l'Océan ✆ 05 56 03 77 87. *Open every day from April to September, and from Friday lunchtime to Sunday lunchtime in March. October and November. Closed from December to late February. Late service in summer until 11pm.* The Pinasse, housed in a charming old villa, welcomes its passengers on board from the Belisaire jetty. Inside, the setting is up-to-date, with natural wood panelling, parquet and scale models of boats all around. In fine weather, the terrace by the water is very popular . The fish dishes and specialities are inventive and sophisticated. Advance booking recommended.

Lacanau-Océan

L'OYAT ** – Front de mer Impasse Emile Lacaze ✆ 05 56 03 11 11. *Website: www.hotel-oyat.com Annual closing from early November to late March. Open every day. Reception from 8am to 11pm. 30 double rooms from 68 € to 112 €, according to season. Breakfast 9 €. Set menus 19 € and 23 €. Salad bar Raconte moi des salades at your disposal.* This hotel on the seafront facing the beach has a fine view of the breakers, surfers and fishermen, yet is only 200m from the town centre. The 30 modern rooms are equipped with bathroom, WC and satellite TV. In the restaurant, seafood has pride of place on the traditional menu with fresh fish every day. You can enjoy them either in the dining room or on the terrace.

Langon

RESTAURANT CLAUDE DARROZE 95 cours du Gén-Leclerc ✆ 05 56 63 00 48 *Fax 05 56 63 41 15.Set menus from 42 € to 76 €, à la carte 80 €. Closed 5-20 January, and 17 October-9 November.* This former coaching inn has known two of post-war French gastronomy's top chefs: Raymond Oliver who was born and later worked here, and Claude Darroze who has been running the place for 3 decades now. His recipes contain the best of regional gastronomy, with personal touches of generosity and good humour. Marbled leeks and foie gras, small salad vinaigrette with chanterelles, creamy scrambled eggs with Bordeaux cepes, sole cooked on the bone and stuffed with cepes and pan-fried foie gras, woodpigeon roasted in a *capucin* (sort of funnel used to *flamber*) and its crouton with stuffing and cepes Bordeaux-style, and pear and apple crumble with a soft white cheese sorbet. The wine cellar is unoriginal but safe, and the service up to standard.

Pauillac

CHÂTEAU CORDEILLAN-BAGES Route des Chateaux ✆ 05 56 59 24 24 *Fax 05 56 59 01 89. Website: www.cordeillanbages.com. Set menus from 65 € to 105 €, à la carte 100 €. Closed Monday, Tuesday lunchtime, Saturday lunchtime and from 10 December to 13 February.* Thierry Marx, ex-Taillevent, Robuchon and Chapel, is one of France's top chefs, yet is sometimes shunned by the region's gourmets who seem to blame him for not conforming to local gastronomic standards.After 10 years in the job, mostly spent receiving honours and collecting awards, local prejudice seems finally to be fading. His 'virtual' sausage, lentil and bacon *craquant*, warm and cold chicken stock, whipped cream with liquorice, transclucid egg with parmesan and stock, bass cooked *à l'unilaterale* (on one side only, usually the side with the skin), rhubarb, onion and grilled sesame seeds, spaghetti with sweetbreads, cepes and truffles, and Aquitaine beef fillet smoked over vine shoots, potatoes conserved in the juice are some of France's finest creations. The cellar is huge and fantastic, and very methodical: the Bordeaux reds are grouped by vintage or by appellation.

Sauternes

LE SAPRIEN Rue Principale ✆ 05 56 76 60 87 *Annual closing during the Christmas holidays and in February. Closed Sunday evenings, all day Monday and Wednesday evening. Service from 12 noon to 1.30pm and 7.30pm to 9pm. Set menus 25 € and 37 €.* Opposite the tourist office, the Saprien takes good care of its customers, seating them in a large stone and panelled dining-room with its Gironde tiles in two colours, comfortable chairs and pretty tables, or on the terrace in good weather, with its view across the Giraud vines. The cuisine is both traditional and inventive, and draws enthusiastic reports from passing gourmets. The chef is an expert with spices; his fresh foie gras escalope pan-fried with apples, Dublin Bay prawns with sweet spices, roast sweetbreads with sauternes and curry, lamprey in sauternes and a dessert such as the 'runny' chocolate cake cannot fail to please even difficult palates. Fine wine list, attentive and efficient service.

LANDES

Aire-sur-l'Adour

CHEZ L'AHUMAT 2, rue Pierre-Mendès-France ✆ 05 58 71 82 61. *Restaurant closed Wednesday and a fortnight in late March and early September. Set menus from 10.50 € to 26 €. Double rooms from 29 € to 43 €. Dish of the day 7 €.* The Labrouches have been attracting gourmets for years. Their steamed Landes confit with pot-au-feu vegetables, sweetbreads in Madeira sauce, woodpigeon salmi and foie gras have become standards on the menu. The wines are mainly local, but include madiran, tursan and saint-mont. Pleasant setting with openwork partitions and plants in hanging baskets.

Amou

LE COMMERCE Place de la Poste ✆ 05 58 89 02 28. *Closed Sunday evening and Monday in low season, a forttnight in November and during February school holidays. Set menus from 14 € to 40 €. Childrens' menu 9 €. Double rooms from 40 € to 55 €. Breakfast 7 €.* The Darracq family is known beyond Amou's borders, for their generous and satisfying cooking. There is foie gras and duck breast, of course, but otherwise the choice is varied, with a selection of fried sea fish, chipirons (calamars or cuttlefish) and seafood kebabs but also game. A wide selection of wines accompanies all these flavours.

Dax

L'AMPHITRYON 38, cours Gallieni ✆ 05 58 74 58 05 *Closed Saturday lunchtime, Sunday evening and Monday. Set menus from 21 € to 38 €.* Eric Pujos runs the family business with energy, and has some to spare, since he also founded, and is chancellor of, the confrérie du foie gras des Landes. The menu changes 5 times a year, so you can safely come back to this pretty dining room with its seaside decorations and find different delicacies on your plate.

Grenade-sur-l'Adour

PAIN ADOUR ET FANTAISIE 14-16 pl des Tilleuls ✆ 05 58 45 18 80 *Fax 05 58 45 16 57. Set menus from 35 € to 85 €, à la carte 70 €. Closed Sunday evening, Monday and Wednesday lunchtime.* Philippe Garret, trained by Jean-Pierre Jacob at the Bateau Ivre, and ex- Million at Labertville, Savoy and Guérard, deserves praise. It isn't easy to keep the attention in such a place, with its marvellous17th. and 18thc. stone buildings and comfortable, shady terrace overlooking the Adour: the food could easily be eclipsed by its setting. Philippe has been running the show since 1994, however, backed up by wife Sophie, and he knows the score. His cold pea soup, parmesan *spuma*, and herb biscuit, Ile de Ré grenaille potatoes and Maine half-lobster en cocotte, falavoured with burnt thyme, crunchy artichokes, pan-fried duck foie gras *piccatas* (small thin escalopes) with seasonal fruits, grilled cider apple polenta, cup of chocolate with bergamot, thyme and lemon ice cream and mango tartlet ensure that the customers will appreciate the *cuisine* just as much as the architecture.

LOT-ET-GARONNE

Agen

LE MARGOTON 52, rue Richard-Cœur-de-Lion © 05 53 48 11 55 *Annual closing 22 December-7 January and 18 August-3 September. Closed Saturday lunchtime, Sunday evening and Monday in winter, and Saturday and Sunday lunchtimes and Monday in summer. Set menus from 16€ to 32€. Air-conditioning.* This gastronomic restaurant in the old town has 6 tables, and some delicious specialities, like the oysters marinière with saffron in cappucino, scallops in *sauce miroir* and sweetbreads. For dessert, you'll love the soufflet with prune kernels or chocolate *coulant.* Pretty tablecloths, old chairs, half-timbering and flowers make for a cheerful, countrified setting. Since this is a well-known address, you would be wise to book in advance.

MARIOTTAT 25 rue Louis-Vivent © 05 53 77 99 77 *Fax 05 53 77 99 79. Website: www.restaurant-mariottat.com. Set menus from 23€ to 60€, à la carte 65€. Closed Saturday lunchtime, Sunday evening, Monday and Tuesday lunchtime, a fortnight in February, and a week at Easter and at Christmas.* Christiane and Eric Mariottat took over this former Capuchin convent in 1987, and it has since become Agen's best restaurant. The marvellous setting and charming welcome from the lady of the house, together with the comfort and space available in the dining room are unequalled in town. Eric Mariottat's cuisine is stylised without excess, accurate and modern, yet with deep roots in the regional soil. Duck foie gras terrine au naturel, exotic fruit chutney, bass steak roasted on its skin, green asparagus, peanut-flavoured creamy mousse, suckling lamb cooked three ways; gigot with anchovies, braised shoulder and chops with tamarind, then waffle 'like a memory' served with orange puree, milk sorbet and caramel juice. Christiane Mariottat looks after a cellar containing over 700 recommended bottles all perfectly sorted, right down to the burgundies and Loire wines.

Astaffort

UNE AUBERGE EN GASCOGNE 9 Faubourg Corne © 05 53 67 10 27 *Fax 05 53 67 10 22. Website : www.uneaubergeengascogne.com. Set menus from 24€ to 70€, à la carte 60€. Closed Sunday evening and Wednesday and Thursday (lunchtimes only in summer), and Friday lunchtime from January to March. Annual holiday first fortnight in January, last 10 days in March and first 3 weeks in November.* Solid and jovial, Fabrice Biasolo is nearing his tenth year of running this ancient inn, housed in its 18thc. building for over a century and quite an institution in the region. Fabrice is not yet 35, but having trained with Daguin, for the basics, and Bras, where he developed his creativity, this young chef won't let himself be shut up in the traditional Gascon foie gras, pigeon and duck trilogy (though there is some on the menu). He is an inkeeper in the modern sense, generous and cheerful with a taste for revelry, and his cooking is simple and contemporary, from the beef tartare to the saddle of lamb. Impeccable service, specialised wine cellar (even outside the region) - let's hope this is the prototype for tomorrow's restaurant.

Casteljaloux

LA VIEILLE AUBERGE ** 11, rue Posterne © 05 53 93 01 36. *Closed 27 February-8 March, 26 June-9 July and 20 November-6 December 2006. Closed Sunday evening, Tuesday evening and Wednesday (Sunday evening and Wednesday lunchtime in summer). Set menus from 18.50€ to 36€. 4 rooms from 30.50€ to 36.60€. Breakfast 5.50€.* This inn dates back to 1852, and is located in one of the town's oldest streets. The four rooms are simple yet comfortable, and above all very quiet. The chef's tastes are regional, and he serves a personalised gastronomic cuisine with foie gras escalope pan-fried with apples, Landes salad, beef fillet with morels and Perigord duck breast. The craqueline with caramel mousse is delicious, as are all the desserts. Fine wine list.

Duras

HOSTELLERIE DES DUCS ** Boulevard Jean-Brisseau © 05 53 83 74 58 *Open all year. 17 rooms, including one with disabled access, from 61€to 90€. Breakfast 8.50€. Set menus 15€ to 58€. A la carte. Swimming pool, billiard room. Restaurant closed Saturday lunchtime, Sunday evening and Monday from October-June, Saturday lunchtime and Monday lunchtime July-September.* This former 19thc. convent has been renovated stone by stone, and is now a comfortable traditional hotel. The contemporary rooms are soundproofed and fully equipped. The air-conditioned restaurant with its covered terrace serves traditional cooking updated for modern tastes, using regional and seasonal produce, accompanied by cotes-de-duras wines.

Nérac

AUX DELICES DU ROY 7, rue du Ch,teau © 05 53 65 81 12. *Closed Wednesday and Sunday evening. Set menus from 23 € to 65 €.* The chef draws the crowds thanks to his classic and creative cuisine, with a preference for seafood. He places great importance on cooking times and his raw materials, seeking to transmit all their flavour in the finished dish. Everything is home made and it's difficult to choose from such a well-filled slate. Warm and cheerful decoration, organised service. There are 77 recommended wines in the cellar, mainly from the South West.

Pujols

LA TOQUE BLANCHE © 05 53 49 00 30 *Fax 05 53 70 49 79. Website: www.la-toque-blanche.com.* Bernard Lebrun had his restaurant built in 1980, and its contemporary architecture is surprising in a region where many restaurants are housed in former coaching inns, each more genuine than the last. It has a panoramic view over the old village and the Mail Valley, and a covered, air-conditioned garden, both greatly appreciated by the customers. They come for the chef's solid reputation, and his classic repertory with some modern touches: foie gras escalope pan-fried with apples, warm lobster salad with herb vinaigrette, truffle julienne with foie gras shavings, roast Dublin Bay prawn tails, vegetables and shellfish juices, farm-bred chicken wing with truffles cooked slowly on the bone, chicken juices and seasonal vegetables, then pear feuilleté with bitter almond cream. The top bordeaux vintages and south-west wines are well represented with over 20, 000 bottles looked after by Christophe Basin, who also runs the dining room.

Puymirol

L'AUBERGADE 52 rue Royale © 05 53 95 31 46 *Fax 05 53 95 33 80. Website: www.aubergade.com. Set menus from 78 € to 145 €, à la carte 90 €. Closed in low season, Sunday evening, Monday and Tuesday lunchtime, and in high season, Monday and Tuesday lunchtimes.* Michel and Maryse Trama had some difficulty getting started when they took on this restaurant. Though only half an hour from Agen by car, the village is tiny, with no particular claim to fame, and Michel Trama had to rely on his talent alone to bring in the customers. All the serious guides now recognise his worth, but Michel continues to search and invent, never completely satisfied with his culinary achievements. He is an innovative technician, and his cooking can be devilishly accurate: lobster in a sweet spice vinaigrette, cereal with mango, Dublin Bay prawns *sautéd* with coconut, ginger and orange oil, celery millefeuille with warm foie gras pan-fried with balsamic vinegar, then the chocolate 'tear' with Morello cherries and vanilla sauce, that mythic dessert of Michel Trama's own invention (like Michel Bras' *moelleux*) now copied (often badly) by all and sundry. This is a wonderful restaurant, where even the bread (about a dozen varieties) is well above the usual standard.

PYRÉNÉES-ATLANTIQUES

Ainhoa

HOTEL ITHURRIA * Place du Fronton © 05 59 29 92 11.** *Website: www.ithurria.com. Châteaux et Hotels de France. Sauna, fitness centre. Gastronomic restaurant. Hotel closed 1 January-6 April and 2 November-31 December. Rooms from 105 € to 136 €. Breakfast 10 €. Apartments from 220 € to 260 €. One suite 150 €-220 €. Half-board supplement 35 €-45 €. Open every day in high season, closed Wednesday and Thursday lunchtime from 15 September-15 July. Set menus 32 € and 48 €. À la carte 48 € to 71 €. Dogs admitted. Pool.* This charming hotel in its traditional local building is hidden in the heart of the village. Inside, there are double and triple rooms, a romantic suite and two superb apartments under the eaves, each with two bedrooms, two bathrooms and a dressing room. The rooms include period furniture, brand-new bathrooms, air-conditioning, double glazing and even electric blinds and loggias overlooking the countryside. A beautiful old-fashioned garden and swimming pool await you outside. Let's not forget the restaurant either, run by the Isabal brothers, Stephan in the dining room and Xavier in the kitchen with his father where they concoct such gastronomic classics as the Ainhoa *piperade* (peppers, onions, tomatoes and eggs) with pan-cooked *pata negra* ham, Landes foie gras, Basque cassoulet with red kidney beans, woodpigeon in autumn, etc.

Anglet

CHÂTEAU DE BRINDOS 1 allée du Ch,teau © 05 59 23 89 80 *Fax 05 59 23 89 81. Website: www.chateaudebrindos.com* This chateau belongs to Serge Blanco, the Biarritz player who was the world's greatest rugby back in the 1980s. It is a magnificent late 19thc.building, overlooking a vast lake with ducks swimming among the lily pads. Romantic, even arrogant perhaps, but home of one of the most specialised Basque *cuisines*. Chef Antoine Antunes has calmed down since coming here from the Hendaye thalassotherapy centre (also owned by Blanco) in 2002, probably helped by his stable team and a new and excellent wine waiter. Among his recent creations are the marinated bass flavoured with ginger, crunchy vegetable filaments, a bread slice spread with aubergine caviar, chipirons cooked *à la plancha* with Espelette pepper, fondant cannelloni with piperade and a ewe's cheese gratin, and Pyrenees suckling lamb fillet pan-fried with the *beatilles* (small morsels of the carcass) in a kebab with rosemary, broad beans, peas and sucrine pumpkin farmhouse-style. The cellar is being developed by Sylvain Desheulles, and the service is perfectly managed by Jean-Jacques Mehats, a fixture from the early days.

Bayonne

AUBERGE DU CHEVAL BLANC* 68, rue Bourgneuf ✆ 05 59 59 01 33 *Set menu du pays 23 €, menu-carte: entre amis 35 € and surprise 75 €. À la carte from 42 € to 75 €.* Chef Jean-Claude Tellechea is described as 'Basque, sporty and a great cook' in the visitors' book, also as 'a real artist in his speciality'. The secret of success is to challenge your own ideas, approach people, and communicate with other chefs, he says. His cuisine is pure Basque updated, with a particular love of truffles and lobster, and an occasional foray into other regions. He believes in associating a 'simple' product with a 'noble' one: scallops with an Ibaiona *tuile*, foamy chestnut and cepe cream with little croutons, lobster soup with artichokes and cockles, bass *à l'unilatéral* and a fennel *fondant*, Xamango parmentier with truffled veal juices, and so on. He does his regular tour of the dining room, and another of the lounge with a Patxarran (Basque *digestif*). Jean-Claude Tellechea is all that, and more besides.

LE GRAND HOTEL * Best Western 21, rue Thiers ✆ 05 59 59 62 00.**
Website: www.bw-legrandhotel.com Rooms from 62 € and 'Comfort' rooms 118 €. Prestige rooms according to category and season. Breakfast buffet 1,50 € Closed garage 12.50 €. Quality restaurant. Business menu. This hotel is housed in a fine residence, with a warm and opulent setting inside, blending earlier style with our modern innovations. Period furniture, a spectacular lift, fine moulding and a vaulted arch in the breakfast room exist alongside electronic locks, fire doors, the Wi-Fi system and modem sockets in all rooms. The brightly coloured carpets and soft furnishings are charming: room 202 in particular is superb, all done out in gold, with very fine hangings and a seductive lounge corner.

Biarritz

LE GALION 17, boulevard Général-De-Gaulle ✆ 05 59 24 20 32. *Closed Monday and Tuesday lunchtime. Set menu-carte 28 €. À la carte from 36 € to 50 €. Overnight break menu with the Hotel Windsor.* Ship's captain Patrick Damman is just what the Galion needed. His charisma, cheerfulness and professionalism have given new life to this marvellous liner moored up on Biarritz beach. Beside him, Jean-Pierre «helps you avoid getting a mouthful by advising you on the best bottles», while first mate Christine handles the service with a smile. The setting is exceptional, Art Deco in spirit with panelled and moulded walls, spectacular frescos on the ceiling and comfortable Louis XIII chairs, and the chef's classic cooking pleases the most demanding gourmet. Scallop tartlet with caviar cream, red mullet fillet in *tapenade*, foie gras with grapes, pineapple carpaccio, and some fine specialities, like the excellent *choucroute de mer.* Perfect!

HOTEL DU PALAIS ** 1, avenue de l'Impératrice ✆ 05 59 41 64 00.** *Website: www.hotel-du-palais.com. Leading Hotels of the World. Prices according to aspect, category and season from 260 € to 1,370 € for the Imperial Suite. Breakfast from 26 € to 35 €. 3 restaurants, L'Hippocampe, La Rotonde and La Villa Eugénie. Hairdressing salon and beauty parlour, sauna, fitness, massage and relaxation 05 59 41 64 18. Heated and filtered seawater pool. Private putting green. Spa. Room service.* The Hotel du Palais is in shameless good health. Apart from the most recent award, 23rd place in the Best Hotel in Europe ratings organised in New York by the Condenast, it has entered a phase of spectacular diversification that should influence its future. It has always had these exceptional rooms and suites, continually refurbished by the house team of brilliant decorators in a whirl of ancient patina, exclusive fabrics and period furniture. This year, the Charles Chaplin and Frank Sinatra apartments were redecorated; the result is pure luxury. Yet no-one had ever imagined a whole new floor, based upon the innovative theme 'An Imperial Cruise'. A few portholes along the facade on the top floor were enough to put this genial idea into the Manager's head; his team had it carried out with a minimum of thinking time. The result is breathtaking. In the main corridor, gangways carved from precious woods lead to luxury cabins, rooms or suites. It's all so realistic, you really feel you're boarding an ocean liner on a luxury cruise, about to confront the raging seas. This year, the grand new spa is to be developed. You can't help but admire this Hotel's creativity and enterprise spirit - even if you can't afford its prices!

LA VILLA EUGENIE 1 avenue de l'Impératrice ✆ 05 59 41 64 00 *Fax 05 59 41 67 99. Website: www.hotel-du-palais.com. Set menus from 55 € to 95 €, à la carte 100 €. Closed lunchtimes in July and August, and 1 February-17 March.* This restaurant, named after Napoleon III's wife Eugénie de Montijo, is housed in an immense and luxurious room in a real palace, with a turbulent history. Built between 1854 and 1856, transformed into a hotel in 1894, it was burnt down in 1903 then rebuilt and extended straight away. The world's most famous citizens have stayed here, from Queen Isabelle to Chancellor Bismarck, including Frank Sinatra and the Duke of Windsor. Chef Jean-Marie Gautier is a celebrity in his own right too, having run the sumptuous kitchens for 15 years, and his cuisine is faultlessly classic as befits the setting, though rather lacking the flamboyant note. Pan-fried Dublin Bay prawns, green vegetables and citrus fruits in a marinade, vinaigrette thickened with mango pulp, red mullet fillets, *chipirons* and creamy rice, ink sauce with Espelette pepper, Challans duck confit then roasted on the spit with spices, turnip, apples and sweet potato purée, and 'royal' caramel chocolate with candied apricots, ice cream and *confiture de lait.* The cellar is strong on bordeaux, but less specialised for other wines, simply collecting the vineyard's greatest names.

Bidart

LA TABLE DES FRERES IBARBOURE Chemin de Ttalienia ✆ 05 59 54 81 64 *Fax 05 59 54 75 65. Website: www.freresibarboure.com. Set menus from 33 € to 95 €, à la carte 60 €. Closed Wednesday all year, Sunday evening (except in August), Monday lunchtime in July, 15 November-5 December and 5-20 January.* Philippe and Martin Ibarboure set about transforming a charming 18thc. house into one of the region's most sought-after restaurants fifteen years ago. They seem to have won their bet: little by little, occasionally camouflaged in traditional South-West garb, they have managed to get their own creative, imaginative and modern cuisine accepted - perhaps because it never strays too far from local tradition. The only improvements made this year concern the outside access to the restaurant, and staff circulation in the dining room. The food remains as delicious and generous as ever: the thick white Landes asparagus served warm with 'Txangurro' crabs, roast bass with fine Salies de Béarn salt and polenta domino, Aquitaine beef tournedos, slice of pan-cooked foie gras, and crusty pineapple tart, pina colada cocktail and pineapple and basil sorbet, would make the most hardened gourmet melt with pleasure. The desserts, especially chocolate, are magnificent, and there are some exceptional jurançons in the wine cellar. Delightful ambiance too.

Cambo-les-Bains

RESTAURANT LE BELLEVUE Allée Edmond-Rostand ✆ 05 59 93 75 75. *Hotel closed, replaced by a residence. Closed Sunday evening and Monday, except public holidays. Bistrot set menu (lunchtime) menu du marché 17 €. Menu-carte from 22 € to 30 € (2 or 3 courses).* In an elegant and luminous setting, the dining rooms looking out onto the countryside are soberly decorated, with one or two contemporary touches. The young chef's gastronomic cuisine is quite remarkable, owing something no doubt to his time at the Jardins de l'Opéra and elsewhere, before coming back into the family business. His red tuna carpaccio and olive tapenade stand out, as does the swordfish fillet cooked *à la plancha* with pan fried vegetables and potatoes *croustilles*, or the caramelised banana crèpe in a terrine. Typical South West wines go well with the food, and the wine list has quite a few old vintages, and wines sold by the glass too. Energetic service.

Ciboure

CHEZ DOMINIQUE 15, quai Maurice-Ravel ✆ 05 59 47 29 16. *Annual closing in February. Closed Sunday evening, Monday and Tuesday all day. Open every day in high season. A la carte 52 € to 63 €. Seafood platters can be ordered in advance.* This well-known restaurant with its terrace stands out from the road, and is equally distinctive inside, its dining room looking for all the world like a boat cabin with brasses and frescoes of daily life on the walls. The cooking fits into this atmosphere too, for chef Georges Piron is an expert with fish: appetizers to start with, then some structured dishes like fresh crab flavoured with cepes au gratin, and truffle and foie gras sabayon, pan-fried scallops, chicory hearts with bitter orange juices, a Granny Smith apple *arlette* (flaky pastry case) cooked in cider, with a Darjeeling tea *mousseux* (soft mousse) and *fleurette* infused with apple. Relaxed service.

CHEZ MATTIN Rue Evariste-Baignol ✆ 05 59 47 19 52. *Closed Sunday evening and Monday. Annual holiday mid-January to late February. No set menu. A la carte from 27 € to 40 €, without drinks.* Typical regional restaurant with rustic dining rooms: the largest, displaying stone walls and half-timbering, runs the length of the bar, and is bright with brass. A decorative *chistera* (wicker basket-like implement used to play pelota) reminds you you're in the Basque country. Whichever dining room you choose (the smaller one is sweet, with its dresser and ancient cupboard) you'll be impressed by the food. The chef serves his regional dishes on striped red and blue plates, with matching napkins. Peppers stuffed with cod, txanguro (stuffed Basque crab) *cassolette* or ravioli, asparagus, mussels and pea cream, the house speciality ttoro, grilled monkfish kebab, grilled rib steak, mutton rib, Basque tripe and some excellent, beautifully-presented desserts like the *crèpe* stuffed with pineapple, pineapple ice-cream and a glass of punch. Impeccable service.

Espelette

HOTEL-RESTAURANT EUZKADI ** ✆ **05 59 93 91 88.** *Logis de France. Closed Monday, Tuesday in low season, and 1 November. Annual closing from early November to Christmas. 32 rooms from 48 € to 83 € (sleeps 5). Breakfast 7 €. Half-board 50 €. Full board 61 €. Dish of the day 10 €. Set menus of the day from 16 € to 30 €. A la carte from 28 € to 40 €. Pool, tennis courts.* This is Espelette's First Magistrate's house, located in the heart of the town where you can't miss it. The beautiful postcard faÁade with its red shutters and lines of hot peppers strung up to dry, catches the attention straight away, and the charm extends to the inside too, where there is a lot of fine old furniture, including a table displaying photos of Dad, Leon, as French pelota champion, and more peppers, of course. The Darraodou family is going to restructure the rooms, but for the moment, GuÈthary, Ciboure (the seaside, all in blue with a thick carpet and a little old desk) Ainhoa, Saint-Jean-Pied-de-Port and Iraty (ideal for families) haven't changed. On the ground floor, the dining room is completely genuine, with its superb period furniture and Amatxi cupboard full of famous Basque linen. The next generation's arrival in the kitchens comes as a breath of renewal, though Michel and Christian, now in charge of the cooking, fully intend to keep family tradition alive.

Hendaye

LE COMPLEXE SERGE BLANCO 125, boulevard de la Plage ✆ **05 59 51 35 35.** *Website: www.thalassoblanco.com* The complex, in the Sokoburu quarter, comprises a seawater therapy centre, and a 3-star hotel with gastronomic restaurant, but the 4-star Hotel Ibaia is only a few metres away, with another restaurant, L'Enbata, and a 4-star residence.

HOTEL IBAIA – CONCORDE HOTEL ET RESIDENCE HOTELIERE **** **76, avenue des Mimosas** ✆ **05 59 48 88 88**. *Open all year. 61 individual rooms from 82 € to 184 € according to number and season. Suites from 198 € to 286 € per person. Half-board from 108 € to 250 € per person per day, according to the category. Price with sea water cures included on request. Residence contains 24 apartments, from 238 € per week (studio). Breakfast from 10 € to 12 €. Half-board available. Discovery weekend with seawater therapy and Hendaye-Fontarrabie boat crossing. Garage.* This complex with its Basque architecture offers you two options: either to stay in the 4-star hotel, or in an apartment in the next-door residence. Both have access to the pool, and its setting with a superb view of the harbour. In the hotel there is a charming little bar with a compass above your head, white wood boards and comfortable armchairs, and a gastronomic restaurant. The rooms are 'traditional' or 'comfortable', and air-conditioned, with a view either of the harbour and Spain, or of the beach. They are equipped with mini-bar, TV and telephone, and marble bathrooms with hairdryer and shaving mirror. The pleasant suite has its own lounge and terrace with a panoramic view of Fontarrabie and the harbour. The residence contains 16 studios and 8 apartments (2-room and duplex), spacious, with a kitchenette in the entrance to leave space for the lounge and bedroom. Private entry and garage. The beach is only 30m away!

Jurançon

CHEZ RUFFET 3 avenue Charles-Touzet ✆ **05 59 06 25 13** *Fax 05 59 06 52 18. Website: www.pyreneesonline.chezruffet.fr. Set menus from 24 € to 110 €, à la carte 80 €. Closed Sunday evening and Monday, no annual closing.* This restaurant in the Pau suburbs, once a Bearn farmhouse, was counted among the area's classics long before Christophe Carrade arrived in 1998. It has had its ups and downs however, and these recent years have surely been some of its best. Christophe Carrade calls his cuisine «progressive regional cooking», and his pan-fried duck liver with citrus zests, steamed peas, carrot, ventreche bacon and lightly mentholated double cream, Bigorre pork, raisins soaked in sweet jurancon, grilled pistachios and braised sucrine hearts and scallops browned in olive oil and interlaced with a melted goat's cheese would seem to bear out this description. His desserts are intricate and inventive, such as the chocolate charlotte in *langue de chat* biscuits, *lait de poule* (egg beaten up in milk) flavoured with Carambar and strawberry ice cream. It's original and amusing, but never becomes 'gadget' food - in short, it's a success. Fine wine cellar for regional vintages, and very considerate service.

Orthez

HOTEL RESTAURANT AU TEMPS DE LA REINE JEANNE 44, rue du Vieux-Bourg ✆ 05 59 67 00 76.** *Website: www.reine- jeanne.fr Rooms from 45 € to 70 €. Breakfast 6.50 €. Seasonal set menu 16 €. Dégustation à la reine 35 €. Large seminar room.* Didier Couture is young, energetic and enterprising, and also very talented. His superb residence is already reputed for its setting, its good food and jazz evenings 'Jazz à la Reine'. An extension incorporating the next-door building has added a separate wing with 10 beautiful rooms and a small original terrace boasting a three-hundred-old olive tree. On the first floor is a charming salon with African colonial ambiance, then two floors of air-conditioned rooms with fine furniture and bathrooms, plenty of space and prettily coloured soft furnishings. You have access to a jacuzzi and a sauna, too, in a dry stone setting. The cooking is done with only the freshest, best quality produce, simply presented and understated: mi-cuit foie gras cooked in a cloth, slice of toast, scallops au gratin, beef steak with sweet potatoes mashed with olives, pistachio rice pudding etc. Faultless service.

Pau

AU FIN GOURMET 24, avenue Gaston-Lacoste ✆ 05 59 27 47 71. *Fax: 05 59 82 96 77. Set menus 16 € and 30 €, menu découverte 59 €, with wine 74 €. A la carte from 40 € to 50 €.* Everyone knows this excellent Pau restaurant by now, since it makes bigger waves every season. A few years ago, a pergola sprang up like a mushroom to extend the traditional family building, located in the listed quarter round the station. Inside, the dining room is decorated soberly but with sophistication, and the whole show is run by the Ithurriague family, including the kitchens. The *cuisine* itself is mature, and presented with style: apart from the classic menus you can try the *menu découverte* (discovery menu), either with a selected wine for each course, or without. The Ithurriagues are country-lovers, so during the mushroom season, they go cepe hunting in the mountains, and when there is game on the menu, you can be sure they brought it down themselves too. A real family business.

HOTEL RESTAURANT CONTINENTAL* Best Western chain. 2, rue du Maréchal-Foch ✆ 05 59 27 69 31.** *Website: www.hotel-continental-pau.com Rooms from 59 € to 90 €, according to number and category. Breakfast from 6.50 € to 9.50 €. Lunchtime formula (starter-main course-coffee) 11 €. Set menu of the day 20 €. Seminar rooms. Room service.* The Continental is under new management, and extensive renovation has been planned. Room 470, for example, has had a face-lift, and now boasts a more contemporary look in gold and bordeaux tones, with modern headboards and desk, original lighting, a small lounge corner with cosy armless chairs (chauffeuses), electric shutters and trouser press, a double door at the entrance to the room, etc. On the ground floor, the hotel has already been fitted out in 19thc. style, with plenty of mouldings, chandeliers, collections of paintings and period furniture, and exclusive tapestries and fabrics, seen to advantage in the seminar rooms. A new chef graces the kitchens; the lunchtime formula was his idea, as was putting up the week's menus on Monday for the increasing number of regulars who appreciate freshly cooked produce. Classic set menu and *à la carte* in the evenings.

Saint-Jean-de-Luz

LE GRAND HOTEL ** 43, boulevard Thiers ✆ 05 59 26 35 36.** *Website: www.luzgrandhotel.fr Open 1 March to 17 November. 52 rooms, suites and apartments. Rooms from 175 € to 710 €. One suite in high season. Breakfast 26 €. Sea water therapy weekend (information from the hotel). Gastronomic restaurant. Private car park 17 €.* The year 2006 will be an important one for this luxury hotel, since a new seawater therapy complex is planned to replace the current fitness centre, opening in 2007. The hotel will be open, but without its fitness club. However, one service less won't worry an establishment of this calibre. Facing the ocean, its magnificent architecture houses a charming lounge, cosy bar and restaurant overlooking the beach, in a hushed setting of period furniture, Veronese chandeliers, thick carpets and old parquet, with a monumental staircase leading up to the rooms and suites: Babylonian suites, 2 two-room apartments, 2 rooms with private swimming pool (no, your eyes aren't playing tricks), balconies, loggias and terraces, air-conditioning, electric roller blinds, luxurious and sophisticated plumbing in the bathrooms, and so on, and so on. Who said "but no fitness centre"?

HOTEL DU PARC VICTORIA ** 5, rue Cépé ✆ 05 59 26 78 78.** *Relais et Chateaux. Hotel closed 15 November-15 March, restaurant closed 1 November-1 April. 18 rooms and suites. 9 rooms from 160 € to 635 €, one suite, according to season. Breakfast 18 €. Dogs 10 €. Half-board supplement 50 € per person. Car park. Restaurant Les Lierres.* This is a truly relaxing place, not far from the beaches, in a marvellous park full of rare tree species. The great Victorian-type house contains a lounge and rooms, while the suites, bar (Pavillon des Chats), restaurant (Les Lierres), games room, seminar room, pergola and pool are spread around the grounds. The prevailing style is Art Deco, and there are some fascinating design elements in the bar and the bedrooms, like the spectacular headboards and old radio sets.

Miniature verandas, marble bathrooms, silver and crystal - and jacuzzis complete the luxury fittings. Proud owners R. Larralde and R. Perrodeau won the Welcome Trophy last year, one of only two hotels in the world to have done so!

Saint-Jean-Pied-de-Port

ETCHE ONA 15, place Floquet ✆ 05 59 37 01 14. *Set menu-carte: starter-main course-dessert 29 €. Menu Dégustation, each course from 11 € to 19 €.* Michel Ibargaray and his wife have come back to the region to take over the family restaurant, after a Tour de France (with the Ibarboure Brothers at Bidart in the Basque Country, and with Alain Dutournier at the Trou Gascon in Paris, etc.) Michel likes to follow his heart and his instincts at market, and his menu-*carte* reflects this, changing two or three times a week. You'll find grandmother's cooking, in fact, with his personal touch, for he excels in handling the produce. Topinambour and cherry tomato vinaigrette, poached egg and pan-fried country ham, mullet roasted on the bone and chicory with Parmesan, shortbread tart with almond cream, apple and walnut marmalade with a sweet chestnut soup, and so on. Beautiful to look at, delicious to taste, served with brio in an old-fashioned panelled dining room with period furnishings, immaculate tablecloths and antique silverware. You get the picture? This is an address to memorise.

LES PYRENEES 19 place du Gén-de-Gaulle ✆ 05 59 37 01 01 *Fax 05 59 37 18 97. Set menus from 43 € to 90 €, à la carte 65 €. Closed Monday evening (November-March), Tuesday (late September-late June), 5-28 January and 20 November-22 December.* Firmin Arrambide settled into this pretty Basque house nearly twenty years ago, and for several years now, has progressively been handing over to son Philippe. This is a traditional hotel, bourgeois, classic and reassuring, but it would make a pleasant change to see a few risks taken, and a little more passion in evidence on the menus, which are faultless, but conservative. Raw salmon marinated with herbs and tomato sorbet, Dublin Bay prawn ravioli with Aquitaine caviar, lobster *fricassée* with woodland mushrooms, roast saddle of lamb with conserved garlic, stuffed vegetables and a haricot bean *mousseline*, with iced coffee parfait and chocolate macaroons to follow. The cellar is well supplied with local wines - iroul eguys and jurançons - and some good bordeaux at reasonable prices.

Malartrie castle, la Roque-Gageac

Auvergne

Pavin lake

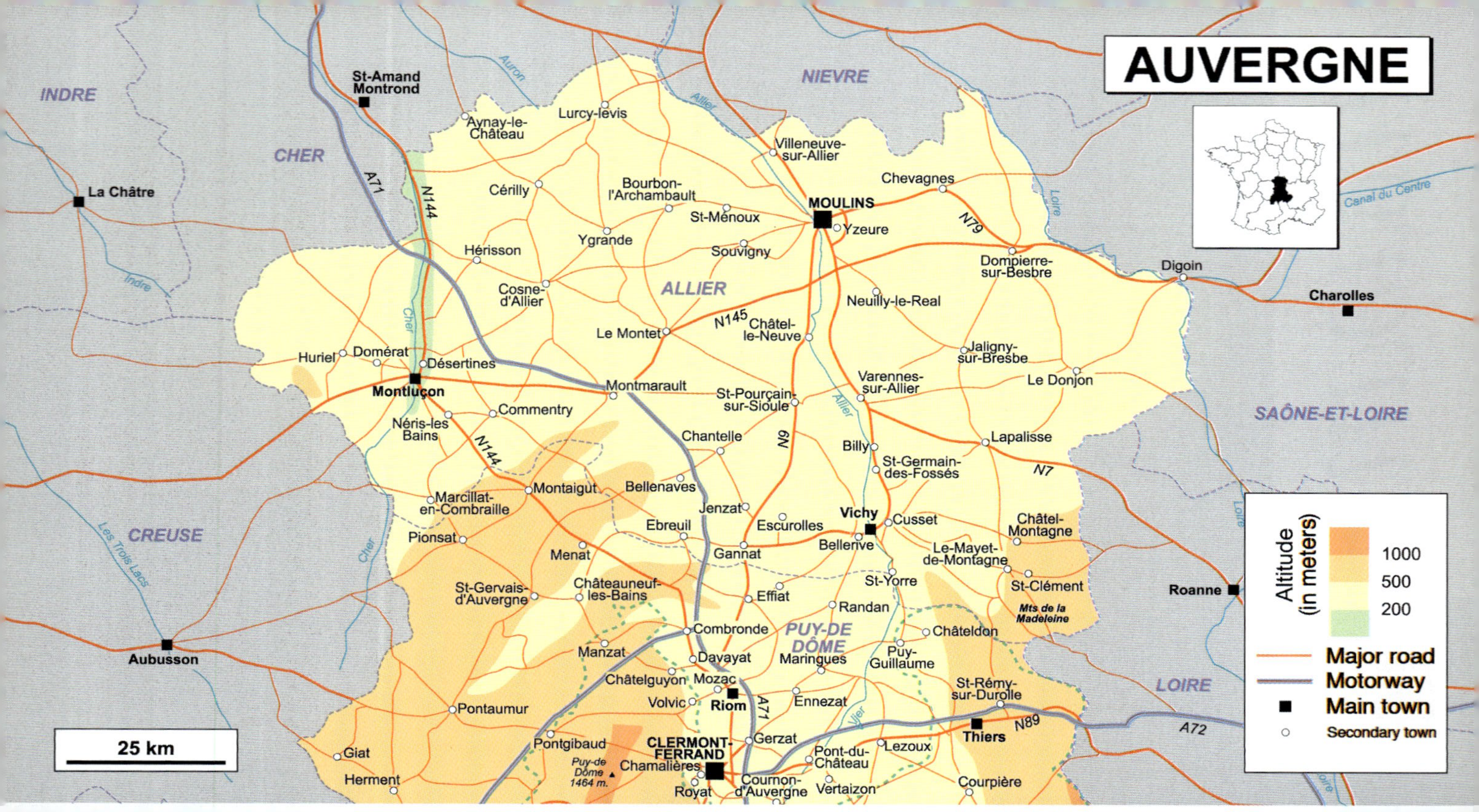
AUVERGNE
Altitude (in meters)
1000
500
200
Major road
Motorway
Main town
Secondary town
25 km
INDRE
CHER
NIEVRE
ALLIER
SAÔNE-ET-LOIRE
CREUSE
PUY-DE DÔME
LOIRE
St-Amand Montrond
La Châtre
Aubusson
Charolles
Roanne
Digoin
MOULINS
Yzeure
Chevagnes
Villeneuve-sur-Allier
Lurcy-levis
Aynay-le-Château
Cérilly
Bourbon-l'Archambault
St-Menoux
Souvigny
Ygrande
Hérisson
Cosne-d'Allier
Le Montet
Châtel-le-Neuve
Neuilly-le-Real
Dompierre-sur-Besbre
Jaligny-sur-Besbre
Le Donjon
Varennes-sur-Allier
Lapalisse
Huriel
Domérat
Désertines
Montluçon
Montmarault
St-Pourçain-sur-Sioule
Commentry
Néris-les Bains
Chantelle
Billy
St-Germain-des-Fossés
Marcillat-en-Combraille
Montaigut
Bellenaves
Jenzat
Escurolles
Vichy
Cusset
Bellerive
Châtel-Montagne
Le-Mayet-de-Montagne
St-Clément
Mts de la Madeleine
Pionsat
Menat
Ebreuil
Gannat
St-Yorre
St-Gervais-d'Auvergne
Châteauneuf-les-Bains
Effiat
Randan
Combronde
Châteldon
Manzat
Davayat
Maringues
Puy-Guillaume
Châtelguyon
Mozac
Riom
Volvic
Ennezat
St-Rémy-sur-Durolle
Thiers
Pontaumur
Pontgibaud
Puy-de Dôme 1464 m.
CLERMONT-FERRAND
Chamalières
Royat
Gerzat
Cournon-d'Auvergne
Pont-du-Château
Vertaizon
Lezoux
Courpière
Giat
Herment
A71
A72
N144
N145
N79
N9
N7
N89
Allier
Cher
Loire
Auron
Indre
Les Trois Lacs
Canal du Centre

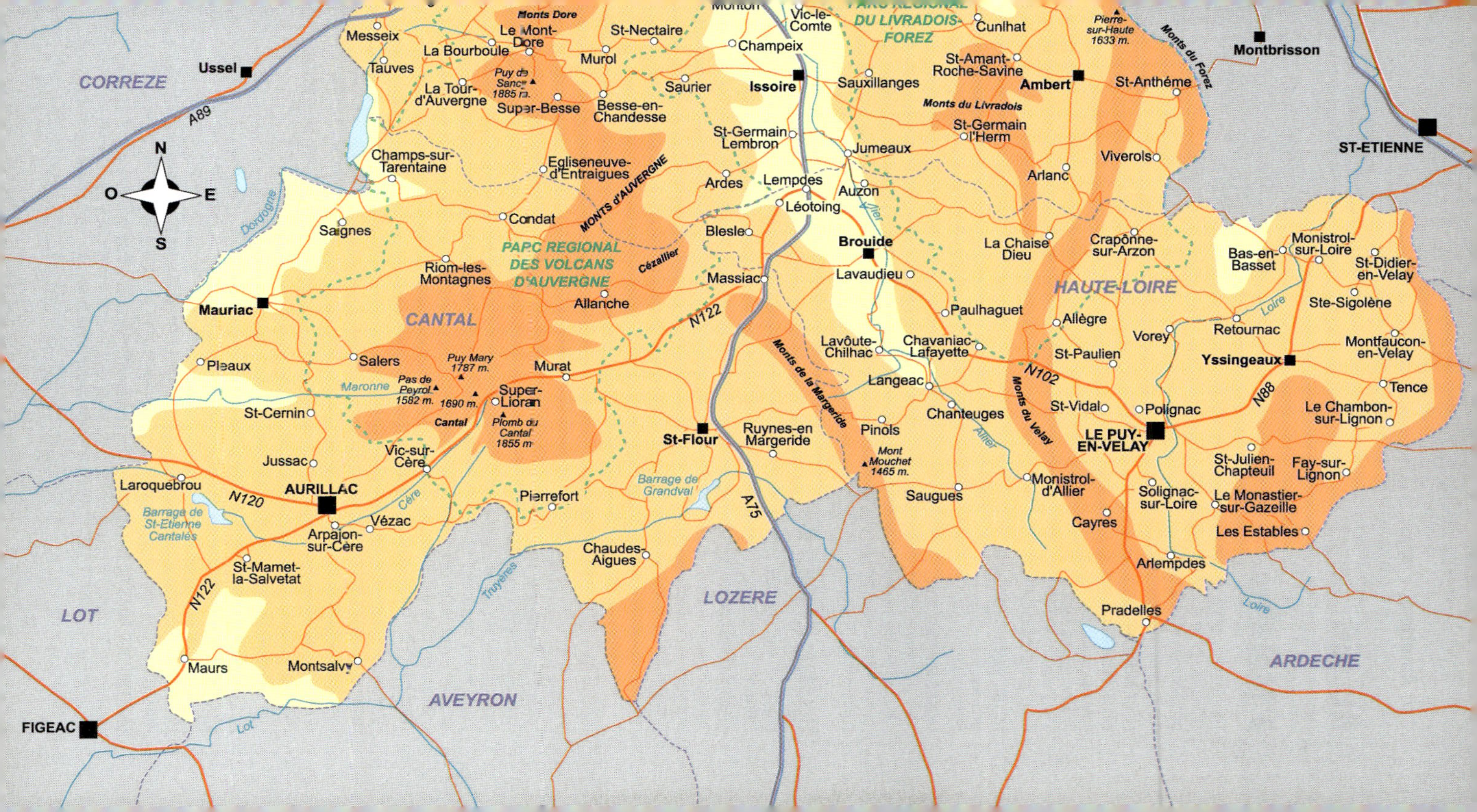

CORREZE
Ussel
A89
N
O
E
S
Dordogne
Messeix
Tauves
La Bourboule
Monts Dore
Le Mont-Dore
Puy de Sancy 1885 m.
La Tour-d'Auvergne
Super-Besse
Murol
St-Nectaire
Saurier
Besse-en-Chandesse
Champs-sur-Tarentaine
Egliseneuve-d'Entraigues
MONTS d'AUVERGNE
Saignes
Condat
PARC REGIONAL DES VOLCANS D'AUVERGNE
Cézallier
Riom-ès-Montagnes
Mauriac
CANTAL
Allanche
Salers
Pleaux
Puy Mary 1787 m.
Pas de Peyrol 1582 m.
1690 m.
Maronne
Murat
Super-Lioran
Plomb du Cantal 1855 m
Cantal
St-Cernin
Jussac
Vic-sur-Cère
Laroquebrou
N120
AURILLAC
Barrage de St-Etienne Cantalès
Cère
Vézac
Arpajon-sur-Cère
St-Mamet-la-Salvetat
N122
Maurs
Montsalvy
LOT
FIGEAC
Lot
AVEYRON
Truyère
Pierrefort
Chaudes-Aigues
Barrage de Grandval
St-Flour
A75
LOZERE
Champeix
Issoire
St-Germain-Lembron
Ardes
Lempdes
Léotoing
Blesle
Massiac
Vic-le-Comte
PARC REGIONAL DU LIVRADOIS-FOREZ
Sauxillanges
Jumeaux
Auzon
Allier
Brioude
Lavaudieu
Paulhaguet
Lavoûte-Chilhac
Chavaniac-Lafayette
Langeac
Monts de la Margeride
Ruynes-en-Margeride
Pinols
Mont Mouchet 1465 m.
Chanteuges
Saugues
Cunlhat
St-Amant-Roche-Savine
Ambert
Monts du Livradois
St-Germain-l'Herm
Arlanc
La Chaise-Dieu
Pierre-sur-Haute 1633 m.
Monts du Forez
St-Anthème
Viverols
Montbrisson
ST-ETIENNE
Craponne-sur-Arzon
HAUTE-LOIRE
Allègre
St-Paulien
N102
Monts du Velay
St-Vidal
Monistrol-d'Allier
Vorey
Polignac
LE PUY-EN-VELAY
Cayres
Solignac-sur-Loire
Arlempdes
Pradelles
Bas-en-Basset
Monistrol-sur-Loire
St-Didier-en-Velay
Ste-Sigolène
Loire
Retournac
Yssingeaux
Montfaucon-en-Velay
N88
Tence
Le Chambon-sur-Lignon
St-Julien-Chapteuil
Fay-sur-Lignon
Le Monastier-sur-Gazeille
Les Estables
ARDECHE

ALLIER

Moulins

This former capital of the Bourbon dukes became the Allier's prefecture after the Revolution. The cathedral, triptych and old town with its half-timbered houses and pink-and-black diamond brick mansions are of historical interest, but Moulins is also a forward-looking town in both industry and the arts.

LE GRAND CAFE 49, place d'Allier ✆ 04 70 44 00 05. *Open all year.* The Grand Café is one of France's most beautiful bar-brasseries, and a listed historic monument. The original 1899 decoration in Art Deco style has been preserved, with its panelled front and walls hung with mirrors reflecting light and space to infinity, and the clock and the barometer, still in marvellous condition. Every second Friday of the month, a jazz evening is held, and there are philosophy discussions the last Thursday of the month, known as cafés philosophiques.

NOTRE DAME CATHEDRAL Place des Vosges ✆ 04 70 20 89 65. Triptych visits every day except Tuesday. Built from 1474 to 1540, the former collegiate church is pure Flamboyant Gothic. In the Bishop's Chapel, you can admire the Triptyque du Maitre de Moulins, a 15thc. wood painting.

MUSEE BOURBONNAIS 4, place de l'Ancien-Palais ✆ 04 70 44 39 03. *Open every day: 10am-12 noon and 3pm-6.30pm (except Thursday). October-March: closes at 5.30pm. Admission: adult 4 €, 4-13s 2.50 €.* The museum is housed in several 17thc. houses, with a maze of galleries, corridors, little rooms, staircases and inside courtyards to find your way through. The guided tour is an opportunity to discover local history.

Bourbon-l'Archambault

Cradle of the Bourbon dynasty, this historic spa town contains one of France's biggest feudal fortresses.

CHATEAU DES DUCS ✆ 04 70 67 02 30. *Open every day, February-15 November: 2pm-6pm. 15 June-15 September: 10am-7pm (except Sunday and public holidays: 2pm-7pm).* This medieval fortress, birthplace of the Bourbon dynasty, has suffered over the centuries, but is still an important feudal ruin. A guided tour reveals the rooms and castle life, with a son et lumière (The Crystal Dagger) in July & August.

Natural sites

FORET DE TRONCAIS. Planted by Colbert in the 17thc. to supply the Royal Navy with timber, Tronçais Forest with its oaks and beeches was one of the biggest in France. Today, it is only a tenth of its original size. You come across lakes, fountains, crossroads and three-hundred-year-old oaks as you walk through the forest, all unobtrusively signposted. Close to the Isle-et-Bardais, there is the Viljot fountain - girls throw in a hairpin so as to find a husband before the year is out – the Carré oak (6m round, 26m high and 300 year old) and the Emile Guillaumin et Charles-Louis Philippe oaks named after two of the region's writers.

MONTAGNE BOURBONNAISE. The Bourbonnais mountain is a hikers' paradise, crossed by a 400 km network of marked-out paths. It is also a conservation area, containing a wealth of plant and animal life. Châtel-Montagne conceals a genuine Romanesque art treasure, hidden by the Cluny monks.

VAL D'ALLIER NATURE RESERVE. One of France's biggest waterway reserves, and an important habitat for European bird life, being home to almost 250 species of nesting bird.

Montluçon

Medieval Montluçon is not only the castle, but also Saint Pierre and Notre Dame Churches, old squares and narrow alleys lined with half-timbered houses where you can enjoy a stroll.

CHATEAU DES DUCS DE BOURBON. Eudes, Comte de Bourgogne, put up the first walls of the present castle in 1250. The old Merovingian ramparts were kept, and the inside courtyard raised to the level of the esplanade. In 1370, Louis II, Duc de Bourbon, came to live in the town, and rebuilt the castle, as did

Jean I and Charles I who followed. The castle now boasted living-quarters on two floors (the upper one under the roof), vast chambers lit by wide mullioned windows, a clocktower and an Italian-style wooden gallery. Montluçon held a strategic position in the Middle Ages, as a border town at the gates of English-occupied territory. Later, the castle was destroyed during the Terror, and after, became a council building, court and stylish cafe before the War Ministry had it fitted out as a barracks in 1913. Mayor Max Dormoy had it restored in 1935, and today it houses the Popular Music and Resistance Museums.

MUSEE DES MUSIQUES POPULAIRES Château des ducs de Bourbon ✆ 04 70 02 56 57. This museum, with its magnificent and extensive music collections, is currently closed for renovation work, but should be open again in May 2006. You'd be wise to check first, before setting out! From the esplanade, you go up a rough stone spiral staircase to the 1st floor of the tower. The museum's grande salle exhibits over 700 instruments, in showcases with sound-tracks. On the next floor, a magnificently renovated triple chamber with a 15thc. fireplace houses some fine earthenware. The last room at the back contains souvenirs of the local Resistance, and the dark days of the Occupation, with its daily sacrifices and acts of cowardice and bravery. The esplanade offers a view over the town and the castle gallery.

Souvigny

Souvigny's religious and historic heritage and medieval festival are attracting more and more tourists to the heart of the Bourbonnais bocage.

SAINT PIERRE AND SAINT PAUL PRIORY CHURCH Place Aristide Briand ✆ 04 70 43 99 75 *www.ville-souvigny.com. Open all year. Guided tours and individual visits every day except Tuesday (enquire at the museum).* In 916, a Bourbon ancestor gave the Souvigny land to Cluny Abbey, to found a priory. Saints Mayeul and Odilon were inhumed here, attracting pilgrims, among them kings and Popes. The biggest and most beautiful religious building in the Bourbonnais.

MUSEES ET JARDINS DE SOUVIGNY ✆ 04 70 43 99 75. *www.ville-souvigny.com. Open every day, except Tuesday: 9am-12 noon and 2pm-6pm (7pm in July & August). Admission: 3.90 €. Guided tour and museums: 6.30 €.* The Musée du Pays is concerned with local archeology, ethnology and monuments. La Grange Sud displays the Romanesque Zodiac column, a 12thc. carved pillar with historiated sides. The priory also boasts reconstructions of formal 17th and 18thc. gardens.

Vichy

MUSEE DE L'OPERA 16, rue Marechal-Foch ✆ 04 70 58 48 20. *Open 3pm-6pm, except Monday.* Opened two years ago for the Opera's centenary, this museum houses a collection of programmes, posters and documents created by the Opera workshop, costumes, accessories, photos of artistes and the building, and architectural plans.

VILLAS & CHALETS. Most of these mansions and chalets date back to the Second Empire, and can be seen along the Avenue des Etats Unis, Rue de Belgique and Boulevard de Russie. They recall colonial-style Louisiana, Haussmann's Paris or Visconti's Venice, and are crying out to be photographed. The

Vichy, hydropathic establishment

chalets round the Parc Napoleon III remind us that the Emperor loved this spa town: the door of the Emperor's Chalet at 107, Avenue des Etats-Unis apparently bore a letter N with an imperial crown above it. Sadly, the house no longer exists. The Emperor also stayed at the Villa Marie-Louise built by the architect Lefaure - you can still admire this chalet.

Ygrande

Prehistoric site and medieval town mentioned in the 12thc., Ygrande has a beautiful Saint Martin Church, part of a Benedictine monastery later grouped together with Souvigny.

SAINT MARTIN CHURCH. Built of local sandstone with a magnificent 14thc. steeple, nearly 36m high, composed of a two-storey octagonal tower topped with a 25m spire.

MUSEE EMILE GUILLAUMIN Les Vignes ✆ 04 70 66 37 90. *Open 1 May-30 October: 3pm-6pm, except Monday and Tuesday.* This family farm belonged to writer Emile Guillaumin (1873-1951), the famous peasant trade unionist who wrote about simple but hard Bourbonnais life in the early 20thc.

CANTAL

Aurillac

Extreme mountain temperatures are often registered here, but Aurillac has other points of interest apart from the weather. Living conditions have not always been easy here (the main industries are dairy and cheese-making), but the town is busy and attractive in season.

MUSEE D'ART ET D'ARCHEOLOGIE Centre Pierre-Mendès-France - 37, rue des Carmes ✆ 04 71 45 46 10. *Open Tuesday-Saturday: 10am-12 noon and 2pm-6pm. Closed December & January.* This museum was set up in a former 17thc. Visitandine monastery in 1990. You discover the Cantal's history from Paleolithic to medieval times, and a bust of Rodin by Camille Claudel, among other works of art.

CHATEAU SAINT ETIENNE. Saint Géraud, founder of the famous abbey, was born in this castle, which has been reshaped many times and now houses a Volcano Museum. It has a 13thc. keep; the rest is mainly 19thc.

TOURS ROMANES. Apart from its fortifications, the town was defended by the Château Saint Etienne and a system of nearby watchtowers. All that remains is Aurillac Castle keep and the Romanesque Saint Simon and de Naucelles Towers (11th or 12thc.)

L'HOPITAL. The town's most interesting Romanesque monument is just opposite Saint Géraud Church tower. It has been converted into apartments: you can live in a genuine Romanesque house for a modest rent!

SAINT GERAUD CHURCH. Originally the abbey sanctuary. Until the Revolution, it was part of the Benedictine abbey founded by Count Géraud in 916. Almost nothing is left of the primitive church.

OLD HOUSES ON THE JORDANNE. One of Aurillac's most picturesque sites. These houses were built in the late 18thc. replacing redundant ramparts which have nevertheless left some traces.

Garabit

VIADUCT. Built four years before the Eiffel Tower, this 500m-long and 120m-high structure was the work of the Eiffel firm. Leon Boyer, the engineer in charge of finishing the Paris-Beziers railway line, drew up the plans.

Mauriac

The old town boasts many 17th and 17thc. buildings.

NOTRE DAME DES MIRACLES BASILICA. *Guided tours available*

The imposing porch with its tympanum depicting Christ's Ascension draws the eye straight away. It is crowned with a jutting archivolt decorated with Zodiac signs. On the building's right flank is a lantern of the Dead, a rare object which used to be in the cemetery between the two churches.

SAINT-PIERRE DE MAURIAC MONASTERY. *Guided tours from May-September. Admission: adults 2.50 €, over-10s 2 €.* Founded in the 6thc. and rebuilt in the 10thc. on the renewing of the Sens priory charters. The 11thc. chapter house pillars are from a Gallo-Roman building. You can see Romanesque and Gothic influences in the cloister, raised in the 17thc. with the Saint Maur reform. Archeological digs have excavated the remains of a Carolingian church built against the 9thc. monastery.

Aurillac, Jordane river

© Iconotec.com

MUSEE MUNICIPAL Rue Emile-Delallo ✆ 04 71 68 07 24. *Ouvert de Pâques à septembre de 10h à 12h et de 13h30 à 18h sauf le mardi hors saison et le dimanche matin. Adultes 2,50 €*. Les prisons de Mauriac, constituées de cellules voûtées, ont été aménagées en 1812 dans l'ancienne demeure des doyens, agrandie de dépendances du monastère. Le tribunal s'étend sur toute la longueur du bâtiment au-dessus des cellules. La pente naturelle de la rue permet toujours un accès en rez-de-chaussée aux deux niveaux. L'ensemble des salles voûtées a été converti par la municipalité en 1984 en un musée remarquable aux thèmes très variés.

Murat

You first see the town from the D926, coming from Ussel. It lights up at dusk, to show off its main sites. Admire Notre Dame des Oliviers Church, the Pavillon Baltard-style covered market, Bonnevie Rock and Bredons Chapel. This superb building has a triple nave roofed in shale and a square belltower. It contains ten very fine Baroque reredos.

MAISON DE LA FAUNE Place de l'Hôtel de Ville ✆ 04 71 20 00 52. *Open July-August: 9.30am-12.30pm and 2pm-7pm; Sunday: 10am-12 noon and 2pm-7pm.* During the other school holidays: 10am-12 noon and 2pm-6pm; Sunday afternoon only. Outside holiday periods: 10am-12 noon and 2pm-6pm; Sunday: 2pm-5pm. This museum boasts 800 different kinds of mammal and bird displayed in their natural habitat, plus 10,000 insects. The 15thc. painted ceilings and pannelling are also of interest.

Salers

You hear cowbells in this pretty village, and learn about the region's history. To see: the Lizet House's Renaissance door with its little pillars; the fine staircase leading up to the Parish Room terrace; the Ronade House's 16thc. framework and the belfry door. You can also admire the Cantal's volcanic landscape from the Barrouze esplanade.

MAISON DE L'ANCIEN BAILLIAGE ✆ 04 71 40 70 59. *Open in season. Guided tour.* This imposing Renaissance building in Place Tissandier belongs to the Comtesse de Lestrade, and contains superb period furniture and some tapestries.

LES BURONS DE SALERS - MAISONS DU FROMAGE DE LA VACHE ET DE GENTIANE SALERS Route du Puy Mary ✆ 04 71 40 70 71. *Open Easter-November, every day: 10am-7pm.* Panoramic view of the summer pastures, guided tours of the Salers cheese-making process, beef cattle and Salers gentian. The cheese was made during summer pasturing by the burroniers, and you can follow the development of burronnier tools, taste and buy cheese and Salers gentian, and take part in a typical burronnier meal in July and August.

MAISON DES TEMPLIERS Rue des Templiers. *Closed Tuesday out of season.* Contains a typical local interior, cultural objects, an exhibition on Salers cattle and cheese-making, all on four floors. A thematic exhibition is organised each summer.

Saint-Flour

The site on its rocky outcrop was probably occupied in the Neolithic era. Today, Saint Flour is known for its various ruins and museums, and carefully-preserved medieval houses. There is still a Middle Ages atmosphere in the narrow streets! The Place d'Armes, now a car-park, is surrounded by monuments, beginning with Saint Pierre Cathedral. In the lower town, you find the Pont Vieux, where a woman, known as the recluse, chose to be shut up. Her prayers protected the town.

SAINT PIERRE CATHEDRAL. Things to see: the mullioned windows, side chapels and a pentagonal chancel, some paintings, a polychrome marble altar, a bronze-and-gold reliquary containing Saint-Flour's relics, a pieta and a 15thc. life-size Christ in black wood, unique in France.

MUSEE DE LA HAUTE AUVERGNE 1, place d'Armes - Palais Episcopal © 04 71 60 22 32. *Open 10am-12 noon and 2pm-6pm every day, 15 April-15 October.* Same opening hours out of season, closed Sunday & public holidays. The museum is housed in a wing of the former Bishops' Palace (17thc.) The rooms are remarkably fine, with their displays of Cantal art.

Vic sur Cère

This former spa town on the Cère is now a rural or ski resort, according to the season. The old town is worth a visit; some of the houses bear plaques explaining their history. It takes 15 mins on foot to reach the Conche waterfall. See the Calvary chapel with its panoramic view, Monaco Princes' house, Cere riverbanks, rocher des Pendus (Hanged Mens' Rock) and the grotte des Anglais (Englishmens' Cave).

LA MAISON DES EAUX MINERALES Ave. de la Duchesse de Fontanges © 04 71 47 57 19. *Open 10am-12 noon and 3pm-7pm, 1 June-30 September.* Other school holiday periods, Monday-Friday: 2pm-5pm. Out of season, open weekends and on request. The town set up this mineral water centre on the old Vic water spa premises. You can taste the water at the fountain in the former bottling workshop; it tastes strongly of iron and comes from the heart of a volcano.

PUY-DE-DOME

LIVRADOIS-FOREZ REGIONAL NATURE RESERVE Saint-Gervais-sous-Meymont © 04 73 95 57 57. Created 20 years ago, and covering the Puy-de-Dôme and Haute-Loire departments, this reserve contains 180 villages and some remarkable environmental sites, boasting a wealth of plant and animal life. The park is situated at middle-mountain height, between the Forez and the Auvergne Mountains, and its natural resources can be discovered via the Maison du Parc, a stone and wooden building covered in vegetation. Inside you find information about the 100 or so guided heritage walks, and films on local history, crafts, know-how and the country's secrets and mysteries.

Clermont-Ferrand

Capital of Auvergne and of the tyre. The town is on a remarkable site at the foot of the Puys range. The Puys are impressive with their 80 volcanos spread over 40km, between the la Sioule and Limagne gorges. Whatever the season, these forests, woods, meadows, moors and lakes provide wonderful scenery.

NOTRE DAME DE L'ASSOMPTION CATHEDRAL. This blackish cathedral with its two spires may be aesthetically controversial, but it is an integral part of the town. Volvic stone is naturally black; the colour does not come from pollution as many tourists still think.

NOTRE DAME DU PORT CHURCH Rue du Port. Listed UNESCO World Heritage. Hemmed in by buildings, this Romanesque church seems rather discreet at first. Wait and see! Built of arkose rather than Volvic stone, it contrasts with the rather dark and sad image of Auvergne's capital. It was built in the 11th and 12thc. on the site of a 6thc. church, and modified in the 19thc., when the blackish stone on the roof and the steeples were added. All the regional Romanesque features can be found here: chevet with radiating chapels, semi-circular vault inside, chancel and transept topped by a cupola. The chancel capitals are exquisite, representing Vice's fight against Virtue and Bible scenes. A Black Virgin exhibited in the crypt attrats pilgrims every summer. Interesting sculptures decorate the south front and the portal, with their original colours. Restoration work planned by the local authorities is underway, to be finished by 2006.

ESPACE ART ROMAN Maison du Tourisme - Place de la Victoire © 04 73 98 65 00. *www.clermont-fd.com and tourisme@clermont-fd.com. Opening hours from the Tourist Office.* A good way to discover medieval architecture, sculpture, painting, lifestyles and habits. The Romanesque Art Centre projects Jean-Michel Mahenc's film 'Le Jeu de la pierre et de la foi' (Game of Stone and Faith), which discusses church-building. You can travel in the region by way of interactive markers, following different routes. The centre also houses temporary exhibitions on medieval themes.

PLATEAU DE GERGOVIE. *Annual closing 15 October-30 April. Open Monday-Sunday: 10am-12.30pm and 2pm-6pm.* The battle between Caesar and Vercingétorix took place here in 52 B.C.

FONTAINE PETRIFIANTE Rue Gaultier de Biauzat © 04 73 37 15 58. These springs are as powerful and mysterious as volcanos, with deep origins indissociable from Auvergne's geological history. Long before they could be scientifically explained, the springs were a basis for legends and superstitious beliefs, and from the 18thc. onwards, human effort sought to exploit them for industrial use. The resulting techniques and know-how led to the development of a new craft incrustation sur moulure: the volcanic water was used to petrify or inlay objects, setting like stone in a mould. You can discover the origins and properties of these thermal and mineral carbonic gas springs and the different stages of the craft – which became a real profession – as well as more recent research into this strange element.

Hérisson

Natural advantages, a rich history and a good dose of human talent have made Hérisson what it is: a marvellous village with oodles of charm. You can admire its castle, medieval streets and Saint Sauveur church steeple; a listed 13thc. square porch tower. Hérisson was founded around the 5thc. A.D. when the inhabitants of the nearby Gallo-Roman oppidum left the site to settle at the foot of a rocky spur with its protective fort overlooking the Aumance. The community developed into one of the duchy's main strongholds and was often beseiged. The old town is still partially surrounded by walls with doors set in them, and has managed to keep its ancient 15th, 16th and 17thc. houses

Saint-Bonnet-de-Troncais

You are in the heart of Troncais Forest, confiscated from the Connetable de Bourbon in 1527. Colbert transformed it into a timber reserve in 1670.

LA FUTAIE COLBERT. This timber plantation contains some superb tree specimens: the Resistance Oak born in 1690 is 41m high; the Twins (from the same stump) date back to 1600, are 22m and 25m high and measure 4.50m around the trunk, and the Sentinel born in 1580 has a 6.55m circumference.

HAUTE-LOIRE

Le Puy-en-Velay

Arriving at the Puy through a snowy pass, you see a marvellous sight : a town circled by volcanos, devoted to God and the Compostella pilgrimage.

SAINT JEAN BAPTISTRY. Baptisms and christenings were held in this 11thc. building opposite the cathedral tower entrance, until the Revolution. The portal displays polychrome lions, Lombard-style.

NOTRE-DAME DE L'ANNONCIATION CATHEDRAL. *Enquiries:© 04 71 09 73 45.* Tradition and legends link the building of an early sanctuary on Mont Anis with the Virgin's 5thc. apparition. The cathedral, dedicated to Our Lady of the Annunciation, was repeatedly modified and rebuilt, until the end of the 12thc., and is rather an original building, since it overhangs a sheer drop. Pilgrimages began developing from the 10thc. onwards and reached their heyday in the 13thc. when pilgrims came from all over Europe to pray in front of 'le devot ymage', a statue of the Virgin in Majesty, Mary, Mother of God. The cathedral was saved from ruin by 19thc. renovation work, and was magnificently restored once more in the late 20thc. In December 1998 it was listed Unesco World Heritage, as one of the churches on the Compostella route. The current statue of the Black Virgin dates back to the 17thc, the one which inspired so much secular veneration having been burnt during the Revolution.

CATHEDRAL CLOISTER. *Open mid May-September: 9am-12 noon and 2pm-5pm. July & August: 9am-6.30pm. Admission: adults 4 €, 18-25s 2.50 €, under-18s free.* One of Christian Europe's finest cloisters (11th & 12thc.).

SACRISTY. Among other treasures, it houses the famous Theodulfe Bible, a remarkable manuscript written by Benedictine monks from 794-798.

ROCHER CORNEILLE - STATUE NOTRE DAME DE FRANCE. *Closed mid November-late January except school holidays, and Sundays: 2pm-5pm. Open mid-March-late April: 9am-6pm. May, June & September: 9am-7pm. July & August: 9am-7.30pm. October-mid March: 10am-5pm. Admission: adult 3 €, students & over-7s 1.50 €. Corneille Rock is 757m high.* The statue was put up in 1860, with the proceeds of donations and a national subscription. Napoleon III gave the Bishop of Puy 213 cannons taken at the Battle of Sebastopol, which were melted down for the occasion. Jean Bonnassieux sculpted this Virgin holding the Child (unusually) on her right arm. It is 22.7m high, weighs 110 tonnes, and contains 262 steps leading up to the crown.

Auzon

Formerly one of the '13 good towns of Auvergne', Auzon stands at the confluence of two streams. Traces of the Middle Ages can be seen round its Romanesque church.

COLLEGIATE CHURCH Contact Jeanine Merlino ✆ 04 71 76 17 85. This 12thc. church (attached to the Chaise-Dieu) boasts several works of art, including a fine 12thc. lime-wood Christ reliquary.

Blesle

Over 40 half-timbered houses, some with corbelling, can be admired in Blesle.

SAINT PIERRE CHURCH. 9thc. majestic church in pure Auvergne style.

HALF-TIMBERED HOUSE. Blesle still boasts some medieval houses with a wooden frame. The faint corbelling and half-timbering filled in with stone are often coated.

Brioude

Both Saint Julien Basilica, and the town with its old houses in the Rue Seguret and Rue de la Chèvrerie, are worth a visit.

SAINT JULIEN BASILICA ✆ 04 71 74 97 49. *Guided tours all year for groups, and individual visitors in high season. Enquiries at the Tourist Office.* Saint Julien Basilica (11th & 12thc.) is Auvergne's biggest Romanesque Church. Its striking architecture is enhanced by the 16thc. pebble paving, Saint Michel Chapel frescoes, 17thc. Vaneau Calvary and statues (Leper Christ, pregnant Virgin and Virgin with Bird).

MAISON DU SAUMON Place de la Resistance ✆ 04 71 74 91 43. Open all year. Discover the river's ecosystem via large aquariums reconstructing the Allier river bed.

La Chaise-Dieu

Known worldwide for its classical music festival, this restored site is green and beautiful.

ABBEY ✆ 04 71 00 05 55. *Open all year. Opening days and times according to season and activities in progress.* The abbey was founded by Saint Robert de Turlande, and its influence was widespread throughout Europe during the Middle Ages. As one of the biggest Benedictine congregations, it was favoured by the Popes, especially Clement VI who had been one of its monks, and who was eventually buried there. The abbey lived through troubled times in the 15th and 17thc., but the arrival of the reformed Saint Maur Benedictine congregation in 1640 brought about a new blossoming of the faith. During the Revolution, the monks left the site, and today, the former abbey church is a local parish church. In 1984, the Brothers of Saint John arrived at La Chaise-Dieu, reviving monastic life. Their first task was to ensure continual silent, religious and liturgic prayer. The abbey contains some sacred treasures, including the white marble recumbent statue of Pope Clement VI and 144 oak choir stalls dating back to the 14thc. Above these stalls, 11 tapestries stretch over 60m in length, portraying Bible scenes that aimed to teach the life of Christ and the Old Testament to those who couldn't read. At the back of the church, the great 17thc. organs have been restored several times.

HISTORIAL ✆ 04 71 00 01 88. *Open Easter-September. In season: 9am-12 noon and 2pm-7pm. Out of season: 10am-12 noon and 2pm-5pm. Admission: adult 2.50 €, child 1.50 €.* Life-size waxworks tell the story of the abbey and the monks' life from Saint Robert to the Revolution.

SALLE DE L'ECHO. *Open every day and all year: 8.30am-6.30pm.* This big room was built for lepers' confessions. Speak in one corner; your voice will follow the groin of the vault and only be heard in the opposite corner. A sort of medieval speaking grill.

MUSEE DU BOIS ET DE LA FORET Rue Saint Martin ✆ 04 71 00 10 35. *Open 1 May-31 October, every day: 10am-12 noon and 2pm-7pm.* A few feet from Saint Robert Abbey Church, you can discover the forest's history, together with traditional forestry activities.

Monistrol-sur-Loire

This medieval town has kept several traces of its prestigious past. The flat-roofed houses have a surprising Mediterranean character. The Château des Evêques, Comtes du Velay, can be seen in the town's old quarter.

CHATEAU DES EVEQUES ✆ **04 71 66 03 14**. *Open all year except Sunday in low season. Guided tours (advance booking only) 1.60 €*. This Episcopal castle was the Bishops of Puy's summer residence from the 17thc. onwards.

URSULINE CONVENT. Founded in the 1630s. The chapel contains the death of Saint Joseph sculpted by Vaneau.

Saugues

ASMUSEE FANTASTIQUE DE LA BETE DU GEVAUDAN ✆ **04 71 77 64 22**. *Open 15 June-15 September every day: 10am-12 noon and 2.30pm-6.30pm.* All year for groups, by appointment. The period atmosphere, landscapes, legends and popular fears concerning this Beast are staged in 22 scenes, with 75 characters to tell the fantastic tale.

TOUR DES ANGLAIS ✆ **04 71 77 64 22.** *Open every day July & August: 10am-12 noon and 2.30pm-6.30pm. Out of season, groups welcome by appointment.* This tower is one of the region's rare examples of 13thc. military architecture.

WATER CURES

The virtues of thermal springs, recognised in Classical Antiquity, were rediscovered in the 18th and 19thc. Watering towns appeared with an eclectic architectural style, aiming for the unexpected and unusual. The idle rich came to take the cure in Auvergne every year, and needed amusing. Napoleon III and the Empress Eugénie patronised Vichy; the Marquise de Sévigné preferred Bourbon-L'Archambault; Maupassant, Chatel-Guyon; General Boulanger, Royat; and the Duchesse de Berry went to the Mont-Dore.

Allier

Bourbon-l'Archambault

This historic spatown is the Bourbon dynasty's birthplace.

LES THERMES ✆ **04 70 67 07 88**. *Open March-November. Water cures April-October.* This establishment, built in 1885, stands in a park. The entrance halls are decorated with beautiful tiles made by the Parvilliers workshops in 1885; they are listed historical monuments. Ask first before going in to admire them, as access is restricted to curists for hygiene reasons.

Néris-les-Bains

The Romans established the first baths at Néris, building swimming-pools, villas, aqueducts, amphitheatre and temples beside them.

LES THERMES 6, place des Thermes ✆ **04 70 03 10 39**. *www.thermes-neris.com. Open April-October.* These waters exploited by the Romans and rediscovered in the 19thc. come out of the ground at 52.8°C, and are used to treat rheumatic, neurological and psychosomatic disorders. The treatment includes thermal pool and natural mud applications. There are also tailor-made options for getting back into shape.

Vichy

Vichy is well-equipped for fitness, relaxation and cultural activities, and gastronomy. You can find it all in the towncentre: watering cure centres, opera, parks, brasseries and restaurants. The queen of spa towns really looks the part, with its Napoleon III buildings, Louisiana-style chalets and salons de thés melling of aniseed confectionary.

SOURCES (SPRINGS). The Hall des Sources was built in 1902 from the plans of wrought-iron craftsman Emile Robert. The inside was modified in 1971 and the roof restored in 1995. It has access to 6 springs: Chomel (43°C) Grande Grille (42.4°C) Source de l'Hôpital, Lucas (28.1°C) Source du Parc (22.5°C) and Celestins (17.8°C).

SOURCE DES CELESTINS. Lucien Woog's elliptic pavillion was built in 1908, to house the Vichy pump room. This spring water was to become the most famous.

COMPAGNIE GENERALE DE L'EAU DE SOURCE 1, ave. Eisenhower ✆ 04 70 97 38 40

SPA VICHY 'LES CELESTINS' 111, bd. des Etats-Unis ✆ 04 70 30 82 35. *www.destinationvichy.com. Closed 4-25 December 2005.* "Undoubtedly one of the best-looking fitness, health and beauty centres in Europe. All your requirements can be metî.

CENTRE THERMAL DES DOMES ✆ 0 800 30 00 63. *www.destinationvichy.com.* Combines effective therapeutic cures Vichy-style with pleasurable getting-into-shape treatment, avoiding the more serious medical balneotherapy.

THERMES CALLOU 30, rue Callou ✆ 04 70 97 98 87. Inaugurated in 1990, this centre has state-of-the-art technology. Therapeutic treatment of arthritis, osteoporosis, rheumatism, diabetes, excess weight, gall-bladder and accident victims etc.

THERMES DE VICHY. *www.vichy-thermes.tm.fr. Open March-October.* Different options are on offer. 'Discovery' and 'Thermal' include the drinking cure and thermal treatment. 'Relaxation' gets you into shape with boiling baths and showers, aquatic gym and body-building.

Puy de Dôme

La Bourboule

This resort specialises in children with respiratory and skin disorders, and is an attractive and pleasant place to stay.

LES GRANDS THERMES Bd. Georges-Clémenceau ✆ 04 73 81 41 00. Ledru designed this fine example of spa architecture in 1877. You can visit the inside.

ETABLISSEMENTS THERMAUX. Opened in 1878. Today, 14,000 adults and children take the waters in its three centres, from February to October. Treatment lasts 21 days.

Mont-Dore

At the foot of the Puy de Sancy in the Dordogne Valley, 1,050m above sea-level, this is not only a spa village, but also a rural tourism and winter sports resort (glide).

THERMES 1, place du Panthéon ✆ 04 73 65 05 10. *Open May-October. Guided tours every hour, May-October: 2.30pm-5.30pm. October-April: 11am-3pm by appointment. Admission 3 €. Open Monday-Saturday: 2pm-5pm.* Already well-known in Gallo-Roman times (Roman bath remains were found under the current building), the benefits of these waters were rediscovered in the 19thc. Siliceous, rich in carbon dioxide and gas, they leave the lava seams inside the centre at 38-44°C. Respiratory and rheumatic complaints are treated with inhalations, drinks, sprays, baths and subcutaneous gas injections. If you just want to get back into shape, there are 1, 3 or 6-day relaxation cures. Tourists can visit the centre, built between 1817 and 1823, later extended and transformed in Neo-Byzantine style. In the waiting hall, there are painted vaults on Vosges sandstone columns, decorated with mosaics. Niches with pediments contain remains from classical antiquity. More mosaics can be seen in the Spring Hall, where the furniture is in ceramic.

VOLCANS D'AUVERGNE

The first eruptions began 56 million years ago, shaping the Auvergne landscape little by little. Europe's biggest volcano took on its present form 6 or 8 million years ago. Compared with this, the Puy-de-Dome is a youngster, appearing only 13,000 years ago. There have been Stromboli-type eruptions in Auvergne, with lava flow; Pelean eruptions with viscous lava forming burning clouds; explosions of strong gas spraying the rock; and phreatomagmatic eruptions where magma combines with water to form lakes, quite often seen in the region.

Chaîne des Puys

The Puys range is 45km long and 4km wide. It is made up of 90 volcanos.

Sites: Puy de Dome, Puys de La Vache and de Lassolas, Gour de Tazenat, Puys des Gouttes and Chopine, Puy Sarcouy, Chaudefour Valley, Puy de Pariou, Royat.

Le Vélay

One single volcano made up of 3 regions, including the Puy basin. The lava has accumulated in domes.

Sites: Saint Michel d'Aiguilhe rock in the Puy, Corneille rock in the same town, Espaly, Denise volcano, Maars du Bouchet, Costaros and de la Sauvetat, Gerbier des Joncs, Mezenc, Meygal, Lake Saint-Front, Lake Issarles.

Monts du Cantal

They form a huge volcano of 2,500 sq.km., rising to 1,854m at the Plomb du Cantal.

Sites: Plomb du Cantal, Puy Mary, La Cère Valley, Mondailles Valley, Falgoux Valley, Pas de Peyrol.

Monts Dore

One of the country's most varied volcanic regions, covering 600 sq.km and reaching 1,886m with the Puy de Sancy.

Sites: Puy de Sancy, Tuilères and Sanadoire Rocks, la Bourboule, Mont Dore, Rochefort-Montagne, Lake Chambon, Saignes. Monton, Chaudes-Aigues, Bort les Orgues.

PARC DES VOLCANS D'AUVERGNE Montlosier - AYDAT ✆ 04 73 65 64 00. Created in 1977, covering the Puys range, Monts Dore, Cezallier, Monts du Cantal and Artense plateau. The headquarters are in the Chateau de Montlosier at Aydat, at the foot of the Puys de la Vache and Lassolas; they house a permanent exhibition on volcanos. The various park centres (maisons) deal with different environmental aspects: information centre at the top of the Puy de Dome; Volvic stone centre at Volvic, cheese at Egliseneuve d'Entraigues, peat bogs at Saint-Alyre-les-Montagne, water and fishing at Besse, flowers at Orcival, burronnier at Lavaissiere, fauna at Murat and Thiezac thatch.

VULCANIA 'PARC EUROPEEN DU VOLCANISME' Route de Mazayes - SAINT-OURS-LES-ROCHES ✆ 04 73 19 70 00. *www.vulcania.com. Open 22 March-8 October 2006. Admission: adult 19.50 €. Call 08 20 82 78 28 to book by phone.* Lava flow was hollowed out to build this 57ha. complex, designed by the Austrian architect Hans Hollein, and constructed with natural materials so as not to spoil the site. The first section, reached by way of a lava tunnel, simulates an earthquake, with rumblings and eruption. You then travel 'to the centre of the earth', learn the history of the universe and the volcanos, which leads you to section two. Different types of volcano are reconstructed and explained here, with post-eruption landscapes. Mythology and religion are touched on in the third section dealing with legends. Next comes the show: 400 spectators can watch Pierre Villemin's film on active volcanos. Another 3-D film is shown in the gallery, telling how the region was shaped. Finally, you come to the volcanic garden with its luxuriant plants. Outside circuits have been set up; a new botanic path and another called 'under the landscape'. This year, you should also be able to walk on Martian volcanos.

VOLCAN DE LEMPTEGY RD941 ✆ 04 73 62 23 25. *www.auvergne-volcan.com. Open February holidays-November (July & August: 9.30am-6pm).* Group bookings all year. See inside a volcano, on foot or in a little train. A typical Auvergne meal is followed by an evening show in June, July and August. Restaurant for groups and individuals.

The Mont-Dore

FOOD AND DRINK

The Auvergne is more than a big cheese platter. This region rich in pasture, and with a few vineyards, has other specialities.

Meat and poultry

Five of Auvergne's beef products have red quality labels: the charolais (Bourbonnais), aubrac (centre and south east Massif Central), salers (Cantal), Hauts Plateaux beef, predominantly charolais (Haute-Loire) and Mezenc fin gras, from two-year-old animals bred on the high Mezenc plateaux.

Puy-en-Velay green lentils

Grown in the region since Gallo-Roman times, from a plant of Mediterranean origin. The microclimate on the high Velay plateaux accelerates the lentil's growth in its red volcanic soil. It is sown in March or April, when the soil temperature is above 5°C, and picked from 1 August to 15 September at 600-1,200m above sea-level; 83,000 quintals are harvested on 5,200 ha. The first dried vegetable to gain an AOC (1996), this green lentil has a fine skin and is never floury, but rather creamy to eat. Four companies produce the sorted, ready-to-cook lentils: the oldest dates back to 1819.

COOPERATIVE DES PRODUCTEURS DE CEREALES ET LENTILLES VERTES DE LA HAUTE-LOIRE La Chartreuse - BRIVES-CHARENSAC ✆ 04 71 04 50 40. The Puy green lentil is sorted, conditioned and marketed in this cooperative.

LA VERTE CONFRERIE DE LA LENTILLE VERTE DU PUY ✆ 04 71 02 99 22

Mineral waters

Auvergne is world-famous for its mineral water. The best-known are from Vichy, Volvic, Vic-le-Comte (Sainte-Marguerite) Châteauneuf and Chateldon. Others are bottled at Mont Dore, in Arviegue. These waters pick up minerals, trace elements and gas on their journey from the depths of the earth to the surface, giving them therapeutic virtues. There are two kinds: still water, like Volvic, and sparkling, either bottled (Saint-Yorre, Vichy, Sainte-Marguerite) or used in thermal treatment. For the latter, they must come out of the ground at a minimum teperature of 35°C, and have a high mineral content with a lot of bicarbonate, calcium and sodium. Chaude-Aigues spring reaches 82 degrees C, while Bourboule is never warmer than 57. All the thermal springs are on faults around the Limagne or at volcanic massif level; there are about 20 of them.

EAUX MINERALES GAZEUSES DE SAINTE-MARGUERITE Thermes de Saint-Maurice-sur-Allier - VIC-LE-COMTE ✆ 04 73 39 99 80

SCBV 70, ave. des Sources - VICHY ✆ 04 70 59 50 00. (Societe Commerciale des eaux minerales du Bassin de Vichy).

SOCIETE DES EAUX DE VOLVIC Le Chancet ✆ 04 73 64 51 24. *Open late March-early November. Admission free. Discover the geology and characteristics of Volvic mineral water at the information centre.*

Cheese

Bleu d'Auvergne

Created in the mid-19thc, this cheese is made in the Cantal, Puy-de-Dome and Haute-Loire. It has a powerful taste, and a crust with green and blue tints. Local brands exist: bleu de Thiezac, Laqueuille, Costaros, Loudes, Langeac, des Cayres and du Velay. It is delicious with nut-oil salad, lentils and rib steaks.

Cantal

Made in its own department, but also in northern Puy-de-Dome, southern Lozere and Aveyron. It gained its AOC in 1956, and used to be made by *buronniers* in the summer pastures. There is cantal jeune (matured 1-2 months, grey-white crust, milky taste) cantal entre-deux (matured 2-6 months, golden lumps on the crust, fuller flavour) and cantal vieux (matured for over 6 months, thick crust scattered with red and orange tints). This cheese goes well with light and fruity wines, walnuts, hazlenuts, grapes and apples, and suits salads, fondues and gratins.

Salers

Made with full, unpasteurised milk between April and November, when the cows go to grass. It got an AOC in 1979, reinforced in 2000. From three months' to 2 years' maturing is required.

La fourme d'Ambert

Made all over the Puy-de-Dome, and in the Loire (fourme de Montbrison). This cheese was already eaten in the 8thc; some insist the Gallic druids knew it. It was given its AOC in 1972. The crust is yellowish, with red and orange stains, and it is traditionally eaten in fine slices or strips, or with a teaspoon. It goes with sweet white wines or fruity reds, and can be eaten with potatoes, cauliflower, pancakes, chicory salads, rabbit and duck breasts, as well as pears and grapes.

Saint-Nectaire

Produced on the Mont-Dore volcanic massifs, in the Puy-de-Dome and the Cantal, this is the best-selling AOC cheese in France. It has quite a firm texture, and is matured on straw; the best are made in August. Try it with a light, fruity red wine, in omelettes and tarts.

The dairy saint-nectaire, which dates back to 1964, is matured for a shorter time.

COOPERATIVE FROMAGERE DU SAINT-NECTAIRE La Ville Tour - BESSE ET SAINT-ANASTAISE ✆ 04 73 79 51 29

ACADEMIE DE LA FOURME D'AMBERT Chambre d'Agriculture et d'Industrie - 4, place de l'Hôtel de Ville ✆ 04 73 82 01 55

COOPERATIVE LAITIERE DE VALUEJOLS Le Bourg ✆ 04 71 73 26 33. This cooperative is open every morning from 11am-12 noon, and specialises in transforming unpasteurised milk cheeses like cantal or tomme.

FROMAGERIE DE LA GENETTE ZA Les Gournets ✆ 04 73 95 40 27. Shop open Monday-Saturday: 8am-1pm. Most Auvergne cheeses are here: tommes, briques, fourmes made on-site, farm-made Saint-Nectaire, bleu d'Auvergne, and goat's cheese, as well as other local produce.

FROMAGERIE JEAN COSTE Le Martinet - Route d'Albepierre - MURAT ✆ 04 71 20 01 71. This cheese dairy has been making cantal, saint-nectaire, bleu d'Auvergne, fourme d'Ambert and laguiole for 60 years.

SOCIETE FROMAGERE DU LIVRADOIS Les Perrines - FOURNOLS - ✆ 04 73 74 60 71. Set up by Jean Thuaire in 1949, this family business operates at different altitudes (700-1,394m: Allanche, Fournols and Tauves). It makes AOC fourme d'Ambert and Montbrison, bleu d'Auvergne; the mountain cheeses brique, tomme, fournols and Le Chabrol raclette; Saint-Nectaire fermiers, salers and cantal. Dispatched throughout France and Europe.

Salaisons (dried and salted pork)

Typically U-shaped, Auvergne's saucissons and saucisses sèches are floury or ash-grey on the outside, dry and spicy inside. They are made from pure pork: the natural casing is filled with a mixture of lean pork meat (80-90%), fat, salt, salpetre, herbs and spices, sometimes other ingredients like wine, pepper or walnut. Having been drained and incubated for 50-72 hours at 24°C maximum, they are dried for 3-6 weeks. They should be flexible, with an ivory bloom, and must be kept in a dry place at 15-18°C.

Country ham

Made from a dried and salted pork thigh, matured for at least 7 months in cellars or drying-sheds. Keep it in the bottom of the fridge, or wrapped in a cloth if whole. It goes perfectly with salads, onion, cabbage, lentils, pears, figs, walnuts and mushrooms.

SALAISONS DU VAL D'ALLIER ZI Chambare - LANGEAC ✆ 04 71 77 17 60. Auvergne saucisses sèches and saucissons secs, dried country ham.

SOUCHON D'AUVERGNE La Croix de l'Arbre - Saint-Maurice-de-Lignon - YSSINGEAUX. Auvergne saucissons secs and saucisses sèches, made by traditional methods since 1948.

SALAISON POLETTE ET CIE Champs Saint-Pierre - TEILHEDE ✆ 04 73 64 31 31. Auvergne saucissons secs and saucisses sèches.

Cheese

Hotels & Restaurants

ALLIER

Bourbon-L'Archambault

GRAND HOTEL MONTESPAN TALLEYRAND* Place des Thermes © 04 70 67 00 24.** *Website: www.hotel-montespan.com. Close late October-late March. 40 rooms from 54 € to 105 € (sleeps 4). Suites 120 € (junior, sleeps 2) 148 € and 160 € 5 large suite, sleeps 2-4). Breakfast 9.60 €. Full board from 58.50 € to 70 € per person. Set menus from 20 € to 45 €. Seminar room, fitness centre, car park and garage, swimming pool. Pets accepted.* Three pretty 16th and 17thc. buildings are linked directly to the spa, with a formal interior garden to daydream in, around the castle ruins. The hotel also has a swimming pool in a fabulous setting, hot baths, a fitness and muscle-stretching centre, lounge, and bar with a fireplace. The rooms range from 30 to 60 sqm. in size, or you can have a suite for greater comfort, or a family apartment with lounge corner, TV, direct phone line and bathroom. In the Talleyrand restaurant, Marcel Livertout invites you to discover his gastronomic cooking in the purest Bourbonnais tradition, with all the natural flavours preserved: smoked duck breast, Charolais beef cuts, regional cheeses and apple and raspberry granité with praline ice-cream; marvellous!

Charroux

LA FERME Saint-Sébastien Chemin de Bourion © 04 70 56 88 83 *Fax 04 70 56 86 66. Set menus from 22 € to 60 €, à la carte 50 €. Closed Monday and Tuesday (except in July and August, Monday only) first 3 weeks in January, last week in June and last week in September.* Everything is home made at Valérie and Philippe Charvet's and they like you to know it. They have been settled in this Bourbonnais farmhouse in one of France's most beautiful villages for about 12 years, and have transformed it into a genuine gastronomic restaurant, where you feel at home and among friends. No easy feat, especially when it comes to keeping up team motivation and customer levels at the end of the season, when villages such as this seem to be miles from anywhere. Philippe welcomes you warmly in his double role as dining room manager and wine-waiter (the cellar is now one of the region's most specialized) while Valérie his wife does the cooking, transformed by her three years with Reine Sammut (La Fénière at Lourmarin in the late 80s-early 90s). Her approach is cheerful and generous, witness the ' three foie gras' with Beaumes de Venise jelly and corn bread, grilled Dublin Bay prawns and gambas, asparagus risotto and asparagus in cappuccino and fine slices, casseroled veal chops with vegetable juices, and macaroon nature stuffed with mascarpone cream, tiramisu ice-cream and coffee sauce. Charroux may boast a population of only 356, but it would stand out on a map of France's Best Places to Eat.

Lapalisse

HOTEL GALLAND * 20, place de la République © 04 70 99 07 21.** *Closed Sunday evening and Monday, except in July and August. Restaurant closed during the same periods, Sunday evening in low season and Monday. 8 rooms from 45 € to 58 €. Breakfast 7 €. Set menus from 24 € to 48 €. A la carte. Children's menu 9 €. Car park. Pets accepted.* The Hotel Galland offers you comfort in a calm setting. The rooms are light, pretty and nicely personalized, overlooking a peaceful square. Jean-Marie Duparc offers an excellent bourgeois *cuisine* that he is always seeking to improve, with even better produce and flavours. His pan-fried duck foie gras escalope rolled in gingerbread crumbs and roast figs with verjus (juice pressed from unripe grapes) is a house classic. Other interesting recipes are the roast Dublin Bay prawns in an olive oil emulsion, sliced Charolais beef in saint-pourçin sediment and the impressive dessert trolley. Exceptionally good service and a very friendly welcome. Unforgettable.

Montaigu-le-Blin

AUBERGE DES TUREAUX Le Bourg © 04 70 43 74 66 *Open from 8am-9pm. Closed Sunday evening, Monday and Tuesday evening, open for bookings only in winter. Set menu of the day 11 €. Set menus 21 €, 25 € and 36 €.* The Auberge des Tureaux run by Didier Neboud provides a warm welcome all year round. You find a friendly, air-conditioned setting decorated in soft colours, and a sophisticated cuisine which includes fresh salmon escalopes with tarragon, Charolais beef, veal sweetbreads, boned quails with grapes and pan-cooked queen scallops with paprika. The wine list offers an interesting choice, and the service is as good as the food. All in all, the sort of place you'll be recommending to friends.

Montluçon

LE GRENIER A SEL *** **10, rue Sainte-Anne et Place des Toiles ✆ 04 70 05 53 79.** *Website: www.legrenierasel.com. 7 rooms from 75 € to 130 €. Breakfast 9 €. Closed Sunday evening, and Monday, except public holidays. Closed Saturday lunchtime in low season. Restaurant closed Monday lunchtime in July and August. Set menus 21.50 € to 65 €, children's menu 13 €.* Hotel-restaurant housed in a 15th and 16thc. bourgeoise residence, in the heart of the medieval city. Garden, terrace and closed car park. The rooms are elegant and spacious, each with its own personality. Carefully-chosen, sophisticated furniture and decor, big, comfortable bathrooms. The restaurant has three dining rooms, where residents can enjoy chef Jacky Morlon's regional cuisine: a little salad from the market garden with chanterelles and sweet and sour seasoning, or a lobster *bohémienne* with Dublin Bay prawns, foie gras and bouillabaisse jelly in citrus fruits, then a farm-bred duck *à la duchambais* or a venison tart with pepper sauce, local cheeses and assortment of chocolate desserts. The wine list is very good. Not to be missed!

Moulins

HOTEL DE PARIS – JACQUEMART *** **21, rue de Paris ✆ 04 70 44 00 58** *Website: www.hoteldeparis-moulins.com Open all year. 27 rooms and 4 suites from 64 € to 122 €. Breakfast 10 €. Pets accepted. Terrace. Swimming pool. Close private garage. Flower garden.* This is a beautiful bourgeoise house, with luxurious, romantic rooms. Please note that the Hotel de Paris stopped running a restaurant in late October 2005, and now only serves breakfast.

RESTAURANT DES COURS 36, cours Jean-Jaurès ✆ 04 70 44 25 66. *Website: www.restaurant-des-cours.com. Set menus from 20 € to 50 €.* Three prettily decorated dining rooms provide 20 place settings among the flowers, where you can taste, enjoy and stock up on gourmet pleasures. New chef Hervé Courtais, trained by Jacky Morlon at the Grenier à Sel in Montluçon, and owner Patrick Bourhy intend to change the Restaurant des Cours' culinary philosophy, by orientating it towards regional produce. Hervé cooks by the book, producing a flavoursome duck foie gras terrine, with marinated mixed dried fruits, or a quail rissole and mushroom duxelles (chopped with shallots) in a Saint-Pourçain wine sauce. The region's best vintages are on the wine list. We promise you won't be disappointed!

Vichy

L'ALAMBIC 8, rue Nicolas-Larbaud ✆ 04 70 59 12 71. *Closed during February school holidays and last 3 weeks in August. Closed Sunday evening, Monday and Tuesday. Set menus from 26 € to 45 €, children's menu 14 €. A la carte.* Jean-Jacques Barbot knows how to mix and match his palette of genuine flavours. Fresh produce selected at the local market makes for tasty and delicate dishes. A few appetisers to start with, then a duck foie gras in its cloth with stewed dried fruit sweet-and-sour style, or roast Dublin Bay prawn tails served hot-and-cold with a lentil and grilled pine kernel salad and tomato cream with carvi seeds, followed by bass filet browned in the oven, and rolled in brioche crumbs, or a steamed farm chicken supreme stuffed with herbs. Then the cheeseboard, and dark chocolate mousse quenelles with red fruit coulis or shortbread tart with pears and almonds. Delicious! The attractive wine list comes in bottles and half-bottles. Service well up to standard.

LES CELESTINS ** 111, boulevard des Etats-Unis ✆ 04 70 30 82 00.** *131 rooms from 170 € to 245 €, and suites. Under-12s free if in their parents' room. Breakfast 20 €. Pets 16 €. Get into shape prices half-board from (double)1,098 € to 1,308 € for 6 days, or golf from (double) 1,086 € to 1,416 € for 6 days. Air-conditioning, cable TV, personal safe, mini-bar, 2 restaurants. Sauna, hammam and jacuzzi. Swimming pool and solarium. Covered parking with guardian, 12 € per day. Set menu 23.50 € for the bistrot, + carte. Menu marché 42 €, menu terroir 56 €, menu dégustation 99 € for the Jardins de l'Empereur. Children's menu (5-12s) 16 €. 12 air-conditioned meeting rooms. Disabled access.* The Sofitel is located on the edge of the Allier lake, facing the prestigious golf course, and right in the heart of town and the Napoleon III parks. It has a direct link to Vichy Les Célestins spa. The rooms are elegantly decorated, warm and spacious with air-conditioning. The bathrooms all have hairdryers and separate WC. There are two restaurants to satisfy all your tastes, whether you're after a gourmet meal or something simpler. The Bistrot des Célestins invites you to savour regional cooking, while Les Jardins de l'Empereur restaurant, run by chef Pierre-Yves Lorgeoux, and opening onto the Napoleon III parks, offers more sophisticated *cuisine*, or balanced health food for those taking the cure. You can also discover Le Bleu Note piano bar, a reading room and French billiards, and a heated panoramic pool and solarium terrace on the seventh floor.

JACQUES DECORET 7 avenue de Gramont ✆ 04 70 97 65 06 *Fax 04 70 97 65 06. Website: www.jacquesdecoret.com Set menus from 40 € to 95 €, a la carte 75 €. Closed Tuesday, Wednesday, 3 weeks during February school holidays and 3 weeks in July and August.* These days, Jacques Decoret is one of the most talked-about chefs. He is considered to be French gastronomy's nicest troublemaker, inventive, innovative and talented. It's hard to believe that one of France's most modern and exciting cuisines is lurking half-hidden down a street totally devoid of charm, in a soulless quarter of Vichy. Jacques Decoret is passionate about culinary technique (rather too much, sometimes) and every dish can surprise you. Grilled *lisette* (mackerel) with juniper berries and fresh anchovies, fresh, lightly salted Concarneau cod, Miéral pigeon cooked two ways, pan-cooked saddle of Auvergne rabbit...the descriptions are a lot simpler than the impression left on your tastebuds! The splendid and highly original dessert called 'potato dynamite' just about sums it up.

CANTAL

Aurillac

GRAND HOTEL DE BORDEAUX* 2, avenue de la République ✆ 04 71 48 01 84.** *Open all year. 33 rooms from 54 €, with shower. 120 €, prestige rooms. Breakfast buffet 10 €.* This hotel is one of the best in town, house in a beautiful 1850s building with its classic rooms, redecorated in 2005. The majority are air-conditioned, and some even have a jacuzzi. The hotel has no restaurant, but can provide a TV meal on a tray served in the rooms. Breakfast can also be served in your room for the same price. Excellent coffee. Excellent welcome from Jacky, a fixture for the last 18 years.

LES QUATRE SAISONS 10, rue Champeil ✆ 04 71 64 85 38. *Closed Sunday evening and Monday. Set menu from 19 € to 35.50 €, à la carte.* With its big aquarium and pale blue walls, this restaurant provides a warm and pleasant setting. The food is presented with care, and looks as good as it tastes; the main regional dishes are given an original and varied presentation. The beef fillet with a morel coulis, and the suckling veal medallion with a cepe coulis are pure marvels, as are the home made desserts; the raspberry gratin with sabayon is simply yummy. What more can we say, except that the discreet and considerate service is up to the same standard as the restaurant and its cuisine. Don't delay - but book first!

Saint-Flour

LE NAUTILUS HOTEL DES MESSAGERIES ** *23, avenue Charles-De-Gaulle ✆ 04 71 60 11 36. Fax: 04 71 60 46 79. Website: www.hotel-messageries.com Closed from 15 October to Easter. Rooms from 45 € to 71 €, and a suite at 97 €. Set menus from 16 € to 55 €.* This hotel has a high reputation in the region, due to its Toque d'Auvergne chef. Le Nautilus is, of course, mainly a fish restaurant, with seaside decoration (including an anchor) in shades of rose. The hotel is comfortable, and the cooking subtle and original. A well-earned reputation, we conclude, and a real pleasure for the customers.

Salers

LE BAILLIAGE * Rue Notre-Dame ✆ 04 71 40 71 95.** *Fax: 04 71 40 74 90. Website: www.salers-hotel-bailliage.com Rooms from 49 € in the annex, and from 55 € to 80 € in the hotel itself. 2 seawater therapy and mountain suites 130 €. Set menus from 14 € to 40 €. Car park. Pool.* You are warmly welcomed in this beautiful and imposing building, a little away from the village. The hotel, which won the Logis de France first prize in 2001, offers very comfortable rooms and the use of a lounge with a stone fireplace. The restaurant has a terrace, and a wide bay window overlooking the park, and you will discover an excellent cuisine drawn from regional standards, with original compositions like the sumptuous pikeperch *fondant* with gentian, the marvellous pan-cooked lamb sweetbreads and snails, and the famous Salers beef fillet. Welcome and service well up to standard.

Vic-sur-Cère

BEAUSEJOUR ** 4, rue Basse ✆ 04 71 47 50 27. *Fax: 04 71 49 60 04. Open late May to 1 October. 35 rooms from 39 € to 62 €. Breakfast 5.80 € and 7 €. Private park, heated pool, car park.* The Beauséjour no longer has a restaurant - it closed last year - and the regulars will be disappointed. However, the hotel is still run by Annie and Alphonse Albouze (a fixture for 28 years) and the atmosphere is as warm and family-orientated as ever. The rooms are comfortably equipped, and the hotel itself is ideally located near the municipal parks, tennis courts, town swimming baths and shops.

Vitrac

AUBERGE DE LA TOMETTE * ✆ 04 71 64 70 94.** *Fax: 04 71 64 77 11. Website: www.auberge-la-tomette.com Open 1 April to 15 November. Set menus from 26 € to 40 €. Rooms from 72 € to 130 €.* This inn, planted in the heart of a chestnut grove, has lots of charm. The hotel is especially pleasant, set in a big, flower-filled garden overlooking the countryside, and its rooms are very comfortable, though a little too modern for our taste. Try to book yours in the oldest part of the inn. The cooking is simply delicious, prepared with fresh local produce. Reading the menu makes your mouth water: chestnut grove salad with foie gras galantine, veal sweetbreads croustade with chanterelles, and pig's trotter and crépinettes (sausage meat in pork membrane) with chanterelles, for instance. A warm welcome adds to the culinary pleasure.

HAUTE-LOIRE

Alleyras

LE HAUT ALLIER Pont d'Alleyras ✆ 04 71 57 57 63 *Fax 04 71 57 57 99. Set menus from 30 € to 85 €, a la carte 65 €. Closed Sunday evening, Monday, Tuesday lunchtime and mid-November to mid-March.* Alleyras? Without a detailed map or a good GPS you'll have trouble sighting this tiny village 30km from the Puy - and there's no mobile phone network! Once you've found it, though, your efforts will be amply rewarded in the hotel-restaurant, entirely rebuilt in 1985 and nestling in the Allier gorges. Total peace and quiet (in low season, you can count an hour between one car going past the hotel, and the next) a very kind welcome from Michèle Brun, lady of the house and rarely flustered, and a charming and well-kept setting. Philippe Brun in the kitchen trained in several prestigious Parisian establishments, before following Régis Marcon as a leader of Haute-Loire gastronomy. He is an expert at composing harmonies: crayfish tails *marinière* thai-style, tapioca balls and *brunoise* (finely-chopped vegetables) in three colours, sweetbread piccata (small thin escalopes), *chénopode Bon Henri* (wild spinach) ravioli, slightly acid tomato, bass rubbed in mountain ham salt, on a Corrent sediment, saddle of local lamb, couscous juice, tender bulgur wheat and small vegetables, and Vellavia beer sorbet, apples in a rose-window and caramelised compote. This cuisine really sets off its region, and it would be a crime not to have a second innings, so meanwhile, why not take advantage of one of the spacious rooms upstairs?

La Chaise-Dieu

HOTEL DE L'ECHO ** Place de l'Echo ✆ 04 71 00 00 45. *Open from Easter to mid-November. Closed Wednesday in low season. Rooms from 45 € to 68 €. Set menus from 16.50 € to 58 €. A la carte.* Located in the Place de l'Echo, this hotel of the same name is embedded in the Abbey. The cooking is honest and not at all disappointing: foie gras, sole, crayfish and truffles are all well cooked and presented, in the hushed atmosphere of a pleasant setting. In summer, gourmets can eat on the beautiful terrace. Choose a room overlooking the cloister, if you can.

Le Puy-en-Velay

FRANÇOIS GAGNAIRE 4 avenue Clément-Charbonnier ✆ 04 71 02 75 55 *Fax 04 71 02 18 72. Website: www.francois-gagnaire-restaurant.com Set menus from 23 € to 75 €, à la carte 60 €. Closed Sunday evening (and lunchtime in summer) Monday, Tuesday lunchtime (in low season) from1-12*

January and first fortnight in November. The other Gagnaire, François, 38 ans, has managed to carve out a place for himself in the great Pierre's shadow (they worked together for 2 years in Saint Etienne, and two others in Paris). After a prestigious career (two years with Chapel as chef de partie, Mionnay, the Imperial Palace in Annecy, two years as second at the Tour Rose in Lyon and then second with Guy Lassausaie at Chasselay) he fixed himself the aim of becoming chef-owner before the age of 35, won his bet (just) and finally managed to establish his 'first name' after 3 years, thanks to a cheerful, updated regional *cuisine*: foie gras civet and grapes served *en cocotte* with aromatic herbs, foie gras de canard poached whole in consommé with autumn truffles, roast sturgeon, its stock in emulsion flavoured with arabica, 'home-made' pike mousse with parsnip purée and pan-fried cepes, lamb knuckle-joint conserved with orange peel and coriander, Cevennes crique (potato galette) with shallots and cepes. The desserts are delicious and creative too, including a variation on the traditional opera cake, panna cotta with Grand Marnier, sweet dumpling candied with sweet spices and Genoa bread with cocoa. One of the finest places to eat in Auvergne.

TOURNAYRE 12, rue Chênebouterie ✆ 04 71 09 58 94. *Website: www.restaurant-tournayre.com Closed Sunday evening, Monday, Wednesday evening and in January. Set menus from 21 € to 65 €.* The Hotel d'Orvy, with its superb 16thc. ceiling provides a sophisticated setting, in which Eric and Ludivine Tournayre welcome you warmly. The cooking is delicate, with regional influences: home-made foie gras, salmon on a bed of green lentils and verbena liqueur sweets all pay tribute to Velay. The pan-fried cepes starter is a classic, and the cheeseboard is well worth investigating. You will love the variety of flavours for dessert: orangettes, madeleines with green tea, and orange tart.

Saint-Bonnet-Le-Froid

AUBERGE ET CLOS DES CIMES ✆ 04 71 59 93 72 *Fax 04 71 59 93 40. Website: www.regismarcon.fr. Set menus from 96 € to 140 €, à la carte120 €. Closed Monday evening (in March, April, May, November and December), Tuesday, Wednesday and from mid-December to late March.* You can easily drive through this Velay village without realising that a great French chef is hiding in its midst. Régis Marcon was born here in Saint Bonnet half a century ago, and has since been an able ambassador for his village, chiefly by communicating his passion for mushrooms. Today, American and Japanese gourmets come to Saint Bonnet, and Régis smiles remembering the days when his restaurant was also a filling station, and he had to give ski-ing lessons to make ends meet. Last October he moved into a new building, 300m from the historic starting point. You now eat comfortably, in a splendid wood and stone setting, which sets off his luxurious yet rural cooking. The menu-*découverte* at 140 € is unbeatable in terms of value for money.

PUY-DE-DOME

Chamalières

LE RADIO 43 avenue Pierre-et-Marie-Curie ✆ 04 73 30 87 83 *Fax 04 73 36 42 44. Website: www.hotel-radio.fr. Set menus from 45 € to 89 €, à la carte 60 €. Closed Saturday lunchtime, Sunday, Monday lunchtime, 2-24 January, 7-15 August and 30 October-6 November.* This famous station on the Clermont gastronomic wavelength has benefited from Frédéric Coursol's talents since he took over from Michel Mioche ten years ago. At barely 30, he is a born innovator, full of good ideas, with a great respect for this magnificent Art Deco hotel built on the theme of radio. Chamalières is perhaps not France's trendiest site, but the cooking is every bit as good as what you taste in Paris. Scallops in ceviche (citrus juice marinade), citrus fruits, San Maurizzio olive oil, dory rolled in bulghur wheat, shellfish *bonbon* (small spiced fritter) with pesto, braised veal sweetbreads and liver, souffléd tome (local cheese) pancake, juice with a herb decoction, and salted caramel tart, milk ice cream and opaline choco-milk feature on the menu. The dining room is delightfully retro, and the cellar has over 1500 recommended wines brilliantly explained by Nicolas Decoulange. A very attractive place to eat.

Châtelguyon

HOTEL REGENCE 31, avenue des Etats-Unis ✆ 04 73 86 02 60.** *Websites: www.hotel-regence-central.com and info@hotel-regence-central.com. Logis de France 2 fireplaces. Open March-late December except for a week in October. 27 rooms with bath, shower and WC, direct phone line. Single room 41 €, double 48 €. All-in spa treatment prices.* English and Spanish spoken. Weddings, seminars. Special overnight rates for sales reps. Children's club and menu. Lift, garage, free closed car park, terrace, garden. This hotel is only 50m from the thermal park, and has plenty of cachet with its extensive, elegant salons and period furniture. Art buffs may be interested in their hostess' paintings, which can also be viewed on the website www.jacqueline-porte.com. A free, private shuttle takes you to and from the spa treatment centre according to your timetable. The owner also offers guided tours of Saint Anne Church.

SPLENDID HOTEL* 5-7, rue d'Angleterre ✆ 04 73 86 04 80.** *Website: www.splendid-resort.com Closed from 17 December to 1 January. 75 rooms with terrace and loggia, Canal +, from 53 € to 110 €. Set menus from 16 € to 60 €. Study days, heated swimming pool open in high season, Le Bel Ami restaurant (seats 250) overnight break from 60 €, direct telephone line, seminars.* This beautiful, late 19thc. hoouse has kept its character. There is a certain charm in its old architecture, so unlike our contemporary straight lines. The restaurant is named after a Guy de Maupassant story, and its setting is superb, all high ceilings and pillars. The cooking is traditional, from 14 €. Special all-in treatment prices are available for the Institut Bien-Etre (Well-Being Centre), either for one person or two.

Clermont-Ferrand

BRASSERIE DANIELE BATH Marché Saint-Pierre ✆ 04 73 31 23 22. *Open Tuesday to Saturday. Set menus, à la carte. Terrace.* This opulent brasserie could do with a slight touch of renovation, but on the whole it is charming. You come in via the shady terrace, go down a small corridor full of wine crates, and finally arrive in the panelled dining room. Mme Bath Hersel welcomes you warmly; the cooking is in Pascal Delayre's capable hands. We recommend the unique aperitif, plant extracts with quince, bitter orange or hawthorn. The food is soberly presented to tease your tastebuds while you guess at the flavours: foie gras, pork cheeks, salmon, whole roast pigeon carved, beef steak, duck aiguillettes (thin strips of breast) and Canada lobster. You should end with the chocolate 'velvet', yummy. A take-away service is available too. For those who are interested, Mme Bath hand paints her own plates.

LE COMPTOIR DES SAVEURS 5, rue Sainte-Claire ✆ 04 73 37 10 31. *Open for lunch from Tuesday to Saturday, for dinner Friday and Saturday evening, take-away service from Tuesday to Thursday, 9am-6pm. Set menus lunchtime 21 €, evening 30 € and 40 €.* This is one of Clermont-Ferrand's recommended haute-cuisine restaurants. The front is very attractive, the decor inside mostly in wood, and the culinary quality excellent. There are two or three starters and main courses at your convenience, with adequate portions. Duck foie gras in its cloth, piquillo peppers stuffed with cod brandade (potato dish), rabbit and foie gras terrine, roast beef with pepper and ginger, roast pineapple and date cream with rhum are some typical examples that you can also taste at home, as take-away dishes. Delicious choice of wines. A cosy room upstairs seats small groups.

RESTAURANT EMMANUEL HODENCQ 6 place du Marché-Saint-Pierre ✆ 04 73 31 23 23. *Fax 04 73 31 36 00. Website: www.hodencq.com. Set menus from 35 € to 130 €, a la carte 80 €. Closed Sunday, Monday lunchtime and from 15 August to 1 September.* Emmanuel Hodencq may well work in a region with a strong culinary identity; he doesn't feel bound to copy his neighbours, by serving traditional Auvergne cooking updated just enough to widen the customer base. Second to the great Alain Passard in his Brussels period, and former chef at the Celadon, Emmanuel, with his charming wife Viviane, has chosen to make his mark with a different gastronomy: duck foie gras escalope pan-fried with Dublin Bay prawns, flavoured with citrus fruit, Dublin Bay prawn tournedos, meat juices, potato cakes, young wok-fried pigeon breast, juice thickened with soy, and red fruit jelly with fresh mint prove his point. Design setting, fine china, pleasant ambiant music and competent service.

Le Mont-Dore

RESTAURANT LE PUY-FERRAND Le Pied du Sancy ✆ 04 73 65 18 99.** Websites: www.hotel-puy-ferrand.com and info@hotel-puy-ferrand.com. Both hotel and restaurant are very reasonable, but the restaurant tends take priority. Your mouth will water on discovering these perfectly-cooked and sophisticated dishes: pounti, salted pork with lentils, cheeses and bilberry tart on the Auvergnat menu; foie gras bonbons with pig's trotters; cress salad; smoked salmon 'frivolities' and snails with cream and blue Auvergne cheese; roast pigeon with seasonal fruit and sweet potato cake; monkfish osso bucco with bacon and spring vegetables; loin of lamb in a gingerbread crust with mountain herb juice (delicious); cheeses, chocolate gourmandise dessert or cherry clafoutis (a kind of baked custard), with a sweet almond milkshake. The choice is yours.

Randan

HÔTEL DU CHÂTEAU DE MAULMONT Maulmont - Saint Priest Bramefant ✆ 04 70 59 03 45 *Fax 04 70 59 11 88. Website: www.chateau-maulmont.com. Set menus from 34 € to 80 €. Closed Sunday evening, Monday (lunchtimes only from mid-July to late August) and Tuesday lunchtime.* Stéphane Roesch didn't need much time to get this château back on the gastronomic rails. Five years after taking the proud residence over, Stéphane has a fine, classic cuisine, which manages to avoid the trap of over-sophistication called for by the setting. Duck foie gras ballotine from the Domaine de Limagne, fig compote, green Cancale oysters, black rice vinegar with shallots and rye bread, roast scallops on a citronella stick, sour apple with lemon, caramelised chicory, Dublin Bay prawns with pan-fried mushrooms and fennel 'foam', roast venison *à la plancha*, pepper sauce, banana kabab and mango 'aeroplane' and exotic fruit sorbet. Average service, cellar well stocked with burgundies and vallée-du-rhone.

Riom

LE FLAMBOYANT 21 bis, rue de l'Horloge ✆ 04 73 63 07 97. *Gastronomic restaurant. Terrace. Disabled access. Open all year from Tuesday to Sunday lunchtime in winter, and Tuesday evening to Sunday evening in July and August. Closed for a fortnight in September. Set menus 19 € lunchtime, seasonal dishes 25 € evenings, except Saturday, coup de coeur 31 €, eveil des sens (awakens the senses) 36 € and 46 €, 42 € for 3 courses, club affaires (business) 19 € to 25 €, tentation gourmande 50 € with 7 courses and 2 glasses of champagne. Wine by the glass 5 €.* If becoming a father made all chefs as calm and inventive, we would advise them to have plenty of children! Hervé Klein manages to mix flavours and surprises on a regular basis. The appetisers are followed by a series of excellent dishes that catch the eye, the nose and the tastebuds in that order: perfectly cooked quail, firm and smooth lobster tail, foie gras with lentils. Even the bread is home made. The setting is up to the same standards, with hand-decorated plates by Elisabeth Monroy adding a colourful touch. Good advice is to be had from the waiter, who knows the good local restaurants and likes to share his love of fine *cuisine* and wine. in summer, you can enjoy the terrace, beside the fountain.

Thiers

L'AIGLE D'OR 8, rue Lyon ✆ 04 73 80 00 50.** *Website: www.aigle-dor.frst. Open all year, restaurant closed Saturday lunchtime and Monday lunchtime in July and August, in low season, Friday evening,*

Saturday lunchtime, Sunday evening, Monday lunchtime. Annual closing last three weeks in November, last week in February and first week in March. 17 rooms from 45 € to 70 €, +10 € per person supplement for a triple room. Overnight break 55 €. Breakfast 6 €. Meeting room 45 sqm. with video projector and broadband connection. Set menu of the day 12 € (weekday lunchtimes), 15 € and 24 €. A la carte. Children's menu 8 €. Pets accepted. Free car park. The Aigle d'Or was created in 1836, and named after Napoleon's passage on the road in front of the hotel. It nestles at the top of the medieval city of Thiers, near the town centre, and is a relaxing place to stay, with comfortable, renovated rooms, all equipped with bathrooms (bath or shower), direct phone line and TV. The restaurant menus are named after famous guests - Balzac, George Sand - who tasted the kidneys in mustard sauce à l'ancienne, and frog's legs with garlic and parsley butter. Seasonal menu often renewed.

Volvic

AU CHAUDRON GOURMAND 6, route de la Nugere–Le Cratère ✆ 04 73 33 57 46. *Website: www.auchaudrongourmand.com Open 7 days a week, except Sunday evening, from Monday to Friday, 6.30am-6pm, Saturday and Sunday 10am-9pm. Dish of the day: 5.50 €, set menu of the day 11 €, express et pachade 9 € truffade 14 €, chaudron 16 €, gourmand 18.50 €, children's 7 €.* Lively, original with a folksy atmosphere. The chef is a woman, clever at resurrecting bygone flavours, which surprises certain customers, and warms the hearts of others who are instantly carried back to childhood. Bourriols - galettes made with three types of flour - omelettes, farinettes - pancakes cooked at the same time as the ingredients - pain perdu (bread pudding) the old-fashioned way, with gingerbread, accompany more classic dishes. Noisy lunchtime ambiance, more hushed and sophisticated in the evening. When you hear the famous 'Allo!' to call over the chef, you'll understand that life is well worth sharing over a simple and tasty dish.

View of Puy of Lassolas

Burgundy

Yonne river in Joigny

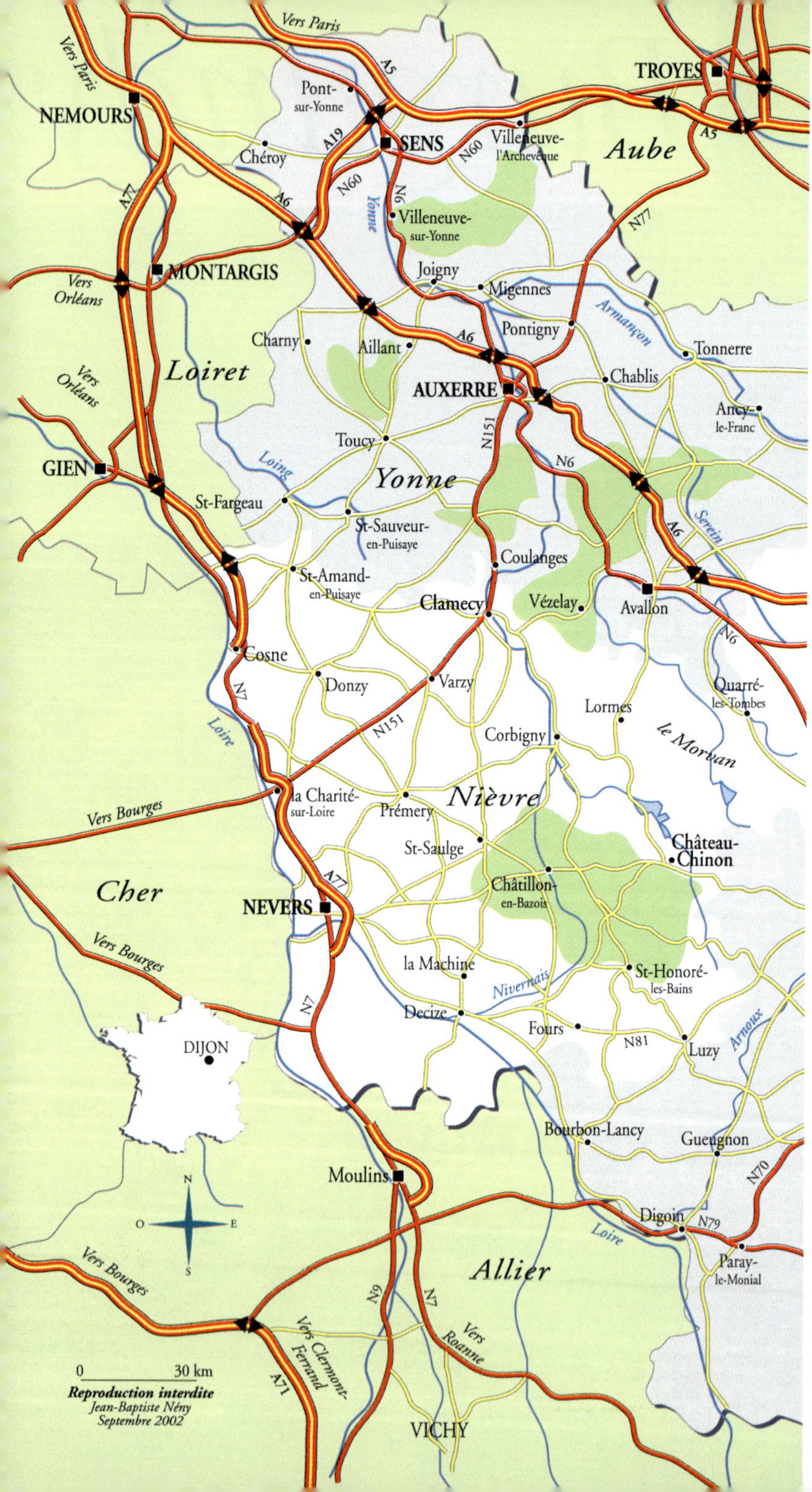

Vers Paris
Vers Paris
NEMOURS
Pont-sur-Yonne
A5
TROYES
SENS
Villeneuve-l'Archevêque
Aube
A5
Chéroy
A19
N60
N60
A77
A6
N6
Yonne
Villeneuve-sur-Yonne
N77
MONTARGIS
Vers Orléans
Joigny
Migennes
Armançon
Pontigny
Charny
Aillant
A6
Tonnerre
Loiret
Vers Orléans
AUXERRE
Chablis
Ancy-le-Franc
N151
Toucy
GIEN
Loing
Yonne
N6
St-Fargeau
St-Sauveur-en-Puisaye
A6
Serein
Coulanges
St-Amand-en-Puisaye
Clamecy
Vézelay
Avallon
N6
Cosne
Donzy
Varzy
Quarré-les-Tombes
N7
Lormes
Loire
N151
Corbigny
le Morvan
Vers Bourges
la Charité-sur-Loire
Prémery
Nièvre
Château-Chinon
St-Saulge
Cher
A77
NEVERS
Châtillon-en-Bazois
Vers Bourges
la Machine
St-Honoré-les-Bains
Nivernais
N7
Decize
Fours
N81
Luzy
Arroux
DIJON
Bourbon-Lancy
Gueugnon
N70
Moulins
N
O
E
S
Digoin
N79
Loire
Paray-le-Monial
Vers Bourges
Allier
N9
N7
Vers Clermont-Ferrand
Vers Roanne
A71
0
30 km
Reproduction interdite
Jean-Baptiste Nény
Septembre 2002
VICHY

Burgundy
Motorway
Major road
Minor road
Haute-Marne
CHAUMONT
A31
LANGRES
Vers Vesoul
Montigny-sur-Aube
Châtillon-sur-Seine
Forêt de Châtillon
Recey
Laignes
Forêt du Grand Jailly-l'Essard et Rochefort
Seine
N71
Aignay-le-Duc
Selongey
Saône
Montbard
Abbaye de Fontenay
Venarey-les-Laumes
Bussy-Rabutin
Is-s.-Tille
Côte-d'Or
Semur-en-Auxois
N74
A31
Mirebeau-s.-Bèze
Haute-Saône
Bierre
Vitteaux
D70
St-Seine-l'Abbaye
N71
Prenois
Sombernon
Pontailler-sur-Saône
DIJON
A38
Marsannay-la-Côte
Gevrey-Chambertin
Clos de Vougeot
Nuits-St-Georges
Saulieu
Bourgogne
N5
Vers Besançon
A36
le Morvan
A6
Abbaye de Cîteaux
DOLE
Arnay-le-Duc
N176
Aloxe-Corton
A36
Archéodrome
Beaune
AUTUN
Meursault
Mercurey
A39
D978
Chagny
A6
Doubs
Verdun-sur-le-Doubs
N73
le Creusot
Givry
CHALON-SUR-SAÔNE
St-Germain-du-Bois
N80
Montchanin
Buxy
N70
Montceau-les-Mines
St-Gengoux-le-National
N6
Lons-le-Saunier
Louhans
Saône-et-Loire
Tournus
Jura
Cormatin
A39
Charolles
St-Bonnet-de-Joux
Grosne
A6
Saône
Cluny
N79
Matour
Vers Genève
Mâcon
A40
Ain
A40
Vers Lyon

AUXOIS

There are plenty of interesting things to see in Auxois. Vercingétorix, scourge of the Romans, looks out across Alesia, site of many archeological discoveries. Fontenay Abbey is listed UNESCO World Heritage, and Flavigny Abbey, in one of France's most beautiful villages, is famous for both aniseed and medieval Christian philosophy - not forgetting Chateauneuf-en-Auxois, with its medieval streets and impressive castle.

Arnay-le-Duc

LE CHATEAU DES PRINCES DE CONDE ✆ 03 80 90 07 55. The Condé Princes bought and restored the castle in the 17thc, but 100 years earlier, it belonged to the finance collector monsieur Merlan de Beaumont. After the Revolution, it was sold off as national property. Today it is a professional training centre, and is open to the public, though the finest parts have been sold abroad. The former portal is in Saint-Germain-en-Laye Museum near Paris. You can see the remains of ramparts in the courtyard, reminders of Côte d'Or's turbulent past.

MAISON REGIONALE DES ARTS DE LA TABLE ✆ 03 80 90 11 59. *Open April to mid-November: 10am-12 noon and 2pm-6pm. Admission: adult 4 €.* Visitors can taste and buy wine and regional produce. This attractive residence, once a 17thc. hospice, has been hosting exhibitions since 1981, concerning the pleasures of the table and culinary arts in general

Bussy-le-Grand

CHATEAU DE BUSSY-RABUTIN ✆ 03 80 96 00 03. *8km north-east of Venarey. Closed Monday. 15 May-14 September: 9.15am-12 noon and 2pm-6pm. Other periods: 9.15am-12 noon and 2pm-5pm. Guided tour 45 mins. Admission: adult 6.10 €, concessions 4.10 €, groups 5.10 €. Gardens only 2.50 €.* Comte Roger de Rabutin wrote (notably to his cousin, Mme de Sévigné) and was written about. His curious castle attracted attention, especially the park, which he designed himself, modelled on Versailles. 34ha. of beautiful formal gardens surround the castle.

Flavigny-sur-Ozerain

Reputed for its beauty and its aniseed. The Middle Ages have left their mark here, and you feel time is standing still. Relax, forget that 21stc. stress, and enjoy Flavigny's gentle lifestyle.

BENEDICTINE ABBEY CRYPT/LES ANIS ✆ 03 80 96 20 88. *Open every day (except between Christmas and New Year): 8.30am-11.30am and 2pm-5pm.* Telephone first in low season. You can visit the aniseed factory Monday to Friday: 10.30pm (maximum 8 people). Admission: adults 1 €. Famous throughout the Western world in medieval times, this abbey greatly influenced the Côte d'Or's development. See the preserved parts of the crypt built after 762, in Saint Pierre Abbey Church. You can join a tour of the aniseed factory at 10.30am.

Sémur-en-Auxois

NOTRE DAME COLLEGIATE CHURCH. The Duke of Burgundy founded a Romanesque church on this site in 1060. Notre Dame was rebuilt around 1225, on slender Gothic lines.

LA PORTE SAUVIGNY. Called after Jean de Sauvigny, the Auxois States' tax-collector. It is the only one of the five gates still intact.

LA TOUR DE L'ORLE D'OR Rue des Remparts ✆ 03 80 97 11 95. Currently closed for renovation work.In the heart of the medieval city, the Keep quarter had its own wall with four big towers: the Prison, Margot, de la Gehenne and Orles d'Or Towers. This last rises to 44m and its walls are 2m thick; it contains an Archeology and Folklore Museum.

Venarey-les-Laumes

LES FOUILLES ET LE MUSEE D'ALESIA ✆ 03 80 96 10 95. 23 *March-28 June: 10am-6pm. 29 June-1 September: 9am-7pm. 2 September-11 November: 10am-6pm. Admission: excavation + museum: 5 €, excavation or museum: 3 €, concessions 4 €, 7-16s 3 €.* After visiting the excavation, you must see the museum, which explains current research, and exhibits part of the findings from oppidum and battlefield (swords, spears and spearheads, cannonballs). The rest are in Saint-Germain-en-Laye Museum.

BEAUNE AND THE CÔTE DES VINS

Vineyard follows vineyard from Dijon to Santenay; Beaune and Nuits-Saint-Georges stick out like islands in a sea of vegetation. Wine-lovers are thrilled with the village names, each one with its history, soil and vintages: Fixin, Gevrey-Chambertin, Meursault, Pommard etc. Enchanting scenery and castles are hidden here too: the Château de La Rochepot at Nolay; Bouilland. Woods and blackcurrant plants (grown for crème de cassis) hold their own among the vineyards.

Beaune

Capital of winegrowing Burgundy, and much more. You come to Beaune for the vintages, but also for its marvellous architecture; the prosperity brought by the first (annual Hospices de Beaune wine auction) enabling the second to be preserved.

NOTRE DAME BASILICA. Easter Monday-end of the annual wine auction. Religious activity was responsible for Beaune's architectural wealth (close on a dozen convents). The predominantly Romanesque and Gothic basilica has its place in the town's history.

HOSPICES DE BEAUNE/HOTEL DIEU ✆ 03 80 24 45 00. *www.hospices-de-beaune.tm.fr. Open all year, every day: 9am-6.30pm, late March-mid November. Other periods: 9am-11.30am and 2pm-5.30pm. Guided tour by appointment.* That inside courtyard, those glazed tiles...Beaune's chief symbol. Stone and framework are Burgundian, but the blend of local and Flemish styles is dazzling. Under its impressive pointed towers, the building was used for medical purposes until 1971! The salle des povres (70m x 15m x 16m high) has a vaulted ceiling like a boat hull; the rows of beams seem to be held in the mouths of sea monsters. Simply magnificent.

MUSEE DES BEAUX ARTS 6, bd. Perpeuil - Porte Marie de Bourgogne ✆ 03 80 24 56 92. *Open April to December. Admission: Adult 5.40 €.* The museum was transferred to the former Calvet wine premises in 2002. The 127 works of art include 12th-20thc. collections, especially 16th and 17thc. Dutch and Flemish paintings. An archeological collection is planned.

MUSEE DU VIN DE BOURGOGNE Rue d'Enfer ✆ 03 80 22 08 19. *Open 1 April-30 November, every day: 9.30am-6pm. 1 December-31 March: 9.30am-6pm, closed Tuesdays, 25 December and 1 January. Guided tour 1hr. Ticket includes BA and Marey Museums.* Discover Burgundy winegrowing's popular traditions. The museum has two exits, one onto Rue d'Enfer (Hell Street), the other onto Rue du Paradis (Heaven Street). A rather apt summing-up of the effects of alcohol.

Famous roof of Hotel-Dieu in Beaune

La Côte des Vins

Nuits-Saint-Georges

Capital of the Côtes de Nuits wines, Beaune's rival. It, too, has its hospices, where its wines are sold in a charity auction.

BELFRY Corner of the Grand-rue and Place de la République. Built in 1619, of Flemish influence, the Belfy was a watchtower in the 17thc. Its chambers were used for the town aldermen's meetings. In the ground-floor guards' room is a huge fireplace. The bells were restored in 1989, and still peal out every day. Nearby is the statue of local sculptor Paul Cabet (1815-1876), who designed the 1870 soldiers' statue on the Nuits Mount.

CASSISSIUM Impasse des Frères Montgolfier ✆ 03 80 62 49 70. *www.cassissium.com. 1 April-19 November: open every day: 10am-1pm and 2pm-7pm. Guided tours 10.30am - 5.30pm, one per hour. 20 November-31 March: closed Sunday & Monday, otherwise: 10.30am-1pm and 2pm-5.30pm. Guided tours at 10.30am, 11.30am, 2pm, 3pm & 4pm. Admission: with audio guide 9 €, adult 6.50 €, concessions 4.50 €, under-12s free (accompanied).* Its cremes and liqueurs are already famous worldwide; now the blackcurrant's secrets are revealed in an interactive tour. You can buy a complete range of blackcurrant products in the Vedrenne shop.

MUSEE DES NUITS SAINT GEORGES 12 rue Camille-Rodier ✆ 03 80 62 01 37. *Open 2 May-31 October, every day except Tuesday: 10am-12 noon and 2pm-6pm.* Some fine Gallo-Roman remains excavated on the Bolard site are on display. The Merovingian room recalls daily life at this little-known period, and different aspects of regional heritage can be viewed in the annual temporary exhibitions.

Chassagne-Montrachet

Famous for its great vintages, though its pink stone is prized and its soil full of truffles. Apart from the grands crus shared with Puligny, les criots is only found in Chassagne.

Gevrey-Chambertin

Not merely wines, but symphonies! You are forgiven for eulogizing in this Mecca of winegrowing.

CHATEAU DE GEVREY ✆ 03 80 34 36 13. *Open by appointment only. Admission: adult 5 €.* Rape and pillage were becoming so frequent in this wealthy winegrowing country that the Sires de Vergy had a fortress built to protect the precious beverage - and the local people too. Later, it was given to the Cluny monks, who did some interior decorating to improve daily comfort. You can admire several rooms and a spiral staircase. Wine-tasting included.

Meursault

The 57m church spire is a landmark for this famous winegrowing village.

ARCHEODROME DE BOURGOGNE Aire de Beaune-tailly ✆ 03 80 26 87 00. *www.archeodrome-bourgogne.com. Access via RN 74 or A6. Open July & August: 10am-7pm, other months 10am-5pm/6pm.* Planet Earth's adventure seen in life-size reconstructions: Alesia's Roman fortifications, a Gallic farm, tumuli, a necropolis. The audiovisual room shows the Earth's beginnings and you can admire its first human inhabitants in the Tunnel of Evolution. Captivating!

Nolay - La Rochepot

The Hautes Côtes' most beautiful stopover point.

CHATEAU DE LA ROCHEPOT. *Open 1 April-31 October, except Tuesday. Admission: adult 6 €. Guided tours available.* A fairytale village set in gently-curving hills, with little houses, woods, the rock, and an incredible castle. Things to see: the 72m-deep well, sumptuous Chinese Room, guard room which could house all the villagers in case of attack, view from the terrace, and of course, the glazed tiles.

MUSEE DE LA MAISON DES PAUVRES Nolay ✆ 03 80 21 80 73. The house dates back to Louis XIV, and houses some fine objects, though you can take in the whole collection at a glance. Notice the Virgin and Child, painted enamels and some signed furniture.

MUSEE DU VIEUX NOLAY ✆ 03 80 21 75 30. Re-opening date depends on the work in progress in the old town centre. This charming little museum contains a bit of everything: the town's rural development, geology, history of the old trades, and so on. You can see collections of tools, old maps, fossils, rocks, minerals and interesting information about the reconstruction work at La Rochepot Château.

Pommard

3km south-west of Beaune, this village gets its name from Pomona, goddess of fruit. She certainly protects these vines!

CHATEAU DE POMMARD ✆ **03 80 22 07 99**. *www.chateau-de-pommard.tm.fr. Visit and tasting, late March-3rd Sunday in November, every day: 9am-6pm. Group bookings.* Ducal privilege established Pommard as a castle in the late 11thc. Only a small part of the grape harvest is entitled to the Monopole Chateau de Pommard AOC. The wine gets even better with age.

Puligny-Montrachet

Alexandre Dumas said montrachet should be drunk 'bareheaded and kneeling'. Without going that far, you have to respect this truly great wine with its 4 grands crus (montrachet, batard-montrachet, chevalier-montrachet and bienvenues-batard-montrachet) and many premier crus.

Vosne-Romanée

The Revolution officially proclaimed this 'the most excellent of all the French Republic's wines'. Judge for yourself, but remember, you are on hallowed ground. In 1760, the Prince de Conti bought Romanee from the Croonenbourg family, thus giving the vineyard a mythical name: Romanee Conti. The six grands crus are romanée-conti, romanée, romanée-saint-vivant, tache, richebourg and grande-rue. Their finesse is remarkable.

Vougeot

This little village has a huge reputation, and is a much-visited place on the wine route, featuring 51 ha. of vines within a walled estate (clos), a famous grille, and the perfect climate for wine growing.

CHATEAU DU CLOS VOUGEOT ✆ **03 80 62 86 09**. *Open every day. April-September: 9am-6.30pm (Saturday 5pm). Admission: Adults 3.60 €.*The monks enclosed their generous heritage with walls between the 12th and 15thc., whence the name 'clos': Clos Vougeot. Its 50.6 ha. area is still the same today. The castle was falling into ruin when the Friends of Clos Vougeot Castle bought it in 1944. That same year, the Chevaliers du Tastevin Brotherhood took the place over for their dinners, held in the spirit of the motto 'Jamais en vain, toujours en vin' ('Where there's a wine, there's a way', perhaps?)

SPIRITUAL BURGUNDY

The medieval Christian Church flourished in Burgundy, its influence reaching across the world. You still feel this in the abbeys, which are so much more than superb stone buildings.

Cîteaux (Côte-d'Or)

CITEAUX ABBEY ✆ **03 80 61 32 58**. *www.citeaux.abbaye.com. Open 1 May-30 June and mid-September-early October: 9.54am-12.45pm, and 2.15pm-6pm. 1 July-15 September: 9.45am-6.30pm, Sunday 12 noon-6.30pm.* The abbey was founded in 1098, but its success began with the arrival of Saint Bernard and his 30 companions. By the late 12thc., the Order owned 343 monasteries; at the end of the Middle Ages, over 3,000. There are still monks living here, defying time and the ephemeral world. You can enter all the historic buildings: the 13thc. copyists' cloister, 15thc. library, 17thc. définitoire and 18thc. Lenoir wing (the monks' living quarters). You are gently but firmly advised to stop in at the shop, where the famous cheese is sold.

Cluny (Saône-et-Loire)

One of Christianity's most influential centres for many centuries. Today, Romanesque stones, gastronomy and green meadows draw lots of tourists, captivated by the medieval streets and marvellous abbbey ruins.

BENEDICTINE ABBEY ✆ **03 85 59 12 79**. *Open every day, 2 May-31 August: 9.30am-6.30pm. 1 September-30 April: 9.30am-12 noon and 1.30pm-5pm. Admission: adult 6.10 €, school parties 5.10 €.* Founded in 909, Cluny Benedictine Abbey had become Christianity's biggest spiritual centre by the late 11thc. It grew and developed until the 18thc., but after the Revolution, was sold off as national property and used as a quarry. It took centuries to build, but only a few years to destroy, and sadly, only a tenth is left today. You can, however, get an idea of its glory from a computerised reconstruction with virtual images (Cluny III in the Archaeology Museum).

Fontenay (Côte-d'Or)

FONTENAY ABBEY ✆ **03 80 92 15 00**. *6km from Montbard, 30km from the A6 exit by the Bierre-les-Semur interchange. Open 11 November-31 March: 10am-12 noon and 2pm-5pm. 1 April-10 November: 10am-5.30pm. Admission: adult 7 €; concessions 4 €.* The Cistercian abbey church is one of the oldest in France; a Romanesque masterpiece listed World Heritage. The architecture is simple and harmonious, true to Cistercian thinking, with nothing to disturb or turn the mind from contemplation. Don't miss the new gardens, reshaped by landscape architect Peter Holmes.

Paray-le-Monial (Saône-et-Loire)

The 10,000 citizens of this 'monk's city' see ten times as many visitors pass through each year. In the late 11thc., Hugues de Semur, Abbot of Cluny, had a great church built here. In 1671, Marguerite-Marie Alacoque entered the Visitation monastery, where she was visited by Jesus three times, thus making Paray's reputation world-wide. Faith and history are linked on every street corner, in remarkable old buildings. Every summer, the Communauté de l'Emmanuel holds international meetings here, grouping together over 20,000 faithful.

SACRE COEUR BASILICA. First a simple priory church, it was given the title Sacre Coeur Basilica in 1875. It is well-preserved, and shows you what Cluny architecture was like. Pope John Paul II prayed there on 5 October 1986.

VISITATION CHAPEL. Also known as the Apparition Chapel. Here, Christ appeared to Saint Marguerite-Marie between 1673 and 1675. The saint's relics are kept in a gilded silver reliquary on the right of the chancel, with Christ's words written around it.

Abbaye de la Pierre qui Vire (Yonne)

A fine Gothic abbey stands south of Avallon at Saint-Leger-Vauban, birthplace of the famous strategist and military fortifier.

LA PIERRE QUI VIRE ABBEY Saint-Leger-Vauban ✆ **03 86 33 19 20.** *www.abbaye-pierrequivire.asso.fr. Open every day. Audiovisual room and bookshop open every day: 10.15am-12 noon and 3pm-5pm. Closed in January. Monastery closed to the public.* The Benedictine monastery was founded in 1850, in this wild and remote corner of the Morvan Forest. The granite Neo-Gothic abbey church is built on two crypts, one above the other. A nearby megalith gave the church its strange name. You can attend prayers with the monks, and see a documentary about their life, before buying their home-made cheese in the shop, and visiting the religious bookshop.

Vézelay (Yonne)

This beautiful village has its group of artists, captivated by the picturesque streets as you will be. From the Middle Ages onwards, Vézelay became an important Christian site, with its basilica containing Sainte Madeleine's relics, and its eternal hill a stopping-point on the Compostella Road. Today, it is part of the Morvan nature reserve, and has plenty to offer: basilica, church, Romanesque (Ursulines) and Renaissance (Theodore de Bèze) houses, and others from the 17th and 18thc. (Town Hall, Pontot House),

Cluny's abbey

ramparts surrounding the town, vineyards and refined but traditional gastronomy.

MAISON DU VISITEUR Place Guillon ✆ 03 86 32 35 65. *www. vezelay-visiteur.com. Open every day, except Tuesday. Closed in January. Admission: adult 7 €, concessions 5.50 €, 6-12s 3.50 €.* The introduction to the basilica is atmospheric: first, a slideshow on a giant screen 'in the shadow of light', followed by the Salle des Symboles where a guide comments on the architecture and light play, and interprets the carved capitals with the help of models.

SAINTE MARIE MADELEINE BASILICA ✆ 03 86 33 39 50. *www.vezelay.cef.fr. Guided tours all year for groups of ten or more, advance bookings only. Enquiries to the Basilica rectorat's tour service: 03 86 33 39 50. Tours with the Brothers and Sisters of Jerusalem, early July to mid-August every day except Monday at 4pm, and Sunday in June and September. Meeting point in the cloister chapel.* Vézelay's prosperity lasted from the 10th to the 13thc. Pilgrims, princes, kings and Popes came to revere Saint Madeleine's relics, before going off to Compostella, or yet another crusade, ensuring a place for Vézelay in Western history. The basilica is an example of Burgundy's Romanesque magnificence, well-proportioned, with sumptuous carving and above all, that fabulous transcendental light.

Taizé (Saône-et-Loire)

TAIZE INTERNATIONAL EUCUMENICAL COMMUNITY ✆ 03 85 50 30 30. *www.taize.fr. Service times: Monday-Saturday: 8.15am, 12.20pm, 8.30pm. Sunday: 10am, 8.30pm.* World prayer centre and Reconciliation Church. Founded by Brother Roger, this community has been growing since the 1960s. Young people from 35 to 70 nations meet here; some weeks, 6,000 of them gather on the hill, and hitch-hikers throng the roads. The landscape is beautiful, with a moving atmosphere of prayer. Not to be missed.

La Boulaye (Saône-et-Loire)

TEMPLE DES 1,000 BOUDDHAS Chateau de Plaige ✆ 03 85 79 62 52. *www.mille-bouddhas.com. Temple open every day: 2.30pm-5pm. Weekends and public holidays: 2.30pm-6pm (winter) or 2.30pm-7pm (summer). July, August and school holidays: 10am-12 noon and 2.30pm-7pm. Admission: about 4 €.* Unique in Europe, this has been a Dashang-Kagyu Ling Centre (meaning 'the happy garden where the soul is linked to Dashang-Kagyu teaching') since 1974. Dashang-Kagyu is one of Vajrayana Buddhism's great schools. The evening ritual is open to everyone, and takes place every day at 6pm (winter) and 7pm (summer), except Wednesday, You can find out more about this religion, which is attracting more and more Westerners, from the bookshop.

DIJON

The Dukes of Burgundy's capital, known for its mustard, gingerbread and creme de cassis, is also a historic city of art, museums and fine civil and religious architecture. You must see Saint Benigne Crypt, Notre Dame Church and its gargoyles, the ducal towers, kitchens and States rooms in the palace, Mansart's architecture and the gardens designed by Lo Nôtre's disciples, the medieval houses and parliamentary mansions - and so much more, as you'll discover on arriving in this elegant town.

PALAIS DES DUCS ET DES ETATS Place de la Liberation ✆ 03 80 74 51 51. The Ducal Palace, which also housed the Burgundy States, now contains the Town Hall and Fine Arts Museum. It is built around three courtyards: the Cour d'Honneur in front, Cour de Bar (and museum) reached by a passage on the right, and Cour de Flore on the left.

MUSEE DES BEAUX ARTS Palais des Etats de Bourgogne ✆ 03 80 74 52 09. *Entrance: Cour de Bar. Open every day except Tuesday. The permanent collections are free; you may have to pay to see a temporary exhibition.* This beautiful museum is worthy of the palace buildings. There are primitive medieval Burgundian, Flemish, Swiss and German works, and 17th, 18th and 19thc. collections. Among the finest are the Salle des Tombeaux with the Dukes of Burgundy's sepulchres, the Maitre de Flemalle's Adoration des Bergers, the Dame à sa toilette (Fontainebleau School), Colson's Repos, and masterpieces by Delacroix, Gericault, Picasso, Bracque, Georges de La Tour, Manet and the Portuguese Maria Helena Viera da Silva.

TOUR PHILIPPE LE BON Hôtel de Ville - Place de la Liberation ✆ 03 80 74 51 51. *Open every day, Easter-3rd Sunday in November. Other periods, Wednesday, Saturday and Sunday (ask about opening hours). Admission: adult 2.30 €, concessions 1.20 €, under-12s free.* This massive tower is 46m high, with 316 steps, and a panoramic view from the top (the snowy Alps can be seen on a clear day).

SAINT BENIGNE CATHEDRAL. Five different buildings were put up on the site of the present Gothic cathedral. All that remains of the Romanesque church can be seen in the crypt. The west front is framed by two big towers; the two octagonal floors on top have cut-off corners and glazed roof tiles.

NOTRE DAME DE DIJON CHURCH. Limited space was available for the builders, who reduced buttress size, flattening the flying buttresses. The decoration is Tuscan-inspired; no other French church has two levels of arcatures and three rows of gargoyles on its front.

MUSEE AMORA 48, quai Nicolas-Rolin ✆ 03 80 44 44 44. *Closed Sundays and public holidays. Open 15 June-15 September: guided tour at 3pm (organised by the Tourist Office). Other periods: guided tour at 3pm Wednesday and Saturday. Admission: 3 €.* Think Dijon, think mustard. The mustard-retailer Amora has worked to associate the two, and you can follow the product from its beginnings and discover its varieties and how it is made here.

MORVAN

A bit of the Massif Central lost in Burgundy. It was known as the 'bad country' producing 'neither good winds nor good people', and the Burgundians were afraid of it. It is, however, a seductive region, with its leafy trees and conifers, bright lakes, ferns and bubbling streams. Made a national nature reserve in 1970, it has been able to keep its environmental heritage intact and develop its tourist infrastructure.

MAISON DU PARC Saint Brisson ✆ 03 86 78 70 16. Set up in 1975 at the crossroads of the four Burgundy departments. The centre boasts a reception and information desk, exhibition centre, the Taureau Lake (former log-floating pool rich in fish), a deer enclosure, a herbularium containing 160 of Morvan's plant varieties and an arboretum with its tree species. There is also a picnic area. A user-friendly place.

Autun

The Romans built this fortified town; many remains can still be seen.

SAINT LAZARE CATHEDRAL. Despite much reshaping and a Gothic spire, this is considered to be one of Burgundy's finest Clunisian Romanesque buildings.

RAMPARTS. Two-thirds of Autun's Roman Wall are still intact; few other Gallo-Roman remains are in such good shape.

TEMPLE OF JANUS. This 3rdc. sanctuary was dedicated to an unknown Gallo-Roman deity; the association with Janus is pure invention. The cella, or place of worship is a squarish tower, 24m high with 16m sides (only two are now left).

ANTIQUE THEATRE. Autun's theatre was the biggest in Roman Gaul: 148m in diameter, holding 20,000 spectators (12,000 today). The seating part is all that is left today (two tiers of the original three).

Château-Chinon

Morvan's capital, perched in the massif close to the highest peaks, overlooking the hilly region.

MUSEE DU SEPTENNAT 6, rue du Château ✆ 03 86 85 19 23. Housed in the former 18thc. Sainte Claire Convent, thie museum contains the objects received by François Mitterand as President, from 1981. You'll enjoy the exquisite and the kitsch, sitting side by side.

COSTUME MUSEUM 4, rue du Château ✆ 03 86 85 18 55. *Closed 1 January until February school holidays 2006. Admission: adult 4 €.* This museum features a collection of French costumes from the 18th to the 20thc., highlighting developments, variations, influences and regional and social differences in type of dress (town and country, the wealthy and the poor, working clothes and Sunday best).

PANORAMA DU CALVAIRE. After the museum, climb up to the Calvary (609m) set up on the site of a Gallic oppidum and the remains of a fortress.

Mont-Beuvray

BIBRACTE. *You can visit the site all year. Guided tours available.* In 52 B.C., Vercingétorix was made Supreme Head of the Gallic armies at Bibracte. He marched on Alésia with his troops, to confront the Roman enemy. After a 2-month siege, he was forced to surrender. Takes you back to school history lessons.

MUSEE DE LA CIVILISATION CELTIQUE ✆ **03 85 86 52 39**. *Open mid-March to mid-November. Admission: adult 5.75 € with audio guide.* Showcase for research currently underway at Bibracte, this museum replaces the site in a European context of Celtic civilisation thanks to scale models, audiovisual documents and interactive screens.

Saulieu

Stopover on the Paris-Lyon road. Saulieu is full of Morvan character and local produce (Charolais beef); an irresistible blend of gastronomy and natural beauty.

SAINT ANDOCHE BASILICA Place du Docteur Roclore ✆ **03 80 64 07 03**. *Opening hours vary according to season.* Characteristic Clunisian style, with its original Romanesque capitals.

MUSEE POMPON Place du Docteur-Roclore ✆ **03 80 64 19 51**. *Open March-December (except Tuesday): 10am-12.30pm and 2pm-6pm. Admission: adult 4 €.* Gallo-Roman remains, medieval statues (an 18thc. angel and 13thc. Christ among others) screens and charters illustrating the town's history, gastronomy and popular arts and traditions.

NIVERNAIS

Right in the centre of France, the Nièvre department contains 215,000ha. of forests, 4,960km of riverbanks, 1,600ha. of lakes and 195km of navigable waterways. Which all adds up to an exceptionally beautiful environment.

Nevers

Proud of its striking buildings and blue earthenware.

BELFRY. This was the former Palais de Justice (law courts), put up from 1398. Two rooms were built under the belfry, hiding a chestnut framework shaped like a boat-hull.

SAINT CYR ET SAINTE JULITTE CATHEDRAL. Containing two chancels for two saints: the west, Romanesque; the east, Gothic.

SAINTE MARIE CHAPEL. Only the chapel is left today, with its amazing Baroque front and witty satiric poem written by Jean-Baptiste Gresset, telling the story of a Nevers parrot: 'Ver-Vert, perroquet de Nevers'.

SAINT ETIENNE CHURCH. This church shows Romanesque architecture at its height. It has changed little over 900 years, though it no longer has a cloister.

SAINT GILDARD CHURCH. Bernadette Soubirous' body is displayed in a reliquary in Saint Gildard Monastery Chapel. She was beatified in 1925 and canonized on 8 December 1933 by Pious XI.

DUCAL PALACE. Built in the 15thc., and now an exhibition centre. It boasts an amazing aquarium of Loire fish.

Nevers, Croux rampart

Clamecy

Vaux d'Yonne's tourist centre. This picturesque old town has narrow, winding streets and ancient, beautiful houses with tiled roofs, and was the birthplace of Jean II of Burgundy, Comte de Nevers (Jean de Clamecy) and the writer Romain Rolland.

MUSEE ROMAIN ROLLAND Ave. de la Republique ✆ 03 86 27 17 99. *Open June-September, every day except Tuesday and Sunday morning (October-May, also closed Monday). Admission: adult 3 €, child 1.50 €, under-16s free.* Housed in the former Duc de Bellegarde's mansion and in Romain Rolland's birthplace, the museum exhibits paintings given to Mitterand, with jewellery and Gallo-Roman and Merovingian sculptures in the Archeology Room, a Fine Arts collection and some good ceramics. Romain Rolland has a room to himself: rare editions, furniture and photos trace the life of this writer, who won the Nobel Prize for Literature in 1915.

SAINT MARTIN COLLEGIATE CHURCH. Built between the 12th and 16thc., hovering between Primitive and Flamboyant Gothic, with nostalgic Romanesque touches.

Cosne-sur-Loire

The Nievre's second-biggest town, at the Loire-Nohain confluence.

MAISON DES CHAPELAINS. This Renaissance mansion is a picturesque spot, with its inside turret joined to a period building.

La-Charité-sur-Loire

On the Loire banks between Nevers and Cosne, this monastic site is culturally important, and has been restored in an attempt to bring back some of its Romanesque greatness.

NOTRE DAME DE LA CHARITE PRIORY CHURCH. Proud under its slate roof, Notre-Dame is the greatest Burgundian church after Cluny.

RAMPARTS. They surround the old town and priory, and offer a magnificent view of Loire, Cher and Sancerre district, notably from the top of the round tower.

MUSEE MUNICIPAL 33, rue des Chapelains ✆ 03 86 70 34 83. *Open April-June and September-November every day except Monday & Tuesday: 10am-12 noon and 2pm-6pm. December-March: weekends: 10am-12 noon and 2pm-7pm, Closed public holidays and January. Admission free.* On two floors, you can see artistic, archeological and ethnological collections. Art Nouveau and Art Deco objects include Lalique, Daum, Galle and Decorchemont glass, Sevres china, and works by Louchet, Deck, Faure and Brateau.

SAÔNE-ET-LOIRE

Chalon-sur-Saône

Once the Merovingian capital, later known for its medieval fairs, Chalon has a famous native son, Nicephore Niepce, inventor of photography (among other things).

SAINT VINCENT CATHEDRAL. The town's most important medieval monument, though the façade and towers are 19thc. Neo-Gothic.

CENTRE HOSPITALIER WILLIAM MOREY 7, quai de l'Hôpital ✆ 03 85 44 65 87. *Guided tours 1 April-30 September, Wednesday & Thursday: 2.30pm (ask about other periods). Admission: adult 3 €, under-15s free.* Founded in 1529 on the Ile-Saint-Laurent by the town aldermen, this historic hospital contains an 18thc, pharmacy with its collection of earthenware pots and 300 herbalist's drawers, a Renaissance building housing the Sainte Marthe Sisters, with a magnificent refectory; and a 19thc, chapel with 16thc. stained glass.

TOUR DU DOYENNE. Put up in the 15thc., later taken to pieces and sold to an American - who then gave it back to the town!

MUSEE NICEPHORE NIEPCE 28, quai des Messageries ✆ 03 85 48 41 98. *www.museeniepce.com. Open 9.30am-11.45pm and 2pm-5.45pm every day except Tuesday and public holidays. July & August: 10am-12.30pm and 1.30pm-6pm. Admission: adult 3.10 €, child 1.55 € (groups & 13-18s), under-13s free. First Sunday of each month (guided tour at 3pm), and Wednesdays free.* A unique photography museum, tracing historical and artistic developments since Niepce's invention, including popular uses and state-of -the-art.

entre CHALON et MÂCON
redécouvrez
le plaisir
CAVE DE
LUGNY
L'ABUS D'ALCOOL EST DANGEREUX POUR LA SANTÉ. CONSOMMEZ AVEC MODÉRATION
AUTOROUTE A6 :
SORTIE TOURNUS
CAVE DE LUGNY
RUE DES CHARMES . BP6 . 71260 LUGNY
TÉL. 03 85 33 22 85 . FAX 03 85 33 26 46
www.cave-lugny.com

Bourbon-Lancy

Saône-et-Loire's only watering-place on the right bank of the Loire, known since Roman times for its therapeutic waters springing from the ground at 58°C.

BELFRY. In the heart of the old quarters, this was formerly the main gate in the town enclosure, put up in 1389. Today, the belfry contains an automaton called the Beurdin, who rings the bells every hour and sticks out his tongue at the passers-by.

Cormatin

CHATEAU DE CORMATIN ✆ **03 85 50 16 55**. *Open every day. Guided tours of the apartments; individual access to the park. No dogs. Admission: park only, 4 €. Château + park: adult 8 €.* This Renaissance château was built in the early 17thc. just after the Wars of Religion, by Antoine du Blé d'Huxelles, governor of Chalon. The sumptuous apartments, six gilded rooms, water-filled moat and recomposed gardens remind you of the Loire châteaux. Every year, there is a theatre festival in July and August, with close on 65,000 visitors. François Mitterand planted an oak here with his friend Mikhael Gorbatchev.

Mâcon

Capital of Southern Burgundy, Mâcon stretches peacefully along the Saone's right bank, convivial with its round-tiled roofs. It has a Mediterranean look about it, and life seems pleasant, especially when you're tasting the local wines or discovering one of its many gastronomic restaurants.

APOTHICAIRERIE. This apothecary's was built around 1775, and is panelled in oak. On the ground floor, you see blue amphora-shaped pots, Empire vases, Mâcon earthenware and two big polychrome vases over a metre high, among others.

SAINT VINCENT CATHEDRAL. Built at the time of Napoleon 1, designed by Guy de Gisors (Palais Bourbon, Madeleine). Lamartine's funeral was held here.

LAMARTINE MUSEUM 41, rue Sigorgne ✆ **03 85 38 96 19** *Open except Sunday morning and Monday: 10am-12 noon and 2pm-6pm. Admission: adult 2.50 €.* On the first floor of the Senecé mansion in the town centre, the museum houses 16th-18thc. furniture, earthenware and paintings (French, Dutch and Flemish schools). Five magnificent 17thc. Aubusson tapestries are also on view. The great salons and former private apartments in the east wing are devoted to the life and works of Alphonse and Marianne de Lamartine.

TOURS DU VIEUX SAINT-VINCENT. You have a unique view over the Mâcon countryside and the Saône Valley from the top of the cathedral tower, which is now at peace, after a turbulent history.

Solutré-Pouilly

ROCHE DE SOLUTRE. Solutré Rock is famous both for its prehistory, and for François Mitterand's annual Whitsun pilgrimage. An impressive site, not to be missed.

MUSEE DEPARTEMENTAL DE PREHISTOIRE ✆ **03 85 35 85 24**. *Open every day, except Tuesday out of season (10am-6pm: check opening times). Closed December & January. Admission: adult 3.50 €, over-6s 2 €, under-6s free.* The Solutré dig began excavating these astonishing prehistoric remains in 1866. For 25,000 years, this had been a hunting-ground, and piles of horse and reindeer bones were dug up, proving that between 35,000 and 10,000 B.C., whole herds had been slaughtered and cut up at the foot of the rock. An instructive and fascinating lesson on prehistory.

Tournus

This cheerful medieval city on the edge of the Saone boasts a majestic abbey church and some pretty good restaurants.

SAINT PHILIBERT ABBEY ✆ **03 85 27 00 20**. *July & August , guided tours except Saturday and Sunday morning: 10.30am and 3.30pm. Admission: adult 4.20 €. Tickets and departure from the Information Point.* This Romanesque abbey managed to survive intact and keep its original character. The apse chapel houses Saint Philibert's relics, while Saint Valerian Sanctuary is in the crypt, site of a remarkable vault and 12thc. fresco.

HOTEL-DIEU 21, rue de l'Hôpital ✆ **03 85 51 23 50**. *Open last weekend in March to the first in November: 10am-6pm every day except Tuesday. Group bookings all year. Admission (including Greuze Museum): adult 5 €, concessions 3.40 €, under-18s free.* This 17thc. building is a fascinating reminder of bygone hospitals. Its ancient rooms are furnished as period wards with the original oak box-beds, pewter dressers and earthenware, and there is a well-stocked apothecary's.

YONNE

Auxerre

Old churches, peaceful streets and the gently-flowing Yonne: tourists love Auxerre and the residents are proud of their town.

SAINT GERMAIN ABBEY 2, place Saint-Germain ✆ 03 86 18 05 50. *Closed Tuesday. Adults 4.50 €.* Saint Germain d'Auxerre Benedictine Abbey stands on a hilltop overlooking the Yonne. It houses the 5thc. Bishop Saint Germain's body. Important building began in the 9thc, taking in the oratory put up by Saint Germain himself and Clothilde's basilica; today only the crypt remains to recall that carved and colourful Carolingian Renaissance period. At the height of its power, the abbey was a flourishing cultural and spiritual centre, influencing the western world. The chapter house and Saint Jean Tower were Romanesque additions; the present abbey church is Gothic. There are some traces of classical architecture: the cloister was rebuilt with the arrival of the Saint Maur Congregation. The monks left during the Revolution, and the monastery became a stud farm and a military hospital (continuing to be used for medical purposes until 1980). Today, an archeological research and restoration programme is under way and the abbey has a new role: it will be housing the town's museum collection.

SAINT-ETIENNE CATHEDRAL ✆ 06 86 52 06 19. *Open Monday-Saturday: 7.30am-6pm and Sunday afternoon: 2pm-6pm.* Though a little short for the Gothic period, its architecture and carved images make it typical of the period.

Ancy-le-Franc

CHATEAU D'ANCY-LE-FRANC ✆ 03 86 75 14 63. *www.chateau-ancy.com. Open April-November. Closed Monday. Guided tours every day. Admission: adult 8 €, concessions 5.50 €, child 4 €.* A square-shaped castle with four corner pavilions, built in the mid-16thc. It was originally surrounded by a moat, and the inside courtyard could only be reached by two gates, defended by drawbridges. This fine example of French Renaissance art contains many treasures.

Avallon

Overhanging the Cousin Valley, this fortified town was once a strategic site. You find 17th and 18thc. bourgeois architecture in the Horloge quarter, with its half-timbered houses and museum, and hidden stairs and paths below the ramparts leading away from the town centre. Continuing between gardens and terraces, you arrive at the Petite Porte with its scented lime trees in summer. From this headland you have a marvellous view of the Panats, Alleux and Alger castles against a background of Morvan scenery.

SAINT LAZARE COLLEGIATE CHURCH. There are religious scenes on the portal, but daily life is also portrayed (the seasons in the centre) and there are centaurs and harpies on the cabled columns. A masterpiece of Romanesque decorative sculpture.

CHABLIS. You visit Chablis to see the cellars, taste the wine, eat well and admire the picturesque alleys lined with 15th and 16thc. houses (if you still can). Various events are organised all year, attracting plenty of interest.

DOMAINE DU VIEUX CHATEAU DANIEL-ETIENNE DEFAIX BP 50 ✆ 03 86 42 42 05 *Website: www.chablisdefaix.com. Email: chateau@chablisdefaix.com. Ouvert every day: 9.30am-12 noon and 2pm-6.30pm. Annual closing in January.* This vineyard covers 25 hectares, and produces the British Royal family's favourite wines. The Princess of Wales, we're told, liked the Vaillon premier cru, while the Queen Mother preferred Les Lys. Daniel-Etienne Defaix uses the 'batonnage' technique, an ancient method adopted by the Pontigny monks: the wine lies are left in the juice and brought up regularly until they destroy themselves, giving the wine special strength and structure and making it suitable for laying down. If you're a fan of old vintages and like to keep your favourite millesimes for a number of years, this wine is definitely for you.

SAINT MARTIN COLLEGIATE CHURCH. Put up in 1160, the collegiate church (community of canons) is a small replica of Sens Cathedral.

SAINT PIERRE CHURCH Rue du Panonceau. A fine example of typical Burgundian Gothic architecture.

PETIT PONTIGNY Rue de Chichee. Chablis holds its folklore events here. Only the cellar is left of the original 12thc. buildings.

Noyers-sur-Serein

This medieval village on the Champagne border is part of Burgundy's rural tradition. It boasts steep, tiled roofs and beautiful 15thc. half-timbered houses with small columns, carved pinnacles and corbelling. The paved main street, once the merchants' quarter, links a series of picturesque squares.

Saint-Fargeau

On the Loing banks, north-west of the forest, this town is well-equipped for tourists discovering the region.

CHATEAU DE SAINT-FARGEAU ✆ 03 86 74 05 67. *Open 1 April-11 November: 10am-12 noon and 2pm-6pm. Admission: adult 8 €, child 4 €.* A fine example of French classicism built on a base dating back to 980. There are richly-furnished apartments and four centuries of craftsmanship intact in the framework, 30m above the ground.

SAINTE ANNE CHAPEL Cemetery. The chapel walls are entirely covered with an amazing collection of 16thc. paintings, Several scenes are displayed, rather like a series of stretched-out tapestries.

FUTURE CHATEAU DE GUEDELON ✆ 03 86 45 66 66. *Visits from March to November. Admission: adult 8 €.* You have to see it to believe it - a 13thc. fortress built all of a piece in the 21stc! In the heart of the forest, 35 'creators' are putting up a fortress that will take 20 years or so, respecting 13thc. techniques and construction materials. This medieval building site is a perfectly serious venture, closely followed by a historical and scientific committee; the plans were drawn up by Jacques Moulin, chief Historic Monuments architect. In 2004, the lord's living quarters and main tower were erected, culminating in a great Gothic hall with intersecting ribs.

Sens

Prestigious medieval archbishopric. Sens has proudly kept its historic buildings safe from the dangers of local rivalry and war.

SAINT-ETIENNE CATHEDRAL. This was the first great 'metropolitan and primate' Gothic cathedral. Its influence within the Christian world was widespread.

MUSEE, TRESOR ✆ PALAIS SYNODAL Place de la Cathedrale ✆ 03 86 64 46 22. *Open Mondays, Thursdays, Fridays: 2pm-6pm. Wednesdays, Saturdays & Sundays all day. Admission: adult 5 €, concessions 2.40 €.* The former Archbishops' Palace now houses the region's historic collections and treasures, including the extraordinary Villethierry treasure: 867 jewels and objects found in a vase. The cathedral treasure contains tapestries (Notre Dame de Pitié, 16thc), 15thc. altar facings ancient cloths for wrapping relics, reliquaries and shrouds.

PARC DU MOULIN A TAN ✆ 03 86 95 38 72. A magnificent park with regional, rare and exotic plants in its greenhouses.

Tanlay

A pleasant stopping-place on the Burgundy Canal, which comes to life in summer with the passing boats. Tanlay boasts a fine Renaissance castle and a contemporary art centre, known to amateurs and professionals alike.

CHATEAU DE TANLAY ✆ **03 86 75 70 61**. *Open April-2 November, every day except Tuesday. Guided tours (1h) from 9.30am and 2.15pm. Admission: adult 8 €, child 3 €. Outside & park only 2.50 €.* This striking 16th and 17thc. castle is surrounded by its moat in a beautiful park. There is a magnificent room painted in grisaille and frescoes in the Tour de la Ligue; furniture and decoration are equally sumptuous. Among the artists who worked here are pupils of the great master Poussin.

Tonnerre

Tradition is preserved in these streets and alleyways, behind the magnificent façades, for Tonnerre is proud of its past.

SAINT PIERRE CHURCH. Composite architecture many-times reshaped, which suits Tonnerre's particular urban style.

LA FOSSE DIONNE. A Vauclusian spring, continually active though its pressure varies. It is deep and narrow, with a strong current, making it difficult to explore.

HOTEL DIEU ✆ **MUSEE MARGUERITE DE BOURGOGNE** ✆ **03 86 55 14 48**. *www.tonnerre,fr. Open every day, except Sunday and public holidays from 1 November-31 March. Admission: adult 3.50 €, child 2.50 €, under-10s free.* Start your tour in the Hôtel Dieu's great hall for the sick, which contains an astronomic instrument traced on the floor in 1784. The museum is housed in an adjoining building and has several theme rooms, one narrating the Hôtel Dieu's history and another reconstructing a 20thc. operating theatre and an 1850 sickroom.

RIVER TOURISM

The current boom in river tourism is simply the latest step in a long Burgundian water transport tradition. The Gauls and Romans developed river trade which flourished until the railway arrived in the 19thc. The waterways were abandoned, until modern holiday trends created a new market, and brought a new kind of sailor to the canals and locks.

Canal de Bourgogne

Linking the Yonne and Saône Valleys along a winding route with a lot of locks. Between the Armançon Valley and Pouilly-en-Auxois, it goes underground for 3,300m, then crosses several tourist regions before reaching Dijon, and journey's end on the Saône Plain.

Canal du Centre

The most active canal in terms of trade, especially on the Saône side between Montceau-les-Mines and Châlon-sur-Saône, where the locks are automated (putting the lock-keepers out of a job). This doesn't hurt the canal's charm, as it wends its way across the Charolais plains to Paray-le-Monial and Digoin.

Canal du Nivernais

Opened in 1843 after 60 years of work, this canal links the Parisian and Loire basins with the help of the River Yonne, and was originally built to supply Paris with wood. Its greenery, steep cliffs and charming villages and lock-keepers' cottages are just waiting to be discovered.

Mâcon, Saône

Digoin

Watering-place and border between the Saône-et-Loire and Allier(marked by the Loire), and crossroads of several canals. Thanks to its geographic position, Digoin was able to develop its trade, and now boasts a much-visited sailing harbour.

CANAL DU CENTRE. 114, 322m long, 14.62m wide and 1.50m deep, with 12 reservoirs and 80 locks, needing 48 bridges and 70 aqueducts. At first, the canal favoured local industrial development (Blanzy-Montceau mines, Schneider factories and Gueugnon forge). After World War II, and the decline in industrial transport, it made a new start in tourism.

PONT-CANAL. This aqueduct spans the Loire from a height of 12 metres, linking the Canal du Centre and the Loire side-canal. Built of stone between 1834 and 1838, it was enlarged in 1870, and measures 243m by 11m, with 11 arches and a lock. You can admire this unusual structure (boats crossing over a river by bridge!) from the towpaths.

Joigny

This pretty medieval town is a good starting-point for a boat-trip on the Yonne. Don't miss the superbly-decorated wooden houses, nor the restaurants: Joigny is reputed for its gastronomy.

LOCABOAT PLAISANCE Quai du Port-au-Bois ✆ 03 86 62 06 14

Saint-Jean-de-Losne

Capital of Burgundy's waterways; visitors from all over Europe stop over in the busy port. The cafes are full of mariners, whose Grand Pardon is held every year, as is a boat fair.

SAINT-JEAN-DE-LOSNE TOURIST OFFICE 5, ave. de la Gare-d'Eau ✆ 03 80 29 05 48

Saone and Yonne boat trips.

The riverbanks are still naturally wild and rather mysterious. You can join up with the Burgundy and Centre canals from the Saone, and the Nivernais from the Yonne. Enjoy the gentle pace of a family barge trip - an opportunity to discover the wildlife, and a host of other environmental treasures.

Bateaux de Bourgogne

Cabin boys and freshwater sailors will be thrilled with these comfortable, fully-equipped barges, the ideal means to discover Burgundy's 1,200 km of rivers and canals. They are so easy to steer that you don't need a licence. Enjoy some magnificent scenery, plant and animal life as you drift gently through the locks. There's no better - or more relaxing - way to spend a family holiday. All aboard, and fair journey! *✆ 03 86 72 92 10. Website : www.bateauxdebourgogne.com; www.tourisme-yonne.com. Combined stay (7 days/6 nights) from 1,277 € for 4. Barge hire from 431 € per week.*

Settons lake

FOOD AND DRINK

Every district has its markets, its craftsmen and its specialities. Burgundians take pride in their culinary know-how and traditions, and the pleasures of the table play an important part in regional culture. Not forgetting the wine, an integral part of every convivial meal, (and of the local economy). Here is what you might find on your plate and in your glass:

Flavigny aniseed

Still made in the abbey. The methods have changed over the years, but the result is the same: sugar syrup slowly wrapped round a grain of aniseed, with a variety of natural flavourings (violet, mint, liquorice, coffee, rose, orange-flower, jasmine and mandarine). The well-known traditional box shows a shepherd courting his shepherdess in front of the Recluse fountain, and offering her an aniseed!

Clamecy and Chablis andouillette

The chitterling sausage (casing filled with chopped intestines) is a Clamecy, Chablis and Mâcon speciality. The intestines are heated, cut into long strips, scraped and prepared, then manually pushed into the casing. The filled sausages are cooked in a court-bouillon for 3-and-a-half to 5 hours. The letters AAAAA found in displays and on menus stand for 'Association Amicale des Amateurs d'Andouillette Authentique'. (Genuine Andouillette-Lovers' Friendly Society).

MAISON DE L'ANDOUILLETTE DE CHABLIS SOULIE 3, place du General-de-Gaulle - CHABLIS ✆ 03 86 42 10 62

MAISON ROUSSELET 15, rue Auxerroise - CHABLIS ✆ 03 86 42 46 93. The legend goes on, thanks to these two traditional andouillette-makers.

Blackcurrant

Like the grapes, this little black berry is the basis of the Côte d'Or local economy. M. Joly, distiller, invented the cassis liqueur recipe, and the fruit is still going strong, despite a slump in the 1980s owing to heavy competition (of inferior quality) from Eastern Europe. Today's production strategy is ' more quality, less quantity', the two principal cassis companies being Vedrenne (Nuits-Saint-Georges) and Lejay-Lagoute (Dijon).

CASSISSIUM Impasse des Freres Montgolfier ✆ 03 80 62 49 70. *www.cassissium.com. 1 April-19 November: open every day: 10am-1pm and 2pm-7pm. Guided tours 10.30am - 5.30pm, one per hour. 20 November-31 March: closed Sunday & Monday, otherwise: 10.30am-1pm and 2pm-5.30pm. Guided tours at 10.30am, 11.30am, 2pm, 3pm & 4pm. Admission: with audio guide 9 €, adult 6.50 €, concessions 4.50 €, under-12s free (accompanied).* Its crèmes and liqueurs are already famous worldwide; now the blackcurrant's secrets are revealed in an interactive tour. You can buy a complete range of blackcurrant products in the Vedrenne shop.

Epoisses

Oldest and most famous of the region's cheeses, and a favourite with Louis XIV. It is made from cow's milk and matured with Bourgogne marc brandy, orangish, soft and creamy. In 1989, the syndicat for the defence of Auxois époisses was created, and the cheese got its AOC in 1991. The chambertin and ami chambertin are similar, and the aisé cendré is an epoisses matured with ashes.

FROMAGERIE GAUGRY Brochon ✆ 03 80 52 45 55. Three generations of family cheese producers, specialised in époisses.

FROMAGERIE BERTHAUD Epoisses ✆ 03 80 96 44 44. One of the most famous producers.

Burgundy snails

Don't confuse them with the vulgar specimens seen on any old wall in damp weather. The glorious local snail is bigger, with a striped yellow shell, and was found among the vines until modern fertilisers began to kill it off. The situation became critical, and the local hunting calendar was modified as a result. Fans prefer snails served in their shells with parsley and garlic butter.

Jambon persillé (marbled ham)

This noble Burgundian recipe is protected by a red quality label, and the ingredients are strictly controlled: only salt, water, stock, brine, edible sugars, and white and grey pepper can go into it, with nutmeg, garlic, shallots, cloves, thyme, bayleaf, carrots, leeks and white wine as flavourings. The ham (born and bred in Burgundy) is presented in a gelée with chopped parsley, traditionally eaten at Easter with a bottle of Meursault.

Kir

Côte d'Or's native aperitif! Originally a means of drinking bad quality white wine, masked by the taste of cassis, it became fashionable with local politicians at banquets and election campaigns. Canon Kir more or less enforced this popularity, signing a contract with local producers. You mix the cassis (one-third) in a flat-bottomed glass with the Bourgogne Aligoté (two-thirds). Red wine can be used instead; this is called a communard and tastes rather strange, though it has its fans.

Cheese

© Ot Le Creusot

Dijon mustard

A mixture of vinegar, white wine and green grape-juice is added to the carefully-sorted mustard grains, popular with connoisseurs who like its strength. There are seven producers, including Amora (formerly Bizouard), Parizot, Grey Poupon, Maille and Bornier. The grains come mainly from Canada, and the resulting yellow paste is supposed to inspire all kinds of qualities (fidelity, reciprocated love) as well as being an aphrodisiac.

MUSEE AMORA 48, quai Nicolas-Rolin ✆ 03 80 44 44 44. *Closed Sundays and public holidays. Open 15 June-15 September: guided tour at 3pm (organised by the Tourist Office). Other periods: guided tour at 3pm Wednesday and Saturday. Admission: 3 €.* Think Dijon, think mustard: The mustard-retailer Amora has worked to associate the two, and you can follow the product from its beginnings and discover its varieties and how it is made here.

BOUTIQUE MAILLE 32, rue de la Liberte ✆ 03 80 30 41 02. *Open Monday-Saturday: 9am-7pm.* A superb shop, with stoneware pots and delicatessen products. Specialises in mustard on tap.

LA MOUTARDERIE FALLOT 31, rue du Faubourg-Bretonniere ✆ 03 80 26 21 30. *www.fallot.com. Tours with professional guides every day: 10am & 11.30am, except Sunday and public holidays. Admission: 10 €.* Learn all about the origins and methods of mustard-making from this traditional manufacturer. Interactive and fun.

Pain d'épices (gingerbread)

In 1900, the Grande Encyclopedie stated 'In France, the pain d'épice most renowned for its delicacy is found in Dijon.', thus placing the official seal of approval on a long-scorned product. Only three producers still have the traditional know-how: Michelin, Bornier and Mulot Petitjean. Rye or wheat flour, honey, spices and a lot of mystery go into it.

WINES

Grapes were already grown for wine in the 1stc. A.D., production being encouraged by the Church, monasteries and the Duchy. The 18thc. bourgeoisie and wine-merchants were good at marketing and and selling: grandes maisons were founded and fortunes made.

Climate, soil, exposure and traditional know-how all play their part in this success; 2,200 houses exploit over 9,000ha. (15 times less than Bordeaux, but then all Burgundy's vineyards are in AOC.) Annual output: 350,000-460,000 hectolitres, three-quarters of them red.

There are three parts to the côte des Vins:

Côte de Nuits: 2,500ha. supplying 15 million bottles (90% red). On either side of Nuits-Saint-Georges, the Côte de Nuits contains almost all the grands crus. The chalky earth (mid-Jurassic) stony soil, slopes, micro-climate and sunshine contribute to these magnificent wines, yet would not be enough without the wine-growers' know-how. Fixin, Gevrey-Chambertin, Morey-Saint-Denis, Chambolle-Musigny, Flagey-Echezaux, Vougeot (with castle and clos) Vosne-Romanée et Nuits-Saint-Georges.

Côte de Beaune: more extensive than the Côte de Nuits (4,800ha. and 25 million bottles), these lazy, confident vineyards were dubbed 'Burgundy's Champs Elysees' by Jean-François Bazin. Their history can be learned in Beaune, on a visit to the famous hospices. The earth is younger: calcareous clay and mid and late-Jurassic marl. Further south, the landscape flattens. 30% of the vinified product is white, and all the wines are prestigious: Chassagné-Montrachet, Meursault, Pommard, Aloxe-Corton and Santenay.

Hautes Côtes: as their name implies, the vineyards overhang the hillside 300-640m up, covering an area of 40km by 10km. The vines are grown together with cereals and fruit, such as blackcurrants. The two AOC are Hautes-Côtes de Nuits and Hautes-Côtes de Beaune (1961). Magny-les-Villers is the border between the two denominations.

BIVB 12, Bd. Bretoniere - BEAUNE ✆ 03 80 25 04 80

MAISON DES HAUTES CÔTES Marey-les-Fussey - NUITS-SAINT-GEORGES ✆ 03 80 62 91 29

ATHENAEUM DE LA VIGNE ET DU VIN 5, rue de l'Hôtel-Dieu ✆ 03 80 25 08 30. *Open every day: 10am-7pm.* An original bookshop, with a section on the art and science of wine, and a 'vinotheque', grouping together the best texts on wine and recent publications on the subject. French and foreign-language reviews available. You can test your newly-acquired knowledge in the bookshop cellar while envying its beautiful bottles.

The right address

YVES NICOT 48, rue Jean-Jacques-Rousseau ✆ 03 80 73 29 88. A small shop for a person of stature. Yves Nicot is a professional oenologist, son of a wine grower and cellarman, considered to be an authority on wine in Burgundy. You can follow his advice without hesitating.

Producers & maisons de vin

MOILLARD GRIVOT La Berchere - RN74 - NUITS-SAINT-GEORGES ✆ 03 80 61 28 13. With over two-and-a-half-centuries of experience as producers and wine-merchants, Moillard Grivot owns 40ha. (half of it in premiers crus and grands crus.) and 30 AOC. Corton Clos du Roi, Clos du Vougeot, Chambertin Clos de Beze: the names speak for themselves.

PATRIARCHE PERE ET FILS 7, rue du College ✆ 03 80 24 53 78. *www.patriarche.com. Open 9.30am-11.30am and 2pm-5.30pm, every day except Christmas and New Year, and All Saints.* One of Beaune's great names, dealing in wine since the 18thc. The cellars represent five Burgundian vineyards: Côtes de Beaune, Côtes de Nuits, Chablis, Côtes Châlonnaises and the Maconnais, from regional AOC to grands crus.

Saône-et-Loire wines

Southern Burgundy is the region's biggest producer, with 13,000ha. of vines in AOC. There are more whites (424,000hl) than reds (317,000hl) in the five established sectors.

The Maranges region is part of the côte de Beaune. Its reds are named after one of the three communes: Sampigny-les-Maranges, Dezize-les-Maranges, Cheilly-les-Maranges, or simply called côte de Beaune village.

The Couchois vineyards stretch between Couches, Dracy-les-Couches, Saint-Sernin-du-Plain, Saint-Jean-de-Trézy and Saint-Pierre-de-Varennes. You find the four great Burgundian cépages here: pinot noir, gamay blanc, aligote and chardonnay. The vineyards produce red wines with the regional appellation (bourgogne rouge and bourgogne passe-tout-grain) and some whites (bourgogne aligoté, bourgogne blanc and cremant).

The Chalon Côte contains four main AOC: rully (mainly whites), mercurey and givry (mainly reds) and montagny (only whites).

The Mâcon district chiefly makes whites. North of the Petite Grosne, you find mâcon villages and mâcon superieurs; the most popular are Lugny and Vire. In the south are the four white grands crus: pouilly-fuisse, pouilly-vinzelles, pouilly-loché and saint-veran.

Finally, in the south of the Arlois district, three of the ten beaujolais grands crus appear in the Saone-et-Loire: saint-amour, moulin-à-vent and chênas.

MAISON DES VINS DE MACON 484, ave. De-Lattre-de-Tassigny ✆ 03 85 38 36 70

MAISON DES VINS DE CHALON Promenade Sainte-Marie ✆ 03 85 41 64 00. *Open 9am-7pm. Closed Sunday and public holidays.*

The right adresses

CELLIER DE JEAN-PATRICE LALY 14, rue de la Grange-Vertu - AUTUN ✆ 03 85 52 24 83. Not to be missed: a mini-museum, some good advice (and adresses) from the master of the house, and of course, the scent (and flavour!) of an excellent cellar.

CELLIER SAINT-VINCENT 12, place Saint-Vincent - CHALON ✆ 03 85 48 78 25. Pascal Laville is a likeable cellarman; his vintages are also well worth getting to know.

LES DOMAINES 36, rue aux Fevres - CHALON ✆ 03 85 93 39 82. All a novice needs to know about wine is explained here by the Revenu family.

VITTEAUT-ALBERTI 16,rue de la Buisserolle ✆ 03 85 87 23 97. The department is known for its sparkling wines, but this has to be the best! Vitteaut-Alberti cremants are winners, in competitions and the best French cellars. Well-deserved success.

CAVE DES VIGNERONS DE BUXY Rue de la Gare ✆ 03 85 92 04 30

CAVE DES VIGNERONS D'IGE Ige ✆ 03 85 33 33 56

CAVE DES VIGNERONS DE MANCEY RN6 ✆ 03 85 51 00 83

CAVEAU DE MONTAGNY-LES-BUXY ✆ 03 85 92 06 85

CAVE DE LUGNY Rue des Charmes ✆ 03 85 33 22 85

CAVE DE VIRE En Vercheron - VIRE ✆ 03 85 32 25 50. The co-operative cellar is particular to Saone-et-Loire, which has a reputation in the field. The groups of winegrowers are efficient in PR, and particularly good at explaining wine to novices. You find a warm welcome and excellent wines.

Nièvre wines

The Pouilly-sur-Loire vineyards stretch along the banks of the Loire and the RN 7 (2 hours from Paris). 1,050ha. are planted; 50ha. of chasselas (pouilly-sur-loire AOC) and the rest sauvignon (AOC pouilly-fumé). 55,000hl is produced on average a year. Pouilly-fumé is a dry white wine with a characteristic smoky aroma. It has a pale gold colour with greenish lights and fruity, mineral or floral notes, and is found on some of the top French and international tables. It goes well with shellfish, fish, white meat and goat's cheese.

Yonne wines

The Yonne vineyards are generally little-known, and their wines can be found at attractive prices. They include, however, the world's most famous white: Chablis. The Yonne had been producing wine for over 12 centuries, and had 40,000ha. of vineyards (the waterway network being useful for promotion and transport towards Paris) when a sudden phylloxera attack killed off almost all the vines in the late 19thc. Today, there are 5,500ha. (4,000 for Chablis alone) and 300,000hl are produced.

Auxerrois wines

Auxerre's vineyard produced wine for kings, then was devastated by phylloxera, leaving only the Clos de la Chainette. The surrounding villages took over: Chitry and Saint-Bris-le-Vineux make excellent whites on 500ha. (chardonnay, aligoté, Saint-Bris or Sacy sauvignon)but the reds are better-known; Irancy (120ha) and Coulanges-la-Vineuse (70ha), made from pinot noir, are prized for their deep colour and red fruit flavours. They can be laid down, and are even better with age.

Chablis wines

These young vineyards contain 7 grands crus: Preuses, Bougros, Vaudesir, Valmur, Grenouilles, Blanchot and Les Clos; and the Montmain, Vaillons and Vaucoupain premier crus, among others. The Petit Chablis is very drinkable too.

Côte Saint-Jacques wines

This tiny plot on the Burgundy wine map is still worth attention. Côte Saint Jacques on the Joigny hillsides is the result of a lot of hard work by a few wine-growers, determined to keep their heritage alive. The pinot gris is one of Saint-Jacques' well-kept secrets, and its wine is unique in the region.

Vézelay wines

Recently-resurrected vineyards flourish at the foot of the basilica. The ancient melon cépage is especially highly rated.

Tonnerre wines

Served long ago at the Kings of France's table, these wines are experiencing a second wind with the new generation of winegrowers.

Crémant de Bourgogne

At Bailly and Saint-Bris-le-Vineux. This sparkling wine is ideal for all kinds of festivities, being made according to the Champagne method. Quite a few reputed restaurant-owners now have it on their wine-lists.

Châtillon wines

Local production has been seeking a new lease of life for 25 years. The AOC was gained in 1975, and official prizes have been coming its way over the last 15 years; an encouraging sign. 60 winegrowers and 23 villages are involved in promoting their dry, light and lively cremant, whose future in this corner of Burgundy looks bright.

Hotels & Restaurants

CÔTE-D'OR

Beaune

LE BENATON 25, rue du Faubourg-Bretonnière ✆ 03 80 22 00 26. *Closed Wednesday, and Thursday and Saturday lunchtimes. Closed Wednesday and Thursday all day in low season. Set menus from 20 € to 48 €.* As its seasonal menu shows, Le Benaton respects the culinary imperatives of French regional cuisine, Burgundian in particular, though not exclusively. Each of the recipes has been reappropriated and can be called original. The setting is bubbling with innovation. An excellent place to eat, where you receive a very pleasant welcome.

HOTEL DES REMPARTS * 48, rue Thiers ✆ 03 80 24 94 94** *Open all year. Rooms from 78 € to 115 € - suites. Breakfast 8 €. Wi-Fi. Parking. Garden.* This hotel is located in the heart of the old town, away from the noise and bustle. It has the advantages of a desirable residence, and the charm: indoor courtyard, French-style ceilings, exposed stones, comfortable setting and rooms (single, family or suite). All the elegance of four centuries of existence, in fact. The hotel ranks highly, due to constant hard work from the staff, together with a sense of duty towards its clients.

LE JARDIN DES REMPARTS 10 rue de l'Hôtel-Dieu ✆ 03 80 24 79 41 *Fax 03 80 24 92 79. Set menus from 30 € to 78 €, à la carte 60. Closed Sunday, Monday, early February -early March, the first week in August and first week in December.* In a region where the great restaurants compete for the most luxurious decor, the thickest carpet, the most prestigious painting and the highest prices, Roland Chanliaud's restaurant - opened in 1990 in a small town house on the circular boulevard - distinguishes itself from the others with its modest setting and surprisingly low prices. The carrot conserve with duck foie gras, cumin and gingerbread, Burgundy truffle risotto with artichokes and anchovies, roast pikeperch with honey, mushrooms and German camomile, saddle of rabbit with cepes, black olives and rosemary and pears rissoled in morel caramel, with chicory ice-cream (an imaginative and successful dessert!) bear the hallmark of a great chef. Few luxury products, then, which means the prices can stay at a reasonable level, but plenty of skill and imagination, ensuring a special moment for each customer. The cellar is run by Laetitia Nicod, and was built on the same principle, offering excellent vineyards at low prices as well as the region's *grand crus*.

Bèze

L'AUBERGE DE LA QUATR'HEURIE ** Rue des Ponts ✆ 03 80 75 30 13. *Fax : 03 80 75 32 92. Website : www.quatrheurie.com. 26 km north-east of Dijon. Open every day. Last order taken 2pm and 9.30pm weekdays, brasserie service all day. Formula 12 €. Set menus from 25 € to 50 €. Rooms from 50 € to 64 €. Indoor terrace.* Next to the small stone bridge, La Quatr'heurie is a half-timbered building with a Hansel and Gretel front and an immemorial look about it. Inside, fireplaces, beams across the ceiling strung with drying hams and sausages and solid, rustic furniture complete the picture. Morning and afternoon, the outside tables welcome passers-by for comforting 'elevenses' (the daily snack is at 4pm in France, hence the name of the inn): charcuterie and cheese spread on thick slices of country bread, washed down with a local wine. The menu pays tribute to both local and Mediterranean produce: chicken livers, foie gras, black pudding, snails, duck breast and veal kidneys, and fish as varied as trout (meunière or with morels) burbot, gambas, salmon and fisherman's stewpot. Follow splendid Burgundian tradition with a tasty beef bourguignon, pork brawn or a pleurotus (mushroom) salad, and for dessert, real Proustian madeleines that melt in the mouth and leave a lasting memory.

Bouilland

HOSTELLERIE DU VIEUX MOULIN 1 rue de la Forge ✆ 03 80 21 51 16 *Fax 03 80 21 59 90. Website: www.le-moulin-de-bouilland.com. Set menus from 40 to 75 €, à la carte 75 €. Closed lunchtimes and 2 January -9 February.* After Jean-Pierre Silva's departure to open a guesthouse in Provence, followed by former second Laurent Andre's interim management, the kitchens in this beautiful house in the Beaune countryside are now in the hands of young Thomas Protot, who trained with David Zuddas (La Charme at Prenois), himself ex- Derbord and Lameloise. In good hands, then, with an elegant, classically inspired cuisine: roast bass matched with broad beans and artichokes, for instance, and some unforgettable fruit desserts. The dining room was refurbished last year, and customers no longer smile at its 1980s-style decoration. The Vieux Moulin has a fine regional wine cellar, though it tends to resort to wine merchants, and the service is well timed.

Chambolle-Musigny

CHATEAU HOTEL ANDRE ZILTENER** Rue de la Fontaine ✆ 03 80 62 41 62.** *Fax : 03 80 62 83 75. Website: www.chateau-ziltener.com. Rooms from 200 €. Suites. Apartments.* One of the region's finest hotels. The main building dates back to the 18thc, above former cellars belonging to the Cistercian monks who made nearby Clos de Vougeot famous. Refined intimity is the watchword, in the rooms, suites and apartments on two floors, with private salons and individual fireplaces, not to mention Louis XVI furniture and marble bathrooms. There is a residents' table (bookings only) and a wine bar serving Burgundian specialities to taste with one of the crus from the chateau cellars.

Dijon

LE BISTROT DES HALLES 10, rue Bannelier ✆ 03 80 49 94 15. *Closed Sunday evening. Last order served at 2pm and 10pm. Lunchtime menu 16 €. À la carte between 13.50 € and 15 €. Chef's suggestion on the blackboard in the evenings. Air-conditioning. Terrace.* This famous restaurant near the Place du Marche is a must. Famous (starred) chef Jean-Pierre Billoux considers it his 'gastronomic recreation' to pay tribute to the region's bourgeoise cuisine, and a certain nostalgia tinges the menu, composed of seasonal produce with a variety of original flavours. Among the house classics are pate in a pastry crust *a l'ancienne*, and more original but just as tasty, courgette stuffed with cod *brandade* (fish and potato dish) and served with a tomato *coulis*. The servings are generous; try the duck leg roasted with spiced wine and fruit or the steamed cod with a mustard cream. The desserts are a pleasant ending to a simple but copious meal, and sweet lovers will enjoy the pear soup with liquorice, vanilla mousse with apricots or dark chocolate fondant with flavoured with mint.

LE CHABROT 36, rue Monge ✆ 03 80 30 69 61. *Restaurant, wine bar and cellarman. Closed Sunday. Last order taken at 2pm and 10.30pm. Set menus 'du marche' at 12 €, lunchtime only. Menu 'affaire' 21 €, menu 'decouverte' 31 €. À la carte from 8 € to 18 €. Terrace. Faire chabrot* means putting wine in your soup, a peasant tradition that has become the house motto, and a sign of conviviality. In an intimate setting inspired by the old bistros, you can meet up with friends to enjoy a glass of good wine (the house speciality) or a meal, or both. Food and wine compliment each other perfectly, the latter recommended by a cellarman of repute. Add sophisticated presentation and service with a smile, and you have a very pleasant set-up. The most memorable starters were the light iced cucumber and grilled chorizo *velouté* and the superb vegetable pistou tart, a matching of original yet familiar flavours. The slice of grilled Charolais beef and herb butter is more traditional, generous, with a delicate taste. You can end your meal with peaches freshened in verbena, or a dessert or homemade *gâteau*. A *pousse-café* - calvados, cognac or marc de Bourgogne - will finally convince you that you came to the right place.

HOSTELLERIE DU CHAPEAU ROUGE 5 rue Michelet ✆ 03 80 50 88 88 *Fax 03 80 50 88 89. Website: www.bourgogne.net/chapeaurouge. Set menus from 38 € to 100 €, à la carte 75 €. No weekly closing, closed the first two weeks in January.* The Chapeau Rouge goes back a long way, in a town where the culinary traditions are among the oldest and liveliest in France. The Burgundian capital has always been spoilt by chefs, with several good restaurants in the town centre and nearby suburbs. Today William Frachot represents Dijon's young guard, rapidly taking over. Settled in this hotel since 1999, he has made his mark among Dijon's top cooks, and is now almost a leader. His cuisine has oriental influences, and is modern and specialised, leaving nothing to chance. Quail brochette (kebab) glazed with spiced caramel Peking-style, and caramelised endives, pan-cooked Lake Leman whitefish, beetroot juice and citronelle, shitake mushrooms and seasonal vegetables, crunchy Burgundy snails, herb purée, seasonal mushrooms and tomato conserve, a pan-fried veal chop with a parmesan crust and small white onions, *ratte* (small new) potatoes and melilot juice, white chocolate and pistachio gateau, red fruit soufflé and iced milk with thyme and lemon feature on his menu. The service is lively and smiling, and the cellar gathers together the region's best bottles. You'll have a great time.

HOTEL SOFITEL LA CLOCHE ** 2, avenue de la Première-Armée © 03 80 30 12 32.** *Fax : 03 80 30 04 15. Website: www.hotel-lacloche.com. Open all year. Hotel-restaurant. Single or double rooms from 125 € to 165 €. Suite from 380 €. Apartment 320 €. Junior suite from 210 € to 230 €. Breakfast 15 €. Animals accepted, supplement 15 €. Fitness centre, sauna.* This is where you spend your luxury mini-break in the Dukes' city. Dijon's grand hotel saw its reputation grow along with the Place Darcy. Its walls are listed in the Historic Monuments Inventory, and have welcomed the rich and famous from all arts and parts: Leopold 1 of Belgium, the sculptor Rodin, Napoleon III and the actress Grace Kelly. Go through the superb reception hall to the famous gardens, where a fountain plays. The piano bar tinkles gently in subdued atmosphere, to encourage conversation. On to the rooms, 68 in all, including 11 suites and 4 apartments. Recent restoration work has set off the Art Deco style. The top floor has been entirely refurbished with new furniture, particularly well adapted to sweet dreams. All the usual services found in luxury hotels are at your disposal, with the added experience of the establishment itself (over 100 years old in its present form) and the elegant setting. La Cloche - named for the superb clock on the roof - has 2 restaurants, including the eponymous Jardins, one of the town's excellent eating-places currently benefiting from a new chef.

LE PRE AUX CLERCS 13 place de la Libération © 03 80 38 05 05 *Fax 03 80 38 16 16. Set menus from 35 € to 90 €, à la carte 70 €. Closed Sunday evenings, Monday, from 20 February to 1 March and from 15 to 26 August.* We knew Jean-Pierre Billoux at L'Hotel de la Gare in Digoin, before the renowned chef left that rather gloomy town for the bright lights of Dijon in 1986. The Place de la Liberation is indeed a lot more *chic* than the Place de la Gare in Digoin, and the elegant Dijon clientele makes no mistake in choosing Le Pré aux Clercs for business lunches and great occasions; more top-of-the-range cars stop outside its door than anywhere else. Jean-Pierre Billoux was trained in cuisine by his wife's family, the Bonnevay, owners of the Hotel de la Gare in Digoin (as was Alexandre Dumaine), and is today one of Burgundy's most respected chefs. You must taste his *paillasson* of langoustines with sherry vinegar, his duck charlotte with gingerbread, and his gingerbread ice cream; once specialities, now true classics.

RESTAURANT STEPHANE DERBORD 10 place Wilson © 03 80 67 74 64 *Fax 03 80 63 87 72. Website: www.restaurantstephanederbord.fr. Set menus from 25 to 78 €, à la carte 75 €. Closed Sunday, Monday and Tuesday lunchtimes and 1-16 August.* Stephane Derbord, 45 this year, was formerly at Le Sévigné at Cosne-sur-Loire in the Nièvre. He left the banks of the royal river to take over from Jean-Paul Thibert, who had upgraded this fine hotel-restaurant in the Place Wilson, a short way from the town centre. Stéphane Derbord has an unusual gastronomic repertory, which surprises, can annoy when he goes too far with certain recipes (too many ingredients) but above all, inspires enthusiasm: pan-fried duck foie gras escalopes, braised cabbage julienne, ginger and cumin; Saône pikeperch barded with steamed bacon, white asparagus and green asparagus julienne with grilled almonds; roast Miéral pigeon deglazed with onion conserve, mashed peas, and the leg in a consommé flavoured with liquorice stick; Genoa bread with roast pineapple; crème brûlée with vanilla pods; mango sorbet and coriander leaf. These dishes are often unruly and innovative; a real breath of fresh air in a region weighed down by its heavy gastronomic tradition. The cellar is excellent for Bourgogne wines, but otherwise, rather limited.

Gevrey-Chambertin

HOTEL LES GRANDS CRUS* Route des Grands-Crus © 03 80 34 34 15** *Website: www.hoteldesgrandscrus.com. Open every day, annual closing from December to late February. 24 rooms at 70 € and 80 €. Breakfast 10 € and 12 €. Animals welcome, supplement 6 €. Walled courtyard.* A beautiful stopping-off place on the *route des grands crus.* This hotel is housed in a Burgundian family mansion, with the typical roof. 3 stars for 24 comfortable rooms right next to the vineyards. The setting is rustic, with exposed stones and fireplace, and an elegant flower-filled decor. Warm, distinguished welcome.

Gilly-les-Citeaux

LE CHATEAU DE GILLY ** © 03 80 62 89 98.** *Fax : 03 80 62 82 34. Website : www.chateau-gilly.com. Located 3km eats of Vougeot. Great French break. Open every day. Restaurant Le Clos Prieur. Set menus from 42 € to 65 €. Cote Terroirs lunch formula, or Cote Terrace buffet in summer, from17 € to25 €. Salon de thé every afternoon: seasonal formula 10 € (drink and pastry).* Once the residence of the abbots of Citeaux, this Chateau is a fine example of 14th and 17thc. heritage, with its thick fortified walls, moat and formal garden. Mr Maniez is the new manager, and has been in charge for several months now. Olivier Dupart has been running the kitchens since 2004, and is specialised in the *grandes étapes.* His gastronomy can be appreciated in the Clos Prieur restaurant, a superb Gothic hall featuring a 14thc.vaulted ceiling with intersecting ribs, where the service is as elegant as the food presented: young braised marsh duck, mullet à *la plancha* and saddle of lamb tandoori vye with more traditional flavours like pan-cooked pikeperch and quail's eggs *en meurette* (in a red wine sauce) with shallots; marbled ham confit, and roast veal sweetbreads. The establishment also proposes the Cote Terroirs restaurant, a chic wine bistro, where you can lunch from Monday to Saturday. In summer, the new restaurant Cote Terrasse provides a buffet lunch and a marvellous view of the garden. The Chateau's cellars contain over 25 000 bottles, served by the glass with the set menu of the day. Those seeking venues for meetings, receptions, cocktail parties or weddings will find small and larger reception rooms for hire, plus a luxurious bar, all recalling chateau life in days gone by.

Ladoix-Serrigny

LES PAULANDS Route de Beaune – RN74 ✆ 03 80 26 41 05. *Fax : 03 80 26 47 56.Website: www.lespaulands.com. 40km south of Dijon and 6km from Beaune. Restaurant closed Monday and Wednesday lunchtimes. Lunch menu 20 €. Set menus from 26 € to 76 €. Rooms from 65 € to 90 €, apartments 100 €. Full and half-board available. Swimming pool and private car park.* This family residence among the vineyards gives priority to its sophisticated *cuisine*, served in an intimate atmosphere. Snail profiteroles and garlic cream with marc de Bourgogne and saddle of suckling veal with Bourgogne truffle juice support the local colours; Marennes d'Oléron oysters sealed with cress and sesame seeds, or cannelloni stuffed with peppers in a *brandade* provide the exotic note. Note that one of the menus includes prestigious Corton vintages. Otherwise, you have a choice of excellent wines at attractive prices from the house cellar.

Levernois

HOSTELLERIE DE LEVERNOIS ** ✆ 03 80 24 73 58.** *Fax : 03 80 22 78 00.Website: www.levernois.com. 15 rooms and 3 apartments. Open 7 days a week. Set menus 28 € and 32 € (Monday to Friday lunchtimes, service until 3pm) and 65 €, 80 € and 98 €.* This Relais ✆ Chateau site is a superb haven of peace and luxury, in its bucolic 4ha. landscaped park close to Beaune and next to a golf course. Elegant manager Jean-Louis Bottigliero has given the hotel a unique prestige, and it deserves its Michelin star. You receive a courteous welcome, and the chance to enjoy a delicate and sophisticated cuisine; the menu changes every two months. Cold crayfish soup with small seasonal vegetables or forest mushroom ravioli with foie gras and celery cappuccino are our recommended starters, followed by *fritto misto* of frogs' legs, or seasoned roast lamb with stuffed vegetables and socca . You would then be wise to take a digestive walk through the formal gardens! This year, l'Hostellerie de Levernois has also opened a warm and pleasantly intimate bistro.

Marsannay-la-Côte

LES GOURMETS 8 rue du Puits-de-Têt ✆ 03 80 52 16 32 *Fax 03 80 52 03 01. Website : www.les-gourmets.com. Set menus from 30 to 80 €, à la carte 55 €. Closed Sunday evenings, Monday, and Tuesday lunchtime, from 16 January to 8 February and during the first fortnight in August.* Joel Perreaut has spent 25 years in this former sheepfold converted into a pleasant restaurant, neither classic nor modern, just comfortable and welcoming. From the produce to the wine list, his choice is made with customer satisfaction in mind, and the dishes are served with tact and precision. Aubergine tart and fillet of sea bream, veal spare ribs and chestnut flour waffles will not revolutionise Burgundy's gastronomy, but you will enjoy eating them, and appreciate the reasonable prices. Why look further afield?

Prénois

AUBERGE DE LA CHARME ✆ 03 80 35 32 84 *Fax : 03 80 35 34 48. Set menus from 23 € to 70 €, à la carte 65 €. Closed Sunday evening, Monday, Tuesday lunchtime, February school holidays and first fortnight in August.* Since setting up his establishment near the famous racing car circuit in 1994, David Zuddas has risen through he gastronomic ranks at Formula One speed. He too seems to be fuelled for top performance, and his cuisine is up-to-date and precise, without sacrificing flavour to technical skill or presentation. Choose from *Culatello de noir de Parme – an exceptional kind of charcuterie – beetroot millefeuille* and smoked eel, cress, delicate Sechouan nougatine and herb salt, asparagus both cooked and raw, polenta *de fonio*, green asparagus and mushrooms, smoked eggs and *feuilletage* dips with black cumin seeds, burbot spiked with conserved lemon, mixed spiced vegetables, thick French veal liver, and daikon pickled in raspberry vinegar, carrot pulp, cumin and juice with mixed spices. The desserts are equally tempting: pineapple ravioli, vanilla panacotta with conserved orange and coriander, or fruit sorbet with black cardamom. The chef's charming wife Catherine manages the service, and the cellars are well equipped with regional wines.

Saulieu

LE RELAIS BERNARD LOISEAU 2 rue Argentine ✆ 03 80 90 53 53 *Fax 03 80 64 08 92. Website : www.bernard-loiseau.com. Set menus from 95 € to 175 €, à la carte 130 €. Closed all day Tuesday and Wednesday lunchtime, from 1 January to 12 April and from 7 November to 20 December. Otherwise open every day, with annual closing from 8 January-10 February.* Three years after Bernard Loiseau's tragic death, this establishment (formerly the Cote d'Or), which now bears his name, is doing as well as can be expected. The delicate question of succession, and how to keep the restaurant running without the great chef who had made it famous, was perfectly handled, thanks to solidarity from Dominique Loiseau's team and also to Patrick Bertron, former second, who took charge of the kitchens three years ago after 21 years with the restaurant. The strategy was to start by keeping most of the master chef's recipes, and little by little, to reduce their number: They are now to be found on a separate menu called simply 'Classics': the famous oyster and langoustine stew, in 'sea juice' flavoured with nettle; pan-fried chicken breast and foie gras with truffled potato purée and *rose des sables* with pure chocolate ice-cream. The rest of the menu offers completely new dishes in harmony with Loiseau's style: foie gras escalope, conserved onion tart and salad of shoots, saddle of Pyrenean suckling lamb with its chops, stuffed piquillo (small conical red peppers) and aubergine purée, crunchy nougatine with a hazelnut mix, grapefruit and soft caramel sorbet. The mood is frank and cheerful, far from the weighty ambiance you find in certain great restaurants, and the cellars are impressively stocked with *grands crus.*

NIÈVRE

Château-Chinon

LE VIEUX MORVAN 8, place Gudin ✆ 03 86 85 05 01.** *Closed Sunday evening and Monday – except July ✆ August – and from mid-December to late January. Set menus from 15 € to 42 €. Rooms from 48 € to 65 €.* This solid *bourgeoise* house is located in the town centre, overlooking the little town and surrounding countryside. Not to be missed if you're looking for a traditional break; François Mitterand was said to be a frequent visitor. Architecture, rooms and furniture are hospitable, not to mention the aromas rising from the kitchens! Burgundian and Morvan gastronomy dominate the menus; the *cuisine*, too, is *bourgeoise*, and well turned out.

La Charité-sur-Loire

HOTEL LE GRAND MONARQUE * 33, quai Clemenceau ✆ 03 86 70 21 73.** *Fax : 03 86 69 62 32. Website : www.le-grand-monarque.fr Formula 18.50 € and set menus from 25 €. À la carte.* Rooms from 72 € to 90 €. The origins of this establishment date back to Louis XIV. It has 15 rooms, including an apartment and a suite, all different, in a pleasant setting with a panoramic view of the bridge and the River Loire. The restaurant offers traditional *cuisine*, with set menus or *à la carte.* James Grennerat is master of the place, and famous for his sauces. Among other specialities are crayfish with champagne and paprika, Bourgogne snails in Tannay wine and a dark chocolate *moelleux* with tea-flavoured cream and pistachio ice cream.

Magny-Cours

LA RENAISSANCE ** 2, rue de Paris ✆ 03 86 58 10 40.** *Closed Saturday lunchtime, Sunday evening and Monday. Annual closing 3 weeks in February and 2 weeks in August. Set menus from 35 € to 85 €. Rooms from 84 € to 150 €.* A haven of peace only metres from the racetrack. Jean-Claude Dray has over 3 decades of experience on the milometer, and has welcomed such illustrious racing drivers as Guy Ligier and Alain Prost at his tables in this pleasant setting. Three menus present a traditional *cuisine*. The Charolais beef steak and the frogs' legs still feature, along with sweetbreads and kidneys, in a series of savoury and convivial dishes.

Nevers

JEAN-MICHEL COURON 21 rue Saint-Etienne ✆ 03 86 61 19 28 *Fax 03 86 36 02 96. Website : www.jm-couron.com. Set menus from 20 € to 45 €, à la carte 60 €. Closed Sunday evening,*

Monday, Tuesday, first fortnight in January and from mid-July to mid-August. When you've been lucky enough to play second to Michel Bras for 4 years (between 1988 and 1992) your culinary baggage is obviously above average. Yet at barely 37, Jean-Michel Couron is not a publicity-seeker. His restaurant near St Etienne Church has a simple front with a wide window, and is just as ascetic inside, with the ancient stones in the small dining rooms left unadorned. The cuisine follows the same precepts, being undemonstrative: duck foie gras terrine, toast and an apple purée with cumin, sea-bream fillet with smoked bacon and green asparagus in a red wine and balsamic vinegar reduction, roast Barbary duck fillet with gingerbread and crusty cauliflower with grilled sesame seeds, biscuit *moelleux* with chocolate and almonds on a foamy bed of white chocolate, and green tea jelly and ice cream. The cellar is small, but selective, with advice given by wife Marie-Hélène.

Pouilly-sur-Loire

LE RELAIS FLEURI ET LE COQ HARDI *** **42, avenue de la Tuilerie** ✆ **03 86 39 12 99** *Closed Tuesday and Wednesday, from October to April. Menus from 25 € to 60 €, à la carte. Rooms 48 € to 80 €. Breakfast 9.50 €.* The Relais Fleuri is peacefully located on the Loire banks, with private access through the park (1ha.) and along the towpath. The ten rooms are shared between two buildings; the 'Cellier' rooms have a sophisticated charm that fits the setting. Bar and lounge are at guests' disposal, and the restaurant, Le Coq Hardi, is widely esteemed and has won several awards. The menu is seasonal, and features black truffles. You can find local specialities in the on-site shop.

SAÔNE-ET-LOIRE

Autun

LES URSULINES *** **14, rue Rivault** ✆ **03 85 86 58 58.** *Website: www.hotelursulines.fr. Open all year. Set menus from 27 € to 85 € (dégustation menu). Rooms and suites.* This former 17thc.convent in the heart of Autun's old quarter is listed by the *Châteaux et Hotels de France*. The formal gardens are magnificent, overhanging the town's Roman ramparts. The rooms, including some with sloping roofs, are either standard comfort or luxury, and all of them have an attractive view across the town or of the Morvan mountains. Breakfast is served in the converted chapel, which still has a feel of olden times. Nothing is missing from the excellent *cuisine*, and the fine wine list pays tribute to Burgundy and elsewhere.

Bourbon-Lancy

LE MANOIR DE SORNAT*** **Route de Sornat Allées des Platanes** ✆ **03 85 89 17 39** *Annual closing during January. Set menus from 18 € to 82 €. Rooms from 58 € to 125 €.* This imposing 19thc. building set in the heart of a green park offers pure enjoyment: a comfortable room in a period house, and a delicious and often surprising *cuisine* that is a real Pantagruelic feast of new flavours. Indulge yourself!

Chagny

LAMELOISE 36 place d'Armes ✆ **03 85 87 65 65** *Fax 03 85 87 03 57.Website: www.lameloise.fr. Set menus from 95 € to 130 €, à la carte 100 €. Closed Tuesday lunchtime, all day Wednesday, Thursday lunchtime and from 20 December to 26 January.* Could this be the most discreet of the great French hotel-restaurants? Lameloise almost seems to be hiding behind the modest face of a respectable Burgundian house with no gastronomic pretensions. Don't be misled by appearances, go in and discover for yourself the smiling welcome (even for passing visitors) well decorated but unostentatious setting and surprisingly relaxed staff. The wine list is encyclopaedic, though the choice of wines by the glass is limited. The loss of its third Michelin star last year must have been a blow, but the food is still excellent in the ultra-classic style: oysters in seafood jelly on a *chaud froid*, salad of herbs with crayfish tails, scallops with green asparagus, hazelnut butter flavoured with black olives, veal cooked two ways, with fresh creamed morels and *à la plancha* with truffle butter. For dessert you must experience the crêpes suzette prepared at your table, flambéd in Grand Marnier and served with vanilla ice-cream - a treat for the eyes and the tastebuds.

Chalon-sur-Saône

L'AIR DU TEMPS 7, rue de Strasbourg ✆ **03 85 93 39 01.** *Closed Sunday and Monday. Lunchtime formula 17 €, set menus at 22.50 €, 28 € and 33 € for the regional menu.* Discreet sophistication outside, gentle warmth in the two restaurant rooms decorated in regional colours. Visitors tend to come back, delighted with the elegantly set tables and blackboard featuring the chef's suggestions in chalk. Excellent cuisine based on fresh produce. The menus are often renewed.

MOULIN DE MARTOREY Saint-Rémy ✆ 03 85 48 12 98 *Set menus from 38 to 78 €, à la carte 55 €. Closed Sunday evening, Monday, Tuesday lunchtime and during February school holidays.* Jean-Pierre Gillot, who has taken over this 19thc.mill with its workings still visible in one of the dining rooms, is not a publicity-seeker. Confident of his skill and experience acquired with Troisgros and Savoy, he manages a half-classic, half-regional repertory with disarming honesty and ease. Pig's trotters stuffed with polenta, roast langoustines and shellfish juice, fillet of dory flavoured with ginger and roasted fish juices, French sweetbreads with Burgundy truffles, browned and blanched salsify, roast pigeon with prunes, calf's stomach with offal, caramel popcorn, corn-flavoured ice cream cornet with *churros* (Spanish fritters). The prices are reasonable, the setting marvellous – cosy but tasteful dining room, charming park with a little river running through it, impeccable service – and the wine list features the best Burgundy wine growers.

LE SAINT-GEORGES * 32, avenue Jean-Jaurès ✆ 03 85 90 80 50.** *Website : www.le-saintgeorges.fr. Hotel, gastronomic restaurant (closed Saturday lunchtime and Sunday evening) brasserie (closed Saturday lunchtime and Sunday). Rooms and suites from 69 € to 125 €.* This establishment is recommended for an overnight stay at Chalon-sur-Saône. Style and comfort are in evidence at reception and in the bar-club, lounges and restaurant. There are 43 standard rooms, 3 lounge rooms and 4 junior suites, of different types, with showers or baths, and a lounge corner as an option. All are soundproofed, with TV, direct phone line, mini-bar and hairdryer. In the kitchen, the chef deserves his stripes for his classic arrangements of regional recipes.

Louhans

MOULIN DE BOURGCHATEAU ** Route de Chalon ✆ 03 85 75 37 12. *Website : www.bourgchateau.com. Restaurant closed Monday, except from March to October. Set menus from 24 € to 60 €. Rooms from 46 € to 105 €.* The Donatelli family runs the Moulin de Bourgchâteau. Apart from daily renovation work, they managed to bring their sunny humour to this beautiful spot. Naturally warm, cordial without being familiar, they attract customers. The setting will encourage you to go full board, and the *cuisine* will confirm your choice. Burgundy has its place on the menu, with frogs' legs and Bresse chicken, but there are Italian dishes too: risotto *arborio* with truffles and tagliatell*i à la trevise* braised in a Parmesan shell, with cubes of pan-fried foie gras. The hot chocolate soufflé with an orange salad is a real delicacy. You'll take pleasure in discovering this restaurant, and note it down in your diary straight away!

Mâcon

HOTEL BELLEVUE * 416, quai Lamartine ✆ 03 85 21 04 04.** *Website: www.ila-chateau.com/bellevue. Hotel closed from late November to mid-December and from 1-15 May. Rooms and apartments from 85 € to 160 €. Breakfast 11 €. Garage 11 €. Bar open 24 hours a day (hotel residents only during the night).* This well run establishment is separated from the River Saône by the main road running along Quai Lamartine. The atmosphere is continental and comfortable, even cosy, and the standard rooms are soundproofed. Excellent welcome.

RESTAURANT PIERRE 7-9, rue Dufour ✆ 03 85 38 14 23. *Closed Sunday evening, Monday and Tuesday lunchtime. Set menus from 26 € to 71 €. Business menu 33 € (starter, main dish, dessert, wine and coffee). Children's menu 12 €.* Isabelle and Christian Gaulin are experts in the art of welcoming guests. The restaurant setting is elegant, with soft tones and lighting, and customers in ties. The service is scrupulously attentive throughout your meal. The menus change with the seasons, and are based on fresh market produce. Fresh and smoked salmon rillettes with mascarpone, a duck leg in *daube*, lobster and foie gras with crunchy sesame *seeds*, and langoustine tails in a tart with sweet spices. The desserts combine visual pleasure with a treat for the taste buds: the homemade sorbets are superb. Talented cooking; the downside is the rather stuffy ambiance.

Mercurey

HOTELLERIE DU VAL D'OR* 140, Grande Rue ✆ 03 85 45 13 70.** *Website : www.le-valdor.com. Annual closing from mid-December to mid-January. Restaurant closed Monday and Tuesday lunchtime. Menu of the day 23 €. Set menus from 20 € to 58 € lunchtimes, 38 € to 68 € evenings. Childrens' menu 12 €. Rooms from 85 € to 110 €. Breakfast 10 €.* Located in the village high street, this well-mannered hotel is used to welcoming both tourists and business guests. The 12 quiet and intimate rooms are stylishly furnished and personalised in the colours of the village seasons: TV, telephone and radio-alarm clock are at your disposal. The cuisine has recently won awards, and you will quite agree with the choice once you have tasted the duck foie gras with figs and brioche with pork rillettes, frogs'legs and snails in a *galette* (pancake) with garlic cream, Charolais beef fillet *maitre de chais* or farm-bred poultry with crayfish. A waffle with honey and 'bachelor' marmalade rounds it off nicely, with a superb selection from the cheeseboard.

Tournus

LE REMPART * 2, avenue Gambetta ✆ 03 85 51 10 56.** *Website : www.lerempart.com. Open every day. Set menus from 25 € to 70 €. Bistro menu 17 €. Rooms from 65 € to 95 €. Apartments and suite from 115 € to 160 €.* We're a long way from the military atmosphere once found in this 15thc. guardhouse. The meals cooked here now follow the traditional gastronomic path, with Burgundy well represented. The menus are delightful, with a generous choice à la carte, and a lot fish dishes in particular. You can order bistro food chez Marion, prepared and cooked according to the day's inspiration. The staff is always well turned out, and deserves its stripes.

AUX TERRASSES ** 18, avenue du 23-Janvier ✆ 03 85 51 01 74 *Restaurant closed Sunday evening, Monday and Tuesday lunchtime. Set menus from 27 € to 60 €.* Henriette and Michel Carette run one of the region's best-loved restaurants on the way into Tournus. You receive an attentive welcome, and can approach the table in relaxed and receptive mood. The elegant chef with his fine moustache and Michelin award cooks a magnificent traditional *cuisine* based on local produce, washed down with a very good wine list.

YONNE

Auxerre

BARNABET 14, quai de la République ✆ 03 86 51 68 88. *Open Tuesday evening to Sunday lunchtime. Set menu 35 € every day except weekends and public holidays, 56 € and 71 €, including wine.* The chef's name is Jean-Luc Barnabet. His restaurant facing the River Yonne has the look of a grand residence, with its gravel walks and well-tended gardens. You won't be disappointed inside, either, where the set menus keep their promises: one of these even accompanies each dish with a different wine. The duck ravioli, trout stuffed with crayfish, potato purée with truffles (in season) and a biscuit *mi-cuit* with chocolate are well worth recommending.

LE MAXIME* 2, quai de la Marine ✆ 03 86 52 14 19.** *Fax : 03 86 52 21 70. Website : www.lemaxime.com. Open all year. Rooms from 75 € to 80 €. Breakfast 10 €. Garage 6 €, and car park. Night watchman. Lift. Seminars. Animals supplement 5 €. Bar.* This converted salt-loft on the banks of the Yonne is now a prestigious hotel with 26 rooms, all intimate and comfortable. You receive a professional, smiling welcome, and the services offered are of a high standard, as is the traditional French cuisine. Elegant dining-room setting and seasonal menu.

Avallon

HOSTELLERIE DE LA POSTE ** 13, place Vauban ✆ 03 86 34 16 16.** *Fax : 03 86 34 19 19. Website: www.hostelleriedelaposte.com Set menus: brasserie from 14 €, restaurant 39 € to 60 €. Rooms from 99 € to 123 €, family room156 € to 196 €, suites 145 € to 181 €.* This hotel has been welcoming guests since 1707, including Napoleon, who stayed here on his return from Elba on 16 March 1815. The calm and spacious rooms combine old-world charm with modern comfort. Furnishings and *cuisine* are equally sophisticated; the set menus show creative use of local produce. Wine is included with some of the meals. The 1707 restaurant bar serves cocktails and champagne.

Chablis

HOSTELLERIE DES CLOS * Rue Jules-Rathier ✆ 03 86 42 10 63.** *Fax : 03 86 42 17 11. Website: www.hostellerie-des-clos.fr. Open all year, except Christmas to mid-January. Rooms from 55 € (single) to 84 € (double). Residence rooms 100 € and 122 €. Apartments 168 € and 183 €. Breakfast 10 €. Set menus from 35 € to 72 €. Children's menu 16 €. Half-board available. Car park and garage. Seminar rooms. Assisted disabled access. Animals accepted.* Michel Vignaud's restaurant is greatly appreciated. He offers his own interpretation of local Burgundian cuisine, such as veal kidneys with Chablis, snail fricassée with a parsley coulis and pikeperch with Chablis. Very pleasant welcome.

Joigny

LA COTE SAINT-JACQUES 14 fg de Paris ✆ 03 86 62 09 70 *Fax 03 86 91 49 70. Website: www.cotesaintjacques.com. Set menus from 78 € to 175 €, à la carte 150 €. Closed Monday and Tuesday* *lunchtime from November to April, annual closing from 2 January to 2 February.* Brigitte and Jean-Michel Lorain's top-of-the-range gastronomic family inn lies peacefully on the banks of the Yonne. Jean-Michel Lorain is among the 10 or 15 most decorated chefs in France. He trained with the best: the Troisgros brothers, Taillevent and Girardet in Switzerland, and of course beside his father, who was already drawing the crowds at the Côte Saint Jacques in the 1970's with his quail and foie gras tart and saddle of hare in pepper sauce. Lorain *fils* offers a technical and innovative cuisine with guarranteed success: oscietra caviar and combava (a kind of small lemon) royale, shellfish taboulé and iced, foamy cauliflower *vichyssoise*, pan-fried ormers, crushed *vitelottes* (potatoes with mauve flesh) with parmesan and butternut, rocket salad, red beetroot and bouchot mussels, sweetbreads with ginger, small onions, rhubarb and radishes. The desserts are as impressive, and include an amazing rose ice-cream in a crunchy tulip with cristallised rose petals. Marvellous wine list, almost unbeatable for great regional bottles.

L'Isle-sur-Serein

LE POT D'ETAIN 24, rue Bouchardat ✆ 03 86 33 88 10. *Fax : 03 86 33 90 93. Website: www.potdetain.com. Set menus from 23 € to 49 €. Rooms from 56 € to 69 €.* This former coaching inn offers 9 comfortable rooms with that particular family *cachet*, and a *cuisine* in the French country inn tradition, created and prepared by Fabien Pechery. The *menu du marché* varies according to the fresh market produce available, and the standard dishes feature seasonal suggestions. The wine list includes some of the finest French wines; father Alain Pechery makes his recommendations.

Montigny-la-Resle

LE SOLEIL D'OR RN77 ✆ 03 86 41 81 21.** *Email: le-soleil-dor@wanadoo.fr. Fax: 03 86 41 81 21. Under 6km south of Pontigny on the Nationale 77. Open all year. Rooms from 51 € (single), 54 € (double) and 62 € (triple). Breakfast 7 €. Set menus 18 € to 66 €. Etoile menu (lunchtime) 12 €. Childrens' menu 10 €. Private lounges. Menus change in April and November.* This top-quality hotel welcomes guests from all over Europe. 16 modern and comfortable rooms (one equipped for the disabled) have been fitted out in an ancient building with Pontigny terracotta tiles, and they are all full of character. Myriam Baujard takes care of everything down to the smallest detail, to make sure you have a perfect stay. Meals are served in two luxurious dining rooms (smoking and non-smoking) with well-spaced tables; the chef is imaginative and original (foie gras pan-fried with bananas and caramel with onions) and you can eat game in season: try the roast venison - or if you prefer, beef fillet with roquefort, or salmon in truffle oil. The desserts are surprising: go for the liquorice mousse. If you want to get out and about, nearby Auxerre, Pontigny and the Chablis vineyards offer plenty to do. Highly recommended.

Saint-Père-sous-Vézelay

L'ESPÉRANCE Route de Vézelay ✆ 03 86 33 39 10 *Fax 03 86 33 26 15. Website : www.marc-meneau-esperance.com. Set menus from 95 € to 195 €, à la carte 150 €. Closed Monday lunchtime, Tuesday, Wednesday lunchtime and from mid-January to early March.* Marc Meneau is a French culinary superstar, and a self-made man. In 1970, in search of adventure, he took on this former bourgeoise residence with its extensive dpark, at the foot of that most touristic of sites, Vezelay. Having won his stripes one by one, with a personal, sensual and ultra-technical *cuisine*, he astonishes observers with the complexity of his preparations. Oysters in seawater jelly, warm crayfish terrine with chive butter, crayfish stock, roast sole with herbs from the 'Simples garden' and grilled spine, pigeon and lobster roasted *en cocotte*, macaroons with raspberries and an iced violet *parfait*. The names of the dishes are concise, the food refined: this is great French cooking at its disconcerting best. The atmosphere in the dining room is delightful, with kind and attentive service, and the cream of Burgundian - and other - bottles on the wine list.

Sens

HOTEL DE PARIS ET DE LA POSTE* 97, rue de la République ✆ 03 86 65 17 43.** *Website: www.hotel-paris-poste.com. Email: contact@hotel-paris-poste.fr. Hotel-restaurant. Open all year. 4 types of room with toilets, bath, Tv and bar, from 61 € to 150 €. Breakfast 12 €. Half-board available. Pets admitted, supplement 8 €. Private garage 8 €.* A comfortable and appetising place to break your journey, with its two restaurants and 25 well-kept rooms. The setting combines tradition and modernity, and is both light and intimate. The services on offer are well up to 3-star standard.

LA MADELEINE 1 rue d'Alsace-Lorraine ✆ 03 86 65 09 31 *Fax 03 86 95 37 41. Website : www.restaurant-lamadeleine.fr. Set menus from 50 € to 90 €, à la carte 110 €. Closed Sunday, Monday and Tuesday lunchtime.* Patrick Gauthier is a sincere and inventive chef. He spends time in the restaurant with the guests, explaining his dishes and culinary philosophy, and guiding his customers' choice, while his excellent second takes charge of the cooking. He is never absent for too long, though: the scallops carpaccio-style, cooked instantly in lime juice and served cold with Isigny cream and avruga eggs must be on time, the slow-combustion roasting of his red mullet fillets with Maussane oil and lime and lemon sauce needs checking, and he wants to make sure that the Quercy lamb is cooked just as the customer at table 4 requested. This is a good-humoured restaurant, due to move to more comfortable premises quite soon.

AD 584550

Brittany

Douarnenez bay

Ile d'Ouessant
I. de Bréhat
Perros-Guirec
Ile de Batz
Roscoff
Plouescat
St-Pol-de-Léon
Lannion
Tréguier
Paimpol
Ploudalmézeau
le Folgoët
Landivisiau
Morlaix
Guingamp
N12
D767
D58
D168
BREST
Elorn
Landerneau
Monts d'Arrée
D789
le Conquet
Plougastel-Daoulas
N165
Finistère
Callac
Côtes
Cahaix-Plouguer
Camaret
le Faou
Crozon
Cap de la Chèvre
Pleyben
N164
Gouarec
Châteaulin
Aulne
Châteauneuf-du-Faou
Pointe du Raz
Douarnenez
Locronan
Noires
Vallée du Blavet
Montagnes
D1
Odet
Audierne
Quimper
le Faouët
Pontivy
D768
Scorff
Morbihan
Rosporden
Fouesnant
Bénodet
Pont-l'Abbé
Concarneau
Quimperlé
Pont-Aven
Blavet
N24
Guilvinec
Hennebont
Pointe de Penmarch
Lorient
Iles de Glénan
Auray
la Trinité-sur-Mer
Carnac
Port-Navalo
Quiberon
Océan Atlantique
Belle-Ile
RENNES
N
O
E
S
0
30 km
Motorway
Major road (4-lane)
Major road
Minor road
Reproduction interdite
Jean-Baptiste Nény
Septembre 2002

BRITTANY

Manche
St-Quay-
Portrieux
St-Cast
St-Malo
Cancale
le Mont-
St-Michel
Dinard
Dol-
de-Bretagne
N176
A84
Vers Rouen
St-Brieuc
N12
Dinan
Antrain
N176
Vers Alençon
d'Armor
Combourg
le Couesnon
Fougères
N12
Vers Mayenne
D700
Ille
Rance
N12
N176
A84
Loudéac
N164
et
Forêt de
Paimpont
RENNES
la Vilaine
Vitré
N24
N157
Paimpont
Vers Laval
Josselin
D163
Ploërmel
N137
Janzé
N24
Vilaine
la Guerche-
de-Bretagne
la Vilaine
Bain-
de-Bretagne
Landes de Lanvaux
N12
la Gacilly
D94
Vannes
Rochefort-
en-Terre
Redon
Vers Angers
Questembert
N165
Golfe du
Morbihan
la Vilaine
Sarzeau
la Roche-
Bernard
Loire
N165
Atlantique
Vers Paris
N137
A11
St-Nazaire
Loire
Loire
NANTES
N249
Vers Cholet
A83
Vers Niort
Ile d'Yeu

BREST AND NORTH FINISTÈRE

Brest

Brest is becoming a popular tourist spot, despite the hurried post-war reconstruction and lack of old buildings. That austere architecture, all straight lines, hides some interesting things if you take the time to notice them.

ARSENAL Tourist Office ✆ 02 98 44 24 96. During the summer season, simply turn up with your identity card or passport (Porte de la Grande Riviere, route de la Corniche). Voluntary guides organise 1h30min tours, every 30mins. You visit a about a third of the town's total area, and board a Navy ship.

CHATEAU. Its majestic walls impress the visitor. The first bridge across the Penfeld was built in 1836; the inhabitants requested it, having had enough of crossing by ferry. This structure was destroyed in World War II, and replaced by today's bridge, which can be raised in less than three minutes, to let ships of over 20m high come through.

MUSEE DE LA MARINE Château de Brest ✆ 02 98 22 12 39. *Closed 15 December-31 January. Open April-September: 10am-6.30pm and October-March: 10am-12 noon and 2pm-6pm (except Tuesday). Admission: adult 5 €.* The medieval castle is built on a rocky spur, overlooking the Penfeld and the harbour - an exceptional, strategic site, quickly recognised and exploited. It is the oldest historic monument in Brest, covering 17 centuries (listed since 1923) and has been reshaped many times during its turbulent past, which is closely linked to the history of both town and seaboard. The National Naval Museum contains a fine collection of ship scale models, paintings and sculptures. Richelieu's Royal Arsenal is remembered, along with the skilled carpenters who built the great seagoing fleets in the heyday of sailing ships. The Grasse fleet was armed in Brest, whose victory over the British fleet at Chesapeake on 30 August 1781 led to the Yorktown victory on 19 October, and ultimately, to American Independence. A significant part of French naval history is commemorated here.

CONSERVATOIRE BOTANIQUE NATIONAL 52, allee du Bot ✆ 02 98 02 46 00. *Access to garden: 9am-7pm. Reception pavilion open to the public Wednesday and Sunday: 2pm-4.30pm. Admission fee for the greenhouses: adult 3.50 €.* 40ha. of natural landscape offering a real breath of fresh air. You cover 6km along the edge of the lakes, without taking the same path twice. The Botanic Conservatory is on the other side of the site, and adds a scientific aspect to this pleasant walk.

OCEANOPOLIS Port de Plaisance du Moulin Blanc ✆ 02 98 34 40 40. *www.oceanopolis.com. Open all year, mid-September-late March (closed Monday): 10am-5pm. Other periods, open every day: 9am-6pm. Admission: adult 15 €, child 10.50 €, under-4s free.* You learn all about ocean movement and underwater life on this scientifically instructive but spectacular site. Three pavilions deal with the different marine environments: temperate, tropical and polar. All in all, the centre contains over 1,000 different species.

PONT ALBERT LOUPPE. This pedestrian bridge has a superb view of the sailing and commercial harbours to the right and Plougastel to the left.

PONT DE RECOUVRANCE. This mythical bridge is a border between the right bank quarters (Recouvrance and Saint Pierre) and Brest; the intersection of town and military bastion; a link between Brest and its economic sector. You sample real Brest life here.

LA RADE. The most famous harbour roads in France. Today, leisure, cultural and sports activities are on offer. See the schooner l'Etoile built in 1932, the Belle Poule, modern warships and submarines.

Camaret-sur-Mer

The 'curved harbour' holds mainly sailing craft today, some of which just do a short round-trip from Brest. The quays look less like workplaces than leisure sites for relaxing and sport.

LAGATJAR ALIGNMENTS. 143 menhirs in a meadow outside the village. These alignments date back to 2,500 or 3,000 years before Christ, and are one of Brittany's biggest sites.

POINTE DE PEN-HIR. The sunsets are splendid, but it's worth going even in a storm. From 70m up, you look down at the jagged cliffs. The waves rush into the gashes, the noise fills your ears as you gaze at the foamy sea. The sight almost makes you forget to admire the warmly coloured moors around you.

Crozon

The peninsula's centre, and a crossing-place for the region's visitors. It is also known for sailing, being perfectly equipped to meet the needs of enthusiasts. Don't forget to admire the 'ten thousand martyrs' reredos in Saint Pierre Church.

ANSE DE DINAN 'KASTELL DINN'. A natural arch links this rock, nicknamed 'le château', to the land. The waves crash against it, raising sprays of foam. Dramatic!

MAISON DES MINERAUX Route du Cap de la Chevre ✆ 02 98 27 19 73. The Crozon Peninsula is of geological interest and rich in minerals. The museum contains a series of rocks explaining its composition.

Morgat

Crozon's seaside resort. Popular in summer, especially for sailing craft, Morgat's reputation comes from its famous sea caves. Over centuries, the sea eroded faults in the sandstone, forming these caves easily reached by boat. They are known as Sainte Marine, Cheminée du Diable, Cormorans and Entonnoir. The most famous is Grotte de l'Autel. The rock walls are coloured with quartz and other minerals. Fabulous!

CAP DE LA CHEVRE 'BEG AR C'HAOR'. One of the peninsula's major sites. At the foot of the headland, the sea has eroded caves in the rock, only accessible by boat. One is called Charivari; a cormorant colony has settled there. From the cliffs, you look over stretches of gorse and heather-covered moor, with the Pointe du Raz so close to the south.

Plougastel

Ten minutes from Brest town centre, Plougastel is fighting for its artistic and historic identity, and its strawberries. A good reason to discover this village, with its maze of little streets.

LE CALVAIRE. Made up of 181 statues representing the life of Christ. Though a mite motionless, it is still fascinating to gaze at the naive-looking little characters, decipher their attitudes and spot symbolic details - for example, the bumps on the cross stand, for plague boils.

CHAPELS. A dozen little 16th and 17thc. chapels are scattered over the peninsula.

MUSEE DE LA FRAISE ET DU PATRIMOINE Rue Louis-Nicolle ✆ 02 98 40 21 18. *www.musee-fraise.org. Open every day June-August (ask about other periods). Admission: adult 4 €, concessions 3.10 €, 10-18s 2.50 €.* The 'Plougastel People' and their peculiarities are on view in this museum. Three centuries of strawberry growing; shellfish catching in Brest harbour; an evening in the reconstructed period interior of an early 20thc. farm. On the first floor, 30 models show developments in local costume. You will be fascinated by the mysterious 'breuriez' ritual!

MORLAIX AND THE MONTS D'ARRÉE

These wild and legendary Breton mountains are protected in the Armorique regional nature reserve.

PARC NATUREL REGIONAL D'ARMORIQUE 15, place aux Foires ✆ 02 98 81 90 08. *www.parc-naturel-armorique.fr.* The reserve covers 172,000ha. (112,000ha on land, 60,000ha at sea) of varied landscapes linked to past and present activity. Otters, dolphins, seals and salmon live in and around the waters. Information and facilities are available all year at 20 different points, to help you get the most from this exceptional environment.

Morlaix

The Penze and River Morlaix estuaries merge in the bay. Morlaix is known for its famous 58m-high viaduct, but it is also a charming old town. Its 15-17thc. 'lantern' houses have corbelled fronts decorated with statues of saints.

CHATEAU DE SUSCINIO GARDENS ✆ 02 98 72 05 86. *Open all year.* Recently, this historic site has been reorganised into contemporary thematic gardens unfolding one after the other, with landscaped scenes featuring ancient trees and collector's plants (Remarkable French Trees label).

MAISON A PONDALEZ 9, Grand-Rue ✆ 02 98 88 68 88. *Open all year. Opening days and times vary with the season. Admission: adult 2.20 €.* This 16thc. half-timbered house has been completely restored and is open to visitors. It has a fine spiral staircase and passages, and an impressive wooden fireplace.

Carhaix-Plouger

Set between the Monts d'Arrée and the 'Black Mountains', this is a good place to start your tour of the region.

MAISON DU SENECHAL Rue de Brizeux. Carhaix-Plouger Tourist Office is housed in this fine building with its 16thc. front, carved granite ground floor and statuettes decorating each storey. Exhibitions take place here all year.

Keremma

MAISON DES DUNES ✆ **02 98 61 69 69**. *Open 8am-12 noon and 2pm-6pm in low season, except Saturday: 10.30am-6.30pm in season. Admission fee for cultural events.* This site stretches over Treflez and Plounevez-Lochrist villages, extending Goulven Bay, and is the north coast's biggest open sandy space: 8km of beach and 200ha. of dunes. 600 plant varieties grow here, and a number of migrating birds stop off every year.

Plouezoc'h

In this delightful place, the winding Rivers Dourduff and Morlaix fill and empty with the tide. Surrounding paths lead through the fields past old farms, copses and fishermen's houses. Saint Etienne Church displays its strange steeple: a massive tower topped by a fine spire next to a turret with stairs. There is a clear view from the top, across to the Monts d'Arrée.

CAIRN DE BARNENEZ ✆ **02 98 67 24 73**. *Open all year except Monday. Admission: adult 5 €*. Europe's biggest cairn (72m x 27m). You see a chaotic heap of stones (14,000 tonnes), but in fact these are carefully built mortuaries, which have survived the centuries without falling apart.

Plouneour-Menez

At the foot of the Monts D'Arrée, a church spire soars proudly into the sky like a needle, bare of pinnacle and balustrade. The triumphal door is sober in design, and the houses round the parish enclosure add a genuine touch.

RELEC ABBEY ✆ **02 98 78 05 97**. *Open all year except January: 10am-7pm. Exhibitions February-December.* The 12thc. Notre Dame du Relec Abbey nestles against the peaty slopes of the Monts d'Arree, upriver f wooded Queffleuth Valley. A departmental restoration programme is underway, and the association Abati Ar Releg looks after the site. Concerts take place on Sundays from May to September, providing a meeting-place for different traditions and cultures. On leaving the abbey, take the sunken lanes across country, where you find typical regional farms and houses. The Monts d'Arrée peaks are silhouetted against the sky in the south. A real breath of fresh air.

Roscoff

This town has kept its character, despite the many tourists and ferry crossings to Britain and Ireland. You can admire beautiful granite houses, with finely carved dormer-windows and delightful gardens.

AQUARIUM STATION BIOLOGIQUE Place Georges-Tessier ✆ **02 98 29 23 25**. 34 smallish tanks house different varieties of fish, including the conger eel. On the first floor, you find some minerals, and exhibition panels on the sea's resources.

MAISON DES JOHNNIES ET DE L'OIGNON ROSE DE ROSCOFF 48, rue Brizieux ✆ **02 98 61 25 48**. *Closed in January. Open July and August: 3pm-7pm, except Saturday. Admission: adult 4 €*. Learn the story of the Johnnies and Roscoff's pink onions. It began in the early 19thc., when Roscoff men crossed the Channel to sell their onion, reputed for its flavour and long life. Others followed them, and the 'French onion-sellers' became known all over the British Isles. Local history only remembers one ancestral Johnny; Henri Olivier. The museum also explains how local onions are grown.

Saint-Pol-de-Léon

The town really began with the Welsh monk Paul Aurelien (future Saint-Pol) who left his retreat to convert the place. A bishopric was established, lasting until 1790, and generating plenty of striking monuments.

BAIE DE PEMPOUL. Cockle-fishers' paradise, and pleasant place to walk, maybe as far as Sainte Anne islet, the village's seaside resort with beach, sailing centre and Kernevez Park (private château).

CATHEDRAL. Built between the 12th and 16thc. The west front first draws your attention, with its two unlike steeples rising to 55m, combining elegance and austerity. The 15thc. chancel is pure Gothic, and the sixty 16thc. choirstalls are carved with different motifs, some funny, others representing local trades.

NOTRE DAME DU KREISKER CHAPEL. This monument rises to 77m - from the ashes of successive Norman and English attacks. In the reign of Napoleon 1, its steeple was a landmark for sailors, ensuring its survival. The northern porch, carved oak altar and 17thc. reredos are not to be missed. You can then climb 163 steps to the balustrade for an amazing view.

VIEILLE VILLE. The old town can be found around the Rue du General Leclerc, between the Kreisker and the cathedral. Several fine houses enhance its medieval character.

CÔTE DE GRANIT ROSE

The unleashed elements sculpted this pink granite coastline, a striking sight along the Tregor seafront.

Lannion

Tregor's capital goes back to the 11thc., and even now you can see 12th-17thc. churches, and half-timbered 15th and 16thc. houses lining its narrow paved streets. The medieval atmosphere has been safeguarded, to the delight of visitors.

CENTRE-VILLE. 16th and 17thc. half-timbered houses with slate sections and caryatids, and others with plain half-timbering, Place Leclerc and Rues des Chapeliers.

CHATEAU LE CRUGUIL ✆ 02 96 48 42 26. *Open inside and outside, weekdays July & August (closed weekends & public holidays): 2pm-6pm. Admission: adult 5 €, under-18s free.* This 16thc. manor, reshaped in the 19thc., belonged to the Comtes de Lannion. You can visit the salon and dining-room, and the park with its formal garden, arbour and lake is an attractive place for a stroll.

BRELEVENEZ CHURCH (Trinité Church). *Guided tours all summer.* Reached by 142 steps. The Templars probably built this Romanesque church. Its second name comes from the south porch's three stone piles representing the Trinity.

STAIRCASE DOWN TO LANNION. The 150-year-old stair had 365 steps for the days of the year. Daily sins could be expiated by climbing them on your knees. Today, there are only 142 left.

Perros-Guirec

A health resort popular with tourists, this pretty little town has majestic surroundings. The coastal paths and Breton coast-road towards Tregastel and Trebeurden are splendid. Kids love the seaside resort. Walk along the Sentier des Douaniers (Smugglers' Paths are here known as Customs Men's Paths!) and admire the dramatic scenery.

NOTRE DAME DE LA CLARTE CHAPEL. The spring filling the fountain gave its name to this Flamboyant Gothic church, built of pink granite in 1445. Pilgrims to the site would entreat the Virgin to cure their eye trouble.

CHEMIN BOISE. You can go back to Saint-Guirec cove this way, and explore the region's sublime granite landscapes.

MUSEE DE CIRE Bd. du Linkin ✆ 02 96 91 23 45. *Open every day, Easter holidays and 15 June-30 September.* This museum groups together life-size waxworks of famous Breton characters like Ernest Renan or La Chalotais. Historical scenes from Breton, Revolutionary and Chouan history are reconstructed.

Pink granite coastline in Ploumanac'h

SEPT-ILES. The Seven Islands mainly shelter birds, though some are inhabited. Rouzic, Malban, Bono, l'Ile Plate, l'Ile aux Moines, l'Ilot du Cerf and the rocky Costans plateau are home to about 18,000 bird couples. You can reach the islands by boat from Perros-Guirec. They cover 44ha. and are protected, with restricted access. A boat trip is the best way to see the whole group, and discover the many types of seabird.

Pleumeur-Bodou

MUSEE DES TELECOMS LE RADOME Cosmopolis ✆ 02 96 46 63 80. *Open every day May-August. Opening days vary during the rest of the year. Admission: adult 7 €.* The photo of the Radôme looming over a small Breton stone house is one of the Pink Granite Coast's symbolic images, combining modernity and tradition. In the 1960s, the Radôme and its aerial ensured the first TV link between the United States and France. No longer in use today, it is a listed historic monument where two shows are held, one of them retracing the telecommunications adventure. The Telecommunications Museum at its foot recalls the people and inventions that made telecom history. A place for encounters and discovery, and a great family experience.

PLANETARIUM DE BRETAGNE - LE CINEMA DES ETOILES Cosmopolis ✆ 02 96 15 80 30 / 02 96 15 80 32 *(24hrs a day). www.planetarium-bretagne.fr. Open every day during school holidays (closed Saturday out of season and Wednesday October-March) July & August: late night opening Tuesday. Admission: adult 6.80 €, concessions 5.44 €, families 21.76 €* . Cosmopolis is a scientific theme park which retraces the region's development from the Neolithic Age via the Gallic village and its menhirs to the modern telecommunications era. The planetarium has one of the biggest cupolas in Europe.

VILLAGE GAULOIS Cosmopolis ✆ 02 96 91 83 95. *Open April-September. 10.30am-7pm in July & August. Otherwise 2pm-6pm. Admission: adult 4 € to 4.50 €.* Discover the daily life of Meem the Gaul in his reconstructed village, with activities that are both educational and fun, and a tavern at your disposal...

STATION ORNITHOLOGIQUE DE L'ILE-GRANDE ✆ 02 96 91 91 40. *Open every day. June & September 2pm-6pm. July & August: 10am-1pm and 2.30pm-7pm.* Stop in here to find out about the different bird species on the Seven Islands. There are explanatory films, and discovery trips with an ornithologist, and you'll end up an expert in seagulls and gannets.

Trebeurden

Suggestive rock and granite shapes are scattered across the moor round Trebeurden, which developed into a seaside resort from the 19thc. onwards. Its 15km coastline is made up of rocky cliffs, dunes, marshes and moors, reached by a number of paths. You find menhirs, dolmen and covered lanes recalling a megalithic past. Enjoy both countryside and watersports: Trebeurden has it all.

Fort La Latte, Frehel

ALLEE COUVERTE DE PRAJOU MENHIR. 14.50m long, with seven covering stones. At the end of the corridor, the funeral chamber contains some interesting examples of wall art.

CASTEL. A chain of dunes link this almost-wild island to the coast.

SAINTE TRINITE CHURCH. 19thc., Latin cross-shaped, containing models of hanging boats.

SAINT-BRIEUC BAY

From Paimpol to Cap Frehel, this bay offers places of interest and a few havens of peace and quiet.

Erquy

Specialising in Saint Jacques scallops, this pretty seaside resort has seven beaches, twelve campsites and a lot of small hotels.

The GR34, or 'smugglers' path'

You can walk down the Goëlo Coast from Roselier headland to Loguivy-de-la-Mer along the GR34, taking about 3 days at a steady but relaxed rhythm, and two days if you hurry and don't stop to bathe too often. The smugglers' path, called chemin des douaniers - Revenue (or Customs) Men's path - in French, is the place for a beautiful and gentle hike accessible to everyone. Sunday walkers can choose to cover a short section only. Braver and more energetic hikers who decide to follow the entire distance discover the whole of Saint Brieuc Bay and beyond, including the Plouha Cliffs, which are the highest in Brittany (104m), and their wide beaches

Fréhel

The moors are sublime: 400ha. of wild gorse and heather-covered land 70m above the sea, with some equally beautiful coastal paths.

CAP FREHEL. Already inhabited in prehistoric times, Cap Fréhel was a Gallo-Roman site around 175-195 A.D., and suffered from the 10thc. Norman invasions. The current lighthouse is 103m above the sea, its beam reaching 110km.

FORT LA LATTE © **02 96 41 40 31.** *www.castlelalatte.com. Open every day July & August: 10am-7pm (other periods: ask about opening times). Admission: adult 4.10 €, under-12s 2.20 €*. This pink sandstone medieval fortress was transformed into a coastal fort between 1690 and 1715. The 14thc. defence system still exists, however; towers, curtain-walls, drawbridge, oubliettes and keep have survived the centuries.

Hillion

MAISON DE LA BAIE Site de l'Etoile © **02 96 32 27 98**. *Closed 16 December-3 January 2006. Admission (permanent exhibition): adult 3 €. Temporary exhibitions free.* The centre informs you about local environmental treasures and maritime activity. Interesting for holidaymakers wanting to know more about the region, but also for those just passing through.

Paimpol

Fishermen set out for Iceland from Paimpol (read Pierre Loti on the subject) and this memorable era is recalled in the town streets and small neighbouring villages, on memorial stones and in ex-votos.

VIEILLE VILLE. The old town is the Latin Quarter, turbulent in the Iceland days, but now a pleasant place, with its ancient alleyways leading to the port.

BEAUPORT KERITY ABBEY Chemin de l'Abbaye © **02 96 55 18 58**. *www.abbaye-beauport.com. Open all year, every day: 10am-12 noon and 2pm-5pm (10am-7pm 15 June-15 September).* This ruined building climbs the hill at the bottom of Beauport cove. You can still see the chaplaincy, press, cellar and refectory, which give you an idea of the abbey in its moment of glory.

MUSEE DE LA MER Rue Labenne © **02 96 22 02 19**. *Open Easter-September. Admission: adult 4.40 €.* Housed in a former cod-drying shed, this museum retraces Paimpol's great Icelandic fising epic. You can also see exhibitions devoted to the Royal and merchant navy, the wreck of the Pourquoi Pas and the lives of sailors' wives.

Plouha

KERMARIA AN ISQUIT (House of Mary the Healer) ✆ 02 96 20 35 78. *Guided tours 1 June-30 September: 9am-12 noon and 2pm-6pm. Admission free. Pardon: 3rd Sunday in September.* This 13thc. chapel was extended in the 15th, 17th and 18thc. Statues of the apostles decorate the south porch. The danse macabre is painted on either side of the nave: 47 characters including a Pope, king, labourer and cord-maker appear in an original dance of death.

PLAGE BONAPARTE ET MAISON D'ALPHONSE. In 1944, 135 allied aviators shot down over France were evacuated from Bonaparte Beach towards England by submarine, commanded from Alphonse's house.

POINTE DE PLOUHA. Take the smugglers' path for a marvellously colourful walk on the Plouha headland.

Saint-Brieuc

Some 17thc. half-timbered houses have survived the town's modernisation, and can be found in the Vieux Saint Brieuc alleys; Rue Fardel, Rue de la Quinquaine, Rue Notre-Dame, Rue du Gouet, Rue Houvenagle, Place au Lin and Place du Martray.

SAINT ETIENNE CATHEDRAL. Several styles are blended in the present cathedral, finally finished in the 18thc. It is one of Saint-Brieuc's few fortified buildings, with its two outside towers. The Renaissance organ dates back to 1540.

MUSEE D'ART ET D'HISTOIRE Cour Francis-Renaud ✆ 02 96 62 55 20. *Open all year. Admission free.* The permanent exhibition illustrates maritime activity, including Icelandic fishing, agriculture, the sailmaking industry and weaving crafts, tourist explosion and social and religious life, through costumes and cultural objects.

Saint-Quay-Portrieux

This deep-water harbour is a popular place for fishing and sailing.

KERTUGAL CHAPEL. Dating back to the 19thc. The pardon is held the last Sunday in July; sailors used to fulfil their vows here, after the fishing season.

PORTRIEUX CHAPEL. This 15thc. chapel was rebuilt in the 18thc. The marble altar was put up with the fishermen's 'tithe', known as 'God's part'.

BEACHES AND PATHS. Take a 5km-walk along the smugglers' path between the Casino beach and harbour. For lazier types, there are five beaches (Casino, Châtelet, Comtesse, Port and Grève Noire), great for sunbathing or strolling in the soft sand.

CÔTE D'EMERAUDE

The Channel looks blue-green from the Emerald Coast cliffs. There are ports of call for sailing trips, and beaches for those unforgettable family holidays.

Cancale

West of Saint Michel Bay, Cancale clings to the granite coastline like any typical Breton fishing village, although its oysters, famous since the 17thc., have placed it in quite a different league. Taste them in the restaurants or directly from the oyster farmers, for a real treat.

FERME MARINE Route de la Corniche ✆ 02 99 89 69 99. *Open 15 February-30 October: tour at 3pm. 15 June-15 September: tours at 11am, 3pm and 5pm. Admission: adult 6.10 €, child 3.10 €.* The oyster farmer's job is explained with its history, and you find out more afterwards, in the workshops. There is a shell exhibition and a film about pearl farming, showing the sea from a different angle.

Dinan

This medieval city on the Rance banks has an old harbour that was once a busy trading port. The waterway brought prosperity, and helped the cloth and leather industries to develop. Steeped in art and history, Dinan is one of Brittany's most beautiful towns.

SAINT SAUVEUR BASILICA. The fine Romano-Byzantine front was built in the 12thc., and Flamboyant Gothic aspects added in the 15th and 16thc. Inside, the architecture, furnishings and stained-glass are remarkable. Joan of Arc's companion Du Guesclin's heart is kept here.

SAINT MALO CHURCH. The building dates back to the 15thc., but was reshaped in the 19thc. Parts of the original are preserved (apse) and the English organ is listed.

MUSEE DU CHATEAU DE DINAN Rue du Chateau ✆ 02 96 39 45 20. *Open all year, except January. 1 June-30 September, open every day: 10am-6.30pm.* The castle's ramparts and machicolated keep, art and history collections, furniture and gold plate reflect local heritage.

GRANDS ET PETITS FOSSES. The fossés are earth ramparts put up in the 15thc. to protect the walls against artillery fire. They stretch from the keep to Jerzual Gate. The Grands Fossés link Saint Malo Gate and Saint Julien Tower, and a garden has been laid out in the moat, giving an unobstructed view of the north towers. The Petits Fossés extend from the Town Hall to the keep.

Dinard

This was a small fishing village until the mid-19thc., when the gentle climate and many sheltered beaches began to attract English aristocrats, who came here for sea bathing and tennis in summer. Today, the resort is still highly rated for traditional seaside holidays.

USINE MAREMOTRICE DE LA RANCE. This kind of dam is unique in France. The idea of exploiting tidal force to produce electricity was attractive on paper, but proved expensive and not at all cost-effective. The sight of Saint-Malo's ramparts from the dam is worth the trip, though.

CLAIR DE LUNE. The most popular of Dinard's four walks. You discover the Grand Hôtel, with its lovely view of Prieuré Beach.

Saint-Malo

The Emerald Coast's jewel, perched on its granite rock at the mouth of the Rance. This famous navigators' town lifts its proud slate and granite walls above the encircling ramparts.

GRAND AQUARIUM Ave. du Général Patton ✆ 02 99 21 19 00. *www.aquarium-st-malo.com. Open every day: 10am-6pm (9.30am-7 or 8pm in season). Admission; adult 13,50 €, 4-14s 9.50 €, under-4s free.* The visit is organised like an underwater dive, where you discover the sea's mysteries first-hand. Meet sharks, turtles and piranhas, before surfacing in a tropical forest. Those in search of excitement can also spend the night in the sharks' ring!

SAINT VINCENT CATHEDRAL Place Jean de Chatillon. Built between the 12th and 20thc., with a magnificent set of contemporary stained glass windows.

DIGUE DE PARAME. You leave the walled part of Saint Malo via this dike, running along Sillon Beach to Rochebonne. In summer, you can watch the birds, and in winter, well wrapped-up, fill your lungs with sea air. Follow this route along the beach, then, and treat yourself to a hot chocolate (or something stronger) at Rochebonne.

FORT NATIONAL. Designed by Vauban and Garangeau like a warship at anchor, the fort was built in 1689 from Chausey granite. It narrates the exploits of corsairs and navigators, naval successes and tragedies. There is an exhibition hall, and you can see the dungeon/ammunition store. The view of the town from the second wall (early 19thc.) is superb.

GRAND BE. From the ramparts, facing Bonsecours Beach, this is the big 'rock' on the left. In fact, it holds Chateaubriand's tomb. Be careful of the tide; it is all too easy to get cut off and be stuck on this island, between sky and water.

COBAC PARC Lanhelin ✆ 02 99 73 80 16. *Open 10 April-26 September, weekends and public holidays; every day in July & August. Admission: from 3 years old upwards, 12 €. Group (20+) and school rates.* This woodland theme park covers 15 ha. and offers a variety of leisure activities: swimming pools and slides, playgrounds (including one under cover) swings, mini-golf, boat trips, go-carts, a 1900 carrousel, Pony Express, Mad Mountains, Rapido (spectacular 80m descent by boat) and so on. You can meet animals (Goat Island; bird sanctuary) and see naturalized ones in the museum. Shady car park (1,000 free places), picnic area, shop, fast food and baby changing facilities on site.

MEMORIAL 1939-1945 Cité Aleth - Quartier Saint Servan ✆ 02 99 82 41 74. *Open April to mid-November. Closed Monday except July & August. Admission: adult 5 €.* This museum covers three floors and 500 sqm, and retraces the history of Saint Malo during the Second World War through photos, objects, articles and documentary film. The memorial was put up by the town in 1994, in the German anti-aircraft defence blockhaus, which is located in the courtyard of Aleth Fort, built according to Vauban's plans in 1759.

RENNES AND THE ILLE-ET-VILAINE

Rennes

At first, this was Condate, 'the confluent', religious and political capital of Armorique, then Brittany. Despite being dogged by fires (the Breton Parliament building was a recent victim) this town is attractive, eternally young and never lacks for atmosphere.

PLACE DU PARLEMENT ET PARLEMENT DE BRETAGNE. The town's finest architectural group, dating back to 1725; several top Parisian architects and decorators of the day had a hand in building it. The most striking rooms are the Salle des Gros Piliers, 36m by 12m, and the Grand'chambre where Parliamentary sessions used to be held, and which boasts two loggias and some magnificent paintings and tapestries. The buildings round the square with their granite arcades, two floors in tuffeau (chalky stone) and Mansart-style roofs are extremely elegant and all made to the same pattern.

PLACE DES LICES. Site of tournaments, festivals and executions in the Middle Ages. One of the two 19thc. covered markets designed by Martenot (Eiffel and Baltard's contemporary) now houses exhibitions and concerts, and the other, the noisy and colourful Saturday market. The Molant and Montbourcher mansions are an unusual blend of wood and granite.

PLACE SAINTE ANNE. To get here, you come down the Rue Saint-Michel, with its half-timbered houses restored in bright colours.

SAINT MELAINE ABBEY. A network of ancient streets busy with shops leading off from the Places Sainte Anne, de la Mairie and du Parlement converges on the Thabor Park and Saint Melaine Abbey.

HOTEL DE VILLE. The Baroque Town Hall has two curved wings, one on either side of the Tour de l'Horloge (Clocktower) capped with a lead onion-shaped dome. The Neo-Classical theatre facing it was built a century later, and is rounded in shape, its façade decorated with Muses. This square is always full of life, which is its chief attraction.

MUSEE DE BRETAGNE 20, quai Emile-Zola © 02 99 28 55 84. *Admission free.* The local collective memory is preserved in this temple to Breton culture from Prehistoric times to the present day - but is to be rehoused at the end of 2005. A few months of closure to put up with; then a new beginning. See you later!

MUSEE DES BEAUX-ARTS 20, quai Emile-Zola © 02 99 28 55 84. *Open every day, except Monday and public holidays. Open all year: 10am-12 noon and 2pm-6pm. Admission: adult 5,30 €, concessions 2.05 €, under-18s free.* The Fine-Arts museum boasts a collection of prestigious paintings, including Georges de la Tour's famous Nativité. These are mostly 17thc. collections, but other periods are represented, including contemporary works.

LE THABOR. Formal gardens, fountains and waterfalls, rare trees and a rose-garden right in the town centre! The Thabor Park's main attraction is its botanical garden, however: an open book on the natural world.

LES GAYEULLES. One of Brittany's biggest leisure parks, stretching over 100ha. The swimming-pool, campsite, grassy areas and playgrounds, minigolf and a children's farm (limited access) and sports pitches and halls are at your disposal. There is even a 'health circuit' and two jogging tracks.

Ille-et-Vilaine

Fougères

Breton, Norman and French conquerors fought over Fougères, strategically placed close to Rennes. Today, it is a charming town.

CHATEAU MEDIEVAL Place Pierre-Symon © 02 99 99 79 59. *Closed in January. Open every day: hours vary according to season. Admission: adult 3.70 €.* Built on a headland above the Nançon Valley, this fine feudal castle is Europe's biggest. Its 13 towers are linked by crenellated curtain walls, forming a 2ha. enclosure.

ATELIER-MUSEE DE L'HORLOGERIE ANCIENNE 37, rue Nationale © 02 99 99 40 98. *Open every day, 15 June-1 September. Open Tuesday-Saturday during other periods. Admission: adult 4.50 €, concessions 3.70 €, families 16.20 €.* Over 200 exhibits trace the development of the timepiece, from the first church clocks to your wristwatch.

BELFRY. This typically Northern French building is only found in Brittany in Fougères and Dinan. This one is the older of the two, and is made of granite, of course.

SAINT SULPICE CHURCH. The church was built in the craftsmen's quarter of the lower town between the 15th and 18thc. Inside, you find two 15thc. granite reredoss and a miraculous 13thc. statue of Notre Dame des Marais (Our Lady of the Marshes).

SAINT LEONARD CHURCH. This church has been reshaped many times; the stained glass is its main attraction. Look closely at the 12thc. medallion on the left, illustrating an episode from Saint Benoit's life. It is Brittany's oldest stained-glass window.

Montreuil-sous-Pérouse

LA ROCHE-AUX-FEES. This Fairies' Rock is the biggest megalithic monument in Brittany. 41 blocks of red shale (some weighing 40 tons) on a 20m x 4m pathway form a vestibule 1.20m high, and a room divided into four. These stones fell from the fairies' aprons, or so the legend goes.

Redon

Crossroads for land and water traffic, Redon has a seaside look about it as you stroll along the quays. Don't miss the fest noz (ceilidh) that is sure to be going on somewhere!

SAINT SAUVEUR ABBEY. A proud reminder of past glories. The 14thc. tower rises to 67m, and is separated from the main church body.

MUSEE DE LA BATELLERIE DE L'OUEST Quai Jean-Bart © 02 99 72 30 95. *Open 15 June-15 September: 10am-12 noon and 3pm-6pm. Open Saturday, Sunday, Monday and Wednesday: 2pm-6pm in low season. Admission: adult 2 €*. This museum illustrates bargee life, with photos, film, scale models and period documents.

PORT. The Vilaine, flowing between its old quays, crosses the Nantes- Brest Canal via a system of double locks. Once full of barges and seagulls, the harbour now houses sailing craft, and is the departure point for river trips.

Vitré

Up on this headland overlooking the Vilaine Valley, you are back in the Middle Ages, in a walled town with ancient alleyways and a fortress. There is a quiet medieval atmosphere in Vitré, lingering around its corbelled houses and paved streets below the church square (Rue de la Baudrairie, Rue d'Embas, Rue Du Guesclin etc).

CHATEAU DE VITRE © 02 99 75 04 54. Open all year, hours vary according to season. Admission: adult 4 €. A fine specimen of medieval military architecture. Corner towers and halfway turrets surround a triangular ground plan. The castle opens onto a drawbridge, with a gatehouse between two machicolated towers.

HOPITAL SAINT NICOLAS. Some of the old town's most striking remains can be found in the Saint-Nicolas quarter. The former hospital chapel dates back to the late 15thc.

NOTRE DAME. Lined with beautiful old houses, Rue Notre-Dame leads to this 15th and 16thc. church, since reshaped. The south front is richly decorated with gables, pinnacles, gargoyles and Flamboyant Gothic windows.

ROMANTIC BRITTANY

Combourg

Combourg is the 'cradle of the Romantic movement', and Chateaubriand's birthplace. The town itself has changed little for centuries, and a most imposing castle overlooks Lake Tranquille, drawing your eyes as you approach.

CHATEAU DE COMBOURG © 02 99 73 22 95. *Open april-october everyday except Saturday, from 10 to 12 pm and 2 am to 5 am (for the parc); from 2am to 5am (interior); in july and auguste for the parc: 10 am to 6 pm and interior: 11am to 5.30pm*. You can admire three centuries of military architecture (13th-15thc) in this perfectly preserved building, restored in 1875. You also discover the atmosphere in which François-René de Chateaubriand grew up. The archive room contains the writer's personal effects and the little iron bed he died in (1848, Rue du Bac, Paris).

Dol de Bretagne

Breton severity meets Norman softness in the border town of Dol. The town is also a link between Mont-Saint-Michel Bay and the first green hills of Cambourg and Antrain, gateway to romantic Brittany.

SAINT-SAMSON CATHEDRAL. First built in the 13thc., and rebuilt on its Romanesque base in the Gothic 'Anglo-Norman' style. The west front, with its 12thc. rectangular door, is framed by two towers; the left is unfinished, and the other dates back to the 15thc. (its bell tower to the 17thc.). Local legend claims an underground passage connects it to Mont Dol.

POINTE DU RAZ

The end of the world; Hell's cooking pot; a powerful dragon sinking into the pebble-filled waves. The Raz headland - marvellously dangerous, evil and beautiful - has fascinated tourists for years. Legends and mysteries have grown up around it: you might spot a gleam of light from the drowned town of Ys, or hear the cries of the shipwrecked, calling you to join them. On a clear day, the more prosaic can glimpse the Ile de Sein and Ar Men lighthouse.

BAIE DES TREPASSES. The dead bodies of the shipwrecked ('trépassés') end up here, brought by strong local sea currents. Celtic tradition claims that here, dead Druids took ship for their tomb on the Ile de Sein, and also that every 2 November, the drowned come back to the bay to seek their loved ones still living.

Audierne

Throughout some difficult times, Audierne has managed to stay a fishing-port. It is also a seaside resort with a sandy beach that attracts plenty of tourists. The town is built like a staircase above the Goyen estuary, with narrow alleyways around the church.

AQUASHOW Rue du Goyen ✆ 02 98 70 03 03. *Open 1 April-30 September, every day: 10am-7pm. Late-night opening July & August. October-March and school holidays, every day: 2pm-5pm. Admission: adult 11 €, child 7.50 €, family 37.50 €.* Like being at the bottom of the sea! Discover 200 species of sea and freshwater fish; touch and feed the skate, and enjoy a magic underwater dive with the help of 3D glasses. There are forty-five minute displays by seabirds and birds of prey, with cormorants diving for fish as the star attraction. Don't leave the region without seeing the show!

Plogoff

The drowned are washed up from the ocean onto this beach. The lake is one of Ys's legendary sites, strangely calm, protected by the Van and Raz outcrops. The west-facing beach is beautiful, but dangerous at certain tides.

NOTRE DAME DE BON VOYAGE CHAPEL. Built in the form of a Latin cross, the chapel houses several statues, an ancient painting and a votive frigate. Nearby are a fountain for making wishes, and a Calvary.

Pont-Croix

This little town on the Douarnenez-Audierne road is not to be missed. The paved medieval streets are lined with ancient houses grouped around the church, recalling village life in bygone days. Cobbled alleys lead down to the calm Goyen; Rue Laennec with its flowers, steep little Rue Chère, big Rue Chère like a staircase, then the old harbour and a quiet walk along the river.

NOTRE DAME DE ROSCUDON CHURCH. *Open every day.* Between 1260 and the present, bays, porches, carvings and stained-glass have been added. Quimper Cathedral copied its spires, and other chapels have used it as a model.

QUIMPER, CORNOUAILLE, PAYS BIGOUDEN

Cornouailles' capital Quimper is not only famous for its delicate lacy crepes, but also for its cathedral, old town and traditional earthenware.

VIEUX QUIMPER. The old town is reached by Rue Kereon, lined with fine medieval houses. Place Terre au Duc is one of Quimper's oldest and most picturesque squares, and nearby is the Saint Mathieu quarter where the old houses are gabled and corbelled.

SAINT CORENTIN CATHEDRAL. The biggest Breton cathedral is Gothic in style, with Norman influence. The marvellous stained-glass in the high windows dates from the 15thc., and represents canons, lords and their ladies surrounded by their patron saints.

NOTRE DAME DE LOCMARIA CHURCH. Overlooking the Odet, this 13thc. Romanesque church was reshaped in the 15thc. and later restored. A robed Christ figures on the beam crossing the transept, and there are fragments of the 12thc. cloister and 19thc. earthenware Way of the Cross (listed).

MONT FRUGY. This hill overlooks the whole town from its 72m, and you have a magnificent panoramic view from the top.

MUSEE DES BEAUX-ARTS 40, place Saint-Corentin ✆ 02 98 95 45 20. *www.musee-beauxarts.quimper.fr. Admission: adult 4 €, concessions 2.50 €. Under-12s free. Open every day except Tuesday: 10am-12 noon and 2pm-6pm. July & August, every day: 10am-7pm.* The Fine Arts Museum is housed in a little Italian-style palace built in 1867, and is one of the richest in France. Brittany's living, original traditions are illustrated in paintings from 1875 to 1905; the region began inspiring both artists and writers, often with real passion, from the 1820s onwards.

MUSEE DE LA FAIENCE 14, rue Jean-Baptiste-Bousquet ✆ 02 98 90 12 72. *Open 15 April-mid October: 10am-6pm except Sundays. Groups by appointment all year. Admission: adult 4 €, concessions for under-25s, children and families.* You mustn't leave Quimper without visiting the Earthenware Museum. Local designers have made ceramic into an art form: three centuries of creation can be viewed here in the former Porquier factory on the banks of the Odet. Religious and historical subjects and scenes from daily life are displayed.

MANOIR DE KERAZAN ✆ 02 98 87 50 10. *15 minutes from the town centre towards Pont-Labbé, then Loctudy. Open April-15 June and 10-30 September: 2pm-6pm, except Monday. 15 June-10 September: 10.30am-7pm.* This large and beautiful house dates back to the 16thc. The Astors were comfortably-off - witness the well-furnished interior - but spent their lives promoting the Bigouden region's economic development. Joseph Astor and his father accumulated an impressive collection of Breton-inspired paintings, and their house boasts a unique collection of local earthenware, including a number of pieces from the Porquier factory. There is also a romantic landscaped park, and an ecomuseum with typical regional animals, and tools used for transforming potatoes and making cider. On Fridays from 4pm-7pm in July and August, an organic produce market is held, bringing together local organic farmers.

PARC BOTANIQUE DE CORNOUAILLE Combrit ✆ 02 98 56 44 93 . *Open every day July & August: 10am-7pm. March-November: 10am-12 noon and 2pm-7pm. Admission: adult 5.80 €, child 2.60 €.* 15 minutes from Quimper. There are 3,500 plant species, including 200 varieties of Japanese maple, and a water garden. You can buy plants in the park, with experienced gardeners to advise you. There is also a mineral museum nearby.

Cornouaille

Benodet

This rather chic seaside resort at the mouth of the Odet is tourist-centred, with its casino and sailing harbour, where a number of yachts are moored. The three sandy beaches are crowded in summer, and all kinds of watersports are on offer. You have spectacular views from the Saint Gilles headland and Cornouaille bridge, 31m above the river, and also from the Pyramide lighthouse, sadly closed to the public. 20km of routes are marked out from Benodet, taking in the Gouesnac'h, Plomelin, Loctudy and Beg Meil loops.

Concarneau

This is the biggest French tuna fishing port, and third biggest in Europe for the quantity of fresh fish unloaded. Known as 'the blue town', Concarneau's Ville-close (old walled quarter) is hemmed in by huge granite ramparts, forming an enclave in the heart of the town.

VILLE-CLOSE. This walled quarter was built on a little island in the Foret Bay, as one of Cornouaille's strongholds. Notice the beautiful fountain in Place Saint-Guenole, and the many small art galleries exhibiting local artists. The port, and its fleet, can be admired from the ramparts.

Traditional costumes

Traditional granite house in Douarnenez

MARINARIUM Place de la Croix ✆ 02 98 50 81 64. *Open February-December. July & August: 10am-7pm.* Exhibition of marine biology, with aquariums containing local flora and fauna.

MUSEE DE LA PECHE 3, rue Vauban ✆ 02 98 97 10 20. *Open 10am-12 noon and 2pm-6pm (except last three weeks in January) 9.30am-8pm in summer, and 10am-6pm during school holidays. Admission: adult 6 €.* This museum located inside the town walls illustrates the world fishing industry's history and techniques, in 1,500 sqm of exhibition space. An hour's visit tells you all there is to know about the subject, which includes shipbuilding and fish conservation methods. You can also access the Hemerica, a 34m-long trawler anchored off the museum quay.

Douarnenez

This legendary town has its own rather Mediterranean character: highly coloured, rich in anecdotes, rough but welcoming. It lies close to the Pointe du Raz, and is known as the 'town with three ports.'

PORT-MUSEE Place de l'Enfer ✆ 02 98 92 65 20. *www. port-musee.org. Open April-November every day except Monday: 10am-12.30pm and 2pm-6pm. 15 June-15 September, every day: 10am-7pm. Admission (museum & boats): adult 6.20 €, 6-15s 3.85 €, families 17.10 €.* A spectacular collection of traditional wooden boats on dry land. Discover sail making, a reconstructed shipwright's workshop, and some old-fashioned sailing craft. You can go inside the big ships on the water, where daily life and work is explained with a sound track and pictures.

PORT DE PECHE. 500 fishermen sail to northern Scotland, the west of Ireland and the Gulf of Gascogne in search of tuna, monkfish, and langoustines. Fishing is still of primary importance in Douarnenez, with bigger quantities being unloaded every day.

Locronan

Locronan's natural scenery has inspired at least 20 filmmakers. The town is firmly anchored in its traditions, a blend of Celtic and Druidic rites and and Christian festivals, and is worth visiting out of season.

GRANDE PLACE. The priory church and 14 elegant 17th and 18thc. residences, with the communal well in the middle. All the old alleys wind off from this big central courtyard.

SAINT RONAN CHURCH AND PENTY CHAPEL. Two Flamboyant Gothic buildings, side by side. The church was built in 1420, with donations from the Dukes of Brittany, and has never been altered.

CEMETERY. Gravestones and sarcophagi, with the church in the background.

Pont-Aven

The bubbly Aven River adds character to this little town, rushing in and out among the rocks in midstream. The colours and light quality are exceptional, and have always attracted artists and painters. The Pont-Aven School was founded in 1886, but the town really became known through Gauguin's paintings, well after his death.

MUSEE Place de l'Hôtel-de-Ville ✆ **02 98 0614 43**. *Open all year, except January. July & August: 10am-7pm. Admission: adult 4 €, concession 2.50 €.* The permanent collection contains works from the Pont-Aven School, with a library on the first floor concerning Breton painters from 1860-1940. An audiovisual centre explains the Pont-Aven group. The museum houses several of Paul Gauguin's zincographies, a pastel drawing entitled Deux tetes de bretonnes, and a painting, Le sabotier (on loan).

PROMENADE DE XAVIER-GRALL, LE BOIS D'AMOUR. A leisurely stroll through some enchanting postcard landscapes and the Wood of Love, in the footsteps of the Pont-Aven painters. Don't forget your sketchbook!

Pays Bigouden

Fouesnant

This seaside resort nestles in a green setting, and has developed a reputation for cider. Fouesnant is also known for its traditional costumes, and the region's tallest and most delicate Breton headdresses. Finally, it boasts three superb headlands: Cap Coz, Beg Meil and Mousterlin, offering pleasant walks and marvellous beaches.

Le Guilvinec

Principal bigouden harbour, ranked fourth among French fishing ports.

HALIOTIKA Terrasse panoramique de la Criee ✆ **02 98 58 28 38**. *Open mid March-late September and school holidays, every day except Saturday: 2.30pm-7pm.* Discover the world of sea fishing in this 730 m^2. exhibition, which explains the life and jobs of the fishermen. Afterwards, you can see the trawlers come in, and take part in the fish auction (criée).

Pont-l'Abbé

These are Bigoudens, a separate Breton clan, whose women wear towering lace caps. The town owes its name to the bridge built from harbour to lake by the Loctudy abbots, and is known for its fine embroidery.

CHATEAU. Still impressive, despite its many transformations. It houses the Town Hall, Tourist Office and Bigouden Museum.

MUSEE BIGOUDEN Hôtel de Ville ✆ **02 98 66 09 03**. *Open Easter-30 September, every day except Sunday: 10am-12 noon and 2pm-5pm. June-September, open Sunday, closing times 12.30pm and 6.30pm.* Souvenirs of local daily life are displayed in four rooms; caps, tools, 19thc. furniture and daily objects give you an idea of long-ago customs and habits in the Bigouden country.

MAISON DU PAYS BIGOUDEN Kervazegan ✆ **02 98 87 35 63**. *Complements the museum.* The farm is built round a courtyard with outbuildings, exactly as it would have been between 1900 and 1920.

LORIENT AND NORTH MORBIHAN

Lorient

'L'Orient: the East'. Once the port for the Indies, Lorient was nearly wiped out in the last war, but was rebuilt and is now a young and busy town. The main activities are still sea-based, with the arsenal, merchant navy and fishing harbour.

SUBMARINE BASE Keroman ✆ **02 97 21 07 84**. *Open June-September and in school holidays; all year for groups (bookings only). Admission: adult 5 €.* Built during German occupation under Admiral Doenitz, this strategic submarine base has been called the 20th century's biggest fortress (1,800,000m3). The French Navy used it for 50 years.

LA THALASSA Quai de Rohan ✆ **02 97 35 13 00**. *Open every day. July & August: 9am-7pm. September-June: 9am-12.30pm and 2pm-6pm (except Saturday & Sunday mornings).* Built in 1960, this was the first trawler with a back ramp, used for oceanographical research. You can visit its three decks, with the fishing sector, cabins and dining rooms, and try out some of the oceanographers' tools.

Etel

Former tuna-fishing harbour, this small coastal community nestles between the port and Kerevin hill. Around Etel, there are little harbours and oyster beds, lakes and woods, wide expanses of dunes and long beaches.

BARRE D'ETEL. Set between the Erdeven headland and Chaudronnier turret, this is a natural phenomenon that developed out of an underwater sandbank during the last century. The sandpile can be seen at low tide, and moves slightly with wind and tides. There is a magnificent view of the sea and the Ria d'Etel entrance.

ILE DE SAINT-CADO. This island's little harbour was the River Etels's biggest sardine-fishing port in the early 1900s. Access by car is reserved for local residents.

Port-Louis

Port-Louis has kept some fine architecture: citadel, beautiful bourgeoise houses and narrow streets.

CITADEL. The Spanish wanted this citadel built in the late 16thc., but it was actually finished on Richelieu's orders over 30 years later. Its imposing military lines are striking seen from the old covered walk. The citadel now houses two museums.

MUSEE DE LA COMPAGNIE DES INDES Citadel ✆ 02 97 82 19 13. *Open every day: 10am-6.30pm, closed Tuesday (mid-September-31 March) and December.* France too had its different India Companies in the 17th and 18thc., and this museum illustrates the links between these companies and Lorient. Historical documents, scale models of boats, furniture, porcelain (400 rare and precious pieces) and many other exotic objets recall that maritime epic, and the trade and cultural relations with Africa, Asia and the Americas established from Lorient, where ships were fitted out and goods were sold for the India Company.

MUSEE NATIONAL DE LA MARINE Citadelle ✆ 02 97 82 56 72. *Closed 16 December-31 January 2006. Hours vary on a monthly basis. Admission: adult 5.50 € , price includes both museums.* Port Louis Citadel houses the Musée de la Compagnie des Indes (India Company Museum) and the Musée National de la Marine (National Naval Museum). The Naval Museum boasts remarkable collections of boat scale models and weapons. The new 'Sea Rescue' rooms, inaugurated in May 2005, contain ex-votos and souvenirs of lifesaving societies, and retrace the development of tools and materials. Human heroism is illustrated with paintings, boat models, archive pictures, interviews, films and soundtracks, round the centrepiece: an amazing 19thc. lifeboat with oars. You should also discover the 'Ocean Treasure Room' devoted to underwater archeology, with an extensive china collection donated by Franck Goddio.

North Morbihan

Le Faouet

Whether religious or secular, Le Faouet's architectural heritage is prestigious, especially from the 15th-17thc. In the late 19thc., a lot of painters were attracted to the region, and the Faouet school began to be talked about in artistic circles. The village is still worth a long visit, with its well-kept houses, covered markets, chapels and museum.

LES HALLES. The magnificent fir and oak framework is supported by a row of short granite pillars on a stone wall, and topped by a slate roof. Notice the octagonal tower, with its eight-sided onion dome.

SAINTE BARBE CHAPEL. Work began on the chapel on 6 July 1489, with splendid results. The chapel overlooks the Elle Valley from its narrow platform, and walkways and staircases link the Gothic sanctuary.

Josselin

The château is Josselin's main attraction, but this discreetly charming little town also boasts some half-timbered medieval houses with corbelling and gables. Walk along the River Oust, under the castle windows; the best place for photos. Josselin is at its liveliest between the basilica and castle, but for peace and quiet, there is the Jardin du Bois d'Amour, a 7ha. park with lake and bamboos.

CHATEAU DE JOSSELIN ✆ 02 97 22 36 45. *April, May & October, open weekends, school and public holidays: 2pm-6pm. June-September, every day: 2pm-6pm. 14 July-31 August, every day: 10am-6pm.* The castle has survived the centuries intact, thanks to its solid structure. Olivier de Clisson put up eight towers; Richelieu later had four of them pulled down, but otherwise, this powerful and harmonious building confronts the third millennium unchanged.

NOTRE DAME DU RONCIER BASILICA. Developed by Olivier de Clisson, the basilica is beautifully situated above the castle. It contains remarkable old furnishings and the recumbent statues of de Clisson and his wife.

Pont-Scorff

MAISON DU SCORFF Bas Pont-Scorff ✆ 02 97 32 50 79. *Open Tuesday-Thursday in summer.* Explore this valley's carefully preserved natural beauty on foot, on horseback, in a canoe or rowing boat. From the Scorff's spring in the heart of Brittany to the Lorient harbour roads, there are over 200 marked-out paths through the woods or along the river. Discover a whole host of environmental treasures, alone, or with a guide.

ZOO DE PONT-SCORFF ✆ 02 97 32 60 86. *Open every day June-August: 9.30am-7pm. Out of season: 10am-5pm. Admission: adult 12.40 €, 3-11s 7.40 €.* With its 700 animals on 11ha., the zoo gets better every year. The environment is pleasant - the animals' living-quarters will surprise you! - and there are four displays, including a seabird show. This zoo is also an important centre for Indian elephant reproduction.

Pontivy

Pontivy country is Rohan country, after the illustrious de Rohan family. You find it in the heart of Brittany, and north of Morbihan.

NOTRE DAME DE JOIE BASILICA. The basilica is the work of Claude de Rohan, fourth son of Jehan II. Its great organ is listed, and frequent concerts are held here, especially in summer.

CHATEAU DES ROHAN Place des Ducs-de-Rohan ✆ 02 97 25 12 93. The present chateau was put up from 1479-1485 by Jehan II, Vicomte de Rohan, and is characteristic of late medieval military architecture: low, massive and squat, with 5m-thick walls. The castle has been completely restored, and today hosts big exhibitions, concerts and plays.

Saint-Aignan

BARRAGE ✆ LAC DE GUERLEDAN. This dam was one of Europe's biggest when it was built between 1923 and 1929, 45m above the Blavet valley towards Saint-Aignan. The 400ha reservoir borders on to Quenecan Forest. A popular site with tourists, where peace and quiet or sports activities are on offer.

FORET DE QUENECAN. Verte et touffue, la forêt dite "la petite Suisse Bretonne" au Nord-ouest du pays, s'étend sur plus de 3000 hectares. Le relief accidenté offre de très belles vues sur la vallée. Deux curiosités sont à voir: le breuil du chêne et le menhir du breuil.

THE ISLANDS

What would Brittany be without islands? There are some magical places to discover off the coast, while respecting the environment, of course.

Batz

Touristy, but genuine, and charming. The island's main resource is still farming (the potatoes are famous!) and you see few cars, but plenty of tractors on the narrow roads; some horses too. Life is leisurely here, and you can take time to enjoy the wild scenery and old stone houses. It only takes 3 hours to go round the island (3.5km x 1.5km). The beaches are found in the south and west, but the water is colder here than elsewhere. In the southwest, you will notice an early 18thc. corsair's house, which housed gunners and customs men in its time. The nearby Beg Seach Fort protected the channel's western entrance, but was reduced to ruins by the Germans in 1944. The lighthouse, built from 1836-1852 (43m high) is now automated, and is closed to the public.

JARDIN EXOTIQUE GEORGES DELASELLE ✆ 02 98 61 75 65. *Open April-September, every day except Tuesday: 2pm-6pm. July & August, every day: 1pm-6pm. October, weekends: 2pm-6pm. Admission: adult 4 €, child 2 €.* Also known as the Colonial Garden, this park is worth the detour for its exotic plants (bamboo, palm trees). Ten Bronze Age tombs and a 17thc. Calvary can also be seen on the site.

ROSCOFF-ILE DE BATZ CROSSING Compagnie Armein ✆ 02 98 61 77 75. *Tickets from the Tourist Office. Yearly service.*

Belle-Ile

The 'Beautiful Island' deserves its name. Take the ferry from Quiberon, and in 45 minutes you'll be landing here, on Brittany's longest island (17 x 9km; 80km of coastline) with its many scenic attractions. There are fertile fields, arid moors and jagged cliffs on the Atlantic coast, with the famous Port-Coton 'needles' and the amazing cave known as the Grotte de l'Apothicairerie. Fine sandy beaches face the mainland. Fig trees, laurels, mimosa, palm-trees and camellias grow in the gentle climate. Writers like Prévert, and painters including Monet, Courbet, Matisse and Vasarely all loved Sauzon fishing harbour. You will be just as keen to come back!

VAUBAN CITADEL, MUSEE HISTORIQUE Le Palais ✆ 02 97 31 84 17. *Open 1 April-31 October: 9.30am-6pm. July & August: 9am-7pm. November-March: 9.30am-12 noon and 2pm-5pm. Admission: adult 6.10 €*. This striking military unit was put up from the 16th-19thc. The museum illustrates Belle-Ile's history, blending the lives of the famous and the daily lot of sailors and fishermen. There is an ancient map collection, and some scale models of ships.

RESERVE ORNITHOLOGIQUE De KOH-KASTELL ✆ 06 72 97 83 25. *July & August, every day except Monday: 10am, 2pm and 4pm. April, May & June: Sunday, 14h. Admission: adult 5 €, child 4 €*. On Belle-Ile's wildest coast, this reserve contains one of Brittany's finest seabird colonies. You can admire tridactylous seagulls, cormorants, oystercatchers and various types of gull.

Ile-de-Bréhat

Set in an archipelago of islets, Bréhat can be reached in 10minutes by boat from the Arcouest headland north of Paimpol. On arriving, you will be struck by the good weather (there is a microclimate) and the absence of cars; this is a pedestrian (or cyclists') island. Walk through the lanes of granite cottages to the rocky cove - but beware of the hordes of rather scary seabirds that will want to join your picnic!

Les Glénans

The archipelago contains 9 little islands and is 20km from the coast (1hr30mins by boat). They are known worldwide for their sailing and diving schools.

Groix

45 minutes off the coast of Lorient, Groix (8km x 4km) has some fine sandy beaches, picturesque villages and geological treasures. Pen Men lighthouse on the western headland warns sailors land is ahead.

GRANDS SABLES. This superb site in the east of the island is the only convex beach in Europe! The sea surrounds the sand, instead of the usual opposite. Not to be missed.

ECOMUSEE DE L'ILE DE GROIX Port-Tudy ✆ 02 97 86 84 60. *www.groix.fr. May-September: open every day. October, November & April: closed Monday. December-March: open Wednesday, Saturday and Sunday*. Ideal for exploring Groix's island heritage. The ecomuseum recreates life in the early 1900s, when this was France's main tuna-fishing port.

Boat in Belle-Ile

Houat

A pretty little island, 5km long, with a string of sandy beaches dug out of the cliffs, and moors where you can camp. The fishermen's village has narrow streets and blue and white houses. Admire the sailing ships bobbing in the clear water.

ECOSOLARIUM ✆ **02 97 52 38 38**. *Open Easter-September.* Study the microscopic underwater world, on the theme of the nurturing sea. You learn about the islanders' lives, and recognise the fragility of the marine ecosystem.

Molène

300 people live on these few windswept hectares, some of them without ever changing their clocks. Sailing is in the blood, but the island's main resource now is tourism. Jo Le Guen put Molène on the map by twice rowing across the Atlantic, once single-handed. Courage and force of character are island qualities. To reach Molène:

PENN AR BED ✆ **02 98 80 80 80**. You can get round the whole island in a day.

DRUMMOND CASTLE MUSEUM ✆ **02 98 07 38 41**. *Open April-October.* This museum bears witness to the famous shipwreck of 16 June 1896. 29 of the 243 victims are buried on Molène. Queen Victoria gave the islanders a tank for collecting rain-water, as a way of thanking the rescuers for their bravery.

Ouessant

Agriculture and breeding are giving way to tourism on Ouessant today. A thousand islanders live on its 8km x 4km. In bygone times, the lack of a sheltered harbour excluded fishing as a source of income, so the men joined the Royal or Merchant Navy, leaving the island to their women. The men take to the sea, the women care for the land: this is the eternal Breton pattern.

BAIE DE PENN AR ROC'H. The coastal path heading southwest, definitely one of the loveliest.

MAISON DU NIOU Hameau de Niou ✆ **02 98 48 86 37**. The Niou house is a typical mid-19thc. island dwelling. Inside, time stands still, as you discover the world of women 'abandoned' by their sailor husbands, and begin to understand the island's fatalistic soul.

MUSEE DES PHARES ET BALISES Créac'h ✆ **02 98 48 80 70**. This museum is housed in Créac'h Lighthouse's former power station. It traces the history of lighthouses and maritime signalling.

POINTE DE PERN. The island's most-visited spot. The northward coastal path reveals a line of jagged rocks, carved out by the waves. Further north, you can't miss Créac'h Lighthouse, with its black and white stripes.

To reach Ouessant: two companies share the daily ferry runs.

FINIST'MER – COMPAGNIE MARITIME ✆ **02 98 04 40 72**. Go from Lanildut or the Conquet to Ouessant with this company. There's no time for sea-sickness: you'll enjoy a quick and magical trip.

PENN AR BED ✆ **02 98 80 80 80**. Crossings all year from Brest (Goulet crossing) or the Conquet. The latter port is quicker, and more comfortable in rough sea!

Ile-de-Sein

Who would be mad enough to settle on this sandy, stony tongue 6m above the waves? The Raz de Sein is turbulent at the best of times, and famed for its storms and shipwrecks. 'Qui voit Sein voit sa fin' goes the proverb, more or less 'See Sein and die'. The islanders cherish their past legends: priestesses, druid cemetery, fairy hole and menhirs; and shun cars, but were also capable of living in the present with acts of heroic resistance in the last war.

CIMETIERE. Le nombre de "péris en mer" est impressionnant. Vous y trouverez la tombe d'Alain Kaminker, frère de Simone Signoret, enlevé par une lame lors du tournage du film "La mer et les jours", en décembre 1958. Son âme erre aux côtés de celle de Marceline Cuillandre, sa mère adoptive sénane.

MONUMENT DE L'ILE DE SEIN (LIEU-DIT " MENEI "). Ce monument rend hommage à la totalité des hommes de l'île qui partirent, du 16 au 24 juin, vers l'Angleterre. L'île de Sein est la seule commune française titulaire à la fois de la Croix de la libération et de la Médaille de la Résistance.

VANNES AND THE GULF OF MORBIHAN

Vannes

Vannes is one of those Armorican towns grown out of a ria, at the meeting of river and sea. In the third century, the Gallo-Romans built a castrum ringed with ramparts against the Germanic threat, thus establishing the basis of a lasting fortified town.

RAMPARTS. Following the machicolated wall from the Porte Prison in the east to the Porte Saint Vincent in the south, you find a series of towers and bastions over 600m, showing the development of military architecture. The 15thc. Tour du Connetable is the most majestic.

SAINT PIERRE CATHEDRAL. The 12thc. north tower on the front is the only remains of the original church, rebuilt in Flamboyant Gothicé style as the portal shows. The Neo-Gothic façade was added in 1857. Inside is an imposing 15thc. nave lined with chapels, including the Holy Sacrament, containing the relics of Saint Vincent Ferrier. A Flemish tapestry (1615) depicts the saint's miracles and canonisation.

PLACE GAMBETTA. Built in the 19thc., this square is in fact a harmonious semicircle facing the harbour, and framing Porte Saint-Vincent which opens onto the old town. Vannes' patron saint is set in a niche above the gate.

MUSEE DES BEAUX-ARTS DE VANNES - LA COHUE 9 and 15, place Saint-Pierre ✆ 02 97 01 63 00. *Open afternoons. Admission: adult 4 €.* The Fine Arts Museum is housed in a medieval market hemmed in by 14th and 15thc. half-timbered houses. It contains a number of paintings on loan, on the theme of light (Boudin, Monet, Cottet) in partnership with Morlaix Museum.

AQUARIUM DU GOLFE VANNES Parc du Golfe ✆ 02 97 40 67 40. *Open February-October: 10am-12.30pm and 2pm-6.30pm. July & August: 9am-7.30pm. December & January: 2pm-6pm.* 40 aquariums, over 200,000 litres of water and 300 varieties of fish recreate the undersea world. There is a new section of marine environments with atmospheric sound, and a true-to-life reconstruction of a coral reef.

Gulf of Morbihan

A huge lake, with forty or so islands floating on it. Some are villages (Ile d'Arz, Ile aux Moines); others have one sole house, and the rest are deserted rocks to avoid when navigating at low tide. You can discover the Gulf by boat, calling in at the islands or going partway up the Auray river.

IZENAH CROISIERES Le Port - L'ILE AUX MOINES ✆ 02 97 26 31 45

VEDETTES BLANCHES 24, rue Pen-Lannic - LARMOR BADEN ✆ 02 97 57 15 27

SOCIETE MORBIHANNAISE ET NANTAISE DE NAVIGATION Quai Bonnelle - LE PALAIS ✆ 02 97 31 80 01

LA COMPAGNIE DES ILES Parc du Golfe - VANNES ✆ 02 97 46 18 19

NAVIX Parc du Golfe - VANNES ✆ 02 97 46 60 00

Auray

Auray is inland countryside on water, a deep sea-arm to the west of the gulf of Morbihan. Oyster farming was developed here, but the area was chiefly known as a port of call for the coasters and bigger ships bringing goods from over the Channel and Northern Europe.

CHARTREUSE D'AURAY. The visit begins in the chapel with the Greek-style Carrare marble mausoleum, put up in 1823 in memory of the Royalist emigrés shot in the region (Carnac, Quiberon, Vannes, Auray) when they returned to France at the height of the Revolution. David d'Angers and his pupil Louis Petitot sculpted the monument. You then go into the big Chartreux Chapel , partly restored after a fire in 1968 that devastated the carved wooden bas reliefs and the chancel and choirstalls dating back to 17thc.

GOELETTE SAINT SAUVEUR Place Saint-Sauveur - Saint-Goustan ✆ 02 97 56 63 38. This 30m-long schooner in the old Saint Goustan harbour on the River Loch was reconstructed from an early 20thc. hull, and recalls the golden age of sailing ships. A small but interesting museum is housed in the hold, with a scale model of the busy port, a slide show and some ancient marine effects. A sailor's life in the 1900's is also illustrated.

Ile-aux-Moines

This cross-shaped island, 6km long and 3km wide, is the biggest and most picturesque in the Gulf. The village with its narrow alleys and low houses is pleasant to explore, or you can hire a bike on the port and go further.

Locmariaquer

'The place where Mary lives', in Breton. Ideally placed at the entrance to the Gulf and River Auray, Locmariaquer was the cradle of oyster farming, producing the famous Belon only found today in Quiberon Bay's deep waters. Megaliths are its other claim to fame, esphecially the Table des Marchand with its carved ogival stone, and the Grand Menhir Brise, which must have been 20m long and have weighed 350 tonnes. At the entrance to the village and in its centre stand the Mane-Lud and Mane-Rethual dolmens.

CENTRE D'INFORMATION ARCHEOLOGIQUE ✆ **02 97 57 37 59.** *Open every day. Admission: adult 4.60 €, concessions 3.10 €, under-18s free.* The Locmariaquer site groups 3 monuments together: the great menhir, Table des Marchand dolmen with its classical mid-Neolithic decorations and the Er Grah tumulus.

Port-Navalo

In the far west of the peninsula, opposite the Gulf narrows. Boats are pushed through like corks in a funnel by the fast ebb and flow currents, especially at high tide. This was an important harbour, chiefly for smuggling and selling the peninsula's wine. We recommend a trip along the lighthouse coast road, between the slipway and Port de Crouesty, to admire this superb site.

PRESQU'ILE DE RHUYS

The Rhuys peninsula is a narrow strip of land stretching 25km between the Gulf of Morbihan and the Atlantic. It gets 2,000 hours of sunshine a year. The north coast is jagged with small creeks; the south has cliffs and wide sheltered beaches. The saltmarshes, Suscinio Castle and Butte de César are historical landmarks, and a scattering of pretty houses, ancient chapels and little harbours colours the landscape. Add a heron or two, some falcons, and of course oysters, and you have the ingredients for a perfect holiday. If you prefer crowds, new buildings and navigating types, then Crouesty is the harbour for you.

CHATEAU DE SUSCINIO ✆ **02 97 41 91 91**. *Open all year. Admission: adult 5 €, child 2 €.* The castle is followed by the Breton History Museum, where the region's history is illustrated by an assortment of souvenirs. Don't miss the room with medieval ceramic floor-tiles decorated with figures and symbols, which used to be in an ancient chapel whose walls and roof fell in. On leaving the château, go towards Suscinio Cove with its lovely view of marshes and castle, taking in the little hamlet with its thatched cottages on the way.

Sainte-Anne-d'Auray

Saint Anne appeared to Yves Nicolazic in July 1623. Two years later, the first stone of a sanctuary dedicated to Mary's mother was laid on the very spot where the Breton peasant saw her. Since then, this religious site has become Brittany's main pilgrimage centre.

Sarzeau

The north coast is jagged with small creeks; the south has cliffs and wide sheltered beaches. The saltmarshes, Suscinio Castle and Butte de Cesar are historical landmarks, and a scattering of pretty houses, ancient chapels and little harbours colours the landscape. From Sarzeau, there are two interesting routes: Suscinio Castle and the Gulf road.

PRESQU'ILE DE QUIBERON

Quiberon used to be an island, but the piling-up of sandy alluvium anchored it to the mainland south of Plouharnel. Today it is a peninsula, 14km by 4km, with varied scenery: in the west, a wild and rocky windswept coast; in the east, beaches and small harbours around Quiberon Bay. Holidaymakers don't lack for activities, with all kinds of beach and watersports on offer.

Carnac

Sheltered by Quiberon Bay, Carnac is world-famous for its menhir alignements, but also as a family seaside resort. Discover the fascinating menhirs, dolmens and other remains of Megalithic times, surrounded by mystery. During your stay in Carnac you'll enjoy relaxing on one of the 5 sandy beaches, or taking part in some of the many activities on offer, on land and sea. Exhibitions, water therapy and casino available.

Plouharnel

The Atlantic starts here! Plouharnel is a beautiful, preserved natural environment with gentle dunes and wide beaches, and a surfers' paradise (the Sainte Barbe spot is supervised by the Surfrider Foundation Europe and attracts surfers from all over the world). You can also go sand-yachting on the beach: lessons and courses are on offer all year round. The old town with its oyster beds and megalithic remains is a popular tourist resort, peaceful and unspoiled, yet full of life and colour. Warm and friendly welcome assured.

La Trinité-sur-Mer

Nestling in the heart of Quiberon Bay, close to Morbihan golf course, La Trinite-sur-Mer has all the charm of a genuine Southern Breton village, yet is also a peaceful family seaside resort. A number of little creeks stretch along the smugglers' path as far as Kervillen and Le Men D°, fine south-facing sandy beaches. Sea-lovers and reputed skippers meet up in the world-famous sailing harbour, close to the town's twisting alleys and quaint old fishermen's houses, and within easy access of the traditional calvary, and fountains concealed along the country paths.

ALIGNEMENTS DE CARNAC ✆ 02 97 52 89 99. Carnac contains 4,000 megaliths on its site, and tourist access to the 'Big Stones' is now limited, to avoid subsidence that could unbalance the menhirs.

MUSEE DE LA PREHISTOIRE 10, place de la Chapelle ✆ 02 97 52 22 04. *Open every day except Wednesday morning (annual closing in January). Admission: adult 5 €, concessions 2.50 €.* Objects found in the sector's tumulus are on display here. A fascinating complement to the megalith visit onsite.

PAYS DE LANVAUX

La Gacilly

An artists' village with paved streets, known for a brand of cosmetics which bears its name.

VEGETARIUM ✆ 02 99 08 35 84. *www.vegetarium.com. Open May-October, weekends and public holidays: 2pm-6pm. Late June and early September, every day: 2pm-6pm. July & August: every day: 10.30am-7pm.* A film sequence on a giant screen explores plant life. There is a huge planisphere, two reconstructed ecosystems (a humid tropical forest and a semi-desert environment) a slide show and interactive walls, to explain the origin and growth of plants. The exhibition covers 650sqm, and is Europe's first on the theme.

Rochefort-en-Terre

Around 1900, tourism appeared in Rochefort, attracting landscape gardeners and various artists. Apart from its well preserved 16th, 17th and 18thc. houses, Rochefort boasts one of the region's most beautiful churches, Notre Dame de la Tronchaye.

PARC DE PREHISTOIRE DE BRETAGNE ✆ 02 97 43 34 17. *www.prehistoire-bretagne.com. Open every day, 1 April-15 October: 10am-8pm (last visitors 5pm). 15 October-11 November, open Sundays, public and school holidays; 1.30pm-6pm.* 2km from Rochefort-en-Terre in 20ha. of wild wooded land with five spectacular lakes and overhanging cliffs, Brittany's Prehistoric Park summarizes prehistory in 30 scenes, illustrated by life-size characters and animals.

CHATEAU ET MUSEE DE ROCHEFORT EN TERRE Le Bourg ✆ 02 97 43 31 56. *Open weekends and public holidays in April and May: 2pm-6.30pm. June & September, every day: 2pm-7pm. July & August, every day: 10am-7pm. Admission: adult 4 €.* The present castle was tastefully restored by American painter Alfred Klots, who added elements brought from outside. It houses period furniture, art objects and painting collections. A newly-opened museum near the castle illustrates local history and traditions.

The Megalith coast... life on the ocean wave !

Play the wind !

Cruises, regattas, light sailing surfing and windsurfing in a safe and enjoyable environment on the Megalith coast !

Enjoy the benefits of the sea !

Fine sandy beaches washed by the warm and limpid waves of the Gulf-Stream... not forgetting the invigorating benefits of seawater therapy !

Discover local heritage !

On foot, by bike, discover the many routes criss-crossing the Megalith coast. The amazing cultural and historic heritage includes dolmen and menhirs, old-world villages, abbeys, chapels and fountains.

Try the local specialities !

Smallbistros, gastronomicrestaurantsandrusticcreperies offer a thousand different flavours fish, seafood, cider, pancakes and Breton pastries are a real treat for gourmets.

Carnac Tourist Office - 74, avenue des Druides - 56342 Carnac Cedex

Tel: +33 (0)2 97 52 13 52 - www.ot-carnac.fr

Plouharnel Tourist Office - Rond-Point de l'Océan - 56340 Plouharnel

Tel: +33 (0)2 97 52 32 93 - www.plouharnel.fr

La Trinité-sur-Mer Tourist Office - Cours des Quais - 56470 La Trinité-sur-Mer

Tel: +33 (0)2 97 55 72 21 - www.ot-trinite-sur-mer.fr

FOOD AND DRINK

Brittany's cuisine was long considered to be heavy peasant cooking, rustic, unsophisticated and filling. Firmly rooted in soil and sea, the traditional products used (buckwheat, cider, and mead) were not refined enough for gastronomic cooks: today, of course, they are very fashionable.

Andouille de Guémené

Made from interwoven pork offal, sliced into regular concentric circles and eaten cold, with the aperitif, for example. This is the best known, but Saint-Brieuc also makes excellent andouille, eaten hot with mashed potato.

Artichokes, cauliflowers and potatoes.

Brittany produces 74% of French artichokes, 72% of cauliflowers and 90% of potatoes. Artichokes are usually boiled and eaten cold with a vinaigrette, but you can eat them braised with bacon rinds, or even fried...

Butter

'Amann' in Breton. Salted butter has been eaten in Brittany since the Revolution, for salt kept the butter from going off, and was available very cheaply in great quantities (thus avoiding the ruinous salt-tax).

Chouchen (Mead).

Nectar of the gods. Mead is usually drunk as an aperitif today - in moderation, since it contains 18 degrees of alcohol. It is made by fermenting honey with water and apple or wine yeast, for 2 to 6 months. There are sparkling, dry, medium-dry and sweet varieties, and even a mead vinegar.

Cider and crepes

Cider

Despite the noticeable improvement in industrial ciders, they have never seen the inside of an oak cask, and owe their bubbles to the addition of carbon dioxide. The most reputed AOC ciders in Brittany are made around Fouesnant; nearby at Quimper, fifteen producers have founded the Cidref association; a quality guarantee. Other versions of the drink come from Pleuhiden (Côtes-d'Armor) and Messac (Ille-et-Vilaine), sparkling and very drinkable. Dry or sweet? It depends on the preparation of the apples. Champagne method or not? That's a matter of taste; purists prefer dry, rather flat cider. There are cider bars in Brittany, where fans can drink a moque or bolée (cider is drunk from a bowl).

Coco de Paimpol

This little white bean now has its own AOC. It is hand-picked; in the region, they talk about 'plucking the coco'. A traditional Breton recipe simmers the beans in a casserole with tomatoes and a green pepper.

Saint-Jacques scallops

The coquilles saint-jacques from Saint-Brieuc contain very little coral, whereas Brest scallops are fleshier, but rarer.

Crêpes and galettes

The term galette à ble noir to designate savoury buckwheat pancakes is used in Upper Brittany. In Lower Brittany, the term crêpe is used for both savoury and sweet pancakes. This is the region's best-known speciality, and there is now a professional diploma. You won't have any trouble finding a crèperie, to taste them.

Seafood and shellfish

Langoustines, lobsters, spider crabs, common crabs, winkles, clams, whelks, shrimp and cockles are the basis of Breton gastronomy. The seafood platter on its seaweed bed is best tasted on a bistrot terrace in a picturesque fishing harbour, to be remembered with nostalgia after your holidays.

Oysters

Of course! Belons, cancalaises, prat ar koum, the ones from Brest harbour; flat or concave, big or small: it's all a matter of taste. The oysters grow in top-quality water, continually stirred up by strong, plancton-bearing currents. The oyster-farmers transmit their know-how from father to son, and each of the twelve grands crus has its own recognised characteristics.

Kouign-amann

Which means 'butter-cake' in Breton. The cake mix contains yeast, with large quantities of salted butter added. The homemade variety is (thankfully) unlike the shop-bought stuff, and is best eaten with tea or cider after a long walk on the Smugglers' Path.

Mussels

They grow near estuaries, where salt and freshwater blend, and are known as bouchot mussels (an old Breton word meaning wooden enclosure). The practice of farming them on wooden posts dates back to the 13thc. Mussels are delicious marinière (cooked in white wine), with french fries if you like, or Saint-Malo-style, with lots of fresh soured cream.

Fish

Brittany has 2,000km of coastline, which means plenty of fish. Anchovies, mackerel, sardines, bream, sole and bass are on all tables, from the poshest to the most humble restaurant.

Pommeau de Bretagne

A mixture of cider brandy (lambig breton) and apple juice, matured in an oak cask. It can be drunk as an aperitif and is excellent with foie gras – or apple tart. The pommeau producers are also part of the Finistère research and development committee.

CIDREF   5, allée Sully – Quimper ✆ 02 98 52 49 07

Gastronomy

Hotels & Restaurants

COTES-D'ARMOR

Binic

LE BENHUYC 1, quai Jean-Bart ✆ 02 96 73 39 00. *Fax: 02 96 73 77 04. Website: www.benhuyc.com* 24 rooms and studios, including 2 equipped for the disabled. Breakfast 9 €. This charming and comfortable hotel facing the harbour boasts a veranda and a terrace with panoramic views. The rooms are well equipped (ask for one overlooking the harbour) with bathroom and WC fixtures, TV and phone.

CHABLIS 7, rue du Quai ✆ 02 96 39 40 17 *Open all year, except in winter. Lunchtime formula 13.90 €. Set menus 15.50 €, 19 € and 25 €. A la carte.* This magnificent and very comfortable restaurant is located on the harbour. The ambience is cheerful yet quiet, and the food marvellous, with seafood specialities served in splendid platters (compose your own!) Cancale oysters and Saint Michel Bay mussels are served with half-salted farm butter - every last ingredient is of prime quality. Grilled fish and fish tartare, cod steak served parmentier-style or beef with snail butter feature on the menus. To finish, choose a red fruit and vanilla millefeuille, or a warm chocolate moelleux. The wine is also good (as the restaurant's name indicates!) with some great vintages served by the bottle or the glass. You have a great view of the Rance from the sunny, heated terrace. Take-away service available, comprising seafood platter and bottle of wine - who could ask for more?

LE COCHON GRILLE Le Hallerais - TADEN ✆ 02 96 39 96 67 *Email: cochon.grille@wanadoo.fr .Open 7 days a week in high season, closed Monday in low season. Set menu of the day 13.50 € (starter, main course, dessert), evening Cochon grille menu 32 €. Extensive car park.* All set to enjoy a pleasant evening with guaranteed ambience? Good, you've come to the right place! Roast pork is the speciality (as the restaurant's name indicates) and the 32 € set menu is perfect for an evening with friends: aperitif, starter, pork, cheese, wine and coffee. Tempting! New this year is the seafood, for the fishier type of customer.

COPAIN COMME COCHON 3, rue du Quai ✆ 02 96 39 88 09. *Close Monday and Tuesday in low season. Formulas 12.80 € and 14.90 €.* A la carte. Open since April 2006, this charming little restaurant is ideally situated on beautiful Dinan harbour with a great view of the Rance. You will be warmly welcomed on the sunny terrace, where you can taste the best ever food chargrilled over the traditional Breton log fire. Grilled meat and fish, Charolais beef ribs, ham on the bone and toasted sandwiches are house specialities. The desserts are made by 'Barnabe', the nearby bakery, and include Antoine's delicious tarts. An excellent place - don't miss it.

PIZZERIA LE MOANA 32, rue Joffre ✆ 02 96 73 65 89. *Closed Tuesday. Open 7 days a week in high season with non-stop service in July and August. Lunchtime formula 12.90 € (except Sunday).* Fresh, home-made pasta is the rule here, and Henri makes a mean ravioli with cheese, served with a Parma ham chiffonnade and walnut sauce. On the pizza side, try the vivaldi, the bulliolini and the parma. The dolce vita is another speciality: an assortment of pasta originally presented in a big dish with an interesting colour mix. For dessert, the traditional tiramisu is always delicious. Cecile and David welcome you in one of the three dining-rooms with their Provencal decor, or on the sunny terrace. Service until midnight. Pizzas to take away until 1am.

Dinan

LE D'AVAUGOUR * 1, place du Champ ✆ 02 96 39 07 49.** *Website: www.avaugourhotel.com. Open 18 February-15 Novembre. 21 rooms from 80 € to 150 € and 3 suites from 140 € to 250 €. Double rooms overlooking street or garden. Disabled access. Pets accepted.* This hotel has a beautiful flower garden on the ramparts, where you can have breakfast or a drink in fine weather. The rooms have recently been renovated, and are bright and colourful, with 3-star comfort levels. There is also a pleasant bar where you can have a rest on the way back from your trip out.

CAFE TERRASSE 2-4, rue du Quai ✆ 02 96 39 09 60. *Open all year. Non-stop service. Set menus 15.20 €, 19.50 € and 25 €. Children's menu 8.50 €.* This charming guinguette can be found on Dinan harbour. The staff are friendly and energetic, and serve you very good bistrot cooking prepared with fresh seasonal ingredients. Delicious Cancale oysters, frogs' legs in fricassee and home-made country terrine are a few suggestions for the starter, followed by bouchot mussels from Saint Michel Bay, with a variety of sauces (mariniere, cream, curry or cider), fusili pasta with scallops, salmon and scallop kebabs with lemon butter, roast loin of lamb with enriched cooking juices and Rossini duck breast. Excellent crepes made with fresh farm milk round off your meal very nicely The superb sunny (and heated) terrace seats 120, and is really the place to drink in the local atmosphere while you eat.

MANOIR DE RIGOURDAINE Route de Langrolay ✆ 02 96 86 89 96 *Fax: 02 96 86 92 46. Web site: www.hotel-rigourdaine.fr Rooms prices from 58 to 82 €. Breakfast 7 €* Near the Emerald Coast with a wonderful sea view This manor house is a confortable old estate just renovated welcome you. In front of your room, a wonderful sea view Near the Emerald coast with an amazing sea view, this old mansion newly renovated welcome you. The 19 bedrooms with century old beams are all comfortables and offer a view on the river Rance. Downstairs,a vast dining room with and old fireplace would be the perfect place to drink a glass at the bar and just relax. Near the hotel, numerous paths are awaiting hiking lovers.This old estate is the perfect place to be if you are looking for quietness and greenery.

CHEZ LA MERE POURCEL 3, place des Merciers © 02 96 39 03 80 *Email: chezlamerepourcel@wanadoo.fr . Formulas 18,90 €, 23,30 € and 33 €. A la carte. Children's menu 8 €.* This magnificent listed half-timbered residence dates back to the 15thc. and is located in the heart of the historic town centre. The cooking is regional and full of character, like the building itself. You can taste the best local seafood - Cancale oysters, delicious home-made fish soup - and country produce like the superbly tender beef steaks. Among the house specialities are buckwheat *croustillant* with crab meat and casseroled meat and fish, and a fresh market produce menu is on offer every day. Don't skip the cheese course; Maitre Bordier's cheese is the cream of the crop. To finish, let yourself be tempted by an excellent home-made ice-cream, or a farm milk crepe. You can enjoy a spot of people-watching from the beautiful sunny terrace, heated in winter.

Etables-sur-Mer

RESTAURANT L'OCEANE 6, rue des Frères-Mahéas © 02 96 70 71 43. *Set menu 12 € (weekday lunchtimes). Dish of the day 7,80 €. Terrace. Car park.* Christelle and Jerome's recently renovated restaurant boasts a large and luminous dining-room, and the ocean salad, frogs' legs and seafood choucroute will please fish enthusiasts. The others can order galettes (savoury pancakes) pizzas or meat dishes. All the desserts and pastries are home made; the tarte Tatin is a must. Bookings for groups of up to 50 taken.

Guingamp

LE RELAIS DU ROY * 42, place du Centre © 02 96 43 76 62.** *Fax: 02 96 44 08 01. Annual closing 1-15 January. The hotel is closed on Sunday and the restaurant on Sunday evening. 7 rooms from 65 € to 130 €. Breakfast 12 €. Set menus from 15 € to 35 €.* You are warmly welcomed in this residence of character, in old Dinan. The decoration is classic and chic, and the seafood cuisine prepared by a creative young chef who excels at pan-fried scallops in a fine tart with leeks fondue and cardamom, served with mashed potatoes with chive oil. You can choose your own lobster from the restaurant tank.

Lamballe

LES ALIZES ** Echangeur de la Ville-Eslan © 02 96 31 16 37. *Fax: 02 96 31 23 89. Annual closing 23-31 December. Weekly closing Sunday, except July and August and for group bookings. 32 rooms from 52 € to 74 €. Breakfast 7 €. Set menus from 17 € to 34 €.* This is a totally modern hotel, but decorated in warm tones all the same. The rooms are comfortable, and there is a billiard table and garden. The restaurant serves dishes concocted from land and sea produce like the assiette terre et mer: duck breasts with ginger, warm oysters with leeks fondue and pan-fried scallops.

Lannion

LA VILLE-BLANCHE La Ville-Blanche © 02 96 37 04 28 *Fax 02 96 46 57 82. Website: www.la-ville-blanche.com. Set menus from 44 € to 72 €. A la carte 60 €. Closed Monday, Tuesday, Wednesday and Sunday evening, 18 December-28 January and 26 June-3 July.* This year, the Jaguin brothers went their separate ways; an event of some importance in this quiet restaurant. Jean-Yves stays put at the helm, while his life-long accomplice Daniel has left to set up his own restaurant La Clarte at Perros-Guirrec. The family business began as a cafe-tobecconist's-grocers opened by the grandparents in the 1930s, and the original spirit still reigns in the revisited regional cuisine: warm oysters in chicken stock and foie gras flan, Breton lobster roast in the oven with salted butter, browned sweetbreads with the deglazing juice, cauliflower and pieds bleus mushrooms, strawberries marinated with passion fruits, iced bergamot mousse and petit beurre biscuit. A delightfully bourgeois and countrified ambiance is one of the most charming things about this white building on the edge of the road, a few minutes from the town centre.

Paimpol

HOTEL DE LA MARNE ** 30, rue de la Marne ✆ 02 96 20 82 16. *Fax: 02 96 20 92 07 Weekly closing Sunday evening and Monday. 11 rooms from 57 € to 77 €. Set menus from 26 € to 70 €, including wine. Children's menu 15 €.* Close to the harbour in a completely renovated traditional residence, with air-conditioning in all the personalised rooms. Classic house dishes are Breton lobster poached in chicken juices, Dublin Bay cappucino with crunchy vegetables, roast dory Rossini-style and the surprising dessert, chocolate trilogy with a kitchen garden flavour.

LA VIEILLE TOUR 13, place de l'Eglise ✆ 02 96 20 83 18. *Annual closing from mid-November to early December. Weekly closing Sunday evening and Wednesday in low season, Monday lunchtime in summer. Set menus from 25 € to 73 € (lobster menu served in summer).* This restaurant serves mainly seafood, in a pleasantly rustic decor, but country produce has its place on the menu. Turbot with Dublin Bay prawn tails and beef fillet marinated in saint-emilion are examples particularly worth mentioning.

Perros-Guirec

HOTEL SPA L'AGAPA** RESTAURANT LE BELOUGA 12, rue des Bons-Enfants ✆ 02 96 49 01 10.** *Fax: 02 96 91 16 36. Website: www.lagapa.com – email: hotel@lagapa.com Rooms140 € to 430 € (prices for two people). Half-board 280 € to 500 €. Full board 380 € to 600 €. Breakfast buffet 18 €. Set menus: lunchtime formula 32 €, evening 55 €, 72 € and 90 €. A la carte.* This hotel overlooks the sea on the Pink Granite Coast, facing the Sept-Iles archipelago. 50 rooms are available, all equipped with mini-bar, safe, TV with DVD drive and free Wi-Fi. Water therapy programmes are also on offer: sauna, hammam, pool, body treatments, fitness training and gym room. The restaurant has a marvellous view of the Sept-Iles and Trestraou beach, which you can access directly. You must taste the bass and scallop tartare with Beluga caviar, lobster with Parmesan, autumn roots and pumpkin, and veal cutlet marinated in cumin. For dessert, go for the rice pudding (the Breton sort is served cold) with mango nem-style, lychees in a half-jelly and mango sorbet.

HOTEL-RESTAURANT LES FEUX DES ILES* 53, boulevard Clemenceau – On the cliff road ✆ 02 96 23 22 94.** *Fax: 02 96 91 07 30. Website : www.feux-des-iles.com – email: feuxdesiles2@wanadoo.fr Closed Sunday evening. 18 rooms from 97 € to 120 € (for two). Breakfast buffet 10 €. Set menus 27 €, 37 € and 62 €. A la carte. Private car park.* Mr and Mrs Le Roux run this hotel, which dates back to 1932. The restaurant and most of the rooms have a view of the sea and the Sept-Iles. All the rooms are equipped with direct phone line, mini-bar, Internet access, satellite TV and hair-dryer. Room service between 6.30pm and 10pm. The chef's specialities are scallops fresh from the bay in a *piperade*, fricassee of wild bass baked on its skin and caramelised apple *délice*. A small door at the bottom of the garden opens on to a path leading to pretty Trestrignel beach, only 300m from the hotel.

HOTEL- RESTAURANT LES STERNES Rond-point de Perros ✆ 02 96 91 03 38. 34 *Fax: 02 96 23 13 01. Website: www.sternes.com – email: bienvenue@sternes.com 20 double rooms from 46 € to 56 €. Breakfast buffet 7 €. Free car park in front of the hotel.* This hotel is located 300m from the yachting

L'AGAPA
HOTEL·SPA
★★★★
RESTAURANT
LE BELOUGA

L'Agapa marie avec élégance le charme discret des années 30 et le confort le plus moderne. Situe à l'aplomb d'un panorama somptueux, l'hôtel joyau de la côte de Granite Rose surplombe la mer et fait face à l'archipel des 7 îles.

Délice du palais au restaurant le Bélouga avec la cuisine d'un jeune chef talentueux formé à l'école de Michel Rostang.

Plénitude grâce aux programmes de soins du corps au spa de l'Agapa (Balnéothérapie, sauna, hammam, sauna, bain à remous et piscine.

UN LIEU DE DÉTENTE ET DE BIEN ÊTRE POUR UNE ESCALE UNIQUE.

L'AGAPA

12, rue des Bons-Enfants / 22 700 PERROS-GUIREC / FRANCE

Tél. : 02 96 49 01 10 / Fax : 02 96 91 16 36 / **www.lagapa.com**

harbour on the way into Perros-Guirec, and is very comfortably equipped. Each room contains shower or bath, WC and hair-dryer, phone, satellite TV and broadband WiFi. Bar, games room and billiard table are at your disposal. Take advantage of the customer fidelity card, and get your tenth night free.

Plancoët

L'ABBAYE * 12, rue Marie-Paule-Salonne © 02 96 84 05 01/0 800 507 513–numero vert.** *Fax: 02 96 84 32 88. Website: www.abbaye-hotel.com. Open every day. Rooms from 50 € to 115 € (apartment). Breakfast buffet 9 €. Pets supplement 5 €. Restaurant Le 18.43 open every day. Lunchtime set menu: 18.43 €. Lunchtime formula 13 €.* What a heavenly place! The Côtes d'Armor's biggest hotel is a former abbey and Trinitaine nuns' convent. It is located between Saint-Malo and Cap Fréhel, 15km from Dinan and 6km from the golf course. In July 2004, M. Chapel from Saint-Malo took on the place, with marvellous results. The 98 rooms, including 3 with disabled access, are comfortable and classic in style, equipped with shower-bath, satellite TV, telephone and hair-dryer. There is a lift, car parks, sauna, Wi-Fi, a superb pool, lounge bar, billiard table and tennis courts. Business customers also have 4 conference rooms at their disposal. The restaurant Le 18.43 provides good semi-gastronomic and traditional *cuisine* with professionally attentive service. If you book in advance, you can have a room opening onto the convent chapel: terribly romantic! The *petits futés* who present our guidebook get a free overnight stay in exchange, in this charming little community full of character. Great!

JEAN-PIERRE CROUZIL 20 les Quais © 02 96 84 10 24 *Fax 02 96 84 01 93. Website: www.crouzil.com. Set menus from 55 € to 105 €. A la carte 85 €. Closed Monday, Tuesday lunchtime and Sunday evening, except in July and August.* Lucky Bretons! With Roellinger, Abadie, Thorel, Jeffroy and others, they account for one of France's biggest concentrations of top chefs. Jean-Pierre Crouzil is one of them, but unlike the others, cannot count on the nearby seaside to attract customers. His restaurant is certainly pretty, and Plancoet has one or two attractive streets, but is off the beaton tourist track. After 35 years of owning and running a restaurant, Jean-Pierre seems to have found the right solution, giving pride of place to fish in summer and meat in winter, and fitting in with customer demand. Too bad that the famous *Guide Rouge* docked him of a star last year; his motivation is still intact. His dory with conserved fennel, mullet with sugar snap pea vinaigrette, and magnificent citrus tart prove he still has plenty of resources. Country fare and childhood vegetables are a feature on his menus, and the cellar contains both great names and the local winegrowers' favourites.

Plérin-sur-Mer

RESTAURANT LA BALNEA 2, avenue du Trégor ✆ 02 96 74 43 57. *Closed Sunday and Tuesday evenings and Wednesday. Weekday lunchtime formula 12.50 €. Set menus from 15.50 € to 28 €. A la carte. Disabled access. Private car park.* Mr and Mrs Schmid took over this restaurant on 1 October 2005. The *cuisine* is mostly seafood, with wines from local wine-growers to go with it. Specialities include oysters in sea water jelly, and scallop profiteroles. A hors d'oeuvres and seafood buffet is at your disposal every lunchtime, and seafood platters are prepared to order. If you're not a fishy person, salads and pizzas are also available. To finish, enjoy a chocolate *croustillant* while contemplating the panoramic view over Saint Brieuc bay.

Pléven

MANOIR DU VAUMADEUC ** ✆ 02 96 84 46 17.** *Fax: 02 96 84 40 16. Annual closing from early November to Easter. Open all year for weddings and seminars. 13 rooms from 95 € to 195 €. Breakfast 10 €.* You break your journey in royal style in this superb 15thc. manor nestling in the Hunaudaye Forest. Furniture and decoration recall the festivities of bygone days - all you need is period costume to feel the part in the park and Renaissance gardens, where you can tease the fish in the lake. Each room is personalised. M. O'Neill treats greeting guests as an art, and you will be very warmly welcomed. The facilities are excellent, and though there is no restaurant, your host recommends the best places to eat and will even book a table for you.

Saint-Brieuc

AUX PESKED 59 rue du Légué ✆ 02 96 33 34 65 *Fax 02 96 33 65 38. Website: www.auxpesked.com. Set menus from 20 € to 90 €. A la carte 65 €. Closed Saturday lunchtime, Sunday evening, Monday, first fortnight in January, last week in April and late August to mid-September.* Jean-Marie Baudic's arrival three years ago certainly shook up the Pesked (fish) who had been dozing comfortably in the traditional atmosphere, although his predecessor Thierry Bernard was already one of the department's best cooks. Having trained with Gagnaire during his Saint Etienne period, and been second for several years to Hélène Darroze in Paris, this thirtysomething took his time before accepting his first chef's job. Working with the two young owners Sophie and Mathieu Aumont, who did well to hire him, he has quickly shown his mettle as one of the very best Breton chefs. His cooking is astounding; his creations superb - the crab tartare with dried crab eggs and Dublin Bay prawns in tandoori and stuffed courgette flowers are unforgettable - and his future looks rosy, with all those gastronomic tributes to collect (the first are already coming in). He is set to become one of the Great West's safest bets.

LA CROIX BLANCHE 61, rue de Genève ✆ 02 96 33 16 97. *Closed Sunday evening and Monday. Set menus from 21 € to 40 €.* A famous restaurant, and rightly so, with a pretty contemporary dining room, elegant presentation and inspired cooking. The menu varies with the seasons; the set menu at 21 € even changes on a weekly basis, and the surprises are always pleasant! Top-quality service and interesting wine cellar.

KER IZEL ** 20, rue du Gouët ✆ 02 96 33 46 29. *Fax: 02 96 61 86 12. Open all year. 22 rooms from 35 € to 55 €. Real breakfast buffet 6.50 €.* Saint-Brieuc's oldest hotel has been entirely restored with a sober, rather classic decoration and comfortable rooms. Guests have a swimming pool and quiet garden at their disposal. Very warm welcome.

Trébeurden

MANOIR DE LAN KERELLEC * 11, allée Centrale ✆ 02 96 15 47 47.** *Fax: 02 96 23 66 88. Website: www.lankerellec.com. Restaurant closed Monday to Thursday lunchtime. 19 rooms from 100 € to 410 €. Breakfast 17 €. Set menus from 46 € to 66 €.* A sophisticated and elegant setting for this 19thc. manor, where each room boasts personalised decoration and a sea view. Some even have a stereo system. Foodies will get a surprise in the dining room, with its boat hull-shaped ceiling. The cuisine is sophisticated too, based on seafood and country produce.

FINISTERE

Bénodet

KER MOOR * Corniche de la Plage ✆ 02 98 57 04 48.** *Fax: 02 98 57 17 96. Website: www.kermoor.com Rooms from 75 € to 130 €. Set menus from 29 € to 57 €.* This hotel in a superb 3 hectares of wooded grounds right in the heart of the town combines seaside charm with a wide range of sporting activities: heated pool, 5 tennis courts and a squash court, with a seawater tharapy centre, golf and sailing nearby. Comfortable, contemporary rooms; good restaurant serving seafood and recipes based on country produce.

Brest

LA FLEUR DE SEL 15 bis, rue de Lyon ✆ 02 98 44 38 65. *Open every day except Saturday lunchtime, Sunday and Monday lunchtime. Set menus 26 € and 38 €.* As delicate as the fine crystals floating on the surface of the saltmarshes that give this restaurant its name, La Fleur de Sel welcomes you in a warm and friendly setting, light and contemporary in design. Chef Yann Plassard of Brest cooks light, bracing recipes to perfection, using Finistere's own fresh ingredients. The service is perfect, and the prices reasonable - that really is the cherry on the cake!

HOTEL LES GENS DE MER 44, quai de la Douane ✆ 02 98 46 07 40**. *Website: www.lesgensdemer.fr Open all year. 20 comfortable rooms at 45 €. Breakfast 7 €. Cheques Vacances accepted. Half-board 55 €. Full board 65 €. Pets 5 €. Weekday lunchtime set menu 9.90 €. Set menus 14.50 €-23 €.* Located in the heart of the old port, this hotel provides reliable services at attractive prices. The town is only a stone's throw away, with its lively bars and busy fishing boats coming and going, and some old vessels to admire. The restaurant is equally pleasant, decorated with frescoes, and the cooking attracts plenty of regulars.

OCEANIA * 82, rue de Siam ✆ 02 98 80 66 66.** *Very comfortable soundproofed rooms, air-conditioned with cable TV, from 58 € to 107 €.* 4 'seawater' rooms with bath and jacuzzi. Breakfast 12 € served in your room or as a buffet. Restaurant. 4 meeting rooms seating 15 to 140. This has always been one of Brest's grandest hotels. It used to be called Le Moderne, when the Branellec ladies ran it with characteristic taste and delicacy. Located in the heart of the town, it is a beautiful place with first-class comfort levels and excellent facilities. The luxury decoration follows an ocean theme. Bar and restaurant deserve your attention, especially the second, which serves superbly prepared seafood. Courteous and considerate welcome

GOLF HOTEL DE BREST IROISE ** Parc de Lann-Rohu ✆ 02 98 85 16 17. *Rooms from 48 € to 66 €.* This hotel is located on a golf course, in a green and restful setting. Both golfers and non-golfers are welcome, though; it is also a popular place for weddings and seminars. You can play a professional round or discover the game, or if you'd rather, go fishing or play petanque! Light meals or more filling menus are available if all this sport gives you an appetite.

Camaret-sur-Mer

HOTEL DE FRANCE ** ✆ 02 98 27 93 06. From Easter to late October. 20 rooms with lift and satelliteTV, including 10 with a sea view, from 48 € to 92 €. Breakfast buffet 7.20 €. You have a choice of menus in one of the two dining rooms, where you can enjoy the house seafood specialities.

Carantec

PATRICK JEFFROY 20 rue du Kelenn ✆ 02 98 67 00 47 *Fax 02 98 67 08 25. Website: www.hoteldecarantec.com Set menus from 32 € to 110 €. Closed Sunday evening, Tuesday lunchtime (mid-September to mid-June) and Monday, Tuesday lunchtime and Thursday lunchtime for the rest of the year.* Patrick Jeffroy insists his cooking is not 'fashionable', yet it is totally unlike those old hat recipes that do nothing for French gastronomy's reputation. Classic and contemporary at the same time, he cooks very good regional and international dishes, which is all that matters to his customers. The menu gets right down to essentials without pretence: flaky buckwheat pastry crust, duck foie gras and roast scallops, and chicken juices, dory fillet with fresh herb butter, carotte de sable and onion marmalade with conserved lemons, Normandy beef with its marrow bone, lacy pancake millefeuille with local red fruit and bergamot cream. The hotel improves a little more with each season, and soon guests will have a new breakfast room, completely redesigned, but still overlooking the sea.

Concarneau

L'AMIRAL 1, avenue Pierre-Guéguin ✆ 02 98 60 55 23. *Website: www.restaurant-amiral.com. Closed Sunday evening in low season, and all day Monday. Open 7 days a week in season. Set menus 14 € (lunchtime) and from 17 € to 38 €.* Contemporary setting, soberly chic with its mahogany panelling and dark blue seats. The cooking is so good here that Concarneau locals almost have to fight to get in. Arnaud Lebossé really knows the regional market stalls and fish market where he gets his raw materials, and the resulting works of art could not be tastier. The wine list covers France and even features Argentinian bottles. Real no-smoking dining room, fine terrace and a bar that hosts regular painting exhibitions and turns into a brasserie at lunchtime, for customers in a hurry. An upstairs room is available for seminars or family parties.

CHEZ ARMANDE 15, avenue du Docteur-Nicolas ✆ 02 98 97 00 76. *Closed Tuesday in low season, and Wednesday. Set menus from 20 € to 35 €.* The oldest restaurant in Concarneau is opposite the sailing harbour beside the walled town. It is a nice place, pleasantly decorated with a pretty Breton cupboard and a shellfish tank in the downstairs dining room. Fish and seafood have pride of place: lightly-smoked tuna fillet, buckwheat pancake and herb cream, Dublin Bay prawn tails pan-fried with chanterelles, bass in a salt crust, mashed potatoes with herbs, mullet with a tomato Tatin and saffron cream with pistou.

HOTEL LES GENS DE MER** **Rue du Port ✆ 02 98 97 04 01**. *Website: www.lesgensdemer.fr Open all year. 20 rooms at 42 €. Breakfast 6.50 €. Half-board 36 € per head per day (based on two people). Pets 5 €. Restaurant closed Saturday and Sunday evening in low season; open 7 days a week in high season. Weekday lunchtime formula 9.50 €. Set menus 15 €-23 €.* This hotel, a former hostel for seagoing folk, is right on the port, and provides reliable services in a pleasant setting with a lively harbour atmosphere. Guests include port workers and sailors as well as tourists and commercial travellers. The restaurant certainly fills up at lunchtime and it is often hard to find a table. Attractive prices.

Douarnenez

LE BORD'EAU **62, rue Anatole-France ✆ 02 98 92 60 86.** *Open all year, closed Tuesday evening and Wednesday in low season, and Wednesday only, in season. Set menus from 17 € to 34 €.* The pun is intended: the dining room is decorated in bordeaux tones, and customers on the terrace almost have their feet in the water (le bord d'eau). The water's edge in question is Rosmeur harbour, and as you'd guess in such a restaurant, seafood and fish are the staples on its menus. The great house speciality is the poêlon de la mer (panful of seafood) that combines cream, mussels, clams, Dublin Bay prawns and shrimps in the same pan. The wine list is very interesting too!

LE CLOS DE VALLOMBREUSE **7, rue Estienne-d'Orves ✆ 02 98 92 63 64.** *Fax: 02 98 92 84 98. Website: www.closvallombreuse.com Open Monday to Sunday, 12 noon-2pm and 7pm-9pm. Set menus from 18 € to 54 €.* Clos de Vallombreuse: what a pretty name! It sounds just like the title of a 19thc. novel. The restaurant serves country produce and seafood, with excellent fish and shellfish that vary according to the day's catch. In summer, gourmets can eat on a terrace overlooking Douarnenez Bay, and at all times, there is the dining room, huge and chic, and some charming private salons (that novel again). You can book into the 3-star hotel if you want to extend your stay.

Morlaix

HOTEL L'EUROPE** **1, rue d'Aiguillon ✆ 02 98 62 11 99.** *Website: www.hotel-europe-comfr 60 rooms from 52 € to 250 € (for the suite). Breakfast 8 €.* These are comfortable rooms in the town centre, renovated, soundproofed and equipped with satellite TV, direct phone line and individual bathrooms. Arlette Paroux welcomes her guests with delicacy, takes care of their comfort, and doesn't forget those thoughtful touches that count for so much, like flowers and art books. You can't help but admire this superb hotel, and the soft sheen on its sculptures. Half-board available in summer (restaurant next-door). Seminar rooms.

Pont-Aven

LA TAUPINIERE **Croissant Saint-André ✆ 02 98 06 03 12** *Fax: 02 98 06 16 46. Website: www.la-taupiniere.com. Set menus from 50 € to 80 €. A la carte 70 €. Closed Monday, Tuesday and 20 September-15 October.* Pont Aven is more than an adorable tourist village famous for its art school, and painters' studios. It also boasts La Taupiniere. Guy Guilloux and his wife Pierrette settled into this charming thatched house in 1975, and it hasn't changed much since. Behind the bourgeois exterior and rather conventional menu lies some good cooking, though years of ups and downs are beginning to take their toll on the chef - and understandably so. Still, discovering the little pan-fried monkfish tails, choucroute with cider, suckling lamb sauté with young vegetables, sea bream tartare, whipped cream with herbs and slices of melon in meringue and marinated raspberries remains one of life's pleasures.

Quimper

L'AMBROISIE **49 bis, rue Elie-Fréron ✆ 02 98 95 00 02.** *Website: www.ambroisie-quimper.com Open Tuesday to Sunday. Set menus from 22 € to 46 €.* Armelle and Gilbert Guyon offer modern Breton gastronomy in an equally contemporary setting, with its design frescos and inlaid lamps. The ingredients are grown in Cornouailles soil by local market gardeners, small farmers and craftsmen, and prepared by a talented chef. The spicy scallops with green asparagus, young pigeon with cider and green peas, and almond craquant with Plougastel strawberries are only samples of what he can achieve. The wine list is subtle, well up to the culinary standards, and covering most vineyards. On the first floor, two little salons seating 20 are available for business meals or family reunions. The owners welcome you with warmth and simplicity. One of the region's best restaurants.

LA FEUILLANTINE **6, rue Haute ✆ 02 98 90 36 37.** *Closed Sunday, except for group bookings. Weekday lunchtime formulas 15 € and 19 €, set menus from 19 € to 28.50 €. Car park Place du Styvel, 2 mins away.* In this elegant 18thc. building the restaurant that gained quite a reputation some years ago is now under new management. Corinne and Frédéric Nédélec have decorated their dining room with taste (artfully crumpled tablecloths and rattan seats) and the courtyard terrace is shady and bright with flowers. They offer a creative, middle-of-the-range cuisine with fish according to the day's catch - we had roast cod with country bacon and Puy lentils - and delicious desserts like melting dark chocolate fondant, a treat for any gourmet. There is a salon seating 30 on the first floor. Absolutely not to be missed, in this charming quarter of Locmaria a stone's throw from the earthenware factories.

HOTEL GRADLON* 30, rue de Brest ✆ 02 98 95 04 39.** *Fax: 02 98 95 61 25. Website: www.hotel-gradlon.com. Annual closing from around mid-December to mid-January. 22 rooms from 69 € to 155 € (doubles), breakfast 10.50 €. Reception every day from 7.30am to 11pm. Garage.* This attractive hotel run by Françoise Liscoet is located in the town centre. The rooms on the garden side have been renovated since 2004. There is a meeting room seating 15 and a room with access for disabled travellers. The indoor garden, bar and reception lounge are still just as elegant in their tastefully redecorated setting.

ILLE-ET-VILAINE

Cancale

A L'ABORDAGE 1, Quai Duguay Trouin ✆ 02 99 89 55 55. *Website: www.creperie-alabordage.com . Email: contact@creperie-alabordage.com. Open all year, 7 days a week: 11am-11pm. Formulas 11.90 €, 12.90 € and 13.50 €. Set menus 15.50 € and 22 €. Children's menu 7.90 €.* Anchored on La Houle harbour, this creperie with its marine decor and friendly atmosphere offers good cooking concocted with excellent regional ingredients. Cancale oysters, Bouchot mussels and fine steaks feature on the menus, together with galettes, the house speciality. They are made from stoneground organic buckwheat flour, 100% Breton, from the Moulin de la Fatigue, and are absolutely delicious! We recommend La Conche (andouille and pan-fried apples), La Pirate and La Flibuste. The crepes are also excellent, and there is a wide choice of salads and grilled meats.You have a marvellous sea view from the sunny terrace.

LE CANCALAIS 12, quai Gambetta ✆ 02 99 89 61 93. Fax: 02 99 89 89 24. *Website: www.lecancalais.com . Open all year. 10 rooms, including 6 with sea view, 45 €-90 € according to season. Breakfast 7 €. Pets accepted. Set menus 16 €, 27 € and 38 €. A la carte.* Arnaud and Jean-Claude Pierpaoli welcome you with a smile in their restaurant. The cooking is seasonal, and the menu changes 3 times a year.

Chef Sebastien Le Basque counts grilled lobster Cancalais-style, generous seafood platters and fresh cod steak Cancalais-style among his specialities. As for the desserts, made with talent by pastrycook Yvan, you must taste the poached Golden Delicious apple, and mini creme brulee with Bourbon vanilla. You'll enjoy your food all the more on the wide south-facing terrace with its sea view. A place to come back to.

LA CANCALAISE 3, rue de la Vallée-Porcon ✆ 02 99 89 71 22. *Closed Monday. Galettes (savoury buckwheat pancakes) and crêpes (sweet pancakes) to take away (order first).*

Located in the old town, this may be Cancale's oldest crêperie. The town's history is exhibited on the walls in photos, and Annette enjoys telling you about it. The pancake mixture is made to an old-fashioned recipe and all the fresh produce used comes from the local soil. Among the house specialities is the marine, a crusty butter galette with home made rillettes and smoked salmon, on a nest of salad. As for the crêpes, the bisquine is stiffed with apple compote and cinnamon then caramelised. Breton cider has pride of place, especially the naturally fizzy Ker Avel. Your welcome is as warm and sincere as the house ambiance.

LA MERE CHAMPLAIN 1, quai Administrateur en chef Thomas & 02 99 89 60 04. *Fax: 02 99 89 71 07. Website: www.lamerechamplain.com. Open 7 days a week all year. 11 rooms, 30 €-65 € according to season. Breakfast 7 €. Pets 7 €. Set menus 14.90 € and 23.90 €. A la carte.* Facing the sea. This restaurant specialises in fish, shellfish and seafood platters of all kinds, including famous Cancale oysters. Breton lobster grilled the chef's way is another house speciality. The menus include mussels en cocotte, crisp golden lemon sole, and a delicious fresh mullet and pan-fried scallop salad. If you're a meat person, you'll enjoy the loin of lamb and beef fillet. For afters, try a pear millefeuille or a chocolate pyramid, both home-made by the pastrycook. Panoramic sea view. Seminar room upstairs.

LE CONTINENTAL * 1, quai de l'Administrateur-Chef-Thomas ✆ 02 99 89 60 16.** *18 rooms from 78 € to 148 € with lift. Breakfast 8.50 €. Pets accepted. Set menu of the day 17 €. Set menus from 23 € to 37 €. Children's menu 11 €* Ideally located on the Houle harbour, this hotel provides comfortable rooms with a view of the superb bay. The restaurant specialities are seafood platters, bouchot mussels, brasserie dishes, tartares and carpaccios. Friendly and efficient welcome.

LA MAISON DE LA MARINE 23, rue de la Marine ✆ 02 99 89 88 53. *Website: www.maisondelamarine.com . Email: courrier@maisondelamarine.com . 3 suites and 2 rooms. All-in Discovery price from 100 € per night on weekdays (starting from 3 nights, and outside French school holiday periods). Tonic weekend from 300 € (2 nights half-board + an afternoon's sand-yachting, riding or aquatonics). Lunchtime market produce menu 19 €. Set menus 30 €, 35 € and 40 €. Sunday brunch 24 € (7 flavours). Weddings and other celebrations organised.* The Maison de la Marine is a top-quality character hotel-restaurant, sophisticated and friendly. Owner Christian Pousset extends a charming welcome to his guests, who will be delighted with the attractive restaurant boasting heated terrace and open fireplace (decorated by talented Erwan Ruffel). Foie gras 'de la mer', duck breast with 5 flavours, lobster cooked in the pot, and chocolate and ginger *moelleux* are just some of the culinary delicacies on offer. The cooking is contemporary and imaginative, using only fresh, seasonal local ingredients. The magnificent rooms are all different - some with a fine sea view - and comfortable (beds to size, marble, English pottery, old-fashioned raised bathtubs). Painting exhibitions, theme evenings (Caribbean, Spanish) aperitif concerts and sea trips are regularly organised. The high point of your stay will be a stroll throught the garden with its palm and olive trees, hydrangeas and lilac. A corner of paradise, between land and sea.

OLIVIER ROELLINGER 1 rue Duguesclin ✆ 02 99 89 64 76 *Fax 02 99 89 88 47. Website: www.maisons-de-bricourt.com. Set menus from 92 € to 160 €. A la carte 120 €. Closed Tuesday and Wednesday in May, June and September, and Monday lunchtime, Friday lunchtime, Tuesday and Wednesday in March, April, October and November, and Tuesday and Wednesday in July and August.* Nearly everyone knows Olivier Roellinger's story. He was a brilliant chemistry student, until a tragic event during his university life led him to change career paths completely and head for the culinary arts. His chemistry studies weren't wasted, though; if you look more closely at his cuisine, you notice that the technical side is highly developed, especially in the use of spices, which he masters to perfection. The Breton soil also plays a big part in his cooking, supplying exceptionally fine market garden produce and seafood. Wild sorrel, flat oysters, foie gras and hazlenut oil, light camembert cream, asparagus and linseed cream, veal sweetbreads and apples, rhubarb and peppercorns, turbot en blanc, almonds, poppy and sesame seed, candied grapefruit and home germinated shoots, saddle of lamb roast on the spit, 'Grand caravan' spices, slightly acid fresh fruit from the tropical isles, and white Malabar pepper ice-cream. The cellar, run by Emmanuel Ackerer, is one of Brittany's most specialised. What a haven of peace and spicy pleasure!

LE ROCHER DE CANCALE Quai de l'Administrateur-Thomas ✆ 02 99 89 53 66. *Open all year except Tuesday. Non-stop service. Set menu from 12 €. Seafood platter from 19.50 €.* From the upstairs dining room, you look right down on the sea, though in fine weather the terrace gets the vote. Cancale oysters from oyster-farmer David Simon, bouchot mussels from Mont-Saint-Michel Bay (July to January), a seafood platter, fish or meat - the choice is yours. In the bar, the Breton beers have pride of place. Non-stop service every day, all year round.

LE SURCOUF 7, quai Gambetta ✆ 02 99 89 61 75 *Closed Monday and Tuesday. Set menus 16 €, 25 €, 32 €, 42 €. A la carte.* Jerome Pierpaoli and his staff welcome you warmly in this restaurant with its view of the harbour, open since April 2005. This talented chef has worked in starred restaurants and is extremely professional, and passionate about his job. Fresh ingredients and organic vegetables are the rule. Among his masterpieces are Breton lobster stew in a buckwheat galette, turbot with andouille in a white butter sauce, pig's cheek simmered in the pot and served with its cooking juices, and liver escalope. For dessert, try the thin stuffed crepes with cider alcohol. The wines are excellent, and the bread made daily the old-fashioned way, with organic flour. A place for connoisseurs!

Châteaubourg

AR MILIN' * 30, rue de Paris ✆ 02 99 00 30 91.** *Website: www.armilin.com. Annual closing late December-early January. Restaurant closed Sunday evening. 32 rooms from 70 € to 200 €, breakfast 12 €. Restaurant, set menus from 27 € to 69 € (dégustation menu).* This hotel-restaurant in an old watermill is part of the Châteaux et Hotels de France and Hotels de charme et de caractère de Bretagne groups, which says a lot about the generous and sophisticated welcome you can expect. Built above the River Vilaine, Ar Milin' is a haven of beauty and peace in a 5 hectare park. The restaurant has white tablecloths and a bourgeois look, and serves a particularly succulent traditional cuisine full of flavour. At the water's edge you'll find the Bistrot du Moulin, which provides a charming setting for lunch - a filling assiette composée, dessert and coffee at a very affordable price.

PEN ROC La Peinière - SAINT-DIDIER ✆ 02 99 00 33 02. *Website: www.penroc.fr Open every day lunchtimes and evenings, in high season, advance booking preferred. Closed Friday, and Sunday evening in winter. Set menus from 29.80. Children's menu 13.80 €. Seats 90. Rooms from 63.50 €-218 € (suites).* This hotel-restaurant offers top-quality services - heated pool, terrace, hydromassage baths and showers, sauna and fitness area. The restaurant has its own kitchen garden. The cooking is sophisticated and the hotel rooms extremely comfortable (Pen Roc belongs to the Hotels of Charm and Character Brittany network, and the Relais du Silence). There are 29 rooms: a single, air-conditioned room costs 67 € per night in low season, and a suite with massage bath and terrace, 183 €. Breakfast is 10.80 € for adults and 9 € for kids. The garage is available at 11 €. Pen Roc's cuisine is excellent: veal, beef, duck, pigeon, lobster, Dublin bay prawns, sea bass, dory, scallops, sole, foie gras, citrus fruits, radishes, cabbage. peas, and strawberry, vanilla and apricot flavours are combined in a variety of different ways on the menus. Talented chefs Joseph Froc and Eric Bouchy choose only the freshest local ingredients as a base for their culinary preparations, and the result is delicious seasonal gastronomy. washed down with your choice from the extensive wine list that includes some rare and ancient vintages.

Dinard

NOVOTEL THALASSA *** **1, avenue du Château-Hébert ✆ 02 99 16 78 00**. *Website: www.novoteldinard.com. Closed in December. Novotel hotel with 104 rooms and 2 suites (bedrooms overlook the sea). Residence Les villas La Falaise, 67 studios sleeping 2 or 3. Rooms from 118 €. Breakfast 13 €, free for under-16s.* This comfortable hotel provides plenty of facilities including 30 rooms with shower, 70 rooms with bath, 2 suites and 4 rooms with wheelchair access. 2 restaurants, La Fregate and La Goelette, facing the sea with panoramic view of Saint Malo Bay. Several festivals are held in the bar: jazz in October, TV in April and reading in January. There is an indoor heated pool to relax in, and besides the seawater therapy, 2 saunas, 2 hammams, jacuzzi, a cardiotraining room and fitness centre. A residence containing 67 studios fitted with kitchenette is linked directly to the seawater therapy centre opposite the hotel.

REINE HORTENSE *** **19, rue de la Malouine ✆ 02 99 46 54 31**. *8 rooms from 190 € to 220 €, sea view. Suite 370 €. Breakfast 14 €. Closed from early October to late March.* This is definitely the queen of hotels, a charming throwback to an earlier time. The villa was put up by an aristocrat, and has kept part of its original furniture and harmonious decoration. You are sure to enjoy a dream break; the smiling staff guarantee it.

VENTS ET MAREES 66, boulevard Albert-Lacroix ✆ 02 99 16 48 74. *Closed Thursday. Formulas 9.50 €, 10.50 € and 14 €. Set menu 13 €, 17 €, 26 € and 35 €. A la carte. Group bookings welcome.* This bar-restaurant-caterer is a friendly place run by Nicolas Petit since 2003. You find it in the centre of Saint-Enogat, a sort of village within Dinard itself. You can't mistake the restaurant, located next to a huge fountain: a Rocca boat, lit up at night, has ended up on the terrace near the entrance (where you can eat). The restaurant seems small, but that's only an impression; it seats 60, so groups are welcome. You can enjoy meat grilled over the fire before your very eyes, or other specialities like choucroute de la mer (fish instead of sausage), seafood platters to eat in or take away, or Breton lobster (order in advance). There is also a fine wine list and a selection of wines by the glass.

Dol-de-Bretagne

DOMAINE DES ORMES ✆ 02 99 73 53 00 *Fax: 02 99 73 53 55 info@lesormes.com Website: www.lesormes.com. The Domaine is a 4-star open-air international hotel in a prestigious green setting stretching over 200 ha., and is part of the 'Castels Campings' chain. 45 rooms, each decorated in its own way, are equipped with bath, shower, direct phone and satellite TV.* There is an 18-hole golf course complete with club house and specialised infrastructure catering for 'events' meetings and seminars. Guests can enjoy a number of leisure activities: tennis, riding, cricket, fishing, an Aquapark, three heated pools for the campsite and one for the hotel. Note that you can even arrive by plane or helicopter, since

the estate also boasts a runway! The staff are like their customers - international, available, discreet and energetic. Non-stop activities, an elegant restaurant - nothing is lacking for a top-of-the-range stay of a day, a weekend, or longer.

LE PORCHE AU PAIN 1, rue Ceinte ✆ 02 99 48 37 57. This attractive restaurant-grill in its beautiful 15thc. merchants' house with granite stall has been under new management since May 2005. You can eat in the ground floor dining room or upstairs. Traditional cooking, dishes chargrilled over the fire.

La Gouesnière

LE CHATEAU DE BONABAN * ✆ 02 99 58 24 50** *Fax: 02 99 58 28 41. Website: www.hotel-château-bonaban.com. Open all year. 19 rooms in the château and 15 in the courtyard pavilion. Double and twin rooms. Château rooms are 120 € to 185 € for superior prestige standard, 125 € to 150 € for prestige standard, 70 € to 125 € for romantic standard, 235 € to 285 € for the Tourelle suite and 160 € to 210 € for the 2 Tourelle rooms. Pavilion rooms are 70 € to 90 €. Set menus 25 € (weekdays only) and 36 €, plus a gastronomic menu 47 €.* The Château de Bonaban dates back to the 17thc, and is on the edge of a lake in 27 hectares of grounds. Its Genoa marble staircase and Gobelins and Aubusson tapestries made to Le Brun's designs qualify it for historic monument status. The comfortable rooms all have private bathroom and WC, hairdryer, telephone and satellite TV. They look onto the park, and the château rooms have a lift. There is a gastronomic restaurant, bar in the château salons, terrace, car park, tennis court, park and of course the lake. It is the ideal place for a wedding, family celebration or anniversary: a personalised estimate is available from reception. Young chef David Lamelyn, trained by the very famous Ducasse, runs the restaurant. He has just obtained excellent marks (and the jury's compliments) in a chefs' competition for his veal sweetbreads recipe in several thicknesses, interspersed with asparagus and artichokes. He mixes Provencale flavours with the best of Breton country produce and seafood, and changes his menus every three months, with the seasons. On the 25 € menu, for example, you can start with Cancale Bay oysters followed by roast lamb *boulangère* with thyme, and for dessert, home made nougat ice cream with honey and a lavender tuile biscuit. Exquisite!

Rennes

L'ESCU DE RUNFAO 11 rue du Chapitre ✆ 02 99 79 13 10 *Fax 02 99 79 43 80. Website: www.escu-de-runfao.com. Set menus from 27 € to 52 €. A la carte 70 €. Closed Wednesday lunchtime, Saturday lunchtime, Sunday evening, during February school holidays and from 5 to 25 August.* This late 15thc. half-timbered house gets it name from the President of the 1720 Breton Parliament. That year, the capital of Brittany was ravaged by a huge fire, and he gave each of the street's inhabitants an ecu in exchange for their help during the blaze. Now one of the region's best restaurants, L'Escu is run by the experienced Alain Duhoux and his wife Nathalie, who supervises the dining room with charm and professionalism. At one point, they planned to move, but have decided against it after nearly two decades in the Rue du Chapitre. The restaurant has been redecorated and modernised, however. Alain Duhoux serves a cuisine created from land and sea combinations: shellfish and green asparagus risotto, roast Breton turbot and cream of green peas, sole fillet, vanilla juice and mashed potatoes, sweetbreads and Breton lobster with Sauternes (the classic house speciality, a real marvel) and Plougastel strawberries, white chocolate and soft white cheese ice cream.

LA FONTAINE AUX PERLES 96 rue de la Poterie ✆ 02 99 53 90 90 *Fax 02 99 53 47 77. www.lafontaineauxperles.com. Set menus from 25 € to 70 €. A la carte 70 €. Closed Sunday evening and Monday.* Rachel Gesbert's restaurant has become the most regular in Rennes over the last twenty years. The basic products are carefully selected, and prepared in a way that sets them off (no showy presentataion) and the prices are reasonable, which probably accounts for a lot. This attractive bourgeois house serves sober and rather predictable but faultless *cuisine*: sweetbread mimosa and foie gras with Dublin Bay prawns, roast Breton turbot with bacon and *andouille* (charcuterie), beef fillet in its pancake Rossini-style and rhubarb *financier* (sort of cake) with country strawberries. If there is a downside, it could be a certain lack of humour; this restaurant tends towards formality, and could do with a few smiles. Good cellar, containing the essential bottles with no surprises.

HOTEL LECOQ-GADBY** 156, rue d'Antrain ✆ 02 99 38 05 55. Website: www.lecoq-gadby.com.** *This hotel in the Châteaux et Hotels de France group offers different types of room. The standard single is 125 €, double 145 €. The superior single is 150 €, double 165 €. The suite (2 bedrooms) is 265 € for one person, 305 € for two. Breakfast from 16-18 €.* This is the only 4-star hotel in the Rennes basin, designed for relaxation, getting into shape and facial care. The customers are mainly stressed-out business people who've forgotten how to relax. There are several all-in prices, combining gastronomic and historical discovery with body treatments and massages, one or two nights' stay, breakfast and dinner (without drinks). Apart from its 11 rooms, there are several different-sized reception rooms. An enchanting place with plenty of atmosphere, charm and character - we especially loved the decoration.

L'OUVREE 18, place des Lices ✆ 02 99 30 16 38. *Open Tuesday to Sunday lunchtime. Monday, Saturday lunchtime and Sunday evening, advance group bookings only (20 or more). Set menus from 14.50 € to 32 €.* A gastronomic halt at the top of the Place des Lices. The 16thc. building with its keel roof houses L'Ouvrée, which means delicate, well-balanced and tasty cooking. The menus vary with the market produce available, and are served in a classic setting. Apart from the excellent food, this restaurant is also reputed for its welcome, warm yet not over the top, and faultless service.

LE SEVIGNE ** 47 bis, avenue Janvier ✆ 02 99 67 27 55. *Website: www.hotellesevigne.fr. Rooms from 56 € to 72 €. Breakfast 7 €.* We feel we can recommend this hotel with our eyes closed. Only a short walk from the station, it boasts several other advantages, like a round-the-clock welcome every day of the year from Marie-Claire Galpin and her team. There are 44 warmly and tastefully decorated rooms, and a generous continental breakfast is served in the bar for 7 €.

Saint-Benoît-des-Ondes

LE DORIS 65, rue du Bord-de-Mer ✆ 02 99 58 76 14 *Closed Friday in low season, and open every day in high season with non-stop service from 12 noon to 11pm. Opens 7am. 10 double rooms, 35 €-38 €. Continental breakfast 6 €. All-in overnight prices for reps.Half-board based on 2 people. Pets accepted, supplement 5 €. Set menus: 14.50 €, 23 €, 42 €. A la carte.* This hotel-restaurant is located between Mont Saint Michel and Saint Malo. Babeth and Pierre have been running it since July 2005, and their kindness will make your stay memorable. Pleasant rooms at affordable prices. The chef concocts traditional dishes of the day including seafood, stuffed shellfish, mussels and french fries, fish and meat, but also some regional specialities from the Aveyron, and delicious home-made desserts like chocolate moelleux and tarte normande flambed with calvados. You can enjoy your food on their attractive sunny terrace.

LE RELAIS DES ONDES 30, rue du Bord de Mer ✆ & fax 02 99 58 77 70 *Open every day in July and August. Closed Tuesday and Wednesday for dinner out of season. Access for disabled people.* Mr and Mrs Soreau welcome you cheerfully in their restaurant in front of Granville's bay.,You will savour a traditionnal cooking. 'A la carte' do not hesitate and try the delicious mussels with fries, and the sea food is also awesome. Enjoy!

Saint-Malo

LE LION D'OR - MAISON HECTOR 1, place Chateaubriand ✆ 02 99 56 36 02 *Open 7 days a week. Non-stop service until late. All the food has its origin traced and identified, and the ingredients are fresh and home-cooked.* The wines are all sold by the glass (discover the Medoc Chateau Loudenne (red), Entre Deux Mers Chateau de l'Hoste (white) and Plo Dalia). You can also taste traditional Munich beer (brewed according to the 1516 Purity Law, the world's oldest law concerning food!). The Lion d'Or chef is a butcher's grandson, and has selected Charolais beef for specialities like beef with pan-fried foie gras. You'll enjoy the bouchot mussels and excellent salmon, scallop or foie gras-based salads. The dishes of the day include *pot-au-feu.* The terrace is heated in winter, and you can eat there until late in the evening. Reasonable prices, bilingual menu (French-English).

BRASSERIE DU CAFE DE L'OUEST - MAISON HECTOR 4, place Chateaubriand ✆ 02 99 56 63 49. *Open 7 days a week. Service 12 noon to 3pm and 6pm-11pm.* This brasserie is located in the historic town opposite the Town Hall chateau. You can have breakfast from 7am; after 8.30am you can enjoy your home-made bread and croissants on the sunny terrace (heated in winter). You'll feel the youthful, energetic atmosphere in this newly refurbished setting. The seafood is excellent here - oysters, shellfish platters, mussels, 'sea choucroute' and pan-cooked scallops - and the dish of the day is often freshly-caught fish. Grilled salmon, pollack fillet, baked sea bass and fish a la plancha are the house specialities. Quick, efficient service and wine sold by the glass. The menu is bilingual French-English. Concert evenings are organised regularly.

L'AMBIANCE MALOUINE 19, rue Jacques-Cartier ✆ 02 99 56 12 04 *Open all year, every day of the week from late April to late September. Non-stop service in July ✆ August.* Mussel, pizza and galette formulas for under 10 €. Open since March 2005, this family creperie-pizzeria is definitely worth discovering. The food is home-cooked and galette specialities include the 'baltique' (smoked salmon, creme fraiche, lemon and chives) and 'rustique' (andouille, cheese, onions and creme fraiche). Ask Jean-Baptiste to serve you an excellent crepe Tatin, with its caramelised apples, caramel, salted butter and vanilla ice cream. The pizza base is home-baked - try the 'mexicaine' - but you may well prefer a salad, omelette or mussels. As you might expect, the Ambiance Malouine is strongly influenced by the sea. You can enjoy the setting all year round, since the terrace is heated in winter.

BRASSERIES

SAINT-MALO IN THE WALLED TOWN

L'ATRE 7, esplanade Commandant-Yves-Menguy ✆ 02 99 81 68 39. *Set menus 17 € and 24 €. A la carte.* The previous owners retired in March 2004, and in January 2005, the new management had the place completely done up. The marvellous view of the Solide tower from the terrace hasn't changed though. A wide choice of fish and seafood is on offer, with seasonal variations. The lunchtime formula is economic and very good: starter and main course or main course and dessert, frequently renewed. Try the fish soup and cod with Dublin Bay prawn sauce, for example - its excellent value for money. Home made bread is included in the price, and the service is polite and attentive.

BEAUFORT * 25, chaussée du Sillon 02 99 40 99 99.** *Website: www.hotel-beaufort.com. Open all year. Château et Hotel de France. Hotel de charme et de caractère. 22 rooms from 75 € to 205 €.* This lovely 1850 house with direct access to the beach has all the charm of a desirable private residence. Mark and Sylvie Peterson have paid a lot of attention to the decoration - pure and simple lines in white and beige tones contrasting with red-brown furniture - and the result is striking. Some of the rooms (recently equipped with Canal +) have private terraces with a truly magnificent sea view. The big panoramic room with its bay windows is a good place to relax, but if you want something more intimate, and feel like a tinkle on the ivories, there is an area with a piano at guests' disposal.

CAFE LICORNE 6, place Chateaubriand ✆ 02 99 40 05 18 *Website: www.cafe-licorne.com . Email: contact@cafe-licorne.com . Open all year: 7am-1am in high season; from 8am in winter. Three breakfast choices: English, French and Breton. Non-stop service all year. Set menu formulas. A la carte. Children's menu 7.90 €.* Friendly staff welcome you only a short distance from the beach, in this pleasant creperie-brasserie-tearoom, facing the chateau.The decor is bright and tasteful, with old posters from the National Lottery and a magnificent traditional zinc bar where you can read the daily paper. The menus feature fresh market dishes, all home-cooked, including galettes and crepes , (Breton specialities made with farm milk), Cancale oysters and bouchot mussels, grilled meat and fish, and salads. The wide terrace with its cane furniture is popular in fine weather - you can watch the painters who set up their easels in the square in summer, while eating your meal, having a drink or even just enjoying a cup of excellent tea.

RESTAURANT LE CHASSE MAREE 4, rue du Grout-de-Saint-Georges ✆ 02 99 40 85 10. *Closed Saturday lunchtime and Sunday in low season. Lunchtime marche du jour (daily market) formula 16 €, set menu 22.35 €. A la carte. Small terrace.* In this restaurant that recently changed hands, Daniel offers a *cuisine* based on fresh, top-quality produce, and his son Sebastien welcomes you and looks after the service. The ground-floor dining-room has a shipyard decor, while on the first floor you find yourself among old rigging. Daniel suggests a scallop salad and lobster tails for starters, and his fish specialities include the *soupiere de chasse-maree*, a tureen of sea produce caught on the tide. Among the meat dishes, try the pot of kidneys, veal sweetbreads and pleurotus mushrooms. To finish, Grandmother's bread-and-butter pudding (French-style) is a must. Top marks for delicious food, generous helpings, and a bilingual menu (English spoken).

DOMAINE DE LA VILLE HUCHET*Parc Hôtelier de Plein Air** ✆ **02 99 81 11 13** *Route de la Passagère. Website: www.lavillehuchet.com . Email: info@lavillehuchet.com . Fax: 02 99 81 51 89.* Within easy access of Rennes, Caen and Dinard: follow directions for Cancale/Saint Malo centre, at the first roundabout (Anciens Combattants) take the first right towards the Grassinais Industrial Zone (Z.I) and follow signposts for Camping Ville Huchet. This campsite is on the edge of Saint Malo, 3 km from the beaches, in a magnificent walled park with 198 spaces, including 56 mobile homes and some apartments. A marvellous place for leisure activities and relaxing in a family atmosphere: the water park, bike hire, table tennis, children's playground and football pitch will delight all ages. A large room with an attractive boat-shaped bar, a pizzeria/snack bar, bread and croissant outlet and minimarket are at your disposal. New in 2006: mini-golf , wide screen TV for sports broadcasts and Internet access. Heaven on earth!

CREPERIE SOLIDOR **7, esplanade Commandant-Menguy** ✆ **02 99 81 64 53.** *Closed from 21 November to 4 December. Non-stop service in season.* What better way to enjoy your pancake made from local flour from the Champinel mill, than while you gaze at Solidor harbour from the sunny terrace. All the galettes are cooked on request, but you can also taste house specialities like the *solidor*, a savoury buckwheat pancake with scallops *flambéd* in cognac and tarragon cream, the *vauban*, with scallops, fresh mushrooms and snail butter, or again the *normande*: warm camembert, salad, apples and lardons, or the *nordique*: salmon and a butter pancake. The sweet pancakes are delicious too: fig with fig compote, whipped cream and fig and cinnamon ice-cream; the *salidou*, salted butter caramel, or the *rance*, frangipane, raspberries, whipped cream and red fruit *coulis*. There are some great salads such as the *briantais*: salad, apples, comté cheese, smoked duck breast, cider vinegar, and chives served with an all-butter buckwheat pancake. Very fast service for the tourist in a hurry.

LE MOULARD D'OGUST La Madeleine Shopping Centre ✆ 02 99 82 48 81. *Open Monday to Thursday: 8am-8.30pm, Friday and Saturday: 8.30am-10pm. Lunchtime express formula 10.90 € (2 courses) and full set menu 14.90 €. A la carte.* This restaurant-pizzeria can be found in La Madeleine shopping centre, and offers fresh, home-cooked food in a rustic country setting. There is a wide range of tasty, generous pizzas like the 'Savoyarde' and the 'Cancalaise', a choice of 9 salads (the Rocamadour, for instance) pasta - you must taste the delicious Fagottini Di Parma - and meat (try it pan-fried). Every day, 5 different suggestions are chalked up on the slate. Sandwiches and paninis are available for the less hungry. Take-away pizzas are another option, especially if you're in a hurry. A customer fidelity card rewards regulars.

GRAND HOTEL DES THERMES ** 100, boulevard Hébert ✆ 02 99 40 75 75**. *Website: www.thalassotherapie.com. Open all year. 178 double rooms from 94 € to 605 € (suite). Breakfast 18 €. Disabled access.* Our team strongly recommends this hotel, in its magnificent setting a stone's throw from the old town and almost at the water's edge. Nearly all the rooms have a sea view. The guests are mainly taking seawater therapy cures, since Saint-Malo's thermal baths are reputed. If you're interested in getting fit and pampering yourself in a bracing seaside atmosphere, then this is the place for you.

LA GRASSINAIS ** 12, allée de la Grassinais ✆ 02 99 81 33 00. *Website: saint-malo-hebergement.com. Open all year except late December to mid-January. 29 rooms, doubles from 58 € to 79 €. Breakfast buffet 8 € from 7.30am to 9.30am. Free car park. Set menus from 20 € to 54 €.* This manor is part of the *Logis de France* group. The site is magnificent, and the rooms are peaceful, despite being right in the middle of a busy town. As for the hotel's gastronomic restaurant, it is reputed for miles around, specialising in fish and seafood. It is closed Saturday lunchtime, Sunday evening and Monday in low season, and seats 35 to 50.

CHAMBRES D'HOTES MANOIR DE LA BARONNIE Avenue du Général-Patton ✆ 01 99 81 95 40. *Website: www.la-baronnie.fr. Email: info@la-baronnie.fr. 5 rooms from 50 € to 110 € according to season, breakfast included.* La Baronnie is a 17thc. *malouniere*, a typical local manor on the way into Saint Malo, near the historic town centre and beaches. Set in 7,000 sqm. of grounds, it still has all the genuine charm of a great family house. The rooms are individually decorated with care, and have bathroom and private WC. Youthful owners Benoit and Sophie Laude go to great lengths to make your stay unforgettable.

HOTEL AMBASSADEURS 11, chaussée du sillon © 02 99 40 26 26.** *Fax: 02 99 40 12 86. Website: www.hotel-ambassadeurs-saintmalo.com. 20 rooms from 60 € to 97 €.* This hotel is set high up, and has an exceptional panoramic view. It is also only 800m from the old town. Mme Nicolas provides a charming welcome, and her comfortable rooms are all equipped with bath or shower, TV and WiFi access. On three floors, they overlook the sea and have balconies. Tea is served from 2pm to 7pm in the *salon de thé*, either in the dining-room or on the small terrace. We warmly recommend the friendly, family atmosphere.

LE PONTON Port des Sablons © 02 99 19 02 19. *Website: www.st-malo-hotel-cunningham.com . Closed Sunday evening and Monday in low season, open every day in high season. Lunchtime dish of the day (until Saturday) 13 €. Set menus 19 € and 25 €.* Le Ponton is located near Saint Malo harbour, and features a charming marine decor, with a genuine dragon (boat shaped in wood) hanging from the ceiling. It is a meeting place for local boating regulars who enjoy traditional cooking: the chargrilled meat, fish and seafood are all delicious. Suggestions are chalked up on the slate, and new dishes from different parts of the world appear on the menu every month. Eat on the terrace in fine weather, overlooking the harbour and facing the old town.

L'ABORDAGE 5, place de la Poissonnerie © 02 99 40 87 53. *Closed Saturday lunchtime, Sunday and Monday. Lunchtime formula from 11 € to 15 €, decouverte menu 50 €. A la carte.* This restaurant and wine bar, open since April 2004, offers wines and spirits from around the world. You can attend tasting classes, and build up your own cellar. The restaurant serves cooking based on fresh seasonal market produce, with a number of tasty local specialities. The lunchtime menu comprises a dish of the day, usually fish, and a glass of wine. Thematic dinners are organised on a regular basis. Don't lose this address!

Saint-Méloir-des-Ondes

LA BELLE DE VILAINE Les Nielles Route du Mont-Saint-Michel © 02 99 89 23 80. *Open from 15 February to mid-November. Set menus from 14 € to 35 €. Large terrace.* Mme Ameline's restaurant is decorated in a most original manner, adding greatly to its charm and conviviality. The cuisine is sophisticated, with seafood specialities. You must taste the grilled Dublin Bay prawns, rouget cooked slowly over a low heat, warm oysters with leeks *fondue*, and cod *aumonière* (in a pastry case) flavoured with *andouille*. The beef fillet with morels is unanimously popular. You'd be wise to book in advance, as the place is often full.

RESTAURANT TIREL GUERIN *   Gare de la Gouesnière** ✆ **02 99 89 10 46.** *Open all year, except mid-December to late January. Single and double rooms from 61 € to 90 €. Set menus from 25 € to 78 €.* This is a pleasant place in the Saint-Meloir-des-Ondes countryside, where customers come to relax. Success is a family affair, with the third generation now running the establishment, and keeping up its excellent reputation with the help of varied and sophisticated restaurant menus. The dining rooms are air-conditioned, and the hotel provides good quality facilities and service. There are 56 comfortable rooms including 9 luxury apartments, with half of them looking onto a pleasure garden. The hotel also has a bar, swimming pool, jacuzzi and tennis courts: quite a programme!

MORBIHAN

Arradon

LES VENETTES*   La Pointe-d'Arradon** ✆ **02 97 44 85 85.** *Website: www.lesvenetes.com – email: info@lesvenetes.com – Weekly closing Sunday evening all year, and Monday in winter. Open all year. 10 rooms from 100 € to 200 €. Half-board for 2: 150 €-200 €. Breakfast 10 €. Set menus 35 €-75 €.* A magnificent hotel almost in the sea, with a great view of the islands whose names feature on the menus. The dining-room is decorated in shades of blue and white, the cooking is seasonal and the wine list well-stocked. The sound of gently clicking golfballs from Morbihan Golf Course is a plus.

Arzon

LE CROUESTY   Rue Croisty** ✆ **02 97 53 87 91**. *Closed mid-November to early February (check opening dates in January). 26 rooms, including 3 family rooms, from 69 € to 90 € in high season. Breakfast 6.90 €. TV and bathrooms with bath in every room. Car park. Bar and Piano.* Located just between Crouesty harbour and Arzon, this contemporary hotel has calm and spacious rooms, and a terrace and bar for residents only.

LA REGATE   3, place d'Artimon–Quai des Voiliers ✆ **02 97 53 91 95.** *Open February-15 November.* The Regate's savoury pancakes are made with genuine Breton buckwheat flour ground in the traditional way. Set menu 13.40 €, with the *petit mousse* (ship's boy) children's menu 8.90 €. Specialities include the Saint Jacques (scallop) salad or Saint Jacques *galette* (savoury pancake) served with leeks *fondue* with cream and lemon, and the black pudding and apple *galette*. The crepes (sweet pancakes) are just as tasty and 100% genuine, being made with organic flour. That Breton classic, the salted butter caramel, is home made. You can however opt for oysters, mussels, fish soup or a salad. The owners are crazy about the place, and provide you with locally brewed cider, a varied wine list and a wide terrace to enjoy it on providing the weather sets fair. You also have a large selection of ice creams to choose from for dessert. Don't miss this restaurant!

Auray

LA CLOSERIE DE KERDRAIN   20, rue Louis-Billet ✆ **02 97 56 61 27.** *Set menus 25 € Tuesday to Friday lunchtime, and 35 €, 46 € and 80 €.* M. and Mme Corfmat welcome you to their 17thc. manor in the town centre, which boasts 2 restaurant dining rooms and tables in the flower garden during fine weather. The cuisine is gastronomic and all very tempting: oysters with green apple juice and cucumber as a starter, gulf mullet sealed in basil oil with crunchy vegetable rolls or a Bertrand Thereaud pigeon

breast roasted in muscadet, melon and fresh mint for the main course, and to finish, Breton shortbread with Saint-Goustan raspberries and pistachio cream sorbet - for instance. Excellent wine list with plenty of appellations. Wine served by the glass. If you're interested, you can visit the aromatic kitchen garden behind the building.

LA TABLE DES MAREES 16 rue du Jeu de Paume © 02 97 56 63 60 *Closed Saturday for lunch, Sunday and Monday. Gastronomic restaurant. Menu 36 €, during the week lunch for 18 €.* You cannot miss the restaurant, all in yellow and black. For lunch, what about some roasted salmon with bacon and lentils. For dessert, try the pear and almond pie or the salt flower shortbread biscuit. Delicious! By the way, do not hesitate to congratulate the chef, he is perfectly fluent in english! A very good adress!

LA LICORNE 15, place Saint-Sauveur – SAINT-GOUSTAN © 02 97 24 06 46. *Closed Wednesday and Thursday. Open all year: 9am-1am (bar). Open every day in July © August. Formula 9.20 €. Dish of the day 8.90 €. Set menus 11 €-27.50 €. A la carte.* The terrace overlooking the harbour is very pleasant in fine weather, and there is a non-smoking dining-room on the first floor with a marvellous view of the harbour. Fish and shellfish are the house specialities (made with fresh ingredients), such as the ocean stewpot or mullet fillets Breton-style. When it comes to dessert, the camembert fondant with salted butter caramel is definitely not to be missed.

L'HOSTELLERIE ABBATIALE-BEST WESTERN * Manoir de Kerdréan ✆ 02 97 57 84 00.** *Website: www.abbatiales.com. Open all year. 67 rooms including 18 in the 14thc. manor (the others are in the modern part of the hotel). Room prices from 65 € to 250 €. Generous breakfast 11 €. 6 meeting rooms available for hire, with up-to-date equipment. Swimming pool, park, terrace, tennis court and private car park. Restaurant open all year. Set menu from 27 €.* The menus are made up of local recipes flavoured with carefully-added spices. Two pleasant dining rooms are available, one in stone with exposed beams overlooking an extensive garden, the other more contemporary, in the recent building, opening onto the pool. Kerdrean Manor is located above the River Auray on the edge of the Morbihan Gulf. Its name means 'stone castle' and it dates back to 1427, though the buildings on the left and the square tower are 13thc. and the central part 16thc. Nowadays, the majestic façade rising proudly from its green setting fronts a comfortable and friendly hotel-restaurant that welcomes both individual guests and groups seeking a *hotel de caractère*. The estate covers several hectares of delightful walks in calm and shady grounds, with a number of rare trees.

Baden

LE GAVRINIS* Toulbroch-en-Baden ✆ 02 97 57 00 82**. *Website: http://gavrinis.com. Closed 8 January-2 February, 19 February-7 March and 27 November-2 December 2006. Weekly closing Saturday lunchtime, Sunday evening and Monday. Open every evening 17 June-17 September. Double rooms from 63 € to 88 €. Breakfast 10.50 €. Pets supplement 7.50 €. Private car park, garden. Lunchtime formula 17 €. Set menu du marche 20 € and lobster menu 75 €.* M. Lignieres' cooking is simply delicious. The food melts in the mouth, revealing a whole spectrum of flavours: Guéméné andouille paté, crunchy salad with hazlenut oil, scallops with fresh coriander juice, and manjari chocolate fondant with saffron sorbet feature on his menus, which change according to the season and the day's catch. The wine list is well-chosen, and includes a 1950 cognac and armagnac. The dining room is non-smoking, and tea fans can choose from a selection of leaves including Japanese and Chinese. A very good restaurant.

LE KERDELAN Port-Blanc ✆ 02 97 57 25 95. *Closed Monday in low season. Set menus from 16 € to 23 €.* This little restaurant a few steps from the Ile aux Moines landing stage takes its name from the nearby bay. New owner Hervé is determined to make it a must for all gourmets, and has repainted and refurbished it as a first step. All the ingredients are really fresh and everything is home cooked. Specialities include mullet with orange caramel, a fish terrine, stuffed clams, *assiette du pêcheur* (a mixed seafood dish), sea bream, duck with mead and loin of lamb. In season, chargrilled fish is very popular. There is also an extensive choice à la carte. The terrace overlooks the harbour, giving you a first-class view of latecomers running in all directions so as not to miss their boat. Simple, friendly welcome and service. Private car park.

Baud

LE CITRON VERT 41, rue Saint-Yves ✆ 02 97 51 03 62. *Closed Monday and Tuesday in low season and during school holidays, open every day in high season.* The tables are prettily decorated with small bouquets of flowers in this warm dining-room with its beautiful exposed beams and large fireplace. Top-quality produce and fresh ingredients are the rule at Jeremy and Manuela's; the galettes are made to a traditional recipe and the crepes prepared with organic flour. Try the 'Seguin' - Lignol goat's cheese, smoked bacon, garlic and parsley butter - or the 'picarde', with leeks, lardons in cream, cheese and an egg, or then again, the 'forestiere', fresh mushrooms, cream and cheese. Salads and meat (of French origin) complete the menu. You can eat on the terrace in the sun - but don't forget to book ahead!

LE RELAIS DE LA FORET 19, rue de la Mairie ✆ 02 97 51 01 77. *Closed Wednesday and Sunday evening. 10 rooms from 39 € to 45 €. Continental breakfast 5 €. All-in overnight stay 50 €. Restaurant lunchtime express formula 10.40 €, set menus 14.50 €-32 €. Childrens' menu 7 €. Rooms equipped with shower, WC and TV.* Pleasant setting, friendly ambience, large character fireplace for chargrilling. The cooking is sophisticated, with seafood specialities. Family meals can be organised with advance booking. **MME ROBIC Kersommer ✆ 02 97 51 08 02.**

Belle-Ile-en-Mer

AUBERGE CHOUK'AZE Chemin du Petit Houx – Locmaria ✆ 02 97 31 79 69. This place is starting to get talked about, thanks to its success with the customers. No hassle or stress here; the staff take time to welcome and advise you peacefully. Fish has pride of place on the menu, but there is meat too, including pork and kid. Everything is home made, and the goat's cheese comes from the neighbouring farm. Customers are offered a four-page newspaper-menu. Chouk'aze is well worth the visit!

CASTEL CLARA GOULPHAR ** ✆ 02 97 31 84 21 – Fax: 02 97 31 51 69.** *Website: www.castel-clara.com Closed until February 2006. Rooms from 183 € to 344 € (suites and split-level). Set menus from 50 € to 65 €.* The Castel Clara is an excellent hotel-restaurant on the charming Goulphar creek, with its little fishing harbour. Plenty of celebrities have stopped off here for seawater therapy and a well-earned rest in a calm and luxurious setting off the beaten track. From 2006 onwards, Goulphar Manor will no longer exist as such, but will be directly linked to Castel Clara.

Billiers

DOMAINE DE ROCHEVILAINE Pointe de Pen-Lan ✆ 02 97 41 61 61 *Fax 02 97 41 44 85. Website: www.domainerochevilaine.com. Set menus 38 € to 95 €. A la carte 65 €. Open non-stop.* This is more than an estate, really a Breton-style complex, located right at the end of the Pen Lan headland. Unostentatious yet magnificent, this comfortable, modern marine spa boasts about 30 rooms, a priest's garden, and one of the region's most experienced and faithful chefs in its kitchens. At fifty-something,

Patrice Caillaut has trained hordes of young cooks, some of whom are now seconding the greats, and his culinary vision has hardly changed since he arrived here in 1984. The restaurant is to be completely renovated this year, to bring its charm and comfort into line with the recent building of the marine spa and the renovation of the bedrooms. Patrice's cooking is based on magnificent produce, faultless technique and little risk-taking: pressed duck foie gras, red beetroot caramel, lobster medallion with poached egg, jardin croquant (crunchy vegetables) dory fillet in a golden crust, combava emulsion, boneless pig's trotter in a poultry membrane and foie gras, *craquante d'opaline* dessert with a creamy dark and white chocolate mousse. The embodiment of luxury *cuisine* in an appropriate setting.

Carnac

LA CALYPSO Le Po ✆ 02 97 52 06 14. *Closed Sunday evening and Monday (except French school holidays). Open February-late November and lunchtimes.* This is a typically low, peaceful Breton dwelling, located among the Po oyster beds. Inside, you find a cosy ambience and a log fire. A few winkles help sharpen the appetite while you're choosing your meal. All the fish - dory, monkfish kebabs, sole - rib steaks and lobsters are chargrilled before your very eyes. The warm oysters are perfect, and the Dublin bay prawns au gratin excellent. A dessert rounds things off nicely. Highly recommended.

LA COTE Kermario ✆ 02 97 52 02 80. *Closed Sunday evening in low season and Monday all year. Set meus from 23 € (weekday lunchtime and evenings) to 52 €.* This pretty Breton house not far from the standing stones might be expected to serve banal food for tourists: well it doesn't! Its young chef has created an inventive menu full of fresh and surprising combinations and personal recipes. All the dishes are home made from the bread to the sorbet. Garden with terrace.

HELENA 1, avenue de la Poste – CARNAC-VILLE ✆ 02 97 52 21 57. *Open every day in high season. Open Friday, Saturday and Sunday evening in low season. Near the church.* M. Treguier knows his stuff when it comes to pizzas and Italian cooking. You can enjoy his home-cooked food in a country setting complete with exposed beams and open fireplace. Two terraces (one covered) are available for fresh air fans. There is a choice of salads, pasta and meat dishes, but pizzas have pride of place on the menu. Try the 'ondata' with squid, gambas and Helena sauce, or the 'bretonne' garnished with andouille, olives, origano, tomatoes and mushrooms.

LE DIANA**   21, boulevard de la Plage** ✆ **02 97 52 05 38.** *Website: www.lediana.com. This magnificent four-star hotel provides 31 rooms with a sea view, from 120 € to 294 € (doubles) according to the season. Breakfast 19 €. Half-board from 156 € to 226 € per person. The restaurant Les Marquises has a set menu du marché renewed every day, 37 €, a menu decouverte 58 € and a lobster menu 66 €. A la carte.* Optimum comfort - pool, hammam, jacuzzi - with a heated freshwater tots' pool, sandy public beach, beach toys at your disposal, cycles of all sizes and a toybox in your room. You can even ask for a babysitter, and look after your offspring better than at home, thanks to the bottle-warmer, changing table and beeper provided. This year, there is a wine and a rum cellar (better ask for the babysitter). Definitely not to be missed.

LA MARINE   4 place de la Chapelle ✆ **02 97 52 07 33** *E-mail: info@lamarinecarnac.com. Website: www.hotel-restaurant-carnac.com. The hotel is open all year; the restaurant is open lunchtimes and evenings in high season. 31 rooms from 39 € to 139 €. Breakfast 6.70 €. WiFi access. Pets accepted 5 €.* Nathalie, Isa, Franck and Laurent welcomr you in this charming, well-run hotel near the beaches, in central Carnac. Fresh ingredients are the keynote when it comes to cooking: the 11 € formula (starter, main course, cheese or dessert) is delicious, and there are others specially suited to all types of budget. Start with a three-fish terrine, followed by the skate with capers in hazlenut butter, and finish your meal with a farandole of home-made desserts. You'll be keen to come back!

LA PLAGE   6, allée du Parc – CARNAC-PLAGE ✆ **02 97 52 12 60.** *Open all year except two weeks in January. Children's menu 7 €. A la carte.* You could call this a polyvalent creperie! All the ingredients are fresh, the vegetables come straight from the farm and the food is home-cooked. The style is regional: mussels with garlic butter, galettes (try *la pitchouse*) Guemenee andouille with rissoled potatoes, crepes, grilled meat, fish, salads and fresh pan-fried scallops. Eat with the breeze in your hair on the wide, sunny terrace.

LE TUMULUS*   31, rue du Tumulus** ✆ **02 97 52 08 21.** *Fax: 02 97 52 81 88. Website: www.hotel-tumulus.com. Open from Easter to late September. Logis de France. Châteaux et Hotels de France, Relais du Silence. 23 rooms from 70 € to 290 € according to season and number of guests.* A short way from Carnac-Plage at the foot of the Saint-Michel tumulus, this hotel offers peace and quiet. The main part of the building dates back to 1900 with a 1940 dining room. A large heated pool, tree-lined park, pleasure garden and fitness centre are at your disposal. The restaurant has painted panelling and a panoramic view of Quiberon Bay, and offers regional cooking with seafood in pride of place.

LA POTION MAGIQUE Rue Saint-Cornely ✆ 02 97 52 63 46. *Email: potmag@aol.com – Open all year. Set menu 9.20 €. Children's menu 6.10 €. A la carte.* The house speciality is the galette, made with traditional buckwheat flour. Scallops flambed with cognac on a bed of leeks; sardine, spinach and tomato and smoked ham are three galette fillings worth checking out. For dessert, try the 'cornelly', with its apples rissoled in butter and home-made caramel. Delicious! Asterix's magic potion turns out to be *chouchen* (mead) with creme de cassis, served as a surprising digestive. While you're tasting it, the kids can take part in a drawing competition, and have their work of art pinned up on the wall afterwards. Note that this place won the gold medal in the Breton Gastronomy Trophy, in September 2005!

LE PLANCTON* 12, boulevard de la plage – BP 86 ✆ 02 97 52 13 65.** *Fax: 02 97 52 87 63. Website: www.hotel-plancton.com – e-mail: onfo@hotel-plancton.com – 30 rooms, including 2 equipped for the disabled and 13 with a balcony, 70 € to 150 € for two, according to season. Breakfast buffet 11 €. Half-board 66.50 € to 99 €. Set menu of the day 32.50 € (evening) and brasserie at lunchtimes. Private car park (closed) 5 €.* This hotel-restaurant is located on the seafront facing Quiberon Bay. The comfortable rooms all have phone, shower or bath, hair-dryer, satellite TV and WiFi access. House specialities include home-smoked fish and grilled Guemene andouilles. Diving enthusiasts please note that Le Padi diving club can be found in the hotel.

Damgan

HOTEL DE LA PLAGE 38, boulevard de l'Océan ✆ 02 97 41 10 07. *Website: www.hotel-morbihan.com – Plenty of charm, facing the ocean, open February to mid-November and during the Christmas holidays. 18 rooms on 3 floors (with lift) from 52 € to 85 €. Suite 125 €, 2 junior suites 85 €. Breakfast 8.50 €, children 6 €. All-in overnight stay 60 €. Dish of the day 6 €. Private car park and large garden at guests' disposal.* The rooms are individually decorated and comfortable, all south-facing and looking onto the sea, with phone, TV and double glazing. The junior suites boast a wide balcony and large bathroom perfect for relaxing. Restaurant Le Solent is open at lunchtime; the menu is chalked up on a slate, and service is quick and efficient. You just have to cross the street and you're on the beach: why not take advantage of low tide for a spot of fishing?

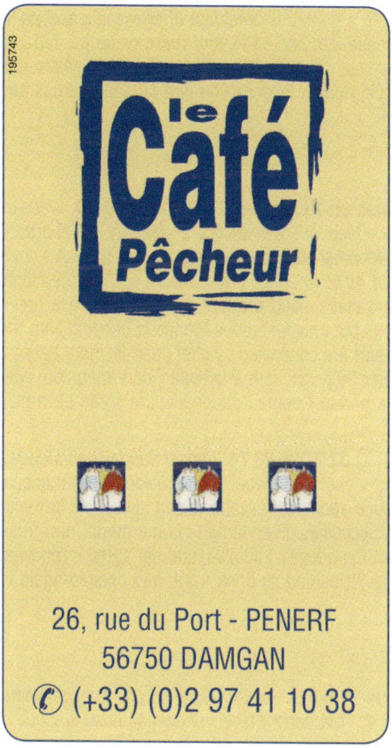

LE CAFE PECHEUR 26, rue du Port ✆ 02 97 41 10 38. *Open every day April-September, closed Monday in low season. Set menus from 20 € to 35 €, children's menu 8 €.* Jean-Marc Da Costa and his team welcome cabin boys and old sea dogs alike in a most original setting, a short distance from the church. Generous helpings of scallop and pan-cooked Dublin bay prawn salad, a magnificent seafood platter made to measure (13 € - 58 €) and apple tart caramelised in salted butter are accompanied by a very attractive wine list. So what are you waiting for? all aboard!

Erdeven

TY GLAZ 22, résidence Loperhet ✆ 02 97 58 31 12 / 06 72 03 03 80. *Website: www.ot-erdeven.fr – 4 chambres 3 ears of wheat, Clés Vacances. 50 € per head per night, breakfast included (tourist tax 0.50 € per head per night). Car park, garden, pets accepted.* Located 1.5km from the beaches, 7km from Carnac, 15km from Quiberon and 32km from Vannes, this residence specialises in comfortable

theme rooms with private bathrooms. Start the day with a generous breakfast of croissants and *pains au chocolat*, various types of bread, fruit and home-made jam served in your room or on the terrace. You're spoilt for choice when it comes to leisure activities: 80km of pedestrian paths for walkers and mountain biking (you can borrow a bike), boules and ping-pong. Indoors, you find TV, DVD, games and local information literature. English spoken.

Hennebont

CHÂTEAU DE LOCGUENOLE** Route de Port-Louis-en-Kervignac © 02 97 76 76 76**. *Website: www.château-de-locguenole.com Relais & Châteaux. Open all year except 2 January-17 February. Restaurant closed at lunchtime except Sunday, and Monday evening in low season. 22 rooms from 112 € to 289 € according to season. Set menus from 49 € to 94 €. Breakfast 17 €.* An exceptional site for this proud Breton castle rising from its mound overlooking the Blavet, in an immense green park sloping down to the river. Beautiful stone, luxurious but unostentatious fittings in keeping with the historic setting, huge, comfortable rooms. Romantic meals are concocted by chef Jean-Bernard Pautrat, who worked with Marc Meneau for quite a time. Lobster fricassée with artichokes, dory meunière with ginger butter, and fatted chicken from the Entillère farm with Guemene *andouille* are some examples of his talent.

LE RESTAURANT DU BLAVET 3, quai de Port-Louis © 02 97 36 28 74. *Closed Sunday and Monday. Set menus 14 € and 24.50 €.* Florise, this restaurant's chef and owner, likes cooking the traditional way: whole veal kidneys pan-cooked in a mustard sauce, monkfish navarin (stew) and apple tart with salted butter caramel and ice cream are among her specialities. Everything is home made from fresh local ingredients. The slate changes daily at the lady of the house's initiative, and her carte is renewed every month. The place was recently closed for a face-lift behind its brick front, and opened again in July 2004 with a brand-new look.

La Roche-Bernard

L'AUBERGE BRETONNE 2 place Duguesclin © 02 99 90 60 28 *Fax 02 99 90 85 00. Website: www.auberge-bretonne.com. Set menus from 55 € to 137 €. A la carte 110 €. Closed Monday lunchtime, Tuesday lunchtime, Thursday, Friday lunchtime and 15 November-20 January.* Jacques Thorel took over this former crêperie 25 years ago, and is now one of France's most interesting chefs. His own interests are diverse - literature, wine, stamp collecting and Breton horses -but he is single-minded about fresh produce: eggs and vegetables come from his own farm, and the fish is the best in the country. The marvellous *dégustation* menu (140 €) contains garden vegetables - courgettes, French beans, carrots etc. - crab *remoulade* with tomatoes, bass, leeks, potatoes and truffles, local lobster with lemon and pepper, sweetbreads, cepes, shallots and Pauillac juice, lamb kebab and Moroccan vegetables, fourme d'Ambert cheese and brioche with cherries, and to finish, the *délice de Solange* (the lady of the house), a dessert composition that'll take your breath away. Don't forget the fabulous cellar (around 3,000 recommended wines), probably one of the five or six biggest in France and a collector's dream.

La Gacilly

LA MAUVAISE GRAINE 16, rue Lafayette © 02 99 08 57 83 *Closed Monday in low season, open every day in July © August. Disabled access.* Sylvain welcomes you in his warmly-decorated and modern creperie, where he uses organic flour and local home-made produce. The 'trappistine' galette (Trappe *fondant*, lardons, onion gratin and potatoes with cream) may tempt you, with a 'beehive nectar' pancake for afters (pear sweetened with honey and mandarine sorbet). You also find mixed salads, meat dishes and home-brewed cider. The creperie is located in a pedestrian street and boasts a sunny terrace and car park. Excellent welcome and service; this is a place to come back to.

Lorient

CONFORT HOTEL ASTORIA** **3, rue Clisson ✆ 02 97 21 10 23. 23** *Fax: 02 97 21 03 55. Website; www.hotelastoria-lorient.com – email: hotelastoria.lorient@wanadoo.fr – 35 rooms from 48 € to 84 €. Breakfast 7 €. Pets 5,50 €. All-in overnight stay: 63 €.* This hotel, located in the town centre near the train station, Palais des Congres, restaurants and cinema has been completely renovated and provides comfortable rooms, all with TV, Canal +, TPS, Internet socket and WiFi. There are adjoining rooms with connecting doors for families, and a lift to all floors. Fully-equipped seminar rooms are available, and there is a car park nearby. Pets accepted. Nordine and Laurence extend a warm welcome to their guests, and the services are excellent.

LE MOLIERE 10, rue Colbert ✆ 02 97 64 25 27. *Closed Saturday lunchtime and Sunday. bar open from 10am. On weekdays, dish of the day 8 €, two courses 10 €, three courses 12 €.* Bistro ambience, excellent cooking from talented chef Jeremy and a warm welcome from Jasmine. You'll appreciate the luminous *commedia del arte* setting and the food, from the cold pork appetisers with your aperitif to the fondue bourguignonne (sold by weight!). A cheerful place.

L'AMPHITRYON 127 rue du Col-Moller ✆ 02 97 83 34 04 *Fax: 02 97 37 25 02. Website: www.amphitryon-abadie.com Set menus from 35 € to 100 €. A la carte 80 €. Closed Sunday, Monday, 1-11 November and 1-17 May.* The affordable prices are the most striking thing about Jean-Paul Abadie's Amphitryon (apart from the unattractive setting!): you can eat à la carte with a bottle of mineral water and a coffee for under 100 €, yet this is one of France's most specialised restaurants. Jean-Paul has collected plenty of tributes in recent years, but it has not altered his democratic ideas: he has kept his feet firmly on the ground and makes sure his exceptional seafood cuisine is accessible to the average customer. Velvet swimming crabs cappucino-style, ginger and lemon, spider crab *royale* with liquorice, dory with artichokes, arabica and cardamom, mullet fillets, winkles and cockles with aniseed, cod half-salted, almonds, avocado and tomatoes, and red tuna in crunchy little tournedos with lovage and sugar snap peas. The desserts from pastrycook Nicolas Multon are superb, especially the baba *bouchon* flavoured with buckwheat and orange, marmalade and rhubarb. Wife Véronique Abadie and wine waiter Anthony Rault manage an exceptional cellar with over 1,000 recommended wines at unbeatable prices.

HOTEL LE VICTOR HUGO** **36, rue Lazare-Carnot ✆ 02 97 21 16 24.** *Fax: 02 97 84 95 13. Open every day all year. 30 rooms from 30 € to 68 €. Breakfast 6 €.* Overnight break from 56 € to 62 €. Ideally located between the sailing harbour, Palais des Congres and town centre, The Victor Hugo provides excellent facilities. Newly decorated with comfortable rooms, it offers cable TV and Canal +, Wi-Fi Internet access, direct phone line and private garage. Special weekend prices. Pets are admitted except in the breakfast room. The Contact-Hotel network gives you a free night after 11 booked in its hotels, which is a pleasant extra.

HOTEL CLERIA 27, boulevard Franchet-d'Esperey 02 97 21 04 59. Fax: 02 97 64 19 10.** *Website: www.hotel-cleria.com. Open every day. 33 comfortable rooms from 55 € to 105 €. Breakfast 8 €.* Laure and Benoit Lesage welcome you discreetly in their town centre hotel, with its tasteful decoration in shades of coffee and vanilla (the white plates and red tablecloths in the breakfast room are most inviting). There is a lift to all three floors, where you find 2 rooms sleeping four, 3 rooms sleeping 3, and some non-smoking rooms. There is wide screen TV with Canal +, TPS and 31 cable channels. Individual closed garages. Air conditioned meeting room. In summer, breakfast is served in the garden. Petit Futé advises you to book in advance.

LE MANOIR DE KERLEBERT Queven ✆ 02 97 80 22 37. *Fax: 02 97 80 20 83. Email: manoirkerlebert@wanadoo.fr – 4 rooms (55 €, and one family room at 80 €). Breakfast included. Under-15s 10 €, under-3s free.* Sophie and Guirec welcome you with fresh locally-produced apple juice, in their 17thc. home 6km from Lorient on the Morbihan-Finistere border. The hotel boasts a billiard table, piano, library and games - and there are some great walks to enjoy in the region. You can order a picnic basket (9 €) the night before, and go off for a whole day's hiking. Dinner is served at the residents' table, or *table d'hotes*, at 8pm, 20 € per head, 10 € for children. The cooking is regional, based on local sea and country produce. Kerlebert Manor also organises wedding nights, with appropriate decoration, and Christmas activities the second weekend in December, with a Provencal creche and Breton storytellers for an evening round the fire.

LES GENS DE MER 14, boulevard Louis-Nail ✆ 02 97 37 11 28.** *Fax: 02 97 37 41 31. Website:: www.lesgensdemer.fr – 31 comfortable, renovated rooms from 36 €. Breakfast 5.50 €. Rooms equipped with satellite TV and telephone. Pets accepted, supplement 5 €.* Just opposite the new fishing harbour, 5 minutes from the town centre by car. This pleasant hotel boasts a restaurant offering a wide choice of home-cooked dishes that are excellent value for money. It also has a meeting room seating 20, and a car park. Banquets and seminars organised on request.

HOTEL LES OCEANES 17, avenue de la Perrière ✆ 02 97 37 14 66.** *Fax: 02 97 37 36 87. Website: www.hotel-lesoceanes.com. 23 renovated rooms including a family suite and 2 triple rooms, from 36 € to 80 € with bathroom, TV and Internet access. Breakfast buffet 6.50 € from 6.30pm (except weekends*

and public holidays). Overnight break 58 €. Pets 5 €. Pierrick and Tanguy Vasseur took over this hotel in July 2005. It is located near the commercial port and fishing harbour, harbour station, Palais des Congrès and town centre, with free, easily available parking along Avenue Perrière. The station is five minutes by bus (line H, Perrière bus stop) and Larmor-Plage is quite close. English and Spanish spoken.

Ploërmel

HOTEL LE THY 8, boulevard Foch ✆ 02 97 74 05 21**. *Website: www.lethy.com. Open all year, 7 days a week.* Seven rooms with 160cm x 200cm beds and TV with Canal +. Rooms decorated in the Van Gogh, Hopper, Hugo Pratt, Tapiece and Klimt style 55 € to 60 €, decoration by Skene Decor. This superb hotel is also a PMU bar (French sports betting is done in PMU cafés), provides a snack service from Monday to Friday (warm and cold sandwiches) and puts on a show in its pub Le Thy'roir every Friday evening (either a dinner concert or a play). Terrace in summer, private car park.

LE ROI ARTHUR – GOLF HOTEL CLUB* Lac au Duc ✆ 02 97 73 64 64.** *Website: www.hotelroiarthur.com. Closed for two weeks in February during local school holidays. 46 rooms from 79 € to 132 €. 12 cottages from 105 € to 172 €. Breakfast 13 €. Set menus from 28 € to 45 €. A la carte.* On the edge of Broceliande Forest, where the Arthurian legends are still alive, Le Roi Arthur has several attractions. Top-quality services, excellent welcome and traditional cooking. 98 (18?)-hole ?? golf course, sports activities on the Lac au Duc site and of course, the forest itself, where you can follow in Merlin's and Viviane's footsteps. Don't forget the Wellbeing Centre for evening relaxation, and theme evenings with talented musicians.

Plumeliau

L'HARMONIC 8, place Général-de-Gaulle ✆ 02 97 51 80 55. *Email: ginesta2@wanadoo.fr – Open every day from 9am. 7 rooms from 25 € to 27 €. Breakfast 5 €. Half-board 40 €, full board 50 €. Formula 10 € every day, set menu 12 € at weekends.* Genevieve and Alain took over this hotel in January 2004. Located 10 minutes from Baud, the Harmonic has a free car park (opposite Plumeliau Church) and offers traditional family cooking. All the rooms have been renovated.

Pluvigner

LE SCAMPI 11, place du Marché ✆ 02 97 24 75 10. *Closed Saturday and Sunday lunchtime. Set lunchtime menu 10.50 €.* Gigi and Jacques have a number of specialist pizzas on offer, including the 'savoyarde' (tomato coulis, mushrooms, potatoes, onions, reblochon cheese and lardons). The menu also features salads, meat and fish dishes and pasta. In fine weather you can eat outside on a wide, sunny terrace. The restaurant is located in the town centre, and is equipped with disabled access and toilets. You can be served very late at weekends, and a take-away pizza service is available. Warm welcome. All in all, a good place to eat.

Pontivy

LE ROHAN 90, rue Nationale ✆ 02 97 25 02 01. *Website: www.hotelpontivy.com – email: contact@hotelpontivy.com – Closed one week in late December. 16 rooms 54 €-136 € (suite, sleeps 2). Breakfast 9 €. Triple, family and nuptial rooms available. Leafy garden, lift, meeting room, bar, closed private car park.* Rather a classy hotel, near Saint Joseph Church and the park. The reception area is decorated in warm reds and oranges, and the breakfast room is particularly attractive. The rooms have a studio flat feel to them: shower room and separate WC, TV with Canal + and a plunging view of Saint Joseph Square or the adjacent gardens.

LA PETITE MARMITE 15, rue des Forges ✆ 02 97 27 94 71. *Closed Sunday, and Monday and Tuesday evenings. Weekday lunchtime formula 10 € and 14 €. Set menus 18 € - 26 €. Children's menu 6 €.* Christophe and David, who took on this restaurant in July 2005, welcome you in a pleasant setting. Breaded camembert on a bed of salad served with a camambert ice-cream makes for an interesting starter, followed by a scallop pot, and a perfect chocolate *moelleux* to finish. You can taste wine by the glass, and take away your bottle! A friendly place, well worth noting.

Questembert

LE BRETAGNE ET SA RÉSIDENCE 13 rue Saint-Michel ✆ 02 97 26 11 12 *Fax 02 97 26 12 37. Website: www.paineaulebretagne.com. Set menus from 40 € to 115 €. A la carte 70 €. Closed Monday, Tuesday, Wednesday lunchtime, 3 weeks in January and 15-24 November.* Georges Paineau's famous restaurant is perhaps less successful today than it was some years ago (he has been running the kitchens in this former coaching inn since 1965, seconded for several years now by tireless Claude Corlouer) but it still makes an impression with its Dublin bay prawns *royale* roasted in tomato butter, lobster in coral butter, *pomme de riz de veau* (sweetbreads and apples) roasted *en cocotte,* and warm apple tart with honey. It's worth making the pilgrimage for the excellent ingredients, perfect combinations and attentive service, even if the menu is not one of Brittany's most up-to-date.

Quiberon

HOTEL BELLEVUE*   Rue de Tiviec ✆ 02 97 50 16 28. Website: www.bellevuequiberon.com.** *Open late April-late September. Large car park at your disposal. 38 comfortable rooms with TV and telephone, 10 have a sea view (over the rooftops) from 51 € to 89 € (singles) according to room and season. Breakfast 9.50 €. Half-board 76 € to 118 €. Heated pool. Set menus 22 €-27 €. Children's menu 11 €.* Though only a few dozen metres from the beach, the Hotel Bellevue is well away from the crowds. Gwenaëlle and Michel Le Mat welcome you kindly in their traditional family establishment, with its pleasant decoration in spring colours and relaxed holiday atmosphere. The restaurant has large bay windows overlooking the sea, and specialises in seafood at reasonable prices. You can drink your coffee by the pool after the meal.

LE ROCH PRIOL   1, rue des Sirènes ✆ 02 97 50 04 86.** *Fax: 02 97 30 50 09. Websites: www.rochpriol.com ou www.hotelrochpriol.fr – email: info@hotelrochpriol.fr – Open mid-February to mid-November. 45 double rooms from 49 € to 89 € per head. Breakfast 7.50 €. Half-board 67 € to 101 € per head. Formulas 12 € and 14.50 €. Set menus 18 €-34 €. The dining-room has just been renovated. Lift, garden and car park. Special offer (according to season): 10% off a 6-day stay. In low season, the shuttle from Auray station to the hotel is free for a minimum stay of 6 nights. Free shuttle to the pier and water therapy centre. Bike hire.* This hotel can be found in a privileged setting a few steps from the ocean and the beaches along the bay. Your welcome is charming yet unobtrusive, just like the interior decor, which confers a certain cachet on the surroundings. Dominique Sellier is an inventive chef: scallop kebab Roch Priol-style, foie gras flavoured with gingerbread, brill fillet with banana butter, Roch Priol sole, fillet mignon with pineapple, and crunchy apple tart flavoured with bitter oranges feature on his menus.

LE RELAIS   64, rue Roch-Priol ✆ 02 97 50 10 56.** *Website: www.hoteldurelais.fr 26 rooms from 46 € to 67 € in season. Breakfast 6.70 €. Weekly all-in prices available, except July and August. Set menus 7.50 € (children's), dish of the day formula + dessert 8.50 €, fish of the day + dessert 11 €, 12 € (except Sunday and public holidays) and 33 €. Couscous (and dessert) every Thursday, order in advance 13.70 €.* Le Relais, which got a new reception area and bar last December, is located near

the beaches and the town, and even in high season, manages to stay peaceful. The personalised rooms are comfortable, and the enormous dining room with its contemporary rose-tinted decor is full of light. Traditional cooking, with seafood specialities and a few tasty, well-simmered meat dishes.

Saint-Pierre-de-Quiberon

L'ORANGE BAR 90, quai de l'Orange © 02 97 30 92 08.4 *Open Easter-September. Bar closed Monday in low season, open all year. Formulas 12 € and 17.50 €. Set menu 25 €. A la carte.* This restaurant has a view of the harbour and the sea, and a terrace overlooking the water. House specialities are mussels with French fries, pan-fried sctallops and seafood platters to order. There are also salads, and some excellent desserts like the apple *chaud-froid*.

LA QUIMPEROISE 15, rue Général-de-Gaulle © 02 97 30 82 83. *Closed Wednesday evening and Thursday.* Open since 12 February and run by Ginette and Guy, this restaurant in the town centre with its sea view is decorated on a cinema theme, with pictures. The galettes are made with 100% Bretin flour: among the specialities you find the 'menhir', two buckwheat pancakes, ham, cheese, mushrooms and cream, and the 'dolmen', three buckwheat pancakes, ham, mushrooms, cream, cheese and egg. For dessert, try a tempting apple crepe with salted butter and home-made caramel. Guy is a master pastrycook, and his profiteroles are delicious.

Vannes

ANNE DE BRETAGNE 42, rue Olivier-de-Clisson © 02 97 54 22 19.** *Fax: 02 97 42 69 10. Website: www.anne-bretagne.com. Open all year. 20 rooms (from singles to rooms sleeping 4) from 43 € to 67 € according to season and number of guests. Breakfast 5.80 €. Closed garage 5 €. Small pets 3 €. Overnight break 55 €.* This hotel, near the station and not far from the town centre, has recently given itself a much-needed face-lift! The rooms have Internet access, mini-bars and TV. M. and Mme Jubert provide guests with a warm welcome and sheafs of brochures with information about the region, so you won't miss out on things to see and do. A very pleasant hotel from every point of view.

LE COMMODORE 3, rue Pasteur ✆ 02 97 46 42 62 *Website (see Vannes tourist office) www.tourisme-vannes.com – look under 'Restaurants'. Closed Saturday lunchtime, Sunday and Monday. Open 7 days a week for groups. Lunchtime formula 11 € (you can compose your own menu). Lunchtime set menu 13.50 €. Childen's menu 8.50 €. Non-smoking restaurant.* You can taste seafood specialities in a merchant navy-style setting in this restaurant, located near Vannes harbour and the post office. Scallop kebab with andouille, warm oysters and monkfish pan-cooked in cider butter feature on the menu, with a few meat dishes like veal sweetbreads and kidneys flambed in Marsala and duck parmentier (a mashed potato dish) with foie gras. For dessert, why not try the delicious Bigouden version of profiteroles, served with home-made salted butter caramel. Simply exquisite.

LE MOULIN A POIVRE 30, rue Thiers ✆ 02 97 47 09 34. *Closed Sunday lunchtime. Formulas 9.90 €, 16 € (Moulin a Poivre) and 21 € (a bit more upmarket). Children's menu 6.90 €. Student menu.* This restaurant and pizzeria specialises in carpaccios and wok cooking, like the penne and scallop with sate, Tha' saute beef with bean sprouts, and monkfish osso-bucco tajine. Original! Along more traditional lines, the pizzas, mixed salads and tartares are equally good: everything is noted up on the slate. The upstairs dining-room is air-conditioned, and both terraces are very pleasant in fine weather. Two bonus points are the friendly welcome and customer fidelity card.

L'OZEGAN 30, avenue Saint-Symphorien ✆ 02 97 54 30 01. *Open Tuesday to Friday, Monday lunchtime and Saturday evening. Lunchtime formulas 8 € to 11 €. Breton set menus 15 € and 18 €* Erwan Conan had had lots of culinary experience in the Caribbean, Switzerland, Basque Country and Savoy before settling in Vannes three years ago. Apart from Savoy fondue and *raclette* (for two) you should try the andouille *fricassée*, savoury buckwheat pancake with goat's cheese, duck breast in honey or roast pork with cider. Well worth discovering.

LE ROOF * Presqu'île de Conleau ✆ 02 97 63 47 47.** *Website: bestwestern.fr (click on Le Roof). Open every day, all year. Set menus from 29 € to 55 €.* You won't get tired of the view over the gulf, and sunset is total magic. Delicate appetisers give you an appetite for the sophisticated dishes to follow, beautifully presented and served in a flower-filled setting. A very attractive restaurant.

VILLA KERASY** 20, avenue Favrel-et-Lincy © 02 97 68 36 83**. *Website: www.villakerasy.com. 12 rooms. Air-conditioning, satellite TV, 2 phone lines per room, mini-bar, private car park. Appointments office and meeting rooms. Pets forbidden.* This is the region's only 4-star hotel, self-nicknamed 'The Charming Small Hotel', and decorated in that style recalling the Compagnie des Indes' heyday (the French India Company). Each of the 12 rooms is unique and ia named after one of the Company's stopping-off places: Pondichery, Moka, and Canton. There is a fireplace in the lounge and an Oriental garden with fountains.

TERROIRS 2, rue de la Fontaine © 02 97 47 57 52. *Email: terroirs.vannes@wanadoo.fr – Closed Sunday and Monday. Set lunchtime menus 12 € and 16 €. Terroir menu 26 €. A la carte.* Jacqueline and Emmanuel are the proud owners of a brand-new restaurant, opened on 10 January 2006. After years spent abroad, with the help of their considerable experience, they have finally found the right place to welcome their customers. Cosily settled by the log fire, you'll be able to make a culinary trip round the world. The head wine waiter will help you choose just the right wine to go with your food, subtlety being the operative word. Try the ravioles and their vegetables as a starter, then lamb in a thyme crust served with *gratin dauphinois* potatoes, with apple crumble and Breton shortbread in a salted butter caramel sauce for dessert. Go on - you can resist everything except temptation!

La Vraie-Croix

CREPERIE L'AUBEPINE 6, place du Palais © 02 97 67 21 50. *Open lunchtime and evenings all year, 7 days a week in July © August. Disabled access.* Sophie and Kristof took on their creperie in 2002, charmingly located in a flower-filled village boasting a European Villages in Bloom gold medal. All the ingredients are fresh and home cooked, and the galette flour is 100% buckwheat. Try the 'langroezienne' (duck breast, egg, mushrooms, chives and cream), the 'paysanne' or the 'montagnarde'. The crepes are also excellent: we recommend the 'gourmande' (caramelised apples, vanilla ice-cream, whipped cream and almonds) or the house Breton caramel. An extensive salad and meat menu is also available. The creperie is a stone's throw from the church and has a covered terrace facing the lake. It is a particularly good place to taste locally-brewed Surzur cider.

Centre

Chenonceaux castle

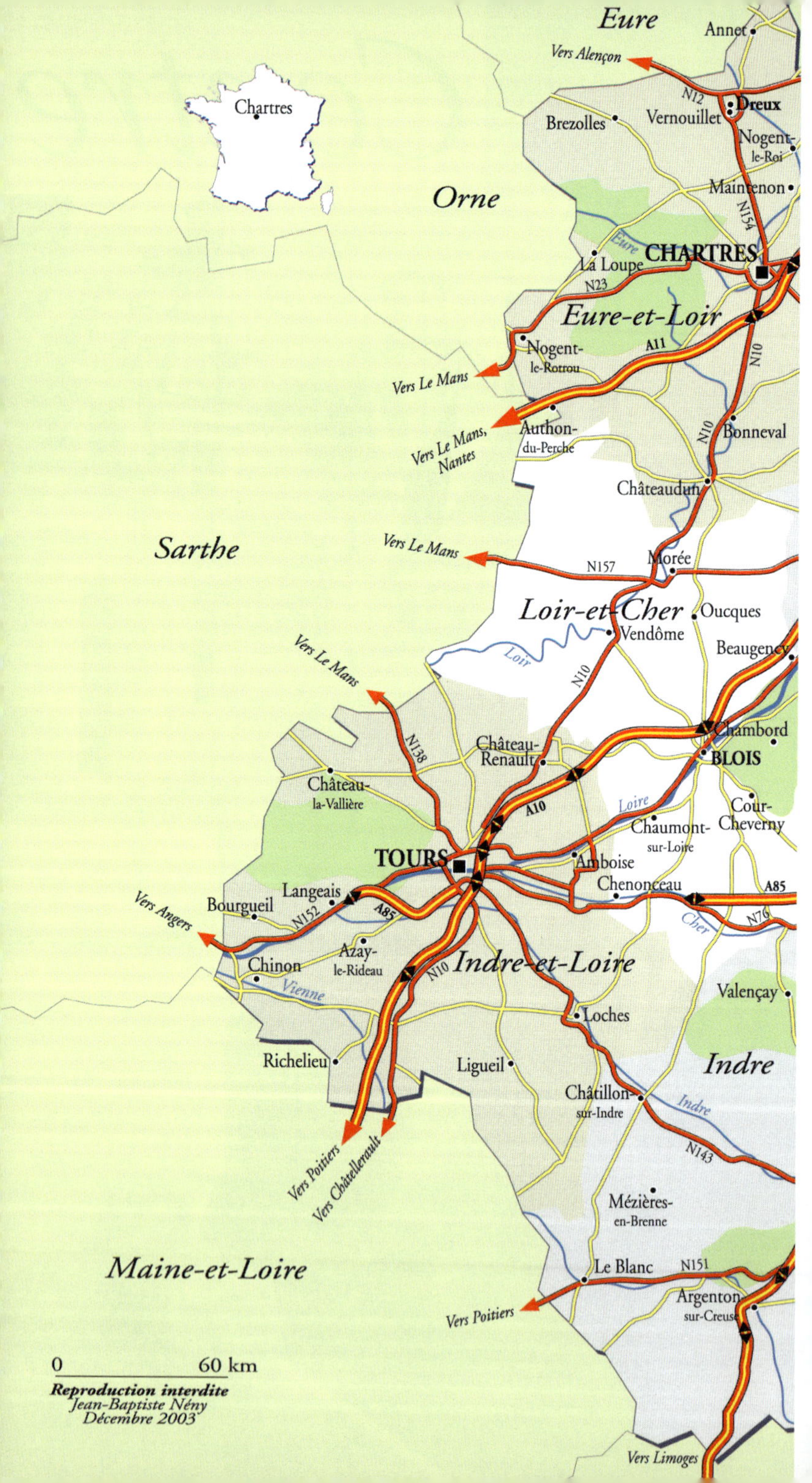
Eure
Annet
Vers Alençon
N12
Dreux
Vernouillet
Brezolles
Nogent-le-Roi
Maintenon
N154
Chartres
Orne
Eure
CHARTRES
La Loupe
N23
Eure-et-Loir
Nogent-le-Rotrou
A11
N10
Vers Le Mans
Vers Le Mans, Nantes
Authon-du-Perche
Bonneval
Châteaudun
Vers Le Mans
Sarthe
N157
Morée
Loir-et-Cher
Oucques
Vendôme
Beaugency
Loir
Vers Le Mans
N138
Chambord
Château-Renault
BLOIS
Château-la-Vallière
A10
Loire
Cour-Cheverny
Chaumont-sur-Loire
TOURS
Amboise
Langeais
Chenonceau
A85
Bourgueil
N152
A85
Vers Angers
Cher
N76
Azay-le-Rideau
Chinon
N10
Indre-et-Loire
Vienne
Valençay
Loches
Richelieu
Ligueil
Indre
Châtillon-sur-Indre
Indre
N143
Vers Poitiers
Vers Châtellerault
Mézières-en-Brenne
Maine-et-Loire
Le Blanc
N151
Argenton-sur-Creuse
Vers Poitiers
0 60 km
Reproduction interdite
Jean-Baptiste Nény
Décembre 2003
Vers Limoges

CENTRE

Motorway
Major road
Minor road
Vers Versailles
Vers Paris
Vers Etampes
Vers Fontainebleau
Vers Paris
Vers Sens
Vers Auxerre
Vers Nevers
Vers Auxerre
Vers Nevers
Vers Montluçon
Seine-et-Marne
Aube
Loiret
Yonne
Cher
Nièvre
Allier
Creuse
A10
N154
N20
N152
Pithiviers
Arthenay
ORLÉANS
Olivet
Jargeau
N60
Montargis
A6
N7
Châtillon-Coligny
Saint-Benoît-sur-Loire
Sully-sur-Loire
Loire
A77
A20
La Ferté-Saint-Aubin
N20
Lamotte-Beuvron
Gien
Argent
Aubigny
Salbris
Romorantin-Lanthenay
Neuvy-Barengeon
Cosne-sur-Loire
Sancerre
Cher
Vierzon
N151
BOURGES
A20
A71
Nérondes
N151
Issoudun
N76
Auron
CHÂTEAUROUX
Saint-Amand-Montrond
La Châtre
Sainte-Sévère-sur-Indre
Aigurande

ORLÉANS AND SOLOGNE

Orléans

Orléans' historical prestige and central position make it the region's capital, though not the biggest town in population terms. In 1429, Joan of Arc liberated the town from English domination, turning the tide of the Hundred Years' War. Orléans was marked by the Wars of Religion, and Condé made it a Fronde stronghold. World War II did not spare it either, but the city has since been rebuilt, the new styles harmonising with surviving ancient monuments.

SAINTE CROIX CATHEDRAL Place Sainte-Croix. *Open every day: 9am-12 noon and 2pm-6pm. Admission free. Entry to archeological basement: enquiries 02 38 24 05 05. Tower visit: 02 38 24 05 05. Basement and towers open 1 May-30 September.* This remarkable example of Gothic art mostly dates back to the 17thc., though earlier parts escaped the destructive Wars of Religion, to remind you that Hughes Capet was crowned here in 987. The majestic nave is 136m long and 33m high, with six bays on intersecting ribs and a perfectly proportioned chancel. Climb to the top of the cathedral for a superb view of the city with its mansions, old quarters and narrow alleys.

SAINT AIGNAN CHURCH. *Crypt open every day, 1 July-15 September: 12pm-6pm (enquire at the Archeological Service 02 38 62 70 56).* The church is in the Rue Neuve Saint Aignan, and boasts a striking 15thc. octagonal bell tower.

MAISON DE JEANNE D'ARC 3, place du Général-de-Gaulle ✆ 02 38 52 99 89. *Open every day except Monday, 2 May-31 October: 10am-12 noon and 1.30pm-6pm. 1 November-30 April: 1.30pm-6pm. Admission: 2 €, students from 16-25 and over-65s half-price, under-16s, school parties and the unemployed free.* Thousands of tourists visit it every year. On the first floor, a son et lumière tells the story of the Siege of Orléans (available in five languages on request). On the second floor, the Maid's life is narrated in 5 models. You can also see some engravings exhibitions, Joan of Arc's standard and a suit of armour and coat of mail made for Luc Besson's film (1998).

MUSEE DES BEAUX-ARTS Place Sainte-Croix ✆ 02 38 79 21 55. *Open every day except Monday: 9.30am-12.15pm and 1.30pm-5.45pm (2pm-6.30pm Sundays). Admission: adult 3 €, under-16s free.* The museum houses a rich collection of paintings, sculpture and art objects, including works by Velasquez, Gauguin, Le Nain, Chardin and Delacroix. There are portraits, a wonderful pastels cabinet, landscapes, still-lifes, religious paintings and mythological scenes leading you from the 16th to the 20thc. over five floors. Regular temporary exhibitions are held.

FORET D'ORLEANS. This huge national forest (45,000ha.) is made up of the Orléans, Ingrannes and Lorris massifs. Leisure park and hunting ground for French nobles during several centuries, it was later left for grazing, and deteriorated fast. In the early 19thc., Scotch pines were planted, and the forest began to be protected. Today you can explore it by car (200km of roads), on foot or by bike (1,000 km of paths), and even on horseback on certain marked-out routes.

Sologne

Briare

This little town on the Loire banks is famous for its 663m bridge-canal. The town's activities are linked to the river: sailing harbour, fishing, and pleasure-boat trips. Other things to see: the 17thc. Canal Lords' chateau, now housing the Town Hall, and Saint Etienne Church.

Chateauneuf-sur-Loire

CHATEAU. Lazing on the banks of the Loire, encircled by its moat. An early 11thc. castle developed into the current 17thc. building, and was lived in by the Capetian Kings and the Valois and Orléans royal families who loved the Loire. Today, it houses the Town Hall and the Loire Naval Museum. The former stables (XVIIthc.) are vaulted in Mansart style, and contain the town library and 18thc. orangery. A collection of flowers and exotic shrubs can be seen in the park, dreamed up by Le Nôtre.

MUSEE DE LA MARINE DE LOIRE Ecuries du Château ✆ 02 38 46 84 46. *Open (except Tuesday) 1 April- 31 October: 10am-6pm; 1 November-31 March: 2pm-6pm. Admission: adult 3.50 €.* A unique collection of over 5,000 objects and nearly 16,000 documents, on several floors. It contains navigation materials, literature connected with the bargees' daily life, local art objects, episodes from the river's history illustrated with scale models (including a 12-metre reproduction of a 19thc. boat) engravings and paintings, etc. There is also a research centre concerning the Loire's navy.

Cheverny

This splendid, magnificently furnished 17thc. residence is the biggest privately-owned Loire chateau still lived-in. Its park covers 100ha. and the forest, 2,000 ha. Cheverny is associated with hunting, and has its own kennels and pack of hounds. A Museum of Hunting reminds you that the castle is on the edge of Sologne, known for this sport.

Lamotte-Beuvron

This pretty town has its own national forest, and lies at the heart of Sologne's walking country, with its wooded scenery and charming villages. Chaumon-sur-Tharonne, Vouzon, Chaon, Yvoy-le-Marron and Nouan-le-Fuzelier smell of woodsmoke and the hunt. Stephanie and Caroline Tatin are the region's heroines, for having invented the delicious Tarte Tatin.

Gien

An elongated village stretching along the river, which lies parallel to two lively main streets. One of these is named after Bernard Palissy from Agen, who founded Gien's world-famous earthenware factory.

CHATEAU. The castle is mainly Gothic but you sense Renaissance influence. Joan of Arc stayed here in 1429, and the present chateau's guests include Henri II, Catherine de Médicis and Charles IX, then Louis XIV and Anne of Austria who came to safety here during the Fronde. From the 14thc., it belonged to the Crown, becoming a state possession during the Revolution, and housing the sub-prefecture, la court and prison. The castle changed hands again in 1823, when it was bought by the department, and now contains the International Hunting Museum.

MUSEE DE LA FAIENCERIE DE GIEN 78, place de la Victoire ✆ 02 38 67 00 05. *Open all year.* The museum is in a former factory cellar, and contains a number of rare pieces. It also traces the history of Gien earthenware, its influences, original production, style and the inventive nature of its plates and services with crests.

MUSEE INTERNATIONAL DE LA CHASSE Chateau de Gien ✆ 02 38 67 69 69. *Open all year, closed Tuesday. 1 July-31 August, open every day: 10am-6pm. Admission: adult 5 €* The museum has been housed since 1952 in the castle built for Anne de Beaujeu, Louis XIth's eldest daughter. 14 rooms are given over to hunting, illustrated through painting, sculpture, decorative arts, arms, trophies and accessories. You can also appreciate the architecture, notably the magnificent oak framework in the Alexandre-François Desportes Room, named after Louis XIV's official hunt and hounds painter (1661-1743).

Jargeau

This modern and simple little town is known for andouille tasting, held twice a year by its confrerie. The Jargeau andouille is not entirely made of tripe, but also offal and meat. You find it in a bladder of large or small diameter.

SAINT ETIENNE CHURCH. *Open every day: 9am-6pm.* First built in the 9thc., this former collegiate church was reshaped several times. You must see its 17thc. choirstalls, listed wrought iron pulpit by Perdoux (1752) and 17thc. carved stone font. Outside is a Renaissance portal.

Lorris

Orléans Forest's chief town, in Gatînais, some 50km from the Loiret prefecture. It dates back to Gallo-Roman times, and was a medieval stronghold.

HALLES. On the Place du Martroi, the covered market has a fine uncovered framework. Thursday has been market day since the Middle Ages.

NOTRE DAME DE LORRIS. This church was built bit by bit during the 10th, 12th and 13thc., and contains an amazing 16thc. organ, not in the chancel but fixed impressively to the wall in the middle of the nave.

MUSEE DEPARTEMENTAL DE LA RESISTANCE ET DE LA DEPORTATION Esplanade Charles-de-Gaulle ✆ 02 38 94 84 19. *Open 1 April-31 October, every day: 10am-12 noon and 2pm-6pm. 1 November-21 March: 2pm-6pm, Wednesday-Sunday (every day for groups). Admission: adult 4 €, 7-18s 1 €.* A must for all World War II fans, this museum is situated in Lorris, an important Resistance town in 1944. The Resistance, deportation, collaboration, daily life during the Occupation and finally the Liberation are explained with the help of images and objects in several rooms. A video document of the period's most significant events closes the visit.

Romorantin

This pleasant sub-prefecture on the Sauldre is the Sologne's capital. You can enjoy a walk around the lake in Fernand-Buisson park, followed by a trip into peaceful old Romorantin where your feet echo on the cobbles. There are ruined fortifications (Porte Braud), Middle Ages houses, Saint Etienne and Saint Aignan churches.

MUSEE DE SOLOGNE Moulin du Chapitre ✆ 02 54 95 33 66. *Open (except Tuesday and Sunday morning) from 10am-12 noon and 2pm-6pm. Admission: adult 4.50 €.* The museum is made up of three different buildings. First, you come to the Chapter Mill, concerned with Sologne landscapes, history, traditional social structure, and economic development through the ages, together with the different kinds of hunting popular with its inhabitants. After crossing the river on a charming footbridge, you enter the Town Mill, where you discover Romorantin's different factories. The visit ends with a tour of the town's oldest building, the Jacquemart Tower, which houses temporary exhibitions.

Saint-Aignan-sur-Cher

You arrive via the Cher's left bank from Saint Romain, and discover a beautiful town, with its castle and old houses. Walking through the medieval alleys, you are back in the time of thick walls and carriage wheels rattling over the paving stones. Old-fashioned serenity is still carefully preserved on the banks of the Cher.

COLLEGIALE ✆ 02 54 75 22 85/02 54 71 22 22. *Open all year: 9am-6pm.* This 12thc. Romanesque building is perfectly balanced: transept, chancel, striking capitals and crypt, with its fine wall paintings.

Saint-Benoit-sur-Loire

SAINT BENOIT ABBEY ✆ 02 38 35 79 00. *Open all year: 8am-9pm, except Sunday morning and public holidays. Admission free.* Stroll to the harbour on the Loire, then back to the Benedictine Abbey in the town centre. In a silent square not far from the river, peace and serenity prevail at the foot of the basilica (11th, 12th and 13thc.), a regional masterpiece of Romanesque art.

Sully-sur-Loire

The town is based around its waterway, and also the castle, which has protected it from agressors since the 10thc., and keeps a lookout for movement up and down the Loire.

CHATEAU ✆ 02 38 36 36 86. *Open every day, 1 February-31 December (except 25 December), 1 February-31 March and 1 October-31 December: 10am-12 noon and 2pm-5pm. 1 April-30 September: 10am-6pm. Guided tours (ask for opening hours). Programme of events on request.* This well-proportioned castle has remarkable towers with pepper-pot roofs, fine keep framework and a covered walk. It is especially pretty in the evenings, all lit up on the Loire. Sully retired here after Henri IV's assassination.

Villeherviers

The church is worth seeing, but the main centre of interest is the Sologne aquarium.

ALIOTIS, AQUARIUM DE SOLOGNE ✆ 02 54 95 26 31. *www.aliotis.com. Open November, December, January & early February, Wednesday, Sunday, school and public holidays: 1.30pm-5.30pm. February holidays-Easter, every day: 1.30pm-5.30pm. 10 April-30 June and 1-30 September: 10am-6pm. 1 July-31 August: 10.30am-7.30pm. Admission: adult 10 €, 3-14s 7 €. Park access free in July & August: 12 noon-7pm.* Modern facilities and intelligent architecture house a hundred tanks big and small, containing aquatic life. The educational hands-on approach (microscope observation) includes watching the sharks, turtles, octopus and moray eels being fed (afternoons). The aquarium contains some rare species such as the steel-jawed Congo Tiger Fish, and a naturalised tiger shark, 4m long.

BEAUCE

France's granary hides treasures in its fields of cereals, like Chartres Cathedral, still drawing thousands of pilgrims every year.

MAISON DE LA BEAUCE Place de la Beauce - ORGERES-EN-BEAUCE ✆ 02 37 99 75 58. *www.terre-de-beauce.com. Open 1 April-14 June and December, Tuesday-Sunday; 2.30pm-6pm. 15 June-15 September: Monday-Friday: 10am-12 noon and 2pm-6pm (weekend afternoons). Admission: adult 4 €, over-6s 2 €, under-6s free.* Right in the heart of France, this region is little known, despite its agricultural significance. There is plenty to learn, however, starting with the meaning of the word paysan (countryman) with its root in pays (country) and paysage (landscape).

Chartres

Chartres Cathedral has been watching over the Beauce for 800 years, like a lighthouse rising above the waves of corn.

CATHEDRAL. From the rose window to its stained glass, green roof, monumental spires and maze, Chartres Cathedral is famous. It is a harmonious Gothic masterpiece, almost untouched since its consecration in 1260 (it was built on an older basilica containing the Virgin's veil as a relic). On entering, the sheer size astounds you (37m high), then you are struck by the Chartres-blue stained glass windows, telling Bible stories and illustrating historic scenes. Above the royal portal is that admirable rose window, with several fine statues nearby. There is a stone maze on the floor; pilgrims had to go through all 291 metres of it on their knees! Whatever your creed, you will appreciate the beauty and harmony of this church.

CENTRE INTERNATIONAL DU VITRAIL 5, rue du Cardinal Pie ✆ 02 37 21 65 72. *Open every day.* Chartres is world-famous for its cathedral's stained-glass windows, lighting up the nave with their marvellous colours, and illustrating the daily lives and spiritual experiences of medieval men amd women. This museum-cum-workshop, housed in a cellar near the cathedral, explains how stained glass is made. There are exhibitions of ancient and contemporary examples, guided tours of the cathedral and courses to learn the techniques. All visitors welcome, whether artistically inclined or merely curious.

MAISON PICASSIETTE 22, ave. du Repos ✆ 02 37 34 10 78. *Open every day except Tuesday and Sunday morning.* Raymond Isidore made a fantastic work of art (naif and brut) of his home, built in 1930. Over 25 years, he transformed the simple house using 15 tonnes of broken crockery as decorative material, and adding courtyards and gardens. Flowerpots, radiogram, his wife's sewing machine, and the bed: the least object became part of his design. The house is a huge mosaic, and can't fail to intrigue you.

Chatillon-Coligny

This town was marked by the Reformation, and the former provost's where the aldermen and later the Protestants met was known as Hell, while the tithe barn housing Catholic canons' meetings was called Heaven.

CHURCH. Built during the 16th and 17thc by Admiral Coligny's father, using one of the towers on the city walls for support and adding the bell tower later. Two other towers remain from this wall, near the castle.

BATEAUX TOURISTIQUES Port de Plaisance - BRIARE ✆ 02 38 37 12 75. *www.bateaux-touristiques.com. Tourist trips on four recent pleasure steamers and two boats with restaurants are on offer.* Enjoy the scenic Gatinais, while going over the famous Briare bridge-canal.

MUSEUM. Housed in the town's former Hotel Dieu, built during the 15thc., and boasting a remarkable porch restored in the 17thc. by an illustrious member of the Montmorency-Luxembourg family. The museum contains findings from archeological digs - notably those concerning the Lete tribe, from Cortrat - holy statues, furniture and paintings representing the Montmorency-Luxembourgs.

Ferrières-en-Gatinais

Three saints made this a place of pilgrimage in the 3rdc. The site's first chapel, Notre Dame de Bethléem, later became a sanctuary.

NOTRE DAME DE BETHLEEM CHAPEL AND SAINT PIERRE AND SAINT PAUL ABBEY CHURCH ✆ 02 38 96 58 86. *Open 7 January-20 December: 10am-7pm in summer; 8am-6pm in winter. Admission free.* Founded in 636, this church was burned down by the Vikings, English (during the Hundred Years' War) and Huguenots in the Wars of Religion. The tower is remarkable; the lower part being the most ancient (Carolingian). In the 13thc. a cupola was added, recalling the one on Charlemagne's palace in Aix-en-

Eure&Loir
Live the French way of life a stone's throw from Paris
Just one hour from Paris, the Eure et Loir region is a haven of the French way of life. Châteaux, manor houses and gardens will transport you back.
Come to Chartres and visit its famous Cathedral, listed as a UNESCO World Heritage site.
Character hotels and gourmet restaurants with fine wine cellars await you for a short stay in the real France, just a stone's throw from Paris.
Eure&Loir
COMITÉ DÉPARTEMENTAL DU TOURISME
10 rue du Docteur Maunoury - B.P. 67 - 28002 CHARTRES CEDEX - FRANCE
Tél 33 2 37 84 01 00 - Fax 33 2 37 36 36 39 - www.chartrescountry.com - infos@tourisme28.com

Chapelle. Louis XIth's godson, the Abbot of Blanchefort, put some finishing touches to the church in the 15thc. The transept vault on its eight columns, choirstalls (17thc.) with Louis de Blanchefort's tomb, and stained glass windows in the apse (16thc.) are worth noticing, as are two interesting sculptures of Saint Pierre and Saint Paul.

NOTRE DAME DE BETHLEEM CHURCH. *Open every day: 8am-7pm in summer and 8pm-6pm in winter.* This is a place of pilgrimage to the Virgin, whose wooden statue is in the chancel.

Malesherbes

The town is linked to the castle and its family, who played host to several monarchs. The most illustrious member was Louis XVI's defending counsel. Chateaubriand also lived in the town.

CHATEAU © 02 38 34 41 02. *Open mid March-mid November, Saturday & Sunday: 3pm-6pm (except reception days).* 40km from Paris, in a 90ha. wooded park, the Chateau de Malesherbes is a unique building. It belonged to highly placed dignitaries at the French Court, and was first put up in the 14thc, then modified in the 18th. Coming up the main avenue, you first notice the chalk-and-brick façade, then the fine panelling and parquet inside, and the dovecote, chapel and 15thc. tithe barn outside, on the estate.

CHATEAU DE ROUVILLE. This medieval building on the banks of the Essonne was restored in the 16thc., with rather too many turrets and watchtowers. Close by is an old washing-place overgrown with greenery. A good reason to come from Malesherbes for a walk along the Essonne.

SAINT MARTIN CHURCH. Built in the 12thc., this church houses some masterpieces, including a 16thc. Entombment from the Cordeliers Monastery, and a statue of Notre Dame de la Pitie from the same period.

MAISON DE CHATEAUBRIAND. The house was built in 1776 (American Independence year), but the estate boasts 14thc. tithe barns and a 15thc. chapel. The imposing dovecote held up to 1,800 pigeons. In season, a son et lumiere pageant brings to life French history, including the story of the chateau.

Montargis

This busy, industrial town has not forgotten its past, and still has plenty of fine remains. Stroll along the Briaré canal and through the old quarters; there are no less than 127 bridges and walkways (Montargis is nicknamed 'the Gatinais Venice').

CHATEAU. The castle was put up in 1160 by Philippe I de Courtenay, on the site of Clovis' watchtower. A few ruins are left of this once-important royal estate: a tower, a postern and the crypt.

HOTEL DURZY. The Durzy mansion estate extends along the Briare canal. Gustave Debrie's famous statue of the Montargis dog is here in the gardens, illustrating an episode in the town's history. There is also a section of 12thc, arcades, called Lorris arcades since they came from a mansion in that town.

MUSEE GIRODET 2, rue de la Chaussée © 02 38 98 07 81. Open all year, every day except Monday and Tuesday: 9am-12 noon and 1.30pm-5.30pm (5pm Fridays). Closed public holidays; 4th Sunday in July. Admission: adult 3 €, child 2 €, under-7s free. Housed in the Durzy mansion since 1864, this museum displays paintings and sketches by the painter Anne-Louis Girodet, and sculptures, bronzes and plastercasts; a bequest from the sculptor Triqueti. There are also paintings from the Northern School, Italian School and Girodet's pupils.

Pithiviers

Pithiviers Church rises from the flat Gatinais landscape - as do some rather less elegant buildings on the left, best forgotten. Inside, the town is prettier, around the Place des Halles, Rue Gourdon, place du Martroi and Rue de la Couronne.

MEDIEVAL FORTRESS. Built by the Lady Héloise in the 10thc. on the town's present site. The inhabitants of 10thc. Pithiviers-le-Vieil (further east) moved into the fortress for greater protection, bringing their trades, and thus establishing a new village around the citadel. A few remains still exist, including the crypt of a collegiate church, excavated during a dig.

MUNICIPAL MUSEUM 17, rue de la Couronne © 02 38 30 00 64. *Museum currently undergoing restruction work. Closed to the public. Regular temporary exhibitions, enquire at the museum.* Located in the old Hotel Dieu, this museum boasts some interesting ethnographic and pictorial collections: you must see the New Caledonia collection, more specifically concerned with the Canaque civilisation, and featuring a fabulous sarcophagus. Local archeology, old crafts and earthenware, pottery (the oldest French potter's wheel is exhibited) and sacred art objects (statues, paintings etc.) are on display in the former Hotel Dieu chapel, dating back to the 18thc.

BERRY

Castles and villages steeped in history and set in buccolic scenery are waiting to be admired in France's historic centre. The region is strongly marked by Romanesque art, with many abbeys dating back to the 11thc. This is also a place of myths and legends, and tales of witchcraft and sorcery.

Bourges

Situated right in the middle of France, Bourges is known above all for its festival and cathedral.

SAINT ETIENNE CATHEDRAL ✆ **02 48 65 49 44**. *Open April-September: 9am-7.15pm. Individual access to the tower. Guided tours of the crypt.* The cathedral stands imposingly on the city heights, a characteristic example of 12thc. architecture with its front, two unequal towers and five portals full of imagery. The great volumes bathed in light, carvings and brilliantly coloured stained-glass windows are harmoniously balanced, there is no transept, and the modelling is surprisingly modern for the period. This Gothic masterpiece is hemmed in by half-timbered houses, as though Bourges were still a medieval town.

HOTEL DES ECHEVINS 13, rue Edouard-Branly ✆ **02 48 24 75 38**. This typically Northern French Town Hall (literally, the Aldermen's Mansion) was built in the late 15thc. against the Gallo-Roman wall. It now houses the works of painter Maurice Estève.

PALAIS JACQUES COEUR 10bis rue Jacques Coeur ✆ **02 48 24 79 42**. *Open every day: 9.30am-12.15 and 2pm-5pm. Guided tours only. Admission: adults 6.50 €, concessions 4.10 €.* Built in the 15thc. by Charles VII's Superintendent of Finance, Jacques Coeur, this is a rare and beautiful example of Gothic civil architecture. The façade overlooking the street is a sophisticated masterpiece.

Châteauroux

PORTE SAINT MARTIN (DE LA VIEILLE PRISON). Apparently the model for the town's arms, with its central archway and tower. It was restored in the 16thc. and served as a prison until 1742.

SAINT MARTIAL CHURCH Rue Grande. Originally an annex to Saint Denis Priory, this church has a single Romanesque nave with a wooden barrel vault. There are 14thc. trefoil bays and a 15thc. tower porch, a gift from one of the town's rich citizens.

SAINT ANDRE CHURCH Place Voltaire. This Gothic-style church was designed by Henri Dauvergne, and consecrated in 1876. The locals like tourists to think it's a cathedral.

PLEUREUSES Place de la Victoire et des Alliés. The statue represents the mother and wife of a soldier killed in the Great War; the faces and posture of the two women are remarkably life-like. Other more discreet sculptures worth noticing are two countrywomen feeding a lamb on the front of the former Breeders' Association building (8, Rue de la Poste), and the return of the mutilated soldier on the war monument, Place Lafayette.

Berrichon Country

Blancafort

MUSEE DE LA SORCELLERIE 'Concressault' ✆ **02 48 73 86 11**. *www.musee-sorcellerie.fr. Open every day, Easter-October. April, May & October: 10am-6pm. June-September: 10am-7pm. Disabled access.* Between Aubigny and Sancerre in the Cher, this museum narrates the history and imaginary universe of the witch, from Greek mythology to peasant superstition. Spells, potions and mandrake root are part of the experience, and you are assailed by colours, smells and sensations.

Mehun-sur-Yèvre

This ancient town on the Yèvre and the Berry canal is known for its porcelain industry. Notre-Dame Collegiate Church is horseshoe-shaped, and the 11thc. chancel has a Romanesque ambulatory (rare in a place of worship) and radiating chapels. The nave, without transept, is a huge rectangle lit by high central windows, covered with a barrel vault rebuilt after the 1910 fire. Don't miss Le Christ en croix by Bourges painter Jean Boucher (1568-1633). Go for a stroll afterwards, along the Rue de la Gargouille, that medieval street below the town by the river, where the Porcelain Centre is now open to the public again after extensive restoration work. The paving stones are 14thc. The watch at the end of the street and old washing-places are also worth a look.

SAINT-AMAND-MONTROND. Several pretty streets in the old town deserve a visit, for this is the 'city of gold' where jewellery is made. Four tonnes of gold a year are worked; 10% of the national market. In 1888, a Parisian jeweller M. Moricault decided to delocalise his factory, and chose to settle in Saint-Amand-Montrond. Other workshops grew out of this first one, and today there are 11 firms with 300 employees.

CHATEAU DE MONTROND ✆ **02 48 96 79 64**. *Open every day except Monday, 15 June-30 September.* From the tower, you have a superb view over the Marmande Valley, the town park and charming bandstand.

CITE DE L'OR Rue Pelletier-Doisy ✆ **02 48 82 11 33**. *www. cite-or.com. Closed 1 January and 25 December. Open every day, 1 July-31 August: 9.45am-6.30pm; otherwise, closed Tuesdays.* This glass pyramid promotes gold for economic and cultural reasons, and for tourism. It contains a theatre, restaurant, museum, shop, showroom, cafeteria and post-office.

Sancerre

Perched on its rocky hillock above the Loire, this lovely little town is known for its wines and goat's cheese, the famous Crottin de Chavignol. Sancerre was built round an early fortress in the 8th or 9thc., and boasts some pretty medieval houses including Clement's logis (15thc.). The Tour des Fiefs is the only remains of the Comtes de Sancerre's castle: the tower escaped when the castle was wiped out in 1621. Climb the 195 steps for a unique view across the rooftops to the outlying hills. The belfry dates back to 1509. Rather rare in this region, it served as a belltower for Notre Dame de Sancerre Church. Another panoramic view is to be had from the Porte-Cesar Esplanade, 150m above the Loire Valley.

BLOIS AND BLESOIS COUNTRY

Blois is in the Garden of France, where the kings built their castles. Tourists come from all over to see the famous Loire châteaux.

Blois

Close to Paris, on the country's biggest river, Blois is a crossroads for several major routes.

CHATEAU ROYAL DE BLOIS ✆ **02 54 90 33 32.** *Open April-September: 9am-6pm. The rest of the year: 9am-12.30pm and 2pm-5.30pm. Admission: adult 6.50 €.* Several centuries of history and dramatic events are condensed in this château, which represents four architectural periods (Romanesque, Gothic, Renaissance and Classical) each inspired by royalty: Charles d'Orléans, Louis XII, François I and Gaston d'Orléans (Louis XIII's brother). Joan of Arc prayed in the chapel, the Duke de Guise was assassinated here and Marie de Medicis, being luckier, daringly escaped from enforced exile. After leaving the chateau, you walk through the pleasant Victor Hugo gardens, under the benevolent gaze of Augustin Thierry whose bust adorns them, and follow Rue Chartraine up to Rue Gallois, then Rue Beauvoir with its half-timbered houses. Like the castle, the town has four principal sectors, marked out on the ground by round brass plaques with symbols (a salamander for the Castle sector, for instance). The Tourist Office provides quiz sheets for the kids, to help them discover each sector.

COUVENT DES JACOBINS. A few 15thc. remains survive, but the original building has been entirely renovated. It houses two museums.

HALLE AUX GRAINS Place de la République ✆ **02 54 90 44 00**. This ancient building (16thc.) has been fitted out to host congresses, concerts and theatrical works, with an auditorium seating 700, a restaurant and ultra-modern facilities.

MUSEUM D'HISTOIRE NATURELLE Les Jacobins - Rue Anne-de-Bretagne ✆ **02 54 90 21 00**. *www.ville-blois.fr. Open Tuesday-Sunday: 2pm-6pm (Tuesday-Friday: 9am-12 noon July & August only). Admission: adult 2.70 €, concessions 1.05 €, under-12s free.* Find out, recognise and understand the Loire's natural environment, the better to preserve it intact. The Natural History Museum is designed principally for young people, to make them aware of the dangers facing our fragile ecosystem. There are thematic exhibitions, children's activities, literature, CD Roms and video films available, to look up facts, prepare a project or just enjoy the discovery.

TOUR BEAUVOIR Rue des Cordeliers ✆ **02 54 90 44 00**. *Open from Easter, 3pm-7.30pm. July & August: 11am-7.30pm.* A vestige of the ancient fortifications. Offers a superb view of town, castle and Loire.

MAISON DE LA MAGIE (MUSEE ROBERT-HOUDIN) Behind the castle, near the Tourist Office. Blois' latest sensation is the Magic Museum. The ground floor illustrates the history of magic and illusion, complete with distorting mirrors, optical illusions and all sorts of tricks, objects and posters. On the first floor you put on special glasses and follow a circuit of images. The next section traces the life of internationally acclaimed magician Robert-Houdin, who was also an inventor in a more serious vein. His ophthalmic instruments, in advance of his day, are now in current use.

Talcy

CHATEAU DE TALCY ✆ 02 54 81 03 01. Castle currently closed for renovation work, until March-April 2006 (subject to change). This castle (15thc-16thc.) is associated with Ronsard, his Cassandre (Salviati) being the owner's daughter. It also inspired the poet Agrippa d'Aubigné, who fell in love with Diane de Salviati (the grand-daughter). This fairly plain Renaissance building has a keep and one wing, (having lost the other in a fire) a press, dovecote and romantic well. The remarkable formal garden, once a sculptural kitchen garden, now contains fruit-trees and flowers.

TOURS AND TOURAINE

Tours

Tours was the kingdom'scapital in the 15th and 16thc., and kept its importance, even when the town council refused the railway in 1845. The old quarters were carefully restored in the early 1960s.

SAINT MARTIN BASILICA 7, rue Baleschoux ✆ 02 47 05 63 87. Near Place de Châteauneuf, this Byzantine-style basilica was put up in the late 19thc. by local architect Victor Laloux, on Saint Martin's tomb.

SAINT GATIEN CATHEDRAL. Its north tower (1507) is 70m high, and the south (1547) 69m. This was done on purpose, the north tower symbolising spiritual power! The great bell ('Christus') weighs 1,850kg. The cathedral measures 97m by 28m (transept 46m) and its vault reaches 29m.

MUSEE DES BEAUX-ARTS 18, place François-Sicard ✆ 02 47 05 68 73. *Open every day except Tuesday: 9am-12.45pm and 2pm-6pm. Admission: adult 4 €, concessions 2 €.* It was a good idea to install the Fine Arts Museum in the Archbishop's Palace, with its serene formal garden. Rembrandt, Rubens, Boucher, Mantegna and Delacroix are displayed in magnificently furnished reception rooms. The smaller, more intimate rooms contain ceramics, and 19th and 20thc. paintings.

Tours castle

MUSEE DU GEMMAIL 7, rue du Murier ✆ 02 47 61 01 19. *Open every day except Monday: 10am-12 noon and 2pm-6.15pm. 1 April-15 November.* The Gemmail, from gemme (gem) and email (enamel) is a modern form of stained glass window; pieces of coloured glass juxtaposed in a collage, and lit from behind. Secular and non-figurative subjects dazzle the eyes beside more classical reproductions of famous works. You can visit a small demonstration workshop and the 12thc. underground chapel: gemmists created the windows.

MUSEUM D'HISTOIRE NATURELLE 3, rue du Président-Merville ✆ 02 47 64 13 31. *Closed Saturday and Sunday mornings, and Monday. Open:10am-12 noon and 2pm-6pm. Admission: adult 2.30 €, concessions 1.10 €.* Fossils, fish, aquatic plants and animals illustrate Touraine's environmental heritage, and the natural world around the Loire. Some retrospectives and a thematic library complete the exhibition.

Touraine

Chinon

Chinon is rich in vineyards, and has a nuclear power station, but also plenty of history. The great 16thc. writer, wit and bon vivant François Rabelais was born here.

CHATEAU ✆ 02 47 93 13 45. *Open mid-March-late September: 9am-7pm. Admission: adults 6 €, concessions 4.50 €.* This royal fortress was put up between the 10th and 15thc., in three distinct parts: Saint George Fort to the east, the castle in the middle (where Joan of Arc met Charles VII for the first time) and Coudray Fort, with its keep where Jacques de Molay and the Templars were imprisoned, and left their graffiti. You must see the towers, Joan of Arc Museum and views over town and valley.

MAISON DE LA RIVIERE 12, quai Pasteur ✆ 02 47 93 21 34. *Open every day except Monday. Admission: adult 3 €, child 2 €.* Discover the Loire Navy, with the help of some fine models. Boat trips are on offer from Wednesday to Saturday in July and August. There is also an annex at Candes-Saint-Martin, departure point for boat and bike trips (bicycles for hire) on the Loire cycle circuit.

Le Grand-Pressigny

500,000 years ago, the Claise Valley dwellers carved flint, and the tradition went on until 4,000 B.C., as did the trade in tools made.

A square keep was built in the 12thc., transformed into a great chateau in Renaissance times. The main buildings on their gallery with open arcades can still be admired, and so can the Tour Vironne and a magnificent covered well.

MUSEE DE LA PREHISTOIRE ✆ 02 47 94 90 20. *Open all year. July-August: 10am-7pm. Admission: adult 4.50 €.* Houses a unique collection of 10,000 objects. flints, weapons, tools. On the ground floor, the Paleontology Museum boasts a rare tree fossil containing an insect cocoon.

Loches

Old houses and cobbled alleys on the River Indre, overlooked by the castle: Loches is another striking medieval town.

DONJON ✆ 02 47 59 07 86. *Open 2 January-31 March and 1 October-31 December: 9.30am-5pm. 1 April-30 September: 9am-7pm. Closed 25 December and 1 January. Admission: adult 5 €, concessions 3.50 €.* This huge Romanesque keep (11th-15thc.) protected the weak lower part of the headland, and its massive towers and underground passages were used as prisons. Near the keep, the Galerie du Champignon (Mushroom Gallery) shows you production techniques.

LOGIS ROYAL ✆ 02 47 59 01 32. *Open 2 January-31 March and 1 October-31 December: 9.30am-5pm. 1 April-30 September: 9am-7pm. Admission: adult 5 €, concessions 3.50 €, family ticket 13 €.* Here, Joan of Arc met Charles VII after the Orléans victory. This fine 13th and 16thc. castle houses Agnes Sorel's tomb and recumbent statue, and Anne de Bretagne's oratory. The 16th and 17thc. Flemish tapestries are also worth seeing.

MAISON LANSYER Rue Lansyer ✆ 02 47 59 05 45. *Closed 2 October-31 March. Admission: adult 4.60 €.* Lansyer (1835-1893) was Courbet's pupil. This was the Vendee painter's family home, and a hundred of his works are exhibited, together with some of Delacroix's sketches and a collection of Japanese objects, including some striking 18thc. Samurai armour. Another section deals with popular traditions.

Lussault-sur-Loire

AQUARIUM DE TOURAINE ✆ **02 47 23 44 44**. *Open every day: 10am-6pm (10am-7pm in summer). Admission: adult 10 €, child 6 €.* 10,000 fish can be viewed in giant tanks, both European (carp, salmon, eels etc.) and exotic (in the mangrove swamp, tropical area and Brazilian crocodile pit). Sensation-seekers will enjoy going through the shark tunnel.

Montlouis-sur-Loire

CHATEAU DE LA BOURDAISIERE ✆ **02 47 45 16 31**. *Open 1 April-1 May, and 1-30 October: 10am-12 noon and 2pm-6pm. 1 May-30 September Admission: adult 7 €.Ticket includes trained bird display, guided tour of castle and gardens and access to park and kitchen garden.* Henri IV's favourite Gabrielle d'Estrées was born in this 16thc. castle. The park is magnificent with its Italian avenue, cedars, rose and kitchen gardens. The latter houses a tomato conservatory, with 400 varieties.

Montrésor

This superb medieval village boasts a fortress put up by Foulques Nerra, reinforced with towers in the 13thc. A Renaissance chateau was built inside the primitive fortress; the main wing is still intact. You meet the past at every corner of the village: the Chancellor's house, picturesque Woolmarket and 17thc. Carders' Market with its Mansart-style roof.

Rigny-Ussé

CHATEAU D'USSE ✆ **02 47 95 54 05**. *Open mid-February-12 November 2006. Admission: adult 11 €.* Sleeping Beauty's castle, so nicknamed because it inspired her creator Charles Perrault. Transformed and improved by successive owners, the castle, gardens, terraces and collegiate church now form a harmonious whole. There are plenty of fairytale towers and pointed roofs, and a well-furnished interior containing tapestries and art objects.

Villandry

CHATEAU DE VILLANDRY ✆ **02 47 50 02 09**. *Gardens open all year, château from February-mid November: 9am-6pm. Admission: Gardens only, 5.50 € (concessions 3.50 €). Gardens & castle 8 € (concessions 3.50 €).* You come for the Renaissance château, but even more for the wonderful gardens on three levels: a kitchen garden, pleasure garden on the 'ground floor' and water garden.

Loches

VALLEY OF THE KINGS: LAND OF CHATEAUX

The Loire Valley is covered in castles, the famous châteaux, but they were not built here for the scenic beauty alone. The river has plenty of advantages, being a natural barrier against invaders and a useful means of transport and trade route. The valley's gentle climate and charming villages seduced the Kings of France during the Renaissance, and they came with their artists and architects, and started to build Renaissance palaces, castles, manors, fortresses, medieval-style towers and cities, fortified farms, churches, abbeys, priories and cathedrals. The best known - those with most architectural and historical interest - are described here. You should visit a few and really take time to appreciate them, rather than sticking to a self-imposed marathon, seeing too much and remembering nothing.

Amboise

Renaissance capital, historic and artistic centre, Amboise reveals its treasures slowly - unlike its many tourists, instantly noticeable!

CHATEAU ROYAL ✆ **02 47 57 00 98**. *Open all year. Admission: adult 8 €.* Built in the 15th and 16thc., this genuinely royal castle introduced Italian tastes to the Loire Valley. The interior contains some marvellous Gothic and Renaissance furnishings, and the fine panoramic gardens are planted with Mediterranean trees. Saint Hubert Chapel houses Leonardo da Vinci's tomb, recently and elegantly restored.

CHATEAU DU CLOS-LUCE 2, rue Clos-Lucé ✆ **02 47 57 62 88**. *www.vinci-closluce.com. Open all year: 9am-6pm (7pm in season). July & August: 9am-8pm. Admission: adult 12 €.* 500m from Amboise, you find Leonardo da Vinci's last residence. The rooms and furnishings are interesting, but the main attractions are the fabulous machines, designed by the artist and mathematical genius and constructed for the museum. You find the biggest in the beautiful park; some are 'hands-on', and very climbable for kids. This château is rather different from the others, and therefore unforgettable. A magical experience.

PAGODE DE CHANTELOUP ✆ **02 47 57 20 97.** *On the D31, 2km south of Amboise. Open every day. July & August: 9.30am-7.30pm. June: 10am-7pm. May & September: 10am-6.30pm. Admission: 6.30 €.* Built by the Duc de Choiseul in 1775, the Pagoda is 44m high, with 7 storeys. There is a magnificent view of Amboise and the Loire, and you can get an idea of the Château de Chanteloup, destroyed in 1823, from the pagoda's pavilion museum. The Pagoda opens on to a magnificent lake (with rowing boats) and extensive gardens.

Azay-le-Rideau

CHATEAU ✆ **02 47 45 42 04**. *Open every day in July & August: 9.30am-7pm. April-October: until 6pm only. Admission: adult 7 €, under-25s 4.50 €, under-18s free.* The castle was built on piles on one of the Indre's islands, from 1518 to 1527, replacing a fortified house burnt down by Charles VII in 1417. The two wings at right angles are a blend of traditional elements and the new Italian style; with its towers and turrets, Azay embodies the Renaissance's brilliant architectural ideal. The furnished apartments set off some fine 15th and 17thc. French and Flemish tapestries.

JARDINS DE LA CHATONNIERE Azay-le-Rideau ✆ **02 47 45 44 40.** *Open 10am-7pm every day, 1 April-2 November. Closed 3 November-31 March. Admission; adult 5 €, under-12s 3 €.* Deep in a secret valley near Azay le Rideau, eight terraced gardens surround a little castle with six towers and a central courtyard. La Chatonnière was first built as a fortress on the Roman road, on the site of a cave dwellers' village, and has an underground church and stables. The gardens stretch over 7ha, and have poetic names: the Garden of Elegance, with statues, copses, mazes and bulbs in spring; the Garden of the Senses, with 150 varieties of scented perennial; Abundance, a leaf-shaped kitchen garden; Croissant de l'Invraisemblance (Crescent of Unlikeliness) with its thousand gold and orange rose-bushes; and the Garden of Silence in the Renaissance living-quarters.

Chambord

CHATEAU DE CHAMBORD ✆ **02 54 50 40 00 / 0 825 826 088**. *www.chambord.org. Open all year: 9am-5.15pm (6.15pm October-March, 6.30pm July & August). Admission: adult 8,50 € (6 € January-March), concessions 5 €, under-18s free.* Biggest and most fascinating of the Loire châteaux, Chambord dates back to the first French Renaissance. François I began it in 1519, but it was only finished in 1685. You discover 5 centuries of history in its remarkable architecture, notably da Vinci's famous double spiral staircase and the walkway on the roof, among a maze of battlements, towers and turrets. On leaving the castle, you can walk in the huge, enclosed forest park, habitat for many wild animals. The whole estate is listed UNESCO World Heritage (1981).

Chaumont-sur-Loire

CHATEAU DE CHAUMONT ✆ **02 54 51 26 26**. *Open all year: 9.30am-6.30pm in high season; 10am-5pm in low season. Admission: adult 6.10 €, 18-25s 4 €, under-18s free.* This attractive site overlooks the Loire, but is less well known than its neighbours. It houses a proud 15thc. castle with a number of round, machicolated towers and keep (also round), once a fortress between Cheverny and Chenonceaux. Inside, there are Brussels and Aubusson tapestries, 15th and 17thc. furniture and a collection of terracotta medallions from Italian Jean-Baptiste Nini's 18thc.factory. The stables are luxurious, having been fitted out for the Prince de Broglie in the late 19thc., and the landscaped gardens were laid out in 1884 by Henri Duchêne. From mid-May to mid-October, the International Garden Festival takes place here (enquiries: Conservatoire des Parcs et Jardins et du Paysage ✆ 02 54 20 99 22).

Chenonceaux

Nearly a million tourists visit this chateau every year!

CHATEAU DE CHENONCEAU ✆ **0 820 20 90 90**. *Open all year: 9am-5pm or 7.30pm according to the season. Admission: adult 8,50 €-12 €, concessions 6.50 €-9.50 €.* Chenonceau is the Loire's pride and joy, with its uniquely beautiful Renaissance architecture. It is the 'Ladies' Castle', built by Katherine Briçonnet in 1513, embellished by Diane de Poitiers and Catherine de Medicis and saved from the Revolution by Mme Dupin. The formal gardens and park surrounding the castle add to this impression of delicacy and grace. There are some rich collections inside; Renaissance furniture, 16th and 17thc. tapestries and great paintings. On summer evenings, you can stroll through the illuminated gardens from 9.30pm to 11pm, to music by Corelli.

Cheverny

CHATEAU DE CHEVERNY ✆ **02 54 79 96 29**. *Open every day, all year. Admission: château & park 6.50 €.* This splendid castle was finished in the 17thc., in a pure, classical style with Renaissance influence. Inside are rich furnishings and sumptuous tapestries, including L'enlèvement de la Belle Hélène (Gobelins). The Salle des Trophées (Trophy Room) contains 2,000 stag heads: the antlers seem to be growing out of the wall as if in a horror film! Outside, you can explore the canal and park in an electric car or boat. Cheverny was Hergé's model for Tintin's chateau Moulinsart, and the exhibition 'Les Secrets de Moulinsart' takes you into the world of Tintin and Captain Haddocks' adventures.

Azay-le-Rideau castle

© Iconotec.com / Pierre Delaguerard

CHATEAU DE TROUSSAY ✆ **02 54 44 29 07**. *Open every day, June-September: 10.30am-12.30pm and 2pm-6pm; all day July & August. Admission: adult 5 €, concessions 3.50 €.* This castle contains many works of art and excellent sculptures. Its painted ceilings, polychrome stained-glass, tiling and period furniture are a pleasure to look at. A regional museum of Sologne's bygone rural traditions is housed in the picturesque outbuildings, encircled by a pretty park with ancient trees.

Langeais

CHATEAU DE LANGEAIS ✆ **02 47 96 72 60**. *Open all year. Admission: adult 7 €.* Charles VIII and Anne de Bretagne were married here in 1491; the scene is depicted in a tableau of realistic waxworks. Admire the tapestries and Gothic furniture, and the 10thc. keep in the courtyard, last remains of the primitive castle.

LOIR VALLEY

Not to be confused with the other one (Loire). The Loir Valley is made for walks and discoveries.

Vendôme

Ronsard met Cassandre here, and the atmosphere is still romantic. You enter the old town by the Rue du Faubourg-Chartrain, then Rue du Change; on the left is the Tour de l'Islette. First port of call is the 15thc. Saint Jacques Chapel, once part of the Oratorians College, where Balzac was a boarder from 1807 and 1813. Today, painting exhibitions are often held there. After the Town Hall, towards Rue Saint Jacques, you come across Ronsard's bust, then the Madeleine Church and its stone belltower. Go up Rue de la Poterie to Rue Saunerie: you will see the Porte Saint Georges, the town's southern gate. You now walk through the covered market with its fine metal framework, and come out at the Tour Saint Martin (16thc.): its bells are a town landmark, pealing out every hour on the hour. You now find yourself in the Place de la République, close to the abbey.

LA TRINITE ABBEY CHURCH ✆ **02 54 77 05 07**. *Admission free all year.* This superb building was part of the abbey founded by Geoffroy Martel. Transept and pillars remain from the 11thc. Romanesque church, but its front (1506) is a fine example of Flamboyant Gothic. The chapter house contains some striking Romanesque frescoes. You go in through the museum in the cloister yard, now mostly destroyed. The steeple dates from the 12thc.

Couture-sur-Loir

There are some pretty houses in the village, and the old Saint Gervais Saint Protais Church (its stone steeple was put up by Loys, Ronsard's father, and the family crest with its three fish is on the bell tower). You then go looking for Ronsard's 'Isle Verte', where he wanted to be buried. It is behind the cemetery, reached by a bridge over the Loir, and must be the region's most poetic picnic site! From the cemetery, a path takes you to the poet's birthplace (Manoir de la Possonniere).

MANOIR DE LA POSSONNIERE ✆ **02 54 72 40 05**. *Guided tours. Admission: adult 6 €.* Loys Ronsard achieved military glory under Louis XII and François 1, and consequently had an elegant Renaissance chateau put up on the family stronghold. A number of maxims recalling common sense and duty are engraved in the stone. Little Pierre was born in the manor in 1524, and spent the first 9 years of his life there, influenced by his father's pious ideas of devotion and courage.

Lavardin

Listed as one of France's most beautiful villages, Lavardin is well worth seeing, for its ruined medieval castle, old houses and superb setting in wooded hills near the Loir Valley. The most picturesque walk in and around the village is to the Grottes aux biques, an enchanting site; another pretty route leads through foliage to the Loir, arriving in Montoire.

CHATEAU ✆ **02 54 85 07 74.** *Open 1 June-20 September, except Monday: 11am-12 noon and 3pm-6pm.* This ruined fortress (11th-16thc.) with original keep, gatehouse and triple wall still stands proudly on its headland. It was the area's main stronghold for many years. Charles VII and Agnes Sorel stayed there in 1448.

Troo

A cave dwellers' village on four levels. This former fortified town offers a splendid view, and contains a 12thc. collagiate church. You can also visit the Petrifying Cave, Louvre, with its 12thc. keep, Talking Well, 12thc. hospice and Stone Cross (14thc.). Climb the spiral steps to the viewpoint indicator, where you squint at the horizon to identify villages, castles and features, and follow the snaking Loir into infinity. Coming down on foot towards the road, you see the cave-dwellings and Romanesque Saint Jacques des Guerets Church, with its remarkable 11th and 12thc. frescoes and 15thc. wall paintings.

FOOD AND DRINK

A fertile region rich in agricultural produce, game and traditional recipes (including the famous Tarte Tatin) - not forgetting the Loire vineyards.

Loire

Goat's cheese

In 1896, Moise Boulay was the first goat's cheese producer in Chavignol, a small village near Sancerre. On his death in 1922, his wife Leontine went on with the cheese-making until her son-in-law Georges Dubois took over.

This delicious little cylindrical goat's cheese is made with unpasteurised full-fat milk, and owes its flavour to the rich pastures around Sancerre. It received an AOC in 1976.

Gourmets enjoy sainte-maure, a soft white goat's cheese with a straw through the middle, covered with salt and ash before maturing. It also has an AOC. The castle museum houses a goat's cheese exhibition, with costumed characters and a tasting.

Tarte Tatin

Sologne pastry-cooks Stephanie and Caroline Tatin perfected this upside-down apple tart, and a Tatin Fair takes place in early September. Other regional specialities are honey and porcelain.

'Real' Pithiviers

It is only logical for this sugar-producing town to have a cake as a speciality. The ingredients, however, have changed since its early days. Today's recipe contains almond paste and flaky pastry, not part of the original version, which was basically glace fruits in a soft textured cake. Almond paste was added as trade developed, and flaky pastry included on its invention in the 18thc.

Vineyards

Sancerre, Menetou-Salon, Bourgueil and Touraine produce fruity whites and light reds, to be drunk chilled.

Bourgueil

MUSEE DES VINS DE TOURAINE 16, rue Nationale ✆ 02 47 61 07 93. *Open all year, every day except Tuesday: 9am-12 noon and 2pm-6pm. Admission: adult 2.60 €, concessions 2 €, under-12s free.* You learn the secrets of Touraine wines and the history of their vinification techniques. A friendly place!

MAISON DES VINS DE BOURGUEIL 18, place de l'Eglise ✆ 02 47 97 92 20. *Open all year. 16 September-14 May: Friday & Saturday only.* In 1991, the Bourgueil winegrowers bought actor Jean Carmet's family house, a 15thc. building in the town centre, and restored it. You can now call in to taste and buy the week's wines, and even have a tasting lesson from a winegrower to develop your palate.

Gastronomy - Le Choiseul, Amboise

© Le Choiseul

Vineyard

ROUTE DES VIGNOBLES DU CŒUR DE FRANCE

This road covers 170km of vineyards. You set out to explore the region's 5 AOC: Sancerre, Menetou-Salon, Reuilly, Quincy and Côteaux du Giennois, and also the Chateaumeillant vineyard. The route follows picturesque little roads with orchards, hills and valleys, joining up with Burgundy to the east, and the Val de Loire wine route (Atlantic to Touraine), in the west.

UNION VITICOLE De MENETOU-SALON 21, rue de la Mairie - MENETOU-SALON ✆ 02 48 64 87 26. Menetou-Salon got its AOC in 1959. The wines are delicate and spicy, fruity roses and perfumed reds, and should be drunk straight away, preferably chilled.

BUREAU INTERPROFESSIONNEL DES VINS DU CENTRE (BIVC) 9, route de Chavignol ✆ 02 48 78 51 07. The BIVC isn't accessible to tourists, but produces literature and has mapped out a tourist route. Sancerre is the best-known AOC in the Loire Valley, and can be drunk at any time, with fish, seafood and goat's cheese. The rose is refreshing and goes well with starters, the red with red meat, game and all cheeses (drink it at 12-14_C).

Chinon

The old medieval cellars hide real treasure: red wines (cabernet franc) that have been maturing there for years.

MUSEE ANIME DU VIN ET DE LA TONNELLERIE 12, rue Voltaire ✆ 02 47 93 25 63. *Open April-September: 10.30am-12.30pm and 2pm-7pm. Admission: 4 €.* The region is proud of its vineyard, and displays its wines in scenes animated by automatons. Tasting on request.

CAVES PLOUZEAU 94, rue Haute-Saint-Maurice ✆ 02 47 93 32 11. *www.plouzeau.com. Open April-late September: 11am-1pm and 3pm-7pm, except Sunday and Monday.* A quality producer, who makes both Chinon and Touraine wines.

Vouvray

Famous for its sparkling white. There are a number of winegrowers.

Cave des Producteurs de Grands Vins de Vouvray 38, vallee Coquette ✆ 02 47 52 75 03. Open every day: 9am-12.30pm and 1.45pm-7pm. 50 producers grouped together reveal the secrets of their cellars, and explain how their wines are made. The last stage of the visit is of course a tasting.

MAISON 15, ave. Léon-Brulé ✆ 02 47 52 71 62. *Open every day, except Sunday: 9.30am-12.30pm and 3pm-6pm. Sunday by appointment..* This family firm owns no vines, but buys the must at grape harvesting, and makes its wine using a traditional method. The different stages of the process are explained while you visit the chalky tuffeau cellars.

Hotels & Restaurants

CHER

Bourges

ABBAYE SAINT-AMBROIX Boulevard de la République ✆ 02 48 70 80 00. *Website : www.alpha-hotellerie.com. Set menu of the week 43 € to 71 €. Average price à la carte : 71 €. 60 place settings. Closed Sunday and Monday.* The 17thc. Abbaye Saint-Ambroix, listed historical monument, is located opposite the Pres-Fichaux garden, only a stone's throw from the station and Bourges town centre. You feel like a time traveller as you go from the pastel-coloured reception hall to the restaurant, down a corridor lined with arcades, remains of an 8thc. cloister destroyed during the Wars of Religion. The dining room is housed in a former chapel with a high vaulted ceiling, decorated in purple and gold to escape from the place's monastic austerity. The chef has created a sophisticated, seasonal cuisine to go with the historic setting; his dishes enchant the tastebuds at each stage of the meal, with never a false note. Loire wines are given pride of place to accompany the Dutruy snails with garlic cream and raifort, roast veal with crayfish, spinach shoots, nantua and meat juices, cheese trolley, poached pear with liquorice, vanilla creme brulee and oak-flavoured ice cream.

LE BEAUVOIR 1, avenue Marx-Dormoy ✆ 02 48 65 42 44. *Website: www.restaurantlebeauvoir.com. Gastronomic cuisine. Closed Sunday evening. Annual closing: 3 weeks in August. Set menus from 17 € to 41 €. Average price a la carte 65 €. Service 12pm-3pm and 7pm-9.30pm. Car park 50m away, near the Marais de Bourges. Catering. Receptions, seminars.* Located near the Bourges marsh canals, Le Beauvoir is a delightful place to eat. The restaurant has been refurbished, and the atmosphere in the dining room is convivial but quiet and comfortable - even the air-conditioning is just right! You are surrounded by glass and pottery cockerels of all kinds (the French emblem), collected by owners Didier Guyot and his wife, who explore their region's culinary wealth with talent and passion to create the fresh seasonal menus personalised by the chef with subtle notes and flavours. Scallops in ravioli with red butter, duck foie gras pan-fried hamburger-style, liquored Banyuls colonel and you won't be able to resist the house speciality, chocolate souffle and creme anglaise with Colombian coffee! This sublime dessert proves yet again that eating well is an art. Both restaurant and kitchens will have been reshaped in early 2006.

Châteaumeillant

LE PIET A TERRE 21 rue du Château ✆ 02 48 61 41 74 *Fax:02 48 61 41 88. Set menus from 39.50 € to 120 €, a la carte 70 €. Closed Sunday evening, Monday, Tuesday, Wednesday lunchtime and from early December to late February.* It all began in the 1980s with a simple creperie owned by Sylvie Piet and Thierry Finet. Then Thierry decided to abandon crepes in favour of something more gastronomic, and developed his personal style; fresh, spontaneous and innovative. Green asparagus cooked in chicken juices, pork rillons, green pea julienne with mint, *cappucino des talons*, warm oyster lasagna, Marenne Oleron fines de claire (fresh oysters), green garlic shoots and small white onions, seawater emulsion with roots, pork fillet barely sealed, Boischaut ham and aromatic herb *roule*, pan-fried cuts of beef fillet, country ham, leeks and carrots, oak-flavoured cream panna cotta, Passau raspberries, lemon and coconut *dentelle* with vanilla seeds and grilled hazlenut feature on his menus. If you look beyond this brilliant cuisine, you'll see that it is part of a whole setting where decoration, crockery (like the amusing sardine tin for serving these little fish, just cooked) and the new flower, vegetable and aromatic herb garden all play their part. An experience unlike any other, and a vision of tomorrow's restaurant.

EURE-ET-LOIR

Bonneval

HOSTELLERIE DU BOIS GUIBERT * N10 Hameau du Bois Guibert ✆ 02 37 47 22 33.** *Fax 02 37 47 50 69.* Set menus from 25 € to 47 €. 14 rooms. Prices from 65 € to 130 €. Murielle and Eric Leluc welcome you into the enchanted setting of their 18thc. manor house. Chef Jerome Lebreton's *cuisine* has a regional accent; taste the subtle notes of his frogs' legs raviole with smoked garlic and parsley *coulis*, pikeperch fillet pan-fried with *andouille de Guemene* and Beauce lentils, and roast, spiced pineapple to finish. In fine weather, you have a magnificent view of the lawns and copses from the terrace.

Chartres

LE GRAND MONARQUE * 22, place des Epars ✆ 02 37 18 15 15.** *Fax 02 37 36 34 18. Gastronomic restaurant Le Georges: set menus from 32 € to 56 €. Brasserie Le Madrigal: formula 20 €. Service until 10pm. Car park. 50 rooms from 95 € to 165 €. 5 suites.* This former coaching inn has been the pride of the country for three-and-a-half centuries, and deserves your admiration. Inside, the cuisine is both traditional and creative: the Chartres pate and Curnonsky veal chop are delicious, and the desserts small masterpieces. The wine list pays tribute to some grand crus, and wine-tasting evenings are organised regularly, for amateurs and connoisseurs. Comfortable and charming rooms.

Châteaudun

AUX TROIS PASTOUREAUX 31, rue André-Gillet ✆ 02 37 45 74 40. *Website: www.aux-trois-pastoureaux.fr. Set menus 21 €, 42.30 € (choice of 2 courses) 63.30 € (choice of 3 courses). The restaurant is now open lunchtimes and evenings, Tuesday to Saturday. Advance booking for groups on Sunday and Monday.* This inn has been welcoming guests for two centuries. Today, after considerable refurbishing, it is a beautiful place for a gastronomic break; the chef mixes tradition and creativity. Jean-Francois Lucchese and his team welcome you warmly, and invite you to taste the home-made Perigord duck foie gras with toast, scallops roasted with celery infusion and sweet pepper, rock fish duos grilled with star aniseed, and roast mallard breast with 5 spices on a vegetable Tatin. Take a look at the medieval menu, which is well worth discovering. Lovely to look at, and quite delicious!

Nogent-le-Roi

LE CAPUCIN GOURMAND 1, rue de la Volaille ✆ 02 37 51 96 00. *Website: www.capucin-gourmand.fr. Closed Thursday evening (except July and August) and Monday all year. Set menus from 25 € to 40 €.* This delightful 15thc. half-timbered house in the heart of the town is decorated inside in blue and yellow tones, an exotic touch recalling a Provencal mas lost in the centre of France.The *cuisine*, too, reveals Provencal influence, though the chef changes his menus to suit local market produce.The dishes are all very savoury, prepared and served with great care and attention to detail. There's every chance you'll fall in love with the Capucin Gourmand; it is really not to be missed.

Saint-Symphorien-le-Château

LE CHATEAU D'ESCLIMONT ** ✆ 02 37 31 15 15.** *Fax 02 37 31 57 91. Website: www.esclimont.com.* Set menus from 69 € to 96 €. 54 rooms from 140 € to 1,280 € (exclusive suite). The Chateau d'Esclimont dates back to the 11thc. It was partially destroyed in successive wars, and rebuilt in the16thc., and in the 19thc. Vicomte de la Rochefoucauld, Duke of Bisaccia, made it a showcase for Renaissance architecture. Since 1980, the Chateau has been a Grande Etape Francaise. It stands by a beautiful lake with its swans and ducks, in the heart of a magnificent, listed 60 ha. park containing some rare tree species. In the 18thc.-style restaurant, you can enjoy a romantic candlelit dinner that will thrill your tastebuds, and there is no lack of active pursuits to work it off later. The chateau boasts a helisurface, and a launching pad for hot-air balloons, but there are also tennis courts, golf, swimming pool, boat trips and a work-out itinerary. Francois de la Rochefoucauld's famous motto «C'est mon plaisir» (It's my pleasure) seems to have been adopted here!

INDRE

Argenton-sur-Creuse

MANOIR DE BOISVILLERS * 11, rue du Moulin-de-Bord ✆ 02 54 24 13 88.** *Website: www.manoir-de-boisvillers.com. Open 7 days a week. 16 rooms from 58 € to 96 €.* The owners welcome you like friends to this charming, 3-star hotel, housed in a remarkably renovated 18thc. residence, in the middle of a small park with swimming pool. It is ideally situated for one of old Argenton's most pleasant sites on the banks of the River Creuse. The rooms are equally pleasant.

Châteauroux

LA CIBOULETTE 42, rue Grande ✆ 02 54 27 66 28. *Closed every other Sunday. Annual closing: August and Christmas holidays. Formula (2 courses)15 € and 20 €. Set menus: 9 € (children's menu) 17 €, 22 €, 27 € or 33 € (with 3 glasses of wine) 42 € (with 4 glasses of wine). A la carte around 30 €.* It is always a pleasure to sit down under the pictures of rounded pumpkins, giant rhubarb, sunflowers in their glory and pretty bottles painted by Alain Bellanger with photographic fidelity. The tables are attractively set too, and the seasonal menu is a harmonious combination of traditional Berry cuisine and more sophisticated flavours. Maurice Garnier buys his fresh produce at market, and is especially considerate towards slinmmers; on the menu, the letters m and g indicate *cuisine minceur* (slimming) or *gourmande* (pile on the calories).We recommend the green Berry lentil terrine with foie gras, and the duck salad with fine herbs, followed by grilled mackerel fillets with mustard and aniseed, and duck breast with spiced caramel. The desserts are delicate: *ganache* with prunes and orange conserve, and seasonal fruit *feuillete* with *creme anglaise.* Courteous and attentive service, selected wines served by the glass on two of the more expensive menus.The cellar holds a careful selection of great names in wine.

ELYSEE HOTEL * 2, rue de la République ✆ 02 54 22 33 66.** *Fax 02 54 07 34 34. Open 7 days a week. 18 rooms. Double room 64 €.* This pretty hotel with its 1900 front is in the town centre, close to theatre and cinemas. The French journalist and newsreader Paul Amar once chose it as a base, while he was writing a book about the average Chateauroux citizen. You certainly feel at home here; the setting is elegant and warm, and the rooms comfortable. The floors have recently been renovated, and the dominant note is blue monochrome.

Issoudun

LA COGNETTE 6 boulevard de Stalingrad ✆ 02 54 03 59 59 *Fax 02 54 03 13 03. Website: www.la-cognette.com. Set menus from 29 € to 66 €, a la carte 50 €. Closed Sunday evening, Monday, Tuesday lunchtime and in January.* This inn dates back to the 1830s, and is well-known in central France. Balzac stayed here often, and was said to be inspired by the setting when he wrote *La Rabouilleuse.* In the 1960s, Alain Nonnet put the inn on the map, and won acclaim for his cuisine. He has now handed over to his son-in-law, Jean-Jacques Daumy, president of the Young Restaurateurs of Europe, and the roquefort *zephyr* with Baumes de Venise wine, fillet of turbot with shallots, duck fillet and liver poached in a *pot-au-feu* and strawberry and fresh fruit basket with raspberry *coulis* would seem to prove him right. A wine cellar rich in regional *crus* adds the final confirmation: the inheritance is definitely in safe hands.

Mèzières-en-Brenne

AU BŒUF COURONNE ** 9, place Charles-de-Gaulle ✆ 02 54 38 04 39. *Closed Sunday evening and Monday except for public holidays. Closed mid-November to early February, and one week in early June. 8 rooms from 30 € to 40 €. Set menus 14 € (weekdays), from 19.50 € to 40 €.* This restaurant was once a 17thc. coaching inn, and its wide porch has seen the world go by. An enlarged postcard on the wall shows the same bustling place in 1910, when it provided not only a restaurant service but also vehicle hire. The set menus feature carp, definitely king fish in this region. Very good traditional cuisine, and excellent desserts.

Saint-Chartier

CHATEAU DE LA VALLEE BLEUE * Route de Verneuil-sur-Igneraie ✆ 02 54 31 01 91.** *Website: www.chateauvalleebleue.com. Closed 15 November-15 March. Hotel closed Sunday evening and Monday in April and May, and from 15 September-15 November. 13 rooms from 100 € to 150 € and 2 apartments from 175 € to 215 €. Restaurant closed weekday lunchtimes apart from group bookings. Set menus 29 € and 39 €. A la carte around 50 €.* This hotel is housed in a small chateau built by Henri Dauvergne for Doctor Pestel, who treated the writer George Sand. You cross a section of the park to reach the magnificent reception area, with its ancient buffet and log fire in the fireplace. Both dining rooms overlook a wide, sloping lawn, with an attractive view of the village and the Chateau des Maitre-Sonneurs' tall silhouette. Curtains, mirrors, candles and freshly-cut flowers on the tables provide the right decor for this prestigious setting. The regional *cuisine* is sophisticated too, and features pan-fried foie gras lobe and a mixed salad of young leaves and shoots with blackberry vinegar, pikeperch George Sand-style, Berry guinea-hen supreme, a fine cheese trolley, spiced pear *croustillant* with vanilla cream, and apple tart.

INDRE ET-LOIRE

Amboise

LE CHOISEUL 36 quai Charles-Guinot ✆ 02 47 30 45 45 *Fax 02 47 30 46 10. Website: www.le-choiseul.com. Set menus from 50 € to 95 €, a la carte 75 €. Closed first fortnight in January. Open for dinner only.* This splendid restaurant was partly destroyed by fire in January 2005, but fortunately without serious consequences; indeed, though forced to close for several months, the time was put to good use for general renovation work. Pascal Bouvier is still in the kitchens, and even if he only exercises his talents for dinner (lunch is now served in the 36, in the same building, which offers a simpler menu), the result is superb. Bourgogne truffles, broad beans and pig's head, ratte potato *rouelles* with truffle vinegar, *cassolette* (shallow oven-proof dish) of crayfish and chanterelles with chopped chicken offal, sauce supreme with shellfish stock, roast bass 'petit bateau' with artichokes, chestnuts and apples, bread spread with duck foie gras, red fruit and wild bilberry *allumette royale*, and white chocolate ice-cream. The cellar is as daringly original as the food, with the region's best bottles well represented. Impeccable service.

LE FLEURAY ✆ 02 47 56 09 25. *Website: www.lefleurayhotel.com. Email: lefleurayhotel@wanadoo.fr. Open every day, bookings only. 14 double rooms from 78 € to 115 €. Set menus 28 €, 38 €. A la carte (varied) 50 €, children's menu 16 €.* The Newington family welcome you in this beautiful old-fashioned residence. All the rooms are individually decorated with a view of the garden; some have a private terrace. Delicate, inventive cooking, and excellent regional wines to go with it. Heated pool to relax in. Dogs welcome. 2006 sees the opening of a new dining-room, providing more space and comfort for guests. Not to be missed!

Chenonceaux

AUBERGE DU BON LABOUREUR 6 rue du Dr-Bretonneau ✆ 02 47 23 90 02 *Fax 02 47 23 82 01. Website: www.amboise.com/laboureur. Set menus 30 € to 75 €, a la carte 65 €. Closed Tuesday lunchtime, from 13 November to 22 December and from 9 January to 11 February.* This old country inn on the road leading to the Chateau de Chenonceau has been handed down through the family Jeudi for over a century. Antoine has been running it for 20 years, with no complaints; the rooms are divided between 5 small but very comfortable houses and the *cuisine* is classic but faultless. The menus feature poached egg with truffle and tuna, haddock and broad bean mousse *rouleau*, sea bream *a l'unilaterale*, balsamic vinegar reduction, fine herbs and beetroot chips and fennel, pan-cooked, beef fillet and ox tail with Bourgeuil wine, potato *galette* (pancake) and grilled shallots, strawberry *galette*, basil *cremeux* and Sechouan pepper sorbet. Classic and modern at the same time, supported by a cellarful of the valley's best bottles - and some from beyond.

Chinon

HOTEL DE FRANCE * Restaurant Au Chapeau rouge 47-49, place du Général-De-Gaulle ✆ 02 47 93 33 91**. *Fax : 02 47 98 37 03. Annual closing from mid-February to mid-March. Restaurant closed Sunday evening and Monday, hotel closed Sunday evening in low season. 31 rooms from 78 €.* An elegant classic in the heart of the medieval quarter. This fine 16thc. residence is comfortable and welcoming, with its up-to-date rooms of character, decorated with wall fabric. Sophisticated cuisine based on seafood and livestock breeding.

AU PLAISIR GOURMAND Quai Charles-VII ✆ 02 47 93 20 48. *Closed Sunday evening, Monday and Tuesday lunchtime. Set menus : 28 €, 39 €, 49 € and 62 €.* Known and remembered far and wide, this restaurant is Rabelaisian in its pleasures. You settle down in an intimate and sophisticated setting, ready to enjoy the subtle flavours of country produce: snail ravioli with garlic cream, pikeperch in white butter, *beuchelle a la tourangelle* (Touraine tart made with kidneys and sweetbreads in a cream and mustard sauce), ox tail with Chinon wine, strawberry *gratin* with almonds. The cellar lives up to the cooking, and offers a wide range of bottles for novices and connoisseurs alike.

Le Petit-Pressigny

RESTAURANT DALLAIS La Promenade ✆ 02 47 94 93 52 *Set menus from 36 € to 78 €, a la carte 60 €. Closed on Sunday evening, Monday, Tuesday, 2 January-1 February and 25 September-10 October.* The Promenade in question surely refers to the successful career of a close-knit and capable duo: Jacky Dallais, who has been in the kitchens for over 20 years now, generous, frank and always good-humoured, like his cooking; and Xavier Fortin, restaurant manager and skilled wine-waiter. This is *grande cuisine*, at more than competitive prices - you can eat *a la carte* for 60 €! Big green asparagus, grilled, truffled chicken with crusty sorrel, *sanguette* (black pudding made from poultry blood), sugar snap peas and Touraine chicken with truffle juice, roast 'petit bateau' dory, mashed potato and small white onions,sweetbreads with anchovies and creamed lettuce, caramel craquant with coffee, hazlenut praline ravioli, and hot chocolate and vanilla ice-cream give excellent value, and as this culinary probity leaves you with a few euros over, why not indulge yourself and dip into the sumptuous (and equally reasonable) cellar? A most enjoyable Promenade, and an address to remember.

Montbazon

LA CHANCELIERE - LE JEU DE CARTES 1 place des Marronniers ✆ 02 47 26 00 67 *Set menu Fax 02 47 73 14 82. Website: www.lachanceliere.fr. Set menu 33 €. Closed Sunday, Monday, 22 January-13 February and 6-22 August.* In a region with a wealth of good restaurants, you need imagination to make any impact, and Michel Gagneux (once chef de partie beside Legay at Ledoyen) has been doing just this since he arrived here in 1982. The results have proved him right: warm oyster ravioles with champagne, grilled langoustine tails with spiced oils, flavoured with pistachio, wild duck roasted with chanterelles and charlotte potato *galette*, and dark chocolate Vesuvius with a raspberry heart. The prices are gentle on your pocket, the service pleasantly relaxed and the wine cellar tempting, though not economic.

CHATEAU D'ARTIGNY Route de Monts ✆ 02 47 34 30 30 *Fax: 02 47 34 30 39. Website: www.artigny.com. Set menus from 50 € to 81 €. A la carte 80 €. Open all year.* Built between 1912 and 1916 by the famous perfumer Coty in pure 18thc.style, this majestic chateau is approached by a long avenue winding through the forest. The gravel crunches under your wheels as you park your saloon car in the huge car park, then step into an immense and luxurious hall, where the staff spring to attention. The dining room is regal, and rather impressive when you're not used to great restaurants. Francis Maignaut has been used to this one for 25 years, and his menu suits the style of the place to perfection, with festive produce, classically and faultlessly prepared, affording discreet pleasure. Red mullet fillets with Salamanca chorizo, green vegetables with basil and Piquillo pepper, pikeperch fillet *contise* with fresh truffles (inserted into cuts under the skin), gnocchi and leek tagliatelli, roast duck confit with sweet spices, peaches and turnips with curcuma, Roussillon apricots flavoured with lavender and soft white cheese sorbet with Genoa bread. The wine list is a book, one of France's heaviest, and features some mythical bottles at unspeakable prices, and other, more affordable young winegrowers.

DOMAINE DE LA TORTINIERE** 10, route de Ballan - LES GUES DE VEIGNE ✆ 02 47 34 35 00.** *Fax 02 47 65 95 70. Annual closing 21 December-1 March. Restaurant closed Sunday evening, 1 November-1 March. 30 rooms from 145 € to 320 € (suites). Breakfast 15 €. Set menus from 40 € to 70 €.* This traditional residence got its 4th star in June 2005, confirming its status as symbol of Touraine's luxury hotel business. The Second Empire chateau has a lot of cachet, and is remarkably well fitted out to provide both comfort and old-world charm. Sophisticated rooms, some air-conditioned, divided between the chateau and its old pavilions. The food is of the same quality, with a cuisine currently based on the classics. Excellent welcome.

Rochecorbon

HOSTELLERIE DE LA LANTERNE 48, quai de la Loire ✆ 02 47 52 50 02. *Annual closing from mid-January to mid-February. Closed Sunday evening, Monday, Tuesday evening in low season. Set menus from 21.90 € to 47 €.* Rene Pommier, Maitre Cuisinier de France, is looking forward to well-earned retirement, but for the moment, and for those customers nostalgic for classic, top-quality cuisine, this great chef goes on preparing those dishes with regional accents: andouillette and rillon *matignons*, Racan country pigeon, pikeperch *en papillote* flavoured with star aniseed, and an iced souffle to finish. A fine wine list goes with them. Thanks, Mr Pommier, for a pleasant evening spent in the elegant setting of this typical Touraine residence; you'll be missed!

Tours

JEAN BARDET Château Belmont ✆ 02 47 41 41 11 *Fax 02 47 51 68 72. Website: www.jeanbardet.com Set menus from 90 € to 180 €, a la carte 120 €. Closed Saturday lunchtime, Monday lunchtime and all day Tuesday from 1 April to 31 October, and Saturday lunchtime, Sunday evening, all day Monday and Tuesday lunchtime the rest of the year.* Jean Bardet is a monument to French cuisine. Working beside Guerard, Blanc, Westermann and Trama, he has proved in 25 years of highly-skilled cooking that you can make a success of top-level gastronomy outside Paris and the Cote d'Azur. He was already drawing the crowds while still at Chateauroux, and things have gone from good to better since he settled in this superb Napoleon III residence in 1987, with his charming and indispensable wife Sophie. Jean Bardet is a specialist in vegetable gastronomy, and maintains a huge kitchen garden where he grows all the aromatic herbs he uses in his cooking (over 1000 plants, including 25 different kinds of basil). His menu is specialised too: cream of leeks, sweet onion juice, duck foie gras cooked whole in a terrine, with black Touraine truffles, crayfish and grilled cocoa bean *cappucino*, farm bred pork belly braised for 18 hours, with Aquitaine caviar, charlotte *mousseline*, red fruit *croquantine*, mascarpone *cremeux* with Jamaica pepper and soft white cheese sorbet. 'Bardet', as his wife calls hin affectionately, in public, has reached retirement age, but still has a firm hand, and a sharp eye.

CHARLES BARRIER 101 avenue de la Tranchée ✆ 02 47 54 20 39 *Fax 02 47 41 80 95. Set menus from 25 € to 70 €, a la carte 60 €. Closed Saturday lunchtime and Sunday.* This mythical restaurant (among the 20 most popular in France in the 1970s and 80s) has kept the name of its illustrious founder, although master chef Charles Barrier departed this earth long ago. Herve Lussault, who trained with Senderens (Lucas Carton in Paris) and at the Chateau d'Artigny did not flinch before the weight of his inheritance, but chose to pay it tribute his way, with a very personal and inextravagant cuisine, much less sumptuous than the great Charles' own. Pig's trotters stuffed and truffled, accompanied by black pudding, chervil cappucino and langoustine tartare, young Challans duck roast with spices or whole sweetbread hearts braised in *vin jaune* feature on a menu well worth the visit. The chef also cooks for a bistro just next door, where you find good value for money too.

HOTEL DE L'UNIVERS ** 5, boulevard Heurteloup ✆ 02 47 05 37 12.** *Website: http://hotel-univers-loirevalley.com. Open all year 24 hours a day. 85 rooms including 8 suites and 3 rooms fitted out for visitors with limited mobility. Single or double room from 193 € to 265 €. Suites from 337 € to 398 €.* In the heart of Tours, near the TGV station, congress centre and commercial and tourist quarters. The hotel is part of the Concorde chain. Large, air-conditioned rooms equipped with mini-bar, wide screen TV, cable, desk, trouser press and bathroom with hair-dryer. Six salons are also available (covering 800 sqm.in all). Bar and gastronomic restaurant La Touraine. The Hotel de l'Univers is ideally situated for discovering this delightful town.

LA ROCHE LE ROY 55 route de Saint-Avertin ✆ 02 47 27 22 00 *Fax 02 47 28 08 39. Website: www.rocheleroy.com. Set menus from 30 € to 65 €, a la carte 55 €. Closed Sunday, Monday and first three weeks in August.* This pretty Touraine manor is outside the town centre and the tourist traps, and so doesn't count on passing customers to fill its dining room. The midday service is mainly taken up with business lunches; a business menu - called 'Affaire' - at 30 € has been created for these customers. Alain Couturier's real fans tend to come in the evening: this chef, ex-Charles Barrier, Ledoyen (in the Legay period) and Gavroche in London, manages to keep prices down even in such a sumptuous place, where VAT is still at 19.6%. His pan-fried foie gras escalope with Puy lentils, anguille *en matelote* with Vouvray wine, roast pikeperch with white butter and gingerbread, roast supreme of young pigeon with foie gras, sweetbreads braised with limeflower and woodland mushrooms, warm lemon souffle, *granite colonel* (a kind of iced sorbet with vodka), chocolate orange *moelleux* and cocoa sorbet are excellent value for money. You find all the region's great wines in the cellar, from Huet to Chidaine. Very professional service.

LOIR-ET-CHER

Blois

AU RENDEZ-VOUS DES PECHEURS Rue du Foix ✆ 02 54 74 67 48. *Fax 02 54 74 47 67. Annual closing three weeks in August. Closed Sunday and Monday. Set menus from 27 € to 75 €.* A little local grocers' with its old-fashioned counter has been converted into one of the most popular places in Blois. The bistro ambiance is pleasant, and the menus feature mostly fish, preferably from the Loire. Quality produce and value for money are the strong points.

L'ORANGERIE DU CHATEAU 1 avenue Jean-Laigret ✆ 02 54 78 05 36 *Fax 02 54 78 22 78. Website: www.orangerie-du-chateau.fr. Set menus from 32 € to 66 €, a la carte 70 €. Closed Sunday evening, Monday lunchtime in high season, Tuesday in low season, Wednesday and mid-February to mid-March.* Jean-Marc Molvaux has become the Loir et Cher's most admired and most decorated chef in the ten years since he set up shop in this 15thc. listed building, ideally situated opposite the chateau. Formerly of the Hauts de Loire, at Onzain, and Bernard Robin at Bracieux, not far from here, Jean-Marc now cooks for the local nobility in this privileged and aristocratic setting. The menu consolidates rather than revolutionising, and is flawlessly executed: open blue lobster ravioli, with juice from the press and Aquitaine caviar, roast scallops on an onion puree and blackcurrant juice, fennel *choucroute*, young Vendome pigeon carcass in a spiced crumble, with quinoa seeds, and the legs confit in cannelloni, with a reduction of cooking juices; mango and Victoria pineapple ravioli *a la passion,* guava sorbet. The service is very efficient, and some of the tables have a fine view of the castle.

Bracieux

LE RELAIS DE BRACIEUX 1 avenue de Chambord ✆ 02 54 46 41 22 *Fax 02 54 46 03 69. Website: www.relaisbracieux.com. Set menus from 40 € to 120 €, a la carte 70 €. Closed Tuesday, Wednesday and from 20 December to late January.* Bernard Robin has been feeding the gourmets in his delightful and opulent coaching inn a few kilometres from Chambord for 30 years now. The horses are no more, on the old Paris-Bordeaux road, but the house is still there, as solid as ever. The dining room can be rather empty some days, owing no doubt to the lack of an on-site hotel, yet Bernard Robin continues to work with his customary generosity. His iced tomato emulsion with celery salt, small Breton sardines and avocado sorbet-style, steamed turbot, white Sologne asparagus, light morel cream with lemon conserve, spit-roast Touraine hazel grouse truffled under the skin, ratte potato puree with salted butter, Sologne strawberry feuillantine, cristallised lavender flowers and *confiture de lait* ice cream are both regional and contemporary, at their best in this discreet bourgeois setting overlooking a charming landscaped garden. Splendid Loire wine list, unadventurous when it comes to other wines, but solidly reputable with its Burgundies and Bordeaux.

Chambord castle

Chaumont-sur-Tharonne

LA CROIX BLANCHE DE SOLOGNE * 5, place de l'Eglise © 02 54 88 55 12.** *Fax 02 54 88 60 40. Restaurant closed Tuesday, Wednesday and Thursday lunchtime. 18 rooms from 65 € to 95 €. Breakfast 9 €. Set menus from 21 € to 55 €.* This has long been a reputed establishment, where the chefs - all women since the 18thc.- have always enchanted visitors to this friendly corner of Sologne. Local specialities, such as carp fillets in Touraine Gamay wine, Albicoco rabbit (a reference to the film-maker who adapted Le Grand Meaulnes by Sologne author Alain Fournier) or *mique royale* (regional recipe based on kind of poached bread dough). Beautiful rooms in authentic regional style complete your stay.

Lamotte-Beuvron

HOTEL RESTAURANT TATIN ** 5, avenue de Vierzon © 02 54 88 00 03. *Hôtel Logis de France - 2 fireplaces. 14 rooms from 58 €. Breakfast 8.50 €. Closed Sunday evening and Monday. Set menus from 27 € to 51 €.* Enter the famous Tatins sisters' lair, where the myth itself was born: one of the sisters, falling behind in her preparation, had to invent a dessert, and thus the celebrated Tarte Tatin was created by accident, like so many culinary successes. Chef Martial Caille has found his place in that atmosphere which seems to linger on from the sisters' era. His cuisine is a delicate combination of condiments and spices, attuned to the seasons. The tarte Tatin is there, of course, golden and melting in the mouth. Why not extend your stay in one of the delightful hotel rooms, maybe still inhabited by the *demoiselles*?

Romorantin-Lanthenay

GRAND HOTEL DU LION D'OR 69 rue Georges-Clemenceau © 02 54 94 15 15 *Fax 02 54 88 24 87. Website: www.hotelliondor.fr. Set menus from 90 € to 130 €, a la carte 110 €. Closed Tuesday lunchtime, 19 February -31 March and 13-24 November.* Coming back to the Lion d'Or at Romorantin is rather like returning to a family home, finding the same unique comforts and seeing the old familiar faces. Didier Clement has been giving of his best for 25 years in this splendid Renaissance mansion, built by one of Francois I's friends. He is always full of new projects (a Napoleon III-style awning with wrought iron guardrail now decorates the entrance) but makes sure his *cuisine* stays close to the natural ingredients without being over-demonstrative: Breton langoustines with saffron, chutney, peas *mousseux*, skate wing with ketchup butter, Malossol vegetables, dory and crab, potatoes with citronelle and sweet peppers, suckling veal chop with chanterelles, curd ravioli with sage, apricot millefeuille and olive oil verdale and fennel prove his point.The cellar is extraordinary for the Loire, having over 1,000 recommended bottles and containing some hitherto untasted vintages, quincy and pouilly fume in particular, specially created for the restaurant.

LOIRET

Combreux

AUBERGE DE COMBREUX ** 35, route de Gâtinais © 02 38 46 89 89. *Fax 02 38 59 36 19. Website : www.auberge-de-combreux.fr. Gastronomic cuisine.Open every day except Monday and Friday lunchtime. Annual closing from mid-December to late January. Service from 12 noon to 2pm and 7pm to 9pm. Set menus 19 € (except weekends) 29 € and 36 €. Average price a la carte 30 €. 19 rooms from 53 € to 79 €. Breakfast 9 €. Swimming pool. Tennis. Cycling. Fixed prices for seminars. Animals admitted. Car park.* This charming old coaching inn is located in the pretty village of Combreux. Manoo and Julien Ozanne welcome you most attentively. After an aperitif in the lounge, you discover the dining room with its exposed beams, straw-bottomed chairs and intimate ambiance, and the veranda opening onto the garden with a view of the trees. Chef Elisabeth Blanchard also plays the piano, an extra personal touch added to her regional cooking skills. The menu is seasonal, renewed three times a year, and deliciously authentic. You'll want to stay longer, so why not sample the comfortable hotel facilities, swimming pool and tennis court and a pleasant walk through the village?

Courtenay

AUBERGE DE LA CLE DES CHAMPS * Route de Joigny-les-Quatre-Croix © 02 38 97 42 68.** *Fax 02 38 97 38 10. 7 rooms from 71 € to 128 €. Set menus from 25 € to 45 €.* This 17thc. inn is located outside Courtenay in a country setting. You'll appreciate the warm welcome and quiet, sunny hours spent relaxing by the outdoor heated pool. Traditional cuisine, carefully prepared with local produce. Fine wine list, including Loire, Bordeaux and Burgundy.

Gien

LE P'TIT BOUCHON 66, rue Bernard-Palissy ✆ 02 38 67 84 40. *Closed Saturday lunchtime and Sunday. Lunchtime set menu 16 €, evenings from 20 € to 23 €.* A friendly place with a relaxed atmosphere, where no-one stands on ceremony. A blackboard suggests some simple, classic dishes to enjoy in the rustic setting.

LA POULARDE ** 13, quai de Nice ✆ 02 38 67 36 05. *Fax 02 38 38 18 78. Annual closing 15 days in January. Closed Sunday evening and Monday lunchtime. 9 rooms from 49 € to 63.50 €. Set menus from 19.50 € to 60 € (Rabelais degustation menu).* An excellent classic hotel-restaurant on the banks of the Loire, facing a large park. Elegant dining rooms, a regional menu with its typical specialities, like pikeperch supreme in Chinon wine, and game in season, such as knobs of venison with spiced pears. The menus are well composed and the service efficient. The rooms are well-equipped, and some have a view of the river.

Orléans

LES ANTIQUAIRES 2, rue au Lin ✆ 02 38 53 52 35. *Website: www.restaurantlesantiquaires.com. Private air-conditioned salons. Closed Sunday evening and Monday. Set business menu Affaires 38 € (except Saturday evening and Sunday lunchtime), Saveurs Gourmandes menu 46 € and Degustation menu 66 €.* In this elegant bourgeoise house, the top-of-the-range setting is a perfect match for Philippe Bardeau's cuisine. As a Maitre Cuisinier de France, he offers sophisticated and tasty dishes, which seem to contribute to the serenity and feeling of well-being that linger in the place - or perhaps that's the wine list. Taste the Sologne venison minute, spread with cepes and stuffings, or wild boar and beef with foie gras. And the hot chocolate in sabayon, served cold. Delicious!

EUGENE 24, rue Sainte-Anne ✆ 02 38 53 82 64. *Fax 02 38 54 31 89. Closed Saturday lunchtime, Sunday and Monday lunchtime. Menus from 22 € to 52 €.* Located between the Place du Martroi and boulevard Alexandre-Martin, this restaurant boasts a pleasant setting and a cosy ambiance. The dining room is prettily decorated in warm tones, and the cooking shows considerable Provencal influence. Come and taste the subtle mix of flavours, creativity and imagination; this is *haute cuisine* at its best.

Champagne-Ardenne

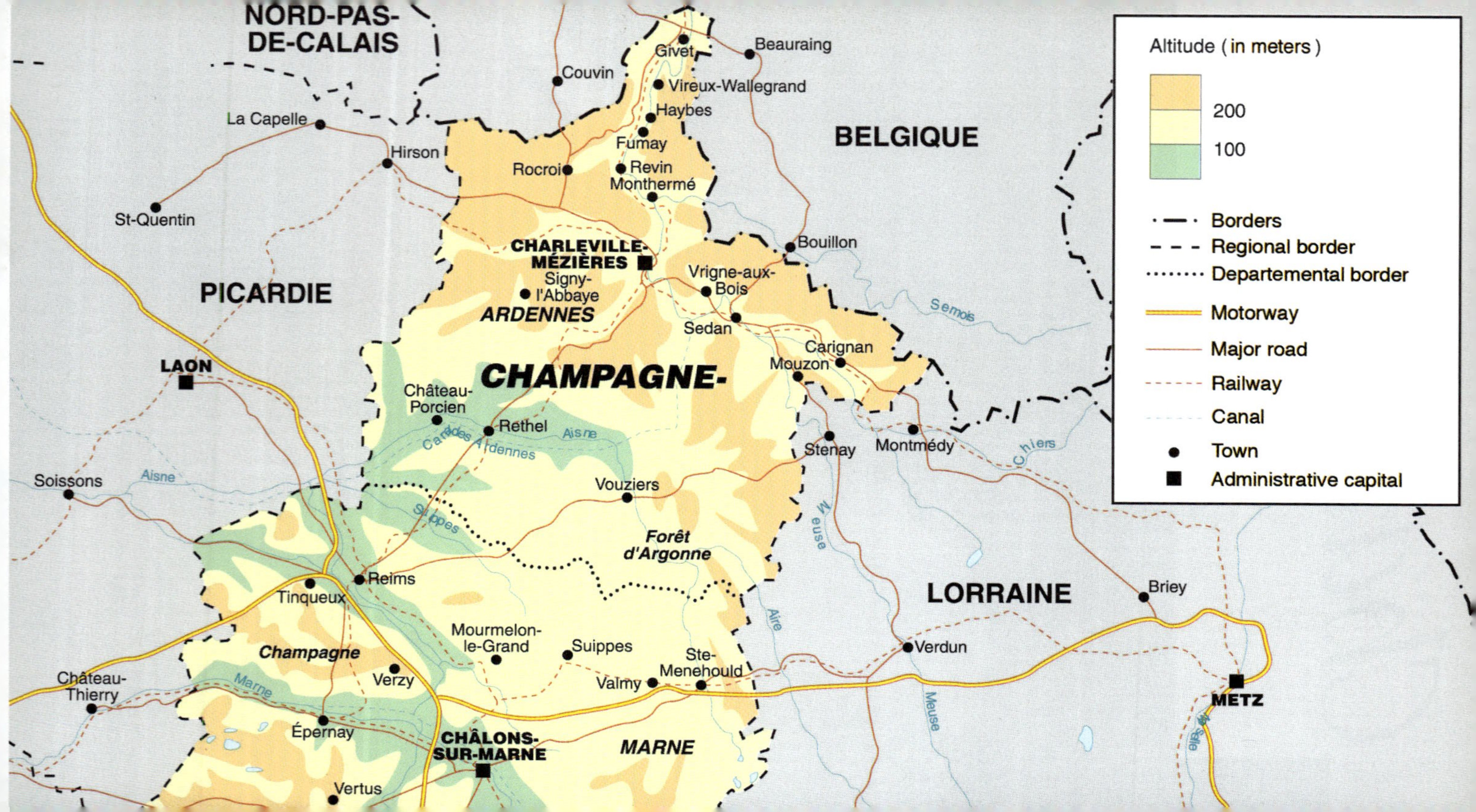

NORD-PAS-DE-CALAIS
PICARDIE
BELGIQUE
CHAMPAGNE-
ARDENNES
LORRAINE
MARNE
Champagne
Forêt d'Argonne
Givet
Beauraing
Couvin
Vireux-Wallegrand
Haybes
Fumay
La Capelle
Hirson
Rocroi
Revin
Monthermé
St-Quentin
CHARLEVILLE-MÉZIÈRES
Signy-l'Abbaye
Bouillon
Vrigne-aux-Bois
Sedan
Semois
Carignan
Mouzon
LAON
Château-Porcien
Rethel
Aisne
Canal des Ardennes
Stenay
Montmédy
Chiers
Soissons
Vouziers
Meuse
Suippes
Reims
Tinqueux
Aire
Briey
Mourmelon-le-Grand
Verdun
Verzy
Ste-Menehould
Valmy
Château-Thierry
Marne
Épernay
CHÂLONS-SUR-MARNE
METZ
Moselle
Vertus
Altitude (in meters)
200
100
Borders
Regional border
Departemental border
Motorway
Major road
Railway
Canal
Town
Administrative capital

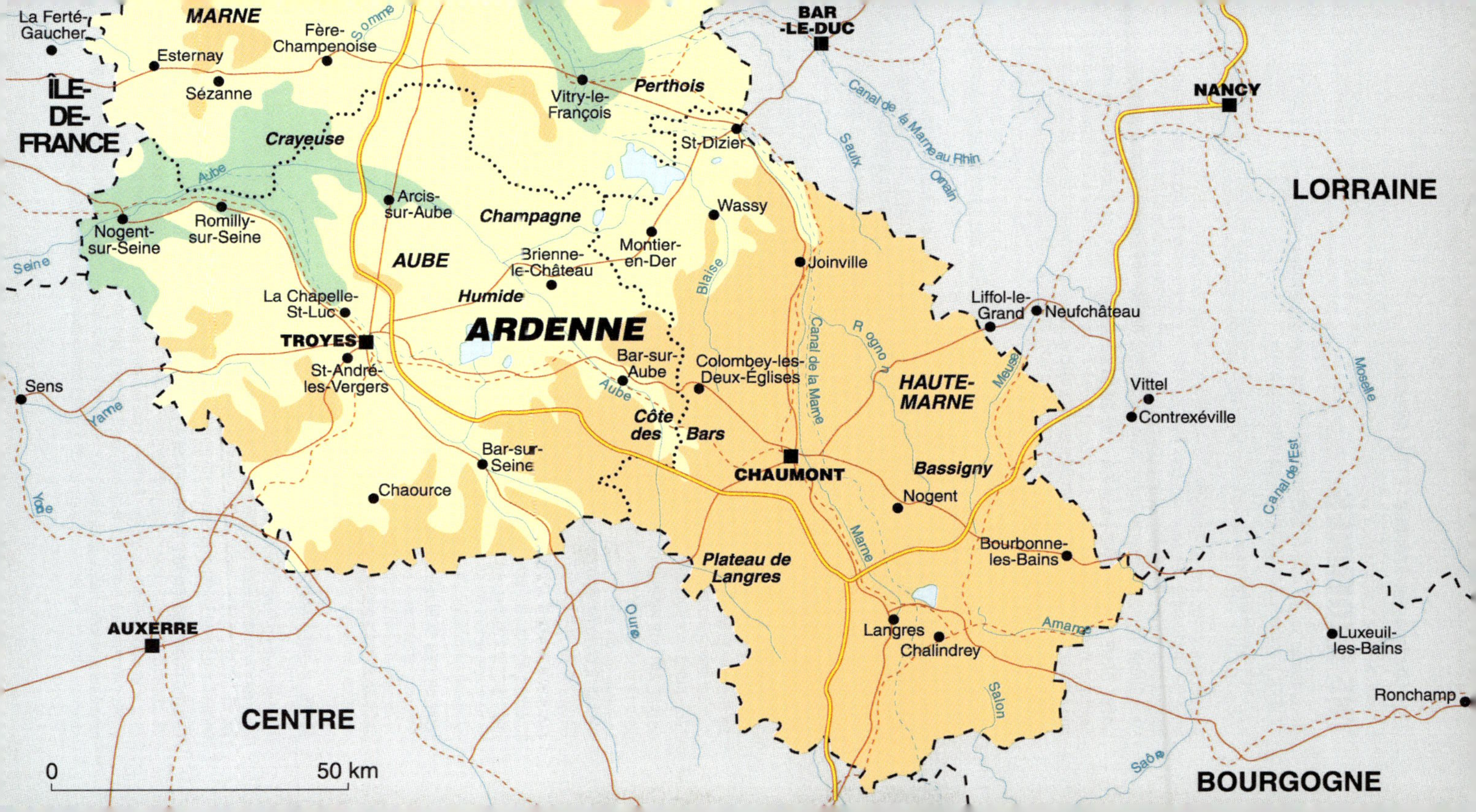

LORRAINE
BOURGOGNE
CENTRE
ÎLE-DE-FRANCE
MARNE
La Ferté-Gaucher
Esternay
Sézanne
Fère-Champenoise
Somme
Vitry-le-François
Perthois
BAR-LE-DUC
NANCY
Canal de la Marne au Rhin
Saulx
Ornain
St-Dizier
Crayeuse
Aube
Nogent-sur-Seine
Romilly-sur-Seine
Seine
Arcis-sur-Aube
Champagne
AUBE
Brienne-le-Château
Montier-en-Der
Wassy
Joinville
Blaise
Humide
La Chapelle-St-Luc
TROYES
ARDENNE
St-André-les-Vergers
Sens
Yonne
Yonne
Bar-sur-Aube
Colombey-les-Deux-Églises
Canal de la Marne
Rognon
Liffol-le-Grand
Neufchâteau
Meuse
HAUTE-MARNE
Vittel
Contrexéville
Moselle
Côte des Bars
Bar-sur-Seine
Chaource
CHAUMONT
Bassigny
Nogent
Canal de l'Est
Marne
Bourbonne-les-Bains
Plateau de Langres
Ource
AUXERRE
Langres
Chalindrey
Amance
Luxeuil-les-Bains
Salon
Ronchamp
Saône
0
50 km

THE ARDENNES

The Ardennes served as a protective rampart in the days of European conflicts, but they are also a romantic place with their gentle hills and extensive forests.

Charleville-Mézières

A prefecture in two halves: Charleville for trade and industry, and historic Mézières, a military site since the 10thc. Arthur Rimbaud was born here (and didn't much care for it), and the town is also the international marionette capital. Set on a peninsula in a loop of the Meuse, it boasts a paved and arcaded Place Ducale, Ardennes Museum, Notre Dame d'Espérance Basilica and a thriving pedestrian sector.

NOTRE DAME D'ESPERANCE BASILICA ✆ 03 24 57 53 92. *Open every day from 9am-6pm except Sunday morning (Mass from 11am-1pm). Guided tours in July & August, Tuesday & Thursday: 3pm or by appointment.* Flamboyant Gothic with Renaissance touches. The contemporary stained-glass windows are by Rene Durrbach.

FORT DES AYVELLES. Built after the Franco-Prussian War (1870), this fort has resisted the onslaughts of time and its enemies. It is in two parts, the battery above the Ayvelles being linked to the fort by a corridor-shaped dugout, defended by towers at intervals down its length, and containing some medieval and Renaissance elements (the look-out on one of the towers).

GRAND MARIONNETTISTE. Designed by monumental clockmaker Jacques Monastier. Every day from 10am-9pm, you can follow the lives of the Four Aymon Sons and their horse Bayart in four tableaux. The puppet master's giant hands work the strings from inside the little castle. Not to be missed!

PLACE DUCALE. Emperor Charles' imperious statue has towered over this beautiful square since 1899. The Place Ducale reminds you of Arras and its Flemish houses.

MUSEE DE L'ARDENNE 31, place Ducale ✆ 03 24 32 44 60. *Open every day except Monday: 10am-12 noon and 2pm-6pm. Closed 1 January, 1 May and 25 December. Admission: adult 4 (includes the Rimbaud Museum). Under-18s free.* Housed in a 17th, 18th and 19thc. building in the Ducal Palace, this museum contains the Charleville region's historical and artistic heritage, including collections from the Neolithic to Merovingian periods. The town's specific treasures are on show: the marionettes (you discover the Grand Marionnettiste's mechanism and some temporary exhibitions), Corvisart Hospital's 120 earthenware pots and a huge collection of 3,000 coins (the museum owns 30,000 in all).

MUSEE ARTHUR RIMBAUD Quai Rimbaud ✆ 03 24 32 44 65. *Open every day: 10am-12 noon and 2pm-6pm. Closed Monday. Admission: adult 4 (includes the Ardennes Museum).* At the foot of Mount Olympus, on the corner of 'his' quay, the town honours Rimbaud's genius with a museum housed in the Old Mill. It contains various documents; writings and photos soberly displayed. You discover the poet's life and work, and his early years in Charleville.

MAISON RIMBAUD 7, quai Rimbaud. Opened in October 2004 (Rimbaud Year) this centre is devoted to writing and travel. Each room represents one of the author's destinations: Brussels, Marseille. London and Harar in Ethiopia, with a film projection and sound track. A resident writers' centre exists in the same place, where young authors can work, and talk about their writing. (Ask at the Rimbaud Museum for opening times, 03 24 32 44 65).

MANOIR DES SORCIERES 55, rue de Montjoly ✆ 06 63 64 75 80. *Open July & August, Saturday & Sunday afternoon.* A real witches' house! The last Ardennes witches have taken over this venerable 1775 residence in the town centre, to hold coven meetings and practise their arts. You can take part in their experiments and learn some herbal remedies, in each of the eight disturbing rooms. Those precious books on the library shelves may well reveal their secrets. Wonderfully creepy.

Bogny-sur-Meuse - Château-Regnault

The Four Aymon Sons' Rock peaks above the town, its four quartzite points calling to mind the four legendary horsemen. Bogny is the first big village on the Meuse downriver of Charleville, and is known for its metallurgy and ironwork. The Metallurgy Museum retraces this industry's development. The Mineral and Fossil Museum is also worth a visit.

CENTRE D'EXPOSITION DES MINERAUX ET FOSSILES DES ARDENNES 32, rue Maurice Louis ✆ 03 24 32 05 02. *Open 15 June-31 August, Tuesday-Sunday: 2pm-6pm. September: open weekends: 2pm-6pm. Admission: adult 2 €, under-12s free.* Local geology is on show in nine exhibition rooms. Samples of the department's biggest mineral and fossil deposits can be viewed: fluorine, quartz (rock crystal) limestone and even native gold. There are some rare and spectacular fossils from the Paleontological Ardennes, and on the first floor, minerals and fossils from national and international sources.

MUSEE DE LA METALLURGIE 103, rue de la Vallée ✆ 03 24 32 11 99. *July & August, open every day: 10am-12 noon and 2pm-6pm. May, June & September: 2pm-6pm. Admision: adult 3 €, child 1.30 €.* Ardennes metallurgy has been the industry's spearhead for centuries. You can see old trades and crafts; nailmakers and smiths, and working machines: for making nuts and bolts; milling machines; reels. You'll be moved by the forge wheel worked by a dog, and fascinated at the complexity of certain ancient tools. Technical instructions, paintings and activities bring this industrial heritage to life.

Fromelennes

This village is known for its caves, but also has some interesting buildings: Saint Laurent Church, Sainte Rolande de Flohimont Chapel (1706), an 18thc. château and Flohimont Fountain. Industrial remains in the form of quarries are scattered through the area.

GROTTES DE NICHET ✆ 03 24 42 00 14 (mairie). *Open every day, 1 June-31 August: 10am-12 noon and 1.30pm-7pm. 1 April-31 May and 1-30 September: 2pm-6pm. Guided tour: adult 5 €, 10-15s 2.50 €, 6-9s 1.50 €.* The Nichet Caves go back to the primary era and are hollowed out of ancient Givet limestone. Twenty rooms are spread over 3 levels, 50m deep. There are a lot of animal traces (mammoths, aurochs and Nichet pheasants), and humans are thought to have lived here in prehistoric times, not to mention the legendary Nutons; underground imps with magic powers.

Fumay

This town used to be known for its slate production, as its colours and Slate Museum remind you. It is also the capital of white pudding with onions, celebrated with a festival every July. Make sure you see the Flemish Gothic Saint Georges Church in beautiful yellow stone, and stroll along the pleasant riverbanks which give the town much of its character.

MUSEE DE L'ARDOISE Rue Martin Coupaye ✆ 03 24 41 10 25. *Open every day, April-September: 10am-12 noon and 2pm-6pm. Monday-Friday, October-March: 1.30pm-6pm. Admission: adult 2.50 €, child 1.50 €. Guided tours 2.50 €.* Fumay slate has been known and used all over the region for 8 centuries. The museum, housed in the former Carmelite convent, retraces the industry's history. Documents, old tools, manufacturing methods and photo exhibitions on the escailleurs' (slate quarrymen's) techniques and daily life. Cellars and wells are reconstructed.

Givet

500m from the Belgian border, Givet has a long and eventful history, well-preserved medieval heritage (thanks perhaps to Charlemont Fortress' deterrent powers) a lively town centre and a river port: plenty of reasons to stop off there.

CENTRE EUROPEEN DES METIERS D'ART 10, quai des Fours ✆ 03 24 42 73 36. *Closed Sunday and Monday morning. Open all year (except Christmas and New Year's Day, and February): 10am-12 noon and 2.30pm-6pm. Admission free for individual visitors.* Showcase for the arts and crafts, from the Ardennes and elsewhere. 5,000 handcrafted objects are displayed, from leather to wooden toys, ceramic, jewellery and table arts.

FORT DE CHARLEMONT ✆ 03 24 42 03 54. *Open 1 July-31 August, Tuesday-Sunday: 1pm-6pm. Guided tours: adult 3 €, child 1.50 €.* In 1555, Charles V had an invincible citadel built on Givet's limestone spur. The fortress became French in 1680, and Vauban, true to type, added a wall in that same year.

Liart

A typical 12thc.Thierache village. The pleasant 16th and 17thc. church was reinforced with a machicolated keep.

MAISON DE LA THIERACHE ✆ **03 24 54 48 33.** *Open every day except Christmas & New Year's Eve. Thematic visit: 2.30pm-5.30pm. Ask for timetable of activities. Admission: adult 7 €, child 3.50 €. Bookings only.* Local life and working habits are on display in this traditional farm, along with agricultural and domestic tools. The activities on offer in the 'teaching' farm include the afternoon snack where you can sample homemade produce (sugar tart, gingerbread, apple juice). There is also a holiday centre, hiking paths, field trips for schools and a children's farm. You can hire mountain bikes (book in advance).

Mouzon

This border town's fortifications have protected the old houses grouped around the big and beautiful church, particularly the 'Spanish Houses', reminders of the 17thc. Spanish siege. Mouzon has a mooring-place on the river and is a listed Green Holiday Resort.

NOTRE DAME ABBEY CHURCH ✆ **03 24 26 56 11.** *Open every day: 8am-7pm. Guided tours (bookings only). Admission: adult 2.50 €, child 0.75 €.* The Benedictines founded this abbey in the 9thc. The present church was begun in the 12thc., burned down then restored, and finished in the 15thc. in fine Gothic style, with typical pointed spires.

MUSEE DU FEUTRE Place du Colombier ✆ **03 24 26 50 76.** *Open April-September. June-August, every day: 2pm-7pm. Admission: adult 3.50 €.* The world's oldest textile is displayed in a working production line, a yurt and some art and design collections.

Rethel

Sadly, Verlaine's old quarters were wiped out during the two World Wars. The town is still as lively, but with wide streets and squares, and reconstructed buildings. The wall paintings in the Town Hall give you an idea of Rethel in the 19thc., and there is still Saint Nicolas Church, hit but saved and restored, with its beautiful Flamboyant Gothic portal.

Revin

Pretty Revin began in a loop of the Meuse, but has spread out into the surrounding country. Plenty of pleasant walks on offer.

MUSEE DU VIEUX REVIN Maison Espagnole, quai Edgar Quinet ✆ **03 24 40 19 59.** *Open May-September: 10am-12 noon and 2pm-6.30pm. Admission: adult 1.80 €, child 1.50 €, under-12s free.* This ancient half-timbered 'Spanish' house is a reminder of past times. The ground floor houses an early 20thc. period room, and there is an exhibition of local history (renewed each year) on the first. Upstairs you discover Revin's casting industry.

Rocroi

This star-shaped fortified town north of Revin is an amazing example of military urban planning. It was built in 1555, and reinforced by Vauban in 1675.

MUSEE DE LA BATAILLE DE ROCROY Place du Luxembourg ✆ **03 24 54 20 06.** *Open 1 may-15 October: 10am-12 noon and 2pm-6 pm (5pm in low season). Admission: adult 4 €, under-12s (accompanied by an adult) free.* The museum retraces the Thirty Years' War that laid waste to Europe between 1618 and 1648, and in particular Condé's rout of the Spanish on 19 May 1643. 2, 500 hand-painted lead soldiers enact the 6-hr battle (10,000 dead) in their respective regiments.

Sedan

Strategically important since its beginnings, Sedan boasts Europe's biggest fortress. It is also known for carpet manufacturing. The town's historical and artistic past lives on in the Town Hall (1822), Turenne Monument (1823) and the Menil quarter's 17th and 18thc. houses.

CHATEAU FORT Place du Château ✆ **03 24 27 73 73.** *www.sedan-bouillon.org. Individual visits with audio guide. 1 January-14 March and 16 September-31 December, weekdays: 1.30pm-4.30pm; weekends, school & public holidays: 10am-12 noon and 1.30pm-4.30pm, closed Monday. 15 March-30 June: 1.30pm-5pm. 1 July-31 August: 10am-6pm. Admission: adult 6.90 €, 6-16s 4.60 €.* Europe's most extensive fortress is residential as well as military. Built by the Ducs de la Marck, it measures 35,000m^2 on 7 storeys. Inside, the Historium narrates its long and eventful story. Beautiful view from the ramparts. A 3-star hotel-restaurant is now open inside the fortress.

MUSEE DU CHATEAU FORT DE SEDAN Place du Château ✆ **03 24 27 73 73.** *Opening hours and ticket prices same as fortress.* Housed in the fortress, the museum contains 16th, 17th and 18thc. tapestries from Brussels, Beauvais, Aubusson and Audenarde, and objets excavated from the fortress. There are paintings illustrating the 1870 war (Etude du panorama de Sedan by Louis Braun), 17th, 18th and 19thc. pewter and art objects made in Sedan: lace, silverware and weapons.

MANUFACTURE DU TAPIS POINT 13, bd. Gambetta ✆ 03 24 29 04 60. *Open all year, Tuesday-Saturday: 8am-12 noon and 2pm-6pm. Individual visitors, admission free.* You must visit this working carpet factory, whose workshops have been using the same techniques since 1878. Instructive and interesting.

Vendresse

This picturesque village is well worth the visit. Things to see: the 1830 blast furnace; a beautiful castle-like farm where the King of Prussia stayed in 1870; and the fortified church and arboretum (Bois de la Vierge) with its oratory. It contains an avenue of Douglas Firs, brought here as seeds by the creator Pol Bouin in 1912.

CHATEAU DE LA CASSINE ✆ 03 24 35 44 84. *www.la-cassine.com.* Louis de Gonzague, Duc de Rethel had a country residence built here in 1571, and founded a Cordeliers monastery on the site in 1585. The Italian-style building was burnt down in 1697. The present ruined castle, put up in 1850, was also the victim of fire in the 20thc. Every summer, the castle's Cultural Association organises son et lumière shows (Saturdays in July and August).

COUVENT DE LA CASSINE ✆ 03 24 35 44 84. *Admission free.* The castle was destroyed by fire for the second time in 1940, leaving only the monastery's cloister and monks' dormitory. The chapel and attic framework is strikingly shaped like an upside-down boat hull. The monastery became a farm during the Revolution, but the whole set-up is still very beautiful, even in ruins.

DOMAINE DE VENDRESSE Rue du Haut Fourneau ✆ 03 24 35 57 73. *Open every day: 10am-6pm. July & August: 10am-8pm. March & October: 2pm-5pm. Open weekends: 10am-6pm. Groups by appointment only: 10am-5pm. Admission: adult 6 €, child 3.50 €.* The Ardennes' casting industry's last witness. This 19thc. blast furnace is open to the public, and you can relive the casting experience through film, computerised images and sound track. The coal hall illustrates metallurgy through the ages, The site also covers fish-breeding, which later replaced casting, with aquariums of fresh-water fish (pike and silurid). Outside, the 6ha. estate contains fishponds, water-gardens and fountains; you can observe the fish in their natural habitat.

Vouziers

This is charming countryside, full of contrasts. Not far from the pre-Ardenne ridges, the land is given over to livestock and forestry, with the wood-panelled Porcian settlement in the Aisne Valley, below the Champagne hills.

AUTORAIL PICASSO ✆ 03 24 71 47 60. *Every Sunday, June-September.* Every summer, the Picasso railcar takes passengers for a trip in the southeast Ardennes. It passes through Voncq, Vouziers, and Saint Morel on the Attigny-Challerange line, at the gentle speed of 40km/h. A relaxing way to spend a day sightseeing.

HAUTE-MARNE

This peaceful department lies between the Vosges and Burgundy, among game forests and fertile valleys. It contains a little town which looms large in French (and international) history: Colombey-les-Deux-Eglises, last home of General de Gaulle.

Bourbonne-les-Bains

Champagne-Ardennes' only watering place. The beautiful scenery with its forests, prairies and solid village houses provides a foretaste of the Vosges.

NOTRE DAME CHURCH. Commissioned in 1160, at a time of great religious trends, this church has survived the onslaught of war and fire. Though built in a transition period, it is more Gothic than Romanesque.

COMPAGNIE DES THERMES Place des Thermes ✆ 03 25 90 07 20. *www.valvital.fr. Bookings 7am-10.30am (except Sunday). Monday: 6.30am-10.30am.* Traditional treatment is on offer (18 days) or an individual formula. These include getting into shape, for a morning (40 €), 3 days (100 -110 €) or a week (190 -215 €). You have four treatments per day: hydromassage; water jets, baths, sauna, etc.

MUSEE MUNICIPAL/MEDIATHEQUE Parc du Château ✆ 03 25 90 69 47. *Open all year, every day except Monday, Thursday and Sunday.* Discover the town's spa past in this museum, with the remains of Gallo-Roman baths. Another room contains paintings by local artists.

Chaumont

A pleasant town half-hidden in greenery.

KEEP. Built in the 11th and 12thc. on a natural outcrop overlooking the Suize Valley, this is the last remains of the Comtes de Champagne's castle. Its terrace provides a magnificent view.

SAINT JEAN BAPTISTE BASILICA. One of Chaumonts' oldest buildings, with its 13thc. nave and 15th and 16thc. chancel and transept. The basilica houses a high altar and pulpit (by local sculptor Bouchardon) that are real works of art.

JESUIT CHAPEL. This 17thc. chapel (1629) is typical of the Jesuit style. The splendid decoration includes Claude Collignon's monumental reredos, where you see Bouchardon's Assumption.

TOURELLES. The fine 15th and 16thc. mansions in the old town are embellished with turrets and corbelling.

MUSEE D'ART ET D'HISTOIRE Place du Palais ✆ 03 25 03 01 99. *Open every day except Tuesday: 2pm-6pm (summer: 2.30pm-6.30pm). Admission: adult 1.50 €, children & students free.* The museum houses an archeology exhibition containing a rare bronze breastplate dating back to the 9thc. B.C.; sculptures including fragments from Claude de Lorraine's tomb by Dominique Florentin (16thc.) and 16th-20thc. paintings from the Flemish, Italian, French and Spanish Schools. Chaumont's glove industry is also represented.

Colombey-les-Deux-Eglises

A national tourist Mecca. The path between the General's home, La Boisserie, and the cemetery where he rests, is well-worn! Colombey is quiet, as befits a presidential village, and boasts an impressive Lorraine Cross in pink granite on the memorial overlooking the plain.

MEMORIAL CHARLES DE GAULLE RN19 ✆ 03 25 01 50 50. Open every day except Tuesday: 10am-12.30pm and 2pm-6pm, 1 April-31 October. Out of season: 10am-12 noon and 2pm-4pm. Admission:

The viaduct of Chaumont

adults 4 €, under-18s free. This pink granite Lorraine Cross is 43.5m high. At the foot, an exhibition displays medals, stamps and other memorabilia concerning the General's life, including his front-wheel drive 15CV.

LA BOISSERIE © **03 25 01 52 52.** *Open 15 April-15 October, every day:10am-12.30pm and 2pm-6.15pm (closed Monday in winter). Admission: Boisserie & Memorial, 7 €, Boisserie alone, 4 €, under-12s free.* You visit the main rooms on the ground floor of Charles de Gaulle's family home: dining-room, living-room, library, study, and the park.

Joinville

A historic town, with an impressive heritage.

CHATEAU DU GRAND JARDIN 5, ave. de la Marne © **03 25 94 17 54.** *www.legrandjardin.com. Open June-August: 9.30am-7pm. Other periods: 10am-12 noon and 2pm-6pm. Admission to gardens: adult 4 €, over-10s 1.50 €, under-10s free.* This Renaissance castle was put up by Claude de Lorraine, for his wife's pleasure and entertainment. The gardens and orchards have been faithfully restored in keeping with the period: fruit trees, flowerbeds, varied and heady scents.

NOTRE DAME CHURCH. The oldest parts date back to the 12thc. The beautiful *Mise au Tombeau* (Burial) with its fine and supple lines is the church's masterpiece.

SAINTE ANNE CHAPEL. Built in 1502 by Gerard d'Allichamp, canon of the castle's Saint Laurent Church. The style is sober (nave with two bays), decorated with windows by local glass artists.

MUSEE DE L'AUDITOIRE Rue de l'Auditoire © **03 25 94 43 51.** *Guided tours (guides on site at weekends; tours by appointment only during the week) Sunday afternoon: 3pm-6pm, mid-May-October; Saturdays and Sundays in July & August (same times). Adult 4 €, concessions 2 €.* Discover the original cachots, reconstructions of a lord of the manor's court, Claude de Lorraine's funeral chamber and the Joinville Princes. Joinville's history is retraced in 24 tableaux. Evening visits take place the last Thursday and Friday in July and first Thursday and Friday in August.

Langres

The walls are impressive, even seen from a distance. A statue of native son Denis Diderot stands proudly in the central square.

FORTIFICATIONS. The 3km covered walk boasts 7 towers and 6 gates (one Gallo-Roman) and a great view. The Petit Saut Tower (1521) has a fine rib-vault above a central pillar at the top of the stairs; the Navarre and d'Orval Towers are of interest too. On hot days, lizards come out of the cracks to bask in the sun and amuse the kids.

SAINT MAMMES CATHEDRAL. 12thc. Burgundian Romanesque building, with a fine nave (23m high). Things to see: Amoncourt Chapel, the font, 16thc. tapestries on both sides of the transept and a 15thc. carved door.

MUSEE D'ART ET D'HISTOIRE Place du Centenaire © **03 25 87 08 05.** *Open every day: 10am-12 noon and 2pm-5pm. 1 April-30 October, until 6pm. Closed Tuesday. Admission free.* Discover the Bacchus mosaic (2ndc. A.D.) and archaeology, prehistory, Gallo-Roman and Egyptian collections. The paintings include Tassel, Michelin and Gillot, with Bouchardon and Petitot's sculptures. Earthenware, pewter and Langres knives grace the Decorative Arts section.

Nogent

Nogent flourished in the 19thc., with its several million craftsmen, replacing older Langres as regional knife-making capital.

MUSEE DE LA COUTELLERIE-ESPACE PELLETIER Place Charles de Gaulle ✆ 03 25 31 89 21. *Open every day, March-November: 10am-12 noon and 2pm-6pm. July & August, 7 days a week. Closed Tuesday, March-May & October. Admission: adult 2 €, child 1 €.* Nicolas Pelletier, skilled 19thc. knife-maker, has given his name to this museum next to the old Georget workshop. He transformed Nogent knives into works of art, giving them a certain style. Fine scissors, surgical instruments and tools are also on show.

MUSEE DU PATRIMOINE COUTELIER 2bis, ave. du 8 Mai ✆ 03 25 31 70 63. *Open every day except Monday: 2pm-6pm.* The Nogent knife industry from its early days: 18th and 19thc. knives, scissors and surgical instruments.

Saint-Dizier

Originally a 13thc. fortified village, now the Haute-Marne's busiest town.

CIRCUIT GUIMARD. Saint-Dizier foundry cast the works of Art Nouveau architect Hector Guimard (Paris metro entrances). About 100 houses proudly show off his window surrounds, balconies etc.

MUSEE MUNICIPAL Allee Jean-François Lescuyer ✆ 03 25 07 31 50. *Open Tuesday, Thursday & Friday: 2pm-6pm. Wednesday, 2nd and 4th Saturday of the month: 10am-12 noon and 2pm-6pm. Admission free.* Housed in the old Post Office, the museum deals with with local history and environment: sea fossils, flying reptiles, and the only Bernissartensis iguanodon ever found in France; Gallo-Roman archaeology and Merovingian treasures, a bird collection (Lescuyer), Fine Arts and cast-iron works, including Guimard.

MAISON DU COMBATTANT Route d'Hoerincourt ✆ 03 29 70 26 86. *Admission free every last Saturday of the month (except in December) 8 May and 11 November: 2pm-6pm.* This new museum next to airbase 113 displays souvenirs from the wars between 1870 and the present day (letters, diaries, aircraft-carrier models, weapons). Thought-provoking.

REIMS AND THE MARNE

Reims cathedral

Reims

Famous for its bubbly, and French Royal history. Clovis was baptised here by Bishop Rémi in 498, and Joan of Arc had Charles VII crowned here too. The Franco-German armistice was signed in Reims on 7 May 1945. The cathedral, Palais du Tau, Saint Remi Basilica and abbey are all UNESCO-listed.

NOTRE DAME CATHEDRAL. *Closed during services. Guided tours (Tourist Office) from Easter onwards, Saturday & Sunday: 2.30pm.* Gothic masterpiece built in 1211, chosen for royal coronations in memory of Clovis' baptism. The north side portal bears the famous Smiling Angel statue; 2,300 statues in all decorate the outside of the church. Many of the 13thc. stained glass windows have been destroyed; those left were saved and restored by the Simon glass-workers. Chagall designed the blue stained glass in the apse chapel (1974) that shimmers in the light.

PALAIS DU TAU 2, place du Cardinal Luçon. *www.monum.fr. Open every day except Monday: 9.30am-6.30pm (in season).* Contains cathedral statuary and the 'Fort Roy Clovis' tapestries (Arras, 15thc.) hanging in the royal banqueting hall. You can also see the 13thc. Archbishop's Chapel, 12thc. cathedral treasure chamber, and Saint Ursula's 'nave' (15thc.). Other rooms cover Charles X's coronation, the last to be held in Reims.

SAINT REMI BASILICA. *Open 8am-dusk (7pm at the latest).* Houses Saint Rémi's body. In 760, a Benedictine community settled on the site built to house pilgrims, and the basilica was extended and consecrated in 852, but disappeared around 1,000. The present Northern French Romanesque church (1049) hosts a *musique et lumière* show every Saturday, 30 June–6 October, at 9.30pm.Listed UNESCO World Heritage.

MUSEE AUTOMOBILE REIMS-CHAMPAGNE 84, ave. Georges Clemenceau © 03 26 82 83 84. *www.musee-automobile-reims-champagne.com. Open all year (except Tuesday): 10am-12 noon and 2pm-6pm (5pm November-March) Admission: adult 6 €, child 4 €(10-18s) family 15 €.* 200 vehicles from 1908 to the present day. Some were limited series (Alba, Meissier, Suère etc.) and there is one local Scar model. 80 pedal cars and motorbikes are on display. These old factory premises also house a period number plate collection and 4,000 miniature and toy cars.

MUSEE DE LA REDDITION 12, rue Franklin Roosevelt © 03 26 47 84 19. *Open all year: 10am-12 noon and 2pm-6pm. Closed Tuesdays and public holidays. Admission: 3 € with the pass découverte. Free every first Sunday of the month.* This technical college was Eisenhower's HQ, and the Third Reich's unconditional surrender was signed here on 7 May 1945. The negotiation room is still as it was then, and there is an exhibition on World War II and the role played by the United States.

MUSEE DES BEAUX ARTS 8, rue Chanzy © 03 26 47 28 44. *Open every day: 10am-12 noon and 2pm-6pm, except Tuesday.* The Fine Arts museum contains paintings, art objects, ceramic and sculpture. There are 25 canvases from 1460-1520, a series of portraits by father and son (Les Cranach) and French 17th and 18thc. works by Poussin, Fragonard and Boucher, while Corot, Millet, Sisley, Pissaro and Renoir's landscapes represent the 19thc.

MUSEE DU FORT DE LA POMPELLE RN44 – Route de Châlons-en-Champagne © 03 26 49 11 85 *Open (except Tuesday) 11am-6pm weekdays and 11am-7pm weekends and public holidays. Admission: adult 3.50 €, over-10s 1.50 €, under-10s free.* The 1914-1918 War Museum is housed in Pompelle Fort, 5km from Reims. Built after the 1870 war as part of the town's new fortifications (1880-1883), the fort contained six 155mm and four 138mm cannons, machine guns and 277 gunners were garrisoned in it. After 40 years of decay, the National André Maginot Federation bought the fort, and the town acquired it in 1968.

SAINT REMI ABBEY MUSEUM 55, rue Simon © 03 26 85 23 36. *Open every day: 2pm-6.30pm. Saturday & Sunday: 2pm-7pm.Admission: adult 3 €.* Learn about the abbey's history, the town's Gallo-Roman and military past, and regional archeology.

CHAMPAGNE. 200km of Gallo-Roman or medieval chalk quarries containing 250 million bottles of champagne are hidden underground. You can visit some of these prestigious cellars.

Foujita Chapel

Notre Dame de la Paix Chapel is an act of faith, of course, but also a gift, made in 1965 by René Lalou, chairman of Mumm champagne, to Japanese Buddhist painterLeonard Foujita. A contemporary of Picasso, Braque, Jacob and Modigliani, Foujita became a Catholic shortly after a mystical experience during a visit to Saint Remi Basilica. He designed the chapel himself, clearly influenced by Romanesque architecture, and decorated the inside. At nearly 80, he could be seen perched on mobile scaffolding, painting his 12 frescoes using a medieval technique that could not be touched up.

The Marne

Châlons-en-Champagne

Prefecture of the Marne and Champagne-Ardennes, Chalons has kept its medieval monuments, though no Gallo-Roman remains are left.

SAINT ETIENNE CATHEDRAL. Mass on Sunday at 9am. Only the crypt and one tower are left of the Romanesque church (1147). The 12th-16th stained-glass windows are exceptional, especially the Redemption (1147).

NOTRE DAME EN VAUX CHURCH. Impressive, with its spires and huge porch protecting the south side portal. inside, you will be struck by the harmonious proportions and diffuse light. There are 56 bells in the 19thc. peal; one of Europe's biggest.

MUSEE DU CLOITRE DE NOTRE DAME EN VAUX Rue Nicolas Durand ✆ 03 26 64 03 87. *Open all year, except Tuesday and public holidays: 1 April-30 September; 10am-12 noon and 2pm-6pm. 1 October-31 March: 10am-12 noon and 2pm-5pm (6pm weekends). Admission: adult 4.60 €, concessions 3.10 €, groups 4.10 €, under-17s free. Guided tour on request.* Behind Notre Dame, this museum houses the remains of the medieval cloister built by collegiate canons in 1170, and pulled down in 1759. Recent demolition work on the site uncovered some interesting finds, and more systematic excavation unearthed the cloister. Admire the column statues and sculptures on the section of reconstructed arcature, and imagine how splendid the whole work must have been.

MUSEE JULES GARNET 13, rue Pasteur ✆ 03 26 69 38 53. *Open all year: 2pm-6pm, except Tuesday and public holidays. Admission: adult 1.70 €, concessions 1.15 €, under-18s free.* This museum is housed in the former Vidâme de Chalons, a charming residence with a 1625 portal. There are a number of 14th-19thc. paintings, and 99 models of French churches and cathedrals, by Dr Mohen.

MUSEE DES BEAUX-ARTS ET D'ARCHEOLOGIE Place Godart ✆ 03 26 69 38 53. *Open all year: 2pm-6pm, except Tuesday and public holidays. Sundays: 2.30pm-6.30pm. Admission: adult 2.50 €, concessions 1.65 €, under-18s free.* This museum in the town centre displays a 19thc. Champagne period room downstairs, then medieval, Renaissance and Rodin sculpture, and paintings by Corot and Millet (among others) on the first floor.

MUSEE SCHILLER ET GOETHE 68, rue Léon Bourgeois ✆ 03 26 69 38 53. *July & August: 2pm-6pm, except Tuesday and public holidays. September-June, Saturday: 2pm-6pm; Sunday: 2.30pm-6.30pm. Admission; adult 1.70 €, concessions 1.15 €, under-18s free.* Schiller's heirs donated his personal effects to the town. You can see china, furniture and other objects belonging to this pacifist writer; Goethe's great friend.

Dormans

A substantial village in the pretty Marne Valley, on the department's western edge.

CHATEAU DE DORMANS. The castle is closed to the public at present, but you can admire it from the shady park. It was built in Charles V's reign (1370), on an earlier 10thc. site, and belonged first to Cardinal Jean II, then to the great Conde, Prince de Conti, and later to the Marshal de Broglie. Many sumptuous receptions have been held here.

MEMORIAL DES BATAILLES DE LA MARNE Parc du Château ✆ 03 26 57 77 87 / 03 26 53 35 86. *Open every day: 2.30pm-6.30pm, Sunday morning 10am-12 noon. Admission: adults and children free.* This national monument to the Great War dead stands in the castle park on the way out of town. The chapel overlooks the Marne Valley, scene of so many battles. There is a crypt, and an ossuary with 130 coffins containing the bones of 1,500 French soldiers killed between 1914 and 1918. The names of those divisions involved in the battles are carved in the cloister. The memorial park is open every day from 8am-7pm.

Lac du Der-Chantecoq

Lake Der is a 4,800ha. reservoir in the Marne and Haute-Marne departments. It was created to protect Paris from potential Seine flooding, then was added to Champaubert Reservoir in 1974 after six years of transforming work (14 bridges, 25km of road and 24km of dykes were built and 3 villages swallowed up). Today, the lake is a leisure site, internationally known for its 270 species of birdlife: herons and duck, not to mention cranes (40,000 at a time may stop off here on their migration route). The villages with their typical houses and half-timbered churches, museums, views and restaurants are attractive in both winter and summer.

MAISON DE L'OISEAU ET DU POISSON CD13 - OUTINES ✆ 03 26 74 00 00. *www.m-o-p.fr.st. Open every day July, August, October & November: 10am-6.30pm. Other periods: open Sunday and public holidays: 10am-6.30pm, weekdays: 1.30pm-6pm. Closed Saturdays. Group bookings. Admission: adult 6 €, child 3.50 €, under-5s free.* Animal ecomuseum. An animated model of Lake Der at reception explains how the Marne dam-reservoir works. Follow the gangway over the pond and enter the birds' universe. Some of them are displayed in their habitat, in a special showcase..

MUSEE DU PAYS DU DER Les Grandes-Côtes - SAINTE-MARIE-DU-LAC ✆ 03 26 41 01 02. *www.museedupaysduder.com. Open every day: 10am-5pm; 6pm Sundays and public holidays; 7pm in summer.. Admission: adult 4,50 €, child 2.80 €, family 13 €.* This museum-village is made up of half-timbered houses rescued from long-gone villages. The Blacksmith's House is a rest and picnic area, and sells regional produce and drinks. The 16thc. Nuisement aux Bois Church has been set up here, and there is a dovecote, bread-oven, washing place and educational pond, simples garden and traditional orchard. Models and temporary exhibitions are on display.

Oger

The church has a square 12thc. porch-tower and contains 48 17thc. stalls, from the former All Saints' Abbey in Chalons-en-Champagne.

MUSEE DES TRADITIONS DE L'AMOUR ET DU CHAMPAGNE 1, rue d'Avize ✆ 03 26 57 50 89. *Open 9am-11am and 2pm-6pm (3pm Sunday) from early March to late November. Open by appointment from December to February. Admission: adults 6 €.* This museum features the ever-popular theme of love and marriage, specifically covering the period 1820-1920. Over 600 original and sumptuous objects are on display: ceremonial jewellery, unusual gifts, and furnishings, together with the rites and customs associated with weddings and married life at this time. After visiting this first exhibition, you can admire a superb collection of 19thc. labels with their explanations, illustrating the history of champagne. There are some rare objects such as a bottle from the Napoleonic vintage, another called Deux Coupes (Two Glasses) and some champagne flutes known as 'impossibles'. Going downstairs, you discover the Old Tools gallery, leading to the carved and vaulted 18thc. cellars.

Pourcy

MAISON DU PARC Chemin de Nanteuil ✆ 03 26 59 44 44. *www.parc-montagnedereims.fr. Open from Easter to 1 November: 2.30pm-6pm.* The regional park centre in its contemporary building offers information, literature and thematic exhibitions. You can discover the Reims Mountain Park in video films, or by going on one of the walks indicated in the guide. Theme days are also organised - mosaics, Romanesque churches, meeting artists, walks by the river - and nature trips, such as mushroom-hunting. An activity timetable is available from local tourist offices.

Sainte-Ménehould

A pretty little town on the edge of the forest. The picturesque upper quarter has kept its medieval style, with Notre Dame du Château Church at the top, overlooking the steep streets and winding alleys. The lower quarter, notably the Place de l'Hôtel de Ville, is typically 18thc. Dom Perignon's statue reminds you that this famous monk, who invented champagne, was born here.

NOTRE DAME DU CHATEAU CHURCH. This 13thc. Gothic church has survived all onslaughts, including François 1's fortification work (against a feared attack by Charles V). Its fine capitals portray rural scenes. Sainte Ménehould's statue overlooks the town from the castle mound.

MUSEE VIARD-MOREL ✆ 03 26 60 85 83 Currently closed for renovation work. Further information from the Tourist Office.

Valmy

A battle against the Prussians took place on this historic plateau, on 20 September 1792, and lead to the proclaiming of the Republic. The windmill marking the site was sadly destroyed in the 1999 hurricane, but there is a statue of General Kellerman, commander of the French armies (his heart is inside the pyramid). The miller's house below was rebuilt for the French Revolution bicentenary celebrations.

Vitry-le-François

NOTRE DAME COLLEGIATE CHURCH. This 17th and 19thc. church boasts an imposing classical front with two towers. Inside are its chapels, a four-poster-style high altar (17thc.) carved tombstones and a superb organ.

PLACE D'ARMES ET LA DEESSE. This square was laid out on a geometric ground plan in 1545, at the junction of four main roads. The Palais de Justice was added in 1548 (housing both law courts and Town Hall), and a wooden church in 1557, replaced by the collegiate church in 1629.

Several houses were built alongside. The central fountain is topped by a wrought-iron statue known as la Déesse (the Goddess), put up in 1842 in honour of the Marne. She holds an oar, symbol of the navigable river, and a horn of plenty representing 19thc. prosperity.

CHAMPAGNE VINEYARDS

The region's main tourist attraction is of course its champagne. This delicate bubbly wine enjoys international prestige, and no celebration is complete without it.

Dom Pérignon (1638-1715), cellarer at Hautvillers Abbey, made the first champagne from black grapes. Since then, this illustrious monk's work has been much developed, and improvements made in the choice of *cépage* and yeast, mix of different wines and fizz control. In 1927, 34,000 ha. of vines came under the AOC. Today, 31,000 are planted, with 30,200 in production. Only three *cépages* are allowed: pinot noir (body and strength), pinot meunier (suppleness and flavour) and chardonnay (delicacy, aroma), and 34 quality standards must be complied with.

Champagne's hillsides have chalky soil and a good geographical position. You can visit the Côte des Blancs, Côte des Bar, Montagne de Reims and Vallée de la Marne, and taste the subtle differences in their products.

There are 320 crus in 5 departments: Marne, Aube, Aisne, Haute-Marne and Seine-et-Marne. Each cru obtains a quotation of 80-100% according to the quality of its grapes. About 300 millions of bottles are produced per year, and both the great champagne houses and winegrowers offer visits and tastings.

SYNDICAT GENERAL DES VIGNERONS 44, ave. Jean Jaures - EPERNAY ✆ 03 26 59 55 00. 99% of local winegrowers are members of this syndicate, covering 320 villages.

CIVC 5, rue Henri Martin - EPERNAY ✆ 03 26 51 19 30. Created in 1941, the Comité Interprofessionnel des Vins de Champagne manages the mutual interests of champagne producers and sellers, together with the profession's technical and economic aspects (oenological research and laboratory experiments; export market studies and statistics).

Epernay

The birthplace of champagne, right in the heart of the vineyards. Avenue de Champagne is the business quarter, where you find the great maisons and dealers in their comfortable 19thc. Renaissance or Neo-Classical-style buildings. Apart from these, and some fine mansions built during the 19thc. business boom, Epernay has few past remains, having been so often attacked and pillaged, and finally almost wiped out in World War One.

MUSEE DE LA CAVE ET DES METIERS DU CHAMPAGNE 57, rue de Verdun ✆ 03 26 51 19 11. *25 March-31 December: 10am-12 noon and 2pm-6pm.Admission: adult 6,50.* A series of scenes explain the process: grape-harvesting, working the wine, mixing, pouring out and bottling. There is a panel of tools used for work on the vines, and a collection of old and recent posters. Associated jobs are also mentioned: basket-weaving, printing, glass and cork-making, and labelling.

Champagne Caillez-Lemaire

Ay

Ay and its vineyard (370ha, all grand cru) are set on a hillside on the banks of the Marne, between vines and forest, in the Montagne de Reims nature reserve. You can see Saint Brice Church with its Gothic portal, and the nearby 'Henri IV' wine press.

INSTITUT INTERNATIONAL DES VINS DE CHAMPAGNE 15, rue Jeanson © 03 26 55 78 78. *Open Monday-Friday: 9am-12 noon and 2pm-6pm, or by appointment (every day).* Get to know champagne - with pleasure! Better known as Villa Bissinger, this Champagne wine school offers introductory courses.

Champagne maisons

In 1729, Nicolas Ruinart founded the first champagne firm in Epernay, then moved it to Reims. He was followed by Moet et Chandon (1743), Cliquot-Ponsardin (1772) and Heidsieck (1785). More firms appeared in the 19thc. The Reims cellars were installed in chalk quarries, which provide ideal storage conditions and are amazing to visit.

Reims

CHAMPAGNE ALAIN THIENOT 14, rue des Moissons-Taissy © 03 26 77 50 10

CHAMPAGNE LANSON 66, rue de Courlancy © 03 26 78 53 89

CHAMPAGNE G.H. MARTEL & Co 17, rue des Créneaux © 03 26 82 70 67. *www.champagnemartel.com. Open every day: 10am-7pm. Guided tour and tasting (5).*

CHAMPAGNE PIPER-HEIDSIECK 51, bd. Henry Vasnier © 03 26 84 43 44

CHAMPAGNE POMMERY 5, place du General Gouraud © 03 26 61 62 56

Epernay

Reims' rival for the title of champagne capital. The following maisons have their cellars here:

CHAMPAGNE JANISSON-BARADON 2, rue des Vignerons © 03 26 54 45 85

CHAMPAGNE CHARLES ELLNER 1 et 6 rue Cote Legris © 03 26 55 60 25

CHAMPAGNE DE CASTELLANE (N.M) 57, route de Verdun © 03 26 51 19 19

CHAMPAGNE MERCIER 68-70, ave. de Champagne © 03 26 51 22 22

CHAMPAGNE MOET ET CHANDON 20, ave. de Champagne © 03 26 51 20 20. Dom Perignon's statue stands proudly before the beautiful house, Avenue de Champagne. Discover its history, champagne-making and the product range.

CHAMPAGNE PERRIER-JOUET 26, ave. de Champagne © 03 26 53 38 10. The firm began in 1811, and settled in this prestigious avenue where it has 10km of cellars.

CHAMPAGNE VRANKEN 42, ave. de Champagne © 03 26 59 50 50

Le Mesnil-sur-Oger

The village may be small, but the whole vineyard is listed grand cru.

MUSEE DE LA VIGNE ET DU VIN 2, rue Eugène Guillaume © 03 26 57 50 15. *Visits by appointment, adult 7 with tasting (3 champagnes).* The wine press room contains examples from all over France (17th, 18th and 19thc.), along with a barrel-washer and scales. A cooperage room has been added, extending the museum. The whole visit and tasting session take about 2 hours.

TROYES AND THE AUBE

Troyes

This opulent city is the historic capital of Southern Champagne. Churches and half-timbered houses stand beside beautiful patrician stone mansions in the narrow streets and picturesque alleys, and the town centre is shaped like a champagne cork (the Montgueux slopes and Cote des Bar vineyards are not far off).

SAINT PIERRE AND SAINT PAUL CATHEDRAL. 114m long, 50m across the transept and 28.5m under the roof vault: this cathedral is one of France's biggest. Begun in the 12thc, continued in the 13th and finished in the 18th, it illustrates these different periods, without losing any of its Gothic purity. The famous stained glass windows (182 panels) bathe the church in beautifully soft light.

SAINT URBAIN BASILICA. One of the world's three perfect Gothic buildings, say the experts. Saint Urbain is slender, light and vertical, and the chancel is all in glass.

SAINTE MADELEINE CHURCH. Mostly 12thc, this attractive old church houses a large rood-screen, brilliantly carved by Jean Guailde between 1508 and 1517. Notice the Creation stained-glass window, with its surrealist panels.

SAINT PANTALEON CHURCH. The only church in Troyes with a wooden vault. Light floods through the clear 17thc. glass in the great upper bays, and illuminates countless statues representing the early Troyes school, and the Italian style of sculpture which replaced it in the mid-16thc.

APOTHICAIRERIE DE L'HOTEL DIEU Quai des Comtes de Champagne ✆ 03 25 80 98 97. *Open every day except Tuesday: 1 June-30 September: 10am-1pm and 2pm-6pm. Other periods: Monday, Wednesday, Saturday and Sunday. Admission: adult 2 €, over-25s 1 €, under-25s free.* Discover the pharmacy as it was in the early 18thc. with its hundreds of pots from the pharmacopoeia of past centuries. 320 painted wood, earthenware and pewter boxes are displayed, along with other apothecary's objects such as 16th and 17thc. bronze mortars.

Houses with timber framings

MUSEE MARGUERITE BOURGEOYS 38, rue Georges Clémenceau ✆ 03 25 73 37 30. *Open every day except Monday: 10am-6pm. Sunday & public holidays: 2pm-6pm. Admission free.* Born in Troyes in 1620, Marguerite founded the Notre Dame Congregation in Canada, in 1653. She was beatified in 1950 and canonised by John Paul II in 1982, for her religious teaching work.

MUSEE DE VAULUISANT 4, rue de Vauluisant ✆ 03 25 73 05 85. *Open every day except Tuesday, 1 June-30 September: 10am-1pm and 2pm-6pm. Other periods, open Monday, Wednesday, Saturday and Sunday. Admission: adult 3 €, over-25s 1 €, under-25s free.* This museum tells the story of hosiery (underwear, stockings and socks), once the town's main industry. It shares the fine mid-16thc. premises with an exhibition of 16thc. Troyes art, including the Vierge de Villenauxe and the Montier-la-Celle Mise au Tombeau.

MAISON DE L'OUTIL ET DE LA PENSEE OUVRIERE 7, rue de la Trinité ✆ 03 25 73 28 26. *Open 10am-6pm every day, including weekends and public holidays.Admission: adult 6.50 €* The Tool and Working-Class Thinking Museum exhibits 10,000 tools (all used) grouped by trade or theme. A library contains 35,000 books on working-class thinking and philosophy.

MUSEE D'ART MODERNE Place Saint Pierre ✆ 03 25 76 26 80. *Open 11am-6pm except*

Monday and public holidays.Admission: adult 5 € Housed in the former Bishops' Palace, the Pierre and Denise Levy Donation is one of Europe's finest modern art collections. Daumier, Corbet, Millet, Degas, Seurat, Matisse, Modigliani and Balthus illustrate developments in French art from 1850-1950. Fauvism is represented by Derain, Vlaminck, Braque and Dufy, among others. You can also discover Troyes painter and glass-worker Maurice Marinot.

Stained glass of Troyes cathedral

© Iconotec.com

Parc de la forêt d'Orient

Orient Forest (70,000ha) lies between copses and meadows, impressively deep and atmospheric, and haunted by the mysterious Templars.

MAISON DU PARC Office de Tourisme des Grands Lacs ✆ **03 25 41 54 09.** *www.pnr-foret-orient.fr. Open January, February, March, November & December every day: 1pm-5pm. April, May, June, September and October: Monday-Friday: 10am-12 noon and 2pm-6pm, weekends and public holidays: 10am-1pm and 2pm-6pm. July & August: every day: 10am-6pm.* Opened in 1973, this centre is housed in the barn, stables and outbuildings of a converted farm, with meeting and exhibition rooms, and a cinema. On the ground floor, the natural world is explained according to 3 themes: earth, water and forest. Upstairs, contemporary environmental initiatives are outlined, including the park's conservation activity. You can discover this regional nature reserve for yourself by choosing a thematic activity from the annual programme of events.

LACS. 5,000ha. of lakes, adapted for water sports (diving, swimming, fishing). There are sailing harbours, clubs and training centres for boat fans; a bird sanctuary and a number of campsites by the lakeside.

Brienne-le-Château

Brienne, with its sumptuous château overlooking the old quarters, is known for its military academy and one old boy in particular; a certain Bonaparte.

SAINT PIERRE AND SAINT PAUL CHURCH. *Open every day: 9am-6pm.* Some 12thc. pillars still exist in the nave: the others are 14thc. Apse and chancel date back to the 16thc: striking grisaille windows illustrate the lives of Saints Crépin, Crépinien, and Agathe; and Noah. Napoleon made his first communion here.

HALLE. This 'new' covered market replaced the ancient (1270) in 1720. The roof is a heavy and imposing structure of flat tiles on wooden pillars.

MUSEE NAPOLEON 34, rue de l'Ecole Militaire ✆ **03 25 92 82 41**. *Open 1 April-30 September: 10am-12.30pm and 2pm-6pm. Ask about other periods. Admission: adult 4.30 €, concessions 2.60 €.* Bonaparte's life at Brienne Military Academy and the 1814 French campaign are described in this museum. The ancient Carmelite Chapel houses statues and gold plate from the town's church treasure.

ECOMUSEE DE LA FORET D'ORIENT 1, chemin Milbert ✆ **03 25 92 95 84**. *www.pnr-foret-orient.fr. Open every day except Monday, 1 May-30 September, weekdays 10am-12 noon and 2pm-6pm, Saturday, Sunday & public holidays: 2pm-6pm. 1 October-30 April, weekdays 2pm-5pm, Saturday, Sunday & public holidays: by appointment. Admission: adults 4 €, students 2.50 €, under-12s free.* This ecomuseum celebrates regional history, know-how and traditions, and is instructive, thought-provoking and fun. 3,000 restored agricultural tools from the 18th-20thc. are on display in the former dairy. There are two magnificent barns, a superb collection of old tractors and a working forge and cartwright's workshop (1900).

Chavanges

This beautiful rural village contains some 18thc. half-timbered houses, typical of the region. The annual Onion Festival is held here on a Saturday in October, an opportunity to meet the market gardeners and taste their produce.

Elsewhere in the Aube

Bar-sur-Aube

An international crossroads in the 12th and 13thc, Bar-sur-Aube hosts the annual Champagne Fair (traces of it can be found in the many underground cellars and storerooms). Admire the ancient houses, some half-timbered, and fine mansions, and take a walk down the Rue des 7 Tournants, a real maze of an alley, that twists and turns before coming out in the Tanneries (tanners') quarter.

SAINT JEAN CHAPEL. This tiny half-Romanesque, half-Gothic chapel has served many purposes since it was built: a chapel for soldier-monks, a barn and an apartment being some of them. The Knights Templars were probably its first owners.

SAINT PIERRE CHURCH. A small Benedictine monastery first occupied the site of this fine 12thc. church, with its covered gallery along the outside wall. The romantic organ has 40 stops on 3 keyboards, and was made in 1845 by the royal organ builder Lete.

OLD HOUSES AND PICTURESQUE TOWN. Wandering through the streets and alleys, you come across these ancient, half-timbered houses, as well as some fine old private mansions. A 17thc. house known as the Château Gaillard, where Louis XIV once stayed, can be seen at 32, bd. Victor Hugo. The ancient ramparts were pulled down in the 18thc, and the Promenade des Chevillottes planted in 1771 instead, with its two lakes. Ducks and swans admire themselves in the water. The Sept-Tournants alley is a genuine maze. Follow its twists and turns, and you'll eventually find yourself in the tannery quarter.

Bar-sur-Seine

Aube champagne capital in the Seine Valley, Bar-sur-Seine was a prosperous town in the 16th and 17thc. Its beautiful half-timbered houses include the Renaissance House with its brick sections, fine pilasters and elegant corner statue of Saint Roch.

SAINT ETIENNE CHURCH. Built from 1505 onwards, on the site of two earlier 10th and 11thc. churches, Saint Etienne is a blend of Renaissance and Flamboyant Gothic styles. Bas reliefs illustrating the saint's life, a fine 17thc. wooden pulpit and bench and grisaille stained glass windows complete its fine interior.

16THC AND RENAISSANCE HOUSES Rue de la République. A large stone house was put up on an earlier residence: the crypt remains but is closed to visitors. The rib vaults on cylindrical pillars mark it out as Jehan Le Martin's building. The Renaissance house is further down the street, on the corner of Rue Victor Hugo.

CHAPEL OF THE PASSION 118, rue des Fossés. Corinthian pilasters, and capitals as fine as Chambord's. This 12thc. chapel had been destroyed several times before starting a new life in 1665.

CHATEAU DU COMTE DE BAR. Jeanne de Navarre, Queen of France in 1273, was born here. The castle was pulled down in 1595, and only the Tour de Lion (or de l'Horloge) is left.

COMMANDERIE TEMPLIERE D'AVALLEUR. *Open once a month in April, May & June; every Saturday in July, August and September. Guided tours: 2.30pm-6pm.* The Knights Templars Order was founded in Jerusalem in 1119 by Champagne-born Hugues de Payns, to protect pilgrims in the Holy Land. This fortress was put up by Manasses, Comte de Bar and Bishop of Langres. Its role was to make profits to support military action and the occupation of the Middle East. A well preserved 12th-13thc. chapel with its original Gothic framework and rainwater tank are the oldest remains; the Renaissance main building and postern were rebuilt by the Hospitallers who lived on the site for 450 years.

Bayel

Not to be missed. Bayel has been a glass-making town since 1300, specialising in the techniques of blowing, hand-cutting, sand and acid engraving, finishing, gilding and enamelling.

CRISTALLERIES ROYALES DE CHAMPAGNE La Voie Basse ✆ 03 25 92 37 60. The Tourist Office organises guided tours of these Royal Crystal Workshops every day: 9.30am and 11am, Monday-Friday (except public and annual holidays), Saturday on request. Factory shop open every day. Murano was the 17thc. capital of glass artistry, so Colbert persuaded the master glass-worker Jean-Baptiste Mazzolay to leave Italy for Bayel, which was particularly well-equipped for this art (castle patronage and plentiful sand, water and wood). From that day on, the town has been making glass, and today 200 people produce glasses, decanters, jugs, vases and other objects; 2,000 in all, requiring 35 different techniques.

ECOMUSEE DU CRISTAL - CENTRE MAZZOLAY ✆ **03 25 92 42 68**. *Open every day: 9.30am-1pm and 2pm-6pm, Sunday: 2pm-6pm (closed Sunday from 1 October to 30 March). Admission: adult 3.80 ; including crystal workshops, 3.10 €.* Discover Bayel crystal's history and manufacturing methods through an explanatory video and exhibition of pieces from 1900 to the present day, including a fabulous collection of 1930s vases.

Chaource

This big rural village nestling in bocage scenery is pleasant to visit, with its half-timbered houses. Its main claim to fame, however, is a pair of amazing 16thc. sculptures by the Maitre de Chaource.

SAINT JEAN BAPTISTE CHURCH. *Open every day: 8.30am-7pm (6pm in winter) until 31 October.*

Champagne and Italian art erge in the parish of Chaource, which houses the Maitre's Mise au Tombeau sculpture and a gilded wooden crib, probably the oldest in France.

MUSEE DU FROMAGE Place de l'Eglise ✆ **03 25 40 10 67**. *1 April-30 September, open every day except Tuesday. 1 October-31 March, open Saturday, Sunday and public holidays. Groups by appointment all year: 10am-12 noon and 2pm-6pm. Admission: adult 4,50 €, under-14s 2 €.* This original museum celebrates the local cheese (chaource) but also contains some curious objects, like the dog collar with spikes to protect the dog's throat when fighting wolves, or the travelling shepherd's hut (demourée) carried on a sledge.

Clairvaux

CLAIRVAUX ABBEY. *www.abbaye-clairvaux.barsuraube.net. Historic buildings: April, May, June, September & October; Saturday: 2pm, 3.30pm and 5pm. July & August; Saturday: 2pm, 3pm, 4pm and 5pm. 14 July-15 August: every day (except Saturday): 4.15pm. Please be there 15 minutes early. Passport/identity card required. No photos.* On the Champagne-Bourgogne border lies the 'silent land', where Saint Bernard built his famous abbey in 1115, and lived until his death in 1153. Today, Clairvaux is shut off by long walls, so you can't even catch a glimpse of it from outside. Once inside, however, you find architectural treasures, with a few remaining walls from Clairvaux I (pulled down in the 19thc.): the *monasterium vetus* (1115-1135), the splendid lay brothers' building (Clairvaux II; 1135-1708) and Clairvaux III's great classical cloister (1708-1792). Restoration is underway on these historic buildings, overseen by the Ministry for Culture.

Essoyes

Auguste Renoir's village. His memory is cultivated here, along with the local vines. He chose to settle in this little village among the vineyards in 1882, and bought a house, staying in it from May to October every year. Today, it belongs to his descendants, and is open to visitors.

ATELIER AUGUSTE-RENOIR 7, rue Extra ✆ **03 25 38 56 28**. *Open all year, except Monday. Every day from 1 May to 15 September.* You find Pierre-Auguste Renoir's studio at the bottom of the garden on the first floor, well away from his noisy children. Today, it houses a collection of personal objects, and the ancestry and works of the painter and sculptor, together with souvenirs of his friends. You can also see the family tomb in the village cemetery, where parents and children now rest. Renoir's self-portrait in bronze decorates the monument, along with a bronze of his wife.

Maisons-les-Chaource

This little village contains two museums in one, with the aim of protecting local crafts.

MUSEE DES POUPEES D'ANTAN ET DE LA TONNELLERIE ✆ **03 25 70 07 46.** *Open every year: 10am-12 noon and 2pm-6pm. Open public holidays and Sundays, 10 March-15 November. Closed Tuesdays. Admission: adult 4 €, child 2 €.* Your every move is being watched by 160 pairs of eyes! This museum contains dolls of all periods, from 1860s wax models to vinyl babies of the 1950s. Beside it, the cooperage workshop is displayed as it used to be; the guided tour really brings it to life. A tasting brings your visit to a close.

Nogent-sur-Seine

SAINT LAURENT CHURCH. In 1650, Louis XIV nicknamed the town 'Nogent la Belle Tour', and the tower is still as beautiful, 37m high, drawing all eyes with its campanile topped by a colossal statue of Saint Laurent.

LES GRANDS MOULINS. To the right of the bridge, these mills ground flour for town and region in the early 20thc, thus continuing a milling tradition dating back to the Carolingian era.

MUSEE MUNICIPAL PAUL DUBOIS ALFRED BOUCHER Rue Alfred Boucher ✆ 03 25 39 71 79. *1st weekend in April-15 June; 15 September-late November; Saturday & Sunday: 2pm-6pm. 15 June-15 September, every day except Tuesday: 2pm-6pm. Admission: adult 3 €.* The sculptor Alfred Boucher (1850-1934) had this museum opened in 1902, on the site of the ancient fortress. Today, a pretty park encircles it, and the town centre is close by. There are 3 themes: archeology, 17th-20thc. painting and sculpture.

Les Riceys

The Riceys is a village community in 3 parts: Ricey-Haut, Ricey Haute-Rive and Ricey-Bas. It is also the only French village with 3 AOCs! Pinot noir is predominant, and champagne is produced, but also the Riceys rosé.

Saint-Pierre and Saint-Paul cathedral, Troyes

FOOD AND DRINK

Champagne's local produce is reappearing on the tables. The Ardennes region is known for its charcuterie, especially the ham, boudin blanc a l'oignon (white pudding) Rethel boudin blanc and Ardennes dry sausage. The Haute-Marne produces cheese, truffles and wine. As for the Aube and the Marne, they have other specialities, apart from champagne.

Andouillette de Troyes

Made exclusively from pork stomachs cut lengthways in strips, then stuffed into a casing taken from the pig's big intestine, seasoned with salt, pepper, chopped onion and white wine (or champagne!) and simmered for hours in aromatic stock. Choose only andouillettes with the AAAAA lable, and grill them on your summer barbecue. The best suppliers are Daniel Thierry (Sainte-Savine) and Patrick Maury (Troyes).

Biscuit rose (Reims)

Taste it dipped in a drop of champagne or red wine. This pink biscuit (bis-cuit means 'cooked twice') goes back to the 17thc, and is made from sugar, wheat flour, eggs, vanilla and cochineal for the pink colour. Even soaked in champagne, it stays crunchy.

Bussy boulettes

This is a white turnip, grown until the 1930s in the Aube and Marne, and now come back into fashion. It is less strong and tastier than the traditional turnip, and is delicious fried or au gratin.

JEAN-LUC GALICHET 2, impasse des Fosses - Bussy-le-Chateau ✆ 03 26 67 56 80

Chaource

AOC cheese with a white crust, creamy centre and nutty taste. You find it at the Fromageries Besnier in Vaudes, Fromagerie d'Armancon in Auxon, Fromagerie ‡ Mussy and the Ferme des Tourelles at Mesnil Saint Georges.

MUSEE DU FROMAGE Place de l'Eglise ✆ 03 25 40 10 67

Langres

Langres' cheese-making tradition goes back to the 18thc. This AOC cheese has an orangish crust (the surface is naturally concave), ivory colour and creamy, nutty taste, and can be matured in Champagne or Bourgogne marc brandy.

Sainte-Menehould pied de porc.

Sounds more elegant in French! This is pig's trotter, simmered all night then rolled in breadcrumbs and grilled in the oven. You eat it with stewed apple. The whole foot is eaten, even the crunchy bones. This dish dates back to 1790.

Cheeses

Hotels & Restaurants

ARDENNES

Bazeilles

L'AUBERGE DU PORT ** Route de Remilly ✆ 03 24 27 13 89. *Fax : 03 24 29 35 58. Website: www.aubergeduport.com.* Restaurant closed Saturday lunchtime and Sunday evening, and Friday evening in winter. 20 rooms, 15 of which have been entirely renovated. Single room 52 €, double 61 €. Breakfast buffet 8 €. Set menu weekdays 17.50 €. Set menus from 23.50 € to 29.50 €. À la carte. Children's menus 9 € and 15 €. Wine on sale. L'Auberge du Port is located at the gates of Sedan on the edge of the Meuse, and is a favourite haunt of gastronomy-lovers. The buccolic surroundings boast a children's play-area with a garden and a shady terrace, and decorative charm merges with culinary quality: dried Ardennes ham and wild boar ham in a salad, cuts of venison in a creamed marinade, chestnuts in butter and a *feuilleté* of apples with bilberries, or the pastrycook's *palette gourmande* with its two *coulis* or fruit sauces. The rooms are fully equipped and very comfortable.

Charleville-Mézières

LA COTE A L'OS 11, cours Aristide-Briand ✆ 03 24 59 20 16. *Fax : 03 24 59 48 30.* Menus from 15 € to 32 €. Closed Sunday evening except July and August. An Ardennes-style brasserie with its typical dishes, meat - lamb knuckle-joint conserved in garlic, grilled rib on the bone - and seafood; try the seafood *choucroute*, for instance. Real foodie ambience, not to be missed.

Fagnon

HOTEL ABBAYE DES SEPT FONTAINES * ✆ 03 24 37 38 24.** *Fax : 03 24 37 58 75. Website: www.abbayeseptfontaines.fr.* 23 rooms from 84 € to 197 €. Breakfast 13 €. 4 set menus at 29 €, 38 €, 46 € and 54 €, and *à la carte*. You'll find spacious rooms and gastronomic *cuisine* in this magnificent residence set in over 30 ha.of land. The menus change weekly to suit seasonal produce. This highly-rated spot is good for relaxing; it even has a 9-hole golf course (with a planned extension to 18 holes). Excellent welcome.

Rethel

AU SANGLIER DES ARDENNES ** 1, rue Pierre-Curie ✆ 03 24 38 45 19. *Fax : 03 24 38 45 14. 12 rooms from 42 € to 46 € with television and telephone. Car park and garage. Set menus from 9 € to 12 € (brasserie) or 17 € to 26 € (restaurant).Children's menu 8 €. One-night stop-off 58 €.*

This classic brasserie has been located in the town centre since the 1920s. It is split into two parts; on the brasserie side you'll find plenty of dishes ranging from the standard - grilled salmon steaks, trout with almonds or sirloin in a pepper sauce - to the regional - salad with fat bacon, Rethel white pudding with apples, stuffed trout Ardennes-style...On the restaurant side, the chitterling sausage in mustard sauce, prime beef cut with shallots and grilled duck confit are well-cooked, if not particularly original.

Sedan

AU BON VIEUX TEMPS 1 et 3, place de la Halle ✆ 03 24 29 03 70. *Closed Monday, Wednesday evening and Sunday evening. Annual closing 15 February - 12 March and last 2 weeks in August. Set menus at lunchtime from 10.50 € to 13 € Tuesday-Saturday, gastronomic set menus from 20 € to 38 €, children's menu 8 €.* Au Bon Vieux Temps is in fact two restaurants: the gastronomic one at number 1 and le Marmiton at number 3.

AUBE

Bar-sur-Aube

LA TOQUE BARALBINE 18, rue Nationale ✆ 03 25 27 20 34 *Closed Sunday evening and Monday, except public holidays. Set menus from 18 € to 50 €. À la carte 40 €.* La Toque Baralbine is certainly one of the Aube's best eating places. Daniel Phelizot's regional cuisine in its highly personalised sophisticated setting is quite sought-after. The dining-room is light and spacious, and you can consult the menu, a glass of local champagne in hand, comfortably seated on padded Louis XV chairs round a prettily-set table. Your taste-buds are quivering already: foie gras, the famous young Onjon pigeon with ratafia, Bernon snails, game, fish, desserts like the *crème brulée* flavoured with lavender (in season). Traditional, gastronomic, balanced in quality and quantity, spices and herbs knowledgeably added without denaturing the product, olive oil a feature...Well-assisted by his wife Sylvie, Daniel is a real professional who has become an ambassador for hemp oil, produced in the Aube of course; you are invited to discover its particular taste. Discover his inspiration and creativity, accompanied by a wine list containing over 200 recommended names from local winegrowers and more than 30 champagnes. Absolutely not to be missed.

Mesnil-Saint-Père

AU VIEUX PRESSOIR AUBERGE DU LAC * 5, rue du 28-Août-1944 ✆ 03 25 41 27 16.** *Fax : 03 25 41 57 59. Website : www.auberge-du-lac.fr.* Hotel closed Sunday evenings from 1 October to 1 March. Restaurant closed Monday lunchtime. Standard double rooms from 67 €, luxury double room with jacuzzi from 118 €, suite 155 €. Set menus 24 € - Tuesday to Saturday only (except public holidays) - and from 35 € to 69 €. This fine hotel ideally located on the way into the village in a typical old Champagne building, has kept all its attractions yet is fitted out to suit modern tastes.A little Art Deco lounge lit by a glass roof opens onto a luminous dining-room. In this elegant setting with exposed beams and yellow walls with inset spaces, you can't help but appreciate the sophisticated *cuisine* concocted by chef Patrick Gublin.Try his foie gras *amusants*, roast turbot with champagne butter, crab and seafood tartar with Oleron oysters, young pigeon flanks roasted with giblets, spiced apples, and for dessert, chocolate *moelleux* with vanilla cream and almond milk ice-cream.

Troyes

HOTEL DE LA POSTE ** 35, rue Emile-Zola ✆ 03 25 73 05 05.** *Fax : 03 25 73 80 76. Website : www.hotel-de-la-poste.com.Open every day, all year. Double room from 105 € to 112 €, bedroom-lounge from 109 € to 130 €, air-conditionned suite from 155 € to 165 €. Breakfast 12 €. Garage 10 €.* Set in the heart of the Bouchon, opposite the Town Hall, this luxurious hotel has plenty of cachet. Its 32 rooms with satellite TV and Canal + include 6 junior and 2 senior suites, all air-conditioned. For Beauty, there's a marble bathroom with a corner bath; for the Beast, a private garage to park that big car, a relaxing corner where he can smoke his cigar in a cosy armchair, and a recently-opened bar, the Art Cafe - for sipping cocktails, champagne or one of a selection of whiskies.

Villemoyenne

LA PARENTÈLE 32 rue Marcellin-Lévêque ✆ 03 25 43 68 68 *Fax : 03 25 43 68 69. Set menus from 26 € to 72 €, à la carte 55 €.Closed Monday, Sunday evening, during February and October school holidays and 10 days in July/August.* We knew the Caironi brothers at Bar-sur-Seine, where their establishment, Le Parc de Villeneuve, was the top-of-the-range chateau-type. Difficult to run and lacking in rooms, it must have become too big for Christophe and Bruno, who decided to exchange it 4 years ago for what used to be the village grocer's, now prettily redecorated. It has open spaces, a modern setting and a lively cuisine every bit as good as their cooking during the Parc de Villeneuve period. Cold langoustine chartreuse, fresh Landes duck foie gras confit, ravioli in cuttlefish ink, supions and parsley, saddle of lamb with a vegetable matignon (diced carrots, onions and bacon) and simple meat juices flavoured with tarragon, praline tartelette chapel-style and vanilla sorbet. Christophe Caironi could talk forever about his cellar, with its 200 recommended wines, including the best of every region.

MARNE

Ambonnay

AUBERGE SAINT-VINCENT ** 1, rue Saint-Vincent 03 26 57 01 98 *Website: www.auberge-st-vincent.com. Closed Sunday evening, Monday and Tuesday lunchtime. Annual closing February, and the second fortnight in August. Rooms from 51 € to 65 €. Set menus from 29 € to 70 €. 'Champagne gourmande' formula - half-board - during the week 152 €, based on 2 nights for 1 person. Weekend 160 €.* Anne-Marie Pelletier welcomes and takes care of her customers round the big fireplace, in a pretty, renovated and skilfully decorated setting, while Jean-Claude concocts some original dishes from regional recipes. The main menu changes twice a year, and the market menu every week. There is a fine selection of wines, especially regional ones.

Châlons-en-Champagne

JACKY MICHEL 19 place Mgr-Tissier ✆ 03 26 68 21 51 *Fax : 03 26 70 51 67. Website: www.hoteldangleterre.com. Set menus from 33 € to 90 €, à la carte 60 €. Closed Monday lunchtime, Saturday lunchtime and Sunday, during the Christmas holidays and from mid-July to 8 August.* Jacky Michel, who took over the Hotel d'Angleterre restaurant in the early 1980s abides by the local rule that serving staff should be in livery, the wine list full of champagne and a meal *à la carte* cost around 60 €. Yet rather than serving only classically cooked luxury produce like most of his colleagues in the area (some with talent, it must be said) he seeks inspiration in the use of citrus fruits, spices and 'peasant' produce - potatoes, artichokes, lovage - that he likes to combine with nobler foodstuffs: potato tart, country asparagus, tomato conserve, truffle oil vinaigrette, turbot breast spiked with conserved lemon, fennel, yoghurt cream with mint and coriander, loin of lamb roasted on the spit, seasonal vegetables with thyme flowers, salted butter shortbread, raspberries, coconut, almond milk ice-cream. The cellar contains some great French wines, but is less daring than the cooking; a pity.

Champillon

ROYAL CHAMPAGNE Champillon-Bellevue ✆ 03 26 52 87 11 *Fax : 03 26 52 86 69. Set menus from 32 € to 100 €, à la carte 85 €. Closed Monday, Tuesday lunchtime and the last week in December.* This former 18thc.coaching inn is one of Champagne's most prestigious stopping off places: its exceptional situation on the Reims Mountain, its protected architecture and recent renovation - which has added a swimming-pool, a fitness centre and a splendid veranda for the restaurant, overlooking the vineyards and Epernay Valley - make it a favourite place to stay for the rich and famous.Management changed last year - Andrea Ricol handed over to fabien Delaffon - but the kitchens are now in a settled phase, after a few difficult years.With four years' experience of orders, Philippe Auge is quite at ease with the repertoire of classic, updated *cuisine* favoured by his well-off customers: foie gras confit marinated in vin de Bouzy, apple and grape chutney, toasted country bread, pigeon in hazlenut pastry, duck legs conserved in their juice, Savoy cabbage *millefeuille* with country bacon, cod fillet roasted in salted butter, penne pasta in cuttlefish ink, octopus stew, shellfish with conserved tomatoes, warm soufflé with the famous pink Reims biscuits and preserved pears, pink champagne sorbet. The cellar is admirable, quite 'Royal', and the service all you'd expect from a grand hotel.

Epernay

AU BACCHUS GOURMET 21, rue Gambetta ✆ 03 26 51 11 44 *Website: www.aubacchusgourmet.com. Closed Monday and Tuesday. Annual closing from 20 December to 20 January. Service 12 noon - 2pm and 7.30pm-10pm. Formula 16.90 €, set menus from 24 € to 89 €. Red and white tones both inside and out and a warm welcome: you are here to enjoy the many flavours of Mediterranean cooking.* This cuisine is based on olive oil and fresh produce; the vegetables are often pan-fried and the sauces delicious. Chef Jean-Paul Fernandès was in fact voted best French sauce-maker. The main menu changes every month, and the set menu at 89 € suggests a meal with champagne, each course accompanied by its flute. The wine list contains 300 recommendations, with bottles from 1918 to the present day.

HOTEL-RESTAURANT LES BERCEAUX 13 rue des Berceaux ✆ 03 26 55 28 84 *Fax : 03 26 55 10 36. Website: www.lesberceaux.com. Set menus from 30 € to 65 €, à la carte 90 €. Closed Monday, Tuesday, during February school holidays and the second half of August.* Former chef for 10 years at the Chateau de Fere in the Aisne, then for 6 years at Aux Armes de Chanpagne, l'Epine, Patrick Michelon settled into this medieval house during summer 1996, firmly intending to stay this time. The annex, inaugurated two years ago, is a sign that the establishment is doing well, despite the difficulties experienced by the restaurant business today. With his 50th birthday under his belt and still full of drive, Patrick's roots are in the pure gastronomic tradition, a master chef if not a modernist. *Aiguillettes* (thin strips) of bass marinated in dill, coriander, pickled lemon and Liguri olive oil, the 'famous' turbot in champagne, gratine on a bed of fresh noodles, suckling calf, veal medallions and crispy calf's head, green asparagus and early chanterelles, a selection of chocolates, cereals and grilled hazlenuts and sweet almond ice-cream feature on his menu.

L'Epine

AUX ARMES DE CHAMPAGNE 31 avenue du Luxembourg ✆ 03 26 69 30 30 *Fax : 03 26 69 30 26. Website: www.aux-armes-de-champagne.com. Set menus from 25 € to 90 €, à la carte 80 €. Closed Sunday evening and Monday.* Two years ago, the Perardel, who had managed this proud establishment for 3 generations, handed over office to chef Philippe Zeiger, now 36, and his associate Pascal Fouassier, who runs the restaurant. They dusted off the business very gently, so as not to upset staff or regular customers, and Philippe introduced a creative and inspired menu worthy of his time at Bernard Loiseau and Bardet. It features a courgette velouté, *ile flottante* with spices and smoked salmon shavings, scallops *au naturel*, lemon-flavoured juice and caramelised onions, farm rabbit kebabs, creamy risotto, risotto with milk and mango cubes. Splendid cellar, worthy of the great regional establishments: Christian Rubler is in charge of over 500 recommended wines.

Montchenot

AUBERGE DU GRAND CERF 50 route Nationale ✆ 03 26 97 60 07 *Fax : 03 26 97 64 24. Set menus from 35 € to 85 €, à la carte 60 €. Closed Tuesday evening, Wednesday, Sunday, two weeks in February and 3 weeks in August.* This Grand Cerf, comfortably settled on the Reims mountain less than 10 minutes from the capital of Champagne and fifteen minutes from the champagne capital Epernay, has been run for nearly 15 years by Dominique Giraudeau. Now nearing fifty, he can boast a superb career: trained by Michel Vignaud - Hostellerie des Clos at Chablis - he moved on to the Auberge Normande at Carentan with Gerard Bonnefoy, and then to Chez Passard. This subtle technician works with a classic menu (his own definition) but is modernising little by little, seconded for over 7 years now by young Pascal Champion, and keeps one eye on tradition and the other on current recipes: Breton lobster in a sweet and sour vinaigrette, roast langoustines with cauliflower semolina and calf sweetbread with truffles satisfy traditionalists and the more adventurous alike, the common factor being a sense of quality. There is a well-stocked cellar - 500 recommended wines with commentary from Herve Lannois.

Reims

BRASSERIE DU BOULINGRIN 48, rue de Mars ✆ 03 26 40 96 22. *Closed Sunday. Last orders taken at 11pm Monday to Thursday, midnight on Friday and Saturday. Brasserie formula 17.50 € except Friday evening, Saturday evening, evenings before public holidays and public holidays themselves. Menu des Halles 24 €.* The Boulingrin has been a favourite meeting place for the Remois since 1925, and has kept the period style. Seafood is served all year except July and August, but the menu harbours plenty of other ideas: bass roasted in Guerande salt - 16 € - seafood choucroute - 14 € - calf's head and brains in *sauce ravigote* with steamed potatoes -12.50 € - and a chocolate *moelleux* with almond milk to finish - 6 €..

GRAND HOTEL DES TEMPLIERS ** 22, rue des Templiers ✆ 03 26 88 55 08.** *Credit cards accepted. 18 air-conditioned rooms, from 180 € to 340 €. Breakfast 25 €.* Not far from the city centre in a quiet district, near the champagne houses and the cathedral. Discover the discreet charm of a19thc. mansion with its carved wooden ceilings and staircase. The period rooms are equipped with marble bathrooms. Faultless service from this four-star hotel, which also offers a heated swimming pool, hammam amd sauna.

Tinqueux

L'ASSIETTE CHAMPENOISE 40 av Paul-Vaillant-Couturier ✆ 03 26 84 64 64 *Fax : 03 26 04 15 69. Site: www.assiettechampenoise.com. Set menus from 60 € to 115 €, à la carte 100 €. Closed Tuesday, Wednesday lunchtime and second two weeks in February.* Succeeding his father, Arnaud Lallement was propelled to the front of the stage no doubt far too young for his liking. Luckily, his supportive mother, wife and sister share the tasks intelligently in this elegant castle where he has received the highest gastronomic honours in only a year, including a second Michelin star and a third chef's toque from the Gault Millau.These distinctions have not turned his head, however, for the young chef is aware that success is transient without self-challenge. Quality produce is still top of his list, simple and superb: blue lobster, herb jelly, shellfish juice with thyme and lemon, Breton dory, sucrine rib served with meat juice, farm-bred pigeon in a lean smoked bacon tart with young spinach, and black Gascon pork roasted and garnished *à l'ancienne*.

Vitry-le-François

HOTEL DE LA CLOCHE ** 34, ruc Aristide-Briand ✆ 03 26 74 03 84. *Fax : 03 26 74 15 52. Website: www.hotel-de-la-cloche.fr. Hotel with 22 rooms from 55 € to 100 €. Breakfast from 7 € to 9 €. Restaurant closed Saturday all year, Sunday evening from 1 October to 31 May.Set menus from 22.50 € to 46 €.* Access to Jacques Sautet's gastronomic restaurant is through the hotel. The round tables are prettily set, and the lighting and coloured curtains give the place style. Specialities such as Pere Sautet's *matelote* (fish chowder cooked in wine) 'cite rose' salad and pork trotter *paupiettes* (rolled and stuffed meat packages) are concocted here. On the same theme, the wine list includes Jacques Sautet's own *cuvee*. Next to the restaurant you find the brasserie Le Vieux Briscard.

HAUTE-MARNE

Bourbonne-les-Bains

HOTEL DES LAURIERS ROSES ** Place des Bains ✆ 03 25 90 00 97. *Fax : 03 25 88 78 02.* Annual closing from 1 November-2 April. 68 rooms from 38 € to 68 €. Breakfast 5.50 €. Set menus from 14 €. This contemporary and well-run establishment opposite the Tourist Office and thermal baths has reasonable prices and can guarrantee you a pleasant stay and a *cuisine* both classic and up-to-date. Garden and terrace. Garage.

Chaumont

HOTEL TERMINUS REINE * Place du Général-de-Gaulle ✆ 03 25 03 66 66.** *Fax : 03 25 03 28 95. Website: www.relais-sud-champagne.com.* Open all year. 63 comfortable rooms with TV and Canal +. Double rooms from 37 € to 110 €. Breakfast buffet 8 €. Set menus from 17.50 € to 39 €. *Dégustation* menu 70 €. A short way from the tourist quarter, opposite the station, this grand establishment extends the Champagne country's traditional welcome.The chef gives of his best: you must taste the roast bass in virgin oil, ratatouille minute, venison fricassee with Alsace wine accompanied by fresh pasta with herbs, and heart of beef fillet pan-fried with mushrooms from local forests. A fine wine list includes the excellent Haute-Marne vin de pays.

Colombey-les-Deux-Eglises

HOSTELLERIE DE LA MONTAGNE * RESTAURANT NATALI Rue Pisseloup ✆ 03 25 01 51 69.** *Fax : 03 25 01 53 20. Website: www.hostellerielamontagne.com Annual closing second half of January and September, and 22-27 December.Closed Monday and Tuesday. 9 rooms, including one suite, from 100 € to 150 €. Breakfast 13 €. Set menus from 28 € weekdays to 85 € for the découverte menu.* This friendly regional stopping-off place has had a new address since July 2005.

In a 19thc. house transformed into a hostelry, Jean-Baptiste Natali suggests tempting specialities which change with the seasons. All agree that this talented young chef has launched an original and inventive *cuisine.* A top quality address not to be missed.

Joinville

HOTEL DU SOLEIL D'OR * 9, rue des Capucins 03 25 94 15 66.** *Fax : 03 25 94 39 02.* Annual closing 2 weeks in February. Closed Sunday evenings, Monday and Tuesday lunchtime. 20 rooms from 70 € to 95 €. Breakfast buffet 9.50 €. Set menus from 20 € to 40 €. The Soleil d'Or is located on the way out of town towards Troyes. It has ancient flagstones, beams and roughcast walls in the monastic style, but also air-conditioning and silverware on the gastronomic restaurant tables where Rudy Robbe hones his talents. His cuisine gives priority to sobriety and highlights quality produce.

Langres

HOTEL DE L'EUROPE ** 23, rue Diderot ✆ 03 25 87 10 88. *Fax : 03 25 87 60 65. Website: www.relais-sud-champagne.com.* Closed on Sunday evening from November to late May. 26 rooms from 62 € to 75 €. Breakfast buffet 7.50 €. Set menus from 15 € to 45 €, including a *menu du terroir* (local dishes) 26 € and children's menu 10 €. Located in the Rue Diderot in the town centre, the Hotel de l'Europe is still the same family establishment it's always been.The traveller's comfort is ensured and the traditional cooking makes for attractively-garnished plates. Try bass *flambée* in pastis, a scallop kebab, crusty poultry fillet *'sous bie',* and a tulip of *flambée* Morello cherries. Wash it down with a Montsaugeon wine to really feel part of a most satisfying regional tradition. The service is kindly and attentive. We recommend the *menu du terroir* for the cheese course, with its well-matured local products.

Corsica

CORSICA
Cap Corse
Rogliano
Macinaggio
Bianco Sagro-di-Santa-Guila
Pietracorbara
Canari
Sisco
Monte-Stello
Nonza
Erbalunga
Nice
Marseille
Genova
Toulon
Piombino
Savona
Golfe de St-Florent
BASTIA
Patrimonio
Désert des Agriates
La Conca d'Oro
St-Florent
Oletta
Bastia Plage
Etang de Biguglia
Le Haut Nebbio
Sto Pietro di Tenda
Murato
Nebbio
Bastia Poretta
Toulon
Genova
Marseille
Nice
Savona
Anse de Peraiola
Marseille
Nice
Lozari
Ile-Rousse
Golfe de Calvi
Belgodère
Balagne
Calvi
N 197
Calenzana
Calvi Ste-Catherine
Forêt de Tartagine
Ponte-Leccia
Vescovato
Castellare-di-Casinca
Fiumalto d'Apugnani
Moriani-Plage
San-Nicolao
Cervione
Golfe de Galeria
Monte Cinto 2710 m
Niolo
Restonica
Galeria
Girolata
Lozzi
Piedicroce
Sermano
Moriani
Calacuccia
Albertacce
Corte
Pianello
Golfe de Porto
Porto
Evisa
Forêt de Valdo-Niello
Sto-Pietro-di-Venaco
Venaco
N 200
les Calanche
Piana
Moïte verde

Capo Rosso
Vico
Guagno-les-Bains
Fôret de Vizzanova
Monte d'Oro
Cargèse
Sagone
Bocognano
Sari-d'Orcino
Tiuccia
Golfe de Sagone
Ghisoni
Kirie Eleison
Monte Renoso
Aleria
Plaine d'Aleria
Etang de Diane
Ucciani
Bastelica
Prunelli-di-Fiumorbo
Ghisonaccia
Fiumorbo
AJACCIO
Cauro
Ventiseri
Aérodrome et base de Solenzara
Punta de la Parata
Marseille
Nice
Toulon
Genova
Porto Torres
Ajaccio Campo-Dell'Oro
Zicavo
Sta-Maria-Siché
Monte? Incudine
Solenzara
Tallano-Scopamène
Sari-di-Porto-Vecchio
Porticcio
Golfe d'Ajaccio
Moca-Croce
Col de Bavella
Aullène
Quenza
Station préhistorique de Filitosa
N
O
E
S
Zonza
Favone
Capo di Muro
Olmeto
Ste-Lucie de-Tallano
Golfe de Valinco
Propriano
0 km
10 km
20 km
Massif de l'Ospedale
Lecci
Marseille
Toulon
Porto Torres
Sartène
N 198
Golfe de Porto-Vecchio
Ortolo
Punta-di-Senetosa
Porto-Vecchio
Mégalithes de Cavria
Sotta
Iles Cerbicales
Pianotoli-Caldarello
Figari
Golfe de Ventilegne
Golfe de Santa Manza
Pta de Capicciola
Bonifacio
Ile de Cavallo
Capo Pertusato
Ile de Lavezzi
Sardaigne

AJACCIO AND THE AJACCIO GULF

Ajaccio

Regional capital of Corsica, and departmental prefecture, Ajaccio is an enchanting town. Stroll through the old streets, or beside the palm trees, or watch the time pass from a sunny cafe terrace. Everyone seems to be on holiday. 300 days of sunshine (95 days above 25_C) is one reason why 500,000 tourists and 20,000 trippers come here every year. The beautiful gulf scenery with its 35km coastline and 15km of natural beaches is another.

COURS NAPOLEON. Perpendicular alleys run off from the town's main road, to the quays. The Grand Café Napoleon was built in 1821 by the architect Carrayol, and is the oldest of the town's establishments. Generations of Ajaccians have spent whole afternoons drinking, chatting and playing bridge in its vaulted rooms. Late night opening Friday in July & August. Admission: adult 5.35 €.

MUSEE-PALAIS FESCH 50, rue Fesch © 04 95 21 48 17. *Open all year. Opening times vary according to season. Late night opening Friday in July & August. Admission: adult 5.35 €.* Cardinal Fesch collected French, Spanish, Flemish, German, Dutch and Italian paintings (16,000 in all), and was especially keen on the Italian Primitives. The museum's collection is second only to the Louvre, with Titian, Cosme Tura, Bellini, (after)Raphael, and Botticelli's 'Virgin and Child' as the masterpiece.

IMPERIAL CHAPEL 50, rue Fesch © 04 95 50 13 84. Inaugurated by Napoleon III in 1860, the chapel is in the palace's left wing. Nine members of the Bonaparte family are buried here. (Napoleon's own ashes are in his Invalides tomb, in Paris).

MAISON BONAPARTE Rue Saint Charles © 04 95 21 43 89. *Open 1 April-30 September: 9am-12 noon and 2pm-6pm. Winter: 10am-12 noon and 2pm-4.45pm. Admission: adult 4 €, 18-25s 2.60 €.* Napoleon was born on the antichamber sofa on 15 August 1769, and spent part of his childhood here. Napoleon III had it restored and refurnished, and opened it as a museum.

SANGUINAIRES. You mustn't miss sunset on these four islets (red or black, depending on the weather) with their 150 different plant species. Go by boat from Ajaccio, for a magical view, and come back via the north coast, with the sailors' cemetery, Greeks' chapel and citadel.

PARC NATUREL REGIONAL DE CORSE 2, rue Major Lambroschini © 04 95 51 79 10. *www.parc-naturel-corse.com. Open 8am-12 noon and 2pm-5pm. 8am-7pm in summer.* This nature reserve's centre provides information about its hiking paths in several languages, and gives sensible advice. The reserve was created in 1972, with two aims: to protect the environment, and develop its potential; and it looks after about a third of the territory. Flora and fauna are carefully monitored, and the fabulous Scandola land and sea reserve, listed UNESCO World Heritage, also comes under its protection.

Around Ajaccio

Cargèse

A small and picturesque fishing harbour, influenced by the Greek colony which settled here in the 17thc. In the village, two churches face each other, one following Latin rites, the other Orthodox. The Cargèse archimandrite leads the service in both alternately. The village is becoming more touristy, but so far, has kept its traditional nautical look and peaceful Mediterranean atmosphere.

Porticcio

Fifteen years ago, this was a big sandy beach. The beach is still there, but so is a busy seaside resort with modern infrastructure and facilities. Don't expect to find peace and quiet, or typical local life: at Porticcio you eat, drink, swim amd sunbathe, go out and have fun, in a lively summer holiday atmosphere.

Sagone

An attractive site, with long and beautiful beaches. You can dive, and do all kinds of watersports. Don't forget to go up the pretty road from Sagone Valley to Vico; about half-way up, leaving the river and about 1.5 km after the bridge, you find a footpath to the Saint Antoine Pass (via Balogna) with its fabulous panoramic view.

Soccia

Soccia is the most beautiful village in the area, hidden far from everywhere, yet busy and lively. It has ancient stonework, panoramic views of the mountains from its balconies, and a quality of life you find nowhere else. If you happen to be there on 15 August, you'll find yourself caught up in the yearly festival, the biggest 15 August celebration in the whole mountain circle.

LAC DE CRENO. 1,300 metres above sea-level, this lake is less famous for its water than for its magnificent setting. It boasts two kinds of water-lily, including the rare red lilies in clusters a few metres from the edge. Don't miss the chance to go right round the lake; from the other side it looks like the Grand Canyon, with its breathtaking peak, red rock, and the mountains beyond. One of the island's most attractive walks: rather steep on the way up, but there is a clearly-marked path and a fountain five minutes from the top. It takes a good hour.

Vico

On the way down from the Saint Antoine Pass, you find this remarkable site. A real Corsican village, warm and lively round its charming little square. Clever holidaymakers stay at Vico and go to the beach at Sagone or in the Liscia Gulf, 30 mins by car.

SAINT FRANÇOIS MONASTERY ✆ 04 95 26 83 83. Put up in 1482, and rebuilt in the 17thc., this still-active monastery contains the oldest wooden Christ in Corsica.

BALAGNE AND CASTAGNICCIA

A rich and picturesque region with agricultural and pastoral traditions, despite being by the sea (La Balagne is known as the Garden of Corsica). The beautiful villages with their shepherds, farmers and craftsmen have strong identities, and there are two lively seaside resorts and two proud rival cities: Calvi and Ile-Rousse.

Calvi

The Genoese founded this fortified town, now an arrival point for ferries and planes, and very full in season. Calvi consists of a citadel, or upper town, and a harbour. The citadel contains the Governors' Palace, a great building with two towers, the powder magazine and the 13thc. Saint Jean Baptiste Cathedral, burnt down then restored in the 16thc. Built in the shape of a Greek Cross, this church is finely decorated. Walk round the citadel, and admire its bastions, and views of the mountains, bay and Revellata Gulf. The port was used in the Provence Landings, on 15 August 1944.

STARESO Pointe de la Revellata ✆ 04 95 65 06 18. If you're a nature-lover, and would like to know more about marine biology, or try diving in a dream setting, then Stareso is for you. The Underwater and Oceanographical Research Station is a scientific base for studying the marine environment. A word to the wise: this isn't a place you stop off at along the road! To get there, you have to follow a 4 km track (a 4X4 vehicle is essential). On reaching the Revellata headland, the sea and wild scrubland (maquis) stretch before

Ajaccio, memorial of Napoleon

you. Divers can pass the FFESSM brevet (certificate) and nature-lovers walk in the maquis between dips in the sea. You can stay in the recently-renovated Revellata lighthouse, but call first, to make sure the place is available.

Aléria

Capital of Roman Corsica, Aléria boasts some fine remains, and excellent oysters farmed in Diana's Pond.

MUSEE DEPARTEMENTAL D'ARCHEOLOGIE (Fort de Matra) ET SITE ANTIQUE ✆ 04 95 57 00 92. Matra Fort was built by the Genoese in 1572, and played an important part in the 18thc. Wars of Independence. The museum inside contains objects excavated during archelogical digs; 8,000 years of Corsica's history, and its relations with the Mediterranean civilisations are on display.

RESERVE DE FAUNE DE CASABIANDA. About 5km south of Aleria. The reserve spreads over 1,748ha., and contains ponds, marshes and pasture, lined with juniper trees. It was created in 1951 to protect certain endangered animal species like the red partridge, hare, heron, Turkish turtledove and mallards. The Corsican stag is thriving, having been recently reintroduced into this habitat.

Belgodère

The name means 'beautiful pleasure', and you won't be disappointed when contemplating the soft blue coast and Balagna hills behind, from the town balcony.

Calenzana

This big village overlooking Calvi was once the bastion of Corsican Independence. Today, it is mainly known for its hikes (GR20 departure point).

Corniche de la Castagniccia

This 5km coast road links Cervione and San Nicolao, running along the ridges between mountain and sea. Santa Maria Poggio is a charming village with a breathtaking panoramic view from the church esplanade. Just before San Nicolao, your drive becomes a rally, as the coast road narrows into a pass hemmed in by two mountain sides.

Ghisonaccia

This strategic tourist spot is half-way between Bastia and Bonifacio (85km each way). Once a transhumance site for Ghisoni shepherds, Ghisonaccia became a prosperous little town with the 1960s agriculture boom. The coast has developed its resort, and now offers 4,000 lodgings in holiday villages that blend in well with the environment.

Ghisoni

Marmanu and Sorba Forests contain paths accessible to everyone on foot or by mountain-bike, making Ghisoni an ideal departure point for hikes and walks, where you discover architectural and natural treasures at the same time.

Ile-Rousse

Red porphyry islets in the northwest, and a wide white sandy beach in the south mark the boundaries of this prosperous and very lively town, modern and yet rooted in its Latin culture. Pascal Paoli's 'Isula Rossa' (called 'Paolina' for a while) is one of the island's most attractive seascapes, with its remarkable colours (water, rocks) and light quality, and truly Corsican character.

Piedicroce

Lively, rather touristy but full of character, this village serves as Castagniccia's capital, being at the crossroads of its two main roads.

Pigna

Corsicans and tourists come up from Ile-Rousse to discover this dream village, faithful to its crafts and customs. Artists and craftsmen have settled in the old alleys, and there is plenty of life and atmosphere, with festivals organised now and again.

BASTIA AND CAP CORSE

Bastia

Prefecture of the Haute Corse department, Bastia is the only town that looks like a city. Corsica's industrial and economic sector lies between Poretta (20km south) and Toga in the northern suburbs (former metallurgy quarter) and the city is full of busy people in a hurry. It also contains some fine religious buildings dating from the 16thc.: churches and monasteries emerge from steep and twisted alleys and tiny hidden squares. This is the French Baroque capital, for both sacred and urban architecture, rich in Mediterranean ochre tints and gardens clinging to sloping hillsides above the sea.

SAINTE MARIE CATHEDRAL. A tastefully restored Baroque art treasure.

CITADEL ('Terra Nova'). The site is attractive with its house and hanging garden overlooking the sea. You can admire different views of the town along the walkway.

CHURCH OF THE CONCEPTION. This striking building has a square of shingle in front, illustrating the cosmos with sun and stars.

SAINT CHARLES CHURCH. Founded in 1635 by the Jesuits, but called SaintIgnace (for Ignatius Loyola), Saint Charles Borromee is one of the town's oldest churches.

SAINT JEAN BAPTISTE CHURCH. This listed historical monument can be seen on the Vieux-Port.

PALAIS DES GOUVERNEURS. Bastia fortress overlooks the old harbour. Its keep has high ramparts and can store huge water reserves, allowing it to withstand siege. The Governors' Palace houses the Corsican Ethnographic Museum, and holds plays and concerts in its courtyard.

PLACE SAINT NICOLAS. A great forum and meeting-place, for exchanging gossip or mananging political intrigues and love affairs.

MUSEE DE BASTIA ✆ 04 95 31 09 12. Regional history illustrated by exhibits of all kinds, from the antique to the contemporary. There is also some mainly Italian pictorial art.

Cap Corse

Stretching gently out into the Gulf of Genoa, the 'Isula di l'Isula' (Island's island) is steeped in tradition. The 40km headland is lined with golden beaches and and dizzy heights, and dotted with authentic picturesque villages.

TOURS GENOISES. These ancient round or square towers along the Cap Corse coastline were look-out posts, designed to signal invasion. They were built in the 16thc. when Genoa was defending Corsica (and its own interests) against Saracen raids. The islanders are proud of them, and they may soon become village property again (apart from the finest which will be listed), a means of protecting them from predatory coastal developers, and saving a trace of the dramatic and tragic events they witnessed.

Centuri

This village is on the Cap's west coast, difficult to reach with its sharp ridges. The rocky scenery is beautiful, but there are only a few rather small and stony beaches. Centuri is a lovely little harbour village, with flowers, secret corners, stone staircases and bright houses with typical serpentine roofs (magnesium silicate with pretty green tints). A perfect seascape for watercolour painters.

Nonza

The village's main monument is Sainte Julie Church (16thc.) with its pretty and delicate steeple, and square tower clinging to the cliff. Inside, a painting depicts the saint's martyrdom, and you can admire a fine 16thc. Baroque high altar. The Mamelles Fountain on the road to Pino is a monument to Saint Julie, who had her breasts cut off: two springs rose from the place where they were thrown.

Saint-Florent and Le Nebbio

Known as the Corsican Saint Tropez! This charming little sailing harbour (often renovated) with its narrow streets of shops and restaurants and suberb buildings nearly falling into the sea is a departure point for boat trips into the Saint Florent Gulf and towards the magnificent unspoilt beaches along the maquis towards the Balagne.

PORTO GULF

Porto

Famous for its sunsets over the gulf, and the Spelunca Gorges (going up to Evisa via Ota). Nestling between Ajaccio and Calvi, Porto links mountain and sea, and is in two parts: Vaita and the harbour. You can visit the square tower with its marvellous view of the gulf.

TOUR GENOISE ✆ **04 95 26 16 27.** *Open April-October.* Houses an exhibition on the 16thc. Genoese towers. Illustrations, commentaries and a wall fresco gives the visitor an idea of local life at this period, organised around the tower.

AQUARIUM Place de la Marine ✆ **04 95 26 19 24**. Ideally situated in Porto Harbour's former powder magazine, this aquarium contains the most typical Mediterranean fish: grouper, moray eel and octopus.

RESERVE NATURELLE DE SCANDOLA. An ecological treasure shared between Cap Rosso Peninsula and Galeria. Created in 1975, it was the first French nature reserve on both land and sea, and aims to protect the rare fauna found in this precious Mediterranean zone: the last ospreys, peregrine falcons, bluebirds and swifts, and in the sea, 450 species of algae, endangered fish and magnificent coral banks.

Evisa

Evisa village is a good place to set off on a forest hike. On the way out of the village, visit the chestnut grove, and discover the Spelunca Gorges (1h30mins there and back).

Girolata

Until recently, this peninsula at the world's end had neither electricity nor telephone, and the postman was its only link with the country. Even today, no road goes as far as the fishing village, but you can reach it by boat, from Ajaccio, Cargèse or Galéria.

Piana

A delightful, authentic village, lively in season, nestling in the calanques. This fantastic mineral landscape seems to have been hacked out of the red granite rocks in surrealist shapes.

THE SOUTH

Bonifacio

The 13thc. citadel was put up by the Genoese (who had captured the town in the late 12thc.), 60m up on the cliffs above Bonifacio which juts out into the sea, thus making it unassailable. They added 3m-thick ramparts, and as a last security measure, installed Genoese in it and in the town, replacing the native Corsicans. No wonder the town is so hostile to invaders, be they French or even Corsican!

Things to discover in Bonifacio: the inhabitants, with their history and customs; 'La Semillante': a tragedy that struck the Lavezzi Islands in the last century; the former Roman slave camp on the same islands; the King of Aragon's staircase; the 'Corsican Rudder'; sea caves; Pertusato Semaphore (105m above the sea); citadel; shops and restaurants; boat trip companies (short trip: 45 mins, long trip: 1h30mins, including the Sperone Gulf and its former Roman shelter, Lavezzi and Cavallo Islands etc.). Bonifacio is enchanting, and you'll be hard put to leave it after your visit.

BASTION DU MEMORIAL. A tour of the fortress, straits and surrounding area is marked out. The underground vaults contain reconstructed scenes of the town's history.

U PALAZZO PUBLICU. Part of Bonifacio's church treasure is exhibited, along with a presentation of its five confréries (brotherhoods).

SAINT ERASME CHURCH. This 13thc. church is dedicated to the patron saint of sailors and fishermen.

SAINT JEAN BAPTISTE CHURCH. Contains the carved wooden polychrome statue: *Beheading of Saint John the Baptist*, carried in processions.

ESCALIER DU ROI D'ARAGON. 187 steps carved out of the rock lead to the citadel, or down to the little shingle beaches (for a fee, and they're steep!). A notice advises against their use by people with weak hearts and pregnant women.

CIMETIERE MARIN. This cemetery has an exotic look, with its slate roofs and mausoleums like little houses. Afterwards, you can walk along the cliffs to the citadel.

SAINTE MARIE MAJEURE CHURCH. The biggest and most richly-decorated of the town's churches, with some fine furnishings. The loggia was used as a chamber by local councillors, and the Podéstat, or chief magistrate, dealt out justice there.

BELVEDERE DE LA MANICHELLA. One of Bonifacio's finest sea views.

AQUARIUM DE BONIFACIO 71, quai Comparetti ✆ 04 95 73 03 69. A natural cave in the harbour, fitted out to reveal the underwater world from the tiniest shrimp to the biggest moray eel.

Olmeto

Stories and legends await you in this village, so strongly Corsican in character. It is also a prehistoric site, with a less thrilling but more scientific history!

SANTA MARIA CHURCH. This big Romanesque Church was first built in the 9thc. It has a lantern tower, and contains a remarkable 19thc. organ.

Porto-Vecchio

Known on the island as the 'salt town': salt is harvested on the marshes every September. Corsica's third-biggest town is picturesque, with the busy modern harbour on one side, with musical entertainment in summer, and the old town on the other, set in its stronghold on the pink porphyry rocks. The ramparts are lively in season, housing a number of shops. Stroll through the alleys and squares; don't forget to take a snapshot of the Genoese gate, still intact. Porto-Vecchio is still delightful, even full of tourist hordes.

GOLFE DE PORTO-VECCHIO. Too many recent buildings and tourist facilities have rather spoilt this site's natural beauty, though it is part of the International Marine Park, and the Pointe de la Chiappa is a protected zone for marine species.

GOLFE DE SANTA GIULIA. A sort of laguna, between a pond and the sea, with very fine white sand. The site is fitted out like a holiday village, with barriers to filter traffic and 'sleeping policemen' which reassure parents. Ideal for learning to windsurf.

PLAGE DE PALOMBAGGIA. A pretty coast road links the beautiful beaches of Asciaghju, with its clear, tropically-blue water, and Palombaggia, facing the Cerbicale Islands. You walk through a pine-grove, and climb a dune before reaching the beach itself.

Propriano

Its little port is lined with pretty terraces in season, and the town boasts good shops, a theatre and some sandy beaches. Inland, there are prehistoric remains, hiking and bridle paths and some well-preserved traditional villages.

Bonifacio's port

POINTE DE CAMPOMORO. A beautiful coastal trip. Follow the Sartène road until just after the bridge over the Rizzanese, where you turn on to the D121. Go past the aerodrome and pretty Portigliolo Beach: you come to some marvellous views across the gulf, notably at Belvédère and Punta di Campomoro. though the best panoramic view can be had from the restored Genoese tower (1586), one of the islands' biggest.

Sartène

Said to be 'the most Corsican of Corsican towns'. Sartène is beautiful, austere and discreet, with its tall fortified houses in grey granite clinging to the rock, and medieval alleys and passages. Sit on a cafe terrace in Place Porta, and watch the world go by. Despite the touristy shops and restaurants, Sartène's atmosphere is still authentic.

The surrounding countryside with its vineyards and wild maquis has some superb routes for discovering prehistoric sites. Sartène also boasts a 33km coastline, from Campomoro to Rocapina.

MUSEE DE LA PREHISTOIRE CORSE Rue Croce © 04 95 77 01 09. *Open May-September, except Sunday: 10am-12 noon and 2pm-6pm. Closed weekends out of season.* All sorts of objects, statues and carved stones give you an idea of the lifestyles, arts and characteristics of the island's different prehistoric civilisations (Neolithic, Megalithic, Torrean and later, Roman).

VIEILLE VILLE. Walk under the Hôtel de Ville arch to Place du Maggiu, and you are in the old town. Close by, the Maison des Artisans displays pottery and gastronomic specialities. From time to time, you come to a staircase, which may lead to a private house, or to another quarter. The shops are grouped round the square and Cours Soeur Amélie, the good food street.

Solenzara

This enviable site with its eucalyptus trees and mountain backdrop was once infected with mosquitoes; today it is a seaside resort on the eastern coast, known as the Cote des Nacres (mother-of-pearl), calm and family-orientated. Solenzara's beaches without currents are perfect for kids, and the fishing harbour is full of big boats, being the only one able to accommodate them.

CENTRAL CORSICA

Corte (Corti)

The island's historic and geographic heart. Pasquale Paoli laid the foundations for a Corsican Nation at Corte in the 18thc, set in the middle of dramatic gorges: Restonica, Scala di Santa Regina, Tavignano; on the western edge of the Castagnaccia and the northern sector of the Vizzavona Pass, east of the Niolo and south of the Nebbio. The region's resources are pastoral and tourist-based, which is understandable, given Corte's vital and genuine beauty.

The town's central position and historical associations make it a real capital for many Corsicans, who reject the beaches' artificial lifestyle in favour of something more authentic. Corte's buildings are modest but full of character, and the old town is well-preserved, seeming to reject all occupants.

PLACE PAOLI. Designed by Victor Huguenin (1864), Pascal Paoli's bronze statue rises proudly in the centre of the square, linking the old quarters and citadel to the more recent town.

SAINTE CROIX CHAPEL. Inside, the chapel is paved with grey Restonica marble, and the single nave has interesting trompe-l'oeil perspectives. You can admire a fine Italian-style organ and Baroque reredos. The famous Granitola penitents' procession held on Maundy Thursday leaves from Saint Croix.

CHURCH OF THE ASSUMPTION. Built in 1450 on the Place Gaffory, extended by Alexandre Sauli, the church contains a fine carved wooden pulpit and a Baroque Christ, also in wood. The tall campanile overlooks the old town, and is its most ancient monument.

PLACE DU POILU. The Arrighi de Casanova's house is on the right: the general was made Duke of Padua, having distinguished himself at Saint Jean d'Acre and Marengo. In 1768, Napoleon's father lived in it, and Joseph Bonaparte (future King of Spain) was born there. On the left is the Palais National. This fine example of Genoese civil architecture was the Corsican Parliament and seat of government under Pascal Paoli, and the first Corsican university was set up here.

CITADEL. The old town's most spectacular building. The citadel was built in the 15thc., 100m up on top of a headland. Unlike the Genoese fortresses, it was built inland, and served first as a political prison, then as barracks for a Foreign Legion regiment until 1984. It now houses the Corsican Regional Anthropology Museum.

NID D'AIGLE. This tower was built in 1419 by Vincentello d'Istria, in the pay of the King of Aragon, who also built the citadel. There is a magnificent view of Corte and its surroundings.

BELVEDERE. Wide panoramic view of the citadel and fine old Corte residences. You can visit the cachots, where Corsicans were imprisoned during the war with Genoa.

MUSEE DE LA CORSE La Citadelle ✆ 04 95 45 25 45. *Open all year. Opening times vary according to season.* Gives a complete picture of rural Corsican culture and traditions. On one side, the Doazan Gallery contains objects collected by the ethnologist Father Doazan, in memory of Corsica's pastoral and agrarian history. On the other side, the 'Museum in progress' gallery illustrates current developments in tourism, industry and the Corsican identity crisis.

PALAIS NATIONAL. The Genoese building at the citadel entrance was the seat of Pascal Paoli's government. The first university was founded in this palace, but then closed down. 200 years later, it has reopened as the University Institute of Corsican Studies.

VALLEE DE LA RESTONICA. This valley is protected by the Corsican Regional Natural Park, and is a listed site with plenty of varied fauna. You can spot birds of prey, great sparrows, and unusual breeds like the Corsican nuthatch; and meet flocks of sheep, proof that pastoral activity is still a reality.

LACS DE LA RESTONICA. These famous lakes are popular in summer. Melo, Capitello and Goria, and the Renoso lakes, are part of the Restonica massif.

Calacuccia

You must explore Calacuccia's alleys and stone staircases to unearth its hidden charms, like the Christ in Saint Pierre Church. The picturesque, old-fashioned monastery on the edge of the village is both a museum and a gite. You can go right round the lake, passing through Casamaccioli village. Valdo-Niello Forest contains clumps of beeches, and laricio pines, leafier than their maritime cousins.

Monte Cinto is the island's highest peak (2,170m), but is quite easily climbed, though you need to be fit! On a clear day, from the top ('Corsica's Roof'), you can see the whole island, as far as the Italian coast.

Levie

PARC NATUREL REGIONAL DE CORSE Sorba ✆ 04 95 78 42 03. Capital of the Alta Rocca, 1,300m above the Ortolo Valley, Levie consists of several UNESCO-listed historic and prehistoric sites, with a few hamlets, and hiking paths winding through oak trees towards Cagna mountain. It is a lively, beautiful village dating back to the Middle Ages, with 16thc. granite houses and the square-towered Saint Nicolas Church, containing a 15thc. ivory Christ.

MAISON D'ACCUEIL DES SITES ARCHEOLOGIQUES du 'Pianu di Livia' ✆ 04 95 78 48 21. CUCURUZZU ✆ 04 95 78 48 21. *Admission fee. Open 1 April-30 October, audioguide (walkman) supplied on entry.* This huge complex consists of an enclosure and an upper monument formed by a pile of rocks, which weigh a tonne. Bronze Age hunter-gatherers lived in the *castellu*, with its craftsmen's huts, basins for grinding cereals and storage spaces.

Citadel of Corte

FOOD AND DRINK

Corsica's insularity and landscapes are reflected in its cooking; a unique mixture of Mediterranean cuisine (olive oil, pasta, seafood) and a more robust mountain diet of charcuterie.

Charcuterie

Corsican cold meats are excellent. Figatelli are pork liver sausages made in winter and eaten until spring; dried and smoked, and flavoured with herbs and seasonings (goat meat is sometimes added). The lonzu is a filet of smoked pork, seasoned and dried for two months only. There are also coppa (rolled pork shoulder, dried for 4 months, with red wine and/or seasonings added) and pancetta (streaky pork belly). The country is also known for its terrines of wild boar and figatellu, and blackbird and thrush pâtés.

SYNDICAT POUR L'AOC 'CHARCUTERIE' Ajaccio ✆ 04 95 29 26 00

Chestnuts

For centuries, the chestnut tree provided Corsican 'bread', with chestnuts as the basic food, life being hard. They were boiled, grilled or ground into flour to make polenta, cakes and even chestnut bread.

In Castagniccia, the chestnut region, 22 different dishes based on the fruit used to be served at weddings.

GROUPEMENT REGIONAL DES PRODUCTEURS ET TRANSFORMATEURS DES CHATAIGNES ET MARRONS DE CORSE Corte ✆ 04 95 48 10 30

Clémentine de Corse

Over 25,000 tonnes of clementines are harvested in the island every year. They must be hand-picked ripe, juice and acidity levels are checked, and no chemical treatment after harvesting is allowed.

APRODEC 15, ave. Jean Zuccarelli - BASTIA ✆ 04 95 31 89 37

Cheeses

These were traditionally made by shepherds and women in spring and autumn, Today, Corsica produces 2,500 tonnes of cheese; 75% from ewe's milk, the rest from goat's. Brocciu, a soft white fromage frais, is the best-known. The others are: niulincu, smooth with a scraped crust (from ewes or goats); round venacesu; artinesu with its pressed, medium-soft texture; calenzanesu, soft and spicy (goat) creamy bastelicaccia cheese and cuscionu, with its coloured crust and soft texture. They are all delicious with country or chestnut bread, and fig jam, watermelon or melon, to soften the strong taste. For more information:

ASSOCIATION REGIONALE 'CASGIU CASANU' (farm cheeses). Mezzavia ✆ 04 95 25 65 74

Olive oil

Back in fashion, along with healthy eating. The mills are working again, with modernised picking and pressing techniques. Corsican oil did not comply with European standards at first, but that is now being seen to. For more information:

SYNDICAT INTERPROFESSIONNEL DES OLEICULTEURS DE CORSE Santa Lucia di Talla ✆ 04 95 78 01 83

Sausage in Bastelica

Honey

Corsican honey is reputed for its rich flavour, which comes from the wide variety of flowers and trees available to the bees (2,835 species, 127 endemic) and resulting palette of nectars. At one time, every family had a hive, some built into the house walls (Venaco rock-wall illustrates the importance of 19thc. bee-keeping). Now you just have to taste it!

SYNDICAT AOC MIEL DE CORSE Mele di Corsica - SAINTE LUCIE DE MORIANI ✆ 04 95 38 54 03

Oursins (Sea Urchins)

Love them or hate them, they are an institution on the island. The sought-after coral is in fact the animal's gonads, or genital glands. They can be cooked in soups, creams, omelettes, soufflés and with scrambled eggs, but fans prefer eating them in the shell, at the water's edge. Families and friends meet up on Ajaccio's beaches at Sunday lunchtime, round a fire. With good bread and a glass of white wine, this is heaven!

Fish and seafood

Fish play a big part in Corsican cuisine. Red mullet, mostelles, sea bream and bass are also bred in fish farms. Fish is often freshly grilled; the langoustines are reputed and can be cooked in a court-bouillon or or grilled in olive oil. Inland, you can eat river trout and eels.

Pasta and polenta

Cannelloni and ravioli are served as an entrée Italian-style, or with meat. The recipes are more highly-spiced than in Italy, and pasta stuffing is usually brocciu. Meat dishes can also be eaten with polenta, made with chestnut flour instead of corn, or slices of thickened polenta as a bread substitute.

Meat, poultry and game

Corsicans eat a lot of pork and kid (fried with garlic, olives, or in a sauce), but also more and more veal (excellent!). There are a number of wild boar recipes (stewed and simmered, to bring out the strong flavour), and pigeons and woodcock in season. Thrush and blackbirds are eaten in pates.

Wine

Vines are as ancient as olive groves in Corsica, and wine has overtaken clementines as the main export force. The 450 winegrowers (7,200ha. of vineyards) go for quality rather than quantity (3,800ha. in AOC, 3,100ha. vins de pays and table wines.).

COMITE INTERSYNDICAL DES VINS DE CORSE 7, bd. du Général de Gaulle - BASTIA ✆ 04 95 32 91 32. *www.vinsdecorse.com*

UNION DES VIGNERONS DE L'ILE DE BEAUTE (U.V.I.B.) Aleria ✆ 04 95 57 02 48. *www.vignerons.iledebeaute.com*

Corsican cheeses

© Xavier Bonnin

Hotels & Restaurants

Ajaccio

LE 20123 2, rue du Roi-de-Rome ✆ 04 95 21 50 05. *Closed Monday. Open evenings only. One set menu 28 €.* A village in the heart of the town! The owner has totally rebuilt his native village (Pila-Canale in Southern Corsica) in Ajaccio, including even the sounds of his childhood, in a fight against nostalgia. He also shares his grandmother's (*minane's*) cooking with visitors, on a single menu with several choices. The dishes are strictly traditional (he insists on it) and the cheese is served with a spoonful of fig jam, sending your palate into raptures. Another world!

A LA FUNTANA 9, rue Notre-Dame ✆ 04 95 21 78 04. *E-mail: afuntana@wanadoo.fr Closed Sunday and Monday all day, except in summer, open every evening. Set menus from 32 € to 52 €. A la carte 40 €.*This restaurant was run by a *Toque d'Or* until 2003, and his successor continues along the same gastronomic lines. The Barazza family has added its personal touch, as well as refurbishing the place. Art is everywhere, even on the plates. Mediterranean cooking is given pride of place, especially with Corsican produce, such as a small local producer's charcuterie, or oysters from Diane's Pool. The result is magic - but if it comes largely from the island's sea and mountain harvest, other regions of France contribute, and the Breton lobster and veal sweetbreads deserve a mention.

Bastia

LA CITADELLE 6, rue du Dragon–Vieille-Ville ✆ 04 95 31 44 70.
Fax: 04 95 32 77 53. Website: www.restaurantlacitadelle.com E-mail: restaurantlacitadelle@wanadoo.fr. Manager: Maurice Bovo. Closed in February, Sunday evening and Monday. Lunchtime formula 24 €, set menu 33 €. A la carte 40 €. There is a new broom at La Citadelle this year; young chef Gilles Maza from Béarn has arrived in the kitchens. This former oil press located within the citadel walls of old Bastia (the press is still intact and preserved in the middle of the dining room) has been converted into a restaurant, specialising in foie gras (prepared three different ways) but also spicy cuttlefish *en cocotte* with Espelette pepper, Corsican veal selected by M. Martinelli, and the Alimea dessert *farandole.* The wine list offers an honorable choice of both Corsican and other French wines. Good luck to the new chef - we'll be following up.

CORSICA HOTELS BEST WESTERN * Avenue Jean-Zuccarelli–Le Fango ✆ 04 95 55 05 10.** *Fax: 04 95 55 05 11. Website: www.bestwestern-corsica-hotel.com E-mail: contact@corsica-hotels.fr* With 71 rooms, from 55 € (single) to 96 € (triple), this hotel is ideally located in the town centre, 20km from the airport, 400m from the station and 900m from the port. The hotel also has a garage with security system (for a fee), if you book in advance. The rooms are simple, clean and tastefully decorated, and snacks are available at any time. Air-conditioning and soundproofing guarantee a peaceful night's rest. A very professional establishment.

Bonifacio

LE VOILIER 81, quai Comparetti ✆ 04 95 73 07 06 fax 04 95 73 14 27 *Set menus from 24.50 € to 29.50 €. A la carte (evening) 50 €. Annual closing January-February, weekly closing Wednesday and Sunday evening in low season only. Management: M. Jean-Paul Bartoli. E-mail: lautrerestaurant@wanadoo.fr* This semi-gastronomic *cuisine* opens the gateway to the Mediterranean, those flavours typical of southern sea and country produce produced by Jean-Paul Bartoli. A fine menu with the day's suggestions, according to what is available at market. We especially liked the scallop carpaccio and Denti tartare with Dublin Bay prawns in filo pastry, courgette flowers stuffed with clams, capon stuffed with capon and its *fumé*, Jean-Paul's bouillabaisse and the red fruit *craquelin* and sorbets. Pleasant and attentive service from Madame. An excellent gastronomic restaurant with competitive prices.

Calvi

LA SIGNORIA ** Luxe Route de la Forît de Bonifato ✆ 04 95 65 93 00.** *Fax: 04 95 65 38 77. Website: www.hotel-la-signoria.com – e-mail: info@hotel-la-signoria.com. Manager: M. Jean-Baptiste Ceccaldi. Annual closing November-March. 24 rooms and suites, from 130 € to 450 €. Half-board supplement 77 € per person. Set menus from 55 € to 95 €. A la carte 70 €.* This sublime 18thc. Genoese residence is marvellously located in a park with Mediterranean trees, on the way into Calvi. The personalised, well-kept rooms and suites are decorated with sophistication; together with the facilities, this makes La Signoria one of the best hotels on the island. You can eat in the gastronomic restaurant in the evening, and have lunch round the pool. The Mediterranean grounds and restaurant terrace sheltered by hundred-year-old palm trees invite you to relax here for longer than planned, and enjoy the new chef's talented cooking. The island's best vintages feature on the wine list, along with others from the French continent.

LA VILLA ** Luxe Chemin de Notre-Dame-de-la-Serra ✆ 04 95 65 10 10.** *Fax: 04 95 65 10 50. Website: www.hotel-lavilla.com – e-mail: reservation@hotel-lavilla.com. Set menus 75 €. A la carte 130 €. Dégustation menu 150 €. Rooms and suites 380 € and 560 €.* This hotel in its beautiful natural environment boasts sophisticated rooms decorated with taste and sobriety. The setting is enchanting, overlooking Calvi Bay. There are four swimming pools, a sports centre and tennis courts at your disposal, and the beach is 5 minutes by car. Prices vary according to season. Chef Christophe Bacquié, holder of a *Meilleur Ouvrier de France* title, concocts delicate Mediterranean dishes in a unique atmosphere marked by Corsican generosity. Note that this magic place is part of the *Relais et Châteaux* chain.

Erbalunga

LE PIRATE Place Marc-Bardon ✆ 04 95 33 24 20. *Fax: 04 95 33 18 97. Website: www.restaurantlepirate.com – e-mail: jeanpierrericci@aol.com. Manager: Jean-Pierre Ricci, chef Gerry Momnessin. Closed Monday, Tuesday and Wednesday lunchtime in season. Set lunchtime menus du marché 35 € and evening menu découverte 55 €. A la carte 50 €. Air-conditioned dining room, terrace on the edge of the small fishing harbour. Mediterranean gastronomic cuisine.* Young Gerry Monmessin and his two acolytes are in charge of the kitchens this year, offering subtle variations on the seafood and country themes. The best ingredients are carefully selected according to season, and skillfully prepared, but there is no point in describing the menu; it is so varied and features so many surprises. Environment and service are well up to the standards set by this picturesque village. It's great to find a place to eat of this quality in the region.

Piana

CAPO ROSSO ** Route des Calanches ✆ 04 95 27 82 40.** *Fax: 04 95 27 80 00. Website: www.caporosso.com – e-mail: infos@caporosso.com Open April to mid-October. 50 rooms from 80 € to 300 €, including 8 luxury and a junior suite. Breakfast included in the room price. Set menus terroir 25 €, pêcheur 35 €, découverte 58 €. A la carte 50 €, half-board from 85 € per person.* Pleasant rooms, calm and full of light, well up to holiday comfort standards. The setting is exceptional, set back from the village towards Porto, with a unique view of the calanches and the sea. The hotel has been completely renovated; the air-conditioned rooms all come with balcony. The gastronomic restaurant Le Neptune lives up to the site, with fine menus featuring local produce, skillfully prepared. House specialities include grilled Dublin Bay prawns and bouillabaisse.

Porticcio

LE MAQUIS** Luxe ✆ 04 95 25 05 55.** *Fax: 04 95 25 11 70. Website: www.lemaquis.com – e-mail: info@lemaquis.com Closed 2 January - 11 February. 25 rooms and 3 suites from 155 € to 1,200 €. A la carte 90 €. Set menu 65 €.* Corsican luxury, in a secret, fairytale place away from the seaside resort. Le Maquis is located on the edge of the coast in an exotic atmosphere full of flowers. Decorated with white stone and Mediterranean furniture, the rooms are superb and luminous, and perfectly equipped, while the apartments come with jacuzzi, plasma TV screen and panoramic terrace. Two pools (one indoor heated) a tennis court and massage parlour complete the facilities at your disposal. M. Lorenzoni-Salini runs L'Arbousier, one of the island's most reputed restaurants, with its fine gastronomic dinner menu and lunchtime grills served on the terrace. Seminar area, seating 30. Extensive wine list with Corsican and Continental vintages.

Porto-Vecchio

BELVEDERE Route de Palombaggia ✆ 04 95 70 54 13 *Fax 04 95 70 42 63. Website : www.hbcorsica.com. Set menus from 50 € to 90 €. A la carte 80 €. Closed 8 January-11 March.* Porto Vecchio tops the list for luxury hotels, above Calvi or Ajaccio. The Belvédère is part of this privileged cast, combining an unforgettable sea view with top-of-the-range *cuisine* at corresponding prices. You have two options when it comes to eating: the grill, Mari e Terra, which offers cabri, lamb and suckling pig, along with fish, vegetables and seafood (June to October only) and the 'gastronomic' restaurant for dinner too, in its magnificent rotunda dining room. The best local ingredients are cooked Mediterranean-style (Dublin Bay prawn ravioli with mushrooms, Corsican veal chops, and bass cooked on its skin). Not quite up to the standards set by the Grand Hotel at Cala Rossa or the Casadelmar, but then the prices are more reasonable.

CASADELMAR Route de Palombaggia ✆ 04 95 72 34 34 *Fax 04 95 72 34 35. Website : www.casadelmar.fr. Set menus from 65 € to 145 €. A la carte 150 €. Closed mid-November to late March.* This luxury hotel giving onto Porto-Vecchio Bay was opened in May 2004, with an explosive effect. Both hotel facilities and restaurant laid claim to the top-of-the-range, and as such attracted a great deal of attention. The prices are rather predictably steep. Davide Bisetto, the Italian chef, trained at the Carpaccio, one of the Parisian Royal Monceau's two restaurants, and promotes an Italian-influenced cuisine: Venetian-style *baccala* (cod), farm bacon and polenta with cress, carnaroli rice risotto with Oristano saffron pistils and Sardinian gambas, lightly-spiced crispy wild duck, citrus sauce and gnocchi with rosemary, and old rum baba, strawberry, basil and lemon. The sumptuous setting with terrace overlooking the gulf and town of Porto-Vecchio, relaxed and efficient service, and fine Southern cellar in the capable hands of Guillaume Bonnaud place the Casadelmar among the Mediterranean's finest restaurants.

Sartène

SANTA BARBARA Route de Propriano ✆ 04 95 77 09 06. *Fax: 04 95 77 09 09. Website: www.sarteneauberge.fr – e-mail: aubergesantabarbara@wanadoo.fr Manager: Mme Gisèle Lovichi. Annual closing mid-October to Easter. Set menus 28 €. Average bill: 35 €. Advance booking recommended.* One of the island's prettiest places to eat, both for the setting - green haven of peace above the town with a superb flowering arbour - and the charming meals. The radiant owner is no doubt proud of her restaurant's excellent ingredients and cooking; you'll appreciate the snail *aumônière* (folded pancake) with tagliatelli and garlic, mutton with haricot beans, roast pigeon with myrtle and polenta, and *pain perdu* (bread pudding) with pears and caramel sauce, if you've room left. The cellar specialises in local wines, the set menus are good, and the service attentive and smiling. This year, for the first time, you can stay overnight here, in one of three superb villas sleeping 8, with private pool.

Côte d'Azur Monaco

Saint-Tropez

Montélimar
RHÔNE - ALPES
Veynes
Bourg-St-Andéol
Pierrelatte
Valréas
Nyons
Rosans
Aygues
Buech
Lez
Barjac
St-Ambroix
Bollène
Pont-St-Esprit
Ouvèze
Baronnies
Vaison-la-Romaine
Bagnols-sur-Cèze
Orange
Mont Ventoux 1910 m.
Comtat Venaissin
LANGUEDOC-ROUSSILLON
Laudun
PROVENCE-
Sorgues
Carpentras
Uzégeois
VAUCLUSE
Forcalquier
AVIGNON
L'Isle-sur-la-Sorgue
Aramon
Gordes
Oraison
NÎMES
Marguerittes
Cavaillon
Bonnieux
Manosque
Bouillargues
Lubéron
Vergèze
Alpilles
Verdon
Fontvieille
St-Gilles
Vauvert
Eyguières
Salon-de-Provence
Lunel
Arles
BOUCHES-
Rians
Aigues-Mortes
Petit Rhône
Miramas
DU-RHÔNE
Camargue
Grand Rhône
Crau
Aix-en-Provence
Istres
Arc
Gardanne
Trets
St.-Maxim
Stes-Maries
Port-Louis-du-Rhône
Port-de-Bouc
Roquevaire
Allauch
GOLFE DU LION
Martigues
MARSEILLE
Cassis
La Ciotat
Bandol
La Seyne-sur-Mer
MER MÉDITERRANÉE
0
50 km

Embrun
UTES-ALPES
ITALIE
Coni
Ubaye
Barcelonnette
La Motte
Mont Pelat
3051 m.
Mont Ténibre
3031 m.
eron
Bléone
Colmars
Isola
Var
Tinée
DIGNE
St-Martin-Vésubie
Mont Clapier
3045 m.
La Brigue
ALPES-DE-HAUTES-PROVENCE
ALPES-MARITIMES
St-André-les-Alpes
Barrême
Roya
Asse
ALPES-CÔTE D'AZUR
Estéron
Vésubie
Sospel
SAN REMO
Moustiers-Ste-Marie
Contes
Tourrette-Levant
Carros
Artuby
Loup
Menton
Lac de Ste Croix
Vence
NICE
MONACO
Cagnes-sur-Mer
Villefranche
Plan de Canjuers
Grasse
Fayence
Aups
Le Cannet
Antibes
Salernes
Juan-les-Pins
Draguignan
VAR
Cannes
Le Muy
Argens
Fréjus
Vidauban
Roquebrune-sur-Argens
St-Raphaël
Brignoles
Le Luc
Ste-Maxime
Maures
St-Tropez
Grimaud
Cogolin
Ramatuelle
Bormes-les-Mimosas
Cavalaire-sur-Mer
ULON
Le Lavandou
Hyères
Îles du Levant
Îles de
rquerolles
Îles de Port-Cros
Îles d'Hyères
Altitude (metres)
1000
500
200
100
Borders
Regional border
Departemental border
Motorway
Major road
Railway
Canal
Town
Prefecture

TOULON, MAURES AND THE ILES D'OR

Toulon

Toulon harbour begins at the Pradet and ends at the Saint Mandrier Peninsula. On a guided boat trip, you discover the arsenal, National Navy buildings, sailors' graveyard, port at La Seyne-sur-Mer, former boatyards, Tamaris' resort coast-road, Lazaret Bay with its mussel beds, the Sablettes, Saint-Mandrier Peninsula, the long dyke closing the harbour to the east, the fortifications, Cap Brun, the smugglers' path and Le Mourillon. Seasickness-sufferers can climb 500m up Mont Faron in the north of Toulon (1944 Provence Landings site) on foot, or go by road or télépherique. The harbour view is marvellous, and you can visit the memorial.

MUSEE DE LA MARINE Place Monsenergue – Quai de Norfolk ✆ 04 94 02 02 01. *Open every day: 10am-12 noon and 2pm-6pm. Admission: adult 5 €, 6-18s 2.30 €* Access via the magnificent old Arsenal gate (1738). The museum illustrates Toulon's seafaring history from the Middle Ages to the present day, with a number of scale models.

RADE (HARBOUR). Several pleasure boat companies on Quai Cronstadt offer tours of the harbour.
CATAMARANS ALAIN ✆ 04 94 46 29 89

SNRTM ✆ 04 94 62 41 14

TMT ✆ 04 94 23 25 36

Maures and Iles d'Or

Giens Peninsula

The isthmus linking Giens to the mainland are unique, Almanarre Beach, famous for its windsurfing championships, borders the western one, which is only 50m wide.

Ile de Porquerolles

A few cable lengths from the coast, the biggest of the Hyères Islands (7km x 3km) is a pleasure to visit. Discover the scenery and village by bike or on foot (there are few cars, and strict regulations apply), then have a swim in the Silver Beach's turquoise water. Note that Porquerolles is very crowded in season!

Toulon's port

Ile de Port-Cros

This is the Iles d'Or archipelago's smallest island (10m²), and a national park: nature lovers can admire the seagulls and cormorants, and clouds of coloured butterflies in spring. The fish are quite tame (perhaps because fishing is banned!) and will swim close to divers, swallowing the air bubbles they make. From mid-June to mid-September (10am-5pm), you can take an underwater trip armed with mask, snorkel and flippers, and discover a wealth of carefully preserved aquatic treasures.

Le Lavandou

This old fishing-village in the south of the Maures massif is now a popular seaside resort, with fine waters and coastline. The harbour holds 1,100 sailing boats, and there are no fewer than 12 beaches. Anglade Beach, the most westerly, is also the most fashionable with lounge lizards.

La Garde-Freinet

This old Provencal village is perched on its Maures massif peak like a sentinel; hence its name. You can still see the 9thc. Freinet fort. Before the coming of tourism, the village lived on its forest resources: woodcutting, chestnuts and cork making. Discover some hamlets hidden in superb scenery by following one of the many marked-out walking paths.

VERDON GORGES AND PROVENCE VERTE

Gorges du Verdon

Over thousands of years, the River Verdon slowly eroded the Provencal plateau's Jurassic limestone, resulting in this huge fault with its 800m canyons, a natural border between the Var and the Alpes de Haute Provence. Intrepid Edouard Alfred Martel was the first man to follow the Verdon into its bed, and fully explore the gorges (alone) in 1905. Today, there are 3 ways to do it. Firstly, by car on the Route des Crêtes, with its superb plunging views (2 hours and 100km there and back). >From the A8, take the RN555 towards Draguignan, go up to Comps on the D955, and follow Sublime cliff road on the D71. Coming from Moustiers Sainte Marie, take the Sublime via Aiguines and the right bank, towards Mayreste Belvédère on the D952. The most spectacular viewpoints are Mescla Balcony, with its panoramic view of the Verdon-Artuby confluence, and Rancoumas Belvédère, 400m above water level. Secondly, you can go on foot, along the hiking paths (10 different routes) Consult the Guide des Sentiers de Verdon, (from Tourist Offices and the Maison du Parc). Finally, why not by kayak (about 7 hours)? There are no safety exits along the route; the only way out is on arrival, in Lake Sainte Croix, so experienced kayakists alone should attempt the descent (technically difficult, with a risk of water rushing in from the Chaudanne and Castillon dams). Make sure you take a practised guide.

Provence Verte

Draguignan

France's main garrison is also the centre of La Dracénie, a group of villages nestling in green countryside, each with its character, history and treasures.

MUSEE DE L'ARTILLERIE, ECOLE DE L'ARTILLERIE Quartier Bonaparte BP 400 ✆ 04 98 10 83 85. *Open Sunday-Wednesday: 9am-12 noon and 1.30pm-5.30pm. Admission free.* Set up by the artillery training school, the museum traces the history and development of the gun. It includes a collection of old cannons (mainly Second Empire), ammunition, historical reconstructions, slideshows and exhibitions. The address is not mere coincidence, since Napoleon began his career as an artillery sub-lieutenant.

Le Thoronet

THORONET ABBEY. Enquiries: ✆ 04 94 60 43 90 *www.monum.fr. Open Monday-Saturday: 10am-1pm and 2pm-5pm. Under-18s and unemployed free. Admission: adult 6.50 € concessions 4.10 € Guided tours for groups (bookings only). Enquiries: ✆ 04 94 60 43 90.* Thoronet (the Var's most visited site) is one of the 3 Provencal Cistercian abbeys (Senanque and Silvacane are the others). Kitchens, scriptorium and refectory have disappeared, but the church, cloister, chapter house, storeroom and dormitory are still intact. Built in the shape of a Latin cross with one nave, the church boasts excellent acoustics, perfect for Gregorian chants. Its harmonious proportions and balanced structure make it on of the finest examples of Provençal Romanesque architecture.

Varages

EARTHENWARE MUSEUM Place de la libération ✆ 04 94 77 60 39. *Open every day July-September. Traces the history of Varages earthenware.*

FACTORY SHOP, VARAGES FRANCE Route de Manosque ✆ 04 94 77 64 79. *Open every day: 9am-6pm.* A good place to buy traditional Provencal pottery tableware at unbeatable prices. The glazed and decorated earthenware is made on the site according to Varages tradition dating back to 1695.

CANNES AND GRASSE

Cannes

Cannes has always attracted stars, celebrities and royalty, transforming it from a small early-19thc. fishing port into a sophisticated resort. In 1946, the town hosted the first Film Festival, now its major event, held every year in May. Today, oil sheiks have replaced the old European dynasties, but Cannes still sparkles with the same cosmopolitan brilliance.

LA CROISETTE. Along this famous esplanade are the palaces (French term for top hotels), where jet set, aristocracy and film world congregate every May. From the Croisette headland you have a panoramic view of l'Estérel and La Napoule to the west, and the Golfe-Juan, Cap d'Antibes and Pre-Alps in the east, along with the Lérins Islands, which seem very close.

ALLEE DES ETOILES DU CINEMA. Around the Palais des Festivals on the Georges Pompidou Esplanade, over 200 of cinema's greatest names have left their handprints in plaster casts.

PALAIS DES FESTIVALS. The pride of Cannes, despite looking a bit like a bunker. Built in 1982, it contains an auditorium (2,500 seats) a theatre (1,000 seats), rooms equipped with simultaneous translation facilities, exhibition halls, and a Salon des Ambassadeurs (standing space for 3,000), and is perfect for festivals and congresses. Don't forget the photo on the red-carpeted steps outside, for instant star status!

PORT SAINT-PIERRE; JETEE ALBERT-EDOUARD. The world's most beautiful yachts, lie at anchor here all year. Boat trips to the Lérins Islands leave from this jetty, just behind the harbour station.

QUARTIER DU SUQUET. The remains of old Cannes are found in this quarter: Mont Chevalier, ancient fortified citadel with narrow, steep and twisting alleys, and Notre Dame d'Espérance Church (Place de la Castre), pure Provencal Gothic.

Iles de Lérins

Even if your stay in Cannes is short, you must at least take a boat trip to Sainte Marguerite, bigger and closer of the two islands.

SAINTE MARGUERITE. Crossing takes 15 mins. Round trip: adult 10 , 4-10s 6.50 . Boats leave every hour from the harbour station (04 92 98 71 30). The island is covered in eucalyptus forest (180ha.), and has a jagged rocky coast with a number of little creeks where you can swim (notably in the channel between the islands).

SAINT HONORAT. The smaller neighbour Saint Honorat houses one of Christendom's oldest abbeys, and still belongs to Sénanque Cistercian Order. The monks who live there observe Saint Benoit's rule. 7 small chapels, also part of the monastery, are scattered across the island.

Mandelieu-la-Napoule

This resourceful little town offers plenty to do: golf, sailing, rowing, diving, water ski-ing, parascending or simply strolling in the park. Its 3 sailing harbours (La Napoule, La Rague and Port-Inland) can hold 3,800 boats.

CHATEAU DE LA NAPOULE ✆ 04 93 49 95 05. *www.chateau-lanapoule.com. 1 February-31 October: 10am-6pm. Guided tour: 6 € concessions 4 €* This ruined castle was bought in 1918 by a couple of American artists, Henry and Marie Clews, who rebuilt it in medieval style. Today it belongs to an association that helps young artists worldwide, and contains a number of paintings (Clews collection and temporary exhibitions).

Théoule-sur-Mer

This pretty village lies at the Pointe de l'Aiguille, where the Estérel's red rocks plunge into a turquoise sea. It offers 3 beaches (with lifeguards) a sailing port (190 places) and a crenellated castle with turrets, which is actually an 18thc. soap factory (closed to the public). From the headland, you have access to the Aiguille Nature Reserve.

PARC DE LA POINTE DE L'AIGUILLE. One of the region's most beautiful nature reserves, with sublime panoramic views of Cannes Bay and the Lérins Islands, and a variety of tree and plant species in an evergreen setting.

Vallauris

This village is associated with pottery, and two artists in particular. Pablo Picasso settled here in 1950, attracting plenty of other artists and visitors, organising and patronising exhibitions, and signing a number of pots. Jean Marais retired here in 1978, after a long career in theatre and cinema, and took up pottery until his death in 1998. He is buried in the village graveyard.

MUSEE MUNICIPAL MAGNELLI MUSEE DE LA CERAMIQUE ET MUSEE NATIONAL PICASSO *Place de la Libération ✆ 04 93 64 16 05. www.musees-nationaux-alpesmaritimes.fr and www.musee-picasso-vallauris.fr. Open every day except Tuesday: 10am-12.15pm and 2pm-5pm. Admission: adult 3,20 € concessions 2 €* Same opening hours and prices for both museums. Vallaris castle museum, an imposing Provencal fortified house rebuilt in the 16thc., now houses the Magnelli Town Museum, Ceramic Museum and National Picasso War and Peace Museum. The latter contains Picasso's La Guerre et La Paix, (1955) a 125m fresco on display in the Romanesque Chapel.

MUSEE DE LA POTERIE Rue Sicard ✆ 04 93 64 66 51. *Open May-October: 9am-6pm, Sunday & public holidays: 2pm-6pm. Closed November-January. Admission: 2 .* This museum contains an interesting retrospective of a potter's work, illustrating all the techniques from clay extraction to firing, and housing some fine period and contemporary pottery.

ESPACE JEAN MARAIS 3, ave. des Martyrs de la Résistance ✆ 04 93 63 46 11. *Closed Sunday, Monday and public holidays. Admission: 1.50 €* Over 100 pieces of pottery, lithographs, drawings, and paintings illustrate the career of Jean Marais, theatre and cinema actor, sculptor, ceramic artist and painter.

MAISON DE LA PETANQUE 1193, chemin de Saint Bernard ✆ 04 93 64 11 36. *Open Monday-Friday: 9am-12 noon and 2pm-6.30pm; all day Saturday in season. Admision: Adult 3* . Mr and Mrs Filiaggi, former boules manufacturers, have created this very individual museum. Even if you're not a boules champion, you'll want to be one after your visit! The way out is through the shop; few visitors leave empty-handed.

Grasse

Grasse, world perfume capital, features further on in 'Gardens and Perfumes'. It is also a little regional capital, set high above the Cannes plain and coastline, with some fine museums.

MUSEE D'ART ET D'HISTOIRE DE PROVENCE 2, rue Mirabeau ✆ 04 93 36 80 20. *www.museesdegrasse.com. Open every day, June-September: 10am-6.30pm. October-May: 10am-12.30pm and 2pm-5.30pm. Closed in November. Admission: adult1,50 € free first Sunday each month.* The thematic collections include prehistory, Roman and medieval architecture, popular arts and traditions, rural life and crafts, olive-oil making, a Provençale period kitchen, the Marquis and Marquise's private apartments (17th & 18thc.) and some fine earthernware.

MUSEE JEAN-HONORE FRAGONARD 23, bd Fragonard ✆ 04 93 36 80 20. *www.museesdegrasse.com. Open every day June-September: 10am-6.30pm. October-May 10am-12.30pm and 2pm-5.30pm. Closed in November. Admission: adult 3 € child 1.50 €* Fragonard (1732-1806) was born in the region. You can admire his paintings in this elegant 17thc. country house.

MUSEE PROVENCAL DU COSTUME ET DU BIJOU 2, rue Ossola ✆ 04 93 36 44 65. *www.fragonard.com. Open every day: 10am-6pm. Closed 1pm-2pm November-January. Admission free.* This private museum belongs to the Fragonard Perfumery, and houses 18th and 19th Provençal costumes and jewellery.

Gourdon

Like most of the villages perched up in the hills, Gourdon has its share of medieval houses and alleys, staircases, vaults and arched passageways, little squares, hidden corners and secret recesses. The central streets are full of craft shops selling Provençal fabric, honey, glass, objects carved from olive wood, pancakes and gingerbread, pottery, and perfume, especially lavender water.

CHATEAU DE GOURDON ✆ 04 93 09 68 02. *Open June-September: 11am-1pm and 2pm-7pm. October-May: 2pm-6pm, closed Tuesday. Admission: adult 4 €*. The chateau's main façade looks directly on to the village square. Inside, you find a collection of ancient weapons and armour, 16th and 17thc. furniture and a painting from the Cologne School dating back to 1500. On the second floor is a museum containing an exceptionally rich collection of naOve paintings, including a portrait by Douanier Rousseau. The terraced gardens - on three levels - were designed by Le Nôtre.

Mougins

A delightful village 'spiralling round its steeple'.

VIEUX VILLAGE. You will enjoy wandering through the cool, narrow streets, so typical of this region.

MUSEE MUNICIPAL Place Sainte Anne ✆ 04 92 92 50 42. *Open 10am-12 noon and 2pm-6pm. Admission free.* A number of objects and remains, illustrating Mougins' history.

MUSEE DE L'AUTOMOBILE ✆ 04 93 69 27 80. Acces via the A8 between Antibes and Cannes; Breguières rest area. Open every day: 10am-6pm (7pm in summer). Closed in November and between 12 noon and 2pm in low season.Admission: adult 7 . 100 vehicles are exhibited (collector's items), with thematic displays, films on automobile history, collectors' events and swaps.

L'ESTÉREL

This volcanic massif covers 32,000ha. (13,000 listed) and its red, rocky landscapes are straight out of a Western - which turned into a disaster movie last summer, when hectares of forests and pine groves went up in careless flames. Please respect the bans, and help preserve these splendid Provençal landscapes with their flora and fauna, and atmospheric little villages perched in the hills.

Fréjus

A thousand years of history have left their mark on this beautiful seaside resort.

AMPHITHEATRE Rue Henri Vadon ✆ 04 94 51 34 31. *Open Tuesday to Sunday.Admission Adult 2 !. Park 5,60 ! for 5 sites (2 museums, 3 monuments), valid for a week.* One of Gaul's biggest amphitheatres, dating back to the 1st or 2ndc. A.D.

EPISCOPAL GROUP 58, rue de Fleury ✆ 04 94 51 26 30. *www.monum.fr. Open all year. 1 October-30 May, except Monday: 9am-12 noon and 2pm-5pm. 10 June-30 September: 9am-6.30pm every day. Admission: adult 5, concessions 3.10 € under-18s free.* Includes the cathedral and cloister, built from the 11th-14thc. The 5thc. baptistry is one of Gaul's oldest Christian monuments. The cloister has a painted ceiling depicting a fantastic bestiary.

ROMAN THEATRE Rue du Théâtre Romain ✆ 04 94 53 82 47. *Open every day, except Monday.* The remains of this Roman theatre date back to the 1stc. B.C. or early A.D. It held 2,000 spectators, and you can still see some radiating walls and remains of the stage in local sandstone. The theatre has been restored, and in 2004, was named Philippe Leotard in memory of the actor.

AQUATICA RN98 ✆ 04 94 51 82 51. *www.parc-aquatica.com. Open June-September: 10am-7pm.* The Cote d'Azur's biggest water park has 10,000m^2 of pools for all sorts of water games.

Saint-Raphaël

OFFICE DE TOURISME Le Stanislas - Rue Waldeck-Rousseau ✆ 04 94 19 52 52. Like its neighbour Fréjus, Saint Raphael's past goes back to antiquity. The site was already a popular summer residence for wealthy Romans; much later, in the Roaring Twenties, it became a holiday resort, complete with casino and luxurious villas.

MUSEE ARCHEOLOGIQUE Rue Vieille ✆ 04 94 19 25 75. *Open every day except Sunday, Mondayand public holidays: 9am-12.30pm and 2pm-5.30pm. Admission free.* Check in advance for out-of-season opening hours. Housed in the old church's former presbytery (church and watchtower are worth a visit) this museum contains objects excavated from Saint Raphael Bay. There is a big Paleolithic and Neolithic collection, along with amphoras and antique crockery rescued from underwater wrecks.

Seillans

This magnificent little village looks like a filmset, with its small houses clinging to the slopes of Mount Auzières. The narrow paved alleys leading up to the castle have a Middle Ages feel, and the ch,teau itself is an imposing medieval building overlooking the plain. This is a typical old Provençal village, with its rustic porches, shady squares and gently splashing fountains. Not far from Seillans, you can visit picturesque Bargemon, known as the olive tree capital.

MAISON WALBERG Place du Thouron ✆ 04 94 50 45 54. *Open all year, 1 October-31 March 2006, Tuesday-Saturday: 3pm-5pm. Admission: adult 2 €.* 70 lithographs by Max Ernst and Dorothea Tanning, and a large number of photographs can be seen here, in the couple's home at Seillans between 1964 and 1976. One of the best-known surrealists, Max Ernst spent the last years of his life, and finished his work, in this peaceful and very pretty village. His famous bronze 'Le génie de la Bastille' stands on the Place de la République, a spot he especially loved.

GARDENS AND PERFUMES

Gardens

The Côte d'Azur is France's main flower-growing region. Its gentle climate and heavenly landscapes are ideal for creating gardens – here are some of the most interesting.

PARC EXFLORA RN7 Antibes. This living plant museum covers 5ha.

PARC GUSTAVE THURET Antibes ✆ 04 93 67 88 00. The Institute of Agronomic Research runs this park, and experiments with acclimatizing rare species.

PARC DE LA VILLA EILENROC Bd. Kennedy – CAP D'ANTIBES ✆ 04 93 67 74 33. *Open Tuesday & Wednesday. Closed July & August.* A huge park, very well kept. The plants and trees are beautifully laid out, as well as rare.

JARDIN EXOTIQUE Eze ✆ 04 93 41 26 00. July & August: 9am-8pm. September: 9am-7pm. October-January: 9am-5pm. Admission: adult 4 €. Discover all there is to know about the world's cacti!

JARDIN DE LA VILLA FORT France Saint-Jean-de-Grasse ✆ 04 93 40 55 93 15 *April-30 June and 15 September-30 October: 9am-10.30am, 11am-12.30pm.* Advance booking only for group visits. Every season has its flowers in this garden containing over 500 varieties. A rare pleasure.

JARDIN BOTANIQUE DU VAL RAHMEH Ave. Saint-Jacques – MENTON. *Open all year, closed Tuesday.* Belongs to the National Natural Histrory Museum. 'Val Rahmeh' boasts a rich collection of edible plants, arecaceas and solanaceas.

JARDIN DE MARIA SERENA 21, promenade de la Reine Astrid – MENTON. An exceptional setting and temperate climate, ideal for acclimatizing rare and delicate plants.

JARDIN DU PALAIS CARNOLES 3, ave. de la Madone – MENTON. Don't miss this one. It contains a complete and beautiful collection of citrus fruits: oranges, lemons, kumquats, grapefruits etc.

JARDIN EXOTIQUE 62, bd. du Jardin Exotique – MONACO ✆ 00 377 93 15 29 80. *15 May-15 September, every day: 9am-7pm. Other periods: 9am-6pm. Closed 19 November and 25 December. Admission: adult 6.90 € 6-18s 3.50 € under-6s free.* Ticket includes Grotte de l'Observatoire and Musée d'anthropologie préhistorique. You can see this extraordinary garden's giant cacti from far off: the fabulous collection contains 6,000 varieties, including these Mexican Candles. You also find euphorbia, balls, unusual tree-trunk shapes, strange flowers and arborescent species, in all shades of green. The garden boasts a sweeping view of Monaco, Cap Martin and Italian Riviera.

ROSERAIE PRINCESSE GRACE Quartier de Fontvieille – MONACO. *1 April-31 October: 9am-7pm. 1 November-31 March 9am-6pm. Admission free.* This magnificent rose-garden spreads 5,500 rose bushes before your admiring eyes. The Grace de Monaco, created by Meilland for Prince Rainier and Grace Kelly's wedding, is one of the most beautiful.

PARC PHOENIX 405, promenade des Anglais – NICE✆ 04 92 29 77 00. *Open all year. 1 April-30 September: 9.30am-7.30pm. Other periods: closes at 5.30pm.* This 7ha park contains Mediterranean flora biotopes, and the Diamant Vert, a huge greenhouse fitted out with seven different tropical and subtropical climates, and thousands of rare plant species. The lake is occupied by a host of tropical and water birds, fish, and insects. A number of diurnal and nocturnal birds of prey have recently been added to the site.

JARDINS DE LA FONDATION EPHRUSSI DE ROTHSCHILD Saint-Jean-Cap-Ferrat ✆ 04 93 01 33 09. *Open in season: 10am-6pm. Out of season: 2pm-6pm.* Baroness Ephrussi de Rothschild designed 7 different gardens: formal, Japanese, Spanish, Florentine, Provençal, exotic and Oriental. An earthly paradise.

Perfumes

Flowers mean perfume, which is made in Grasse, according to different production methods with natural fragrances.

MUSEE INTERNATIONAL DE LA PARFUMERIE 8, place du Cours Honoré Cresp - GRASSE ✆ 04 97 05 58 00. *Re-opening planned for 2008 (subject to confirmation).* Closed since September 2004 for two years of extension work. The exhibitions go on, however, both on the building site and in town.

FRAGONARD USINE HISTORIQUE 20, bd. Fragonard - GRASSE ✆ 04 93 36 44 65. *Open 9am-6.30pm. Closed November-January: 12.30pm-2pm.*You can visit the 18thc. factory and private Perfume Museum, where a collection of objects illustrates 5,000 years of history. The shop products are sold at factory prices.

FRAGONARD LA FABRIQUE DES FLEURS Les Quatre Chemins - GRASSE ✆ 04 93 77 94 30. *Open all year: 9am-6.30pm. Closed 12.30pm-2pm, November-January.* This contemporary factory makes perfume, soap and scented products, and is set in a garden of sweet-smelling plants. On-site shop.

GALIMARD 73, route de Cannes - GRASSE ✆ 04 93 09 20 00. *www.galimard.com. Open every day: 9am-6pm.* Free guided tour of the factory and workshops. On-site shop. This famous perfumery explains the extraction of precious fragrances. Galimard also offers to create your own perfume, at the 'Studio des fragrances' (route de Pégomas 04 93 09 20 00).

MOLINARD 60, bd Victor Hugo - GRASSE ✆ 04 93 36 01 62. *www.molinard.com. Open April-September: 9am-6.30pm, 7 days a week. October-March, Monday-Saturday: 9am-6pm.* Founded in 1849, this is one of France's oldest perfumeries. You must see the collection of Lalique and Baccarat bottles. On-site museum shop.

SAINT-TROPEZ AND THE SAINT-TROPEZ GULF

Saint Tropez blends superficial summer pleasure-seeking and traditional heritage. The Gulf brings an international clientele every year, seeking sunshine and a friendly sea, but the resort is at its most attractive later, with its paved streets basking in a peaceful out-of-season atmosphere.

Saint-Tropez

Although this peaceful little fishing port owes its reputation to a few cinema and pop stars, why not forget the yachts, restaurants and nightclubs for a while, and discover the authentic town with its museums and traditions?

MUSEE DE L'ANNONCIADE Place Grammont ✆ 04 94 97 04 01. *Open every day: 10am-12 noon and 2pm-6pm, except Tuesday and public holidays. Admission: adult 5 € under-12s free.* This museum, housed in a former chapel at the end of the port, displays paintings of Saint Tropez, including pointillist, fauvist and nabis works.

CITADELLE, MUSEE ✆ 04 94 97 59 43. Building work in progress may affect opening days and hours: please phone first to check. Open every day, 1 October-31 March: 10am-12.30pm and 1.30pm-5.30pm. 1 April-30 September: 10am-12.30pm and 1.30pm-6.30pm. Closed Tuesday & public holidays. For centuries, this citadel was the main defence structure between Antibes and Toulon. Today, it is all that is left of the town's fortifications, and houses a maritime history museum containing amphorae, statues, scale models of ancient and modern boats (Greek galley, Commander Cousteau's Calypso), documents, pictures and weapons.

MAISON DES PAPILLONS 9, rue Berny ✆ 04 94 97 63 45. *Open every day: 10am-12 noon and3pm-6pm, except Tuesday Admission: 3.50 €* The painter Dany Lartigue set up this museum in his family home. 20,000 brightly coloured butterflies are exhibited, including rare and exotic specimens from the Solomon Islands and Amazonia.

Gulf of Saint-Tropez

Cogolin

This is an arts and crafts town, known for its genuine Maures heather pipes, and fine wool carpets made since the 1920s in Jacquard and Oriental styles - and found on the Elysée and White House floors!

MUSEE RAIMU Ave. Georges Clemenceau ✆ 04 94 54 18 00. *Open every day except Sunday morning and Tuesday. Out of season: 10am-12 noon and 3pm-6pm. In season: 10am-12 noon and 4pm-7pm. Admission: adult 3.50 € over-11s 1.75* . The talented Var actor's life and career, traced through unique and authentic documents, objects, clothes and furniture. If Raimu is new to you, you can discover him in Marcel Pagnol's Marius film trilogy.

Gassin

One of France's most beautiful villages, as you realise, strolling through streets and alleys hung with bougainvillea and plumbagine. The Dei Barri Promenade offers a panoramic view over Cavalaire Bay, with the Isles d'Hyères in the distance. Notre Dame de l'Assomption Church on the corner of the Passage des Bénédictins was finished in 1558, and contains a Saint Laurent reliquary, gilded Virgin, ancient stoup and several paintings. After the church, take the Passage du Guet (Porte des Sarrasins), go up the central street, turn right and come back down the Rue du Puits, then Rue du Moulin, where olive oil used to be made. On the left is the village's narrowest street, the Androuno, where you have to walk in single file - perhaps the narrowest in the world?

Grimaud

This typical village is set high on a hill between land and sea, and its oldest stones date back to the 7thc. B.C! Its narrow flower-filled alleys contain a number of ancient wooden doors, porticos and stone staircases. Climb up to Grimaud Castle overlooking the village, with its pretty view of village and harbour. In the early 1960s, an architect had the bright idea of turning Grimaud's marshy area into a lakeside quarter. You reach it on foot via fortified gates, and the islets are linked together by Venetian bridges with arcades and pillars. Port Grimaud is thus known as the Cote d'Azur's Little Venice!

Ramatuelle

Ramatuelle's arrow alleys are filled with jasmine, geraniums, bougainvillea and honeysuckle. Opposite the square, 14thc. Notre Dame Church backs onto the ancient ramparts, with its serpentine door dating back to 1620. A number of artists and actors have stayed here, and there are festivals in summer: Musique et Liberté, Les Temps Musicaux, Thé,tre et Variétés, Jazz ‡ Ramatuelle. Saint Tropez's best beaches are here too, notably Pampelonne (5km of soft sand).

Sainte-Maxime

A fine sandy beach runs along a shady promenade with its palm-trees and umbrella pines: this is Saint Maxime town centre! To the east lie the Garonette, Elephants and Nartelle beaches, while Croisette Beach on the western side is the best for swimming. Saint Maxime is known for its sailing harbour and the pleasures of sea cruising.

Saint-Tropez

MUSEE DU PHONOGRAPHE ET DE LA MUSIQUE MECANIQUE Parc Saint Donat - Route du Muy ✆ 04 94 96 50 52. *Open every day except Monday and Tuesday, Easter-late September.Admission: adult 3 €.* A unique collection of 300 musical machines, from the phonograph to the mechanical piano, including barrel organs, automatons and music boxes, and the first wirelesses and televisions.

Saint-Maximin

A big Provencal village, with a magnificent basilica built on the crypt where Saint Mary Magdalene was buried in the 1stc. A.D.

This basilica is Provence's most beautiful Gothic building.

SAINTE MARIE MADELEINE ROYAL BASILICA. Charles II, Comte de Provence and King of Naples decided to put up this basilica in 1295, but the actual building took several centuries. The shrine containing Saint Mary Magdalene's remains immediately became a place of intensive pilgrimage - at the time Saint Maximin was an important stopping place on the Compostella road. The Basilica boasts an apse, two apsidioles, a great nave and sixteen side chapels. The nave reaches 29m high and is

81m long, laid out in the Gothic style, most unusual for Provence where the Romanesque style tends to predominate.

The Great Organ. This organ is the work of organ-builder Jean-Marie Isnard, and has an exceptionally rich melodic quality, boasting no less than 43 stops spread over 4 keyboards, and 2,962 pipes.

The Crypt. This 4thc. Christian vault contains the sarcophagi of Saint Maximin, Saint Sidoine, Saint Marcelle and Saint Suzanne. The furniture is ornate, and includes a magnificent carved wooden pulpit dating back to 1756, and a reredos by Antoine Ronzen (1520) on the theme of Christ's Passion, in 16 tableaux. It depicts the oldest known view of the Palais des Papes in Avignon. The 17thc. choir stalls are extremely beautiful.

SAINTE BAUME MASSIF Hikers: enquiries to 04 94 50 55 50. This massif between the Var and Bouches-du-Rhone is covered with exceptional forest facing both north and south. To the north, the vegetation features beech and holly, maples and lime trees, such as you find several hundred kilometres higher up the country; in the south, it is more typically Mediterranean. Over 110 bird species nest on the site, including sparrowhawks, woodpeckers, tawny owls and tits of all kinds. In the undergrowth you might spot badgers and stone martens, but also foxes, boars and deer.

NICE AND THE ARRIERE-PAYS

The Greek Nikkaia is now France's fifth biggest town, deceptively lazy in the sun, for in fact Nice is an active place, with plenty of museums and monuments to add some interest to your seaside holiday.

PROMENADE DES ANGLAIS. Following the Baie des Anges curve along 5km of seafront, the promenade got its name in the 19thc. from the English winter colony that paid for the building work. Only the Hôtel Négresco and Palais de la Méditerranée façade (a listed monument) are left of that Belle Epoque period, with its Rococo villas. You can still enjoy a leisurely stroll, however, and watch the swimmers who continue the sea-bathing tradition in all seasons.

VIEILLE VILLE. The old, twisting alleyways in the heart of Nice are lined with tall buildings, spanned by arches with several storeys above and linked by staircases without apparent logic, and the tiny squares are crowded with pedlars and restaurant terraces. Start your tour on the Quai des Etats Unis, and go under the arcades to the Cours Saleya. In the 18thc. this was Nice's main elegant thoroughfare, almost on the seafront with the old town crowding behind. Today, you can feast your senses on the colours and scents of its famous flower, fruit and vegetable market.

CATHEDRAL. The glazed tiles on its magnificent Genoese-style dome shine in the sun, and can be seen from any quarter of the town. Inside, the cathedral is splendidly Baroque.

PALAIS LASCARIS 15, rue Droite ✆ 04 93 62 72 40. *Open every day except Tuesday and some public holidays. Admission free.* This 17thc. palace is built round two inside courtyards, with a monumental staircase leading to the upper storey. The vaults in the public apartments are decorated with frescos (one wall with beautiful stucco cariatids and atlantas) and those on the ceilings have a mythological theme, including a superb 'Phaeton's Fall'. There is 17th and 18thc. furniture, and Flemish tapestries, and an 18thc. pharmacy with its vases and phial. The third floor is soon to house Nice's antique instrument collection.

SAINT NICOLAS RUSSIAN ORTHODOX CATHEDRAL Ave. Nicolas II ✆ 04 93 96 88 02. *In season: 9am-12 noon and 2.30pm-6pm. Out of season: 9.30am-12 noon and 2.30pm-5pm. Closed to visitors Sunday and Russian Orthodox festival mornings.* Built in 1912, this imposing cathedral (the biggest outside Russia) calls to mind Saint Basil Basilica in Moscow's Red Square.

ARENES DE NICE. This Roman amphitheatre has been enlarged several times since it was built in the 1stc. B.C. Today, the Nice/Cimiez Jazz festival is held here every year in July.

THERMES. Built in the 3rdc. A.D., this assortment of hot and cold baths and pools is housed in a huge building. Some of the bathrooms were fitted out for worship by the first Christians, and there is even a cathedral; the chancel is in the former frigidarium and the baptistry in a rotunda.

CIMIEZ FRANCISCAN MONASTERY AND MUSEUM Place du Monastere ✆ 04 93 81 00 04. *Open every day: 8am-6.30pm. Museum open every day except Sunday and public holidays: 10am-12 noon and 3pm-6pm Admission free.* Cimiez Franciscan Monastery is a listed building. Its 15th-17thc. church contains Gothic and Renaissance reredos by Louis Brea, a great carved and gilded Baroque reredos, vaulted ceilings painted with fresces and a marble recumbent statue and cross (1477). The museum itself occupies one floor of the monastery buildings with their painted walls, overlooking the cloisters. A number of documents illustrate Franciscan history and spirituality, along with a reconstructed 17thc. chapel and cell.

MUSEE MATISSE 164, ave. des Arènes de Cimiez ✆ 04 93 81 08 08. *Open 10am-6pm. Closed Tuesday and some public holidays. Admission: adults 4 € concessions 2.5 €* This museum houses the collection given by Matisse to the Town of Nice: 68 paintings and gouaches, 236 drawings, 218 engravings, 57 sculptures, 14 illustrated books, 95 photos and 187 of the artist's personal effects.

MUSEE DES BEAUX-ARTS JUKES CHERET 33, ave. des Baumettes ✆ 04 92 15 28 28. *Open 10am-6pm. Closed Mondays and some public holidays. Admission: adults 4 € concessions 2.50* . Admire the many 17thc. Italian paintings, and 18thc. works by Van Loo, Hubert Robert and Fragonard. Upstairs are 19th and 20thc. artists: Boudin, Monet, Sisley, Bonnard, Dufy, Marie Laurencin, Van Dongen and Picasso; Impressionists, Post-Impressionists and Carpeaux and Rodin's sculptures. The museum also displays the works of Jules Chéret, one of the modern poster's founding fathers.

MUSEE NATIONAL MESSAGE BIBLIQUE MARC CHAGALL Ave. Docteur Menard/Corner Bd. de Cimiez ✆ 04 93 53 87 20. *www.musees-nationaux-alpesmaritimes.fr and www.musee-chagall.fr. July-September: 10am-6pm. October-June: 10am-5pm. Closed Tuesdays, 1 January, 1 May and 25 December. Admission: adult 5,50 € concessions 4* . Contains Chagall's 17 great Bible message paintings, expressing his wish for human peace, happiness and harmony.

MUSEE D'ART MODERNE ET D'ART COMTEMPORAIN Promenade des Arts ✆ 04 93 62 61 62. *Closed Monday and some public holidays. 1 May-15 October: 10am-6pm (5pm 16 October-30 April). Admission: adult 6 € concessions 2.50* . The MAMAC, built by architect Yves Bayard, is a sort of fortress with four grey marble towers linked by transparent walkways. You can see works from the recent Nice School and avant-garde European and American artists (1960s to the present).

MUSEE DES ARTS ASIATIQUES 405, promenade des Anglais - Arenas ✆ 04 92 29 37 00. *www.arts-asiatiques.com. Open every day except Tuesday. 1 May-15 October: 10am-6pm. 16 October-30 April: 10am-5pm. Admission: adult 6 €* The Asian Arts Museum is a living link with Indian, South-East Asian, Chinese and Japanese art forms. Built by the Japanese architect Kenzo Tange in white marble and glass on a lake of aquatic birds, the museum represents both the courtly and popular aspects of these cultures, and there are displays of music and dance, and demonstrations of traditional techniques (Chinese calligraphy, Japanese floral art) and the Tea Ceremony in the Tea Pavilion, all year round.

Inland

When you turn your back on Nice to go inland to the arrière-pays, the hills around the town soon give way to pre-mountain scenery with narrow valleys and isolated villages perched high on the slopes. These are worth a day's visit, for the contrast with the big town below; the way of life is almost autarkic, still based on mountain agriculture.

Contes

This medieval village has grown out of its original limits, with recent buildings running down the valley slopes, yet it is still just as pretty.

SAINTE MARIE MADELEINE CHURCH. Built in the 16thc., the church was enlarged and given 3 naves after the River Paillon flooded in 1530. Its Sainte Madeleine reredos (François Brea) narrates the life of the famous sinner in several pictures. In front of the church is the Renaissance Fountain, on two levels.

MUSEE DE LA VIGNE ET DU VIN ✆ 04 93 79 19 17. *ww.musee-contes.fr. Open second and fourth Sunday of the month: 10.30am-12.30pm and 2pm-5pm. Admission: adult 1.50 € under-18s free.* Contains all the traditional tools needed for winemaking.

MOULIN DE LA LAOUZA Quartier Le Martinet ✆ 04 93 79 28 73. This genuine Genoese oil mill is typical of the Paillon Valley. Open November-March, Monday-Saturday. Produce sold on site.

Lucéram

Lucéram is a fortified medieval village; its alleys, covered passages and bridges across the streets are well worth seeing. The 12thc. wall, crenellated and fortified, has a round machicolated tower and walkway in one corner.

SAINTE ROSALIE AND SAINTE MARGUERITE D'ANTIOCHE CHURCH. This Romanesque-Gothic church was reshaped in Baroque style in the 18thc. Inside is the sacred art treasure, and some beautiful reredos by Canavesio. Don't miss the extraordinary reliquary showing Saint Marguerite, swallowed whole by a dragon, escaping alive from its belly. There is also a 13thc. pieta in carved polychrome wood, incense-burners, monstrances, candelabra and processional lamps.

Puget-Théniers

A small regional capital, at the Var-Roudoule confluence. In the 19thc., the town contained a number of little factories: tanneries, weavers, oil and flour mills, until these industries declined. The opening of a road and railway brought new life to Puget-Théniers, now a tourist rather than an industrial town. Visit the old town, with its ancient houses and shops, their lintels bearing signs of the different trades, and Templar inscriptions. There is still one town gate in the ruined ramparts, and you can see the Rue Gisclette ghetto, once closed at each end every night.

ECOMUSEE DE LA ROUDOULE Rue Calade © 04 93 05 07 38. *Open every day, 15 April-15 November: 9am-12 noon and 2pm-6pm. Out of season: weekends only. Admission: 5.50* . Learn more about the region's geological composition, with guided walks and the exhibition of everyday objects. Souvenir and local craft shop.

TRAIN DES PIGNES. Information and bookings: Chemins de fer de Provence ‡ Nice 04 97 03 80 80. At Digne 04 92 31 01 58/04 97 03 80 80. On the Nice-Digne line, this steam train is pulled by a 1909 locomotive, restored and kept up by a voluntary team of former railwaymen. It runs from Puget-Théniers to Annot and back on Sundays and public holidays in July and August.

Saint-Paul-de-Vence

TOURIST OFFICE 2, rue Grande © 04 93 32 86 95. This artists' paradise has been immortalised by painters, poets and singers, and overrun by tourists. The Colombe d'Or restaurant is used to celebrities; artists little known at the time left paintings to pay for their meal, making the family's fortune years later. Avoid the village in July and August if you can, but don't hesitate to visit at other times: Saint-Paul-de-Vence is an authentic beauty spot.

MUSEE D'HISTOIRE LOCALE Place de la Castre © 04 93 32 41 13. *Open every day: 10am-12.30pm and 1.30pm-5.30pm. Admission: 3 €*. This fun museum tells the story of Saint Paul with life-size waxworks in historical tableaux, made by the Musée Grevin.

FONDATION MAEGHT Colline des Gardettes © 04 93 32 81 63. *Open early July-late September: 10am-7pm. Early October-late June: 10am-12.30pm and 2.30pm-6pm. Admission: adult 11 €* . The Maeght Foundation was created by the art dealer Aimé Maeght (1906-1981) and built by architect Jose-Luis Sert, Le Corbusier's disciple and collaborator. This 'Modern Art Temple' is a museum of contemporary painting and sculpture, but also a meeting-place for artists and research centre, and its white concrete and pink brick blend naturally into the Provençal landscape. You can view works by Giacometti, Soulages, Bazaine, Léger, Kandinsky, Adami, Viallat, Zadkine, MirÛ, and others, along with thematic exhibitions. On-site library, bookshop and cinema.

Sospel

Set at the foot of the mountains on the banks of the Bévéra, this delightful little town is a historic site. Merchandise travelled through Sospel between Turin and Menton on the Salt Route, and you can still see the old tollbridge with its two arches and defensive tower on the central pile (now housing the Tourist Office). Sospel made a fortune from this toll until the 18thc.

SAINT MICHEL CHURCH. This church was once a cathedral, in the days of the Avignon Popes. A new chapel was built in Sospel during each plague epidemic, to attract divine protection. The front has three doors and two storeys, the upper one decorated with statues in their niches, and there is a very fine 13thc. Lombard Romanesque steeple. The side aisles are without chapels, and there is no cupola on the transept, but false loggias containing portraits of saints surround the chancel, and the high altar is topped by a dais.

PENITENTS BLANCS CHAPEL (KNOWN AS THE SAINTE CROIX CHAPEL). This 16thc. chapel re-used the apse from a medieval church, so its Baroque style is only visible inside. The single nave has a low vaulted ceiling and the chapel is decorated with frescoes. The Baroque aspects are noticeable around the high altar, in the column shape and trompe l'oeil painting.

FORT SAINT ROCH © 04 93 04 00 70. *Open April, May, June & October; Saturdays, Sundays and public holidays: 2pm-6pm. July-September(every day except Monday): 2pm-6pm. Admission: adult 5 € child 3 €*. 1km from town centre, follow signs to Escarene on D2204. After the cemetery, follow arrows indicating military route. This Maginot Line fort was built in 1932 to guard the Italian border, using 5,000 cubic metres of concrete and 385 tonnes of steel. It was equipped for comfort with its own electricity generator, complete with air filtering and ventilation. You can see the original 13-tonne cannon, and rooms fitted out as museums explaining the daily life of the Chasseurs Alpins troops.

ORIENT EXPRESS Gare de Sospel © 04 93 04 20 95. *Open 10 am-12 noon, except Wednesday and Saturday lunchtime. Meal 22.50 € and 29 €. Visit only (without meal) 2 €.*Information about visits from Sospel station.. Four carriages from the mythical 1929 train immortalised by Hercule Poirot are stationed here. You can spend a day at Sospel with a meal on the Orient Express, guided tour of the town and visit to Saint Roch Fort.

Vence

Despite the seasonal tourist crowds, Vence has kept the authentic style and charm of a typical inland Cote d'Azur town.

NOTRE DAME DE LA NATIVITE CATHEDRAL. The cathedral is a blend of Romanesque, Gothic and Baroque, and contains Carolingian stones finely set into the pillars. The stalls in the tribune are carved with funny or naughty miséricordes, by Jacques Bellot of Grasse (1460).

ROSAIRE CHAPEL (MATISSE CHAPEL) D2210 - Route de Saint Jeannet © 04 93 58 03 26. *Open Mondays, Wednesdays, Saturdays: 2pm-5.30pm. Tuesdays & Thursdays: 10am-11.30am and 2.30pm-5.30pm. Sunday: 10.45am (after Mass)-12 noon. Admission: 3 .* Convalescing in Vence in 1948 at the end of his life, Matisse designed this chapel with the architect Perret, decorating it from 1949 to 1951. Thought to be controversial, it is still one of Matisse's major works, illustrating the development of 20thc. religious art.

CHATEAU NOTRE DAME DES FLEURS *Galerie Beaubourg - 2618, route de Grasse, between Tourettes-sur-Loup and Vence © 04 93 24 52 00. Open every day except Sunday: 11am-7pm. Closed 15 January-15 March. Admission: 5 €* In the yellow gallery on the ground floor, and outside, is a contemporary art collection including Cesar, Nikki de Saint-Phalle, Schnabel, Beatrice Cussot, Louis Can etc. From above (reached via the terraces) you have a superb view of the mountains.

CHATEAU DE VILLENEUVE - FONDATION EMILE HUGUES Place du Frêne © 04 93 58 15 78. *Open every day except Monday: 10am-12.30pm and 2pm-6pm. July-September: 10am-6pm. Admission: 5 .* Built by the Seigneurs de Villeneuve in the 17thc., this castle is known for its modern and contemporary art, with an annual programme of thematic exhibitions.

THE RIVIERA

The French Riviera consists of a string of towns along the N7, offering sunshine, beaches and the perfect holiday. Postcard scenery and an azure sea attract senior citizens seeking a warm climate, but France's favourite tourist destination suits all ages.

Antibes

Old Antibes, huddled round the castle, is a kind of village within a town, sought after for its pedestrian streets lined with old-fashioned shops, whose craftsmen and shopkeepers have been there for generations. The Promenade Amiral de Grasse runs beside the old town on the ruined ramparts (preserved since the 17thc.) to Port Vauban, with the town's main monuments above.

MUSEE ARCHEOLOGIQUE Bastion Saint-André © 04 93 34 00 39. *www.antibes-juanlespins.com. Open all year. Closed Mondays and public holidays. Admission: adult 3 € child 1.50 € Under-18s free. Combined ticket 10 €* Housed in the Saint-Andre-Bastion, a military fortification built by Vauban in the late 17thc., this museum has a panoramic view of the old town and Cap d'Antibes. Its two vaulted galleries contain the town's archeological collection: ceramic, amphorae, mosaics, coins and daily objects going back to Antiquity.

MUSEE PICASSO Château Grimaldi © 04 92 90 54 20. *www.antibes-juanlespins.com. Open every day except Monday. Admission: adult 5 € concessions 2.50 €* This museum contains 175 of Picasso's works. The town having placed part of the castle at his disposal during his stay (1946-1947), he donated most of the paintings, sketches and drawings exhibited. The ground floor display includes Biot pottery, fountains and works by Leger and Modigliano, and on the second floor, Nicolas de Stael, Magnelli and Ernst are exhibited in Picasso's former studio. Sculptures by Miro, Amado and Germaine Richier can be seen on the terrace.

PORT DE PLAISANCE. The Cote d'Azur's biggest sailing harbour can take boats of more than 165m.

MARCHE PROVENCAL Place Masséna. The Baltard-style covered market is typical of the region. A plaque marks the house where Maréchal Masséna lived, with his Antibes wife, Marie-Rosalie Lamarre.

FORT CARRE © 06 14 89 17 45. Open Tuesday-Sunday: 10am-11.45am and 1.45pm-4pm (May-September-6pm). Admission: 3.50 . This typical star-shaped fortress was gradually built over the years on Saint Jaume Rock: the central tower in 1550, four bastions - France, Corse, Nice and Antibes - added

20 years later. Vauban finished the fortified wall. Supposed to be impregnable, the fort was taken once, by surprise and the Duc d'Epernon for Henri IV, in 1592.

MARINELAND RN7 - Route de Nice - 306, ave. Mozart ✆ 04 93 33 49 49. *www.marineland.fr. Open every day from 10am. Evenings in season, with son et lumière. On-site restaurant. Admission: adult between 28 € et 33 €* Enjoy dolphin, sea-lion and orc displays in this marine theme-park with its panoramic underwater views. The aquariums contain brightly-coloured exotic fish and jellyfish, and sharks swim through a 30m transparent tunnel.

Biot

Pronounced Biotte, this delightful coastal village is perched on a hill in a sea of mimosa, roses and carnations. It is known for its ceramics and 'bubble' glass-blowing.

VIEUX VILLAGE DE BIOT. The traditional old village has been preserved, with its paved alleys bridged and almost covered by houses.

VERRERIE DE BIOT Chemin des Combes (at the foot of the village, on the D4) ✆ 04 93 65 03 00. *www.verreriebiot.com. Access: follow the fuschia-pink signposts. April-October: 9.30am-7pm. July & August: 9.30am-8pm. Sunday & public holidays: 10am-1pm and 3pm-7pm. November-March: 9.30am-6pm. Sunday and public holidays: 10.30am-1pm and 2.30pm-6.30pm. Admission free.* Watch with fascination while blown 'bubble' glass objects grow before your eyes.

Cagnes-sur-Mer

This medieval fortified village surrounding the Grimaldi Castle is so high up it has been nicknamed 'the Cote d'Azur's Montmartre'. It has also been well-preserved and restored.

CHATEAU-MUSEE ✆ **04 92 02 47 30** *Open every day except Tuesday: 10am-12 noon and 2pm-5pm (6pm in summer). Admission: adult 3 €, concessions 1.50 €.* Built in 1309 by an earlier Rainier Grimaldi, this fortress now belongs to the town. The massive keep has battlements and is machicolated, with a triangular courtyard inside. Notice the staircase with its double bannister and the marble Louis XIII portal. There is a beautiful view of Cagnes, the sea and the Alps from the top of the tower.

Eze

This village perched in the mountains spreads over three cliff roads. The old village is 429m above the sea, its narrow alleys in the shadow of the ruined medieval castle. The cellars and ground floors, once stables, now house a number of artists and craftsmen.

NOTRE DAME DE L'ASSOMPTION CHURCH. This original church was rebuilt in the mid-18thc. It has a single Baroque nave, some 18thc. paintings and furniture and a striking Assumption statue by Muerto. The emblazoned font dates back to the 15thc., and the square tower has two floors. The French comedian Francis Blancho is buried in the little graveyard, and his inscription reads: 'Let me sleep, it's what I do best'.

PENITENTS BLANCS CHAPEL. Built in 1300; the only Middle Ages building still intact.

Golfe-Juan

Napoleon I landed on the beach here after escaping from Elba in 1815, so it is the Route Napoleon's real starting-point. There is a fine, sheltered sandy beach sought-after by swimmers, and fishing and sailing harbour.

Menton

The only town in Europe where lemons grow all year round. A micro-climate ensures clement weather and luxuriant plants and flowers; a good reason for the town's many parks and gardens, and the long list of crowned heads and stars who have stayed here (among them Queen Victoria, Elizabeth of Austria, Winston Churchill and Katherine Mansfield). Gateway to Italy and border town, Menton has its own definite atmosphere, which can be felt in the old town and monuments.

VIEILLE VILLE. Follow Rue Saint-Michel, lined with orange-trees and shops, beside the Place aux Herbes where the market is held. Then take Rue des Logettes and Rue Longue to Saint Michel Church, paved in front with beautiful grey and white mosaics bearing the Grimaldi arms (Prince Honoré's 'H'). Chamber music concerts are held here in season.

SAINT MICHEL ARCHANGE CHURCH. Biggest and finest Baroque church on the Cote d'Azur. It includes a 15thc. clocktower, only remains of the two sanctuaries formerly built on this site, later covered with a glazed tile campanile. The present Genoese campanile (53m) was put up in the 18thc. The Baroque front has two storeys and a harmonious arrangement of columns, pilasters and pediments. The beautiful organ case dates back to 1666, and there is a Puppo reredos, Crucifixion and a 17thc.Virgin and Child.

CIMETIERE DU VIEUX CHATEAU. Reached by the Rue du Vieux Château, this graveyard occupies the site of a long-gone medieval castle. Each terrace belongs to a particular religion or nationality. The architect Tersling, who built most of the region's late 19thc. villas, is buried here.

PORT DE MENTON. The Quai Napoleon III and Imperatrice Eugenie jetties were built in the late 19thc., and a fine view is to be had from the end of each, over the Jean Cocteau Museum, Promenade du Soleil, arcades and old town round Saint Michel Church, with the mountains behind.

MUSEE JEAN COCTEAU Quai Napoléon III ✆ 04 93 57 72 30. *Open every day except Tuesday: 10am-12 noon and 2pm-6pm. Admission: adult 3 €.* Housed in the 17thc. Bastion Fortin buit by Prince Honore II of Monaco. Cocteau designed his museum, calling it his 'sarcophagus and golden mask'. Pebble mosaics, ceramics, tapestries, pastels (including the famous Innamorati series) and drawings are on display, along with sketches of Menton's Salle des Mariages (registry office) and Villefranche Chapel.

MUSEE DES BEAUX-ARTS 3, ave. de la Madone ✆ 04 93 35 49 71. *Open every day except Tuesday: 10am-12 noon and 2pm-6pm. Admission free.* This was the Monaco Princes' former summer residence, when Menton was in the Principality. Today it contains modern paintings on the ground floor (Forain, Dufy, Suzanne Valadon, Sutherland) and French and Italian Primitives upstairs (Louis Bréa, da Vinci, Maineri). The gardens have some fine citrus fruits: oranges, lemons, grapefruit and kumquats.

Saint-Jean-Cap-Ferrat

Somerset Maugham, F. Scott Fitzgerald, King Leopold II of Belgium and Gregory Peck all had luxurious villas well hidden from prying eyes on this prestigious peninsula. You can tour it by boat or on foot (a 3-hour walk) over the rocky headlands: Pointe de la Ganivette, Pointe de la Coisse, Pointe de Crau de Nao and Pointe Malalongue with its 33m lighthouse. After climbing 164 steps, you can look out over the whole coast, from the Estérel to Pointe de Bordighera (Italy). The path then crosses the most jagged section, going round the Baie des Fosses and Pointe Saint Hospice, passing Maurice Rouvier Harbour and Promenade and coming to Pointe Baratier and the Beaulieu-sur-Mer entrance. This is a spectacular seaside walk, with really beautiful scenic sites.

Once a fishing port, Saint-Jean-Cap-Ferrat Village is now a sailing harbour. A few carefully restored houses can be seen in the old village.

TOURIST OFFICE 59, ave. Denis-Demeria ✆ 04 93 76 08 90 *Fax 04 93 76 16 67*

VILLA EPHRUSSI DE ROTHSCHILD ✆ 04 93 01 33 09. *Property & gardens open 15 February-1 November: 10am-6pm (7pm July & August). Admission: adult 9,50 €.* In 1905, Baronness Beatrice Ephrussi (nee Rothschild) fell in love with Cap Ferrat. She bought 7ha. of land and had a palace built, calling to mind Renaissance mansions in Florence and Venice. She had 7 gardens laid out overlooking the sea: formal, Spanish, Florentine, lapidary, Japanese, Provencal and a rose-garden with a Temple d'Amour. You can wander from one to another, with a different sea view each time; an enchanting experience.

Villefranche-sur-Mer

The beautiful harbour between Mont Boron and Cap Ferrat was originally a fishing port, but also housed the French Navy in its time. Today, it has gone back to fishing and sailing. The tall old town houses round Quai Courbet and the port have brightly-coloured Italian-style fronts, reflected in the water. Rue du Poilu is the main thoroughfare in the twisting mass of little alleys, and Rue Obscure with its vaulted roof sheltered the villagers during bombing attacks.

CITADEL. This listed building houses the Town Hall, and is surrounded by huge ditches carved out of the rock. Vauban admired it, as did Louis XIV, who allowed it to stand, while having all the Comte de Nice's other fortifications pulled down. Today, gardens and walks have been laid out in the ditches.

SAINT PIERRE CHAPEL (JEAN COCTEAU CHAPEL) Le Port ✆ 04 93 76 90 70. *Open: 9am-12 noon and 2pm-6pm, except Monday. Admission: 2 €* Cocteau lived in Villefranche for several years, and wrote Orphée there. He offered to decorate this little chapel, used by fishermen for storage. The fresces are surprising: dense and detailed pictures on freely expressed religious themes.

Villeneuve-Loubet

The medieval village round its castle up in the heights contrasts with the seaside buildings below, especially the four Marina Baie des Anges pyramids, huge staircases built for giants. These controversial structures designed by Andre Minangoy are 1960s architectural experiments.

THE PRINCIPALITY OF MONACO

The name probably comes from the Monoikos, who occupied the rock before it was conquered by the Romans in the first century B.C. It fell into the hands of the barbarians, then the Saracens, until the Comte de Provence chased them from the Côte d'Azur. Emperor Barberossa placed the rock under Genoese supervision. Today, it has been in the Grimaldi family for 700 years (since the 13thc.). Monaco is a tax haven and a millionaires' paradise; 4 in 5 hotels are 3-star or above. There are more Rolls per m^2 than anywhere else in Europe, luxury boutiques line the streets and there is a jet-set colony. It is however very hard to get Monagasque nationality. There are five quarters: the Rock (Monaco Town), with the palace; the old fortified town; the cathedral and Oceanographic Museum and the new districts built into the sea.

CASINO DE MONTE CARLO Place du Casino ✆ 00 377 92 16 20 00. The Casino was designed by Charles Garnier (Paris Opera) in the late 19thc., a sumptuous building recalling all the luxury and sophistication of the Belle Epoque, when Russian Grand Dukes arrived in shining torpedoes (the cars parked outside today are no less impressive). It has been the setting for several films, and is still a gaming temple where fortunes are lost and won on the green baize.

MONACO CATHEDRAL 4, rue du Colonel Bellando de Castro ✆ 00 377 93 30 87 70. This late 19thc. Neo-Romanesque cathedral is built of white Turbie stone, on the site of the old Saint Nicolas Church. Inside is a marvellous 16thc. reredos by Louis Brea and a high altar in white Carrare marble incrusted with mosaics, with a glimpse of the Penitents Blancs Pieta just behind. The Monaco Princes' tombs are in the crypt.

GRANDS APPARTEMENTS DU PALAIS PRINCIER Place du Palais - Monaco-Ville ✆ 00 377 93 25 13 31. *www.palais.mc. Closed 1 November-31 May. 1 June-30 September, every day: 9.30am-6pm. 1-31 October, every day: 10am-5pm. Admission: adult 7, 8-14s and students 3 €. Guided tours with audio-guides in 10 languages. Napoleon Museum 4 €.* This is a private palace (only the Grands Appartements are open to the public) built in the late 13thc. on the site of an earlier castle (1215) then extended and embellished during the Renaissance. It is luxuriously decorated: the Cour d'Honneur boasts a Carrare marble staircase and geometric figures containing 3 million stones, and the Palatine Chapel has a fine high altar. When the Prince is in residence, the flag bearing his coat of arms flies above the Tour Sainte-Marie's white Turbie stone. The south wing houses a museum of Napoleon memorabilia and the Palace's historical records, including the Independence Charter signed by Louis XII.

MUSEE OCEANOGRAPHIQUE DE MONACO - Ave Saint Martin ✆ 00 377 93 15 36 00. *www.oceano.mc. January, February, March: 10am-6pm. April, May, June: 9.30am-7pm. July & August: 9.30am-7.30pm. September: 9.30am-7pm. October, November, December: 10am-6pm. Closed the day of the Monaco Formula 1 Grand Prix. Adult 11 € 6-18s 6 €* Albert I (1848-1922) was an oceanography fan and a great promotor of arts and sciences. He founded this museum in 1910, to exhibit his research findings from all the planet's seas. The spectacular aquarium contains 90 tanks and 4,500 types of fish, a coral reef and shark lagoon, and you can learn about the history of oceanography in the museum itself.

COLLECTION DE VOITURES ANCIENNES DE SAS LE PRINCE DE MONACO *Monaco Top Cars Collection - Le Terrasses de Fontvieille ✆ 00 377 92 05 28 56. www.palais.mc. Open every day: 10am-6pm, except Christmas & New Year's Day.* HRH Prince Rainier III has been collecting and restoring vintage cars for 30 years. He has about 100 famous European and American vehicles, each of which had a particular impact on its era.

MUSEE NATIONAL DES POUPEES ET DES AUTOMATES 17, ave Princesse Grace ✆ 00 377 93 30 91 *26. www.musee-national.com. Open 15 April-30 September, every day: 10am-6.30pm. Other periods: 10am-12.30pm and 2.30pm-6.30pm. Closed Christmas & New Year's Day, 1 May and 19 November. Admission: adult 6 €, 6-14s 3.50 €.* This museum, housed in a magnificent villa built by Charles Garnier, displays 400 dolls in scenes from elegant daily life: drinking tea, meeting friends, doing their hair, shopping. A huge 18thc. Neopolitan crèche contains 200 characters.

FOOD AND DRINK

South East French cuisine is based on garlic, oil, salads, herbs and fish (which 'lives in water and dies in oil' according to a Mediterranean proverb). The French chef Alain Ducasse calls it 'sunshine cooking'. Playwright Jean Racine wrote to la Fontaine from Uzes in 1661, "Oil replaces butter here, and I was apprehensive about the change, but I have tasted some in sauces today, and honestly, there is nothing better".

Anchoiade

An anchovy purée containing crushed capers and olive oil. Delicious on toast with an apéritif.

Farcis Niçois

You can stuff (farcir) what you like, usually aubergines, courgettes and peppers, though tomatoes and even onions are an idea. The stuffing contains a little pork; the other ingredients vary to suit the chosen vegetable.

Olives

Olives are green when they fall off the tree, and go black later. Olives from Nice are small, crunchy and full of flavour, which they give to the salade niçoise. The traditional handpicking by curvy peasant girls immortalised in 19thc. paintings is long gone; today a wide net like a spider's web is thrown over the tree as if to catch sardines, and with the first breath of mistral, the olives fall into the basket at the bottom of the net.

Bagnat bread

An huge sandwich containing lettuce, sliced tomatoes, anchovies, hard-boiled eggs, capers and olives, moistened with a few drops of olive oil. Hold it firmly flat with both hands; if you stand it on end you lose the filling out of the bottom.

Pissaladière

This traditional Nice recipe is onion tart garnished with anchovies and small black olives. You can eat it hot or cold, with drinks or as a starter.

Fish and seafood

You will enjoy them all the more having seen them at dawn on the market stall. Sardines, red mullet, swordfish and bass (best eaten barbecued with fennel), decorative orange scorpion fish and sea urchins. Sea bream and dory are delicious grilled or in fish soup.

Ratatouille

This is a dish of vegetables simmered in olive oil (the secret is never to use water). Onions, peppers, aubergines, courgettes and tomatoes are added to the pan in that order, and left to cook slowly with plenty of garlic and herbes de Provence.

Salade Nicoise

A mixed salad containing sliced tomatoes, olives, hard-boiled eggs, anchovies, radishes and tuna. You more or less add what you want.

Seafood

WINE

The côtes de provence wines go well with local cuisine. The best *cépages* are at Bandol, Pierrefeu, on the Var slopes, in the Maures and Argens valley, and on the Saint Tropez heights at Grimaud, Cogolin, Collobrières and Bormes-les-Mimosas. The most reputed wines are Bellet, Sainte Roselyne, La Gaude, Saint Jeannet and Menton. The rosé (made by white wine vinifying of red grapes) is popular in Provence, and should be drunk cool but not cold. The rather dry white wine goes well with fish and seafood. You can follow a kind of Côte d'Azur wine route, and visit the storerooms, cellars and co-operatives.

COMITE INTERPROFESSIONNEL DES VINS D'APPELLATION COTES DE PROVENCE Maison des Vins LES ARCS ✆ 04 94 99 50 10. Provence has had 5 AOC since 1978, the result of local winegrowers' efforts to comply with quality standards.

Bandol

This *cépage* covers 150ha. around Bandol, Sanary, Six-Fours-les-Plages, La Cadière d'Azur, Le Beausset and Le Castellet. Bandol reds are powerful wines which must be kept for three years before drinking. Whites and rosés do not age well, and can be drunk young.

We recommend the Château de Pibarnon, especially the red, from the sunny, sheltered Cadière d'Azur slopes.

Bellet

What a pity the vineyard area is so small: the white wine is elegant, fruity, and delicious to taste. 14 winegrowers blend carefully chosen *cépages* (the grapes have had 2,700 hours of annual sunshine) to produce 125,000 bottles a year. The experts consider the bellet to be one of the best scenty whites. Try a Château de Crémat, both light and powerful.

Côtes de provence

The dry rosés and strong reds from the Maures vineyards add great flavour to Provencal cooking. 19,000ha. cover the Var, Bouches-du-Rhône and Alpes-Maritimes departments, placing the region sixth in the national production league (80% rosé, 15% red and 5% white).

Tibouren *cuvée spéciale* pleases the most jaded gastronomic palates, and the traditional rosés (cinsault, grenache and syrah) are reputed for their fruitiness. Provence is the world's main rosé producer.

We recommend Château Galoupet, and Domaine de la Courtade, with its incomparable bouquet. The grapes ripen in the Ile de Porquerolles sunshine, unharmed by either frost or drought.

Palette

Whites, reds and rosés grown east of Aix-en-Provence, and featuring on local wine lists. Palette wines are full-bodied and fruity: we recommend the Rousset cellar, whose maitre de chais Gilbert Estienne will show you around.

French gastronomy

Hotels & Restaurants

ALPES-MARITIMES

Antibes- Cap d'Antibes- Juan les Pins

LES STRELIZIAS * and RESTAURANT LE PATIO Rue Pierre Commanay, Juan les Pins ✆ 04 92 93 64 00** *Fax 04 93 61 17 89. Website : www.lesstrelitzias.com. Open all year. Hotel or hotel residence formula. Double room 92 € to 143 € according to season, single 60 € to 89 €. Apartments let from 301 € per week (studio sleeping 2) in low season to 693 € per week in high season. Consult the website for online special offers. Car park 5 € per day, breakfast buffet 11 €. Half-board 29 € per person.* Complex located outside the town centre, yet close to beach and shops. Exceptional setting in a vast walled and tree-lined garden. The newly-renovated rooms are extremely spacious for a 3-star hotel, functional and well-decorated with a big cupboard and terrace, bathroom and all the creature comforts - TV, hairdryer, telephone. Families and business people can choose the residence option, and rent a large apartment with a kitchenette. The studio (40sqm) with balcony sleeps two; the 3-room apartment sleeps 6. The restaurant Le Patio serves creative Provençal cuisine in excellent taste, compared with some hotels. In fine weather, it's very pleasant to have lunch on the outdoor terrace. The pastis bar 'L'Anis Club' is a hotel speciality, a cosy lounge where you can taste over 130 different aniseed drinks. Another positive point (especially in high season) is the private underground car park with direct access to the upper floors. The complex also has seminar rooms with convertible salons. Comfort and good value for money together make this an address worth noting.

LA GAROUPE BEACH 823 bis Chemin de la Garoupe, 06160 Cap d'Antibes. 04 93 61 40 51. *Website : www.garoupe.com. Open 1 May to 5 September, 10am-8pm. Restaurant open for dinner Thursday, Friday and Saturday in June, July and August.* Garoupe Beach is a top-class restaurant on the edge of the famous Cap d'Antibes beach - such a beautiful place that you could be in some exotic setting on the other side of the world. The beach is made up of natural rocks, sand and landing stages suspended directly over the water. The lilos are laid directly on the ground, or on sunloungers. You can have lunch with your feet in the water, so as not to lose a minute of sunshine. On the menu, you find very good salads, attractively presented, fish of the day and pasta. If you come by boat, you'll be met by a small annex.The staff are very attentive. Upstairs there is a magnificent terrace where you can have a drink before dinner. It's better not to bring small children, as the landing-stages can be dangerous if they are running around.

LES VIEUX MURS 25, Promenade Amiral-de-Grasse – Vieil-Antibes ✆ 04 93 34 06 73. *Fax 04 93 34 81 08. Website : www.lesvieuxmurs.com. Email:lesvieuxmurs@wanadoo.fr. Car park 5 minutes on foot. Disabled access. Annual closing Monday 13 November-Sunday 3 December inclusive. Open every day 11 April-12 November: 12 noon-2.30pm and 7pm-10.30pm, 11pm in high season. Restaurant closed Mondays and Tuesday lunchtime from December to mid-April. Car valet service. Lounge bar. Set menus: gourmets 39 €, dégustation 60 €, children's menu 20 €. Chef Thierry Grattalora suggests his Breton Lobster menu (3 courses), 75 €. A la carte around 60 € without wine. Lunchtime bistrot suggestions 17 €-25 €. Located on the Old Antibes ramparts, facing the sea.* Philippe Bensimon has been running this charming restaurant since April 2002, and has transformed both the interior design and the *cuisine*! The decor - by De Tonge - is all warm, sophisticated tones. In summer, you can have lunch on the outdoor terrace facing the Mediterranean. Old walls, certainly, but youthful cooking, full of talent and inventiveness, thanks to Thierry Grattarola, former chef at the Hotel Belles Rives in Juan-les-Pins. The menu-carte is renewed every month to suit the seasonal market treasures available. Thierry's big successes are the veal chop with cepes, polenta and crunchy Golden Delicious apples; scallops with the juices just sealed, pumpkin and chestnut stock with truffles; pan-fried foie gras served with autumn fruits, port and balsamic vinegar reduction, and for dessert, brioche bread-and-butter pudding, pears and hot chocolate, and apple crumble with calavados, cinnamon ice-cream and salted caramel.

Beaulieu-sur-Mer

LA RESERVE DE BEAULIEU 5 boulevard du Mal-Leclerc ✆ 04 93 01 00 01 *Fax: 049301899.Website: www.reservebeaulieu.com. Email:reservation@reservebeaulieu.com Open every day. Annual closing 9 November-19 December. Rooms from 170 € in low season to 2,745 € in high season. Top-of-the-range Mediterranean cuisine. Lunchtime dish of the day . Average bill 150 €. Set menus 60 € and 105 €. Establishment created in 1880.* A superb Renaissance villa, rooms with frescoes, a peaceful patio and a dining-room that recalls the upper deck of a boat provide the setting where Olivier Brulard (ex-La

Pinède, Saint Tropez, Pré Catalan and Trois Marches, Versailles) concocts his sophisticated cooking, a blend of seafood and Provençal country dishes. The menu includes blue lobster vinaigrette with local citrus fruits, seasonal salads dressed with Comté de Nice olive oil, and Normandy scallops baked in their shells with lemon and a fresh herb and pine cone *marinière*. A marbled truffle dish with organic pumpkin emulsion and smoked bacon will please truffle fans. The three citrus fruit tarts delicately flavoured with violet and maritime pine round off a perfect meal. Creativity and professionalism are the rule, together with a royal welcome and impeccable service. The cellar is well-stocked: all in all, the place deserves its 2 Michelin stars.

Biot

LES TERRAILLERS 11, route du Chemin-Neuf ✆ 04 93 65 01 59. *Fax 04 93 65 13 78. Website : www.lesterraillers.com. Closed Wednesday and Thursday. Air-conditioned dining room. Private car park. Set menus 35 €, or 42 € with drink and coffee included, weekday lunchtimes, 49 €, 59 € and 70 €. A la carte 80 € evenings.* First class restaurant, with a Michelin star, housed in a genuine 16thc.pottery with vaulted ceilings, ancient beams and old exposed stonework. Period furniture, shady terrace - all in all, an enchanting setting. Owners Pierre and Chantal Fulci and chef Claude Jacques have managed to create a suitable climate of top-quality comfort and gastronomic excellence.

Cagnes-sur-Mer

LE CAGNARD** 1, rue Pontis-Long ✆ 04 93 20 73 21**. *Fax 04 93 22 06 39. Website : www.le-cagnard.com. Open all year. Restaurant closed Tuesday and Thursday lunchtime. Member of the Relais et Châteaux chain. 20 rooms and 5 suites. Single rooms 135 € to 200 €, doubles 170 € to 280 €. Breakfast 15 €.* Watch out - you're in the lap of luxury here. Jean-Yves Johany and Didier Anies have managed to transform a superb 13thc, residence with large fireplace and painted coffer ceilings into an extra-comfortable air-conditioned hotel with all mod cons. All the spacious rooms have a marvellous sea view. The gastronomic restaurant will satisfy the most difficult gourmet. Set menus 46 € (lunchtime only), 60 € and 81 € evenings. Excellent cooking, with top-quality fresh market ingredients.

LA FLEUR DE SEL 85, montée de la Bourgade - Les Hauts-de-Cagnes ✆ 04 93 20 33 33. *Website : www.restaurant-fleurdesel.com. Annual closing 1 November-20 December and 2-20 January. Weekly closing Wednesday, and Thursday lunchtime. 4 set menus: Saveur 21 €, Passion 30 €, Gourmet 39 € and Dégustation 52 €.* M. and Mme Loose run this restaurant with considerable talent. The dining room is prettily decorated with paintings and watercolours of Provence landscapes. You find a warm welcome, as well as gastronomic cuisine at reasonable prices. Every dish can be ordered from the carte and is regularly renewed.

LE GRIMALDI* 6, place du Château - Haut-de-Cagnes ✆ 04 93 20 60 24.** *Fax: 04 92 02 19 47. Website: www.hotelgrimaldi.com - Email: reservation@hotelgrimaldi.com. Open all year. Character hotel and restaurant. 4 rooms and suite on 2 floors. Double rooms 115 €-165 €. Breakfast included. Comfortable.* Located in the main square of the old town, next to the Grimaldi chateau. The hotel is accessible via the restaurant. The whole place was renovated 2 years ago, and the result is a blend of the modern and the picturesque: the rooms are tastefully decorated in pastel shades with a rustic look, and well-equipped with small hi-fi sets just like at home. Chef Franck Manenq's fresh and creative cooking is chiefly Mediterranean, especially enjoyable served in the restaurant's 'cute' and rather intimate interior dining room (seats 30 only). You'll probably choose to eat on the terrace in fine weather, overlooking the chateau square.

Cannes

HOTEL 3-14 5 Rue François Einesy ✆ 04 92 99 72 00 *Fax 04 92 99 72 12. Website: www.3-14hotel.com. Standard room 170 € to 300 €, superior room 250 € to 400 €, and 350 € to 1,500 € a night for a suite. Breakfast 23 €, garage and parking valet 23 € per day. 96 rooms, including 15 suites on 5 floors.* This is the huge new achievement from the Partouche group. How can we describe this totally atypical hotel, having visited almost all the rooms? 'It doesn't matter where you're from: here, you're somewhere else!' seems to be the concept. The project's two creators, Karine Ellena Partouche and her interior designer sister Alexandra, have added a very personal multicultural and ethnic touch to their work, influenced by years of worldwide travel. On entering the hall, Shanti (Peace in Hindi) the garden gnome perched on a Murano fountain smiles a greeting. Each floor corresponds to a continent, and as you step out of the lift, you are in another world: colours, scenery, music...Unbelievable.

HOTEL DE PARIS* 34, boulevard d'Alsace ✆ 04 93 38 30 89**. *Fax: 04 93 39 04 61. Website: www.hotel-de-paris.com - Email: myriam@hotel-de-paris.com. Close to the town centre and station, in the heart of Cannes, 10 minutes on foot from the Croisette and Palais. Annual closing 8-20 January and 7-28 December inclusive. Single room 90 € (low season)-250 € (high season). Double 95 € (low season)-250 € (high season). Breakfast buffet 13 €.* An attractive hotel with plenty of charm, and a typically Mediterranean ochre facade, nestling in a leafy setting. This magnificent garden contains a swimming pool with solarium (a 'plus' for the hotel) and there are also a sauna, hammam and jacuzzi. The 50 rooms have recently been renovated and are decorated in Louis XVI style; soundproofed, air-conditioned, some with balcony or terrace and a view over the garden or the town. Every room has a large desk, WiFi or modem socket, and satellite TV for your own choice of programmes. Garage and private car park. Private beach Le Rado only 10 minutes away on foot. Conference room with direct access to pool and terrace. Lounge and residents' bar with international library. All in all, top-quality setting and service.

IL RIGOLETTO 60, boulevard d'Alsace ✆ 04 93 43 32 19. *Closed Sunday and Tuesday evening out of season and congress periods. Special lunchtime set menu: starter + main course + dessert 15 €. Set menus Verdi 32 €, Gourmand 49 €.* Italian-influenced Mediterranean gastronomic cuisine, with succulent specialities like veal medallions with foie gras Milanese-style, fresh home made pasta, wild bass, Parma ham *chiffonade* with Parmesan shavings, and stuffed pigeon with foie gras and dried fruit. An excellent restaurant with no weak points.

LA PALME D'OR 73 la Croisette ✆ 04 92 98 74 14 22 *Fax 04 93 39 03 38. Website: www.hotel-martinez.com. Set menus 55 €-160 €. A la carte 150 €. Closed Sunday and Monday, 6 November-5 December and 13 December-20 December.* The Palme d'Or goes on holding its own, season after season. The Martinez hotel has an international reputation to keep up, and the slightest false step would be a disaster. Both Christians - Willer, executive chef, and Sinicropi, kitchen chef - are well aware of this, and are quick to capitalise on their advantages: a first-floor dining room with a splendid view of Cannes Bay, a recent change of decorative image by a famous designer (it looks wonderful) and a professional team in kitchens and dining room working to keep the competition (neighbour Le Majestic) at bay. The two rival hotels are currently drawing in the success stakes, in both the Michelin and Gault Millau.

38, THE PLACE- On the Hotel GRAY D'ALBION premises. 38, rue des Serbes BP 295 *) 04 92 99 79 79. Fax: 04 93 99 26 10. Website: www.gray-dalbion.com.* This is a new and trendy concept in Cannes - 38, The Place, open since 17 January 2006, and bringing together restaurant, bar, terrace and kitchen accessories shop all in one place. Open every day except Sunday and Monday outside festival time. Philippe Starck designed the crystal lighting and some of the accessories. You notice the same attention to detail on the tables with their orchid bouquets and state-of-the-art objects - how about an atomiser spray for vinaigrette? The tableware is Limoges china, made to measure so as to go with the designer cutlery. Alain Roy cooks world cuisine: have you ever tasted cepes in a 'cappucino' with woodland mushroom dips?

Eze

LE CHATEAU DE LA CHEVRE D'OR Rue du Barri ✆ 04 92 10 66 61 Fax 04 93 10 86 94. *Website: www.chevredor.com.* Philippe Labbé, who trained with Loiseau, Boyer and Michel Lorain, and was initiated into Mediterranean cooking by Roger Vergé and Christian Willer, seems to be blossoming in this marvellous restaurant, where he replaced Jean-Marc Delacourt two years ago. The magnificent staggered gardens, terrace overlooking Villefranche harbour 300m below, and panoramic dining room are part of a whole experience, including rather aristocratic but justifiable prices. The lobster and chicken macaroni timbale with truffled lait de poule (sort of egg nog), braised turbot with shellfish juice, served with an artichoke and orange 'garden', clams au gratin , casseroled veal rib with verbena and a sweetbread kebab, carrots flavoured with orange, vegetable stock served in a separate glass dish with foamy lait de poule flavoured with lemon juice, roast fillet with exotic pepper, lotus chips and aubergine tempura with sesame seeds, foie gras with passion fruit juice and sliced mango, exotic fruit in a traditional passion-fruit soufflé, fruit sorbet and 'minestrone' with a cloud of Malibu granita are exclusive creations: in fact the key word for this place is perfection, both on your plate and before your eyes.

CHATEAU EZA** Rue de la Pise ✆ 04 93 41 12 24.** *Fax 04 93 41 16 64. Website : www.chateaueza.com. Annual closing 2 November-19 December.* This is a real medieval castle (with plenty of modern comfort!) where you could almost imagine meeting Joan of Arc herself. Down in the village, two donkeys with packsaddles are loaded with your luggage, a parking valet takes charge of your car, and you go into the castle on foot, just like in the olden days. This used to be the home of H.R.H. Prince William of Sweden, so there's plenty to see and to marvel at. The 10 rooms are all very comfortable, and there is a superb view from the castle terrace. Prices range from 150 € to 290 € for a double standard room. Continental breakfast 20 €. Various formulas. The gastronomic restaurant offers the Château menu at 35 € and the Saveur menu at 45 € for lunch, and the Dégustation menu à 90 € for dinner. A la carte. Young chef Laurent Le Cann has already made a gastronomic name for himself on the Côte d'Azur.

HOTEL RESTAURANT HERMITAGE* 1951, avenue des Diables-Bleus - Grande corniche) 04 93 41 00 68**. *Email: ezehermitage@wanadoo.fr. Logis de France. Single rooms 59 €-99 €, doubles 59 €-119 €, breakfast 8 € per head per day, half-board 28 € per head per day. Restaurant closed Tuesday, and Wednesday lunchtime. Set menus 20 €-45 €. A la carte around 30 €.* Imagine a haven of peace in a garden full of blooms: a small but charming hotel with a magnificent view of the sea and Mercantour National Park mountains. The 16 Provençal-style rooms (including one for reduced mobility guests) have recently been renovated and are very comfortable, with TV, Internet access and air conditioning. In summer, you can enjoy a swim in the pool. The restaurant is open seven days a week for hotel guests and non-residents alike.

Grasse

LA BASTIDE SAINT-ANTOINE 48 av Henri-Dunant ✆ 04 93 70 94 94 *Fax 04 93 70 94 95. Website: www.jacques-chibois.com. Set menus 55 €-180 €. A la carte 115 €. Open every day, all year.* Jacques Chibois is a modest chef, who has never tried to make the magazine covers, yet he can be proud of his career. Having served a 5-year apprenticeship with Michel Guérard, who greatly influenced him, he spent time with Jean Delaveyne, Roger Vergé and Louis Outhier, some of the great Seventies chefs, and has twice managed to rise to the heights of gastronomic success - the first time at the Royal Gray Hotel in Cannes, the second in his own magnificent bastide in the Grasse countryside (where the rich and famous were already regular visitors in the 19thc). His *Découverte* menu (170 €!) is one of the best of its kind: potato royale with cream and olive oil, asparagus with morels, pasta and truffle caviar with a conserved marron coulis, bass in breadcrumbs with horn of plenty mushrooms and celery, Dublin bay prawns in a spicy rice fricassée, Limousin veal, tuberous vegetable purée, a pancake 'symphony', apple and pear, chocolate and praline, marshmallow with orange flower, mandarin sorbet and woodland strawberries.

Mandelieu – La Napoule

AZUR HOTEL ARCANTIS* 192 Avenue du Maréchal Juin ✆ 04 93 49 24 24**. *Fax: 04 92 97 68 36. Website: www.azurhotel06.com. Email: reception@azurhotel06.com. Air conditioning, garden, swimming pool, car park (English, German, Italian, Dutch). Double rooms 57 €-96 € according to season. Breakfas buffet 8 €.* New owners the Vanderstichelens have had the hotel entirely renovated, and extend a warm welcome. The 48 rooms are all comfortable, and there is a pleasant and relaxed family atmosphere. Excellent value for money.

L'OASIS Rue Jean-Honoré-Carle ✆ 04 93 49 95 52 *Fax 04 93 49 64 13. Website : www.oasis-raimbault.com. Set menus from 50 € to 150 €. A la carte 110 €. Closed Monday lunchtime and from mid-December to mid-January.* The great Louis Outhier raised this restaurant to gastronomic heights thirty-five years ago, before causing a stir on his retirement in 1988, when he gave Michelin back his 3 *macarons*. The Raimbault brothers, chef Stéphane, François and Antoine took over 15 years ago, and have managed to keep the place well up in the Côte d'Azur's gastronomic stakes. The *cuisine* interprets the great classics with flair, rather than pursuing innovation for its own sake: bass in a golden crust with tarragon, veal fillet mignon and foie gras with ginger, baked mango, roast loin of Alpilles lamb with parsley and a snail dish with stuffing. Well-trained yet relaxed service. Superb, classic cellar.

Menton

LE DARKOUM 23, RUE Saint-Michel ✆ 04 92 07 34 72. *Open every day lunchtime and evening. A la carte from 16 €, children's formula 7.50 €.* After almost 2 years of renovation work, extensions, restoration and a change of owner, Le Darkoum is once more ready to welcome fans of Moroccan

cuisine. Apart from the new decor - stonework, glass ceiling, mosaics, wrought iron and new colour scheme - nothing has changed: same concept, same flavours and same staff! The menu offers variations on the Oriental salad theme; couscous and of course, tajines. All the flavours of North Africa slide across your palate: eat slowly and you'll be transported to the other side of the Mediterranean - though the quality and quantity of the food, and typical warm welcome can already be found right here. Friday and Saturday evenings are Moroccan dance nights; the atmosphere is extraordinary.

LE DAUPHIN* 408, promenade du Soleil ✆ 04 93 35 76 37**. *Fax 04 93 35 31 74. Website: www.hotel-ledauphin.com. Closed mid-November to mid-December. 3 types of room: sea view, mountain view or junior suite, from 59 € to 92 € for a double and 51 € to 79 € for a single. Breakfast 8 €. Half-board 18 € per head.* The Dauphin is remarkably situated just above the sea, and has been completely renovated. You will be charmed by the setting on arrival, especially the beautiful terrace facing the sea - an invitation to relax! The rooms are quite large, decorated in restful shades of beige and pink, all soundproofed and air-conditioned, and equipped with cable TV, mini-bar and safe. The 'sea view' ones have a wide balcony where you can eat breakfast. The suites are designed for families. The restaurant is open every evening, with a la carte meals and half-board menus. The owner extends a particularly warm welcome. Public and private car parks nearby. Excellent value for money.

RESTAURANT LE PARIS-ROME 79, porte de France ✆ 04 93 35 70 45. *Fax: 04 93 35 29 30. Website: www.paris-rome.com - Email: info@paris-rome.com. Open every day except Monday, and Tuesday lunchtime. Annual closing 1 November-28 December. Weekday lunchtime formula 26 €. Set menu-carte 36 €. Decouverte menu ('wake up your taste buds and your senses') 75 €.* This cosy setting in warm Mediterranean colours offers a blend of seasoning and spices from around the world, and a thousand sunshine flavours. The Castellana family and chef Yannick Fauries have developed a creative, top-quality gastronomic menu including seawater terrine with avocado and crab foam; bass steak with raw fennel shavings, Limoncello sorbet and French caviar, crusty sweetbreads in their reduced 'coffee with cream' cooking juices, and rose marshmallow with rosemary and an assortment of different cherries. The wine list is most attractive, featuring Provence, Corsica, Italy and Bordeaux, at reasonable prices, with certain wines served by the glass. A friendly, welcoming place, and very good value for money.

LA RIVIERA 1 563, promenade du Soleil ✆ 04 93 35 25 75. *Italian specialities. Weekly closing Wednesday evening and all day Thursday, except July and August, open every day. Annual closing in January. Average bill 26 €. Set menu 20.50 € (starter, main course, cheese or dessert).* Dish of the day 10.50 €. Menton's best transalpine restaurant, featuring home made Italian country recipes. Wide choice à la carte. Escalopes; fish grilled, fried and in a carpaccio; pasta with seafood - and the inevitable tiramisu for dessert. Fine selection of reasonably-priced Italian wines. Your meal is served on a dream terrace facing the sea. Professional and rapid service.

Mougins

L'AMANDIER DE MOUGINS Place des Patriotes ✆ 04 93 90 00 91. *Fax: 04 92 92 89 95. In the village. Open every day: 12 noon-2pm and 7pm-10pm. Gourmand lunch 25 €. Set menus: Saveurs 34 € (evenings), Christophe 44 €. A la carte. Terrace and parking facilities.* This very pretty restaurant is housed in a former olive oil mill press; you eat in the original vaulted room. The terrace nestling in its green landscape is superb, and the food sumptuous. Try the cold aubergine caviar soufflé, piquillo pepper coulis, dried tuna, sea bass christophade braised in the oven and served with tapas and courgette flower fritters, and to finish, almond ice-cream in a peach velouté. The christophade is a speciality invented by chef Christophe Ferre - an elaborate dish of the day such as Challans duck stuffed with spices under the skin, or Christophe mullet on a tapenade crust. The desserts are perfect, and the wine list contains a few treasures. Not a single false note!

LA BROCHE DE FER 427, avenue Saint-Basile ✆ 04 92 92 08 08. *Fax: 04 92 92 88 54. Website: www.labrochedefer.com. Email: info@labrochedefer.com. Weekly closing Monday and Sunday evening. July & August: open evenings only until 11pm, seven days a week. Private car park. Amex cards accepted. Average bill 50-60 €. Weekday lunchtime formula 23 €. Set menus: Tradition 29 €, 'from the spit' 39 €, children's menu 10 €.* La Broche de Fer (The Iron Spit) is reputed on the Cote d'Azur, though some of its former glory had worn off over the last few years. The restaurant changed hands in early 2006, and suddenly all the old panache is back! The decor has been tastefully renovated: the inside dining room with its exposed beams and corner fireplace has lost none of its cachet, but the tables are prettily set and the magnificent shady terrace has a new look, not to mention a bar in summer. The cooking is definitely in a superior category, prepared with fresh market ingredients, and the roasted meat - a feature - is excellent. A genuine pastry cook concocts home-made sweets. The wine list thrills connoisseurs, with over 200 top names, and 30 chateaux available in half-bottles.

LE MOULIN DE MOUGINS 424 chemin du Moulin ✆ 04 93 75 78 24 *Fax 04 93 90 18 55. Website : www.moulindemougins.com. Set menus 48 € to 160 €. A la carte 120 €. Closed Monday. No annual holiday period.* In January 2004, Alain Llorca took over the reins from the great Roger Vergé (who had been running the restaurant for 35 years), and has no reason to regret leaving the Negresco. His new restaurant gets more attractive every season, and he has kept his faithful Nice clientele, as well as Vergé's regulars. The menu is more modern than they were used to, although plenty of legendary dishes are still there, like the *poupeton* (kind of bread pudding soufflé) with black truffles, and locally-caught whole fish. Apart from the tapas menu - always fun - there are Dublin bay prawns cooked with thyme and new potatoes with shellfish, an aubergine and fresh market vegetable merenda, turbot in artichoke *barigoule* and casseroled Dublin bay prawns, with courgettes. Brother Jean-Michel is a faithful partner and skilled pastrycook; his desserts are original and elegant. Iced lemon served in a glass Italian meringue-style, foamy exotic mango, praline *croustillant* and vanilla ice cream. Business is generally good, but although the Moulin has four suites and three rooms, it lacks the real hostelry facilities needed to back up a restaurant of this level.

Nice

HI HOTEL 3, avenue des Fleurs ✆ 04 97 07 26 26. *Fax : 04 97 07 26 27. Website: www.hi-hotel.net. Double room from 180 €, including breakfast.* The Hi is a new luxury concept and a total break with tradition. 200m from the sea, designed by Matali Crasset (who has worked with Philippe Starck), Hi offers 38 rooms with 9 concepts. Each concept involves a particular way of organising space. Inside, everything works with state-of-the-art technology: remote-controlled lights and shutters, cordless cell phone, broadband Internet, flat screen and hi-fi equipment. Communication and user-friendliness are the keywords, with automatic bars on each floor, a bar in the heart of the hotel, indoor garden, the 'hi food' self-service area open 24 hours a day, and hammam, with massage on request; roof terrace with a small swimming pool - contemporary design again! - and giant water beds to lie in the sun on. We recommend you to try this new experience!

CAFFE DELL'ARTE 6, cours Saleya (Vieux-Nice) ✆ 04 93 62 30 37. *Website : www.caffe-dellarte.com. Open every day except Monday and Tuesday lunchtime. Non-stop service from 8am to 12.30am. Tearoom, breakfast (7.50 €) wine bar. Average bill 30 €.* Exotic teak decoration and parquet on the floor, outside terrace (heated in winter), first-floor dining room with a cosy adjacent lounge, and original toilets located in an old wardrobe! This restaurant-gallery idea is very trendy, the point being to link the culinary and pictorial arts. Temporary exhibitions of local artists' works – painters, mosaics designers, sculptors and glassworkers – and private viewings are to the fore. As for the cooking, the Caffe dell'Arte has two talented chefs, Pierre Thet helped by Sandrina Monchy. Their menu features various salads, crêpes, meat dishes, fish and pasta. The day's suggestions are often original, blending sweet and savoury flavours. You must taste the home-made pastries, especially the chocolate fondant! Beautiful wine list, boasting an excellent choice of *appellations*.

CHANTECLER 37 promenade des Anglais ✆ 04 93 16 64 00 *Fax 04 93 88 35 68. Website : www.hotel-negresco-nice.com. Set menus from 45 € to 130 €. A la carte 120 €.* If 2004 was an unsettled year for the Negresco - Alain Llorca left for the Moulin de Mougins, Michel del Burgo replaced him for only a few months, then in the summer Bruno Turbot arrived from Clovis in Paris - then 2005 will have been the consolidation period. The ambient luxury hasn't changed, nor the rather dated decoration, but the moment is still unique, especially if the owner Mme Augier is there, at her little table facing the huge mirror. The cooking remains classic: avocado gaspacho with crayfish in spicy vinaigrette, bass in a golden herb crust with rocket juice and melting aubergines, grilled saddle of Sisteron lamb and tomato millefeuille, and rose-flavoured macaroon with stewed rhubarb. The service is formal, ties are worn for dinner, and there is a vast but costly cellar.

L'ESQUINADE 5, quai des Deux-Emmanuel, sur le port. ✆ 04 93 89 59 36. *Closed Saturday lunchtime, all day Sunday and Monday lunchtime. Annual holiday 5 January-5 February, and one week in late June. Set menus: Premier 19.50 €, Gastronomic 45 €. A la carte 35 €-60 €.* If you consider yourself a connoisseur of quality meat, then don't miss this place! Marcel Béraud is a roast meat specialist by trade, and prepares an absolutely sumptuous spit-roasted shoulder of suckling lamb with rosemary sauce - among other delicacies. The 'Simmenthal' beef rib on the grill, sauce Béarnaise, and grilled beef fillet with a 5-varieties-of-peppercorn sauce will also tempt your taste buds. Spit-roasted poultry is on the menu too, calling up images of medieval castle fireplaces: partridge served with sautéed potatoes and rosemary, and a slice of toast spread with foie gras; mallard duck garnished with woodland mushrooms; and pheasant with cranberries, in grand veneur sauce. As we're on the harbour here, fish is not forgotten, and scallops, Dublin bay prawns, lobster with truffles, and whole sea bass seasoned with fennel and thyme have their place with the rest.

FOUR POINTS SHERATON** and its restaurant LE CAPRICE. 59 Promenade des Anglais, entrance rue Sauvan (perpendicular street). ✆ 04 93 97 90 90** *Fax 04 93 44 06 55 Website: www.elyseepalace.com. Email reservation@elyseepalace.com.* Located on the famous Promenade des Anglais, a few minutes on foot from central Nice, this hotel can be singled out by its spectacular contemporary architecture and monumental bronze statue sculpted by Nice artist Sosno. It was entirely redecorated in 2001, and provides top-quality comfort levels and service. The 143 rooms and suites are decorated and

furnished in Art Deco style, with view of the sea or the town, king-size bed, 24-hour room service, individual air conditioning, safe, marble bathroom, satellite TV and video games, and broadband Internet access. The roof boasts a panoramic terrace with an exceptional all-round view over sea, town and neighbouring hills. You can relax at the open-air pool and bar, well away from the usual tourist bustle. Le Caprice is a gastronomic restaurant run by chef Olivier Richard, who concocts subtle Mediterranean cooking that manages to combine professional precision with creative fantasy. The menu follows the seasons and market availability: nothing could be fresher. Quick weekday lunchtime formula 19 €.

HOTEL LES CIGALES* 16, rue Dalpozzo +33 (0)4 97 03 10 70** *Fax +33 (0)4 97 03 10 71. Website: www.hotel-lescigales.com.†Email: info@hotel-lescigales.com.* Open all year.19 comfortable, soundproofed and air-conditioned rooms with bathroom, mini-bar, satellite TV, telephone with outside line and modem socket, safe, hairdryer and WiFi access. Double room 120 €-160 € in high season (according to category, standard or superior) 90 €-130 € in low season. Single room 100 €-115 € in high season. Near the Promenade des Anglais behind the Palais de la Mediterranée and Ruhl Casino. Former private mansion tastefully renovated, with top-of-the-range comfort. The rooms are brightly decorated in red and yellow. Excellent welcome and service; no private car park, but then this is a great luxury in the centre of Nice! Several public car parks nearby.

LE PALAIS MAETERLINCK** 30, boulevard Maurice-Maeterlinck ✆ 04 92 00 72 00** - *Fax : 04 92.04.18.10. Website : www.palais-maeterlinck.com. 40 rooms.* Gastronomic restaurant , Le Mélisandre. Rooms from 245 € to 790 € (junior suite with terrace) according to category and season. Le Palais can be found in the east of Nice, hanging between earth and sky on the lower cliff road. Once the home of poet Maurice Maeterlinck, it was converted into a hotel in 1989. Charm and luxury are everywhere: in the 3 ha. park, outdoor heated pool and extremely comfortable rooms. Romantic atmosphere.

LE RESTAURANT DES VIVIERS. **22, rue Alphonse-Karr ✆ 04 93 16 00 48**. *www.les-viviers-nice.com. Open every day except Sunday. Annual closing in August. Average bill between 45 € and 50 €. Set menus 35 € and 50 €, lobster special 65 €. Air-conditioning throughout the restaurant.* Renaud Geille has handed over to Jacques Rolancy this year, but you don't change a winning team, so chef David Vaqué is still running the kitchens. The dining room is cosy, and carefully decorated, with nothing left to chance. David is one of the new generation of gastronomic chefs behind a simply creative, light and sophisticated cuisine, and has developed the carte with his culinary expertise: the menu changes with seasonal variations in market produce. Fish has pride of place on the menu: try the small monkfish baked in lettuce cream, bass with sauce vierge, the house bouillabaisse, and Breton lobster in all its forms. On the meat side, there is Puntoun Farm duck, or duck breasts with honey. The desserts are all deliciously light. Some of the best crus around feature on the extensive wine list. Unobtrusive, professional service. An excellent place to eat.

LE RIVE DROITE **22, avenue Saint-Jean-Baptiste. ✆ 04 93 62 16 72**. *Closed Sunday. Set menus : dégustation 33 €, lunchtime 19 €, or dish of the day 10.80 €. A la carte around 25-35 €.* This restaurant boasts100% old-fashioned local cooking! Le Rive Droite won the Nice Cuisine prize in 1995 (sadly it no longer exists) and is a veritable sanctuary of local gastronomy. Pissaladière, aubergine fritters, pan-fried sardines and mullet, beef tripe Nice-style, a sublime daube and equally delicious polenta, pan-cooked scampi with garlic, fish soup from the local rocks with pistou, ravioli with cepes, aubergines au gratin, Saint-Etienne-de-Tinée goat's cheese, Saint-Martin-Vésubie cow's milk tome, and a very good fig tart feature on the menus. The chef is especially proud of his gnocchi, made from potatoes and flour in the traditional way to a 100-year-old recipe!

Peymeinade

RESTAURANT LA GARGOULETTE **70 Av de Boutiny ✆ 04 93 66 22 88**. *Closed Wednesday, except in July & August. Set menus 15 € (except Sunday and public holidays) 22 €, 28 €, 34 €. A la carte.* Local specialities bouillabaisse and bourride made to order. Terrace, car park. Patrice Orhant is the chef; his wife runs the dining room. The cooking is reliable: fish soup, quail salad with grapes, dory in flaky pastry on a leek fondu, shellfish sauce and Sisteron pieds paquets. These excellent traditional dishes are attracting a growing number of regulars.

Roquebrune-Cap-Martin

VISTAERO **1 551, route de la Grande-Corniche ✆ 04 92 10 40 00.** *Website: www.vistapalace.com - Email: info@vistapalace.com.* This is the hotel Vista Palace's gastronomic restaurant. Open every day lunchtime and evenings, except 1 June-15 September evenings only, to make way for summer restaurant La Corniche le Midi. A la carte around 53-57 €. Car parking valet. This restaurant overlooks the entire coast from its privileged position up on the Grande Corniche. Exceptional view, romantic atmosphere and sophisticated cuisine – who could ask for more? In summer, La Corniche le Midi offers simple Provençal and Mediterranean cooking, but Vistaero is something else, especially since chef Charles Semeria left the Royal Riviera at Saint-Jean-Cap-Ferrat to settle here and explore local quality produce. The result is a blend of Mediterranean, Italian and Provençal influences: violet artichokes barely tossed in hot olive oil; a few ravioli with ricotta and Menton lemon; dory fillet braised on an onion fondue with anchovies and polenta with Pantenegra ham. Not forgetting the chocolate arch flavoured with chicory and cream of confiture de lait (a milk-based preserve). The wines are perfect, suiting all tastes, budgets and dishes.

Saint-Jean - Cap-Ferrat

LA VOILE D'OR** 7, avenue Jean-Mermoz - Port de Saint-Jean ✆ 04 93 01 13 13.** *Website : www.lavoiledor.fr - Email: reservation@lavoiledor.fr. Open mid-April to mid-October. Other set menus 60 €, 80 € and 100 €.* Car valet service. Chef Georges Pélissier's cooking is worth going out of your way for – taste his scallop kebab with sesame seeds, roast cepes, green aparagus tartare with seasonal mushrooms, chicken juices in a truffle vinaigrette, and iced chocolate velouté and hot and cold banana macaroon dessert. Tremendous wine list, plus a dream setting opposite the harbour: this place is a real find!

Saint-Paul-de-Vence

LE CLOS DES ARTS** 350 Route de Saint Paul ✆ 04 93 32 40 00** *Fax 04 93 32 69 98 - Website: www.closdesarts.com† Email: info@closdesarts.com – New in 2006. Open all year. 9 rooms, 220 €-570 €. Breakfast 14 €-22 € according to season. Half-board +82 € per head per day. Restaurant open every day, lunchtime and evenings. Air-conditioned, non-smoking dining room. Set menus 40 €, 65 € and 85 €. Children's menu 21 €. A la carte 64 €. Car park, bar, private lounge, terrace, panoramic view of Saint-Paul Village and the region.* This charming hotel-restaurant is located in 2 ha. of enchanting leafy grounds. Its shady terrace, sublime view of the surrounding landscapes and elegant, air-conditioned rooms are great assets, as is its position, on the way into the famous artists' village. The cuisine, managed by Hervé Gély, is inventive, and suits all tastes, thanks to the grill where crayfish, lobster and red meat can be cooked to customer requirements. There is also a typical Provençal bistrot (seats 30) open all hours, that welcomes tea and coffee-drinkers, champagne-lovers and foodies seeking simple fare: tasty Spanish ham, for instance, or goat's cheese with a glass of local wine (Var/Provence).

HOTEL LE HAMEAU* 528, route de La Colle (Face au village de St Paul) ✆ 04 93 32 80 24.** *Fax: 04 93 32 55 75. Website: www.le-hameau.com - Email: lehameau@wanadoo.fr. A magnificent hotel with lots of charm. Annual closing mid-November to mid-February. Single or double room 120 €-220 €. Breakfast 12.50 €. 17 rooms, apartments and suites, all different and comfortable. Air-conditioning, mini-bar, outside phone line, TV, Internet socket, room service, genuine antique Provençal furniture, traditional red tommette floor tiles.* This is an 18thc. Provençal farm, remarkably well restored in its leafy setting. The rooms display a perfect blend of ancient and modern in their soft furnishings, colours and flowers. The pool (with wave machine) is located on a breathtaking site with a beautiful view of Saint-Paul. Nearby, you have the relaxation area with jacuzzi, sauna and hammam; massages are available by appointment. Petit Futé readers get 10% off the price of their stay in low season. Pets accepted. Secure car park.

LE SAINT-PAUL** 86, rue Grande ✆ 04 93 32 65 25.** *Fax 04 93 32 52 94. Website : www.lesaintpaul.com. 15 rooms from 190 € to 310 €, 4 suites between 280 € and 580 € according to season. Continental breakfast 22 €. Set menus 48 € to 85 €.* The Saint Paul is a charming hotel composed of several houses, terraces and passages put together in the heart of old Saint Paul. It makes you think of a sophisticated Renaissance palace, drawing atmosphere from its surroundings. You find comfort, decoration, a marvellous panorama, ambience and gastronomy: chef Frédéric Buzet is already well-known for excellence. One of the most attractive Relais et Châteaux hotels.

Théoule-sur-Mer

RESTAURANT CHEZ PHILIPPE Port de Théoule ✆ 04 93 49 87 13. *Open all year, closed Tuesday in winter. Set menus 25 €, 38 €. Seafood menu 38 €. Royal seafood platter (for 2) 89 €. A la carte.* Bouillabaisse to order. Seafood and fish specialities, shellfish. The enchanting setting and Philippe's delicious cuisine make advance booking essential. Small shellfish flan with Sancerre coulis, lobster cooked in the oven, crayfish tails and Bouchot mussels au gratin in a belle aurore sauce, and beef fillet with pepper flambed in cognac feature on the menus.

Vence

LES BEATILLES 8, rue du Marché ✆ 04 93 58 04 17. *Website: www.lesbeatilles-vence.com - Open all year . Closed Tuesday and Friday lunchtime in summer. Closed Thursday, and Friday and Saturday lunchtimes in low season. Set menus 29 € and 36 €. A la carte.* Contemporary cuisine. This charming restaurant has recently been taken over by Guillaume Ollivier and his partner Jelena. The terrace facing the Town Hall and cathedral seats 20 in season. This talented young chef works with fresh ingredients: on the menu you find fennel fondue with courgettes, shellfish juice with peppermint, Mediterranean dory confit in olive oil, and baked pineapple with its Tahitian vanilla parfait. Guillaume was trained by Christophe Dufau, chef at Les Bacchanales, Tourettes-sur-Loup, and his future looks very promising.

HOTEL MIRAMAR*** **167, avenue Bougearel✆ 04 93 58 01 32.** *Website: www.hotel-miramar-vence.com - Email: resa@hotel-miramar-vence.com. Open all year, round-the-clock service. Double room 78 €-128 € in low season, and 88 €-148 € in high season. Breakfast 10 €-12 €.* This former mansion has been converted into a character hotel with plenty of charm. The Miramar has an impressive panoramic view of the Vence coast and mountains, and is only 200m from the town and historic centre. Recently renovated, it offers comfortable rooms, equipped with bathrooms (bath or shower, WC) telephone and TV. Each is named after a Provençal flower – cornflower, nasturtium, and so on - and is decorated in the region's colours. Superb panoramic terrace. Swimming pool set in a leafy garden. In fine weather you can have breakfast on the terrace overlooking the sea and the Baous. Top-quality services, peace and quiet and comfort guaranteed. Private onsite car park. Note that Petit Futé readers who come with their guide get a free breakfast.

Villefranche-sur-Mer

LE CARPACCIO **Promenade des Marinières ✆ 04 93 01 72 97.***Website: www.restaurant-carpaccio.com. Facing the sea. Open every day in season. Special lunchtime set menu 25 €. A la carte around 35 €-40 €. Children's menu 13 €.* Car valet and boat service: you are collected from your boat from June to late September. The restaurant is located at the end of the harbour, almost in the sea, with its small terrace and private lounge. It is known for its fish specialities, and has a lobster and crayfish tank. Start with the dégustation dish - a series of delicious little starters – follow on with fish and octopus carpaccio and to finish, choose the crème brulée with lavender honey. If you're a pasta fan, you'll be spoilt for choice. There is also a range of meat dishes, not forgetting the pizzas. Excellent cooking, in short, and very professional service to go with it. Cigar cellar for amateurs. Car park right at the restaurant door. Yves Pannard and his staff have made this restaurant one of the places to eat in Villefranche.

LA MERE GERMAINE **7, quai Amiral-Courbet ✆ 04 93 01 71 39.** *Open every day in season. Annual closing 14 November-24 December. Special lunchtime and evening set menu 37 €. Children's menu 20 €. A la carte 50 € to 60 €, without drinks.* This is a chic place, despite its name, with an attractive dining room and elegant tables with flowers. The staff are well-trained and the cooking skilful, right down to the presentation - each dish is a small work of art. Inventive garnishes and sauces. The stuffed and grilled fish deserve a special mention; the seafood and shellfish too. Try the loin of Sisteron lamb, which is perfect. This culinary quality is reflected in the prices, but it's good value for money all the same.

HOTEL-RESTAURANT LA FLORE*** **5, boulevard Princesse-Grâce-de-Monaco – Basse corniche ✆ 04 93 76 30 30.** *Fax 04 93 76 99 99. Website : www.hotel-la-flore.fr. Logis de France. Open all year. Price for 2 people in high season 46 € to 257 € (suite). Breakfast buffet 10 €. Private garage with CCTV 9 € per day, with a few free parking spaces in front of the hotel.* Magic view of Villefranche Bay, one of the world's finest panoramas. Located only 5 minutes from the beaches. This former 19thc. residence was renovated in 1994 in keeping with its original Provençal style. The rooms vary from luxury mini-suite to standard, on the car park side, which explains the price difference. Most have balconies or terraces overlooking the harbour. All come complete with bath, shower or jacuzzi, WC, mini-bar, hairdryer, telephone and satellite TV. Pool with solarium. Restaurent open early March to late October, except Wedneesday. Excellent value for money in its category.

VAR

Agay-Anthéor

LES FLOTS BLEUS Avenue Eugene Brieux. Antheor ✆ 04 94 44 80 21. *Fax: 04 94 44 83 71. Website: www.hotel-cote-azur.com. Email: contact@hotel-cote-azur.com. Open mid-March to late October. 18 rooms sleeping 1-4, from 50 € to 79 € according to season and number of guests. Breakfast 6 €. Half-board 70 €-171 €. Full board 81 €-231 €. Set menus 15 €-34 €.* Snack meals available June-September. Private car parks (one closed, for motorbikes). Bright, comfortable rooms with private terrace overlooking Antheor Bay and the beach below. Dining room with panoramic view and shady terrace under the plane trees, where you can enjoy traditional dishes and fresh fish, with home-made bread and desserts.

Bandol

HOTEL ILE ROUSSE ** 25, boulevard Louis-Lumière ✆ 04 94 29 33 00**. *Fax 04 94 29 49 49. Website: www.ile-rousse.com. Open every year. 55 rooms from 112 € to 368 €. Private, closed garage.* Car park outside. Outdoor seawater pool. Internet access. Wi-Fi. 5 restaurants, including one gastronomic, Les Oliviers. 2 private beaches in season. A stone's throw from the town centre, right on the Rènecros Bay with its fine sandy beach, this hotel offers comfortable air-conditioned rooms, all individually decorated with terrace or balcony. Room-service, laundry, secretarial assistance and car-hire are available, and guests can enjoy the on-site Héliovital-Thalgo seawater therapy centre facilities (outside access for non-residents), offering a variety of revitalising seawater treatments, relaxation and fitness areas - jacuzzi, hammam and cardio-training - and beauty treatment booths. Ask about the range of special all-in prices.

Bormes-les-Mimosas

LE DOMAINE DU MIRAGE * 38, rue de la vue des îles ✆ 04 94 05 32 60**. *Fax 04 94 64 93 03. Website: www.domainedumirage.com Open late March-early November. 35 double rooms from 120 € to 175 €, according to season, breakfast included. Apartments to let, from studio to 2-room flat, 445 € to 1,020 € for a week. Closed car park and garages. 2 heated pools. Children's play area. Fitness pavilion. Balinese rest room. Tennis and table tennis. Boules pitch. Flower garden. Private beach.* This hotel with its colonial-style façade overlooks Lavandou Bay and the Iles d'Or, and is located on an estate with over a hectare of land. You can lunch under the palm trees or by the pool: the asiettes composed of fresh market produce are irresistible. In the evening, you choose your dinner from four starter, main course and dessert suggestions.

L'ESCOUNDUDO 2, ruelle du Moulin. Old village ✆ 04 94 71 15 53. *Annual closing 15 February-15 March. Closed Tuesday and Wednesday. Set menus 40 € - lunch - 58 € and 78 €.* The talented Dandine brothers are a breath of fresh air in this restaurant, with their youth and enthusiasm. Mathias looks after the regional yet modern cooking, and Fabien runs the dining room. They may be moving on elsewhere soon - so you'd better get there quick!

Cogolin

LE GRAIN DE SEL 6, rue du 11-Novembre ✆ 04 94 54 46 86. *Closed Sunday and Monday. Open evenings only in July and August, closed Monday. Set menu of the day 33 €. A la carte around 50 €.* Philippe Audibert's fresh and spirited coooking is a pleasure to eat, though with only 22 place settings, it is also quite a privilege! All the experience gained at Byblos in Saint Tropez and his own natural talent go into Philippe's cuisine.The menu changes regularly, alternating little Nice-stule stuffings, saddle of venison with pepper sauce, part-dried tomato and polenta au gratin, Mediterranean capon stuffed with Savoy cabbage, cepe risotto and to finish, warm chocolate tart or autumn fruit poached in spicy juice.

Draguignan

L'AUBERGE PIERROT 773, avenue maréchal Galliéni, route de La Motte ✆ 04 94 68 35 37. *Fax 04 94 68 67 97. Closed Sunday evening, Monday and Tuesday evening. Annual closing in February. Set menus 10 € - weekday lunchtimes - 22 € and 28 €. Children's menu 10 €. A la carte around 40 €. Closed car park.* Jean-Paul Pierrot gained a star from the *Académie nationale de cuisine* in 2003, for his top-quality regional cooking. His menus vary from day to day, following market produce availability, with game in season. Chicken with crayfish, roast leg of lamb, tournedos Rossini, seafood pot-au-feu and the house *dessert Pierrot gourmand*. It's especially pleasant to eat on the terrace in summer.

HOSTELLERIE DU MOULIN DE LA FOUX ** 941, chemin Saint Jean, quartier de la Foux ✆ 04 98 10 14 *14. Fax 04 94 68 70 10. Website: www.moulindelafoux.fr. Open all year. Inter Hotel. 27 rooms, 8 twin, 2 triple, 17 double, from 54 € to 78 €. Breakfast buffet 6.90 €. Restaurant closed Saturday lunchtime and Sunday. Set menus 16 € and 30 €. Children's menu 10 €. Car park.* This recently renovated hotel is located on the way into the town from the south, in a converted 18thc. watermill surrounded by a leafy park with the River Foux running through it. Francine Marchal serves traditional cuisine with foie gras, gambas flambéd in pastis and beef fillet with mushrooms.

Fayence

LA TABLE D'YVES 1357, Route de Fréjus ✆ 04 94 76 08 44. *Fax 04 94 76 19 32. Website: www.latabledyves.com Closed Wednesday and Thursday lunchtime. Set menus 28 €, 40 € and 50 €. A la carte 35 € and 40 €. Private, closed car park.* Isabelle and Yves Merville have patiently renovated this former tennis club among the vines on the Fayence plain, giving it a pretty facelift. The dining room is decorated in warm shades, and there is an attractive terrace with a flowering arbour and wrought-iron furniture, overlooking the village. Pastoral chic! The menus change on a monthly basis, depending on what seasonal produce is available, and the resulting dishes are delectable: cepe ravioles in mushroom stock, fillet of Barbary duck roasted in lavender honey, cod and brandade de morue (cod and potato dish) with spiced oil, and chocolate moelleux *minute* to finish with.

Flayosc

L'OUSTAOU 5, place Joseph Brémond ✆ 04 94 70 42 69. *Fax 04 94 84 64 92. Website: www.loustaou.net Closed 15 November-15 December, Sunday evening, Monday and Tuesday. Set menus 28 €, 33 €, 44 €. A la carte 55 €.* Lydie and Mathieu Cassin took over this 1732 coaching inn only a short time ago, and have made sure of the place's traditional rustic look. The chef trained with Gérard Vié, ex-Mesclun in Cannes, and prepares gastronomic cuisine with a Provençal influence. His carte changes every three months, suggesting gambas carpaccio with lime and shellfish oil, dory with aioli and grilled vegetables, roast farm suckling veal and Taggiasche olives - among other delicious things.

Fréjus

L'ARENA 145, rue du Général de Gaulle ✆ 04 94 17 09 40. *Fax 04 94 52 01 52. http://www.arena-hotel.com. Logis de France. Châteaux Hôtels de France. Closed 15 December-15 January. 36 rooms, from 65 € to 145 €. Breakfast 11 €. Restaurant closed Monday and Saturday lunchtime. Menus 23 € - weekday lunchtime - 43 € and 55 €. A la carte 60 €. Private car park. Swimming pool.* This hotel in the heart of town is full of Southern atmosphere, with its luminous dining room, decorated in warm yellow ochre tones, and air-conditioned, soundproofed rooms overlooking a pleasant flower-filled patio. Chef Loïc Belanec, formerly with the Pourcel brothers in Montpellier, excels at sunshine cooking, like artichoke barigoule with coriander and fresh mussels, roast fillet of veal, sage juice, polenta with butter, asparagus fricassée and citron gratin, with red fruit coulis.

Hyères

LA COLOMBE 663, route de Toulon. RN 98 La Bayorre ✆ 04 94 35 35 16. *Fax 04 94 35 37 68. Website: www.restaurantlacolombe.com. Closed September toJune: Saturday lunchtime, Sunday evening and Monday. July and August: Saturday lunchtime, Monday and Tuesday lunchtime. Set menus 25 € and 33 €. A la carte 45 €.* Member of the *Varois Maîtres Restaurateurs* association. The beautiful split-level dining room in beige and ochre and the leafy patio are Nadège's domain. Pascal Bonamy looks after the kitchen, where he cooks Provencal and Mediterranean dishes, such as scallop and shellfish pot, pan-fried bass with summer vegetables and young pigeon fricassée with foie gras and port.

La Croix-Valmer

HOTEL SOULEIAS Plage de Gigaro ✆ **04 94 55 10 55**. *Fax 04 94 54 36 23. Website: www.hotel-souleias.com. Open mid-April to mid-October. 41 rooms, 1 suite and 6 junior suites from 93 € to 433 €, sleeping one to three people, prices according to the season. Breakfast buffet 17.50 €. Set menus 46 €, 64 € and 77 €. A la carte around 64 €. Children's menu 17 €. Closed car park with surveillance. Tennis courts. Swimming pool overlooking the sea. 18m yacht with skipper.* The hotel nestles in a 2ha. park giving onto Gigaro beach, with a panoramic view of the Iles d'Or and Calvaire Bay. The sophistcated rooms have all the essential comforts, are located in the park or round the pool, with a privated terrace, and look south, towards the sea. Chef Gérard Ferri prepares delicious light recipes for the lunchtime fraîcheur menu and creative Provençal gastronomic cuisine in the evenings. He uses country produce and seafood to produce dishes like cold sole aioli, pan-fried bass tournedos, stewed fennel, conserved tomatoes and saddle of lamb in a herb crust.

Les Arcs-sur-Argens

LE LOGIS DU GUETTEUR * Quartier médiéval du Parage**. *Place du Château & 04 94 99 51 10.Fax 04 94 99 51 29. Website: www.logisduguetteur.com. Member of the Varois Maîtres Restaurateurs association. Open every day. Annual closing in February. 13 rooms from 108 € to 195 €. Breakfast 15 €. Set menus 34 €, 56 € and 76 € (all truffle).* Private car park with CCTV. Swimming pool. History lovers will admire this 11thc. fortress, a former home of the Comtes de Provence, where Max Callégari's feasts are served in winter in marvellous dining-rooms with vaulted ceilings and a crackling log fire, and in summer, on terraces above the poolwith a panoramic view of the Argens Valley, Rocher de Roquebrune and Maures massif. Before going up to your air conditioned room, taste the pasta risotto with saffron, pan-cookes pistes (little squid) with citrus fruits, cod with lemon and capers, fennel, Taggiasca olive coulis, sesame seed croustillant, citrus fruit soup with rose water and warm pistachio financier.

Le Lavandou

HOTEL L'OUSTAOU ** 20, avenue du Général de Gaulle ✆ **04 94 71 12 18**. *Fax 04 94 15 08 75. Website: www.lavandou-hotel-oustaou.com. Open all year. 20 double rooms from 44 € to 59 €. Breakfast 5.50 € downstairs, 5.70 € in your room. Half-board available with a partner restaurant nearby, 21 € extra per adult, 14 € extra per child.* This small family hotel near the port and vast Lavandou beach has recently been fully renovated. Some rooms have a sea view or terrace.

Porquerolles

L'OLIVIER Le Mas-du-Langoustier ✆ **04 94 58 30 09** *Fax 04 94 58 36 02. Website : www.langoustier.com. Set menus from 52 € to 82 €. A la carte 80 €. No weekly closing, closed from mid-October to mid-April.* This Olive Tree is the Mas du Langoustier Hotel's exclusive restaurant, nestling at one end of the Ile de Porquerolles. Most of its customers are hotel residents, since there are no boats running back to the mainland in the evenings. Chef Joël Guillet was second to Dominique Le Stanc at the Negresco in the late 1980s, then chef at the Vallon de Valrugues in Saint Rémy de Provence. His langoustine tails pan-cooked with dried green apple powder, reduced juices, green salad and sweet potatoes with vanilla oil, courgette fritters, tomato chutney and figues in black sugar, grilled bass fillet, cannelloni made from black olive pasta stuffed with aubergines, and vegetable juice with mustard, then seaweed croustillant with coconut milk rice pudding, candied exotic fruit and rum and raisin ice cream all have a deliciously select taste (which goes well with the prices). Idyllic setting, marvellous sea view and perfect service.

Ramatuelle

LA FORGE Rue Victor-Léon ✆ 04 94 79 25 56 *Open every day in season. Annual closing 15 November-15 March. Closed Wednesday. Formula 25 €. Set menu 35 €.* This is a real forge, where you can still see the old anvils, bellows, hammers and iron ingots. Chef Henri Fazio's cuisine doesn't seem out of place in this craftsman's decor, though: his delectable specialities would go down a treat anywhere. Open Dublin bay prawn ravioles with shellfish cream, veal shin parmentier in its juice, crispy *galette*, and for dessert, a warm chocolate *moelleux* (rather like chocolate pudding with a runny middle), vanilla ice cream and butter caramel are on the menu.

YELLOW VILLAGE LES TOURNELS. Route de Camarat. Tel 04 94 55 90 90. *Fax 04 94 55 90 99. Website: www.tournels.com . Email: info@tournels.com. Open 1 March-10 January. 960 spaces: 16 €-38 € for 2 according to season and type. Chalets and cottages sleeping 4-6, 48 € -140 € per night according to season. Heated pool, mini golf, tennis, volleyball and basketball courts. Shopping centre. Restaurant, tobacconist, newsagent, laundry, shuttle to beach in July & August.* This camping and caravanning site overlooks the Pampelonne beaches, and has a wide choice of accommodation on offer, scattered through a 20ha, pine grove. There is also a 1,000 sqm. 'well-being' area with pool, hammam and fitness centre.

Saint-Aygulf

PARC CAMPING DE SAINT-AYGULF PLAGE 270, avenue Salvarelli ✆ 04 94 17 62 49. *Fax 04 94 81 03 16. Website: http://www.camping-cote-azur.com. Email: info@camping-cote-azur.com. Open 1 April-31 October. 1,100 spaces. 11.50 €-25.50 € per night for 2 people, 1 vehicle, 1 tent or caravan, price according to season. Chalets (sleep 4) 220 €-670 €per week, according to season. Mobile homes (sleep 4) 260 €-670 €. Multi-sports ground. Children's playground. Restaurant. Bar. Grocery.* This campsite among the umbrella pines in 22 ha. of parkland has direct access to the sea and some fine sandy beaches.

Sainte-Maxime

LA BELLE AURORE 5, boulevard Jean Moulin ✆ 04 94 96 02 45. *Fax 04 94 96 63 87. Website: www.belleaurore.com Closed mid-October to mid-March. Member of the Varois Maîtres Restaurateurs association. Restaurant closed Wednesday in low season. 17 rooms from 160 € to 314 € according to* *the season. Continental breakfast 15 €. Set menus 35 €, 52 €, 76 €. A la carte 45 €. Car park. Pool. Solarium. Private beach.* This hotel almost floating on the waves offers rooms with a Provençal feel, and balconies or private terraces overlooking the sea. Chef Jérôme Zuéras is an expert at cooking seafood, served in the circular restaurant or on the terrace: Dublin bay prawn tempura with conserved tomatoes, gambas kebab and supions (calamars) with artichokes, and grilled dory fillet with anchovy cream.

Saint-Maximin

HOTELLERIE DU COUVENT ROYAL * Place Jean-Salusse ✆ 04 94 86 55 66**. *Website: www.hotelfp-saintmaximin.com. Open all year. 67 rooms from 80 € to 140 €. Breakfast buffet 12 €.* A Provençal Gothic setting with rib vaulted ceilings, cloister and medieval garden for this hostelry: you are in an old royal convent adjoining the basilica, built between 1295 and 1315 to house Dominican monks, on the orders of the Prince of Palermo, future Charles II of Anjou. Today, the rooms are - fortunately! - equipped with all modern comforts.

Saint-Raphaël

HOTEL RESTAURANT LES AMANDIERS 874 bd Alphonse Juin ✆ 04 94 19 85 30. *Fax 04 94 19 85 31. Website: www.les-amandiers.com. Email: sarljr@aol.com. Open all year. 11 rooms 35 €-76 € according to season. Furnished studios sleeping 3-5, 165 €-530 € per week according to season. Bar, restaurant. Sert menus. Half-board 23 € per day per head (breakfast, dinner and drink). Heated pool, private car park. Logis de France.* All the rooms are non-smoking, air-conditioned and equipped with bath or shower. The hotel is located between Santa Lucia sailing harbour and the water therapy centre.

L'AMANDINE Espace Oméga 100, boulevard du Cerceron ✆ 04 94 51 33 41. *Fax : 04 94 40 49 03. Lunchtime formula 12 €. Set menus 19.50 €, 25 €, 34 €. Children's menu 8 €. Car park.* Chef Hervé Allibert, who is also a 'Recevez sans cuisiner' caterer, prepares semi-gastronomic, traditional Provençal cuisine from fresh ingredients: pan-cooked scallop kebab with sesame seeds and its peppermint juice, mullet and crab lasagna with dill, foie gras marinated in dandelion nectar and redcurrant jelly with Espelette pepper.

L'ARBOUSIER 6, avenue de Valescure ✆ 04 94 95 25 00. *Fax 04 94 83 81 04. Website: www.arbousier.net. Annual closing during the last 10 days in Decemberand first week in January. Weekly closing Monday and Tuesday. Set menus 27 €, 35 €, 45 € and 58 €. A la carte around 70 €.* Member of the *Varois Maîtres Restaurateurs* association. You need to climb a few stairs to reach this gastronomic haven, which is a warm-coloured dining room in winter and a flower-filled, shady garden in summer, at the foot of the Templars Church. Chef Philippe Troncy, one of Michel Guérard's disciples, prepares seasonal dishes respecting the ingredients' natural flavours - witness his Dublin bay prawn carpaccio with marjoram vinaigrette, veal shin confit with a woodland mushroom raviole, foamy sauce with truffles and red fruit gratin with all flower honey, caramelised with cane and brown sugar.

Saint-Tropez

HOTEL DES LICES Avenue Augustin Grangeon ✆ 04 94 97 28 28. *Fax: 04 94 97 59 52 . Website: www.hoteldeslices.com . Email: contact@hoteldeslices.com. Open 1 April-11 November and 27 December -6 January. 42 rooms from 75 €-355 € per night, according to the season.* Continental breakfast 13 €. Private car park, pool, heated jacuzzi. Bar, WiFi. Located in the town centre in a cosy family setting 300m from the harbour, close to the famous Place des Lices.

HOTEL SUBE * 15, quai Suffren ✆ 04 94 97 30 04. Fax : 04 94 54 89 08.** *28 comfortable and well-equipped rooms from 65 €. Breakfast 10 €.* This hotel is located right on the harbour, so you can watch the Tropezian world go by and really feel in the thick of things.A balcony overloking the *vieux port* is more than a dream; it's absolute heaven.

RESIDENCE DE LA PINEDE Plage de la Bouillabaisse ✆ 04 94 55 91 00 *Fax 04 94 97 73 64. Website : www.residencepinede.com. Set menus from 60 € to 145 €. A la carte 100 €. No weekly closing, closed mid-October to Easter.* A year after Olivier Brulard's departure for the Réserve de Beaulieu, Arnaud Donckele, only just 30, seems very much at ease in his new role. He is familiar with the world of top restaurants, having spent three years at Lasserre, the Plaza Athénée and the Louis XV, and quite used to superb settings and top-of-the-range customers. His cuisine lives up to all expectations, though the prices *à la carte* make it impossible to forget this is Saint Trop. Garden peas and soft-boiled egg with French caviar and pea shell emulsion with almonds, cod heart with a *grenobloise* flavour, creamy garlic and parsley risotto, casseroled back and loin of 'Rex du Poitou' rabbit, garden pea gnocchi, carrots with coriander and rosemary, apple and lemon soufflé, apple emulsion and a Menton lemon tartelet feature on the menu. The cellar boasts a lot of aristocratic recommended wines - champagne, great bordeaux - as you'd expect. Plenty of competent service.

Toulon

LE JARDIN DU SOMMELIER 20, allées Courbet ✆ 04 94 62 03 27. *Fax 04 94 09 01 49. Website: www.le-jardin-du-sommelier.com Open every day, except Saturday lunchtime and Sunday. Set menus 32 €, 39 €, 49 €.* Wine waiter Christian Scalisi created this restaurant in 1992, with the aim of offering simple dishes to go with wine-tasting - the wines in question were to be grands crus at lowish prices. Today, his garden has become a Mecca of Toulon gastronomy, serving shellfish and sweetbread cassolette, vegetables and the stock cappucino; pikeperch with chicory fondue, ginger and orange, and carrot cream; and crêpes stuffed Suzette-style, flambéd with Grand Marnier. You can discover different French wines by ordering wine by the glass, one of our favourite services 3 glasses for 15 € or 5 € a glass. Open every day.

NEW HOTEL AMIRAUTE * 4, rue Adolphe Guiol ✆ 04 94 22 19 67**. *Fax 04 94 09 34 72. Website: www.new-hotel.com. Open all year. 58 rooms from 78 € to 85 €. Breakfast 9 €.* Wi-Fi. This hotel, located near the Place de la Liberté, Boulevard de Strasbourg and the SNCF train station, provides comfortable air-conditioned rooms.

Franche-Comté

Besançon

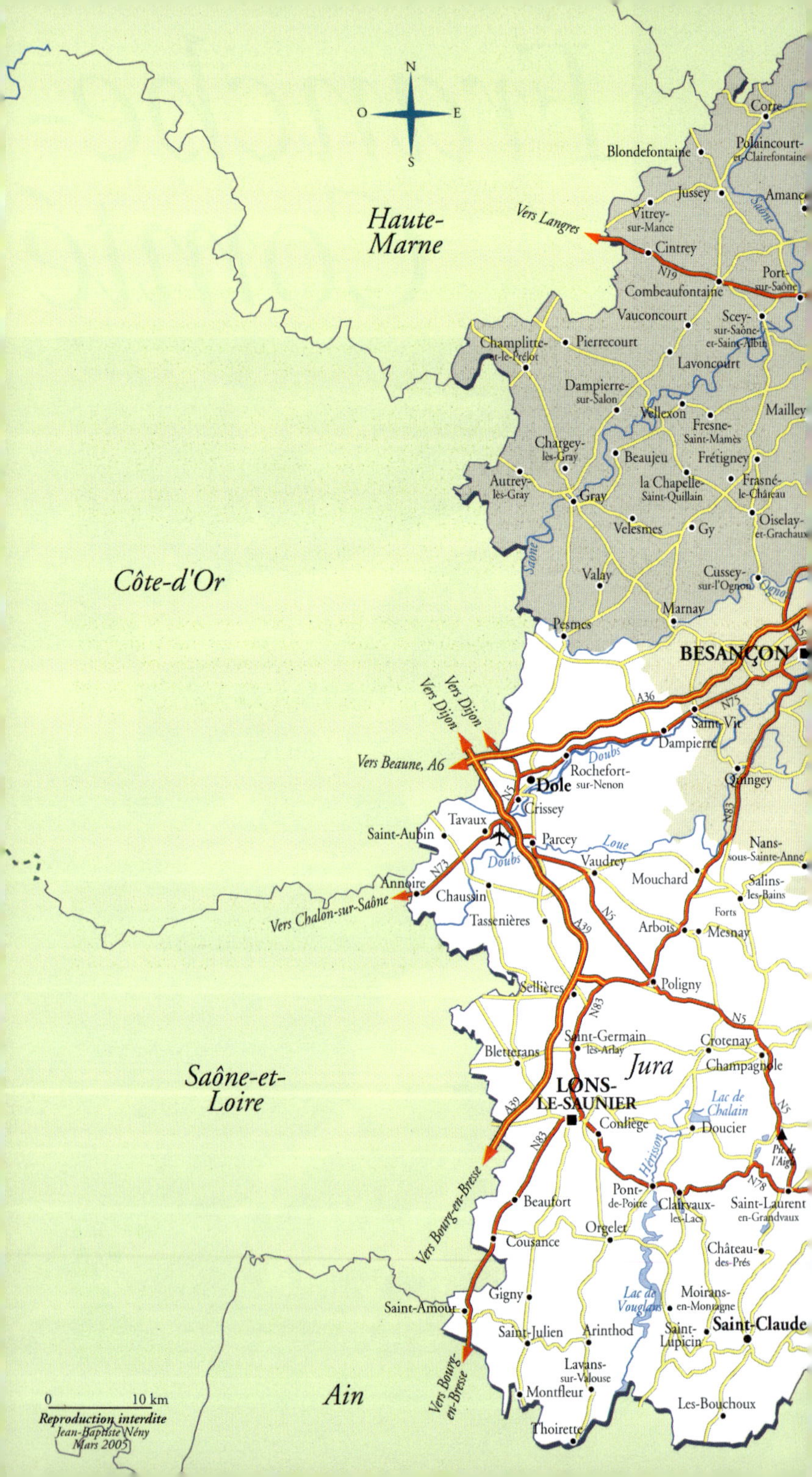
N
O
E
S
Haute-Marne
Côte-d'Or
Saône-et-Loire
Ain
Jura
Corre
Blondefontaine
Polaincourt-et-Clairefontaine
Jussey
Amance
Saône
Vitrey-sur-Mance
Vers Langres
Cintrey
N19
Port-sur-Saône
Combeaufontaine
Vauconcourt
Scey-sur-Saône-et-Saint-Albin
Champlitte-et-le-Prélot
Pierrecourt
Lavoncourt
Dampierre-sur-Salon
Mailley
Vellexon
Fresne-Saint-Mamès
Chargey-lès-Gray
Beaujeu
Frétigney
Autrey-lès-Gray
Gray
la Chapelle-Saint-Quillain
Frasné-le-Château
Velesmes
Gy
Oiselay-et-Grachaux
Saône
Valay
Cussey-sur-l'Ognon
Ognon
Marnay
Pesmes
BESANÇON
A36
N75
Saint-Vit
Vers Dijon
Vers Dijon
Vers Beaune, A6
Dampierre
Doubs
Rochefort-sur-Nenon
Dole
Quingey
N5
Crissey
N83
Tavaux
Saint-Aubin
Parcey
Loue
Nans-sous-Sainte-Anne
Doubs
Vaudrey
N73
Mouchard
Salins-les-Bains
Annoire
Chaussin
Vers Chalon-sur-Saône
Forts
Tassenières
N5
Arbois
Mesnay
A39
Poligny
Sellières
N83
N5
Saint-Germain-lès-Arlay
Crotenay
Bletterans
Champagnole
LONS-LE-SAUNIER
Lac de Chalain
A39
Conliège
Doucier
N5
N83
Hérisson
Pic de l'Aigle
N78
Vers Bourg-en-Bresse
Beaufort
Pont-de-Poitte
Clairvaux-les-Lacs
Saint-Laurent-en-Grandvaux
Orgelet
Cousance
Château-des-Prés
Gigny
Lac de Vouglans
Moirans-en-Montagne
Saint-Amour
Saint-Julien
Arinthod
Saint-Lupicin
Saint-Claude
Lavans-sur-Valouse
Vers Bourg-en-Bresse
0
10 km
Montfleur
Les-Bouchoux
Thoirette
Reproduction interdite
Jean-Baptiste Nény
Mars 2005

FRANCHE-COMTÉ
Vosges
Vers Epinal
Ailleviller-et-Lyaumont
Vauvillers
Corbenay
Saint-Loup-sur-Semouse
Fougerolles
Fontaine-lès-Luxeuil
Faucogney-et-la-Mer
Raddon
Servance
Conflans-sur-Lanterne
Luxeuil-les-Bains
Faverney
Mélisey
Giromagny
Rougemont-le-Château
Vers Mulhouse
Vers Mulhouse
Champagney
Rougegoutte
Saulx
Lure
BELFORT
Fontaine
Haut-Rhin
Canal de la Haute-Saône à Montbéliard
Mollans
Lyoffans
Montreux-Château
Vaivre
VESOUL
Haute-Saône
Danjoutin
Territoire-de-Belfort
Héricourt
Châtenois-les-Forges
Villersexel
Grandvillars
Bethoncourt
Courchaton
Sochaux
Delle
Montbéliard
Beaucourt
Rougemont
Montbozon
Valentigney
Seloncourt
Loulans
l'Isle-sur-le-Doubs
Mandeure
Vers Delémont
Rioz
Clerval
Pont-de-Roide
Doubs
Villars-sur-Dampjoux
Glère
Baume-les-Dames
Saint-Hippolyte
Marchaux
Roulans
Trévillers
Cour-Saint-Maurice
Nancray
Pierrefontaine-les-Varans
Maîche
Charquemont
Vercel-Villedieu-le-Camp
Mamirolle
Le Russey
Tarcenay
Valdahon
Orchamps-Vennes
Epeugney
Ornans
Vers la Chaux-de-Fonds
Morteau
Amancey
Mouthier-Haute-Pierre
Villers-le-Lac
Doubs
Déservillers
Levier
Doubs
Vers Neuchâtel
Boujailles
Pontarlier
Grand Taureau 1 323 m
Frasne
Lac de Saint-Point
Bonnevaux
Malbuisson
SUISSE
Nozeroy
Métabief
Jougne
Mont d'Or 1 460 m
Vers Lausanne
Mouthe
Les-Planches-en-Montagne
Chapelle-des-Bois
Morez
Bois-d'Amont
Les-Rousses
Vers Nyon
Vers Genève
0
30 km
Motorway
Major road
Minor road

LAKES AND FORESTS

The Franche-Comte is all blue and green. Forestry covers 700,000ha. of this middle-mountain region, which is half its territory. A network of rivers and torrents flows across plains and plateaux, and in between the valleys: the Doubs, Saone, Ognon, Ain, Loue and Dessoubre are the principle waterways and their tributaries. The region also contains 80 lakes and 1,000 big ponds; the Lake Country in the centre of the Jura has been likened to a little Scotland. Paleontologists have discovered Neolithic cities here, showing that the nomadic tribes were beginning to settle close to water, and develop fishing and agriculture. Two houses on piles have been reconstructed on the edge of Lake Chalain.

Route des étangs

There are 14 places to stop off at as you go through this 'Country of a Thousand Ponds' in the heart of the Saone Vosges, with its stone, sandstone and granite buildings.

MAISON DU TOURISME DE VESOUL 6, rue des Bains ✆ 03 84 97 10 70. Route des lacs

The Lakes Route covers 150km between the Jura lakes Chalain and Vouglans, including Lakes d'Antre, Bonlieu, Chambly, Clairvaux and Ilay, along with belvederes, to admire the bridges and waterfalls from a height.

PAYS DES LACS TOURIST OFFICE Clairvaux-les-Lacs ✆ 03 84 25 27 47

Route des sapins

This route links Levier (Doubs) with Champagnole (Jura) through 10,000ha. of forest. You go through the Levier, Joux and Chapois conifer plantations, where the trees can be huge. Some are over 45m high and 1.2-1.3m in diameter.

CHAMPAGNOLE TOURIST OFFICE ✆ 03 84 52 43 67

ONF ✆ 03 81 46 29 00

BESANÇON AND THE DOUBS

Besançon

The Doubs prefecture and regional capital is also a watchmaking town (close to Switzerland); a pleasant place with many green spaces and a citadel built by Vauban, overlooking the river. There is plenty to see here: Saint Jean Cathedral and its astronomical clock, the Fine Arts and Archeology Museum and the banks of the Doubs (stroll along the Grande Rue and lively Rue Bersot). On the opposite bank near the citadel is the picturesque old Battant quarter, with its many cafes and restaurants.

SAINT JEAN CATHEDRAL 10ter, rue de la Convention. The two apses are Carolingian, and there is no main fa¡ade. You enter the church on the north side via an 18thc. side portal. Inside, the nave with its great arcades is 12thc. Romanesque and the rib vaults (also 12thc.) are Gothic.

HORLOGE ASTRONOMIQUE Saint Jean Cathedral ✆ 03 81 81 12 76. *Guided tours every hour: 9.50am-11.50am and 2.50pm-5.50pm. Closed Tuesday (and Wednesday, October-April) and in January.* This astronomical clock is 6m high, 2.5m wide and has 60 dials. 21 automatons chime the hour, and the dials show the tides, phases of the moon days of the week etc. The guided tour lasts 20 mins and is well worth it.

CITADEL ✆ 03 81 87 83 33. *Open every day except Christmas and New Year's Day.*Admission: adult 7.50 € to 8 €.Vauban's design took 48 years to build, before today's version was reached at. It houses several museums: the Comtois Museum with its popular arts and crafts; the Resistance and Deportation Museum; a little children's farm; an Aquarium with different fish species and an open-air tank; a Noctarium (local nocturnal animals); an Insectarium with its many legs and a Climatorium, explaining the changes in our climate and its effects. There is also a beautiful wildlife park, set out to recreate the natural habitat. A small train takes you to and from the town, with a free bus service in season.

FORTIFICATIONS. Apart from the famous Citadel, there are a number of forts (Griffon, Bregille, Chaudanne) and ruined ramparts, mostly dating from Vauban's time.

PALAIS GRANVELLE 96, Grande Rue. A French Renaissance-style palace. The elegant three-storey front has Tuscan, Ionic and Corinthian columns, and the steep roof is decorated with three Gothic-shaped skylights.

MUSEE DU TEMPS Grande Rue - Palais Granvelle ✆ 03 81 87 81 61. *Admission adult 3,50 €, valid 2 days. Concessions 1.5 €. Admission free on Sundays, with guided tour at 3pm.* 3 floors of exhibitions are set out as a series of 'moments to experience' with a sensory approach: games, models, videos, soundtracks and a contemporary bronze wall frieze; you can travel through the history of clockmaking from the 16thc. to the present day. This unique museum will eventually be adding to its displays, with 4,300 m^2 of exhibition space in all.

MUSEE DES BEAUX-ARTS ET D'ARCHEOLOGIE Place du Marche © 03 81 82 39 89. *Open every day except Tuesday. Wheelchair access.* One of the oldest and most impressive French museums, containing Roman mosaics, Egyptian sarcophagi and 14th-20thc. paintings. Courbet, a Titian, Rubens, Matisse, Géricault, Cranach and Bellini have left a trace here.

MUSEE DES MAISONS COMTOISES © 03 81 55 29 77. *www.maisons-comtoises.org. Open every day mid March-mid November. Admission: adult 7.50 €, 6-16s 4 €, under-6s free.* Discover the Franche-Comte, 15km from Besancon. The museum contains 30 examples of typical Comtoise rural architecture, pulled down and rebuilt on the site using old-fashioned techniques. There are hands-on activities: breadmaking, animal-tending, cancouillotte-tasting, a trip in a carriage.

HOPITAL SAINT-JACQUES 2-4, place Saint Jacques. The Parisian architect Royer designed this classical building just after the French Conquest (1674). It contains a beautiful 17th-18thc. pharmacy. On the right, you can see the Chapelle du Réfuge dome with its glazed tiles from far away; this was local architect Nicolas Nicole's first work (18thc.).

Elsewhere in the Doubs

Baumes-les-Dames

Leaving Besan¡on, on the old Alsace road, you come to Baume-les-Dames, a small town full of character, set among seven green hills at the Doubs-Cusancin confluence and known for its religious orders. The ladies in its name are the nuns of the abbey founded by Saint Germain, Bishop of Besan¡on, between the 5th and 8thc., which kept its influence in the region for many years.

ABBEY CHURCH. Rebuilt from 1738-1760 by Nicolas Nicole on the site of an earlier church (11th or 12thc.), this is a beautiful though unfinished building (the front, intended to be temporary, became permanent). It was pillaged and deconsecrated during the Revolution, and now hosts concerts and exhibitions.

SAINT MARTIN CHURCH. This 17thc. Gothic church contains paintings, reredos and sculptures including a 16thc. pieta and and polychrome wooden statues (Sainte Barbe, 16thc.). The great organs (Callinet 1839) are among France's finest.

Houses in Besançon

Montbéliard

Montbéliard country is France's main industrial region, having inherited its character from the old Protestant comté. It also has some marvellous scenery, up on the Jura plateaux crossed by the Doubs and Allan rivers.

MUSEE DU CHATEAU DES DUCS DE WURTEMBERG Cour du Château ✆ 03 81 99 22 61. *Open every day except Tuesday: 10am-12 noon and 2pm-6pm. Admission: adult 1.50 (winter) €, concessions 0.75 €, under-18s free.* Building began on the castle in the 15thc., and took 300 years! Its various architectural styles are German-influenced, for the town was part of the Principality of Wurtemberg from 1397-1789. Today, it houses the Conservatoire and a museum covering Wurtemberg history, and paleontology (Cuvier, who invented this science, was a native of the region).

Ornans

Gustave Courbet's birthplace has of course devoted a museum to him, but it is also worth stopping here for the beautiful old houses on the riverbanks, and fishing tradition.

MUSEE GUSTAVE COURBET Place Robert Fernier ✆ 03 81 62 23 30. *Open July & August: 10am-12.30pm and 1.30pm-6pm. Other periods: 10am-12 noon and 2pm-6pm, except public holidays. 1 November-31 March: closed Tuesday. Admission: adult 6 €.* Housed in a fine 18thc. mansion near the bridge in the centre of Ornans, with a hanging garden along the river, this museum contains Courbet's paintings, drawings and sculptures, and a number of works by his friends and contemporaries, other Comtois landscape painters, and photographers.

Pontarlier

The Haut Doubs' capital has been an important trading centre since the Middle Ages, due to its links with Switzerland. Despite losing many of its old buildings in several fires, it is still a pretty town, with a striking castle (Joux) - and is also known for Comte cheese. Absinthe was developed here by Henri-Louis Pernod, from 1805, using an 18thc. Swiss recipe, and such artists as Baudelaire, Rimbaud, Verlaine and Van Gogh believed it to be a creative stimulus. The aniseed drink was however outlawed by the Government in 1915, to protect the soldiers at the front from health risks and decadence.

CHATEAU DE JOUX La Cluse-et-Mijoux ✆ 03 81 69 47 95. *www.chateaudejoux.com. Open all year. July & August: 9am-6pm. Admission: adult 5.50 €, child 2.80 €.* Perched on its rock on the way out of Pontarlier towards Switzerland, this castle is not to be missed. Many legends have been woven around its walls since they were first built against the limestone ridges 1,000 years ago. The site illustrates developments in military architecture from the Middle Ages to Vauban and even Joffre. Plays and shows are held in the castle in summer, and Lelouch's Misérables was filmed there.

HAUTE-SAÔNE

Parc Natural Regional du Ballon des Vosges

The Ballons des Vosges Regional Nature Reserve contains 203 villages in 3,000 km^2, covering 4 departments (Haut-Rhin, Haute-Saône, Vosges and Territoire de Belfort) and three regions (Franche-Comte, Alsace, Lorraine). It offers a variety of natural landscapes, with different features and climates: between the forests (67% of the surface) lie high pastures, cliffs and rocks, peat bogs, beech, conifer and oak plantations, limestone hills, lakes, ponds and rivers.
www.parc-ballons-vosges.fr

Champlitte

MUSEE D'ARTS ET TRADITIONS POPULAIRES ALBERT DEMARD Chateau de Champlitte ✆ 03 84 67 82 00. *Open 1 October-31 March: 2pm-5pm. 1 April-30 September: 9.30am-12 noon and 2pm-6pm. Closed Saturday and Sunday morning, and Tuesday. Ticket includes 1900 museum. Admission: adult 6 €, under-16s free.* In the castle's beautiful setting, this museum illustrates technical progress in the late 19th and early 20thc. A whole village with its bakery, dairy, farm, chemists', school, doctor's surgery, hospice, cafe and social and cultural activities, is displayed in 40 rooms.

MUSEE 1900 DES ARTS ET TECHNIQUES Rue des Lavières ✆ 03 84 67 62 90. *Ticket includes Popular Arts & Traditions Museum. Admission: adult 6 €, under-16s free. Open all year (until 6pm in season, 5pm out of season). Closed Tuesday mornings & Sunday (except summer)* A reconstructed village with two streets, craft workshops (cobbler, baker, cartwright, smith) and the 'new' 20thc. trades (steam engine, garage with its vintage cars).

Gray

One of the region's three strongholds. The town has plenty of tourist attractions: the banks of the Saône, a beach, a picturesque old town with Gothic housefronts and some friendly cafe terraces in the lower quarter.

NOTRE DAME BASILICA Place de la Sous-Préfecture ✆ 03 84 65 69 10. Building started on this beautiful Flamboyant Gothic building in 1481, but stopped five years later, and was not finished until the 19thc. A superb Neo-Gothic porch was added at this point, noticeably different from the original style. You need to take time to appreciate the architectural detail inside the basilica.

CHATEAU DU MUSEE DU BARON MARTIN Rue Pigalle ✆ 03 84 65 69 10. *Open every day except Tuesday. 1 November-30 April: 2pm-5pm. Summer: 10am-12 noon and 2pm-6pm. Admission: 3.50 €.* Housed in the Comte de Provence's 18thc. mansion on the site of the old fortress, this museum contains 17thc. Dutch and Flemish paintings, some 19thc. pictures and sculpture and Pierre Paul Prud'hon's unique drawings. Temporary exhibitions all year.

Jonvelle

This charming village is at the far end of the Haute-Saône department in the Jussey canton. In 1968, the local priest discovered the baths belonging to a Gallo-Roman villa on the edge of the village. A dig was organised, and three mosaic-decorated baths were excavated: cold, tepid and hot. In the Middle Ages, Jonvelle was part of a barony closely linked with Burgundy, and sharing the same turbulent history, though well-protected by the River Saône and a solid defensive wall. The listed church has a 12thc. Romanesque nave, 13thc. Gothic chancel and a second 17th-18thc. nave in Flamboyant style.

Discover Malans, Acey and Marnay in the surrounding Ognon Valley, and visit Gy castle at Gray. Montmirey la Ville, Dole and the Serre Forest are also well worth a visit.

Luxeuil-les-Bains

Luxeuil in the north of the Haute-Saône has been a spa town for two thousand years. At that time, the Gallic gods Lussoius and Brixta regulated the twelve hot springs; the Romans later confirmed their reputation for purifying, and granting long life and fertility. A number of Gallo-Roman wooden figures found near the springs seem to be ex-votos left there by grateful sufferers. Dwellings, workshops and funeral steles have been excavated, showing that this was an important 'resort' in the 5thc., when the Barbarians (Burgonds and Francs) invaded. In 1768, a thermal establishment was built on the Gallo-Roman site, in a 5ha. park.

Montbéliardes

MAISON DU TOURISME ET DU THERMALISME 1, rue des Thermes ✆ 03 84 40 06 41

SAINT COLOMBAN ABBEY ✆ 03 84 40 13 38. *Guided tours by appointment all year for groups (book in advance).* This was first a Colombanian then a Benedictine abbey, founded in the 6thc. and rebuilt in the 15th, 17th and 18thc. Saint Colomban Chapel was put up between 1812 and 1854, with stained-glass windows depicting regional saints (Desle, Eustaise). There is an oak high altar in the chancel and a 19thc. monumental tableau to the monastery's founder Saint Colomban. The cloister, like the rest of the abbey, was rebuilt in the 15thc. During the Revolution, it was used as a covered market. You can see Saint Colomban House, and the saint's statue in the silent courtyard.

SAINT PIERRE BASILICA ✆ 03 84 40 06 41. *Visits on request.* Built on the site of the first Saint Colomban Chapel (the abbey church), this 13thc. Gothic basilica has a Romanesque look about it. It was carefully restored by Viollet-le-Duc, and contains a fine 17thc. organ case, Renaissance stalls and a pulpit from Notre Dame de Paris.

CONSERVATOIRE DE LA DENTELLE DE LUXEUIL-LES-BAINS Le Thiavaux - Salle des Moines (under the cloister) ✆ 03 84 93 61 11. *Open Tuesdays & Fridays: 2pm-5.30pm.* Watch lace being made. Courses in lace making techniques (luxovian stitch) are held for beginners and the more experienced, twice a week.

TOUR DES ECHEVINS. This 15thc. Town Hall and watchtower now houses the museum. Climb the spiral staircase to the tower for a view of the town.

MUSEE DE LA TOUR DES ECHEVINS 36, rue Victor Genoux ✆ 03 84 40 00 07. Open April-October, *Wednesday-Sunday: 2pm-6pm. Admission*: adult *2,10* Paintings by local artist Jules Adler, 19th and 20thc. works, and a Gallo-Roman archeological collection, partly representing the water cult and including seven of the sculptures excavated in 1865.

MAISON DU BAILLI. The 15thc. Hôtel Thiadot is a fine Flamboyant Gothic building; admire the windows, crenellated tower and balcony. It houses the town library and Maurice Beaumont Museum.

Pesmes

This picturesque village is perched above the Ognon Valley in the south of the Haute-Saone. It was pillaged, burned down and attacked by plague but managed to overcome these trials. You can still see the ruins of its troubled past in the narrow flower-filled streets: fortified gate, 16thc. mansions and imposing castle (1519). The 12thc. church has a glazed-tile roof and the chancel contains a magnificent wooden triptych by local painter Jacques Prévost, one of Raphael's pupils. Walk along the castle ramparts with their superb panoramic view of the valley and Jura beyond. They are lit up by a son et lumiÃre on summer evenings.

CHATEAU ✆ 03 84 31 21 92. *Private residence. Access to the outside and 14th & 15thc. guardroom. Visits in July* only, *August & September.* The oldest parts of the castle date from the 10thc.; the Sires de Pesmes, descendants of the Counts of Burgundy, go back to the 11thc. Since then, several buildings have been put up on the site.

MAISON ROYALE ✆ 03 84 31 23 23. *Easter-15 June and 1-30 September, weekends and public holidays: 3pm-6pm. 16 June-31 August: every day except Tuesday: 3pm-6pm. Groups by request. Admission: 4 €.* This former fortified house with its original architecture was restored 10 years ago. It belonged to a travelling salesman, and contains curiosities from all over the world.

Ronchamp

NOTRE DAME DU HAUT 13, rue de la Chapelle ✆ 03 84 20 65 13. *Open April-September: 9.30am-6.30pm. October & March: 10am-5pm. November-February: 10am-4pm. Admission: 2 €.* This chapel on Bourlemont Hill owes its contemporary shape to Le Corbusier. It blends perfectly into the scenery, its concrete curves catching the light in a peaceful atmosphere of spirituality and prayer.

MUSEE DE LA MINE 33, place de la Mairie ✆ 03 84 20 70 50. *Open all year, except Tuesday. July & August: 10am-12 noon and 2pm-7pm (other periods: 2pm-6pm). Admission: adult 3.05 €, child 1.52 €.* The region was strongly marked by this industry not so long ago. The museum illustrates mining techniques and the miners' daily life with documents, tools and instruments, and contains a fine collection of lamps.

Route through the villages fleuris

This brightly-coloured route through the Haute-Saône and Territoire de Belfort takes you to traditional flower-decked hamlets like Rougegoutte and Anjoutey. You will make other discoveries along the way: the Negritude Museum in Champagney, Etueffont Forge Museum and Champagnole Church with its 25-bell peal.

Vesoul

Made famous by a Jacques Brel song! Vesoul is in fact worth seeing for its chapel overlooking the town, and museum.

SAINT GEORGES CHURCH Place de l'Eglise. *Open Monday-Saturday afternoons in July & August, and some mornings.* Information about guided tours from the Tourist Office & 03 84 97 10 88.

PALAIS DE JUSTICE Place du Palais. The former law courts were built in 1771. The Barberousse house (No. 3 on the square) has a basket-handle arch and a sundial. On the corner of Rue Gevrey, the 18thc. Petremant house bears its builder's initials on the balcony rail, above the Cafe Français.

LA MOTTE. This small hill overlooks Vesoul; from the top, you have an interesting view over the Langres Plateau, Jura and Vosges. Francis Panaget's bronze viewpoint indicator (1979) and the pretty Virgin Mary Chapel built in 1857 are worth the climb!

GROTTE DE SOLBORDE. 3km south on the Besançon road, reached by a path via the Rocher des Douze Apôtres (12 Apostles' Rock). The River Emeline flows through this cave, thought to have miraculous properties since a statue of the Virgin was discovered there in 1663.

Villersexel

CHATEAU-MUSEE DE VILLERSEXEL ✆ 03 84 20 51 53. *Now a hotel.www.villersexel.com. Open Wednesday-Sunday: 2pm-5pm. Guided tours at 2.30pm, 3.30pm & 4.30pm.* This 19thc. Neo-Gothic castle is one of the region's finest buildings. The frontal pavilion has two alternating stone columns, a style reflected in the farm that dates back to an earlier 18thc. castle, almost totally destroyed in the 1870 war.

LOCAL JOBS AND CRAFTS

Timber and woodcrafts

The Franche-Comte is covered in 700, 000 ha. of forest (42% of the surface area), so it is only natural that the industrial production of wood should have developed over the years. The region produces 2 million cubic metres of wood per year, 5% of the national product, and the timber industry employs 6,400 people despite inadequacies in the paper goods field and the sawing-up of trees (70% of the wooded surface area and 35% of the total volume of commercialised timber). It provides the raw material for woodcutters, village sawmills and traditional wood-transforming crafts (the Haut Jura wood turners and marquetry craftsmen, pipes, wooden toys etc.). In the furniture sector, a few restructured companies (Sanijura, Parisot Meubles) also contribute to the daily life of local country villages and small towns.

Toys

Jura toys, which account for a quarter of national production, grew out of wood and water. The rivers turned the vanes, providing energy for the wood turners' workshops, where the first tops, whistles, skittles, and yo-yos - those simple but eternal shapes found every year under the Christmas tree - were made. The 1950s saw the arrival of synthetic materials, and the toy industry adapted marvellously well to one in particular: plastic - flexible, brightly-coloured, less expensive and usable for any new idea. Today 95% of toys made in those Jura factories located between Saint Claude, Moirans and Oyonnax (in the Ain department) are the result of that radical mid-20thc. modernisation, even if wooden toys still enchant us all.

LE MUSEE DU JOUET 5, rue du Murgin - MOIRANS ✆ 03 84 42 38 64. *Open 10am-12.30pm and 2pm-6pm (except Saturday morning, Sunday morning, public holiday mornings and Mondays from 15 September-15 April). Admission; adult 5 €.* Located in the heart of the Haut Jura nature reserve and French toy capital, this Toy Museum is purpose-built, and contains over 15,000 toys - the oldest dating back to Antiquity. The permanent exhibition is interactive, and you can't help but feel quite emotional, whether your taste runs to wooden horses or miniature cars. In 2003, the museum acquired an exceptional collection of 3,500 toys, including antiques, dolls and mechanical and optical toys. All kinds of game and toy can be found in this collection, which covers 4,000 years of human history. A fascinating journey through time, different cultures, and childhood.

Horlogerie

In the Haut-Doubs between Morteau, Charouemont and Damprichard, clock-making has been the principle craft since the 17thc. The famous Comtoise grandfather-style clocks with their iron or copper pendulum visible through a small window in the front of the case were first made of fruit tree wood, then later, in the 19thc., of coniferous wood. Wood and enamel craftsmen - who created the faces - combined their talents with the clock-maker's know-how, and the reputation of Franche Comte clocks was made. The first watches were the work of the Dumont brothers in Besancon, and in 1767, Frederic Japy set up a prototype watch factory at Monbeliard. Following the Swiss-French road linking the twin towns of Besancon and Neuchatel - N57 towards Pontarlier, across the border, then back via Le Locle, Villiers-Le Lac, Morteau and Les Fins - you'll notice plenty of signs of this clock-making history, with its intricate know-how and elegant casing. This is a fascinating world, still full of energy even today, as advanced technology and fashion go hand-in-hand towards harnessing time.

Saint-Claude, pipes and Diamonds

Early pilgrimages to the miraculous Saint Claude Cave led to local manufacturing of holy objects made first of wood, then decorated with marquetry. A new speciality was born: lapidairerie, or stone-cutting (all stones except diamonds). In the 1830s, many new industries grew up, such as paper goods, nail factories and wireworks, using the region's plentiful hydraulic energy. Diamond-cutters appeared after 1840, and pipe-makers in 1850, who gave the town its national claim to fame. Different museums describe this craft process, and also how diamonds are cut. A Master Pipe-makers' Brotherhood was created in 1967: it 'enthrones' famous personalities every year.

MUSEE DE LA PIPE ET DU DIAMANT 1, place Jacques Faizant ✆ 03 84 45 17 00. *Open 20 December- 30 April and October, every day: 2pm-6pm, except Sunday and public holidays. May-September, open every day: 9.30am-12 noon and 2pm-6.30pm. Admission: adult 4.80 €.* Some of the finest pieces made by Saint Claude's traditional craftsmen are on display in this Pipe and Diamond Museum. All sorts of pipe - long and short, intricately worked and rustic - illustrate that diversity and quality so highly valued by pipe-lovers. The museum also features diamonds and other precious stones, a local industry that is rather less well-known but just as interesting.

Franche-Comte's techniques and culture route

From Belfort in the north to Moirans-en-Montagne in the south, you travel from one museum or exhibition to the next, following a route which illustrates the region's technical and craft traditions in 11 stages. The journey takes you to Rochere crystal and glassmaking factory, Ronchamp Mining Museum (Haute-Seine), Ettuefont Forge Museum in Besancon, Morez Spectacle Museum, and Moirans-en-Montagne Toy Museum, not forgetting the Salins-les-Bains Saltworks.

JURA

Green forests and pastures, blue rivers, lakes and waterfalls, yellow wine and white snow: the Jura is a colourful holiday spot for nature-lovers.

Arbois

Capital of Jura winemaking for centuries, Arbois hides the region's most impressive cellars under its paved streets. A square, ochre-coloured steeple rises above hilly vine and orchard-covered slopes, and large, solid winegrowers' houses with coloured fronts and gardens line the passages and alleyways. The local stone's golden tints can be admired in the sober 12th-13thc. Saint Just Church, fine Pécauld Castle and medieval Pont des Capucins beside the imposing Tour Gloriette.

MUSEE SARRET-DE-GROZON 9, Grande-Rue ✆ 03 84 66 55 55. *Guided tours. Open June-September, weekends: 3pm-6.30pm. Open every day except Tuesday in July: 3pm-6.30pm. In August, the museum is included in a guided tour of the town. Admission free.* The Sarret de Grozon family donated their mansion to the town. It now houses a Far Eastern earthenware and porcelain collection, 17th and 18thc. paintings and works by Courbet and local painter Pointelin.

Arlay

Recent discoveries in a cave show the region was inhabited in the Magdalenian era. Some imposing ruins are all that are left of the Middle Ages, and an 18thc. château (owned by the de Laguiche family) has replaced the ancient castle. Part of the estate is open to the public, as is the magnificent park. Arlay is also an important winegrowing area.

CHATEAU D'ARLAY M. et Mme. R. de Laguiche ✆ 03 84 85 04 22. *15 June-15 September, every day: 2pm-6pm. Admission: adult 6.10 €, under-12s 4.60 €. Bird of prey display at 4pm & 5pm.* The Chateau d'Arlay was the Princes of Orange and Comtes de Chalon-Arlay's medieval fortress. The present building was put up by the Comtesse de Lauraguais in 1774, on the site of a Minimes monastery (the vaulted cellar is still visible). Birds of prey fly low over the romantic 18thc. park; their wings almost brush against you. The kids will love it!

Cascades du Hérisson

This series of beautiful waterfalls spreads over a 4km walk, climbing from 515 to 780m above sea-level. The River Hérisson falls (from the Greek heri, sacred and Celtic onn, water) come from two streams rising in the Bonlieu and d'llay lakes. At the foot of the Grand Saut, Lacuzon Cave takes its name from the famous captain who fought for the Franche-Comte's independence. The place is bewitching, but can be slippery and dangerous underfoot.

Dole

Louis Pasteur's birthplace is a historic town, also known for its artistic heritage.

NOTRE DAME COLLEGIATE CHURCH. *Admission free every day: 7am-7pm. You can climb up the tower (260 steps).* This 16thc. church is a symbol of Hapsbourg Catholic resistance. The porch-tower is 75m high, and Karl-Joseph Riepp's carved wooden organ with its 3,500 pipes (18thc.) is one of the few still intact.

MAISON NATALE DE PASTEUR ET MUSEE ✆ 03 84 72 20 61. *Open April-October, except Sunday morning and public holiday mornings: 10am-12 noon and 2pm-6pm. July & August: 10am-6pm. Admission: adult 4.50 €, concessions 2 €. Under-12s free.* Follow the development of Pasteur's work, from his crystallographic research to his defeat of rabies. You can see the machines he used for his bacterial experiments, and the continuity of his ideas in the research carried out by 22 Pasteur Institutes on 5 continents.

MUSEE DES BEAUX-ARTS - 85, rue des Arènes ✆ 03 84 79 25 85. *Open 10am-12 noon and 2pm-6pm. Closed Monday and 24 December-2 January. Admission free. Book your guided tour at the Tourist Office.* The Fonds Regional d'Art Contemporain (Regional Contemporary Art Collection), is housed in Dole Fine Arts Museum. 400 works are on display on the third floor. The figurative style is predominant, with Pop Art and the New Realists well represented. Apart from the FRAC, the museum covers ancient Egypt and archeological discoveries made in the Jura, from the Neolithic to Merovingian ages, and owns a picture by Dole artist Attiret, painted in China where he did many portraits of Imperial dignitaries. Four exhibitions a year are held on the ground floor.

Saint-Point's lake and Port Titi

Lons-le-Saunier

A picturesque and historic town in the heart of Jura's winegrowing region, known for its thermal baths.

MUSEE DES BEAUX-ARTS Place Philibert-de-Chalon ✆ 03 84 47 64 30. *Open Monday-Friday (except Tuesday): 10am-12 noon and 2pm-6pm. Saturday, Sunday and public holidays: 2pm-5pm. Admission: adult 2 €.* Discover paintings from the 17th, 18th and 19thc. French (4 Courbets) Italian (Della Vecchia) and Flemish (Breughel the Younger) Schools, and 19thc, sculpture (stone composition by Perraud).

MUSEE D'ARCHEOLOGIE 25, rue Richebourg ✆ 03 84 47 12 13. *Open Monday-Friday 10am-12 noon and 2pm-6pm. Saturday, Sunday & public holidays: 2pm-5pm. Closed Tuesday. Admission: adult 2, students & groups 1 €, under-18s free. Wednesdays & first Sunday of the month free.* France's oldest dinosaur, Plateosaurus (210 million years B.C.) and the Chalain dugout are on display here, with thematic exhibitions from the museum's collections, often changed.

MUSEE ROUGET DE LISLE 24, rue du Commerce ✆ 03 84 47 29 16. *Open from 3rd weekend in June to the Journées du Patrimoine (Heritage Days) in September. Admission free.* The room where the Marseillaise's composer was born is on the first floor above a little courtyard, in an arcaded street. It has been reconstructed from documents, with period furniture and personal effects (sabre, bust, paintings). The influence of his major work is explained in a series of panels.

THEATRE. An early 20thc. masterpiece, all painting, gilding, red velvet and stucco.

SAINT DESIRE CHURCH. This splendid Romanesque church was built in 1083. The outside, restored in the 19thc., is disappointing; but nave, transept and crypt are pure 11thc. Pre-Romanesque.

PUITS SALE. Lons stopped producing salt in 1966, but the salt water is used for thermal treatment, and underground pipes link the Salt Well to the baths, near the Archeological Museum.

Molain

MOIDON CAVES Route d'Arbois ✆ 03 84 51 74 94. Open April-late September. Admission: adult 6 €. Discover the Jura's finest stalactites only a stone's throw from Arbois. There are too many to count, and they are all impressive. A spectacular son et lumiere highlights the pools. An exceptional site.

Poligny

This is a characteristic village with its bells, towers and ancient rooftops. You can follow the ramparts on foot, round the Sergenterie. Known for Comté cheese, Poligny has a number of maturation cellars, a National Dairy Industry School and a Comté Museum (see Food & Drink). Its wine is well up to the standard of its cheeses.

SAINT HIPPOLYTE COLLEGIATE CHURCH. *Open to the public until 7pm.* This Gothic church still holds services, and contains 15thc. Burgundian School statues, and an organ restored by Dominique Lalmand. Admission free until 7pm. Summer visits Tuesday & Thursday: 10am-12 noon and 2.30pm-5.30pm.

URSULINE CONVENT. The former monastery courtyard displays 19 arches. It is near the Tourist Office.

HOTEL-DIEU Hôpital ✆ 03 84 37 24 21. *Monday-Friday: 9.30am-4.30pm.* You can admire the former pharmacy with its fine earthenware pots on the premises of the local hospital (still in action).

Salins-les-Bains

The department's only cluse is 50km from Lons-le-Saunier in the Furieuse Valley. Salt was extracted by the Romans, then by 15thc. monks, and is still one of Salins' sources of wealth. Visitors come to take the waters in the thermal centre built on the little saltworks. These waters are rich in potassium, calcium, magnesium and trace elements, and contain 330g of salt per litre. Rheumatism, growth and gynaecological problems are treated from March to November, and every summer, a specialised children's centre looks after enuresis sufferers and children with eating and behavioural disorders. You can get into shape and pamper yourself in the Relaxation Area.

THERMES DE SALINS LES BAINS Place des Alliés ✆ 03 84 73 04 63. *www.thermes-salins.com. Open all year, except January.*

HAUT-JURA

Parc Natural Regional du Haut-Jura

Spreading its 145, 580 ha. over the Doubs, Jura and Ain departments, this regional nature reserve took shape in 1968 after the regrouping of 100 villages. The different natural habitats - mountain forests, high meadows, woods, peat bogs, lakes and deep valleys - give rise to varied flora and fauna. Traditional farming and forestry methods ensure the protection of this environmental beauty.

MAISON DU HAUT-JURA Lajoux ✆ **03 84 34 12 30**

Morez

Morez stretches out at the bottom of a cluse (transversal valley) crossed by the Bienne. Claude Girod had a hydraulic mill built to harness the river as an energy source, thus promoting the development of small industries like pit sawyers, edge-tool makers and nail factories. In the 18thc., watch-making appeared, and later, the manufacture of spectacles (which began with an 18thc. craftsman putting together a wire frame for nailmaking). Today, Morez is the capital of this industry, and has a reputed research and study centre.

BELVEDERES. Four of these surround the town, giving exceptional views of the cluse.

MAISON DE L'EMAIL 171, rue de la République ✆ **03 84 33 31 29**. *Open Tuesday, Thursday, Friday and Saturday: 3.30pm-6.30pm. Admission free.* Enamel was Morez's main industry for over a century, from the 18thc. manufacture of grandfather clock faces to signs and advertising. In June 2006, an international meeting will take place here on the subject of enamel.

VISEUM - MUSEE DE LA LUNETTE Place Jean Jaurés ✆ **03 84 33 39 30.** *www.jura.com. Open all year except December, every day except Tuesday: 10am-12 noon and 2pm-6pm. July & August: 10am-1pm and 2pm-6pm. Admission: adult 5.* Housed in a contemporary building opposite the Town Hall. This exhibition illustrates local spectacle-making history, from basic techniques to fashion design, including the role of vision (correction and optical illusion). There is an original collection of optical instruments from different societies throughout history.

Morbier

Between 900 and 1,200m above sea level, Morbier is best-known for its AOC cheese.

FROMAGERIE DE MORBIER Col de la Savine ✆ **03 84 33 59 39**. *Open Monday-Thursday: 8.30am-12 noon and 4.30pm-7pm. Friday & Saturday: 8.30am-12 noon and 3pm-7pm. Sunday: 8.30am-12 noon.* You find this cheese dairy at the Savine Pass, after leaving the N5. Climb the wooden staircase to the first floor, to view the exhibition 'From grass to milk', overlooked by the reproduction of a proud Montbéliard cow.

Premanon

CENTRE POLAIRE PAUL-EMILE VICTOR 1, rue de la Sambine ✆ 03 84 60 77 71. *Open every day (except Tuesday in school holidays): 10am-12 noon and 2pm-6pm. Closed 15 November-15 December. Admission: adult 5.* Polar explorer Paul-Emile Victor has not been forgotten by his native Jura. The Polar Centre illustrates his experience, with a huge polar bear, some penguins and his sledge on display.

Les Rousses

Best-known of the Jura resorts. The development of tourism has not altered the quality of life here, and it is within easy reach of a Northern French clientele.

CAVES A COMTE JURAFLORE Fort des Rousses ✆ 03 84 60 02 24 *www.juraflore.com. 2-15 July, every day except Saturday: 2pm, 4pm & 6pm. 16 July-19 August: every day: 10am, 2pm, 4pm & 6pm. 20 August-2 September, every day: 2pm, 4pm & 6pm. Admission: adult 4.60 €, child 3.20 €.* This fort is no longer in military use, but its fortifications are ideal for maturing cheese. Wear warm clothes! On-site sale of cheese.

MUSEE DU SKI ET DE LA TRADITION ROUSSELANDE Centre d'Accueil Le Grand Tetras - 705, route des Rousses d'Amont ✆ 03 84 60 51 13. *Open in season, Tuesday & Thursday: 5pm-7pm.* Voluntary contributions welcome. Roger Tinguely has an impressive collection of sledges, sleighs, bobsleighs and skis in his basement (the oldest date back to 1850). Village life is illustrated with farming, forestry, stone cutting and even spectacle making. A surprising museum!

Arc-et-Senans Royal Saltworks

This UNESCO-listed monument dates back to the 18thc. when Louis XV's engineers were trying to increase salt production. It was built by the architect Claude-Nicolas Ledoux between 1775 and 1779, but stopped working in 1885, when its profitability fell.

SALINE ROYALE D'ARC ET SENANS ✆ 03 81 54 45 26. *Open all year except Christmas and New Year's Day. November-March: 10am-12 noon and 2pm-5pm. April, May & October: 9am-12 noon and 2pm-6pm. June & September: 9am-6pm. July & August: 9am-7pm. Admission: adult 7 €, 16-25s 4.50 €, 6-15s 2.80 €. Under 6s free. Bookshop, souvenir shop, restaurant.* Claude-Nicolas Ledoux imagined a utopian community - Chaux - where workers and managers would live together. In fact, living and working conditions were not easy in this supposedly ideal town, with its 11 buildings (workshops and lodgings) in a semi-circle round the Director's house, intended as an integrated factory. The Royal Saltworks was to exploit salt, but the project never got past the Revolution, though the factory was in use for over a century until the introduction of new techniques closed it down. The history of salt and the story of the ideal town are both illustrated in this unusual and fascinating place.

MUSEE CLAUDE-NICOLAS LEDOUX ✆ 03 81 54 45 45. An insight into this architect's uncommon personality and ambition (and the only European museum devoted to the work of one sole architect). Admission is included in your saltworks entry ticket.

TERRITOIRE DE BELFORT

France's smallest department came into being after the heroic Siege of Belfort in 1871. Though Alsace was annexed by Germany, the Belfort Territory remained in France, and became a real department in 1922. It covers 609 km^2 with 134,000 inhabitants, and has some remarkable natural scenery: the Ballons des Vosges Regional Nature Reserve (including the Ballon d'Alsace), Malsaucy Reserve and the Belfort Sundgau in the south on the Swiss border.

Belfort

Mentioned for the first time in 1226, in a non-aggression pact between the Counts of Montbéliard and Ferrette. Belfort is a small town but was fortified by Vauban in 1675, and became a border fortress guarding the passage between Vosges and Jura. This job was well done until the 19thc.; three German sieges were successfully resisted. The last saw the creation of the territory, and made Denfert-Rochereau famous. Belfort remained in France, and welcomed refugees from Alsace, among them the founders of the mechanical construction company that became Alstom, specialised in railway technology such as high-speed trains (TGV).

CHATEAU DE BELFORT ✆ **03 84 54 25 51.** From June to September, a guided tour will show you the different fortification systems used from the Middle Ages to the 19thc. including Vauban's. The underground passages, powder magazines and fusiliers' gallery are quite spectacular.

SAINT CHRISTOPHE CATHEDRAL Place d'Armes ✆ **03 84 28 01 59**. This massive structure is built of pink Vosges sandstone, a local speciality.

LION DE BELFORT At the foot of Belfort Castle ✆ **03 84 54 25 51**. Open every day. June-September: 9am-7pm. Belfort's symbol has earned the town its nickname, «Cité du Lion». The lion was designed by Bartholdi (Statue of Liberty) in pink sandstone, 22m long and 11m high, and represents Belfort's resistance in the 1870-71 siege. Together with the inhabitants of Bitche and Moselle, they were the only French to overcome the mighty Prussians, and the lion is in dominant position, holding an enemy arrow in its paw. This colossal statue had already left its mark on the nation's collective memory when it was finished in 1880, as its Parisian counterpart indicates.

MONUMENT DES TROIS SIEGES Place de la Préfecture. A monument to the three officers who refused to surrender Belfort in the 1814, 1815 and 1870-71 sieges. It is known as the monument des trois menteurs (three liars' monument) in Belfort: Legrand (the big) is the smallest of the three, Lecourbe (the bent) is standing up straight - and Denfert-Rochereau? Well, «en fer» means 'made of iron', and the statue certainly isn't.

DONATION MAURICE JARDOT 8, rue Mulhouse ✆ **03 84 90 40 70**. *Open every day except Tuesday. Admission: adult 4 €*. Maurice Jardot was art dealer D.A. Kahnweiler's business partner in pre-war days. His personal collection, donated to the town, includes works by Picasso, Braque, Léger, Laurens and Masson. Others were added on his death in 2002, including some Matisses.

MUSEE D'ART ET D'HISTOIRE Château de Belfort ✆ **03 84 54 25 51**. *1-31 March, every day except Tuesday: 10am-12 noon and 2pm-5pm. Other months, every day except Tuesday: 10am-6pm.* The basement contains prehistoric and Gallo-Roman remains, then a series of showcases follows the region's conflicts from floor to floor, ending with the last World War. A special 19thc. display illustrates the three sieges and Belfort's separation from Alsace.

The Trans-Jurassian Ski-ing Race

This ski-ing race is held on the third Sunday in February between Lamoura and Mouthe in the Doubs (76km for men and 46km for women, starting from the Rousses). Every year, over 90,000 skiers from all over the world come for the race, and around 2,500 enter the competition. Two cross-county ski-ing fans, Georges Berthet (1924 Chamonix Olympics) and Jacky Mandrillon (journalist) dreamed up the race in 1979. Sadly, they didn't see their idea take shape, since the first version of the 'Progressime du Jura' had to be cancelled owing to bad weather, and both men died in 1980. A year later, Marc Dole took over the organisation, continuing to run the competition until 1993, and the newly-named 'Transjurassienne' was born. Every year, thousands of skiers and hundreds of voluntary organisers take part in what has become a successful cross-country race from village to village. The crowds applaud; cowbells ring; the mood is generally festive. There is also a 'Mini-Trans' (7 to 25km) and a 'Transjeune' (Young Trans) for 5 to 10-year-olds (1.5-16km). See it - or even better, try it!

Other sites - around Saint Claude, Saint Laurent-en-Grandvaux, Morez, Nozeroy, Mouthe, Morteau, Gilley, Montbelliard - also offer opportunities for cross-country skiers to race through the forests in the tracks of local Olympic champion Fabrice Guy. This sport clearly owes its regional fame and popularity to the Trans-Jurassian.

TRANS'ORGANISATION Espace Lamartine - MOREZ ✆ **03 84 33 45 13.**

FOOD AND DRINK

A simple but generous cuisine, reminding you that the region is rich in natural resources and local produce.

Charcuterie

Smoked meat is typical of the region, the best-known being Morteau and Montbeliard sausages. Other products are: Doubs smoked ham, Luxeuil-les-Bains ham (marinaded in red wine, rubbed with salt and left for a month before being smoked over a conifer sawdust fire) brisi (dried smoked beef) and Fougerolles gandeuillot (pork giblets kneaded and crushed with kirsch before being smoked in a pocket made of intestine lining).

Morteau sausage is made from top-quality local pork and smoked in a great pyramid-shaped chimney typical of the Haut Doubs, over a coniferous wood and sawdust fire.

Montbeliard sausage is made from the same meat, smoked over a fir, spruce and juniper fire using traditional methods. Garlic and cumin give it a particular flavour.

Cheese

Comté (AOC) and Emmental grand cru (Label rouge) are the best known, but you can also try Morbier (Label regional), creamy Mont d'Or (AOC), Bleu de Gex (AOC), Cancoillotte, Edel de Cléron, a mild, creamy cheese, and Septmoncel, a cow's milk cheese with mould inside, from the Jura.

The Bleu du Haut Jura (Gex): a matured cheese made from unpasteurised milk, either soft and mild with a definite flavour, or stronger with a woodland aftertaste. Visit these dairies in the Haut Jura Regional Nature Reserve (03 84 60 01 59)

Cancoillotte: used to be called 'melted cheese', and goes back to the 16thc. at least. This soft, fermented homemade cheese is eaten hot or cold, on bread or with sausage or rostis.

Comté: dates back to the Middle Ages, when the long, hard Jura winters forced villagers to think ahead and make a long-lasting cheese. They pooled their cows' milk in cooperatives (fruitiÀres) and made this unpasteurised cheese, pressed, cooked and matured (4 to 24 months) to acquire its flavour and 'personality'. This was the first cheese to have an AOC, and is still traditionally made in 200 or so fruitiÀres.

MAISON DU COMTE Ave. de la Résistance ✆ 03 84 37 23 51. *www.comte.com. Open all year, Tuesday-Friday: 2pm-5pm. July & August, Tuesday-Sunday: 10am-11.30am and 2pm-6pm. Admission: adult 4 €, concessions 3 €*. Learn how to make Comte cheese in this brand-new centre, which takes you from pasture to maturation cellar and finally to the tasting.

SYNDICAT DES FABRICANTS AFFINEURS D'EMMENTAL TRADITIONNEL. *Besançon ✆ 03 81 83 46 13.* The Mont d'Or or Haut Doubs Vacherin (AOC): a gourmet fromage, with its woody flavour redolent of spruce trees, and corrugated crust. It is made in winter at an altitude of 700m, and can be tasted between 10 September and 10 May. Don't hesitate!

SYNDICAT INTERPROFESSIONNEL ✆ 03 81 82 89 68. Morbier: this pressed but uncooked cheese is split into two by a blue line, for economic reasons. A single milking was often not enough for a whole cheese on the modest Haut Jura farms, so the amount made in the morning was protected with a layer of charcoal (vegetable charcoal is used today), and finished off after the evening milking. Farmers and cheese-makers all like to share their know-how, and the secret of making a truly great Morbier.

SYNDICAT INTERPROFESSIONNEL DU MORBIER ✆ 03 81 53 22 30. For about ten years, these producers have been developing cheese making on the farm, and farm-gate sales, and invite you to discover a top quality cheese made in perfect conditions thanks to their know-how. You can meet them on the farm or at market; don't hesitate to ask them about their work.

INFORMATION FROM THE MAISON DU HAUT JURA Lajoux ✆ 03 84 34 12 30

Honey and sweets

The region is rich in dairy products and fruit trees, which makes for excellent cakes and pastries in all four departments. The galette de Goumeau is a buttery brioche-type cake flavoured with orange flower, while the 'Belflore' (from the Belfort Territory) is an almond shortbread pastry filled with raspberries and decorated with almonds and hazelnuts. Montbozon biscuits are soft-centred with different flavours, and Oyrieres is famous for its traditional gingerbread. Beaume-les-Dames specialises in 'eights' (their shape) or craquelins, tasting of hazelnut butter. Honey is made in each department, and has different and distinctive plant flavours: fir tree, acacia, clover and dandelion.

Morille

At the end of winter, mushroom experts and fans rush to the region's woods in search of the famous morels (white, brown and grey). Careful: this mushroom can be poisonous if eaten raw! You wash them in vinegar water, cook them and enjoy them with a local wine.

WINE

Arbois

Capital of Jura winemaking for centuries, Arbois hides the region's most impressive cellars under its paved streets. A square, ochre-coloured steeple rises above hilly vine and orchard-covered slopes, and large, solid winegrowers' houses with deep cellars, coloured fronts and gardens line the passages and alleyways. The local stone's golden tints can be admired in the sober 12th-13thc. Saint Just Church, fine Pécauld Castle and medieval Pont des Capucins beside the imposing Tour Gloriette.

CHATEAU PECAULD ✆ **03 84 66 40 45**. *Vine and wine museum. July & August, every day: 10am-12.30pm and 2pm-6pm.* Once the last of Arbois' defences, this castle now houses the Jura Wine Institute, along with the Franche-Comte Vine and Wine Museum. Outside, you can identify different *cépages* on small vines. There are old presses and tools, a film about vin jaune and vineyard history, winegrowers' portraits, and a cooperage exhibition, with tastings for groups of 10 or more. In season, you can develop your oenology skills at an introductory wine-tasting evening, and the FÕte des Vins at Arbois is held in July.

Vin jaune; vin de paille

The Franche-Comte and Jura are proud of their **vin jaune (yellow wine)** first made from the Savagnin *cépage* on the Château-Chalon slopes, but now also found at Arbois, l'Etoile and on the Jura slopes. Harvested in mid-October, vinified as a white wine, it matures in an oak cask for at least 6 years 3 months. Part of the wine evaporates through the permeable barrel, and a veil of indigenous yeast forms on the surface, giving the wine its characteristic aroma and golden colour. A 62.5cl bottle was specially created for this wine (supposed to be what is left of a litre after long ageing).

Vin de paille (straw wine): the grapes used to be dried on a bed of straw, and are now left six weeks on racks, giving 80% dehydration and increasing sugar content. On pressing, these sugar-filled grapes yield 15 ot 18 litres of must (for 100kg of grapes) which ferments slowly then ages in oak casks for at least 2 or 3 years. Naturally sweet, the wine's resulting crystallized and exotic fruit aromas (prune, honey, caramel, orange) develop fully after many years in the cellar.

Macvin and Crémant du Jura

macvin : this liqueur wine is obtained from unfermented grape juice with a third of marc added. It is matured for twelve months in an oak cask, and has an amber colour, and a complex and remarkable perfume. Fans like to drink it chilled, as an aperitif, and gourmets appreciate it served with melon and a slice of smoked Haut Jura ham, as a starter. Chefs and cordon bleus reduce it to a liquid caramel that goes well with foie gras. Finally, caramel and vanilla ice cream with raisins are a perfect dessert match for the Macvin.

Cremant du Jura : a long tradition of sparkling wines gave the Jura vineyards access to the appellation Cremant du Jura in 1995. This wine is essentially made from chardonnay, poulsard and pinot noir grapes, following the same strict rules as its Champagne cousins. The result is delicate: a rare and elegant bubbly to drink at celebrations with family and friends, as an aperitif or dessert wine, or even right through a festive meal. The cremant comes in dry or demi-sec, white or rose, and there is one for every taste.

Local cheese

Hotels & Restaurants

DOUBS

Besançon

MERCURE PARC MICAUD* 3, avenue Edouard-Droz ✆ 03 81 40 34 34.** *Fax : 03 81 40 34 39. Open all year. 95 air-conditioned rooms complete with mini-bar from 104 € to 134 €, buffet breakfast 12.50 €. Parking free.* The hotel provides all the comfort and service you'd expect from the Mercure name. Located on the edge of the loop, it has an unbeatable view of one of Besançon's most beautiful parks, the Micaud, bordering onto the River Doubs. The casino close by provides entertainment for hotel visitors. Note that the hotel restaurant was entirely renovated at the end of April 2005.

LE MUNGO PARK 11 rue Jean-Petit ✆ 03 81 81 28 01 *Set menus from 35 € to 95 €, à la carte 65 €. Closed Sunday, Monday and from 25 July to 15 August.* Jocelyne Lotz-Choquart et and her partner Gérard Lotz can sigh with relief at last The building works that made life difficult are finished, and the district is newly attractive, as well as convenient – thanks to the brand-new car-park in front of the restaurant. The dining–room also has a brand-new carpet – gone is the old blue one with its darns and creases – and you instantly feel better. The cuisine has not lost the ingredients of its charm; quality products, generous portions and a discreet but real inventiveness: millefeuille of conserved potatoes with foie gras and morteau sausage, a morel velouté with Morteau pork grillons, steamed cod, pak-choi leaves with garlic juice, scallops in a fricassée with leeks and curcuma, black Nyons olive oil, fillet of farm pigeon, rocket salad with almonds, red wine sauce with kaloupilé leaves, warm cream made with nuts and the local vin jaune caramelised with brown sugar, wine-flavoured ice-cream. Gérard Lotz watches carefully over his cellar with its 350 excellent wines, including all those that count in the Jura.

Montbéliard

HOTEL BRISTOL 2, rue de Velotte ✆ 03 81 94 43 17.** *Website: www.hotel-bristol-montbeliard.com. 43 rooms: singles from 38 € to 68 €, doubles from 41 € to 70 €. Breakfast 6.50 €. annual closing in August and during Christmas week. Garage and parking facilities.* The Bristol Hotel is located in Montbéliard town centre, 300m from the station. Situated in a 19thc. town residence, it has plenty of old world charm, and is pleasant and well cared-for, with standard prices for its category. Its wine and champagne bar could be another advantage!

Villers-le-Lac

HOTEL-RESTAURANT LE FRANCE* 8, place Cupillard ✆ 03 81 68 00 06.** *Closed in January and 1 week in November. Restaurant closed Sunday evenings, Monday and Tuesday lunchtime.14 rooms from 55 € to 100 €. Breakfast 9 €. Set menus 20 € for lunch, between 25 € and 68 € for dinner.* A beautiful hotel set high in the Haut-Doubs mountains. No surprises here; quality service and a peaceful stay have been key words for several generations. The rooms are decorated in sober style, modern yet cosy. In the kitchen, Hugues Droz shakes up expectations with his specialities: the morel mushroom set menu with…morels, the nibbles for dessert, or Jura snails in an absinthe infusion. Don't forget the cellar, one of the region's richest.

JURA

Arbois

JEAN-PAUL JEUNET 9 rue de l'Hôtel-de-Ville ✆ 03 84 66 05 67 *Fax 03 84 66 24 20. Website : www.jeanpauljeunet.com. Set menus from 32 à 130 €, à la carte 100 €. Closed Tuesday and Wednesday out of season, Tuesday and Wednesday lunchtime from July to mid-September and in December and January.* What a beautiful place! This is the perfect French-style hotel just as you imagine it, full of good humour and generosity. Jean-Paul Jeaunet loves his region and the family house where he grew up before taking over from his father, who was just as well known in his time. Imaginative, passionate and up-to-date, his cuisine, though difficult to classify, is as appealing as he is himself behind his big moustache. Oysters fondant poached in vin jaune with tarragon, galette de gaude (pancakes made with grilled cornflour and eggs), frothy juice and ficelle pancakes with rye and seaweed, Breton lobster in a carapccio on a rare herb fondue, an almond-milk blancmange, warm crayfish in jelly, crayfish in emulsion with a rare herb salad, Bresse poultry served in two ways, stuffed leg and and the supreme contisé (superficial cuts made, then filled with slivers of liver), loin and leg of suckling lamb, a vegetable and warm herb fondue, lamb's trotters, nut macaroons stuffed with blancmange floating on apples and cinnamon, apple juice sorbet. This cooking is both deeply rooted in its regional soil and ultra-modern like the establishment itself, traditional yet forward-looking.

Dole

LE BEC FIN 67, rue Pasteur ✆ 03 84 82 43 43. *Closed Tuesday and Wednesday ; Monday and Tuesday lunchtime in summer. Seasonal dishes 17 €. Seasonal set menus 26 €. Bec Fin set menus 43 € and 52 €. Découverte set menu 65 €.* Congratulations are due to young chef Romuald Fassenet, holder of a *Meilleur Ouvrier de France 2004* award. Creative and thorough, he offers an original and evolutive cuisine using fresh seasonal produce. There are three dining-rooms and a seminar room seating 30 people: the dining-rooms are located in one of Rue Pasteur's beautiful vaulted cellars, near the scientist's birthplace. In summer, you can eat on one of two small terraces at the water's edge. Among the Bec Fin's dishes are game in season, *petit Mercey* snails, river fish – including the wild pikeperch – and poultry *façon percée du vin jaune.* Excellent welcome.

HOTEL* RESTAURANT LA CHAUMIERE 346, avenue du Maréchal-Juin ✆ 03 84 70 72 40.** *Closed Saturday lunchtime, Sunday and Monday lunchtime. Set menus from 30 € to 70 €. 19 rooms from 77 € to 120 €. Breakfast 10 €. Wifi, covered terrace, car park, swimming pool, garages.* This magnificently restored farm provides all the comfort you could wish for, and an irresistible charm. The soundproofed rooms open onto the garden and the pool; the decor is both rustic and elegant. Discover chef Joel Cesari's delectable cuisine; creativity, sophistication and taste combined with brio. Nearby Chaux forest offers relaxation, and the Aquaparc is only a few hundred metres away.

Lons-le-Saunier

LA COMEDIE Place de la Comédie ✆ 03 84 24 20 66 *Annual closing during Easter school holidays and first 3 weeks of August. Closed Sunday and Monday. Set menus 18 € and 30 €. Suggestions and à la carte.* La Comedie, located in the old winegrowers' quarter in the heart of the town centre, welcomes you with ten or so tables, a private lounge and an indoor garden where you can eat in summer. The dining room with its soft tones and winegrowing motifs is in art deco style. The service is attentive and the *cuisine* light and sophisticated, specialising in fish. Chef Bernard Hemery's *tour de France* of the culinary arts has won him acclaim; his menus change from day to day depending on the fish available. Deserts also have a special place on his menus, like the iced coffee truffle and the rum baba with pineapple salad accompanied by a glass of old rum. Not forgetting a wine list that pays tribute to the region.

Vineyard

Salins-les-Bains

RESTAURANT DES BAINS Place des Alliés ✆ 03 84 73 07 54. *Closed until February 2006 for renovation work. Restaurant closed Sunday evenings and Mondays. Brasserie formula. Set menus from 17.60 € to 47.60 €.* Set between the arcades of the hydropathic establishment and the entrance to the thermal pool in the pretty little Place des Allies, the Restaurant des Bains is often recommended for its excellent table. Salads and a brasserie menu are on offer on the terrace during the summer.

GRAND HOTEL DES BAINS ** 1, place des Alliés ✆ 03 84 37 90 50. *Annual closing in January. 32 rooms from 60 € to 80 €. Full breakfast buffet 9 €.* The hotel has direct access to Salins-les-Bains thermal swimming pool, and offers comfortable rooms in a quiet and sophisticated atmosphere.

HAUTE-SAÔNE

Luxeuil-les-Bains

HOTEL BEAU SITE* 18, rue Georges-Moulimard ✆ 03 84 40 14 67.** *Website : www.beau-site-luxeuil.com. Closed Friday evening, Saturday lunchtime and Sunday evening in winter. 33 rooms from 60 € to 80 €. Breakfast 8 €.* This typical spa hotel in the fine Logis de France style has managed to move with the times, yet has not broken with tradition. The rooms are fairly spacious, completely renovated and comfortable. The outdoor swimming pool is heated in summer, and there are non-smoking bedrooms and a pretty park. Excellent *cuisine* with a tasty regional menu. The orange walls are Provencal in style; the welcome is warm and the service efficient.

Vesoul

LE CAVEAU DU GRAND PUITS 3, place du Grand-Puits ✆ 03 84 76 66 12. *Set menus from 17.50 € to 37 €.* This traditional carefully-prepared *cuisine*, one of the Vesulians' favourites, is better-quality than the simple brasserie, and good value for money. Among the specialities you find filet of pikeperch, veal kidneys and foie gras. The restaurant is a former coaching inn, and you'll be comfortably seated in a beautiful vaulted cellar with its exposed stones.

Dole

TERRITOIRE-DE-BELFORT

Belfort

L'AMBROISIE 2, place de la Grande Fontaine ✆ 03 84 28 67 00. Service until 10.30pm. *Closed Sunday evening and Monday. Credit cards and luncheon vouchers accepted.* Located on the way into the old town. The decor shows good taste and confidence; you can sit in the window - ideal during snowy evenings for the fairytale atmosphere - or in the raised part of the restaurant if you're after a romantic dinner for two. The dishes of the day according to the season are written boldly up on the blackboard. In autumn, game is tastefully cooked, and simply but exquisitely presented. This is one appetizing dish your palate will never forget; so take time to enjoy it in peace.

GRAND HOTEL DU TONNEAU D'OR * 1, rue Reiset ✆ 03 84 58 57 56. 52** *Website : www.tonneaudor.fr 52 rooms from 87 €, breakfast 11 €, restaurant.* The Tonneau d'Or takes you back to earlier times with its sophisticated and sumptuous decor; to the magic of Paris in 1900, the year it was built. The staircase in the entrance is a listed Historic Monument, but the welcome you get from the staff is every bit as impressive as the magnificent building. There is a free car park with about 10 spaces adjoining the hotel. The restaurant is open from Monday to Friday evening, from 12 noon to 1.30pm and from 7pm to 10pm, and offers set menus from 15 €.

LES SAVEURS Centre Atria 1, avenue de l'Espérance ✆ 03 84 58 85 00. *Open every day until 10.30pm. Set menus from 15 €. Just after the ramparts on arriving at Belfort via motorway exit 13.* Chef Bernard Treil adds his personal touch, which is greatly appreciated. Among the best choices, the Comte dishes offer you a sample of regional know-how with a glass of Arbois wine to go with it, and dessert included. On the *à la carte* menu, which changes twice a year, you find home-made duck foie gras with soft figs and *assiettes du lion* comprising mountain and Montbeliard sausages, Haut-Doubs country ham, comte and morbier cheese: a meal in itself. The chef prepares this feast himself, with most communicative pleasure; so don't miss the chance to enjoy it. Bon appetit!

Languedoc-Roussillon

Pont du Gard

LANGUEDOC ROUSSILLON
Altitude (metres)
2000
1000
500
200
Major road
Motorway
Prefecture
Main town
Secondary town
CANTAL
AURILLAC
Fournel
Nasbinals
LOT
Lot
CAHORS
RODEZ
AVEYRON
MILLAU
A75
A20
ALBI
A68
TARN
TOULOUSE
CASTRES
A61
La Salvetat-sur-Agout
Lamalou-les-Bains
Olargues
Roquebrun
St-Pons-de Thomières
St-Chinian
Puisserguier
Capestang
HAUTES-PYRENEES
Saissac
Caunes-Minervois
Minerve
Castelnaudary
Ouveillan
Salles-sur-l'Hers
CARCASSONNE
Rieux-Minervois
Canal du Midi
Coursan
Belpech
Capendu
NARBONNE
Gruissan Plage
Fanjeaux
A61
Aude
Lagrasse
Limoux
Sigean
AUDE
Durban-Corbières
Port-la Nouvelle
ARIEGE
Chalabre
Couiza
Mouthoumet
A9
Leucate
Rennes-les Bains
Quillan
Tuchan
Salses
N
O
E
S
Belcaire
Axat
St-Paul-de Fenouillet
Latour-de France
Estagel
Rivesaltes
Le Barcarès
Sournia
Millas
Têt
PERPIGNAN
Canet
Prades
Vinça
Ille-sur-Têt
Thuir
St-Cyprien
Elne
ANDORRE
Olette
PYRENEES-ORIENTALES
Le Boulou
Argelès
Collioure
Banyuls
Font-Romeu
Mont-Louis
Amélie-les-Bains
Céret
Saillagouse
Prats-de-Mollo
Arles-sur-Tech
Tech
Bourg-Madame
ESPAGNE
ESPAGNE

LE PUY-EN-VELAY
HAUTE-LOIRE
ARDECHE
30 km
DRÔME
Le Malzieu-Ville
St-Alban
Grandrieu
Langogne
Aumont-Aubrac
St-Amans
LOZERE
Châteauneuf-sur-Redon
Marvejols
Bagnols-les-Bains
MENDE
Chanac
Le Bleymard
Villefort
Ste-Enimie
Le Pont-de-Montvert
Florac
Génolhac
Bésseges
Barjac
Pont-St-Esprit
Barre-des Cévennes
La Grand-Combe
St-Ambroix
Meyrueis
St-Germain-de-Calberte
Lussan
Bagnols-sur-Cèze
ORANGE
St-André-de-Valborgne
ALES
VAUCLUSE
Trèves
Valleraugue
Vézénobres
GARD
Roquemaure
Lasale
Uzès
Sumène
St-Hippolyte-du-Fort
Le Vigan
Lédignan
Remoulins
AVIGNON
Alzon
Ganges
Sauve
Quissac
Aramon
Claret
NÎMES
St-Martin-de-Londres
Sommières
Beaucaire
Lodève
Aniane
Gignac
Les Matelles
Castries
Vauvert
Lunel
St-Gilles
A54
Clermont-l'Hérault
MONTPELLIER
Mauguio
Aigues-Mortes
HERAULT
Paulhan
La Grande-Motte
Grau-du-Roi
BOUCHES-DU-RHÔNE
Pézenas
Montagnac
A9
Palavas-les-Flots
Servian
Mèze
Frontignan
Bessan
Sète
Agde
BEZIERS
Cap d'Agde
Valras-Plage
A7
Tarn
Gard
Hérault
Rhône
MER MEDITERRANEE
GOLFE DU LION

CANAL DU MIDI

The Romans had thought about linking the Mediterranean to the Atlantic, but nothing was done until 1666, when Louis XIV signed an edict 'for the building of a canal communicating between the waters of the two seas Ocean and Mediterranean'. Pierre-Paul Riquet, who first suggested the idea to Colbert, was given the task. Work began in 1667 and ended in 1681. 12,000 labourers dug 254km of trenches, 80km of channels, 150 bridges and tunnels and over 60 locks. Vauban called it 'the finest and noblest work of its kind ever undertaken'. After Riquet's death in 1680, fortunes were made on his canal, but eventually railways replaced waterways. Today, the locks work for pleasure boats and tourists, and walkers, joggers and cyclists use the banks for their leisure. The canal crosses a region rich in history and legends, and holidaymakers follow it through vineyards and cypresses in the Mediterranean sunlight, in search of picturesque villages and fortified towns with their traditions and festivals.

Practical information

You can navigate freely on the Canal du Midi and the Robine from March to October (except for Christmas and New Year's Day, 1 May, 14 July, All Saints' and 11 November). The locks are open from 8am-12.30pm and 1.30pm-5.30pm or 7.30pm, depending on the month. From November to February, you can use the canal on request. Speed limit: 6-8km/h (to protect the banks) reduced to 3km/h on approaching locks, bridges, ports and stops, and when passing or overtaking another boat. You are expected to slow down near small boats and canoes, and riverside fishermen. You do not need a licence to steer a boat hired through a boat hire company.

DIRECTION REGIONALE 2, port Saint Etienne - TOULOUSE ✆ 05 61 36 24 24

SUBDIVISION LANGUEDOC-OUEST Port du Canal - CARCASSONNE ✆ 04 68 71 74 55

CARCASSONNE AND THE AUDE

Carcassonne

France's second-most-visited site (after the Mont-Saint-Michel). This model of military architecture built, preserved and restored by man is also a lively and charming town; its lower quarter follows on from the 13thc. bastide and still contains traces of fine old houses. You need to stay a while in Carcassonne, to fully appreciate its historic, religious, architectural and tourist attractions.

CITE Listed World Heritage since 1997, these fortifications were restored by Viollet-le-Duc who rebuilt 3km of walls and the 13thc. Narbonnaise gate with its two spur-shaped towers. Come early in the morning, on foot (the route from town to cité crosses a delightful bridge) and take time to visit the monuments and museums.

MUSEE DE L'ECOLE 3, rue du Plo Cité médièvale ✆ 04 68 25 95 14. *Open all year: 10am-6pm (7pm in July & August). Admission: adult 4 € students 3 € under-12s free.* In the heart of the medieval city. Housed in a former primary school, this museum reconstructs the atmosphere of an old-fashioned classroom, with the smell of chalk and ink. An amazing schoolbook library is available to all.

MUSEE DE L'INQUISITION La Cite ✆ 04 68 47 00 09. *Open all year.* This controversial exhibition shows the extent of human intolerance, fanatism and barbarity. Its impressive collection of torture instruments and engravings of man-made horrors leave you feeling uneasy. Not suitable for the ultra-sensitive.

CHATEAU COMTAL ✆ 04 68 11 70 77. *Opening hours depend on the season (open every day). Admission: adult 6.10 € 18-25s 4.10 €.* Built in the 12thc. by the powerful Trencavel family. Don't miss the collection of stone works: religious art, ancient sculptures and funeral exhibits such as sarcophagi, Merovingian steles, capitals and Calvary.

SAINT NAZAIRE BASILICA. *Open 9am-12 noon and 2pm-7pm (5pm in winter). Mass on Sunday, 11am.* The only remains of the 11thc. Romanesque building are the crypt and some pillars in the nave; figures with raised arms, topped with plants, feature on the capitals. The six-bay nave was put up in the 12thc. and the chevet dates back to the late 13thc. while transept and Gothic chancel are early 14thc.

IMAGINARIUM 3-5 rue Saint Jean ✆ 04 68 47 78 78. *www.art-hist.com/imaginarium. Open Easter-All Saints. Opening hours on recorded message: 04 68 47 77 71. Admission: adults 7 € concessions 4.75 €.* July 1209: Simon de Montfort's army invades Languedoc in its crusade against the Cathares... A spectacular museum with its historical show, gallery of 13 illuminations fitted with soundtrack, multimedia and kids' areas.

MEMOIRE DU MOYEN AGE Espace Pont-Levis Chemin des Anglais ✆ 04 68 71 08 65. *Open every day: 10am-7pm. Admission: adult 5 €, students 4 €, under-12s 3 €.* A foretaste of your visit to the fortress. You can see a video of weapons, costumes and architecture from the 5th-15thc. and a son et lumière tracing the Gallo-Roman and 13thc. periods, including the last attack on the fortress (1240). Miniature figures re-enact this last siege in an impressive scale model.

MUSEE DE LA CHEVALERIE Place Saint Jean ✆ 04 68 72 75 51. *Open April-September. By appointment out of season. Admission 3 € kids 1.50 €* Weapons and archery fans will love this little museum opened by a collector, with plenty of Middle Ages arrow-points, armour and costumes to admire.

MUSEE DU SENECHAL 6, rue Viollet-le-Duc ✆ 04 68 47 35 06. *Open every day: 10am-6pm. Closed Wednesday. Admission 3 €, kids 1.50 €.* Scenes from medieval life displaying weapons, costumes and characters: dancers, musicians, a jester, a troubadour, jugglers etc. Regional anecdotes and stories complete your visit.

CATHA-RAMA Domaine de Sautes N113 ✆ 04 68 78 77 98. *www.catharama.d-av.com. Open Easter-All Saints. Admission: adult 5 € child 4 €* An excellent way to discover local history through this audio-visual display, while tasting the property's wines.

SAINT MICHEL CATHEDRAL. Built between 1262 and 1283, pulled down in 1355, rebuilt and knocked down again in 1840, finally restored by Viollet-le-Duc. This superb Languedoc Gothic building has beautiful stained glass and a rose window. Its treasure contains master paintings and sculptures from Carcassonne's diocesan churches.

MUSEE DES BEAUX-ARTS 1, rue de Verdun ✆ 04 68 77 73 70. *Open 15 June-15 September, every day: 10am-6pm. Other periods, Tuesday-Saturday: 10am-12 noon and 2pm-6pm. Admission free.* A collection of 17th, 18th and 19thc. paintings (Chardin, Subleyas, Courbet, Corot, Poliakof) is housed in the former Présidial, along with earthenware, tapestries and art objects. The ground floor rooms are kept for 20thc. collections and temporary exhibitions.

CHATEAU D'AGUILAR Tuchan ✆ 04 68 45 51 00. The castle ruins can still be seen on a rocky spur. This fortress on the border between France and Aragon was originally a 12thc. polygonal-shaped hideout, built in the middle of a hexagonal enclosure with six towers (13thc)

Carcassonne and its five sons

Carcassonne was considerably reinforced by Louis IX and his successors from 1240 onwards, after the disposessed Vicomte Trencavel's failure to reconquer the city. Five fortresses outside Carcassonne were fitted out and fortified, to form an impressive defensive line facing the Aragon border. The city's 'five sons' were kept in a defensive state until 1650 and the Pyrenees Treaty, when the border was pushed back beyond Roussillon, and they lost all their strategic importance.

Carcassonne, ramparts

CHATEAU DE PEYREPERTUSE Duilhac-sous-Peyrepertuse ✆ 06 71 58 63 36/04 68 45 40 55. Languedoc's most beautiful example of medieval military architecture. Built on a mountain ridge overhanging a breathtaking sheer drop, the castle has three sets of surrounding walls over 300m in length, with over a hectare of ruined buildings inside: main building, chapels and garrison quarters. From the plateau overlooking the Saint Jordi keep, there is a magnificent panoramic view; on a clear day you can see as far as the Mediterranean shores.

CHATEAU DE PUILAURENS Lapradelle ✆ 04 68 20 65 26. Perched 697m above sea-level, Puilaurens fortress is one of the best-preserved in Cathar country. Louis IX had it fortified, and it was the most southerly citadel in France for over 400 years - and the last Cathar site to fall. This defensive castle *par excellence* is both architecturally interesting and instructive.

CHATEAU DE QUERIBUS Cucugnan ✆ 04 68 45 03 69. This former royal fortress standing on its impressive rocky spur marks the beginning of Cathar Country if you arrive from the coast. It is an excellent example of military architecture, famous for its polygonal keep and Primitive Gothic hall with the vault supported by a strong circular pillar opening out into a palm shape. Today, a spiral staircase leads to a terrace on the roof of the keep, 728m above the ground, with its view of the imposing Fenouilledes landscapes, Roussillon plains and Corbieres.

CHATEAU DE TERMES ✆ 04 68 70 09 20. Termes Village clings to the hillside in a most picturesque staggered manner. The last remains of its castle can be found on an imposing, protected site at the top of a rocky slope with a view of the Hautes Corbieres. It is hard to imagine that these ruins were once one of the Bas Languedoc's most powerful medieval domains, held by the Termes family until 1228.

Aude

Fontfroide Abbey

FONTFROIDE ABBEY RD613 ✆ 04 68 45 11 08. *www.fontfroide.com. Open every day. Admission: adult 6.50 € 7-15s 3 €* Nestling in a valley 15km from Narbonne, Fontfroide was first mentioned between 1080 and 1095. The heart of the abbey dates from the 13th and 14thc. and links the main buildings. The galleries have rib-vaults, and the capitals are decorated with bunches of leaves. The chapter house is over the cloister's east gallery, as in all Cistercian monasteries, and was put up in the early 13thc. It has three bays covered by nine rib-vaults on four marble columns. The abbey church and its 12thc. nave are the building's oldest parts.

Alet-les-Bains

Formerly an episcopal town, now a watering place, Alet is on the edge of the Haute Vallée, and boasts a considerable historic and architectural heritage in a fine natural setting. A 12thc. rampart reinforces the environmental defences, and the village has kept its medieval look, with streets running off from a central square, superb half-timbered and corbelled facades and ancient shopfronts.

ABBEY ✆ 04 68 69 93 56. *Open all year. July & August: 9am-8pm. 1 October-30 June: 8.30am-12.30pm and 2pm-6pm. Admission: adult 2,50 € child 1 €* Founded in 813, the abbey was at the height of its influence in the 12thc. After the troubled Cathar period, it was made a bishopric to keep control of the region.

CATHEDRAL. Though ruined, this is a fine example of Languedoc Romanesque art. Six buttresses support the Romanesque apse, topped with columns and superb capitals decorated with acanthus. The cloister was on the north of the church; only the chapter house is visible now, with its richly carved Romanesque front.

Castelnaudary

Castelnaudary is the department's third biggest town, and boasts a beautiful setting, a number of tourist attractions and a world-famous speciality; the cassoulet.

VILLE MEDIEVAL. Ramparts were built round the town during the 12thc., and modified as the population grew. The last wall was put up in 1366, while the town was being rebuilt after a whirlwind visit from the Black Prince in 1355.

APOTHICAIRERIE. The Bishop of Saint-Papoul built Castelnaudary hospital in 1772. Now the Jean-Pierre-de-Cassabel Hospital Centre, it has inherited a magnificent apothecary's with a collection of 18thc. Moustiers pots.

COLLEGIATE CHURCH. Built in the 13thc. in Southern Gothic style, Saint Michel Collegiate Church began life as a temple and fortress, and was raised to collegiate status in 1318. It boasts the South of France's finest peal of bells (35), a majestic single nave and some beautiful works of art in its side chapels.

GRAND BASSIN. Pierre-Paul Riquet and François Andréossy built this 7ha. dock from 1666 to 1681, enabling Castelnaudary to become a major trading port. Today, it is a sailing harbour, and a reservoir supplying the four Saint Roch locks.

MUSEE DU PRESIDIAL 10, rampe du Présidial ✆ 04 68 23 00 ??. *July & August: Tuesday-Saturday: 10am-12 noon and 3pm-7pm. Sunday & Monday: 3pm-7pm. Admission: adult 3 € child 0.80 €* The seneschalsy headquarters were built in 1585 and pulled down on the orders of Louis XIII in 1623. The façade is of more recent date, with interesting mullioned windows, for the remains of the building were restored and have served as a prison, lodgings and (nowadays) the Archeological Pottery Museum.

Caunes-Minervois

The town's upper quarter is worth a visit for its architecture: decorative housefronts with Gothic and Renaissance doors, windows and moulding; the remains of the city wall.

ABBEY ✆ 04 68 78 09 44. *Open every day April-September; otherwise, weekends and school holidays only. Guided tour: adult 3 € child 1.50 € groups 2.30 €* Founded in 780, the abbey became a place of pilgrimage and holy processions, which still continue today. In the 17thc. Jean d'Alibert, Abbot of Caunes had the main body built. The abbey joined the Saint Maur Congregation in 1659; as a result, some of the buildings were restored.

Gruissan

Gruissan is chiefly characterised by its vast sandy beaches stretching down to the sea.

VIEUX VILLAGE. This old fishermen's village has its souvenirs: Barberousse (Redbeard)'s Tower recalls the famous medieval pirate, and is encompassed by a castle (1246); the church, also dating back to the Middle Ages, was recently restored. Local sailors pray in Notre Dame des Auzils Chapel on stormy evenings, and have their own graveyard.

CHALETS. Fans of Jean-Jacques Béneix's cult film 'Betty Blue' (1986) will recognise the blue sky over white sand and the strange chalets built on piles dotted across the beach. Gruissan-Plage is still as surreal, with the same sun and chalets.

Lastours

The present village takes its name from its four castles, which can be seen from the many panoramic viewpoints on local walking paths.

LES QUATRE CHATEAUX ✆ 04 68 77 56 02. *Closed in January. Open October: 10am-5pm. April, May, June & September: 10am-6pm. July & August: 9am-8pm. Open weekends and school holidays in February, March, November & December: 10am-5pm. Groups by appointment. Admission; adult 3 €*

child 1.50 € On the top of a 300m ridge, Cabaret, Surdespine, Quertinheux and Tour d'Espine illustrate the development of 11th and 12thc. military architecture. The castles gained in importance during the crusade against Albi. Don't forget to wear stout shoes!

CASCADE DE CUBSERVIES. One of Europe's most dramatic waterfalls (90m high). You get the best view from Cubserviès hamlet.

Leucate

There are four Leucates, each with its own character: Leucate Village, Leucate Beach, Port Leucate and La Franqui.

Leucate-Village: 2km from the sea (witness the oysters and seafood served in its restaurants) and full of Mediterranean charm.

Leucate-Plage: well-sheltered from headwinds, this seaside resort goes back 80 years. The countryside is only a few minutes from the beaches and creeks, up on the lighthouse plateau, where paths lined with low dry stone walls wind through vines and almond-groves.

Port-Leucate: an oyster-farming centre, with delicious produce. This is also Languedoc-Roussillon's biggest sailing harbour (1,100 moorings).

Narbonne

This Roman capital is now the departmental centre of tourism, winegrowing and rugby. You can also laze on its fine sandy beaches, and enjoy that holiday feeling of doing nothing in the sun.

SAINT PAUL BASILICA Rue Arago. This church was built on the site of a 4th and 5thc. necropolis around the tomb of the town's first bishop. The chancel is striking with its great arcades, double triforium and high windows, and elegant vaults. The early Christian crypt is part of a large necropolis built in Constantine's time (4thc.)

PALAIS DES ARCHEVEQUES, SAINT JUST CATHEDRAL. Saint Just and Saint Pasteur Cathedral and the Archbishops' Palace are an exceptional blend of Romanesque and Gothic architecture.

JARDIN ET SALLE DU PILIER. This remarkable 14thc. ensemble houses some medieval sculpture, inscriptions, bas reliefs, capitals and statues from the Visigoth era to the 15thc.

MUSEE ARCHEOLOGIQUE Ancien Palais des Archevêques ✆ 04 68 90 30 66. *Open every day, except Monday in winter. Admission: adult 5.20 € concessions 3.70 € (ticket valid for 4 museums in 3 days).* Discover Narbonne's remarkable Roman paintings. A large lapidary collection brings Roman Narbonne to life, with its daily activities, institutions, places of worship and business.

MAISON NATALE DE CHARLES TRENET 13, ave Charles Trénet ✆ 04 68 90 30 66. *Open every day except Tuesday, 1 October-31 March: 2pm-6pm. Admission: adult 5.20 € concessions 3.70 € Guided musical tour of Charles Trénet's birthplace.* The popular French music-hall and varieties singer was born into a musical family in 1913. The souvenirs of his enchanted childhood are just as he left them, before the town bought his house.

Rennes-le-Château

What is Rennes-le-Château's secret? A fascinating legend has grown up around this little village perched on its headland. At the end of the 19thc., newly-arrived parish priest Béranger Saunière discovered a run-down church. Suddenly, he had an apparently endless source of money; decorated the church, bought land, built himself a fine house with a Neo-Gothic tower (Tour Magdala) and led a life of luxury. 'The priest has found buried treasure' went the rumour - but what treasure? Cathar, Templars, Blanche de Castile, parchments concerning the Kings of France, revelations of the true story of Christ: all these ideas were put forward from the 1960s onwards. Today, Abbé Saunière's estate is run by the town council, and houses a museum of village history including his own curious story.

ESPACE BERANGER SAUNIERE Mairie ✆ 04 68 74 72 68. *Closed 11 January-20 February 2006. Open 10am-7pm in high season (closes 6pm mid-season, 5pm low season). Admission: adult 4,25 €.*

Sigean

This little Corbières town has plenty to interest the tourist, apart from its African Reserve. Saint Felix Church (17thc.) boasts a listed organ, and you can enjoy a stroll through the streets to the ramparts.

RESERVE AFRICAINE. *Open all year. 300ha of naturally humid zones and limestone hills are home to 3,500 animals, mostly African, living quite freely in wide-open spaces.* As you drive through the Brousse and Savane Parks (with your windows up) you catch sight of Tibetan bears, white rhinos, giraffes and the famous lion kings.

PERPIGNAN & THE PYRÉNÉES-ORIENTALES

An imposing Catalan mountain known as the Canigou overshadows this region, where Romanesque art once flourished, and each small village church has its magnificent Baroque reredos.

Perpignan

No-one goes to Perpignan by accident. This isolated city is 30km from Spain to the south, bypassed in the north by the Narbonne road and hemmed in by the Pyrenees. Its citizens thus lived in a state of autarky for many years – though in a beautiful setting.

CASTILLET Place de Verdun ✆ 04 68 35 42 05. *Open every day except Tuesday, 1 October-31 April: 11am-5.30pm. 1 May-30 September: 10am-7pm. Admission: 2 € and 4 €.* This 14thc. red brick fortress is part of the ramparts; a gate known as the Porte de France was added in Louis XI's time. At one time a prison, it now houses the Catalan Popular Arts and Traditions Museum (Casa Pairal).

CITADELLE ET PALAIS DES ROIS DE MAJORQUE 2, rue des Archers ✆ 04 68 34 48 29. *Open summer: 10am-12 noon, winter: 9am-5pm. Admission: adult 4, 2 € and 3 €* The Kings of Majorca's residence (13th-14thc.) was housed in this citadel overlooking the town. Inside, the elegant Gothic architecture makes up for a rather austere exterior.

Boat, Argeles-sur-Mer

© OT Argeles-sur-Mer

SAINT JEAN BAPTISTE CATHEDRAL Place Gambetta. One of the finest Southern Gothic cathedrals. Each chapel has its Baroque reredos, and so has the white marble high altar. A Moorish King's head hangs from the great organ in carved and sculpted wood.

Ille-sur-Têt

L'HOSPICE D'ILLE. This is one of the few preserved hospices in Southern France. It was founded by Marie d'Ille in the 13thc. to house the region's poor and Compostella pilgrims. The present buildings and Baroque pediment date back to the 16th and 18thc. The 11thc. Romanesque Rodona Church, built of big river pebbles, is typical of Roussillon medieval architecture, and blends in well with the former Hospice buildings.

MUSEE DU SAPEUR POMPIER 116, ave Pasteur ✆ 04 68 84 03 54. *Open every day except Tuesday:10am-12 noon and 2pm-6pm (7pm in season). Admission: 3 €.* This Firemen's Museum contains several rooms displaying old helmets, medals, ladders and 19thc. hand pumps; and a cinema where you can see a very realistic video on fire-fighting.

SITE DES ORGUES 2km north of Ille-sur-Têt ✆ 04 68 84 13 13. *Accessible all year. French school holidays 10am-5.30pm. October-March:10am-11.45am and 2pm-5pm. April & May: 10am-11.45 am and 2pm-6pm. June-September: 9.30am-7.30pm. July & August: 10am-6pm. Admission 3,50 €* The amazing rock formation on this site is the result of years of erosion: the fairytale chimneys and magical soft rock towers overhung by harder terraces fascinate both adults and kids. A small ochre canyon sculpted by wind and water that will leave a lasting impression in your mind's eye.

Côte Vermeille, Vallespir

The sea seems bluer along the Catalan beaches, where the sea winds offer ideal surfing conditions for the Mediterranean coast, and the mountains are so close.

Argelès-sur-Mer

This family resort nestles at the foot of the Albères (last of the Pyrenees range).

AIGLES DE VALMY Château de Valmy ✆ 04 68 81 67 32. *April-October: 11am-6pm. Closed Monday, except June, July & August. Admission: adult 8 € child 6 €.* Perched in the Albères foothills, the castle is a magnificent setting for birds of prey displays. The park contains local flora, including the famous Albères cork oaks, which supply a good many corks for your wine bottles.

ARGELES-PLAGE. One of the oldest coastal resorts, between Pyrenees and Mediterranean.

Banyuls-sur-Mer

A picturesque fishing harbour, all old-fashioned charm and typical staircase alleys. Banyuls has an aperitif named after it, and is the birthplace of sculptor Aristide Maillol. Inland is just as interesting, with its fantastic views over the Mediterranean, and sun-drenched, vine-covered hillsides sliding into the sea.

MUSEE MAILLOL Valle de la Roume ✆ 04 68 88 57 11. *Open all year except public holidays. October-April: 10am-12 noon and 2pm-5pm. May-September: 10am-12 noon and 4pm-7pm. Admission: adult 4 € under-14s 3 € under-7s free.* A modest museum has been set up in Maillol's beloved farmhouse, where eminent artists of the early 20thc. came to stay. One of the sculptor's major works stands on his tomb in the pretty garden: La Méditerranée, ode to woman.

AQUARIUM DE BANYULS Ave du Fontaulé ✆ 04 68 88 73 39. *www.obs-banyuls.fr. Open all year: 9am-12 noon and 2pm-6.30pm. Closes at 9pm in July & August. Admission: adult 4.40 € 6-12s 2.10 €.* 250 animal and plant species from local waters inhabit the 40 tanks on display. Founded in 1883, this is one of France's oldest aquariums.

RESERVE NATURELLE MARINE 18, ave de Fontaulé (reception) ✆ 04 68 88 56 87. *Reception points along the harbour and Peyrefite Beach, open every day: 10.30am-12.30pm and 4.30pm-6.30pm.* A 250m underwater discovery path in the protected zone between Banyuls and Cap Peyrefite. You can see marine wildlife in action by swimming on the surface or just under it with flippers, mask and snorkel. The five observation stations are each marked by an information buoy (never deeper than 5m).

Céret

Home of Catalan folklore and tradition. You'll often see the red and gold flags flying from all windows, and the espadrille is worn with pride in Céret. Bullfighting is an ancient custom, and the feria in July is the high point of the year. Céret is also a Mecca of 20thc. art: Picasso, Matisse, Soutine, Manolo, Dufy, Cocteau and the composer Saint-Saens all stayed here.

MAISON DE L'ARCHEOLOGIE Place Picasso ✆ 04 68 87 31 59. *July-September, open every day: 10am-1pm and 2pm-5pm. Other periods, Monday-Friday: 10am-12 noon and 2pm-5pm. Closed in January. Admission: adult 2.50 € concessions 1.50 € under-12s free.* This little museum of local archeology is housed in the Tour d'Espagne (part of the old ramparts) on the delightful Place Picasso.

MAISON DE MUSEE D'ART MODERNE 8, bd Maréchal Joffre ✆ 04 68 87 27 76. *www.musee.ceret.com. Open every day, 1 May-30 September: 10am-7pm. Admission: adult 5.50 € concessions 3.50 € under-12s free.* A collection of paintings and sculptures that marked the early 20thc.: Chagall, Dali, Dufy, Picasso, Matisse, Manolo, Herbin and Miró are all here. The parallel events and temporary exhibitions are always interesting.

Collioure

This historic town has been famous since the days of the Majorcan Kings, and immortalised by the 20thc.'s great painters. Picturesque alleys full of charm, a church with its symbolic tower, Mediterranean colours and light, and a powerful castle lined with marvellous little beaches all go to make Collioure the jewel of the Catalan coast.

VIEILLE VILLE. This medieval quarter has kept its authentic charm despite the many tourists. The alleys round the harbour are full of life and Catalan seaside atmosphere.

CHATEAU ROYAL ✆ 04 68 82 06 43. *Open every day, summer: 10am-6pm, winter: 9am-5pm. Admission: 4 €.* The Kings of Aragon chose this as their Roussillon residence; later, it belonged to the Majorcan Kings and finally to the French, after the Pyrenees Treaty. It hosts pictoral and ethnographic exhibitions of local crafts and popular traditions.

CHEMIN DU FAUVISM Espace Fauve - Quai de l'Amirauté ✆ 04 68 98 07 16. Henri Matisse and Andre Derain came to live at Collioure in the first years of the 20thc. The Fauvist Path runs through the town's alleyways seeking out places that inspired these artists, or featured in their paintings.

The mountain

Les Angles

Huddled round its pretty Romanesque church, Les Angles has kept its traditional old mountain village charm: rustic houses with slate roofs and the remains of a castle. Les Angles is now a major winter sports resort with 50km of downhill ski slopes and over 100km of cross-country tracks on the Capcir plateau, ideal for this sport.

PARC ANIMALIER DES ANGLES Pla del Mir ✆ 04 68 04 17 20. *Open all year. July & August: 10am-7.30pm. Other periods: 10am-12.30pm and 2pm-6pm. Admission: adult 8 €,4-14s 6.50 € under-4s free.* You can see boar, moufflons, izards, marmots, ibex, wolves, bears, stags, reindeer and roe deer in their natural habitat in this well-known wildlife park.

Le Canigou

You cannot help but admire this impressive but rather frightening peak. Its snowy summit (2,784m above sea-level) served as a beacon for Greek sailors in antique times. Climbers have a splendid view; from the top, you can see the whole Pyrenees range and on a clear day, the Mediterranean as far as Marseille.

Font-Romeu

This resort is well known in France, rising in tiers from 1,600 to 1,800m above sea-level. It is ideal for winter sports, with its 52km of slopes, 28 lifts and hundreds of snow blowers; Font-Romeu pioneered this technique, as a means of countering 3,000 hours of annual sunshine.

FOUR SOLAIRE D'ODEILLO Rue du Four-Solaire ✆ 04 68 30 77 86. *Open every day, July & August: 10am-7.30pm. Other periods: 10am-12.30pm and 2pm-6pm. Admission: adult 6 € 8-18s 3.50 €, under-8s free.* This typical little mountain village holds the world's biggest solar furnace (40m high and 54m wide). Odeillo's new exhibition Le soleil apprivoisé (the Taming of the Sun) explains solar energy and its use with models, interactive experiments (both instructive and fun) and a film about the solar furnace.

Mont Louis

After the Pyrenees Treaty of 1659, Louis XIV decided to have a stronghold put up at the crossroads between Capcir, Cerdagne and Conflent. Vauban chose this strategic site, which became France's highest fortified town, named Mont Louis in honour of the Sun King.

Fortunately, Mont Louis didn't see much action, and is still intact, so you can see how it looked in the 17thc.

LA PLACE FORTE. Having never withstood a siege in its life, Mont Louis' fortifications are still in perfect condition. The well, worked by a wheel, is intact, and the tree-lined ramparts are pleasant to walk on with lovely views of the town and neighbouring mountains.

Les Bouillouses: a jewel in the Catalan Pyrenees

Bouillouses Lake and its surroundings is one of the Pyrenees-Orientales' most beautiful nature reserves, listed since 1976. The site includes several Capcir villages at the foot of the Carlit Peak, grouped around Lake Cune, a vast artificial reservoir containing 15 million cubic metres. Located 2,017m above sea-level, it offers an immense mirror (164ha) to the deep, immaculate blue of the Catalan sky. Walking round the lake is a marvellous experience, in the midst of this pure natural environment, with the sharp scent of pines in the fresh air (pine woods run down the Peric slopes). The place is also heaven for fishing and hiking, since the Bouillouses is the departure point for climbing Carlit Peak (2,921m), the highest in the Eastern Pyrenees. Other, easier routes are available for the less energetic, such as the path linking the lakes. The Conseil Regional limits access by car during the summer, and has provided a car park (with surveillance) where you can take a shuttle to and from the site. You can also get to the Bouillouses by cable car from the surrounding resorts (information 04 68 04 24 61).

FOUR SOLAIRE DE MONT LOUIS Résidence Vauban ✆ 04 68 04 14 89. *www.four-solaire.fr. Open every day: 10am-12.30pm and 2pm-5pm. July & August, closes at 7pm. Admission: adult 5.50 €, over-7s 4 €, under-7s free.* Have fun learning about solar energy through fascinating experiments, like solar concentration (the furnace's 3,500 facets provide a temperature of 3,000 degrees C). Grown-ups and kids alike can understand how a solar furnace works, and will enjoy the shop with solar-fired ceramic and bronze, various objects connected with the sun, and literature on the subject.

Pradès

This big, inland town contains some fine stone and brick houses, and others built from River Têt pebbles. The great cellist Pablo Casals lived here for 20 years and invited a number of artists. He *has a museum and a festival to his name.*

SAINT PIERRE CHURCH. Built from 1606-1750, on the site of a 12thc. Romanesque church (only the elegant Lombard steeple remains from this early period). Inside, the mass of Baroque colour and gilding is impressive.

MUSEE PAU CASALS 33, rue de l'Hospice ✆ 04 68 96 28 55. *Open Tuesday-Friday in season: 9am-1pm and 2pm-5pm. Saturday: 9am-1pm. Tuesday-Saturday out of season. Admission free.* The great composer, cellist and humanist Pablo (Pau) Casals had a house in Pradès. It is full of souvenirs: his piano, cello, photos and stage costumes. You can hear his recordings in the museum (moved to the mediatheque) set up in homage to the Master.

Thuir

Economic and winegrowing capital of the Aspres, a small area of wild countryside between Canigou and the Roussillon plain. Thousands of tourists come here to see the Byrrh cellars, and the world's biggest oak vat, but Thuir itself is a charming town with shady squares and narrow alleys. Events take place here all year round.

CAVES BYRRH 6, bd Violet ✆ 04 68 53 05 42. *www.byrrh.com. Admission: 1.70 € Open all year; November-March by appointment only.* These cellars have been making wine-based aperitives since 1892. Discover kilometres of tuns and vats containing 20,000 to 200,000 litres of drink, including the giant oak vat that holds 1,200,000 litres of liquid. Don't forget to look up and admire Gustave Eiffel's gigantic hall (1892). The tour ends with a tasting session: Byrrh, Cinzano, Ambassadeur and Dubonnet are the most famous names.

MUSEE DE LA NATURE ET DE LA CHASSE Bd Violet ✆ 04 68 84 67 86. *Open mid-June to mid-September. By appointment at other periods.Admission: 2,40 €* The Pyrénées-Orientales are home to a large number of animals, thanks to their varied scenery and climate. Deer, foxes, boar and izards are displayed in their natural habitat, enabling you to consider the fragility of our ecosystem from a viewpoint that is educational as well as fun.

Vernet-les-Bains

This reputed watering place was known as the Pyrenees Paradise by the celebrities who came here for treatment in the early 20thc. It boasts a superb natural setting at the foot of the Canigou, but also a Mountain Museum and wildlife park, where local trades and crafts and everyday objects are on display, as well as flora and fauna.

SAINT MARTIN DU CANIGOU ABBEY Casteil ✆ 04 68 05 50 03. *Opening hours vary (information from the abbey or Casteil Syndicat d'Initiative). Closed January. Admission: adult 4 €, over-12s 3 € Access on foot or by 4x4.* After the hike from Casteil over rising ground, you see the abbey clinging to its rocky outcrop 1,100m above sea-level. This awesome religious site deserves appropriate dress and a respectful attitude.

Elsewhere in the Pyrénées-Orientales

Le Barcarès

This fishing village is a faithful reconstruction of traditional Salanque dwellings before 1960s town planning took a hand. At that time, Saint Laurent-de-la-Salanque was a hamlet of a harbour with some dwellings built of reeds and a few huts. On the beach lies the silted-up ocean liner Lydia, only one of its kind in the world. You can visit the restaurant, disco and shell and coral exhibition on board: the view and the experience are magical.

Canet-en-Roussillon

Canet is Perpignan's beach. The old village is attractive with its narrow streets, pretty steeple and castle (renovation in progress). There are flamingos on the lake's wild, natural banks, and some fishermen's huts, rebuilt in local style.

AQUARIUM Bd de la Jetée ✆ 04 68 80 49 64. *July & August, every day: 10am-8pm. Other periods, closed Monday, open 10am-12 noon and 2pm-6pm. Admission: adult 5.60 €, child 3.50 €.* 54 tanks containing 350 species from all 5 continents, including some strange tropical fish.

MUSEE DU BATEAU ET DE L'AUTOMOBILE Parking des Balcons du Front de Mer ✆ 04 68 73 12 43. *July & August, open every day: 2pm-8pm. Out of season, closed Tuesday, open 2pm-6pm. Admission: adult 4 €, child 3 €.* One of these museums illustrates automobile development in the 20thc. The other deals with sailing history, from the brightly coloured Catalan boat to the aircraft carrier Clemenceau. The scale models are remarkably accurate and true-to-life.

Elne

The upper town overlooks the plain from its mound, and boasts one of France's most elegant cathedrals and cloisters.

ELNE CATHEDRAL & CLOISTER ✆ 04 68 22 70 90. *Open every day except 1 January, 1 May and 25 December (opening hours vary according to season). Admission: 5 € including cloister and Terrus museum.* Built from the 11thc. onwards, and reshaped several times to add Gothic decoration, this is a massive and austere cathedral, overshadowed by its tower with open bays on two storeys. It contains some interesting medieval works by Catalan artists, like the richly worked marble stoup. The beautiful 12thc. cloister's southern gallery is Romanesque; the other three sides are Gothic. The capitals sculpted in white, blue-veined marble, depict fantastic animals, plants and flowers and Biblical characters.

MUSEE TERRUS Rue Porte-Balaguer ✆ 04 68 22 88 88. *Open every day, June-September:10am-7pm. April & May: 10am-6pm. October-March: 10am-12 noon and 2pm-5pm.Admission: adult 1,80.* Maillol's friend and an excellent watercolour artist, Terrus was born in Elne in 1857. He loved this region, and drew his inspiration from its landscapes.

VIEILLE VILLE. The remains of the upper town date back to the 14thc. Steep and pretty streets, quiet squares and ancient houses can be found round the cathedral, by following the discovery trail. A few galleries near Rue Porte-Balaguer recall the town's artistic associations.

Tautavel

This Corbières village lies in a pretty valley on the Aude border, 30km north-west of Perpignan. Its steep alleys, ruined feudal castle perched on a headland and blue limestone cliffs are charming, but Tautavel's claim to fame is the discovery 30 years ago of Europe's oldest skull, dating back about 450,000 years. A museum was opened, along with an international university research centre specialising in archeology and paleontology, changing Tautavel's face and opening the door to mass tourism.

LA CAUNE ARAGO. Tautavel Man's excavation site is 3km from the village, open to the public from April to late August. You have a beautiful view of the valley from its heights. In season, a little tourist train links the village with the cave and picturesque Gouleyrous Gorges.

MUSEE DE TAUTAVEL Ave. Leon-Jean Grégory ✆ 04 68 29 07 76. *www.tautavel.com. Open all year. Opening hours vary according to season:10am-7pm in high season. Admission (museum & exhibition): 7 €* Meet Tautavel Man, and learn about his hostile environment and way of life via 800,000 objects and tools, scenes of prehistoric life and a film about savage prehistoric survival shown on a giant screen.

CATHAR CASTLES

Quéribus castle

The word 'Cathar' comes from the Greek katharos, meaning 'pure'. The Cathars were partisans of a purer Christianity, closer to Gospel teaching than the corrupt Catholic church of the time. They rejected the sacraments of baptism, marriage and even communion, not believing in Christ's resurrection nor his incarnation in the bread and wine. The Gospel forbids swearing, so they refused to take the oath on which the whole feudal society was based. This attitude challenged the established powers, who pronounced it to be heresy, and Rome launched a crusade 'against Albi' in the early 13thc. In 1233, Pope Gregory IX undertook to wipe out Catharism, by founding the Inquisition, a whole penal and legal system. It was so methodical and effective that in barely a century, the new religion had disappeared. The Church had succeeded in enforcing one single power and religion...for the time being.

Lastours

You come across some impressive ruins along this footpath; proud-looking but sadly damaged. Quertinheux is the first castle: one tower and a bit of wall are left. The second, Fleurdespine, is totally ruined; few remains of its fortifications are to be seen. Next comes the Tour Régine, whose round tower stands erect, despite the section of wall crumbled at its feet. The last castle is Cabaret, a squat keep behind a fairly well-preserved wall.

Château de Villerouge-Termenes

This striking 13th and 14thc. castle has been perfectly restored: the towers in particular are superb. It was built round a quadrangle, with a tower at each corner; the biggest served as a keep. An audiovisual guided tour explains Catharism and local life in the 14thc.

Château de Termes

It is hard to believe that these ruins were once a family stronghold, belonging to the powerful Termes seigneurie. The ticket office in the village houses a photo exhibition on illuminated texts, and you find objects excavated on the castle site upstairs.

Château de Puivert

Little remains of the original building; the imposing keep was put up two centuries later. It was owned by the Congost family, strongly Cathar and protector of troubadours. The village museum near the castle contains a restored medieval kitchen and examples of Middle Ages crafts. Upstairs are medieval musical instruments.

Château de Puilaurens

Perched 700m above sea-level, this is one of the best-preserved Cathar castles. Louis IX had it fortified, and for 400 years it was France's most southerly citadel - and the last Cathar stronghold to fall. You climb up through the forest (about 15 mins) to reach the fortress, and admire its machicolation, battlements and loopholes.

Château de Peyrepertuse

This must be Languedoc's finest medieval military building. It looks impossible to reach, up on those breathtaking cliffs, and you don't fancy driving up such a narrow road on the edge of a sheer drop! Once there, however, you have a panoramic view as far as the Mediterranean coast from the plateau overhanging Saint-Jordi Keep.

Château de Quéribus

Built on a rocky spur reaching 750m, this fortress has three surrounding walls and a massive keep, containing the fine'Pillar Room'. The vault has superb intersecting ribs.

MONTPELLIER

This regional capital has plenty of character, and is deeply attached to both the inland winegrowing country and the sea.

ANTIGONE. Catalan architect Ricardo Bofill designed this modern quarter for 1980s Montpellier, enabling the town to grow beyond its limits.

SAINT PIERRE CATHEDRAL. *Open every day: 9am-12 noon and 2.30pm-7pm (Saturday: 6.15pm).* Pope Urban V had a chapel added to Saint Benoît College in 1363, which became Saint Pierre Cathedral when Montpellier was made a bishopric in 1536. Devastated during the Wars of Religion, it was rebuilt in several stages (17th and 19thc.) contrasting with its stark front and 14thc. porch.

JARDIN DES POTIERS Rue du Faubourg de Nîmes. Before starting work on the tramway, an archeological dig was held, and the base of a 12thc. chapel (Saint Esprit Order) was excavated. You can see it in this archeological park (by the big staircases along the Corum), along with a rebuilt Pila Saint-Gély Royal Gate, in the shade of cypresses and an olive tree.

AGROPOLIS MUSEUM 951, ave. Agropolis © 04 67 04 75 00. *www.museum.agropolis.fr. Open every day except Tuesday: 2pm-6pm. Admission: adult 5 €, concessions 3 €, under-10s free. Group tour every afternoon by appointment, or first Thursday of the month at 3pm (6.50 € each).* Learn about the role of food in human culture with the exhibition 'Food and agriculture in the world', leading to 'Humanity's Banquet', a scientific and artistic presentation of different diets around the world. This scientific museum, closely linked to the Agropolis scientists, houses both permanent and temporary exhibitions, with activities for adults and kids, conferences and a cyber-museum.

MUSEE FABRE 39, bd Sarrail © 04 67 14 83 00. Work in progress! By 2006, the museum will have trebled in size, housing 900 pictures compared to 600 today.

CH'TEAU DE FLAUGERGUES 1, 744 ave. A. Einstein © 04 67 65 51 72. *Gardens open every day in summer, except Sunday and public holidays June-September: 8.30am-10.30am and 2.30pm-6.30pm. Guided tour inside by appointment. Admission: adult 7,50 €.* This beautiful 'folly' was reshaped in the early 18thc. to look like an Italian villa. A monumental staircase takes up a quarter of the inside, decorated with 17thc, tapestries and leading to ancient rooms full of precious things. The gardens stretch out below, lined by the property's vines.

JARDIN DES PLANTES 163, rue A. Broussonnet © 04 67 63 43 22. *www.jardindesplantes-montpellier.com. Open every afternoon. Closed Monday. Admission free.* A real historic monument, created by Henri IV's edict of 1593, to grow medicinal plants for use by the Faculty of Medicine. Restoration work is underway, but the part still open to the public contains the Archaeological Mountain and its Phillyrea with the hollow trunk, once a lovers' letter-box; Ecole de Candolle; arboretum; Bambouseraie (bamboo garden) and Jardin Anglais (landscape garden) with the Nelombos Pool. Well worth the trip, especially for romantics.

PARC ZOOLOGIQUE DU LUNARET Ave du Val de Montferrand © 04 67 54 45 23. *www.zoo-montpellier.fr. Open every day, 15 May-15 September: 9am-7pm. Winter: 9am-5. pm. Admission free.* Lions, bears, rhinos, zebras, buffalo, ostrich, antilopes, stags, panthers and birds live in these 80ha. of

Uncommon sites

LAC DU SALAGOU. Not far from Montpellier, Salagou Lake lies in the middle of a fabulous landscape featuring red mountains, vineyards and wooded scrubland. This deep red mountain colour against the intense blue of sky and water seems almost unreal.You have a marvellous view of the lake from Liausson Village on the hillside. On the nearby Lieude site, some mysterious animal prints have been uncovered.

CIRQUE DE MOUREZE. A short distance from Lake Salagou's red banks you find Moureze Village, surrounded by some surprising scenery extending over 8km. Gigantic limestone pillars (dolomites) strike up into the sky, some of them very oddly-shaped. This stone forest was sculpted by erosion, and is the most extensive one of its kind in France. Moureze itself, located at the bottom of the moon landscape, is also well worth a visit.

PIC SAINT-LOUP. Overlooking the scrubland, this majestic peak rises to 658m above sea-level, and boasts some original and interesting plant and animal life. If you manage to climb the southern face, you'll be rewarded by an immense panoramic view from the Cevennes to the sea, and from Mont Ventoux to the Caroux Massif. Breathtaking! You can also go rock-climbing, gliding and potholing. At your feet lies Matelles, a medieval village with a fascinating past. The site is listed as being of 'superior interest'.

Mediterranean forest. Discover some rare species, such as the bongo, Tibetan takin and Iberian wolf, with the help of the explanatory panels. There are regular guided tours of the wildlife park and nature reserve.

Villeneuve-les-Maguelone

MAGUELONE CATHEDRAL. Admission free (there is a car-park fee). A music festival takes place here in June. Maguelone Cathedral stands on an islet of vines and pine trees between the Prévost lake and the sea. Montpellier's bishopric had its headquarters in this Romanesque building from the 5th-11thc. The primitive church was pulled down in the 8thc. after being retaken from the Saracens, and rebuilt in the early 12thc. The polygonal chevet and vaulted apse date back to this period. From 1158-1178, the original nave was replaced by the present barrel vault with its conchiferous limestone walls. The tympanum on the west portal is carved in pure white marble representing Christ in His Majesty surrounded by the Evangelists. The cathedral was recently given some contemporary stained glass windows in a refined style that suits the architecture.

HERAULT AND LANGUEDOC COAST

Hérault

Béziers

Capital of a winegrowing region, Béziers also made its fortune from the Canal du Midi in its heyday. The canal is now only a tourist attraction, but the vines are still going strong. You can make out Saint Nazaire Cathedral from far off, up on the town heights. Beziers is also characterised by the River Orb, and the growing fame of its annual feria.

SAINT APHRODISE BASILICA Place Saint Aphrodise. This pre-Romanesque basilica was reshaped in Gothic times, and named after a Bishop of Béziers. Inside, the font has been made in a 3rdc. sarcophagus representing a lion hunt. In the chancel, Christ on the Cross was sculpted by Injalbert.

SAINT NAZAIRE CATHEDRAL Plan des Albigeois. The imposing, fortified cathedral overlooks Béziers from its rocky headland.

SAINT JACQUES CHURCH Place Saint Jacques. Former Augustinian abbey church, and a masterpiece of pure Romanesque art.

HOTEL FABREGAT Place de la Révolution & 04 67 28 38 78. *Open Tuesday-Friday:9am-12 noon and 2pm-6pm. Closed Sunday morning and Monday. Admission: 2.50 €. Guided tour by appointment. Ticket including Musee Biterrois and Espace Riquet: 3 €.* The Fine Arts Museum contains paintings and sculptures from the 15thc. to the present, but also a gallery of Jean Moulin's drawings, this being the famous resistant's birthplace. The museum's oldest pieces are upstairs: a Greek cup (4thc. B.C.) and some Merovingian sculptures.

MUSEE DES BEAUX-ARTS Place de la Révolution ✆ 04 67 28 38 78. *Open Tuesday-Friday; 9am-12 noon and 2pm-6pm. Admission: adult 2.45 €. Ticket 5.20 € includes the Biterrois Museum and Espace Riquet.* The Fine Arts Museum contains a beautiful collection of paintings and sculpture from the 15thc. to modern times. There is a gallery of Jean Moulin's drawings, the famous wartime Resistance hero being a native of Beziers. The oldest exhibits are on the first floor: a Greek dish dating back to the 4thc. B.C. and some Merovingian sculptures.

Lodève

This historic town with its architectural treasures is on the N9, just after Montpellier. Carpet weaving brought prosperity, as you can see from the many magnificent private mansions.

SAINT FULCRAN CATHEDRAL. Lodève was a bishopric from the 4thc. to the Revolution, and has a striking fortified cathedral.

MUSEE FLEURY Square Georges Avric ✆ 04 67 88 86 10. *Open Tuesday-Sunday: 9.30am-12 noon and 2pm-6pm. Admission: adult 4, 6 € during the summer exhibition.* Housed in the Cardinal de Fleury's beautiful mansion, this museum has some interesting regional geology and paleontology collections. Gallo-Roman remains and disc-shaped steles are on display, along with Paul Dardé's sculptures. Works by Dufy, Caillebotte and Poliakof were added in 2002, on loan from a private collection. Every summer, the museum organises two big temporary exhibitions of paintings.

ATELIER NATIONAL DE TISSAGE DE TAPIS DE LODEVE Ave. Du Général de Gaulle ✆ 04 67 96 40 40. *Open Tuesday, Wednesday & Thursday:1pm-3.30pm. Admission: adult 3,20 €, concessions 3 €.* This is the Manufacture des Gobelins' only annex, opened in 1966 as part of the Manufacture de la Savonnerie. The models are made from artists' cartoons for State collections and exhibitions.

Lunel

Lunel is not far from the Gard border, in open countryside full of vineyards, fruit trees (apples) and market gardens.

NOTRE DAME CHURCH. This is a remarkable building, both for its Jesuit front and its outside steeple, raised at the end of the church on a former medieval watchtower. Inside, don't miss the 19thc. font and listed organ built in 1856 by A. Cavaillé-Coll.

HOTELS PARTICULIERS. The town has kept several of these mansions: the 18thc. Hôtel du Bernis (Rue Emile Zola), 18thc. Hôtel de Brignac façade (near the Cours Gabriel Péri) and houses of different periods along the Rue de la Libération.

Minerve

One of Hérault's finest sites. The village is built on a rocky outcrop between the Cesse and Brian Gorges. Start at the foot of La Candela, a ruined octagonal tower; go through the low gate and down to the Cesse. The river has dug out two natural bridges (110m and 200m long with a 40m-high opening) at this point; it is nearly always dry, so you can walk along the bed, facing the elements and feeling small.

MUSEE DE FIGURINES HUREPEL 5, rue des Martyrs ✆ 04 68 91 12 26. *Open every day, April-September. By appointment out of season. Admission: adult 2.50 €, 14-18s 2 €* The Cathar story told by figurines in strikingly realistic scenes. Each santon is hand-made and details are added to the scenery every year. Commentary available in eight languages. Instructive and fun.

Olargues

One of France's finest villages, Olargues is extremely picturesque, perched in the hills with its 13thc. Pont du Diable (Devil's Bridge) and castle church tower. Time stands still in the narrow alleys lined with pretty medieval houses.

MUSEE DES ARTS ET TRADITIONS POPULAIRES Escalier de la Commanderie Mairie ✆ 04 67 97 71 26. *www.olargues.org. Open every day in summer:15h-18h. Admission free, contributions welcome.* Olargues' agricultural and trading past is illustrated on several floors of a town house.

Pézenas

Not to be missed on a visit to Languedoc. This little town's private mansions are architecturally striking, and hide some remarkable courtyards (just push open the doors!) Molière stayed here in the 17thc. and has never been forgotten.

PLACE GAMBETTA. The Tourist Office is housed in Gély's barbers' shop, where Molière liked to eavesdrop, no doubt finding inspiration for his plays! The consul's house opposite is now the Maison des Métiers d'Art; the 18thc. front hides an earlier building (1552).

The province States were held here several times during the 17thc.

HOTELS PARTICULIERS. Scattered through the town centre, each house has its own particular charm and striking architecture.

MUSEE DE LA PORTE 7, Rue Montmorency ✆ 04 67 98 35 05. *Open every day (Sunday afternoon only). July & August, late night opening Wednesday & Friday: 9pm-11pm. Admission free.* Discover a collection of 15th-20thc. doors of all shapes and sizes, with their ironwork: locks and bolts, catches, strap hinges, knockers, wrought-iron nails.

Roquebrun

This little medieval village is nicknamed 'Little Nice', and seems to be climbing up the mountain side from the Orb river banks, shared by some old 17thc. mills and the square. The ruins of an earlier village and feudal tower overlook the Mediterranean garden laid out below.

JARDIN MEDITERRANEEN ✆ 04 67 89 55 29. *Open mid-February to mid-November. Admission: adult 4.50 €.* This magnificent plant reserve displays over 400 Mediterranean and exotic species on its terraces. A superb site.

The Languedoc Coast

The Catalan blend of land and sea makes this an especially lively coastal area.

Agde

Known as the Mediterranean's Black Pearl, Agde is France's oldest town after Marseille. It was a medieval fortress and wealthy Renaissance bourg, and has several different faces to offer the visitor. Across the Hérault lies Grau d'Agde and the end of Richelieu Beach, reached by a ferry.

SAINT ETIENNE CATHEDRAL. This 12thc. fortified Romanesque church on the banks of the Herault is surprisingly black, built of volcanic stone with 2-3m-thick walls, machicolation and battlements.

Cap d'Agde

A typical 1970s seaside resort, bringing the coast within everyone's reach. 140,000 people spend their summer holidays here, against 3,000 inhabitants in winter. There is a huge marina with 2,234 moorings, surrounded by shop and restaurant-lined quays catering for every tourist need.

AQUARIUM 11, rue des Deux Frères © 04 67 26 14 21. *www.aquariumagde.com. Open every day: 2pm-6pm. July & August: 10am-11pm. Admission: adult 6.50 €, 6-12s 4 €* Meet seahorses, octopus, sharks, jellyfish, moray eels and groupers in the Mediterranean and Tropical sections. Their 30 seawater pools are filled with rocks and coral, and the water is regularly changed. On-site cinema.

FORT BRESCOU © 04 67 94 29 68. *Organised tour for groups by appointment, from April onwards. 15 June-10 September, open every day.* You reach this volcanic islet off the Cap by boat from the Cap or Grau d'Agde. It is mostly taken up with a 17thc. fortress built from Vauban's plans, which served as a prison in the 18thc.

MUSEE DE L'EPHEBE Mas de la Clape © 04 67 94 69 60. *Open every day: 9am-12 noon and 2pm-6pm. Admission: adult 4 €, concessions 1.60 €, under-8s free.* A museum to please fans of underwater archeology. Ephèbe is a Greek bronze statue, 2,300 years old, discovered in the Hérault in 1964, and adopted by the the town as its symbol.

Etang de Thau

Between this lake and the sea, a narrow strip of coast holds the town of Sète, its Mont Saint Clair and harbour. Lake Thau itself is huge, with plenty of room for oysterbeds, the Canal du Midi (running through it), and leisure activities like sailing and windsurfing. There are fishing villages all around the lake: Bouzigues, Mèze, Marseillan and Balaruc, a small spa reflected in the water.

La Grande-Motte

Built in 1962 by architect Jean Balladur in avant-garde style (pyramids rising from an ocean of greenery), this resort aims to be up to date. An ideal holiday site for sports fans and the geometrically-minded.

AQUARIUM PANORAMIQUE Le Port © 04 67 56 85 23. *Open every day. Admission: adult 5 €, under-14s 3.50 €, under-5s free.* A number of tanks contain over 400 fish and invertebrates from the Mediterranean and tropical seas (especially sharks).

Marseillan

Originally a fishing port, Marseillan made its fortune in the wine trade in the early 20thc. Today, it is a Canal du Midi outlet, and a pleasant port of call for sailors and yachtsmen. The beach is magnificent, and can be reached by train (the department's only resort with a rail link); it is 1.6km from the nearest station.

NOILLY PRAT 1, rue de Noilly © 04 67 77 20 15. *Open every day, 1 March-31 December: 10am-12 noon and 2.30pm-6pm. Tour and tasting session 3,50 €* You pass impressive rows of bottles on your way through the storeroom where secret mixtures are made. The tasting starts with the traditional dry, then the red (made for export) and amber.

Palavas-les-Flots

This well-known resort falls victim to the popular family holiday stereotype, with lots of huge campsites. Don't believe all you hear: Palavas is a pleasant place, with lively canal banks and plenty of atmosphere.

MUSEE DU TRAIN Parc du Levant ✆ 04 67 68 56 41. *Enquire about opening hours.* The Train Museum was opened in 1996, and recalls the days of the railway line linking Palavas to Montpellier from 1872-1968. An exhibition of train illustrations by artist Albert Dubout brings back the memories. Guided visit for groups (10+ people).

PHARE DE LA MEDITERRANEE. The 'lighthouse' is in fact a mushroom-shaped water tower now housing the Tourist Office. The walkway on top provides a splendid view of the region, and a revolving panoramic restaurant invites you to eat while admiring it.

Sète

One of the Mediterranean's most promising towns, 183m up on Mont Saint Clair, reputed for its heritage, gastronomy, tourism and sport, among other things. Writer Paul Valéry and singer-songwriter George Brassens were born here. The traditional Saint Louis jousting, where red boats oppose blue like modern-day knights, is a highlight of the social calendar, and a family ritual, handed down from father to son.

VILLE BASSE. Sometimes called the Languedoc Venice, for its canals linking Lake Thau to the sea.

MONT SAINT CLAIR. Overlooking the lower town, with a clear view in all directions over Thau and the Cévennes. You reach the top via the steps, to find a viewpoint indicator among the pines, and some small footpaths.

ESPACE BRASSENS Bd Camille Blanc ✆ 04 67 53 32 77. *Open every day, except Monday out of season. Admission: adults 5 €, over-10s 2 €.* Brassens himself guides you through headphones, telling you the secrets of his life and career. The first part of the exhibition is biographical, the second in the video room projects documentary material, and the third takes a thematic look at the artiste's songs.

MUSEE PAUL VALERY Rue François Desnoyer ✆ 04 67 46 20 98. *Open every day: 10am-12 noon and 2pm-6pm, closed Tuesday and public holidays out of season. Admission: summer,3 to 4.60 € (including temporary exhibition), out of season 3 €, under-12s free.* The setting is marvellous, above the sailors' graveyard overlooking the sea. Sète and its artists (18th and 19thc) are exhibited on the ground floor. Upstairs, in the Paul Valéry Room, the writer's artistic talent is on display. Temporary exhibitions and local contemporary artists are also given space on this floor.

M.I.A.M. 23, quai Maréchal de Lattre de Tassigny ✆ 04 67 18 64 00. *Open every day except Tuesday out of season: 10am-12 noon and 2pm-6pmClosed Monday from 2006 onwards. Admission: adult 5 €, over-10s 1.50 €, under-10s free, first Sunday of the month free for all.* The acronym is a joke (French for 'yum yum'), and stands for 'Musée International des Arts Modestes', exhibiting those simple examples of graphic art (wrappings, promotional free gifts, etc) that our post-modern age takes for granted.

Sète, houses near the port

NÎMES AND THE GARD

This little region is caught between Rhône and Vidoule, garrigue and marsh, a rich past heritage and an industrial and technological future.

Nîmes

Capital of the Gard, this Roman town hosts three bullfighting ferias a year, but is also an elegant and sophisticated cultural centre.

MAISON CARREE. *Open summer: 9am-12noon and 2.30pm-7pm, winter: 9am-12.30pm and 2pm-6pm. Closed 1 May, 25 December, 1 January. Admission free.* Built in 5 A.D., dedicated to Caius and Lucius Cesar (Emperor Augustus' son and grandson) this Square House was the consuls' meeting place. Its geometric shape is strict but harmonious, and Corinthian capitals decorate the columns. The pronaos ceiling and entrance are both 19thc.

CARRE D'ART Place de la Maison Carrée ✆ 04 66 76 35 35. Designed by architect Sir Norman Foster, the Carré d'Art covers 13,000 m^2. and like the Pompidou Centre in Paris, houses a library, mediatheque, workshops and the Contemporary Art Museum, containing 300 works, from the 1960s to the present day.

ARENES. *Open summer: 9am-7pm, winter: 9am-6pm.* Nîmes amphitheatre was an architectural feat in Roman times, seating 25,000 spectators on 34 tiers. They came to watch gladiators; since the late 19thc. the public has been filling the amphitheatre again, to see Spanish bullfighting.

JARDINS DE LA FONTAINE Quai de la Fontaine. *Open 8am-8pm. Admission free.* Maréchal and Dardaihon laid out these gardens in the 18thc. and in doing so, found Gallo-Roman remains, still visible today. Decorated with marble, thermae and statues, this is one of Europe's most beautiful walks.

TOUR MAGNE Jardin de la Fontaine - Chemin Guillaume Laforêt ✆ 04 66 67 65 56. *Open summer: 9am-7pm, winter: 9am-5pm Admission: adult 2,60 €.* Only remaining tower of the 80 once positioned round the ramparts. It looks like a lighthouse, permanently lit up, and can be seen from all roads leading into the town. It has lost its top floor, reaching 32m nowadays.

TEMPLE DE DIANE Jardin de la Fontaine. Was this a temple, sanctuary or library in antique times? Diana's temple keeps its secret, content to be beautiful, and to inspire so many architects.

CASTELLUM Rue de la Lampèze. This Roman monument is unique. It used to channel water from the Pont du Gard through lead pipes, for the town's consumption. You can still see the circular reservoir.

Nîmes, Maison Carrée

CATHEDRAL Place aux Herbes. Take time to admire the tall friezes on this 900-year-old façade, bearing traces of different periods. Inside, each passing civilisation has left a small chapel as its mark.

MUSEE DES BEAUX ARTS Rue Cité-Foulc ✆ 04 66 67 38 21. *Open every day: 10am-6pm except monday.* The museum contains Roman mosaics found in Nîmes (in the covered market) and paintings from the 17th-19thc. French, Flemish, Italian, and Dutch schools. Two of Henri Bouchard's statues frame the entrance. Temporary painting exhibitions, Classical and Baroque concerts and activity workshops for kids take place here too.

Southern Cévennes

This magnificent region stretching from the Gard to the Haute-Loire is of great historical interest, and boasts a variety of landscapes and tourist attractions.

Alès

This former mining town has turned its slag heaps into green, wooded hills. Under its peaceful bourgeois cover, Alès is a Protestant working-class community: France's first Reformed Church was founded here in 1560.

COLLINE DE L'HERMITAGE. Imposing ruins of a Pre-Roman oppidum wall can be seen on the top of this hill, along with Notre Dame des Mines Chapel, which is a pilgrimage site.

SAINT JEAN CATHEDRAL. Built on the ruins of a Roman temple in the old town centre, the cathedral chancel boasts a superb grand organ.

FORT VAUBAN. The citadel began as a prison for Protestants, and is still in use as the current Alès Prison. Though you can't visit the fort, you can always stroll on the terraces and admire the Bosquet gardens.

MUSEE PIERRE ANDRE BENOIT 52, montée des Lauriers ✆ 04 66 86 98 69. *Open 1 September-30 June: 2pm-6pm (closed Monday). July & August, every day: 2pm-7pm. Closed in February. Admission free.* The Modern Art Museum is really fascinating, thanks to editor and collector Benoît's donation. His collection includes works by Braque, Picabia, Picasso, Miró And the Pre-Cubists.

ESPACE DE LA MINIATURE Montee des Lauriers - Rochebelle ✆ 04 66 55 63 32. *Open 1 October-31 May: 10am-12 noon and 2pm-5pm (closed Tuesday). 1 June-30 September: 10am-12 noon and 2pm-6pm.* Housed in the Verrerie de Rochebelle, a disused industrial site near two big local museums. 17,000 miniatures are exhibited in the stables: 50 or so showcases of trains, planes and cars to thrill the imaginations of both big and little boys (and girls!)

MINE TEMOIN Chemin de la Cité Saint Marie - Rochebelle ✆ 04 66 30 45 15. *Open April, May, September, October & November: 9.30am-12.30pm and 2pm-5.30pm. June: 9am-6.30pm. July & August: 10am-7.30pm.? Admission: adult 6.70 €, child 3.50 €* The history of Cévennes mining from 1230 to the present, in 650m of galleries dug out of Montaud Hill. A 20-minute video gives you an idea of what life was like here in the past.

Anduze

The town has kept the fountains in its alleys and its Tour de l'Horloge (Clocktower), and the central square is pleasant in summer, under the terrace parasols.

MUSEE DE LA MUSIQUE 4, route d'Ales ✆ 04 66 61 86 60. *July, August & Easter and autumn school holidays: open every day. Other periods: open Sundays and public holidays: 2.30pm-6pm. Closed in January & February.* Over 1,000 instruments are exhibited, with a number of training courses and concerts on offer. You can learn to beat the bamboos in a lively atmosphere, which promotes the world's music.

TRAIN A VAPEUR DES CEVENNES ✆ 04 66 85 13 17. *Runs every day: 26 March-11 September; every day except Monday: 13 September-1 November. Train leaves from Anduze at 9.30am, 11.30am, 3pm and 5pm. Disabled access. Admission (round trip): adult 11 €, 4-12s 7 €* This friendly and colourful little train runs between Anduze and Saint Jean du Gard (13km), via the Vallee du Gardon's tunnels and bridges. You can stop off at the bamboo garden between two trains (admission not included in the ticket price),

Champlauson

FORET DE FOSSILLES ✆ **04 66 60 34 65**. *Open April-September and Sunday in low season. Disabled access to site and train.* Only site of its kind in the Cevennes. Open since July 2005. Come and visit the Fossil Forest by little train. The trip starts in the museum, where you can see fossilized plants and tree trunks, and continues by train through a Mediterranean forest with a beautiful panoramic view. Once in the Fossil Forest, you'll be amazed by the trees fossilized in life-like positions.

Générargues

This authentic village in the Cévennes heights contains two traditional museums, and is in itself well worth a visit.

LA BAMBOUSERAIE ✆ **04 66 61 70 47**. *www.bambouseraie.fr. Open 9.30am onwards all week. Closed 15 November-1 March. Admission: adult 7,50* This bewitching corner of the Far-East was designed in 1855. You need at least 2 hours to see the whole bamboo garden: the luxuriant forest of greenhouses full of colourful flowers; Oriental cabins; purple lotuses; water garden and of course, shops; but once under its exotic spell, you will surely want to stay longer.

MUSEE DU SANTON Place du Tilleul ✆ **04 66 61 66 74**. *Open school holidays, June & September: 2pm-7pm. July & August: 10am-7pm. Other periods, Wednesday, Saturday & Sunday: 2pm-6pm.* After the Bambouseraie's Far Eastern exotic atmosphere, you rediscover Provence, and its traditional carved santons. This animated museum contains over 200 of them, and you can take back some original Christmas presents from the souvenir shop..

Uzès

Cool streets and charming inland scenery, between sea and Cévennes.

VIEILLE VILLE Office de Tourisme ✆ **04 66 22 68 88**. *15. June-15 September. 2-hr tour starts from the Tourist Office.* Uzès has been completely restored, and this tour takes you through its alleys, streets and squares with a commentary from the Ministry of Culture-approved guide. Medieval towers and mansions with their hidden courtyards and gardens give you an idea of Uzès' importance in regional history.

SAINT THEODORIT CATHEDRAL. Rebuilt several times since the 17thc., the cathedral gained a Neo-Romanesque façade in 1873. Inside, a listed classical French organ framed with 17thc. painted volets benefits from excellent acoustics.

LE DUCHE. The Ducs d'Uzès go back to the 10thc.; their castle is a huge, four-sided fortress with three towers.

JARDIN MEDIEVAL Impasse Port-Royal ✆ **04 66 22 38 21**. *Open 1 April-1 November.* A sumptuous medieval-style herb garden, housed in the Château Raynon (one of Uzès' two 11thc. castles) at the foot of the Tour du Roi and Tour de l'Evêque.

MUSEE HARIBO Pont des Charettes ✆ **04 66 22 74 39**. *www.haribo.com. Closed Monday out of season, and January. Admission: adult 4.50 €, concessions 3.50 €, 5-15s 2.50 €* Known to all local kids, this sweet museum known has been updated (to keep abreast of new production methods) and has a hands-on approach to the history of sweetmaking, with waxworks, collectors' items, explanatory panels and demonstrations (why not try your hand?) Great fun as well as instructive

Pont du Gard

Now World Heritage-listed, the Pont du Gard became a site in 2000. Discover its archeological, historical and natural aspects in the museum (2,500 m^2) which explains the role of urban architecture and water in Roman civilisation, the building of the aqueduct and its influence. In the kids' area (Ludo), the youngest can become Gallo-Roman pupils, engineers trying to master water and budding archeologists. The film 'Le vaisseau du Gardon' shows you some beautiful pictures of the bridge on a giant screen. You can also follow a 1.4km marked-out path known as 'Mémoires de garrigue' through vineyards, olive groves, cereal plots and oaks with their dry stone walls, and learn about this 2,000-year-old Mediterranean landscape shaped by man. In summer, fans of swimming and leisure activities can try out the beach.

SITE DU PONT DU GARD Route du Pont du Gard - Vers Pont du Gard ✆ 08 25 01 30 3

Le Vigan

Life is gentle in the Southern Cévennes' 1,000 year-old capital, where fountains play in the medieval streets and gardens.

MUSEE CEVENOL 1, rue des Calquières ✆ 04 67 81 06 86. *Open 1 April-30 October: 10am-12 noon and 2pm-6pm (closed Tuesday). Other periods: Wednesday only. Admission: 4.50 €.* Thousands of exhibits on 3 floors recall past times in the Cévennes. Local history, environment and trades (basket-weaver, glassworker, cobbler, cooper), are on display in one room; some fabulous 18thc. costumes in another.

Petite Camargue

The dyking of river and sea has created these briny shallows choked with reeds, and made a habitat for flamingos, little black bulls and white Camargue horses.

Aigues-Mortes

This medieval harbour is linked to the sea by a 6km-canal. Built as a bastide, it attracts plenty of tourists in season.

REMPART AND TOUR DE CONSTANCE ✆ 04 66 53 61 55. Aigues-Mortes' powerful fortifications are intact, thanks to the surrounding lagunas. You should see them in the evening, melting into the light on the lakes...most striking from the Plan, on the Grau-du-Roi road.

PLACE SAINT LOUIS. This is the village square; the heart of the medieval city. Saint Louis (king from 1226-1270) had Aigues-Mortes built for its port, to set sail for the Holy Land. The second trip was fatal, since he died of plague in Tunis. His bronze statue can be seen in the square.

CAPUCHIN CHAPEL Place Saint Louis ✆ 04 66 53 38 60 *Open Tuesday, Wednesday and Thursday in winter: 11am-12.30pm and 4pm-8pm. Open every day except Tuesday in season.* This 17thc. exhibition centre mostly houses contemporary works: Viallat, Nîmes Fine Arts School and many others.

PENITENTS CHAPEL Place Saint Louis ✆ 04 66 53 73 00. Contains a magnificent stucco reredos, a Carrare marble altar and some striking stained glass windows.

SALINS DU MIDI ✆ 04 66 70 40 24. *www.salins.com. Open every day March-October.* 'Saunier de Camargue' sea salt comes from a magnificently wild natural site in the heart of the Camargue. The saltmarsh's flora and fauna can be discovered from a little train or open-topped bus, with the ecomuseum and souvenir shop for later.

Le Grau-du-Roi

Before to Saint Louis' harbour at Aigues-Mortes, where he took ship for the crusades. The village developed round its fishing harbour before tourist attractions were thought of, but now the amazing 'town' of Port-Camargue, Boucanet Beach and Espiguette dunes have made this grau popular as well as royal.

MUSEE DE LA MER Ave. du Palais de la Mer ✆ 04 66 51 57 57. *www.seaquarium.fr. Open every day. January-April: 10am-7pm. May, June & September: 10am-8pm. July & August: 10am-midnight. Entrance via the Seaquarium. Admission: adult 10* This museum recalls Grau-du-Roi's fishing village history, and the sailors who put happily out to sea. It contains a number of treasures brought up from the depths: amphorae, shells, wrecks etc.

SEAQUARIUM Ave. du Palais de la Mer ✆ 04 66 51 57 57. *www.seaquarium.fr. Open every day. January-April: 10am-7pm. May, June & September: 10am-8pm. July & August: 10am-midnight. Free car-park. Disabled access. Caters for groups. Activities & events.* Twinned with the Sea Museum, to create a marine complex. Includes Aagiant tank holding sea mammals, shark tunnel, panoramic amphitheatre for sea-lions and seals and an underwater observatory. Complete and modern.

OBSERVATOIRE DES OISEAUX DE CAMARGUE Route de l'Espiguette ✆ 04 66 73 52 05. *Guided tours by appointment.* Watch some superb birds (terns, flamingos, herons, oyster-catchers and egrets) from this typical Camargue house.

Saint-Gilles

'Gateway to the Camargue', Saint Gilles is an attractive and historic town, with resources in tree- and winegrowing. Its classified costières-de-Nîmes vintages are particularly reputed.

Unusual Gard Sites

CIRQUE DE NAVACELLES. This giant funnel was hollowed out by the Vis, between the Blandas and Larzac causses. The village is hemmed in with its ditch 300m below ground level, making this an extraordinary site. The Navacelles Circus and Vis Gorges are among the region's most spectacular natural attractions.

Follow the River Bonheur (which means 'happiness') from Camprieu. Close to Camprieu Village, you can walk along the lake with its dam holding in a little Bonheur. The rock becomes chalky, turning to limestone, and the stream rushes into a fault. The Bonheur seems to have disappeared, but comes out again 600m further on in the famous Bramabiau Chasm, where the torrent carves out the rock into amazing shapes. The river now changes its name and becomes the Bramabiau. You'll be impressed by the great, dark fissure marking the entrance. When the high-flowing water rushes out of this breach, a subdued rumbling echoes up in the mountain: it's an astonishing sight. Immense halls lead one out of the other through narrow winding corridors, with natural wonders to gaze at round each corner. The pedestrian access path running along the mountain side is splendid too. Bramabiau Chasm is the only active underground river of its kind open to the public in France.

ABBEY CHURCH ✆ 04 66 87 41 31. A fine example of regional medieval art, with its Romanesque treble portal, 'Saint Gilles spiral' staircase and France's biggest crypt. This 12thc. church is listed UNESCO World Heritage, as part of the Compostella pilgrimage routes.

MAISON ROMANE ✆ 04 66 87 40 42. *Open all year, except January. Admission free.* A 12thc. listed historic monument, housing the town's Ethnology Museum, The Old Saint Gilles Room contains tools and objects illustrating daily life in the early 19thc.; there are also Camargue, ornithology and Romanesque archeology rooms. On the top floor, you can see a 14thc. statue of Saint Gilles and a medieval fireplace.

On the Rhône route

Beaucaire

SAINT ROMAN ABBEY Route de Nîmes ✆ 04 66 59 52 26. *Open every day April-September; weekend afternoons only in winter.* This abbey, clinging to its rock between Nîmes and Beaucaire, existed in the 5thc. It is fitted out as a monastery, with chapel, necropolis and monks' cells.

NOTRE DAME DES POMMIERS ✆ 04 66 59 26 57. There are bas reliefs on the front, and a frieze narrating Christ's Passion. The guided tour of the town includes this imposing collegiate church.

ESPLANADE DU CHATEAU ✆ 04 66 59 26 72. *Displays in the afternoon, midi-March-early November. Closed Wednesday.* Some impressive birds of prey give a colourful display of flying in the Château de Beaucaire's enchanting setting. Master-falconers in Roman dress take you back in time by making eagles, falcons and hawks fly just over your heads, to music.

VIEUX MAS Route de Fourques ✆ 04 66 59 60 13. *Open every day. Closed in January.* Life in a traditional early-20thc. mas is recreated here, with its animals, agricultural tools and old-fashioned trades. An exhibition traces the development of country life from 1900 to 1950.

Pont-Saint-Esprit

Heavy 13thc. traffic led to a decision to build a bridge where three kingdoms met. 20 arches span 900m of Rhône riverbed. It took 40 years to carry out the work, with the help of the Holy Spirit - hence the name.

MUSEE D'ART SACRE DU GARD *2, rue Saint Jacques ✆ 04 66 39 17 61.* Open every day except Monday. Closed in February.Admission: adult 3 Pont Saint Esprit's major attraction is this religious art museum, not without charm. Housed in a 12thc. mansion, it contains gold and silver plate, reliquaries, pastoral robes, earthenware pharmacist's pots (15th-18thc.), crèches and santons.

Roquemaure

THE COLLEGIATE CHURCH Tourist Office ✆ 04 66 90 21 01. *Open all year, by appointment at the Tourist Office.* This Provençal Gothic collegiate church has been a place of pilgrimage for lovers since it began housing Saint Valentine's relics in 1868.

A reconstruction of the relics' arrival (in traditional dress) is staged on Saint Valentine's Day.

LOZÈRE

A sparsely-populated region, rich in natural produce.

Aubrac

Magnificent, almost deserted landscapes, rough pastures, cows and tomme cheese: this high plateau is also famous for its many plants and flowers.

Lozere castles, fortresses, cathedrals, churches and temples

In 1724, Father L'Ouvreleul counted 136 castles in the Lozere. Even if some of them have disappeared with the passing years, the Cevaudan still has some fine buildings on display, like the Chateau de la Baume at Prinsuejols, Coucoussac, Saint Alban, la Caze, Canilhac, Tournel, Saint Germain, Calberte, Saint Saturnin, Tartaronne, la Garde de Guerin and Chanac - not to mention Villaret Tower and Malzieu, nicknamed 'The pearl in the valley'. As for Lozere's religious monuments, there are a number on both sides of the Tarn Gorges divide - Catholic in the north and Protestant in the south - considered to be real architectural treasures. Don't miss Mende Cathedral, the remains of the early Benedictine monastery at Saint Enimie (refectory and Saint Madeleine chapel), Saint Martin de la Canourgue Church sanctuary (one of the region's finest) Aumont Aubrac Church and the powerful Nasbinais Church in the Cevennes.Only two Protestant temples have resisted the ravages of the Cevennes' turbulent history, at Collet-de-Deze and Vialas.

Prinsuéjols

CHATEAU DE LA BAUME ✆ **04 66 32 51 59.** *Open 10am-12 noon and 2pm-6pm in July & August. By appointment at other periods.* The 18thc. Chateau de la Baume is 17km from Marvejols and is nicknamed 'The Cevaudan Versailles'. It is one of the Lozere's finest castles, beautifully decorated according to Louis XIV's wishes, with Italian influence from the Montpellier painters.

Sainte-Lucie

Thirty years ago, a wildlife park was set up in this unknown hamlet, bringing it suddenly into the public eye. The fantastic site overhangs the Crueize Gorges and Val d'Enfer (Hell Valley).

LOUPS DU GEVAUDAN Sainte-Lucie ✆ **04 66 32 09 22.** *www.loupsdugevaudan.com. Open every day. Summer: 10am-7pm, spring & autumn: -6pm, winter: -5pm. Closed in January. Admission: adult 6.50 €, 5-12s 3.50 € November-March: reduced prices for all. Gevaudan Wolf Park opens 7 of its 22ha. to the public, and offers guided tours (in the admission price) every day.* You can see Canadian, Polish, Siberian and Mongolian wolves in semi-liberty, and finish your tour with the museum exhibition, a blend of myth and reality.

The Cévennes

For centuries, this was Lozère's richest countryside. Terraces (or bancels) mark the landscape; a sign of local efforts to exploit poor soil. Chestnut trees glow yellow and orange in autumn. The violent conflicts provoked by Protestantism united the Cévennes, and forged a particular identity apart from the rest of the region.

Florac

Follow the marked-out route (laid out by the town and Cévennes National Park) through Florac's old alleyways to discover its character. A good starting-point for your tour of the region.

CHATEAU DE FLORAC Maison du Parc National des Cévennes ✆ **04 66 49 53 00**. *www.cevennes-parcnational.fr. Open in summer every day: 9am-6.30pm. Out of season, weekdays: 9.30am-12.30pm and 1.30pm-5.30pm; weekends during school holidays. Admission: adult 3.50 €, concessions 2.50 €.* Cévennes National Park HQ is housed here. Inside, the park's work is illustrated, with maps, guides and information about events and exhibitions on offer, to satisfy all centres of interest.

Gorges du Tarn

The Tarn Valley hesitates between Central and Southern France, with its cool forests and close-cropped grass. Fast-flowing rivers carved imposing gorges out of the rocks, sometimes as deep as 500m, separating bare and arid plateaux known as causses.

Meyrueis

Meaning 'in the middle of the streams', Meyrueis is one of Lozère's southern gateways.

L'AVEN ARMAND Hures-la-Parade ✆ 04 66 45 61 31. *Open mid-March-early November. Admission: adult 8,30 €, under-12s and students 5 €.* This immense aven (cave) - 120m long, 65m wide and 45m at its highest point - could hold Notre Dame de Paris. Instead, it contains the biggest known concentration of stalagmites (the highest reaches 30m).

FERME CAUSSENARDE D'AUTREFOIS Hyelzas ✆ 04 66 45 65 25. *www.ferme-caussenarde.com. Open every day, Easter-All Saints. Admission: adult 5 €, 7-14s 2.10.* On the Causse Méjean, you discover country people's daily life until the 1950s in this typical 18th and 19thc. farm. Furniture, linen, utensils, tools and agricultural machines, old photos and films are on display, along with an animated miniature santon village and some farm animals.

GROTTE DE DARGILAN D139 ✆ 04 66 45 60 20. *www.dargilan.com. Open every day, spring-autumn school holidays. Admission: adult 8 €, 6-18s 5 €.* Martel explored this cave in 1888, it was fitted out for visitors in 1890 and got electric light in 1910. The scene is as beautiful with modern lighting: your path (1km) passes between active concretions in pinkish tones (from their crystallization).

Le Rozier

Gateway to the Lozère causses when you arrive from the Languedoc Plain.

LES ARCS DE SAINT PIERRE Saint Pierre des Tripiers. This community with its many hamlets is a geological site, with amazing shapes formed by erosion. The 'arcs' are 3 arches sculpted in the dolomite. You'll find them along the marked-out path.

BELVEDERE DES VAUTOURS Le Truel ✆ 05 65 62 69 69. *Open mid-March-mid-November, every day: 10am-5pm (July & August 6pm). Admission: adult 6,50 €, child 3 €.* Cevennes National Park and the LPO designed the Vulture Belvedere together: an ideal place to watch and learn about these great birds, thanks to an attractive exhibition using modern technology. The observation terrace is equipped with telescopes, and live images are transmitted from cameras concealed in the vultures' nests. Explanations and commentaries by specialised ornithologist guides.

GORGES DE LA JONTE. From these gorges, a winding road set into the cliffs leads to Saint Pierre des Tripiers, with its Caussenarde architecture (often in pretty bad condition).

Sainte-Enimie

This little village rises in tiers on the steep slopes of two cliffs, in a loop of the Tarn. Walk along the old ramparts, through narrow streets, under vaulted passages and past beautiful restored housefronts in the Place au Beurre or Rue de la Privadenche.

DOMAINE DES BOISSETS Champerboux ✆ 04 66 48 50 73. *Open Easter-October: 10am-5pm every day except Tuesday. 15 June-15 September: 10am-6pm every day. Out of season: groups by appointment. Admission: adult 6 €, under-12s 3 €.* The Boissets hamlet overhangs the Gorges du Tarn, 400m above Sainte Enimie on the edge of the Sauveterre Causse. This departmental centre illustrates and explains gorges and causses, with 6 theme 'houses', each one audioguided. Inside, up-to-date exhibitions go well with the 17thc. architecture. The Petit Train des Causses takes you from Sainte Enimie centre to the site (train and visit 8) and there is a moufflon park nearby.

MUSEE DU VIEUX LOGIS ✆ 04 66 48 53 44. *Open Easter-September, every day: 10am-12 noon and 3pm-5pm, except Monday and Tuesday. July & August, every day: 10am-12 noon and 4pm-8pm, except Saturday and Sunday morning.* One of the Gorges du Tarn's first ecomuseums, housed in a Presbytery outbuilding. Everyday objects throughout the ages are on display, and a video shows you the medieval town, past and present. There is also an exhibition of religious art.

La Margeride

Europe's least-populated region. A low mountain range forms a north-south barrier with high passes, separating the Loire from the Garonne tributaries.

Langogne

For centuries, Langogne's chief resources were forestry and livestock but also wool-weaving.

SAINT GERVAIS ET SAINT PROTAIS CHURCH. The primitive Burgundian Romanesque church dates back to the 11thc. but was reshaped in the 16th and 17thc. following damage in the Wars of Religion. The front has a monumental Flamboyant Gothic portal, and inside, 85 12thc. granite capitals are carved with flower motifs and historic scenes, each different.

FILATURE DES CALQUIªRES 23, rue des Calquières ✆ 04 66 69 25 56. *Open all year, Monday-Saturday: 9am-12 noon and 2pm-6pm. Sunday: 11am-12 noon and 3pm-5pm. Admission: adult 5,50 €, child 3 €*. This old mill in full working order still contains its 19thc. machines worked by paddle wheel.

MUSEE D'ART SACRE. On the first floor of the former presbytery adjoining the church, you find a sumptuous collection of sacerdotal ornaments and objects used in religious rites, all in perfect condition.

Sainte-Eulalie

EUROPEAN BISON PARK ✆ 04 66 31 40 40. *Open all year. Admission: adult 11 €, child 6 €*. European bisons appeared 10,000 years ago, and became extinct in France 1,500 years ago. Here in Margeride, 1,250m above sea-level, they have found exactly the right kind of climate and habitat. 200 hectares of forest and moorland house 35 specimens living (almost) wild. You can visit this nature reserve by barouche, or by sleigh in winter. The Maison du Bison provides information about this impressive animal's history and lifestyle.

Vallée du Lot

Mende

Mainly a business and administrative centre, Mende is lively in summer with its influx of tourists. Start with the imposing cathedral, then Place Urbain V with the Pope's statue, Hôtel Plagnes on the right and the former Bishop's Palace on the left (destroyed by fire in 1887 and rebuilt in Mansart style). From here, wander through the narrow streets and little paved squares with their fountains and houses of character.

NOTRE DAME ET SAINT PRIVAT CATHEDRAL. This huge cathedral recalls the tremendous power of medieval bishops. The chancel contains 18thc. Aubusson tapestries.

MONT MIMAT AND SAINT PRIVAT HERMITAGE. Mont Mimat and its hermitage overlook the town. The belvedere contains a viewpoint indicator, and a huge cross seems to protect local inhabitants.

PONT NOTRE DAME AND TOUR DES PENITENTS. The town's oldest monuments. Notre Dame Bridge and the Penitents' Tower are the remains of Mende's ancient fortifications.

Monts Lozère

With the Rivers Lot and Allier to the north, and the Tarn in the south, these Lozere mountains overlook the department named after them. The Tarn's springs rise in them, while the other two rivers have their sources further north. The granite mass with its gently rounded shapes rises to Finiels Peak at 1,702m above sea level. Further east, Finiels Pass (1,541m) and Cassini Peak (1,680m) mark the ridge, which plunges down into the Cevennes. The massif is part of the Cevennes National Park, particularly rich in plants and wildlife, and the granite tops show above chestnut and fir groves and low-level vegetation. You can hike in any season, or ski in winter, and the mountains are also a good place for nature walks, and water therapy at Bagnols-les-Bains thermal and health resort (04 66 47 60 02).

FOOD AND DRINK

Split between sea and Massif Central foothills, the region has the best produce of both: Mediterranean fruit and seafood; Cevennes meat (lamb and Aubrac beef). The vineyards in the middle get better every year.

Collioure anchovies

Collioure's claim to fame. Fresh anchovies are salted whole, and left in their brine for several days. Heads and guts are removed, and they are stocked in barrels between layers of salt for 3 months. They can be eaten like this, or cleaned, dried, and packed in oil.

Aubrac

This hardy breed of Massif Central cattle used to work in the fields, and is able to withstand the hard winters. Dark brown, with black-ringed eyes, they are easy to recognise. Extensive breeding in pastures for 2-4 years results in tasty red beef, further improved by crossbreeding with Charolais cattle. Note that cantal and laguiole cheese are made with milk from these cows.

Bourride

Baudroie (the Mediterranean name for angler) is cooked in white wine on a bed of vegetables. Before serving, the sauce is thickened with aioli, and the dish is eaten with croutons spread with the fish liver and steamed potatoes.

Cassoulet

The capital is Castelnaudary, but you find it round Carcassonne and in the Pyrénées. It is a mixture of white beans, pork and sausages, cooked for a long time in a 'cassole' (earthenware dish). The more you heat it up, the better it gets! The Grande Confrérie de Castelnaudary (gastronomic society) makes sure cassoulet's origins and quality are respected.

Cheese

The best are from Lozère

The bleu des Causses and bleu d'Auvergne are veined cheeses made from cow's milk, matured 3-6 months. The laguiole is like cantal, made from tomme fraiche. This is known as fourme d'Aubrac, when it has no AOC, and was traditionally made by shepherds in the burons (small dairies in the summer pastures), a practice now dying out.

Roquefort, a veined cheese from ewe's milk, is made in the neighbouring region. The milk comes from several southern departments (including the Lozère causses), but the maturing process takes place in the town itself.

Cassoulet

Fruit

One of France's main fruit suppliers, producing peaches and nectarines (185,000 tonnes), apples (145,000 tonnes), apricots, grapes and cherries.

There is a boom in apricot-growing: Roussillon's red apricots are small, sweet, scented orange fruit with dark red spotted skins, and new varieties are being grown in the Gard.

Cherries are grown in Ceret (Pyrénées-Orientales), Remoulins (Gard) and Olargues (Hérault), but labour costs and the fruit's sensitivity to weather changes are threatening production.

The reinette apple is traditionally grown in the Roussillon and Cévennes Valleys. In the 1960s and 70s, other apple orchards (Golden Delicious etc.) were planted in converted vineyard soil. Roussillon's production of 'Confluent' apples is slowing down, though the Vigan pomme-reinette (Cévennes) is resisting, thanks to the fashion for local produce.

In the 1950s, the Hérault was a big grape-supplier, but massive imports from Italy and Spain and the consumer taste for bigger grapes have hit production badly. The Clermont-l'Hérault sector continues to grow grapes with their collective regional label, but the traditional chasselas only accounts for 40%, and has competitors among the new varieties from the Gard.

Loup

The Atlantic sea bass is sought after for its taste and texture. The fish hatch out in the Languedoc lakes, fatten in summer and reach the sea in November. They are caught using several methods including trawling. A new technique of breeding the fish in ponds ensures regular and calibrated production.

WINE

These vineyards cover a huge surface area (the world's biggest). The winegrowers have made tremendous efforts over the years to improve quality and diversity, and today there are 32 AOC in Languedoc-Roussillon.

CONSEIL INTERPROFESSIONNEL DES VINS DU LANGUEDOC *www.languedoc-wines.com.*

Blanquette de Limoux

In 1531, in the Saint Hilaire Abbey cellars, a monk noticed his corked wine making bubbles - the world's first brut! Limoux wines are even thought to have inspired Dom Perignon. Their pale yellow colour and green apple, acacia flower and hawthorn notes are characteristic.

Cabardès

Aromatic and balanced wines. The powerful reds and rosés have a bouquet of red and exotic fruit, with tobacco, coffee and prune notes developing as they age.

Collioure

Grown in the same soil as banyuls, these vines cover four villages: Collioure, Port-Vendres, Banyuls-sur-Mer and Cerbere. The wine stays in the vat for 6 months, then is bottled and matured in air-conditioned storehouses. The young wine is purple, with a red fruit and spice bouquet. In time, it darkens to mahogany, and venison, leather and truffle notes can be detected; it now goes well with red meat and game.

Corbières

The highest levels of the massif are limestone and shale, then come wide terraces of pebbles, sandstone and marl. Carignan, grenache noir, syrah, mourvedre and cinsault grapes grow here, for red wines: the whites combine grenache, macabeu, bourboulenc, marsanne and rousanne. Languedoc's biggest AOC includes 87 villages and 19,000 classified hectares.

Costières de Nîmes

The reds are rounded and generous, the rosés full of sunshine, and the whites go well with fish or make wonderful apéritifs. In time, the reds gain body and can be eaten with casseroled meat and game.

Coteaux-du-Languedoc

One of the oldest vineyards, stretching from the Gard to the Aude and covering much of the Herault from the hills overlooking Lake Thau to the first Larzac Causse foothills.

Côtes du Roussillon

The main cépage for the reds is carignan (70%) along with grenache. The whites come from macabeu and the local malvoisie du Roussillon grape (tourbat), and are often made from fresh, scented grapes picked before they are ripe. The grape soaking time is reduced for the rosés (called the saignée, or bleeding) and they are very fruity. The reds are made by carbonic soaking; their raspberry and redcurrant aroma, becomes spicy with age. Those that are traditionally macerated have higher tannin content, with Morello cherry, prune and roasted almond notes.

Fitou

Fitou wines have a red fruit aroma, with spicy, peppery and woody notes, maturing into ripe fruit, prune, roasted almond and leather. Full-bodied and rich, they stay long on the palate.

Limoux

These white wines should be made from handpicked grapes and casked straight away. The burnt oak barrels give them a particular flavour, but you can still taste the chardonnay grape. A mixture of three cépages goes into these rich and ample wines.

Malepère

South West and Mediterranean grapes go into these powerful AOC, perfect with red meat, strong cheese and cassoulet. Merlot, cot and cinsault are the chief cépages, with cabernet, grenache and syrah added in lesser proportions.

Maury

Shale soil, 50% grenache and traditional maceration give a richly aromatic wine, full of colour and tannin. Powerful and full-bodied, it develops cooked fruit and cocoa notes with age.

Minervois

The grapes are grown on tiered terraces between the Montagne Noire and Canal du Midi, producing an extraordinary variety of wines. The structured reds contain blackcurrant and violet aromas, developing crystallized fruit notes with age. Red fruit aromas characterize the rosés, and the elegant whites have a certain finesse.

Muscat de Rivesaltes

A natural sweet white whine, made from small muscat grapes and Alexandria muscat, in Banyuls, Maury and Rivesaltes soil. These wines are fruity, light and delicate, the typical muscat aroma blending with mint, broom and acacia notes.

Carcassonne, vineyard

Hotels & Restaurants

AUDE

Bages

LE PORTANEL La Placette ✆ 04 68 42 81 66. *Fax : 04 68 41 75 93 Open all year. Closed Sunday in low season. Set menus from 17 € (lunchtime) to 38 €. Children's menu 12 €. Air-conditioning.* Perched on the rocky headland overlooking the lake, the restaurant has an exceptional view across to the Ile Saint Martin. Inside, this former fisherman's house retains all its charm. The menu, based on freshly-caught lake produce, suggests delicious fish dishes like the crab soup cappucino, crab bisque, whipped cream and a pinch of cinnamon.The foie gras menu is divine, with its foie gras and green cabbage terrine and apples conserved in wine jelly. If you choose the eel degustation menu, you have seven different eel dishes just out of the lake; eels in a terrine with sage, smoked, *en bourride* (with onions, carrots, leeks and orange peel) or stewed with old Fitou wine, for example. For dessert, try the pear and caramel *marronnier*, or the milk chocolate and grilled hazlenut *feuillantine*. The wine list features the region's best crus. Strong points: the sophisticated table setting and attention to detail (nibbles to start with; warm bread rolls), and Lisettes's professional welcome.

Carcassonne

AU COMTE ROGER 14, rue Saint-Louis - La Cité ✆ 04 68 11 93 40. *Website: www.comteroger.com. Closed Sunday. Annual closing 15 February-15 March. Menus from 30 € to 40 €. Average price a la carte 50 €. Children's menu 12 €.* Pierre Mesa's restaurant gathers together all the flavours of Languedoc. You can taste fresh Mediterranean fish, or a Lauragais guinea-hen, cooked with all the chef's creativity and invention. The Cathar lamb and goose confit, duck and sausage cassoulet are naturally there too. Enjoy this fresh and flavoursome cuisine in the Art Deco dining room or on the terrace, in the shade of the pergola. The region's most delicate wines are available to accompany your choice.

HOTEL DU DOMAINE D'AURIAC ** Route de Saint-Hilaire ✆ 04 68 25 72 22.** *Website : www.relaischateaux.com/auriac. Relais et Chateau rooms. Rooms from 150 € to 450 €. Swimming pool, tennis and 18-hole golf course. Bistrot d'Auriac. Set menus from 60 to 80 €. Winter grills served on the terrace.* A stone's throw from the medieval city, far from the noise and bustle of the town, this luxury hotel can be found in its immense park, among a number of rare tree species. Ideal for relaxing, and enjoying a range of sports and nature activities. Gourmets can choose half-board and benefit from the adjoining restaurant's gastronomic cuisine. The prices obviously correspond to the number of stars, though.

HOTEL DE LA CITE ** Place Saint-Nazaire - La Cité ✆ 04 68 71 98 71.** *Website : www.hoteldelacite.com. Rooms from 250 € to 900 € (winter) and 325 € to 1,250 € (summer). Under-16s free. Breakfast buffet 24 €. Enclosed car park. Rooms with satellite TV, VCR and mini-bar. Set menus from 48 € in low season, in La Barbacane restaurant.* This hotel is a historic monument, and has been welcoming showbiz, art and political stars for over a century. Its fine old stones add charm to the luxury comfort that goes with 4 stars; magnificent furniture, distinguished reception. There are a swimming pool and formal gardens outside, and a piano bar for music and relaxation inside. In summer, you may meet artists staying for the Festival de la Cite.

HOTEL DU DONJON -LES REMPARTS * 2, rue du Comte-Roger ✆ 04 68 11 23 00.** *Website: www.hotel-donjon.fr. Open all year. Double rooms from 100 € to 160 €. Suite from 145 € to 200 €.* If you're looking for luxury, it's here! In the heart of the medieval city, too. You can relive the dramatic Middle Ages atmosphere while still enjoying all the sophisticated modern comfort of spacious rooms and a shady garden.

LE LANGUEDOC 32, allée d'Iéna La Bastide ✆ 04 68 25 22 17. *Website : www.languedocrestaurant.com. Open mid-January to mid-December. Closed Sunday evening and Monday, out of season. Set menus from 22 € to 40 €.* Didier Faugeras is following family tradition, and offers an excellent *cuisine* in this beautiful restaurant. In fine weather, you can eat on the patio, with its trees, statues and varnished vases, or in the pretty dining room's country setting. The menu does justice to local fish, like angler and bass, but the cassoulet with its duck confit is not forgotten, and neither are the poultry fricassees and Lauragais quails. Long life means quality, in the case of this excellent eating place.

Castelnaudary

RESTAURANT LE TIROU 90, avenue Monseigneur-de-l'Angle ✆ 04 68 94 15 95. *Website: www.letirou.com Open lunchtimes and Saturday evenings. Closed Monday. Set menus from 16 € to 30 €.* You come across Le Tirou just behind the filling station on the road to Carcassonne. The setting is chic and welcoming, with its ochre walls and superbly set tables, so you tell yourself this is going to be an exceptional meal. And you're right - the chef prepares duck, confits and other local produce to perfection. We chose that standard dish, the cassoulet de Castelnaudary, unoriginal, it's true, but a safe bet. It was divinely cooked, and truly delicious. This excellent restaurant has nothing to hide; even the kitchens are visible behind glass. Don't forget to book in advance.

Cucugnan

AUBERGE DE CUCUGNAN ** 2, place de la Fontaine ✆ 04 68 45 40 84. *Closed from January to mid-March, and Wednesday in low season. Set menus 16 € to 40 €. Rooms from 43 € to 56 €.* This famous village at the foot of the Chateau de Queribus is proud of its inn, known as a specialist in traditional Aude cuisine. You find charcuterie, grilled meat, game in season and tasty dishes simmered at length, like the cockerel in Corbieres wine. 3 litres of wine, in fact, forming the basis of the sauce, plus an aromatic mixture of tomatoes, white onions, garlic, mushrooms, bouquet garni and olive oil, which fills the dining room with the heady flavours of Cathar country. 6 modest but pretty rooms are available for those who don't feel like getting behind the wheel straight away...

Fontjoncouse

RESTAURANT GILLES GOUJON Avenue Saint-Victor ✆ 04 68 44 07 37 *Fax 04 68 44 08 31. Set menus from 49 € to 100 €, a la carte 115 €. Closed Sunday evening, Monday, Tuesday and in January and February.* Without Gilles Goujon, who settled in this little Corbieres village in 1992, Fonjoncouse would never have had a claim to fame. The early days weren't easy, though; Gilles Goujon can smile about it now, but he lived through months of empty dining rooms on weekdays. Former second at the Petit Nice (in the Jean-Paul Passedat period), Goujon now enjoys himself immensely in the Narbonne countryside, and has been backed up by his alter ego Andre Mancuso in the dining room for the last 5 years. The ewe's brousse ravioli with a few morels and country asparagus, pot-au-feu with liquorice, pikeperch, herbette cannelloni, pine kernels and petit gris snails in aigo boulido cream, roast black pork, rind and fat juices with Lucques olives, chickpea puree and galette with fat, garriguette strawberries with conserved black olives and thyme flower sorbet with vanilla-flavoured olive oil are a few of his successes. The cellar contains all the best Corbieres domaines, and the wine waiter seems to be on first name terms with every vine in the region. Very thoughtful service.

La Pomarède

HOSTELLERIE DU CHATEAU DE LA POMAREDE * ✆ 04 68 60 49 69** *Website: www.hostellerie-lapomarede.fr. Open all year except November. Closed Monday and Tuesday. Set menus from 24 € to 68 €. PMC 70 €. Rooms from 85 € to 110 €. Suites 150 € and 170 €. 1 apartment 170 €. Breakfasts 12 €.* Gerald Garcia opened his *hotel de charme* in 1998 in this little village, La Pomarede. All 6 rooms and one of the suites are devoted to famous Lauragais personalities, like Riquet, Comte de Toulouse, and Pope John XXII. The charm lies in the elegant cherry wood furniture and soft wine, mauve and cream tones, and also in the dining room, in Gerald's sensitive cuisine. Young pigeon cooked two ways, with chanterelles, pan-fried foie gras and vanilla-flavoured juices, and Breton lobster in a golden spaghetti risotto with red berries and a shellfish sauce are just two examples.The desserts don't lag behind either; nougat ice cream with Bizes lucque olives and Minervois *granite* with tomato.

Lastours

LE PUITS DU TRESOR 21, route des 4 Châteaux ✆ 04 68 77 50 24. *Website : www.lepuitsdutresor.com. Open all year. Set menus from 15.50 € to 49 €.* This little village wth its four ancient castles has been home to chef Jean-Marc for 3 years now. He has set up his restaurant in carefully converted textile factory, where a small, privileged clientele - local and foreign - can enjoy the elegant and sober setting and Jean-Marc's undisputed knack for good cooking. The dishes are original and light, and feature oyster liegeois, foamy cauliflower cream with cumin, snail *crepinette* (stuffed pork caul) with herbs and garlic cream, sea bass *croustillant*, artichokes pan-cooked with rosemary, roast saddle of Cathar lamb and stewed cocos (white beans) and pequillo peppers. The cheeses, either freshly-made or matured, are delicious, with a shortbread tart with Cabardes nuts to finish.

Narbonne

LA TABLE SAINT-CRESCENT 68 Avenue du Général-Leclerc ✆ 04 68 41 37 37 *Fax 04 68 41 01 22. Set menus from 34 € to 70 €, a la carte 65 €. Closed Saturday lunchtime, Sunday evening and Monday.* Claude Giraud officially handed over to his son Lionel in 2003. Lionel is only 25, yet already has a solid career behind him: The Crillon in Paris with Christian Constant, the Ritz with Guy Legay, the Bastide Saint-Antoine with Jacques Chibois, then back to the family business as chef de partie for fish, with later, a new Tour de France, including Chez Guerard, la Cabro d'or and...Romania, before returning to go. This Table is an excellent restaurant, housed in an 8thc. oratory full of inspiration for a cook: fresh cod and fine mousseline, vegetable mirepoix with Muscat vinegar, crab tartare with summer vegetables and cold bisque with argan oil emulsion, line-fished bass cooked in the sautoir, cocos and grilled almonds in a cassoulet and meat juices with sherry vinegar, braised bull's cheek and steamed seasonal vegetables in port are the result. The father's hallmark is still there, but the son's is making itself felt. Plenty of Languedoc wines in the cellar, and reasonable prices everywhere.

GARD

Aigues-Mortes

LES TEMPLIERS* 23, rue de la République ✆ 04 66 53 66 56.** *Rooms from 100 € to 130 €. Breakfast 10.50 €. Two restaurants. Lunchtime set menu 12 €, and a la carte.* Aigues-Mortes certainly hides some marvels, and Les Templiers is an example. Luxury discreetly in evidence, warm colours and 13 personalised rooms explain its growing fame. The hotel building dates back to the 17thc. and its green setting boasts plenty of cachet, reinforced by owners Anne and Igor Alary. There are two restaurants; one, overlooking the street, where lunches are served (shaded tables can be added outside), and the other with patio and solarium used for dinners. Exposed beams, fireplace and a series of delightful alcoves make for a sophisticated yet intimate ambiance. A place to discover, absolutely.

Alès

LE BELLINI 23, place Henri-Barbusse ✆ 04 66 52 30 40. *Closed on Sunday. Dish of the day and coffee 8.50 €.* This restaurant fitted out in bistro style with marble tables and a long counter lined with stools is a convivial place. The owners look after you on arrival, and are attentive to your comfort throughout the meal. One of Djorkaeff's jerseys has been carefully framed above the bar, leaving the owner's passion for football in no doubt. The a la carte dishes feature on a large blackboard: assiette Bellini, salads, roast salmon with mango, brushetta and the popular sausage with aligot (cheese and potato puree). At lunchtime, dining room and terrace are monopolised by the locals, welcomed as friends. Excellent address.

Beaucaire

HOTEL DES DOCTRINAIRES * Quai du Général-de-Gaulle ✆ 04 66 59 23 70** *Rooms from 51 € to 78 €, on two floors, all with bathroom and separate WC. Set menus 18 € to 40 €, children's menu 10 €. Restaurant closed Saturday lunchtime from mid-December to mid-January. Lift to all floors. Private car park.* The Hotel des Doctrinaires in its green setting harks back to the noble Doctrinaire's College that occupied the site in1650. A vaulted entrance opens onto the dining-room, superbly restored in wood and stone. Ancient wall hangings add a medieval note. Against a backdrop of discreet, top-quality service by candlelight, chef Jean-Francois Faure prepares delicate and flavoursome dishes; the set menus at 18 €, 30 € and 40 € are accompanied by a wine list comprising both great regional wines and *grands crus*. The extensive cheese trolley reveals some new finds. Enjoy your breakfast or a fresh-air *aperitif* on the patio, or even a starlit dinner.

Garons

RESTAURANT ALEXANDRE 2 ruc Xavier-Tronc ✆ 04 66 70 08 99 *Fax 04 66 70 01 75. Website: www.michelkayser.com. Set menus from 39 € to 88 €, a la carte 85 €. Closed Sunday, Monday (July & August) Wednesday evening (September-June) and during February school holidays.* This beautiful restaurant, opened in the 1960s on the edge of Nimes, was completely renovated in 2003. Michel Kayser is also modernising his menus, but progressively, still focusing on the Mediterranean: pan-fried duck foie gras, gingerbread and polenta tart with Costieres apples and a Maury reduction, thickened with cocoa bean, fillet of dory and roast squid, flavoured with condiments and a vegetable mosaic, *churros* in cuttlefish ink, sauce made with crushed pine kernels, capers and tomato conserve, jugged hare with its roast saddle, thickened with Vigan apples, pan-fried foie gras and pumpkin cream with game fat. The sumptuous dessert trolley often draws applause, and the cellar covers the region.

Nîmes

IMPERATOR CONCORDE** Quai de la Fontaine ✆ 04 66 21 90 30.** *Website : www.hotel-imperator.com. 62 rooms from 121 € to 368 € (suite). Breakfast 16 €. Restaurant L'Enclos de la Fontaine, set menus from 45 € to 60 €. A la carte.* The Imperator Concorde is a legend in Nimes. Centrally-located, yet only a stone's throw from the magnificent La Fontaine gardens, it has its own huge and superb flowering garden planted with exotic trees - sequoia, gingko, biloba - and is famous for its early 19thc. lift. The locals like to have a drink here in the Hemingway bar, do business in the salons, and celebrate the feria. A place for bullfighters and artists, which gives the impression that living is easy. Colourful and comfortable rooms, impeccable service and services - flowers and champagne in your room - to please even the most demanding guests. If all else fails, a few moments' relaxation in the garden should put things right.

LISITA 6 rue des Arènes ✆ 04 66 67 29 15. *Website: www.lelisita.com. Closed Sunday and Monday. Set menus at 26 €, 42 € and 65 €, and a la carte.* This sought-after restaurant benefits from an exceptional setting, close to the bullring. Chef Olivier Douet and wine-waiter Stephane Debaille are responsible for the elegant interior and acknowledged culinary excellence.The *cuisine* is traditional; its specialities are foie gras and scallops, but you can also try Camargue bull meat. Good local wines feature on the wine list, along with a selection of great French classics.

Pont-du-Gard

LA BEGUDE SAINT PIERRE RD981 – Vers Pont du Gard ✆ 04 66 63 63 63 *Fax : 04 66 22 73 73. Website : www.hotel-saintpierre.fr Set menus from 29 € to 49 €. Children's menu 15 €. Garage, disabled access, half-board, outdoor swimming-pool.* La Begude is a *mas*, and a former17thc. coaching inn on the road between Remoulins and Uzes, covering a 14 ha.natural site. You can almost see the coaches-and -four galloping up to the door, as you arrive. The big fireplace in the reception hall always smells faintly of woodsmoke, from the winter log fires. The Griffoul family are well known in the area, and have worked wonders with the *mas*. Wood - room 29 has superb exposed beams -stone and old earthenware match the Provencal fabric furnishings. The rooms are air-conditioned, with satellite TV, mini-bar and safe, and there is a sauna and fitness centre. The garden with its beautiful swimming pool invites you to relax in the shade of the hundred-year-old olive trees. When it comes to eating, there are two dining rooms, which often display painting exhibitions, including the works of Nimes artist Laurent. The menu offers plenty of sophisticated dishes, with all the flavour of fresh regional produce, vegetables and herbs. You can hire the site privately for a special occasion, but even an overnight stay is memorable.

Port-Camargue

LE SPINAKER* LE CARRE DES GOURMETS Pointe de la Presqu'île ✆ 04 66 53 36 37.** *Website : www.spinaker.fr Open weekends 11 February-20 March. Open every day except Monday and Tuesday 21 March-1 July and 29 August-13 November. Open evenings and Sunday lunchtime 2 July-28 August. A la carte 60 €-100 €. Hotel open all year, every day 11 February-14 November, otherwise Thursday, Friday and Saturday only. 21 rooms from 109 € to 230 €. Garage, terrace, outdoor swimming pool.* What solitude, all alone at the far end of the island, in the middle of Europe's biggest sailing harbour! Pines and palm trees surround this charming seaside hotel with its own pool. You could call it a haven of peace, in the heart of Port Camargue seaside resort, and an excellent base for nature walks and sports activities, starting with your large and comfortable room, overlooking the pool. The restaurant, Le Carre des Gourmets, is widely known and appreciated for its top-level gastronomy.

The hotel can accommodate up to 70 people, for reunions and celebrations of all kinds.

Uzès

LES 3 SALONS 18 Rue du Docteur Blanchard ✆ 04 66 03 36 80. *Open Wednesday-Sunday. One-course lunchtime formula 17 €. Evening set menu 39 €.* You'll find this restaurant at the corner of an alley; a 17thc. mansion in the town's historic centre. Sophisticated beige and grey tones, old fireplaces and parquet decorate both dining rooms and the bar, and a leafy indoor courtyard welcomes you in fine weather. Sophisticated and creative cuisine, prepared with seasonal produce. Faultless service and presentation.

Villeneuve-les-Avignon

AUBERTIN 1, rue de l'Hôpital ✆ **04 90 25 94 84** *Closed Sunday evening and Monday, except in season. Set menus from 35 € to 49 €. A la carte. Air-conditioned. Terrace.* It's quite a mystery, why Jean-Claude Aubertin isn't in higher favour in the 'red book'. After all, he deserves to be; you'll taste one of the region's best *cuisines* under these arcades in the heart of Villeneuve. Marbled foie gras confit with figs, woodland cream, roast scallops with pistou and Camargue bull fillet pan-fried with red wine and served with ratte potato puree are among his recent proposals. As for the chestnut and rhum souffle, let's just say he's hard put to satisfy the demand!. Two private rooms on the first floor can host lunches and dinners, for groups or seminars. Service on the terrace in fine weather.

LA MAGNANERAIE** 37, rue Camp de Bataille** ✆ **04 90 25 11 11** *Fax 04 90 25 46 37 Website : www.hostelleriela-magneraie. Closed late October to 20 November. Set menus from 33 € (weekdays) to 80 €. Business menu 25 €. A la carte. 32 rooms from 100 € to 450 € (apartment). Breakfast: buffet 18 €, served in your room 20 €. Private car park.* This calm and classy hotel is now part of the Best Western chain. The building dates back to the 15thc. when it was used by a cardinal's staff, and is surrounded by a luxuriant flower garden. The rooms are peaceful, some with a view of the garden, and there is a swimming pool available in summer. You can taste delicious Provencal specialities in the elegant pastel-coloured dining room; the restaurant is famous for its regional *cuisine.*

Le Prieuré 7 place du Chapitre ✆ **04 90 15 90 15** *Fax 04 90 25 45 39. Website: www.relaischateaux.com/leprieure. Set menus from 36 € to 95 €. Closed Tuesday, Wednesday and November-March.* Le Prieure at Villeneuve-les-Avignon is a safe bet; one of those great French restaurants that defies trends and keeps its standards high, whatever the season or time of day, and whether chef Serge Chenet (who arrived in 1988) is working or on holiday. So many great chefs have done a stint here, knowing they'll benefit from the training, and the place inspires confidence in the customers too. You can almost order with your eyes shut! The Catalan lamb with Oriental flavours and aubergine conserve, langoustine kadaif and pork belly roasted in honey and sesame seeds, herb salad with grilled corn oil, will be up to their usual standard without a doubt. The dining room has some fine vaulting, and a handy indoor courtyard for fine weather: what more proof do you need?

HÉRAULT

Béziers

HOTEL IMPERATOR * 28, allées Paul Riquet** ✆ **04 67 49 02 25** *Website : www.hotel-imperator.fr. Open all year. Rooms from 49.50 € to 82 €. Breakfast 7 €.* This 3-star hotel in the town centre offers top quality B&B, with impeccable service. Easy access, enclosed car park, 45 quiet and comfortable rooms with air-conditioning, telephone and computer socket. Pretty indoor garden.

Cap d'Agde

CALADOC Ile aux Loisirs ✆ **04 67 26 87 18.** *Annual closing January. Closed Sunday and Monday except in high season. Set menus from 26.50 € to 46 €. A la carte.* The Hotel du Golf restaurant is well named; like the Caladoc, a hybrid grape found only in Languedoc, Jean-Claude Fabre's *cuisine* is elaborate and cross-bred, despite its deep regional roots. The interior subtly mixes and matches contemporary Japanese style and Mediterranean warmth. The greenery, teak furniture and wrought iron, and stone vase with floating flowers give the patio a touch of Feng Shui. The menu pays tribute to both Mediterranean and regional produce: wild mushroom terrine, warm foie gras escalopes, Mediterranean white bream fillet grilled *a la planxa* and served with a creamy risotto and little vegetables, and nougat ice-cream with a nougatine *chemise*, for instance. Wine-waiter Laurent Saint-Dizier can always find the perfect wine to go with your meal, among the 300 bottles in the cellar.

La Grande-Motte

ALEXANDRE Presqu'île du Port ✆ **04 67 56 63 63.** *Website : www.alexandre-restaurant.com. Closed Sunday evening and Monday. Set menus 20 € (Bistrot d'Alexandre) 35 € and 67 €.* This gastronomic restaurant facing the sea is one of La Grande-Motte's recommended addresses. Dany and Michele Alexandre welcome you with simplicity and good humour. The dining room in Mediterranean colours is fitted out with taste, and has a great view of the port. The chef is an expert with sophisticated marine flavours; try his clam risotto and frog's legs in a frito, monkfish medallion with broad beans, or saddle of rabbit stuffed with pine kernels and aubergine cannelloni. The region's best vintages accompany these original and delicious dishes to perfection.

Montpellier

CASTEL RONCERAY 130, rue du Castel-Ronceray ✆ 04 67 42 46 30 *Closed Sunday and Monday. Set menus from 25 € to 60 € (degustation menu).* With its awning and marvellous bougainvillea, the Castel Ronceray symbolises an art of living and a gastronomy which is classic yet never old-fashioned. Chef Patrick Guittat is not afraid to suggest stripped gambas cooked in the tandoori, marinated salmon and shelled lobster with Sechouan pepper served with stuffed piquillo peppers with goat's cheese or, more classic, a medallion of monkfish tail, sweetbreads with cepes or a venison steak with foie gras. In the dining room, wife Nathalie puts you at your ease, and gives you expert advice on choosing your wine, so that you quickly forgive the rather pompous service.

LA COMPAGNIE DES COMPTOIRS 51, avenue de Nîmes ✆ 04 99 58 39 29. *Open every day, lunchtime and evening. A la carte 40 €* The Pourcel brothers have set up their brasserie in this family house, decorated in wood and colonial fabrics. The cuisine reveals Southern, Oriental and Asian influences. You start with the *mise-en-bouche* (nibbles before the starters): goat's cheese and anchovy mousse then chanterelle toast with honey and nuoc-mam, which could easily be starters in themselves. We tried the autumn mushroom ravioli on a pumpkin *mousseline*, country ham and chestnuts, and it was a delight, full of surprises.For dessert, sliced, poached pears, lemon sorbet and ginger. Each product is excellent, and there is real genius in the cooking!

HOTEL LE GUILHEM* 18, rue Jean-Jacques-Rousseau ✆ 04 67 52 90 90** *Website : www.leguilhem.com Rooms from 71 €. Breakfast 11 €.* This hotel in one of Montpellier's old streets welcomes its customers in a building dating back to the 17thc. The 34 rooms are all different sizes; the most pleasant overlook a terrace with a small, tree-filled garden underneath. They are all air-conditioned, and attractively decorated. The whole set up is peaceful, welcoming and ideal for a relaxing stay or a business trip. The car park is extremely useful in the town centre!

LE JARDIN DES SENS 11 avenue Saint-Lazare ✆ 04 99 58 38 38 *Fax 04 99 58 38 39. Website: www.jardindessens.com. Set menus from 50 € to 190 €, a la carte 130 €. Closed Sunday, Monday, Tuesday and Wednesday lunchtime (except in summer, Sunday, Monday and Wednesday lunchtime only) and the first fortnight in January.* The Pourcel brothers would feature in any Top Ten of the most mediatic French chefs. Jacques and Laurent Pourcel are hyper-active, always between two flights: an opening in Asia, a seminar in the USA, or a new Comptoir in Paris. At barely 40 years old, after 15 years of running the Jardin des Sens, they have become stars in the world of great gastronomy, turning Montpellier into a 'balancing metropolis' on the map of top French restaurants - even if the prestigious Guide Rouge demoted them last year. They have been criticised for taking the easy option, but their cooking is still the best in Languedoc-Roussillon: their pan-fried Breton lobster tail, mixed green salad of young leaves and shoots in olive oil with balsamic vinegar pearls, feet and claws in an oriental roll, small squid stuffed with ratatouille and langoustine tails, cooking juices spiced with soya, sliced courgettes in a salad, roast pigeon fillets with the offal in a pastilla, pan-cooked pear quarters, raspberry fricassee, jesuit biscuits and iced parfait with Sicilian pistachio are still unequalled elsewhere. The cellar contains mainly Languedoc wines, with more and more 'low prices' (just as well) even if the majority of the crus are inaccessible to most pockets.

CELLIER-MOREL La Maison de la Lozère ✆ 04 67 66 46 36 *Fax 04 67 66 23 61. Site: www.celliermorel.com. Set menus from 46 € to 59 €, a la carte 80 €. Closed Sunday, Monday lunchtime, Wednesday lunchtime and the first three weeks in August.* Chef Eric Cellier and wine waiter Pierre Morel (in charge of a cellar with around 500 recommended wines, including the most specialised and attractive in Languedoc) are definitely in second place behind the inevitable Pourcel brothers, in terms of competition bretween top restaurants in Montpellier alone. Their fine 18thc.mansion is especially known for its excellent value for money: you must try the pan-fried escalope of duck foie gras pressed with cinammon flavoured potato and mousse de lait fume sanguin with vinegar, the saddle of hare croustillant in an emulsion of civet sauce and chocolate cannelloni with butternut, the fillet of sea bream, frothy bacon, crunchy vegetables and marinated endives, Morello cherry crumble, and semolina and vanilla biscuit with a soft white cheese sorbet. The cellar is magnificent, of course, and the service extremely pleasant, managed with talent by Pierre Morel.

Saint-Martin-de-Londres

LES MUSCARDINS 19, route des Cévennes ✆ 04 67 55 75 90 *Closed in February, and Mondays and Tuesdays. Set menus 29 € (lunchtime) and from 39.50 € to 67.50 €.* Traditional recipes are enriched with unusual ingredients and cooked with imagination in this restaurant, which deserves its well-established reputation.The fish and seafood are especially well prepared, like in the lobster salad with truffle butter, the bass with aromatic herbs and the monkfish kebabs with chorizo. A foie gras and gingerbread escalope, braised sweetbread with truffles, lamb and goat all feature on the menus among the land produce, as opposed to sea.

Saint-Pons-de-Thomières

LES BERGERIES DE PONDERACH – Relais et Châteaux Route de Narbonne ✆ 04 67 97 02 57. *Open mid-March to early November. Rooms from 84 € to 105 €, breakfast 11 €. Set menus 29 € to 45 €. A la carte.* This beautiful 17thc. farm has been converted into a *hotel de charme,* with large rooms opening onto a terrace and overlooking a meadow with magnificent cherry trees amd magnolias. This setting matches the gastronomic *cuisine*, variable according to the market produce available.The food is studied, the delicate preparations seasoned with pepper and spices, and only the best local produce is chosen. Gilles Lentin likes to cultivate an intimate ambiance, and make his guests feel special, so he invites them to relax in the piano-bar or on the summer patio, and organises frequent classical music concerts and exhibitions in his art gallery.

Sète

LE GRAND HOTEL* 17, quai de Lattre-de-Tassigny ✆ 04 67 74 71 77** *Website: www.sete-hotel.com. Open all year, except Christmas and New Year.* This beautiful 1900 hotel facing the Canal Royal attracts customers with its luxurious yet unostentatious setting, sophistication and faultless service. The reception hall leads into a conservatory with Baltard-style glass walls. The rooms are reached by a winding staircase on three floors, all different and stylishly furnished, huge and comfortable. The warm welcome and quality services live up to the hotel's three stars; you can't fail to appreciate your stay.

LOZÈRE

Aumont-Aubrac

CHEZ CAMILLOU* 10, avenue du Languedoc ✆ 04 66 42 80 22.** *Website : www.hotel-camillou.com. Open April-October. Rooms from 55 € to 83.50 €. Set menus from 16 € to 60 €. A la carte.* Comfortable rooms and suites, with a regional cuisine defying all competition. In this sophisticated setting, you discover real gastronomy. Every product is chosen with care and presented to advantage: the cepe fricassee and pan-fried foie gras, roast pikeperch and tomato fondu, with fennel and cockle juice, and lamb confit with onion in lasagna, carrot puree with cumin are all examples of culinary excellence.

La Garde-Guérin

AUBERGE REGORDANE La Garde Guérin ✆ 04 66 46 82 88** *Website : www.regordane.com Open Easter-September. Set menus from 17 € to 32 €. Rooms from 49 € to 60 €.* This 16thc. seignorial estate in the heart of the medieval village, with its courtyard set between massive stone walls and its sunny terrace, is now the home of Philippe and Pierre Nogier, whose inventive cuisine thrills the most jaded palates. They are skilled at matching local produce to the subtlest flavours, and serve their dishes in the inn's historic setting under vaulted ceilings and behind latticed windows. The traditional Garde-Guerin hospitality is respected, with comfortable rooms - TV, VCR and telephone - and a hikers' dormitory.

Langogne

DOMAINE DE BARRES* Route de Mende ✆ 04 66 69 71 00**. *Website : www.domainedebarres.com. Open April to mid-November. Rooms from 68 € to 92 €.* Overnight break (low season only) 68 €. Set menus from 25 €. A la carte. From April onwards, the golf clubhouse provides a formula at 15 €. This 18thc. residence was converted into a superb 3-star hotel by the talented architect Jean-Michel Wilmotte. It offers golf, getting into shape sessions and top-quality cuisine at affordable prices. The clubhouse becomes a lively centre of activity from springtime onwards, with a relaxed lunchtime menu available, enabling you to really make the most of the country setting.

Mende

LA SAFRANIERE Chabrits ✆ 04 66 49 31 54 *Closed Sunday evening and Monday. Set menus from 18 € (weekday lunchtimes) and 42 € evenings and weekends.* This remarkable restaurant is worth the visit, even though you have to climb up above Mende to reach the village, where saffron used to be grown for dying. Today, you make the climb to sit down in a pretty dining room in pastel tones, partitioned in wood, behind a small garden, and to sample a simple and harmonious cuisine. The menu of the day, like the more elaborate meals, offers quality meat and fish, from local meadows or express coastal services. This modern Safraniere is also well named, mastering as it does the use of aromatic herbs and spices.

Meyrueis

CHATEAU D'AYRES* Les Ayres ✆ 04 66 45 60 10**. *Website: www.chateau-d-ayres.com. Open mid-March to mid-December. Rooms from 88 € to 136 €, breakfast 12 €, set menus from 19 € to 43 €.* This chateau, formerly a monastery, now lords it over a 5 ha. park planted with giant sequoias and hundred-year-old oaks. The renovated rooms are furnished in the old-fashioned style, and there are period salons available. New chef Jacky Jubin masters the mixing and matching of local produce: home-smoked salmon, roast lamb with Causse juniper berries and young farm-bred pigeon en cocotte with garlic cream feature on his menus. Jean-Francois de Montjou and his wife Helene have placed a swimming pool and tennis courts at their guests' disposal, and watch over their comfort discreetly but continually.

Sainte-Enimie

CHATEAU DE LA CAZE** La Malène ✆ 04 66 48 51 01. Website : www.chateaudelacaze.com.** *Open from mid-April to mid-November. Restaurant closed Thursday lunchtime and Wednesday outside the summer season. Rooms from 108 € to 162 €, suite from 190 € to 220 €, apartment from 230 € to 260 €. Breakfast 14 €. Set menus from 30 € to 76 €.* This romantic chateau was built in the 15thc. to house the illicit pleasure of a Soubeyran lady, so the story goes. The inside is enchanting, with its vaulted ceilings, frescos, and an immense Gothic fireplace, and luxury of luxuries! even a bathroom nestling in one of the towers.The rooms are all comfortable, furnished in wrought iron and warm-coloured fabrics, and you'll only want to leave yours for a sunlounger in the garden, or to sit down to a meal. Jean-Paul and Sandrine Lecroq have undertaken some renovation work in order to combine modern comfort with the charm of old-world stone. In this setting, they serve a gastronomic *cuisine* which will enchant your tastebuds.

PYRÉNÉES-ORIENTALES

Argelès-sur-Mer

RESTAURANT L'AMADEUS Avenue des Platanes - ✆ 04 68 81 12 38 *Website : www.lamadeus.com Closed in December and January. Set menus from 23 € to 33 €. Lunchtime formula 15.50 €.* Set back from the noise and bustle of the beach, facing the Tourist Office, the Amadeus is Argeles' specialist in fish and seafood. Tourists and locals crowd into the summer patio or the large air-conditioned dining room to taste Marc Ryngert's zarzuela with lobster from his tank, rock fish soup or Bouzigues oysters, fish of the day or mussels with saffron in a cassolette. You can even take away your seafood. Apart from the fish, there are salads and pasta, and regional dishes like the *freginat de Baixas* (beef saute minute). A good seaside restaurant, which isn't such a common find.

Banyuls-sur-Mer

HOTEL LES ELMES ** RESTAURANT LA LITTORINE Plage des Elmes ✆ 04 68 88 03 12 *Website : www.hotel-des-elmes.com Closed mid-November to mid-December. Rooms from 44 € to 107 € according to season, comfort and view, breakfast 8.50 €. Set menus from 23 € to 55 €. A la carte 27 € and 34 €.* A kilometre before Banyuls-sur-Mer, round a turning, you come upon the delightful Elmes cove, which provides the setting for one of the most reputed hotel-restaurants along the Roussillon coast. It has 30 simple and elegant rooms, six of them renovated with a sea view. The cuisine is marked out by the freshness of its produce and chef Jean-Marie Patrouix's mastery and creativity. Try the succulent fresh cod steak with garlic cream or the tasty cold courgette cream with Bouzigues oysters and ice cream quenelles with olive oil and basil.

Céret

HOTEL RESTAURANT LES FEUILLANTS ** 1, boulevard Lafayette ✆ 04 68 87 37 88** *Website : www.feuillants.com.* Closed from 20 December to March, Sunday and Monday during the winter and Monday the rest of the year. Rooms from 66 € to 140 €, breakfast 12.20 €. Set menus 23 € (brasserie Le Carre) and 32 € to 46 €. When the Banyols left for the Bordeaux region, this hotel- restaurant rather lost its role as one of regional gastronomy's strongholds. After a few false starts, it finally regained its place thanks to Robert Abraham. David Tanguy is now ship's captain, and the restaurant is always full. The recent creation of the Le Carre brasserie enables customers to benefit from the luxury hotel setting - and shady terrace - yet eat at affordable prices.

Collioure

HOTEL CASA PAIRAL * Impasse des Palmiers ✆ 04 68 82 05 81**. *Open April-October. Rooms from 75 € to 175 €, breakfast 10 €.* The Casa Pairal hotel is an old Catalan residence with an ochre front, and a sumptuously decorated hall behind it. There is a superb Mediterranean garden with fountain, hundred-year-old cypresses and palm trees and a delightful swimming pool nestling in greenery. The 28 spacious rooms all have air-conditioning and mini-bar. Peace and quiet are rare in this touristic spot, so don't hesitate to take advantage of it here, at just 100m from the beach.

Molitg-les-Bains

CHATEAU DE RIELL ** ✆ 04 68 05 04 40 Website : www.relaischateaux.fr/riell.** *Rooms from 134 € (with bathrooms and private terraces) to 285 €. Apartments from 315 € to 365 €. Breakfast 17 €. Set menus from 42 to 64 €. Closed November-March. Closed Monday to Friday lunchtime.* Molitg is a charming little spa resort nestling in greenery on the banks of the Castellane. The Chateau de Riell is a 4-star luxury hotel, and an elegant and sophisticated place for a short break. Its sumptuous 19thc.Catalan building is set in the heart of a magnificent wooded park, and contains 19 spacious and personalised rooms, with top-quality services. The gardens boast two swimming pools, tennis courts and a fitness centre. The cuisine is well up to the same standard, thanks to talented chef Lionel Migliori. In the baroque dining room, you can enjoy flavoursome Mediterranean dishes at your leisure, such as roast pepper cremeux with lobster stock or the formidable pork confit with pig's trotter and vegetables peasant-style. A memorable meal in a spectacular setting.

Perpignan

CHAPON FIN 18 boulevard Jean-Bourrat ✆ 04 68 35 14 14 *Fax 04 68 35 48 18. Website: www. parkhotel-fr.com. Set menus from 25 € to 100 €, a la carte 55 €. Closed Sunday, first fortnight in January and second fortnight in August.* Pascal Borrell, who had put the Park Hotel's fine restaurant back on the rails, has recently left Perpignan for Switzerland, and his replacement came right across France to take up the place, still warm. Alexandre Klimenko had in fact been managing the kitchens in the Hotel de la Chartreuse du Val Esprit at Gosnay in the Pas-de-Calais. The task might have seemed daunting, but the cooking has lost none of its quality or persuasive force: sole roule with citrus fruits and blancmange with oysters, lamb *epigramme* and honey-glazed vegetables, and an amazing dessert, fennel conserve, tomato sorbet, olive oil and aubergine chips.The cellar contains a wealth of relatively inexpensive Roussillon wines. If there is a small defect, it has to be the rather banal decoration in the dining room.

CHATEAU LA TOUR APOLLINAIRE 15, rue Guillaume Apollinaire ✆ 04 68 92 43 02. *Email: elena.wood@wanadoo.fr – Website: www.latourapollinaire.com 90 € per night for 2 people.* The Tour Appollinaire is a real castle, luxurious and quiet, set in a garden of palms and exotic trees. It is owned by English writer Robin Wood and his Russian head-hunter wife Elena, who fell in love with the place (which dates back to 1826) and decided to restore it in the original style, with some discreet modernisation. The resulting building, with its Art Deco touches, is one of the most beautiful in the Pyrenees Orientales, and conveniently situated as well, only a stone's throw from Perpignan's medieval centre. To cap it all, the recently-built swimming pool will be at guests' disposal this summer.

EL XIRINGUITO 10, rue Pierre Rameil ✆ 04 68 34 39 51. *Open all year, closed Sunday, Monday evening and Saturday lunchtime. Formula with* *starter, main course and dessert, 11 €. Main course only 8.50 €. Choice of combinations 7.50 € to16 €.* Don't pass up this typically Catalan restaurant, where you can taste local specialities like parillade, fish *a la planxa* and real tapas, deliciously and uniquely prepared with products brought across the border by the restaurateur himself at regular intervals. Usap supporters can follow the fortunes of their favourite warriors on a wide screen, while enjoying a catalan cream, *rousquilles* (round, sugar-coated biscuits) or *croquants de saint-paul* (almond biscuits) with a glass of muscat for 6 €, or *churros* with chocolate for 5 €. From time to time there is a flamenco evening, adding southern dance to the attractions of sport and *cuisine.*

LA VILLA DUFLOT **** **3 Rond-point Albert-Donnezan – vers Porte d'Espagne – ✆ 04 68 56 67 67** *Website : www.villa-duflot.com Open all year. 25 single and double rooms from 120 € to 160 €, suite 200 €, breakfast 13 €. The rooms are soundproofed and air-conditioned. Refrigerator bar. Vinotheque. Restaurant. Menu-a la carte 30 €. Banquets. Private car park and bus park with disabled access. Dogs accepted. Swimming pool, terrace, garden.* Located outside the town, the Villa Duflot is the only 4-star hotel-restaurant in Perpignan. The main building, Mediterranean in style, houses the air-conditioned bedrooms, and the pool has an adjacent terrace for topping up your tan.The gastronomic restaurant has an air-conditioned dining room and a patio, and there are several rooms seating 10 to 120 people, suitable for weddings and business meetings. It only remains to add that the hotel has full wheelchair access, and the town centre is 5 minutes away by car.

Rivesaltes

AUBERGE DU DOMAINE DE ROMBEAU Avenue de la Salanque ✆ 04 68 64 35 35. *Website: www.domaine-de-rombeau.com Open every day, lunchtime and evening. Set menus from 22 € to 42 €.* On the way out of Rivesaltes towards Perpignan, the Domaine de Rombeau is a reputed winegrower's property, producing muscat de rivesaltes, cotes-du-roussillon and excellent vins de pays. It is also a restaurant, popular with the Perpignanais for their weddings, communions and anniversaries, since it boasts 5 personalised rooms seating 30 to 450 people. It really is a charming spot, with its fine old residence and attractive pool. In summer, you can eat grilled meat on a vine shoot barbecue outside, accompanied by one of the Domaine's own wines, then visit the superb vaulted cellars afterwards. The master of the estate, Pierre-Henri de la Fabregue is a great art-lover, and sometimes lets young regional artists exhibit their work in the Domaine.

Saint-Cyprien-Plage

L'ILE DE LA LAGUNE, RESTAURANT L'ALMANDIN **** **Boulevard de l'Almandin-Les-Capellans ✆ 04 68 21 01 02** *Website: www.hotel-ile-lagune.com* Closed in February. Rooms from 143 € to 170 €, suite from 190 € to 255 €, breakfast 15 €. Set menus from 43 € to 95 €. South of Saint-Cyprien, on an islet in the laguna facing a wide beach, you find this luxurious hotel-restaurant. A little wooden bridge provides access, through luxuriant greenery, and there is a small private harbour with a shuttle to the village, a magnificent pool and a park; in short, an idyllic setting. The huge, personalised rooms are equipped with bath and shower, mini-bar, air-conditioning, lounge and satellite TV, and boast every comfort. The cuisine is well up to standard, with a delicate Mediterranean influence; we feel the high prices are justified by exceptional quality produce and the chef's unique mastery of flavour. A must.

Limousin

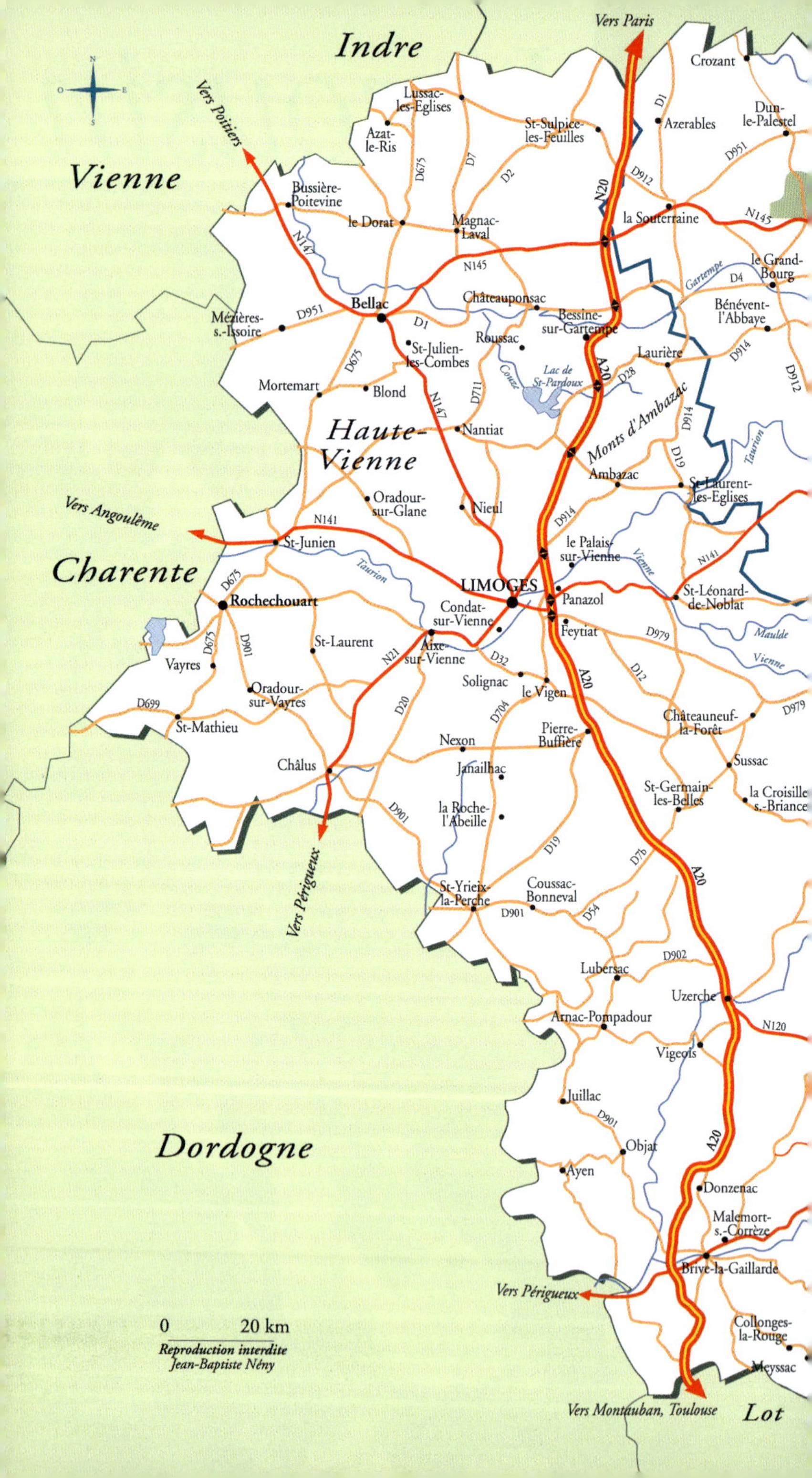

Indre
Vers Paris
Crozant
Vienne
Vers Poitiers
Lussac-les-Eglises
Azat-le-Ris
St-Sulpice-les-Feuilles
Azerables
Dun-le-Palestel
D1
D951
D675
D7
D2
D912
N20
Bussière-Poitevine
le Dorat
Magnac-Laval
la Souterraine
N145
N147
le Grand-Bourg
Gartempe
D4
Bellac
Châteauponsac
Bénévent-l'Abbaye
Mézières-s.-Issoire
D951
D1
Bessines-sur-Gartempe
St-Julien-les-Combes
Roussac
Laurière
D914
D912
Lac de St-Pardoux
Couze
A20
D28
Mortemart
Blond
D711
Monts d'Ambazac
D914
Haute-Vienne
Nantiat
D19
Taurion
Ambazac
St-Laurent-les-Eglises
Vers Angoulême
Oradour-sur-Glane
Nieul
N141
D914
St-Junien
le Palais-sur-Vienne
Vienne
Charente
N141
Taurion
LIMOGES
D675
St-Léonard-de-Noblat
Rochechouart
Condat-sur-Vienne
Panazol
Feytiat
Maulde
D979
D901
St-Laurent
Aixe-sur-Vienne
Vayres
N21
D32
Vienne
D12
Solignac
le Vigen
A20
Oradour-sur-Vayres
D699
D20
D704
Châteauneuf-la-Forêt
D979
St-Mathieu
Pierre-Buffière
Nexon
Sussac
Châlus
Janailhac
St-Germain-les-Belles
la Croisille-s.-Briance
D901
la Roche-l'Abeille
D19
D7b
A20
Vers Périgueux
St-Yrieix-la-Perche
Coussac-Bonneval
D901
D54
D902
Lubersac
Uzerche
Arnac-Pompadour
N120
Vigeois
Juillac
D901
Dordogne
Objat
A20
Ayen
Donzenac
Malemort-s.-Corrèze
Brive-la-Gaillarde
Vers Périgueux
0
20 km
Reproduction interdite
Jean-Baptiste Nény
Collonges-la-Rouge
Meyssac
Vers Montauban, Toulouse
Lot

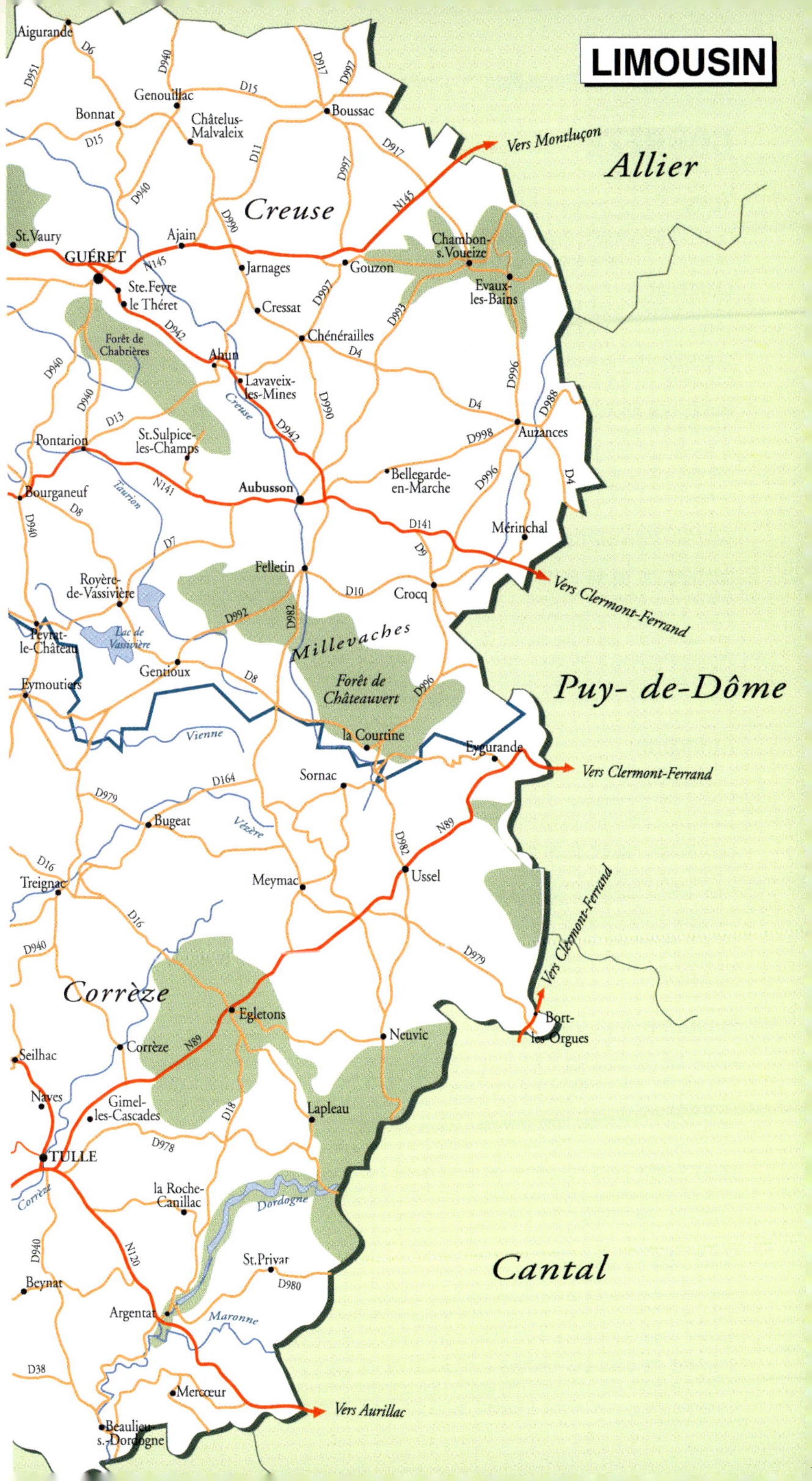

LIMOUSIN
Allier
Creuse
Puy- de-Dôme
Corrèze
Cantal
Millevaches
Forêt de Chabrières
Forêt de Châteauvert
Vers Montluçon
Vers Clermont-Ferrand
Vers Clermont-Ferrand
Vers Clermont-Ferrand
Vers Aurillac
Aigurande
Genouillac
Bonnat
Châtelus-Malvaleix
Boussac
St.Vaury
Ajain
GUÉRET
Jarnages
Gouzon
Chambon-s.Voueize
Evaux-les-Bains
Ste.Feyre
le Théret
Cressat
Chénérailles
Ahun
Lavaveix-les-Mines
Auzances
Pontarion
St.Sulpice-les-Champs
Bellegarde-en-Marche
Bourganeuf
Aubusson
Mérinchal
Felletin
Crocq
Royère-de-Vassivière
Lac de Vassivière
Peyrat-le-Château
Gentioux
Eymoutiers
la Courtine
Eygurande
Sornac
Bugeat
Treignac
Meymac
Ussel
Egletons
Neuvic
Bort-les-Orgues
Corrèze
Seilhac
Naves
Gimel-les-Cascades
Lapleau
TULLE
la Roche-Canillac
St.Privat
Beynat
Argentat
Mercœur
Beaulieu-s.Dordogne
Creuse
Taurion
Vienne
Vézère
Dordogne
Maronne
Corrèze

CORREZE

Tulle

Corrèze's prefecture is a pleasant place to discover. The Middle Ages and Renaissance houses (maison de Loyac) and Enclos and Alverge quarters are definitely worth seeing.

CATHEDRAL. A 12thc. masterpiece. Its magnificent nave is vaulted with intersecting ribs, and some superb stained glass windows by Jean-Jacques Cruber of Strasbourg were added to the chevet in 1979.

CLOISTER. The northern part is mutilated, but the pure 13thc. Gothic arcades are still striking. The chapter house wall paintings are combined with carved bas reliefs, which is rare.

MUSEE DES ARMES ANCIENNES Place Albert Faucher ✆ 05 55 26 22 05. *Open Monday-Friday: 9am-12 noon and 2pm-6pm. Admission free.* This museum in the Souilhac quarter illustrates the history of French and foreign weapons. Pride of place is given to Tulle's industrial heritage: pre-1822 flints of different types and models, repeaters, automatics and guns firing blanks. A cultural and scientific project is underway, started after reorganization in 2003.

Arnac-Pompadour

CHATEAU. 05 55 98 51 10 *Guided tours every 30 mins. 1 October-9 February: 2pm-4.30pm. 10 February-30 March: 2pm-5pm. 1 April-30 June: 10am-11.30am and 2pm-5pm. 1 July-30 September: 10am-11.30am and 2pm-5.30pm. Race days: 10am-11.30am. Admission: 4 €* . Only the terraces can be visited, since the inside houses the National Stud Farm's offices, but a guide tells you all about this imposing fortress, a gift from Louis XV to Mme de Pompadour in 1745. Arrow-slits, machicolations, a well, stele, training yard etc. can be seen, with a view of the deep moat and 25ha. racetrack (you may catch site of the horses). Your imagination will do the rest!

Aubazine

This rural village is known for its monastic life, and some exceptional architecture. In the 12thc. Saint Etienne had a monastery built at Obazine (for monks) and a convent in the Coyroux Valley (for nuns). These two sanctuaries came under the Cistercian Order in 1147.

CISTERCIAN ABBEY. 05 55 25 79 93. *Guided tours every day except Monday: 11am, 3.30pm and 4.30pm. Admission: 3.25 €* . Meeting-point: the beautiful village square. A Romanesque building, built of three different materials: gneiss foundations, sandstone walls and shale roof (later replaced by slate).

The abbey church contains Saint Etienne of Obazine's limestone tomb: a remarkable piece of 13thc. carving. Notice the strange staircase that the monks used to reach the sanctuary. The liturgical oak cupboard is one of France's oldest, and the Virgin of Piety in polychrome limestone dates back to the late 15thc.

Beaulieu-sur-Dordogne

Admire the fine buildings in these well-restored medieval alleys: the Clarisse house with its balconies, and another with a dovecote now housing the Youth Hostel. You'll see a magnificent Renaissance mansion in Place de la Bridolle, and half-timbered houses, Place du Marché and Rue Sainte-Catherine, along with an old tower from François 1's time. Beaulieu has a gentle climate, and offers water sports and leisure activities on the Dordogne. Strawberry-lovers can try the locally-grown fruit.

SAINT PIERRE ABBEY CHURCH.: 05 55 91 09 94 This Romanesque church is the biggest in Corrèze: cross-shaped, with a treble nave and ambulatory, and fine 12thc. Limousin sculpture on its portal. The tower keep was added in the 14thc.

Bort-les-Orgues

Bordering on Corrèze and the Cantal, Bort's attractions are the Romanesque Saint Germain Priory Church and a dam. The church contains a 15thc. statue of Sainte Anne de Bort and a modern bronze Christ by sculptor Louis Chavignie. The old cornmarket houses an archeological museum.

BARRAGE DE BORT-LES-ORGUES ✆ 05 55 96 02 49. *Open all year. Admission free.* Visitor's circuit inside the hydro-electric plant. This dam on the Limousin-Auvergne border is 120m high and forms the Dordogne's biggest reservoir. A special tourist circuit has been set up (open all year).

Brive-la-Gaillarde

If you haven't time for museums, but want to discover Brive, don't miss the Saturday morning market. You'll find plenty of cepes and chanterelles here at mushroom time.

SAINT MARTIN COLLEGIATE CHURCH. The old (mainly) pedestrian streets run off from this church in the historic town centre. It was built in 1280; transept, octagonal cupola and part of the chevet are left of the Romanesque original.

MUSEE LABENCHE 26bis, bd Jules Ferry ✆ 05 55 24 19 05. *Open every day except Tuesday. 1 April-30 October: 10am-6.30pm. Other periods: 1.30pm-6pm. Admission: adult 4.50 € concessions 2.50 € under-16s free.* Brive's museum is housed in this beautiful and noble Renaissance Labenche mansion. Archeology, history, local people, art, numismatology, popular arts and tradition and natural history are on display in 17 rooms. The museum also contains a collection of 17thc. tapestries made in Mortlake, England.

MUSEE EDMOND MICHELET 4, rue ✆ 05 55 74 06 08. *www.centremichelet.org. Open every day except Sunday: 10am-12 noon and 2pm-6pm. Admission free.* The Michelet family's former residence houses this museum, devoted to the deported Resistant, several times minister under de Gaulle.

Collonges-la-Rouge

Red sandstone gives Collonges a luminous beauty, attracting over 300,000 visitors a year.

You reach the Place de la Fontaine via Rue de la Barrière. Around the square, the Ramade de la Serre and 'Sirene' (mermaid) houses and Town Hall are quite striking. Lower down are the Porte du Prieure and Ramade de Friac residence, with its often-photographed towers; still lower, the Saint Jacques de Compostella inn, where pilgrims stayed. Beautiful Benge Manor is close by, with its turrets and Renaissance window. Going back up Rue de la Barrière, the Porte Plate (flat, having lost its towers) leads to Place de la Halle and Saint Pierre Church with its Penitents' Chapel. You take Rue Noire to see the remarkable Castel de Maussac, then the Ch,teau de Vassinhac, Manoir de Beauvirie and Ch,teau du Martret, overlooking the town.

MAISON DE LA SIRENE. Built in the 16thc., this house takes its name from a mermaid holding a comb and mirror carved in the stone. Today, it houses the Popular Arts and Traditions Museum with hundreds of objects, furniture and documents (05 55 25 41 04)

LA HALLE. The old village bread oven complete with utensils can be seen under the covered market framework, held up by massive pillars.

CHATEAU DE VASSINHAC. Built in 1583, this was the Vicomté de Turenne governors' residence. Powerful yet sophisticated, it boasts hexagonal towers containing wide spiral staircases, pepperpot turrets, mullioned windows and a Gothic door.

MUSEE VIVANT DE L'OIE Ferme de la Veyrie ✆ 05 55 25 31 40. *Open mid-July-late August: 10am-7pm. Easter-November: 10am-12 noon and 2pm-7pm. Admission free. Guided tour: 2.50 €* . Learn all about wild and domestic geese in this renovated barn: mythology, literature, craft and culinary traditions.

MUSEE DE LA SIRENE DES ARTS ✆ TRADITIONS POPULAIRES. *Open every day, Easter-November: 10.30am-12 noon and 2.30pm-7pm. Out of season, by appointment. Admission: 1.50 €, under-10s free.*

Admire the spiral staircase, old-fashioned kitchen and trade tools (baker, farmer, winegrower) in this fine old house.

Donzenac

Each alley has its medieval, Renaissance and 17thc. remains. Twisting streets wind round the 18thc. church tower.

SAINT MARTIN CHURCH. Contains 13th and 14thc. enamel reliquaries in a showcase, among other treasures.

PENITENTS' CHAPEL. Worth seeing for its rich furnishings and beautiful gilded wooden Baroque reredos.

MAISON DU XIIIe SIECLE ✆ 05 55 85 65 35. Limousin's oldest house is in Rue du Puy-Broch

Gimel-les-Cascades

This village's history is bound up with water. Legend has it that the waterfalls were made by a magician for love of a beautiful lady, who lived in the Ch,teau de Gimel, and gave him impossible tasks to fulfil if he wished to win her hand. Every night he succeeded, and every day she found a new task: a majestic waterfall, deep chasm and magnificent castle appeared by magic. Then the magician, growing weary of her other suitors, made her vanish. They say she walks out of the castle and through the waterfall at full moon.

LES CASCADES ✆ **05 55 21 26 49**. *Early March-late October, every day. July & August: 10am-7pm. Out of season: 10am-6pm. Wednesday: 11am-6pm.* The Montane makes its way among the gorge rocks, and tumbles into the ravine as a spectacular waterfall. There are 3 falls: Grand Saut (45m), Redole (38m) and Gouttatière or Queue de Cheval (60m), but first come the Cascadelles, falling into the Inferno chasm. Legend has it that these dark waters hide a drowned village, and you can sometimes hear the church bells ringing. Picturesque, magical, poetic and breathtaking in parts.

SAINT PARDOUX DE GIMEL CHURCH. Built in 1486, its treasure includes a 12thc. Limoges enamel shrine containing Saint Etienne's relics and shaped like a house (20cm by 29cm).

Gorges de la Dordogne

Also known as the High Valley, this is one of France's wildest natural sites. The gorges can be 150-350m deep, and many birds of prey make their home there, including peregrin falcons, kites and eagles.

Meymac

Mont Bessou (976m) and the Mas Chevalier (965m) are the department's highest peaks and Meymac, its biggest community, where mountain strength blends with the gentler lowland lifestyle.

CENTRE NATIONAL D'ART CONTEMPORAIN Abbaye Saint André ✆ **05 55 95 23 30**. *Open September-June, every day except Monday: 2pm-6pm (mornings by appointment). July & August, open every day: 10am-7pm. Annual closing: Christmas holidays. Admission: adult 4 €, concessions 2 €.* Housed in Saint Andre Abbey since 1979, this contemporary art centre hosts thematic exhibitions covering the main trends from 1970 to the present and displays monographs and the work of young artists. The abbey's cultural importance (Meymac was refounded here by the Benedictines in the 12thc.) has thus been restored along with the building.

SAINT ANDRE ABBEY CHURCH ✆ **05 55 95 18 43**. *Guided tours all year on request.* Built in stages during the 12thc., this Romanesque church's size and former outbuildings recall its monastic origins. Admire the fine façade, semi-circular vault and carved granite capitals. Inside are a 12thc. black wooden Virgin, 15thc. stone pieta and splendid Baroque organ. The contemporary art centre is in the south wing.

Sarran

Known for its 'President Jacques Chirac' Museum and Ch,teau de Bity, owned by the Chiracs and thus closed to the public.

CHURCH. Dates back to the 15thc., and contains a listed reredos. Floodlit on Saturday evenings.

MUSEE DU PRESIDENT JACQUES CHIRAC ✆ **05 55 21 77 77**. *www.museepresidentchirac.fr. Admission: adult 4 €. Open January & February, Saturday & Sunday: 10am-12.30pm and 1.30pm-6pm. March-June, September-December, every day except Monday: 10am-12.30pm and 1.30pm-6pm. July & August, every day: 10am-12.30pm and 1.30pm-6pm.* Native of Corréze, Jacques Chirac chose to live at Sarran, and the museum designed by architect Jean-Michel Wilmotte displays gifts received by the President during official visits and international meetings. A second room houses temporary exhibitions.

Saint-Nazaire

Saint-Nazaire village and church used to stand on this headland at the Dordogne and Diege confluence, considered to be the Dordogne Valley's most striking viewpoint. From the far end, you have a wonderful view over the Dordogne Gorges (Mareges dam reservoir) and the River Diege.

Turenne

The powerful Vicomtes de Turenne's medieval stronghold contained 3,000 inhabitants in the 11th and 12thc.; now there are less than 800! The road to the castle is lined with fine houses, including the 'Tournadour House', once the town's salt loft. After the Calvary, you reach the fortified gate in the second of three walls. Right, is the Seneschal's house; left, the Capuchin Chapel with the Saint Paul quarter below. Other beautiful residences surround the Place de la Halle.

CHATEAU ✆ **05 55 85 90 66** *April-June, September & October: 10am-12 noon and 2pm-6pm. July & August: 10am-7pm. Admission: adult: 3.50 € € 7-18s 1.50 €* . Two towers with a garden between are all that is left of the fortress. The Tour de l'Horloge is a 13thc. keep; you can visit the guards' room, where objects and furniture are on display in a reconstruction of medieval life. The round Tour de Cesar is probably 11thc. Climb the spiral staircase to the watch room, and the terrace with its viewpoint indicator.

CHURCH. This late 16thc. collegiate church was only finished in 1668. Shaped like a Greek cross, it contains a high altar topped with a carved and gilded wooden reredos depicting Jesus' Passion.

Uzerche

Originally a fortress, then a residential town with noble mansions where neighbouring lords spent the winter. Rising in tiers with its towers and spire, Uzerche has been likened to a sea-and sand-less Mont Saint-Michel!

Varetz

A small shady square awaits the tired tourist in the village centre, while Castel Novel stands proudly on the hill. Its main buildings date back to the 14thc. but it has a 13thc. tower. Turrets and galleries are 16thc.

CHURCH. Partly Romanesque, this 12thc. church was reshaped over the centuries. High cylindrical columns split the nave into two; the 12thc. capitals are decorated with plants in one nave and animals in the other. The recently restored high altar has a Crucifixion table and 12thc. gilded wooden reredos.

CREUSE

Ahun

A town full of interest for the visitor. The old houses with their discreet charm, stone bridges and exuberant natural environment are enchanting.

CHURCH. Guided tours all year on request: 05 55 62 53 93. Its patron is the local martyr Saint Sylvain. Part of this church is Romanesque (apse, apsidiole, and 10thc. crypt built on a former Gallo-Roman temple). The nave, topped by an octagonal steeple, is an identical 18thc. reconstruction. This restoration work was undertaken from 1777-1781, by episcopal architect Joseph Brousseau. You reach the crypt from the outside. Inside the church are some interesting furnishings: a 12thc. baptismal tank carved with a palm-leaf garland; 16thc. Christ of Mercy; 15thc. pieta depicting Saint John, Mary Magdalene and the Holy Women at Mary's side and a 17thc. reliquary in gilded wood. The chancel contains some striking 17thc. panelling by master-sculptor Jean Pavillon.

Aubusson

Six centuries of tapestry-making have left their mark on this famous place. Most of the workshops were in the Rue Vieille quarter.

MAISON DU TAPISSIER 05 55 66 32 12 Rue Vieille. *Open Monday-Saturday. July & August: 10am-7pm (ask about opening times for other months) adult 4 €.* This 16thc. master-smoother's residence illustrates the history of tapestry-making: origins, development, techniques and life in a weaving workshop.

MUSEE DOM ROBERT Rue Saint Jean ✆ **05 55 66 10 08.** *Open Easter-November, every day: 10am-12 noon and 2pm-6pm.* Other periods by appointment. Admission: 4 . In the 10thc. chapel, you can see the work of Dom Robert, prestigious contemporary tapestry cartoonist and Benedictine monk. His tapestries are a hymn to creation and the glories of nature.

MUSEE DEPARTEMENTAL DE LA TAPISSERIE 10 Ave des Lissiers ✆ **05 55 83 08 30**. *Open July & August every day except Tuesday morning: 10am-6pm. Guided tours included in admission price: 11.30am, 2pm and 4pm. September-June: every day except Tuesday: 9.30am-12 noon and 2pm-6pm. Admission: 4 €. 'Passport' price: 3 €.* This museum (only 20 years old) illustrates the story of Aubusson-Felletin tapestry. A 17th, 18th and 19thc. tapestry collection depicts country, mythological, historical, Biblical and romantic scenes. The 20thc. renovation period, lead by Jean Lurçat is also represented. Contemporary works, cartoons and models are added each year, and temporary exhibitions are held.

Aubusson tapestries

It is difficult to be exact about these tapestries' origins. Some say they were brought to France by the Saracens, who settled on the banks of the Creuse after their defeat in 732, finding both soft water and a favourable climate for sheep breeding, to provide wool. Whatever the story, the records establish certain facts: in the 15thc. tapestry-weavers were living in Felletin.

In the 17thc., Colbert granted the title of Royal Tapestry Workshop (Manufacture royale) to the Aubusson (1665) and Felletin (1689) workshops. In order to tell them apart, Aubusson tapestries were given blue selvage, while Fellatin tapestries had brown. The smoothers worked from Le Brun's cartoons, among others. Everything went well until the Edict of Nantes was revoked in 1685, and many Protestant tapestry-weavers left Aubusson for Germany, weakening the town's industry. The state of the French economy up until 1730 did nothing to improve tapestry-making in the country as a whole.

In the 18thc. during the reigns of Louis XV (letters of patent in 1732) and Louis XVI, the state renewed its interest in the tapestry industry. Verdure was fashionable, as were Boucher's, Lancret's and Watteau's cartoons. A wider range of brighter colours was used, and carpets using the new French knot stitch technique on high-smoothing looms created work for women around 1743.

The 1789 Revolution and the fashion for wallpaper hit the tapestry workshops hard. In the 19thc. tapestry-makers had run out of imagination and new cartoons, and were reduced to making copies of existing models, changing only a few details, like the costumes. Fortunately, the manufacture of carpets (Aubusson short pile) and furniture saved what had become a switchback situation.

In 1937, a meeting between painter Jean Lurcat and Francois Tabard, the young manager of a family workshop, led to the rebirth of tapestry making. Future creations were limited to 40 colours, and the cartoons were no longer painted but numbered, with each number corresponding to a shade or tone. In 1939 the Quatre Saisons (Four Seasons) was produced in conjunction with Gromaire and Dubreuil. This powerfully lyrical work, together with Lurcat's 'public relations' initiatives encouraged a number of artists to create designs for tapestry-making.

Today, large orders are few and far between, given the current economic situation and price of tapestries, but contemporary works designed by artists (some trained by the Enad) are still made locally, and the Aubusson Museum attracts plenty of visitors every year.

Aubusson tapestries, Tapisserie d'Achille (detail) - XVIIe

Bourganeuf

A 19th and early 20thc. porcelain and tapestry industry boom led to the transport of water from the Jarrauds waterfall to the town, for hydraulic energy. Bourganeuf was the first French town to have electric light.

SAINT JEAN CHURCH. Formerly a chapel for the Knights of Saint John of Jerusalem, the church was built in the 12thc. and enlarged by adding north and south chapels in the 15thc., forming a corner of the priory. The 19thc. wall decorations and stained glass windows have just been restored. Notice the 15thc. reliquary and a superb statue of the Angel Gabriel holding a stoup shaped like a Saint Jacques scallop.

MUSEE DE L'ELECTRIFICATION Route de la Cascade ✆ 05 55 64 26 26. *Open every day except Sunday, 1 July-31 August: 10am-12 noon and 2pm-6pm (Saturday 5pm). Admission: adult 4 €, 11-15s 3 €, under-11s free.* Discover the history of electricity in France, including recent developments.

TOUR ZIZIM. *Tower closed indefinitely for renovation work.* Built from 1484-86 by Prince Djem, the 3-storey framework is remarkable. It contains archeological findings, illustrations of local life and Bourganeuf's old industries, Resistance memories, ethnography, and documents about the Knights of Malta and Prince Djem.

Boussac

Once Boussac-le-Château, at the Petite Creuse and Beroux confluence, its history is closely linked to the 12thc. castle.

CHATEAU ✆ 05 55 65 07 62. *Open all year: 9am-12 noon and 2pm-6.30pm (5.15pm in winter). Admission: adult 8 €, child 4 €.* This castle on its imposing headland once housed the famous *Dame à la Licorne* tapestries, and played host to George Sand who set part of her novel Jeanne here. A powerful fortress, richly-furnished inside.

Crozant

The village is chiefly known for its ruined fortress' past glory. Built on a rocky headland at the Creuse and Sedelle confluence, this medieval stronghold was destroyed by Richelieu, yet the ruins still recall the luxury and excess of those days. They consist of three towers, a 15thc. keep and Isabelle d'Angouleme's tower. Painter Armand Guillaumin, leader of the Ecole de Crozant, has his bust in the square near the church.

Felletin

Felletin has fountains, chapels, ruined fortifications, a medieval bridge on the Creuse and some fine 15th, 16th and 18thc. houses. It is also known for tapestry-making (15thc. birthplace; 17thc. Royal Tapestry Workshop) diamond-cutting (19thc. Imperial Factory) and today, the Ecole Nationale des Métiers du Batiment; a building and construction school.

CHATEAU D'ARFEUILLE ✆ 05 55 66 40 40 *Open June-September 2006 (subject to confirmation): 10am-12 noon and 2.30pm-6.30pm. Guided tours: 10.30am, 3.30pm and 5pm. Admission: 3.50 €. 'Passport' price (afternoon only) 2.5 €.* Originally a 12thc. fortress, the present building dates back to the late 15thc., and has always been in the same family. Don't miss the marvellous 18thc. park.

Guéret

The town's origins go back to 690, when the local population was grouped round the monastery. Today it is the Creuse's prefecture.

MUSEE D'ART ET D'ARCHEOLOGIE DE GUERET Hôtel de la Senatorerie Ave de la Senatorerie ✆ 05 55 52 07 20. *Open every day except Tuesday and public holidays: 1 May-31 October: 10am-12 noon and 2pm-6pm (other periods: 2pm-6pm). Admission: adult 2.50 €, passport 1.90 €, child 0.80 €.* This museum in its green park illustrates the region's history from Prehistoric times to the Middle Ages with everyday objects (ceramic, glass, tools). There are Egyptian collections (the gods; funeral rites) and Oriental art. You can also see Limoges enamel and 17th-20thc. painting and decorative arts.

Peyrat-le-Château

Overlooking beautiful Vassiviére reservoir, the big 11thc. square tower with a spiral staircase is all that is left of this castle.

MAISON DES MOULINS Moulin de l'Eau ✆ 05 55 69 26 05. *Guided tour 7 days a week in July & August.* 14 scale models (1 in 10) of local stone mills are on display in this former watermill on the banks of the Maulde. They all work, and the commentary is provided by their designer Jean-Claude Mareau. Beautiful and educational.

Sainte-Feyre

The 13thc. church (fortified in the 14thc, reshaped in the 15th and 16thc.) contains the fine 15thc. polychrome stone group Sainte Anne Trinitaire, and the lords of Sainte Feyre, la Valette and Chatres' tombs. There is an 18thc. reredos with painted panels. On the other side of the road is a chapel to Saint Hubert, patron saint of hunters, rebuilt in 1512 by Pierre de Sainte-Feyre.

CHATEAU DE SAINTE FEYRE © 05 55 81 15 52. *Open every day, 15 June-15 September: 10am-12 noon and 2pm-7pm. By appointment out of season. Admission 5 €, passport 3 €* . An 18thc. castle built on medieval foundations, to architect Brousseau's plans. The remains include a defensive tower, and you can visit 10 rooms. This classical structure is unique in Creuse.

PARC ANIMALIER DES MONTS DE GUERET © 05 55 81 23 23. *www.loups-chabriéres.com. 1 April-31 May: 10am-6pm. 1 June-15 September: 10am-7pm. 16 September-31 March, Wednesday, Saturday, Sunday, public and school holidays: 1pm-5pm. Admission: adult 7 €, concessions 5.5 €*. You can see wolves in their natural habitat in this extraordinary wildlife park, in different enclosures according to their origins. A pack of European wolves lives in the Roches enclosure (13,000 m^2). Two others are kept for old, solitary wolves and animals adapting to their surroundings. This legendary creature is explained in three thematic displays: mythical wolves, real wolves and modern-day wolves and their environment.

HAUTE-VIENNE – VASSIVIERE COUNTRY

Limoges

From antique times to the present, Limoges' history is fascinating, and not only connected with porcelain. Known for revolutionary combat and later, Resistance, (de Gaulle called it 'the capital of the maquis'), it now likes to be seen as an artistic and cultural town in central France.

AQUARIUM DU LIMOUSIN 2, boulevard Gambetta © 05 55 33 42 11. *Open 10.30am-6pm. Admission: adults 6.50 €*. 600 sqm. of underwater world to discover. Built in the town's former water reservoir, this aquarium contains over 300 kinds of seawater fish from all over the world, together with European freshwater fish. You can admire some amazing specimens, such as electric fish, clown fish, longhorn trunkfish, stonefish and piranhas.

SAINT ETIENNE CATHEDRAL. Gothic masterpiece, built on the site of a temple remaining from Roman Augustoritum (the original Limoges). Building started in 1273, but wasn't finished until the late 19thc. when Viollet-le-Duc had the steeple attached to the nave.

CITY QUARTER Bd de Fleurus © 05 55 34 46 87. This is the old episcopal city quarter, built round the cathedral.

PETIT TRAIN TOURISTIQUE Bd de Fleurus © 05 55 34 46 87. *Admission: adult 5 €, under-12s 3.5 €.*

Hôtel de ville, Limoges

MUSEE MUNICIPAL DE L'EVECHE-MUSEE DE L'EMAIL Place de la Cathedrale ✆ 05 55 45 98 10 *October-June: open every day except Tuesday: 10am-12 noon and 2pm-5pm (6pm in June). July-September: all week-6pm. Admission free. Guided tour by appointment with the Tourist Office 05 55 34 46 87.* From 2005 onwards, the museum is renovating its contents over a 2-year period, but will stay open. Set up in 1912, the Musee de l'Evêché contains 5 collections in 23 rooms (enamel, painting, Egyptian, Gallo-Roman and medieval archeology and lapidary) the first including over 500 pieces of Limoges enamel from the 12thc. to the present. There are a number of bronze and terracotta Egyptian figurines, works by the region's painters (Renoir, Suzanne Valadon, Guillaumin), sarcophagi and funeral furnishings. Kids' activity brochures are available free.

CITE DES METIERS ET DES ARTS Jardin de l'Evêché (lower part) - 5, rue de la Regle ✆ 05 55 32 57 84. *Winter closing November-Easter. Admission: adult 4 €, concessions2 €.* Discover guild history, its customs and traditions (compagnonnage).

Porcelain

Only princes and lords could afford real (hard) china from the Far East or Saxe: French attempts were pretty, but too soft, through lack of kaolin. In 1766, this mysterious earth was found at Saint Yrieix, and used first in foreign and Parisian factories. Then Turgot, steward of Limoges, had Massie convert his earthenware factory to porcelain, and the first Limoges china appeared. The Revolution checked expansion for a while, but factories mushroomed in the 19th. The 'Blancs de Pouyat', for instance specialised in perfect whiteness and technical skill. Limoges was soon exporting 50% of production to Paris and its decoration workshops, and 50% to the USA, via importers like David Haviland. In the later 19thc. the porcelain-makers became competitive, and production was modernised. Progressive social ideas were gaining ground; the CGT trade union was born in Limoges in 1895, and there were violent strikes in 1905. By the 20thc., Limoges had a sure reputation in Europe and North America. New factories sprang up: Bernardaud, Raynaud, Camille Tharaud. Quality and prestige have been preserved through the century's strikes, wars and economic crises, thanks to exceptional skill and know-how, and the artists' and ceramic engineering schools founded for the industry.

MUSEE NATIONAL ADRIEN DUBOUCHE 8, place Winston-Churchill ✆ 05 55 33 08 50. *www.musee-adriendubouche.fr. Open every day except Tuesday: 10am-12.25pm and 2pm-5.40pm. July & August: 10am-5.40pm. Admission: 4 €, under-18s free. Ticket including Manufacture Bernardaud: 5.60 €.* Built in 1900, this superb building contains an extraordinary 12,000 pieces of earthenware and china.

BERNARDAUD LA MANUFACTURE 27, ave. Albert Thomas ✆ 05 55 10 55 91. *www.bernardaud.net. Open every day (and public holidays) 1 June-30 September: 9am-11.15am and 1pm-4.15pm. Admission: adult 4 €.* Founded in 1863, this is one of Limoges' oldest working factories.

PAVILLON DE LA PORCELAINE Ave. du President Kennedy - ZI Magre ✆ 05 55 30 21 86. *www.museehaviland.com. Open every day: 8.30am-7.30pm. Admission free.* The Pavillon tells an American story, about the Haviland brothers who came to export from Limoges and stayed to make reputed china in their huge factory.

GARE DES BENEDICTINS. This 1929 building replaces an earlier station, opened in 1856 with the first railway line. It is a symbol of architectural skill (the first French station to be built overhanging the platforms) and of Limoges' prosperity before the economic depression.

QUARTIER DE LA BOUCHERIE. *Guided tours for all during school holidays, and for groups all year by reservation at the Tourist office 05 55 34 46 87.* A medieval quarter with its own history, architecture, traditions and atmosphere. The Rue de la Boucherie is one of Limoges' most picturesque streets, housing butchers from the 13thc. onwards in wooden houses with stone ground floors. The present houses had their half-timbering renovated in the 1970; the oldest go back to the 14th and 15thc. Meat was originally sold in the Place des Bancs; the butchers didn't open shops on their ground floors until the Revolution.

MAISON TRADITIONNELLE DE LA BOUCHERIE 36, rue de la Boucherie. *Open every day, July-September. Admission free; commentary. Guided tours for all during school holidays and for groups all year by reservation at the Tourist Office & 05 55 34 46 87.* Set up jointly by the town council and association Renaissance du Vieux Limoges, this ecomusee reconstructs the life of an 18thc. butchers' family in one of the 58 houses where members of this powerful guild lived and worked.

AQUARIUM DU LIMOUSIN 2, bd. Gambetta ✆ 05 55 33 42 11. *Open every day: 10.30am-6pm. Admission: adult 6 € 4-15s 4.50 €, concessions 5.50 €.* Set up in the town's former reservoir, the aquarium contains over 300 species of fish, with some amazing specimens: electric fish, clown fish, piranha, etc.

Haute-Vienne

Bellac

A picturesque setting on a Vincou Valley slope; Ch,teau Barthon de Montbas with its watchtowers and the old houses in Rue de Belfort are Bellac's main attractions.

BELLAC CHURCH. Notice the Romanesque apse capitals, and the little serpentine capitals on the Limousin portal with its 4 archivolts. The remarkable shrine is the Limoges workshops' oldest existing piece.

TANNERIE GAL 1, rue des Tanneries ✆ 05 55 68 06 25. *Groups only, by appointment.* This working tannery (Bellac's last) houses a living museum in one of its oldest buildings.

Chalus

French comedian, author and songwriter Pierre Desproges (1939-1988) was born here.

CHATEAU DE CHALUS-CHABROL ✆ 05 55 78 56 61. *www.chateaudechalus.com. Open every day, 1 July-31 August: 10am-7pm. April, May, June & September: 10am-12 noon and 2pm-6pm. Admission: adult 6 €, 6-15s 3 €.* Richard the Lionheart was mortally wounded besieging this castle in 1199. You can visit the ruined 11thc. church, 11th-12thc. Chalus-Chabrol keep, 11th-13thc. living quarters (corner tower and two 11thc. rooms), 17thc. wing (oak staircase, furnished 17th and 18thc. rooms), medieval garden, 17thc. gardens and Feuillardiers museum.

MAISON DU CHATAIGNIER 28, ave. François Mitterrand ✆ 05 55 78 51 13. *Open every day.* Explains the associations and trades associated with chestnut trees, their life, seasonal rhythm and circuit. Regional produce on sale.

Eymoutiers

This prosperous tannery town has preserved its houses with openwork attics used for drying, like the master-tanner's house on the edge of the Vienne.

SAINT ETIENNE COLLEGIATE CHURCH. Built on the site of hermit Saint Psalmet's sepulchre. The composite architecture is striking: Limousin portal, fortified tower, chnacel rebuilt in the 15thc. and 16 windows dating from 1460-1485.

Mortemart

Two feudal mottes can be seen at the village entrance; the Dukes' feudal castle is in ruins, partly covered by the former moat. Mortemart is listed one of France's finest villages.

Nexon

Nexon is famous for the breeding of Anglo-Arab horses, and is also the capital of circus arts. The castle - now the Town Hall - was built in the 17thc. by Leonard de Gay, then restored and extended in the 19thc. Nexon's breeders and owners are great horse-lovers, and the stud farm, authenticated in the early 16thc., was reputed for its elite pedigree mounts.

JARDIN DES SENS. *Admission free.* May be visited as a one-off, or included in the Tourist Office programme of discovery trips in and around Nexon: 05 55 58 28 44. Located on the edge of Nexon Chateau Park. The sense of touch has priority in this garden of the senses, which boasts a varied selection of trees, a bamboo maze designed to look like a circus big top, an orchard containing a number of different fruit trees, a therapeutic garden and a flowering wall on a rainbow theme.

Oradour-sur-Glane

On 10 June 1944, the SS division 'Das Reich' massacred 642 people, including 300 children, and burned down the village. It happened at 2pm. The men were sent into the barns, to be shot or burned to death. The women and children were killed in the same way, shut up in the church. Oradour's conservation is unique for symbolic reasons, and the State rebuilt the new town (finished in 1953). One of Limousin's last lanterns of the dead can be seen in the graveyard.

CENTRE DE LA MEMOIRE ✆ 05 55 43 04 30. *www.oradour.org. Open every day. Annual closing 16/12-31/01. Admission: adult 6 €; students, unemployed and war veterans 4 €.* This centre traces the events leading to the Oradour massacre and its outcome: the rise of Nazism, French defeat, collaboration, Resistance, policy of terror, 8 and 9 June 1944, national recognition, trials and amnesty. It bears witness, informs and pleads for peace between nations. Books, catalogues, postcards and videos are available from the bookshop.

Rochechouart

Ancient ramparts, towers, a 16thc. fountain and the Consuls' House can be seen on a stroll through the town.

CHATEAU DE ROCHECHOUART. The present building has kept its 13thc. corner tower and keep, but is otherwise 15thc. Admire the magnificent gallery with its twisted columns and 15thc. framework, and the wall fresces tracing Hercules' story (16thc. grisaille wall-paintings) and early 16thc. hunting scenes depicting Rochechouart and his ramparts.

SAINT SAUVEUR CHURCH. Houses a religious art museum conatining 12thc. paintings and sarcophagi.

ESPACE METEORITE 16, rue Jean Parvy ✆ 05 55 03 02 70. *Open July & August, Monday-Friday: 10am-12.30pm and 1.30pm-6pm. Weekends and public holidays: 2pm-6pm. Out of season: open afternoons, closed Saturday. Admission: adult 3 €.* 200 million years ago, a huge meteorite crashed in the area. You can learn more about it from the panels, samples, video, model and trips to the site in summer.

Le Vigen

The 12th-13thc. church (reshaped in the 19thc.) built on the site of Saint Theau's monk's cell, has a striking west front with a Limousin portal and a flat, two-storey tower. The beautiful Ligoure and Du Reynou castles are close by.

PARC PAYSAGER ET ANIMALIER DU REYNOU Le Reynou ✆ 05 55 00 40 00. *Open every day, April-mid November: 10am-8pm. Other periods: 10am-5.45pm, except Mondays & Tuesdays. Open every day during school holidays: 10am-6pm. Admission: adult 9.50 € 3-12s 6 €.* Built by the porcelain manufacturer Charles Haviland, Le Reynou castle park is landscaped according to Impressionist and Japanese theories, with 132 varieties of plant. The 1999 hurricane caused a lot of damage, but it is still beautiful, and now houses a 30ha, wildlife reserve with mammals and birds sharing different open spaces.

Vassivière Country

Limousin's main sailing and tourist resort is based on Lake Vassiviére and villages around: Feniers, Faux-la-Montagne, Gentioux-Pigerolles, Royere-de-Vassivière, Saint-Martin-Ch,teau in Creuse; Beaumont-du-Lac, Nedde and Peyrat-le-Ch,teau in Haute-Vienne.

MAISON DE VASSIVIERE ✆ 05 55 69 76 70. *Open all year: 9am-1pm and 2pm-5pm. Saturday & Sunday: 2pm-5pm. June-September: 11am-1pm and 2pm-7pm. www.vassivière.com.* Things to see on the Ile de Vassivière: Raymond Poulidor exhibition, Centre National d'Art et du Paysage with its sculpture park, footpaths, animals and summer events.

CENTRE NATIONAL D'ART ET DU PAYSAGE Ile de Vassivière ✆ 05 55 69 27 27. *Open April-September, every day: 11am-1pm and 2pm-7pm. October-March, every day except Monday: 2pm-6pm. Admission: adult 3 €, concessions 1.50 €.* Built by architect Aldo Rossi, with Xavier Fabre, this is an exhibition, creation and training centre. The Contemporary Art Centre houses temporary exhibitions, and the sculpture park brings together artists and landscapes, with the resulting works (temporary and permanent; monumental and discreet).

Plateau de Millevaches

Millevaches means 'a thousand springs' and not 'a thousand cows' as you might think. The plateau reaches its highest point at the Mont de Bessou (976m). The department's eastern border is formed by the wild and beautiful gorges of the Chavanon, which flows into the Dordogne at Confolent-Port-Dieu. The long, hard winters are followed by splendid springs, short summers that are never too hot, and warm Indian summers often lasting well into October. The massif is well-watered, with over 1,300 mm of annual rainfall, and thus represents one of France's biggest water towers. This landscape provides a strong contrast to the wild and austere heather-covered moors scattered with pine forests and valleys hidden in the hollows or on the edge of the plateau, where small slate-roofed villages nestle. The region is perfect for trout fishing, mushroom-picking, hiking or simply admiring the beauties of nature.

FOOD AND DRINK

Unfairly known as 'rape and chestnut eaters' for many years, the Limousins have proved that you can do wonders with such ingredients.

Most of the region's typical dishes are a simple alchemy of natural produce. There's nothing better than a delicious *cul-noir* flavoured with Brive mustard and served with potato pate, and a *flognarde* for afters.

Mushrooms

The woods are full of edible mushrooms...if you know where to look. Morels in spring, meadow mushrooms in April, chanterelles in May, parasol mushrooms in September and horns of plenty in October for your omelettes and fricassées. The most prized is the cepe.

Chestnuts

Before the arrival of potatoes, this was the basic foodstuff. You find them in soup, terrines, blood puddings, garnishes, cakes, liqueurs and sweets. The Maison du Chataignier in Chalus gives examples of this rustic fruit's various uses.

Massepain

A speciality from Saint-Leonard-de-Noblat, made of crushed almonds, sugar and egg-whites. The five local patissiers keep the recipe to themselves!

Moutarde violette

This 14thc. condiment is one of Brive's specialities, made from black grapes seeded, cooked and sieved, then added to the mustard flour. Used in the making of highly-flavoured sauces.

Apples

There are 50 varieties, including the famous Sainte Germaine. Delicious raw or cooked, with fish, foie gras and blood pudding.

Truffles

Three types of truffle are found mainly in Corrèze: the black, winter and summer (or Saint Jean) truffles. They grow well-buried in chalky soil, in oak woods, and are now also grown artificially in truffle oak plantations.

Limousin meat

Beef

Limousin cattle are delicious and robust (the butcher's guild in Limoges was prosperous and powerful from the 13thc.) but their reputation really dates from a local breeder's decision not to cross-breed them, about 100 years ago. They are fed on their mothers' milk, then graze in pastures, giving tender lean meat of excellent quality (Blason-Prestige label).

Culs-noirs

This ancestral 'free-range' pork is definitely better than the hybrid sort you tend to find today. The black-bottomed pigs come from Saint Yrieix, and give thicker bacon and tastier meat.

Veal

The main French producer of sucking veal (one Corrèzian farmer in two breeds them). The animal fed by its mother gives a pinkish-white meat with a nutty taste.

Hotels & Restaurants

CORRÈZE

Aubazine

HOTEL-RESTAURANT LE SAINT-ETIENNE ** Le Bourg © 05 55 25 71 01 *Fax : 05 55 25 71 37. Site Internet : www.lesaintetienne.com 42 rooms from 39 € to 43 €. Breakfast 7 €. Children's menu 10 €. Set menus from 16 € to 21 €. Dogs admitted.* This former priory belonging to the12thc. Cistercian Abbey is located in Aubazine centre, and boasts some intimate and sophisticated private salons.From its genuine Corrèze interior, with fireplace and exposed beams, you can contemplate the abbey through the dining-room windows. Your gaze will surely be distracted however, by the local specialities delicately concocted in the kitchens. Burbot kebabs, local trout pan-fried with langoustines and tornedos *sautéed* with a foie gras escalope fix all your attention on your plate. The restaurant offers an original formula which lets you choose your own set menu by selecting a starter, garnished meat or fish course, cheese platter and dessert from the main menu. In summer you can also choose your own tan, by deciding between the shady terrace or the one in the sun. The park is pleasant; the rustic rooms opening onto the garden comfortable and the annex rooms in small maisonettes surrounded by hydrangea gardens provide a real change of scene. Access to the hotel car park gets you into the mood of the place straight away.

Beaulieu-sur-Dordogne

LE TURENNE * 1, boulevard Saint-Rodolphe-de-Turenne © 05 55 91 10 16. *Open March to mid-November. Closed Monday lunchtime. Set menus from 12.90 € to 40 €. 17 rooms from 50 €. Breakfast 8.50 €.* This charming, former 17thc.abbey was taken on three years ago by the Lefevre family. To reach the restaurant you cross a magnificent terrace, where you're strongly tempted to choose a table and enjoy the sunshine. The restaurant opening onto this terrace and the shady garden has a warm and rustic atmosphere, the tables are skilfully set out and the cuisine is delicate and original. You won't forget these flaversome dishes for a long time...Spacious rooms, decorated with taste.

Brive-la-Gaillarde

CHEZ FRANCIS 61, avenue de Paris © 05 55 74 41 72 *Open every day except Sunday, Monday and public holidays. Set menus from14 € to 21 €.* The least you can say is that Chez Francis has an original setting. The restaurant walls serve as a visitors' book, and the writers from the Book Fair don't wait to be asked before inscribing their impressions, right up to the ceiling. The owner has collected many unusual objects from the four corners of the globe, which make you feel you're in a 1930s flea-market. Except that the cuisine is sophisticated and gastronomic and the welcome warm.

LA TRUFFE NOIRE * 22, boulevard Anatole-France © 05 55 92 45 00** *Open all year. Menus from 19.50 € to 90 €. 27 rooms from 75 € to 130 €. Breakfast 9.15 €. Seminars, touristic stop-offs and birthdays catered for.* This old Flemish-style building has kept its original front door, and breathes old-world charm and warmth. Set in the heart of Brive, the Truffe Noire was a rotisserie in 1873. It continues the region's gastronomic tradition by preferring local produce served on menus called Cantou or Pais. Duck, lamb and beef with the famous Brive violet mustard are at home here, as is the 'black diamond' which flavours the truffle menus, a house speciality. The restaurant's big dining room opens onto a shady terrace much appreciated in summer, and frequented by celebrities taking part in the town's annual events, such as the Book Fair in November. The rooms are soundproofed and air-conditioned.

Collonges-la-Rouge

L'AUBERGE DE BENGES © 05 55 85 76 68 / 06 18 52 85 82. *Open Saturday evening and Sunday lunchtime only, until April, or weekdays with advance booking. Set menus from 8 € to 23 €.* The Chateau de Benges' former barn was fitted out for this *auberge* or inn, run by Isabelle and Philippe, ex-owners of the Triskel at Brive.They've kept the warm atmosphere from their former establishment in a red sandstone setting, with whitewashed walls and sheeny woodwork.The *cuisine de terroir* is based on local produce and varies from week to week but you'll always find a top-quality foie gras or confit not too far from your plate. We recommend the Cantal fondue with cepes for fondue fans; it's a house speciality.

Tulle

LE CENTRAL 32, rue Jean-Jaurès ✆ 05 55 26 24 46 *Set menus from 20 € to 40 €.* Le Central is a real Tulle institution, set up in 1927 by Angele and Antonin Poumier. Since then, three generations have worked hard to make the establishment a success, and today grandson Raymond does the cooking, helped by his parents Jean, at reception and in the brasserie and Yvette, who looks after the patisserie. The dishes are original, made from irreproachable produce. *Salade du marche* with pan-fried foie gras, sweetbreads and scallops *au gratin* with conserved fennel, chanterelles and cepes in a crust with foie-gras and truffles. Michelin have awarded Le Central three forks, and Raymond Poumier has recently been singled out as Regional Chef 2005 by the Gault-et-Millau guide, thus confirming his already recognised skill.

Varetz

LE DOMAINE DE CASTEL NOVEL** ✆ 05 55 85 00 01** *Fax : 05 55 85 09 03. Site Internet : www. castelnovel.com. Open all year. 37 rooms from 90 € to 340 €. Set menus served lunchtime only, from 22 € to 29 €. Evenings, from 37 € to 62 €. Children's menu (under-12s) 15 €.* This superb fortified chateau built of red Collonges stone, with its three pointed towers, dates back to the Middle Ages. In 1289 it belonged to Geraud and Bernard Pida de Castel Novel, then towards the end of 1500, to the Aubusson family, who kept it for three centuries. One of the last owners was Henry de Jouvenel, journalist and politician, who married the writer Colette.She became a baroness, and chatelaine of the estate, writing some of her novels here, and the menus recall this period: the Bel-Gazou and its duck foie gras with sweet wine and sweet-and-sour rhubarb, and the Colette with steamed lobster and mushroom ravioli followed by pigeon roasted on the bone and country bacon chips. The setting, like the cuisine, is prestigious, in its 40 ha. tree-filled park with heated swimming pool, tennis courts and a 3-hole and practice golf-course. Weather permitting; you can enjoy your drink or coffee under the trees, while admiring the superb view of the valley. Still in a literary vein, it's all luxury, calm and voluptuous pleasure, to quote the poet Baudelaire.

CREUSE

Bénévent-l'Abbaye

HOTEL DU CEDRE Rue de l'Oiseau ✆ 05 55 81 59 99.** *Closed Friday and Sunday evening. Annual holiday in February. Set menus from 18 € to 40 €. 16 rooms from 48 € to 96 €.* The old farm buildingsin the heart of the village have been rehabiliated to provide two reception rooms, terrace, swimming-pool and a park overlooked by a majestic cedar many hundreds of years old.The rooms are very comfortable; the seminar room is under an ancestral vault.The menus change with the seasons and include local produce like leg of Limousin lamb with chanterelles. For dessert you can savour an excellent *crème brulée* or raspberries *au gratin.*

Chénérailles

LE COQ D'OR 7, place du Champ-de-Foire ✆ 05 55 62 30 83 *Open Tuesday to Sunday lunchtime. Annual holiday early January, late June and late September.* Menus from 12 € to 41 €. 6 rooms at 38 €. Breakfast 6 €. The setting, quality of the food and warmth of the welcome harmonise in a recipe for success. A real diversity of dishes is offered according to the season, notably the warm foie gras escalope prepared as the moment dictates, as are the pikeperch and Limousin sirloin steak. The chocolate fondant is a must.

La Souterraine

CHATEAU DE LA CAZINE * Domaune de la Fôt, Noth ✆ 05 55 89 60 00** *Website: www. chateaulacazine.com.* Open all year. Set menus from 18 € to 55 €. 22 rooms from 75 € to 95 €. This magic place has a history: the Vicomte Pierre de Curel bought the estate while travelling through the region in 1890, together with the little manor La Fot - built in the 6thc. on the site of a former castle - and the Cazine lake. He had the great chateau put up in 1894. The rooms are luxuriously fitted out. The menu suggests an appetizing choice to suit the prestigious setting, the dishes varying with the seasons. Horse riding, mountain biking, tennis, swimming pool and lake fishing are on offer.

HAUTE-VIENNE

La Roche l'Abeille

AU MOULIN DE LA GORCE ✆ **05 55 00 70 66.** *Fax : 05 55 00 76 57. Website: www.moulingorce.com.* Closed Monday to Wednesday lunchtimes, except October and November: closed Monday and Tuesday to Friday lunchtimes. 9 rooms from 70 € to 150 € - single or double - and 1 apartment in a converted oil mill: 206 €. Set menus 40 € (main course, dessert) 48 € (starter, main course) 59 € (starter, main course, dessert) 80 € or 105 € (with wine) and 95 € or 190 € (with wine). This renowned establishment in its enchanting setting beside a beautiful lake offers service of the highest level. Chef Pierre Bertranet prepares sophisticated dishes accrding to season: here are some examples. Scrambled eggs with truffles. Duck foie gras duo. Carpaccio of langoustines, potato and chive cream farinettes. Bar spiked with garlic cloves and cress and scented oil mousseline. Veal kidneys cooked in a salt crust with Brive violet mustard. Figs roasted with blackcurrants Melba-style and Bourbon vanilla ice-cream. Note the superb cheese platter and the wine cellar where grand crus rub shoulders with original yet more accessible bottles. Attentive service, quiet and comfortable rooms.

Limoges

AMPHITRYON 26, rue de la Boucherie ✆ **05 55 33 36 39.** *Closed Sunday and Monday. Set menus : 19 € (lunchtime formula) 24 € (lunchtime menu) 36 €, 60 € (6 dishes à la carte). À la carte around 48 €.* Under new management with the arrival of chef Richard Lequet and his partner Eglantine who looks after reception and service in a most friendly manner. Behind the half-timbered facade you'll especially enjoy the cosy setting, comfort and pretty tablecloths. The cuisine is traditional with an innovative accent, and always carefully presented. Here are some examples from the current menu. The foie gras trilogy, prepared in 3 ways. The half-lobster *a la plancha*, with seasoned *herbettes* and tomato sorbet. Pigeon breast with thighs *en tartine* and Savoy cabbage with bacon. Bass steak accompanied by raw and cooked cepes, parsley juice and chicken juices. Chocolate and Morello cherries. Home-made ice-creams and sorbets. Pleasant nibbles are included with all the menus. Everything we ordered was excellent, and the wine cellar suits all tastes. Service discreet but alert.

HOTEL MERCURE ROYAL LIMOUSIN * Place de la République 05 55 34 65 30.** *Fax : 05 55 34 55 21. Website: www.mercure.com.* 77 rooms from 88 € to 117 €. Canal + and satellite chains. 8 adaptable salons can take 10 to 150 people (meetings) or up to 250 people (cocktail parties). Breakfast 10 €. Restaurant catering for seminars (advance bookings). Room-service Monday-Thursday evenings. Supplement for animals 9 €. Located in the heart of the town, this hotel provides quality services. A charming welcome is ensured; the comfortable rooms are air-conditioned and equipped with WiFi. Most of them have recently been renovated, or shortly will be. There is no quiet season here, what with passing VIPs and all those congresses and seminars to organise.

PHILIPPE REDON 3 rue d'Aguesseau ✆ **05 55 34 66 22.** *Fax 05 55 34 18 05. Closed Saturday lunchtime, Sunday, Monday lunchtime, first 2 weeks in January and first 3 weeks in August. Set menus from 25 € to 60 €, à la carte 70 €.* The Limousin cannot boast many excellent restaurants: there are three or four of them at the most, and Philippe Redon is the only one in Limoges, fifteen years after the start. These few brave cooks deserve support at a time when the 'gastronomic' restaurant is experiencing difficulties, especially in the provinces. Lively and modern, Philippe's recipes are worth calling in for, especially the langoustine and celery *croustillant*, pan-fried foie gras and asparagus, juice *extrême* with vegetables, or the turbot steak with sesame and green tea and leeks pureed with lemon, or again the young pigeon breasts caramelised Oriental-style, with lime and mango sticks, and his crunchy turban of wild strawberries and caramelised cream. Rumour says that Philippe Redon might move somewhere more comfortable, on the edge of Limoges, maybe in summer 2006. Watch this space...

Magnac-Laval

LA FERME DU LOGIS La Thibarderie ✆ **05 55 68 57 23.** *Fax : 05 55 68 52 80. Website : www.resa-france.com. Closed Sunday evening and Monday in low season, and from January to mid-February. Open all week from 15 June-15 September. 2 mobile homes (sleep 5-6) available for rent: 320 €/week in low season, 435 €/week in July & August. Set menus 15,50 € (except Sunday and public holidays) 25 €, 32 €. Children's menu 8 €. À la carte around 32 €.* Ancient stonework, fireplace, exposed beams, red hexagonal floor-tiles: you don't get more rustic than this. Etienne Muller is a bon vivant, and when you stay with him and his charming wife, you discover what conviviality really means.The cuisine pays tribute to local produce: trout fillet in saffron sauce, Limousin sirloin with fine salt and seasoning, regional cheese platter, chestnut *moelleux*. These specialities feature among others on a generous menu at 25 €. if you prefer to go *à la carte,* don't miss the excellent home-made foie gras, confits and the venison steak. The farm-produced cheeses and desserts are worth a special mention - chestnuts and local fruit. Pleasant shady terrace and lake with free fishing close by, for customers.

Saint-Léonard-de-Noblat

HOSTELLERIE LE GRAND SAINT-LEONARD ** *Route de Clermont-Ferrand & 05 55 56 18 18. Fax : 05 55 56 98 32. Closed Monday, Tuesday lunchtime and 15 December-15 January. 14 rooms from 54 € to 59 € (single or double). Cable TV. Breakfast 10 €. Set menus 25 € (except weekends) 42 €, 60 €. À la carte around 57 €. Private garage.* Inside you find a brass collection, elegant tablecloths, fine bone china and glassware in a rustic setting. Jean-MarcVallet is a remarkable cook. A fine Saint-Jacques scallop tart on a chopped mushroom bed with a parsley *coulis*. Home-made duck foie gras. Beef fillet and oxtail in Cahors wine, with poached marrow. Turbot fillet roated in salted butter with artichoke slices and pan-fried foie gras. Duck supreme with apples in a balsamic vinegar sauce. Not forgetting the *farandole* of truly exquisite desserts: iced coffee soufflé or chocolate *biscuit moelleux* with vanilla. This chef is a perfectionist down to the last detail, and it shows in both the cooking and presentation of his dishes. Attentive service and fine wine cellar with classified bottles and crus millesimes. Comfortable rooms.

Saint-Yrieix-la-Perche

LA BONNE CAVE 7, place Pierre de l'Homme ✆ 05 55 75 02 12. *Closed Monday in season, Monday and Tuesday out of season. Set menus : children 8 €, weekday lunchtimes 10 € à 12 €, 19 €, 25,50 €. À la carte around 24 €.* In a pretty setting both modern and countrified, and a good-humoured ambience, the Bonne Cave offers a cuisine that combines originality with tradition.The menu is *seasonal*: we could choose from an aubergine mousseline with fresh tomato coulis, an avocado cocktail with prawns in an Aurore sauce, smoked and fresh salmon rillettes, a shark steak with nettles (delicious), a piece of beef with woodland flavours and many other dishes, well-prepared and served on attractive plates. For dessert, we were won over by the chocolate and Morello cherry *marquise*. The prices are reasonable and you won't be disappointed. Service is quick and attentive, and the terrace is pleasant in summer.

Typical landscape of Creuse

Lorraine

Haroué castle

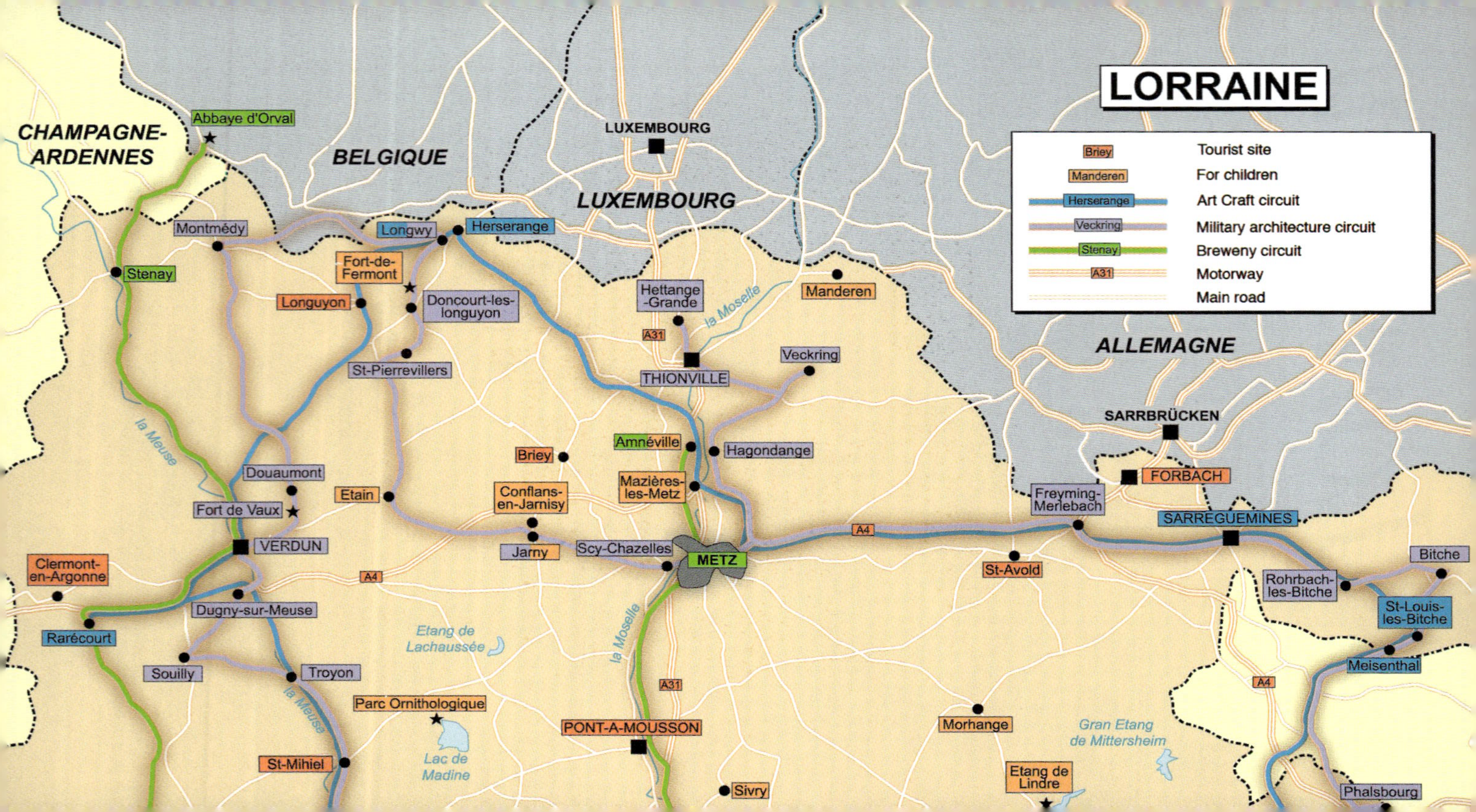
LORRAINE
Briey Tourist site
Manderen For children
Herserange Art Craft circuit
Veckring Military architecture circuit
Stenay Breweny circuit
A31 Motorway
Main road
CHAMPAGNE-ARDENNES
BELGIQUE
LUXEMBOURG
LUXEMBOURG
ALLEMAGNE
SARRBRÜCKEN
Abbaye d'Orval
Stenay
Montmédy
Longwy
Herserange
Fort-de-Fermont
Longuyon
Doncourt-les-longuyon
St-Pierrevillers
Hettange-Grande
A31
la Moselle
Manderen
Veckring
THIONVILLE
Amnéville
Hagondange
Briey
Mazières-les-Metz
Conflans-en-Jarnisy
Jarny
Scy-Chazelles
METZ
Etain
Douaumont
Fort de Vaux
VERDUN
Clermont-en-Argonne
Rarécourt
Dugny-sur-Meuse
Souilly
Troyon
la Meuse
la Meuse
A4
Etang de Lachaussée
Parc Ornithologique
Lac de Madine
St-Mihiel
la Moselle
A31
PONT-A-MOUSSON
Sivry
FORBACH
Freyming-Merlebach
A4
SARREGUEMINES
St-Avold
Bitche
Rohrbach-les-Bitche
St-Louis-les-Bitche
Meisenthal
A4
Morhange
Gran Etang de Mittersheim
Etang de Lindre
Phalsbourg

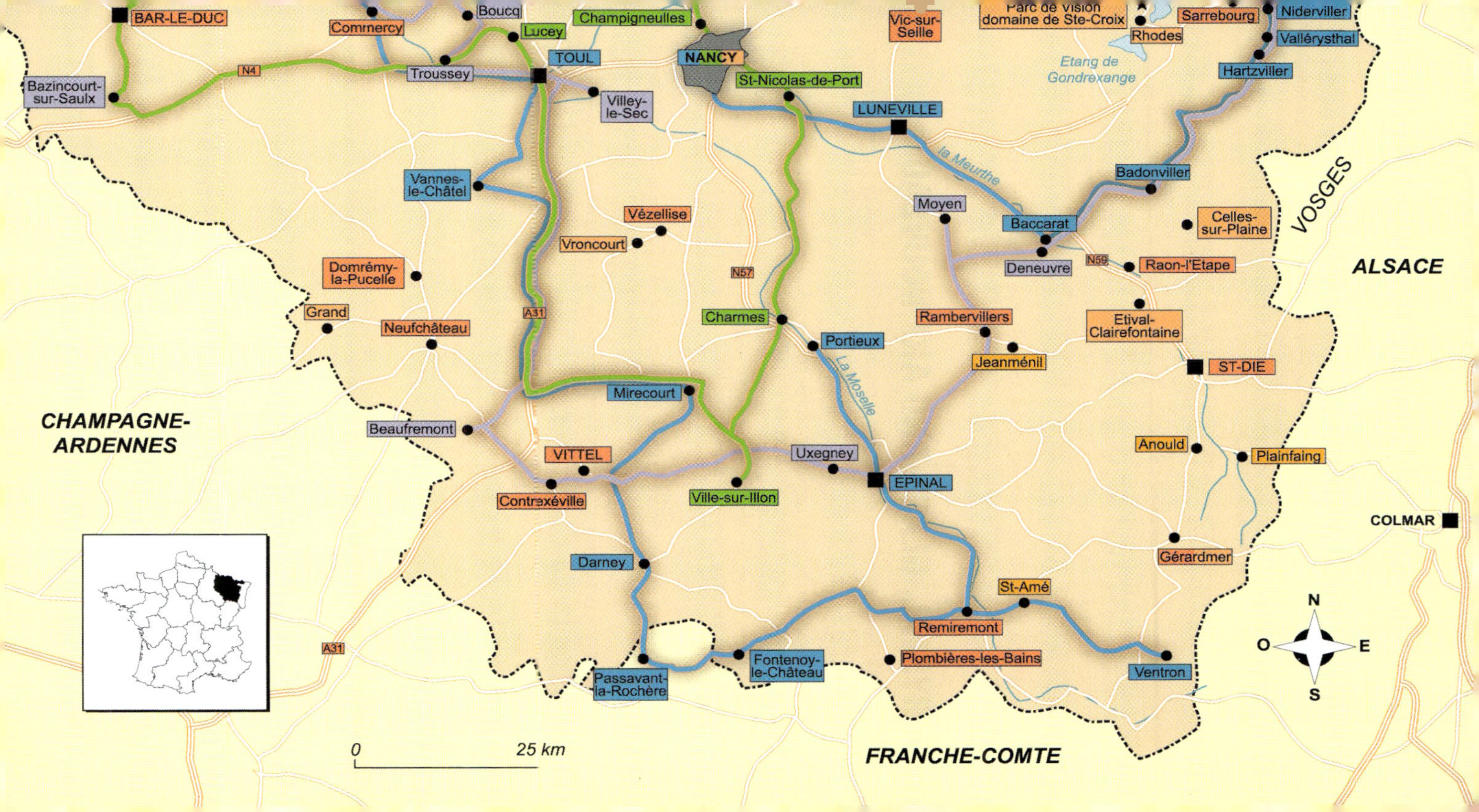

BAR-LE-DUC
Commercy
Boucq
Lucey
Champigneulles
NANCY
Vic-sur-Seille
Parc de vision domaine de Ste-Croix
Rhodes
Sarrebourg
Niderviller
Vallérysthal
Hartzviller
Etang de Gondrexange
Bazincourt-sur-Saulx
N4
Troussey
TOUL
Villey-le-Sec
St-Nicolas-de-Port
LUNEVILLE
la Meurthe
Badonviller
VOSGES
ALSACE
Vannes-le-Châtel
Vézelise
Vroncourt
Moyen
Baccarat
Celles-sur-Plaine
Deneuvre
N59
Raon-l'Etape
Domrémy-la-Pucelle
N57
Grand
Neufchâteau
A31
Charmes
Portieux
Rambervillers
Etival-Clairefontaine
Jeanménil
ST-DIE
La Moselle
Mirecourt
CHAMPAGNE-ARDENNES
Beaufremont
Anould
Plainfaing
VITTEL
Uxegney
EPINAL
Contrexéville
Ville-sur-Illon
COLMAR
Gérardmer
Darney
St-Amé
N
O
E
S
Remiremont
Plombières-les-Bains
Fontenoy-le-Château
Passavant-la-Rochère
Ventron
0
25 km
FRANCHE-COMTE

Pont-à-Mousson

The town developed from 1850 onwards, with the discovery of iron minerals at Marbache, the arrival of the railway, setting up of the Foundries (1866) and refugee industries from Prussian-occupied Alsace-Lorraine (1871). Pont-à-Mousson, the eternal border town, became an important economic centre until 1914, when it came under fire for 4 years.

PREMONTRES ABBEY 9, rue Saint Martin ✆ 03 83 81 10 32. *www.abbaye-premontres.com. Open every day except Tuesday: 9am-6pm. Sunday & public holidays: 2pm-6.30pm. Admission: 5 €, concessions 3 €, under-6s free.* Built from 1705-1735 in classical style, this superb listed monument is surrounded by gardens and a park running down to the Moselle. Abbey and church were founded by the Prémontrés Order (1,300 monasteries in Europe). After the Revolution, the abbey became a diocesan seminary, then a field hospital in the Great War. Mostly destroyed in September 1944, it has been restored and is now a cultural centre. Things to see: the cloister with garden inside, walled in by 3 galleries; Baroque-style abbey church; chapter house; refectory; and 3 striking monumental staircases (Petit rond, Majestueux Ovale and Grand Carré).

PARC NATUREL REGIONAL DE LORRAINE Logis Abbatial – Rue du Quai ✆ 03 83 81 67 67. *www.pnr-lorraine.com.* Discover some amazing plants and wildlife in this nature reserve with the Clés de la découverte (Keys to Discovery), available from the central address (see above).

CRYSTAL, GLASS AND ART NOUVEAU

Lorraine has plenty of forests, useful for energy-consuming industries, especially glass and ceramics. Sandstone soil and lots of water also gave the region a head start in the table arts. Gallo-Roman traces of this activity exist, but factories began to spring up from the 18thc. onwards.

Bohemian glassmakers settled in Lorraine, and dukes, bishops and noble families in France and the Holy Roman Empire had their arms engraved on goblets and bottles, causing a boom in glass engraving. In the late 19thc., Emile Gallé developed certain techniques at Meisenthal, engraving on superimposed layers of coloured glass treated with acid to obtain a cameo effect. He in turn trained master glassmakers, some of whom (the Daum brothers) became famous too.

Baccarat crystal

In 1764, Monseigneur de Montmorency-Laval, Bishop of Metz set up the Sainte-Anne-de-Baccarat glassworks with a master glass-maker from Saint-Louis. Converted into a crystal glassworks in 1817, it soon had a worldwide reputation for excellence. Unlike glass, crystal contains lead oxide, but the craftsmen's fine work also gives it that luxury cachet. Baccarat is the only glassworks capable of making large pieces (crystal being much heavier than glass). Among them are a 3.85m candelabra ordered by Tsar Nicholas II, and some crystal furniture.

MUSEE DU CRISTAL Rue des Cristalleries ✆ 03 83 76 61 37. *Open all year, every day. Admission: adult 2.50 €, group 2.50 €.* You find it on the Baccarat industrial site, in the former directors' residence. The museum contains 1,100 artefacts in 4 rooms, including a 'technical' room which traces its history from 1764, and illustrates crystal-making: working under heat, cutting, engraving, gilding, paperweights, etc. reflecting the glassmakers and cutters' skill from the early 19thc. onwards.

Emaux de Longwy

During the 1798 earthenware boom, a factory was opened in the Carmelite monastery at Longwy-Bas. It managed to survive changing fashions and economic slumps, and continued to develop over two centuries, up to the present. The earthenware is known for its blue colour obtained from copper oxide and cobalt fusing at high temperature and producing a range of blues from turquoise to lapis-lazuli. The crackled look and cloisonnement giving depth to the motifs are characteristic of Longwy enamelwork.

Faiences de Sarreguemines

Sarreguemines earthenware industry began in 1790 with Nicolas-Henri Jacobi, who settled in the suburbs. After a rocky start, Bavarian Paul Utzschneider took over and developed the factory. He registered a patent for his red and black clay, a favourite with Napoleon I. The factory produces Art Nouveau and Art Deco artefacts for the table, but also tiles to decorate buildings and stoves. You can admire this earthenware in Paris, at the Brasserie Mollard (Rue Saint Lazare) and Potée des Halles (Rue Etienne Marcel).

MUSEE DES TECHNIQUES FAIENCIERES Sarreguemines ✆ 03 87 98 93 50. *www.sarreguemines-museum.com. Open all year.*

EPINAL AND THE VOSGES

Epinal

The industrial boom in this town came after the 1871 defeat, with the arrival of spinners and weavers fleeing Alsace. Epinal is famous for its coloured prints (images), and also boasts some fine architecture.

SAINT MAURICE BASILICA. The basilica seems to protect old Epinal, having come through so many wars without a scratch. The serene and solemn atmosphere inside is striking.

CITE DE L'IMAGE 42bis, quai de Dogneville ✆ 03 29 31 28 88. *Open Monday-Saturday: 9am-12 noon and 2pm-6.30pm. Sunday & public holidays: 2pm-6.30pm. Guided tour every day: 9.30am, 11am, 3pm and 4.30pm (3pm & 4.30pm Sunday & public holidays). Exhibition gallery: admission free. Ecomuseum admission: adult 4.70 €, student 3.15 €, 6-16s 1 €*. The new Cité de l'Image includes the Print Museum and the Imagerie d'Epinal.

IMAGERIE D'EPINAL ✆ 03 29 31 28 88. *www.imagerie-epinal.com.* In 1796, Jean-Charles Pellerin set up in the coloured-print trade, just as you see today. The picture is engraved on a wooden board, then printed by means of a Gutenberg Press. The colourist applies different paints with stencils and a round brush for the finish. Over the years, Epinal coloured prints have diversified and modernised. Learn stencil, printing and colouring techniques on old machines, in a series of instructive workshops. A real pleasure.

MUSEE DE L'IMAGE ✆ 03 29 81 48 30. *www.epinal.fr.* The Print Museum contains over 20,000 French and foreign prints and woodcuts, along with temporary exhibitions illustrating coloured prints past and present.

NOTRE-DAME AU CIERGE CHURCH Rue Maréchal-de-Lattre de-Tassigny. This building is an example of modern architecture (1956-1958) alternating concrete and coloured glass paving slabs. The great glass ceiling, one of the biggest in France, was created in the Chartres master glassmakers' tradition, and depicts scenes from the Virgin Mary's life

The Vosges

Domrémy-la-Pucelle

This famous little village was Joan of Arc's birthplace.

BOIS-CHENU BASILICA ✆ 03 29 06 93 47. *Open 8am-7pm.* Located 1km from the village. You can easily believe Joan heard saintly voices in this enchanting landscape: of such things is History made.

CENTRE D'INTERPRETATION Rue de la Basilique ✆ 03 29 06 95 86. *Open 1 October-31 March, every day except Tuesday: 10am-12 noon and 2pm-5pm. 1 April-30 September: open 9.30am-12 noon and 1.30pm-6.30pm. Admission: adult 3 €, child 1.50 €, under-6s free.* Joan of Arc's life, history and mythical status. A video traces the Maid of Orléans' history, and her many different personae are illustrated with a slideshow. She has served as a model for a number of art forms, and her story has been re-examined and reinterpreted. The Gallery of Faces takes you back to the historical context.

MAISON NATALE DE JEANNE D'ARC ✆ 03 29 06 95 86. *Open 1 October-31 March, every day except Tuesday: 10am-12 noon and 2pm-5pm. 1 April-30 September, open 9.30am-12 noon and 1.30pm-6.30pm. Admission: adult 3 €, concessions 1.50 €, under-6s free.* Joan of Arc's birthplace, bought and restored by the Vosges departmental council, is overwhelmingly simple. Three coats of arms on the wooden door pediment recall its history; otherwise, it seems to contain no memories.

Gérardmer

Better known as the Vosges Pearl, Gérardmer's setting is remarkable: on the edge of a lake with a morainic dam, in a valley hemmed in by conifer and prairie-covered mountains. The village has no trouble attracting visitors; in fact France's first Syndicat d'Initiative (forerunner to the Tourist Office) was set up here in 1875, known as the Walks Committee. Gérardmer could almost be Swiss, with its wooden chalet-like houses and mountain scenery.

LAC 660m above sea level, this was originally a glacial lake, so you might prefer boating, pedalo or windsurfing to swimming (only for the toughest). Part of the perimeter is along the road, but a cycle track has recently been added.

MUSEE DES METIERS DE LA FORET ET DU BOIS 11, rue de l'Eglise ✆ 03 29 60 82 02. *www.expoforet.com. Sign up for the daily tours: 9am and 2pm.* Discover all the different aspects of forestry: jobs, industrial sites for woodcutting, skills etc. Part of the visit is outside, on a guided excursion.

Mirecourt

Capital of the Xaintois region, known for its stringed instrument-making (17thc.), lace-making, and organ-building. These industries made Mirecourt one of Lorraines' richest villages.

MAISON DE LA MUSIQUE MECANIQUE 24, rue de Chanzy ✆ 03 29 37 51 13. *Open every day, except Tuesday and first three weeks in January. Admission: adult 4.60 €, under-10s 0.75 €.* Mirecourt is the birthplace of mechanical music. You can see some of France's finest old (working) machines in this museum.

MUSEE DE LA LUTHERIE ET DE L'ARCHETERIE FRANCAISES Hôtel de Ville ✆ 03 29 37 81 59. *Open 1 May-30 September, Monday-Saturday: 10am-12 noon and 2pm-6pm. Sunday: 2pm-6pm. Other periods: ask for opening hours. Closed January, Tuesday & public holidays. Admission: adult 4, child 1.50 €.* Learn how to transform wood into music in this Stringed Instrument and Bow Museum. A selection of stringed instruments illustrates different periods and manufacturing methods, along with their craftsmen (Lupot, Vuillaume, Derazey, Pecatte) who made Mirecourt famous in the 19thc. The art has survived in present-day violin, guitar, mandolin and bow-makers, and the apprentices at the Ecole Nationale de Lutherie.

Remiremont

One of the Vosges' finest towns, gateway to the Hautes Vosges and Ballons des Vosges Regional Park. This marvellous setting is linked to an eventful past: the Lady Canonesses' influence is still felt in the town.

ABBEY CHURCH. Mostly 13thc; the 11thc. underground crypt is the only remains of an earlier Romanesque church. The chapter's treasure includes the Virgin given (it is said) by Charlemagne who came to hunt in the region. Gothic Saint Pierre Abbey Church was consecrated in 1299. Its bulb-shaped steeple and tower date back to 1804.

ARCADES. Lining the main shopping street full of elegant boutiques. The first rays of sunshine really bring the town to life.

PLACE HENRI UTARD AND PALAIS ABBATIAL. The Abbey Palace houses the law courts and Town Hall. The noble Canonesses' splendid houses can be seen around the square.

Saint-Dié-des-Vosges

Neolithic tribes lived on the Bure massif overlooking the town some 4,000 years ago. The Celts came next, developing work and iron trading, while Saint Deodat, Bishop of Nevers, had foundations laid in 669 to extend the town. A remarkable literary, artistic and scientific movement grew up in Saint Die in the 15th and early 16thc.

PINK CATHEDRAL Guided tours in summer: 10.30am and 4pm (except Sunday morning). This superb pink sandstone building has been burnt down several times. Its front and two imposing towers are by Italian Giovanno Betto. The nave is the only Romanesque part, typical of southern Lorraine; chancel, apse and transept are Champagne Gothic. The church boasts 53 windows on the theme 'Death and Resurrection', designed in 1987 by 10 different artists.

MUSEE CHARLES-DE-BRUYERES 70, rue Charles-de-Gaulle ✆ 03 29 62 59 14. *Open every day except Tuesday. Admission: adults 1,80 €.* In 1905, Charles de Bruyeres donated his house and art collections to his native town. He had accumulated a number of aristocratic portraits, religious paintings and souvenirs of Remiremont Abbey. Remiremont Town Council added other paintings, and popular art objects like pottery and glass (including some Ecole de Nancy pieces, notably by Emile Galle). A reconstructed 19thc. Vosges bedroom and kitchen illustrate daily life as it used to be.

METZ AND THE MOSELLE

Metz

Built on a hill at the Moselle-Seille confluence, Metz was an important Gallo-Roman town (the baths and one of France's oldest churches are visible traces) but really became influential in the Middle Ages with the Carolingian dynasty. Many churches and cloisters of the period have survived successive German wars with relatively few scratches. Discover the town's pleasant atmosphere by boat or on foot.

SAINT ETIENNE CATHEDRAL ✆ 03 87 75 54 61. *Open every day: 9am-6.30pm. Guided tours all year.* Built between 1220 and 1520, but modification went on until the 20thc. The nave is 123m long and 42m high, and contains Chagall's Old Testament windows, part of 6,500m of stained glass incorporating designs by a number of other artists. The cathedral is nicknamed 'God's Lantern'.

SAINT PIERRE AUX NONNAINS CHURCH ✆ 03 87 39 92 00. *Open 3 May-17 September, every day except Monday and public holidays: 2pm-6.30pm. 19 September-30 April, Saturday & Sunday: 2pm-6pm.* One of France's oldest churches, built from 380-395 as a Gallo-Roman gymnasium, part of the thermal baths. War and politics have reshaped the church many times over 1,000 years!

MUSEES DE LA COUR D'OR 2, rue du Haut Poirier ✆ 03 87 68 25 00. *Open Monday-Friday: 9am-5pm, Saturday & Sunday: 10am-5pm. Closed Tuesday and public holidays. Admission: adult 4.60 €, senior citizens 3.30 €, students under 25 2.30 €, under-18s free.* The Cour d'Or groups together the Archeology, Architecture and Fine Arts Museums on the same site. The name comes from the Kings of Austrasia's palace, installed in the old thermal baths (now under the museums). The Gallo-Roman period is well represented, as are regional sculptures and Metz School artists.

PLACE DE LA COMEDIE. The square, with its 18thc. theatre (oldest in France still in use), is built on an island. The Protestant Temple Neuf on the edge of the square is magnificently lit up at night.

PLACE SAINT LOUIS. Italian bankers who settled here in the 13thc. designed the arcaded houses, and sixty money-changers set up shop under the vault in the 14thc. The square is full of charm, especially during the Christmas Market.

Gorze

Metz's Little Switzerland, nestling in the Gorzia Valley among superb forests. A good starting point for a hike.

ABBEY. Founded by Chrodegang, Bishop of Metz in 749, according to Saint BenoÓt's rules, it became one of Christendom's most famous Benedictine abbeys, notably for its teaching and plain-song, ancestor to the Gregorian Chant.

AQUEDUC ROMAIN. The Romans had Metz supplied with Bouillons spring water via this aqueduct linking Gorze to Metz. The town was thus able to fill the thermal baths and swimming pool.

PALAIS ABBATIAL DE PHILIPPE EBERHARD DE LOEVENSTEIN. Built from 1696-1700 by Prince-Abbot Philippe Eberhard de Loevenstein. The Baroque palace's fountain statues are mythological gods, and there are remarkable bas-reliefs on the two staircases. The building became a hospice in 1811, and is now run by the Departmental Treatment and Accommodation Centre.

Moselle

Amnéville-les-Thermes

Most recent of Lorraines's spas. Saint Eloy Spring was discovered in the early 20thc., and put into use fifty years later. The water has a high iron and mineral content (salt, calcium, magnesium) and comes out of the ground red, at 41 degrees C. The centre specialises in respiratory and rheumatic disorders, and thousands of visitors benefit from it every year.

AQUARIUM IMPERATOR Centre Thermal et Touristique ✆ 03 87 70 36 61. *Open weekdays: 2pm-7pm, weekends & public holidays: 10am-7pm. Admission: over 12s (adult) 9 €, 3-11s 5.50 €.* Round the world in 37 aquariums. You'll enjoy the sharks bay, tropical greenhouse (piranha tank) and reconstructed white shark.

THERMAPOLIS Centre Thermal et Touristique ✆ **03 87 70 36 61**. *Open Monday-Wednesday:10am-10pm, Thursday: 9am-10pm, Friday & Saturday: 10am-midnight, Sunday: 9am-8pm. Annual closing 1st week of September, Christmas & New Year. Prices: 9 € for 2 hrs; 11.50 € for 3hrs etc. (other options: 16hrs, 30hrs & 60hrs). Over-4s accepted.* This lakeside centre has an indoor freshwater pool (32_C) and a thermal pool (37_C). Feast your eyes on the sumptuous interior decoration while pampering your body.

PARC ZOOLOGIQUE Centre Thermal et Touristique ✆ **03 87 70 25 60**. *www.zoo-amneville.com. Open April-September:9.30am-7.30pm (8pm Sundays & public holidays). October-March: 10am-dusk. Admission: over-12s (adult) 20 €, 3-11s 11 €.* Amnéville zoo contains over 1,300 animals (200 species) in an 11ha. forest. You can see parrots flying freely, African elephants, giraffes and gazelles, and polar bears whose pool contains 800,000 litres of water. All the animals are in their natural habitat, living in pairs or groups in huge enclosures.

Bliesbruck

BLIESBRUCK-REINHEIM EUROPEAN ARCHEOLOGICAL PARK ✆ **03 87 02 25 79**. *Open March-October: 10am-6pm. Admission: adult 4.60 €.* Blies Valley archeologists have unearthed a Celtic necropolis, a villa and a little Gallo-Roman town on this site. An original museum circuit leads you from the Princess of Reinheim's famous reconstructed tomb to pavilions containing the remains of public baths and craftsmen's houses. Activities are regularly organised to show what Gallic and Gallo-Roman daily life was really like.

Maizières-lès-Metz

PARC WALIBI-SCHTROUMPF ✆ **03 87 51 90 52**. *www.sixflagseurope.com. Open April-end October ; July & August every day, other periods, open weekends at least (check first). Admission: 3-11s 16.75 €, over-12s 21.80 €.* Between Metz and Luxembourg. The park is family-orientated, with 19 amusements - including fairground rides (Anaconda, Comet Space, Zig Zag) for sensation-seekers with strong stomachs, a mini-farm and a number of shows.

Marsal

The Seille Valley contains rock salt, once the only preservative and condiment, and thus worth a fortune. Marsal abandoned its salt industry in the 1970s.

MUSEE DU SEL Porte de France ✆ **03 87 01 16 75**. *www.museedusel.org. Open every day:2pm-6pm. Sunday and public holidays: 10am-12 noon and 2pm-6pm. 15 June-15 September, open Thursday, Friday and Saturday mornings: 10am-12 noon. Weekends only in December. Closed 22 December-7 January. Admission: adult 3 €, child 2.30 €* The story of 'white gold'. The region's subsoil contains huge rock salt deposits, 200 million years old. The museum illustrates the different uses of salt and displays some fine rocks, along with 500 saltcellars. In season you can visit the village and salt marshes, and taste and compare different types of salt.

Metz

Sarrebourg

One of Lorraine's oldest urban sites (2,000 years).

CORDELIERS CHAPEL Place des Cordeliers. *Open every day, May-end September, Monday-Saturday:10am-12 noon and 1.30pm-6.30pm € Sunday & public holidays: 2.30pm-5.30pm. October-end April, Monday-Saturday: 10am-12 noon and 2pm-5pm.* This 13thc. Gothic chapel was rebuilt in the 17thc. Marc Chagall designed the immense stained glass window (Biblical scenes on the theme of peace) and west front. The monumental tapestry 'Peace' transposes the window he made for the United Nations in New York.

MUSEE DU PAYS DE SARREBOURG 13, ave. de France © 03 87 03 27 86. *Open Monday-Saturday:10am-12 noon and 2pm-6pm. Sunday: 2pm-6pm. Closed Tuesday and public holidays.* These interesting collections come from the region's archeological sites: jewellery and sepulchre ornaments (1,900-50 B.C.) and everyday objects found in excavated Gallo-Roman villas (Saint Ulrich). Medieval and modern sculpture, Niderviller earthenware and china (18thc.) and Lorraine furniture are also on display.

Rhodes

SAINTE CROIX WILDLIFE PARK © 03 87 03 92 05. *Open 19 March-12 November 2006. Admission: adult 12.50 €.* 1,200 animals from 80 European species live on these 120 ha. of Moselle countryside, and you can see some of our greatest wild forest mammals wandering freely in their natural habitat. The park will be welcoming new inhabitants - vultures and marmots - for its 25th birthday.

MEUSE

Bar-le-Duc

The town's origins go back to the 1stc. A.D., but it developed in the 10thc. when Duke Frederic I of Haute-Lorraine built his castle, and the local nobility settled in the upper quarters, which were thus preserved until the 16thc. Streets, squares and church constitute an open-air museum. You go down the staircase known as the '80 steps' to reach the lower town (in fact there are 143). Raymond Poincare's birthplace, Gilles de Trèves College (admired by Montaigne), the Michaux monument (they invented the bicycle) and a number of churches are found in this quarter.

SAINT ETIENNE CHURCH. Built between the 12th and 14thc., its front is a blend of Flamboyant Gothic and Renaissance. Inside, three private 16thc. chapels complete the main nave, which contains two major works by Ligier Richier. The ultra-realistic Transi depicts Charles V's favourite Rene de Chalon 3 years after his death, and the polychrome wood Calvary shows Christ and the two thieves, one peaceful, the other rebellious.

MONUMENT DES MICHAUX. This little monument to the Michaux is on the corner of Rues Maginot and du Bourg. They invented the pedal velocipede.

MUSEE DU BARROIS Esplanade du Château © 03 29 76 14 67. *Open Wednesday-Sunday: 2pm-6pm. Admission: adult 2 €.* Archeology, Fine Arts, Ethnology, History and the decorative arts feature together at this unusual cultural crossroads. The Barrois Museum is housed in a 16thc. ducal chateau boasting the fine Chartes treasure room and a wide esplanade. Discover archeology with the antique Nasium collections, and admire some14th and 17thc.Lorraine sculptures, and Flemish, Italian and French paintings. There is an interesting ethnography section; and the pedal velocipede invented by Pierre Michaux is on display. You have a view over the lower town and Bar-le-Duc area from the esplanade in front of the chateau. Not to be missed.

Avioth

This modest little village contains a dazzling Gothic basilica.

BASILICA © 03 29 88 90 96. Guided tours every day except Monday, May-end September: 3pm & 5pm. Built from the 13th-15thc., this impressive Gothic basilica has some fine carved decoration. Outside is the Flamboyant Gothic Recevresse, where pilgrims put their offerings (nowadays it only attracts attention). An annual international pilgrimage ends here on 16 July, and the Avioth Artistiques, a medieval festival orgnised by artists and craftsmen, is held on the last Sunday in July.

Commercy

The town has a luminous quality, reflecting off the white stone fronts of its buildings: this local stone from Euville Quarry was reputed in the 19thc, and used to build the Paris Opera. The madeleine sponge cake immortalised by Proust in Remembrance of Things Past was invented in Commercy.

CHATEAU. First a medieval fortress, then the Cardinal de Retz's home after 1662; he wrote part of his memoires here. King Stanislas of Poland, Duke of Bar and Lorraine made it his summer residence in 1744, turning the region into a literary and scientific centre. The majestic horse shoe-shaped esplanade in front offers a fine view towards the forest.

MUSEE DE LA CERAMIQUE ET DE L'IVOIRE 7, ave Carcano © 03 29 92 04 77. *Open 1 May-30 June and 1 September-1 October, weekends and public holidays: 2pm-6pm. 1 July-31 August: every day except Tuesday: 2pm-6pm. Admission: adult 3 €* Housed in the former municipal bains-douches (public baths), this museum contains several collections in its Art Deco interior. You can admire 17thc. European and Oriental ivory, learn about techniques and substitution materials, and also see some 18th and 19thc. ceramic. The museum grew out of an early 20thc. legacy from a Dr. Boyer.

NANCY AND ITS REGION

Nancy

Nancy starts with the Middle Ages, and the old town round Saint Epvre Basilica, Porte de la Craffe and the Grande-Rue. Next comes the 18thc., with the Place d'Alliance - Place de la Carrière - Place Stanislas tryptich. The last of these squares was built by Stanislas as the Place Royale, and now bears his name. Admire the gilded wrought-iron railings designed by locksmith Jean Lamour, Neptune and Amphitrite fountains and five surrounding pavilions. At night, the square is beautifully lit up. The three squares are UNESCO-listed. The 1900s saw the influence of master-glassmaker Galle and the famous Ecole de Nancy. This artistic movement left its mark on the whole town: ten artists who shared the same vision (associating natural elements and technical innovations) produced buildings, villas and private houses of exceptional character.

Nancy is also the Art Nouveau capital. Houses with wrought-iron railings and pine cone or ginkgo leaf - shaped stones can be seen all over town, and even public buildings have their Art Nouveau touches. Visit the 1900 Villa Majorelle to get an idea of the inside (ask about opening hours at the Tourist Office).

SAINT EPVRE BASILICA Place Saint Epvre © 03 83 32 12 99. *Open every day, Easter-October: 2.30pm-6pm. Guided tours according to calendar.* This superb Neo-Gothic building in the old town was put up in 1864 by architect Prosper Mary. It contains Klem furnishings, four remarkable windows and an organ with a sumptuous case.

NOTRE DAME CATHEDRAL Place Monseigneur Ruch. *Open every day: 8.30am-12 noon and 1.30pm-6.45pm.* Duke Leopold started work on the church, finished in 1759. Nancy became a bishopric in 1777, and the church a cathedral. The fine classical three-storey front is typical of the 18thc., and the organ with its striking case dates back to 1756.

CORDELIERS CHAPEL 66, Grande-Rue © 03 83 32 18 74. *Open every day, 1 January-30 April and 1 October-31 December: 10am-12 noon and 2pm-5pm (6pm Sundays). 2 May-30 September: 10am-6pm. Admission: adult 1.50 €, under-7s free.* Built by René II in the late 15thc. to give thanks for his victory over Charles the Bold. The church contains some fine sculptures and the ducal chapel houses all the Dukes of Lorraine's sepulchres, rather like the Villa Medicis in Florence.

MUSEUM AQUARIUM DE NANCY 34, rue Sainte-Catherine © 03 83 32 99 97. *Open every day, April-August: 10am-12 noon and 2pm-6pm. September-March: 2pm-6pm. Admission: adult 3.80 €, under-6s free. Special admission prices during the period of 1st floor renovation work.* 300 species of tropical fish are housed in 72 tanks recreating their natural habitat. This aquarium in the centre of Nancy is one of France's finest - after Monaco, of course!

MUSEE DES BEAUX-ARTS 3, place Stanislas © 03 83 85 30 72. *Open every day: 10am-6pm, except Tuesday. Closed 1 January, 1 May, 14 July, 1 November and 25 December. Adult 6 €, students and senior citizens 2.50 €, under-12s free.* Start with the 18thc. pavilion, housing works from the Court of Lorraine's artistic circles and other great French painters like Delacroix. Follow that with 16thc. Italian paintings, 17thc. Northern School and 20thc. works on the ground floor. The impressive Daum collection is displayed in the Haussonville Bastion, remains of the town's fortifications.

MUSEE DE L'ECOLE DE NANCY 36-38 rue du Sergent Blandan © 03 83 40 14 86. *Open Wednesday-Sunday, 10.30am-6pm. Admission: adult6, concessions 2.30 €* Housed in the Maison Corbin with its park and circular aquarium, this extraordinary museum exhibits the Ecole de Nancy's greatest designers: Majorelle, Gallé, Hestaux, Gruber, Vallin, Daum, Walter, Friant etc. Their works illustrate the concepts of French Art Nouveau: Gallé's incredible autumn and twilight bed, Majorelle's waterlily furniture, Masson de Vallin's dining-room, and some amazing molten glass.

MUSEE LORRAIN ET PALAIS DUCAL 64-68 Grande-Rue ✆ 03 83 32 18 74. *Open every day except Tuesday: 10am-12.30pm and 2pm-6pm. Admission: Palais Ducal & Couvent des Cordeliers Arts and Popular Traditions section, 4.60 € One site only: 3.10 €* Housed in the Dukes of Lorraine's 16thc. palace, this museum traces regional history from Prehistoric times to the First World War (earthenware, ceramic, tapestries, miniatures). Admire works by engraver J. Callot and the 17thc. Lorraine painters Georges de la Tour, Deruet and Bellange. One room illustrates Jewish religion and culture. The Arts and Popular Traditions Section in the former Cordeliers Monastery covers 19thc. rural Lorraine: village, fields, homes and furniture. Period rooms are displayed with traditional furnishings, pottery and kitchen utensils. In Nancy's oldest church you can see Rene II's tomb by Mansuy Gauvin, Gueldre's recumbent statue (Ligier Richier) and the Ducal Chapel where the Dukes of Lorraine were laid to rest.

PEPINIERE. Nancy's favourite park nestles between the old town and Place Stanislas. Don't miss the rose-garden in the middle - or the delicious bergamote and mirabelle ice-creams!

Around Nancy

Baccarat

Baccarat is famous for its crystal (see 'Crystal, glass and Art Nouveau') but it also features one of France's most beautiful modern art churches. Saint Remy Church was built between 1953 and 1957, and contains Baccarat crystal stained glass windows (20,000 pieces in 52 different colours) symbolising life and light, and an organ with 40 stops and 3,660 pipes - not forgettting the 55m tower and visible wooden framework. The interesting old town is worth a visit, as is Deneuvre, overlooking Baccarat, with its Hercules Springs and archeological musuem. You follow in the footsteps of pilgrims hoping to find solace with Hercules: the sanctuary is just as it was in the late 4thc.

Haroué

CHATEAU ✆ 03 83 52 40 14. *www.Chateaudeharoue.fr. Open May and September, except Tuesday, Sunday and public holidays: 2pm-6pm. June: Wednesday-Sunday: 2pm-6pm. July & August, every day: 10am-12 noon and 2pm-6pm. Admission: 2 adults + 2 under-16s, 8 €, adult 8 €, child 2.50 €.* This superb building is still the Princes of Beauvau-Craon's home. Admire the formal garden opening onto fields, surrounded by a carp-filled moat, and four medieval towers with their tall windows under pointed slates. The comparison with Chambord is most apt when the castle is filled with light from its 365 window panes. You can visit all the rooms with their period furniture, including the 12 Malgrange tapestries depicting the life of Alexander the Great, ornamental painter Jean Pillement's 'Chinese decoration' in a corner tower and the recently restored 'Salon Herbert' featuring the Princesse de Beauvau and Comtesse Delphine Potocka, great friends of Chopin, amid much gilding.

Nancy, Saint-Epvre basilica

Lunéville

Stanislas Leszczynski, King of Poland and Duke of Lorraine, settled his prestigious court at Lunéville in the 18thc; Voltaire stayed here often. A reputed earthenware factory was set up in the town at the same period.

CHATEAU ✆ 03 83 76 04 75. *Open 1 May-30 October: 10am-12 noon and 2pm-6pm, except Tuesday. Free access to park all year.* Built in the grand tradition of classical art, with rocaille touches. Temporary exhibitions and events illustrate the castle's 18thc. Lumières heritage. In spring 2005, restoration work on the zone destroyed by fire will accelerate, with guided tours of the site for visitors. The imaginary world of Stanislas' period is recreated in the Parc des Bosquets.

CONSERVATOIRE DE LA BRODERIE PERLEE ✆ 03 83 73 56 86. *www.broderie-luneville.com. Open every day except Tuesday: 2pm-6pm. Closed 13 November to March 2006. Admission free.* Luneville was famous for its beaded and sequined embroidery in the late 19thc. The museum traces its history from 1850 to the present, with a collection of dresses, outfits and pieces of embroidery. May-September: thematic embroidered costume exhibition. Every year, a public embroidery demonstration is given by a member of the Ecole de Broderie d'Art, as part of the Point de Lunéville, Perles et Paillettes collection.

SAINT JACQUES CHURCH. *Open every day: 9am-12 noon and 2pm-5pm.* The elegant pink Vosges sandstone front and Rococo towers were designed by Emmanuel Here.

MANUFACTURE DES FAIENCERIES DE LUNEVILLE ET SAINT CLEMENT. ZA des Faienceries - 1, rue Trouillet ✆ 03 83 74 07 58. *www.manufacture-luneville.com. Open all year except Sunday and Monday: 10am-12 noon and 2pm-6.30pm. Admission free.* Housed on the first floor of the factory warehouse, in the former workshops (now closed), this pottery collection (Lunéville, Saint Clément, Lille, Sarreguemines and even Delft) traces the development of earthenware through the ages in a dazzling patchwork of colour.

Saint-Nicolas-de-Port

Originally called Port, due to its position on the last navigable stretch of the Meurthe. Already a trading crossroads, it became a place of pilgrimage after local pilgrims brought one of Saint Nicholas' finger joints from Italy. In the late Middle Ages, the town ranked as one of the most important European holy sites and business centres, and that energy can still be felt in its modern commercial and tourist infrastructures.

BASILICA ✆ 03 83 46 81 50. *Open 8am-6pm in season, 5pm in winter. Guided tours all year for groups (10+) with audio guide for individual visitors. Group 3 €, child 1.50 €, visit with auto guide 2 €* This basilica was completely restored thanks to a local woman, Camille Croué-Friedman, who married an American millionaire. It is a Flamboyant Gothic building built in curious broken cross shape, the uneven ground resulting in a crooked nave.

MUSEE DU CINEMA ET DE LA PHOTOGRAPHIE 10, rue Georges-Rémy ✆ 03 83 45 18 32. *Thursday, Friday & Saturday: 2pm-6pm; Sunday: 2.30pm-6.30pm. Closed 20 December-5 January. Admission: adult 3.50 €, child 2 €* Magic lanterns, optical toys, shadowgraphs, early daguerreotypes and manual cameras are on display, with a number of demonstrations tracing the development of the moving image.

Saxon-Sion

Pilgrims came here in the Middle Ages to pray for the Crusaders in the Holy Land, which explains the 'Zion'. The Celts had already worshipped their gods on this hill, and the Romans Mercury; the Christians came to adore the Virgin. Writer Maurice Barrès called it the 'inspired hill. One of those places where the spirit breathes'.

BASILICA. Dates back to the mid-18thc. Its 48m-high monumental tower topped with a 7m Virgin overlooks the plain, and attracts large numbers of pilgrims.

COLLINE DE SION. One of France's spiritual centres. Well before the Roman Conquest, the Gauls had already traced out a triangular nemeton (sacred wood) on the north headland, dedicated to the fertility goddess Rosmerta. This made way for a temple to Mercury under Roman rule. When the Franks arrived in the 5thc. three villas were built: Sion, one owned by Wado, and an earlier one called Saxon. The porch tympanum features Saint Gérard de Toul, Duke Charles IV, Tiercelin (guardian of the site before the Revolution) Monseigneur Foulon and Père Michaux, who built the tower, and an anonymous oblate representing the future. Inside, you can see the 14thc. apse with its fine gilded statue of the Virgin, and Jean Lamour's railing (1753), along with the Reconciliation Altar where French and Germans shook hands in 1973. Don't miss the Pourtour path, with its panoramic view between earth and heaven, which moves believers and sceptics alike.

Toul

The name comes from the old Gallic word 'tol' meaning 'stone', which shows how old Toul is. Neolithic tribes settled there long before it became the fortified Leuques capital described by Caesar. After Roman colonisation, the town was a bishopric, then came under the Germanic Holy Roman Empire. Saxon emperors seeking Church support against secular rivals, and Bishops chosen by the Emperor used their power and gifts to make Toul a rich and influential place.

SAINT ETIENNE CATHEDRAL. Built between 1221 and 1500, this cathedral is built to a Romanesque plan but on Gothic lines. The 13thc. chancel and cloister and 16thc. nave recall Toul's episcopal period; a richly-decorated front contrasts with the building's austerity. Inside you can admire a magnificent window depicting the Crowning of the Virgin, dating back to 1503, a fresco and some carved pillars. Saint Etienne is being restored but remains open.

SAINT ETIENNE CLOISTER. France's second biggest Gothic cloister was built in the 13th and 14thc. Notice its fantastic animal gargoyles.

VIEILLE VILLE. Vauban's ramparts are almost intact round the old town, with its buildings of all periods from the Middle Ages to 18thc. Admire the Portes de Metz, de France, Jeanne-d'Arc and Moselle: the latter is the town's main entrance and is used for the mediatheque. To see inside: Saint Etienne Cathedral and cloister, Saint Gengoult Collegiate Church (13th-16thc.) with its stained glass windows and 16thc. Flamboyant Gothic cloister, and the museum in the former Bishops' Palace. Toul contains several Art Nouveau houses (Rues Albert Denis and du Marechal Foch); be sure not to miss them.

MUSEE D'ART ET D'HISTOIRE DE TOUL 25, rue Gouvion-Saint-Cyr ✆ 03 83 64 13 38. *Open every day except Saturday: 10.30am-12 noon and 2pm-6pm. Closed Sunday morning from November-late March. Admission: adult 3 €.* The Art and History Museum is housed in the former Maison Dieu. The 13thc. patients' room contains lapidary collections and historic monuments. Toul's entire history is illustrated by this archeological and artistic wealth displayed in about thirty rooms. including a big room devoted to popular arts and traditions and a fine ceramic collection, mostly from the former Bellevue earthenware factory, featuring some remarkable Cyffle pieces. Look out for the nine prestigious 16th and 17thc. tapestries and the gallery with its many European paintings (19thc. in particular).

THE WAR YEARS

Lorraine's border with Prussia (later Germany) brought invasions and endless war, marking both civil and military buildings. Over the centuries, forts but also fortified farms and churches were built, to shelter the inhabitants in wartime. The region's museums explain this military architecture.

Verdun

The name calls up images of hell. In 1914, France's most powerful fortress became an entrenched camp, focal point of the Great War.

The impossible living conditions and lack of hygiene in the trenches cost 163,000 Frenchmen and 143,000 Germans their lives - not counting the mutilated survivors. A number of forts, monuments and cemeteries in the north east of Verdun recall these horrors.

In 1987, the UNO awarded Verdun the title 'World Peace Capital'. The main courtyard of the Bishops' Palace bears this inscription: 'War is born in the minds of men; peace must also be born in their minds'.

CITADELLE SOUTERRAINE ✆ 03 29 86 62 02. *Open every day except in January: 10am-12 noon and 2pm-5pm. 1 February-31 March. April, May, June & September: 9am-6pm. July & August until 7pm. October-December: 9am-12 noon and 2pm-5.30pm. Admission: 6 €* During the First World War, the citadel's underground gallery served as a civilian refuge and soldiers' barracks. 10,000 men and women lived there. Today it is a museum, recalling memories of battles and ruined villages by means of documents, weapons, military equipment, photos and portraits.

CENTRE MONDIAL DE LA PAIX, DES LIBERTES ET DES DROITS DE L'HOMME Palais Episcopal, Place Monseigneur Ginisty ✆ 03 29 86 55 00. *www.centremondialpaix.asso.fr. Open every day, 1 June-15 September: 9.30am-7pm. Other periods: 9.30am-12 noon and 2pm-6pm. Closed January.* Housed in the superb 18thc. Bishops' Palace, the World Peace Centre hosts lectures, conferences, concerts and films promoting peace and human rights and liberties, along with temporary exhibitions (notably on the Great War). The permanent exhibition 'From war to peace' invites you to reflect on ways of limiting war: the UNO, Europe etc.

THE VERDUN MEMORIAL Fleury-Devant-Douaumont ✆ 03 29 84 35 34. *Open every day 1 February: 15 December. Spring & summer: 9am-6pm. Autumn & winter: 9am-12 noon and 2pm-6pm. Admission: adult 7 €.* Located in the heart of the battlefield, the Verdun Memorial is one of Europe's main First World War museums. It was set up in 1967, under the aegis of veteran Maurice Genevoix of the French Academy, and is a historic sanctuary and place of memory bearing witness to the suffering of those soldiers who fought in this sector of the Western Front from 1914 to 1918. The museum area is organised round a striking reconstruction of the battlefield, with planes, vehicles, heavy weapons and uniforms illustrating the industrial war, and personal objects from the trenches recalling the men's everyday lives. There are thematic and educational exhibitions; films, photos, lithographs and posters from the period remind us of the war's social, economic and and cultural aspects. The Research and Study Centre with its documentary area and educational service is a place for exchanging ideas and information, open to all (access to archive documents by appointment only).

Douaumont

FORT DE DOUAUMONT ✆ 03 29 84 41 91. *Open every day: 10am-6pm. Adult 2.50 €, child 1.30 €.* You can't fail to be moved by this fort. It was taken by the Germans in 1916, despite being the Meuse's best-armed and defended site. Inside are three floors of galleries and blockhouses, lookout posts and turrets, machine guns and cannon. A 2,50m-thick concrete shell covered the fort, and yet it fell to the Germans in the early stages of the Battle of Verdun (25 February 1916). The ossuary containing unidentified remains of 130,000 soldiers fallen in combat and the lines of crosses in the national cemetery are heart-wrenching.

Souilly

MUSEE DE LA VOIE SACREE 22, Voie Sacrée ✆ 03 29 80 52 76. *Open all year: Monday-Friday: 9am-5pm.* An exhibition of written documents and photos tracing the Voie Sacree's essential role in transporting supplies, ammunition and soldiers to the Verdun Front in the Great War.

Other war sites

Bitche

MUSEE DE LA CITADELLE ET DU PAYS DE BITCHE ✆ 03 87 96 18 82. *Open: 1 March-15 November: 10am-5pm. Adult 6 to 7 €, child/student 3.50 €, under-7s free.* Built on a steep-sided rock 308m long and 30-60m wide, this military masterpiece of Vauban's design was built from 1680-1683, 336m up, overlooking above the town. The underground passages contain blockhouses, a stable, hospital, kitchen and bakery dug out of the rock and sheltered from bombing.

Fermont

FORT ✆ 03 82 39 35 34. *Open weekends and public holidays, April, May & September; June, July & August everwork.y day. Adult 5 €, 7-12s 3 €* One of the Maginot Line's finest forts, Fermont was a 27ha. underground stronghold with 7 blockhouses, now a museum of defence work. The exhibition, with its reconstruction, is 30m below ground.

Montmedy

MUSEE DE LA FORTIFICATION ✆ 03 29 80 15 90. *Open every day, May-September: 10am-6pm (July & August, 7pm).* Check opening times for other periods. A museum of military architecture in the Meuse, from Prehistoric times to Vauban. Instructive!

CITADEL ✆ 03 29 80 15 90. *Open every day, 1 February-30 November. Admission: adult 4 €, child 2 €, under-6s free.* Built in the reign of Charles V, the Citadel is quite a village. It has a fine rampart walk, and houses the Fortification and Bastien-Lepage Museums.

Thionville

FORT DE GUENTRANGE Chemin du Fort ✆ 03 82 53 33 18. *Open May-September, 1st & 3rd Sundays of the month. Tour at 3pm. Admission: 2 €.* The Germans built this huge fortified unit from 1899-1906. It consists of two artillery batteries each with 4 revolving turrets, and can hold 1,844 troop soldiers and 54 officers.

Military cemetery of Verdun

© Iconotec.com / Pierre Delaguerard

Troyon

TROYON HISTORIC FORT. *Open every day, March-end November: 2pm-7pm.* Built from 1878-1879, this fort had its moment of glory in the early days of the Great War, when a mere 450 soldiers held 10,000 men of the Kronprinz's 5th Army in check.

Uxegney

FORT D'UXEGNEY ✆ 03 29 38 32 09/03 29 82 53 32 *Open mid June-mid September, Saturday & Sunday afternoons. July & August, every day. Guided tours: 2pm, 4pm. Admission: adult 5 €, under-14s 1.50 €.* Uxegney Fort was an important part of Epinal operations base in General Sere de Rivières' fortified system, set up in 1870 from Belfort to Epinal and Toul to Verdun. Built from 1882-1884, it is one of the few French forts modified right up until 1914. Today it is a listed monument, thanks to restoration and re-equipping by voluntary workers.

Villey-le-Sec

FORT DE VILLEY-LE-SEC 2, place de l'Eglise ✆ 03 83 63 90 09. *Guided tours May-September, Sundays & public holidays: 3pm. 14 July-15 August, every day except Monday. Admission: adult 6 €, 7-16s 2.50* Sere de Rivières' defence system was set up on all French borders after 1870. Villey-le-Sec Fort enclosed the existing village within a 3.5km-wall and garrisoned 1,300 men and 79 pieces of ordnance. After the tour, you can ride in the kind of little train used to provision the fort.

VOSGES WATERING PLACES

Water has always been important in Lorraine. Celts, Romans and Gauls worshipped water gods and goddesses. In Roman times, some hot springs were used to treat soldiers' wounds, then offered for relaxation to the general public.

Even today, some of the region's waters have recognised therapeutic qualities. Lorraine has 5 spas, made fashionable again by the current trend for thermal treatments.

Bains-les-Bains

In the heart of the Vosges forest between hills and plain. Bains' hot springs go back to Gallo-Roman times. when they were used to heal Roman soldiers. In 1864, they were state-approved for the treatment of cardio-vascular illness and rheumatism. The water leaves the ground at 25-51_C from 11 different springs, siliceous, sodic and rich in bicarbonates. Mineral content is low, but it contains a lot of rare gas.

The thermal park welcomes visitors with leisure activities: tennis courts, minigolf and fishing.

THERMES 1, ave du Docteur Mathieu ✆ 03 29 36 32 04

Contrexéville

Everyone knows Contrex and its benefits to slimmers: this is the 'Thermal Slimming Capital'. The water is rich in calcium and magnesium and contains a lot of minerals and trace elements. It is recommended for liver and kidney disorders as well as weight problems. Five springs produce water at 11_C. The resort goes back to the 17thc., when Stanislas had the water's qualities examined, but it became fashionable during the Belle Epoque when Queen Isabel of Spain and the Shah of Persia stayed there.

Two centres offer spa treatments: the Etablissement Thermal and Aquarius in the Hôtel Cosmos.

ETABLISSEMENT THERMAL Galerie Thermale ✆ 03 29 08 03 24

Plombières-les-Bains

The Romans discovered these waters in the 2ndc. A.D. Montaigne, Verlaine, Alfred de Musset, Napoleon III, and Berlioz all came here for treatment, bringing Plombières into fashion. Beaumarchais even had the very first Mariage de Figaro performed here! The 18th and 19thc. houses with wrought-iron balconies are an added attraction: the resort is known as the Town of a Thousand Balconies. 27 springs are worked, at 23-81_C, and the water has low mineral content but a lot of trace elements, good for digestive and rheumatic disorders and relaxation.

SOCIETE THERMALE DE PLOMBIERE-LES-BAINS Place Maurice Janot ✆ 03 29 30 07 00

Vittel

The best known of Lorraine's spa towns. In its 700ha. of parks and forests, Vittel welcomes patients and tourists alike. A simple glass of Vittel from the spring does you good, with its sulfates, bicarbonates, calcium and magnesium. Once fit and energetic, you can choose from the resort's many sports activities (the town has an Olympic Preparation Centre) or try the casino or races.

ETABLISSEMENT THERMAL Parc Thermal - VITTEL ✆ 03 29 08 76 54.

FOOD AND DRINK

Lorraine is definitely for the sweet-toothed! The home of the madeleine offers you delicious confectionery and liqueurs. Though springs abound, the locals prefer their beer and regional wines.

Nancy Bergamot

In the mid-19thc. a Nancy confectioner added a few drops of bergamot essence to one of his recipes. The resulting sweets were instantly successful, and are still as popular today. The blend of boiled sugar and essential oil can be cut by hand or with an industrial blade: the cooking gives it a transparent golden look.

Woippy Strawberries

Rather surprisingly, Woippy was France's second-biggest strawberry producer in 1945. Village fêtes are still held at strawberry-picking time, all over the region.

Langres

This AOC cheese goes back to the 19thc. and has a fine, wrinkled, pale yellow or brown crust. You recognise it by the hole in its upper part, which gets bigger on maturing (15-21 days with repeated washing). Temperature and humidity levels, along with the cheesemonger's skill, define its taste and texture.

Madeleine de Commercy

During one of King Stanislas' great banquets, the pastry-cook lost his temper and resigned. A young cook called Madeleine took over, and concocted a little shell-shaped cake made from eggs, butter sugar and flour. The form may vary slightly, but the cake's basic shape is still the same, as is the delicate orange-flower smell.

Mirabelles

What are sunshine yellow, weigh 15g and can only be eaten for a few weeks every summer? Mirabelles, of course! This fruit is identified with Lorraine, which produces 70% of the world's supply. You can eat them off the tree (small with knotty branches), or as a garnish on sweet and savoury dishes. The eau de vie is exported as a digestive aid (it warms the heart at the same time!)

MAISON DE LA MIRABELLE 16, rue du Capitaine Durand - Rozelieures ✆ 03 83 72 32 26

Potée

This dish is simmered, and keeps you warm during harsh winters. Ingredients for 6: 500g of smoked fat bacon, 2 Lorraine cooking sausages, 7 manchons confits (duck) half a cabbage, potatoes, carrots, turnips, 2 handfuls of white beans, onions, bayleaf, salt and pepper. Put the bacon, manchons, peeled vegetables salt and pepper in a casserole dish. Cover with water and cook for about 2hr 30mins over a low heat. Add the sausages 20 mins before serving.

Quiche

Who can imagine Quiche without Lorraine? Ingredients: 200g flour, 100g butter, 4 eggs, 1 bowl of fresh cream, 250g smoked bacon, salt and pepper. A real Quiche Lorraine contains no milk or cheese. Make the shortcrust pastry. Cut up the bacon and brown in butter. Beat the eggs with the cream and seasoning. Add the bacon, pour into the pastry case and cook for 30-40 mins at 180_C.

Hotels & Restaurants

MEURTHE-ET-MOSELLE

Lunéville

LES BOSQUETS 2, rue des Bosquets ✆ 03 83 74 00 14.
Closed Sunday evening, Tuesday evening and Wednesday. Express formula lunchtimes. Set menus 15 € and 32 €. After your pleasant stroll through the chateau park just opposite, you'll find the same refreshing, spring-like atmosphere in this restaurant, located in a typical old Luneville house. The walls are yellow, the tables prettily set with Luneville plates, and the seasonal cuisine is original and makes talented use of fresh market produce. The smiling service, family atmosphere and good advice about your choice of food are other positive points. The chef's speciality is fish, so you must taste his recipes. This is one of the town's oldest restaurants, and the owner is extremely proud of its success.

CHATEAU D'ADOMENIL Rehainviller ✆ 03 83 74 04 81 *Fax 03 83 74 21 78. Website: www.adomenil.com. Set menus from 45 € to 90 €, à la carte 85 €. Closed Sunday evening (except mid-April to late October, Monday, Tuesday lunchtime and January).* This chateau is one of Eastern France's most impressive; restful, luxurious, sumptuously fitted out, and surrounded by a vast estate, falling away to a river. It attracts amateur photographers in all seasons. Chef Cyril Leclerc, the owner's son-in-law, manages to eclipse the setting, though, with his menu: Dublin Bay prawn tails from Loctudy, mango *craqueline*, sweet and sour vegetables, muscat-flavoured oil, small white onions and ginger, frogs' legs, potato *churros, petite piche* cod (refers to the type of fishing), an organic egg poached in shrimp *consommé* with bean sprouts, veal kidneys, Langres *parmentier* (potato dish) with chives and the juice flavoured with sherry, shallots and bitter cocoa, an assortment of apricots, gingerbread, rosemary-scented crème brûlée and soft white cheese sorbet. The cellar isn't too expensive, even when it comes to the great Alsace wines. Faultless service.

HOTEL DES PAGES * 5, quai des Petits-Bosquets ✆ 03 83 74 11 42.** *Fax: 03 83 73 46 63. Website: www.hotel-les-pages.com.* 37 rooms from 61 €, breakfast 8.50 €. This is the only hotel in the town centre, located opposite the chateau on the other side of the water, and set back from the main street. The rooms are quiet and comfortable, and the more expensive are decorated with period furniture. The others are more classically furnished.

Nancy

LE CAP MARINE 60, rue Stanislas ✆ 03 83 37 05 03 *Open lunchtime and evening, Monday to Friday and Saturday evening. Set menus from 31 € to 46 €. A la carte 60 €.* This pretty setting with its boat theme (on the walls and tables) is just the place for a gourmet cruise. Fish and seafood have pride of place on the menu, and the food is presented on large plates, pleasing to the eye as well as the taste buds, and unfussy, so you can really smell the mixture of flavours. The desserts are carefully prepared too; the crunchy parts are a harmonious contrast to the melting bits. Discreet service from the crew.

LE CAPUCIN GOURMAND 31, rue Gambetta ✆ 03 83 35 26 99 *Closed Saturday lunchtime, Sunday evening and Monday. Set menus from 33 € to 60 €. Average price à la carte 64 €.* The setting has been completely redone in beige monochrome, with woodwork, tablecloths, Louis XV chairs, remarkable parquet and mouldings. The kitchens are new as well, and are now a fitting place for the sophisticated and exquisite *cuisine*. The detailed description of the dishes is quite poetic, and wakes up the taste buds most effectively. Chef Hervé Fourrière is immensely talented, as his marvellous recipes confirm.

GRAND HOTEL DE LA REINE ** 2, place Stanislas ✆ 03 83 35 03 01** *Fax: 03 83 32 86 04. Website: www.hoteldelareine.com. Double or single rooms from 140 € to 270 €. Breakfast 14 €. Le Stanislas restaurant: set menus from 30 € to 43 €. A la carte.* This is Nancy's only 4-star hotel, housed in an 18thc. palace on the majestic Place Stanislas. The rooms are all furnished in Louis XV style, with top-quality services on offer. The gastronomic restaurant serves meals in its dining rooms with their high ceilings or on the sheltered terrace, according to the season, and the *cuisine* is as sophisticated as the setting. A bar completes the picture. The Grand Hotel has welcomed some distinguished guests in its time, being a favourite haunt of passing celebrities. Queen Marie-Antoinette and Zinedine Zidane are just two examples in the last 250 years.

Le Grenier à Sel. (A) 28 rue Gustave-Simon ✆ 03 83 32 31 98 *Fax 03 83 35 32 88. Website: www.chez.com/grenierasel. Set menus from 30 € to 55 €, à la carte 85 €. Closed Sunday, Monday, last week in July, first fortnight in August and Christmas.* That dining room! It's spacious and quite well decorated, but terribly noisy (due to the restaurant's success, which is a good thing) and not very welcoming. This is the only flaw in Patrick and Frédérique Fréchin's establishment. After setting up shop in 1997, they had a few teething problems before the restaurant really took off two or three years ago, helped by word of mouth and a gastronomic guide's recognition. You don't forget Patrick Fréchin's forceful and surprising *cuisine*, which is always a success. His red mullet cooked at low temperature and spring vegetable tartlet, roast Dublin Bay prawns *à la diable*, green asparagus spread on bread with conserved shallots, pigeon with grilled cocoa beans and juice, and bitter chocolate with Japanese coconut balls and pineapple emulsion, chestnut flour and Tonka bean cake leave the local and even regional competition far behind. The cellar is full of fine bottles at attractive prices. What a pity there isn't a sunnier setting!

MEUSE

Verdun

HOSTELLERIE DU COQ HARDI * 8, avenue de la Victoire ✆ 03 29 86 36 36** *Fax: 03 29 86 09 21. Website: www.coq-hardi.com.* Open all year. 35 rooms and 3 apartments. Rooms from 93 € to 130 €. Bistrot du Coq Hard, set menus from 19.50 € to 35 €. Coq Hardi gastronomic restaurant, set menus from 43 € to 92 €. Very pretty hotel dating back to the early 19thc., located on the banks of the Meuse near the Victory monument. The Coq Hardi is almost an institution in Verdun, with its rich decoration recalling a period filmset. The rooms are luxurious and very comfortable, with private bathroom and all mod cons. A cockerel lords it over the dining room, of course, where chef Frederic Engel concocts his delicate and sophisticated recipes with the very best regional produce. If your budget is tight, the bistrot offers more traditional dishes at affordable prices.

Etain

LA SIRENE ** 22, avenue Prud'homme-Havette ✆ 03 29 87 10 32. *Fax 03 29 87 17 65.* Closed from 23 December to 1 February. 22 renovated rooms from 45 € to 60 €, breakfast 7 €. Restaurant closed Sunday evening and Monday. 6 set menus from 13 € to 50 €. A la carte. Napoleon III stopped here in 1870, after the Battle of Gravelotte. Your stay will be pleasant, with seasonal, local *cuisine* in the restaurant and some sweet-savoury mixes, where the region's mirabelle has pride of place.

MOSELLE

Baerenthal

L'ARNSBOURG 18 Untermuhlthal ✆ 03 87 06 50 85 *Fax 03 87 06 57 67. Website: www.relaischateaux.com. Set menus from 105 € to 130 €, à la carte 100 €.* Closed Tuesday, Wednesday, January and a fortnight in September. Arnsbourg features among the region's greatest and most isolated restaurants: you think you've arrived when you see the signs for Baerenthal, but you've still got several kilometres to go through the magnificent Muhl Valley, before finding it. This former forester's house was converted in the early 20thc. by Cathy and Jean-Georges Klein's grandmother, and the lonely setting has probably encouraged them to open the hotel rather sooner than planned (in 2006). Jean-Georges' cooking is full of personality, and reveals Oriental and Spanish influences, since this Lorraine chef is a great friend of Ferran Adria, the Spanish genius from El Bulli. His pan-fried Dublin Bay prawns, potato *croustillant*, herb salad, frogs' legs with herbs and coriander, lobster, lobster cream and nem with ginger, or pigeon breast seasoned with Japanese horseradish and coffee sauce are really inventive. The service is relaxed and smiling, and very efficient too, and the cellar boasts over 800 recommended bottles from Alsace and elsewhere.

Metz

GRAND HOTEL DE METZ 3, rue des Clercs 03 87 36 16 33.** *Fax: 03 87 74 17 04. Website: www.hotel -metz.com 62 rooms. Double room 59 € to 70 €, single room 52 € to 70 €, family room (sleeps 3-5) 85 € (free for under 12s), prestige room 90 €. Breakfast buffet or served in your room 7 €. Garage 10 € (book in advance). 5 € supplement for pets. Logis de France.* A top-of-the-range hotel located in a semi-pedestrian street right in the town centre, close to the cathedral and the Arsenal.

The building dates back to the 18thc. and has 62 charming rooms, all light and quiet. Each room is individually decorated and well furnished, and you'll note the 'welcome' tray served on your arrival. The Prestige rooms are the most luxurious, with bathroom opening onto the bedroom and separate toilet. The hotel offers an all-in Escapade Gourmande (165 € for two) combining a night in a Prestige room and a gastronomic dinner at the Pampre d'Or, one of Metz's top restaurants. The Logis de France and Membres des Relais de la Mirabelle quality labels mean that staff are in a good position to give you a little inside advice about local restaurants! Seminar room and showroom available. Pleasant, friendly welcome.

HOTEL DE LA CATHEDRALE * 25, place de Chambre © 03 87 75 00 02** *Fax: 03 87 75 40 75. Website: www.hotelcathedrale-metz.fr. 20 rooms from 68 € to 105 €. Breakfast 11 €.* This hotel nestles in a charming 17thc. residence at the foot of the cathedral. On the first floor, residents can have breakfast on a patio facing the cathedral. The comfort level is simple, but the rooms are period and full of charm. The decoration is original too, with nothing standard or merely functional about it: the ancient wooden furniture, fireplaces, and exposed beams make for a most romantic setting. A word of advice: there are only 20 rooms, and the hotel is full most of the year, so you'd be wise to book in advance.

RESTAURANT MAIRE 1, rue du Pont-des-Morts © 03 87 32 43 12 *Website: www.restaurant-maire.com. Closed Tuesday and Wednesday lunchtime. Set menus from 23 € to 61 € (dégustation menu).* Yves Maire is one of Metz's stars. Sophistication is the word that comes to mind to describe both his restaurant setting, with a magnificent view of Metz, and his *cuisine*. You do rather get fed up seeing *Maire* written all over the place, however (napkins, tray, etc). The menu changes often, so it's not easy to mention his specialities. Anyway, the descriptions certainly make your mouth water, and you won't be disappointed with the reality!

Thionville

L'HORIZON* 50, route du Crève-Cœur © 03 82 88 53 65** *Fax: 03 82 34 55 84. Website: www.lhorizon.fr.* Rooms from 96 € to 148 €. Breakfast 18 €. Restaurant closed Monday and Saturday lunchtimes. Set menus from 32 € to 58 €. The Speck family welcomes you in their beautiful residence a few minutes from Thionville. This listed hotel de charme is rustic in style and setting, with old wooden wardrobes and a view of the magnificent park. The restaurant has plenty of charm as well, offering delicate and varied dishes for your enjoyment.

VOSGES

Epinal

LES DUCS DE LORRAINE 5 rue de Provence © 03 29 29 56 00 *Fax 03 29 29 56 01. Set menus from 34 € to 74 €, à la carte 60 €. Closed Sunday evening and exceptionally, during the second fortnight in August for renovation work.* Five years ago, Stéphane Ringer and Claudy Obriot swapped the town centre for this splendid, late 19thc. bourgeoise residence, slightly outside Epinal. The setting isn't exactly cheerful, with its Grand Siecle style and Louis XV furniture, carved woodwork and moulding, so different from the ultra-modern decor you find nowadays in many restaurants. The important thing, however, is the food, and in this field, Stéphane Ringer certainly masters his subject. Warm scallop carpaccio, green Mallemort asparagus and basil emulsion, Marennes oysters served iced in iodised stock, roast pikeperch with thyme, bayleaf and rosemary, pan-roasted frogs' legs, dovecote pigeon fillet in a sesame crust and pan-fried liver, les beatilles en espumo (bits of the offal in froth) with the leg, and cabbage, and mirabelle soufflé with its coulis and sorbet are examples of his recipes. This is cuisine with a bourgeois influence, revisited and rectified according to current standards, and at prices that leave you a little something over for the wine list.

LA FAYETTE *** **Parc économique le Saut-le-Cerf** ✆ **03 29 81 15 15** *Fax: 03 29 31 07 08. Website: www.bestwestern-lafayette-epinal.com. 62 rooms. Double room 78 € to180 €. Breakfast 10.80 €. Swimming pool, water therapy, sauna, fitness centre. Tennis courts on the edge of the forest and municipal golf course close by. Theme weekends. Set menus from 18.50 € to 41.50 €.* The service is excellent, and the staff, in their red and black uniforms, most attentive. Comfortable and spacious rooms, especially the most recent. Colourful restaurant, cosily fitted out with modern furnishings.

Gérardmer

AUBERGE DU BORD DU LAC ** **166, chemin du Tour-du-Lac** ✆ **03 29 63 44 98** *Fax: 03 29 63 21 21. Website: www.auberge-bord-lac.fr.* Rooms from 60 € to 80 €. Breakfast 10 €. Restaurant closed Sunday evening. Set menus from 15 € to 30 €, dish of the day 10 €. A la carte. This auberge overlooks the lake at the opposite end from Gérardmer. This is an ideal and very peaceful spot. Wide lawns run down to the lake, and you feel rather as if it's your private pool! You can eat on the restaurant terrace or veranda, too, adding the fine view to your enjoyment of the meal. The cooking is good, though unexceptional.

Neufchâteau

HOTEL EDEN ** **Rue de la Première-Armée-Française** ✆ **03 29 95 61 30** *Fax: 03 29 94 03 42. Website: www.leden.fr.* 25 rooms, from 47 € to 69 €. Restaurant closed Sunday evening and Monday. Set menus from 22 € to 42 €. This hotel is unremarkable from the outside, with its modern architecture, but you get a very different impression inside. The rooms are spacious and prettily decorated, some with water massage or jacuzzi bath The French gastronomic *cuisine* is faultless, and the cellar full of new and interesting bottles to discover.

Plombières-les-Bains

LA FONTAINE STANISLAS ** **1, Fontaine-Stanislas** ✆ **03 29 66 01 53** *Fax: 03 29 30 04 31. Closed 15 October-1 April. 16 rooms from 38 € to 56 € (the most expensive rooms are small apartments). Breakfast 7 €. Set menus 17.50 € and 39 €.* At Plombières, Place de l'Eglise, follow signs to Epinal-Xertigny for 2 km, then take the forest road. This hotel is half-hidden in the woods, in a beautiful natural setting, with a view across magnificent Plombières Valley. The owners are the Bilger family, who welcome you with open arms. You can look forward to a restful and invigorating stay, in a comfortable room or annex apartment with a balcony overlooking the valley, and enjoy sophisticated regional *cuisine*. This is a good address to note, with extra points for the setting, the cooking and that kind welcome.

Vittel

L'OREE DU BOIS ETRESTAURANT LA FORET ** **Face au golf** ✆ **03 29 08 88 88** *Fax: 03 29 08 01 61. Website: www.loreeduboisvittel.fr. Rooms from 59 € to 80 €. Set menus from 16 € to 35 €.* The forest is all around you, with wide windows overlooking the racecourse. Inside, the restaurant is soberly decorated in beige tones, and rather distinguished, a fitting setting for the sophisticated seasonal cuisine. The hotel services are of the same quality: the spacious rooms are decorated in either traditional or modern style, and there is even a surprising 'organic' room. You can choose from different kinds of break, 2 to 5 days, and a selection of thermal treatments at Vittel spa.

Midi Pyrénées

Valentré's bridge on the Lot, Cahors

MIDI-PYRENEES
Dordogne
N
O
E
S
Payrac
Gourdon
Lot
Lavercantière
Catus
Puy-l'Évêque
Lot
CAHORS
Sauzet
Montcuq
N20
Montaigu-de-Quercy
Lauzerte
Lot-et-Garonne
Vers Agen
Vers Bordeaux
Tarn-et-Garonne
Valence
N113
Moissac
Lafrançaise
Golfech
N20
Landes
Castelsarrasin
Tarn
A62
MONTAUBAN
Lavit
Barbotan-les-Thermes
La Romieu
Saint-Avit-Frandat
Gers
Montréal
Condom
N21
Gramont
Montech
Larressingle
Lectoure
Beaumont-de-Lomagne
Garonne
Cassaigne
Eauze
Valence-sur-Baïse
Saint-Clar
Fronton
Fleurance
Grisolles
Vers Mont-de-Marsan
Vic-Fezensac
Saint-Puy
Monfort
Nogaro
Miramont-Latour
Grenade
Lavardens
N124
Barcelonne-du-Gers
Aignan
Lupiac
Mauvezin
Cologne
Laurac
N20
A62
Riscle
Termes-d'Armagnac
Gers
AUCH
Castelnau-Rivière-Basse
Plaisance
N124
L'Isle-Jourdain
Blagnac
Gimont
TOULOUSE
Cazaux-Savès
Marciac
Saramon
Mirande
N21
Maubouguet
Samatan
Muret
Gers
Pyrénées-Atlantiques
Rabastens-de-Bigorre
Espaon
Rieumes
Canal de Saint-Martory
A64
Garonne
L'Isle-en-Dodon
Vic-en-Bigorre
N21
Vers Pau
Castelnau-Magnoac
Boulogne-sur-Gesse
Carbonne
TARBES
N117
Séméac
Aurignac
Montesquieu-Volvestre
Cazères
Saint-Martory
Martres-Tolosane
Lannemezan
Lourdes
A64
N117
N21
Montréjeau
Saint-Gaudens
Bagnères-de-Bigorre
Saint-Bertrand-de-Comminges
Argelès-Gazost
Saint-Girons
Hautes-Pyrénées
Neste
Garonne
Saint-Béat
Cauterets
La Mongie
Bourg-d'Oueil
Le Mourtis
Oust
Massat
Mont Né
2 147 m
Luz-Saint-Sauveur
Saint-Lary-Soulan
Ariège
Peyragude
Vignemale
3 298 m
Bagnères-de-Luchon
Aulus-les-Bains
Gavarnie
Pic d'Estats
3 145 m
Pic des Crabioules
3 116 m
0
10 km
Reproduction interdite
Jean-Baptiste Nény
Mars 2005
ESPAGNE

Vers Brive-la-Gaillarde
Corrèze
Cantal
Lozère
Martel
Sarennac
Dordogne
Souillac
Castelnau
Sousceyrac
Saint-Céré
Rocamadour
Lacapelle-Marival
Vers Aurillac
N140
N20
Livernon
Cardaillac
Labastide-Murat
Figeac
Célé
Capdenac-Gare
Vers
Lot
Saint-Cirq-Lapopie
Villefranche-de-Rouergue
Lalbenque
A20
Montpezat-de-Quercy
Caylus
Najac
Saint-Antonin-Noble-Val
Caussade
Bioule
Mur-de-Barrez
Sainte-Geneviève-sur-Argence
Truyère
Saint-Amans-des Cots
Entraygues-sur-Truyère
Laguiole
Conques
Estaing
Saint-Chély-d'Aubrac
Prades-d'Aubrac
Decazeville
Saint-Côme-d'Olt
Aubin
Marcillac-Vallon
Espalion
Bozouls
Sainte-Eulalie-d'Olt
Saint-Geniez-d'Olt
Rignac
Onet-le-Château
Laissac
Campagnac
Vers Montpellier
Belcastel
Aveyron
RODEZ
N88
Pont-de-Salars
Sévérac-le-Château
Baraqueville
Vézins-de-Lévézou
Sauveterre-de-Rouergue
Peyreleau
A75
Naucelle
Lac de Pareloup
Salles-Curan
Cassagnes-Bégonhès
Saint-Beauzély
Millau
Cordes-sur-Ciel
Tarn
N9
Carmaux
Réquista
Nant
La Cavalerie
Saint-Affrique
Roquefort
Brousse-le-Château
la Couvertoirade
ALBI
Aiguelèze
Gaillac
Ambialet
Saint-Sernin-sur-Rance
Cornus
Lisle-sur-Tarn
Alban
Rabastens
Rance
Camarès
Saint-Sulpice
Réalmont
Belmont-sur-Rance
Vers Montpellier
Graulhet
Brusque
Lautrec
N112
Lacaune
Murat-sur-Vèbre
Montastruc-La-Conseillère
Lavaur
Vielmur-sur-Agout
Agout
Brassac
Castres
Cuq-Toulza
N126
Puylaurens
Haute-Garonne
Caraman
Labruguière
Anglès
Hérault
Saint-Félix-Lauragais
Escoussens
Mazamet
Dourgne
Vers Béziers
A61
N113
Villefranche-de-Lauragais
Revel
Saint-Amans-Soult
Auterive
Canal du Midi
Cintegabelle
Vers Carcassonne
Mazères
Saverdun
A66
Pamiers
Mirepoix
Aude
FOIX
Lavelanet
Mer Méditerranée
Roquefixade
Montségur
Tarascon-sur-Ariège
Vicdessos
Ax-les-Thermes
0
30 km
Pyrénées-Orientales
Motorway
Major road
Minor road
Andorre
Vers Andorra la Vella

ALBI AND THE TARN

This is Cathar country. The town and surrounding villages are particularly beautiful.

Albi

SAINTE CECILE CATHEDRAL 6 bd. Sibille ✆ 05 63 43 23 43. *Admission free except the choir, 1. Chancel visit 1 € (over-12s). Audio guides in French, English, Spanish, Italian, German and Dutch: 3 € Treasure: adult 3 €, 12-25s 2 € Guided tours: ask at the Tourist Office for times and price. Open 1 June-30 September: 9am-6.30pm. 1 October-30 May: 9am-12 noon and 2pm-6.30pm. Closed to visitors during services.* This towering pink brick church is a Southern Gothic masterpiece (no flying buttresses; single nave). Built between 1282 and 1480 as a cathedral-fortress, it could house the town's entire population of 6,000 at need. The biggest Last Judgement and statuary collection in Christendom have been kept from this medieval period. The frescoes under the vault constitute France's oldest and most extensive group of Italian paintings.

SAINT SALVI COLLEGIATE CHURCH & CLOISTER. *The cloister is open all year: 7am-8pm. The collegiate church is open all year: 8.30am-12 noon and 2pm-6pm, except Wednesday (2.30pm-5pm) and Sunday (2-4.30pm).* Visitors tend to pass over the architectural interest and delicacy of this group in favour of Albi's other monuments, though the Romanesque church, topped by an amazing watchtower-steeple, and harmonious Romanesque-and-Gothic cloister are well worth seeing.

PALAIS DE LA BERBIE ✆ 05 63 49 48 70. *Gardens open 1 September-30 June:8am-12 noon & 2pm-6pm. July & August: 9am-6pm.* La Berbie (from the Occitan bisbia, bishopric) is an impressive palace-fortress, built in the 13thc. by the Bishops of Albi, the oldest parts dating back to 1240-1245. Bernard de Combret and Bernard de Castanet developed the fortifications between 1254 and 1307, as a show of strength for the Albigeois, heretics and King's officers. A massive keep, the Tour Mage (restored in the 18thc.) rose 50m above the Tarn. Louis d'Amboise later added Renaissance living-quarters, with wide openings and slate roofs. The 17thc. bishops transformed the ramparts into a walkway with a view of the Tarn, and laid out formal gardens in the old military courtyard. In 1922, the building became the Toulouse-Lautrec Museum, to house the collection left to the town council by the artist's mother, Countess Adèle.

MUSEE TOULOUSE-LAUTREC Place Sainte Cécile – Palais de la Berbie ✆ 05 63 49 48 70. *www.musee-toulouse-lautrec.com. Open every day (except Tuesday, October-March). July & August: 9am-6pm. Admission: adult 5 €, concessions 2.50 €, families 12.50 €.* The museum owns over 1,000 of Henri de Toulouse-Lautrec's works (including 214 paintings and a number of drawings, posters and lithographs) donated by his mother. The collection traces the artist's life and professional development: he is best known for creating the 'modern poster' in Montmartre in 1886. Works by some of his contemporaries (Bonnard, Vuillard, Valadon) and the Paris School (early 20thc.) are also on display.

Sainte-Cécile cathedral, Albi

MUSEE DE CIRE 12, rue Toulouse-Lautrec ✆ 05 63 54 87 55. *Open 15 June-15 September:10am-12 noon and 2.30pm-6pm. Other periods: 2.30pm-5pm. Closed Sunday & Monday and January & February. Admission: adult 3.20 €, 6-12s 1.40 €* This Wax Museum portrays the characters who made old Alby's history, in 18 scenes (Bernard de Castanet, Antoinette Salvan de Saliès, Rochegude and Jaurès) along with former trades (pastel and hat industries; mining etc.) now died out.

MUSEE LAPEROUSE Square Botany Bay ✆ 05 63 46 01 87. *Open every day except Monday outside July & August). Admission: adult 2.50 €, concessions 1.50 €, under-12s free.* Documents and personal effects from this brave Albi navigator's last voyage. He was wrecked on the Vanikoro reefs in 1788.

PARC ROCHEGUDE. A beautiful plant universe, living and breathing in the heart of town. Admiral Henri Paschal de Rochegude gave this 4 ha. park to the town in the 19thc. It boasts a number of natural wonders such as 'Bird Island', and visitors out for a stroll can admire the 17thc. private mansion, stream and pool filled from a waterfall, maze and magnificent classical and zoological gardens.

Elsewhere in the Tarn

Looking south towards the Mediterranean from its Black Mountains, the department still identifies with its Cathar history.

Ambialet

The Tarn twists its loop round a shaly peak, forming France's finest isthmus (according to a 19thc. geographer). It is certainly striking!

AMBIALET MONASTERY & CHAPEL. The 11thc. Romanesque chapel is built of shale with few apertures. In 1507, Frotaire, Bishop of NÓmes and brother to the Vicomtes d'Albi and d'Ambialet gave the church and its little monastery to Saint Victor Abbey in Marseille. (This Benedictine monastery played an important role in the Albigeois conflict). The removal of unnecessary parts, along with the plaster covering the inside walls, left the chapel bare in its Romanesque purity. The monastery is now part of the Congregation of Saint John. Notice the 17thc. statue of Notre Dame de l'Oder, and the strange copper censer shaped like a Romanesque chapel. A devil burns in the pan.

SON ET LUMIERE. *July & August, Thursday: 10pm. Admission: adult 5 €, 7-12s 2.50 € Seating below the Town Hall (follow indications).* The son et lumière takes you back to the days when Ambialet was the region's most important stronghold.

Castres

Sous-prefecture of the Tarn, and Jean Jaures' birthplace. The textile industry brought prosperity to Castres: the old wooden houses with their coloured galleries overhanging the River Agout recall the drapers, dyers and tanners who used the water in their work.

ARCHEOPOLE Parc de Gourjade ✆ 05 63 59 56 41. *Open 2pm-6pm except Sunday and public holidays. Admission: adult 2 €* The Archeopole is an archeological study and research centre in the Parc de Gourjade. You can see the furniture excavated on the neighbouring Gallo-Roman site in the exhibition gallery, follow a guided tour, and be introduced to experimental archeology: dig, flint-carving, work with clay, etc.

SAINT BENOIT CATHEDRAL. Built between 1680 and 1718, the cathedral houses a collection of 18thc. Toulouse School paintings and an elegant Baroque group.

MUSEE GOYA Hôtel de Ville ✆ 05 63 71 59 27. *Open every day, July & August: 9am-12 noon and 2pm-6pm. September, April, May & June: 9am-12 noon and 2pm-6pm. 1 October-31 March: closes 1hr earlier on weekdays and opens 1hr later on Sundays and public holidays. September-June: closed Monday, 1 May, 1 November & 25 December.* Housed in the 17thc. Bishops' Palace, the Goya Museum contains an impressive collection of Spanish painters: Velasquez, Murillo, Ribera, Valdes Leal, Alonso Cano, Beruete, Fortuny, Rusinol, Zuloaga, Anglada-Camarasa.The 3 Goyas are Self-portrait with spectacles, Portrait of Francisco del Mazo and The Philippines Junta. The arms room displays 300 old guns, privately donated.

Cordes-sur-Ciel

Cordes, 13thc. *bastide*, is a medieval eyrie on its rocky spur, with its feet in the fortified village and its rooftops in the sky.

GOTHIC HOUSES DE CORDES. Many of these Gothic houses are representative of the style; a few in particular are worth close attention. Maison du Grand Veneur. This is the only 3-storey house. It owes its fame to the hunting scene on its façade (some see this as symbolic of Cathar persecution). Maison de Grand Fauconnier. A more recent ochre sandstone Gothic residence. The columns are thinner, capitals longer, tympana less crowded and Gothic arches more accentuated than on the other houses. Maison du Grand Ecuyer. This is Cordes' most finely decorated façade, with its 14thc. sculptures intact (hybrid characters, winged woman with webbed feet, dragon, false gargoyles, etc.) Could this eclectic decoration be a symbol of alchemy?

MUSEE CHARLES PORTAL 27, Grand Rue Raimond VII ✆ 05 63 56 00 40. *Open every day July & August: 2pm-6pm. 1 April-31 October, Sunday & public holidays: 2pm-5pm.* The remains of Prehistoric, Gallo-Roman, Merovingian and medieval Cordes, together with various objects, documents and archives.

REPERE MEDIEVAL 4, place Charles Portal ✆ 05 63 56 00 78. Open every day, April-September. Other months: 2pm-6pm. Giant animated models of the medieval period tell the story of Cordes and the Comtes de Toulouse.

Gaillac

This thousand-year-old town seems full of the joy of living - which comes, perhaps, from its well-known wines.

SAINT MICHEL ABBEY CHURCH Place Saint Michel. An impressive brick building, overhanging the Tarn.

CHATEAU AND PARC DE FOUCAUD Ave. Dom Vaysette ✆ 05 63 57 18 25. Built in the 17thc. from plans inspired by the Villa d'Este, this castle now houses the Fine Arts Museum. Its tree-filled park blends Italian and French styles - perspective, terraces, fountains, orangerie, pavilion - and has always been open to the townspeople. It is one of the biggest gardens of its kind in the South of France.

MUSEE DES BEAUX ARTS Château de Foucaud ✆ 05 63 57 18 25. *Open November-April, Friday, Saturday & Sunday: 10am-12 noon and 2pm-6pm. May-October, every day except Tuesday: 10am-12 noon and 2pm-6pm. Admission: adult 2.50 €, child 1.20 €, under-12s free.* The Fine Arts museum exhibits 19th and early 20thc. regional artists, portraits and landscapes (Classical, Romantic, Post-Impressionist and Expressionist) on two floors of the superb 17thc. Château de Foucaud. Pendaries' sculptures have a room to themselves. Temporary exhibitions are housed on a floor apart.

FONTAINE DU GRIFFOUL Place Thiers. A remarkable 16thc. bronze group depicting four characters and a cockerel. The red Caunes marble basin and fittings were added in the 17th and 18thc.

Giroussens

Known as the Balcony of Languedoc, for its extraordinary view of the Agout Valley and Vaurais plain, this village is known for its pottery tradition.

JARDIN DES MARTELS ✆ 05 63 41 61 42. *Open May-August, 11am-7pm. 15 March-1 May and September-November: 2pm-6pm. Weekends & public holidays 15 March-15 November: 10am-6pm. Admission: adult 6 €, 10-18s 4.50 €, 4-10s 3.50 €.* Admire 2,500 plant varieties in 3.5ha. of landscaped park; this exhibition changes with the seasons! The kids will love the mini-farm with its deer, Ouessant sheep, Chinese pigs and decorative ducks.

Lavaur

This medieval stronghold saw 400 heretics burned to death during the Albi Crusade against the Cathars; eight centuries later it has not forgotten. A stele on the Plo Esplanade recalls the event. The old town's ancient tangle of streets hides some surprises worth discovering.

SAINT ALAIN CATHEDRAL. A truly striking Southern Gothic building. The hour is struck on a side tower by an oak jacquemart wearing a Phrygian cap.

Monestiès

This delightful medieval village in the Cerou Valley is as round and beautiful as a pearl in its oyster shell.

SAINT JACQUES CHAPEL-ENTOMBMENT ✆ 05 63 76 41 63. *Admission: adult 3.50 € Chapel + Bajen-Vega museum:5 €.* This chapel, a former pilgrims' hospice on the Compostella road, has contained one of the region's wonders since 1774. This almost life-size collection of 20 polychrome limestone statues represents the last three episodes in Christ's Passion: the Crucifixion, the Pieta and the Entombment. The delicate features and contained suffering on the faces of those ten people converging towards Christ's altar are overwhelming. A work of art unique the world over.

MUSEE BAJEN-VEGA Place de la Mairie ✆ 05 63 76 19 17. *Admission: adults 3 €*. This residence where the Lord Bishop use to stay now houses a museum illustrating the life and work of two artists: Martine Vega and Francisco Bajen, who donated the house and many of their paintings to the community. The museum was inaugurated in 1999.

Montans

Not far from Gaillac, hidden among the vines, Montan is a national archaeology centre, known for its 1st and 2ndc. Gallo-Roman ceramic.

ARCHEOSITE ✆ 05 63 57 59 16. *Open April-October: 10am-12 noon and 2pm-6pm. Out of season, Saturday, Sunday & public holidays: 2pm-6pm; weekdays by reservation for groups. Admission: adult 4 €, concessions 3 €, 6-12s 2 €* Lifesize reconstruction of a Gallo-Roman street (unique in France) with bakery, potter, tavern, house and atrium all remarkably true to life.

Montalet Peak and Lacaune Mountains

Montalet is the highest of the Lacaune Mountains, reaching 1 259 m. From the top, you can see the Aubrac, and sometimes as far as the Pyrenees and the Mediterranean. Its Virgin was put up in 1882. This region of southern Massif Central foothills including Mont Barre, Mont Grand and others, has become famous for its pure air and water (Mont Roucous, La Salvetat). Be careful if you're there in winter: there is a risk of heavy snowfall.

Puylaurens

A pretty balcony overlooking the Pyrenees, with a pleasant view of the region. Stroll through the ancient quarters, stretching from bridge to bridge, and see 17thc. corbelled houses (11, Rue Cap de Castel), a 16thc. covered passage running off from Place de Fouyssac, the Corneilhan mansion, Rue du Four and fine 17thc. housefronts (Rue Foulinou) including the Roque Buisson mansion.

CHATEAU DE PUYLAURENS. This 13thc. brick fortress on its rocky outcrop was an Inquisition prison in Cathar crusade days.

Rabastens

This 'little Albi' is known for its ancient vineyards (AOC gaillac) handcrafted furniture and brick architecture.

NOTRE DAME DU BOURG CHURCH. This church shows the influence of Toulouse art in the Albi region. The 14thc. decorative painting in nave and chancel is remarkable.

MUSEE DU PAYS RABASTINOIS 2, rue Amédée de Clausade ✆ 05 63 40 65 65. *Open Tuesday-Friday: 10am-12 noon and 2pm-6pm. Saturday, Sunday & public holidays: 3pm-6pm. Admission: adult 2 €, children free*. Collections of art and local history on three floors, including some unique glazed pottery (Giroussens, 17th and 18thc.).

CAVES AND CHASMS

Caves and grottes come in all shapes and sizes in the Midi-Pyrénées (3,000 on record) with their limestone cathedrals, stalactites and stalagmites, and Paleolithic wall art. 20 caves are open to the public, namely among the rich prehistoric deposits in the Ariège and Lot.

Ariège

GROTTE DE NIAUX ✆ 05 61 05 88 37 or 05 61 05 10 10. *www.sesta.fr. Open all year except Monday, November-March, except (public & school) holiday Mondays. Admission: adult 9.40 €, child 5.70 €, concessions 7.50 €*. A large and beautifully-decorated prehistoric cavern, with polychrome frescoes and black-line drawings (probably made from a mix of charcoal and manganese oxide with added grease). Commander Mollard and his son discovered them almost by accident in 1906; other discoveries followed. The amazing 'Black Salon' (which has been reconstructed in the Prehistoric Art Park) is definitely not to be missed.

GROTTE DU MAS-D'AZIL Ave. de la Grotte ✆ 05 61 69 97 71. *Open every day, June & September: 10am-12 noon and 2pm-6pm. July & August: 10am-6pm. Check opening times for other periods. Admission: adult 6.10€, over-5s 3.10€* Impressive underground scenery in tunnel form – and that's not all. A number of archeological remains have been excavated: tools, small flints, tiny scrapers, stag-antler harpoons and strange little flat coloured pebbles.

Lot

GROTTES DE PECH-MERLE Cabrerets ✆ 05 65 31 27 05. *Open 4 April-1 November:9.30am-12 noon and 1pm-5pm. Groups all year, by appointment (except 15 December-15 January) Admission: adult 6 to 7. Admission 15 June-15 September: adult 7€, 5-18s 4.50€ Cave visit 1hr approx., exhibition & film, 40mins. Book first (limited to 700 visitors per day).* Over 1,200 galleries and 7 chambers containing the 'Mammoths' Chapel'; disc chamber with its strange concretions and human footprint; enigmatic 'bison women' ceiling, bears' gallery and horse fresco surrounded with mysterious signs and hands in negative position.

GROTTES DE COUGNAC ✆ 05 65 41 47 54. Admire thousands of stalactites and stalagmites and 25,000 year-old wall paintings in a single visit. The second cave contains the oldest dated figurative animal paintings accessible to the public.

GROTTE DES MERVEILLES L'Hospitalet ✆ 05 65 33 67 92. *Open every day, April-October:10am-12 noon and 2pm-5.30pm. July & August: 10am-7pm. Admission: adult 5€, 5-12s 3€*. This cave is covered in beautiful concretions, formed by continually running water. Paleolithic artists left their work on the walls 20,000 years ago: you can identify a horse, a stag, felines and six 'negative' hands.

GOUFFRE DE PADIRAC ✆ 05 65 33 64 56. *www.gouffre-de-padirac.com. Open Easter-November. 11 July-31 July: 9am-6pm; August: 8.30am-6.30pm (check times for other periods). Time your visit for before 10am on weekdays and avoid weekends in high season. Admission: Adult 8.50 Free car park.* This naturally-excavated chasm opened up the Lot Causse's surface. You go down 103m by lift or stairs to the underground river, and travel along it to the Lac de la Pluie (Rain Lake) chamber, continuing on foot to the Grand Cours and Grand Dome chambers with their 94m vaulted ceiling, and Lac Supérieur, 28m above the riverbed.

GERS – GASCONY

Foie gras, armagnac: this is good food country - and the scenery is just as satisfying!

Auch

Gers' prefecture and capital of Gascony, Auch is divided in two by the River Gers. The right bank is modern, busy and low-lying; the left is the ancient cité, built like an amphitheatre on a rocky outcrop.

SAINTE MARIE D'AUCH CATHEDRAL. This huge cathedral has a Gothic nave with Renaissance and Classical decoration. Five radiating chapels and four in the straight sides surround the vast chancel. The ambulatory's 18 stained-glass windows were made by 16thc. master-glassmaker Arnaud de Moles. The great chancel stalls are Flamboyant Gothic in style.

ESCALIER MONUMENTAL Place Salinis, with its marvellous view across the Gers and surrounding country, is linked to the lower town by a 19thc. monumental (and listed) staircase built into the hillside. On these six flights (370 steps) stands the statue of Charles de Batz, better known as d'Artagnan; his famous energy should help you reach the top! A good digestive exercise.

POUSTERLES. Medieval streets, once linking the upper and lower towns, with their steep staircases (hard on 21stc. legs, so no longer used much). Discover their old houses, then notice the differences between 18thc. perspective and Second Empire decoration in the Allées d'Etigny.

MAISON DE GASCOGNE. The 19thc. cornmarket is a pleasant and lively place with its arcades: in summer it displays local produce and crafts. Out of season, it hosts events like the Antiques Fair. The post office opposite is housed in a fine 18thc. building, once Hôtel de l'Intendance, then the prefecture.

Condom

Former bishops' city, now a showcase for Gascony's treasures. From July to September, the town council organises a temporary condom exhibition (called a préservatif in French) in the Lannelongue Clinic, to capitalise on British giggles.

SAINT PIERRE CATHEDRAL. Late Gothic, with a light and luminous nave, and a fine 16thc. cloister. Take a walk through the town to admire the old 18thc. mansions (Hôtels de Polignac and Cugnac).

MUSEE DE L'ARMAGNAC 2, rue Jules Ferry ✆ 05 62 28 47 17. *Open April-October: 10am-12 noon and 3pm-6pm. November-March: 3pm-5pm. Closed Tuesday & public holidays.* Learn all about this famous drink: history, secrets and anecdotes. You can also admire a collection of winemaking utensils and an 18-tonne monumental press.

GASCOGNE NAVIGATION ✆ 05 62 28 46 46. *Open every day, 1 April-30 October. Admission: 23 /hour, 54 /half-day, 92 /day.* Motor boat hire (no licence needed) and trips on the D'Artagnan, on the Baise.

Larressingle

One of France's smallest fortified villages, this *castlenau* has one 270m rampart encircling houses squeezed up against the curtain walls, with castle and church in the middle. Larressingle also houses the Pilgrims' Halt Museum (where 50 characters illustrate village life at the time of the Hundred Years' War), an enameller, goldsmith and artist. On the edge of the fortified village is a 13th and 14thc. siege camp, with three working war machines. The footpaths in this peaceful place lead to the Compostella Road, and the Pont d'Artigue (between Larressingle and Beaumont-sur-l'Osse) is one of the last Romanesque bridges, specially built between the 12th and 13thc. for pilgrims to pass.

Lavardens

A pretty, oval-shaped village, fitting the outcrop it is built on. Its wall has gone, but five of the towers remain. To the west, the Comtes d'Armagnac's 17thc. castle proudly overlooks the valley, with a remarkable view. The paved rooms are huge, and regularly host exhibitions. Each year,'petits marches du soir' (small evening markets) are held in this lively and inventive village.

CHATEAU DE LAVARDENS ✆ 05 62 64 51 20. *Closed 15 January-15 February. April, May, June, September & October: every day: 10.30am-12.30pm and 2pm-6pm. July & August: every day, 10am-7pm. November, December, February & March: every day: 10.30am-12.30pm and 2pm-5pm.* This feudal castle was the Comtes d'Armagnac's stronghold, taken and and destroyed by royal troops in 1496. Later, it came into the House of Navarre, and was rebuilt around 1620 by Antoine de Roquelaure, Marshal of France, and companion of Henri IV, who made him a gift of it. Sold to 12 families during the Revolution, it fell into ruins from lack of common management, but was rescued by a handful of castle-lovers in the 1960s.

Lectoure

This is one of the oldest Gers communities, with over 100 sarcophagi (found on the plain), thousands of Gallo-Roman remains and a Gallic well. During the barbarian invasions, the town moved onto the heights, where it stays to this day, proud and elegant, overlooking the Gers Valley. Start at Saint Gervais Saint Protais Cathedral, then follow the Bastion walk past the statue of Marechal Lannes, where the viewpoint indicator shows you the grey-blue line of the Pyrenees. Visit the Lapidary and Pharmacy Museums and the Musee Lannes (to find out more about this local Marshal), ending up with the Fontaine de Diane, Tour du Bourreau (Executioner's Tower) and 18thc. mansions.

Montréal-du-Gers

The first of the Gers bastides, founded in 1255 along a rocky peak. The square has arcades on three sides, and the Gothic church was built in line with the ramparts. Half-timbered houses and a 13thc. gate complete this remarkable site.

A kilometre away, the luxurious Gallo-Roman Villa Séviac spreads out its sumptuous 3ha. carpet of polychrome mosaics, containing 32 different motifs.

VILLA GALLO-ROMAINE DE SEVIAC ✆ 05 62 29 48 57. *www.seviac-villa.fr.st. Open March-November, every day: 10am-12 noon and 2pm-6pm. July & August: 10am-7pm (ticket includes museum). Admission: 4 €, under-12s free.* The villa has preserved its unique mosaics: millions of tiny cubes arranged in geometric figures, composing a series of superb decors. In the south west part, a courtyard separates the main residence from a huge thermal bath complex.

Tillac

CHATEAU DE PALLANNE GOLF COURSE ✆ 05 62 70 00 06. *Fax: 05 62 70 00 01. www.Chateaugolfdepallanne.fr. E-mail: golfcpallanne@infonie.fr.* This 18-hole course is open all year. Par 72, 6,341m. Green fee: weekdays 30 €, weekends 35 €. Senior citizens 2 €. (weekdays), under-18s 15 (weekdays). Restaurant April-October (menu from 13 €, assiette golfeur 8 €.) Pro shop in clubhouse. This hilly course among oaks and conifers surrounds a pretty 18thc. castle, with the Pyrénées as backdrop. The first six holes are flat (two water features) and the climb gentle, until the 10th hole with its steep par 3. The Broqueville family offers accommodation in the 4-star (max. 18 people) 2-star Orangery (6 people) and 3-star Dovecote (4 people). Enquire at the golf club.

Valence-sur-Baïse

This bastide perched in the hills boasts a fine square and 14thc. church with two towers. Sailing craft can moor in the harbour: Valence is useful as well as decorative.

FLARAN ABBEY ✆ **05 62 28 50 19**. *Open except January. Admission: adults 4 €.* Built by Burgundian monks in pure Cistercian style, with marvellous craftsmanship.

Lourdes

The town is universally known for its pilgrimages, and contains a number of religious monuments: the sanctuary (impressive despite its controversial architecture), huge, underground Saint Pie X Basilica (holds 20,000), Byzantine Rosary Basilica with its 15 chapels and upper Neo-Gothic basilica overlooking the grotto. In this small cave are many plaques, each giving thanks for a miracle. Saint Bernadette's museum opposite the castle completes the religious tour.

MUSEE GREVIN 87, rue de la Grotte ✆ **05 62 94 33 74**. *Open every day, April-June and September-October: 9am-11.40am and 1.30pm-6.30pm. Sunday, opens 10am. July & August, same opening hours plus evenings: 8.30pm-10pm every day. Admission: adult 5.50 €, child 2.75 €.* 100 waxworks arranged in 18 different scenes, illustrating the lives of Christ and Bernadette Soubirous, local girl turned saint.

MUSEE DE LOURDES Parking de l'Egalite ✆ **05 62 94 28 00.** *Open every day, 1 April-31 October: 9am-11.45am and 1.30pm-6.45pm. Admission: adult 5 €, child 2.50 €.* The apparitions happened in 1858. Lourdes Museum illustrates the historical context, with the period's costumes, shops and trades (4,000 exhibits plus son et lumière).

PETIT LOURDES 68, ave. Peyramale ✆ **05 62 94 24 36.** *Open every day, 1 April-20 October: 9am-12 noon and 1.30pm-6.45pm. Free car park. Adult 5 €, child 2.50 €* Lourdes in 1858 in realistic miniature.

MUSEE PYRENEEN ✆ **05 62 42 37 37.** *Open every day. Summer: 9am-12 noon and 1.30pm-6.30pm (mid-July-mid August, open non-stop). Winter: 9am-12 noon and 2pm-6pm. Adult 5 €, child 2.50 €* 18th and 19thc. rural life, art and popular traditions in the Pyrenees. The museum is housed in Lourdes Fortress (11thc.).

HAUTES-PYRÉNÉES

Climbing from plain to mountain, towards the Pyrénées National Park with its fantastic scenery.

Argelès-Gazost

Located between ski resorts, Argelès-Gazost is a pleasant place for a stroll, between staircases, gardens and terraces in the pure mountain air.

COLLINE DES MARMOTTES - Pyrenees Wildlife Park ✆ **05 62 97 91 07**. *Open every day, April-end October (June-August: 9am-7pm). Admission: adult 9 €, child 6 €.* See marmots, deer, brown bears, squirrels, wolves and otters on this wildlife trail. You can make your favourite animal's pawprint in the Trail Workshop afterwards.

ETABLISSEMENT THERMAL ✆ **05 62 97 03 24**. This classified resort treats respiratory and phlebological disorders, in the middle mountains at an altitude of 400m.

Arreau

Strategically placed between the Aspin and Peyresourde Passes, Arreau is the starting-point for a number of hikes and cycling trips. This charming mountain hamlet is worth a visit for its architecture and Rivers Neste d'Aure and Neste de Louron.

AIGLES D'AURE ✆ **05 62 40 10 35**. *Open every day, April-mid September, from 2.30pm. Display at 3.30pm. July & August, display at 3.30pm & 5pm. Admission: adult 6 €, 5-12s 4 €.* 25 kinds of diurnal and nocturnal birds of prey go through their paces. The discovery circuit (eagles, vultures, falcons, owls etc.) has been set up in the birds' natural environment, with explanatory panels.

Bagnères-de-Bigorre

This spa resort has attracted the fashionable world throughout history. Henri IV's mother Jeanne de Navarre came to cure her sterility (!) Later, Mme de Maintenon, Lamartine and George Sand took the waters here. Today, a range of activities is on offer, including a casino and local museum.

MUSEE SALIES Bd. de l'Hyperon ✆ 05 62 91 07 26. *Open 1 May-31 October. Closed Monday & Tuesday. Admission: adults 4 €, students 3 €* Housed in a fine Art Deco building, the museum contains 17th and 18thc. earthenware, Barbizon landscape painters, oriental art, a Blanche Odin collection, religious art and processional lights.

GRANDS THERMES - AQUENSIS ✆ 05 62 95 00 23. *www.thermes-bagneres.com.* This City of Water offers a choice of options, combining leisure, relaxation and getting fit. The water is rich in trace elements and mineral salts, naturally hot and does you good!

Cauterets

A pretty village 967m above sea-level, set in a valley among conifer forests, known for its icy torrents and hot springs (Cauterets spa water leaves the ground at 55 degrees C). The surrounding country is delightful for walking, with spectacular views.

PONT D'ESPAGNE. 7km from Cauterets, in the Pyrenees National Park. This is an exceptional, carefully-preserved site on the Waterfalls Route, with wildlife and flora unique in Europe.

LA FERME BASQUE Route du Cambasque 05 62 92 54 32. *E-mail: fermebasque@wanadoo.com. http://fermebasque.free.fr.* Restaurant and farm gate sale. Specialising in farm mutton, cassoulet, civet, navarin and pâtés, also lamb with prunes or piperade, duck, confits, gizzards, foie gras, magrets, sausages, pork, cheese and jams. Gift baskets available.

Luz-Saint-Sauveur

Framed by narrow, rather sinister gorges, Luz basin spreads as far as the Gavarnie and Bastan mountain stream confluence.

PONT NAPOLEON. Napoleon III decided to have this monumental bridge built in late summer 1859, over the Pau mountain stream. The structure has one arch (42m) resting directly on the gorge. The roadway (67.5m) is made of shale and the stone balustrade weighs 24,000kg. Nowadays, the site attracts tourists and also bungy-jumpers.

TEMPLARS' FORTIFIED CHURCH. This ancient and striking church is not to be missed. The building was raised and given 6m-high ramparts with 87 crenels, and a wide ditch. The clocktower was also a look-out post.

Parc National des Pyrénées

GAVARNIE. The department's highest and most isolated village (1,375m) nestles close to the Gavarnie Circus, part of a high limestone massif culminating in Mont Perdu (3,353m). The Circus forms an amphitheatre with 3 concentric tiers, at 1,500-1,700m, and the Grande Cascade (Great Waterfall) falls from a height of 420m. The whole family can climb to the Circus (1hr approx), or get there on donkey- or horseback.

MAISON DU PARC NATIONAL ✆ 05 62 92 42 48. *www.parc-pyrenees.com. Open July & August, every day: 9.30am-12.30pm and 1.30pm-6.30pm.* The Pyrenees National Park is an animal and plant sanctuary, sheltering endangered species and those already extinct in other parts of Europe. It covers 5,700ha. and 100km east-west in the Aspe Valley, with high massifs and impressive peaks.

MUSEE 1900 Boulevard Latapie-Flurin ✆ 05 62 92 02 02. *Open except 15 October-15 December. Admission: adult 6 €.* This museum

Gavarnie river

The underground world of the Hautes-Pyrénées

The underground world fascinates most of us. Here are a few sites absolutely not to be missed. Bétharram Caves - Saint-Pé de Bigorre: 05 62 41 80 04. These caves had been open for 102 years in 2005, and still boast a fantastic circuit over 5 floors - among draperies, calcites, excentrics, stalactites, stalagmites and marmites - including a boat trip and little train journey.

Gargas Caves - Aventignan: ✆ 05 62 39 72 39. You can admire engravings and animal paintings illustrating the secret art of Stone Age hunters who came here 27,000 years ago. Marvellous lighting.

Loup Caves - Lourdes: ✆ 05 62 94 20 91. Rooms full of strange shapes, modelled by thousands of years of crystallisation.

Médous Caves: ✆ 05 62 91 78 46. Extensive calcite slides have created capricious shapes recalling waterfalls, organs, draperies and strange architecture.

Vieille Aure Mines - Route du Pla d'Adet: ✆ 05 62 39 46 19. Another place with more recent memories. This museum is the only one of its kind in the Pyrenees, and a Mecca of French mineralogy. You discover an old manganese mining site, with the outside preserved and fitted out for visitors, and a genuine restored mountain mine with a son et lumiere circuit in several languages.

is housed in the Hotel d'Angleterre's luxurious Louis XV setting. You can see a magnificent collection of regional costumes from 1750 to1850, and some elegant dresses from 1850 to 1930. Popular, traditional objects, old photos of Cauterets, and a grand hotel kitchen dating from the early 20thc. complete this superb exhibition on two floors.

GAVARNIE, ESTAUBE, TROUMOUSE, ET HEAS. Gavarnie is located in the high valley crossed by Pau's mountain stream, 1,375m above sea level, making it the highest village in the department and the most isolated in France. It nestles close to Gavarnie Circus, Europe's highest limestone massif (Mont Perdu 3,353m) and a listed World Heritage Site. This circus forms a magnificent natural amphitheatre with three concentric tiers, stretching out at the top over 14km, and rising to 1,500 or 1,700m. The Grande Cascade is the highest in Europe (420m) with its magnificent snow walls and levels, know all over the world. The whole family will quite easily manage the climb, but you can also go right to the top on horseback, or donkey (for hire): it takes about an hour on foot from village to circus. Gavarnie is the best known, but Troumouse Circus is also a pleasant site for a hike, starting out from Gedre village, and Estaube offers a unique view of Mont Perdu and Tuquerouye Gap from its depths. It is also an exceptional place for marmot-watching.

Pic du Midi

You arrive at the top (2,877m) after a 15 min. cable-car ride, to discover a breathtaking panoramic view of the Pyrenees and southern plains, as far as the Massif Central foothills. 600m^2. of terraces have been fitted out with viewpoint indicators, so you can enjoy the scenery and identify the region's natural features at the same time.

INFORMATIONS ACCES PIC DU MIDI 6, rue Eugene Tenot ✆ 05 62 56 71 11. *www.picdumidi.com. Site open all year, except November. Admission varies with season (low/high): adults 20/23 €, concessions 18 €, under-18s 12 €, family 55/60 €.* The Pic du Midi has been exploring the universe since 1880. Today it is an astrological observation and research centre, with an area where you can discover this science.

VAISSEAU DES ETOILES - Pic du Midi - GAVARNIE ✆ 05 62 56 71 11. www.picdumidi.com

Saint-Lary-Soulan

MAISON DE L'OURS ✆ 05 62 39 50 83. *Open every day. In season: 10am-12 noon and 2pm-7pm. Out of season: 10am-12 noon and 2pm-6pm. Closed Tuesday. Closed in November. Admission: adult 5 €, child 3.50 €.* An educational and ecological centre, housing the exhibition 'Bears: from myth to reality' and a video documentary. Grown-ups and kids alike will love the lodgers, Apollon and Bingo, rescued from cruelty and the abattoir and now cared for on site.

PIC DE NEOUVIELLE. This panoramic peak (3,091m) is quite esay to climb. It takes about 3 hours to reach the top.

RESERVE NATURELLE DE NEOUVIELLE. This nature reserve was set up in 1936, and contains a carefully-conserved wealth of flora, wildlife, lakes and scenery.

Tarbes

Capital of and gateway to the Bigorre region, Tarbes is an important town, linking valleys and plain. Discover the lively town centre, with its atmosphere of southern douceur de vivre.

DE LA SEDE CATHEDRAL. 12thc. Romanesque cathedral, topped by an octagonal steeple.

HARAS NATIONAL, MAISON DU CHEVAL Chemin du Mauhourat ✆ 05 62 56 30 80 *www.haras-nationaux.fr. Open Monday-Friday, guided tours at 10am, 11am, 2pm, 3pm, 4pm. Last Sunday of the month: 2.30pm and 4pm. Admission: 5.50 €.* Napoleon set up this National Stud Farm in 1806, forming a classical and harmonious architectural group. Genetic selection produces several breeds, including the Anglo-Arab. You can stroll through the 9ha. park with its wide, shady avenues, see the stables, tack room and smithy, reproduction section and educational Maison du Cheval, a centre presenting the horse's life and image.

JARDIN MASSEY Rue Massey ✆ 05 62 93 11 74. *Open to the public, winter: 8am-6pm. Mid June-mid August: 7am-9pm.* This landscape park in the town centre was designed by horticulturist Placide Massey (director of Versailles' Trianon Park), who made it a garden of rare botanic species.

PARC NATIONAL DE PYRENEES 59, route de Pau ✆ 05 62 44 36 60. *www.parc-pyrenees.com.* Based at Tarbes. You can find information on the National Park's 7 centres and its environmental conservation work.

Col du Tourmalet

The best-known of the Pyrenees passes, between the Pic du Midi and Neouvielle massif. It is a difficult climb: 18km with an average 8% slope rising to 14% over the last 500m! Keen cyclists still insist on trying.

TOULOUSE AND HAUTE-GARONNE

Toulouse

Known as the Ville Rose, Toulouse is the regional capital, but you'll fall in love with its village warmth and simplicity. Lifestyle and architecture are equally attractive: sunset on the Capitole lights up the bricks; the Grave cupola changes colour like a chameleon with a full moon over the Garonne. A late evening stroll through the pink brick streets is absolutely not to be missed.

Toulouse Violets

Toulouse violet s were immensely successful during the Second Empire, but had already been widely popular since the 18thc. They have fuller flowers than other species, and are grown under glass, flowering from October to March, and displayed in round bouquets or as pot plants. They are also used in perfume and sweet making, liqueurs and cocktails, and are found on the most prestigious tables.

LA MAISON DE LA VIOLETTE Canal du Midi ✆ 05 61 99 01 30/06 22 05 38 33. Facing 2bis, boulevard Bonrepos. The 'Maison de la Violette' barge features violets in all their forms, together with their history. Exhibition, with produce on sale.

SAINT SERNIN BASILICA. Built over several centuries, the basilica consists of both Romanesque (11thc, chevet) and Gothic elements. It was put up for the hosts of pilgrims come to worship at Saint Saturnin's tomb in nearby Notre Dame du Taur, and has been recently renovated and relit.

CAPITOLE. Gilded coats of arms hang from the balconies, recalling the days of the Consouls, (town consuls). The building still plays a role in local government, now housing the Town Hall. Go through the Capitole via the main portal, to the Place Henri IV featuring the king's statue, and the Occitan Cross with the 12 Zodiac signs at its ends.

JARDIN DES PLANTES. Ancient trees stand among the flowerbeds and fountains. A walk past the swans brings you to the former town gates, and an islet adding a touch of wildness. Going back up to Rue Ozenne, you find the antiques dealers quarter, with its narrow streets, mansions and medieval atmosphere. Saint Etienne Cathedral is worth a visit, if only for its 15thc. portal out of line with the 13thc. rose window.

CITE DE L'ESPACE Ave. Jean Gonord (exit 17, rocade Est) ✆ 05 62 71 64 80. *www.cite-espace.com. Closed Monday (out of school holidays). Open Tuesday-Sunday, 9.30am-6pm (9am-7pm during school holidays). Admission, high season: adult 18.50 to 20 €, 13-25s 13 €, 6-12s 11.50 €, including planetarium and terr@dome (low season, 14 €, 11.50 € and 10.50 € respectively). Special rates for groups and families ; guided tours available.* Located on the edge of town, but not far from the centre, this is your chance to see those mythical machines responsible for man's conquest of space. In the 4ha. parc are a replica of the Ariane space rocket, a genuine space engine (Soyouz), life-size MIR space station and Exhibition Pavilion. Between April 2004 and December 2005, you can travel into the future on the space ship Tsiolkovski, in search of aliens, discover the inside of your body in 3-D, or be teleported (Mission Biospace).

JACOBIN CONVENT BUILDINGS Rue Lakanal ✆ 05 61 22 21 92. *Open every day: 10am-7pm.* The 13thc. Southern Gothic monastery has a single nave and superb cloister where concerts are held, together with exhibitions from local museums in the refectory.

FONDATION BEMBERG Hôtel d'Assezat-Place d'Assezat ✆ 05 61 12 06 89. *Closed Monday. Open 10am-12.30pm and 1.30pm-6pm (9pm Thursday). Guided tours every day: 3.30pm.* Argentinian millionaire Georges Bemberg chose this setting for his paintings and bronzes. Admire the Renaissance paintings and modern French School, with 28 of Bonnard's works.

CHATEAU D'EAU 1, place Laganne ✆ 05 61 77 09 40. *www.galeriechateaudeau.org.* Open every day. France's oldest public institution exclusively concerned with photopgraphy was set up in 1974. Housed in a 19thc. building on the Garonne, it hosts monographic and thematic exhibitions and boasts 4,500 original prints.

MONUMENT DE LA RESISTANCE Allées Frédéric Mistral ✆ 05 61 55 03 84. *Open every day: 10am-12 noon and 2pm-5pm. Closed Saturday, Sunday and public holidays. Admission free.* The memorial is hidden underground, and explains the Resistance and the tragic events of 1939-1945. Images, sound and music are blended in this tunnel lined with crypts, recalling the victims of deportation, torture and execution. An astronomical setup commemorates the liberation of Toulouse on 19 August 1944.

ESPACE D'ART MODERNE ET CONTEMPORAIN 76, allées Charles-de-Fitte ✆ 05 34 51 10 60. *www.lesabattoirs.org. Closed Monday. Open Tuesday-Sunday: 12 noon-8pm.* Known as 'the Abattoirs', Toulouse art centre attracts plenty of contemporary art lovers. It includes the municipal modern art museum, regional contemporary art centre and art fund, with 2,000 works on display, and also plays a heritage conservation role. There is a cafe, youth club, picnic area and research and documentation site with auditorium, bookshop and art workshops for kids. The exhibitions cover 3,000 m^2; the salle Picasso contains the remains of the Minotaur in Harlequin costume, the famous stage curtain made in 1936, and on display for 6 months a year to protect its fragile fibres.

MUSEE DES AUGUSTINS 21, rue de Metz ✆ 05 61 22 21 82. *www.augustins.org. Open 10am-6pm, except Tuesday and 25 December, I January and 1 May. Wednesday evening-9pm, with organ concert, entry free with museum ticket.* Under-18s free. Built in the 14thc., this Augustins monastery is one of the region's finest. It houses works from the Middle Ages to the present, Romanesque Gothic and 19thc. sculpture (Rodin, Claudel), Flemish, Italian and French paintings.

MUSEE GEORGES-LABIT 17, rue du Japon ✆ 05 61 22 21 84. *Open 1 June-30 September: 10am-6pm. 1 October-31 May: 10am-5pm. Admission: adult 3 €, concessions 1.20 €.* On the edge of the Canal du Midi in a 19thc 'Moorish Pavilion', this museum houses Far Eastern art collections covering 3,000 years and including India, Cambodia and South East Asia. It also contains Egyptian antiques and Coptic art. A Mediterranean garden has been laid out round the museum.

MUSEE PAUL DUPUY 13, rue de la Pleau ✆ 05 61 14 65 50. *Open 1 June-30 September: 10am-6pm. 1 October-31 May: 10am-5pm. Admission: adult 3 €, concessions 1.20 €.* Housed in a 17thc. mansion, the Paul Dupuy Museum specialises in Toulouse and Languedoc's decorative and graphic art from the Middle Ages to the present. Prestigious art objects seized during the Revolution (ivory, gold and silver work, earthenware) a 17thc. Jesuit apothecary's and one of Europe's biggest clock collections are also on display. You can visit the cabinets of etchings, drawings and coins, and the library, by appointment. Temporaray exhibitions are held twice a year.

PORT SAINT SAUVEUR - CANAL DU MIDI. The harbour has been completely renovated, and provides all modern port services, including moorings for pleasure craft passing through.

AFRICAN SAFARI 41, rue des Landes ✆ 05 61 86 45 03. *www.zoo-africansafari.com. Open every day: 1 October-31 March: 10 am-6pm. 1 April-30 September: 9.30am-8pm.Admission: adult 9.50* This wildlife park 15mins from Toulouse offers an African reserve, traditional zoo, sea-lion displays in summer and a domestic animal farm.

Haute-Garonne

Grenade

12thc. bastide south west of Fronton near the Tarn et Garonne border. The Toulouse Gothic Assumption Church has a fine front and 47m-high steeple. Don't miss the 18thc. covered market with its superb framework, in the village centre.

URSULINE CONVENT 56, rue Roquemaurel ✆ 05 61 80 81 23/05 61 82 61 51. *Open 5-12 July, 12-30 July, 1-14 August, 19 & 20 August and 14 & 15 September: 9am-12 noon and 2.30pm-5.30pm. Guided tours in small groups every hour: 9am, 10am, 11am, 2.30pm, 3.30pm and 4.30pm. Group visits can be booked at other times. Admission: adult 4 €, 12-18s 2 €.*Grenade Convent was founded in 1626 by the Toulouse Ursulines. It was one of the bastide's main religious buildings, near the Garonne-Save confluence. You can visit the former convent, introduced with a video presentation. The ground and first floors have painted ceilings and 17thc.fresces; there is a panoramiv view of the bastide and Garonne Valley from the second and third floors, and an inside courtyard and gardens.

Luchon

Europe's main watering place for ear, nose and throat troubles and rheumatology. The resort has its tourist attractions too: Château Lassus-Nestier (housing the Tourist Office and Pays de Luchon Museum) built in 1772 by Baron Marc de Lassus; the casino, (designed in 1880 by the architect Castex and transformed by Martin in the 1930s) with its Second Empire-style theatre, and the Villa Julia, where Edmond Rostand spent part of his life. Its balcony may have inspired the famous scene in 'Cyrano de Bergerac'.

MUSEE DU PAYS DE LUCHON 18, allée d'Etigny ✆ 05 61 79 29 87. *Saturday, inside: 9am-12 noon and 2pm-6pm. Outside: 9am-12 noon and 2pm-6pm. Sunday: inside: 9am-12 noon and 2pm-6pm. Outside: 9am-12 noon and 2pm-6pm. Admission: adult 1.60 €.* The region's character is condensed in this museum: Greek, Roman and Gallo-Roman antiquities, ethnology, local, regional and thermal history and the Pyrenees.

LUCHON FORME ET BIEN ETRE Les Thermes ✆ 05 61 79 22 97. *www.luchon.com/bien-etre.html.* In Luchon's beautiful spa, this centre offers two approaches to getting into shape: Vitalene and Sourcea. The first includes vapour baths, in underground galleries with swimming pools, massage baths, jet showers and hand massage. The second is softer, with personalised relaxation and beauty treatment (from 40 €). You can even book a tailor-made stay linking the spa benefits with fresh air and leisure activities.

Martres-Tolosane

On the Garonne's left bank, at the foot of the Pyrenees, Martres-Tolosane is a 13thc. bastide chiefly known for its earthenware. It was fortified in the Middle Ages, and you can still see the ramparts flanked with a square keep. A necropole was discovered in the church some time ago, with two sarcophagi bearing the Christian alpha and omega, and an acanthe leaf of Syrian design.

MUSEE ARCHEOLOGIQUE Rue du Donjon ✆ 05 61 98 80 00. *Open 1 July-mide September, every day: 10am-12.30pm and 2.30pm-6pm.* Most of the exhibits are marble copies (the originals are in Saint Raymond Museum in Toulouse), but the antique statuary collection is still worth a visit.

Montmaurin

Montmaurin boasts some astonishing Gallo-Roman architecture. It was a princely town from the 2nd-4thc. A.D., and has left traces of luxurious living: the Villa Urbana with its 200 rooms is the biggest excavated in France, while the commoner Villa Rustica housed 500 clerks.

MUSEE ET VILLA GALLO-ROMAINE DE MONTMAURIN ✆ 05 61 88 74 73. *Open 1 April-30 September: 9.30am-12 noon and 2pm-6pm. 1 October-31 March: 9.30am-12 noon and 2pm-5pm.* Two of the museum's three rooms contain the remains excavated at Montmaurin, and the third covers prehistory and paleontology.

Valentine

SITE ARCHAEOLOGIQUE DE VALENTINE Lieu-dit Arnesp ✆ 05 61 88 74 73. *Admission free. Guided tour by appointment..* Gallo-Roman villa; temple; mausoleum; Early Christian, Merovingian and Pre-Romanesque church; Roman church, priory and necropoles: the remains excavated on Valentine archaeological site date from the 4th-13thc. The villa includes a main courtyard, semi-circular swimming pool and traces of a pagan temple beneath a Christian church. The Gallo-Roman temple contained 18 Saint Beat marble monuments dedicated to Jupiter and a local god named Boucous. A large pagan necropole with thirty steles and marble incineration troughs surrounds it.

Revel-Saint-Ferréol

This delightful preserved bastide has acquired a reputation for handcrafted furniture, accounting for much of local income.

CONSERVATOIRE DES METIERS DU BOIS 13, rue Jean Moulin © 05 61 27 65 50. *Open Tuesday-Sunday, 9am-12 noon and 2pm-6pm, except Friday and Sunday morning. Concessions for groups, under-20s, students and under-14s.* Discover woodwork's many facets in over 20 trades: pit sawyer, carpenter, cabinet-maker, cartwright and chair-maker, sculptor, etc. This fascinating permanent exhibition explains skills now rare or forgotten.

MUSEE NATIONAL DE SPELEOLOGIE Centre Culturel © 05 62 18 01 62. *Open Tuesday-Saturday: 2pm-6pm.* This unique museum illustrates pot-holing techniques and its underground environment, with documents, models, photos, lithographs and other archeological exhibits.

Saint-Bertrand-de-Comminges

Perched on its hill at the foot of the Pyrenees, Saint Bertrand began as a Celtic oppidum, then a Roman town and medieval city. The village's many historical traces and monuments are interesting, and you will be struck by the natural beauty of the site.

Saint-Gaudens

This village has few remains, but those that are left are quite remarkable.

SAINT GAUDENS COLLEGIATE CHURCH. The church boasts an impressive group of Romanesque sculptures from the late 11thc. The most interesting capitals are in the sanctuary.

MUSEE MUNICIPAL DU COMMINGES 6, place du Mas Saint Pierre © 05 61 94 78 70. *Open Tuesday-Saturday: 9am-12 noon and 2pm-6pm. Admission: adult 2.90 €, under-15s 1.10 €.* You start with the prehistoric section, and end with local crafts and costumes. Popular arts and traditions are particularly well-represented: a period room on a Comminges farm, for instance, or Valentine's typical and stylised blue earthenware.

ARIÈGE

This department stretches towards the Pyrénées, with protected mountain areas and Cathar castles overlooking the plain.

Ax-les-Thermes

There are few remains of the town's spa past here, yet thousands come each year to treat their rheumatism and respiratory problems. The Ladres bassin still exists though, built in 1260 by Saint Louis to treat soldiers with leprosy returning from the Holy Land.

MAISON DES LOUPS Les Forges d'Orlu © 05 61 64 02 66. *Open 1 April-November. April, May, June: 10am-5.30pm. July & August: 10am-7pm. September & October: every day except Monday & Tuesday: 11am-5pm. Admission: adult 6,20 €, child 4 €.* In this 6ha. wildlife park are wolves from France and Canada, living in packs. You visit the park along a specially laid-out path, through a beech and conifer forest; the wolves can be observed from special wooden hides, with explanatory panels.

Foix

The town developed round Saint-Volusien Abbey and the castle built in the year 1000, linking its history to theirs.

CHATEAU DE FOIX © 05 34 09 83 83. *www.sesta.fr. Open every day; guided tours available. Admission: adult 4.20 €, child 2.10 €, concessions 3.10 € Family Pass: 2 adults (parents) + 2 children: 12 €* The only castle in Foix Country spared by Richelieu! (1630s). It was built in the 10thc., and really seems to be hanging from the clouds. This strategic position caused a lot of envy, and some fearsome sieges. Today, you can still see its beauty, and feel the Comtes de Foix's power and defiance in its stones.

SAINT VOLUSIEN CHURCH. Guided tours in summer: 10am-12 noon and 2pm-6pm. Volusien Abbey in Toulouse territory was first mentioned in 870. Several centuries later, Roger II, Comte de Foix rebuilt it, and it was inaugurated on 18 January 1112. Sadly, a portal with two raised arches, brick and stone foundations and a few capitals are all that is left today.

LABOUICHE ✆ 05 61 65 04 11. *Open every day: 10am-11.15am and 2pm-5pm, until end June. July & August, every day: 9.30am-6pm. Admission: adult 8 €, under-12s 5.50 €* This long underground boat trip (1.5km) is sensational! It takes place in two stages, with a guide's commentary.

Montgailhard

A few remains of ancient Montgrenier Fortress can be seen on the knoll overlooking this village.

FORGES DE PYRENE Musee des Vieux Metiers d'Autrefois Ave. de Paris ✆ 05 34 09 30 60. *Open all year, except January. Admission: adult 7 €, 6-18s 5.50 €*. 125 traditional rural trades are on display: agricultural, domestic, clothing and interiors (furniture). Some of these crafts no longer exist; the museum illustrates and preserves their heritage.

Montségur

Symbol of Cathar resistance to northern oppression, this proud castle is perched in an eyrie at an altitude of 1,216m. It lives in the local collective memory as painful proof of freedom struck down, and faith broken by iron and fire. The castle suffered 4 sieges, holding out against three, but in March 1244, it fell. It is said that a few Cathars left Montségur just before, taking fabulous treasure that they buried in a cave in the Ariège Valley.

CHATEAU DE MONTSEGUR ✆ 05 61 01 06 94. www.montsegur.org

MUSEE DE MONTSEGUR ✆ 05 61 01 06 94. *www.montsegur.org*. The Ariège Pot Inding Society set up this museum in 1965. It contains mainly 13th and 14thc. exhibits illustrating daily life on the mountain in medieval times.

Pamiers

The Castella mound, with its castle, Carmel Chapel, Bishops' Palace and Tour de la Monnaie. Stop for a rest on the Milliane Esplanade in the shade of the plane trees, and listen to the Sainte Natalene fountain playing.

NOTRE DAME DU CAMP. Only the west portal is left of the original 12thc. church. Inside, you can admire a 17thc. painting of Saint Natalene and another by Latour depicting the Virgin and Child.

Saint-Lizier

The ancient Couserans capital boasts some dazzling architecture. It was first a Roman oppidum, then a bishopric, and has kept ramparts, churches, monuments and remains to illustrate its luxuriant past.

GALLO-ROMAN RAMPARTS. 750m of ramparts surround the old city, 4-6m high, reinforced by 12 round and square towers. This wall was built in the 3rd or 4thc. A.D.

CHURCH (KNOWN AS CATHEDRAL). This 12thc. church has some remarkable Romanesque fresces in the nave.

ROMANESQUE CLOISTER. The cloister is topped by a gallery with wooden pillars (rare) and consists of 32 arcades on alternate simple and gemelled columns.

Tarascon-sur-Ariège

Around Tarascon, many sports, leisure and cultural activities are on offer.

PARC PYRENEEN DE L'ART PREHISTORIQUE ✆ 05 61 05 10 10. *www.sesta.fr. Open April-October, every day: 10am-6pm. Admission: adult 9.40 €, child 5.70 €* Prehistoric art like you've never seen it, in an enchanted park of rocks and water. A huge facsimile of the Niaux Cave reveals all the artwork as it was 12,000 years ago. Discover the Magdalenians via modern techniques: films, giant light shows, multilingual infrared headsets and others for kids. One day seems too short - but then it takes time to travel back 14,000 years without leaving the site.

AVEYRON

Around Rodez, the country consists of small regions forming a province with a strong identity.

Conques

This village is a peaceful canton capital, listed Grand Site de France and UNESCO World Heritage.

ABBEY CHURCH. *Open every day: 8.30am-8pm.* Romanesque masterpiece, built from the 11th-14thc. Two square towers frame the porch with its superb tympanum depicting 124 characters in the Last Judgement. At the other end, the chevet rises in pyramid fashion. The roof recalls piled-up Saint Jacques scallops. Inside is all pure lines, height and austerity.

CLOISTER. You reach it via a small, open staircase leading to a courtyard containing a huge green serpentine pool. Not much is left of the Romanesque cloister, apart from a few capitals in the Dr. Fau Museum. Go down the arcaded corridor (once a refectory for the Benedictine monks) to the wing housing the treasure.

TRESOR DE SAINTE FOY ✆ 05 65 72 85 00. *Open every day.* Closed New Year's Day. Faithful pilgrims bringing gifts to enlist Saint Foy's help gradually built up this treasure over 12 centuries. There are gold, silver and alabaster masterpieces decorated with enamel, but the most prestigious is the saint's gold reliquary, inlaid with precious stones.

Espalion

This village was one of the Compostella road's main stopping places, and was also known for its big fairs. Follow the riverbank to the old palace, a fine 1572 Renaissance building with mullioned windows, pepperpot tower and loggia overlooking the river.

MUSEE DU ROUERGUE Place Pierre Frontin ✆ 05 65 44 19 91. *Open every day July & August: 10am-12.30pm and 2pm-7pm. Closed Saturday morning. Admission: adult 3 €, concessions 2 €.* Housed in Espalion's old prison, this is one of several Popular Arts and Traditions Museums in the region. Traditional costumes (with period photos to provide the original context), Jacquard weaving looms, fashions and social differences in caps, pottery and copperware are on display, and there are regular temporary exhibitions.

Laguiole

A famous name throughout the world, hidden in the depths of your pocket. What is so special about this penknife? It has a characteristic blade that folds up into a frame by means of a metallic spring, caught between the frame's two plates, and ending in the famous fly or bee symbol. The handle is fixed to the plates, and can be made from a variety of materials. It usually has other tools attached, such as a bodkin and a corkscrew - the finishing touches to a perfect Laguiole.

Najac

COUTELLERIE DE LAGUIOLE 15, allées de l'Amicale ✆ 05 65 51 50 14. *Open every day. Guided explanatory tours for groups.* Honore Durand has a passion for knives, and an eye for quality. The blades are forged close by, and the modelling and assembly take place here in the workshop, which you can visit.

Millau

Life is pleasant in this Mediterranean town. Relax on a shady cafe terrace or stroll along the plane tree-lined boulevard around the old quarters.

VIEILLE VILLE. Place Marechal Foch is picturesque with its fine 12th-16thc. arcades and fountain. Originally Romanesque, Notre Dame Church was rebuilt in the 17thc. with a single nave and magnificent modern fresces (Crowning of the Virgin, Jean Bernard, 1939) in the chancel.

BELFRY. Rising 42m above the old town centre, and consisting of a square tower (12thc.) used as a prison in the 17thc.,and a strange octagonal 18thc. tower. The view from the top is marvellous.

MUSEE DE MILLAU Hôtel de Pegayrolles - Place Foch ✆ 05 65 59 01 08. Open all year: 10am-12 noon and 2pm-6pm. Closed Sunday and public holidays, 1 October-1 May. July & August, open every day: 10am-6pm. Millau's traditional industries (leather and gloves), and regional collections - geology, prehistory, Gallo-Roman pottery - are on display, along with some temporary exhibitions.

SITE ARCHEOLOGIQUE DE LA GRAUFESENQUE. *Open every day: 9am-12 noon and 2pm-6.30pm.* Well-located at the Tarn-Dourbie confluence, the Gallo-Roman town of Condatomagus (Millau) was able to exploit alluvial clay in the 1stc.A.D. Failed works were thrown into a ditch, enabling archeologists to catalogue Graufesenque's output.

VIADUC DE MILLAU. Technical skill and architectural creativity are to be found in this gigantic bridge designed by Lord Norman Foster. It is 2,460m long, and 343m high at the top of its pylons (higher than the Eiffel Tower). The roadway (36,000 tonnes of steel) suspended 270m above the Tarn is 32m wide. The whole structure is extremely graceful, and fits well into the landscape.

Najac

A characteristic Rouergue bastide built along a mountain ridge with castle at one end and recent buildings at the other.

FORTERESSE ROYALE DE NAJAC ✆ 05 65 29 71 65. *Open every day, 1 April-30 September, Sundays in October and November holiday (All Saints). By appointment out of season.* Built by the Comtes de Toulouse on a rocky headland, this fortress saw action during the Cathar crusade and Hundred Years' War. The keep is 200m above the River Aveyron, and it has the world's highest archery slits. Impressive.

Rodez

Buildings of architectural interest can mainly be found in the town centre; walk through Rodez's narrow alleys to seek them out.

CATHEDRAL. A majestic Northern Gothic building: the vault with its intersecting ribs rises to 30m. The inside is vast, but bare, contrasting with the 27 richly-decorated radiating chapels.

MUSEE DENYS PUECH Place Clemenceau ✆ 05 65 77 89 60. *Open Wednesday-Saturday: 10am-12 noon and 2pm-6pm. Tuesday & Sunday: 2pm-6pm.Admission: adult 2.50* The works of local sculptor Denis Puech (known for his melancholy female portraits) are exhibited beside a large collection of contemporary art.

MUSEE FENAILLE 14, place Eugene Raynaldy ✆ 05 65 73 84 30. *Open every day except Monday. Admission: adult 3€, concessions 1.50€, under-18s free.* Rouergue's archeology and history collections are chronologically divided into 4 themes: the menhir statues; Segodunum, capital of the Ruthenes; medieval Rouergue (everyday objects and remains of the Romanesque cathedral); 16thc. and Renaissance (tapestries and stained-glass windows).

Saint-Léons

MICROPOLIS Cite des insectes ✆ 05 65 58 50 50. *www.micropolis.biz. Open all year, except mid November-end January. 10am-6pm (7pm in summer). Admission: adult 9.80€, 5-17s 7.10€, under-5s free.* Micropolis, Insect City, takes you on a magical trip through 15 exhibition areas. Watch the fascinating behaviour of live insects and take part in experiments involving contact between insect, plant and human. In 2005, the theme park will include a complementary outside circuit, the Pavillons de la Cite, and an exhibition on the five senses.

Séverac-le-Château

You reach Séverac via the Portes du Latazou and du Peyroux in the ramparts. Inside is one of the region's oldest houses (12thc.).

CHATEAU. 05 65 47 67 31 *Guided tour 15 June-15 September.* The 17thc. castle's kitchens and chapel alone are still intact (though restoration campaigns are often planned for the latter). You can imagine how splendid it must have been from the remains, and textual descriptions (rich furnishings; paintings by the masters).

CITE MEDIEVALE. 1 July-31 August. The *Passeport Estival* also gives you access to Jeanne's house, the Consuls' House, castle and Archeological Museum. Ask at the Tourist office.

Villefranche-de-Rouergue

The town developed like a typical bastide, round Notre Dame Collegiate Church.

CHARTREUSE SAINT SAUVEUR. Open every day, July, August & September. There are 2 cloisters: the smaller in Flamboyant Gothic style; the bigger enclosing a huge garden. Chapel, vestibule and chapter house are equally fine.

NOTRE DAME COLLEGIATE CHURCH. This white stone Languedoc Gothic building was finished in 1519. The imposing porch tower is 58m high, overlooking the square. Inside are 62 late 15thc. carved stalls and some fine stained glass from the same period.

CAHORS AND THE LOT

The river meanders through charming medieval towns and reputed vine-covered slopes.

Cahors

Prefecture (Lot) and capital (Quercy), Cahors grew up on a peninsula. The old quarters are enclosed in a loop of the River Lot, stretching out along its banks.

SAINT ETIENNE CATHEDRAL. Rises imposingly above the medieval town centre. The 12thc. Romanesque north portal portrays Christ's Ascension on its tympanum. The cloister is a Flamboyant Gothic masterpiece.

RUE DU CHATEAU DU ROI. This was the main medieval street, and still contains half-timbered houses with corbelling, Gothic arched doors and 13thc. fronts.

QUARTIER DE LA DAURADE. Having crossed Place de la Liberation, you arrive in Rue Clement Marot (Cahors poet born in 1496, a master of epistles and sonnets). Number 12 housed another local poet,

Cahors, Saint-Etienne cathedral

Olivier de Magny (1529-1561). Half-timbered and corbelled houses can be seen on the corner of Rue de la Daurade.

PONT VALENTRE. France's last medieval fortified bridge. Cahors had three of these in the 14thc. while Paris only had one! Valentre Bridge was finished in the late 14thc. - with the devil's help, they say.

MUSEE HENRI MARTIN 792, rue Emile Zola © 05 65 20 88 66. *Open every day except Tuesday: 11am-6pm. Sunday & public holidays: 2pm-6pm. Admission: adult 3 €, child 1.50 €, under-6's free.* Housed in the old Bishops' Palace. 18,000 works and documents concerning pointillist painter Henri Martin are on display, together with 3 or 4 excellent and unusual temporary exhibitions a year.

MUSEE DE LA TRUFFE ET DU VIN 05 65 36 58 26 - La Chantrerie. 35, rue de la Chantrerie © 65 23 99 70. *Open every day, 1 July-31 August, Tuesday-Saturday: 9.30am-1pm and 2.30pm-7pm. Admission free.* The wine tithes owed to the canons were collected, vinified, matured in a cask and traded in this superb 14thc. building. A collection of tools and utensils illustrates the winegrowers' skills and know-how. On the ground floor was the warehouse (opening on 2 arcades); upstairs, the wine dealer's family had its reception room, now an exhibition area. Introductory tasting sessions are on offer.

Lot

MAISON DE LA DORDOGNE QUERCYNOISE Château © 05 65 10 91 56. *Open 1 April-31 Octobre, every day: 10am-1pm and 2pm-7pm (non-stop in summer).* Geology, flora and fauna, prehistory, art history and navigation are illustrated using modern audiovisual methods.

Cajarc

Medieval village in its circle of cliffs, Cajarc goes back to Gallo-Roman times. President Georges Pompidou and writer Francoise Sagan spent their summers here. The 13thc. church is stem-shaped, to hold out against floods. Walk up to La Capelette (11th and 15thc.) and see the Romanesque chapel which served as a lazar-house. Below, on the banks of the Lot, a curious triangular tower with spiral staircase is all that is left of Coimbre fortified mill. Stone shepherds' houses called *caselles* are dotted along the road up to Plogne viewpoint, which overlooks the whole valley. At Roc-de-Conte, you can see a little cave-dwelling in the rockside (the Maison des Anglais) last Protestant hide-out. Going back down to Cajarc on the GR65 you pass the 25m-high Lacauhne waterfall.

Carennac

One of France's most beautiful villages, and the pride of the Dordogne Valley, this medieval community began as a Cluny priory founded in the 10thc. The ruined hamlet of Taillefer stands out against the skyline above - you take the hiking path opposite the signpost for Taillefer, turn left 300m further on, and follow the yellow markings. A magnificent spot.

EGLISE SAINT-PIERRE. A magnificent 12thc. Romanesque church, famous for its historiated tympanum representing Christ in majesty. There is a remarkable 16thc. entombment in the chapter house, and the cloister is partly Romanesque, partly Flamboyant Gothic.

Figeac

Figeac's exceptional medieval architecture is protected in a conservation sector, and the town has been a listed Ville d'Art et d'Histoire since 1990.

TOUR OF THE TOWN. Start at Place Vival and the 13thc. Hôtel de la Monnaie with its arcades and gemeled bays. Rue Gambetta, you find the 14thc. Hôtel de Livernon, along with other beautiful half-timbered houses, one with a corbelled front. Rue Baduel boasts a splendid 12thc. Romanesque window, and Rue Roquefort, the Galiot de Genouillac mansion: corner bartizans, spiral staircase tower and portal with a Renaissance pediment. In the Place Gaillardy, you find two 15th and 16thc. half-timbered houses, with a *soleilho*, or open loft for drying wool and skins and preserving food. Notice one of Figeac's oldest houses on the corner of Rue Tomfort (12thc.) like the Romanesque house Rue Delzhens. Another Romanesque residence, the beautiful 12thc. Griffon house stands in the Place Champollion, with its treble bays on the first floor. The Hôtel de Crussol is a fine medieval mansion, with its staircase and Renaissance loggia. Climb up to the Cingle-Haut viwpoint, and discover the amazing mosaic of town roofs and valley beyond.

SAINT SAUVEUR CHURCH. Built from the 11th-13thc. The 17thc. painted wooden panels depict Christ's Passion.

MUSEE CHAMPOLLION 4, rue des Frères Champollion ✆ 05 65 50 31 08. *Closed for renovation work until June 2007.* Champollion's birthplace houses a museum illustrating the famous Egyptologist's life and work (notably the deciphering of hieroglyphics).

Gourdon

This medieval town perched on a mound on the Quercy-Perigord border was the Comte de Toulouse's last fortified town.

You enter the old town via the 13thc. fortified gate in the Rue du Majou. The little Neo-Gothic chapel Notre Dame du Majou has lost its drawbridge but you can admire the tiers and 18thc. gilded wooden tabernacle. The prestigious Seneschal's House (now an exhibition centre) has three shields on its door, and fine frescos and fireplaces. Place de l'Hôtel de Ville, you see the former 13thc. consulate; the ground floor with its vaulted ceiling is used as a covered market. Imposing fortified Saint Pierre Church (1302) takes up much of the square, with its machicolations and 35m tower.

Gramat

This crossroads at the junction of several Roman roads was not badly marked by the Hundred Years' War, and fought on the Protestant side during the Wars of Religion. In 1580, the Protestant lord of Gramat guided Henri de Navarre (later Henri IV) across the causse, and helped him take Cahors. Only the 16thc. Tour de l'Horloge, is left from this period. Notre Dame du Calvaire convent was founded to help the disinherited, working with Africa and South America.

PARC ANIMALIER ✆ 05 65 38 81 22. *www.gramat-parc-animalier.com. Open all year. Easter-30 September: 9.30am-7pm and 1 October-Easter: 2pm-6pm. Admission: adult 8 €, 5-14s 4.50 €*. This wildlife park is managed by the Association for the Study and Protection of Causse Flora and Fauna. It houses European otters and those wild animals now dying out (aurochs, bisons, wolves and bears) and the endangered woodland species (badger, ferret, owl, fox and boar). There are also domestic animals threatened by extinction: Basque pigs, Pyrenean goats four-horned sheep and Poitou donkeys. Over 1,000 animals live here in peace and security, and hundreds are born every year.

Lalbenque

This is the Truffle Capital, hosting the South West's biggest truffle market on Tuesday afternoons from later November to late March. 'Black diamond' seekers can meet professional dealers and gastronomy fans. A number of events take place during the winter on the truffle theme.

Don't miss the Gothic Saint Quirin Church (15thc.) with its five-sided apse. The single nave has a splendid reredos and 17thc. panelling. On the way out of the village in the Place du Mercadiol, you can admire a superb 18thc. cross in sculpted stone, a dovecote, gariottes and the Peyrelevade dolmen (1km away).

Martel

This town with its seven towers rises from a limestone plateau. You can learn more of Martel's history from its monuments.

SAINT MAUR CHURCH. A 13th and 14thc. Gothic building (bartizans, machicolations, 48m belltower with arrow slits and a 12thc. Romanesque tympanum depicting Christ at the Last Judgement) leaning against the ramparts.

PALAIS DE LA RAYMONDIE. *Open I July -30 August, except Sunday & public holidays.* The belfry is 33m high. You can see Elias in his fiery chariot over the fireplace in the guard room, along with a collection of Prehistoric and Gallo-Roman objects, ancient postcards and pharmacy pots.

REPTILAND Puy Lombry - RN 140 ✆ 05 65 37 41 00. *www.reptiland.fr. Closed in January and Mondays (except July & August). Open 10am-12 noon and 2pm-6pm. July & August: every day, 10am-6pm € Admission: adult 7, 4-12s 4 €* Reptiland is in a marvellous setting, with a fine view over Martel. It is Europe's only conservation centre for endangered daylight reptile species: lizards, iguanas, turtles, crocodiles and snakes. 250 fascinating living animals to discover!

Puy-l'Evêque

Set on a rocky headland overlooking the Lot. The town's ancient quarters are best viewed from the bridge: tiers of castles, churches and large 14th and 15thc. houses running down to the river. The last remains of the Bishops' Palace with its square 3-storey keep (13thc.) can be seen in Place de la Truffière, with the 13thc. Lychairie at its feet (chapter house and former outbuilding used as an audience chamber for the Bishops' Palace). Walk throught the steep streets to the 15thc. Penitents' Chapel and Château

Bovila at the Porte Renaissance. The old harbour is in the Cale quarter. Fortified Saint Sauveur Church (14thc.) is part of the town's defence system; its powerful porch tower with bartizan and round turret dates back to the English occupation. Don't miss the remarkable carved portal. In the nearby graveyard is an ancient covered Calvary (late 15thc.).

Follow the GR36 from the Tourist Office to Martignac hamlet, with its 12thc. Romanesque Church containing magnificent 15th and 16thc. wall paintings on the Seven Deadly Sins, opposing the Virtues in the Gothic nave.

Rocamadour

France's second most popular tourist site, after Mont-Saint-Michel. This ancient Christian site is still a place of pilgrimage on the Compostella Road, and the number of visitors has trebled in 25 years (from 500,000 to 1.5 million a year). Seen from the Couzou road, this unbelievable site is almost a shock: houses built on the river, churches above the houses, rocks above the churches and the castle above the rocks (as the locals describe it). The fortified village seems to cling to the causse cliff, 150m above the sumptuous Alzou Canyon.

GROTTE DES MERVEILLES L'Hospitalet © 05 65 33 67 92. *www.grottes.des.merveilles.com. Open every day, April-October: 10am-12 noon and 2pm-6pm. July & August: 9.30am-7pm. Admission: adult 5.50 €, 5-12s 3 €.* 100m from Rocamadour, this site was discovered in 1920 and listed 5 years later. You see some delicate concretions and admire the illuminated reflections of stalactites. Continually running water eroded these shapes, and Paleolithic artists decorated the walls with paintings of horses, stags, felines and 6 negative hands, 20,000 years ago.

MUSEE D'ART SACRE FRANCIS POULENC Parvis des Eglises © 05 65 33 23 30. *Closed 1 November-31 March. July & August: 10am-6pm. Admission: adult 4 €, child 2 €, under-8s free.* Panoramic lift. Housed in the Bishops' Palace, the museum covers five floors, ranging from 12th and 13thc. medieval art to the 19thc. Notre Dame de Rocamadour Renaissance. The 17thc. wooden statue of the prophet Jonas (Flemish School) and various Virgins (pietas) in polychrome stone and wood (the oldest go back to the 14thc.) are well worth a look. The museum is dedicated to composer Francis Poulenc who was inspired by N.D. de Rocamadour's 12thc. Black Virgin in 1936.

RAMPARTS DE ROCAMADOUR © 05 65 33 23 23. These ramparts are the remains of a 14thc. fort built to protect the sanctuary. They overhang site, valley and canyon, and offer a breathtaking view.

Saint-Céré

In 1611, a Dutch engineer divided the riverbed running through Saint Cère into several canals to reduce the risk of flood damage. The town was known as 'Little Venice of the Lot', until the canals were covered over in the late 19thc.

Rue Saint Cyr, you find a group of 15th and 16thc. houses with corner turrets, carved portals and Renaissance doors and fronts. The Hôtel Dauzies (Rue Mazel) is a magnificent 17thc. residence, with a splendid stone staircase. It contains the current owner's works of art. The Place du Mercacial contains 15th, 16th and 17thc. dwellings, with the superb Consuls House. On the quays is the Recollets Church (1658) with its striking carved wooden reredos and 800 painted wooden caissons in the ceiling. Sainte Sperie Church was built on a crypt. This Carolingian masterpiece contains the spring of the same name.

GROTTES DE PRESQUE Saint Céré © 05 65 38 07 44. *Open 15 February-15 November: 9am-12 noon and 2pm-6pm (9am-7pm July & August). Admission: adult 7 €, 7-11s 3 €* Admire the view from Presque Cliff, across the Dordogne Valley to the Auvergne Mountains. Next, visit the cave with its stalactites and stalagmites of various shapes and shades, shown to advantage by modern lighting techniques.

Saint-Cirq-Lapopie

Located 80m above the Lot, facing a circus of high cliffs, Saint-Cirq-Lapopie is a marvellous site, stretching from valley to plateau.

Discover the village on foot, and admire the fortified Gothic church (1522), castle terraces with their fine view, Rignault House on the cliff-edge, Peyrolerie and Rocamadour (Pelissaria) Gates, Places du Carol and du Sombral and Auberge des Gabariers (the Lot's freshwater sailors) where André Breton stayed. Don't miss the Bancourel and Cirque de Venes Belvederes at the village entrance; the view is spectacular.

MUSEE RIGNAULT ✆ **05 65 31 23 22**. *Open April-30 September, every day except Tuesday: 10am-12.30pm and 2.30pm-6pm. Adult 2* Saint-Cirq-Lapopie has inspired a number of artists, and this exhibition space houses contemporary art exhibitions: graphic arts in spring and sculpture during summer, displayed in gardens overlooking the Lot.

Saint-Jean-Lespinasse

The Chateau de Montal at Saint-Jean-Lespinasse is a Renaissance jewel. Saint Jean Baptiste Church is a fine example of 12thc. Poitevin Romanesque architecture, and boasts a Gothic vault and 14th. and 15thc. wall paintings uncovered only a few years ago.

CHATEAU DE MONTAL ✆ **05 65 38 13 72**. *Open (subject to confirmation) from Palm Sunday to November, except Saturday: 9.30am-12 noon and 2.30pm-6pm. Admission: adults 6 €.* It was here that the Mona Lisa and many other paintings from the Louvre were stored between 1942 and 1945. Perched on a leafy knoll, from the outside this is simply a rather rough medieval manor. Inside, however, the courtyard gives you a foretaste of the building's real nature, and the influence of Jeanne de Balzac who had the chateau built in 1523. The formal gardens boasting four mazes, monumental carved fireplaces, and 16th and 17thc. period furniture are well worth seeing. The facades in the main courtyard are decorated with family portraits and allegorical statues of Prudence and Strength, with some admirable ignudi (naked young people in the style of antiquity) on the skylight pediments. The monumental staircase with its vaults and delicate decoration under the steps has no equal in France. The Chateau de Montal had been sold in pieces to the world's museums, but regained its possessions thanks to patron Maurice Fenaille.

Souillac

It is said that Saint Eloi founded Souillac Abbey. The beautiful 12thc. Saint Marie Church, shaped like a Latin cross, is now all that remains. Souillac is also known for its automatons; after your museum visit, don't forget to follow the circuit of animated signs through the town.

MAISON DE LA DORDOGNE QUERCYNOISE Ave. de Sarlat ✆ **05 65 27 11 68.**

MUSEE DE L'AUTOMATE Place de l'Abbaye ✆ **05 65 37 07 07.** *Open all year. July & August: 10am-7pm. April, May & October: 10am-12 noon and 3pm-6pm, except Monday. Admission: Adult 5.* This collection of 19th and 20thc.automatons and mechanical toys is unique in Europe. You can admire over 300 moving automatons in Souillac Abbey grounds, designed in the Roullet and Decamps workshops from 1865 onwards, and grouped according to 6 themes (theatre, music, the town, etc).

MUSEE DES ATTELAGES DE LA BELLE EPOQUE Rue Paul Chambert ✆ **05 65 37 07 75**. *Open April, May and October: 10.30am-12 noon and 2.30pm-5pm, except Monday. July & August: 10.30am-1pm and 2pm-6.30pm. June -September: 10.30am-12 noon and 2.30pm-5pm.* Sixty horse-drawn vehicles, including Tsar Nicolas's barouche, the Comtesse de Segur's berlin and an old fire engine. Connoisseurs of upholstery will be impressed.

TARN-ET-GARONNE

This small department has plenty of interesting - and delicious - sites.

Auvillar

Overhanging the Garonne, Auvillar has a harbour where boats are moored and artists settle to paint the town. The Tour de l'Horloge, circular market and square with its half-timbered and corbelled houses all deserve notice.

SAINT PIERRE CHURCH Fairly heteroclite on the outside, this church is surprisingly harmonious inside. Notice the red marble stoup (Louis XV), even if you don't use it. The 17thc. pulpit and reredos behind the high altar are both remarkable. You can access the Treasure Chapel via the Rosary Chapel; it dates back to the 15thc. and once housed the clergy's sepulchres.

MUSEE D'ART ET TRADITIONS POPULAIRES Place de la Halle ✆ **05 63 39 89 82** *Open 1 May-31 October, except Tuesday. Other periods: Saturday & Sunday.* This museum was partly set up with the villagers' donations. It contains craftsmen's tools and models and some archeological finds, together with an earthenware and pottery collection on the first floor, made in Auvillar in the 18th and 19thc. (moulds also displayed).

Bruniquel

A fortified village on an exceptional site above the river, at the mouth of the Aveyron Gorges. Its old houses, belfry and remains of medieval gates and fortifications are built in tiers, with an imposing fortress above. The castles were put up on an earlier 6thc. building, and consist of the 12thc. Queen Brunehaut's Tower, knights' room with its fine gemelled windows, Baroque door and Renaissance gallery with its view of the Aveyron Valley.

The Maison Payrol is worth a visit: this former bourgeois residence contains three monumental fireplaces, a cellar with arcades and columns, wall paintings and a superb 15thc. ceiling). Five rooms on three floors exhibit local history, with 300 souvenirs from private collections.

Donzac

CONSERVATOIRE DE LA RURALITE ET DES METIERS D'AUTREFOIS ✆ 05 63 29 21 96. *Annual closing in January. Open every afternoon: 2pm-6pm, groups by reservation. Closed Monday out of season. July & August: every day: 9.30am-12 noon and 2pm-7pm. Admission: under-10s free, 10-14s 3.50 € adults 5 €.* 10,000 objects displayed in a 2,000m space: this elongated building is shaped like the local farms. The crafts of bygone days are exhibited in a lively setting, with period shops (grocer's, haberdasher's, cafe and tobacconist's) set up as they were. Outside, you can see old varieties of fruit tree and vines, recalling the region's fruit-growing tradition.

Ginals

BEAULIEU ABBEY ✆ 05 63 24 50 10. *Open 1 April-30 June and 1 September-30 November: 10am-12 noon and 2pm-6pm, except Tuesday. July & August: 10am-12.30pm and 2pm-6.30pm every day. Admission: adult 6.50 Groups by appointment (all year).* Founded in 1144, Beaulieu Abbey was a prosperous place for several centuries. Much later, it was bought and restored to house the first Midi-Pyrénées contemporary art centre. The 13thc. church is pure Gothic - (single nave, octagonal cupola, high openings, rose windows) The chapter house pillars spread out into massive square arches. This overall harmony is typical of Cistercian philosophy.

Gramont

CHATEAU DE GRAMONT ✆ 05 63 94 05 26. *Open 2 May-30 June and 1-30 September: 10am-12 noon and 2pm-6pm, except Mondays. July & August: open every day. Closed in January. Admission: adult 5* The Château de Gramont is one of the region's finest castles. Built over several centuries, it is a blend of styles (Gothic chatelet, Renaissance wing). The terraced gardens are beautiful, with a view of the Lomagne hillsides.

Lauzerte

This 13thc. *bastide* overlooks the Barguelonne and Londou Valleys, with a remarkable view of the surrounding country. It is amazingly beautiful: the Place des Cornières, Barbacane viewpoint, half-timbered houses with Romanesque facades, Seneschalsy cellars, former Clarisses convent, Saint Barthélemy and Carmes churches and remains of the ramparts are definitely not to be missed. Alleys and hidden corners contain a wealth of detail if you take the time to look: wrought-iron shop signs, ceramic street signs, fountains, carved and sculpted decoration, the Blue Penitents' great leather cross, Baroque reredos, organs. Stopping-place on the Compostella Road, Lauzerte also boasts an amusing introductory garden, designed for pilgrims.

Moissac

Known for its AOC chasselas grapes, Moissac shares itself between the Compostella Road and Canal du Midi, hillsides and Tarn banks. Its abbey is a masterpiece of Romanesque art.

SAINT PIERRE ABBEY CHURCH 6, Place Durand de Bredon. The Cluny ideal of Romanesque architecture, with a marvellous portal.

CLOITRE DE MOISSAC ✆ 05 63 04 01 85. *Open every day, July & August: 9am-7pm (ask about other periods).* The 76 late-11thc. capitals decorating this beautiful cloister are Romanesque sculptural treasures.

Montpezat de Quercy

In the heart of the Quercy vineyards, this medieval village has some lovely Middle Ages houses, a 14thc. Southern Gothic collegiate church and half-timbered houses belonging to the former Canons' College; an Ursuline Convent (now a state school) and Notre Dame de Saux, a fine Romanesque church.

Montauban

Pinkest of the pink towns, the Tarn-et-Garonne prefecture was built as a *bastide* in chessboard style round the Place Nationale. Enter the town via the Pont Vieux, built for Philippe le Bel in the 14thc. Opposite is the Bishops' Palace, put up on the lower rooms of an earlier castle built by the Black Prince during the Hundred Years' War (now the Ingres Museum).

CATHEDRAL. Original, because built of stone, contrasting with all that pink brick. The cathedral obviously stands out from the surrounding buildings, and its size and shape can be admired from far off.

PLACE NATIONALE. Its outline reproduces the primitive ramparts' trapeze-shape, and it lies at the centre of the chequered bastide plan. Place Nationale is the perfect medieval square (6,500m with the couverts) and the first to be enclosed (2 streets at each corner give it 8 access points). Around the square are the couverts, Southern-style arcaded shopping galleries, originally in wood, but today, two fires and three rebuildings later, a fine example of classical brick architecture.

PONT-VIEUX. Planned in the foundation charter of 1144, ordered by Philippe le Bel in 1304 and built from 1311-1335 by Etienne de Ferrières and Mathieu de Verdun. This pink brick bridge has seven Gothic arches with high openings to let out Tarn flood water, and is flat, rather than curved, which was a new concept. It simplified communication between the Comte de Toulouse and what was then France, and the development of the two banks, besides resisting the Tarn's spectacular floods.

MUSEE INGRES 9, rue de l'Hôtel de Ville ✆ 05 63 22 12 91. *Open in July, August & September: 10am-6pm. Other periods, every day except Monday: 10am-12 noon and 2pm-6pm. Adults from 4 to 6 €*This classical painter who opposed Romanticism and excelled at female nudes was born in Montauban. His museum is housed in the old Bishops' Palace.

Saint-Antonin-Noble-Val

Saint Antonin boasts the oldest Town Hall in France. The fortified village grew up around a Benedictine abbey, and its beautiful 13th, 14th and 15thc. residences are signs of medieval prosperity. You can visit a genuine oil press, and a museum housed in France's oldest civil building (1125) containing local and regional arts and traditions collections (Place de la Halle; look for the belfry!).

Roquefort

FOOD AND DRINK

The land of foie gras, truffles, cepes and cassoulet - and they seem all the better for it!

Lautrec's pink garlic

Grown since the Middle Ages, this garlic has become quite famous. Use it raw, finely chopped or rubbed on bread croutons, to season salads, vegetable and fish soups. It can also be fried, simmered, steamed and roasted peeled, or in its skin.

ALINEA Route de Castres - LAUTREC ✆ 05 63 70 81 81

Armagnac

White wine is distilled in an Armagnac still, giving a colourless alcohol between 52-72%. Many years of ageing, first in a new oak cask, then in an older one, bring the alcohol content down to 40%-48%. The maitre de chai then creates harmonious and skilful mixtures (coupes) ending up with a product for the market. Today, Gers vineyards account for 15,000ha. with an annual output of 6-8 million bottles. 4,000 winegrowers and 40 dealers are involved. Further information: *www.armagnac.fr*

Cassoulet

There are several recipes, and the debate recalls the Wars of Religion! In Toulouse you use mutton and (Toulouse) sausages, in Carcassonne pork chops, in Castelnaudary, goose or duck confit and a small garlic sausage, and in Corbières, salted pig's tail and ear.

Cèpe

You find them more easily in Tarn-et-Garonne at the markets or in restaurants than in the woods, the best places being closely-guarded secrets. Cepe-picking is in fact regulated; the Vaissac variety is listed 'French Culinary Heritage'.

Foie gras

Geese have long been identified with the Gers: in the early 19thc. there were 140,000 in the department. Duck-breeding now follows a close second, and these two feathered friends are the basis of Gascon gastronomy and its holy trinity: foie gras, magret (breast) and confit.

SAMATAN (Gers). Every Monday a crowd of buyers and sellers from all over France meet in this covered market among the tonnes of foie gras. You can even have your fatted duck cut up into pieces in a room set aside for that purpose.

Tarbes haricot

The bishop of Poudenx first planted these beans on the Tarbes plain, in the early 7thc. Long, flat and white, slightly curved and always picked by hand, they melt in the mouth. ,

Cheeses

Cheeses

© Phovoir

Roquefort

There are three steps to making Roquefort cheese. First, the milk is collected from the Lacaune ewes within the AOC limit. This is transformed into curds, the penicillium roqueforti is added, and the mixture is worked in a vat, put into moulds, drained and salted. These fourmes can now be matured in Roquefort. After 20 days, they are hermetically wrapped in tinfoil to stop the penicillium developing. The cheeses are matured for 90-350 days in all, which explains differences in flavour in the same brand of Roquefort.

Truffe

Quercy's 'black diamond' grows under oak and walnut trees - but no-one will tell you which ones! You will find them more easily at Caussade market (late November-early December) Mecca of truffle-trading.

Vieille prune de Souillac

The plums are carefully selected, and the making of this brandy has been a Roque family secret since 1905. Amber-coloured, mellow to the taste, it has a bouquet of fruit aromas and a real plum flavour.

DISTILLERIE ROQUE ✆ 05 65 32 78 16

Vineyards

This is a land of wines, and wine-growing is deeply rooted in the local culture. There is a vast collection of *cépages* and AOCs: Cahors, Gaillac, Madiran and many more.

Vin de Cahors AOC

This wine can be laid down; a Cahors made in the valley and on the terraces gains body after 3 years; one from the plateau needs at least 5, and the best keep in the cellar for over 15 years. A mature Cahors with its subtle, sophisticated flavour goes perfectly with truffles, red meat with cepes, and game. Rocamadour and cantal cheese suit a great Cahors; Roquefort goes better with a younger, full-bodied and tannic wine.

CHATEAU EUGENIE Albas ✆ 05 65 30 73 51

CHATEAU LEGREZETTE Gaillac ✆ 05 65 20 07 42. *www.Chateau-legrezette.tm.fr*

CHATEAU DE CHAMBERT Les Hauts Coteaux - FLORESSAS ✆ 05 65 31 95 75. *www.chambert.com. Open every day, except Sunday: 8.30am-12.30pm and 2pm-6.30pm.*

CHATEAU DE MERCUES Mercues ✆ 05 65 20 00 01

CHATEAU DU CAYROU Puy-l'Eveque ✆ 05 65 22 40 26. *Open Easter-November, Monday-Saturday: 10am-12 noon and 2pm-7pm.* Nestling in a park with 200-year-old trees, the Château du Cayrou stands among 30ha. of vineyards. They were planted in 1971 by the Jouffreau family, winegrowers for several centuries at the Clos de Gamot in Preyssac, and are traditionally grown on a graves soil. After the cellars, you can visit the exhibition of old winemaking tools, and see the castle's painting and sculpture collections.

DOMAINE DU PRINCE **Cournu - Saint-Vincent-Rive-d'Olt ✆ 05 65 20 14 09**

DOMAINE DES SAVARINES **Trespoux ✆ 05 65 22 33 67**

CHATEAU DU CEDRE **Bru - VIRE-SUR-LOT ✆ 05 65 36 53 87.** *Open Monday-Saturday: 9am-12 noon and 2pm-6pm.*

CLOS LA COUTALE **Vire-sur-Lot ✆ 05 65 36 51 47**

Côtes-du-frontonnais

This ancient vineyard (4thc. A.D.) developped in the Merovingian era on cleared land in Agre Forest. One ancient and exclusive cepage is used: the negrette. The reds are fruity, supple and delicate, ruby-coloured with blackcurrant and prune aromas (older wines have a more varied bouquet). The roses are light-coloured and scented. These are balanced and distinguished wines that go well with fish and charcuterie.

CHATEAU BEL AIR **Fronton ✆ 05 61 82 45 75**

CAVE COOPERATIVE DE FRONTON **Fronton ✆ 05 62 70 97 79**

CHATEAU LE ROC **Fronton ✆ 05 61 82 93 90**

DOMAINE MATABIAU **Fronton ✆ 05 61 82 96 01**

Côtes-de-gascogne

The neat rows of vines on the Gers slopes produce côtes-de-gascogne vins de pays, pleasant, fruity, festive and friendly.

Vins de Gaillac

The Tarnais are proud of their ancient vines, and their improved quality. Red or white, Gaillac wines go with any menu.

DOMAINE DE PIALENTOU **Brens ✆ 05 63 33 00 80**

CAVE DE TECOU **Tecou - GAILLAC ✆ 05 63 33 00 80.** *www.cavedetecou.fr. Free tasting, open 8am-12 noon and 2pm-6pm, every day except Sunday and public holidays.* Tecou groups together 100 winegrowers on 900ha. As befits the leader in direct on-site sales, it has a new air-conditioned reception area, with a wide bay window looking into the storehouse. A huge oval bar suggests plenty of tasting in friendly surroundings.

DOMAINE DE LAGARRIGUE **Lagarrigue - Senouillac ✆ 05 63 41 70 83**

Madiran

The Hautes-Pyrénées have only one classified vineyard: the Madiran, grown in the north of the department on acid soil in the Adour Valley. This coloured, tannic wine with its raspberry flavour ages well, and suits confits, farm lamb, cepes, Tarbes beans, fish and cheese.

CHATEAU DE CROUSEILLES **Crouseilles ✆ 05 58 68 10 93.** *Tasting cellar open every day.* This Château has an impressive history, and an exceptional Madiran vineyard.

MAISON DES VINS DE MADIRAN **Rue de l'Eglise ✆ 05 62 31 90 67.** *Open every day: 9am-6.30pm in summer. Closed Sunday in winter.* Free tasting: Madiran and Pacherenc du Vic-Brilh. Information on the AOC.

DOMAINE PICHARD **Soublecause ✆ 05 62 96 35 73.** *www.domaine-pichard.com. Open Monday-Saturday: 9am-6pm.* Auguste Vigneau was the first Madiran winegrower to sell his wine in bottles.

Marcillac

This is Aveyron's best-known vineyard. Stretching over 11 villages and almost the whole Marcillac-Vallon canton, it exploits 160ha. and produces 5,000-6,000 hectolitres, 90% red, 10% rose. The wines are full-bodied with a deep colour.

DOMAINE DU CROS **Goutrens ✆ 05 65 72 71 77**

DOMAINE LAURENS **Clairvaux ✆ 05 65 72 69 37**

FRANCIS COSTES **La Baronie - Combret - NAUVIALE ✆ 05 65 69 83 05**

Pacherenc AOC

The original, ancient name means 'vine in line' which is now the usual way of planting vines. Overripe grapes are hand-picked and sorted on the sunny slopes from late October to 31 December. This Saint Sylvestre (New Year's Eve) grape harvest is excellent publicity, since it is shown on the world's TV screens.

PRODUCTEURS PLAIMONT ✆ 05 62 69 62 87.

Hotels & Restaurants

ARIÈGE

Audressein

L'AUBERGE ✆ **05 61 96 11 80.** *Website: www.auberge-audressein.com. Closed Sunday evening and Monday outside school holiday periods. Annual closing 3 weeks in January. Set menus: 16 € (weekday lunchtimes) 33 €, 46 €, 65 € and 85 €. Excellent menu. Coffee menu from 2.50 € to 3.80 €. Closed terrace on the river. 9 rooms from 45 € to 65 €.* Full or half-board available if you stay more than 3 days. The Auberge d'Audressein lies at the foot of the Bellongue Valley, where the film *The return of Martin Guerre* was made, starring Gérard Depardieu. It is without doubt one of the best restaurants in Couserans and Ariège. Stéphanie and Yves Atelin welcome you in this stone house, a former 1870s forge: their establishment was awarded a star in the Bottin Gourmand 2004 and a mark of 15/20 by the Gault-et-Millau 2005. In 2003, Yves graduated from the Ariège Chamber of Commerce and Industry. The chef offers traditional regional cuisine; the main and set menus change regularly. Try the Audressein trout souffléed with Bamalou cheese in *sauce sambuc*, or the pigeon leg with an endive pancake and Fronton sauce. An address to remember!

Ax-les-Thermes

L'ORRY LE SAQUET *** **RN 20 Route d'Espagne** ✆ **05 61 64 31 30.** *Website: www.auberge-lorry.com Open all year except October half-term. Closed Tuesday and Wednesday. Set menus from 21 € to 69 € and à la carte. «Tables gourmandes d'Ariege-Pyrenees». Restaurateur de France label and member of L'Euro toque association. 15 rooms from 59 €. Breakfast 8 €.* Marc and Sylvie Heinrich are happy to welcome you to their chalet. Cooking is done only with genuine local produce, and the fish are from the nearby Mediterranean. Follow your mood and your appetite, and taste one of the following marvels: foie gras served in various ways, grilled bass, old-fashioned farm-bred duck, shelled crab *croquant* with cuttlefish, pineapple carpaccio in passion jelly... The hotel has been recently renovated and is now in the 3-star category. Each room is named after a mountain flower, and is decorated in its colours.

Foix

HOTEL-RESTAURANT LONS ** **6, place Georges-Dutilh** ✆ **05 61 65 52 44.** *Website : www.hotel-lons-foix.com Hôtel open all year. Annual closing from 20 December to 5 January. 38 rooms starting from 49 €. Restaurant open every day except Friday evening and Saturday lunchtime; closed from 20 December to 20 January. Set menus from 14 €.* This establishment belongs to the "Logis de France" family. Located on the left of the Pont Vieux, overlooking the Ariège, this former coaching Inn has been run by the Lons family for nearly 40 years. Some of the rooms have a view of the river and the others of the Place Duthil, on the town side, as is the entrance. The reception lounge, bar and seminar rooms attract the business world, come to negotiate with the "Foix merchants". The restaurant, extended by a glassed-in terrace, is on a level with the riverbank and has room for 250 place settings. Choose from several different set menus, or go à la carte. Cassoulet or confit, duck breast kebab, rabbit stew, seafood, frogs' legs and snails follow an appetising salad buffet. Local cheeses go well with glowing ruby bordeaux or burgundy wine. The *croustades*, amandines, flans and other pastries are homemade, as are the ice creams.

Mirepoix

HOTEL-RESTAURANT LE COMMERCE & 05 61 68 10 29. *20, cours Docteur-Chabaud. Website: http://le-commerce.fr Email: lecommerce@chez.com Restaurant closed Saturday, except July & August. Annual closing 16-30 October 2006 and January. Set menus 16 €, 19 €, 21 €, 24 €, 28 € and 30 €. Children's menu 7 €. Menu of the day 12 €, except weekends and public holidays. 32 rooms from 36 €-54 €. Breakfast 7 €.* Tradition is important in this hotel-restaurant, where recipes are handed down from generation to generation. The latest of these respects 'fundamentals' like the cepe omelette, duck breasts and confit and of course, cassoulet, foie gras, gizzards and other timeless classics found in Ariege cooking. You can, however, also try the ostrich steak with raspberry vinegar, monkfish with hippocras, salmon, frogs' legs Provencal-style, and scallops with young vegetables. The desserts change every day. There are 32 different rooms, all very comfortable. Breakfast and other meals are served on the shady terrace in fine weather, under sumptuous trees - very welcome in the hot Ariege sunshine. A hotel-restaurant just waiting to be discovered.

LA MAISON DES CONSULS * 6, place des Couverts ✆ 05 61 68 81 81.** *Website: www.maisondesconsuls.com Open all year. 7 rooms and one suite. Rooms from 85 € to 140 € (the Astronomer's Suite) depending on number of occupants and location.* Mirepoix's poshest hotel, with its 3 stars, can be found in the former 'house of justice' (medieval law court), now listed and famous for its carved joists. French-style ceilings with their exposed beams and fine period woodwork characterise the medieval architecture. The rooms have been given historic names, and carefully personalised and stylised decoration. The Marshal's, Marquis' or Monseigneur's rooms live up to their noble titles, and Dame Louise's room, set apart, is as discreet as a boudoir. The Writer's and Academician's rooms ensure poetic nights. As for the Commercial Traveller's room, it is dazzlingly sober. The Astronomer's Suite looks out at the stars and over a wide terrace with a view of the rooftops. It contains an imposing bed of 2.80 sqm. with 4 pillows! All the rooms have a bath, TV and minibar. Customers are welcomed in a big reception lounge, and a wide-screen TV is equipped with Canal Satellite. Start your day with a choice of breakfast: Parisian or special Ariégeois with a plate of local *charcuterie* (cold pork meats).

LES MINOTIERS & 05 61 69 37 36. *Avenue Maréchal Foch. Website: www.lesminotiers.com Email: info@lesminotiers.com Weekly closing Saturday lunchtime. 22 rooms from 45 €-65 €. Breakfast 5.50 €. Set menus 15 €, 23 €, 28 € and 34 €. Shady terrace seating 60, private car park, dining room seating 70. Air-conditioning.* This former mirror factory facing the town swimming pool has been skilfully restored with exposed stone and a wrought iron decor, and was opened on 9 July 2005 by Gilles Riveslange and Alain Fuffo. The chef cooks with fresh, local ingredients; the recipes are regional. You will have difficulty choosing, faced with lamb in a morel crust, sirloin steak mountain-style with Balmalou fondue, veal chop with morels, mullet with ginger, scallops in orange butter, smoked salmon charlotte, and foie gras pan-cooked with apples or figs.

LE RELAIS ROYAL & 05 61 60 19 19. *8, rue maréchal Clauzel. Website: www.relaisroyal.com Email: relaisroyal@relaischateaux.com Closed January. Hotel rooms 150 €-180 € for 1 or 2 people, according to season. Restaurant set menus 22 € 29 €, 48 €, 59 €, 65 € and 82 €. The 22 € menu is served on Wednesday, Thursday and Friday lunchtime only.* This historic 18thc. residence has become the Ariege's top 4-star hotel, thanks to Gerwin Rutten and Rogier Van Den Biggelaar. The building was completely renovated in 2004. Five rooms and three suites combine luxury, comfort and innovation. The hotel restaurant Le Ciel d'Or offers top-of-the-range service and cuisine: spiced 'Adventure' monkfish, bass cooked on its skin, foie gras carpaccio with pepper, pork fillet mignon and Ariege black pudding, and Savoy cabbage fricassee with walnuts and conserved lemons. The menu changes with the seasons. The wine list reinforces that impression of good taste and competence. New, attractive and delicious!

AVEYRON

Belcastel

LE VIEUX PONT ✆ **05 65 64 52 29** *Fax: 05 65 64 44 32. Website: www.hotelbelcastel.com. Set menus from 28 € to 80 €, à la carte 60 €. Closed Sunday, Monday, Tuesday lunchtime and from 1 January-15 March.* The Vieux Pont is the story of two sisters, Nicole and Michele Fagegaltier, the first in the kitchen, the second in the dining room, who have spread the fame of their family inn beyond the Aveyron borders through sheer tenacity and generosity of spirit. Value for money is about the best in the region: sucking lamb sweetbreads pan-fried with cuttlefish and ginger, several vegetables with grilled ham, foamy and crispy soup with cepes, spinach leaves, a piece of Aveyron and Segala veal with parsley *au gratin*, potatoes pureed with almond milk and *fromage blanc* with powdered orange, pineapple and fennel conserve with ginger, orange and coriander ice-cream, green apple juice with dill. This gastronomy, anchored in the local soil yet modern, conveys a certain image of happiness underlined by discreet and smiling service and a wine cellar with deep roots in the region.

Creissels

CHATEAU DE CREISSELS** **Route de Saint-Affrique** ✆ **05 65 60 16 59** *Website: http://château-de-creissels.com. Closed from 26 December to early March. 30 rooms from 58 € to 88 €, according to whether they're in the recent building or the chateau. Breakfast 8.30 €. Set menus from 23 € to 52 €.* This residence has 12thc. foundations, and successive centuries have left their mark on it. A crenellated tower rises above the main body of buildings set around a flower-filled courtyard, while the inside rooms are elegantly furnished with rugs and crystal chandeliers. The bedrooms hark back to their period, some with a balcony overlooking the garden. The restaurant harmonises with the setting, in a vaulted dining room in winter and on the terrace in summer, with a view over the town. The tables are perfect, with a *cuisine* of classic alliances and sophisticated flavours. Sweetbreads and Roquefort cheese-based dishes are the house specialities.

Espalion

LE MEJANE 8, rue Méjane © 05 65 48 22 37. *Closed Sunday evening and Monday in July and August, closed Sunday evening, Monday lunchtime and Wednesday from September to June. Menus 16 € (lunchtime) 22 €, 32 € and 38 €.* If you feel like an especially tasty meal, this restaurant with its snug decor, entirely given over to good food, is for you. The lunch menu consists of a main course followed by the cheese platter and the dessert of the day, and you will discover an imaginative cuisine, aiming to spice up the taste and quality of regional produce. Thus the little cabbage is stuffed with crab in shellfish juice, and the lamb sweetbreads are served on a *pascade* (kind of thick pancake) with bread and herbs. The foie gras and guinea-hen terrine, conserved in red wine and bacon is a frank success, the young stuffed pigeon *ballotine* seasoned with juniper berries leaves a pleasantly memorable taste in your mouth. And since you wouldn't want to leave the table without a superb full stop, you'll hesitate between iced parfait with Velay verbena and dark chocolate and a slice of golden pineapple with its crunchy caramel cornet on caramel milk. It's a difficult choice, but once made, sure to be absolutely delicious.

Estaing

AUBERGE DE SAINT-FLEURET 19, rue François-d'Estaing © 05 65 44 01 44.** *Website :www.perso.wanadoo.fr/auberge.st.fleuret Closed 15 November-15 March. Rooms from 44 € to 48 €. (low season) and 47 € to 51 € (high season). Breakfast 7 €. Set menus from 17 € to 50 €.* The recent addition of a swimming pool has done nothing to disturb the old-fashioned charm cultivated in this inn, housed in its period building. You find it in the two halves of the restaurant; one well furnished and cosy as a bourgeois dining room, the other light and spring-like, with walls covered in Monet-style iris and large windows opening onto the garden. Gilles Moreau treats you to regional dishes with that extra creative touch: pork trotters in Estaing's own white wine, asparagus tartare with marinated pink trout, foie gras pan-fried with apple puree and chicken *fricassee* with local honey and hazelnuts are on the menu this year, as are one or two fruit-based desserts. Alexandrine has redecorated the 14 rooms in harmonious blue and yellow. The quieter ones overlook the garden, others have TV and they all come equipped with bath or shower, W.C. and telephone. Look forward to a pleasant stay.

Laguiole

MICHEL BRAS Route de l'Aubrac © 05 65 51 18 20 *Fax: 05 65 48 47 02. Website: www.michel-bras.fr. Set menus from 54 € to 160 €, à la carte 140 €. Closed Monday, Tuesday lunchtime, Wednesday lunchtime (except July and August, closed Mondays only) and from late October to early March.* This huge house was built in 1992 on a plateau in the heart of the Aubrac countryside that Michel Bras promotes with such passion and energy. Its ultramodern architecture - all light stones, glass and metal - will surprise you, standing out against, yet somehow harmonising with, the superb desolation of the natural setting. The long dining-room was dreamed up to set off the magnificent landscape: the well-spaced tables are all turned towards the immense bay windows and the countryside beyond. Warm and up-to-date at the same time, with a cheerful little stream running through it, this is a theatre for the most exquisite *cuisine*, now increasingly taken care of by son Sebastien, who at nearly 35 will soon be expected to take his father's place. Extraordinary technique goes into dishes like the famous fresh vegetable *gargouillou*, yet the procession of savoury, crunchy vegetable looks so simple! The same goes for the poached and grilled chicken breast in foamy stock, *rumex patienta* and young artichokes and the chocolate *coulant* (perfected by Michel Bras 25 years ago) regularly served as variations on a theme. This first-rate restaurant is one of the five or six in France that you really have to have tried: the service is frighteningly efficient (a little distant, perhaps) and the wonderful rooms look on to equally fine scenery.

Millau

CAPION 3, rue Jean-François-Alméras © 05 65 60 00 91 *Closed Tuesday evening, Wednesday and all July. Set menus from 17 € to 38 €. Lunchtime formula 12.50 €.* Created by a family known in the region for its culinary art, the Capion establishment keeps up the tradition. Fabien and Christian Aveline ensure customer satisfaction in premises where the aroma of bygone recipes gone still lingers. These old-fashioned dishes - such as braised shin - are once more among the chef's specialities, and he even joins you at the end of your meal for feedback - generally very positive. Which isn't surprising considering you are facing a trolley of homemade desserts, where the charlotte made with three types of chocolate vies with seasonal tarts and Millau *faune*.

Najac

L'OUSTAL DEL BARRY Place du Bourg ✆ 05 65 29 74 32.** *Closed 11 November-23 December and 1 January-late March. Rooms from 50 € to 73 €. Breakfast 8.50 €. Set menus from 23 € to 48 €.* On the way in to the bastide, in the 'barry', or suburb from which it gets its name, this house -or oustal - looks most promising, with its lounge, terrace and small garden. Its pleasantly decorated rooms overlook the village or towards the Aveyron valley and provide all the comfort you need. Apart from its welcome, the Oustal's reputation comes from its cuisine. With considerable mastery, chef Rémy Simon knows how to match a fillet of bass in a spinach crust with a soft broccoli cream, or lamb with a garlic and thyme juice served with a potato *brochette* (kebab) and tomato conserve. The desserts are just as sophisticated; like the rest of the menu they are made with fresh market produce and garden herbs.

Rodez

GOUTS ET COULEURS 38, rue de Bonald ✆ 05 65 42 75 10. *Fax: 05 65 42 75 10. Menus from 32 € to 70 €, à la carte 45 €. Closed Sunday, Monday, Tuesday evening (except in June, July August and December) 9 January to 1 February, 30 April to 9 May and 4 to 18 September.* 15 years after setting up his restaurant in this house in the old town, Jean-Luc Fau remains one of the region's most enthusiastic and engaging chefs. Good humour and good food go together here, reinforced by excellent produce and smiling service. Despite his obvious success, the prices have decided to stay reasonable (you'll have difficulty spending over 45 € à la carte). So *en route* then, for the foie gras *crème renversée*, sweet potato coulis, herb salad with argan oil and spiced caramel; for the lobster stew and veal kidneys, rice in cuttlefish ink with pepper touches; for the *hochepot* of ribs, rind and calf's head, vegetables, stock and mustard and for the apple meringue stuffed with quince and flavoured with pine, and honey, gingerbread and vanilla ice-cream. You leave fulfilled (and feeling full) determined to come back, and in doing so, to pick out a few new bottles from a wine cellar that's specialised yet affordable, with intelligently advice from wife Emmanuelle.

Sauveterre-de-Rouergue

HOTEL-RESTAURANT LE SENECHAL * ✆ 05 65 71 29 00.** *Closed January to mid-March, Monday, Tuesday lunchtime, Thursday lunchtime (except public holidays), Monday lunchtime in July and August. Rooms from 105 € to 148 €. Breakfast 15 €. Set menus from 25 € to 110 €.* The Senechal is in fact 3 establishments in one: the 3-star 'luxury' hotel, the traditional two-star and a restaurant, run by MichelTruchon. The grand hotel can be found outside the bastide ditches, and is a mixture of traditional and contemporary architecture. In front of the establishment, a sort of raised patio lets you choose between sun and shade for your breakfast table. The restaurant is on the bastide's perimeter, on the ground floor of the inn. Behind the small window panes, a large bar leads on to a country-style dining room where the tables are carefully set with crystal and decorative plates. Michel Truchon's *cuisine* is a gastronomic promenade between the fertile Rouergue country and Mediterranean influences, a tune composed with sweet-and-sour chords. This memorable feast comes with a fine wine list, and the fleeting pleasure of a choice coffee and a cigar from the cellar. A delectable top-of-the-range break in your journey.

Villefranche-de-Rouergue

L'ASSIETTE GOURMANDE Place André-Lescure ✆ 05 65 45 25 95 *Closed Sunday all year round, Tuesday and Wednesday evening out of season. Menus from 14 € to 32 €.* Your eyes anticipate the pleasure to come as they take in the medieval dining-room behind its 13thc.door, built entirely of stone, with the original exposed beams running across the ceiling. The tables are tastefully set, and the walls decorated with menus from great French restaurants to whet your appetite. The 'real' menu is full of local delicacies. Among the chef's successes are foie gras pan-fried with fresh apples and the classic but tasty *aligot* (mashed potato cooked with cheese) and *tripoux* (small bundles of stuffed sheep tripe). The set menus give you a choice of meat or fish, served according to the rules of culinary art in a quiet atmosphere where you can concentrate on your taste buds.

GERS

Auch

ROLAND GARREAU ***LE JARDIN DES SAVEURS Place de la Libération ✆ 05 62 61 71 71. *Hotel closed Sunday evening, except Whit Sunday and in summer. Restaurant open every day except Sunday evening. Lunchtime and evening service. Last order taken around 10pm. Tradition menu 25 €. Club menu 42 €. Gourmand menu 49 €. 29 rooms from 63 € to 126 €. 2 suites 195 €, 298 €. All-in price for under-10s 20 €.* The *Concours National du Meilleur Ouvrier de France Cuisine* is an exceptionally difficult competition, yet Roland Garreau wears a victor's collar in the French national colours on his white coat, a sign that his *cuisine* belongs to the great tradition of French gastronomy rooted in exceptional soil and rich in farm produce and wines. Like the multiple variations on a duck foie gras theme, the roast pigeon supreme with thin bacon (the taste of bygone days) or the veal sweetbreads and duck foie gras *en cocotte*. The fish might be (*à la carte*) slice of roast turbot with fine seasoning, with the juice of Gers poultry. As for the personalised rooms in this former coaching inn, they combine old-world charm and modern comfort: satellite TV, mini-bar, Internet access etc.

Castera-Verduzan

LE FLORIDA Rue du Lac ✆ 05 62 68 13 22. *Closed Sunday evening and Monday, except public holidays. Annual closing February school holidays. Set menus: weekdays from 13.50 € (lunchtime) to 34 €, Sunday from 27 € to 50 €. Dinner on the terrace in summer.* In the heart of the village, near the church, behind a stone facade, lies a cosy room where a log fire crackles in winter. Bernard Ramouneda is one of those inventive Gers chefs in love with the culinary arts and a member of the Ronde des Mousquetaires. He cooks local produce with respect and daring, inventing subtle combinations. The Angèle menu, in memory of his grandmother, offers fresh truffles, cepes and game in season. The cellar specialises in first-rate local wines, but also holds every wine-lover's favourite *grands crus*. One of the great places to eat in the Gers region.

Condom

LE LOGIS DES CORDELIERS ** Rue de la Paix ✆ 05 62 28 03 68. *Website : www.logisdescordeliers.com Annual closing in January. Rooms from 45 € to 68 €. Breakfast 7 €. VRP break from 60 €. Swimming pool.* There are 21 rooms in this haven of peace and greenery in the town centre.Most of them have a private terrace, a full bathroom, direct phone line and TV, and open onto the swimming pool. Some of them are non-smoking. Private car park available for guests.

L'Isle-Jourdain

HOSTELLERIE DU LAC ** ✆ 05 62 07 03 91. *Annual closing one week at Christmas. Last order taken at 10pm in summer, 9.30pm in winter. Menus from 14 € to 35 €. 29 rooms from 38 € to 45 €. Terrace.* In a sunny setting, d'Artagnan's statue proudly shows the way in to l'Hostellerie du Lac, which is both an institution and a place for a break that smells of holidays. Mme Rabassa welcomes you kindly in the great restaurant with its stone pillars or on the vast shady terrace, and serves you with regional *cuisine*: crayfish and fresh liver in pastry, pigeon confit with foie gras, and a *cassolette* (small, shallow ovenproof dish) of scallops. The rooms are tastefully decorated and equipped with a direct telephone line and colour TV. There are 2 seminar rooms for groups of 20-25 people. Pleasant swimming pool with a view of the lake.

Lectoure

HOTEL DE BASTARD **Rue Lagrange ✆ 05 62 68 82 44. *Annual closing 20 December-1 February. Restaurant closed from 1 September to 14 July, Sunday evening, Monday and Tuesday lunchtime, then from15 July to 31 August at Monday lunchtime only. Set menus15 €, 28 €, 60 €. Rooms from 46 € to 70 €. Swimming pool, terrace, private lounges and meeeting rooms.* This is a huge 18thc.building with a fine façade, and proves to be the Mecca of Gers gastronomy and hostelry. Jean-Luc Arnaud at the piano is one of the talented performers from the Ronde des Mousquetaires, and he sets the scene for an inventive and original *cuisine* created from local produce. Hostess Anne Arnaud provides a charming welcome, and the 27 rooms are comfortable and modern.

Montréal-du-Gers

CHEZ SIMONE ✆ 05 62 29 44 40. *Restaurant closed Sunday evenings, Mondays and Tuesdays in low season, except public holidays. Lunchtime and evening service. Last order taken between 9.30pm and 10pm. Set menus from 15 € to 50 €. Credit cards and American Express and luncheon vouchers (Ticket- Restaurant and Chèque-Repas.) accepted. Terrace.* The Daubin restaurant embodies Gascon virtues: authenticity, kindness and *finesse.* You'll enjoy fine cooking in a sophisticated, tastefully decorated setting: hake caught with a rod and line, free-range veal with conserved garlic or liver with *tarbais* (Tarbes beans) *en cocotte* (casseroled). You're allowed to choose and savour other dishes, too. Wooden bread plates and sloping water glasses make for an unusual table setting, and there is no wine list: you choose your wine from the central buffet display. Service is attentive and smiling. In summer, the tables are set up under a quiet and shady flowering arbour, on the Place des Champions-de-France-de-Rugby.

Pujaudran

LE PUITS SAINT-JACQUES Place de la Mairie ✆ 05 62 07 41 11. *Closed Sunday evening, Monday and Tuesday. Annual closing last fortnight in August. Set menus 22 € weekday lunchtimes, 32 €, 50 € (découverte menu) and 70 € (dégustation menu). Credit cards and American Express accepted. Private rooms for family receptions. Terrace. Last order taken 10pm.* Once again boasting a star in the Guide Rouge, Bernard Bach has become the standard-bearer for the great Gers restaurant business. His dining room is elegantly rustic, with brick walls, carved woodwork, silver and crystal in evidence; Mme Bach's welcome is top-quality, like the service. Each dish is presented with timing and conviction, so that a simple meal becomes a feast. The menu changes with the seasons. When we were last there, it was offering truffles. Bernard Bach calls it "a *cuisine* altered and adapted in search of flavour, rather than simple to prepare and cook". Wine waiter Patrick's wine list is sumptuous. In summer, you can eat on the terrace, near the well where thirsty pilgrims once drank on the road to Compostella. During the *décades gourmandes* chefs with stars from other regions are invited to come and treat the customers to their specialities.

HAUTE-GARONNE

Colomiers

L'AMPHITRYON Chemin de Gramont ✆ 05 61 15 55 55. *Fax : 05 61 15 42 30. Website : www.lamphitryon.com Menus de 30 € to 95 €, carte 80 €. Open all year.* Who's the talk of Toulouse at the moment? Michel Sarran of course, in the town centre, and Yannick Delpech, the rising star of Colomiers and the Midi-Pyrenées region. Comfortably settled in this beautiful countryside dining-room near the Airbus buildings, you let yourself be spoilt by staff who are visibly happy to work with such a pilot: fresh sardines with thick cream and herring caviar; crème prise with foie gras and pumpkin pulp; scallops à la poutargue, noodles and Chinese artichokes with conserved lemon, roast Mont-Royal pigeon with pear and mango and fresh mint; and perles de Japon (oriental semolina balls) and coconut in a milk-chocolate bar - what a number of delicious dishes! The cellar is specialized though expensive, and the service efficient, coached with charm by owner Sandrine Btard.

Saint-Félix-du-Lauragais

AUBERGE DU POIDS PUBLIC Faubourg du Poids-Public ✆ 05 62 18 85 00 *Fax: 05 62 18 85 00. Set menus from 27 € to 67 €, à la carte 50 €. Closed Sunday evening, in January and one week in November.* Claude Taffarello can be proud of his accomplishments. 15 years ago, he took over a former stopping-off place for lorry drivers, which also served as filling station and village inn. He has just had the restaurant entirely renovated and the panoramic view of the Lauragais Mountains from the large bay windows is all the more impressive. There are still one or two annoying details: loud noise from the kitchens, and service with a tendency to simply dispose of day-to-day matters, which is a pity. Claude Taffarello's cuisine is fortunately still full of sap and good humour: crunchy langoustines, small pan-fried broad beans with shellfish vinaigrette, tuna with its juices just sealed in, conserved lemon paste and cucumber puree, braised Lauragais veal shank and its juice reduced and simmered with vegetables, and *millas* (a kind of clafoutis) caramelised in the pan, orange butter and vanilla ice-cream. There is a fine wine cellar specialising in the Southwest, and a family atmosphere.

Toulouse

LES CAVES DE LA MARECHALE 3, rue Jules-Chalande ✆ 05 61 23 89 88. *Closed Sunday and Monday lunchtime. Set menus from 13 € to 14.50 € (lunchtime) and from 23 € to 26 € (evening). À la carte 35 €. Dish of the day 13 € and 14.50 €. Last order taken at 10.30pm. Credit cards and luncheon vouchers accepted. Meals for groups of up to 120. Advance booking recommended.* Even those Toulousains who have never set foot in the place know these Caves by repute. The setting is the former Dominican priory of Saint Romain, abandoned in the 13thc. It suffered various fates before M. Chanzy exchanged the pulpit for gastronomic pleasure, by notarial deed in 1975. You might even hire the premises to organise your party: the regional cuisine is blamelessly traditional and the bill won't strike fear into you. Duck breasts with peaches, tournedos Hyppolite -your host's name - salmon with leek fondue and fresh pasta, home-made cassoulet and *Délice de la maréchale*, a dessert not for the under-18s: the menu stays faithful to its standards. A sure thing, in fact, and one of the *petites futees'* favourite places.

CROWNE PLAZA ** 7, place du Capitole ✆ 05 61 61 19 25.** *Website: www.crowneplaza-toulouse.com. 162 rooms from 245 €, promotional offers on the Internet. Weekend prices. Breakfast 22 €. Restaurant l'Autan-Tic: set menus from 18 € to 39 € and à la carte. Summer restaurant Le Grand Patio open from mid-April to mid-October. Bar du Plaza open every day until 1am. 8 meeting rooms seating up to 100. Rooms for the handicapped.* The Crowne Plaza is one of Toulouse's most prestigious hotels, ideally situated in the town centre, Place du Capitole. All the rooms combine space, comfort and practicality, and have been completely renovated. Apart from the usual hotel services there are car and concierge services at your disposal, a customer rep to deal with your requests, a fitness club with jacuzzi and sauna, a business centre and a Wi-Fi system. The Autan-Tic restaurant offers a trendy cuisine with subtle menus and modern à la carte combining regional dishes and exotic flavours. The Grand Patio is a real haven of peace, where you can savour light, summery cooking on a sunny Florentine terrace. Finally, don't miss out the Plaza bar, if you like jazzy ambiance; Tuesday and Thursday are piano bar evenings.

MICHEL SARRAN 21, boulevard Armand-Duportal ✆ 05 61 12 32 32. *Fax : 05 61 12 32 33. Website: www.michel-sarran.com. Set menus from 45 € to 140 €, à la carte 95 €. Closed Saturday and Sunday all day, Wednesday lunchtime, August and Christmas week.* The restaurant everyone's talking about, Midi-Pyrenees' rising star, can be found In Toulouse, outside the historic centre in the business district, and In a rather charmless street. Michel Sarran has been working In this late 19thc. building for 10 years now: at 44 he has already proved himself with Ducasse, Guérard and Lorrain. Though no attention-seeker, he works on, researches, Invents, perfects and serves one of the South West's most Innovative and enthusiastic cuisines. Foie gras Soupe tiède (tepid soup) with Belon oysters, scallops In an allumette feuilleté with sea-urchin cream and Aquitaine caviar, grilled sole fillets and sweet potato purée with hazelnut oil, tomato caramel with salted butter, tarbais beans In emulsion wiith rhum, and marrons glacés, conserved strawberries, caramel and salted butter Ice-cream, cooked cream with cinnamon (Sarran's desserts are some of France's most Innovative and successful). Good humour reigns In the dining-room, the service Is as cheerful as the cooking, and likely to stay that way.

HAUTES-PYRÉNÉES

Argelès-Gazost

LE MIRAMONT *** **44, avenue des Pyrénées ✆ 05 62 97 01 26.** *Website : www.hotelmiramont.com. Open every day. Closed mid-November to mid-December and 10 days in January. 27 rooms (including 2 suites) 58 € to 76 €. See also Les Jardins du Miramont rooms, 52 € to 66 €. Half-board for stays of three nights or longer. Breakfast 8 €. Disabled access. Restaurant closed Wednesday and Sunday evening except in July and August.* This elegant hotel is located in the lower town, near the thermal park. Its rooms are comfortable, spacious and well-equipped. Marcelle Pucheu greets you with warmth, while her son Pierre, a 'young European restaurant-owner' awaits you in the restaurant, Le Casaou (garden in patois). You've a choice of set menus from 19 € (except Sunday and public holiday lunchtimes) to 50 €, with fresh market produce. The Art Deco-style dining room is air-conditioned and as sophisticated as the service. The food is superb, meticulously prepared and well presented. When it comes to the wine, you are invited to broaden your horizons with a world tour: we suggest you try the vin de pays de Bigorre, quite a surprise. Wine is available by the glass for the more abstemious customers. Add a pleasant garden as a finishing touch, and you have a restaurant to recommend in Argelès.

Bagnères-de-Bigorre

L'AUBERGE GOURMANDE 1, boulevard d'Hypéron ✆ 05 62 95 52 01 *Open Wednesday to Sunday evening. Set menus: gourmand 25 €, chef 35 €, gastronomique 50 €.* Located in the heart of Gerde Village, the Auberge Gourmande offers regional gastronomic cuisine with Mediterranean overtones. Monsieur Beal concocts delicious dishes like veal sweetbreads with cepes, or spinach with aniseed calling up visions of Catalan lanscapes.For dessert, don't miss the golden brioche with almond butter, served with salted caramel ice-cream. Friendly atmosphere and efficient service.

Barèges

LA MONTAGNE FLEURIE ** **21, rue Ramon ✆ 05 62 92 68 50.** *Open from mid-December to late March, depending on snow conditions, and from mid-May to mid-October. 14 rooms sleeping 2-4; 44 € for a double. Breakfast 5.50 €. Half-board from 37 €, according to season. Small dogs admitted. Lobby for skis, with a shoe-dryer.* This hotel is 50m from the thermal baths and has been well known since 1924. Today, Fabienne and Jacques Lapeyre welcome you warmly into its family atmosphere. Both furniture and fittings are rustic yet sophisticated, and pleasant to look at. You'll admire the staircase banister running up through three floors, a real *bigourdane* curiosity. The rooms are quiet and restful, all equipped with a lovely bathroom, separate toilet and cupboards. Some of them overlook the mountains and the torrent, le Bastan. The *cuisine* is varied, carefully prepared and served in a pretty dining room. All in all, a great place to unwind.

Capvern-les-Bains

LE MIRAGE ** ✆ **05 62 39 04 13.** *Website : www.lemirage.fr* We were really taken with the Mirage hotel-restaurant, located just near motorway exit 15. To start with, it is beautiful, with top-quality service. Surrounded by gentle countryside, with the Pyrenees as a backdrop, Le Mirage is a remarkable place, firstly for its contemporary architecture outside, and then for the luxury and hushed comfort inside. All 20 rooms are on the garden floor with private terrace and direct access to the park. They have a bathroom, direct phone line, satellite and Canal + TV, Internet access, automatic alarm call...in short, top-of-the-range comfort. The hotel was well designed for meetings and seminars, but also for leisure breaks, with indoor and outdoor pools (the latter offers swimming against the current or in an eddy, on a natural site) a fitness centre, sauna, hammam, solarium, hairdresser and beautician with treatments and massages. After relaxing, you sit down to eat, and discover sophisticated French cuisine, with music if you wish, or a simpler and quicker brasserie formula. In fine weather, all sorts of salads and grills are served round the pool. Who could ask for more? Well, there is one extra detail: Le Mirage is the casino's hotel-restaurant.

Cauterets

HOTEL-RESIDENCE LE LYS Rue de la Féria ✆ **05 62 92 11 11.** *Website : www.hotelresidencelelys.com Studio for 2 from 212 € - 465 €, studio for 4 from 236 € to 599 €, apartment for 5 from 362 € to 818 €: weekly prices. Half-board available for groups.* Right opposite the Cauterets ski-lift and close to shops, this establishment has 70 apartments for rent, with balcony and mountain view. Whether you're on a summer hike or a ski-ing holiday, you'll be very comfortable, with TV, direct phone line and kitchenette at your disposal. You can relax in the jacuzzi, sauna or hammam after a day's hard walking, while the kids play in the garden or games room, or spend the long winter evenings by the fireside with a good book (you can borrow books free of charge from the library). Enjoy your breakfast in bed or in the communal room, and warm up your muscles in the fitness centre before putting on your skis.

Lourdes

GRAND HOTEL DE LA GROTTE **** **66, rue de la Grotte** ✆ **05 62 94 58 87.** *Website : www.hotel-grotte.com Individual room 68 € to 116 €. Suite 230 €.* This hotel is located below the fortified castle and 5 minutes from the sanctuaries, and has an enchanting view of the basilica, park, mountain stream and the mountains themselves. You'll appreciate the comfortable, rather luxurious apartments, suites and rooms decorated in Napoleon III style. As for eating, choose between the traditional gastronomic restaurant with its elegant decor and set menu at 28 €, or the brasserie with its contemporary setting and terrace, set menu 17 € or à la carte. The same family has been running the place for four generations, and are continually updating the standards of comfort.

Saint-Lary-Soulan

LA PERGOLA *** **25, rue Vincent-Mir** ✆ **05 62 39 40 46.** *Website : www.hotellapergola.fr Closed in November and 10 days in May. Open every day. 20 rooms from 60 €. Breakfast 9 €. 3 family residences (sleeps 3-4) from 80 €. Private car park. Set menus 21 € to 38 €. Seminars. Ski and bike lockup. No admittance for animals.* La Pergola is on the edge of Neouvielle national park and nature reserve; an exceptional setting in the heart of the tourist sites, for summer breaks, and the snowy slopes for winter sports. The hotel gained its third star after a lot of renovation work, and is also recognised by the Tables Gourmandes des Sites Pyreneans, and well known at a national level. Only two of the department's establishments have the *Hotellerie de charme et de caractere en Midi-Pyrenees* label, La Pergola and Le Lion d'Or at Cauterets. The rooms are well equipped with TV, Internet, hair-dryer, and terrace or balcony. The chef cooks superb portions with great care, and you can expect both quality and quantity in two restaurants: L'Enclos des Saveurs, open evenings, Sunday lunchtime and public holidays; a sophisticated *cuisine*, or La Pergola, closed Monday and Tuesday lunchtime, and offering typical regional cooking. The menu changes and develops. The terrace and small adjoining garden, with its deck chairs, are extremely pleasant. The Pergola team will make sure you have an excellent stay in these peaceful surroundings. Not to be missed.

Tarbes

L'AMBROISIE 48, rue Abbé-Torné ✆ **05 62 93 09 34.** *Website : www.perso.wanadoo.fr/lambroisie. Set menus 34 € to 70 €, 24 € weekday lunchtimes. À la carte.* Housed in the Tarbes bishopric's former presbytery, L'Ambroisie is the only Michelin star in the department (it also has two stars in the Bottin Gourmand). Daniel Labarrere cooks dishes dear to his heart, that vary with the seasons: the flowers, vegetables and fine herbs come from his garden. The maitre d'hotel watches over the dining room with an expert eye, while the chef's creations waft under your nose: scallops with green grapefruit and chicory fondue, in a lime sauce, roast woodpigeon in an onion and olive *pissaladière* (a Provençal vesion of pizza) deglazed with its own olive juice, *Chibouste* (a pastry cream confection) *au gratin* with caramel, pear pieces and mint syrup. It's hard to know what to recommend; the 'menu gourmand' is served with 4 main dishes, a cheese platter and 2 desserts, composed according to the season and the moment's inspiration. The cellar is well stocked and affordable even for modest budgets. As an occasional treat it's much less expensive than you would think, especially the set menus. What's more, Daniel Labarrere has fitted out two luxurious rooms at 95 €. Book yourself into a great night.

HOTEL HENRI IV * 7, avenue Bertrand-Barère © 05 62 34 01 68.** *24 rooms including 2 suites from 58 € to 98 €. Breakfast 7 €. Closed garage 6 €. Indoor garden, lift. 24 rooms including 2 suites from 60 € to 98 €. Breakfast 8 €. Closed garage 6 €. Indoor garden, lift.* The Henri IV is one of Tarbes' hotels of character. 20 or 30 years ago, it was the only hotel in town with 3 stars, and all those celebrities who've stayed in the Bigorre capital know it well. Ask for the visitors' book out of curiosity, and you'll see all the famous signatures. Today, its charm and beauty are still in evidence: just take a look at the facade. Inside, the hotel is exquisite, the rooms are sound-proofed with bathroom, hair-dryer, direct phone line, mini-bar, TV, Canal +, Canal Satellite and Internet plugs. One of the best hotels in town, and a safe bet.

LOT

Cahors

LE BALANDRE 5 avenue Charles-de-Freycinet © 05 65 53 32 00 *Fax: 05 65 53 32 26. Website: www.balandre.com Set menus 57 € to 85 €, à la carte 65 €. Closed on Sunday, Monday and the second week in November.* This restaurant is housed in the comfortable Hotel Terminus (close to the station) and so tends to go unnoticed. There is no arrogant facade, no huge park around the building, no mediatised chef: Gilles Marre and the staff work from day to day with the same modesty and seriousness. Gilles is a fervent supporter of his local cuisine and regional gastronomy, and it shows: Tarbais beans cooked in walnut oil in a vinaigrette stock, black pudding and bacon ravioli, duck foie gras duo, home-made chutney and toasted *croustilot*, macaroni stuffed with cepe and crayfish mousse, *au gratin*, pigeon supreme with the thighs *en caillette*, potato and cepe *rostie*, and a roquefort *mendiant* with salad. The service is kindly, managed with tact and distinction by Laurent, the chef's brother.

Gramat

LE LION D'OR * 8, place de la République © 05 65 38 73 18.** *Website: www.liondorhothel.com. 15 rooms from 50 € to 85 €. À la carte: 40 €. Shady terrace under the vine. Dogs admitted.* This imposing three-storey residence in Gramat Grande Place conceals treasures. The magnificent dining-room is a perfect setting for Jerome Roseau, trained for years in Michelin-starred establishments. His cuisine is top of the range, regional yet evolutive, and follows the seasons with his own personal touch, served with the best crus in Cahors country. Don't miss the chef's speciality: lobster tagine with Albenque truffles and bourbon vanilla. The Lion d'Or is also a 3-star hotel with air-conditioned, fully equipped rooms.

Lacave

LE PONT DE L'OUYSSE © 05 65 37 87 04. *FAX: 05 65 32 77 41. Website: www.lepontdelouysse.fr Set menus from 46 € to 120 €, à la carte 70 €. Closed all day Monday in early and late season, otherwise Monday and Tuesday lunchtime. Annual closing 15 November-early March.* This Lot village boasts not only the Pont de l'Ouysse but also the Chateau de la Treyne (see opposite), making it the only community of its size to possess two remarkable restaurants since Lourmarin lost Edouard Loubet. Daniel Chambon has been settled in this family house for 30 years, and we recommend you book an evening in each place. The menu is regional but light, and promises moments of sheer pleasure while you are enjoying the beauties of the site and the splash of the river. Duck foie gras pan-fried with asparagus, duck juices with balsamic vinegar and truffles, bass roast in its skin with artichokes and tomato conserve, braised sweetbread tournedos, langoustine tail with spinach and lemon butter, warm apple tart and orange butter, caramel sauce and cinnamon ice-cream. The attractive cellar has everything, and competent Patrick Limonta gives you excellent advice. Kindly and efficient service.

CHATEAU DE LA TREYNE © 05 65 27 60 60. *Fax: 05 65 27 60 70. Website: www.chateaudelatreyne.com. Set menus from 43 € to 120 €, à la carte 100 €. Close Tuesday to Friday lunchtime and mid-November to late March.* Despite getting off to a tricky start two years ago, Stephane Andrieux finally stayed faithful to this splendid chateau overlooking the Dordogne, and continues to amuse himself in the kitchens of this ultra-select establishment (if the beautiful site, majestic chateau, formal park and 120 ha. forest aren't enough to convince you that this is no simple tourist canteen, just count the huge cars competing with their gleaming chrome in the car park). The cooking is absolutely classic, embodying the image of great French cuisine lightly touched up with modernity that foreigners tend to have: chicken soup with milk and truffles, duck foie gras from the Lot en cocotte, salsify, raisins and wild pear, cooking juices with Montbazillac, scallop shortbread with parsley butter and cepes, parsley root, roast venison cuts, *bricelet* (small waffle) with green cabbage, pan-fried chanterelles and chestnuts in their juice, assortment of 'Grand Cru' chocolate (served as a log and in tube shapes) with mandarin sorbet. You'll experience castle highlife, at least for a few hours!

Loubressac

RELAIS DE CASTELNAU*05 65 10 80 90.** *Website: www.relaisdecastelnau.com.* Open from 1 April-1 November. Closed Sunday evening and Monday from April-October. 40 rooms from 60 € to 100 €. Menus from 15 € to 45 €. À la carte. The village is built on a headland; from the panoramic restaurant you can admire the valley, hills, towers and two castles, including the magnificent Castelnau fortress. Needless to say, the rooms also benefit from this natural environment. Thierry welcomes you in the cool, light, pastel-coloured dining room. Laurent is in the kitchen. He's a champion with fish, being from Brittany, but he also cooks local Quercy dishes to perfection, and his suppliers are excellent local producers. The wine list features some fine Cahors millesimes.

Martel

RELAIS SAINTE-ANNE ***05 65 37 40 56. *Website: www.relais-sainte-anne.com Closed during the winter until March. 16 rooms from 70 € to 245 € (suites).* This restful place is housed in a former 19thc. religious boarding-school for young girls. A magnificent flower garden planted with trees offers peace and intimity unspoilt by the swimming pool, carefully placed a short distance away. The rooms are as comfortable as you could wish. The sumptuous breakfast is served in a room opening onto the park (notice the majestic fireplace), or on a sunny terrace. Once a year in summer, the hotel organises a concert.

Mercuès

CHATEAU DE MERCUES **** ✆ **05 65 20 00 01** *Annual closing from November to Easter. Closed Monday, Tuesday, Wednesday and Thursday lunchtime. 24 rooms from 170 € to 260 € and 6 suites from 270 € to 400 €, for 2 people. Breakfast in your room 20 €, buffet (dining-room) 22 €. Set menus, renewed every season, from 60 €. À la carte.* Terrace (exceptional view), swimming-pool, tennis courts, formal gardens. Helisurface, car hire. Disabled access. Visit the splendid *chai* (wine storehouse) with tasting sessions in July and August. On a listed site, the former count-bishops of Cahors' summer residence (from the 12thc. onwards) is now a *Relais et Chateau* offering prestigious services in the heart of the Cahors vineyards. In the kitchen, Philippe Combet has kept a zest of Provence in his Mediterranean fish dishes, but Quercy gastronomy is not forgotten, and is served in rustic style, like this loin of Quercy lamb in a bacon *papillote* with roast vegetables. There is a fine choice of Cahors on the wine list and excellent dining room service: carving, *flambèeing*...The rooms are surprising; the one in the tower looks onto a superb roof, and the Bishop's Room has a bronze sundial inlaid in the parquet.

Puy-l'Evêque

LE BELLEVUE *** **Puy-l'Evêque** ✆ **05 65 36 06 60** *Closed 15-30 November and 10 January-10 February. Rooms from 62 € to 87 €. Menu of the day 12.50 € weekdays.* The hotel has 11 rooms available in an ancient, recently modernised building. Christophe Lasmaries exercises his skill in the kitchen, creating gastronomic menus from 25 € to 62 € which are difficult to describe since they change every day. We can safely mention the chestnut *velouté*, though, and the duck *chartreuse* (duck and and cabbage encased in stuffing) with foie gras, since this is traditional fare. There is an excellent wine list based on Cahors. The big, modern dining room is air-conditioned and overlooks the valley with a view of the Lot and a brasserie menu for modest budgets.

Souillac

LA VIEILLE AUBERGE *** **1, rue de la Recège** ✆ **05 65 32 79 43.** *Website: www.la-vieille-auberge.com. Closed Sunday evening and Monday from early January to 31 March. 19 rooms from 55 € to 70 €. Consult our website for promotions. Set menus from 25 € to 65 €. À la carte.* Robert Veril 's cuisine is based on traditional recipes that he develops, mixing and matching flavours in his *coulis* and *papillotes*. He also knows how to get the best out of the sea. For special occasions, the prestige *dégustation* (tasting) menu at 60 € is a must: the chef composes it using four house specialities as a basis. A word to gourmets; the wine list is complete and well balanced, and the desserts personalised.

TARN

Albi

HOSTELLERIE SAINT-ANTOINE** - RESTAURANT COTE JARDIN 17, rue Saint-Antoine ✆ 05 63 54 04 04**. *Fax 05 63 47 10 47. Website : www.saint-antoine-albi.com. Garden. Double rooms from 100 € to 220 €. Breakfast 12 €. Set menus from 24 € No children's menu. Restaurant closed from Saturday lunchtime to Monday lunchtime, and Monday evening in low season.* The Hostellerie Saint-Antoine is a prestigious establishment only a few steps from the Place du Vigan. It was founded in 1734 (one of the first in France!) on the site of a former monastery of the same name. It has been entirely modernised, and offers all the comfort you'd expect from a 4-star hotel: bath, W.C., mini-bar, air-conditioning, and so on. The decor in each room is unique, but they are all luxurious and beautiful, with excellent nights guarranteed. The garden is a carefully preserved haven in the town centre. The restaurant offers a choice of three menus for amateurs of sophisticated flavours. Regional specialities are cooked with delicacy, two examples being the duck foie gras pan-fried with Morello cherry vinegar and the stuffed lamb chop in its own juices with sage and garlic.

LE JARDIN DES QUATRE SAISONS 19, boulevard de Strasbourg ✆ 05 63 60 77 76. *Closed Sunday evening and Monday except for group bookings. Last order taken at 10pm. Set menus between 17 € and 31 €. Children's menu 8 €. Terrace and veranda.* A stone's throw from the Pont Neuf, Muriel and Georges Bermond welcome you in an intimate and tastefully decorated setting. The food is well up to the place's reputation. You'll rediscover the taste of fresh market produce and home-grown flavours in tune with the season: prawn ravioli with truffle velouté, *transparence* d'oranges with Beaumes-de-Venise muscat, seafood pot-au-feu, langoustine *velouté*, salmon fillet cooked in the oven, tomato conserve with clams, warm foie gras with apples, the juices reduced with muscat and sultanas, matured cheeses and wicked desserts like the strawberry *coulis* with sweet wine or the coffee *marnissimo* with gingerbread sauce. "When I'm cooking, I often think about the wine that should go with the dish", says the introduction to the impressive wine list, and it's easy to believe that the chef is passionately keen on his job. Epicurians, amateurs and connoisseurs should book their table and not leave before discovering the list of brandies and whiskies, and the cigar cellar. And indulge with moderation, of course!

Castres

HOTEL RENAISSANCE* 17, rue Victor-Hugo &✆ 05 63 59 30 42. Fax 05 63 72 11 57** *20 rooms from 55 € to 72 €. Breakfast 7 €. Garage 5 €. Short break 70 €. Bar. Air-conditioning. Disabled access. Animals accepted. Carte Bleue and travellers' cheques accepted.* Bathrooms equipped with hair-dryers, direct phone lines in all rooms, Internet connection, satellite TV. You'll really fall for this 17thc. mansion's sophisticated comfort, with its hangings, carpets, rugs, four-poster beds and alcoves.

Cordes-sur-Ciel

LE GRAND ECUYER** Grand-Rue Raymond VII ✆ 05 63 53 79 50.** *Website: www.thuries.fr. Closed from October to Easter. Restaurant closed Monday in high season, every day at lunchtime in low season. Menus from 38 € to 105 €. 13 rooms from 77 € to 151 €. Suite 200 €. Breakfast 11 €. All credit cards accepted. Advance booking recommended.* In 1980 Yves Thuries took over this former hunting lodge, which had been listed Monument Historique in the 19thc. Many feasts must have taken place here before it became the fine example of regional gastronomy it is today. Sophisticated preparation and presentation, exceptional cuisine varying with the seasons, and charming desserts from Jean-Francois Arnaud are the rule. The 12 charming rooms and suite mostly have period four-poster beds and overlook the valley.

Garrevaques

CHATEAU DE GARREVAQUES * ✆ 05 63 75 04 54.** *Website: www.garrevaques.com. Restaurant closed Tuesday and Wednesday. Rooms from 100 € to 200 €. Breakfast 10 €. Restaurant prices from 15 € to 55 €. Tuesday and Wednesday, residents' table from 30 €. Coffee- and tea-making facilities. Rooms for hire (seminars, weddings).Park. Swimming pool. Jacuzzi. Spa. Tennis. Billiards. Disabled access to hotel and spa. Cookery, pottery, bookbinding, language and furniture restoration courses available. English German and Spanish spoken.* The chateau was built in the 15thc. and reshaped after being burnt down during the Revolution, yet it is still in the same family. Mme Barande de Gineste and her daughter Marie-Christine are the descendants of Count Henri de Gineste. Today the chateau contains 8 comfortable rooms, luxurious and genuine - no lifts or TVs! Facing the chateau, in the converted stables with the spa, are 15 more sophisticated rooms, equipped with Internet connection, satellite TV, DVD players, air-conditioning and safe. The former barn (400 sqm.) can be used as a reception or conference room. There are also the steward's pavilion, which holds 12, two restaurants - one regional, the other gastronomic - and a park with 100-year-old trees, which adds the magic touch to weddings and other family celebrations.

Rabastens

LE PRE-VERT ** 54, promenade des Lices © 05 63 33 70 51. *Fax 05 63 33 82 58. Website: www.leprevert.com. Annual closing in January. Restaurant closed Sunday evening and Monday lunchtime. 13 rooms from 34 € to 85 €. Menus from 12 € to 30 €.* The Pre-Vert is housed in a former17thc. mansion. The cuisine is regional, including Tarn ewe's milk curd with chives, pork fillet with turnips and roquefort and knuckle of lamb confit with the famous Lautrec pink garlic.Unless you prefer sweet-and-sour, in which case the duck breast with Gaillac wine confit and pears or aiguillettes (long strips of duck) with ginger caramel are not to be missed. All the pastries and desserts are home made. The hotel offers comfort and sophistication in its 13 rooms. It also offers photography courses for groups of 4 to 8; choose from weekends, a full week or one day, full or half-board.

TARN-ET-GARONNE

Auvillar

HOTEL-RESTAURANT DE L'HORLOGE ** © 05 63 39 91 61. *Closed 8 December - 8 January. Restaurant closed Friday except in July and August, and Friday and Saturday lunchtime from 15 october -15 April. Set menus from 24 € to 65 €. Terrace. 10 rooms from 35 € to 65 €.* There are two establishments in one, to please all kinds of appetite and budget. The bistrot side has à la carte from 5 € to 14 € (except Sunday and public holidays) with salads, grilled meat and a dish of the day. On the gastronomic restaurant side, the chef serves seasonal local produce with ingenuity: aubergine *mille-feuille* and langoustine tartare with grilled, spiced sweetbreads, Marasquin summer fruit simmered in the pan, mascarpone ice-cream, Pyrenean lamb to taste, seasonal starters, lampreys *à la bordelaise*, grilled bass with Nyons olive oil. On fine days, you'll be tempted by the shady terrace under the plane trees.

Moissac

LE PONT-NAPOLEON 2, allées Montebello © 05 63 04 01 55 *FAX: 05 63 04 34 44. Website: www.le-pont-napoleon.com. Set menus from 25 € to 70 €, à la carte 45 €. Closed Sunday (evening only in July and August), Monday and January.* Located at the foot of the famous bridge spanning the Tarn, Michel Dussau's hotel-restaurant would not win any design prizes (the establishment's heavy facade and retro style are rather unattractive) but it could beat all records for conviviality. The difficulties experienced in the kitchens in recent years are a thing of the past, and customers come from far and wide to taste the deserving chef's flavourful cuisine. Free-range poultry tourtelette, braised seasonal vegetables, black Caussade chicken, spit-roasted with braised summer vegetables and meat juices from the carcass, grilled duck breast or duck leg confit, seasonal mushroom garnish and the goose with semi-conserved plums, braised summer vegetables and Quercy croustade with seasonal fruit trilogy. The region's best wines share the cellar (Plageolles or Da Ros to mention the best-known) and the service is relaxed but efficient.

Montauban

HOTEL ORSAY – RESTAURANT LA CUISINE D'ALAIN 31, rue Salengro © 05 63 66 06 66. *Closed 24 December-6 January and 8-23 August. 20 rooms from 47 €. Restaurant closed Saturday lunchtime, Sunday and Monday lunchtime, and public holidays. Private car park and garage (closed). Terrace. Set menus: children's 11 €, lunchtime 23 € wine and coffee included, 32 €, 58 €. Short break prices. Holiday vouchers.* This 2-star hotel is just near the SNCF railway station, and has carpeted, soundproofed and air-conditioned rooms. Fully equipped seminar rooms are available. Alain Blanc, Maitre Cuisinier de France, runs the restaurant, and composes a delicious regional *cuisine* which gives the desserts their due. A pastry trolley appears at the end of the meal; everything on it is terribly tempting and it proves difficult to choose. The dishes aim for sophistication: *tourin* (garlic and goose-fat soup) with white garlic, pan-fried liver escalope with caramelised apples and scallops in a grapefruit salad.

Nord Pas-de-Calais Picardy

Sunset in Authie bay

Dunkerque
Malo-les-Bains
Vers Bruges
Grande-Synthe
Coudekerque-Branche
Calais
Gravelines
Bergues
Hondschoote
Côte d'Opale
Bourbourg
Guemps
Wissant
Guînes
Ardres
Audruicq
Esquelbecq
Wormhout
Watten
Guémy
Marquise
Tournehem-sur-la-Hem
Steenvoorde
Cassel
Wimereux
Boulogne-sur-Mer
Saint-Omer
Arques
Bailleul
Manche
Outreau
Lumbres
Hazebrouck
Armentières
Desvres
Hardelot-Plage
Samer
Thérouanne
Aire-sur-la-Lys
Merville
Pas-de-Calais
Isbergues
Laventie
Haubourdin
Fauquembergues
Norrent-Fontes
Hucqueliers
Lillers
Béthune
La Bassée
Le Touquet-Paris-Plage
Etaples
Maresville
Fruges
Cambrin
Wingles
Heuchin
Douvrin
Montreuil
Fressin
Divion
Barlin
Courrières
Azincourt
Lens
Berck-sur-Mer
Campagne-lès-Hesdin
Le Parcq
Saint-Pol-sur-Ternoise
Liévin
Maintenay
Hesdin
Vimy
Fort-Mahon-Plage
Aubigny-en-Artois
Vron
ARRAS
Rue
Crécy-en-Ponthieu
Frévent
Dainville
Auxi-le-Château
Avesnes-le-Comte
Le Crotoy
Gueschart
Nouvion
Beaumetz-les-Loges
Maizicourt
Lucheux
Cayeux-sur-Mer
Saint-Valery-sur-Somme
Doullens
Pas-en-Artois
Croisilles
Saint-Riquier
Bernaville
Ault
Friville-Escarbotin
Abbeville
Ailly-le-Haut-Clocher
Fienvillers
Beauval
Bapaume
Le Tréport
Fressenneville
Domart-en-Ponthieu
Beauquesne
Acheux-en-Amiénois
Pozières
Vers Dieppe
Canal de la Somme
Puchevillers
Toutencourt
Gamaches
Saint-Maxent
Condé-Folie
Flixecourt
Villers-Bocage
Albert
Combles
Oisemont
Airaines
Flesselles
Franvillers
Bray-sur-Somme
Blangy-sur-Bresle
Picquigny
Querrieu
Péronne
Somme
Camps-en-Amiénois
AMIENS
Corbie
Vers Rouen
Hornoy-le-Bourg
Villers-Bretonneux
Longueau
Liomer
Athies
Boves
Chaulnes
Orival
Saint-Sauflieu
Rosières-en-Santerre
Vers Neufchâtel-en-Bray, Rouen
Poix-de-Picardie
Moreuil
Nesle
Ailly-sur-Noye
Conty
Flers-sur-Noye
Roye
Formerie
Feuquières
Grandvilliers
Montdidier
Seine-Maritime
Breteuil
Crèvecœur-le-Grand
Vers Forges-les-Eaux, Dieppe
Marseille-en-Beauvaisis
Noyers-Saint-Martin
Maignelay-Montigny
Lassigny
Songeons
Cuvilly
Elincourt-Sainte-Marguerite
Crillon
Juvignies
Oise
Ribécourt
Thérain
Saint-Just-en-Chaussée
Bulles
BEAUVAIS
Fouquerolles
Remy
Compiègne
Saint-Germer-de-Fly
Etouy
Estrées-Saint-Denis
Allonne
Bresles
Clermont
Auneuil
Flavacourt
Noailles
Liancourt
Verberie
Trie-le-Château
Mouy
Morienval
Nogent-sur-Oise
Les Ageux
Béthisy-Saint-Martin
Sainte-Geneviève
Crépy-en-Valois
Eure
Chaumont-en-Vexin
Villeneuve-les-Sablons
Méru
Montataire
Creil
Précy-sur-Oise
Senlis
Serans
Lierville
Chantilly
Betz
Ermenonville
Nanteuil-le-Haudouin
Val-d'Oise
Vers Paris
Vers Paris
Vers Paris
Vers Paris
Vers Paris
Le Plessis-Belleville
Vers Meaux
Hauts-de-Seine
Yvelines
PARIS
Seine-Saint-Denis
Seine-et-Marne

NORD PAS-DE-CALAIS PICARDIE
Autoroute
Nationale 4 voies
Nationale
Départementale
Préfecture
Sous-préfecture
Ville, village
Sortie d'autoroute
Aéroport
Forêt domaniale
BELGIQUE
Vers Gand
Vers Tournai
Vers Bruxelles
Vers Mons
Vers Dinant
Vers Chimay, Couvin
Vers Charleville-Mézières
Vers Rethel
Vers Reims
Vers Reims, Strasbourg
Vers Épernay
Vers Montmirail, Sézanne
Vers Meaux
Tourcoing
Wattrelos
Roubaix
Villeneuve-d'Ascq
Cysoing
Orchies
Marchiennes
Saint-Amand-les-Eaux
Vieux-Condé
Anzin
Valenciennes
Somain
Denain
Bouchain
Nord
Bavay
Maubeuge
Hautmont
Le Quesnoy
Berlaimont
Solre-le-Château
Cambrai
Carnières
Solesmes
Avesnes-sur-Helpe
Caudry
Le Cateau-Cambrésis
Landrecies
Eppe-Sauvage
Trélon
Le Nouvion-en-Thiérache
Fourmies
Wassigny
Oisy
Le Catelet
Bohain-en-Vermandois
Etreux
La Capelle
Hirson
Saint-Michel
Fresnoy-le-Grand
Guise
Etréaupont
Lesdins
Saint-Quentin
Sains-Richaumont
Vervins
Aubenton
Gauchy
Origny-Sainte-Benoite
Le Hérie-la Viéville
Seraucourt-le-Grand
Ribemont
Brunehamel
Rozoy-sur-Serre
Marle
Crécy-sur-Serre
Montcornet
Tergnier
La Fère
Bucy-lès-Pierrepont
Liesse-Notre-Dame
Dizy-le-Gros
Chauny
Saint-Gobain
Crépy
Athies-sous-Laon
Ardennes
Sinceny
LAON
Sissonne
Coucy-le-Château
Anizy-le-Château
Saint-Erme-Outre-et-Ramecourt
Lor
Urcel
Epagny
Chavignon
Corbeny
Neufchâtel-sur-Aisne
Vailly-sur-Aisne
Soissons
Beaurieux
Berry-au-Bac
Bourg-et-Comin
Braine
Aisne
Hartennes-et-Taux
Chéry-Chartreuve
Oulchy-le-Château
Fère-en-Tardenois
Marne
Neuilly-saint-Front
Coincy
Le Charmel
Château-Thierry
Crézancy
La Chapelle-Monthodon
Charly-sur-Marne
Condé-en-Brie
Nogent-l'Artaud
Artonges
Viels-Maisons
0
30 km
Reproduction interdite
Jean-Baptiste Nény
Mars 2006

LILLE

This lively European capital, Flemish in feeling, lies at the hub of an extensive communication network. The best time to come is the first weekend in September, when the famous braderie takes place, probably the biggest flea-market in Europe. Strolling through Lille, you discover the beautiful stones of its 17thc. faÁades, which take on a festive air in the sunlight.

LILLE BELFRY. *Currently closed to visitors.* The bell tower, built between 1924 and 1932 by the architect Dubuisson, is 105 metres high. Climb its 100 steps to the top, then get your breath back while admiring a view of 50 km round. This unique panorama of the capital of Flanders and its surroundings is not for vertigo sufferers!

NOTRE-DAME DE LA TREILLE CATHEDRAL Place Gilleson. ✆ 03 20 31 59 12. Building started on this neo-Gothic church in the middle of the 19thc. and was finished in for the time being in 1947. The main faÁade has only just been completed, by an amazing marble veil. The rose window at the top and the door at the bottom are its only decoration.

CITADELLE Avenue du 43e-Régiment-d'Infanterie. Built by Vauban on existing fortifications, the 'queen of citadels' is the biggest and one of the best kept-up in France, hence its nickname.

PLACE DU GENERAL DE GAULLE. This historic square is always teeming with life. It was the scene of various shows of force by the German armies, and of Gustave Delory's funeral in 1925. The mythical Big Wheel is set up here at Christmas, to the delight of children and adults alike.

PETIT QUINQUIN Square Foch. At the entrance to the square, a poor lacemaker is trying to lull her baby to sleep. The baby is none other than the Petit Quinquin, from Alexandre Desrousseaux's anthem of the same name, written in local dialect in 1853. Eugène Déplechin's statue commemorates this illustrious character.

PALAIS DES BEAUX-ARTS 18bis, rue de Valmy ✆ 03 20 06 78 00. *Closed on Tuesdays. Open Monday: 2pm-6pm, Friday: 10am-7pm, other days: 10am -6pm. Admission: 4.60 € (adult) 3 € (child); yearly subscriptions: single 18.60 € , concessions 10.80 € , double 27.90 € , young person 10.80 € , family 38.80 €* . Built in the 19thc., the Fine Arts museum contains Dutch and Flemish paintings from the 15th to the 17thc. (Rubens, Van Dyck), Spanish (Goya), French (David, Delacroix, Monet, Renoir) and Italian collections. There are also historical collections (Middle Ages, Renaissance plans in relief of fortified towns) pottery and drawings.

The coal mines

It may not be tourism in the usual sense of the word, but these grass-covered slag heaps are a moving reminder of past industry, and a way of life now gone for ever.

Early deposits were discovered in the Hainaut, near Valenciennes and Douai, in the 18thc., but they were surface deposits, and easily reached. The Industrial Revolution brought the mining craze, and with it the first boring and sampling attempts. This research was fruitless for a long time, but in 1846, 'black manna' was discovered at Oignies in the Artois Basin.

The first mine shafts were dug, and rudimentary working methods were progressively modernised. For the miners, it was a dangerous job, with a risk of firedamp, rock fall, walls caving in, and fatal accidents. The whole family worked at the mine, and could earn a decent living: the men went down the pit, the women cleaned and maintained the lamps, and the children, known as galibots, wriggled into the corners that were hard to reach, and worked diligently until they were old enough to go down the pit and dig for coal themselves. The mine owners realised that a profitable yield depended on the workers' wellbeing, and built the famous corons, communities of back-to-back brick houses where the miners and their families lived.

Little by little, life developed, with shops and bistrots opening up around these streets. The local festivals involved everyone, and were great annual events. The mining industry survived through booms and slumps until the 1970s. By then, 7 to 8 metric tons of coal were being brought up per day, compared with only one in the early 1900s. Working practices had changed, and the miners were more often specialised workers, or technicians manipulating mechanical diggers. With progress came unemployment, and by the early 1980s the situation was critical: foreign competition with lower production costs had destroyed the profitability of Northern French mines. The last mine closed on 21 December 1990 at Oignies, where the story began - a story that cannot fail to strike a chord in the hearts of visitors from across the Channel.

MUSEE DE LA MAISON NATALE DU GENERAL DE GAULLE 9, rue Princesse © 03 28 38 12 05. *www.maison-natale-degaulle.org. Open every day except Monday, Tuesday and public holidays: 10am-12 noon and 2pm-5pm. Undergoing restoration work until June 2005. Admission: adults 5 € , concessions 3 € , free for the under-9s.* De Gaulle's birthplace houses a collection of documents and personal belongings.

LEWARDE HISTORIC MINING CENTRE Fosse-Delloye - LEWARDE © 03 27 95 82 82. *Open all year. Admission: adult 9.90 € to 10.90 €.* Built on an 8 hectare site, over a former pit, this is the biggest mining museum in France. Ex-miners guide you through the salle des pendus, or cloakroom, lamp store, tavern and stables, then you travel on through 450m of galleries and coalface in the pit train. This museum is one of the region's most popular sites, so it's a good idea to book ahead.

MUSEE DES CANONNIERS Rue des Urbanistes © 03 20 55 58 90. *Open mid-February to mid-December (except first three weeks in August) Monday-Saturday: 2pm-5pm. Admission: adult 5 €.* This Gunners' Museum is housed in an 18thc. wing of the former Urbanist Sisters' convent, and contains over 1,500 collector's items illustrating five centuries of battalion history. It was set up in 1849 around General Negrier's cenotaph, and traces the lives of the Lille Gunners, created in 1483. Among the chief exhibits are two out of the three remaining Gribeauval cannons; the third is at Les Invalides in Paris.

Roubaix

The industrial revolution brought prosperity to this simple weavers' community, which lasted until the textile crisis in the mid-20th century. Today it is the capital of the mail-order business, which thrives among the building sites that are a sign of cultural renewal, and the tall buildings that even Lille cannot rival.

There are several remarkable monuments typical of an early 20thc. eclecticism aiming to fuse the most important architectural styles. Places to see are the Town Hall, built by Victor Laloux, the architect who designed Orsay station in Paris, and Pierre Cateau's mansion, built by an industrial group.

HOTEL DE VILLE 17, Grand-Place. A visit to Roubaix starts with the magnificent Town Hall, opened in 1911. A 2.4-metre frieze decorates the faÁade, its 40 characters demonstrating the different stages of textile manufacturing.

MUSEE D'ART ET D'INDUSTRIE/ SWIMMING POOL Rue de l'Espérance © 03 20 69 23 60. *Open Tuesday to Thursday: 11am-6pm, Friday: 11am-8pm, Saturday and Sunday: 11 am-6pm. Closed on Monday and some public holidays. Admission: adults 5 € , free for the under-18s..* Former swimming pool, now a museum with an avant-garde programme presenting town history and economics, the textile industry and fashion.

Tourcoing

This busy town is centered on its Town Hall, an early 19thc. building which is a rather heavy blend of various influences. It replaced the first Town Hall built a century earlier in a more elegant style, with

Lille, Grand'Place

a pinnacle. Saint Christophe neo-Gothic Church (13th- 16thc.) has just been restored; there is some beautiful stained glass and a church bell museum (open the first and third Sunday of the month from May to October, 2pm-6pm).

MUSEE DES BEAUX-ARTS 2, rue Paul-Doumer ✆ 03 20 28 91 60. *www.musenor.com. Open every day except Tuesday and public holidays, 1.30pm-6pm. Admission free.* Works of classic and contemporary art are shown to advantage in this interesting art gallery.

Villeneuve-d'Ascq

The first French New Town, created in 1970 by merging three communities: Ascq, Anappes and Flers. Flers Chateau was built in 1661, and acquired by the Lords of Flers. It is typically Flemish in style, with brick walls and stone seams, and has belonged to the town since 1970. It houses the Tourist Office, an archeological museum and temporary exhibitions.

MUSEE D'ART MODERNE 1, allée du Musée ✆ 03 20 19 68 68. *Open (except Tuesday): 10am-6pm. Admission: adult 6.50 €*. This museum was opened in 1983, and contains a permanent exhibition of significant works by great 20thc. artists (Braque, Picasso, Modigliani, Miro).

DUNKERQUE AND FLANDERS

With its North Sea, forests and hills, bordering on Belgium, beautiful Flanders has inspired great artists.

Dunkerque

This important industrial town is the country's third port, with its dockyards, refineries and harbour where giant ships of 300,000 to 450,000 tonnes put in. It was bought from the English in 1662 by Louis XIV, whose corsair Jean Bart (France's saviour) was born here. The town was almost totally wiped out by bombing during the last war.

BELFRY. The belfry was put up in 1440, and by a miracle was not destroyed in the 1940 bombing. The bells date from 1962 - the great bell Jean Bart weighs 7 tonnes - and they chime the 'Jean Bart cantata' every hour on the hour. Climb to the sixth floor for a view of the town from 58 metres up.

HOTEL DE VILLE. A rather solid building with a 75-metre-high belfry, put up in the late 19thc. and partially destroyed during the war.

MUSEE DES BEAUX ARTS Place du Général de Gaulle ✆ 03 28 66 21 65. *Open Monday to Sunday: 10am to 12.15pm and 1.45pm to 6pm. Closed on Tuesday, 25 December, 1 January, 1 May and 1 November. Admission: adult 4.50 €* This contemporary building in a central square contains paintings from the French, Italian and Northern schools, plus scale models of warships and some precious gold and earthenware objects. In the basement is a reconstruction of the Battle of Dunkerque.

Villeneuve-d'Ascq, mills

DUNKERQUE GOLF COURSE Route du Golf ✆ 03 28 61 07 43. *Website: www.golf-dk.com – email: golf@golf-dk.com. 210 €-945 € to enrol, depending on the type of subscription and players' ages, plus a 25 €-55 € green fee (18 holes).* The Tourist Pass, available from the Dunes de Flandre Tourist Office, gives you reductions in the green fee. November-March: 9am-6pm every day, opens 8.30am at weekends. April-October: 8.30am-7pm every day, opens 8am. at weekends.

Dunquerque golf course has been laid out inside Vauban's fortifications, Fort Valieres.The pleasant setting is green and hilly, with plenty of water obstacles, and greens open all year. The club house provides a friendly and relaxed atmosphere where players can meet. There are two covered practice courses for beginners and experienced players, in case of rain (not unusual in this part of France). A yearly subscription is financially advantageous, since you no longer have to pay an entrance fee.

Flanders

Bergues

This quiet little coastal town was reinforced successively by Baudouin the Bald, Guy de Dampierre and Philippe the Bold, then fortified by Vauban. The poet Lamartine was MP for Bergues at the end of the last century.

BELFRY Place Henri Billiaert. *Admission: 2 € per person, 1 € half price and groups.* Though built quite recently, this is one of the town's chief attractions, with its 193 steps leading to the top, 47 metres up. Well, almost the top, for safety's sake.

MUSEE LE MONT DE PIETE 1, rue du Mont-de-Piété ✆ 03 28 68 13 30. *Open every day except Tuesday: 10am-12 noon and 2pm-5pm.* The 17thc. Mont-de-Piete (pawnbrokers'), designed by Wenceslas Cobergher, houses collections of objects recalling the past, some inherited from Lamartine. There are also paintings from the great Flemish schools of the 17th and 19thc., and from regional studios. Saint Winoc Tower deserves a visit, as does the bird sanctuary near the canal. This pretty town is a listed holiday resort, with fishing on the banks of the Colme.

Cassel

The Romans built a fortified town here, at the junction of seven roads. Today, with its fine paved square and attractive site, Cassel deserves to be called the prettiest town in Flanders.

CASTEEL MEULEN. *Open all year at weekends and during school holidays: 10am to 6pm, guided tours for groups every day by reservation only.* The original castle windmill, one of many in the area, burned down in 1911, leaving only the big stone used to attach the sails. The current 18thc. mill, known as Moulin Ruytoor, was brought 7km from neighbouring Arneke in 1947. The miller explains how the mill works and the flour is made. Places to see: the ancient Notre Dame Collegiate Church, first built before the 11thc. Close to the town, the 16th century Roome windmill at Terdeghem, preserved and worked by an association that organises guided tours (Tel: 03 28 43 35 81).

Steenwerk

At the foot of the Flanders hills, not far from Lille, La Gorgue, Nieppe, Sailly sur la Lys and Steenwerk stretch out along the River Lys. The local Tourist Office groups them together and offers activities based on the valley's traditions and environment. Time stands still in the old towns full of architectural treasures, and the museums house a rich and authentic heritage.

SAINT JEAN BAPTISTE CHURCH Grand'Place. This church was rebuilt after the Great War. Its font dates back to 1567, and the fine stained glass windows illustrate Saint John the Baptist's life.

NOTRE DAME DES SEPT DOULEURS CHURCH La Croix du Bac. The parishioners had this church built, and it houses 27 statues of saints, either the patron saints of guilds, or those known to be healers.

MAISON FLAMANDE Rue de Nieppe ✆ 03 28 44 20 04. Admire the fine, neo-Gothic exterior of this 19thc. Flemish house, designed by the architect who restored the monuments in Bruges.

HAINAUT

The history of this ancient province is bound up with its mines, and its strong commercial traditions, which led to the industrial development of its towns.

Cambrai

Cambrai is chiefly famous for three things: a sweet known as the Bétise (silliness), andouillette a la fraise de veau (calf's caul chitterling sausage) and handkerchiefs.

MUSEE MUNICIPAL 15, rue de l'Epée ✆ 03 27 82 27 90. *www.villedccambrai.com. Open every day except Monday and Tuesday: 10am-12 noon and 2pm-6pm, guided tours by reservation. Admission: adults 3 € , 6 to 18s 2 €* . This functional and educational museum in the Hôtel de Francqueville houses collections of archeology and French, Flemish and Dutch paintings. There is a local heritage section with an audiovisual presentation of the town's history, a fibreoptic relief layout and works of art from monuments destroyed during various wars. Other places to see: the belltower with its 31 bells, the remains of Charles V's citadel built from 1543 (royal gate and Balagny arsenal) and the Ch,teau de Selles, with its 13thc. wall; all that is left of the former fortifications put up by the Count, Bishop of Cambrai.

Douai

Douai, ancient capital of Flanders, is a historic and artistic town as well as a centre of the textile industry. It kept its layout and noble 18thc. residences throughout the 1940 bombing. The famous belfry (1380-1475) houses 62 bells and rises to a height of 54 metres including its steeple with the 50kg Lion of Flanders weathercock on the top. There is a fine view over the town.

MUSEE DE LA CHARTREUSE 130, rue des Chartreux ✆ 03 27 71 38 80. *www.musenor.org. Open every day except Tuesday: 10am-12 noon and 2pm-6pm. Groups by reservation only. Admission: adults 3 € , groups of 15 or more, 1.50 €* . This former Carthusian convent built of 16th and 17thc. brick and stone has a striking cloister, refectory and chapter house. Among the remarkable collections it houses are Northern School reredos, Flemish Renaissance paintings and French and Italian works (Veronese, Carrache).

Valenciennes

Valenciennes was formerly known for its mines and steelworks, but also for cloth and lace. The town began to specialise in lacemaking with FranÁois Badar, from the 17thc. onwards. The painter Watteau, the chronicler Froissart and the father of advertising Jean Mineur were all born here. The town has been nicknamed 'The Athens of the North' because of its artistic tradition dating back to the late 18thc., when the Académie des Beaux-Arts was founded. The school has since produced fifty or so winners of the Prix de Rome.

MUSEE DES BEAUX-ARTS Boulevard Watteau ✆ 03 27 22 57 20. *www.valenciennes.fr. Open every day except Tuesday: 10am-6pm, Thursday until 8pm. Admission: adult 3.50 to 4.50 €, concessions 1.75 €* . Valenciennes Museum was built in the early 20th century, and is a spacious building with monumental proportions ideal for showing its prestigious collection. This starts with Gallo-Roman archeology and ends in the 20th century, including 17thc. Flemish painting and great works of 19thc. sculpture.The museum has a conference room, shop, educational rooms and even a place to relax, the Cafe Carpeaux.

AISNE

This rural department with its traditional houses and magnificent landscapes has had its moments in French history.

Château-Thierry

The southern part of the Aisne offers a range of pleasures, from champagne, produced in the Marne valley and Tardenois plateaux, to literature, with souvenirs of Paul Claudel and La Fontaine at the Ch,teaux de Condé-en-Brie and Fère-en-Tardenois.

Ch,teau-Thierry boasts medieval remains such as the Saint Pierre and Saint Jean Gates (13th-14thc.) Balhan Tower (12thc.) reached by a genuine spiral staircase, and the ch,teau (11th-13thc.), which retains traces of its fortifications. There are medieval activities in summer.

MUSEE JEAN DE LA FONTAINE 12, rue Jean de la Fontaine ✆ 03 23 69 05 60. *Open every day except Tuesday: 9am-12 noon and 2pm-6pm, from April to September: 10am-12pm and 2pm-5pm from October to March. Admission: adults 3.50 € , 6 to 18s 1.60 €* . Housed in the author's birthplace, this collection comprises documents, old editions, engravings and 17th to 20thc. paintings concerning La Fontaine, his life and times. He was born in 1621, spent his early life here, and the surroundings inspired his animal fables.

GOLF DU VAL SECRET Le Val Secret ✆ 03 23 83 07 25. *Fax: 03 23 83 92 73. Website: www.golfvalsecret.com – email: accueil@golfvalsecret.com – 18 holes. Par 72 from 5,703m. Architect Paul Lenaerts (1984). Record round 64 Laurent Percherancier. Green-fee (one week) 31 €, weekend 46 €. Small car 22 €. All-in price including green-fee + meal (weekdays) 46 €, weekend 58 €. No basic level requested for beginners. Pro-shop and golfers' meals in the club. Slope markers: white gentlemen 141, yellow gentlemen 133, blue ladies 132, red ladies 115.* The golf course was built on the site of the former Val Secret Abbey. Today, only one farm building remains, now turned into the clubhouse. The first 9 holes were laid out in 1987, then another 9 added in 1994. The whole course is short but technical, being hilly and wooded; the holes are named after characters from La Fontaine's fables. Number 7 is the Stag, par 5 (406m) with an elevated green, which must be played to the left. Number 10 is the Heron, par 4 (305m), with a slight dog-leg to the left and a pretty pond to cross - the ideal place to take a superb photo late on an autumn afternoon. Careful of the out-of-bounds on the right, and the glittering water with its jumping carp and mocking ducks! Then comes Number 13, The Fly?, par 3 (167m) with a high start and elevated green, very long, shallow and rolling. After your round, Bruno Regnard offers a golfer's menu at 20 € in the clubhouse, and a cold buffet. The 3-star Hotel Ile-de-France (03 23 69 10 12) 1.5km away, and the Hotel Campanile (03 23 69 23 23) less than 1km, will put you up for the night.

Chemin des Dames

The Great War has fixed this name in our memories, like Verdun and Douaumont. It actually comes from the 18th century, when Louis XV's daughters took this path to visit their wetnurse. The route runs between Malmaison Fort and the National Tank Monument at Berry-au-Bac, through stone quarries which sheltered combatants. Like a modern Lascaux, the walls are covered in 'cave paintings' left by these soldiers. Along the path you re-live a sombre episode of history via thematic panels illustrated by documents of the period.

Condé-en-Brie

CHATEAU DE CONDE - DEMEURE DES PRINCES ✆ **03 23 82 42 25**. *www.chateauconde.com. Open 15 April to 15 October, every day except Monday: 2.30pm-5pm. Admission: adults 9 € , 6-12s 3.60 €* . The castle is privately owned, listed and lived-in all year round. It was sumptuously decorated in the 17th and 18thc. by Watteau, Boucher, Oudry and other prestigious artists, at the request of the Bourbons, the Princes of Savoy and the Marquis de la Faye. A family visit is fun, with lead soldiers, educational games and a treasure hunt in the park for the kids.

Guise

The Guise family was determined to make their home one of the best fortified in the realm, and one of the most spacious and elegant in Renaissance Europe. The region was well defended by a network of fortified churches, and Vauban worked on the fortress, which came under State ownership and was gradually given over to the army (the title of Duc de Guise did not include the ch,teau). The worst damage inflicted on this castle was ironically from French bombs in 1917, when the town was freed from German occupation.

CHATEAU Club du Vieux-Manoir ✆ **03 23 61 11 76**. *http://Ch,teaudeguise.free.fr. Closed between Christmas Day and New Year's Day. Open every day: 10am-12 noon and 2pm-7pm (5pm in winter, 6pm in spring). Admission: adults 5 € , 8 to 14s 2 €* . Admire the listed 12thc. keep, visit the subterranean passages and blockhouses, inspect the 3-D plan with its thousand figurines. The 17-hectare site houses an archaeological museum.

FAMILISTERE DE GODIN ✆ **03 23 61 11 76**. *Open every day from 1 April to 31 October, guided tour at 2.30pm and 4.30pm. >From November to March, open on Saturday, guided tour at 2.30pm and 4.30pm, and Sunday, at 3pm. Admission: 4 € , free for the under-10s.* The 'familistere' was an ambitious undertaking: a workers' housing estate of more than 2 000 people, where the families wre helped from birth to bring up their children. In 1862 Godin's ideas, though utopian, still had an impact on the public education system. The project's historic, human and sociological dimension can be felt on the premises, which are now deservedly part of French cultural heritage.

La Ferté-Milon

The Ferté has two reasons to be proud: Louis d'Orléans' unfinished ch,teau and Jean Racine, who no doubt felt the first stirrings of tragedian talent in his native town. You can still stroll along the Ourcq and the canal; the island between them is called the Mail. The iron bridge linking it to the Hericart property (where La Fontaine got married) was the work of an unknown designer called Gustave Eiffel.

MUSEE JEAN RACINE 2, rue des Bouchers ✆ 03 23 96 77 77. *Open early April to late October, on Saturdays, Sundays and public holidays: 10am-12.30pm and 3pm- 5.30pm. Admission: adult 4 € , child 2 €* . Racine lived with his grandmother in this house, which contains valuable documents and objects, like the sculptor David d'Angers' marble statue.

Laon

Laon has often marked French history since Charlemagne, and the town's historic and religious renown can be seen in its architecture, and its extensive conservation area. Victor Hugo said "A Laon, tout est beau".

Places to see: first, Notre Dame Cathedral, Primitive Gothic in style (1155-1235) with its five historiated towers and sumptuous interior (organs, stained glass). The magnificent quarter with its Canons' Cloister was redesigned in the 12th and 13thc. Saint Remi Church was rebuilt in the 1500s, then destroyed in the 19thc.; only part of it remains.

MUSEE D'ART ET D'ARCHEOLOGIE 32, rue Georges-Ermant ✆ 03 23 20 19 87. *Open every day except Monday: 11am- 6pm June to September, and 2pm-6pm October to May. Admission: adult 3.30 € , child 2.45 €* . This museum in the old town houses regional and Mediterranean archeology, including Egyptian antiquities; a superb collection of Greek vases; 15th and 19thc. paintings with the famous Annunciation reredos, sculpture and furniture.

Saint-Quentin

Named after a 3rdc. martyr, Saint Quentin was destroyed in 1917. The town's principle style is therefore Art Deco, contrasting with medieval Laon, although there is also some Gothic left: the basilica with its striking chancel is a site of pilgrimage. Climb up to the top and admire the panoramic view. The outside is brightly lit after dark.

HOTEL DE VILLE. This Flamboyant Gothic model is a listed building. The 1643 campanile was rebuilt in 1769; the Town Council room is listed Art Deco. The belltower holds 37 bells.

RESERVE NATURELLE DES MARAIS D'ISLE Maison de la Nature ✆ 03 23 05 06 50. *Open Monday to Friday: 10am-12 noon and 2pm-5.30pm. Closes at 5pm on Saturday and Sunday.* The lake and nature reserve are close at hand, beyond the station, after the rue d'Isle. You can learn about their biotopics, flora and fauna in the on-site Maison de la Nature by means of documents, books and audiovisual material. Visit the site via its peripheral path, with guided tours the first Sunday of the month.

Soissons

Soissons was France's first Christian capital, thanks to Clovis. Later, in the early Carolingian era, the region was the site of conflict over the division of land between Charlemagne's sons, and from then on, Soissons was a favourite ground for monarchic pillage and power struggles. The Great War destroyed a large part of the town, leaving only ruins, and the old quarter that can still be visited.

Places to see: the Hôtel de Barral, very valuable French Regency and still lived in, with its fountain, sundial and main staircase. On the other bank of the Aisne lies Soissons' oldest monument, the crypt of former Saint Médard Abbey, built by Charles the Bald in 841.

SAINT JEAN DES VIGNES ABBEY. The abbey has a 13th to 15thc. church with soaring spires, a striking refectory, fine cloister (13thc.) and loggia (16th-17thc.) containing the abbey church's statuary.

SAINT GERVAIS ET SAINT PROTAIS CATHEDRAL. This Gothic cathedral (12th-14thc.) suffered during the Great War, but despite having been damaged in an explosion in 1815, the stained glass windows are splendid, as are most of the furnishings. Look out for one of Philippe de Champaigne's works, and an Adoration of the Shepherds by Rubens.

Le Vase de Soissons

Grégoire de Tours put this story into his 6thc. 'Histoire des Francs'. Clovis had invaded the town and was pillaging the churches with his troops as usual. He coveted a magnificant vase, which he asked to keep over and above his share of the booty. Only one soldier disagreed, and struck the vase in two with his axe. Clovis stayed calm, and left with his half. Some months later, the future King of the Franks decided to review his troops. Arriving in front of the jealous soldier, he seized the man's axe and threw it to the ground, for it was in bad condition and thus unworthy of combat. The soldier bent to pick it up, and Clovis, who took care of his own axe, split his head open.

Villers-Cotterêts

Best-known for its decree, made by FranÁois 1 in 1539, stating that French should be the official language for legal and administrative orders and separating civil and religious justice.

CHATEAU RENAISSANCE FRAN«OIS-1ER. *Open May to October every day except Monday: 11am-3pm, and November to April every day except Sunday and public holidays: 11am-3pm (open all year). Admission: 4 € , cultural passport: 3 € , free for the under-twelves.* This hunting lodge with its sculpted ceiling above the staircase is Villers-Cotteret's main attraction. It was used by FranÁois 1 (and the Dukes of Orléans), as the salamander decorations remind us.

OISE

This agricultural department at the gates of Paris is one of its lungs, and an escape route for suffocating Parisians.

Beauvais

Beauvais, the departmental prefecture, was almost completely rebuilt after the War, and there are few monuments left of its original architecture, apart from the much-visited cathedral.

SAINT PIERRE CATHEDRAL. The gothic vaults of the chancel are the world's highest, rising to 47 metres. Building was started in 1225, and never finished, since the nave still has not made its appearance. There is a fine reredos, the Genesis Rose, and two remarkable clocks: a 14thc. chiming clock and a 19thc. astronomical clock whose movement contains 90 000 pieces and 70 automatons. Showings at 10.40am, 11.40am, 2.40pm, 3.40pm and 4.40pm every day in summer, and from 1 November to 31 March at 11.40am, 2.40pm and 3.40pm (admission: adults 4 €).

SAINT ETIENNE CHURCH. This church has very fine 16thc. windows, with historical and religious motifs. It also has a hospice, the Saint-Lazare maladrerie (11th-13thc.), the biggest of its kind in Northern Franco.

GALERIE NATIONALE DE LA TAPISSERIE 22, rue Saint-Pierre ✆ 03 44 15 39 10. *Open every day except Monday. Admission free* . Louis XIV's minister Colbert put Beauvais' tapestry on the map in the 17thc. This gallery, a modern building of sober design near the cathedral, follows the development of tapestry from the Middle Ages, with priority given to examples from the various French manufacturers. There are contemporary works too, including some from the current Beauvais tapestry workshop.

MANUFACTURE NATIONALE DE LA TAPISSERIE 24, rue Henri Brispot ✆ 03 44 15 39 10. *Open on Tuesdays, Wednesdays and Thursday afternoons: 2pm-4pm. Admission: adult 3.20 € , child 1.10 €* .The tapestry workshop is still turning out magnificent pieces today.

Chantilly

Famous for the great names linked with its ch,teau, notably Condé and Montmorency; equestrian sport and sweet whipped cream.

CONDE MUSEUM ✆ 03 44 62 62 62. *www.ch,teaudechantilly.com. Open every day except Tuesday, April-November: 10am-6pm. Out of season: 10.30am-12.45pm and 2pm-5pm. Admission: adult 8 € , child 5.50 €* . Housed in the Ch,teau itself, and one of the richest French museums, the Condé includes collections of major French and Italian works (Poussin, Delacroix, Ingres, Fra Angelico, Raphael) porcelain (Sèvres, Chantilly) and rare books and manuscripts, such as the Duc de Berry's Tres Riches Heures, grouped together in a superb library. Some of these collections came from that wealthy and enlightened amateur, the Duc d'Aumale. Don't forget to visit the park, one of the finest formal gardens laid out by Le Nôtre.

MUSEE VIVANT DU CHEVAL ✆ **03 44 57 40 40**. *www.musee-vivant-du-cheval.fr. Open every day except Tuesday, April to October: 10.30am-6.30pm (7pm at weekends). Out of season, open during the week: 2pm- 6pm, weekends 10.30am-6.30pm. Open also on Tuesdays from May to August: 2pm-6.pm.* This museum for horse-lovers, the world's biggest and finest, is housed in the 18thc. stables facing the ch,teau and the racecourse. You can discover a variety of species among the 30 or so 'boarders', and also what being a stable hand, vet or blacksmith involves.

Compiègne

Compiègne, town of kings and emperors. Joan of Arc was captured here, and part of the medieval town still lends its historic charm to the present-day pedestrian centre. Visit the remarkable Town Hall with its 16th-century belfry; its Picantins, or jacquemarts, strike the Bancloque, an ancient bell dating back to 1303. The annex houses the Historic Figurine Museum.

CHATEAU Place du Général de Gaulle ✆ **03 44 38 47 00**. *Open every day except Tuesday: 10am-6pm, 1 April to 30 September. From 1 November to 28 February, the Grands Appartements are open from 10am-3.45pm. The other museums are open at the usual times. Admission: 5.50 € /2-museum pass, 4.50 € /Grands Appartements.* Visit the Great Apartments, whose architects were famous in their time (Girodet, Marcion). The Motor and Tourism Museum traces the history of cars, from the first horse-drawn vehicles to steam cars and internal combustion engines. The grounds of the ch,teau, laid out by Berthault, are quite spectacular.

CLAIRIERE DE l'ARMISTICE MEMORIAL Route de Soissons ✆ **03 44 85 14 18**. *Open every day except Tuesday (closed mornings January and February). Admission: adult 3 € , child 1.50 € , under-7s free.* Historic monuments and a museum in the heart of the forest. The chief attraction is the famous Armistice Carriage of 11 November 1918 and 22 June 1945. Uniformed figures, scale models, trench craft and weapons tell the story of two World Wars.

COMPIEGNE FOREST. The royal forest covers 15 000 hectares, joining up with the forests of Laigue and Villers-Cotterêts. It contains the first paths marked out for pedestrians in France, making it easier for walkers to discover historic sites and places of interest.

Crépy-en-Valois

The castle and Saint Arnoud Abbey were put up in the 10th century. A village quickly grew up around them, and was fortified in the 11thc. Kings settled into the castle up until the Hundred Years' War, which did a lot of damage to the community.

MUSEE DU CHATEAU ✆ **03 44 59 21 97**. *Open from the end of March to 11 November, every day except Tuesday: 2.30pm- 6.30pm (3pm-7pm on Sundays and public holidays). Admission: adult 4 € , child 2.50 €* . The Archery Museum in the keep houses a unique collection of documents, bows, arrows, targets and other objects tracing the history and traditions of archery.

Ermenonville

Close to Paris, with the benefits of a natural environment perfect for tourism.

MER DE SABLE Centre attractif Jean Richard ✆ **03 44 54 00 96**. *www.merdesable.fr. Open early April to late September. Admission: adult 16.50 € , child 13.50 €* . This theme park with its shows and attractions calls to mind the Wild West. Three new activities in 2004: you can play cowboys on the mechanical horses of the Piste de l'Ouest, ride the panoramic Big Wheel and try out the simulators in the games room. Fun for all the family.

Gerberoy

This is the smallest medieval town in France, containing some fine old houses. The 11thc. fortifications defended the town solidly, keeping it pretty much intact for posterity. Visit the ruined ramparts, Charlemagne Tower and Saint Pierre Collegiate church, containing an Aubusson tapestry and a vestry where the Collegiate treasure is kept. The Town Hall has an archeological collection on the first floor. Gerberoy has inspired countless artists, as one of France's finest villages.

Noyon

This is a beautiful medieval town, with its half-Gothic, half-Romanesque Cathedral. Take a walk through the genuine cobbled streets around it, as far as the boulevard, and enjoy the many 15th and 16thc. houses with their towers and roofs sticking up proudly above the old stone walls.

CATHEDRAL. Proud of its nickname 'The Parthenon of Christian architecture', the 12th-15thc. cathedral boasts fine Romanesque capitals in the chancel, complex decoration and a Primitive Gothic exterior with chapels surrounding the nave. One of the best-preserved canon and episcopal units in France.

Pierrefonds

The impressive feudal castle renovated by Viollet-le-Duc in the 19th century, with its many crenellated towers and steep roofs calls to mind the Baroque or the operetta.

CHATEAU NATIONAL DE PIERREFONDS © **03 44 42 72 72**. *www.monum.fr. Open every day from 15 March to 15 September: 9.30am-6pm (check opening times for the rest of the year). Admission: adult 6.10 € , reduced price 4.10 € , under-18s free.* First built early in the 15thc., left to fall into ruins, it was rescued by Napoleon III. Viollet-le-Duc was asked to turn it into an imperial ch,teau while keeping its original character. The great 19thc. builder never saw his work completed, for he died 20 years later, but it went on until interrupted in 1885.

Plailly

PARC ASTERIX © **03 44 62 34 34**. *www.parcasterix.fr. Access from Paris: by car: A1 motorway towards Lille, direct exit for Parc Asterix. By RER (suburban train), line B3 from Ch,telet or Gare du Nord, direction Roissy. Get off at Roissy 1, take the Parc Asterix shuttle from the coach station. Admission: adult 33 € for the day (60 € for 2 days), child 23 € (42 € for 2 days) under-3s free. Car park: 3 €* . Only 30 km from Paris, the successful Parc Asterix has been welcoming visitors for 10 years. The magic potion really works here, the many attractions - a looping-the-loop machine, flying chairs, the Trojan Horse, a giant bobsleigh - are tremendous fun, and the shows are excellent. There are six restaurants and 40 snackbars on the site, with hotel accommodation at the Trois Hiboux in the heart of the forest, if you find that one day is not enough to enjoy this very Gallic theme park.

Pontpoint

MONCEL ROYAL ABBEY Club du Vieux Manoir ✆ **03 44 72 33 98**. *Open every day except Monday and Wednesday morning. Admission: adult 5.50 € , child 2 € .* Worth visiting for Moncel Royal Abbey (14th century) and the remains of Philippe le Bel's 13thc. castle.

Senlis

Senlis is a Gallo-Roman, royal, medieval and modern town all at once. Walk through the charming old town, where mansions, medieval houses and little churches bask in history half-an-hour from Paris.

NOTRE DAME DE LA VICTOIRE ROYAL ABBEY ✆ **03 44 53 00 72**. *Open 20 August to 30 September every day except Sunday morning. Admission free.* These ruins lie in a fine English-style park, with its chestnut tree-lined walk. Philippe-Auguste had the abbey built in 1222, Joan of Arc passed through here, and Louis XI, who considered it his favourite place to stay. The buildings you can see are from various periods: the 13thc. abbey church remains and monks' eel pond, a 15thc. farm, 18thc. central building and 19thc. orangery.

CATHEDRAL. Built between the 12th and 16thc., it has an impressive Flamboyant Gothic faÁade, majestic with its peaks and spires.

CHATEAU ROYAL. Overlooking the town, this royal ruined castle goes back to Hugues Capet, first king of the Capetian dynasty at Senlis. The present remains are 12thc, supported by a Gallo-Roman wall. Saint Louis had a priory built next to the castle; you can still admire its convent buildings. They house a Hunting Museum, unique in Europe, containing trophies, costumes and objects relating to the hunt, but also works of art and historical documents.

COTE D'OPALE

The Opal Coast, between Boulogne-sur-Mer and Calais, is one of the most beautiful French coasts. To discover it, take the D940 coast road, 40 km linking Boulogne and Calais. To the south of Boulogne, the Opal Coast goes on to that famous oh-so-chic resort Le Touquet-Paris-Plage.

Arras

CAVES ROQUILLAS 3, rue d'Achicourt ✆ **03 21 23 00 43** *Open Tuesday-Saturday: 9.15am-12.30pm and 2.15pm-7.30pm.* An excellent place for wine-lovers. There is an impressive choice covering all domains and origins, from small producers to the most famous vineyards, in red, white and rose. The same goes for the alcohols, including some rare bottles, and brands chosen to suit customer tastes.You'll love the gift packs and accessories for opening and keeping your wine.

Berck-sur-Mer

A seaside resort for the sporty, but also for family holidays. The climate is bracing and therapeutic; visitors came to take the cure in the 1840s, along with many artists.

DUNES DE L'AUTHIE. Near Berck, more like sand cliffs than dunes, they are the work of wind and tides, and quite spectacular. Follow the path for 24 km, and you will come across sheep, and if you look carefully, orchids, which grow in this environment.

Boulogne-sur-Mer

This is France's main fishing port, supplying a quarter of national production. British tourism has influenced the town's commercial style, with bilingual menus, many pubs and signs in Union Jack colours. The most popular beer, though, is Facon, a local brew you can find everywhere, not to be outdone by Guinness or MacEwans.

CHATEAU-MUSEE Rue de Bernet ✆ **03 21 10 02 20**. *Open every day except Tuesday: 10am-12.30pm and 2pm-5pm, Sundays: 10pm-12.30pm and 2.30pm-5.30pm. Admission: adult 1 € .* Without a doubt the best preserved fortified medieval castle in the North of France. The museum houses collections from antiquity, paintings, sculpture and ceramics (Boudin, Rodin), not to mention the various exotic objects brought back from far-off trips by Boulogne sailors.

NAUSICAA Boulevard Sainte Beuve ✆ 03 21 30 98 98. *www.nausicaa.fr. Group bookings for more than 20 people. Open every day: 9.30am-8pm, 1 July to 31 August. Closed on Christmas Day and at 2pm from 1 September to 30 January. Admission: adult 13 €, 3-12s 9 € in high season.* A mixture of the educational and the magical, with plankton, jellyfish and sharks in their different acquariums, and a 'hands-on' pool where you can get friendly with a skate. By the end of your visit you will have seen over 10 000 marine animals swimming in the 4.5 million litres of water that fill the tanks.

Eperlecques

LE BLOCKHAUS Rue du Sart ✆ 03 21 88 44 22. *Website: www.leblockhaus.com. Open March : 2.15pm-6pm, April and October : 10am-12 noon and 2.15pm-6pm, May-September : 10am-7pm, November 2.15pm-5pm. Closed December- February. Admission adult 7 €, child 4.50 €, student 5.50 €.* From 1943 onwards, one of the biggest blockhauses ever built by the German Army lay hidden in Eperlecques Forest . It was intended to be used as a liquid oxygen factory and a V2 missile launch base. On the other side of the forest massif was a V1 missile launch base. Today you can discover the secrets of Nazi weapons during a visit with soundtrack commentary.

Hardelot

A chic and sought-after resort. Hardelot offers the visitor exclusive wooded surroundings, 13km of beach and a large sports centre. The wind is ideal for sand yachting.

Romelaere

This 82-ha. Nature Reserve in the heart of the Saint Omer marshes shelters a number of nesting and wintering birds, with paths specially fitted out so you can watch them at your ease. An environmental paradise, now accessible by boat trip from Nieurlet.+

Le Touquet

Le Touquet's long sandy beach and dunes host the Cervoling, an international kite competition, but the town also boasts a listed nature reserve in the Canche estuary.

AMIENS AND THE BAIE DE SOMME

Amiens

Regional capital, the Somme's main town miens is pretty and busy. Stroll through the pedestrian quarter round the splendid cathedral towards the Saint-Leu district along the River Somme, where trendy bars and classy restaurants abound.

CATHEDRAL. Notre Dame is closely linked to Amiens' history. The city became a religious capital in the 6thc, due to its first wooden cathedral, Romanesque in style and built to house Saint Firmin's relics. Ravaged by war and fire, this wooden building was replaced in the 13thc. by an impressive stone cathedral. Extraordinary means were made available, thanks to divine inspiration, and the will to build something really imposing, and a gigantic building site was set up in 1220. The work, though, was not really finished until the early 17thc., in the reign of Louis XIII! The cathedral was spared during the two World Wars, by a miracle - or the Pope's influence with the German Army - but a different battle began in 1992, when the faÁade underwent restoration by laser, and the statues found their colour again. The façade includes a statuary of portals, the three tympana above showing biblical scenes, with the Last Judgement over the central porch. (The lost colours in these tympana came back after the laser treatment). The nave soars to 42 metres from paving to vault (Notre Dame de Paris is only 35 metres high, and in fact the entire nave could fit inside the one in Amiens!)

The whole length of the vault is ribbed, except for the transept square. The chancel has 7 radiating chapels, the axial chapel with its windows comprises two bays. The chancel enclosures show scenes from the life of John the Baptist. The stalls were ordered by 16thc. canons, and it took the craftsmen and painters 11 years to finish them and install them in the chancel. There are 110, showing scenes from everyday life in the 16thc., and Biblical, evangelical and historical episodes. The spire is the highest and oldest cathedral spire in existence, despite being shortened in 1627.

LES HORTILONNAGES Boarding: 54 bd. de Beauville ✆ 03 22 92 12 18. *Guided tours by boat, 1 April to 31 October every day: 2pm-6pm. Price: adult 5.30 € , teenager 4.20 € , 4-10s 3.50 €* . 300 hectares of garden on the river could have inspired the great Impressionist painters. 55 km of channels criss-cross these fertile little islets in the heart of the city. Visit them in the traditional boat called a barque à cornet. These former marshes have been there since Gallo-Roman times, but market gardening really took off in the 19thc, and still goes on. Not to be missed.

PARC ZOOLOGIQUE DE LA HOTOIE Allée du Zoo - Esplanade de la Hotoie ✆ 03 22 69 61 00. *Open April to September.* Organised into geographical and climatic zones, this 6-ha. safari park provides a natural green setting for nearly 300 animals of 70 different species, from all the continents. Each species lives in an environment close to its natural habitat. The park contains hundred-year-old trees and its own network of waterways.

Baie de Somme

The bay extends across 70 square metres, where the Somme flows into the Channel, known chiefly for its flora and fauna, its marshes and wide stretches of sand. This part of the land was under water a few centuries ago; enclosing dykes were built, halting the tides' advance inland. These tall dykes or 'royons' dried out the land, allowing it to be used for agriculture. Channelling the Somme and the bigger streams took centuries, and unstable underwater sandbanks held up the work still further. The resulting environmental conditions proved to be an unexpected haven for bird life, whether nesting or migratory. Watch out for the tides, which can be dangerous.

Abbeville

The capital of Ponthieu was heavily bombed, particularly on 20 May 1940. Its architecture is mostly recent, with some historic remnants. A few pretty houses here and there in the alleyways and cul-de-sacs, such as the Haberdashers' or the Commander's, once home to an order of Knights Templars. See also the Place du Pilori, where the condemned were publicly punished.

BELFRY (13thc.). The former Town Hall belfry is one of the oldest (1209) and best preserved in the region. With good eyesight or binoculars, you can make out a weathervane in the form of a horseman (none other than the Comte de Ponthieu) 20 metres up on the top of the tower. You also find the interesting Boucher-de-Perthes Museum, devoted to the French prehistory specialist.

SAINT VULFRAN COLLEGIATE CHURCH. One of the town's most striking monuments, Flamboyant Gothic in style (and unfinished), your eyes are drawn to its two 55.8-metre towers, its opulent variety and harmony. In 1853, Victor Hugo visited this " old faÁade, eaten away by the North Wind and the moon, which one leaves with a tear, having entered with a smile."

The Somme Lakes

This department is named after the river running through it, with its winding tributaries flowing in meanders, and forming thousands of lakes. Follow the Somme, and you go back in time to prehistoric Samara, relive the Hundred Years' War at Picquigny, and understand the dark days of the Great War at Peronne, with its Historial as a living memory. Your path is strewn with castles, churches and mills - and suprises.

Cayeux-sur-Mer

MAISON DE L'OISEAU Carrefour du Hourdel Lancheres ✆ 03 22 26 93 93. *Open every day from 1 April to 12 November. Closed on Tuesdays in February, March, October and November. Admission: adult 6 € to 9 € , child 4.30 € to 6.40 €* . 3km from the village, coming from Saint Valéry, you can discover the local fauna, the various breeds typical of the Baie de Somme, and learn how to recognise them with picture montages, slide shows and a hut for watching ducks in their habitat. A resting place for duck species and sand dwellers, and a wintering refuge for teal. There is also an exhibition of birds of prey in flight, between September and November.

PARC ORNITHOLOGIQUE DE MARQUENTERRE. *www.marcanterra.fr. Open every day from 15 March to 11 November; Sundays and holiday periods during the rest of the year. 1 April to 30 September, open 9.30am-7pm (admission until 5pm), 1 October to 31 March, 10am- 6pm (4pm). Admission: adult 9 €, child 6 €.* This 250-hectare coastal conservation site near Saint Quentin-en-Tourmont is the department's best-known bird sanctuary in the Baie de Somme. It is a favoured observation post for migratory birds (sandpipers, barnacle geese), and for discovering the Picard coastline's rich ecosystem. Educational guides welcome you, and you have a choice between the initiation route, with its explanatory notice boards and the observation route with access to certain restricted paths.

Amiens, The Hortillonnages

FOOD AND DRINK

This region has taste! Choose a brasserie or an estaminet (tavern) to enjoy a beer and the dishes that go with it: potjevlesch, a typical meat dish, or the inevitable chicken waterzoi (a kind of stew). The chicory makes a pale contrast to the local cheeses, among the strongest in France.

Bétises de Cambrai

Grandfather Afchain didn't know his silly mistake would create the Nord-Pas-de-Calais' most famous sweet, or he'd have made it earlier. Back in the 19thc., he was only an apprentice in the family sweetshop when he messed up a recipe, which gave the sweets their typical mentholated taste. They sold so well that they became the house speciality and were a huge success. Don't forget the sottises de Valenciennes, either, which are trying to compete.

Chicon

Chicory, in local dialect. The roots of this widespread vegetable are roasted like coffee beans. It is eaten au gratin or in a salad, rather than boiled.

Sweets

Best known are the little quinquins from Lille, the pain de Cassel or tartine flamande (slice of brioche with brown sugar), desserts made with cassonade (brown sugar), various tarts. *Pain perdu* (bread-and-butter pudding), *craquelins* (bread rolls with sugar and cinnamon) and *gaufres* are other favourites. In Picardy, you can try pumpkin waffles and the *gateau battu*, made chiefly in the Abbeville area on religious feast-days, a sort of fluffy brioche containing a lot of beaten eggs - hence its name. It is served with rhubarb or gooseberry jam. Filled waffles are found everywhere in the North of France, and are also homemade.

Cheese

Known for their strength; also for their delicacy and flavour. The boulette d'Avesnes (pungent) is served in sealed terrines. The coeur d'Avesnes, or Rollot, is rather like a maroilles, that king of Northern cheeses made in the Avesnois and the Aisne, and which is often compared to the vieux-lille (wicked, but what flavour!) that comes from the cellars of Lille. The maroilles goes back to the 7thc., but the monks really started making it from the 11thc. onwards. It is made from cows' milk, and stocked for 2 to 3 months in the cellars before being eaten. It exists in three sizes, sorbais (540g) mignon (380g) and quart (180g)

Northern beers and brasseries

The word brasserie means brewery. This historic sector is expanding: new beers, but also new mirobrasseries, where the local product can be tasted, sometimes with food. Hops are a feature of the

North Gastronomy

Flemish landscape, inspiring watercolour artists, but brasseries can be found in other parts of Northern France, like Artois, or the Douai area.

BRASSERIE LEPERS 4, Grand-Place - ANNOEULIN © 03 20 41 58 48. Small brewery whose beer, the Angelus, is made from barley malt and wheat, and has a subtle taste.

BRASSERIE CASTELAIN 13, rue Pasteur - BENIFONTAINE © 03 21 08 68 68. This brewery makes Northern France's most famous beer, the ch'ti. Cordial and full of character, it has really helped to put local brews on the map.

LES BRASSERIES DE GAYANT V 63, Faubourg de Paris - DOUAI © 03 27 93 26 22. *Fax: 03 27 93 26 20.* An industrial brewery, producing, among others, la biere du demon, supposedly the strongest in the world.

BRASSERIE LA CHOULETTE 16, rue des Ecoles - HORDAIN © 03 27 35 72 44. Nice name, nice beer - either blonde (pale ale) or ambrée (light brown ale), but better known in the latter form. This powerful beer has an aromatic, lightly caramelised flavour.

BRASSERIE DUYCK 113, route Nationale © 03 27 49 70 03. Beer-loving France was shaken up in the seventies by Jenlain, in blonde, ambrée and Christmas versions. The brewery also offers a March beer, the Sebourg, a light blonde, and an organic beer, la Fraiche de l'Aunelle. In 2004, two new beers flavoured with ginger and absinthe came onto the market.

BRASSERIE JEANNE D'ARC 38, rue Anatole France - RONCHIN © 03 20 16 92 92. *Fax: 03 20 88 26 01.* This big brewery makes a blonde of repute, an aromatic ambrée, the Belzebuth (a devastating blonde), and some interesting mixtures, such as the Latina, flavoured with tequila, as well as Christmas and March beers.

LA BIERE DES TROIS MONTS 121, route de la Chapelle - SAINT SYLVESTRE-CAPPEL © 03 28 40 15 49. In the heart of French Flanders, one of the North's best-known beers, the Trois Monts.

DISTILLERIE CLAEYSSENS 1, avenue des Châteaux - WAMBRECHIES © 03 20 14 91 91. *Guided tours every day except public holidays: 9.30am-12.30pm and 1.30pm-5.30pm, bookings only. Admission: adult 6 € , 12-18s 4 € , under-12s free.* Tasting after the guided tour. Known already for a homemade juniper liqueur, you can now discover the wambrechies, an excellent light-brown ale.

BRASSERIE TERKEN 3, quai d'Anvers - ROUBAIX © 03 20 76 15 00. One of the two most important industrial breweries in the North, the other being Heineken, at Mons-en-Baroeul. The Terken, blonde or brune, is found everywhere.

© Cdt Aisne / Dessirier

Hotels & Restaurants

NORD

Bergues

LE BRUEGEL 1, rue du Marché-aux-Fromages © 03 28 68 19 19. *Open every day. Set menus 18.90 € to 29.50 €. Children's menu 6.90 €.* This tavern is a wide building stretching along the river bank, and the town's oldest house, actually dating back to Bruegel's time. No-one would guess that it is a real restaurant on entering; it looks like a bit of a dive with its counter and scattering of tables. Going further in, you catch site of a big dining room, open kitchens, washing hanging up and waiters dressed in 16thc. peasant costume. The pleasant folksy atmosphere goes with a well-filled menu of regional specialities, like *flamiche* (a sort of quiche) with maroilles cheese, Bergues beef steak and a pudding with raisins soaked in rum. There are also more local dishes, Bergues cheese and sausage, that you don't find anywhere else. For the last 10 years, this has been a great place to stop for a meal.

Bondues

AUBERGE DE L'HARMONIE 36, place de l'Abbé-Bonpain © 03 20 23 17 02 *Closed Monday, Tuesday evening, Thursday evening and Sunday evening. Annual closing in July. Set menus from 23 € (weekdays) and 33 € (Sunday). A la carte 40 €.* The brotherhood of Auguste Escoffier's disciples was right to extend its membership to Didier Tharin. In a superb decor combining comfort and a harmonious colour scheme, and attentive waiters (no waitresses) L'Auberge de l'Harmonie serves classic cuisine - veal sweetbreads, rock lobster etc. - including culinary finds like crunchy scallops served in their shells, flavoured with star aniseed. Excellent advice is given to help you choose your wine. The restaurant also organises theme evenings, with découverte menus offering new and different dishes..

© Cdt de l'Oise / D. Cry

Cambrai

CHATEAU DE LA MOTTE-FENELON* Square du Château ✆ 03 27 83 61 38.** *Fax: 03 27 83 71 61. Website : www.cambrai-château-motte-fenelon.com. Rooms 55 € in the park (breakfast 10 €) château 85 €, 90 €, prestige 130 €, 190 € and 230 €. One room in the orangery 80 € a night. In high season 230 €, orangery and château rooms 100 €, park 60 €. Set menus 22 € to 32 €, Friday evening and Sunday lunchtime 23 € and 37 €, Sunday set menu 33 € including drinks. Always open.* This hotel-château-restaurant has 40 top-of-the-range rooms, fully equipped with bath, shower and TV. Tennis courts available for sporty types. Private car park for peace of mind.

Douai

LE TURBOTIN 9, rue de la Massue ✆ 03 27 87 04 16. *Closed Saturday lunchtime, Sunday evening and Monday. Set menus 16 €, 26 €, 30 € and 42 €. A la carte 30 €.* Le Turbotin is definitely one of the town's best restaurants, specialising in fish, seafood and shellfish, simply cooked and full of flavour. A pleasantly convivial atmosphere completes the picture, along with staff experienced in the culinary and table arts.

Dunkerque

LE BISTROT DE LA PLAGE 24, digue de la Mer ✆ 03 28 65 01 11. *Open every day. Set menus from 12,50 € to 22 €, children's menu 5,80 €.* This restaurant is well-named, since its covered terrace looks directly onto the sea. The talented chef prepares beautifully presented fish specialities like prawn croquettes, cod steak with maroilles cheese, and grilled gambas with sauce gribiche. If you're not a fishy person, there are meat dishes and salads on the menu, and a full and varied slate suggests original dishes of the day - Norwegian poached egg, fish lasagna - and local specialities like prunes in *chuche mourrette* (a local aperitif made from *crème de cassis* and juniper berries) and Flemish *carbonade* (meat cooked in beer). If you've time for a leisurely meal, this is the place for you!

DUNKERQUE GOLF COURSE Route du Golf ✆ 03 28 61 07 43. *Website: www.golf-dk.com – email: golf@golf-dk.com. 210 €-945 € to enrol, depending on the type of subscription and players' ages, plus a 25 €-55 € green fee (18 holes).* The Tourist Pass, available from the Dunes de Flandre Tourist Office, gives you reductions in the green fee. November-March: 9am-6pm every day, opens 8.30am at weekends. April-October: 8.30am-7pm every day, opens 8am. at weekends.

BEST WESTERN WELCOME HOTEL * 37, rue Poincaré ✆ 03 28 59 20 70** *Fax: 03 28 21 03 49. Website : www.hotel-welcome.fr. Rooms from 66 € and buffet breakfast 9 €. 40 rooms in all, including a VIP suite. Bathrooms and individual WC. Canal + and cable TV, Wi-Fi .connection available. Disabled access. Seminars.* The 'world's first name in hotels' in Dunkerque town centre also meets the international Best Western chain's additional standards of service and facilities. The rooms are equipped with satellite TV and modem -you'll have no communication problems! - and hot dishes are available from room service until 10pm. There is a room designed for seminars, meetings and family get-togethers. The adjacent Ecume Bleue restaurant serves a 13 € formula, with fish so fresh you can see its tail still wriggling. Private parking for customers.

HOTEL-RESTAURANT LES GENS DE MER Quai Risban ✆ 03 28 66 15 22. *Fax: 03 28 63 74 85. 42 rooms at 49,50 €, breakfast 6,50 €.*When you're staying in Dunkerque, it's pleasant to wake up to a view of the harbour, the sea and its spray, only 5 minutes from the town centre. Contemporary architecture and quiet rooms, where you can hear the ropes flapping against the masts of boats lying at anchor not far away. At the Gens de Mer, you feel like a real sailor. Before putting on your red cap and joining the crew, you need to fill up on iron rations.You choose your ship - each menu bears a name, from the frail dinghy (7.10 €) to the brigantine (18.50 €) - and your route, a channel crossing (brasserie side) or the Flanders banks (restaurant side). Attentive staff serve a selection of varied and tasty regional dishes. Ideal for playing old sea dogs.

Lille

CARLTON ** 3, rue de Paris ✆ 03 20 13 33 13**. *Website : www.carltonlille.com. Rooms from 165 €, junior suite 252 €, breakfast 17 €. Cupola suite 1,180 €, car park 17 €. Disabled access. pets accepted. Groups welcome. Bar. Lift. Garage. Car parking valet service. Weddings, seminars. Hammam, Jacuzzi, sauna, UV lights. Service after midnight. No cheques.* Soundproofed and air-conditioned rooms. Broadband Internet at reception. The Carlton lives up to its image: Art Deco façade and copper dome, distinguished reception and magnificent rooms. The suites are sumptuously decorated in the purest Louis XV and Louis XVI style, and have marble bathrooms. View over the town centre; facilities up to the expected standard. Beautiful period bar and reception rooms.

LE CLUB CLEMENT MAROT 16, rue de Pas ✆ 03 20 57 01 10. *Fax: 03 20 57 39 59. Website : www.lestablesgourmandes.com. Open Monday to Sunday, 12 noon-2.30pm and 7pm-10.30pm, except Sunday evening. Set menus 32.50 € and 42.50 €, including wine, 54 € with champagne (a half-bottle per head) and 50 €. Lunchtime formulas 16 € (2 courses) or 23 € (3 courses). A la carte 45 €.* Chef Clément Marot is a culinary artist, and a poet in his own way, in his restaurant, and as godfather to others like the Auberge de la Creûle at Hazebrouck. He only works with the freshest of local market ingredients to prepare his specialities, recognised and loved by all: Dublin bay prawn salad, Licques poultry with maroilles cheese and chicory, venison sauté with apples and red cabbage. Iif the ingredients aren't up to his high standards, the dish is off the menu. The desserts - variations on a classic theme - are equally delicious: chicory cream and crêpes Suzette flambéd, which is quite rare nowadays.

L'HUITRIERE 3 rue des Chats-Bossus ✆ 03 20 55 43 41 *Fax 03 20 55 23 10. Website: www.huitriere.fr. Set menus 47 € to120 €. A la carte 70 €. Closed Sunday evening and 22 July-24 August.* L'Huîtrière is a real institution, the kind you only find in provincial cities, one per town. The challenge is to keep the regulars interested and satisfied, and also to attract the type of customer who collects top restaurants like others collect paintings. Jean Proye thus decided to hand over to his oldest son Antoine this summer, partly to meet this challenge, but also to keep up with increasing local competition in Lille and its north suburb. Of course there's nothing revolutionary about this change; L'Huîtrière is still the North of France's finest fish shop and the recipes cooked there are inimitable: scallop parcels with green cabbage and truffles, slice of turbot cooked in beer, and remarkably fresh seafood. A must for fish lovers.

LE SEBASTOPOL 1, place Sébastopol ✆ 03 20 57 05 05. *Website: www.restaurant-sebastopol.fr. Closed Monday lunchtime, Saturday lunchtime and Sunday evening. Set menus 30 € to 65 € (musée and gourmandise). A la carte.* A remarkably unassuming restaurant, considering its luxury standards and success record. Chef Jean-Luc Germond changes his menus every season, giving a new and original slant to his cuisine: contrasting Landes duck foie gras in a dried fruit nougat, the warm part in a beetroot syrup, roast scallops, chicory fondue with orange juice and aniseed, shortbread with candied quince, chicory cream, ginger ice cream and Grand Marnier soufflé, with an exotic fruit salad. Good food without too many explanatory speeches!

Valenciennes

LE GRAND HOTEL * 8, place de la Gare ✆ 03 27 46 32 01**. *Website: grand-hotel-de-valenciennes.fr. Open all year. Standard room 78 € single, 88 € double, comfort 85 € and 93 €, prestige 99 € and 109 €, breakfast 10 €. Garage let 7 €, 10% reduction weekends. Staff speak English, German and Spanish.* The Zielinger family has been running this hotel since 1938, with its 93 rooms and 5 comfortable suites including hairdryer, trouser-press, TV, mini-bar and courtesy tray ; six of them are even equipped with water therapy. Relaxation fans will love the sauna. Seminars and receptions can be organised (very professionally) on request. Gastronomic restaurant, traditional brasserie. Pets welcome.

Villeneuve d'Ascq

ASCOTEL Avenue Paul-Langevin ✆ 03 20 67 34 34. *Email: ascotel@club-internet.fr. 83 rooms, single 70 €, double 75 €, twin 79 €. 2 triple rooms 95 €, 2 family rooms sleeping 4 with lounge and TV 120 €. Breakfast 10 €. Tourist tax 0.75 €. Credit cards accepted. Holiday and restaurant cheques. English, German, Italian and Spanish spoken. 2 rooms equipped for disabled guests. Pets 10 €. Groups welcome. Seminars, weddings. Lift. All-in overnight price for sales reps. Private car park under surveillance. Vegetarian menu, children's menu. Bar open 8am-11pm. Late room service available. Shoe-shining machine in the corridors. All rooms have bathrooms (bath & shower), hairdryer, and TV with Canal Satellite. WiFi access. Iron and ironing board can be provided.* The town's only 3-star hotel is located in the Cite Scientifique. Guests arriving by car can access Ascotel easily; if you're coming by metro (Cite Scientifique station) you follow the footpath (signposted) through a wooded area. You'll notice the fresco featuring the town of Villeneuve d'Ascq, painted by a local artist. The hotel adjoins Le Melantois restaurant (well worth the trip!) which has just been renovated, and boasts pleasant new interior décor in muted tones. Apart from its functional bedrooms, Ascotel also has a large meeting room, making it particularly suitable for business customers. The hotel-restaurant-amphitheatre (seats 385) complex constitutes the biggest congress centre in town.

PAS-DE-CALAIS

Arras

HOTEL DE L'UNIVERS * 5, place Croix-Rouge ✆ 03 21 71 34 01**. *Website: www.hotel-univers-arras.com. Rooms from 75 € to 130 €. Breakfast 12 €.* This old monastery converted into a hotel has undergone some recent refurbishing to update its comfort standards. You can choose from three kinds of room according to your budget. There are seminar rooms and the facilities that go with them, and the Clusius restaurant , still just as luxurious. The reception staff welcome you in a variety of languages, ideal for a tourist town like Arras. The theme evenings in the wine cellar are definitely worth discovering!

CAVES ROQUILLAS 3, rue d'Achicourt ✆ 03 21 23 00 43 *Open Tuesday-Saturday: 9.15am-12.30pm and 2.15pm-7.30pm.* An excellent place for wine-lovers. There is an impressive choice covering all domains and origins, from small producers to the most famous vineyards, in red, white and rose. The same goes for the alcohols, including some rare bottles, and brands chosen to suit customer tastes.You'll love the gift packs and accessories for opening and keeping your wine.

LA FAISANDERIE 45, Grand-place ✆ 03 21 48 20 76. Closed Sunday evening and Monday. *Set menus 25 € to 60 €. A la carte.* You go down a few steps into this gastronomic den, where traditional dishes are served with a modern touch to suit today's demanding taste buds. The atmosphere is hushed, barely disturbed by the clatter of knives and forks. Sliced scallops and foie gras shavings, lobster and chestnut fricassée, roast venison with stewed sweet peppers, matured cheeses on the cheeseboard and desserts like the citrus fruit refreshment with redcurrants and chocolate and almond *croustillant.* Arguably the best place to eat in Arras.

LE PAIN GOURMAND 9, rue de la Housse ✆ 03 21 23 17 88 *Open every day except Sunday: 7am-1.15pm and 3pm-7.15pm.* You're welcomed with a smile (which is important!) and faced with a range of breads, seasonal fruit tarts, home-made waffles filled with vanilla or brown sugar, and original sandwiches that you really feel like eating (how many other bakeries roast their own meat to fill their sandwiches?) The Musialowskis are on to a great thing - let's hope it continues. English spoken, too.

HOTEL IBIS 11, rue de la justice ✆ 03 21 23 61 61. *Website: www.ibishotel.com. Email: H1567@accor-hotels.com. Double rooms 69 € weekdays and 51 € or 59 € weekends. Supplement for 3rd person 10 €. Pet supplement 5 €. Breakfast buffet 6.50 €. Reception 24 hours a day, 7 days a week. Ideally located near the two squares, with 63 rooms including 3 fitted out for disabled guests.* The bar offers a snack service 24 hours a day, and a breakfast formula for early and late risers, served from 4am to 12 noon. Close to underground public car park.

Avion

RESTAURANT LYONNAIS Parc de la glissoire ✆ 03 21 70 04 03. *Closed Saturday lunchtime, Sunday evening and Monday. Set menu from 22 €. Plaisir du Lyonnais menu 42 €.* Native of Lyon, Yves Primpoer settled in the Pas-de-Calais in 1989, and has developed a culinary style that blends influences from the two regions. His menus offer a choice of warm and cold starters: snails with garlic cream, duck foie gras escalope, melon stuffed with crayfish tails and smoked salmon petals. The main courses include tripe with cepes, and duck breast with a blackcurrant sauce and red fruit. For afters, try the home-made ice-cream, or crunchy raspberry dessert. A take-away service is available on request for some of the dishes.

Boulogne-sur-Mer

CHEZ JULES 8-10, place Dalton ✆ 03 21 31 54 12. *Closed Sunday afternoon in low season, 15 September-5 October and 23 December-8 January. 4 set menus 18,30 €, 22,10 € (except weekends and public holidays) 25,10 € and 34,50 €.* Chez Jules, the ambience is friendly with top-quality service. The waiters in their black aprons and green checked waistcoats are attentive to your every need; here, customers soon become regulars. The ground floor is the brasserie with its period brasses and country panelling, a few sketches of the old harbour and a lobster tank to remind you you're at the seaside. Upstairs the decor changes to early 20thc.style, but the food is still excellent. "The secret of good cooking is working with fresh ingredients" declares the chef to all and sundry, so it's not surprising to find so many different fish on the menu. The house also specialises in pizzas and welsh rarebit, chargrilled on the fire before your eyes. Book ahead to avoid disappointment.

HOTEL-RESTAURANT LES GENS DE MER Quai Chanzy ✆ 03 21 31 73 20 *Fax: 03 21 30 40 46. Open all year. Restaurant closed Sunday evening. 41 two-star rooms from 45 € to 79 €. Breakfast 6.50 €. Set menus 9.50 €-19 €. Car park. Meeting room.* This modern, recently renovated hotel can be found near the sailing harbour. It welcomes guests all year round; the customer base includes sailors, tourists and regulars, all seaside enthusiasts.

LE MIRADOR ** 2-4, rue de la Lampe ✆ 03 21 31 38 08. *Fax : 03 21 83 21 79. 18 rooms from 26 € to 35 €. Breakfast 5 €. Set menus from 9 € to 28 €. Closed in January.* Blue and green stones, and pebbles set into the walls create a seaside theme, which continues on the menu where fish have pride of place: monkfish flambéd with cognac, sole pan-fried in butter, swordfish au gratin, spaghetti with seafood and scallops. If you're in a hurry, we advise traditional welsh rarebit or the Napoleon omelette - bacon, onions, fried potatoes and cheese - for quick service.

Gavrelle

LE MANOIR 35, rue Nationale ✆ 03 21 58 68 58. *Hotel open every day. Restaurant closed saturday lunchtime and Sunday evening. Rooms from 48 €. Set menus 19 €-35 €.* Near Arras, in a peaceful country setting ideal for relaxing. All rooms have WiFi Internet socket and are very comfortable. Weddings, communions and family reunions can be organised. The restaurant serves traditional dishes, with a lunchtime set menu of the day at 18 €, and express formula at 15 €, both excellent value for money. The foie gras with port or gizzards *confit* are good starters, followed by lamb with garlic cream or haddock flavoured with maroilles. Leave room for the home-made nougat ice cream or chocolate and mandarin *imperial*.

La Madelaine-sous-Montreuil

LA GRENOUILLERE ✆ 03 21 06 07 22 and 03 21 86 36 36. *Website : www.lagrenouillere.fr. Annual closing in January. Closed Tuesday and Wednesday except July and August. 4 rooms from 75 € to 95 €. Breakfast 10 €. Set menus 20 € (weekday lunchtimes) 30 € (except Saturday evenings and public holidays), 50 € and 70 €.* This hostelry in its perfectly lovely setting is well worth the trip. A sophisticated cuisine combining seafood and country dishes is served in a panelled dining room with period brass, old-fashioned buffets and 1930s frescoes on canvas depicting frogs at the table. Chef Roland Gauthier is a culinary artist, witness the beef carpaccio millefeuille-style, parmesan, reggiano, cebette onions and peppers; Salers beef, lime, and anchovies, and woodland strawberries with goat's milk faisselle (curd-like dairy speciality) for dessert. Everything is delicious, and you're really spoilt for choice.

Le Touquet-Paris-Plage

FLAVIO "LE CLUB DE LA FORET" 1, avenue du Verger ✆ 03 21 05 10 22. *Website: www.flavio.fr. Closed Monday, except in July and August. Set menus from 20 €. Children under 6 free.* Chez Flavio is an institution, known for its celebrity customers. The food is exceptional, of course - Guy Delmotte knows his job. His menus include ingenious recipes using local seafood, like trout or turbot, and the famous lobsters that you eat with a serviette tucked under your chin. The wine list is up to scratch, and musicians play unobtrusively while you eat. Sober but charming setting; a classic coastal restaurant.

WESTMINSTER HOTEL ** 5, avenue du Verger ✆ 03 21 05 48 48** *Website: www.westminster.fr. Double rooms from 135 € to 575 €. Breakfast 16 €.* This imposing and rather majestic hotel can be found on the way into Le Touquet. The antique central lift takes you up to one of 115 luxurious rooms, with a 1930s feel. The gastronomic restaurant Le Pavillon, open every evening except Tuesday, offers menus from 45 € to 115 €. William Elliot's carte gives pride of place to fish specialities and seasonal produce. The brasserie Le Cimaise has recently been renovated in the same between-the-wars style as the rest of the hotel. Buffet lunch and set menus from 24 € to 31 €. The bar offers over 100 whiskies, and traditional chocolate.

Montreuil-sur-Mer

CHÂTEAU DE MONTREUIL 4 chaussée des Capucins ✆ 03 21 81 53 04 *Fax 03 21 81 36 43. Website: www.chateaudemontreuil.com. Set menus from 60 € to 79 €. A la carte 60 €. Closed Monday, Tuesday lunchtime - July to September - and from mid-December to mid-February.* British customers tend to like this restaurant, once the Fould-Springer (Rothschild) family's country house. Christian and Lindsay Germain have been running it for a quarter of a century, and the peace and quiet, protected setting, warm welcome and comfort standards are very pleasant. Christian Germain knows this clientele, having spent some time training in England with the famous Roux brothers, and his menu combines luxury, a little affectation, and plenty of talent: St Vaast oysters, served warm in beer foam with sorrel, slice of bread and salted butter, mullet cooked à la planche, chutney and red beetroot juice, suckling veal, the thick side pan-fried with salsify and the cooking juices, chicory *meunière*, garriguette strawberries on rhubarb poached with Bourbon vanilla from Madagascar, and tomatoes and strawberries in compote with olive oil and basil ice cream. The cellar specialises in white burgundies and red bordeaux, rather unexciting but suiting customer tastes.

Noeux-les-Mines

LE CARREFOUR DES SAVEURS 94, route Nationale ✆ **03 21 26 74 74.** *Closed Monday. Set menus from18 € to 50 €. A la carte 35 €.* At first sight, this restaurant isn't much to look at: an unobtrusive building by the side of the road, and a few signposts. A glance through the windows reveals something very different, though. Freshly-set tables, service in uniform, hushed atmosphere - and a *carte* well up to the chef's ambitions. His vichy cream with salmon rillettes, and salmon with chorizo are particularly successful, along with desserts like crème brûlée and chicory ice cream - classic, but very welcome. You'll enjoy your meal here - especially if you taste the home made marshmallow!

Saint-Laurent-Blangy

LES JARDINS DE SAINT- LAURENT 1, rue Laurent Gers ✆ **03 21 50 81 00.** *Open every day except Sunday. Set menus from 17.50 €.* This restaurant overlooks a leafy park with a duckpond. M. Basdevant and his new chef Remi Hautecoeur make sure you enjoy an excellent gastronomic meal, which might include salmon and beetroot tartare with horseradish sauce or Perigord sweetbreads. For afters, don't forget to leave room for the crusty chocolate biscuit and its citrus fruit *coulis.*

Saint-Nicolas-lez-Arras

CAMPANILE ZA les Alouettes ✆ **03 21 55 56 30** *Email: arras.stnicolas@campanile.fr. Rooms 58 €-62 €, supplement for 3rd person 8 € (under-12s free in the double room). Weekend prices at certain times, 49 €-51 €. Breakfast buffet (full and attractive) 7.20 €. All-in overnight stay 79 €. Set menus 9.90 €-17.70 €. Two children's menus, 5.95 € and 8.95 €.* The Campanile has 39 rooms with bath, including two fitted out for reduced mobility guests, and a pair of connecting rooms. Pets welcome without a supplement. The seminar room seats 30. Huge car park. The restaurant has an open fireplace and a cosy atmosphere, for breakfast and dinner. You get a 'courtesy tray' with hot drinks and biscuits in your room. Friendly reception.

Saint-Omer

LA COUPOLE Rue du Monts-Cars ✆ **03 21 12 27 27.** *Site: www.lacoupole.com – e-mail: lacoupole@lacoupole.com. Open every day: 9am-6pm all year, 10am-7pm in July & August. Admission: 9 €, concessions 6 €, groups 7.50 €. 4.50 € reduction for groups of 20 or over.* This V2 missile firing bunker is protected by a huge 70m-diameter dome in reinforced concrete, poured directly over backfill which was then cleared away so as to put up the walls. The whole construction is almost indestructible. Today, this underground launch base contains a museum illustrating Hitler's secret weapons - which foreshadowed the conquest of outer Space - and Northern France's suffering under German occupation.

Vendin

LENSOTEL* Vendin 2 shopping centre ✆ 03 21 79 36 36.** *Website: www.lensotel.com – email: lensotel@wanadoo.fr. Rooms 60 € and 67 €. Breakfast 9 €. Set menus 16 €, 22 € and 30 €. A la carte. Restaurant open every day. 70 single or double rooms with mini-bar and TV, plus an attractive view of the ornamental pond and swimming pool (open in summer).* The restaurant is excellent, with original menus (featuring casseroled game) and a warm and friendly setting. The private salons ensure your meetings remain confidential.

Wimereux

HOTEL DU CENTRE ** 78, rue Carnot ✆ 03 21 32 41 08. *Fax : 03 21 33 82 48. Website : www.hotelducentre-wimereux.com. Closed 20 December-20 January. Restaurant closed Monday. Set menus 16.50 € to 29.50 €. A la carte around 25 €. Rooms from 53 € to 75 €. Breakfast 7 €.* This residence dates back to 1890, when it was the stables for a coaching inn. At that time, during the Belle Epoque, Wimereux was a luxury holiday resort. The Boulanger family has managed to keep the best of the period decor; the 25 rooms are richly and comfortably decorated, with shower, bath and TV. The restaurant serves traditional dishes like grilled bream with fennel, chicken cooked with quince and citrus fruit terrine with orange jelly.

EPICURE 1, rue de la Gare ✆ 03 21 83 21 83 *Set menus from 25 €. Advance bookings only.* L'Epicure is located at one of the first turnings in the Rue Carnot, coming from Boulogne. It has an unassuming look, and the inside decor is equally modest, but the cuisine makes up for this, being flamboyant and innovative. Chef Philippe Carrée has created the 'grand couvert' and 'petit couvert' menus: the first features roast Dublin bay prawns on a bed of onions conserved in lemon, and curry sauce, chopped crab in a vegetable marinade, and a side dish of tomatoes (original!) and the second is also surprising, with sea bream fillets and artichoke flavoured with aniseed. You'll realise why booking ahead is the rule here.

PICARDY

AISNE

Berry-au-Bac

LA COTE 108 1, rue Colonel Vergezac ✆ 03 23 79 95 04 *Closed 25 December-11 January; Sunday evening, Monday and Tuesday. Set* *menus 23 € to 68 €.* The chef masters his cooking perfectly, working only with top-quality ingredients that he prepares with talent. The cuisine is served in an attractive dining room, decorated in modern style.

Chamouille

MERCURE*** ✆ **03 23 24 84 85**. *Fax: 03 23 24 81 20. Website: www.ailette.fr - Email: hotel.mercure@ailette.fr - 58 rooms from 89 € to 99 €. Breakfast 12.50 €. set menus 17 €-42 €. Free car park. Swimming pool.* The Mercure Ailette's 58 3-star rooms all have a splendid view of the 150 ha. lake. Piano bar, restaurant with air-conditioned veranda, pool, 18-hole golf course nearby. Quiet country setting.

Chauny

LA TOQUE BLANCHE 24, avenue Victor-Hugo ✆ **03 23 39 98 98** *Website : www.toque-blanche.fr. Closed Saturday lunchtime, Sunday evening and all day Monday. Set menus 32 € to 70 €. 5 rooms from 60 € to 87 €. Breakfast 12 €.* This is forest and pasture countryside, rich in all kinds of natural produce: game in season, and autumn truffles from the Renansart territory; asparagus, chicory and carrots; pork and Charolais beef from the Amiens herds. Véronique puts together the wine list, featuring burgundies from small domaine winegrowers – consumption here tends to be moderate, judging by the number of half-bottles! La Toque Blanche has been the proud owner of a star for 15 years now –make sure you follow it!

Fère-en-Tardenois

CHATEAU DE FERE Route de Fismes ✆ **03 23 82 21 13** *Fax 03 23 82 37 81. Set menus 50 € to 90 €. A la carte 75 €. Closed Monday lunchtime (from January to March and November to Christmas) and 2 January-10 February.* The château's recent gastronomic history has been rather eventful. Several top chefs have passed through, staying only for a season or two, to be replaced by others not necessarily up to scratch, and the image of this splendid 18thc. residence in its 12 ha. park has suffered. Dominique Quay, former chef at the Goyen in Audierne, seems to have brought stability to the restaurant at last: - he arrived in 1997 and is still holding the fort. Having trained in Brittany, fish have pride of place on his menus, including turbot in a herb crust, dory, and bass carpaccio. The château is gaining a reputation for consistent quality, which you also appreciate in the majestic hotel rooms with their high ceilings.

Laon

HOTEL DU COMMERCE **11, place des Droits-de-l'Homme** ✆ **03 23 79 57 16**. *Fax: 03 23 79 63 90. – Website: www.hotel-commerce-laon.com Email: hotel-commerce-laon@wanadoo.fr. 24 rooms, pets accepted 5 €, private garage 5 €. Rooms 29 €-39 €. Breakfast 5 €.* After much-needed renovation, the Hotel du Commerce offers singles, doubles and rooms sleeping several people, all with bathroom. It is conveniently located in the heart of the lower town near the railway station. Welcome and service with a smile, pleasant setting - you can't help but feel at home.

Reuilly-Sauvigny

AUBERGE LE RELAIS 2 rue de Paris ✆ **03 23 70 35 36** *Fax 03 23 70 27 76. Set menus from 29 € to 75 €. A la carte 85 €. Closed Tuesday, Wednesday, 29 January-2 March and 20 August-7 September.* The first time you set foot in this little town in the Aisne, you have difficulty believing that the modest *Logis de France* façade with no particular charm hides one of the region's top restaurants. Chef Martial Berthuit's talent is well-known in these parts, however: after 25 years at the Auberge Le Relais he is still constantly innovating, and spoiling his customers with the region's best ingredients, as well as

produce from farther afield. Try his beetroot jelly and cauliflower cream, Dublin bay prawn carpaccio with olive oil, lobster pan-cooked with grapefruit, capers and broad beans, served with its *raviole*, and slightly acid deglazing juice, pan-fried turbot, white onion *fondue*, asparagus and fennel sauce, chilled cream of garden peas, dried parmesan and olivettes, and young pigeon supreme, with its leg confit in crusty *kadaif* (fine spaghetti-like pastry) with mushrooms and cress, and the excellent desserts to follow, including one of the best millefeuilles in France. Great champagne list, and relaxed service in a pretty dining room on a veranda overlooking valley and vineyards.

Saint-Quentin

LE GRAND HOTEL* 6, rue Dachery ✆ 03 23 62 69 77. 24 rooms from 69 € to 90 €. Breakfast 8 €.** *A top quality hotel, with spacious rooms fully-equipped for a comfortable stay.*

HOTEL DES CANONNIERS * 15, rue des Canonniers ✆ 03 23 62 87 87** *www.hotel-canonniers.com. 5 rooms from 50 € and 2 suites at 105 €. Breakfast 8 €.* This beautiful hotel was once a private mansion, now fully renovated. It has few rooms, but they are marvellous, especially the ones overlooking the park, which is open for walks.

LE VERT GOUTEILLE 80, rue d'Isle ✆ 03 23 05 13 25 *Open every day, except Saturday lunchtime and Sunday. Set menus from 15 €. A la carte.* You find a warm and friendly atmosphere in this restaurant specialising in Lyonnais *cuisine*. Produce and wines are equally well chosen. The day's suggestions vary according to season and the chef's mood. You can eat on the terrace in fine weather.

Vervins

LA TOUR DU ROY* 45, rue du Général-Leclerc ✆ 03 23 98 00 11**. *Fax: 03 23 98 00 72. Website: www.latourduroy.com - Email: latourduroy@wanadoo.fr - 22 rooms from 65 € to 230 €. Breakfast 15 €. Restaurant closed Monday and Tuesday lunchtimes. Set menus 35 €-65 €.* This amazing pink building with its twin towers stands proudly on Vervin's 10thc.ramparts, and is run by Annie Desvignes. It is in fact a real chateau, in brick and white stone, and has several salons and a pleasant interior garden. The elegant wood and marble decor is reflected in a perfectly classic *cuisine*, using only the best and freshest regional products: foie gras terrine with truffles, suckling pig with beer and cherries, eel *au vert*, and game stuffed with cepes or morels. You can enjoy confiture de lait (a caramel-like preserve) for dessert. The rooms have been entirely done up, and all have a superb view of the valley. Four of them boast a jacuzzi.

Villers-Cotterets

LE REGENT* 26, rue du Général-Mangin ✆ 03 23 96 01 46**. *Fax: 03 23 96 37 57. Website - www.hotel-leregent.com - Email: info@hotel-leregent.com - 26 rooms from 38 € to 80 €. Breakfast 8 €. Open every day. Foam baths, garage.* This former coaching inn has kept its old-fashioned charm and 18thc. style. A log fire crackles in the monumental fireplace, an old clock ticks away time, and the beautiful interior courtyard recalls the days of coaches and horses. The rooms are comfortable and elegant with plenty of charm; each has its bathroom (bath or shower), WC, and colour TV with satellite channels. Some have a balcony.

OISE

Apremont

LA GRANGE AUX LOUPS 8, rue du 11-Novembre ✆ 03 44 25 33 79 *Open every day except Sunday evening and Monday. Set menus from 25 €. Dégustation menu from 50 €. A la carte. Rooms 80 €, breakfast 10 €.* This auberge is a must in the department, probably the most reputed of its kind. It is located on the edge of Chantilly Forest, and decorated in an elegant yet rustic manner with beams and a superb central fireplace. Gastronomic cuisine, using prestigious ingredients, with traditional recipes revamped Nouvelle Cuisine-style.

Beauvais

HOTEL KYRIAD 26, rue Gay-Lussac ✆ 03 44 02 55 15**. *Website: www.envergure.fr/template. Open all year. 48 rooms from 50 €. Breakfast 8 €. Two rooms fitted out for disabled visitors. Set menus 13 €-19 €.* M and Mme Leveaux welcome you warmly with tray of sweets and hot drinks. The 48 rooms are all different and are equipped with bathrooms and all the usual comforts. Relax in the sauna (you can borrow a bathrobe) and enjoy regional cooking in the restaurant, which offers local speciality menus and excellent dishes of the day. Great value for money!

CITY-HOTEL 227, avenue Marcel-Dassault ✆ 03 44 15 38 38. *Fax: 03 44 15 38 00. Website: www.cityhotel.fr. Rooms 60 €, extra bed 10 €. Breakfast 7.50 €. All-in overnight price 79 € (room, dinner in the Grand Chêne and breakfast). Private car park with CCTV. Free parking available in the car park during a stay beginning in Beauvais.3 mins from the airport, 5 mins from town centre, close to Marcel Dassault Park in its green setting.* The City Hotel offers 44 comfortable, soundproofed rooms, all equipped with bathroom, WC, washbasin, flat screen TV (TPS, satellite, Canal +) and free WiFi connection. Bar, terrace and billiard room are at guests' disposal.

HOSTELLERIE SAINT-VINCENT ** Rue de Clermont ✆ 03 44 05 49 99 Fax: 03 44 05 52 94. *Website: www.vincent-h.com. 48 rooms at 62 €. Set menus 16 € to 33 €. A la carte 25 €. Breakfast 8 €. Last order taken at 10pm. This modern, family-run building is ideal for a convenient and pleasant* *stay in Beauvais. Classic but varied cooking, with game in season. Two rooms equipped with water therapy.*

Chantilly

CAMPANILE RN 16 Gouvieux ✆ 03 44 57 39 24 *Open all year, 44 rooms from 65 € on weekdays. Breakfast 7.20 €.* Discover Chantilly with its international reputation, only 45km from Paris. The owners welcome you warmly; the rooms are all comfortable and equipped with bathrooms. The restaurant offers dishes of the day and buffet formulas for starters and desserts (as much as you can eat) for 13.80 €. A seminar room is available for business trips or meetings, and guests have a private car park at their disposal. Pets accepted.

HOTEL DU PARC BEST WESTERN* 36, avenue du Maréchal-Joffre ✆ 03 44 58 20 00** *Website: www.hotel-parc-chantilly.com/ <http://www.hotel-parc-chantilly.com/> . Email: bwhotelduparc@aol.com. Open all year, 7 days a week, 24 hours a day. 57 rooms and 4 suites from 80 € to 180 €. Breakfast 11 €. Pets allowed. Four rooms fully-equipped for disabled guests. Beauty parlour next-door.* This hotel is in the centre of Chantilly, a few minutes from the racecourse, near the station. It will please even the most demanding guests, who find a faultless welcome and spacious, comfortable rooms - all individually decorated; some with private terrace. The private car park at residents' disposal has CCTV, but the Hotel du Parc's major attraction is its interior park, where you can have breakfast in fine weather, or go for a stroll. Don't forget this address!

Compiègne

CAMPANILE Avenue de Huy ✆ 03 44 20 42 35 *Located 10 minutes from the town centre on the edge of the woods. An original motel-style hotel (all rooms are accessible from the car park). Open all year, 53 rooms (2 reserved for guests with reduced mobility) from 66 € weekdays and 49 € weekends in low season. Breakfast buffet 8 €.* Within easy reach of the town centre, yet close to the forest. Warm welcome. Suitable for business travellers or family holidays. All the rooms have a balcony. The restaurant offers a buffet formula from 13.50 €, with unlimited starters and desserts. A la carte formulas and dishes of the day (fish and meat) available. The menus change on a regular basis.Car park at guests' disposal. Pets accepted.

HOSTELLERIE DU ROYAL-LIEU * 9, rue de Senlis ✆ 03 44 20 10 24.** *Website www.hostellerie-du-royal-lieu.com. Open all year, 7 days a week, 24 hours a day. 12 rooms and 3 suites from 83 € to 105 €. Breakfast 9 €. Set menus from 35 € and 46 €. A la carte.* Every room and suite in this huge, half-timbered house is individually decorated with period furniture. The cosy bar and spacious Louis XIII-style dining room overlooking a leafy, flower-filled park have their own particular timeless atmosphere. Chef Angelo Bonechi prepares classic but inventive gastronomic *cuisine. Covered terrace; meals served in the garden during* summer.

LA PART DES ANGES 18, rue de Bouvines 03 44 86 00 00. *Open every day except Saturday lunchtime, Sunday evening and Monday. Set menus from 35 €. A la carte. Children's menu 16 €.* Located in the town centre, in a warm and friendly rustic setting with period furniture. Sophisticated *cuisine.*

Gouvieux

CHATEAU DE MONTVILLARGENNE ** Avenue François Mathet ✆ 03 44 62 36 36. Site: www.chateaudemontvillargenne.com.** *Theme menus 36 €. Set menus from 18 € for 5-12 year olds. Local specialities. Rooms 170 € to 300 €.* You reach this prestigious chateau by crossing a sumptuous leafy courtyard leading to a wide avenue lined with beautifully-kept hedges and magnificent flowerbeds. A number of 19thc. poets and writers - de Musset, Hugo, Lamartine and Chateaubriand - used to meet here: you can imagine them being inspired by the setting. Today, the site is protected by CCTV outside. Inside, a series of luxurious corridors are lined with display cases containing jewellery, ornaments and locally symbolic figurines, like horses and stags. Gourmets will enjoy the fine cuisine. Ideal for honeymoon couples (whose budget can stretch to it!).

Pierrefonds

LE CHALET DU LAC 1, chaussée Deflubé ✆ 03 44 42 03 33. *Email: chalfonds@aol.com Open every day during French school holidays. Closed Monday and Thursday in term time.* Opposite the chateau at the water's edge, this delightful and rather imposing inn offers traditional French cooking which includes grills and more gastronomic dishes. There is a *salon de the* where you can taste crepes and delicious ice-creams, comfortably settled by the lakeside.

Noyon

LA DAME JOURNE 2, boulevard Mony ✆ 03 44 44 01 *Fax: 03 44 09 59 68. Closed Sunday evening, Monday, Tuesday evening and Wednesday evening. Set menus from 19 €. A la carte.* Located in the historic heart of the town, this reputed restaurant has a name for excellence. A meticulously-prepared *cuisine* based on local, seasonal ingredients is served in a classic and intimate setting: snails, scallops (in season), beef fillet with snails, a red fruit 'conversation' and trolleys boasting 14 cheeses and 14 desserts feature on the menus.

Senlis

LE SCARAMOUCHE 4, place Notre-Dame ✆ 03 44 53 01 26. *Site: www.le-scaramouche.fr Closed Tuesday and Wednesday. Set menus 26 €. Children's menu 11 €. A la carte.* This attractive restaurant facing the splendid cathedral may seem rather steep for your budget, but it's the place to treat yourself to a special meal - a romantic dinner for two, perhaps – with pig's trotter in *tarte Tatin*, roast onions and mustard-flavoured juice, or game in season. The charming terrace and luminous decor add something to the culinary pleasure.

SOMME

Abbeville

AUBERGE DE LA CORNE 32, chaussée du Bois ✆ 03 22 24 06 34 *Closed Saturday and Sunday. Set menu 15 €.* Yves Lematelot does catering too. Rather than hesitating too long between the marbled foie gras with figs and the veal sweetbread escalope with chanterelles, you could trust his respect for natural flavours, and choose the day's suggestion instead. Quick, unobtrusive service in a pleasant little dining room.

Amiens

LE BOUCHON 10, rue Alexandre-Fatton ✆ 03 22 92 14 32. *Open every day except Sunday evening. Set menus 22 € to 42 €, lunchtime express menu 13 €.* Two dining rooms welcome you, in this restaurant overshadowed by the Tour Perret. The setting is elegant and modern, with contemporary paintings on the walls and wooden designer chairs. The seasonal cooking is faultless too: taste the foie gras mi-cuit with a glass of tariquet (white wine) or the caramelised pear with gingerbread ice cream and glass of coteau du layon.

BEST WESTERN – GRAND HOTEL DE L'UNIVERS * 2, rue de Noyon ✆ 03 22 91 52 51** *Website: www.bestwestern.com/fr/grandhoteldeunivers 41 rooms from 78 € to 102 €. Breakfast 10.80 €.* This Grand Hotel has managed to keep its opulent but cosy and welcoming style through several periods of refurbishing and renovation. The huge rooms are all differently decorated, with cable TV and mini-bar. Room service. Four rooms available for meetings and seminars.

Fort-Mahon-Plage

HOTEL DE LA TERRASSE ** Avenue de la Plage ✆ 03 22 23 37 77. *Website: www.hotellaterrasse.com Logis de France 56 rooms with bathrooms, most with a sea view. Double room (2 people) from 37 € in low season at the back of the hotel to 85 € with sea view and bath with bubble machine, in high season. Set menus from 12.90 € to 48.95 €.* The hotel has a brasserie corner and a restaurant, and its speciality is fish. Seafood platters, live lobster, monkfish, turbot and bass fillets feature on the menu.

Le Crotoy

LES TOURELLES ** 4, rue Pierre-Guerlain ✆ 03 22 27 16 33. *Website: www.lestourelles.com 27 rooms from 57 € to 75 €. Breakfast 8 €.* The hotel with its two turrets can be seen from Saint-Valéry. Inside, it has an exceptional panoramic view over the Baie de Somme. This is a classy place, right down to the last detail, and the food is of the same quality, beautifully prepared and served.

Péronne

HOSTELLERIE DES REMPARTS ** 23, rue Beaubois ✆ 03 22 84 01 22. *Fax: 03 22 84 31 96. 16 rooms from 55 € to 85 € (single or double). Breakfast 7.50 €. Set menus from 22 € to 40 €. Pets accepted. Carte Bleue credit card.* This hotel, located on the town's ramparts, welcomes you warmly. The setting is attractive, and the rooms comfortable and tastefully decorated. You are served classic and personalised cuisine, rooted in the local soil: warm Haute Somme smoked eel, Picard matelote (fish in white wine) and other regional culinary pleasures.

Roye

LA FLAMICHE 20 place de l'Hôtel-de-Ville ✆ 03 22 87 00 56 *Fax 03 22 78 46 77. Website: www.flamiche.fr Set menus 32 € to 125 €. A la carte 75 €. Closed Sunday evening, Monday, Tuesday lunchtime, first week in January and last 3 weeks in August.* Marie-Christine and G Borck Klopp's place is a typical provincial restaurant, cosily warm and friendly, though you may feel rather cramped in the dining room, which is small and usually full. The serving staff can seem cold and rather haughty, but then again, the master of the house is a passionate type, and a great wine connoisseur. In the kitchen, Marie-Christine steers her way easily through an ultra-classic repertory, where game has pride of place in season, served with magnificent mushrooms and rich, plentiful sauces. Some of the dishes may be slightly overcooked to your taste, and the prices are high, but this Flamiche is still one of the most attractive restaurants north of Paris.

HOTEL CENTRAL-LE FLORENTIN ** 36, rue d'Amiens ✆ 03 22 87 11 05. *Fax: 03 22 87 42 74. Website: www.leflorentin.com Closed Sunday evening and Monday. 8 rooms from 37 € to 52 €. Set menus from 14 € to 36 €. A la carte 35 €.* This restaurant in its Florentine-style setting serves varied but traditional *cuisine*, with Picardy *ficelle* (savoury pancakes) duck confit with mushrooms and fisherman's stewpot on the menu, and poached pear in caramel sauce for dessert. It is also an hotel, with individually decorated rooms.

Saint-Valéry-sur-Somme

L'HOTEL-RESTAURANT DU CAP HORNU 2, place Guillaume-le-Conquérant ✆ 03 22 60 24 24. *Site Internet: www.hotelcaphornu.com 9 gîtes sleeping 6-8 (480 € to 980 € a week) and 66 rooms (49.50 € and 114 € a night). Breakfast 9 €. Advance bookings only. Open February to early January. 3 big car parks.* 2 km from Saint-Valéry-sur-Somme, Le Cap Hornu looks towards Le Crotoy and the Hourdel headland. It is a peaceful place, nestling in greenery, ideal for family breaks and small groups of friends. On site, you find a top-quality restaurant, outdoor heated pool, two tennis courts, bikes for hire (9 € -13 € for ordinary cycles, and 10 €-17 € for electric bikes) and free access to the Belle Dune aquaclub from September to May. The late 17thc.-early 18thc. manor is also a good place for weddings, seminars and family parties - anniversaries, christenings etc. You absolutely must climb up to the sailors' chapel, via the path towards old Saint-Valéry-sur-Somme, and enjoy the exceptional view of the Baie de Somme and Cap Hornu.

LE QUAI DES ARTS 3, quai Perrée ✆ 03 22 60 80 18. *Fax: 03 22 60 86 81. Closed Monday evening and Tuesday in low season. Set menus between 16 € and 32 €.* Covered terrace and upstairs dining room overlooking Saint-Valéry harbour. Traditional cuisine, excellent value for money. Ask for a window table, so as to enjoy the panoramic view.

BELGIQUE

La Panne

DONNY** Donnylaan, 17 ✆ 058/41 18 00.** *Website: www.hoteldonny.com – email: info@hoteldonny.com – Single room 65 €-80 €, double 75 €-185 €.* This is the town's most attractive hotel, only 2 minutes from the sea. The services are top-of-the-range, with excellent value for money. The standard family room (sleeps 4, plus breakfast) is 125 € in low season and 145 € in high season, and the standard double room costs only 75 € in low season and 85 € in high season. The indoor pool, sauna, Turkish baths and fitness room are at guests' disposal. If you're after something more luxurious, the junior suites with lounge or private terrace have a view of La Panne nature reserve or towards the sea: prices range from 100 € for two in low season to 125 € in high season. The all in 'sano' offer (3 hours) costs 40 € for a hotel resident and 50 € for a non-resident, and includes a relaxing seawater therapy bath with seaweed, a back massage and the sanoclub: the offer is a must for plenty of managers who organise top-class seminars here. The WiFi Internet access in the rooms is new this year, and complements the Internet area in the bar.

Oostende

BOTTARGA Albert I promenade, 64 ✆ 059/80 86 88. *Website: www.bottarga.be – Lunch: 14 € (soup, main course and coffee, for example) Set menu 38 €. A la carte 35 €.* We love this modern bistro facing the sea, with its cosy interior. The atmosphere is trendy but quiet, and you'll quickly feel at ease. There is a vegetarian menu, and you can also try 'world food'. The cooking is certainly inventive, whatever you eat: even the simplest scampi kebab has its touch of originality. Add a warm welcome, and you have the ingredients for success.

CELTIC IRELAND Langestraat, 67 ✆ 059/51 85 99. *Website: www.celticireland.be – email: oostende@celticireland.be – Open every day. Single rooms 90 €-130 €, doubles 120 €-150 €, suite 180 €. A la carte 30 €.* A genuine piece of Ireland in Belgium. With a little imagination, you feel you're really in shamrock country. Wall and ceiling decoration is inspired by the Book of Kells, and there are several floors: the main bar with theme areas, the restaurant (local gastronomy) Wild Celt's Bar in the basement and the biggest terrace in Ostend. You can have a traditional meal or a pint of Guinness in one and the same place. There are live concerts every evening. The menu is varied, featuring Irish Stew and Indian chicken curry with coriander. For dessert, Baileys' Irish ice cream seems an obvious choice, followed by one of the many Scotch, Irish and Japanese whiskies. If you overdo it, a luxurious room is available for sleeping it off.

EUROPE HOTEL** Kapucijnenstraat, 52 ✆ 059/70 10 12/059/70 48 48.** *Fax: 059/80 99 79. Email: info@europehotel.be – Single rooms 47 €-87 €, doubles 62 €-102 € in low season, 68 €-108 € and 83 €-123 € in high season. Breakfast included. Half-board available. 55 tastefully-decorated rooms with all mod cons - TV, telephone, safe, bathroom with bath/shower and WC. Pleasant lounge, meeting room, bar and restaurant with breakfast buffet, sauna, Turkish baths, solarium and fitness room.* The hotel is located in a quiet part of the town centre, 50m from the seafront, promenade and beach, and 300m from the casino. Car park or garage at your disposal. Dogs admitted.

IMPERIAL BEST WESTERN* Van Iseghemlaan, 76 ✆ 059/80 67 67.** *Fax: 059/80 78 30. Email: info@hotel-imperial.be – Single rooms 55 €-90 €, doubles 65 €-120 €, breakfast included. Extra bed 25 €. Car park 15 €.* Opposite the beach and the casino, this hotel has 60 rooms equipped with bathroom (bath or shower), WC and hairdryer, cable TV, radio, and telephone with outside line. Internet connection available. You can ask to have a small fridge or cot in your room, and a high chair in the breakfast room. Every effort is made to guarantee you a pleasant stay.

OSTEND HOTEL* Londenstraat, 6 ✆ 059/70 46 25.** *Fax: 059/80 46 22. Email: ostend-hotel@oostende.net – Rooms 56.50 €-61.50 € for one, 79 €-89 € for two. Half-board supplement 21 €, breakfast 8 €.* 123 recently-renovated rooms are at your disposal, including 40 comfortable fa ily rooms and junior suites. Fully-equipped bathroom, phone with direct outside line, colour TV and internal video network which lets you watch two films a day for free. The family rooms measure 30 sqm. and can be separated in two parts by a folding door; they also have a second TV, mini-fridge and a bigger bathroom with bath, as do the junior suites. The bar is pleasant and the restaurant huge, with a 1950s-style setting and buffet. There is a games room for the kids, meeting rooms fron banquets and seminars, a fitnesss centre, sauna, and two solariums. The beach and fish market are just nearby.

TER KADE*** **Visserkaai, 49 ✆ 059/50 09 15.** *Fax: 059/51 04 87. Email: info@terkade.be – Single rooms 49 €, twin 93 €.* Forty-two rooms with a view of the sea between beach and harbour. Both rooms and studios are elegant and comfortable, with bathroom, TV, telephone, fridge and hairdryer. Free tea and coffee are at your disposal. The restaurant menu is varied. An ideal place to spoil yourself.

THERMAE PALACE**** **Koningin Astridlaan, 7 ✆ 059/80 66 44.** *Fax: 059/80 52 74. Email: info@thermaepalace.be – Rooms 170 €-220 €, suite 320 €, breakfast 14 €.* Most of the 153 rooms and 6 suites in this monumental hotel have a sea view, and also provide 4-star comfort. The hotel itself is Art-Deco in style, facing the golf coures and racetrack, and offers a fitness centre and Olympic pool nearby. When it comes to eating you have two options: the gastronomic restaurant Perigord with its original menus, or the Paddock Bistrot for simpler meals (terrace for fine weather). 18 rooms are at your disposal for organising congresses and other events.

176291

OSTEND HOTEL

*Ostend*** Hotel*
Located on the seafront and
in the heart of the town,

ACCES **** HOTEL

*Acces**** Hotel*
Unique access
to the sea,
and so much more!

176292

Looking for a romantic
week-end for two ?
A breath of fresh air
on the beach ?
Consult the special deals
on our website.

Acces****Hotel,
we do our best
to make your feel at home !

Normandy

NORMANDIE

Autoroute
Nationale 4 voies
Nationale
Départementale
Préfecture
Sous-préfecture
Ville, village
Sortie d'autoroute
Aéroport
Forêt domaniale
Normandie
Manche
Cap Lévy
St.Pierre-Eglise
Cherbourg
Barfleur
D901
Pointe de Barfleur
Quettehou
D904
N13
D902
Valognes
Bricquebec
Plages du Débarquement
Ste.Mère-Eglise
Grandcamp-Maisy
St.Sauveur-le-Vicomte
D514
Arromanches-les-Bains
St-Aubin-sur-Mer
Houlgate
Douve
D903
Carentan
Bayeux
Ouistreham
Cabourg
Douvres-la-Délivrande
D900
D24
D971
St.Jean-de-Daye
D5
D572
Tilly-sur-Seulles
D7
A13
Balleroy
CAEN
Périers
Vire
D9
D2
D13
Troarn
Dives
ST-LÔ
N175
N13
Moult
D972
Calvados
Coutances
Manche
N174
A84
D562
N158
D40
Aunay-sur-Odon
D7
N175
Potigny
D6
Gavray
D6
Clécy
D511
Granville
Condé-sur-Noireau
Vire
Vassy
N512
D577
D511
Falaise
Villedieu-les-Poêles
Brécey
Orne
N158
D909
D973
D999
Sourdeval
Tinchebray
Flers
Putanges-Pont-Ecrepin
Argentan
Avranches
Sée
Ecouché
Briouze
le Mont-St.Michel
D5
Messei
D924
Mortain
D962
N175
N176
Domfront
D908
la Ferté-Macé
Carouges
St.Hilaire-du-Harcouët
Sélune
Pontorson
A84
N176
Bagnoles-de-l'Orne
D21
Vers Fougères
Vers Rennes
Vers Mayenne
Vers le Mayenne
Ille-et-Vilaine
Mayenne

le Tréport
Vers Abbeville
Criel-sur-Mer
Eu
Vers Abbeville
Gamaches
Dieppe
Envermeu
le Bourg-Dun
St.Valery-en-Caux
Arques-la-Bataille
D925
Fontaine-le-Dun
Béthune
D1
Bresle
Vers Amiens
A28
Fécamp
D925
Cany-Barville
D142
Longueville-sur-Scie
Neufchâtel-en-Bray
Aumale
Etretat
Valmont
D940
D926
Fauville-en-Caux
Yerville
St-Saëns
Criquetot-l'Esneval
Goderville
D915
Forges-les-Eaux
Oise
D925
A29
Yvetot
Seine-Maritime
Buchy
Montivilliers
N15
Caudebec-en-caux
Barentin
A150
Andelle
Argueil
Vers Beauvais
Lillebonne
Duclair
A15
Seine
ROUEN
Gournay-en-Bray
Honfleur
Boos
N175
A29
Fleury-sur-Andelle
Pont-Audemer
Montfort s./Risle
Pont-l'Évêque
Pont-de-l'Arche
Etrépagny
A13
N138
Elbeuf
Gisors
Lieurey
le Bec-Hellouin
les Andelys
Blangy-le-Château
Louviers
Vers Pontoise
Brionne
Lisieux
Thiberville
le Neubourg
Seine
Val-d'Oise
A13
A28
la Rivière-Thibouville
Eure
N13
Iton
A13
Vernon
Bernay
Eure
Livarot
Orbec
EVREUX
Touques
Broglie
Beaumesnil
D140
Vers Paris
Pacy-sur-Eure
Vimoutiers
Conches
St-André-de-l'Eure
D916
D819
la Neuve-Lyre
Ivry-la-Bataille
D979
N138
Damville
N154
Breteuil
Risle
Yvelines
Exmes
Gacé
l'Aigle
Iton
Nonancourt
D932
Verneuil
Vers Dreux
Nonant-le-Pin
le Merlerault
Moulins-la-Marche
Avre
Courtomer
N12
Sées
D932
Tourouvre
Orne
N
N138
N12
Mortagne-au-Perche
D918
O
E
S
D938
Rémalard
Vers Chartres
Bellême
D955
Eure-et-Loir
Vers le Mans
le Theil
N23
Vers le Mans
0
30 km
Sarthe
Loir et Ch
Reproduction interdite
Jean-Baptiste Pény
Mars 2006

ROUEN

ROUEN-NORMANDIE TOURIST OFFICE 25, place de la Cathédrale © 02 32 08 32 40. *www.rouentourisme.com - E-mail: rouen@tourisme.fr - Open May-September: 9am-7pm. Sunday & public holidays: 9.30am-12.30pm and 2pm-6pm. Octobre-April: Monday-Saturday: 9am-6pm, Sunday & public holidays: 10am-1pm. Free brochures (Rouen & department) available, with information about evening entertainment. Tickets on sale here for town tour in the little train.* Old stone and modernity co-exist pleasantly in Rouen. The historic centre with its busy shops is undergoing renovation, so that future tourists will be better able to enjoy the town and its river.

SAINT OUEN ABBEY CHURCH Place du Général de Gaulle. *Open 16 January to 14 March, and 1 November to 14 December, Wednesday, Saturday and Sunday: 10am-12.30 pm, and 2pm-4.30pm; 15 March to 31 October every day except Tuesday: 10am-12.30pm and 2pm-6pm.* This is a masterpiece of its kind, if you manage to forget the rather heavy neo-Gothic façade. Founded in the 7th century, the abbey church contains unique, predominantly yellow, stained glass (14th to 16thc.) set off by the light flooding the nave.

AITRE SAINT-MACLOU 186, rue Martainville. *Open every day: 8am-8pm. Admission free.* This charnel house was built in 1526, to bury plague victims.

GROS HORLOGE BELFRY Rue du Gros-Horloge. 'Le Gros' as it is known is the town emblem, one of the oldest working clocks in Europe (16thc. face, 14thc. workings). Under its 16thc. arch, the clockface overlooks the busiest street from its belfry, and the people of Rouen used to set their watches by it.

NOTRE DAME CATHEDRAL Place de la Cathedrale. *Open every day: 8am-6pm, except public holidays and Monday morning (opens at 2pm).* May not be visited during services (Sunday morning before 1pm). The cathedral is a real patchwork of styles; building started in 1150 and went on until the 15thc., even longer for the spire (the highest in France at 150m) which was rebuilt in the 19thc. after the previous one had been destroyed by lightening. Monet loved it, among others.

GRANDMONT CHAPEL. Last remains of Grandmont Abbey, founded by Henry II of England, Duke of Normandy in the 12thc. for the Grandmont order. The chapel was rebuilt in the late 15thc.; parts of it date back to the 12th, 13th and 14thc.

JEANNE D'ARC CHURCH Place du Vieux Marché. *Open 10am-12.15pm and 2pm-6pm except Friday morning, Sunday morning and during services.* War damage compensation for Saint Vincent Church, destroyed by bombs, was offered on one condition: another church had to be built. So Louis Arrechte designed Jeanne d'Arc, inheriting Saint Vincent's 15thc. stained glass which he set off beautifully. Today, the church is considered as one of the town's chief monuments.

Rouen, historical house

SAINT MACLOU CHURCH Place Barthélemy. *Open Monday to Saturday: 10am-12 noon and 2pm-6pm (5.30pm in winter) and Sunday: 3pm-6pm. Admission free.* Rouen's third church is a late Gothic masterpiece, sadly damaged by bombing, which made a hole in the chancel and weakened the neo-Gothic spire (still unbalanced). The striking portal has 5 porches; its wooden doors were sculpted by Jean Goujon.

HOTEL DE BOURGTHEROULDE 15, place de la Pucelle. Inside courtyard open Monday to Friday: 9am-12.30pm and 1.30pm-6pm. Saturdays: 2pm-6pm. The town's oldest and finest private mansion (16thc.).

JARDIN DES PLANTES 114ter, avenue des Martyrs de la Résistance. *Open every day, 8am to nightfall (8pm* *in summer, 5.30pm in winter). Greenhouses open from 9am to 11.30am and from 1.30pm to 4.45pm.* One of the town's most beautiful walks, with its ornamental ponds and gardens, equatorial greenhouses, seasonal flowers and leisure facilities.

MUSEE DES BEAUX-ARTS Square Verdrel ✆ 02 35 71 28 40. *Closed on Tuesdays and some public holidays. Open 10am-6pm. Admission: adult 3 €* . A 19thc. building renovated in 1994, housing 16thc. to contemporary works of art. These include the great names in painting: Caravaggio, Rubens, Velasquez, Poussin, Fragonard, Ingres, Géricault, Delacroix, Corot, Degas, Monet, Renoir and Sisley. Admire Rouen Cathedral in grey weather by Monet, or the tapering face of a Modigliani.

Forges-les-Eaux

There is a craze for this pretty watering town, supposed to have therapeutic virtues. The earthenware industry also left its mark, thanks to the Englishman George Wood who settled here in 1797. Today, one man, Alexandre Audel, goes on making it; otherwise, Forges pottery is only a memory.

COLLECTION DE FAIENCES XIXe Hôtel de Ville ✆ 02 35 90 52 10. *Open all year on request (enquire at the Tourist Office).* Forges earthenware is famous for its naive decoration: houses, flowers, fish and birds, on 'black bottoms' and 'brown bottoms' (a reference to the colour coating the pottery underneath). There are over 100 19thc. exhibits to admire in Forges Town Hall Wedding Room.

GIVERNY AND THE BANKS OF THE SEINE

A corner of Paradise along the Seine between Paris and Normandy drew the Impressionist painters. Normandy contributed greatly to the development of the Impressionist movement, revolutionary in its time.

Giverny

Charles Monet's village is a place of pilgrimage. The painter settled there in 1883, and stayed until his death in 1926, painting his famous 'Waterlilies' in the meantime. It is a pleasant place to idle, among artists' studios and craft shops opening up like poppies in the sun.

MUSEE ET FONDATION CLAUDE MONET ✆ 02 32 51 28 21. *www.fondation-monet.com. Open every day except Monday, 1 April to 31 October: 9.30am-6pm. Open holiday Mondays. Admission (house and gardens): adult 5.50 €, 7-12s 3 €.* The painter's property has been restored in the style of the period, and his collection of Japanese prints reframed and hung as he used to have it. There are none of Monet's original paintings on the site (the nearest can be seen in the Alphonse-Georges Poulain Museum at Vernon); the attraction is the gardens laid out identically. The straight lines of the Clos-Normand, with its cleverly mingled essential oils, is followed by the oriental watergarden where the Japanese bridges creak under tourists come to admire the waterlilies. A useful tip: avoid Tuesdays and Thursdays when groups tend to come.

MUSEE D'ART AMERICAIN 99, rue Claude Monet ✆ 02 32 51 94 65. *www.maag.org. Open every day except Monday, 1 April to 31 October: 10am-6pm. Admission: adult 5.50 €, 13-18s 3 €, under-12s free.* The contemporary shape and careful lighting are a complement to the Monet Foundation, and the original works of American painters influenced by Monet contrast French and American views on 19th and 20thc. painting.

Les Andelys

Château Gaillard proudly defends the Andelys on their beautiful site in the Seine valley with its superb view. The towns are linked by parallel roads, Petit Andely to the west and Grand Andely to the east. The former is especially attractive, boasting half-timbered houses and a yachting harbour.

CHATEAU GAILLARD ✆ 02 32 54 04 16. *Open 10am-1pm and 2pm-6pm every day, except Tuesday, 15 March to 15 November. Outside access free. Guided tour of the keep: 3 € (40-minute tours at fixed times*). Richard the Lionheart had the castle built in 1196, so as to keep watch over the Seine and protect Rouen. The ruins are quickly seen; history fans then tour the keep, and learn that it held out eight months during Philippe Auguste's siege.

MUSEE NORMANDIE NIEMEN Rue Raymond-Phelip ✆ 02 32 54 49 76. *Open every day, except Tuesday, 1 June to 15 September: 10am-12 noon and 2pm-6pm; 16 September to 31 May: 2pm-6pm. Admission: adults 3.50 €.* Created by the General de Gaulle in 1942 to fight on the Eastern Front. Of its 96 pilots, 42 never came back, and the museum retraces that period with its extensive collection of souvenirs, documents, photos and objects like the Mirage F1 in front, reminding us that the Normandy-Niemen adventure goes on, 60 years later.

LE HAVRE – CÔTE D'ALBATRE

Le Havre

The town's history is of great interest. It was built by François 1 for military reasons; later the maritime link Le Havre-New York opened it up to the outside world. During World War II, the town was wiped out. It was reconstructed by Auguste Perret in reinforced concrete, from 1946 onwards. Though strongly criticized, this reconstruction has become the symbol of a new town resolutely facing the future.

NOTRE DAME CATHEDRAL Rue de Paris. The church was built between 1539 and 1630 and bombed during the war, much of its furnishings going up in flames. It has a fine, classic 17thc. façade and a Gothic side tower.

SAINT JOSEPH CHURCH Boulevard François 1er. The architects Perret and Audigier rebuilt this church. Its 106m tower is hollow from 84m up, and dedicated to victims of the World War II bombings.

ESPACE MARITIME ET PORTUAIRE DES DOCKS VAUBAN Quai Frissard ✆ 02 35 24 51 00. *Open Saturday, Sunday, Tuesday and Wednesday: 2.30pm to 6pm, or every day for groups (bookings only).* Originally built in 1846, these are France's oldest docks. Today they house a maritime museum, where you can discover those techniques and activities, from ocean liners to whale fishing, which are part of the port's history.

GRAVILLE PRIORY 1, rue Elisée-Reclus ✆ 02 35 24 51 00. *Open Wednesday to Sunday: 10am-12 noon and 2pm-6pm, except public holidays. Adults and children over 12, 3 €.* Le Havre's oldest monument. The 11th and 13thc. church is listed. Together with the convent buildings, it has a magnificent view over the town and Seine bay, and is surrounded by gardens. Its Romanesque part contains some interesting thematic capitals. Having been a museum since 1929, the church houses a collection of religious art from the 16thc. to today (parts of reredos; Madonnas; pieta) a history of urban dwelling contained in 100 or so scale models and collections of decorative art: coffers, wood, furniture, panels, and so on.

PONT DE NORMANDY. The Normandy Bridge has linked Upper and Lower Normandy since January 1995, and is an essential part of the Estuary road joining the Alabaster and Floral Coasts. You can be in Le Havre in a few minutes, and from there, discover the region. You can also cross the bridge on foot in about 2 hours, to admire the view over the bay - but you need to be fit!

Côte d'Albâtre

The Alabaster Coast stretches from Dieppe to Etretat. Its famous cliffs have been painted by great artists, and taken part in the most beautiful sunsets.

Dieppe

Dieppe began to flourish with William's conquest of England. From the 14th century, many expeditions left the town on voyages of discovery. The beach is the nearest to Paris, and attracts a fair number of artists.

LE BOUT DU QUAI. One of the town's oldest quarters. The rue des Cordiers, rue des Veulets and Place du Moulin à Vent all boast listed houses.

NOTRE DAME DE BONSECOURS CHAPEL. Dieppe's sailors made a pilgrimage here before putting to sea. In the Pollet quarter, a staircase leads up to the clifftop towards the chapel. The view and the military semaphore are worth seeing.

CHATEAU-MUSEE ✆ 02 35 06 61 99 *Open every day: 10am -12 noon and 2pm-6pm in season, every day except Tuesday: 10am-12 noon and 2pm-5 pm (6pm Sundays) out of season.* Built on the cliffs, Dieppe's castle has housed an ivory museum since 1923. Ivory is the town's speciality, and there are over 1 500 pieces to see. There are also paintings from the 16th to 20thc. and a marine room. The Camille Saint-Saens room contains the composer's personal belongings, such as his first piano, and another room is devoted to Braque's engravings.

SAINT JACQUES CHURCH. A blend of styles, from classical to High and Flamboyant Gothic. The outside looks more like a cathedral, given its size.

ESTRAN CITE DE LA MER 37, rue de l'Asile-Thomas ✆ 02 35 06 93 20. *www.estrancitedelamer.free.fr. Open all year, every day: 10am-12 noon and 2pm-6pm (except 25 December and 1 January).* This scientific and technical study site is divided into five areas, covering 1650 square metres on three

Pont de Normandie

levels, and dealing with fishing technology, ship building, cliffs and shingle and marine biology. This last topic is illustrated with aquariums containing flora and fauna from the Norman coasts. The museum is full of explanatory material, scale models and videos, accessible to all ages. Outside, you can discover the coast or visit the port and the fish auction.

MAISON MIFFANT. Built in 1624, this typical half-timbered Normandy residence is listed. The house has escaped the ravages of time and wars, thanks partly to the impressive skill of its carpenter.

Etretat

Etretat's hollow needle is the postcard to send from Normandy! This surprising geological phenomenon has been captured by Monet and others, and owes them its fame to an extent.

CLOS ARSENE LUPIN 15, rue de Maupassant ✆ 02 35 10 59 53. *www.arsene-lupin,com. Open every day: 10am-6pm, 1 April to 30 September and during French school holidays. Open the rest of the year Friday, Saturday and Sunday: 11am-5pm. Admission: adult 6 €, concessions 5 €, 6-16s 3.50 €.* Maurice Leblanc's house, where his famous character Arsene Lupin helps you discover the secret of the hollow Noodlo. Educational and fun.

CLIFFS. Etretat is shaped like a crescent moon, and features white cliffs, a white pebble beach and blue sea. Little has changed since Maupassant said this. The little houses huddle together under their slate roofs in the shelter of the cliffs. In fact, Etretat needs to be seen from above, with a pair of stout shoes and some willpower for the climb. The Aval (downstream) is the best known of the cliffs but can only be approached at low tide. Beyond the oyster beds, is the 'trou a l'homme' (manhole), the cave believed to have saved a shipwrecked man from a watery grave. Climbing towards the bay gives you a good view of the Porte d'Aval and 70-metre hollow Needle, followed by the second 'door' or Manneport, 90 metres high. At the other end of the beach, a staircase dug out of the cliffs leads up to Notre Dame de la Garde Chapel, together with the monument to aviators Nungesser and Coli. Superb view!

Eu

You'll enjoy visiting Eu, for despite its average size, it has so much of historical interest to see.

CHATEAU D'EU AND PARK. ✆ 02 35 86 44 00 *Open Easter to late October: 10am-12 noon and 2pm-6pm (tills close at 11.30am and 5.30pm.) except all day Tuesday and Friday morning. Admission: 4 €.* The first castle on the site is mentioned in the account of William the Conqueror's marriage to Matilda of Flanders in 1050, but it was knocked down on Louis XIth's orders in 1475. More building followed, notably due to Anne Marie Louise d'Orléans, known as the Grande Mademoiselle, who had formal pleasure gardens added to the estate in 1665. The town of Eu bought the castle in 1964 and installed the Town Hall and a museum in it. Today, it is open to the public, after renovation work which has given it back some of its former brilliance: the caisson ceiling in the Guise gallery has been reconstituted and the main staircase restored.

NOTRE DAME AND SAINT LAURENT COLLEGIATE CHURCH. *Open 9am-12 noon and 2pm-6pm (5pm November to March) except during services.* The Archbishop of Dublin, Laurent O'Toole, died at Eu in 1180, and the existing church was rebuilt in his name between 1186 and 1226. It contains a 30-metre Romanesque crypt where his tomb was placed. The recumbent statues of the Comtes d'Eu and the d'Artois family have been keeping him company since the 19thc. The nave has not been touched since it was first built.

Fécamp

Its inhabitants are known for their adventurous spirit, braving the seas in search of spices, foodstuff or new materials. In the 19thc, cod fishing off Newfoundland became lucrative, and Fécamp flourished.

HOLY TRINITY ABBEY CHURCH. The current Primitive Gothic abbey church goes back to the early 13thc, though the façade was rebuilt in the 18th and the axial chapel is 15thc. Flamboyant Gothic. A sanctuary already existed on the site, however, in 665. The church boasts a 127-metre nave and a lantern chapel typical of the region that casts a surprisingly clear light on the stones. The Dukes of Normandy's sepulture is worth seeing, in the south transept, and in the north transept, an astronomical clock (1667) with the tides marked on its face.

TERRE NEUVAS AND FISHING MUSEUM 27 boulevard Albert 1 (on the beach) ✆ 02 35 28 31 99. *Open every day except Tuesday: 10am-12 noon and 2pm-5.30pm. Open every day in July and August including Tuesday: 10am-7pm.* Facing the sea, the museum tells you about the cod fishermen who left for Newfoundland in the last century. Objects, scale models of boats and seascapes recall the harsh living conditions, herring fishing, shipbuilding and the industrial transforming of the fish, as well as lighter subjects like the port, the beach and sea-bathing. Fecamp's own souvenir album.

BENEDICTINE PALACE 110, rue Alexandre Le Grand ✆ 02 35 10 26 10. *www. benedictine.fr. Can be visted every day except in January and on 25 December. Admission: adult 5.80 € over-12s 2.80 €, under-12s free. Tasting for adults after the visit.* This neo-Gothic and Renaissance-style palace offers several thematic visits: a Fine Arts museum with collections of religious art; an exhibition of essential oils with plants and spices from all over the world, the distillery and cellars where the famous liqueur is made, and a contemporary exhibition centre.

Le Tréport

ILLUMINATED CLIFFS. Le Tréport wouldn't be the same without its cliffs, which give the resort its charm. They are among Europe's highest, peaking at over 100 metres, and the town lights them up between nightfall and 2am from October to May on Friday, Saturday and Sunday, and from June to September every evening.

Fécamp, palais Bénédictine

MUSEE DU VIEUX TREPORT 1 rue de l'Anguainerie - Former prison ✆ 02 35 86 13 36. *Open Easter to late September weekends and public holidays: 10am-12 noon and 3pm-6pm. Admission: adult 2 €, child 1 €. This former prison, built against a 16thc. vaulted door, now houses Le Tréport's museum.* The lives of seafarers, their fishing material, wrecks, scale models of boats, even a whale's rib and the skeleton of a skate are collected here. Fossils, drawings and engravings recall their harsh lives, but also the holiday Tréport with its 'pleasure trains', sea bathing and beach-huts; the old trades, such as marine carpenter and shingle-gatherers are mentioned. This is the town's memory, in fact.

DEAUVILLE AND CÔTE FLEURIE

The Côte Fleurie, or Floral Coast, is known throughout France for its beaches, its fashionable resorts (Deauville, Cabourg, Trouville), traditional restaurants and marvellous countryside.

Cabourg

This resort still calls to mind the Belle Epoque, though it has renovated its tourist facilities.

GRAND HOTEL. Charles Bertrand, Mayor of Cabourg and owner of the Baths and Casino, had the current Grand Hôtel built in 1907, blending Renaissance and 1900 style. It was the third to be built on that site. Marcel Proust spent his summers there until 1914.

Deauville

Deauville grew out of its sand dunes in the 19thc. thanks to the Empress Eugénie and the Duc de Morny, to become one of France's most luxurious resorts. It is also famous for its horses; the annual sale of yearlings at the end of August is an event, as are its races and polo matches. Deauville also means cinema, with its festival staged around the legendary boardwalk.

PLANCHES. The world-famous planks form an 800-metre boardwalk, built in 1923. Ladies thus avoided dirtying their shoes in muddy places.

SAINT LAURENT CHAPEL Rue du Moulin Saint Laurent. A mysterious chapel near Touques, with its early 12thc. vault and small fortress-like loopholes - why it needed this protective measure is anyone's guess. Well worth the trip.

CALOUSTE GULBEKIAN PARK Domaine des Enclos ✆ 02 31 14 40 00. *Open every afternoon, 1 July to 31 August: 2pm-6pm.* 24 hectares of peace and quiet, among black walnut and white ash trees from the Americas, Dutch plane trees, albizzias, and other rare trees. The park has belonged to the town since 1973, and is situated between Deauville and Mont Canisy.

Honfleur

This picturesque port at the far end of the Côte Fleurie is mentioned in documents going back to the 11thc.

Le port de Honfleur

SAINTE CATHERINE CHURCH AND TOWER Quartier Saint-Catherine © 02 31 89 11 83. *Open 9am-6pm in summer; 9am-12 noon and 2pm-5pm in winter. Closed during services. The tower is open every day except Tuesday: 10am-12 noon and 2pm-6pm.* Built of oak in the mid-15thc. by the town's naval carpenters, to thank God for ousting the English, this is the biggest church in France. The tower is separate.

SAINT ETIENNE CHURCH Quai Saint Etienne - Rue de la Prison © 02 31 89 14 12. The former church houses both the Naval and Ethnography Museums. The former boasts scale models of boats, and objects telling the story of the port. The latter contains reconstructed interiors from olden times, clothes and objects from local life.

SALT LOFTS Rue de la Ville The lofts are huge 17thc. stone buildings, built by the ferme generale des gabelles, (salt-tax farming) under Colbert, to stock the salt (up to 10 000 tonnes) needed for fitting out the cod-fishing expeditions. One burned down in 1892; the two left are listed monuments. The town authorities use them for exhibitions, concerts, conferences, etc.

LIEUTENANCE. It stands out among the others in the harbour. The King's Lieutenant and Governor of Honfleur lived here; before that, in the Middle Ages, it was a city gate.

MAISONS SATIE 67, boulevard Charles V © 02 31 89 11 11. *Open 1 May to 30 September: 10am-7pm; in winter, 11am-6pm. Closed Tuesday. Admission: adult 5.20 €, child 3.50 €*. A trip to the heart of Erik Satie's world. The composer was born here in 1866.

MUSEE EUGENE BOUDIN Place Erik-Satie © 02 31 89 54 00. *Open 15 March to 30 September: 10am-12 noon and 2pm-6pm. 1 October to 14 March: 2.30pm-5pm. Saturday and Sunday: 10am-12 noon and 2.30pm-5pm. Admission: Adult 4.50 € to 5.20 € child 2.80 €*. Admire the works of Monet, Courbet, Jongkind, Isabey, and 92 paintings and drawings by Boudin himself, in this modern building.

NATUROSPACE Boulevard Charles V © 02 31 81 77 00 *Open every day, late January to late November. Admission: adult 7.25 € , 3-14s 5.50 €, family 27.50 €*. You've never seen the natural world like this! In a temperate greenhouse (28° C), 200m. of paths wind through a tropical universe of plants and butterflies, recalling Binot Paulmier de Gonneville, who left Honfleur for the tropics in 1503, and discovered Brazil. You'll be captivated by the exotic beauty of this place. Bon voyage!

Houlgate

The architecture is amazing: beautiful 19thc. villas of coloured brick with wooden beams face the sea. The town's name was only definitively adopted in 1905.

BELVEDERE. Leave Houlgate on the coast road to reach this panoramic viewpoint, where an indicator set up in 1958 helps you identify local sites of interest.

HOULGATE CASINO 41, rue Henri-Dobert ✆ 02 31 28 75 75. *Website: www.groupe-vikings.fr - Open every day: 10am-2am, Sunday to Thursday, 10am-3am Friday, 10am-4am Saturday and evenings before public holidays. Set menus from 16 €.* This splendid casino on the seafront is quite the most impressive on the Normandy coast. Built in Belle Epoque style, with sophisticated colonial interior decor, it manages to avoid both tastelessness and ostentation. Even the one-arm bandit room is not as kitsch as usual in this kind of establishment (fans please note the arrival of some new machines in 2006). You'll even notice some greenery, intended to provide a little oxygen. There's always something going on at Houlgate Casino: concerts, all kinds of show, and theme evenings with the appropriate decoration and cocktails (last year the Le Tanka lounge bar transformed its dance floor into a beach with several cubic metres of sand!). The restaurant is now in the capable hands of chef Virginie Dupille - good news for gourmets, who can discover her culinary talent in the hushed intimacy of the Pondichery dining-room or on the terrace in fine weather (direct view of the beach). To sum up, this is a great vintage casino. Take your Petit Fute guide along and say we sent you - you'll get a pleasant surprise.

Ouistreham-Riva-Bella

LOCKS. Caen canal ends here in the port of Ouistreham, so locks were built to make navigation easier. The first appeared in the late 18thc, the second in 1903 and the last in 1963. Ships of 30,000 tonnes can pass through its 225m by 28m.

MUSEE DU MUR DE L'ATLANTIQUE - LE BUNKER Avenue du 6 Juin ✆ 02 31 97 28 69. *Open every day, 11 February to 1 May and 30 September to 15 November: 10-6pm; 1 May to 30 September: 9am-7pm. Admission: adult 6.50 €, child 3.10 €.* This 17m building was a former headquarters, surveying all navigation in the Baie de Seine within a radius of 40 km with a powerful rangefinder. The original blockhouses, rooms, machine room and ammunition depot are reconstructed on five floors.

MUSEE No4 COMMANDO KIEFFER Residence Jean-Bart - Place Alfred-Thomas ✆ 02 31 96 63 10. *Open every day, 31 March to 30 September: 10.30am-6pm. Admission: adult 4.50 €, over-10s 2.50 €.* You learn about Major Kieffer who landed with his French soldiers on 6 June 1944, as part of the liberating Franco-British 4th Commando. There are weapons, uniforms and badges.

Pont-Audemer

This former river port was named after Audemar, Comte de Poitiers, sent by King Eudes to fight off Viking attacks. Discover its canals, picturesque alleys and old houses by following the helpful historic tour directions.

Trouville

Separated from its twin, Deauville, by the Touques, Trouville remains a peaceful town, despite the tourists and many artists who've been coming since the 1800s. You'll find it lively, though, even out of season.

NATUR'AQUARIUM 17, rue de Paris ✆ 02 31 88 46 04. *Open all year. July & August: 10am-7.30pm, September & October 10am-12 noon and 2pm-7pm. November to Easter: 2pm-6.30pm. Easter to June: 10am-12 noon and 2pm-7pm. Admission: adult 7 , 5-16s 3.50 €. The ticket also gives admission to the Sea Museum and Villerville Desert.* This 600m^2 aquarium contains a huge variety of flora and fauna from the planet's seas and oceans. Sharks, turtles, scorpion- fish and groupers can be viewed in close-up; snakes, lizards, and frogs follow in a large vivarium.

CAEN

Caen, verdant town with its thousand-year-oldpast and William the Conqueror, who perhaps made the town what it is today; capital of Lower Normandy and Calvados, prefecture, university town, centre for sport and the arts. There is even a yachting harbour. This is really a pleasant town to visit and to live in.

PLACE SAINT SAUVEUR. Oldest square in Caen, trapeze-shaped, between the Palais de Justice and Saint Sauveur Church. 18thc. residences surround the central statue of Louis XIVth.

RUE FROIDE. Notre Dame de Froiderue stands proudly at the head of this 15th and 16thc. street, going over a branch of the River Odon. The church has two naves side by side, and was built between the 14th and 16thc.

HALF-TIMBERED HOUSES 52-54, rue Saint Pierre. These two houses huddled together date back to the 15th century. The overhanging storey made them roomier inside, while sheltering the shop stalls downstairs from rain and sun. They are finely sculpted, especially No. 54, with its 7 statuettes on the first floor and three left on the second. No. 52 houses the postal museum.

ABBAYE AUX HOMMES and ABBAYE AUX DAMES. Their history is linked; they were founded by William and Matilda in 1060 and 1062 as penitence, Pope Leon IX having judged their marriage illegal on the grounds that they were fifth cousins. The church forgave them, and the abbeys are the pride of Caen, standing as they do for eternal love, which appeals to everyone.

ABBAYE AUX HOMMES Esplanade Jean Marie Louvel ✆ 02 31 30 42 81. *Guided tours every day at 9.30am, 11am, 2.30pm and 4pm (except 1 January, 1 May and 25 December). Admission adult 1.50 €, child 1 €. The 11am tour includes the convent buildings, press and waiting-room; the others tours, the convent buidings and abbey church.* The abbey was founded in two parts; Saint Etienne Church and the convent buildings for the Benedictine monks, which now house the Town Hall. Saint Etienne was begun in 1066 and consecrated 11 years later. It is both Romanesque and Gothic in style; 90m high and 124m long.t

ABBAYE AUX DAMES Place Reine Mathilde ✆ 02 31 06 98 98. *Guided tours every day at 2.30pm and 4pm (except 1 January, 1 May and 25 December). Reception every day: 2pm to 5.30pm. Admission free.* Duchess Matilda of Flanders founded this sister abbey in 1060, with its convent buidings and Trinity Church. The former date back to the 18thc. and house Lower Normandy's Conseil Regional. Coming here is like time-travelling; the cloister, whose 4th side was never built, and the great staircase are in themselves worth a visit. Matilda's tomb is in the Romanesque chancel of Trinity Church, built from 1060 to 1080. Don't miss the crypt!

CAEN MEMORIAL A museum for peace. Esplanade Dwight Eisenhower ✆ 02 31 06 06 44. *www. memorial-caen.fr. Open every day, 9am-7pm. Closed during the first two weeks of January and 25 December. Admission low season: adult 16.50 to 17.50€, child 14€. Admission high season: adult 17.80€, child 15.50€*. This isn't really a museum, but a place for understanding why, in the hope that it will never happen again. "Pain broke me, brotherhood raised me, from my wound sprang a river of freedom" is engraved on the white façade, which just about sums up the Memorial. Inside, you are swallowed up by the War, from Occupation to Liberation; you hear voices from the past and see unbearable images. Afterwards, the events which followed on - Cold War and other conflicts - are commented on. There is a mediatheque, bookshop, restaurant and children's garden on the site. Not to be missed.

DUCAL CHATEAU. *www.chateau.caen.fr. Open all year: 6am-1am, Tuesday to Saturday and 6am to 7.30pm (winter) and 6am to 9.30pm (summer). Admission free*; the castle is being restored but the museums remain open. The castle is difficult to miss, occupying a central place in the town, from which point it has witnessed several centuries of history and been somewhat shaken up by them. Inside, you can visit Henry I Beauclerc's Exchequer Room, which served as a ceremonial room for the Dukes of Normandy who lived in the castle. The Governors' Rooms (17th and 18thc.) now house the Musée de Normandie.

Bayeux

Not only the Tapestry. Bayeux was the first large town to be liberated on 7 June 1944, and has managed to preserve its typical half-timbered houses and manors. It has a peaceful atmosphere, watched over by its beautiful cathedral.

NOTRE DAME CATHEDRAL Presbytery ✆ 02 31 92 01 85. *Guided tours every day in season. Open every day: 8.30am-6pm, 1 October to 30 June and 8.30am-7pm, July to September.* Beautiful Norman Gothic building, of amazing height. The 11thc. towers are 75 metres high (the central one is 15thc.). Little remains of William's first cathedral, inaugurated in 1077.

CONSERVATOIRE DE LA DENTELLE DE BAYEUX 6, rue Lambert Leforestier ✆ 02 31 92 73 80. *Admission free. Closed on Sunday. Open 10am-12.30pm and 2pm-6pm. Inside the 18thc.* Hôtel Doyen, its aim is to conserve the know-how and skill of Bayeux's lacemakers from the 17th century. You can see modern-day lacemakers at work.

MUSEE MEMORIAL 1944 DE LA BATAILLE DE NORMANDIE Boulevard Fabian Ware ✆ 02 31 51 46 90. *Open all year except the last two weeks in January. Closed for renovation work. Should reopen in May 2006. From 16 September to 30 April. 10am-12.30pm and 2pm-6pm. 1 May to 15 September: 9.30am-6.30pm. Admission: adult 6€, OAP 5€, students 3€.*This museum retraces the events of summer 1944; those 77 days that shook the world, known as the Battle of Normandy. A short film with original footage tells the story (French and English showings). Next to the museum is the British Memorial Cemetery, with its 4 868 tombs of Commonwealth soldiers.

BAYEUX TAPESTRY Rue de Nesmond ✆ 02 31 51 25 50. *Open all year except 25 and 26 December, 1 and 2 January. 15 March to 30 April, and 2 September to 3 November: 9am-6.30pm. 4 November to 14 March: 9.30am-12.30pm and 2pm-6pm. 1 May to 1 September: 9am-7pm. Admission; adult 5.10€, OAP 5€, student 2.60€. Audioguide* *(headphones): 1 €*. The audioguide tells the story of the Tapestry, an 11thc. masterpiece rather like a comic strip, embroidered to commemorate the Battle of Hastings in 1066. The work is extremely precise, and the tiny details of everyday life are fascinating.

NORMANDY LANDINGS BEACHES

Having celebrated the 60th anniversary of the Normandy Landings in 2004, Normandy continues to pay tribute every year to those who made history (see the Caen Memorial, or The Longest Day). All year long, the huge cemeteries remind us to say "Never again!" while making sure we don't ever forget.

Arromanches

ARROMANCHES 360 Chemin du Calvaire ✆ 02 31 22 30 30. *www.arromanches360.com. Open February & December: 10.10am-4.40pm. 1 April-14 May, 15-30 September & October: 10.10am-5.40pm. 15-31 May and 1-14 September: 10.10am-6.10pm. March & November: 10.10am-5.10pm. June, July & August: 9.40am-6.10pm. Film shown at 10 and 40 minutes past the hour. Admission: adult 4 €, students and children: 3.50 €*. One of the 3 French circular cinemas. Surrounded by 9 screens, you are totally immersed in the 18-minute documentary 'The Price of Liberty', which narrates the events of 1944 with original footage. On the way out, admire the view over Arromanches les Bains' artificial port and the cliffs from the panoramic room

Douvres-la-Délivrande

BRITISH CEMETERY. The first casualties of 6 June 1944 were buried here, as were those who fell between Caen and the sea. There are 1,123 graves in all: 923 British, 11 Canadian, 3 Australian, 1 Polish, 180 German and one unidentified.

Gold Beach

The central beach, onto which the British landed 25,000 men, with 413 killed and wounded by nightfall on 6 June 1944. 89 barges were sunk.

MUSEE DU 6-JUIN-1944 D-DAY Place du 6 Juin – ARROMANCHES-LES-BAINS ✆ 02 31 22 34 31. *www.normandie1944.fr*. The museum was built on the very site of the artificial harbour. Animated scale models containing war souvenirs reproduce the landing conditions, facing a bay window looking out on the real theatre of operations.

PEGASUS BRIDGE ✆ 02 31 44 62 01. *Admission free. Guided tour: adult 3 €, child 2.50 €*. Freed during the night of 5-6 June by the Vth Parachutist Brigade, the bridge took the name of their emblem, Pegasus. The current bridge is a copy of the original, preserved on another site. The exact place where Major Howard's glider Horsa landed on 6 June is marked by a stele.

Juno Beach

This 7km beach between Gray-sur-Mer and Saint Aubin-sur-Mer, in the middle of the British sector, was taken by the Canadians. 3,200 vehicles, 2,500 tonnes of material and 1,500 men landed here; 1,074 of them were killed or wounded.

GERMAN CEMETERY La Cambe ✆ 02 31 22 70 76. 1,160 German graves; smaller than the famous American cemetery, but just as poignant a reminder.

CENTRE JUNO BEACH Voie des Francais Libres - COURSEULLES-SUR-MER ✆ 02 31 37 32 17. *www.junobeach.org. Open every day: 9.30am-7pm, 1 April to 30 September; 10am-1pm and 2pm-5pm, 1 October to 31 March. Closed in January. Admission: adult 6.50 €, child 5 €, under-8s free*. The museum has been put up on the very site of the Canadian landing. It gives an account of Canada's part in D-day and the War in general, as well as a view of the country today. Not to be missed.

Omaha Beach

Situated between Vierville-sur-Mer to the west and Colleville-sur-Mer to the east. This was the American sector, taken by the 1st and 29th Infantry Divisions. The 6km beach is lined by 30m cliffs on both sides, notably the Pointe du Hoc, attacked by the Rangers. Unfortunately, owing to poor visibility, the Allied bombers missed their targets, leaving the German guns intact. The 8 companies in the first wave of landings found themselves in hell, facing these cannons and machine-guns, picked off without even having stepped into the water. There was no shelter to be had on the smooth beach, and no way of getting off it.

Yet they made a breach, and the attack was a success despite the heavy losses. Only 100 of the 2,400 tonnes of material were landed, and 3,881 of the 34,000 men were killed. Hence the beach's sad nickname 'Bloody Omaha'.

MUSEE OMAHA BEACH Avenue de la Liberation - SAINT-LAURENT-SUR-MER ✆ 02 31 21 97 44. *www.musee-memorial-omaha.com. Open 15 February to 15 March: 10am-12.30pm and 2.30pm-6pm; 16 March to 15 May and 1 October to 15 November: 9.30am-6.30pm; 16 May to 30 September: 9.30am-7pm, 7.30pm in July and August. Admission: adult 5.40 €, under 16s 2.80 €.* Costumes, insignia and weapons are organised around panels explaining the Omaha landings. The life-size figures placed in situation are very realistic. The museum has recently doubled in size, the better to house this large military collection.

AMERICAN CEMETERY Colleville-Saint-Laurent ✆ 02 31 51 62 00. *Open all year: 9am to 5pm, except 25 December and 1 January. Admission free.* A huge cemetery overlooks Colleville beach, one of 14 American World War II cemeteries. We are in the United States, since the French government made them a permanent grant of the land. The 9,387 white crosses line up on a well-kept green lawn: of the soldiers beneath, three received the Congress Medal of Honour, and four are women. On the circular arch of the wall are the names of the 1,557 missing in the region. An emotional experience.

Ranville

Ranville's bridge was taken in the night of 5-6 June , making it the first French village to be freed.

MEMORIAL PEGASUS BRIDGE Avenue du Major Howard ✆ 02 31 78 19 44. *Open 1 May to 30 September: 9.30am-6.30pm; 1 October to 30 November and 1 February to 30 April; 10am-1pm and 2pm-5pm. Annual closing 1 December to 31 January.* Dedicated to the 6th British Airborne Division, the first liberators to land in the region during the night of 5-6 June. The Pegasus Memorial, officially inaugurated by Prince Charles on 4 June 2000, boasts an impressive collection of authentic documents and objects. The actual bridge is in the park, and another major attraction is a life-size model of the glider Horsa.

RANVILLE MILITARY CEMETERY. The biggest after Bayeux, with 2,563 graves: 2,152 British, 76 Canadian, 3 New Zealand, 1 Australian, 5 French, 1 Polish, 1 Belgian. 322 German and 2 unidentified. The youngest was not yet 16!

Sainte-Mère-Eglise

Liberation, parachutists and a famous church tower: the town does however have other interesting features.

THE CHURCH. Begun in the 11thc. in Romanesque style and finished in the 15th. On 6 June 1944, American soldiers machine-gunned it, there being German soldiers sheltering inside. You can still see the marks today. Fine stained-glass windows commemorate the American divisions.

MUSEE AIRBORNE 14, rue Eisenhower ✆ 02 33 41 41 35. *Open every day, 1 February to 31 March and 1 October to 30 November: 9.30am-12 noon and 2pm-6pm; 1 April to 30 September: 9am-6.45pm. Admission: adult 6, 6-14s 2 €.* The real story of the Longest Day told through the pictures and souvenirs of the 82nd and 101st American Airborne Division operations. A moving experience.

FERME DU COTENTIN ECO MUSEE Chemin de Beauvais ✆ 02 33 95 40 20. *April & May: 2pm-6pm; June & September: 11am-6pm, July & August: 11am-7pm. French school holidays (except Christmas): 2pm-6pm. Admission: adult 4 €, child 1.60 €.* Discover the way peasant farmers used to live, in this lovely 17th and 18thc. farm museum containing costumes and furniture. Local breeds of donkeys, sheep and hens, and an orchard of old varieties of cider apple complete the visit.

Sword Beach

The British Sector between Lion-sur-Mer and Ouistreham saw 28, 845 men and 2,603 vehicles land on 6 June. 630 were killed or wounded.

MUSEE No4 COMMANDO KIEFFER Place Alfred Thomas - OUISTREHAM-RIVA-BELLA ✆ 02 31 96 63 10

Utah Beach

The most westerly sector (in the Manche). The Americans who took it were going for Cherbourg, as quickly as possible. At nightfall on 6 June, 20,000 men and 1,700 vehicles had landed, with 'only' 197 casualties.

MUSEE DU DEBARQUEMENT Plage d'Utah Beach ✆ 02 33 71 53 35. *www.utah-beach.com. Open all year, except January. June to September: 9.30am-7pm. (ask about opening times the rest of the year). Admission: adult 5 €, 6-16s 2 €.* Set up in a former blockhouse at operations base WN5, exactly where the American troops set foot on Norman soil on 6 June. Contains a remarkable collection of photos, archives, models and other objects belonging to veterans.

MUSEE DE LA LIBERTE 18, avenue de la Plage - QUINEVILLE ✆ 02 33 21 40 44. Museum in a blockhouse. You relive German Occupation through posters, ration cards and old radio sets.

MEMORIAL DE LA LIBERTE RETROUVEE (FREEDOM REDISCOVERED) ✆ 02 33 95 95 95. *Website: www.memorial-quineville.com Open 1 April-13 November, every day : 10am-7pm. Group bookings all year. Admission: adult 6 €, students and groups 5.50 €, under12s 4 €.* After closing briefly for renovation work, the memorial now includes a new 1,000 sqm. museum space, with fresh collections and 80 life-size models taking part in a staged setting. Located on the edge of the beach beside a blockhaus, this fine and rather unusual museum recreates life during the German Occupation, and retraces events from the exodus to the Liberation in a most up-to-date manner. The film 'From Utah Beach to Cherbourg', projected in a real cinema completes the story. It's all there: the Vichy Government's propaganda posters, ration cards, old wireless sets confiscated to stop the French people listening to 'Ici Londres' and the anti-Nazi broadcasts, and a moving assortment of personal possessions found on the landings beaches. You discover daily life at this time in the superbly reconstructed street, with its shops and life-size model people. If you didn't live through that tragic period between the declaration of war and Armistice Day, 8 May 1945, this museum will help you understand the events leading up to the immense deployment of Allied forces that arrived to free Europe at dawn on 6 June 1944. Overwhelming.

COTENTIN

This peninsula stretches into the Channel just before Brittany. The Allied landings also left their mark on its gentle countryside.

Avranches

Scene of the famous breakthrough allowing the advance of the Allied front. There are, however, other things to see apart from the artificial harbour. Avranches has a fine historic centre, and the Mont-Saint-Michel is nearby. Visit the beautiful Jardin des Plantes, best seen in the deepening light of late afternoon.

MONT SAINT MICHEL MANUSCRIPTS Mairie ✆ 02 33 58 00 22. The Mont Saint Michel manuscripts will be moving to new quarters in 'Le Scriptorial' from May 2006. Not to be missed! The museum is open all year, except January. Open every day, 1 June to 30 September: 10am-12 noon and 2pm-6pm. July & August: 10am-6pm. Guided tours available. Admission: 3.10 , under-10s free. One ticket for all 3 sites (manuscripts, town museum and Saint Gervais treasure): 4.60 . The library boasts over 14,000 ancient manuscripts, revealing the patience, accuracy and skill of calligraphers from the 14thc. onwards.

SAINT GERVAIS TREASURE Basilique Saint-Gervais ✆ 02 33 58 00 22. *Open 1 June to 30 September every day except Sunday morning: 10am-12 noon and 2pm-6pm. Open every day in July and August.* The striking 74-metre granite tower contains 23 bells. Inside the basilica, one of the treasure's relics is the skull of Saint Auber, founder of the Mont-Saint-Michel.

Barfleur

A picturesque little fishing port, called the 'pearl of the Val de Sair', which suits it.

SAINT NICOLAS CHURCH. It took two centuries (17th-19th) to put up this church, on the rock in the middle of a sailors' cemetery. The tower was knocked down in 1767, after bad weather damage, giving it a squat look, but the octagonal dome on one chapel, and the shale roofs are worth noticing.

Bricquebec

A big Monday market is the chief attraction of this pretty town.

NOTRE DAME DE GRACE CISTERCIAN ABBEY ✆ 02 33 87 56 10. *Open every day. Illustrated video commentary in summer at 3.30pm, in winter on request. The shop is open during the week from 9.30 am to 12 noon and 2pm- 5.30pm; Sunday 4pm-6pm.* Ascetic Cistercian life proved harsh for Abbot Onfroy, founder of Bricquebec Abbey in 1824, having been a priest in the Coutances diocese. 25 Trappist monks still live in the Abbey, breeding milch cows and making their own charcuterie; their produce, including the famous trappe de Bricquebec cheese, is sold in the shop. Individual or group retreats can be organised with the hotelkeeper; you estimate the price yourself.

CHATEAU ✆ 02 33 52 21 65. *Open every day except Tuesday, 1 July to 31 August: 10am-12 noon and 2pm-6pm.* A wealth of beautiful architecture comprising the 14thc. polygonal keep (23m high), Tour de l'Horloge (clocktower), 12thc. crypt with superb rib vaults and the former main door.

MUSEE A LA RECHERCHE DU TEMPS PERDU Les Brecqueries ✆ 02 33 52 26 48. *Open 1 April to 31 October, weekends and public holidays: 2pm-7pm. July & August, 7 days a week: 2pm-7pm.* Open in the morning by arrangement for groups. This museum 'in remembrance of things past' stages peasant life in the last century: the farm, school, grocer's shop...souvenirs from grandad's day that may well bring back memories for you too. A real Time Machine.

Cherbourg

Cradled in the world's greatest artificial harbour, Cherboug is proud of its naval leanings. Over the last century, hundreds of submarines have been made in the military port; the fishing harbour shows off its pretty trawlers and Chantereyne marina is France's second biggest. Ferry transport is expanding too, with deliveries to Britain and Ireland. The town's fine sandy beaches can be reached by car, bus or bicycle. A lively, busy town wedded to the sea.

NOTRE DAME DU VOEU ABBEY Opposite the naval hospital ✆ 02 33 87 88 89. *Admission free to the grounds.* Founded in the 12thc. by the Empress Mathilde, who had vowed to build a monastery wherever she could land during a storm at sea, the abbey has been pillaged many times and was damaged during World War II.

SAINTE TRINITE BASILICA Place Napoleon. *Open every day: 8.30am-7pm.* Built out of a 5thc. church, this is one of Cherbourg's oldest monuments, with a fine high altar and reredos sculpted by Armand Fréret, a 14thc. font, stone Virgin and 19thc. double polychrome pillars.

LA CITE DE LA MER Gare Maritime Transatlantique ✆ 0 825 33 50 50. *Open 1 June to 31 August: 9.30am-7pm (tills close at 6pm). 1 September to 31 May: 10am-6pm (tills close at 5pm). Admission: high season, adult 14 €, child 10 €, under-6s free (but not allowed in the submarine for safety reasons). Annual closing in January.* Human adventure in the undersea world is the theme, on the site of the former transatlantic Harbour Station. The submarine visit takes 45 minutes, and the 16 pools grouped round the highest cylindrical aquarium in Europe reproduce that silent universe which fascinates us so much.

Digulleville

ANDRA CENTRE DE LA MANCHE ✆ 02 33 01 69 13. *Public reception open Monday-Friday: 8.30am-12 noon and 1.30pm-5pm. Guided tours by appointment.* The ANDRA is the national agency for radioactive waste management. The Manche centre stocks waste with low and average radioactivity and a short lifespan, and is about to enter a surveillance phase that will last several centuries. This is a world premiere – and don't forget the regular exhibitions.

Granville

Perched on its rock like a mermaid, the former citadel, now the Haute-Ville, spreads up the cliffs. Fishermen's houses and private mansions alike recall a history relatively spared by World War II; gargoyles, cornices and sculpted lintels are untouched, and a cannon ball from a much older conflict is still stuck in a turret at 14, rue Notre-Dame.

AQUARIUM DU ROC AND MUSEE DU ROC 1, boulevard de Vaufleury ✆ 02 33 50 19 83. *Open February to late October: 10am-7pm. Admission: adult 7 €, child 3.50 €.* This aquarium complex on the rocky headland contains collections of shells and minerals, the aquarium itself and a butterfly garden.

Pour en savoir plus...
sur le Centre de stockage de la Manche...
visitez-le.
Centre de stockage de la Manche
Z.I. de Digulleville
50440 Beaumont-Hague
N° Azur 0810 120 172
Coût d'une communication locale
www.andra.fr
ANDRA
Agence nationale pour la gestion des déchets radioactifs
Conception graphique

MUSEE D'ART MODERNE RICHARD ANACREON Place de l'Isthme ✆ **02 33 51 02 94**. *Open every day in season: 11am-6pm. Out of season, from Wednesday to Sunday: 2pm-6pm. Admission: 2.70 €* for the collection and temporary exhibitions. This modern art museum in the Haute-Ville contains bookseller and art-lover Richard Anacreon's collection of antiquarian books and paintings. Famous artists and writers called at his bookshop in Saint Germain, and he kept their rare books, letters, autographs, drawings and manuscripts. There are paintings by Derain, Dufy, Picasso and Utrillo. Unique in Lower Normandy.

MUSEE CHRISTIAN DIOR Villa 'Les Rhumbs' - Jardin public ✆ **02 33 61 48 21**. *Open 15 May to 30 September every day: 10am-12.30pm and 2.30pm-7pm. Admission: adult 5 €.* You're invited into a great French designer's house! This was Dior's childhood home, in the centre of the park; a museum since 1997.

La Hague-Goury

The headland, the sea, so many little villages and ports: this is La Hague, once a pirates' lair, now better known for the lobsters, common and spider crabs in their cages.

PHARE DES TEMPETES. Firmly fixed to the Gros du Raz, this lighthouse is the department's biggest, together with Gatteville. They were built of granite by the same engineer, de la Rue, between 1834 and 1837. The stones fit into each other and are pegged to the rock with bronze girders for greater solidity. The sea is rough round here.The beam has an 18-mile reach, in which Goury is said to dine by candle-light every night!

Villedieu-les-Poêles

A picturesque town with smart little houses, known for eight centuries for its copper manufacturing.

COPPER WORKSHOP 54, rue Général-Huard ✆ **02 33 51 31 85**. *Open all year except Sunday and public holidays. Open on Sunday in July & August. Guided tours available.* At Villedieu-les-Poeles as in the Viaduc des Arts in Paris, the copper workshop is keeping alive a tradition. Copper, brass and even silver objects are created, restored and made on request. A fascinating glimpse inside the craftsman's world.

CORNILLE-HAVARD BELL FOUNDRY 10, rue du Pont-Chignon ✆ **02 33 61 00 56.** *Open February to 30 May and 1 September to 20 November, Tuesday to Saturday and Easter Day: 10am-12 noon and 1.30pm-5.30pm. 1 June to 10 July, 7 days a week: 10am-12 noon and 1.30pm-5.30pm. 11 July to 30 August, 7 days a week: 9.30am-6.30pm. Admission; adult 4.30 €, under-12s 2.50 €.* Built in 1832, this workshop has kept its beaten earth floor, huge oven, copper tools and wooden travelling crane in perfect working condition. the guided tour explains bell workings, with templates to engrave the motifs.

MAISON DE L'ETAIN 15, rue du Général-Huard ✆ **02 33 51 05 08**. *Open all year Monday to Friday: 9am-12 noon and 1.30pm-5.30pm, Saturday: 9am-12 noon and 2pm-5.30pm. Guided tours. Admission: adult 3.50 €, over-10s 2.30 €.* Discover the history of tin in this foundry-workshop, with its unique collection of moulds.

Saint-Lô

Saint-Lô is an equestrian capital, at the junction of the Cotentin peninsula and the 'mainland' in the Vire basin.

RAMPARTS. They mark the limits of today's town centre. Walk along them to the pretty park overlooking the River Vire. If you want an even better view, climb the Beaux Regards Tower, reminder of the city's fortified past.

BELFRY Place du Général-de-Gaulle. Standing proud with its unicorn on the top, sign of the town's Renaissance, the belfry's vertical lines contrast with the horizontal covered market Town Hall, forming an axis with Notre-Dame and Saint-Croix Towers.

MADELEINE CHAPEL ✆ **02 33 77 60 35.** *Visits all year round by reservation only. Open Saturday and Sunday: 2pm-6pm, July to September. Out of season for groups and tours.* Major Howard was brought into this chapel after being mortally wounded on 17 July 1944, and it is devoted to the events of World War II, with an exhibition of trophies and war photos telling the story of Saint-Lo's liberation.

SAINTE CROIX ABBEY CHURCH ✆ **02 33 77 60 35.** *Open every day: 8.30am-7pm.* This Romanesque building is the oldest in Saint-Lô. It was consecrated in 1204, and has been altered many times, with the convent buildings being transformed into stables in the early 19thc. The portal and the first bays alone remain from the Romanesque period. The tower, rebuilt in 1860, was knocked down in 1944 and replaced by a concrete campanile with lattice-work.

NOTRE DAME CHURCH ✆ **02 33 77 60 35**. *Visits all year round by appointment only.* Badly marked by the 1944 bombings, this Flamboyant Gothic building bears signs of war damage despite its restoration.

NATIONAL STABLES Avenue du Maréchal Juin Visiting Service ✆ 02 33 55 29 09. *Guided tours June to September. Admission: adult 4.50 €, 12-16s 2.50 €*. The National Stables is part of Saint-Lô's history and culture, with its 19th-century architecture touched by the War. It houses 70 stallions from 7 different breeds, including the Normandy Cob, favoured for teams, the French Selle, famous competition champion, the French Trotte, and ponies.

Saint-Martin-de-Landelles

L'ANGE MICHEL LEISURE PARK ✆ 02 33 49 04 74. *Open Easter-September* . This landscaped historic site in its natural amphitheatre is the only one of its kind in Normandy. It offers over thirty fun activities: aquasplash (descending the rapids by boat), tourist train, summer sledging, dodgem boats, and the new arrival, aquatics (heated water). You find a warm and friendly 'chalet' atmosphere and splendid scenery. Altogether a magic spot.

Saint-Vaast-La-Hougue

This magical place saw the arrival of the English Kings in the Middle Ages and the naval battle of 1692 in which Admiral de Tourville was beaten by the English (them again). Fortified in the 16th century, it is now a fishing port and marina, with granite quays and houses.

TATIHOU ✆ 02 33 23 19 92. From the port of Saint-Vaast-la-Hougue you can reach the island in a strange amphibious boat with 43 seats. There are trips every day from 1 April to 30 September, every 30 minutes between 10am and 6pm, during school holidays (except Christmas) every day from 2pm to 5pm. The rest of the year, it is open at weekends, 2pm to 5pm. Annual closing is from 11 November to mid-February. The crossing costs 7.60 € (with admission to the museum and Vauban Tower). Round trip to the island without the museum visit: 4.60 €, 4-11s: 1.50 € . This pretty little 28-hectare island with the exotic name is cradled in the sea a stone's throw from Saint-Vaast and can be reached on foot at low tide. It used to be forbidden to visitors, for soldiers and sailors in quarantine lived there in the days of the great epidemics. The former lazar-house is now the Tatihou Naval Museum, which boasts objects from wrecks sunk at the Battle of La Hougue in 1692, between French and Anglo-Dutch vessels. During the visit, you can discover daily life on board ship for sailors in the reign of Louis XIV.

MONT-SAINT-MICHEL

A much-visited and legendary site, where Saint Michael slew the dragon and still keeps watch, in case the devil is buried underneath. The former dyke that led tourists to the door of the citadel has been destroyed, in the hope that the bay would resist the invading sands. It is the bay that makes the Mont; the waves rush in like galloping horses and the sinking sand shifts underfoot, while the sheep graze in the saltfields. Whether drawn to the mystical or not, you must go there at least once in your life, preferably at low season when the site is at its least commercial.

Mont Saint Michel and its high tides

The Mont Saint Michel is one of the wonders of the western world, and the scene of some of continental Europe's highest and most dramatic spring tides. These tides go out to a distance of 15 kilometres from the coast and come in again at a speed that increases during the last hours of the flow. You are advised not to adventure out on the strand without first checking the tide timetable.

ABBEY ✆ 02 33 89 80 00. *Open 7 days a week. 2 May to 30 September: 9am-5.30pm. 1 October to 30 April: 9.30am-4.30pm (5pm during school holidays). Guided tours available. Admission: adult 6.40 €, reduced-price 4 €, under-18s free. Supplement for guided tour: 4 €, student 3 €. Free the first Sundays, October to May. Son et lumière every evening from spring onwards.* The ancient Benedictine Abbey church spire rises to over 150m on the top of Mont Saint Michel rock. It was founded in the early Middle Ages, after the archangel Michael had appeared three times to Bishop Aubert. Its architecture covers five centuries, for 10th to 15thc. builders were inspired by the Carolingian, Romanesque, Gothic and Flamboyant in turn. The result is a rich assortment of crypts, churches and exceptional buildings. Visit at night to get the full effect of sumptuous illumination. Unforgettable. Enquiries 02 33 89 80 00. Mass is held every day at 11am, Saturdays at 6pm, in the Abbey and Saint Pierre Church.

ARCHEOSCOPE ✆ 02 33 89 01 85. *Admission: adult 7 €*. Learn the history of the intriguing Mount, through magical tales and legends, sacred stories about the Abbey and the mysteries of tides and sinking sands.

LOGIS TIPHAINE © **02 33 60 23 34** *Open every day: 9am-6pm.* As Captain of Pontorson, Bertrand Du Guesclin made the town a place of jousting and tournaments. In 1365, he had a house built on the heights of the Mount to protect his wife Tiphaine de Raguenel, his "gentle fairy". The house still belongs to the Duguesclin family.

MUSEE HISTORIQUE © **02 33 60 14 09.** *Admission: adult 7 €.* Travel back through a thousand years of history, and discover the Abbey-builders. The cells, oubliettes and famous periscope are impressive.

MUSEE MARITIME © **02 33 60 14 09.** *Admission: adult 7 €.* A place for science and the environment. Find out all about the strongest tides in Europe and the biggest natural and cultural French site of the late 20thc. There's also a great collection of scale models of boats. You'd need to be patient to sew all those sails!

Courtils

MAISON DE LA BAIE DU MONT-SAINT-MICHEL © **02 33 89 66 00.** *Open April to late May: 2pm-6pm. June & September: 10am-6pm, July & August: 10am-7pm. School holidays: 2pm-6pm. Admission: adult 4 €, child 1.60 €, group 2.50 €.* Together with your visit to the Mount, you can penetrate the secrets of the bay, and find answers to such questions as: does the bay silt up? is conservation work planned for the Mount and its bay? The visit takes about 45 minutes.

PAYS D'AUGE

Right in Normandy's geographic centre, this is a little heaven: perfect landscape, gentle climate and excellent natural products.

Le Bec Hellouin

This little village attracts plenty of tourists, being a typical Normandy beauty spot, but they also come for its famous abbey.

NOTRE DAME DU BEC ABBEY. *www.abbayedubec.com. Open every day: 8am-9pm. Guided tours by the monks every day except Tuesday: 10.30am, 3pm and 4pm.* Majestic and peaceful, the splendid abbey buildings spread across the Bec Valley. A knight named Herluin founded the abbey, making of it an influential spiritual and intellectual centre for 11thc. Europe. The classical cloister was built between 1640 and 1660, one of the first in France with its Italian-style terrace. You mustn't miss Saint Nicolas Tower: he is one of the saints sculpted on the buttresses. The original tower was destroyed by fire; this one was built in its place in the 15thc., almost all that is left of the former abbey church. You can make a retreat here, or hear Mass with Gregorian chants.

Bernay

Another little town typical of the region, built round its 11thc. abbey. A few old quarters escaped the

World War II bombings.

ABBEY CHURCH Place Guillaume de Volpiano ✆ 02 32 46 63 23. Romanesque art in Normandy began with this abbey, in the reign of William the Conqueror. It was rebuilt in the 17th and 18thc., lost its monastic life for good during the French Revolution, and now houses the Town Hall, municipal museum and law courts. The passing years have not spoilt this majestic and beautiful building.

NOTRE DAME DE LA COUTURE BASILICA. Built on the site of a very ancient place of worship. This church has 3 naves in the shape of a Latin cross, with a huge transept and an apse in ambulatory form. It was built as a basilica in 1950, and contains fine 15th, 16th, 17th and 19thc. stained glass windows, 17thc. pulpit and stalls, and a crypt, probably the remains of the primitive church.

Cormeilles

This charming little village among its pastures and orchards is best-known for its 13 second-hand dealers.

SAINTE CROIX CHURCH. *Open every day: 9am-7pm.* Cormeilles church, originally Romanesque but altered in the 15th and 19thc, is unique in Normandy for its floor, which follows the ground's incline, making the chancel several metres higher than the back of the nave! Curious and striking.

Harcourt

Church, covered market and half-timbered houses form a picturesque site. Enjoy it before going to see the castle.

DOMAINE D'HARCOURT rue du Ch,teau ✆ 02 32 46 29 70. *Open 1 March to 15 November. 15 June to 15 September, every day: 10.30am-6.30pm; 1 March to 15 June and 15 September to 15 November, every day except Tuesday: 2pm-6pm. Admission: adult 4 €, 6-16s 1.50 €, under-6s free.* Wheelchair access. Art exhibitions. On the same site, you have medieval architecture, art and a 95-hectare forest park. The castle bears traces of 12th and 14thc. medieval art, with a 13thc. tower, 15thc. keep and fortified walls. During the Hundred Years' War, it was captured by the English in 1418 and freed by Dunois in 1449. One of the oldest arboreta in France surrounds the castle, created by the Agricultural Academy in 1840. It boasts over 400 species of tree and bush, including leafy, conifers, and sequoias.

Lisieux

Capital of the Pays d'Auge.

MEDIEVAL ROUTE ROUND THE TOWN CENTRE. *Leave from the Tourist Office - 11 rue d'Alencon. Approximate time: 2 hours.* The Tourist Office has marked out a route with 14 panels and arrow indicators that can be followed on foot or by bicycle. You travel through time from the year 1,000 to the French Revolution. Lisieux was a prestigious medieval city, run by Count-Bishops linked with the Dukes of Normandy and Kings of England and France.

LISIEUX BASILICA Avenue Jean XXIII ✆ 02 31 48 55 08. *Visitors welcome. The basilica is open all year except during services. May-October: 8.30am-8pm, November to April: 9am-6.30pm. The dome can be visited in July and August only: 9.30am-12 noon and 2pm-5.30pm. Film on the life of Saint Thérèse shown 3 times a day. Admission: 2.50 €.* Up in the town heights, this imposing monument draws Catholic pilgrims from all over the world. The young Carmelite Thérèse was canonized in 1925, and Pope Pius XI had the basilica put up in her honour.

LES BUISSONNETS-MAISON DE THERESE DE LISIEUX 22, chemin des Buissonnets ✆ 02 31 48 55 08. *Summer: 9am-12 noon and 2pm-6pm; winter: 10am-12 noon and 2pm-4pm.* The family furniture and Therese's bedroom can be seen, with the family's objects. Among the 85,000 yearly visitors are faithful Catholics who come here to feel close to the saint.

SAINT PIERRE CATHEDRAL Place François Mitterand. *Open 9.30am-7pm in summer and 9.30am-6pm in winter. Visitors welcome. Disabled access on the south side.* The present 110-metre building is Lisieux's third cathedral. It was built by Bishop Arnoult (1170-1182) and is one of the first Gothic cathedrals in France. This was Thérèse Martin's parish church for 11 years, before she became Saint Thérèse of the Infant Jesus. Wheelchair access on the south side.

CARMEL CHAPEL 37, rue du Carmel ✆ 02 31 48 55 08. *Open (except during services) 7.15am-7pm in summer, 7.15am-6.30pm in winter. Contributions welcome. Guided tours all year; 9am-12 noon and 1.30pm-6pm.* The chapel opened in 1877 and was partly transformed in 1923. It houses Thérèse's shrine, where she lies dressed in her Carmelite nun's homespun.

Orbec

Busy and rural at the same time, this town in the heart of the Pays d'Auge has a rich past.

L'H'TEL DIEU SAINT REMY CHAPEL Grande rue. Founded in 1290 and rebuilt in the 15thc. The brick porch is topped by an elegant Renaissance belfry, and inside, you can admire some fine 19thc. stained glass windows.

NOTRE DAME CHURCH Rue grande. Rebuilt after the Hundred Years' War, the church tower is a tall, defensive Renaissance structure, with the bells on top. It also has beautiful stained glass, including two 15thc. windows.

THE PERCHE

Part bocage, part farmed plains, the Perche is on hilly ground: the Ecouves signal rises to 417 metres, the highest peak of western France. Visit Sées, Mortagne and BellÍme, small towns whose heritage is untouched by war. The hero of these parts is the horse, be he a thoroughbred, a trotter or a solid Percheron.

Alençon

Situated on the Sarthe, on the 'border' of the Orne department, Alençon is none the less its prefecture. Saint Thérèse of Lisieux was born here, as was the 'point d'Alençon', that fine lace placed on the map by Colbert's Royal Workshop. Stroll throught the old quarters to see Saint Thérèse's birthplace, the former Hôtel de Guise and the Dukes' castle.

Alençon has a number of parks and gardens. The oldest, rue Balzac, is the aptly-named Parc des Promenades, dating back to the late 18thc. Camelia-lovers must visit the Espace Aveline garden, Rue du College, listed as a garden of reference for the flower. There is an arboretum (boulevard de Koutiala) with aquatic plants, and the Maison d'Oze's orchard with its fruit trees, simples and old rose bushes.

CHATEAU DES DUCS Place Foch. The remains of the castle are impressive: a 14thc. building following on from the 12thc. keep. It has become a prison, convenient for the nearby Palais de Justice (19thc.). Two massive towers frame the present prison door.

Parc Natural Regional du Perche

Covering the Lower Normandy and Centre regions, the nature reserve contains four types of natural environment: forests, bocage (farmland criss-crossed with hedges) and prairies, lakes and marshes, and hills and moorland. Next are the cultural treasures; while exploring the countryside, you may come across an old manor or a proud castle. The region's customs and arts and crafts have their place here too, the Percheron draught horse being an example. Several associations organise hikes through the park all year round.

PARC NATURAL DU PERCHE Maison du Parc Courboyer - NOCE ✆ 02 33 25 70 10 *www.le-perche.org*

Bellême

On the edge of the beautiful forest bearing its name, Bellĺme is a picturesque historic capital with its medieval remains, 15thc. porch, vaults and many 17th and 18thc. mansions, such as the Hôtel Bansard-des-Bois (18thc.) near the ancient fortress. The presbytery garden is also worth seeing, for its 17thc. wrought-iron balconies and view over the forest.

Mortagne-au-Perche

An appealing region, with its diverse hilly landscapes, picturesque villages and gentle way of life.

HOTEL DU RECEVEUR DES TAILLES. The elegant residence of the Parisian banker Jean-Hyacynth Hocquart, at 3, rue des Tailles. Louis XV style and pink roughcast walls.

HOTEL DE LA RUE SAINTE-CROIX. This magnificent mansion with its curved fronts goes back to the 18thc.

NOTRE DAME CHURCH. The vault is finely-sculpted, and the stained glass windows tell the story of Mortagne and its characters.

MUSEE PERCHERON Porte Saint-Denis ✆ 02 33 25 25 87. *Open July & August, Tuesday to Sunday: 3pm-6pm. Admission free.* Opposite the Maison des Comtes de Perche, housed in a 12th-16thc. building, the museum presents the history of the Perche and its noble line of Counts. Jules Champlain, medal engraver and native of Mortagne, has some of his works here too.

Mortrée

CHATEAU D'O ✆ 02 33 39 55 79. No fantasies please, this castle has nothing to do with the famous Histoire d'O! It is rather a blend of Gothic and Renaissance, grafted onto an older fortress by Jehan d'O after the Hundred Years' War. The castle is surrounded by a moat and a splendid 22-hectare park with a fine orangerie. There are furniture restoration workshops in the former stables (courses available).

HORSES

A living tradition in Normandy, and the Orne in particular. Horse breeding has long been the department's most prosperous industry. Between the 14thc. Royal stud farm at Domfront, owned by the Valois, and the Pin stud farm set up in 1714, the Orne made great strides in the field. From 1859 onwards, mainly racehorses were bred, including many prizewinners. All through the 19th century, great names in stud farms appeared in the department, from 'La Genevraie' in 1813 to the 'Haras de Tellier' in 1892.

Stud farms

Lower Normandy owns two of the finest French stud farms: the Haras du Pin in the Orne and the Haras National de Saint-Lô in the Manche. The Pin stud farm was built between 1715 and 1730, and is the oldest of the 23 stallion depots run by the Ministry for Agriculture. Set up on a 1,100-hectare estate, it includes the Institut du Cheval, the Ecole Professionnelle des haras nationaux and the Bergerie racecourse. Napoleon III favoured the development of equestrian sport, racing and improved breeding, and Society came to the Pin stud farm races, at the Bergerie au Pin-au-Haras racecourse established in 1823.

As for Saint-Lô stud farm, it supplied 20% of French production. There are breeding and showing competitions promoting the horse, to which Saint-Lô owes its international reputation, confirmed every August at the Normandy Horse Show.

HARAS DU PIN **Le-Pin-au-Haras ✆ 02 33 36 68 68**

HARAS NATIONAL **Avenue du Marechal-Juin - SAINT-LO ✆ 02 33 55 29 09**

The Percheron

The 19thc. was the golden age of the Percheron, the Orne peasant's working companion. He was appreciated throughout the French countryside and abroad, notably in the USA. A cross between the cob and the Arab, this draught horse goes back to the Crusades, and has been used for agricultural work, courrier service, transporting Army equipment and even for drawing Parisian omnibuses. Today, he is still a great worker, and is much in demand for forest unloading.

Saint Céneri-le-Gérei

A fairy tale village , one of the most beautiful in France. Set on a granite spur, its charm and peaceful atmosphere come from its old houses and alleyways and 12thc. bridge across the Sarthe. The Romanesque parish church is built of sandstone and granite, with some interesting 12th and 14thc. frescoes. Well worth seeing.

Sées

The town's religious history pervades its alleys and monuments, attracting filmmakers: Luc Besson's Jeanne d'Arc, Sade and Saint Cyr were filmed here.

SAINT MARTIN ABBEY. The first 7thc. abbey was destroyed in the Norman invasions, then rebuilt in the 11thc. by the Bishop of Sees, Today it is a medical institute, but it occasionally houses exhibitions, or serves as a backdrop for film-makers.

CATHEDRAL. *Guided tours in July and August: 11am-12.30pm and 2.30pm-6,30pm, except Saturday and Sunday morning and all day Monday. Reservation only. Admission: 2 €.*186 spotlights and 26,250 kw/h a year are needed to illuminate the cathedral. A sound and light show with pictures takes place inside from 1 July to 16 September. Enquiries and bookings at the Tourist Office.

Soligny-la-Trappe

Best known for its abbey. The Romanesque church Saint Germain d'Auxerre (11th and 12thc.) was built on a feudal motte, with a fine view all around.

GRANDE TRAPPE ABBEY ✆ 02 33 84 17 00. *la.trappe@wanadoo.fr.* This is the last men's abbey in the Orne. Notre Dame de la Grande Trappe was founded around 1120 by Rotrou III, Comte du Perche, for the eternal rest of his wife's soul (she was the King of England's daughter and had perished in a shipwreck). Towards the end of the 16thc., the abbey went into decline. In 1663, after a dissolute life, Armand-Jean de Rance asked permission of Louis XIV to reform his abbey, adopting the Cistercian regime. The monks were also asked to devote some time to field labour. The abbey flourished and regained its influence; James II of England and Saint Simon made retreats there. The Trappists fled to Switzerland and then Russia during the French revolution, and only got back their ruined abbey in 1814. Since then, they have remained faithful to their past, updating it for today's lifestyle. The abbey houses 35 monks between 24 and 90. They originally made dairy produce; now they offer the public a range of monastic objects and regional products, with a religious bookshop as well. The book 'Happiness in God' by father abbot Dom Marie-Gerard Dubois tells the story of this community, and can be bought on site. Only the park and the church are open to the public; you can watch a video to discover the abbey itself, and attend services (12.30pm, 2.30pm).

FOOD AND DRINK

Normandy is famous for its orchards, cider and Calvados, but offers other specialities, such as Camembert.

Andouilles and andouillettes

Whatever you might expect, an *andouillette* isn't a small *andouille*! The Vire andouille, best-known of its kind, is pork-based, and eaten cold and sliced, while the andouillette, from Alencon, is veal-based and enclosed in waxy fat rather than smoked. It is delicious charcoal-grilled.

ASSELOT ET FILS Rue de l'Alliere - VIRE ✆ 02 31 68 21 69. Homemade prize-winning andouille, one of the town's top names. You can see it being made (except Saturdays).

CHARLES AMAND 5, rue Andre-Halbout - VIRE ✆ 02 31 67 01 79. Another famous name in andouille-making.

Isigny butter

Isigny has been making butter for ages, already supplying the capital in the 17thc., and exporting abroad to England, Holland and even the Americas. The quality and flavour of this butter is widely recognised.

The boudin noir (black pudding)

Mortagne-en-Perche (Orne) is the black pudding capital. Made from pork blood, onions and lard (fat bacon), the boudin mustn't be too dry or too crumbly. it is eaten hot, but some like it sliced cold; delicious with the apéritif. The whole region from Perche to Ouche produces top-quality boudin.

Canard à la Rouennaise

Duck Rouennaise-style, cooked in its blood, is a great traditional recipe. The duck is crushed in a press, and the blood collected to make the sauce, which is poured over the aiguillettes.

Cider, Calvados

There are different kinds of cider; *doux* (sweet) artificially made by stopping fermentation at 2.5° or 3° of alcohol, or *brut* (dry), up to 4-5°. Witnin these two categories are the *sec* (under a year old), the pur jus (has no water added), the *boucher* (goes on fermenting when bottled) and the mousseux (naturally fizzy). Home producing is getting more and more difficult, which is why producers are diversifying into the *poiré*.

A Domfront invention, *poiré* is to pears as cider to apples, but little is made, so it isn't easy to find. *Pommeau*, a blend of cider and calvados has had its AOC since 1991; at 16-18 it is served cold, without ice, often as an aperitif.

CIDER ROUTE. East of Caen, this mapped-out tourist route winds through the picturesque Auge landscape, linking Beuvron-en-Auge, Bonneboscq, and Beaufour-Druval, villages in the Cambremer canton. Ch,teaux, manors, half-timbered houses and apple orchards give the marvellous scenery a picture-postcard look.

Caramels de Normandie

© Floriane Ravard

Calvados is a spirit best tasted in an unfinished cup of coffee or with a sugar cube (canard). It is the by-product of cider distillation, first mentioned by Gilles de Gouberville in the 16thc. at Mesnil-au-Var in the Manche. There are 2 production zones, 'Calvados' and 'Calvados du Pays d'Auge' and one AOC dating from 1942.

DOMFRONT. Famous for its calvados and especially for its poiré. Thanks to them both, the region is listed as a quality flavour site ('Site remarquable du gout').

MUSEE DU CALVADOS ET DES METIERS ANCIENS Route de Trouville ✆ 02 31 64 30 31. *www.pere-magloire.com. Open Easter to late October. Call for information about opening hours.* The museum is in the Père Magloire distillery; 2,000 casks have been stored here since 1821. You learn a lot from visiting the storehouse and the museum, and can taste and buy the calvados.

Seafood

One of the main advantages of being on the coast. The seafood platter is one of Normandy's specialities: oysters, prawns, winkles, common crabs, spider crabs, mussels, clams and other shellfish. Isigny-sur-Mer is known for its oysters as well as its butter and caramels. At Grandcamp-Maisy, 2,100 tonnes of scallops are caught; this is Normandy's second fishing harbour, after Port-en-Bessin. Port may be a small village, but its 250 fishermen and 55 boats bring in 11,000 tonnes of fish of 50 different species. You can hardly avoid mentioning lobsters, small 'demoiselles' of 250-400g, or Cosqueville prawns called 'bouquet'. Finally, at Barfleur, the *moule blonde* is the village's own gastronomic mussel.

Tripes à la mode de Caen

Tradition insists you taste this early in the morning! Early risers in Caen enjoy breakfasting at 9am on a dish of tripe with a glass of white wine. Tempted?

LE CAFE TROUSSEL Route de Lisieux - CABOURG-FORMENTIN ✆ 02 31 61 11 15. Full of tripe-lovers. They are homemade here, you won't find better. To prove it, they've been winning prizes since 1979.

Cheese

Normandy is France's most prolific cheese-producing region, thanks to both the natural environment and a healthy tradition. The dominant areas are the Pays d'Auge (Calvados, Orne and Eure) and Pays de Bray (Seine-Maritime).

Boursin

Invented at Croisy-sur-Eure in 1957, made from pasteurised milk with cream, garlic and fines herbes added, the boursin was the first cheese to appear in the ads.

Bricquebec

Little-known, looking rather like a pont-l'eveque or a livarot, but pressed rather than cooked (cantal; tomme de Savoie) and thus unlike the better-known Normandy cheeses. Originally made by monks, its flavour is constant.

Camembert

Most famous of all, the everyday cheese, soft under its strong-flavoured crust. The name, however, offers no guarrantee; camembert is made industrially all over France and even abroad, some brands managing to turn out a decent quality despite the lack of standards.

LA FERME PRESIDENT Camembert ✆ 02 33 36 06 60. All you need to know about camembert; taste it and buy some.

Livarot

Known as 'le colonel', Livarot has had its AOC since 1975; round, 12cm in diameter and 5cm thick, with an orange-yellow crust wrapped in five bands of sedge. It is soft, made from unpasteurised milk; one of Normandy's oldest cheeses. It comes in four official sizes. The mignot, made near Vimoutiers, is rather like the livarot.

LE VILLAGE FROMAGER Fromagerie de Livarot - 42, rue du Gal Leclerc - LIVAROT ✆ 02 31 48 20 10. *Open 1 April to 30 September: € 9.30am-12 noon and 1.30pm-5pm.* Discover Normandy's cheeses in these dairies where you can taste livarot and pont-l'Évíque.

Neufchatel

Going back to the 11thc., maybe the oldest, certainly the most romantic of cheeses. It is heart-shaped; you can't help but love it!

The heart can weigh 600g. It also exists in other shapes and sizes, but its AOC (1969) fixes the production zone at 30km around Neufchatel, including 30 producers, 28 of them farmers. It is made exclusively from cow's milk, and spends 10 days drying before being eaten, but for full flavour, one more month is needed to complete the maturing process: fans insist on three to four months for a really strong cheese.

SYNDICAT DU FROMAGE ✆ 02 32 97 53 01.

Pont-l'Évêque.

Square (11 cm sides, 3cm thick), weighing 350-400g, it has a greyish-white crust striped with fine reddish lines. It may have been the monks of a Pays d'Auge abbey who first made it. It is mentioned in the 13thc. Roman de la Rose, and had a poem written to it in 1660!

FABRICATION DU PONT-L'EVEQUE ✆ 02 31 64 12 77

Hotels & Restaurants

CALVADOS

Bayeux

HOTEL-CHATEAU DE BELLEFONTAINE* 49, rue Bellefontaine ✆ 02 31 22 00 10**. *Website: www.hotel-bellefontaine.com 21 rooms, suites and apartments sleeping 4, from 92 € to 153 € in low season, and from 110 € to 220 € in high season. Breakfast 11 €.* This splendid 18thc. residence surrounded by a lake is the ideal place for a romantic weekend, or simply an exceptional stay. You can enjoy a walk through the leafy park only a short distance from Bayeux centre.

HOTEL LE LION D'OR* 71, rue Saint-Jean ✆ 02 31 92 06 90.** *Website: www.liondor-bayeux.fr - 24 rooms and one suite. Rooms from 86 € to 162 € in low season and 108 € to 194 € in high season. Breakfast 11 € in low season, 12 € in high season. Half-board 69 € to 123 € according to season. Market produce menu 20 € (lunchtime) and 26 € (evening). Set menus from 35 € to 46 €. Children's menu 13 €.* The Lion d'Or can be found in a former coaching inn that dates back to the 18thc., set back from its portal behind a paved courtyard. Take time to admire the small salon beside reception, in the footsteps of Churchill and the Kennedys who also stayed here - sadly too soon to appreciate Patrick Mouilleau's cooking. His recipe for success is a combination of solid regional basics and perfect mastery of produce and flavours, with a dash of inventiveness thrown in for good measure. Vire andouille charlotte with chestnuts and scallops with dried Bayeux Pig bacon are only two delicious examples. Wind down in the the lounge bar before a good night's sleep in one of the comfortable rooms, so close to the busy town centre yet surprisingly quiet. This hotel has recently changed hands and is experiencing a new lease of life as a result. Make sure you keep abreast of special offers, such as theme weekends for tourists or romantics - or both.

HOTEL REINE MATHILDE 23, rue Larche ✆ 02 31 92 08 13**. *Closed in December and January. Rooms from 50 € to 74 €. Breakfast 6 €.* One of the best-known hotels in the area, and with good reason: its 16 rooms are all equipped with shower and private WC, telephone and colour TV, with a little writing desk, and the quality standards are generally high. Between May and December, you can go down to the Brasserie Guillaume and enjoy some of Normandy's delicious specialities. You'll be doing the right thing, staying here.

Bénouville

LA GLYCINE 11, place du Commando-n°4 ✆ 02 31 44 61 94.** *Website: www.la-glycine.com. Closed between Christmas and New Year. 35 rooms, from 48 € (single) to 73 € (sleeps 4). Half-board 46 € to 71 €. Breakfast 7 €. Overnight break 58 €. Set menus from 18 € to 42 €.* M and Mme Decker took over this hotel in 1991, and have since developed the restaurant. The outside is lovely when the famous wisteria (glycine) is in flower, and now the inside is all set to match it. Mme Decker has decorated it in warm tones; brick-coloured walls, organdie, and a jungle note in the lounge and reception with its zebra-striped seats. The rooms are full of light, one opening onto an indoor garden. Sophisticated cooking - especially the sauces - combining country recipes and seafood. The lobster in coral sauce is the house masterpiece of long date.

Cabourg

LE BEAU SITE 30, avenue Foch ✆ 02 31 24 42 88. *Website: www.lebeausite.fr. Closed 1-28 December. Closed Monday and Tuesday in low season. Set menus 17 €, 25 € and 35 €. Children's menu 10 €.* Enjoy lunch or dinner in a postcard setting overlooking the sea, surrounded by the beautiful architecture typical of these coastal residences on the Promenade Marcel Proust. There is a car park at the entrance, and a charming old hallway up a few steps, with the usual display of brochures about the region. The huge dining room has a view of the waves, and the passers-by; you can watch them at leisure through the large bay windows while eating your Breton lobster (cooked 'their way') or Auge Valley duck breast with rosemary, saffron and herbs smelling of the South. A most attractive site.

GRAND HOTEL DE CABOURG** RESTAURANT LE BALBEC Promenade Marcel-Proust ✆ 02 31 91 01 79.** *Website: www.cabourg-web.com/grandhotel. Open all year. Double room from 130 € to 260 €. Suite from 336 € to 500 €. Fixed price in low season from 4 nights, 242 € to 282 € for two people par night. Set menus from 42 € to 48 €. Buffet with music on Sundays and public holidays, 46 €, including drink and coffee.* This fine, historic hotel is marked with the town's past as well as its own. A blend of Renaissance and 1900 styles, it was the third one to be built on this site, in 1907. It stretches majestically along the seafront beside the casino, as though showing off its architecture. Cross the hall to the side of the hotel overlooking the sea, and you'll be able to measure the luxury. The ghost of Marcel Proust seems to hover in what is almost a museum, yet strangely timeless. You can take tea looking out at the sea, or amuse yourself during a concert-dinner or in the piano bar. The same charm can be found in Le Balbec's sumptuous dining room, and the sophisticated dishes full of flavour featuring on the menus. The Sunday lunch buffet (46 €) offers a profusion of seafood and is marvellous value for money.

LA CLOSERIE-RESIDENCE HOTELIERE – Jardins du Casino 11, avenue Jean-Mermoz ✆ 02 31 24 25 26. *Website: www.lacloseriecabourg.com. 30 apartments from 2 to 4 rooms, 30-70 sqm. sleeping 4 to 8. One weekday night from 70 € to 100 €. Weekends and public holidays from 90 € to 150 €. One week from 370 € to 840 € depending on the season and number of people.* This little corner of heaven is just opposite the Casino and a few yards from the sea. What could be better? La Closerie specialises in charm, tradition and the art of living. The reception part of the hotel is housed within the elegant walls of an old Cabourg residence; the more recent apartments are in the new building. There is a heated pool (May-September) and a garden to relax in, with Isabelle's smile as a cheerful extra. Add a beautiful staircase and a lounge corner near the bar, and the picture is almost complete. The apartments are huge, bright and very comfortable, decorated in shades of blue, and each has its own dishwasher. The ones overlooking the garden with a view of the casino and Grand Hotel are naturally the most sought-after. A top-quality address.

Caen

LE DAUPHIN* 29, rue Gémare ✆ 02 31 86 22 26.** *37 rooms, including 5 suites, from 65 € to 150 €. Breakfast 10 €. Label Normandie Qualité Tourisme.* This is perhaps the hotel with most going for it, in Caen. Le Dauphin (Best Western) belongs to the Pugnat-Chabredier family, and is housed in a former priory, which explains its architectural wealth. Stained-glass windows, a small raised courtyard, period furniture, wall hangings, panelling, exposed beams and ancient stonework harmonise in a decorative rustic style with plenty of cachet. The rooms have a similar ambiance. For your pleasure and relaxation, the 21st century is present in the form of a sauna and fitness centre, and there is a corner for smoking cigars. The restaurant is one of Caen's best.

L'INSOLITE 16, rue du Vaugueux ✆ 02 31 43 83 87. *Open 7 days a week in high season, closed Sunday and Monday in low season. Closed 3 weeks in January and one week in October. Captain's formula 15 €, captain's menu 22 €, admiral's menu 22 €, prestige autour du terroir normand 45 €. Vegetarian set menu 14.94 €, children's menu 6.86 €.* This restaurant is well named ('unusual') with its cosy setting and variety of objects - paintings, old photos, cat and fish statuettes - shellfish tank and period wine bottles against a backdrop of exposed beams and ancient stonework. Brigitte and Philippe Delannoy have faithful regulars eager to recommend their cooking to friends, but passing customers are welcomed just as warmly. The menus are mainly seafood: emperor fillet with crayfish, lobster, fish *papillote* in a fresh mint infusion, seafood, shellfish and a scallop formula. Superb wine list (Philippe is an enthusiast) and an impressive collection of spirits, with separate showcases for the rums and the whiskies. Friday lunchtime, there is a *table d'hôtes*, where everyone eats together, and the Cigar Club meets once a month on a Thursday evening. This year, L'Insolite is treating itself to new terrace. Enjoy to excess!

LA PETITE MARMITE 43, rue des Jacobins ✆ 02 31 86 15 20. *Closed Saturday lunchtime, all day Sunday and Monday evening. Set menus from 18 € to 26 €.* This is definitely one of our favourite places to eat in Caen, with its pleasant setting, large, well-spaced tables and menus offering traditional luxury foods - home made foie gras, Dublin Bay prawns, sole, monkfish - cooked with an inovative zest. The wine list is excellent, and the service discreet and respectful without being stuck-up. Jean-Luc Barthélémy takes the orders, makes sure your dessert comes, serves the wine, advises you on your choice of dish, and explains the chef's combinations. His energetic and professional team second him perfectly. On the plus side: the whole set-up, with its culinary art on your plate, and floral art on the walls. Minus points? We can't find a single one!

Deauville

LE GARAGE 118, avenue de la République ✆ 02 31 87 25 25. *Set menus 16.50 € and 26.0 €, quick formulas 10.50 € and 11.70 €.* Le Garage is on the corner of Rue Gambetta and Avenue de la République, a stone's throw from the Place Morny. The cooking is traditional, using local produce with a wide choice of seafood. We thought the real Auge Valley chicken was delicious. You get a friendly welcome, with natural smiles, and quick service even when there's a full house. Dining room tables separated with mid-height partitions is a good idea, giving customers a sense of privacy. Photos of movie stars (the Deauville film festival) and old car posters (after all, this is a former garage!) decorate the walls. Extensive choice of wines, by the glass or the bottle: the burgundy aligoté is excellent.

HOTEL NORMANDY BARRIERE ** RESTAURANT LA BELLE EPOQUE 38, rue Jean-Mermoz 02 31 98 66 22.** *Open all year. 291 rooms, suites and apartments from 262 € to 414 €. Breakfast 24 €. Menu du marche 47 €.* The Normandy is part of Deauville's history, so we felt we should include it, even though you'd have to take out a loan to stay there! The blue-grey half-timbering, salons and bar deserve a visit, and if the local cuisine isn't to your taste, go and have brunch there at least once, to the sound of the piano. That's all, but you shouldn't miss it...

LE SPINNAKER 52, rue Mirabeau ✆ 02 31 88 24 40 *Website: www.spinnaker-deauville.com. Closed Monday and Tuesday. Set menus du marché 30 € and 40 €.* Pascal Angenard started the Deauville Chefs' Club, so as to keep traditional Normandy *cuisine* alive: duck foie gras with four spices, hot andouille de Vire *parmentier* (with potato), rabbit stuffed with rosemary, and crab parfait with cream are just a few recipes that certainly deserve saving! You'll swoon with pleasure as the pastry cook describes the desserts.

Dives-sur-Mer

CHEZ LE BOUGNAT 25bis, rue Gaston-Maneville ✆ 02 31 91 06 13. *Website: www.chezlebougnat.fr. Open 7 days a week for lunch, and Thursday, Friday and Saturday evenings. Annual closing between Christmas and New Year. Set menus from 14.90 € (lunchtime, except Sunday), menu découverte 19.90 €, gastronomic menu 24 €. A la carte.* Somewhere between junk shop and restaurant, François Tessonnière's lair is a curiosity in itself. Among the objects on the walls, shelves and in display cases, you'll find the menu, specialising in meat, from home made charcuterie to pot-au-feu. You can trust the good quality of the food, while rummaging through any amount of second-hand treasures. The Rabelaisian wine list matches the dishes perfectly. Book in advance if you can!

Falaise

L'ATTACHE Route de Caen ✆ 02 31 90 05 38. *Annual closing two weeks in late September-early October. Closed Tuesday and Wednesday. Set menus from 18 € to 34.50 €, plus a menu-carte 42 €.* Monsieur Hastain's words on the menu sum up L'Attache very well. "Man has made music with cooking, Nature has provided the score, the seasons a stave and tempo, and I have added notes and colours that crackle, crisp and crunch, and end up singing on your plate". What more can we say, except that you must try it at least once - you'll be back!

HOTEL DE LA POSTE 38, rue Georges-Clémenceau ✆ 02 31 90 13 14. *Closed Sunday evening and Monday, Friday evening from 1 October-30 April, and Saturday lunchtime from 1 May-30 September. Closed one week in October and 2-15 January. Double room 49 €. Breakfast 7 €. Half-board for 2 from 3 nights, 50 € per person per night. Set menus 15 €, 23.50 € and 30 €, gastronomic menu 36 €.* The Hotel de la Poste faces the Château de la Fresnaye, and has 17 comfortable rooms, a dining room (seating 70) refurbished in pastel colours, and a small salon seating 20 for family reunions and other celebrations. Chef Mme Boutmy worked in several of Canada's top restaurants before settling in Falaise. She is one of Escoffier's disciples, with a great respect for culinary tradition; among her specialities are duck *ballotine* stuffed with foie gras, served with an onion and rhubarb conserve; snail *feuilleté* (in pastry) with pleurotus mushrooms and a light Pernod cream; grilled rib steak with shallots and a Bordeaux wine sauce; and trout fillet in cider sauce. Delicious!

Honfleur

L'ABSINTHE*** *Website : www.absinthe.fr. Includes hotel, restaurant and brasserie La Grenouille on three sites. Restaurant 10, rue de la Quarantaine 02 31 89 39 00. Set menus from 30 € to 49 €. Hotel 1 rue de la Ville 02 31 89 23 23. Rooms from 98 € to 129 €. Suite 220 €. Breakfast 10 €.* Located in the town centre, a stone's throw from the fishing harbour, this charming hotel has 7 rooms including a very attractive suite, and is decorated throughout in warm wood panelling. The restaurant has its back to the hotel, facing the harbour, and boasts two magnificent dining rooms, with exposed beams and fireplace. The cooking is sensational: pan-fried foie gras with ginger caramel, and lobster millefeuille with Nantes butter are two tasty examples.

LA FERME SAINT-SIMEON Rue Adolphe-Marais ✆ 02 31 81 78 00 *Fax 02 31 89 48 48. Website: www.saint-simeon.com. Set menu 120 €. A la carte 110 €. Closed Monday and Tuesday lunchtime.* Exclusive, chic and very sought-after, La Ferme Saint-Siméon went through a difficult patch in 2002, being forced to close for several months after extensive damage caused by fire. It opened after repairs and renovation, more beautiful than ever, with talented and inventive chef Patrick Ogheard at the helm. Having been Alain Ducasse's second for a year at the Louis XV in Monaco, then employed in the National Education system, this native of Auvergne launched the new-look restaurant with a minimum of fuss but plenty of regularity. Foie gras with *pommeau*, (regional apple drink) apple condiment and sultanas, pommeau jelly, scallops meunière, Polish-style cauliflower in raw shavings, Iranian royal oscietre caviar, slice of turbot braised in mustard-flavoured stock, half-dried tomatoes and bread with crusty thyme, lamb casseroled with small broad beans, piquillos and salad shoots, a walnut, hazelnut and almond *dacquoise* gâteau, and Tanariva chocolate mousse. An exceptional address for privileged customers.

HOTEL CASTEL ALBERTINE* 19, cours Albert-Manuel ✆ 02 31 98 85 56**. *www.honfleurhotels.com. Open all year. 27 rooms, from 75 € to 150 €. Breakfast 8 €.* This splendid 19thc. residence belonged to historian Albert Sorel of the Academie Française, who would surely have approved of his old house today. There is a real haven of peace on the other side of the blue wrought-iron gate, where Veronique Renouf welcomes you warmly. The rooms are spacious and comfortable, smaller in the modern part of the hotel, and more affordable. Veronique's pride and joy is the magnificent park with its hundred-year-old trees; a truly restful place. The harbour and Honfleur centre are a short walk away.

HOTEL DU CHEVAL BLANC* 2, quai des Passagers ✆ 02 31 81 65 00**. *Website: www.hotel-honfleur.com. 32 rooms and 2 suites. Double rooms from 70 € to 230 €. Suites (sleep up to 4) from 300 € to 425 €. Breakfast included. Private car park (bookings only). Public car park 100m away. Label Normandie QualitéTourisme.* In 2004, the Dubosts took over this magnificent 15thc. building on the harbour, with its enchanting view at all times of the day. A wooden horse presides over the entrance lounge; there are old leather armchairs, and a fine wooden staircase - no lack of cachet, in fact. The rooms have been renovated and are very comfortable; the suites even come complete with jacuzzi. A second seminar room is planned, along with general refurbishing here and there - but this doesn't affect the guests: you'll be warmly welcomed and wish you could stay longer. Ideal for a peaceful break near the pedestrian thoroughfares and restaurants.

LA TERRASSE ET L'ASSIETTE 8 place Sainte-Catherine ✆ 02 31 89 31 33 *Fax 02 31 89 90 17. Set menus from 27 € to 45 €. A la carte 45 €. Closed Monday, Tuesday and from mid-November to 10 December.* Gérard Bonnefoy used to run two restaurants in Honfleur, the gastronomic Assiete Gourmande on the quays, and La Terrasse de l'Assiette, more of a bistrot , in the town's prettiest square. Three years ago, he gave up, and put all his eggs in the second basket, renaming it rather cleverly. The gastronomic awards he won on the quays followed him up to his new address, and rightly so: formerly chef at l'Auberge Normande in Countances, Gérard cooks simple yet bracing dishes. His sea bream tartare with ginger, ratatouille sorbet and grilled potatoes; pan-fried Dublin Bay prawn tails, sweet onions in a cold *mousseline*, aromatic vinaigrette; chicken supreme with Vire andouille, potato *blanquette* flavoured with lemon, sweet and sour veal loin, little chocolate *moelleux* (gâteau) and pistachio *coulant* will convert you to his point of view. The dining room has become gentrified with the years, but the delightful ambiance remains unspoilt. White wines have pride of place in the cellar, to go with the house fish specialities.

EURE

Bourneville

RISLE SEINE Le bourg ✆ 02 32 42 30 22. *Closed one week in March, Tuesday evening and Wednesday. Express formula 10.90 €. Set menus 16 €, 20.50 € and 28 €.* In the heart of the Boucles de la Seine Normande nature reserve, you come across this restaurant with its two dining rooms, one boasting fireplace and half-timbering, the other a veranda with a garden view. The cuisine is traditional and regional, and everything is home made. Very reasonable prices. You can order from the express menu at any time, as the locals know to their advantage.

Evreux

HOTEL DE FRANCE 29, rue Saint Thomas ✆ 02 32 39 09 25.** *Website: www.hoteldefrance-evreux.com. Hotel open all year. 16 rooms including a family room, from 40 € to 70 €. Breakfast 6.50 €. Restaurant closed Saturday lunchtime, Sunday evening and Monday. Set menus Saveur and Terroir 23 € and Gourmand 38 €. Children's menu 16 €.* This hotel-restaurant is located in a quiet part of the town centre, not far from the cathedral. A peaceful atmosphere fills the sober and elegant rooms, and the restaurant with view of the Iton and its little bridge. You are served a flavoursome regional *cuisine* that manages to be original. Don't miss the house speciality: Auvergne *estoufinado* with summer truffles. The pot of snails and grilled mullet or lamb fillet are also well worth trying.

NORMANDY HOTEL* 37, rue Edouard Féray ✆ 02 32 33 14 40.** *Fax: 02 32 31 24 74. Restaurant closed Sunday. 20 double or triple rooms from 59 € to 83 €. Breakfast 8.30 €. Set menus from 20 € to 31 €. A la carte 45 €.* This former coaching inn smothered in geraniums knows how to please demanding appetites, whether in the dining room for a chic lunch, or after quick service in the bar. The chef's classic recipes - whole braised kidney and roast turbot in olive oil - are served and eaten to music. Big selection of home made desserts, and efficient service. French and foreign customers.

Gisors

LE CAPPEVILLE 17, rue de Cappeville 02 32 55 11 08. *Closed Wednesday and Thursday. Set menus from 25 € to 43 €.* Fans of Normandy's cuisine like to eat in this near-institution, with its seasonal dishes: game in winter and little fresh vegetables in spring. The menus change every 3 or 4 months with the seasons. You find the restaurant in one of the town's busiest streets - just follow the delicious local cooking smells wafting towards you.

HOTEL MODERNE 1 place de la Gare ✆ 02 32 55 23 51.** *Open all year. Restaurant closed Friday evening, Saturday and Sunday evening. Set menus from 12.80 € (weekdays) to 24 €. A la carte 26 €. 3 children's formulas. Rooms from 42 € to 62 €. Breakfast 8 €.* This old posting inn has recently been renovated, and a warm, flower-scented welcome and family atmosphere await you. Mme Gavoué also organises a *table d'hôte*. Old-fashioned cooking prepared the same day with fresh ingredients is the rule, witness the fondue Normandy-style, and crusty fatted chicken with camembert cream. If you're here Sunday lunchtime, don't miss the seafood menu, 26 €.

Giverny

ANCIEN HOTEL BAUDY 81, rue Claude Monet ✆ 02 32 21 10 03. *Annual closing 1 November-30 March. Closed Sunday evening and Monday, except public holidays. Set menu 20 €. A la carte.* This was the inn where the American painters stayed, come to find inspiration in their master's works. The building dates back to 1890, and is set in the heart of a garden featuring an ancient rose-garden and a period artist's studio, five minutes from the Claude Monet Museum. On the menu are Baudy omelette with duck confit, Landes salad, warm goat's cheese with salad and *sautéed* potatoes and chicken in a cream and mushroom sauce with potatoes *au gratin*. The terrace is pleasant in fine weather.

Louviers

MANOIR DE LA HAYE LE COMTE* 4, route de La Haye-le-Comte ✆ 02 32 40 00 40.** *Website: www.manoir-louviers.com. Restaurant closed Sunday evening and Monday. Set menus from 20 €. A la carte. Rooms from 70 € to 100 €. Breakfast 11 € in the dining room, 12 € served in your room. Access D133 going towards Neubourg, then the D113.* Still Louviers, but real countryside; what a good place for a peaceful luxury break! The16thc. manor in its extensive grounds (5 ha.) can't fail to please, whether you stay for a meal or a few nights. Excellent regional gastronomy, terrace in season, and plenty of activities are on offer: golf, hard court tennis, mountain biking, *boules* and table tennis.

Pont-Audemer

BELLE ISLE SUR RISLE** 112, route de Rouen ✆ 02 32 56 96 22.** *Website: www.bellile.com. Annual closing early January to mid-March and mid-November to late December. Closed Monday or Wednesday in low season. Set menus from 32 € to 62 € (dégustation menu served for 2). 20 rooms from 112 €. Breakfast 13.50 €.* This charming hotel-restaurant on an island in the Risle dates back to 1856, and is set among trees and flowers in a 2ha. park. Elegant style and atmosphere, comfortable rooms with a view of the park and the river. The gastronomic restaurant is well up to the general standard. Toboggan, tennis, table tennis, heated indoor pool, fitness centre and sauna keep you occupied during your stay.

Vernon

LES FLEURS 71, rue Carnot ✆ 02 32 51 16 80. *Closed Sunday evening and Monday. Set menus from 21 € to 42 €. A la carte 41 €.* The menu adapts to seasonal ingredients, changing three times a year, and the gastronomic menu at 42 € gives you a mouth-watering idea of the chef's talents. After all, this restaurant has a long-standing reputation: it existed as such on the site in a former private mansion in 1912!

HOTEL D'EVREUX 11, place d'Evreux ✆ 02 32 21 16 12.** *Restaurant closed Sunday, except public holidays. Set menus from 21 € to 27 €. A la carte 40 €. 14 rooms from 33 € to 59 € according to season. Breakfast 6 €.* 14 comfortable rooms are available in this 18thc. hotel, with its cheerful decoration typical of Normandy, and excellent traditional and seasonal cooking. We recommend the foie gras in its cloth, followed by beef fillet Rossini and warm apple tart with calvados sorbet. Trustworthy.

MANCHE

Avranches

LA CROIX D'OR ** 83, rue de la Constitution ✆ 02 33 58 04 88. *Closed January. 31 rooms from 55 € to 90 €. Breakfast 8 €. Lunchtime formula 16 €, except Sunday and public holidays. Set menus from 24 to 53 €. Pets accepted. Car park.* All the rooms in this former 17thc. coaching inn with its period furniture and brass overlook the landscaped garden. A peaceful spot in the heart of the town, with fine, sophisticated cuisine rooted in the Normandy soil.

Barneville-Carteret

LA MARINE Rue de Paris ✆ 02 33 53 83 31 *Fax 02 33 53 39 60. Website: www.hotelmarine.com. Set menus from 30 € to 89 €. A la carte 60 €. Closed Sunday evening, Monday and Thursday lunchtime in March, October and November; Monday and Thursday lunchtimes in April, May, June and September. Annual closing from mid-November to early March.* This Marine has had the wind in its sails for the last couple of years. Laurent Cesne had already made this family business work well before that, but recent renovation work has given it a rejuvenating face lift, enabling it to sail ahead of local competition. At 45, Laurent is an excellent technician and fish expert, one of the best chefs in north-western France. His Denneville oysters in shrimp consommé or on a foie gras *royale*, bass fillet barded with marjoram on a courgette conserve, cappucino with parmesan, mullet on a tomato and Taggiasca olive shortbread tart, pan-fried cuttlefish, pink grapefruit terrine with bergamot, citrus sorbet and a lacy orange-flavoured *tuile* biscuit will easily persuade you of that. The recently-redecorated dining room overlooks Barneville harbour. Accurate but relaxed service.

Cherbourg

LE FAITOUT 25, rue Tour-Carrée ✆ 02 33 04 25 04. *Seats 50. Open every day, except Sunday and Monday. Orders taken until 9pm. Set menu 20 €.* This little restaurant serves traditional cooking made from fresh ingredients, at affordable prices. Only one menu, but an extensive carte featuring fish, and grilled and casseroled meat dishes. The serving staff don't hang about, so if you're in a hurry at lunchtime, this place is for you. Don't forget to book in advance.

Granville

LA CITADELLE 34, rue du Port ✆ 02 33 50 34 10. *Open all year. Set menus from 16 € to 31 €.* Well located for watching the fish being brought in for cooking: this might be why La Citadelle has such a good reputation for fish and seafood. The Chausey lobster is the house speciality, closely followed by the seafood platter.

HOTEL GRAND LARGE* 5, rue de la Falaise ✆ 02 33 91 19 19**. *Open all year. 52 rooms from 75 € to 99 €, breakfast 8 €. Most of the rooms have a balcony with sea view.* All have direct access to the seawater therapy centre and beach. Car park, garage, terrace and pool (for water treatment customers only), lift, hammam, jacuzzi and bodybuilding room.

Heugueville-sur-Sienne

LE MASCARET 16 rue Sienne ✆ 02 33 45 86 09 *Fax 02 33 07 90 01. Set menus from 19 € to 85 €. A la carte 65 €. Closed Sunday evening, Monday and Wednesday evening, from early September to mid-July, and Monday only from mid-July to late August. Annual closing 25 November-2 December and 2-28 January.* Heugueville sur Sienne? It's a town on the Manche's west coast a few kilometres from Coutances, facing the Sienne bay. Philipe Hardy has been settled in this former 18thc. presbytery for ten years, and is a most sought-after chef, by the culinary guides and Alain Ducasse who had him take part in his Food France - Fou de France initiative this year. Now 37 years old, and helped out in the dining room by his delightful Bulgarian wife Nadia, he has managed to assert his own ideas of a very personal and creative *cuisine*: large pan-fried Dublin Bay prawns with basil serum, crab cannelloni with a touch of lemon, Blainville lobster rissoled in ghee, Delhi powder, Pays d'Auge duck en cocotte, hot chocolate nectar, soft white cheese sabayon and a cardamom *tuile* biscuit. Behind these simple names lie precision techniques and an impressive respect for cooking times. Nadia creates her own particular ambience in the dining room; perhaps the care taken with place settings, cutlery, crockery and even the bread is rather over-the-top, with everything just so like a doll's tea party, but none the less, a meal at the Hardys' is a great experience.

Le Mont-Saint-Michel

LA CROIX BLANCHE* ✆ 02 33 60 14 04**. *These two establishments are one and the same, in fact. 30 rooms, including 8 with a sea view. La Croix Blanche is closed from 11 November to 15 February. Luggage service. Breakfast 10 €. Set menus from 20 € to 30 €.* Regional cooking, from leg of lamb to river trout. Located on the rock under the ramparts, in a beautiful 15thc. house, with a magnificent view of the bay.

LA MERE POULARD * (C) 02 33 60 14 01**. *Inside the walled town. Open all year. 27 rooms.* Hard to miss this restaurant; you have to pass it when you get to the Mont. World-famous for its omelettes, La *Mere* Poularde has taken on top starred chef Michel Bruneau, ex-La Bourride in Caen, to run the kitchens. And he's cooking... omelettes! Beautiful dining room, terribly expensive omelettes..

Saint-Vaast-la-Hougue

CAFE DU PORT 5, quai Vauban Saint-Vaast-la-Hougue ✆ 02 33 23 42 42 *Website: www.cafe-du-port.com Closed late November-late January. Rooms from 45 € to 51 €. All-in overnight price 40 €. Set menus 17 € to 29 €.* 'A welcoming and fraternal establishment' goes the house motto. The reality behind these words is lady of the house Madame Lefilliatre, who takes real care of her guests. Show her your Petit Fute guide, and you'll find yourself with a free aperitif. The beautiful dining room on the first floor overlooks the harbour, and meals are served on the terrace in summer. Seafood, shellfish and fish have pride of place on the menu.

HOTEL DE FRANCE DES FUCHSIAS ** 20, rue Maréchal-Foch ✆ 02 33 54 42 26. *Closed January and February, and Monday, except full-board, in summer, and Monday and Tuesday lunchtime except in November, December and March (closed all day). 36 rooms from 52 € to 116 €, breakfast 11 €. Set menu 18 € weekday lunchtimes, and 25 € to 35 €. Children's menu (moussaillon) 11 €.* A very pretty and opulent residence, embellished with a magnificent fuchsia. You'll enjoy spending time in the attractive - and unexpected - garden. Excellent cooking and a warm welcome as well as oodles of charm.

Villedieu-les-Poêles

LA FERME DE MALTE 11, rue Jules-Tétrel ✆ 02 33 91 35 91. *Open all year. 2 rooms from 130 €. Set menus from 25 € to 60 €.* The oyster stew and grilled sea bream with conserved lemons, among other specialities, are prepared with skill and experience. The rooms are spacious, sophisticated and full of charm. La ferme de Malte itself is a pretty building nestling in an attractive park complete with pool, tennis and a lake. Classy.

LA POMME D'OR 57, rue Général Huard ✆ 02 33 61 01 13.** *Open 7 days a week in season. Closed Sunday evening out of season. 12 rooms from 39 €. Set menus from 14.90 € to 34.90 €.* La Pomme d'Or changed hands in August 2005. M and Mme Tafary have taken on the restaurant and are doing very well, with their creative and personalised gastronomic *cuisine*. Philippe Tafary is an imaginative professional, who knows how to bring out the best in tasty local foodstuffs, and his excellent *carte* is quite out of the ordinary.

ORNE

Bagnoles-de-l'Orne

BOIS JOLI* 12, avenue Philippe du Rozier ✆ 02 33 37 92 77.** *Website: www.hotelboisjoli.com. Annual closing 2 January-13 February. 20 rooms from 65 € to 140 €. Set menus from 20 € to 50 €. Breakfast 11 €.* This Anglo-Norman style villa dates back to the late 19thc. The greenery is charming, and the rooms have a French Regency or Norman look to them, with views of the ancient sequoia trees in the 3,000 sqm. park lying right on the edge of Andaine Forest. The restaurant serves sophisticated cooking characterised by an astute blend of country flavours and spices. Parmentier with black pudding, egg *caillet* with cider cream and fresh cod carpaccio with saffron vinaigrette are on the menu.

LE MANOIR DU LYS* Route de Juvigny ✆ 02 33 37 80 69.** *Fax: 02 33 30 05 80. Website: www.manoir-du-lys.fr. Open 12 February-1 January. 30 rooms from 60 € to 240 €, breakfast 6 €. Pets accepted, supplement 8 €. Set menus from 27 € to 76 €, children's menu 13 €.* This former hunting lodge boasts light and spacious rooms, ranging from classic to modern in style. They are decorated in cheerful colours and fully soundproofed; some have a terrace, and the smaller rooms overlook the orchard where you may catch sight of a stag or a doe. For family parties, the Manoir du Lys has also built 7 wooden pavilions in the forest clearing, each complete with terrace, lounge, bedroom and large bathroom. Ideal for discovering the natural environment! The chef offers locally-based gastronomic cuisine, served on the terrace in summer and by the fireside in winter.

Flers

AUBERGE DU RELAIS FLEURI 115, rue Schnetz ✆ 02 33 65 23 89. *Annual closing early January and early August. Closed Sunday, Monday and Friday evening. Set menus from 19.50 € to 37 €. A la carte 45 €.*

A pleasant place, housed in a former coaching inn. The dining room with its exposed stonework is both rustic and elegant, and the cooking well-prepared and up-to-date, using only the most carefully-selected and freshest ingredients. Good, varied cellar, excellent welcome, and an attractive garden sheltered by an old lime tree.

Mortagne-au-Perche

HOSTELLERIE "GENTY HOME" - RESTAURANT "LA GRILLADE" Place de la République - 4, rue Notre-Dame ✆ 02 33 25 11 53.** *8 rooms from 40 € to 46 €, breakfast 6.50 €. Set menus from 19 € to 27.50 €. Closed Sunday evening and Monday, except public holidays.* The Genty Home and La Grillade are among Mortagne's best establishments. The chef cooks traditional dishes that you can sample on the terroir menu: black pudding feuilleté with apples, and chicken fricassée Normandy-style, followed by warm apple tart with a calvados sorbet. Top quality food and an enchanting setting make this hostelry a must.

HOTEL DU TRIBUNAL 4, place du Palais ✆ 02 33 25 04 77.** *21 rooms from 48 € to 100 €. Set menus from 17 € to 35 €. A la carte 32 €.* Impeccable, comfortably equipped rooms in an attractive traditional hotel. Elegant regional *cuisine* featuring the famous Mortagne black pudding.

Sées

LE CHEVAL BLANC 1, place Saint-Pierre ✆ 02 33 27 80 48.** *Annual closing 2 weeks in February and 3 weeks in November. Hotel closed Friday evening. Restaurant closed Thursday evening and Friday. Rooms from 27 € to 44.50 €. Breakfast 4.50 €. Set menus from 10.50 € to 38 €.* A classic setting for this hostelry, with fairly small but very clean rooms. The restaurant serves specialities like snail feuilleté, vire steak with pommeau and veal sweetbreads, beautifully presented with generous helpings.

L'ŒLE DE SEES Macé ✆ 02 33 27 98 65.** *Website: www.ile-sees.fr. Closed Sunday evening and Monday. Double room from 55 € to 65 €. Breakfast 8 €. Set menus from 23 € to 34 €.* This is a peaceful place, well away from town noise and bustle. The summer terrace and fireside corner in winter welcome gourmets for an excellent meal cooked with local ingredients: foie gras, home made smoked salmon and the Œle de Sées' famous tripes. The rooms are furnished in pastel shades, and very comfortable.

SEINE-MARITIME

Caudebec-en-Caux

LE CHEVAL BLANC 4, place René-Coty ✆ 02 35 96 21 66.** *Website: www.le-cheval-blanc.fr. Formula 14.20 (main course + dessert or starter + main course). Set menus 15 € to 35 €. Rooms from 45 € to 63 €. Children's menu 10 €. Breakfast 6.50 €. Closed Sunday evening, except days before public holidays and from 22 December - 31January.* All kinds of tasty dishes feature on the menu, and it's often hard to choose between fish and meat - when it comes to dessert you'll throw caution to the winds! Maxi-salads are available on weekdays at very reasonable prices. A comfortable and welcoming hotel.

Dieppe

LE BISTROT DU POLLET 23, rue TÎte de Bœuf ✆ 02 35 84 68 57. The Pollet is the authentic old fishermen's quarter, and this bistrot is well worth the trip, with its fresh fish and simple, expert recipes. Xavier Hericher is a talented chef, and Florence manages the service with skill. You'll be recommending this place to friends - and coming back.

HOTEL AGUADO* 30, boulevard de Verdun ✆ 02 35 84 27 00.** *Website: www.hoteldieppe.com. Rooms from 62 € to 90 €. Breakfast 9 €. Pets are not accepted.* This attractive hotel links town and sea with its monumental arch. Each of its 56 rooms is personalised and renovated, providing the most up-to-date and sophisticated comfort. You have a breakfast room, lounge facing the sea and English-style bar at your disposal. Delightfully cosy atmosphere.

Etretat

DOMAINE SAINT-CLAIR LE DONJON* Chemin de Saint-Clair ✆ 02 35 27 08 23.** *Website: www.hoteletretat.com. Open all year. Gastronomic set menu 39 €, gourmet set menu 49 €. Seasonal menu 100 € (including drink). A la carte 70 €. Children's menus under-8s 8 €, 8-12s 25 €. 21 double rooms from 90 € to 330 €, breakfast included, Breakfast 10 € for under 10s. 25 € supplement for over-12s, breakfast included.* Nestling high on its rocky spur, this magnificent site overlooks the village, sea and Etretat cliffs. Choose between two charming residences in the heart of the estate, le Donjon (the Keep) and la Villa; the Donjon's chef Wilfrid Chaplain concocts sophisticated gastronomic *cuisine*, blending local produce with exotic flavours from all over the world. The estate wine waiter runs the select Wine Cigars Club, where fans can taste both, by the glass and the item. An ideal place to escape from the rat race and enjoy the art of living - even the luxurious rooms have a cultural theme, being dedicated to famous characters in literarature and painting from the Second Empire and Belle Epoque periods.

LE DORMY HOUSE* 40, route du Havre ✆ 02 35 27 07 88.** *Website: www.dormy-house.com. Menu-carte. Children's menu 10 €. Rooms (including 2 with disabled access) from 85 € to 200 €. Breakfast 14 €.* This hotel in its wooded 4ha. park has a well-earned reputation for satisfying its guests. Every year brings some new fittings or renovation work, to improve the already excellent facilities. Peace, quiet and comfort best describe the environment, with direct access to beach and village, and a golf course only 2 minutes away. The English-style terrace has a panoramic view of the cliffs. The rotunda restaurant serves local specialities, changing its menu every three months; the fresh fish and shellfish are guaranteed to thrill your taste buds. Choose the Maupassant break from 150 € to 200 € a night for two, including room, breakfast and dinner. Note that some of the rooms can be converted into apartments sleeping families. The Rayon Vert bar plays jazz on Friday and Saturday.

LA FLIBUSTE Front de mer ✆ 02 35 29 23 25 *Open 7 days a week. Closed for a fortnight in November and January. A la carte.* This is where you should come to taste meat or fish cooked *à la plancha*, or a home-made pizza, facing the sea with a fine view of the harbour and Yport cliffs. All the dishes are made with fresh ingredients and home-cooked. In addition to the menu you can choose suggestions like salted or Fécamp cod, and pan-fried mussels and shrimps, from the slate. Interesting wine list (bottles from 13.40 €) and wines by the *pichet* (jug) or glass.

Forges-les-Eaux

AUBERGE DU BEAU LIEU 2, rue du Montadet – Route de Paris ✆ 02 35 90 50 36. *Website: www.auberge-du-beau-lieu.com. Hotel and restaurant closed Monday evening, Tuesday and Wednesday lunchtime. Closed the last three weeks in January and first week in February. Set menus 17 € (except Saturday evening, Sunday lunchtime and public holidays) 34.25 € and 53.50 €. A la carte 60 €. Children's menu 13 €. 2 double rooms 55 € and one single room 39 €. Breakfast from 6 € to 11 €.* This inn can be found on the way out of Forges, about a kilometre from the centre on the D915 towards Paris. Poultry and fish have pride of place, producing classics like roast duck with Rouennaise sauce and neufchatel *croquant*. The chef is a duck expert, but his desserts are every bit as delicious - the pineapple au gratin, for instance. His menus change with the seasons and his imagination, and the result is absolutely not to be missed. Impeccable service, with advice on your choice of food and wine, and rooms available if you decide to take second helpings.

Frichemesnil

LE SOUPER FIN 1, route de Clères ✆ 02 35 33 33 88. *Website: http://souper.fin.online.fr. Closed Sunday in low season (October to Easter). Annual closing 3 weeks in summer and 21 December-5 January. Set menu 'Tradition' 29 €, set menu 'Surprise' 43 €, chef's suggestion 47 € (on the slate Friday evening, Saturday and Sunday, and depending on what's available at market the other days). A la carte 50 €. Children's menu 10 €. Terrace. 2 rooms 44 € single, 50 € double. Extra bed 12 €. Breakfast 8 €.* Chef Eric Buisset and his wife Véronique (in the dining room) welcome you to their charming little restaurant in Frichemesnil, 4 km from Clères. The cooking is sophisticated and carefully prepared with local colour dishes and menus that change every week. You only find out what you're getting on the Surprise menu as it is actually served, but we recommend it! Two quiet and comfortable rooms have been fitted out for latecomers. Don't miss it.

Le Havre

LES GENS DE MER 44, rue Voltaire ✆ 02 35 41 35 32. *Email: agismlehavre@wanadoo.fr Rooms from 48 €. Breakfast buffet 6.50 €.* This two-star ‚flagship' is located near the commercial docks, facing the central covered market, a short distance from the Town Hall. 95 spacious, renovated rooms are available, providing exceptional value for money.The restaurant can seat 250, and specialises in home cooking, with an extensive choice of menus at attractive prices. The Seamen's Club for sailors offers an evening's relaxation. Two meeting rooms holding 35 and 150 and a private car park are also available. Seminars and banquets are organised on request.

HOTEL DE BORDEAUX* 147, rue Louis-Brindeau ✆ 02 35 22 69 44**. *Website: www.bestwestern.com/fr/debordeaux. 31 rooms from 62 € to 78 €. Breakfast 10 €. Garage 10 €.* Spacious and comfortable rooms are on offer in this town centre hotel, popular for its friendly welcome and attractive decor. Parking is no problem in this commercial district, so you can enjoy a leisurely wander through the nearby pedestrian streets. A place that attracts the rich and famous, and is used to putting up (with) celebrities.

HOTEL VENT D'OUEST* 4, rue de Caligny ✆ 02 35 42 50 69**. *Website: www.ventdouest.fr Rooms from 80 € to 120 € or two communicating rooms for families 140 €. Breakfast 9 €.* Located near Saint Joseph's Church, one of Auguste Perret's architectural works of art, this hotel is rather British in style, sober and luxurious. Faultless welcome and rooms on three floors named Marine, Campagne and Montagne. Hushed atmosphere in the bar, and meals on a tray for guests who prefer to stay in; room service is available. Just the kind of hotel Le Havre needed - this 'West Wind' seems to be blowing it a lot of good.

LA VILLA DU HAVRE 66 bd Albert-1er ✆ 02 35 54 78 80 *Fax 02 35 54 78 81. Set menus from 32 € to 185 €. A la carte 100 €. Closed Sunday and Monday, 17 July-31 July and 3-31 January.* 2006 will be an eventful year for Jean-Luc Tartarin, who at barely 40 is becoming a chef to be reckoned with. The first floor of writer Armand Salacrou's former home is to undergo extensive renovation with an air-conditioned veranda planned for the housefront facing the sea. The dining rooms are also to be redecoated. This is good news for the Partouche group's leading restaurant, since it means Tartarin is staying on. This vintage car fan serves an ultra-contemporary, inventive *cuisine* including dishes like wholegrain rice and cepe *velouté*, Paimpol coco beans cappucino-style, redcurrant juice, slice of Iberian palette (pork shoulder), duck foie gras sliced thickly and cooked *à la plancha,* 'virtual' *choucroute*, acidic salad, balsamic vinegar juice and juniper berries, wild bass on a warm turnip and Campari jelly, mussel emulsion with fennel, roast grouse poached in a pure malt whisky stock, praline *croustillant* with panna cotta and plums in jelly with balsamic vinegar and hibiscus. Powerfully innovative, excellent culinary technique.

Rouen

L'ECAILLE 26 Rampe-Cauchoise ✆ 02 35 70 95 52 *Fax 02 35 70 83 49. Set menus from 30 € to 45 €. A la carte 80 €. Closed Saturday lunchtime, Sunday and Monday.* This restaurant is modestly located Place Cauchoise, in a rather cheerless quarter of Rouen. Nevertheless, those in the know will tell you Marc Tellier is a real specialist in seafood *cuisine*, concocting dishes like Dublin Bay prawns grilled with thyme, light butter with fresh herbs, roast cod with cream of smoked cod roe, scallop *fricassée* and lobster with shellfish and Beaumes de Venise coulis with incredible talent. Those allergic to fish can choose a Landes duck confit with charlotte potatoes *sautéd* with lardons before making room for a chocolate *moelleux* with pistachio ice cream.

LE BISTROT DU CHEF EN GARE – GILL 26, rue Verte – En gare ✆ 02 35 71 48 66. *Closed Saturday lunchtime, Sunday and Monday evening, except for bookings. Orders taken between 11.45am and 2.30pm and 7.30pm and 10.30pm. 'Vite garcon' formula 15.50 € (not served Friday or Saturday evening). Weekend formula 24 €. A la carte 27 €.* This is a chic restaurant on the first floor of the station building, with a business customer base. Old-fashioned decoration, objects connected with the railway - plaques, wagons and little trains - tablecloths and red velvet banquettes make for a comfortable setting, and the cooking is excellent, presented on a short but efficient menu, regularly renewed. We recommend the weekend formula, a tour of Normandy's gastronomy. The downside is being in the station - but then you forget that with your first mouthful of delicious food.

GILL 9 quai de la Bourse ✆ 02 35 71 16 14 2 *Fax 02 35 71 96 91. Website: www.gill.fr. Set menus from 40 € to 85 €. A la carte 80 €. Closed Monday.* Since Michel Bruneau (ex-La Bourride, Caen) left for La Mère Poularde at the Mont-Saint-Michel, Gilles Tournadre's restaurant has become the most prestigious in Normandy. He has since redoubled his efforts to keep this leadership, aware that you can't rest on your laurels, and sensing attack from Jean-Luc Tartarin in Le Havre and Christophe Ogheard in Honfleur. This summer, his place on the quays was entirely destroyed, rebuilt and then re-opened in mid-October with a totally new contemporary look, and slightly fewer place settings, leaving more personal space for his customers. Though we haven't yet eaten in this new Gill, we have every faith in Gilles Tournadre's culinary talents and are sure his *cuisine* is still the city's finest.

Yvetot

AUBERGE DU VAL AU CESNE ✆ 02 35 56 63 06. *Closed Monday and Tuesday. Set menu 25 €. 5 rooms 80 €. Breakfast 9 €.* This charming spot on the D5 between Yvetot and Duclair has quite a reputation in the Pays de Caux. They like tradition in this inn, welcoming their guests warmly. Once upon a time the villagers came here at Easter to eat the hard-boiled eggs they had given up for Lent. Hence the name 'Val au Cesne', in Latin 'Valley of the Meal'. The custom still continues today. If eggs aren't your thing, go for the terroir set menu at 25 € with its Roy d'Yvetot leg of lamb as a speciality and apple feuilleté for dessert. The rooms are beautifully cosy.

Paris Ile-de-France

Notre-Dame and the Seine

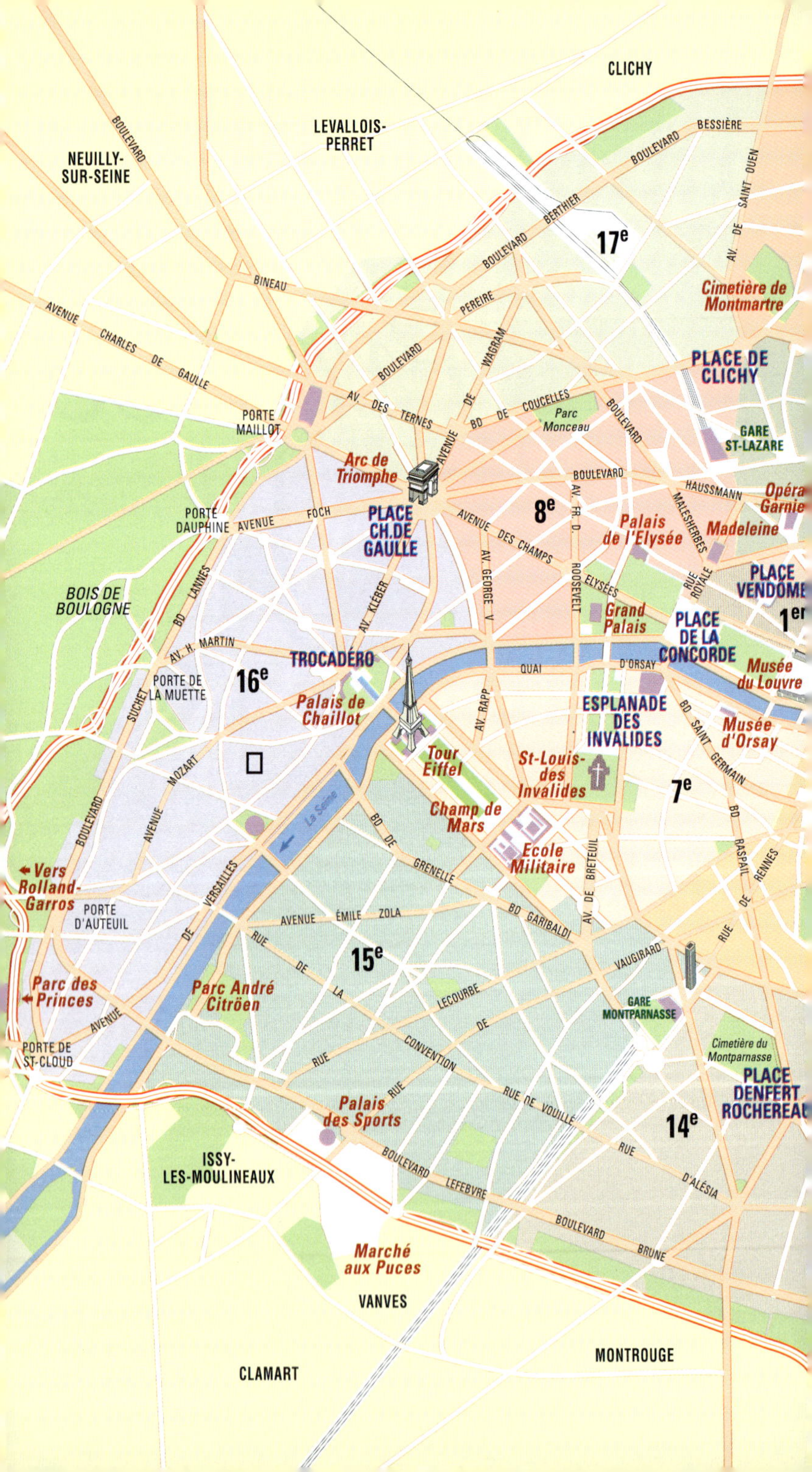
CLICHY
LEVALLOIS-PERRET
NEUILLY-SUR-SEINE
BOULEVARD
BESSIÈRE
BOULEVARD
AV. DE SAINT OUEN
BOULEVARD BERTHIER
17e
Cimetière de Montmartre
BINEAU
PEREIRE
AVENUE CHARLES DE GAULLE
BOULEVARD
DE WAGRAM
PLACE DE CLICHY
AV. DES TERNES
BD DE COUCELLES
Parc Monceau
BOULEVARD
PORTE MAILLOT
AVENUE
GARE ST-LAZARE
Arc de Triomphe
BOULEVARD HAUSSMANN
Opéra Garnie
PORTE DAUPHINE
AVENUE FOCH
PLACE CH.DE GAULLE
8e
AVENUE DES CHAMPS ELYSÉES
AV. FR. D. ROOSEVELT
Palais de l'Elysée
MALESHERBES
Madeleine
RUE ROYALE
PLACE VENDÔME
BOIS DE BOULOGNE
BD LANNES
AV. KLÉBER
AV. GEORGE V
Grand Palais
PLACE DE LA CONCORDE
1er
AV. H. MARTIN
TROCADÉRO
QUAI D'ORSAY
Musée du Louvre
PORTE DE LA MUETTE
16e
SUCHET
Palais de Chaillot
AV. RAPP
ESPLANADE DES INVALIDES
BD SAINT GERMAIN
Musée d'Orsay
Tour Eiffel
St-Louis-des Invalides
7e
AVENUE MOZART
La Seine
Champ de Mars
BD RASPAIL
BOULEVARD
AVENUE
BD DE GRENELLE
Ecole Militaire
AV. DE BRETEUIL
RUE DE RENNES
← Vers Rolland-Garros
PORTE D'AUTEUIL
DE VERSAILLES
AVENUE ÉMILE ZOLA
BD GARIBALDI
RUE DE LA CONVENTION
15e
VAUGIRARD
Parc des Princes
Parc André Citröen
LECOURBE DE
GARE MONTPARNASSE
AVENUE
PORTE DE ST-CLOUD
Cimetière du Montparnasse
RUE
PLACE DENFERT ROCHEREAU
Palais des Sports
RUE
RUE DE VOUILLÉ
14e
RUE D'ALÉSIA
ISSY-LES-MOULINEAUX
BOULEVARD LEFEBVRE
BOULEVARD BRUNE
Marché aux Puces
VANVES
MONTROUGE
CLAMART

PARIS
Puces de St-Ouen
ST-OUEN
Vers Stade de France
ST-DENIS
BOULEVARD NEY
BOULEVARD NEY
BD MAC DONALD
PORTE DE LA-VILLETTE
BD ORNANO
RUE DE LA CHAPELLE
18e
Zénith
Cité des Sciences et de L'Industrie
PANTIN
AVENUE DE FLANDRE
PORTE DE PANTIN
BD BARBÈS
Basilique du Sacré-cœur
AVENUE JEAN JAURÈS
BD DE ROCHECHOUART
BD. DE LA CHAPELLE
BOULD.
19e
PLACE PIGALLE
GARE DU NORD
RUE LA FAYETTE
BD DE MAGENTA
Canal St-Martin
BD DE LA VILLETTE
Parc des Buttes Chaumont
BD SÉRURIER
9e
RUE LA FAYETTE
RUE DU FG. POISSONNIÈRES
GARE DE L'EST
10e
RUE DE BELLEVILLE
BD DE MAGENTA
BOULEVARD MORTIER
2e
PLACE DE LA RÉPUBLIQUE
AV.
AVENUE DE LA RÉPUBLIQUE
BD DE
Palais Royal
Forum des Halles
BOULEVARD DE SÉBASTOPOL
3e
PARMENTIER
BOULEVARD
Cimetière du Père Lachaise
20e
Centre G. Pompidou
BD DES FILLES DU CALVAIRE
RUE DE RIVOLI
Île de la Cité
Hôtel de Ville
PLACE DES VOSGES
AV. PHILIPPE AUGUSTE
BOULEVARD DAVOUT
11e
6e
4e
Notre-Dame
PLACE DE LA BASTILLE
VOLTAIRE
Île St Louis
QUAI HENRI IV
BD HENRI IV
BD
ST-GERMAIN
BD ST MICHEL
Opéra Bastille
RUE DE LYON
Jardin du Luxembourg
Panthéon
La Seine
BOULEVARD DIDEROT
PLACE DE LA NATION
COURS DE VINCENNES
AVENUE
Jardin des Plantes
12e
BD SAINT
5e
GARE DE LYON
BD DE PICPUS
BD DE L'HÔPITAL
DAUMESNIL
BD
GARE D'AUSTERLITZ
BOULEVARD SOULT
BD DE PORT ROYAL
BD ST MARCEL
Palais Omnisports de Paris-Bercy
AV DAUMESNIL
Observatoire
BOULEVARD ARAGO
AV. DES GOBELINS
BD VINCENT AURIOL
Vers Parc Floral
Bibliothèque Nationale de France
PLACE D'ITALIE
BD AUGUSTE BLANQUI
BOIS DE VINCENNES
VINCENNES
RUE DE TOLBIAC
AVENUE D'ITALIE
13e
MASSENA
BOULEVARD
Parc Monsouris
IVRY-SUR-SEINE
CHARENTON
0 1 km
Reproduction interdite
Jean-Baptiste Nény
Juillet 2002
LE KREMLIN-BICÊTRE
GENTILLY

The quarters

Paris has no less than 80 districts, each with its own history. They were grouped into 20 arrondissements in 1860, yet Parisians are still attached to their vie de quartier which represents a human and urban identity.

La Bastille

The heart of popular Paris has been beating between Bastille and Nation since the start of the Revolution on 14 July 1789, when the hated Bastille prison was taken by force, heralding the end of absolute monarchy. In 1871, with the Prussian army laying siege to the capital, the starving Parisians opposed Thiers and set up the Commune, which was to end in a bloodbath. On 8 February 1962, towards the end of the Algerian war, 9 people were killed in violent police repression of a demonstration against the far-right O.A.S, at Charonne metro station. Today, this rebellious quarter has become quite bourgeois, following renovation work centred on the Bastille Opera, but is still the place for popular demonstrations and celebrations.

Bercy

Traditionally a wine storage site, with its warehouses and Port de la Rapée on the Seine close by, Bercy is now a developing quarter. The omnisports stadium hosts sports events, rock concerts and shows, and the Finance Ministry blends classic and contemporary styles.

Les Champs-Elysées

Le Notre had this elm-lined route built in 1670, extending the central avenue throught the Jardin des Tuileries to the current roundabout. During the Second Empire, the avenue became one of high society's favourite haunts, and is now a cosmopolitan and tourist quarter.

Grands Boulevards

They surround what used to be old Paris, on the right bank, from Concorde to Bastille via République, but the northern boulevards (Madeleine, Capucines, Italiens, Montmartre, Poissonniere) are the busiest, with the Opera and the big department stores nearby on Boulevard Haussmann.

Les Halles

Former marshland drained for agriculture. Louis VI (the Fat) set up a public market here in the 12th century, and the site gradually became a bazaar selling everything. In 1854, the Halles were demolished to make way for Baltard's 10 pavilions, put up in 1866 and described in Victor Hugo's *Le Ventre de Paris*. By 1950, the Halles were supplying food to 20% of the French population, but in 1965 the market was transferred to Rungis and La Villette. The current Forum des Halles, a huge leisure and shopping centre, was designed by Vasconi and Pencreach, and inaugurated in 1979.

Statue in front of the Eiffel tower

Ile de la Cité

The Roman city Lutèce was built on this island; medieval Paris grew out of it. The Parisii were only a peaceful tribe of boatmen until the Romans arrived to teach them civilisation, but they gave their name to the city four centuries later, when the population was beginning to settle on the banks of the Seine, having resisted several invasions with their customary energy and the help of patron Saint Genevieve. The Cite is still the capital's centre, and with Notre Dame and its charming neighbour the Ile Saint-Louis, well worth the visit.

Montmartre

Sacre Coeur Basilica was put up in 1876, when Montmartre was becoming notorious for its bohemian life: poets and Impressionists, freedom of thought and creativity, and Sunday painters, who can still be seen sketching a few portraits. This picturesque quarter is for artists and lovers, and tourists the world over who've seen *Moulin Rouge* or *Amélie*.

Montparnasse

The butte (rise) was given this pompous name by 17thc. students from the Latin Quarter, when it was a meeting-place for poets. Around 1725 it disappeared to make way for a road and a cemetery, opened in 1824, but the quarter kept its artistic associations, and its cafes were popular with the Surrealists in the '20s and '30s.

Quartier Latin

In the 12thc., Paris University moved from Notre Dame to the left bank, and established a student tradition (Panthéon, Sorbonne, Jussieu, Censier) which was often nonconformist and rebellious, even giving rise to national power struggles like in 1968. Latin was the quarter's official language until 1793, hence the name. Formerly home of culture and booksellers, the Latin Quarter is now better-known for its shops and fast food bars.

The Marais

Originally a huge swamp, this quarter became part of Paris inside Charles V's fortified wall. Building began on Henri IV's Place Royale (now Place des Vosges) in 1612, and the elegant and sophisticated Marais was born. Talented architects, stone-cutters, carpenters, cabinetmakers and roofers of the period produced the beautiful buildings that make this quarter special. Its narrow streets are home to creators and fashion designers, and the many cafes and nightclubs have become meeting-places for the capital's gays.

Saint-Germain-l'Auxerrois

Today, this is the Louvre quarter, the royalist heart of Paris, close to Saint Germain church (the third to be built on the site since the 7thc.). Rue Saint Germain l'Auxerrois is one of the oldest in Paris, already traced out in 820.

Saint-Germain-des-Prés

The quarter is named after Saint Germain, Bishop of Paris, who had a basilica built in the fields close to Paris, to house Saint Vincent's tunic which his king, Childebert 1, had taken at Saragossa. The quarter is not famous for its church, however, but for its literary cafes (Les Deux Magots, Le Flore) where post-war artists and intellectuals met. The first jazz clubs sprang up in the quarter's cellars, for partying existentialists.

What to see

Certain Parisian monuments have captured the world's imagination; the Eiffel Tower, the Arc de Triomphe...some of the most-visited sites on earth.

ARC DE TRIOMPHE Place Charles de Gaulle (8e) ✆ 01 55 37 73 77. *www.monum.fr M° Charles de Gaulle-Etoile. Open every day. April-October: 10am-11pm and October-April: 10am-10.30pm. Tills close 30 minutes before. Admission: adult 8 €, 18-25s, groups, large families and teachers 4 €50, under-18s accompanied by an adult and first Sundays of each month free.* The Arc de Triomphe offers visitors a marvellous view, the Louvre and the Place de la Concorde on one side and the Arche de la Defense on the other, with viewpoint indicators to help you identify other landmarks. The monument was built for Napoleon 1 in 1806, and is 50m high and 45m wide, with France's greatest military victories engraved on the sculpted parts. The tomb of the Unknown Soldier has been here since 28 January 1921, representing the 1,500,000 victims of the Great War. The flame of memory never goes out, and is revived every evening at 6.30pm. Baron Haussmann was responsible for the 12 avenues radiating from the Place, and thus indirectly for the giant traffic-jams they tend to create.

MONTMARTRE, SACRE COEUR BASILICA Parvis du Sacré-Coeur (18e) ✆ 01 53 41 89 00. *www,sacre-coeur-montmartre.com. M° Anvers or Abbesses (you can take the funicular railway). Open every day. Basilica: 6am-11pm (last admission 10.15pm). Dome: 9am-6.50pm (admission: 5 €) and crypt: 9am-6.30pm (admission free).* The basilica was built on top of Montmartre hill, 129m above the city. Building started in 1875, and and was finished just before World War 1, consecration being put off until 1919. This Romano-Byzantine church with its 83m dome is world-famous, attracting fleets of visitors. Stunning view over Paris

Luxembourg park

SAINT MARTIN CANAL (10e). Louis XIV dreamed it up, Napoleon started building it; the Saint Martin Canal with its nine locks, two swing bridges and walkways is very popular. It links the Arsenal dock to La Villette dock, where it meets up with the Ourcq Canal. It has always inspired poets, writers and artists: its banks are busy, creative places. At night It becomes rather sinister; the shadows hide all kinds of thieves and thugs. Marcel Carne's 1938 film Hôtel du Nord immortalised the quarter, reflecting real life at the time (it was completely filmed in the studios). The quarter's village feel is still there, despite inevitable changes, which tend to be gradual.

THE CATACOMBS 1, place Denfert-Rochereau (14e) ✆ 01 43 22 92 38. *M° and RER Denfert-Rochereau, Open Tuesday to Sunday: 10am-4pm (10am-12 noon for guided group tours, except Sunday) Admission: adults 5 €, concessions 2.50 € to 3.30 €. In 1786, the Catacombs were*

Sacré-Cœur

opened to take the overflow from Parisian cemeteries (and the contents of those that had been closed). The network of galleries covers over 100km, proving a useful hiding-place for the Resistance on the eve of the Liberation of Paris. It contains the remains of 6 million Parisians from the late 18th century to Haussmann's era.

NOTRE DAME CATHEDRAL 6, place du Parvis (4e) ✆ 01 44 32 16 70. *Open every day: 7.45am-7pm. Admission free. Access to towers, April-October: 9.30am-7pm; November-March: 10am-5.30pm.* This is the centre of Paris and of France. Maurice de Sully, 12thc. Bishop of Paris, decided to put up the cathedral on the ruins of a basilica. Building started in 1160, to be finished 170 years and three kings later, around 1330. It has seen great moments in French history: Henri IV's conversion to Catholicism because ´Paris is worth a Mass[a]; Napoleon 1's coronation. The Gothic front with its three sculpted portals is instantly recognisable, as are the 28 statues on top representing the Kings of Judea and Israel and dating back to the building's restoration after damage during the Revolution. Above is the magnificent rose window, between its two 70m towers (387 steps). The church's dimensions are not imposing, but the architecture is very beautiful.

CHATELET (1er). A central fountain decorated with sphinx and statues commemorates Napoleon's victories, framed by two theatres.The Thé,tre du Chatelet, Paris' current musical theatre, faces the Thé,tre de la Ville, bought by Sarah Bernhardt in 1899. The poet Gérard de Nerval was found hanged on this site in 1855. The quarter's dozens of little restaurants fill up at lunchtime with employees from neighbouring department stores. The Saint Jacques Tower in its square is the last remnant of Saint Jacques de la Boucherie Church, place of pilgrimage on the road to Compostella. It is 52m high, and houses a weather observatory at the top. The alchemist Nicolas Flamel is thought to have got up to mischief here, and Pascal worked on the effects of gravity.

CONCIERGERIE 2, boulevard du Palais (1er) ✆ 01 53 40 60 97. *Open every day, 1 March-30 October: 9.30am-6pm, 1 November-27 February: 9am-5pm. Closed on Easter and Whit Mondays, Ascension Day, 8 May, 14 July, 15 August. Admission: 6.50 €.* First Parisian Royal Palace, enlarged and transformed into a sumptuous residence by Philippe le Bel. It became a law court, and was partly converted into a prison in the 15thc. The dungeons recall the Revolution's sadder moments; Queen Marie Antoinette was imprisoned here for two and a half months (her reconstructed cell can be seen), Robespierre spent a night here; Danton and Camille Desmoulins, heroes of the first hour, awaited their sinister appointment with the guillotine. The medieval rooms are beautiful, recently restored and newly-lit.

OPERA BASTILLE 120 rue de Lyon (12e) ✆ 01 40 01 19 70. *Guided tour of the Opera by appointment. Admission for visits: adult 10 €, concessions 8 €.* This big modern theatre is Carlos Ott's work. It has 2,700 seats with homogeneous acoustics, unique stage equipment, integrated workshops for costumes, accessories and scenery, and practice and rehearsal rooms.

OPERA GARNIER Place de l'Opéra (9e) ✆ 01 40 01 25 99. *Open every day for visits: 10am-5pm. Admission: adult 7.* Napoleon III had the architect Charles Garnier build the Opera; already imposing outside, the staircases and decoration inside are a luxurious blend of the baroque and the neo-classical. Chagall painted the ceiling of the red and gold theatre in 1964.

Dôme des Invalides

PLACE DE LA CONCORDE (8e). The Place de la Concorde opens onto the Champs-Elysees, the Jardin des Tuileries and the Seine, and is closed off by the Naval Ministry and the Hôtel Crillon. Over 1,200 people were guillotined here during the Reign of Terror, including Louis XVI, Marie-Antoinette and Robespierre. Louis-Philippe had a 3,300-year-old obelisk put up in the centre, matching the one at the Temple of Luxor in Egypt. The Chevaux de Marly leading to the Champs-Elysees are reproductions; the originals are safe from pollution in the Louvre.

PLACE VENDOME (1er). Designed by Jules Hardouin on the site of César de Vendôme's destroyed mansion and gardens. It became the Place Vendôme in 1799, and gave its name to the Austerlitz column put up in 1806 to commemorate Napoleon's victory. It is now famous the world over for its luxury jewellers and hotels. In the middle is a statue of Louis XIV on horseback.

PLACE DES VOSGES (4e). Louis XIII on horseback graces this square, with its rural atmosphere among the trees and arcades. Henri IV's architects had 36 pavilions arranged rather like a chessboard, with the King's pavilion in the south facing the Queen's, in the north. First called Place Royale, it became Place des Vosges as a reward for being the first department to pay its taxes.

QUAIS DE SEINE. The city's backbone: both banks of the Seine have their habituees who come for a romantic walk, to sunbathe or to rummage in the bouquinistes' green boxes on the lookout for a first edition or an old engraving. Some old-world shops still exist around Pont Neuf and the Pont des Arts, a pedestrian bridge between the Louvre and the Académie Francaise from which you can admire the river traffic.

SAINTE CHAPELLE Quai de l'Horloge (1er) ✆ 01 53 40 60 97. *Open 9am to 6pm. Admission: adult 6.50 €.* Pierre de Montreuil put up the Sainte Chapelle from 1245-1248 for Saint Louis, who wanted a church to house Christ's Crown of Thorns and a fragment of the Holy Cross he'd just bought from the last Frankish Emperor of Constantinople. It has one nave, with two chapels one above the other (lords upstairs). There are great windows (15m by 4m) instead of walls, bathing the church in wonderful light. Over half the stained glass is original; it depicts 1,000 scenes from the Testaments, among the finest in France. Don't miss the statues of the 12 Apostles fastened to the columns.

EIFFEL TOWER Champ de Mars (7e) ✆ 01 44 11 23 23. *www.tour-eiffel.fr. Visits every day: January-June 9.30am-11pm (9am-midnight from mid-June-late August). Admission: adult 4.10 € (first level), 7.50 € (second level), 10.70 € (top); child 2.30 €, 4.10 €, 5.90 €; stairs to the second floor, over-25s 3.80 €, under-25s 3 €.* Concessions for groups. The most-visited monument in France is as impressive as ever; the view still changes surprisingly from level to level. You can eat in one of the two panoramic restaurants (first or second level). Gustave Eiffel built his tower for the 1889 Universal Exhibition; its destruction was planned for 20 years later, but it was finally kept for scientific reasons. Its feet are placed at the four points of the compass, it weighs over 10,000 tonnes and was the highest monument in the world until 1929 (324m today).

MONTPARNASSE TOWER Place Raoul Dautry (entrance 33 av. du Maine) (15e) ✆ 01 45 38 52 56. *www.tourmontparnasse56.com. Open every day: 9.30am-11.30pm, 1 April-30 September; 9.30am-10.30pm, 1 October-31 March. Admission: adult 8.50 €, students and 14-18s 7.50 €, 5-14s 5.80 €.* 38 seconds in Europe's fastest lift, and you are on the 56th floor of the Montparnasse Tower, in the panoramic bar 'Le Belvédère', with a unique view. The capital stretches out 210m below you; with the help of the exhibition panels you can gen up on Paris ancient and modern. A helicopter's-eye view of the city can be viewed in the audio-visual room. On a clear day you can see for 40km from the roof terrace, but the perfect moment to catch is the sun setting and the city lights coming on.

TROCADERO (16e). Between 1826 and 1880, this quarter, once deserted marshland and fields, became one of the most luxurious in Paris. Haussmann flattened the hilltop on which Daviout built the Palais du Trocadero for the 1878 Exhibition, replaced by the Palais de Chaillot between 1935 and 1937. Opposite the Eiffel Tower, with its Place des Droits de l'Homme and its monumental fountains, the Trocadero's museums (Musee de la Marine, Cité de l'Architecture et du Patrimoine) and cinematheque attract the crowds.

Museums

Paris is proud of its Louvre (the world's biggest museum), and of the diversity of its museums in general.

MUSEE DU LOUVRE Cour Napoleon - Place du Carrousel(1e) ✆ 01 40 20 50 50. *Recorded information: & 01 40 20 51 51. www.louvre.fr. Open every day: 9am-6.45pm except Tuesday and some public holidays. Open until 9.45pm Wednesdays and Fridays. Admission: 8.50 € before 6pm, 6 € after 6pm and Sunday. Under-18s and unemployed free. First Sunday every month free. Keep the whole day free for your visit.* This former residence of French Kings has become the world's foremost museum, for its size and the treasures it houses. There are 7 departments: Oriental, Egyptian, Greek, Etruscan and Roman antiquities; painting, sculpture, art objects and graphic arts from the Middle Ages to 1850. You go in through the big Pyramid in the Cour Napoleon, and reach the reception via an escalator.

- **Sully wing**

This is the Louvre's original architecture, with the remains of Philippe-Auguste's fortress (ditch and keep). In the Sphinx's crypt (ground floor, Porte des Arts, Seine side) is the Egyptian antiquities collection with the Crouching Scribe, a painted chalk statue with a strangely life-like face. Champollion, one of the first Egyptologists and decoder of hieroglyphics put together the primitive collection. The renovated rooms house the Greek antiquities, where you can see the Venus de Milo, one of the Louvre's stars.

French painting is on the second floor, shared between the Sully and Richelieu wings. The Sully wing contains 17th-18thc. works: Watteau, whose personal and delicate style can be seen in his *Pélerinage à Cythere* and *Gilles, Portrait d'un adolescent. La Pompadour* by Quentin de la Tour, Chardin's *La fontaine de cuivre*, Fragonard's *Les baigneuses* and Boucher's *Le déjeuner* are other brilliant examples of the period.

- **Denon wing**

The Samothrace Victory, the Louvre's major work of art, is here, as is Etruscan art: painted terracotta, ceramic, jewellery and funeral decorations all skillfully made. Don't miss the Cerveteri sarcophagus showing husband and wife at a banquet of the gods. On the first floor are major 19thc. French paintings: Géricault's *Le Radeau de la Meduse* and *La Liberté guidant le peuple*, painted by Delacroix after the 1830 July uprising. David's academic style is represented by *Le Sacre de Napoleon*.

Italian painting, newly restored to chronological order, includes frescoes by Botticelli (15th century) and Luini (16th century), and Fra Angelico's Calvary. The 16thc. works are the best-known: the *Mona Lisa* (La Joconde) and other paintings by Leonardo da Vinci, Veronese's *Noces de Cana* (the story of the Renaissance, with its major figures), The Louvre has extended to include more Italian and Spanish paintings (El Greco, Murillo, Goya) and an icon room.

- **Richelieu wing**

French portraits and religious paintings from the 14th to 17thc. are exhibited here, including Clouet's portrait of François I, Fouquet's of Charles VII, *Orphée et Eurydice* by Poussin, Georges de la Tour's L'*Adoration des Bergers* and *Le Repas des paysans* by the Le Nain brothers. You come across the works of Claude Gellée (Le Lorrain), and de la Tour's *Tricheur à l'as do carreau* (you'll notice the artist displays the same eye for light and colour as in his religious scenes). Breughel, Rubens, Rembrandt and Franz Hals are grouped together in a great cathedral-like room; Vermeer's *Lacemaker* is here too. Various art treasures and furniture are also here in this new part: religious art going back to the Franks, from Saint Denis Royal Basilica, and Gothic furniture, crosses, paintings, jewellery, earthenware and inlaid work. The East is on the ground floor, collected by 19thc. French archeologists from the antique sites of Babylon, Niniveh or Lagash, relics of the Sumerian, Assyrian and Phoenician civilisations. This floor also houses sculpture, with religious art from the Middle Ages onwards; funeral monuments and masterpieces by Puget, Girardon, Houdon and Pigalle. The Cours Marly and Puget are two symmetrical aisles displaying large works of sculpture (Marly de Coustou's horses) in an open space.

MUSEE D'ORSAY 62, rue de Lille (7e) ✆ 01 40 49 48 14. *www.musee-orsay.fr. Open Tuesday, Wednesday, Friday and Saturday: 10am-6pm, Thursday: 10am-9.45pm, Sunday: 9am-6pm. 21 June-30 September, open from 9am. Admission: adult 7.50 € first Sunday each month free.* This great national museum opened in 1986, in the former station built by Victor Laloux for the Universal Exhibition of July 1900. The huge glass building houses 19thc. national collections, plus donations, including the world's biggest Impressionist collection, sculptures, graphic arts, furniture and objects, architecture and photography. You can see Renoir's *Le bal du moulin de la Galette*, Monet's *Gare Saint-Lazare*, *Les nymphéas bleus* (Blue Waterlilies) and *Les Coquelicots*, Cézanne's *Les joueurs de cartes*, *L'étoile* and *La repasseuse* by Degas, Sisley's *L'inondation à Port-Marly* and Pissarro's *La jeune fille à la Baguette*. Some of Van Gogh's work is here, namely La chambre de Van Gogh a Arles, L'*Autoportrait* of 1889 and L'*Eglise d'Auvers-sur-Oise*. There follows a collection of Fauvist paintings, and some forerunners of more radical movements: Matisse, Derain, Vlaminck. To end a very pleasant visit, the Pont-Aven School, Douanier-Rousseau's naive exotism and foreign works from the turn of the 20thc.

CITE DE LA MUSIQUE 221, avenue Jean-Jaures (19e) ✆ 01 44 84 44 84. *www.cite-musique.fr. Open Tuesday to Saturday: 12am-6pm and Sunday: 10am-6pm. Admission: adult 7 € concessions 2.30 €, under-18s free.* All kinds of musical activities grouped together under one roof: concerts, music museum, workshops for playing an instrument, information centre. You find all styles: classical, jazz, song, world music. There are over 300 concerts a year and shows for young music fans.

DALI ESPACE MONTMARTRE 11, rue Poulbot (18e) ✆ 01 42 64 40 10. *M° Abbesses and Anvers – Website: www.daliparis.com – Open every day: 10am-6pm. Admission: adult 10 €, student 6 €, seniors and teachers 7 €, under-8s free.* Audio guides for hire. This is a real jewel of a museum, exclusively devoted to the Spanish artist. The exhibition is cleverly staged in a theatrical manner, with sequential lighting, music and Dali's voice off, as befits the surrealist world he loved so much. Over 300 original graphic works and a large number of sculptures are on display, with 3-D creations of the most famous surrealist images. You can also discover the art gallery, where limited series of Dali's sculptures, engravings, lithographs and seriographs are on sale. Condensed essence of Dali!

MUSEE DE LA MUSIQUE. A fascinating collection of around 1,000 instruments and works of art, from the early 17thc. to today, including a Galerie Contemporaine of contemporary music.

MUSEUM NATIONAL D'HISTOIRE NATURELLE - JARDIN DES PLANTES - GRANDE GALERIE DE L'EVOLUTION 36, rue Geoffroy-Saint-Hilaire (5e) ✆ 01 40 79 57 79. *www.mnhn.fr. Open 10am-6pm, Wednesday to Monday. Admission: adults 7 €, concessions 5 €.* The Grande Galerie de l'Evolution houses collections inherited from the Galerie de Zoologie (1889). The animals and birds are grouped according to their natural habitat under the big glass roof: African savannah, tropical forest, coastal, etc. There are rooms containing precious specimens of endangered and extinct species. Visitors of all ages enjoy wandering among these life-like animals, and learning more about them. Not to be missed!

INSTITUT DU MONDE ARABE 1, rue des Fossés Saint Bernard (5e) ✆ 01 40 51 38 11. *www.imarabe.org. M° Jussieu. Open every day except Monday: 10am-6pm. Admission: adult 10 €, concessions 4 €.* Jean Nouvel's imposing glass, aluminium and concrete building opened in 1987. It was created on the initiative of 19 Arab states, to foster the many aspects of Arab culture through its library and museum. The collections come from French national museums and gifts or loans from Arab countries who are members. The museum itself is on 3 levels devoted to Arab-Islamic art, with illuminated manuscripts, carpets, precious fabrics, ceramics and scientific instruments, reminders of an ancient and brilliant civilisation. The well-publicized temporary exhibitions are usually excellent. Finish your visit on the top floor for a panoramic view over the Seine.

MUSEE D'ART MODERNE DE LA VILLE DE PARIS 11, avenue du Président-Wilson (16e) ✆ 01 53 67 40 00. Open Tuesday to Sunday. Closed public holidays. Open: 10am-5.30pm except Saturday & Sunday: 10am-7pm. Tills close 40 minutes before. Please note that current renovation work has temporarily closed the site, and exhibitions are planned in various Parisian venues. More information on 01 53 67 40 00. This museum was inaugurated in 1961, housed in part of the Palais de Tokyo built for the 1937 Universal Exhibition. It contains mainly French 20thc. works, from Fauvism to contemporary creation, with private donations from collectors and artists. Different artistic disciplines are represented.

MUSEE CARNAVALET 23/29, rue de Sévigné (3e) ✆ 01 44 59 58 58. *Open Tuesday to Sunday: 10am-5.40pm. Permanent collection: admission free. Temporary exhibitions: adult 7 €, concessions 4 €, young people 2.50 €, under-13s free.* This 16thc. mansion has been illustrating Parisian history since 1880. In 1989 it doubled in size, annexing the Le Peletier de Saint-Fargeau mansion (no. 29) now housing important collections concerning the Revolution and the 19th and 20thc, with archeological works in the orangery. At no. 23, the story of Paris is told through its painting, drawings, sculpture, engraving, decorative arts and furniture, from Lutèce's origins to the present day. There is a calendar of activities animated by lecturers, musicians and actors, with concerts, lectures and plays. As if all that weren't enough, the gardens are magnificent in summer.

MUSEE GREVIN 10, boulevard Montmartre (9e) ✆ 01 47 70 85 05. *www.grevin,com. Open Monday to Friday: 10am-6.30pm, Saturday and Sunday and public holidays: 10am-7pm. Admission: adult 17 €, 6-14s 9 €.* The place to keep up with current French celebrities and meet those who have made history. 300 characters are staged in tableaux with appropriate backdrops, and a new feature, the 'Spirit of Paris', combines tradition and modernity to narrate the great moments of the 20thc: the comic strip, first man on the moon, Berlin Wall, 1998 Football World Cup...Have your picture taken with the stars of your choice for posterity.

MUSEE JACQUEMART-ANDRE 158, boulevard Haussmann (8e) ✆ 01 45 62 11 59. *www.musee-jacquemart-andre.com. Open every day: 10am-6pm. Tills close at 5.30pm. Admission: adult 9.50 €, 7-17s 6.50 €, families 26.50 €. The Café Jacquemart-André is open from 11.45am-5.30pm.* These are remarkable collections, particularly the Italian Renaissance. The great house is unique with its antechambers, private apartments, monumental staircase and winter garden. Discover the great 18thc.

painters: French (Boucher, Chardin, Fragonard, Greuze, Vigée-Lebrun) and English (Gainsborough, Reynolds); the French sculptor Houdon, and the Flemish masters in the Andrés' former library (Rembrandt, Van Dyck, Hals, Ruysdael). On the first floor, the 'Italian Museum' is second only to the Louvre for Renaissance works. A chic salon de thé awaits you after the visit, with its tapestries and ceiling by Tiepolo.

MUSEE MARMOTTAN-MONET 2 rue Louis Boilly (16e) ✆ 01 44 96 50 33. *www.marmottan.com. Closed Monday. Open: 10am-6pm. Tills close 5.30pm. Admission: adult 7 €, students and under-25s 4 €, under-8s free. Guided tour by appointment.* 100 of Monet's Impressionist masterpieces, with a number of works from his personal collection including Gauguin, Renoir and Degas. A large and very fine collection of paintings, objects and Empire furniture.

MUSEE NATIONAL D'ART MODERNE-CENTRE GEORGES POMPIDOU Rue Saint-Martin (4e) ✆ 01 44 78 12 33. *www.cnac-gp.fr. Open every day except Tuesday and 1 May: 11am-10pm (tills close at 8pm). Admission: adult 7 €, 18-25s 5 €, first Sunday each month free (supplement for the temporary exhibitions).* The 20thc's artistic life, traced through 1,400 contemporary works of art by painters, architects, stylists, photographers and even film-makers. On Level 5 you discover 900 works covering the period 1907 – 1960, from Fauvism, Cubism (Braque, Picasso, Léger) and Surrealism. Level 4 contains the post-1960 period, with the last ten years well-represented. On the three terraces extending the exhibition space, the imposing sculptures of Henri Laurens, Joan MirÛ and Alexandre Calder are displayed.

MUSEE PICASSO 5, rue de Thorigny (3e) ✆ 01 42 71 25 21. *Open every day except Tuesday: 9.30am-6pm in summer and 9.30am-5.30pm in winter. Admission: adult 6,70 €, concessions 4 € (and for everyone on Sunday) under-18s free.* Housed in the beautiful Hôtel Salé, the largest collection devoted to Picasso contains 200 paintings, sculptures and papers. You can trace his artistic development through the melancholy pink and blue periods of the early 20thc, 1920s cubism and neo-classicism, and a brush with surrealism. The artist's personal collection (Braque, Rousseau, MirÛ and Renoir) reveals his own tastes.

MUSEE RODIN 77, rue de Varenne (7e) ✆ 01 44 18 61 10. *www.musee-rodin.fr. M_ Varenne. Open April-September: 9.30am-5.45pm, park close at 6.45pm. October-March: 9.30am-4.45pm, park closes at 5pm. Admission: adult 5 €, 18-25s 5 €. Admission to park only: adult 1 € , under-18s free. Closed Monday.* The 18thc. Hôtel Biron with its splendid park has always welcomed artists: Cocteau, Matisse, Rainer-Maria Rilke, Isadora Duncan and Rodin himself stayed there. It has housed Rodin's works and collection since 1919. The 6,600 works of art and the furniture belonged to the sculptor: the famous marbles (including *Le Baiser*) bronzes and terracottas, shown to advantage in this sober building, and the sculptures in the garden which include *Le Penseur* and *Les Bourgeois de Calais*. Don't miss sculpture by Rodin's pupil and mistress Camille Claudel.

PALAIS DE LA DECOUVERTE Avenue Franklin D. Roosevelt (8e) ✆ 01 56 43 20 21 *www.palais-decouverte.fr. Open Tuesday-Saturday: 9.30am-6pm, Sundays and public holidays: 10am-7pm. Admission: adult 6.50 €, concessions 4 €, family 13 €, planetarium 3.50 €.* Make your own scientific discoveries; find out about the speed of time, or the composition of DNA through real-time experiments, animation and scale models. The new astronomic projector in the Zeiss planetarium reveals an amazingly clear and luminous sky.

Parks and greenery

Paris is an island surrounded by forest; the city has kept its beautiful royal gardens and added modern ones, blending Art and Nature.

BOIS DE BOULOGNE. The woods are out of bounds from 10pm to 5am the last Sunday in March to the last Sunday in September, and from 8pm to 6am the last Sunday in September to the last Sunday in March. Napoleon III had the Bois laid out, and the 863-hectare forest with its Inferior and Superior lakes linked by a waterfall became the fashionable outing for Parisians of the Belle Epoque. At night, it became the haunt of rather less savoury characters. Today, walkers, cyclists, horse riders, fishermen and boating fans enjoy the Bois, which suffered serious damage during the 1999 storms, and is still healing its wounds.

BOIS DE VINCENNES Parc Floral de Paris - 16, route de Brasserie ✆ 01 43 43 92 95. Since 1969, the Parc Floral has been famous for its landscaping, frequently renewed, its horticultural exhibitions and thematic gardens. 200 varieties of tulip bloom in spring, and a host of dahlias brighten the flowerbeds in autumn. The butterfly garden, Maison de la Nature, bird sanctuary and free classical concert on Sundays from June to September are its the main attractions.

JARDIN D'ACCLIMATATION. ✆ 01 40 67 99 16. *Access via Bois de Boulogne. Open every day: 10am-6pm October-May, and 10am-7pm June-September. Entrance fee.* This 20-hectare park was laid out by the Imperial Zoological Society and its President, Isidore Geoffroy Saint-Hilaire, in 1860. The public was treated to a riot of luxuriant plants in greenhouses, exotic animals and 'savages' as they were then called: Laps, Hottentots and Indians. Today, the gardens are simply botanical, with horticulture and childrens' workshops in the greenhouses. In fact, the trampolines, puppet-show, picnic area, merry-go-round and pony club make this a great place for kids.

JARDIN DU LUXEMBOURG. Entry via the boulevard Saint Michel and rues Vaugirard, Guynemer and Auguste Comte. Open 7.30am-5.15pm in winter and 8am-9.45pm in summer. A harmonious park, sheltering under 100-year-old plane trees. Students laze on the grass; there are ponies, an ornamental pond to sail model yachts on and a playground for kids, and an orchard and beehives where you can learn horticulture or beekeeping.

JARDIN DES PLANTES. *Entry via rues Buffon, Cuvier and Geoffroy Saint Hilaire. Open: 8am-5.30pm in winter, 8am-8pm in summer. The zoo, greenhouses, alpine garden and botanical school garden are open 8am-11am and 1.30pm-5pm every day except Saturday, Sunday and public holidays. The alpine garden is open April-September. Admission free.* There are many attractions here, from the rose garden containing over 300 varieties to the Grand Labyrinthe, a birdwatcher's paradise with its 75 different species. The alpine garden is celebrating its 50th birthday; mountain and rock plants from all over the world bloom in this quiet corner.

JARDIN DES TUILERIES ET JARDIN DU CARROUSEL Place du Carrousel. *The Carrousel is open 24 hours a day. The Tuileries: April-September, 7.30am-9pm; € July-August until 11.45pm, Saturday & Sunday until 12.45am; October-March, 7.30am-7.30pm.* Access via the Place de la Concorde, Place du

Le jardin du Louvre

Carrousel, Rue du Rivoli and the Quai des Tuileries. Opens onto the Louvre, Orangerie, Jeu de Paume and Decorative Arts museums. Over 20 species of tree live in this park; yews, limes, Laricio pines, white mulberry, to name but a few. Merry-go-rounds, cycle and roller-skating tracks amuse the kids, and a funfair is held in July and August.

PARC DE BAGATELLE. Bois de Boulogne - access via the allee de Longchamp, the route de Sevres at Neuilly, the Point-du-Jour and the Bagatelle lakes. Open every day: 8am-5.30pm or 8pm according to the season. Entrance fee. Bagatelle Park continues to charm generations of Parisians with its hundred-year-old trees and iris garden, its clematis collection and the famous rose garden scented with over 8,000 rose bushes (1,300 varieties).

PARC GEORGES-BRASSENS. Access via the rues des Morillons, Brancion and des Périchaux. Open 7.30am (9am Saturday and Sunday)-5.30pm (9.30pm in summer). Modern yet beautiful, this park is a recent success. A scented garden with 80 perfumed, aromatic and medicinal plant species vies with the rose garden. There are beehives (which you can learn about with the Société Centrale d'Apiculture), a pinot noir vine, grass you can lounge around on; it's just like the countryside! For kids, there's a playground with games and climbing frames, a sandpit, a belvedere and a puppet theatre.

PARC ANDRE CITROEN. Access via the Quai André-Citroen, the rues Leblanc, Saint-Charles, de la Montagne-de-la-Fage and de la Montagne-de-l'Esperou.Open 7.30am (9am Saturday and Sunday) to 5.30pm (9.30pm in summer). This modern conceptual park is divided into thematic gardens, with greenhouses, waterlilies and rare acquatic plants.

PARC MONCEAU. Access via the boulevard de Courcelles and the avenues Ruysdael, Velasquez and Van Dyck. Open 7am-10pm in summer and 7am-8pm in winter. This Anglo-Chinese folly was laid out in 1778 by the Duc de Chartres. The grotto with its stalactites is classic Haussmann; there is an Italian bridge, a Rotunda and an ornamental pond to surprise you. The 8 hectares of hilly lawns are dotted with trees including a fig tree, a 35-metre maple sycamore, a purple maple and a 180-year-old Oriental plane tree in the south west of the park.

PARC MONTSOURIS. Access via boulevard Jourdan, avenue Reille and rues Gazan, de la Cité-Universitaire, Nansouty and Emile Deutsch de la Meurthe. Open 7.30am (9am Saturday and Sunday)-5.30pm (9.30pm in summer). Haussmann had this vast park built on former quarries. Take time out for a pleasant stroll past the lakes and waterfalls, over green lawns with here and there a sculpture. There is a kiosk, and playgrounds and a merry-go-round for tots.

PARC DE LA VILLETTE. Paris's biggest park here in the 19th arrondissement is always open. It covers the former national meat market between Porte de Pantin and Porte de la Villette, and contains the Cité des Sciences, the Cité de la Musique, the Grande Halle and the Zenith venue. Ten thematic gardens stretch alongside 3km of walks, cycle and roller-skating tracks.

Paris from the air, on water and by bike

The best way to see Paris is on foot, but you can discover it from other angles too.

Paris from the Seine

There's a river running through it - under the pont Mirabeau, as the poet tells us. The Seine is the city's main artery, and France's biggest commercially navigable river, besides transporting tourists in the *bateaux-mouches*. Comfortably seated in one of these barges, you have time to admire the bridges and monuments, and can even enjoy a good dinner or a dance.

Paris by bike

More and more Parisians are taking to their bikes these days, either to go to work or as a leisure activity. You can ride through peaceful leafy lanes in the Boulogne and Vincennes woods and the Buttes de Chaumont park, or follow one of the many cycle paths set up alongside the wide Parisian avenues. Watch out for roller skaters though!

The boats

BATEAUX VEDETTES DU PONT-NEUF Square du Vert-Galant ✆ 01 46 33 98 38. *www.pontneuf.net. March-October, trips every day: 10.30am-10.30pm. November-February: Monday-Friday, 10am-10pm; Saturday, 10am-10.30pm. Trips last an hour. Tickets: adult 10 €, under-12s 5 €, under-4s free.* How romantic to discover Paris from the water. Go down the staircase from the Pont-Neuf to the very end of the Ile-de-la-Cité to reach your boat. The hour-long guided trip explains the buildings and monuments you pass, from the Cité and Saint-Louis to the Eiffel Tower.

Bir Hakeim bridge

BATEAUX PARISIENS 08 25 01 01 01 Port de La Bourdonnais - *At the foot of the Eiffel Tower* © **01 44 11 33 44.** *www.bateauxparisiens.com. Open every day. Trips every hour, 10am-10pm November-March, and every half-hour, 10am-11pm April-October. Tickets: adult 9.50 €, under-12s 4.50 €.* Embark near the Eiffel Tower for your guided trip as far as the new Bibliothèque Nationale de France. Lunches and dinners are organised all year round, for a magic and romantic journey (from 50).

VEDETTE DE PARIS Pont de Suffren © **01 47 05 71 29**. *www.vedettedeparis,com. Open every day. Tickets: adult 9 €, 3-12s 4 €.* You'll enjoy this unique view of Paris floating and rocking to the rhythm of the barges, from the Eiffel Tower to the Ile Saint-Louis. There are trips for the petits matelots (little sailors) on Wednesdays and every day during French school holidays.

The bridges

36 of them link the capital's left and right banks, each with its own story to tell. Here are a few:

PASSERELLE SOLFERINO. 36th and last of the Parisian bridges, 105m wide, it was put up in Septembre 1999 so pedestrians could cross from the Louvre to Orsay via the Tuileries.

PONT ALEXANDRE III. Perhaps the most famous of the bridges with its statues, gilding and period streetlamps, it was inaugurated with the 20thc.

PONT DES ARTS. Having linked the Louvre to the Institut since the early 19thc., this romantic pedestrian walkway suits its name. It marks a turning point in engineering history, being built of iron instead of stone.

PONT DE GRENELLE. It is not so much the bridge that is famous, but its statue; the scaled-down model of Bartholdi's Statue of Liberty.

PONT NEUF. The oldest bridge in Paris despite its name, built from 1578. Henri IV opened it in 1607, and is still there, on horseback in statue form.

PONT DES ARTS. Built in the early 19thc. this bridge suits its name, linking as it does the Louvre and the Institute. It was built of metal rather than stone, marking the arrival of iron as the major new construction material. Today, it is a pleasant and romantic pedestrian footbridge.

Paris from the sky

AEROPARIS Parc André Citroën - 2, rue de la Montagne de la Fage © **01 44 26 20 00**. *Open every day, 9am-6.50pm weekdays, 9am-8.50pm weekends. Tickets: adult 10 € (weekends 12 €), 12-17s 9 € (weekends 10 €) 3-11s 5 € (weekends 6 €). Free for little Parisians aged 3-11.* The Eutelsat balloon (the world's biggest, bright blue like the satellite operator) was planned to celebrate the year 2000, but the Conseil de Paris voted to keep it five more years. Don't miss the unique experience of looking down on Paris from 150m up, along with 29 other passengers. Popular and fun; for 10 minutes you have a magnificent panorama all around, no noise, no bumps, perfectly safe.

Hotels

ARTS ET VIE 39, Rue des Favorites (15) ✆ 01 44 19 02 69 *Open Monday-Saturday*
This travel agency offers get-away-from-it-all trips to the 4 corners of the the world, at any time of year. Arts et Vie also has holiday residences to let in France (Haute-Savoie, Vaucluse, Landes, Gironde) from 240 € for two, for a week in low season. Theme weeks are organised on the subject of wine-tasting, bridge or keep fit. Successful holidays guaranteed !

1st arrondissement

HOTEL DUMINY VENDOME * 3, rue du Mont-Thabor ✆ 01 42 60 32 80**. *M° Tuileries – Fax: 01 42 96 07 83 – Website: www.hotelduminyvendome.com. Single rooms from 125 €-170 € (according to season). Double rooms 157 €-217 €. Triple Privilege rooms 195 €-245 € (plus 30 € supplement). Tourist tax included. Breakfast 15 €. Direct outside phone line, TV, safe, trouser-press, mini-bar and room service. Air-conditioning in some of the rooms.* This hotel was built in the 19thc. on the site of the former Feuillants convent gardens. Despite their historic setting, the 78 rooms are resolutely modern. A quiet place, with a friendly atmosphere, and a lot of little extras provided to sweeten your stay. Check out the hotel website for one of the many special offers online.

HOTEL LE LOIRET * 5, rue des Bons-Enfants ✆ 01 42 61 47 31**. *M Palais-Royal Musée du Louvre-Fax: 01 42 61 36 85 Website:www.hotelleloiret.com –3-star hotel.Single rooms from 96 €, doubles from 130 €. Continental breakfast 7 €. Car park 20 € per day.* Le Loiret (31 rooms) is a discreet but surprising hotel, in the shadow of the Palais Royal and its gardens, a stone's throw from the Louvre. The rooms are simple but of excellent quality, some overlooking the street, others the leafy garden. They have either shower or bath - or both, depending on your budget.

HOTEL DE LA PLACE DU LOUVRE * 21, rue des Prêtres-Saint-Germain-l'Auxerrois ✆ 01 42 33 78 68. M° Louvre-Rivoli.** *Fax : 01 42 33 09 95. Website : www.esprit-de-france.com. Rooms from 132 € to 158 €. Continental breakfast 11 €.* From this ancient house, a short distance from the Pont des Arts and Ile de la Cité, you have a plunging view of the Louvre's colonnades and Saint Germain l'Auxerrois Church with its rib vaults and Gothic spires. Rooms giving onto the street are best, the ones overlooking the courtyard are no doubt quieter, but have no view. Each one is named after the modern painter whose lithographs decorated the walls. They are very pleasant, in shades of beige and white, with air-conditioning. Breakfast is served in amagnificent vaulted room known as the Salle des Mousquetaires, which at one time provided access to the Louvre.

HOTEL DES TUILERIES *** **10, rue Hyacinthe** *M° Tuileries or Pyramides* ✆ **01 42 61 04 17** *E-mail: htuileri@aol.com. Site: www.hotel-des-tuileries.com.* An exceptional situation for this charming hotel located in a small peaceful street, between the garden of Tuileries, the Louvre and Orsay museums and place Vendôme, in the heart of historical Paris, and also in the area of business and shopping. (see p.)

2e arrondissement

HOTEL APPI 158, rue Saint-Denis ✆ **01 42 33 35 16.** *M° Châtelet Rooms from 48 € for two. Breakfast 5 €.* This little hotel in the heart of Paris is located in the Halles Montorgueil pedestrian area, only a short distance from museums, historic monuments and the huge Forum des Halles shopping centre. Recently opened and very simple, it has 19 quiet, clean and comfortable rooms. You'll find plenty of places to eat in the neighbourhood. Internet access free!

HOTEL ASCOT OPERA *** **2, rue Monsigny** ✆ **01 42 96 87 66.** *M° Quatre-Septembre. Fax : 01 49 27 06 06. Website : www.ascot-hotel-paris.com. Rooms with bath from 100 € to 150 €. Breakfast 8 €. Wi-Fi access in the downstairs lounge, hairdyer, safe and mini-bar in each room. Ironing board on 3rd and 6th floors. Private car park 18 € for 24 hours.* Difficult to find a hotel quieter than this one, a stone's throw from Opéra and the Grand Louvre in the business, tourist and shopping quarter! It boasts 36 rooms on six floors, with sophisticated decoration in a variety of styles. Here you find a four-poster bed in pastel shades, there exposed beams, wooden furniture and a countrified atmosphere. Each bathroom is different too, depending on which room you choose. The staff is most attentive. History fans will like to know that this place was formerly the composer Offenbach's private mansion: he later had the Bouffes Parisien theatre built just next door.

PARISIAN HOME 9, rue Mandar ✆ **01 45 08 03 37.** *Website: www.parisianhome.com* Junior, executive ou deluxe. Parisian Home offers a choice of over 200 furnished apartments, with size and fittings to suit your requirements, and length of stay. All the apartments we let are top-of-the-range, and are located in the capital's central districts. We provide excellent value for money and made-to-measure service. You can choose between Grand Louvre, Bohemia, Amour and Nouvelle Vague according to your mood and taste. Longer stays benefit from price reductions! Parisian Home lowers the rate for lets of over a fortnight, and hands you the keys to Paris from only 55 € per night.

HOTEL DE NOAILLES **** **9, rue de la Michodière 01 47 42 92 90.** *M° Opéra – Fax : 01 49 24 92 71 – Website : www.paris-hotel-*

noailles.com. Double room 190 € to 225 €, double superior 230 € to 265 €, luxury 250 € to 285 €. Suite 390 € (new). Breakfast 15 €. Near the Louvre, the Opera and major department stores. This hotel is a calm and comfortable refuge from the city bustle. It is built round a pretty garden and second-floor terrace in Japanese style. The contemporary decoration is smooth and efficient, without being cold or impersonal, and the comfortable, air-conditioned rooms are well equipped, with Wi-Fi access - the top floor rooms have a balcony. Each floor has a different colour, grey-black, midnight blue, and yellow. Friendly welcome.

HOTEL VICTOIRE OPERA ** 56, rue de Montorgueil ✆ 01 42 36 41 08** - *Fax: 01 45 08 08 79. Website : www.paris-hotel-opera.com.* Metro Sentier and Les Halles. Standard room 214 €, superior 244 €, luxury 275 € and junior suite 335 €. Ideally situated in the heart of the busy and picturesque Rue Montorgeuil, this is one of the trendiest hotels in Paris. The decoration is New York chic, contrasting with the street atmosphere, and will appeal to fans of contemporary design. The low-level furniture in dark wood, consoles and harmonious and relaxing colours are very pleasant. The prices might put you off, though!

3e arrondissement

HOTEL DU PETIT MOULIN ** 29, rue de Poitou ✆ 01 42 74 10 10.** M° Filles-du-Calvaire. *Rooms from 180 € à 350 € a night.* How do you fancy a hotel entirely decorated by Christian Lacroix? This new adventure appealed to the famous designer, who had carte blanche to fit out the 17 rooms one by one, along with the rest of the hotel. The result is a magnificent blend of Baroque and contemporary, in keeping with the spirit of the place. The façade belonged to a former listed bakery.

MURANO URBAN RESORT 13, boulevard du Temple ✆ 01 42 71 20 00. *M° République or Oberkampf. Website : www.muranoresort.com. Breakfast buffet 28 € from 7am-12 noon. Brunch 38 €, Sunday 11.30am-4.30pm.* Another trendy temple, opened in late summer 2004 near République. Individually air-conditioned rooms, LCD screen, light variator, and swimming pool in some suites. Facilities include spa with heated indoor pool, hammam, jacuzzi, and fitness centre. Otherwise, you can simply have a drink or a meal here; it's worth the visit. No menu: à la carte around 50 €.

5e arrondissement

FAMILIA HOTEL ** 11, rue des Ecoles ✆ 01 43 54 55 27. *M° Jussieu – Fax: 01 43 29 61 77 Website: www.hotel-paris-familia.com – Single room 80 €, double from 97 €, superior room from 107 €, luxury room with balcony 117 €. Breakfast included.* This hotel has plenty of charm, and is worth seeking out. It has been in the Gaucheron family for two generations, and is located in the heart of the Latin Quarter. The antique furniture, exposed stonework and sepia frescoes designed by Gerald Pritchard give a medieval feel to the rooms. Ask for one on the 5th or 6th floor with balcony, and have your breakfast on it - there is a marvellous view over the rooftops of Paris, and the towers of Notre Dame are breathtaking.

GRAND HOTEL SAINT-MICHEL * 19, rue Cujas © 01 46 33 33 02.** *M° Cluny-La Sorbonne and RER Luxembourg – Fax : 01 40 46 96 33. Single room 120 €, double 160 €, triple 220 €. Breakfast 12 €.* Apart from its privileged location in the heart of the Saint Michel district, this hotel boasts sophisticated decoration based on contrasts: Empire style in the salon, contemporary in the rooms. These are all air-conditioned with Internet access, and very elegant. You get a polite welcome. Don't miss the breakfast buffet served in the basement; it's generous and attractively presented with home made viennoiseries - pain au chocolat, pain au raisins, etc.

MINERVE HOTEL *** **13, rue des Ecoles ✆ 01 43 26 26 04.** *M° Maubert-Mutualité, Jussieu et Cardinal-Lemoine – Fax: 01 44 07 01 96 – Email: Réservation: info@hotel-paris-minerve.fr – Website: www.hotel-paris-minerve.com – Single room 86 €-116 € (with view of Notre Dame) double 98 €-130 € (with balcony and private patio), triple 150 €, quadruple 170 €. Breakfast 8 €.* You notice the little balconies full of greenery straight away. Inside, the atmosphere is both cosy and sophisticated , with flowers everywhere. A number of rooms have a view of a giant wall fresco. Pretty marble bathrooms; air conditioning in all rooms and two seminar salons. Car parks 20 € per day.

HOTEL DU LEVANT *** **18, rue de la Harpe ✆ 01 46 34 11 00.** *M° Saint Michel – Email: hlevant@club-internet.fr. Website: www.hoteldulevant.com – Single room 69 €, standard 100 € (sleeps one) and 145 € (sleeps 2). Superior room from 135 € (sleeps one) to 160 € (sleeps 2).Twin room 160 €. Triple 175 €-215 € (sleeps 3). Family room 235 €-250 €. Suite 300 € and 320 € (sleeps 5). Breakfast included.* All the charm of Old Paris seems to be here in this haven of peace, right in the centre of the picturesque and busy Latin Quarter. Four generations of the same family have run the hotel, updating comfort standards to suit their guests without sacrificing the old-world atmosphere. You can reach many of the city's attractions on foot – the Ile de la Cité, Seine quays, Notre Dame, the Jardins du Luxembourg, and the Saint Michel and Saint Germain quarters. The nearby RER train links up with the airports and stations. The hotel has 47 elegantly decorated rooms, each with privatel bathroom, satellite TV, individual safe, mini-bar, Internet socket and phone. A great place for tourists and business people alike.

HOTEL DU COLLEGE DE FRANCE ** 7, rue Thénard ✆ 01 43 26 78 36. *M° Maubert-Mutualité and Cluny-La Sorbonne. Fax : 01 46 34 58 29 Website: www.hotel-collegedefrance.com. Single room from 70 € to 83 €, double from 78 € to 110 €. Breakfast 8 €.* This charming hotel is located in a very quiet street. Behind its 17thc. façade you find thirty or so rooms, all very light and decorated in warm shades. Shower or bathroom, TV, radio and alarm-clock. Internet access is also available in your room. Pleasant welcome.

HOTEL DE NOTRE-DAME * 1, quai Saint Michel ✆ 01 43 54 20 43.** *M°/ RER: Saint-Michel. Website: www.paris-hotel-notredame.com Room with a view from 199 €. Breakfast 7 €.* This charming hotel is in the heart of the Latin Quarter, facing legendary Notre Dame Cathedral. The staff are very friendly and welcoming. All the rooms have contemporary furniture, while at reception, the fireplace corner and bar are decorated in 1930s Parisian style. This hotel is ideally situated for exploring Paris on foot, being close to Saint Germain's cafés, restaurants and nightlife, as well as the Sorbonne and the Panthéon.

AU ROYAL CARDINAL HOTEL ** 1, rue des Ecoles ✆ 01 43 26 83 64. M° Jussieu and Cardinal-Lemoine. *Fax : 01 44 07 22 32 – Website: www.hotelroyalcardinal.com –Single or double room 81 €-92 €, twin 92 €-103 €, triple 110 €-126 €, quadruple 115 €-130 €. Tourist tax 0.78 €.* This hotel is located in the mythical Rue des Ecoles, yet the prices are still reasonable, attracting crowds of customers every year. It boasts thirty-six prettily-decorated rooms with double glazing - if you stroll through the quarter on Saturday evening you'll see why! Wi-fi Internet access. Warm and friendly welcome. if you're booking in advance, ask for a room with a small balcony.

HOTEL SUNNY MOUFFETARD ** 48, boulevard de Port-Royal ✆ 01 43 31 79 86. *M° Les Gobelins and RER Port-Royal – Fax: 01 43 31 36 02 –Website: www.hotel-sunny.com Single room 64 €-66 €, double 74 €-77 €, twin 78 €-80 €, triple 105 €. Breakfast 6 €.* This hotel lies between the 5th and 13th arrondissements, or districts, and is a charming place, simple and friendly. The rooms are softly decorated in pastel shades, and have shower or bath, cable TV and phone. You also have Internet access in your room if you wish. For guests who appreciate comfort and a family atmosphere, this is a real home from home.

6e arrondissement

HOTEL AVIATIC * 105, rue de Vaugirard ✆ 01 53 63 25 50**. *M° Falguière – Fax : 01 53 63 25 55 – Website : www.aviatic.fr Rooms: Tradition 132 €, Supérieure 159 €, triple 195 €, Millenium 169 €.* Satellite TV, double glazing and air conditioning, safe, mini-bar and hairdryer. This hotel between Saint-Germain-des-Prés and Montparnasse has been open since 1856, but was best-known in the Roaring Twenties, when aviators from Issy-les-Moulineaux stayed here, hence the name Aviatic. The setting is a typically Parisian blend of chic and classic elegance, with a charming little garden at the heart of it. A hushed Empire-style atmosphere fills the lounge, while the rooms are warmly decorated. All have old-fashioned mosaics in the bathroom. Breakfast is served in your room - with the newspaper! - or in the 1900 bistrot-style dining room. You'll positively fly round thc capital after this.

LE CLOS MEDICIS * 56, rue Monsieur-le-Prince ✆ 01 43 29 10 80**. *M° Odéon. Website: www.closmedicis.com. 38 rooms: classic room from 150 €, superior 205 €, deluxe 225 € and suite 470 €. Breakfast 12 €.* This charming 3-star hotel extends a warm welcome, located in a quiet street between Saint-Germain-des-Pres and the Latin Quarter. All the rooms are very comfortable, and equipped with WiFi. Why not come and have an evening drink in the lounge, with its antique furniture and log fire? In fine weather, breakfast is served in the garden - a luxury in the capital.

HOTEL DES 2 CONTINENTS * 25, rue Jacob ✆ 01 43 26 72 46**. *M° Saint-Germain-des-Prés – Fax: 01 43 25 67 80 – Email: continents.hotel@wanadoo.fr – Website: www.hoteldes2continents.com – (special offers online). Single room 138 €, double (sleeps 1 or 2) 147 €-160 €, twin (sleeps 1 or 2) 160 €, triple 195 €. Breakfast 10 €, served in your room 11 €.* This charming hotel in the shadow of Saint-Germain-des-Pres Church is a breath of fresh air during your stay in Paris. The atmosphere is cosy, blending the styles of two continents; we like the flowers dotted around the rooms, and the modern bathrooms. There are 40 rooms on 6 floors, each a model of elegance.

HOTEL FERRANDI SAINT-GERMAIN * 92, rue du Cherche-Midi ✆ 01 42 22 97 40.** *M° Vanneau – Fax: 01 45 44 89 97 – Email: hotel.ferrandi@wanadoo.fr – Rooms 145 €-230 €. Suite 260 €. Breakfast 11 €. Car park 25 €.* WiFi access, business corner. The Rue du Cherche-Midi is one of the quarter's most fashionable streets, a mixture of chic bohemia, artists and classic Parisians. The prices are therefore very reasonable, given the hotel's location and quality. The rooms are a skilful blend of period furniture and modern comfort - some have a four-poster bed! Plenty of charm, sophistication and warmth, just like the lady of the house (who also looks after the Hôtel de l'Elysées in the 8th arrondissement).

HOTEL DES MARRONNIERS * 21, rue Jacob ✆ 01 43 25 30 60.** *M° Saint-Germain-des-Prés or Mabillon – Fax: 01 40 46 83 56 – Email: hotel-des-marronniers@wanadoo.fr – Website: www.hoteldesmarronniers.com – (special offers online) Single room 110 €, double 153 €-168 €, triple 208 €, quadruple 248 €. Breakfast 10 €, served in your room 12 €.* Tourist tax included. Internet access. Air conditioning. Telephone, satellite TV. Hairdryer. You imagine this hotel under the chestnut trees, but in fact it is set back off the fashionable Rue Jacob, and has a rather extraordinary landscape garden! The decor is impeccable, as befits a hotel in the antiquarian and publishing district. Ask for a room with a view of the garden, and you'll catch a glimpse of Saint-Germain Church spire!

HOTEL LE PETIT TRIANON 2, rue de l'Ancienne-Comédie ✆ 01 43 54 94 64. *M° Odéon, Saint-Michel or Mabillon. Single room from 38 €, double 62 €, triple 75 €.* A genuine, typically Parisian hotel with very attractive prices, in the heart of bustling Saint-Germain-des-Pres. 13 rooms nestle on several floors just above the terrace of the popular Cafe de Comti - an ideal starting point for discovering Paris on foot. At the end of the street, cross the Seine, and you're already on the Right Bank. The rooms are decorated in Provencal, English or Oriental style; take your pick. Real human contact and a family atmosphere are de rigueur here.

HOTEL SAINT-ANDRE-DES-ARTS 66, rue Saint-André-des-Arts ✆ 01 43 26 96 16. *M° Odéon – Fax: 01 43 29 73 34. Single room from 66 €, double from 85 €, twin 90 €, triple 108 €, quadruple 119 €. Breakfast free.* This is the kind of place that feels like home. Smiling welcome and family atmosphere in an old house with secret corners, exposed beams and half-timbering, and large, rather old-fashioned rooms. Ideally located in the heart of nostalgic Saint-Germain-des-Pres, it still has plenty of unspoilt charm, and will ensure you a perfect stay. Internet access.

HOTEL DE SEINE * 52, rue de Seine ✆ 01 46 34 22 80.** *M° Mabillon, Saint-Germain-des-Prés and Odéon – Fax: 01 46 34 04 74 – Email: hotel-de-seine@wanadoo.fr – Website: www.hoteldeseine.com – (special offers online) Internet terminal – WiFi in the lounge.Single room from 138 €, double from 158-168 € and triple from 203 €.Continental breakfast 10 €, served in your room 11 €.* An ideal starting point for doing the Parisian antiques shops and art galleries - stop off at the corner of Rue de Seine and Rue de Buci, and discover the 'real' Paris. This period hotel is a haven of peace, with something magic in its atmosphere. Each room is different, all are warmly decorated in predominating red and yellow tones. Classic and carefully kept up, plus impeccable service with a smile.

LES JARDINS DE PARIS SAINT-GERMAIN * 28, rue Saint-Benoît ✆ 01 44 39 71 00.** *M° Saint-Germain – Fax : 01 44 39 71 29 – Single rooms from 125 € to 155 €, doubles from 145 € to 175 €. Suites from 210 € to 250 €. Breakfast 9 €.* This area is famous for intellectual and political upheaval, and the philosopher Diderot lived in the street where you find this charming hotel, ideal for discovering the Latin Quarter, Carré des antiquaires and Paris by night. Contemporary character and traditional charm blend well together in its 17 air-conditioned rooms, all with Internet access.

LE LUTETIA **** **45, boulevard Raspail ✆ 01 49 54 46 46.** *M° Sèvres-Babylone – Fax : 01 49 54 46 00 – Website : www.lutetia-paris.com. Online bookings. Superior or luxury rooms, junior suite, executive junior suite, suites (1 bedroom or sleeping 2), Arman suite. From 290 €. Air conditioning, double glazing, direct phone line, hairdryer, safe, computer sockets, mini-bar, radio, satellite TV, non-smoking bedrooms.* Built in 1910, Le Lutetia is Paris' main Art Deco hotel. As a privileged witness to the new artistic movements that sprang up between the wars, the hotel welcomed artists like Picasso and Matisse, and the writer André Gide. American singer Josephine Baker stayed here with her many children, and the General de Gaulle spent his wedding night here. The rooms are done out in 1930s luxury chic, with contemporary touches in honey and mahogany bringing them right up to date. The Arman suite is recommended for special (crazy) nights, decorated by the sculptor himself and dedicated to African music and art, with his famous violin-shaped bed and flying notes on the soft furnishings. Majestic and unobtrusive, retro and modern all at once.

HOTEL TRIANON RIVE GAUCHE *** **1 bis, rue de Vaugirard ✆ 01 43 29 88 10**. *M° Cluny, Odéon or RER Luxembourg (direct from CDG – Parc des expos. Villepinte) – Fax: 01 43 29 15 98 – Website: www.hoteltrianonrivegauche.com – (special offers online) Single or double room 120 €-180 €, triple 215 €-225 €.* Extra bed *23 €. Breakfast buffet 12 €.* A stone's throw from the Jardins du Luxembourg (ideal for a morning jog), this hotel is decorated in Empire style, cosy yet flamboyant in a riot of brightly-coloured flowers. 110 rooms offer comfort, sophistication and genuine charm, each with its own individual character. Telephone and satellite TV. Laundry service open every day except weekends.

VILLA DES PRINCES SAINT-GERMAIN ** **19, rue Monsieur-le-Prince ✆ 01 46 33 31 69.** *M° Odéon – Fax: 01 43 26 30 04 – Email: villadesprinces@wanadoo.fr – Website: www.villa-des-princes.com – In low season, single room 80 €, double 95 €, triple 125 €. In high season, single 90 €, double 109 €, triple 149 €. Breakfast buffet 10 €. Tax not included. Internet, WiFi.* Recently renovated, this hotel is housed in a freestone building dating back to the reign of Louis XIII in the XVIIthc. The Prince of Conde acquired it in 1612. Warmly welcoming and full of charm, with lots of wrought iron and a cosy Mediterranean-style decor, the hotel offers personalised rooms, all furnished with antiques. Ideally located for a first visit - and what cachet!

WELCOME HOTEL ** **66, rue de Seine** ✆ **01 46 34 24 80**. *M° Odéon or Saint-Germain-des-Prés – Fax: 01 40 46 81 59 – Email: hotelwelcomeparis@wanadoo.fr – Website: www.hotelwelcomeparis.com - Single room 70 € 85 €, double 98 €-108 €, triple 123 €. Breakfast 9 €. TV and phone. Tourist tax included.* The name is already appealing, and the hotel itself charming. The rooms overlooking the Rue de Seine reflect some of its characteristic Parisian bustle, and there is one small room with a sloping ceiling that is most attractive. Partial air-conditioning, and double glazing.

7e arrondissement

EBER MARS ** **117, avenue de la Bourdonnais** ✆ **01 47 05 42 30** *M° Ecole Militaire. Website: www.hotelebermars.com. Double rooms from 75 €, up to 200 € for the family room. Breakfast 10 €.* Within (short) walking distance from the Champs de Mars and legendary Eiffel Tower, this 2-star hotel is located i+n one of Paris' most prestigious quarters. All the rooms are tastefully fitted out, and have indvidual bathrooms. Some have a view of the Eiffel Tower. Breakfast is served in a pretty lounge next to reception, where you can see photos tracing the Tower's history. (See p. 641)

HOTEL DE L'ACADEMIE *** **32, rue des Saints-Pères** ✆ **01 45 49 80 00**. *M° Saint-Germain-des-Près, Rue-du-Bac – Fax: 01 45 44 75 24 – Website: www.academiehotel.com – Email: academiehotel@wanadoo.fr – Standard double rooms 199 €, deluxe 229 €. Junior suite 299 €. Suite apartment 459 €. Breakfast buffet 14.50 €.* Close to all those cafes, restaurants, boutiques and musuems that put Paris on the map. Empire style, dating back to the 18thc., this hotel offers 33 soundproofed and double-glazed rooms with exposed beams. Some have marble bathrooms, and the junior suites boast a jacuzzi. All are equipped with mini-bar, phone, hairdryer, private safe, radio with alarm and satellite TV. Internet access available. Private car park (23 € for 24 hours). Petit Fute readers get up to 50% off the price of their room and some welcome gifts - chocolates, map of Paris, free invitations to fashion shows and free, unlimited broadband WiFi internet access. Bravo!

HOTEL BEAUGENCY **21, rue Duvivier** ✆ **01 47 05 01 63** *Fax: 01 45 51 04 96. Website: www.hotel-beaugency.com. M° Ecole-Militaire or La-Tour-Maubourg. Room 125 €.* This hotel nestling in a little residential street is well away from the heavy traffic in Avenues de La Motte-Picquet and Bosquet, yet just behind Rue Duvivier you find the Rue Cler, which is great for shops. Inside, a large reproduction in the reception area depicts the River Loire at Beaugency. The comfortable rooms are done out in pastel shades, and all have satellite TV, Canal +, mini-bar, hairdryer, individual cafe and air conditioning. A valet and dry-cleaning service are available at need.

HOTEL DU PALAIS BOURBON ** **49, rue de Bourgogne** ✆ **01 44 11 30 70.** *M° Varenne / Invalides. Fax: 01 45 55 20 21. Website: www.hotel-palais-bourbon.com. Single rooms with bathroom and breakfast 98 €, double 120 €, triple 140 €, quadruple 155 €.* The prices are on a sliding scale depending on your choice: shower or bath, private or communal WC, and mini-bar (only in the largest rooms). You're only a stone's throw from the National Assembly, Invalides, Rodin Museum and Orsay Museum in this quiet, historic and very safe quarter, known for its political institutions. An ideal address for discovering Paris. Highly recommended.

HOTEL SAINT-DOMINIQUE ** **62, rue Saint-Dominique ✆ 01 47 05 51 44**. *M° Invalides or La Tour-Maubourg – Fax : 01 47 05 81 28 – Website : www.hotelstdominique.com. Standard room from 80 €, double from 93 € (sleeps one) or 113 € (sleeps two). Executive and superior rooms from 121 €. Breakfast 8 €. Online bookings and promotions. Bathroom or shower, cable TV, direct phone line, Wi-Fi access and mini-bar.* This former 18thc. convent provides an attractive setting for the art of living Parisian-style. You'll like the courteous welcome, flower-filled patio and new breakfast-room with wide bay windows. The 37 character rooms have a countrified feel, due in part to the Liberty prints and flower motifs on the wall fabrics. Discover historic Paris by following in the poets' footsteps - this must be one of the capital's most romantic hotels.

HOTEL LINDBERGH ** **5, rue Chomel ✆ 01 45 48 35 53**. *M° Sèvres-Babylone – Fax : 01 45 49 31 48 – Website : www.hotellindbergh.com. Double room 98 € to 132 €, triple 152 € and quadruple 162 €. Breakfast 8 €.* Bath or shower, hairdryer, telephone, satellite TV, Wi-Fi access (flat screen computer at your disposal) in the superior rooms. This contemporary hotel harmonises shades of cream and dark panelling. Its 26 rooms are very light, done out in different colours: purple tones, or blue, moss green and chestnut (the most recent). The lounge has big sofas, lamps and books, just like at home. If you like chic yet subtle interior design, the Hotel Lindbergh is for you. What's more, the owners are likeable and very warm. Ideal location for Saint-Germain-des-Prés.

8e arrondissement

ASTORIA *** **42, rue de Moscou ✆ 01 42 93 63 53.** *Fax: 01 42 93 30 30. Website: www.astotel.com. M° Rome, Liège or Europe. Rooms 157 €.* This three-star hotel offers you a city holiday in optimum conditions, with faultless comfort and service and a stylish setting. The rooms are all equipped with air conditioning, safe, min-bar, satellite TV and hairdryer. The Batignolles car park 100m away solves parking problems in this residential district.

CONCORTEL HOTEL *** **21, rue Pasquier ✆ 01 42 65 45 44.** *M° Saint-Lazare or Madeleine – Fax : 01 42 65 18 33 – Website :*

www.hotelconcortel.com. Standard single room from 110 €, superior standard from 125 €. Continental breakfast 8 €. Air-conditioning, Wi-Fi access, mini-bar, safe, hairdryer. Baby sitting service. The Concortel is only a short walk from the Faubourg Saint Honoré's luxury boutiques and the big department stores at Opéra. The soundproofed rooms are done out in yellow touched up with white, simple and chic, and very up-to-date. An outdoor patio provides a pleasant change after frantic shopping trips.

HOTEL DE L'ELYSEE * 12, rue des Saussaies © 01 42 65 29 25**. *M° Madeleine, Miromesnil. Website: www.France-hotel-guide.com/h75008efshhtm. Email: hoteldelelysee@wanadoo.fr Standard air-conditioned rooml with WiFi access from 140 €, de luxe from 225 €, suite 265 €. Breakfast 11 €.* Art and culture fans will find this 19thc. residence a convenient address, close to the Grand Palais, Madeleine and Champs-Elysées. The entrance hall has been renovated with talent, revealing superb original mosaics set off by well-placed mirrors. The rooms are all personalised, and look rather like bourgeois apartments with their period furniture, long, draped curtains and harmonious wall fabrics. The hotel is also near the Elysée Palace, and you can dream of spending a presidential night in the suite under its sloping roof, with a view of the Eiffel Tower.

HOTEL ELYSEES MERMOZ * 30, rue Jean-Mermoz © 01 42 25 75 30.** *Fax 01 45 62 87 10. M° Champs-Elysées-Clemenceau. Single room from 144 €, twin from 179 €, suite 235 €.* This is a magnificent hotel with tremendous charm. Once in the entrance hall with its Mediterranean feel - red-tiled floor, veranda and cane furniture - you forget you're only minutes from the Champs Elysées. The rooms are done out in Provençal style too, painted in restful colours with light wood furniture. Take a break; open your window, lean over your balcony and watch the Parisian world go by.

HOTEL PAVILLON MONTAIGNE * 34, rue Jean-Mermoz © 01 53 89 95 00.** *Fax 01 42 89 33 00. M° Saint-Philippe-du-Roule. Single room with shower 131 €, double 147 €.* We like this hotel, located in a quiet street away from the bustle. The skilful blend of contemporary style and period furniture - Persian carpets and wall fabrics - is very attractive. The top-floor rooms have sloping ceilings, but they are all full of character, painted in soft shades of blue or yellow.

LES JARDINS DE PARIS SAINT-LAZARE ** 53, rue d'Amsterdam © 01 48 74 79 74. *M° Liège – Fax : 01 48 74 83 00 – Website : www.hotelsjardinsdeparis.com. Rooms from 95 € to 105 €. Breakfast 6 €. Wi-Fi Internet access.* Like all the hotels in the Jardins de Paris group, the Saint-Lazare is modern and very welcoming, and only a stone's throw from the station. It even boasts an indoor flower garden. The 58 rooms have bath or shower, Canal + and satellite TV, and a direct phone line. A good starting-point for visiting this busy quarter of Paris with its shopping facilities.

9e arrondissement

HOTEL DE LA CITE ROUGEMONT ** 4, cité Rougemont © 01 47 70 25 95. *M° Grands-Boulevards. Fax. 01 48 24 14 32. Internet: www/hotel-paris-rougemont.com. Single room from 74 €, double from 88 €, triple 108 €, quadruple 124 €. Breakfast 6 €* 33 comfortable and well-kept rooms, shower or bath, with or without TV. Close to the Grands Boulevards, Folies Bergeres and Place de la Republique. Quiet setting with plenty of charm, and friendly welcome from staff always ready to help and advise. Seasonal special offers.

JARDINS DE PARIS MORNY – SAINT-LAZARE * 4, rue de Liège © 01 56 02 66 00.** *M° Liège et RER Auber ou Saint-Lazare – Fax : 01 40 16 44 84 Website: www.hotelsjardinsdeparis.com. Single room from 105 €, double from 125 €, triple from 140 € and quadruple from 155 €. Breakfast buffet 10 €.* 41 air-conditioned rooms with a country chic atmosphere are available in this surprising hotel offering total escape (though the desert island fresco in the lounge probably appeals more to stressed-out Parisians than tourists!) An extraordinary garden in the heart of Paris, only a stone's throw from the

Opera and big department stores. The Jardins de Paris Morny is described as an 'establishment with local colour'. Attractive rooms, newspapers available at reception, laundry and dry-cleaning service.

10e arrondissement

HOTEL LOUXOR ** 4, rue Taylor ✆ 01 42 08 23 91. M° Jacques-Bonsergent or République. *Fax : 01 42 08 03 30. Website : www.hotels-paris-hotel.com Single room 58 €, single with wide bed 77 €, double 87 €, twin 89 €, triple 107 €. Online bookings. Regular Internet promotions, depending on availability. Breakfast 5 €.* Peace and quiet is the main luxury provided by this two-star hotel, located in a busy - and noisy - district. You find it in a little one-way street with limited traffic, between République and the Gares du Nord and de l'Est, near the Grand Boulevards and the Marais. Opéra is a ten-minute walk. The fully-renovated rooms are modern and contain direct phone line, automatic alarm-clock and TV, as well as double glazing and air conditioning. Pleasant and friendly atmosphere, attractive late19thc. setting, and attentive staff. Free Wi-Fi and Internet access available for guests.

11e arrondissement

GRAND HOTEL FRANCAIS * 223, boulevard Voltaire ✆ 01 43 71 27 57.** *M°Nation/ Rue- des-Boulets. Fax: 01 43 48 40 05. Website: www. grand-hotel-francais.fr Single room with shower 95 €, with bath 105 €, twin room 120 €, triple 135 €. Breakfast 8 €.* Located in a busy quarter, with lots of shops and shady cafe terraces, not far from the Gare de Lyon and the Gare du Nord. The 40 rooms have been completely renovated, each one with its own personalised decor and oodles of cosy charm, not to mention soundproofing. The entrance and bar are in granite and solid oak, examples of traditional French elegance. Ideal for relaxing with a drink. The hotel also hosts seminars.

HOTEL BEAUMARCHAIS ** 3, rue Oberkampf ✆ 01 53 36 86 86. *M° Filles-du-Calvaire and Oberkampf – Fax : 01 43 38 32 86 – Website: www.hotelbeaumarchais.com. Rooms from 90 €.* Continental buffet breakfast 10 €, served in your room 12 €. This rather cute and very modern hotel has had its 31 rooms done out in contemporary style, making a change from the usual flowered fabric and pine furniture. They are equipped with air conditioning, double glazing, individual safes, Canal + and satellite TV, bathrooms with shower or bath, WC, hairdryer, the lot. The Beaumarchais also boasts a pleasant lounge and flowers on its patio. It is right next to the Cirque d'Hiver, neither too near nor too far from the lively Oberkampf-Jean-Pierre-Timbaud quarter.

HOTEL BEAUSEJOUR ** 71, avenue Parmentier ✆ 01 47 00 38 16. *M° Parmentier, Saint-Maur ou Saint-Ambroise – Fax : 01 43 55 47 89 Rooms 60 €. Breakfast 5 €.* The Hotel Beauséjour awaits you with its breakfast room, lift, press and theatre, restaurant and taxi booking service, fax and Internet. 31 recently redecorated rooms come complete with colour TV, cable and telephone. Night birds will like being so close to the Rue Oberkampf with its mass of cafés, bars and restaurants.

HOTEL INTERNATIONAL ** 6, rue Auguste-Barbier ✆ 01 43 57 38 07. Fax 01 43 55 21 95. *Website: www.parishotels.com. M° Goncourt or République. Rooms 70 €.* The Hotel International is located in a quiet and sunny street, close to the Saint Martin Canal and several lively districts in the Marais and at République, and is ideal for walks. The charming hotel front is shaded by a small glass and wrought-iron awning, and has a veranda-style entrance with painted walls, garden chairs and plants. Warm and relaxed welcome; comfortable, well-equipped rooms, elegantly decorated in the same style with plenty of wood, wrought-iron and plants.

HOTEL MONDIA ** 22, rue du Grand-Prieuré ✆ 01 47 00 93 44. *M° Oberkampf or République – Fax : 01 43 38 66 14 – Website : www.hotel-mondia.com. Room from 58 € to 69 €. Breakfast 6.50 €.* Top-quality welcome, attractive prices. This 1900 Parisian building with its white shutters and rounded bay windows is close to the Marais and the Oberkampf quarter, a short walk from the Place de la République. Inside, the setting is pleasant, especially the pretty dining-room with its stained glass window effect. The 23 rooms have been renovated and are equipped with bathroom and WC, hairdyer, individual safe, direct phone line and TV with Canal + .

HOTEL DE NEMOURS ** **8, rue de Nemours ✆ 01 47 00 21 08.** *M° Parmentier or Oberkampf – Fax : 01 47 00 01 53. Single room 50 €, double room 68 €. Breakfast 6 €.* The rooms are all equipped with bath or shower and WC, top-of-the-range furniture and beds, colour TV and mini-bar, direct phone line and automatic morning alarm. The bathrooms have been entirely renovated. Services on offer: typing and photocopying, fax, various translations, bookings, taxis, cleaning. This is a lively, cheerful quarter close to shops, busy during the day and full of nightlife. Ideally situated for a first visit to Paris.

HOTEL DU NORD ET DE L'EST ** **49, rue de Malte ✆ 01 47 00 71 70.** *M° République or Oberkampf – Fax: 01 43 57 51 16 – Website: www.hotel-nord-est.com – Single or double room 75 €-85 €. Suite 160 €. Continental breakfast 7 €. Credit cards accepted: American Express, Diners, CB, Visa.* Easy access to airports Roissy-CDG and Orly, the Stade de France and Disneyland Paris. Located on the Right Bank near Place de la Republique, between Opera and Bastille, a short distance on foot from the Grands Boulevards, the business quarters, and the major stations. This quarter, centering on the Rues Oberkampf and Jean-Pierre Timbaud is busy in the daytime, with plenty of nightlife after dark. 45 comfortable rooms are at your disposal, with Canal + and satellite TV, WiFi access, individual air conditioning at your request, and personal safe. Nearby car park. You can relax or have breakfast in the small, flower-filled interior courtyard.

HOTEL DU PRINCE EUGENE ** **247, boulevard Voltaire ✆ 01 43 71 22 81**. *M° Nation or Rue-des-Boulets. Website: www.hotel-prince-eugene.com – Fax: 01 43 71 24 71 – Single room from 67 €, double room from 75 € with shower and 78 € with bath. Twin room 81 €. Extra bed 21 € (free for under-12s) Breakfast 6.10 €. Telephone 0.30 € the unit.* The friendly welcome and relaxed atmosphere make you feel right at home. 35 rooms are available, with bath or shower, WC, colour and satellite TV, Canal +, mini-bar, direct phone line, automatic alarm, and hairdryer. They are comfortable, clean and air-conditioned. A good place to stay on a trip to Paris, with very attractive prices.

HOTEL VOLTAIRE REPUBLIQUE 10, boulevard Voltaire ✆ 01 47 00 21 47. *M° République or Oberkampf – Fax: 01 47 00 88 28 – Website: www.hvr-paris.com – Rooms 55 €, 60 € and 78 € (all with double bed). Twin rooms 67 € and 80 €. Triples 78 €, 84 € and 90 €. Junior suite 100 €. 'Apparthotel' (sleeps 5) with kitchenette 160 €. Breakfast 6 €. Pets accepted.* Ideally located 200m from Place de la Republique, near the main tourist spots in the heart of Paris. Belleville, the Marais, Bastille and the busy streets Oberkampf and Jean-Pierre Timbaud are all close. The rooms are equipped with double glazing, bath or shower, toilets, direct phone line and TV. Some have a balcony, mini-bar and hairdryer. Internet access at reception (for a fee).

13e arrondissement

HOTEL DES ARTS ** 8, rue Coypel ✆ 01 47 07 76 32. *M° Place-d'Italie – Fax : 01 43 31 18 09 – Website : www.escapade-paris.com. Single room from 52 €, double from 65 €, twin 69 €, triple 85 €. Breakfast 6.50 €.* One stay is never enough, according to the receptionist, and you're bound to come back! When you see the warm welcome given to guests, often regulars, you can well believe it. All the rooms have been recently renovated, and they are comfortable, light and well-equipped: families will appreciate the triples. Faultless bathrooms and showers. telephone, TV and Canal +, Wi-Fi.

LA DEMEURE * 51, boulevard Saint-Marcel ✆ 01 43 37 81 25**. *M° Les Gobelins – Fax : 01 45 87 05 03 – Website: www.hotel-paris-lademeure.com. Room with kingsize bed and massage shower 145 €, with bath 175 €, suite with separate lounge 230 €. Breakfast 12 €. Car park 17 € for 24 hours.* Well located between the Manufacture Royale des Gobelins (historic tapestry workshop) and the very lively Rue Mouffetard, this Demeure is an attractive blend of luxury and serenity. Its 43 rooms are double-glazed and equipped with satellite TV, Canal +, broadband modem socket, hairdryer and direct phone line. The corner rooms are beautiful, spacious and light (three big windows), and the ones on the second and fifth floors have balconies. Suitable for families and executives alike. The two stars are well deserved, witness the increasing number of foreign visitors.

14e arrondissement

CECIL HOTEL ** 47, rue Beaunier ✆ 01 45 40 93 53. *M° Porte-d'Orléans or Alésia. Fax : 01 45 40 43 26. Website : www.cecilhotel.net. Single room with shower 65 €, double 78 €. Extra bed 15 €. Breakfast buffet 7 €.* Petit Futé readers get a free breakfast in the price of a night. 2 car parks nearby. The Cecil Hotel is located in a quiet street with a terrace garden overlooking the Petite Ceinture (former railway line encircling Paris). You can have breakfast, tea or a drink here, and enjoy the peace and sunshine. The 25 non-smoking rooms are decorated on a travel theme, and each is personalised: the Romantic with its 1900 vanity table, Marrakech, Ile de Ré, Kenya, and so on. Furniture and ornaments were collected by the owners from flea markets. All rooms have shower or bath, TV, cable, Internet socket and hairdryer. Cots and baby equipment are available. Pets accepted without a supplement. Sophie and François welcome you warmly, and do all they can to make your stay a pleasant one. Excellent value for money from this superb, well-kept hotel.

LES JARDINS DE PARIS ALESIA MONTPARNASSE ** 147 ter, rue d'Alésia ✆ 01 45 42 06 37. *M° Alésia or Plaisance – Fax : 01 45 42 44 56 – Website : www.hotelsjardinsdeparis.com Single room 80 €, double 89 €. Prices vary according to the time of year. Continental breakfast 6 €.* This is an ideal place for business people, though tourists are welcome too! The hotel has 70 functional rooms, light and comfortable, and contemporary in design. There are two meeting rooms with a view of the garden, and you are only a short distance from the Exhibition Park at Porte de Versailles and the lively Montparnasse district. All mod cons, including outside phone line, Canal + TV and Wi-Fi access. Pets accepted.

15e arrondissement

CARLADEZ CAMBRONNE ** 3, place du Général-Beuret ✆ 01 47 34 07 12. *Fax 01 40 65 95 68. Website: www.hotelcarladez.com. M° Vaugirard. Rooms from 73.50 € to 91 €. Breakfast 7.50 €.* Each soundproofed room is individually decorated, and comes complete with bathroom, WC, satellite TV and Canal +, mini-bar and hairdryer. The hotel also has a furnished apartment for four, with two communicating rooms opening onto a patio, ideal for a family. It has been recently renovated, and is located in a lively district, near the Eiffel Tower and Porte de Versailles.

HOTEL AJIEL ** 237, rue de la Convention ✆ 01 55 76 31 31. *M° Convention. Fax: 01 48 28 34 13 - Website: ajiel.hotel@wanadoo.fr- Single room 76 €, double 85 €, triple 108 € and quadruple 130 €, Breakfast buffet 8 €.* Located in a busy shopping street with its restaurants and cinemas, a stone's throw from the Parc Georges Brassens and its second-hand book market, this hotel has an elegant white facade set with small red bricks. The 67 rooms are comfortable and soundproofed with direct phone line and satellite TV; spacious and pleasantly fitted out. The decor is colourful, the bathrooms large and attractive. Charming, efficient welcome and service: the staff will book restaurants and shows for you.

HOTEL BEAUGRENELLE SAINT-CHARLES ** 82, rue Saint-Charles ✆ 01 45 78 61 63. *M° Charles-Michels – Fax : 01 45 79 04 38 – Website: www.hotel-beaugrenelle.com Rooms from 83.50 € to 109 €.* Online special offers and bookings. Breakfast buffet 10.50 €, Low season prices for Petit Futé readers. This hotel, only a few minutes from the Eiffel Tower and Porte de Versailles exhibition park, has a brick façade and plenty of charm. The staff do all they can for your comfort and wellbeing, already ensured by the big, bright breakfast room in shades of orange-yellow, and a small but peaceful courtyard overlooked by at least half the 51 rooms. These are soundproofed and air-conditioned, equipped with cable TV, phone and answerphone, mini-bar, Wi-Fi access, modem socket and trouser press. The ones in

the little pavilion at the back of the courtyard are the nicest. The owners are concerned about the quality of your stay, and make sure no detail is forgotten, including Internet access in the hall. Great welcome and excellent value for money.

HOTEL MIRAMAR * 6, place Bienvenue ✆ 01 45 48 62 94.** *Fax 01 45 48 68 73. M° Montparnasse -Website: www.hotelmiramar75.com - Email: hotel-miramar2@wanadoo.fr. Single room 79 €, double 86 €, triple 130 €. Breakfast 7 €.* This quarter is known for its fashionable cafes, restaurants and a number of cinemas, strategically close to the Montparnasse Tower. The hotel itself is delightful, however, and its tastefully decorated, soundproofed rooms all have direct outside phone lines, cable TV and hairdryer. The elegant, unobtrusive setting, warm decorative tones and subdued light add a certain charm to the place. Pleasant breakfast room. The prices are attractive for a 3-star hotel: all the more reason to stop off here on your next trip to Paris.

HOTEL DES PROVINCES * 192, rue de la Croix-Nivert** *M° Porte-Maillot* **01 45 58 16 08**. *M° Boucicaut. Fax : 01 40 60 19 04. Website: www.hoteldesprovinces-paris.com. Single rooms from 100 € to 130 €, double rooms from 120 € to 150 €, triple rooms 170 €. Breakfast buffet 9 €.* All the French provinces' charm and originality can be found in this cosy 3-star hotel, entirely renovated and air-conditioned. Each of its seven floors has been designed and decorated to represent a French region: Savoie, with its mountains and pine trees; Brittany in marine blue with its boats; Alsace, the Antilles, and so on. Breakfast is served in Provence, or at least in a warm and welcoming setting that feels like it! The 49 rooms are equipped with all mod cons, including cable TV and broadband Internet. A word of advice: book online first, as there are attractive special offers all year round.

16e arrondissement

HOTEL D'ANGLETERRE ETOILE ** 21, rue Copernic ✆ 01 47 27 80 67. *M° Victor-Hugo. Fax : 01 47 27 34 71 – Website: www.hotelangleterre-etoile.com. Single room 78 €, double 86 €, triple 105 €. Breakfast 7.50 €,* served in your room with no supplement. Special offers all year round: don't hesitate to ask for details. Round-the-clock service, satellite TV, private safe, hairdryer, Internet available at reception. You'll be hard put to find better value for money elsewhere in the capital. This is a simple, unobtrusive hotel, with pleasant, spacious rooms and an indoor Spanish-style patio. Nearby Place Victor Hugo offers plenty of culinary and cultural pleasures.

HOTEL ETOILE RESIDENCE IMPERIALE* 155, avenue de Malakoff ✆ 01 45 00 23 45** *M° Porte-Maillot E-mail: res.imperiale@wanadoo.fr. Site: www.bestwestern-etoile-imperiale.com.* Between the business district of the DEFENSE and the CHAMPS-ELYSEES nearby, in front of the Convention Center Gateway MAILLOT, come and discover the Hotel Best Western Etoile Résidence Impériale. A hotel with a lot of character that will seduce you with its serene, warm, and refined atmosphere.

HOTEL HAMEAU DE PASSY ** 48, rue de Passy ✆ 01 42 88 47 55. *M° La Muette or Passy – Fax : 01 42 30 83 72 – Website : www.hameaudepassy.com. Single room 109 €, double 119 € twin 124 €, triple 142 €, quadruple 158 €, breakfast free, Wi-Fi.* This charming hotel is nestling in the depths of an extraordinary private garden, right in the heart of the chic 16th arrondissement. All the rooms overlook the garden, providing guests with a restful break among the greenery, before rushing off to discover Paris. The fashionably busy Rue de Passy lies just in front of this green haven. (See p. 641)

HOTEL BOILEAU ** 81, rue Boileau ✆ 01 42 88 83 74. *M° Exelmans – Fax : 01 45 27 62 98 – Website : www.hotel-boileau.com. Single rooms from 70 €, doubles from 79 €, twins 90 €, triples 125 €. Breakfast 8.50 € (10 € in your room). Tourist tax included. Cable TV, Wi-Fi. One ground-floor room with disabled access.* A charming hotel blending comfort and good taste. We especially like the red tiled floor and panelling in the entrance, and the pretty breakfast room with its glass wall sections. Cosy atmosphere; bright, attractive rooms, some overlooking a flower-filled patio. This upmarket quarter is reputed for peace and quiet, so your stay should be very pleasant.

HOTEL KLEBER * 7, rue de Belloy ✆ 01 47 23 80 22.** *M° Kléber, Boissière, Charles-de-Gaulle-Etoile – Fax: 33 (0)1 49 52 07 20 – Email: kleberhotel@wanadoo.fr – Website: www.kleberhotel.com – Standard room 199 €.*

Double Jacuzzi 229 €. Deluxe (hydro or jacuzzi) 259 €. Jacuzzi Suite 299 €. Breakfast buffet 14 €. This Second Empire -style hotel boasts panelling, marble fittings and exposed stonework, and is located near the Champs Elysees with its haute couture shops, and the Eiffel Tower. All the rooms are air-conditioned with mini-bar, satellite TV, phone with outside line and modem socket. Private car park (23 € for 24h). Petit Fute readers get up to 50% off the price of their room and some welcome gifts - chocolates, map of Paris, free invitations to fashion shows and free, unlimited broadband WiFi internet access. Bravo!

HOTEL VILLA D'AUTEUIL ** 28, rue Poussin ✆ 01 42 88 30 37. *M° Michel-Ange-Auteuil or Porte-d'Auteuil – Fax : 01 45 20 74 70 –Website : www.hotel-villa-dauteuil.com . Single room from 56 €. double from 64 €, triple from 78 €. Breakfast 5.50 €. Tourist tax included. Telephone, TV.* This hotel is located in a quiet residential quarter, and provides a restful setting. Though not in the centre of Paris, there are two metro stations and buses - and above all, it is excellent value for money. The rooms are smart and comfortable; some look out on the garden. The Parisians go for their morning jog in the Bois de Boulogne - why not start the day off on the right foot, and join them?

LES JARDINS DU TROCADERO ** 35, rue Benjamin-Franklin ✆ 01 53 70 17 70.** *M° Passy or Trocadéro – Fax: 33 (0)1 53 70 17 80 – Email: jardintroc@aol.com – Website: www.jardintroc.com – Superior rooms (with jacuzzi) 299 €, Deluxe and Executive 399 €, Napoleon Suite 499 €, suite -apartment 599 €. Breakfast buffet 18 €.* This relaxing and rather luxurious hotel is not far from the Trocadero and Champs Elysees. It boasts elegant salons with exposed stonework, and the rooms are hung with Napoleonic draperies. Most have a view of the Place du Trocadero and Eiffel Tower, and are very comfortable, with jacuzzi, marble bathroom, mini-bar, satellite TV, direct phone line and air conditioning. Internet access. Petit Fute readers get up to 50% off the price of their room and some welcome gifts - chocolates, map of Paris, free invitations to fashion shows and free, unlimited broadband WiFi internet access. Bravo!

17e arrondissement

HOTEL PALMA * 46, rue Brunel ✆ 01 45 74 74 51. M° Argentine.** *Fax : 01 45 74 40 90. Website : www.hotelpalma-paris.com. 37 rooms from 95 € to 145 €, Breakfast 9 €.* This rather exotic Hotel Palma recalls colonial days, with its cane armchairs and wooden tables and bar. You can almost hear the sea! Don't worry, though: once outside, you find yourself near the Palais des Congrès and Place de l'Etoile, only a few minutes from La Défense and the Champs-Elysées. The comfortable rooms are charming with their high ceilings and big windows. Each is equipped with bathrooms or showers, hairdryers, telephone with computer socket and cable TV.

18e arrondissement

HOTEL DES ARTS * 5, rue Tholozé ✆ 01 46 06 30 52.** *M° Blanche or Abbesses – Fax : 01 46 06 10 83 – Website: www.arts-hotel-paris.com. 50 rooms, singles 75 €, doubles 95 €, triples 115 €. Satellite TV and telephone in every room. Breakfast 8 € served in your room.* This pretty hotel lies in the heart of Montmartre, and has been entirely renovated. We can assure you that gests are never dissatisfied with their stay. The rooms are simply done out in sunshine colours, and the ones on the top two floors have a view over the city (if it's free, ask for number 63, which has the best view). The breakfast room is in the basement, but the exposed stonework and careful decoration are charming. The staff too! Internet Wi-Fi connection.

HOTEL REGYN'S MONTMARTRE ** **18, place des Abbesses** ✆ **01 42 54 45 21**. *M° Abbesses – Fax: 01 42 23 76 69 – Email: hrm18@club-internet.fr – Website: www.paris-hotels-montmartre.com – Single room 72 €, double 84 €. Tourist tax included. Breakfast 8 €, or 9 €* served in your room. This is a comfortable place to put down your bags, facing Saint-Jean-l'Evangéliste Church, with a plunging view of the pretty Place des Abbesses. All the rooms are equipped with telephone, TV and Canal +, Wi-Fi, safe and hairdryer. They are attractively decorated, with their pink Liberty print soft furnishings. Most of the fifth floor rooms have a fine view of Paris, notably numbers 56 and 58, more expensive for this reason (single 92 €, double 104 €).

LE TERRASS HOTEL **** **12, rue Joseph-de-Maistre** ✆ **01 46 06 72 85**. *M° Blanche – Place-de-Clichy – Fax : 01 44 92 34 14 – Website : www.terrass-hotel.com. Standard single room 208 €, superior 236 € and de luxe 250 €; standard double 248 €, superior 275 € and de luxe 290 €. Junior suite 336 €.* Continental breakfast in your room or buffet 13 €. Panoramic terrace open from mid-April to mid-September. This hotel is right beside Montmartre Cemetery, at the foot of the hill, and boasts other advantages, apart from its location, like a fireplace and piano in the bar, and comfortable, well-kept rooms (some of the standard category have just been renovated) complete with TV, mini-bar and bathroom. The furniture is period or contemporary, and some of the rooms have disabled access. There are whole non-smoking floors. Apart from the terrace on the 7th and top floor, which serves as a gastronomic restaurant from April/May to September - 50 place settings, à la carte, starters from 13 € to 18 €, meat, grills and other dishes from 18 € to 35 €, cheese 6.50 €, desserts 7.50 € - there is also a restaurant open all year, seating 90, on the ground floor.

20e arrondissement

NADAUD HOTEL **8, rue de la Bidassoa** ✆ **01 46 36 87 79.** *M° Gambetta exit Martin Nadaud. Fax : 01 46 36 05 41. Closed in August. Single or double room with washbasin 44 €, with shower or bath and WC 54 €. Breakfast on request served only in your room. 7 €. Tourist tax included. TV in all rooms. Closed in August.* You find this little brick hotel in a charming quarter near leafy Père-Lachaise Cemetery, away from the noise and bustle of the capital. Warm welcome and clean, well-kept rooms, accessible by lift. Some of the corner rooms bask in radiant sunshine, with a clear view of Paris that you really shouldn't miss. The staff's kindness is a rare quality indeed.

SUPER HOTEL ** **208, rue des Pyrénées** ✆ **01 46 36 97 48**. *M° Gambetta – Fax : 01 46 36 26 10. Website : www.superhotelparis.site.voila.fr. Rooms from 58 € to 70 €. TV, Canal Satellite, telephone, safe, hairdryer, double and triple glazing. Breakfast 6 €.* Car park with guardian 50m away. This hotel is not far from the district Town Hall, and only a stone's throw from the lively République-Bastille Opéra-Nation triangle. The rooms are quiet and comfortable, protected from the ambient noise, and the bar contains some rare Seventies furniture - banquettes, light fixtures and frames - that are fast becoming collector's items. Excellent welcome: a hotel that lives up to its name, in fact!

Restaurants

PARIS

1er arrondissement

L'ANE ET LA MULE 74, quai des Orfèvres ✆ 01 43 54 16 71 M° Pont Neuf *Set menus 25 €, 'L'ane et la mule' 40 €, formulas and à la carte.* Located at the far end of the Ile de la Cité, near the Quai des Orfèvres, this charming, prettily-decorated restaurant welcomes you warmly, and serves sophisticated *cuisine* blending flavours from the Auvergne and the Ile de Ré. The chef concocts top-quality dishes with fresh, natural and seasonal produce. Cream of Jerusalem artichokes with cepes, bacon chips and vegetables is a good starter, followed by a *gauloise blanche* (poultry) with vegetables in flaky pastry, and a white chocolate mousse to finish. Unobtrusive service. A very promising place to eat.

AU CHIEN QUI FUME 33, rue du Pont-Neuf ✆ 01 42 36 07 42. *M° Châtelet or Les Halles – Website: www.au-chien-qui-fume.com – Email: auchienquifume@club-internet.fr – Open 7 days a week: 12 noon –2am. Set menus 'Chien Coquin' 22 € and 28 € (starter, main course, dessert), 'Bazil' 28 € and 34 € (three courses) and 'Agathe' with seafood, 34 €.* This place has existed since 1740, and is a landmark to many Parisians. You'll love the counter, opulent décor and atmosphere of bygone days, even before tasting the traditional quality *cuisine* and excellent seafood platters. The set menu 'Bazil' (34 €) is very good value for money, and includes salmon *mousseline* with a shellfish coulis, chicken fricassee and a delicious tarte Tatin.

AUX DELICES DE MANON 400, rue Saint-Honoré ✆ 01 42 60 83 03. *M° Concorde – Fax: 01 49 27 02 51 – Open every day from 7am-10pm,, except Sunday. Formulas 14 € to 19 €, from assorted salads to a hot buffet.* This place is a restaurant, bakery, pastrycook's, tearoom and caterer all rolled into one! Located in a historic corner of Paris - where Robespierre lived – it is heaven for gourmets, specialising in both sweet and savoury flavours. Two dining-rooms are at your disposal, one elegant, with round aluminium tables, the other decorated in pastel shades, with square tables. You can call in for breakfast before the office (to give yourself a little Dutch courage) or for tea and sympathy with your girlfriends – or why not take the time to enjoy a full meal, and discover some fresh and inventive seasonal dishes? You won't leave without a bagful of goodies either: the take-away service is a real plus.

Other addresses: AUX PAINS DE MANON 31, rue de l'annonciation (16) 01 42 88 36 89. AUX DESIRS DE MANON 129 rue Saint-Antoine (4e) 01 42 72 32 91 (closed Sunday) • MISS MANON 87, rue Saint-Antoine (4e) 01 48 87 87 59 (closed Monday) • AUX DELICES DE BAGATELLE 1, rue Ernest-Deloison – NEUILLY-SUR-SEINE (92) 01 46 24 61 84 (open every day) • AUX DELICES DE MANON 79 bis, avenue Jean-Baptiste-Clément – BOULOGNE-BILLANCOURT (92) 01 48 25 22 69 (closed Monday).

AUX TROIS OLIVIERS 37 bis, rue de Montpensier ✆ 01 40 20 03 02. *M° Bourse ou Palais-Royal – Open lunchtime 11.30am-3.30pm, except Sunday. Open evenings 6.30pm-1.30am, except Sunday. Lunchtime formula from 10.75 € (main course, dessert, glass of wine). Pre-theatre formulas 15.50 € and 19.50 €, a la carte 25 €.* This restaurant gives you a foretaste of the holidays. Tempted? The cooking is Mediterranean-influenced and seasonal, with bouillabaisse made to order. Try the house cocktails: their mojito is the best in Paris. Friday and Saturday evening are swing nights, with bossanova and jazz from 9.30pm to 1.30am. in the lounge-dining room. Note that a delicious appetiser starter is served free when you order. The owner is a colourful character, who enjoys surprising his customers.

AU PIED DE COCHON 6, rue Coquillière ✆ 01 40 13 77 00. *M° Châtelet les Halles. Website : www.pieddecochon.com. A la carte 48 €. Open day and night. Privilege evenings with show and restaurant*

"Au Chien qui Fume"
Bar Restaurant
Groups - Receptions
Banquets - Seminars
Oysters, seafood, dishes with traditional sauces and grilled fish washed down with delicious wines
Tel: +33 (0)1 42 36 07 42
Fax: +33 (0)1 42 36 36 85
7 days a week from 12 noon - 2 am
www.au-chien-qui-fume.com
33, rue du Pont-Neuf - 75001 Paris
189497

AUX TROIS OLIVIERS
Aux Trois Oliviers
Specialities:
Mediterranean specialities season after season
185639
37 bis, rue Montpensier - 75001 Paris • Tel: -+33 (0)1 40 20 03 02
Open from 12 am to 3 pm and from 7 pm to 1 am 30 - tapas and mojito 18 pm 30
Closed on Monday and Sunday evenings

from 52€. This famous Halles restaurant has been open non-stop since 1946, and is one of the last witnesses of the old, pre-war Paris. The *cuisine* is a subtle blend of tradition and modernity: seafood, onion soup and all sorts of meat. You can enjoy a meal here day or night, and taste the best Saint-Vaast, Marennes-Oléron or Belon River oysters, or the house speciality and main claim to fame: pork. Trotters, ears, snout and tail all have their own recipe

LE CAFE RENARD Jardin des Tuileries ✆ 01 42 96 50 56. *M° Concorde ou Tuileries. Website: www.caferenard.com. Restaurant - salon de thé open every day till 11.30pm in summer and 7pm in winter. The Cafe Renard menu has something to suit both busy shoppers from the rue de Rivoli and tourists strolling through the Parisian streets: salads from 8.80€, grilled meat or fish from 9.60€, and some deliciously tempting desserts, waffles, crepes, lemon meringue pie and creme brulee, ice-creams and sorbets, all at very reasonable prices, especially for this quarter of Paris!* Salads, sandwiches and croque monsieur are served until 7.30pm. Whether you rush through at top speed with the express formula or take your time, you'll admire the magnificent setting and appreciate the friendly service.

CARRE DES FEUILLANTS 14, rue de Castiglione ✆ 01 42 86 82 82 *Fax 01 42 86 07 71. Set menus from 65€ to 150€. A la carte 105€. Closed Saturday, Sunday and in August.* This restaurant's critics used to call it a luxury canteen for fans of South West *cuisine*, but its renovation two years ago seems to have given it a new lease of life. Designer Alberto Bali produced a modern, pared-down setting - a wee bit trendy, you might say - for the dining room, matching Alain Dutournier' new menus to perfection. Marinated cepes, pan-fried caps and stalks served in a warm pâté, chestnut cappucino with Alba truffles, monkfish in a potato crust, caviar, horseradish stock, Marennes oysters in seafood jelly with caviar, dark chocolate *fondant*, foamy chicory and moka *crème brûlée* are among the choices. The service is relaxed, though sometimes a bit distant. Serious, almost excessive wine cellar.

CHEZ FLOTTES 2, rue Cambon ✆ 01 42 60 80 89. *M° Concorde – Open 7 days a week lunchtime and evening, last orders taken at 12.30am. A la carte around 15€.* Near Place de la Concorde. This pretty brasserie with its purple velvet banquettes and matching tablecloths has a beautiful Art-Deco glass conservatory with a pleasant terrace. The owner comes from Aveyron, so it isn't surprising to find a few delicious specialities from this region on the menu: the famous aligot (potato puree cooked with tomme cheese) or a tender Salers beef steak served on a hot plate. You also find the brasserie classics though: tagliatelli with foie gras or smoked salmon, swordfish fillet, salmon tartare and a number of enormous assorted salads, or a panful of mushrooms. The desserts are equally tempting: warm tarte Tatin with a fruit coulis, pineapple carpaccio, and a chocolate terrine with vanilla cream. Excellent service. You won't be disappointed - and you'll be back, just like us!

L'ESCARGOT MONTORGUEIL 38, rue Montorgueil ✆ 01 42 36 83 51. *M° Les Halles. Open every day from 12 noon to 2.30pm and 7pm to 11pm, except Sunday and Monday. Business menu 48€ (starter, main course, 2 glasses of wine, mineral water and coffee).* Opening directly onto trendy Rue Montorgueil, this restaurant is now in Laurent Couegnas and Denis Jamet's capable hands. It was founded in 1832 as L'Escargot d'Or, and is a listed Historic Monument, thanks to its beautiful Second Empire setting. Over the years, the rich and famous have fought to get a table under the huge brass snail which serves as its sign: Sarah Bernhardt, Marcel Proust, Picasso, Dali, Lauren Bacall, and many others. Of course snails have pride of place on the classic menu - the 12-snail spiral at 22 € and the snail gueusaille with garlic cream at 13 €, for example - but there is also home made foie gras cooked in salt for 19 €, fresh frogs' legs sautéd Provençal-style at 17 €, pork trotter *croquettes* at 19 €, and spit-roast Gatinet duck with orange sauce for 2 at 52 € , washed down with something from the extensive wine list. The desserts include an irresistible chocolate and fresh mint soufflé known as the Etienne Marcel soufflé (13 €) and crêpes Suzette sautéd the old-fashioned way (18 €).

L'EXOTIKAL 20,rue de la Reynie ✆ 01 42 71 40 57. *M° Châtelet-Hôtel de Ville. Car park: Beaubourg - Hôtel de Ville. Website : www.lexotikal.com. Open 12 noon-2am every day.* This restaurant-bar-cabaret can be found in the heart of Paris, a stone's throw from the Pompidou Centre in a pedestrian precinct. Thierry and his staff welcome you in a rather glamorous red velvet décor, or on the terrace in fine weather. A number of generous lunchtime formulas are on offer: prices start from 12 €. Between 4pm and 8pm, trendy customers meet up for a Happy Hour (or four…). Dinner is served with a Full Monty, in a festive cabaret atmosphere (the 'stripper boys' are chosen from among the best dancers in Paris) which should please the ladies. An ideal place for a hen night, or just a good night out with the girls. Theme nights are organised every month (Brazilian, Oriental, etc.).

LE GRAND VEFOUR 17, rue de Beaujolais ✆ 01 42 96 56 27 *Fax 01 42 86 80 71. Set menus from 80 € to 255 €. A la carte 175 €. Closed Friday evening, weekends and 31 July-29 August.* What defines a great restaurant? Reception, service, choice of ingredients, kitchen staff (from the commis to the chefs de partie) and a setting that's up to scratch are all important aspects, and Le Grand Véfour has all of these worked out. The setting is almost too perfect, being an 18thc. architectural masterpiece that has seen the likes of Victor Hugo, Lamartine, Mac Mahon, and later Colette and Cocteau come through as regulars, towing a crowd of stunned gourmets in their wake. Top chef Guy Martin is also a successful cookery-book author, courted by all the culinary guides like no-one else. Why? All his classic recipes are a huge success: lightly-browned frogs' legs, green sage juice, soft garlic bread slice with marrow bone on a tomato fondue, turbot meunière with white truffle oil, green pea and radish purée, Bresse chicken supreme 'Miéral', lemon with salt, pan-cooked tofu and foie gras. The desserts try to be different, like mango and passion fruit with five spices, for instance, or grapefuit fritters and sorbet lightly flavoured with saffron. The cellar contains all the great names in French wine. Unfortunately few of them are affordable - but then Le Grand Véfour has never claimed to be democratic.

LA POULE AU POT 9, rue Vauvillers ✆ 01 42 36 32 96. *M° Châtelet – Website: www.lapouleaupot.fr – Open every day : 7pm-5am. Set menu 30 €, à la carte around 45 €.* This place is well worth the visit ! Parisians and visitors have been eating well here for over 70 years, and enjoying traditional fare like beef fillet with foie gras (33 €), home-made duck confit (21 €) veal kidneys with mustard cream (21 €) and of course, the chicken in the pot (set menu). The desserts are just as delicious, with the chocolate *délice* and *crème anglaise* (thin custard, served cold) at 9 €, or a dream of a *crème brulée* made the old-fashioned way (9 €).

SUBITO 33, rue Danielle Casanova ✆ 01 49 26 01 66. *M° Opéra Open every day non-stop: 8am- 10.30pm except Sunday. Formula 12.70 €. A la carte 17 €.* Subito ('quickly' in Italian) is still brand-new, and its subtitle 'Il piacere della pasta' (the pleasure of pasta) tells you what to expect: deep orange walls and dark tables for fast food Italian-style and a shop: they say 'tavola calda' in Italy. From breakfast to dinner you have a choice of pasta, salad, rizottos, focaccias and various sandwiches, with desserts and ice-creams to follow. There's music on Thursdays and a DJ on Fridays. Subito is also a caterer with take-away dishes and office and home delivery (free in the quarter).

2e arrondissement

AUX LYONNAIS 32, rue Saint-Marc ✆ 01 42 96 65 04. *M° Grands-Boulevards Open Tuesday-Thursday, from 7.30pm to 10.45pm, Friday and Saturday evening until 11.30pm and lunchtimes, 12 noon -2pm. Closed Saturday lunchtime, Sunday and Monday. A la carte around 50 € per person.* This hundred-year-old bouchon lyonnais has been polished up and made fashionable by Alain Ducasse. Customers come from all over Paris to enjoy traditional Lyon cuisine, and you have to book 2 or 3 days ahead for a weekday, and a week for Friday or Saturday evening! The Dombe crayfish, Bresse poultry, and charcuterie from the Lyon covered markets wake up tired tastebuds, and you toast the food from Duralex glasses, so as to be really authentic. As for the wine, same quality, with a white bourgogne aligoté 2002 at 25 €, or a red côtes-du-rhône, Vienne wine 2003 at 30 €.

TIR-BOUCHON 22, rue Tiquetonne ✆ 01 42 21 95 51. *M° Etienne-Marcel. Open every day 12 noon-2.30pm and 7pm-11pm. Set lunchtime menus 14.50 € (starter + main course or main course + dessert and a quarter bottle of wine per person) and 20 € (starter, main course and dessert). Evening set menu 28 €.* This restaurant nestling in the heart of the Montorgueil quarter serves simple, top-quality cuisine. Rustic ambience in wood and stonework, equally pleasant welcome. The cooking is a delicious blend of flavours and scents: the salmon tartare is wonderful, as is the *pièce du boucher* (red meat cuts). The 20 € menu will satisfy even the most demanding foodies.

3e arrondissement

L'AMBASSADE D'AUVERGNE 22, rue du Grenier-Saint-Lazare ✆ 01 42 72 31 22. *M° Rambuteau – Website : www.ambassade-auvergne.com. Open every day lunchtime and evening until 10.30pm. Set menu 28 €. A la carte around 30 €.* Auvergne's regional cuisine now has its embassy, and about time, when you consider the region's culinary wealth. A rustic 'country inn' setting complements the variety of Massif Central dishes on offer: cheese and potato *aligot*, of course, with sausage, warm Puy lentil salad, farm pork *potée* (casserole) with braised cabbage, Salers beef fillet, duck foie gras *mi-cuit*, and Laguiole profiteroles for dessert. If your mouth waters while you're waiting, a glass of saint-pourçain (red or white) is the thing.

AU BASCOU 38, rue Réaumur ✆ 01 42 72 69 25. *M° Arts-et-Métiers. Open Monday to Friday, 12 noon-2pm and 8pm-10.30pm. Closed weekends.* Delicious cooking smells overwhelm you as you come into this restaurant. The Basque owner welcomes you with open arms, and has so many regulars that you really must book ahead. Basque Country flavours have pride of place on the menu, as you'd imagine. The starters (9 €) include Basque ham *au couteau*, Ciboure anchovy *millefeuille*, and chestnut soup with a duck foie gras *raviole* (sort of pasty) - in season, of course. Fish and meat come next (16 €): gambas with aniseed and an artichoke *barigoule* (vegetables in olive oil), Pyrenees suckling lamb and country black pudding served in thick slices. There is only one cheese - but what a cheese! Ardigasna with cherry jam, 7.50 €. Desserts are 8 €. All in all, excellent regional cooking, for around 35 € per head. Rustic setting.

LE PAMPHLET 38, rue Debelleyme ✆ 01 42 72 39 24. *M° Filles-du-Calvaire. Closed Saturday lunchtime, Sunday and Monday lunchtime. One menu only 33 €. Dégustation menu 50 €.* In a quiet corner of the Marais, Alain Carrère, a former rugby player from Pau, welcomes you warmly, even if he can be grumpy. His dining room is quaint but pleasant, with a rather nice old-fashioned feel to it. The cooking, on the other hand, is bang up-to-date with a bistrot basis and excellent ingredients, notably the poultry and beef. The menu changes every day. His Saint-André onion fondue with foie gras, Dublin Bay prawns and coppa roasted in sea-urchin juice alone is worth the visit. Some forgotten puds appear on the dessert menu, like rice pudding and stewed pear with vanilla. Traditional cooking updated and upgraded.

4e arrondissement

BENOIT 20, rue Saint-Martin ✆ 01 42 72 25 76 *Fax: 01 42 72 45 68. M° Chatelet. Open every day 12 noon-2pm and 8pm-10pm, bookings only. Annual closing in August. Set menu 38 €. A la carte 80 €.* In this very lively Châtelet and Halles quarter, this restaurant is almost an institution, having only changed hands twice since 1912! Red velvet banquettes, copper coat pegs, bronze light fittings and posters leave you in no doubt about your surroundings: this is a stylish Parisian bistrot, with high society and foreign tourist customers. You come to Benoît to enjoy excellent traditional bourgeois cooking, lovingly prepared by chef David Rathgeber. Sophistication and delicacy are the watchwords. A good browse through the wine list will show you how well the cellar is run.

BOFINGER 5-7, rue de la Bastille ✆ 01 42 72 87 82. *M° Bastille. Open every day until 1am. Set menus 23.50 €, 33.50 € (including wine), children's menu 13.50 €.* This attractive brasserie, first opened in 1864, and still decorated in pure Belle Epoque style - glass ceilings and carved wood - is one of the district's classic venues, with a mixed bag of customers (local regulars and tourists). You'll enjoy your fresh seafood platter, sweetbread terrine with foie gras and artichokes in a truffle vinaigrette, or seafood *choucroute* all the more in this very Parisian ambience. Excellent service, fast and professional.

LE TASTEVIN 46, rue Saint-Louis-en-l'Isle ✆ 01 43 54 17 31. *M° Pont-Marie. Website: www.letastevin-paris.com. Open every day except Monday lunchtime, 12 noon-2.30pm and 7pm-11.30pm. Set menus 30 €, 33.50 €, 41 € and 59 €.* This restaurant is housed in a beautiful 17thc. building, whose ancient stonework and exposed beams give it tremendous cachet. The talented chef cooks traditional, seasonal dishes that will please even the most demanding gourmet. The house speciality is Dublin bay prawns, but we especially liked the Salers rib steak with its marrow, and the scallops (in season). For dessert, the home-made *moelleux* and profiteroles are well worth lingering over. An excellent place to start your tour of Parisian restaurants! Incidentally, you can prepare your menu online via the website, which is rather fun.

5e arrondissement

L'ECLUSE 15, Quai des Grands-- Augustins ✆ **01 46 33 58 74** *Open 7 days a week : 11.30am-1am. Set menu from 42 € (wine included), à la carte.* L'Ecluse boasts 6 wine bars in Paris. You are warmly welcomed in a bistro ambience, where the wine waiter is always delighted to advise you on your choice of wine and food. Some excellent menu formulas link the two – a plate of charcuterie (cold sausage etc.) with a Listrac, or a red bordeaux to accompany tagliatelli with foie gras and Serrano ham, for instance. And what better way to enjoy a wedge of roquefort cheese than with a glass of sweet wine? To finish, go straight for the award-winning chocolate cake. Cheers!

Other L'Ecluse wine bars:

L'ECLUSE FRANCOIS 1er 64, rue François 1er (Paris 8) ✆ 01 47 20 77 09
L'ECLUSE MADELEINE 15, place de la Madeleine (Paris 8) ✆ 01 42 65 34 69
L'ECLUSE BASTILLE 13, rue de la Roquette (Paris 11) ✆ 01 48 05 19 12
L'ECLUSE CARNOT 1, rue d'Armaillé (Paris 17) ✆ 01 47 63 88 29
L'ECLUSE ST- HONORE 34, place du Marché St- Honoré (Paris 1) ✆ 01 42 96 10 18

LA METHODE 2, rue Descartes ✆ **01 43 54 22 43.** *M° Monge. Open every day until 2.30am. Tuesday-Saturday; midnight Sunday and Monday. Set menus 12.50 € (weekday lunchtimes), 20 €. Dishes of the day.* In this charming quarter where students rub shoulders with civil servants, there is often a party atmosphere - you could say it's traditional. La Méthode may have changed hands, but memories of famous customers like comedian Coluche (who worked here as a waiter) and singer Georges Moustaki linger on. Today, traditional French cuisine is served, prepared with the best fresh ingredients bought at market by the chef himself, and you can eat very, very late. The party often goes on into the early hours, with concerts and theme evenings to jolly things up. The menu changes several times a year, but you can enjoy the avocado millefeuille with prawns or crayfish at any time, and salmon tartare with white truffle oil on the terrace in summer. "Please yourself", says La Méthode.

LE MOULIN A VENT 20, rue des Fossés-Saint-Bernard ✆ **01 43 54 99 37. M° Jussieu.** *Website : www.au-moulinavent.com Open Tuesday-Friday, 12 noon-2.15pm and 7.30pm-11pm. Open Saturday lunchtime. Lunchtime formula 35 €. A la carte from 40 €.* This genuine bistrot goes back a long way. Today it is run by a woman, and has kept the zinc sheen on its walls and its original flavour by offering the same specialities: among them, Salers beef rib, and fresh frogs' legs. The impressive cellar is full of excellent beaujolais. It's always a great pleasure to eat here, especially in summer when you can have a drink on the terrace.

LES PAPILLES 30, rue Gay-Lussac ✆ **01 43 25 20 79.** *RER Luxembourg. Open Monday-Saturday, 8am-midnight. Set lunch and dinner menus 28.50 € (starter, main course, cheese, dessert). A la carte 25 €.* Welcome to this dining-cellar with its 400 recommended wines, including M. Baral's faugères, M. Navarre's saint-chinian and David Duband's burgundy. As we all know, good wine leads to a feast, but first the bottles are sold at shop prices plus 6 € (cork duty). On the menu you find braised veal, pan-cooked tuna and panacotta with wild strawberries. The cost is reasonable (dishes around 12 €) and the setting cosy and pleasant. The place is full up at lunchtime - so don't forget to book two days ahead at least!

AU PORT SALUT 163 bis, rue Saint-Jacques ✆ **01 46 33 63 21**. *RER Luxembourg. M° Cluny-La-Sorbonne. Website : www.leportsalut.com. Open all year Tuesday-Saturday, 12 noon-3pm and 7pm-11pm. Closed Sunday lunchtime and Monday. Set menu (starter, main course, dessert) 14 €, weekdays only, and 25 € , weekdays and weekends. Formula 20 €.* This restaurant near the Luxembourg Gardens dates back to the 17thc. In the 1950s it was a prestigious cabaret where the greatest French singers of the period made their first appearance. Today the Port Salut is a pleasant restaurant under a stone arcade, in the heart of the Latin Quarter. Customers can be sure of a warm welcome and excellent regional cooking including foie gras, beef cheek *parmentier*, onion gratin, Provencal-style gambas, bass fillet flambéd in pastis and rabbit with Meaux mustard. The desserts are home made; don't miss the marvellous Tarte Tatin. Very good value for money, with smiling, polyglot service - the Port Salut team speaks English, Spanish and Italian. We love it.

6e arrondissement

LA BASTIDE ODEON 7, rue Corneille ✆ **01 43 26 03 65.** *M° Odéon Open every day except Sunday and Monday, orders taken until 10.30pm. Formulas 29.50 and 35.50 €. A la carte around 40 € to 50 €.* This sunny place serves Mediterranean cooking with a Riviera taste, bathed in olive oil, like the raw salmon anchoïade and warm ratte potato salad, grilled aubergine millefeuille, creamy Dublin Bay prawn risotto, *chipiron* (Basque calamars and cuttlefish) fricassée and honey and salted caramel *mendiants* (dessert with dried fruit and nuts). There is more sunshine in the colourful, rustic setting and smiling service. Provence in Paris!

BOUILLON RACINE 3, rue Racine ✆ **01 44 32 15 60.** *M° Cluny-La Sorbonne or Odéon. Website: www.bouillon-racine.com – Car parking service in the evenings. Open every day, service until 11pm. A la carte around 30-35 €, lunchtime formula, fresh market produce set menu 15.50 €, menu bouillon 26 €.* The Bouillon Racine is a listed historical monument. The decoration is sumptuous 1900 Art Nouveau, with bevelled mirrors, opalines, stained glass and gilded lettering. Chef Alexandre Belthoise simmers some classic dishes including traditional 'bouillons' (old-fashioned stock soup) like the vegetable-grower's soup and the bouillon au gratin *à l'ancienne* as starters; stuffed, spit-roasted suckling pig and home-made puree or whole sea bass with balm and wild rice for the main course, and a real cafe liegeois for dessert, served in a jug. Note the jazz evenings, held on two Tuesdays every month. A parking valet is available from Tuesday to Saturday evening.

LE CAFE CASSETTE 73, rue de Rennes ✆ **01 45 48 53 78**. *M° Rennes. Website: www.cafecassette.com. Open every day 7am-1am. Special formula 13.20 €.* Ideally located in the heart of Saint-Germain-des-Pres, the Cafe Cassette is a cosy place serving simple and tasty traditional dishes: grilled rib steak with fine salt, Milanese veal escalope or bass fillet baked in Guerande salt. The desserts are home-made - you must try the apple and salted caramel *feuille a feuille.* A generous brunch (20 €) is available, and an American or French-style breakfast. You'll be easily tempted by a lemon meringue tart or an old-fashioned hot chocolate on the terrace, between two bouts of frantic shopping.

LA CLOSERIE DES LILAS 171, boulevard du Montparnasse ✆ **01 40 51 34 50 Fax: 01 43 29 99 94** *RER B Port-Royal. Open every day 12 noon-3pm and 7pm-midnight. A la carte around 60 € and 80 €.*

This prestigious, almost mythical restaurant is elegantly camouflaged behind a row of shrubs in pots, with a terrace in summer. Famous for its tartare, it also serves excellent fresh fish and tender meat, after a beautifully prepared starter. The decoration is rather antiquated - probably just as it was in Hemingway's day -but it suits the restaurant's style and reputation as a gastronomic institution.

LA TABLE DE FES **5, rue Sainte-Beuve ✆ 01 45 48 07 22.** *M° Vavin Open every evening except Sunday. A la carte around 36 €.* This Moroccan restaurant is one of the oldest in Paris, opened in 1961, and also one of the best. The decor is rather dated now, but who cares? the main thing is the food. Moroccan cooking is supposed to be the women's affair, and that seems to be the case here. Everything is prepared with taste, using fresh ingredients, and the couscous vegetables and tajines are perfectly spiced. Only the lightest and fluffiest couscous and most carefully-skimmed stock are served, setting off the meatballs and kebabs. Refined and thoughtful service go with it. Don't forget this table!

VAGENENDE **142, boulevard Saint-Germain ✆ 01 43 26 68 18**. *M° Mabillon or Odéon. Open 7 days a week, non-stop service from 12 noon to 1am. Set menu 19 € (lunchtime) and formula 23 € lunchtime and evening. A la carte around 35 €. Website:www.vagenende.fr* This restaurant is an amazing monument to Parisian daily life: an early 20thc. brasserie with splendid Art Nouveau decor. Today, it serves traditional regional and fresh market cuisine, rotating on a weekly basis according to the seasons. Another typically Parisian attraction is its chilled oyster stall and seasonal seafood (freshly-caught every day). Varied menu, excellent wines. A private salon seating 50 is available for private evening parties.

LE WADJA **10, rue Grande Chaumière ✆ 01 46 33 02 02.** *M° Vavin. Open Monday-Saturday, 12.15pm-2.30pm and 7.30pm-11pm. Closed week of 15 August. Formula 14 € lunchtimes and evenings, starters and dishes of the day. A la carte, starters from 9 €, main courses from 23 €, desserts from 8 €.* You don't in fact find Eastern European specialities here, though you might think so from the name. Once owned by a Polish family, this trendy local bistro is now in the capable hands of Mme Denise, who serves excellent traditional French cooking, and has just celebrated its 10th anniversary. You are warmly welcomed with a menu of delicious dishes and a very pleasant wine list. Try the stuffed piquillo peppers, pressed lentils, foie gras and home-smoked duck breast, or a dozen oysters (26 €).

Follow on with baked scallops in butter, with ginger and savory, or leg of lamb with garlic and olive oil puree. Marvellous. Ewe's milk cheese with black cherry jam is suggested at 8 €, and the desserts are difficult to resist: chocolate terrine with orgeat and cocoa sorbet must be the pick of the crop. 'It's our pleasure to welcome you - and to see you again!' runs the house credo. You'd best book in advance, since the customers are mostly regulars. We heard that Thierry Coue, formerly with Sandrens, was to take over the kitchens. They couldn't do better.

7e arrondissement

BISTRO B' 81, avenue Bosquet ✆ 01 47 05 36 15. *M° Ecole-Militaire. Open 7 days a week, from 7am to 11pm.* This brasserie opened in January 2005, and serves generous regional cuisine in an Art Deco-style 1930s setting. Formerly Le Bistrot de Papa, it is now Le Bistrot B'; the manager is ex-Wepler, and the chef was Le Bistrot de Papa's former second. The menu mainly features meat dishes, but there are also suggestions of the day on the slate. Wepler (Place Clichy) regulars get 15% off. Aveyron recipes have pride of place, notably those made with Aubrac red meat. You can choose from several set menus, with starter and main course or main course and dessert (19 €-22 €). If you go for the full menu (28 €) you'll taste the excellent house duck terrine, followed by calf's head with traditional sauce gribiche, and to finish, Bistrot B's own tart. You should also try the lunchtime terrine-salad formula, from 6 € to 9 €. The first Wednesday of every month is seafood evening, and the third is devoted to the provinces: the chef chooses a French region and cooks a typical meal - from starter to dessert - for 25 €. A final note: you really *must* try the pear in wine and soft white cheese ice cream for dessert

CINQ MARS 51, rue de Verneuil ✆ 01 45 44 69 13. *M° Rue-du-Bac or Solferino. Open Tuesday-Saturday. Formula and set menu 17 € (lunch) and 21.50 €. A la carte around 35 €.* This new restaurant is unobtrusive yet charming, in the chic bistrot style, neither quaint nor artificially trendy. You are warmly welcomed in a pared-down and sober setting- an old telephone, a blackboard -and served simple yet sophisticated cooking with a few nice surprises. If you go for the country terrine, for instance, it will be served the old-fashioned way at your table, golden-brown on top with the knife stuck in it. The chocolate mousse is served in the same way, so you can have second helpings and even thirds...Between the two, there are some delicious dishes like the scallop carpaccio with olive oil (18 €) and grilled tuna with crunchy salad. The banquettes at the back of the dining room are the most comfortable! Wine *à la ficelle*. Well-off thirty-something clientele. Why Le Cinq Mars, you ask? Look at the wide bar facing the door, and you'll see the Marquis du Cinq-Mars' name engraved on a red *tomette* tile.

D'CHEZ EUX 2, avenue de Lowendal ✆ 01 47 05 52 55. *Website:www.chezeux.com. M° Ecole-Militaire. Set menus 35 € and 40 €. A la carte around 50 € to 70 €.* You quickly feel at home in this friendly place, with its warm reception and tables spread out just enough for customer privacy. The setting is chic and countrified with red-and-white checked tablecloths. If you go for the pork selection (cochonailles) at 24 €, you can choose from pâtés, sausage, black pudding and many kinds of ham, all equally tasty. The *auberge* hors d'oeuvre trolley (17 €) Burgundy snails (16 €) and Provençal-style frogs' legs compete for the limelight with home made goose foie gras (26 €), cassoulet, veal liver with sherry vinegar and a final dessert assortment. It's really hard to make a choice: everything is so delicious.

LE JULES-VERNE Champ-de-Mars ✆ 01 45 55 61 44. *Fax 01 47 05 29 41. Set menus 58 € and 130 €. Open all year.* Paris spread out 123m below your feet, a Slavick interior, and chef Alain Reix: eating at the Eiffel Tower is a magic moment. The Jules Verne was opened in 1983, and remains one of the capital's most exclusive restaurants, not really for its almost-affordable prices, but because it is so difficult to get a table, especially for dinner. Alain Reix was faced with an impossible challenge when he arrived in 1992: how to make customers look at their plates rather than at the breathtaking view outside. He proved equal to it, thanks to11 years' experience with Jacques Le Divellec at La Rochelle, and a series of fresh and original dishes, mainly - though not only - fish. Souffléd bread rolls, one with crab, the other lobster, shrimp cream, turbot baked in the oven, celery and green mangoes, combava juice, Bresse chicken with chanterelles and 'seven-hour' leg, woodland strawberry tart, lemon cream and ginger, litchi emulsion feature on his menus. If you add the Belle Epoque atmosphere, impressive service and privileged feeling -you're eating in one of the world's top monuments, after all! - you'll see why the Jules Verne has the edge over those more mundane restaurants with their feet on the ground!

8e arrondissement

APICIUS 20, rue d'Artois ✆ 01 43 80 19 66 *Fax : 01 44 40 09 57. Set menu 140 €. A la carte 130 €. Closed Saturday, Sunday and in August.* After 20 years spent at Avenue de Villiers in the 17th, Jean-Pierre Vigato finally opened his restaurant in the chic 8th arrondissement last year - big news in the small world of top Parisian restaurants. He chose a particularly fine 18thc. private mansion, built for the Comte d'Artois and formerly owned by a well-known French film producer-director. The dining rooms are terribly stylish, which appeals to the important business customers. Vigato's cooking is a blend of classic and modern: barely grilled Dublin Bay prawns, pan-fried duck foie gras with conserved black radishes, bass with spring onions seasoned with black pepper then caramelised, skate *au naturel*, ketchup tutti frutti and spinach leaves, calf's head with tongues and brains in *sauce ravigote*, pigeon breast with country ham casseroled with beetroot. Distinguished chocolate and caramel desserts share the menu with almond milk blancmange and its fresh and candied fruit. Marvellous interior design; shame about the rather haughty service.

L'APPART 9, rue du Colisée © 01 53 75 42 00. Website : www.lappart.com. *Open 7 days a week, 12 noon-3pm and 6pm-2am. Menu Marché de l'Appart (starter + main course or main course + dessert) 18 €, starter, main course and dessert 23 € at lunchtime. Evening menu on the slate 30 € (starter, main course and dessert). Brunch formula on Sunday. Happy hour every day from 6pm to 8pm. Baking workshop for children over 4 on Sunday.* This restaurant a short distance from the Champs Elysées has its regulars, who always book their table in the same place: the small salon, wine cellar (business lunches) or in a corner of the bar with its library for a cosy, romantic dinner. The atmosphere is convivial and relaxed, and chef Samuel Le Torrielec's new menus are as light and delicate as you could wish: aubergines conserved with rosemary, fresh duck foie gras terrine with orange chutney and a gingerbread tuile biscuit, grilled scallop kebab, creamy carrots with walnut oil and brioche bread pudding-style with caramel.

LE BRISTOL 112, rue du Faubourg-Saint-Honoré © 01 53 43 43 00 *Fax : 01 53 43 43 01. Website : www.hotel-bristol.com.Set menus from 80 € to 175 €. A la carte 150 €. Open all year.* Eric Fréchon's career makes one think of a Ferrari speeding down a German motorway, Having trained at the best school for luxury hotels (commis at the Grande Cascade - the Bristol already - 20 years ago, chef de partie at Taillevent, second at the Tour d'Argent then chef at the Crillon) he has been running the Bristol's kitchens for 6 years now, putting his perfect technique into practice to create the capital's most specialised menus. With all those indispensable luxury ingredients at his disposal - turbot, Dublin Bay prawns from Guilvinec, Challans duck and suckling veal sweetbreads - he hardly needs to use everyday produce, but Fréchon's talent lies in transforming these ordinary foodstuffs into something special. Mackerel in escabeche, tomato flavoured with horseradish and garlic, Saint Gilles Croix de Vie whiting in a breadcrumb crust, green tetragon, served raw and cooked, chargrilled country bacon, green asparagus *à la plancha* and mustard leaves. The prices are out of reach for many, but if you can afford it, you'll be more than happy with your meal. Impeccable service, of course, run by Raphaël Courant, and a magnificent cellar in the care of Jérôme Moreau.

CAP VERNET 82, avenue Marceau © 01 47 20 20 40. *Open every day from 11am-11pm, except Saturday lunchtime and Sunday. Set menus from 50 € to 60 €.* This mythical restaurant located in the Avenue Marceau has a newly-decorated interior in light, poetic shades, and a new menu featuring fresh seafood. The quality is constant, and the cooking simple so as to bring out the natural flavours: bass with creamy celery risotto, rocket with pistou and mature Parmesan cheese shavings, sole cooked two ways - grilled then baked - and green vegetables steamed with angelica. Jean-Marc Lemmery is an expert with seawater, river and exotic fish, but also cooks meat and vegetables with talent. You can also have tea et the Cap Vernet, or a drink after work: wine is served by the glass with home made tapas and appetisers. Excellent welcome; an address to note and remember.

FLORA 36, avenue George-V © 01 40 70 10 49. *M° George-V or Charles-de-Gaulle-Etoile. Closed Saturday lunchtime and Sunday. Orders taken until 11pm. Lunchtime formula 28 €. Set menus 36 € and 65 €.* The cuisine chez Flora is delicate and sophisticated; after the Provençal adventure with Les Olivades, this is a new and very different restaurant. Marbled goat's cheese and aubergine, grilled dory fillet with an artichoke *barigoule* and gnocchi with conserved lemons, followed by red fruit and melon with hibiscus syrup and red granita, are served in a minimalist setting. The technique is fresh and accurate, with a sprinkling of nostalgia for the Mediterranean.

PIERRE GAGNAIRE 6, rue Balzac © 01 58 36 12 50. *Fax 01 58 36 12 51. Website : www.pierre-gagnaire.com. Set menu 230 €. A la carte 200 €. Closed Saturday, Sunday lunchtime and second fortnight in July.* Pierre Gagnaire has always done things his way. Born in the Saint Etienne suburbs over half a century ago (his father ran the Clos Fleuri at Saint-Priest en Jarez) he first took over the family kitchens, then set up on his own in the 1980s, determined to make this town as famous for gastronomy as for football. He quickly managed this, and was awarded his third Michelin *macaron* in 1993. His critics claimed this was the beginning of the end, and his delusions of grandeur had finished him, when, weary of too much success too soon, he gave up his golden 'charms', and came to Paris. Five years later, he got all three of them back, in his new restaurant in Rue Balzac, where his inventive cooking has reached new peaks: Cevennes onions au gratin, browned celery, green apples and young leeks, no. 2 special oysters stiffened in the oven, little Dublin bay prawns in olive oil, spinach shoots and white dandelions with seaweed, cepe *mousseline*, royal sea bream with parsley butter and Lautrec garlic, braised hake with peppered butter, lacquered with grapefruit juice, chicory fondue with Guiness, and pumpkin with Campari are proof of his skill. Today, he is among the four or five most creative and talented chefs of the moment. His friendship with the INRA physical chemist Hervé This has enabled him to take his culinary research even further.

STELLA MARIS 4, rue Arsène-Houssaye ✆ 01 42 89 16 22. *M° George-V or Charles-de-Gaulle-Etoile. Closed Saturday lunchtime and Sunday. Last orders taken 10.30pm. Lunchtime formula 43 €. Set menus 85 € and 130 €.* Stella Maris attracts the gourmets; the Japanese chef has fallen in love with French cuisine, and prepares exquisite dishes with regional ingredients: red tuna *millefeuille*, risotto, roast Breton lobster and guanaja *fondant*. Inventive and attractive cooking, served in a neo-classic setting.

9e arrondissement

BOUILLON CHARTIER 7, rue du Faubourg-Montmartre ✆ 01 47 70 86 29. M° Grands-Boulevards. *Website : www.bouillon-chartier.com Open every day 11.30am-3pm and 6pm-10pm. A la carte around 15 €.* This restaurant could almost go unnoticed, if it weren't for the queue outside. In fact it is world famous, and the dining room can take 300 place settings, yet it is often full. The building itself dates back to the Belle Epoque and is a listed historic monument. A mixed bag of young and older customers, Parisian and foreign, comes here to eat simple, tasty cooking with good value for money. The cucumber salad is 1.70 €, rump steak 9.90 € and pot-au-feu 9.70 €. The waiter scribbles your (reasonable) bill on a corner of the tablecloth. What more could you ask for? Just a free table!

CHARLOT 12, place Clichy ✆ 01 53 20 48 00. *M° Place-Clichy – Website : www.charlot-paris.com Open every day from 12 noon to 3pm and 7pm to midnight (Thursday, Friday and Saturday till 1am).* Set menus lunchtime 19.50 € (starter + main course or main course + dessert with a glass of wine or mineral water) and 25 € (starter, main course, dessert and a glass of wine or mineral water). Privilege evenings with show and restaurant from 52 €. This corner of Place Clichy speaks with a Provençal accent, thanks to Charlot. The king of shellfish gives his seafood preparations Mediterranean flavours, with bouillabaisse coming out top of the list, though the aioli is almost as evocative. The tuna carpaccio and sea bream royale cooked to your taste are equally delicious. Mediterranean cuisine in a Parisian restaurant is one of those heady mixtures good holidays are made of.

LE VIKING 55, rue du Faubourg-Montmartre ✆ 01 42 80 39 02. M° Le Peletier. *Website: www.restaurantleviking.com. Open Monday to Friday from 7am-midnight, Saturday from 6pm-midnight. A la carte 17 €.* A good meal is guaranteed for all in this family restaurant, a genuine brasserie with efficient service and a warm and friendly atmosphere. The cooking is traditional and seasonal, prepared with fresh market ingredients. We recommend the hot sausage *feuilleté* with currants; or steak tartare and home made duck confit if you prefer something simpler. Your meal is served with a smile - in fact the place is so welcoming that regulars enjoy just dropping in for a drink. Customers can book a private corner for birthday celebrations; the atmosphere tends to be generally festive anyway. What a pity there are so few places like this in Paris!

10e arrondissement

BRASSERIE FLO 7, cour des Petites-Ecuries ✆ 01 47 70 13 59. *M° Château-d'Eau. Open every day from 12pm-3pm, evenings from 7pm. A la carte around 45 €.* You reach this local brasserie via the Rue du Faubourg Saint-Denis, and discover the car parking service - a welcome if original touch in Paris, where it is often so difficult to park. The atmosphere is late 19thc. with Alsace country landscapes on the walls; a mechanical piano adds a musical touch. Share a whole beef rib cooked for two, or try the traditional Alsatian dishes, with the inevitable well-garnished choucroute. If you like Oriental food, the Japanese menu is for you.

CHEZ MICHEL 10, rue de Belzunce ✆ 01 44 53 06 20. *M° Poissonnière or Gare-du-Nord. Open 12noon-2pm and 7pm to midnight, bookings only. Closed Saturday, Sunday and Monday. Set menu 30 €.* A la carte dishes are counted as menu dishes with a supplement. Chez Michel is an excellent regional restaurant located just behind Saint-Vincent-de-Paul Church in a very pleasant quarter. It is wise to book in advance, this being a small but popular place. Excellent food is served in a classic setting, with Breton cuisine to the fore, betraying the chef's origins.

TERMINUS NORD 23, rue de Dunkerque ✆ 01 42 85 05 15. *M° Gare-du-Nord. Open 7 days a week from 11am to 1am non-stop. Set menus 22.90 € (11am-5pm and after 10.30pm) and 32.90 € (11am-1am).* This late 19thc. Alsatian brasserie has kept its magnificent Art Deco decor. The high ceilings, counter bar and frescoes are a delight, ditto the lovely 1900 Belle Epoque salon. Inside you find business people between two trips, and trendy waiters. The restaurant seems to reflect the bustle outside, and is always busy. Excellent, classic cuisine, including Marseille bouillabaisse (21.90 €), fish soup with rouille paste and croûtons (9 €) and duck foie gras escalope (23 €). Wide variety of oysters. Very decent wine list.

11e arrondissement

LES AMOGNES 243, rue du faubourg Saint-Antoine ✆ 01 43 72 73 05. *M° Faidherbe-Chaligny or Reuilly-Diderot. Closed Sunday and Monday. Open 12 noon-2pm and 8pm-11pm. A la carte around 33 €.* This restaurant looks like a little stone house with its ivy climbing round the windows. Inside you find low ceilings, stone walls, white beams and panelling, cotton napkins and tablecloths, and serviette-rings - what luxury! One wall is kept free to exhibit paintings. Classic ingredients are well-prepared by a very skilful chef, and served with wines from the Loire Valley, Rhône, South-West, Languedoc, Burgundy, Jura, Corsica and Auvergne. Excellent place to eat; let's hope it'll stay that way.

JACQUES MELAC 42, rue Léon-Frot ✆ 01 43 70 59 27. *M° Charonne. Open 11.30am-3.30pm and 7.30pm-10.30pm. Closed Sunday and Monday. Closed at Easter and in August. A la carte around 25 €.* Jacques Melac's place is better known in Paris as a wine bistrot than a restaurant, yet these days, it is always full of customers come to taste both his wines and his Aveyron *cuisine*, and to meet Jacques himself, born in Bozouls and known for his drooping moustache. He is President of the *Vignerons de Paris* (Paris Winegrowers), an association that collects grapes grown on vines planted by the capital's private citizens. He has been running his bistrot for over 30 years, and conviviality, regional flavours and the good life are still in the air.

12e arrondissement

DE LACAZE 33, rue de Lyon ✆ 01 43 41 97 70. *M° Gare-de-Lyon – Corner of Rue de Lyon and Avenue Ledru-Rollin. Closed Saturday lunchtime and Sunday. Set menus 14 €, 21 € and 23 €, morning and evening. A la carte around 40 €.* This attractive restaurant near the Gare de Lyon welcomes you warmly. The dining room is spacious, with its elegant tables spread out to ensure customer privacy. De Lacaze offers rich menus featuring seasonal game specialities like woodpigeon confit - an exceptional dish that gives the place its originality - served with mashed potato and fine herbs. Fish specialities include cod, grilled bass, seafood casseroles and shellfish. The stuffed mussels are a house classic. For dessert, don't hesitate: have the delicious profiteroles! The atmosphere is pleasant, and the clientele - travellers passing through and regulars - come here for the traditional, top-quality French cuisine. You'd be wise to book ahead.

LES ZYGOMATES 7, rue de Capri ✆ 01 40 19 93 04. *M° Daumesnil and Michel Bizot – Website: www.auxzygomates.com – Closed Sunday and Monday. Open 12 noon-2pm and 7.30pm-10.45pm. Menu-carte 24 € or 30 €, lunchtime formula 14.50 €.* This small restaurant in its beautiful listed street has been burnished by time, and with its huge mirror, flowered tiles and marble, is certainly not lacking in charm. The menus recalls that this was once a pork butcher's; a certain nostalgia lingers in the 30 € (starter + main course + dessert) and 24 € (two courses) menu formulas. The cooking is inventive but respects individual flavours: Dublin bay raviole, stuffed pig's tail, duck foie gras salad with pine kernels; tuna, leg of lamb or chicken *croustillant*; the dishes are all perfectly timed, and served with the right veg. The lunchtime formula gives you starter, main course, dessert and coffee for 14 €! The menu changes every 3-6 months, and the chef's suggestions are renewed on a daily basis. Chic, romantic ambience in the evenings.

O REBELLE 24, rue Traversière ✆ 01 43 40 88 98. *M° Gare-de-Lyon. Open Monday-Friday, lunchtime and evenings till midnight, and Saturday evening only, till midnight. Lunchtime Formulas 19.50 € (lunchtime), 35 € lunchtime and evening.* The interior design here makes a change from checked tablecloths and bordeaux walls, being done out in peaceful shades - a daring green on the walls - light-coloured banquettes, chairs with elegant covers and a sober arrangement for the place-settings. It's chic, and the cooking is trendy too. Big china plates provide plenty of room to present the food, which is hot on exotic smells and new flavours. Snail *galette* on crusty leeks with vanilla, white kidney bean *velouté* with cardamom, buffalo steak on a sweet potato gratin with stuffed mushrooms, caramelised duck breast with poppy seed and yam purée, chibousts with mandarins and a sesame seed *tuile* biscuit are some examples.

13e arrondissement

L'ANACREON 53, boulevard Saint-Marcel ✆ 01 43 31 71 18 *M° Gobelins. Open 12 noon-2.15pm and 7.30pm-10.30pm. Annual closing in August. Closed Saturday lunchtime, Sunday and Monday. Set menus 20 € to 30 €.* André Le Letty trained at the Tour d'Argent. He concocts his menus on a basis of seasonal and market availability. Starters include rabbit terrine with foie gras and small vegetables, snail feuilleté with nettle cream, fresh goat's cheese with conserved tomatoes and basil, with cod in Greek-style vegetable stock, chicken fricassée with salsify, and casseroled pork loin with curry. Fresh, simple and delicious.

L'AUBERGE ETCHEGORRY 41, rue Croulebarbe ✆ 01 44 08 83 51. *M° Les Gobelins or Corvisart. Open 12 noon-2.30pm and 7.30pm-10.30pm. Closed Sunday and Monday. Lunch Set lunch menu 19.30 €, lunchtime and evening formulas 26 €, 32.50 € and 37.60 € (menu gourmand) including a half-bottle of wine per head. superb dégustation menu 47.80 €.* Located behind the Square Le Gall, this former cabaret with its charming rustic façade was one of Victor Hugo's haunts, at a time when the River Bièvre still flowed through Paris. The restaurant now specialises in South-West and Basque Country cuisine. The Labordes, also owners of the Vert Galant hotel with its beautiful garden next door, greet you warmly and settle you in the romantic 19thc. dining room, where you can eat warm or cold foie gras, with cooked apples or grapes - or even take some away, at 45.80 € for 400g. Other specialities are stuffed chipirons (Basque calamars or cuttlefish) in their ink, cassoulet, paella, duck breast and goose neck stuffed with black pudding. Apart from this South-West speciality base, the Auberge also offers seasonal dishes. The wine list is magnificent, with jurançon, irouléguy and madiran wines, among others. A stroll down Rue Croulebarbe will brighten up a grey Parisian day with instant sunshine.

LE TEMPS DES CERISES 18, rue de la Butte-aux-Cailles ✆ 01 45 89 69 48. *M° Corvisart and Place-d'Italie. Open Monday-Friday from 11.45am-2.10pm and 7.30pm-10.45pm, Saturday 7.30pm-10.45pm. Lunchtime set menu 10.50 € (starter, main course and dessert). Lunchtime and evening formulas 14.50 € (starter, main course) or 22 € (starter, main course, dessert). A la carte 25 €.* This restaurant is a workers' co-operative dedicated to the memory of the Paris Commune, and one of the Butte-aux-Cailles' best bistrots. It was opened in 1976, and the service is still as friendly. You can eat cassoulet, grilled andouillette (chitterling sausage) Normandy black pudding and a few foreign dishes like cod acras. If you feel the wait for a table is too long, you'll be advised to have a drink in the Merle Moqueur bar opposite. And make sure you comply with the explicit notice: «SVP, coupez vos portables, bordel», something like «Please switch off your bloody mobile!»

14e arrondissement

L'AMUSE-BOUCHE 186, rue du Château ✆ 01 43 35 31 61. M° Mouton-Duvernet and Gaîté. *Closed Sunday and Monday. Open Tuesday-Saturday, 12pm-2pm and 7.30pm-10.30pm. Set menus 17 € (main coursee + dessert) and 24 € (starter + main course). Menu-carte 30 €.* This restaurant used to be a butcher's and has kept the shop front, adding some rather bright lights. Inside, it is done out in more modern style, with a cosy ambience. Fresh ingredients and some skilful mixing and matching of flavours are typical of the *carte*: Dublin Bay prawns, snail fricassée with mushrooms, foie gras terrine, fresh cod and cress cream, roast duck fillet, the juice reduced with green pepper, and dark chocolate square with hazlenuts. A simple, tasty meal, perfect for a romantic or friendly *tête à tête.*

DE BOUCHE A OREILLE 34, rue Gassendi ✆ 01 43 27 73 14 . *Closed Saturday lunchtime and Sunday.* Chef Benoît Chagny and Sandy at reception welcome you to their newly-decorated restaurant, all done out in Southern colours and warm pastels. Delicious, original cooking.

LA MAISON COURTINE 157, avenue du Maine ✆ 01 45 43 08 04. *M° Mouton-Duvernet, Alésia or Pernety. Open Monday 7.30pm-11pm, Tuesday to Friday 12 noon-11pm and Saturday 7.30pm-11pm. Set menu 36 €.* This restaurant earned itself a reputation years ago, and its sophisticated South-West cuisine is only rivalled by the equally polished welcome and setting. Owner Yves Charles manages an impressive wine list with 200 recommended bottles. Don't miss the chocolate soufflé, whatever you do!

LE PAVILLON MONTSOURIS 20, rue Gazan ✆ 01 43 13 29 00. *RER Cité-Universitaire. Open every day 12 noon-2.30pm and 7.30pm-10.30pm. Set menu 49 €. Gourmet menu 75 €.* This restaurant is housed in an artistically-decorated 1900 pavilion where Mata-Hari and Lenin lunched in their time (though probably not together). In winter, you are snugly settled inside, by the big bay windows opening onto the landscaped garden, but come the summer, you can eat on Haussmann's terrace in a pastoral setting overlooking the park. Seasonal cuisine, including monkfish carpaccio and Dublin Bay prawn *ravioles.* A real breath of fresh air.

LA REGALADE 49, avenue Jean-Moulin. ✆ 01 45 45 68 58. *M° Alésia. Open Monday 7pm-11pm, Tuesday to Thursday 12 noon-2pm and 7pm-11pm, Friday 12 noon-2pm and 7pm-midnight. Set menu 30 €.* South-West cuisine, good value for money. This is one of the capital's best places to eat. Boss Bruno Doucet greets customers warmly in this relaxed setting, but you have to book well ahead - and once here, find a table in the crowded dining room. That's the only downside to this restaurant's success, so we advise you to book for the second service, which tends to be quieter.

VIN ET MAREE 108, avenue du Maine ✆ 01 43 20 29 50. M° Gaîté *Open 7 days a week, 12 noon-2.30pm and 7pm-11.30pm. Lunchtime formula 26.50 €.* This restaurant is located in the heart of Montparnasse, and will please fish and seafood fans. It has plenty of charm, with its pretty blue-and-white marine decor and the slate where menus are written up. The produce changes with the seasons and the day's catch, but you're sure to enjoy the grilled sardines with fine salt as a starter, followed by baked dory, and a delicious Zanzibar Baba for two, to finish. The shellfish and oysters are especially fresh. All aboard!

Other adresses:

183 boulevard Murat (16 ème) ✆ 01 46 47 91 39

276, boulevard Voltaire (11 ème) ✆ 01 43 72 31 33

71, avenue de Suffren (7 ème) ✆ 01 47 83 27 12

15e arrondissement

LA CAVE DE L'OS A MOELLE 181, rue de Lourmel ✆ 01 45 57 28 28. *M° Lourmel. Closed Monday. Table d'hôtes 20 €* This restaurant serves popular cooking with the dishes chalked up on a blackboard: they include terrines, soups seafood, roast veal with purée, cheese, dessert and coffee. Second helpings are available - this is a *cuisine* which suits big appetites. You serve yourself bread and wine, a convivial idea developed by chef Thierry Faucher, ex-Crillon, who also thought up the *table d'hôtes* concept, one common table with 10 place settings and another with 6. If you want to take your time eating without being hurried along, come for the second service at 9.30pm. It's a nice and innovative system, but so successful that you sometimes have to book a week ahead.

JE THE ME 4, rue d'Alleray ✆ 01 48 42 48 30. *M° Vaugirard. Open Tuesday to Saturday, 12 noon -2.30pm and 7.30pm-10.30pm. Dish of the day 18 €. Set menu 33 €.* This restaurant was originally a grocers', and the period decor - panelling, tiled floor, slates and well-stocked shelves - was kept when the shop was converted into a Parisian bistrot. The menu is seasonal: pollack with a vegetable compote (light and tasty), scallops and tagliatelli, and salmon tartare. The desserts are just as nice: rum baba with whipped cream, or chocolate *mi-cuit* with *crème anglaise* (custard served cold like cream); delicious. The varied wine list features some excellent little wines at reasonable prices from 15 € to 35 €. Pleasant welcome; good advice; prompt and efficient service. The chef is a real epicurean, and there are few of them left in Paris. Don't forget to book in advance.

LE QUINZIEME 14, rue Cauchy 01 45 54 43 43. *M° Javel. Open every day 12 noon-2.30pm and 7pm-11pm, except Saturday lunchtime and Sunday. Lunchtime menu 40 € (starter + main course or main course + dessert, glass of wine and water, coffee). Dégustation menu 80 € (starter, fish, meat, cheese and dessert). A la carte from 50 € to 80 €. Parking valet lunchtime and evening.* This is Cyril Lignac's restaurant, a media darling who featured on the TV programme *Oui chef!* a few months ago. This young fan of Mediterranean cuisine set up on his own in February 2005: the interior is simply designed with no flourishes, and the kitchens can be seen from outside. All the subtlety of sunshine cooking can be found in his dishes: to start with, sea bream and mango tartare, coriander and Espelette pepper (17 €) duck foie gras terrine with fine salt, gingerbread and pan-cooked fruit (20 €) Jajugo ham and Lomo Bellota (25 €), crusty tart with chanterelles, sweet onions and herb salad (17 €), just to work up an appetite. Then the main courses: creamy risotto with dried fruits, pan-fried gambas (25 €) scallops cooked in bacon on a foie gras carpaccio (28 €) or chicken burger with mozarella au gratin (20 €). A tiramisu with coconut and exotic flavours is the perfect finish. On the upside, this young chef is full of creative enthusiasm and it comes out in his cooking. The downside: the prices are steep, given his lack of experience.

LE R 6-8, rue de la Cavalerie – 8e étage 01 45 67 06 85. *M° La Motte-Picquet. Website : www.le-r.fr. Open Monday-Saturday, 8pm-2am. A la carte, around 55 € (without drinks).* Nestling on the eighth floor of a building hiding in an empty alley, near the busy Motte-Piquet quarter, this restaurant has a view of the Eiffel Tower illuminated at night. Opened in January 2005 in the New York spirit, this is a cosmopolitan and cosy place, a blend of Colonial and Oriental styles, with filtered light, candles, bamboo, bonzais and Tibetan statues.The atmosphere is relaxed -you could say zen. You are warmly welcomed and settled in a deep, squashy armchair at a black, white and gold lacquered table, ready to choose from a selection of chef David Buinand's culinary inventions. Foie gras 'lollipop' with gingerbread, nem and a foie gras *bonbon* (23 €) or snail fricassée and *sot-l'y laisse* in acidic juice with balsamic vinegar (19 €). The main courses feature *ravioles* in a vegetable and olive oil *barigoule* with ewe's milk curds and Madagascar pepper (21 €), lamb with fine spices and an artichoke *millefeuille* (28 €) or duck with citrus fruits, mango chutney and tamarind sauce (27 €). Terrace (with flowers) heated in winter.

LE RESTAURANT DU MARCHE 59, rue de Dantzig ✆ 01 48 28 31 55. *M° Convention, Porte-de-Vanves or Porte-de-Versailles. Closed Saturday, Sunday and Monday evening. Service until 11pm. Formulas 22 € and 29 €.* This bistrot has a well-filled slate and some culinary marvels, like the quail with olives, which has a flavour you'll find nowhere else. It found a new lease of life with the arrival of Francis Lévêque, who took over the place in September 2003. Next to the daily suggestions on the slate, with their South-West flavour, you'll find Francis' personal favourites which are bound to become classics: tarte Tatin with aubergines and tomatoes, *fondant* leg of lamb, foie gras with steamed herbs and the unforgettable madeleines with raspberry ice cream. The retro bistrot ambience and comfortable terrace are charming.

LE TROQUET 21, rue François-Bonvin ✆ 01 45 66 89 00. *M° Sèvres-Lecourbe. Open Tuesday to Saturday, 12 noon-2.30pm and 7pm-11pm. Menu-carte 30 €, dégustation menu 37 €.* Rugby fans will feel right at home here, Christian Etchebest being from Pau, a local team supporter and a great enthusiast of the game. He has even managed to get the brother-in-law of Imanol Harinordoquy, talented player for Biarritz and the French XV, working in his kitchens ! South-West specialities fill the upper part of the slate, with classics like duck breast stuffed with foie gras, saddle of Pyrenees suckling lamb and the famous home made Basque cake, washed down with a pretty decent jurançon or madiran. You can also taste pan-fried mullets with dried lemon, oxtail and cheek ravioles and stewed orange with a chocolate quenelle, time of year permitting. Excellent value for money.

16e arrondissement

L'ASTRANCE 4, rue Beethoven ✆ 01 40 50 84 40. *Set menus 70 € to 250 €. A la carte 100 €. Closed Saturday, Sunday and Monday, one week in November, over Christmas, one week of the February school holidays and in August.* Everyone has been talking about young chef Pascal Barbot for the last two years, and as a result, it is difficult to get a table at L'Astrance (the dinner waiting lists are almost as long as the district's yellow pages!) Try booking for lunch instead (the marvellous surprise menu is available at lunchtime too) if you'd like to discover this talented chef who trained with Alain Passard (L'Arpège). His foie gras marinated in verjus, button mushroom galette, strips of elm, warm foie gras, seaweed stock and green radishes, mackerel with onion fondue, peppers, capers, coriander and ginger, grilled veal kidney and sweetbreads, morels and melted parmesan, lamb and aubergine slice glazed with miso, and foamy rhubarb with spiced yoghurt will astonish you . The Astrance's success is partly due to competent Christophe Rochat's skilful running of the dining room. Even if the prices, originally very low, have caught up with the 21st century, this cuisine is still worth the cost.

BISTROT DE L'ETOILE LAURISTON 19, rue Lauriston ✆ 01 40 67 11 16. *M° Charles-de-Gaulle-Etoile. Open Monday-Friday lunchtime and evening, Saturday evening only. Formulas 21 €, 26 €, 47 €. A la carte 35 €.* In this attractive contemporary interior in light wood and metal, the cooking is classic, with plenty of new ideas. Christophe and Maria Lacombe run the place, and since they are Guy Savoy's culinary accomplices, surprises are in fashion here. Cod with basil in a *brick* (sort of North African pancake) piperade and mushrooms, pan-fried beef rib steak, gratin dauphinois with bacon and morels and *crêpes* stuffed with strawberry compote, vanilla ice cream or mango and raspberry cappucino and mascarpone emulsion with kiwis are just a few delicious dishes you might like to try.

LE PASSIFLORE 31, rue de Lonchamp ✆ 01 47 04 96 81. *M° Boissière or Trocadéro. Open Monday to Friday evening. A la carte around 70 €.*This is one of those restaurants that really wakes up the tastebuds. Chef Roland Durand prepares gastronomic meals with mischievous pleasure. You'll be struck by his duck terrine with aubergine and almond chutney (tasty!), fried codling sauce tartare with green asparagus (crunchy!) Auvergne cheeseboard (melting!) and coconut and marrow clafoutis (astonishing!), all pleasantly served in a bewitching setting. Well done M. Durand!

17e arrondissement

LA BRASSERIE LORRAINE Place des Ternes ✆ 01 56 21 22 00. *M° Ternes. Open every day till half-past midnight. Privilege evening with show and restuarant from 52 €. A la carte 60 €. Car valet service.* La Brasserie Lorraine has become a meeting place for Eastern France's 'expatriates' in Paris. Located in the pretty Place des Ternes, this historic place with its elegant decor and traditions manages to show a young, lively and welcoming face to customers. The scent and colour of the many flowers filling the Place des Ternes add a harmonious note, especially when tables and chairs are brought out onto the terrace in the first fine days of spring. Here you find the biggest oyster and shellfish selection in Paris, always fresh, and a whole host of dishes like Morteau sausage with warm potatoes, majestic rib steaks, the famous *aiguillette* (thin stips of duck breast) tartare and poached skate wing in hazlenut butter. They don't make brasseries like this anymore!

L'ENTREDGEU 83, rue Laugier ✆ 01 40 54 97 24. *M° Villiers. Closed Sunday and Monday. Set menu 20 € or 28 €. A la carte 40 €.* In this sober bistrot, Basque chef Philippe Tredgeu makes sparks fly - we'd like to see them turned into a star! He definitely deserves one, with his friendly waitresses and very pleasant menus. The foie gras, scallops in their shells with fine herb butter, Savoy cabbage au gratin with Parmesan, duck with turnips and to finish, delicious rice pudding are well worth testing. Attractive, reasonably priced wine list, good choice of bottles under 20 € - which means booking ahead, of course!

RESTAURANT GUY SAVOY 18 rue Troyon ✆ 01 43 80 40 61 *Fax : 01 46 22 43 09. Website : www.guysavoy.com. Set menus 230 € to 285 €. A la carte 160 €. Closed Saturday lunchtime, Sunday, Monday and in August.* Recently promoted Commander of Arts and Letters at just over 50, Guy Savoy is the nicest 'innkeeper' in Paris. His restaurant is all you'd expect from a great establishment: modern, warm and distinguished, and well-heeled customers almost have to fight for a table (and there are plenty of them), to discover French gastronomy at its highest level. Guy Savoy likes amusing his guests, and suggests a few surprise dishes, like the turbot with eggs in salad and soup: the fish is presented on a plate with little holes in it, for the fish sauce to run through. Once this is finished, a waiter takes away the first plate to reveal a second underneath containing fish stock, now mixed with the creamy turbot sauce. Inventive rather than gimmicky, as are the rissoled sweetbreads and small truffle and potato pasties, or grapefruit terrine with tea sauce. The service is supervised by talented Eric Mancio, and includes an Internet menu at 100 € for online orders. The cellar is carefully renewed on a yearly basis.

STUBLI 11, rue Poncelet ✆ 01 42 27 81 86. *M° Ternes. Open 9am-6.30pm, lunch served 11.30am-3pm (Tuesday-Saturday) and Sunday brunch 9.30am-12.30pm. Closed Monday.* Stübli is the Parisian showcase for Austro-German gastronomy. On the right-hand pavement, the pastrycook's and tearoom where you can lunch on the first floor, and where delicious creamy cakes are displayed in the window. On the left-hand pavement is the delicatessen with its generous German cold meats. Appetising! Try the herrings with aniseed, rollmops and *matjes* with rye bread, Stübli salad (potato salad served with a hot beef sausage) salmon koulibiac, sauerkraut, *fleichstrudel* (minced beef, smoked bacon, tomatoes, onions and cumin rolled in strudel pastry and served with a yoghurt and chive sauce, rice and French beans) German-style sweet *choucroute* garnished with a slice of smoked bacon, and Nurnberg and Frankfurter sausages with potato purée. If you've room left, treat yourself to an exquisite home made dessert: Black Forest gateau or strudel. Viennese brunch at weekends 25 €.

18e arrondissement

LA GROLLE DE MONTMARTRE 28, rue de Vieuville ✆ 01 42 57 36 15. M° Abbesses. *Open every day 7pm-11pm, except Wednesday. A la carte 30 € to 40 €.* This Savoyard restaurant has every right to the name, since the owners ran a restaurant for 14 years in the Grand-Bornand, and still get all their supplies in and around this town. Even the beer! Massive beams and natural stone walls set off the mountain decor with its 30 place settings, and your welcome is sincerely warm. You really feel you're in Savoie, rather than Montmartre, transported by magic wand. The 3-cheese fondue (15 € per head) is delicious, and excellent value for money. That's already a good reason to try this place - you won't be disappointed, we can promise you!

LA FAMILLE 41, rue des Trois-Frères ✆ 01 42 52 11 12. *M° Abbesses. Open Tuesday-Saturday evening. A la carte 45 €.* This restaurant has become a must in the quarter. Its small but often-renewed menu features culinary treasures like saddle of lamb, and smoked eel with potatoes, olive oil and cress. A selection of rare wines is available. Interior design in warm shades; equally warm customer welcome. One of Montmartre's most inventive *cuisines*.

LE MOULIN DE LA GALETTE 83, rue Lepic ✆ 01 46 06 84 77. *M° Abbesses. Closed Sunday evening. Open 12.45pm-2pm and 7.30pm-11.30pm. Set menu of the day 20 €. A la carte 45 €.* This famous Montmartre artists' haunt was a windmill first, then a mythic dance hall, and afterwards an Italian restaurant with several celebrities for regulars. Its reconversion has been a great success, and it is especially popular in summer: 80% of its customers are foreign tourists. The dining room is chic and minimal, with an attractive patio, and the delightful terrace overlooks Montmartre's backyards and staircases, invisible from the street. The cooking lives up to its promises, especially Sunday brunch (25 €): choice of hot drink, fresh fruit juice, croissants and bread, scrambled eggs with smoked salmon or bacon, served with sautéd potatoes and salad, citrus fruit salad, brownie or soft white cheese with Morello cherries.

REFUGE DES FONDUS 17, rue des Trois-Frères © **01 42 55 22 65**. *M° Abbesses – Website: www.lerefugedesfondus.com – Open evenings 7pm-2am. Single menu 16 €* You find a gap, and elbow your way in to sit at one of the two large tables, where the glass you are handed turns out to be the 'cocktail' included in the single menu! Next, you have to choose your fondue - meat or cheese? - and wine - white or red? You drink your wine from a 240ml baby's bottle, which obviously adds to the ambience. The customers are young, local or foreign, the atmosphere a cheerful hubbub and the service quick, efficient and watchful. You are invited show your talent with a crayon on the wallpaper, and leave an artist's impression or joke for posterity. A fun place, where you take your friends like you'd go to a show.

RENDEZ-VOUS DES CHAUFFEURS 11, rue des Portes-Blanches © **01 42 64 04 17**. *M° Marcadet-Poissonniers. Closed Sunday and Monday. Open 12 noon- 2.30pm and 7.30pm-11pm. Set menus 10 € and 14 €. A la carte 20 €.* Coco and Christian have replaced Jeannot, but this 'taxi drivers' meeting place' has not lost any of its charm. You still find the good bistrot cooking and convivial spirit of an earlier Paris, that existed here when the G7 company taxi drivers made it their cantine (their garage was just opposite). A new starter + main course or main course + dessert formula at 10 € has been thought up, proving that new ideas also have their place. The cook prepares some excellent dishes hard to find elsewhere, including a few ever-popular classics: herring fillet in oil, grilled mackerel with white butter sauce and steamed potatoes, and à la carte, veal liver deglazed with raspberry vinegar and shallots, and the house speciality, sautéd veal kidneys with Madeira. Recipes made with fresh market produce, that change every day, are also available. As for the desserts, they are all home made: tarts, rice pudding gâteau and chocolate mousse. Culinary simplicity puts a chef's talent to the test - and this one has plenty of it. Don't miss this rendez-vous.

19e arrondissement

AU BŒUF COURONNE 188, avenue Jean-Jaurès © **01 42 39 94 44**. *M° Porte-de-Pantin. Open every day 12 noon-3pm and 7pm-midnight. A la carte 45 € to 50 € without drinks, full menu 32 € (aperitif, starter, main course, cheese, dessert, drink and coffee). Parking valet service.* This restaurant used to be La Villette covered meat market, and certain aspects of the decor, like the period tiles, recall that era. Nowadays it is a bourgeois Parisian bistrot, with wide-backed chairs and faultless, professional service. The owner is a former butcher, so top-quality meat is a house tradition. *Blonde d'Aquitaine* is his favourite beef, served in 300g slabs, rump, and 350g sirloin steaks sautéd *à la mignonnette,* or grilled beef rib for 2 (1.2 kg!). The vegetables come in generous helpings too: charlotte potato gratin, French fries or souffléd potatoes. There are even starters to suit big appetites, like marrow bone with Guérande salt, calf's head and tongue salad, *sauce ravigote*, and slice of calf's liver pan-cooked English-style. Three fish dishes feature on the menu as well. Pure happiness! The wines are all you could hope for: good, affordable bottles, with *grands crus* for the specialists.

MON ONCLE LE VIGNERON 2, rue Pradier © **01 42 00 43 30.** *M° Pyrénées, Belleville or Buttes-Chaumont. Open every day, except Thursday and Sunday, 11am-2.30pm and from 6pm, bookings only. Call early afternoon at the latest for the same evening. Around 25 €.* This restaurant is a real table d'hôtes, like you find in the provinces. The owner makes sure everyone will be there at the same time, so as to simplify the job. Kitchen and dining-room are thrown together open-plan, the tables are big, and everyone rubs shoulders. The starter is often a salad (everyone shares) with 'the best vinaigrette in Paris'. Then ratatouille which is more like piperade, and a duck leg confit. The menu changes every day, depending on the chef's mood and the number of guests to feed. There is a 5 € cork duty on the wines. No bordeaux or burgundy, or grands crus, but no plonk either.

20e arrondissement

LES ALLOBROGES 71, rue des Grands-Champs © **01 43 73 40 00**. *M° Maraîchers or Buzenval. Annual closing August and one week at Easter. Closed Sunday and Monday. Set menus 19 € to 32 €.* Consistent standards, pleasant atmosphere, plenty of regulars encouraging you to have faith in this apparently simple cooking, based on fresh market ingredients. In fact, the chef pays great attention to precision cooking, product quality and presentation. Examples of his skill are the raw salmon with rock salt, aubergine caviar with tarragon, dry cepe risotto, fried monkfish, braised lamb knuckle, garlic conserved in olive oil, and bread pudding and soft white cheese sorbet, composing a great menu at 32 €. Energetic service; good cellar.

L'AMARANTE 233, rue des Pyrénées © **01 43 66 40 21**. *M° Gambetta. Open every day except Sunday; and Monday and Saturday lunchtimes. Formulas 8.50 € and 10 € (lunchtime), and 17 € (evenings).* Here, French and Greek cooking come together in a very happy marriage, on a menu with a number of Mediterranean specialities such as stuffed vine leaves, tzatziki, grilled peppers and Provençal-style gambas. To round off your meal, why not try a honey and almond pastry?

DISNEYLAND

DISNEY RESORT PARIS **Marne-la-Vallée © 01 60 30 53 05 (bookings)**. *www.disneylandparis.com . Open every day: 9am-8pm, except 31 December, 9am-1am. Admission: ticket 1 day, 1 park: adult 49 € , 3-11s 39 € ; (opening hours vary: enquiries at the entry gate) 1 day, 2 parks: adult 49 € , 3-11s 39 €* . Call for information about package prices with hotel included. The Disney Resort is Europe's first tourist destination. It caters for all the family, from its comfy hotels right next to the park to the magical attractions inside. Even three days seem too short to see everything! You'll have heard about Main Street, the castle, the roller-coasters (Space Mountain; not for the faint-hearted), the steamboat trip and the Haunted House. You can also go down a mine on a little train, or be shipwrecked on the Caribbean Pirates' beach. Visit the Small World with its singing, dancing dolls, Peter Pan and Pinocchio, among them. Above all, don't miss the parades of Disney characters.

The Walt Disney Studio Park is just as exciting. Find out what happens on a film set, and how stunts are set up, or take a trip on the Rock'n'Roller ride if you've the stomach for it! This new park is aimed at teenagers and adults, and despite its sharp shows and fabulous film sets, the queues are often shorter than in the other park (you can visit attractions at set times with the Pass system). The Disney village surrounds the park, with its shops, restaurants and disco where you can party all night. You'll be welcome any time of year; Mickey Mouse with his childhood magic is just the same, come rain or shine.

FONTAINEBLEAU, BARBIZON, MILLY-LA-FORET

Not so far from the Parisian hurly-burly, you're suddenly in the countryside, among thick forests, fields of cereal crops, farms and historic castles.

Fontainebleau

Château, forest and rocks are equally famous. Successive Kings of France turned the 12thc. hunting-lodge into the palace it is today, and in François 1's reign (1515-1547), the town grew with it. The kings adored hunting and riding, and established an equestrian tradition in the area. Napoleon 1 founded the Centre Sportif d'Equitation Militaire to train top riders, and it is still there, part of the Senarmont riding school in the English garden. There have been riding competitions and displays of excellence in the hippodrome since Napoleon III.

CHATEAU DE FONTAINEBLEAU **Musée et Domaine nationaux © 01 60 71 50 70**. *www.musee-chateau-fontainebleau.fr. Museum open every day except Tuesday: 9.30am-5pm (6pm in summer). Gardens open every day (free). Admission: under-18s free, adults 5.50 € , concessions 4 € . Free activity booklet for children.* Home of French kings from the 12th to 19thc., the chateau is now a national museum. Philippe le Bel was born here, then Louis X and Louis XIII. Louis XIV signed the Edict of Nantes here in 1685, and Napoleon said goodbye to his Old Guard before going into exile. You'll be amazed by the splendid interior with its huge ballroom, royal apartments and Marie-Antoinette's boudoir. Diane's gallery is 80m long, and the Galerie des Assiettes displays 128 Sèvres china plates, while a Chinese museum holds booty won in the 1860 war. Louis XV has his very own wing. Outside, in the 84-hectare park with its canal, there have been carp in the pond since 1605.

MUSEE NAPOLEONIEN D'ART ET D'HISTOIRE MILITAIRE 88 rue Saint-Honore ✆ 01 60 74 64 89. *Closed Sundays, Mondays and public holidays. Open 2pm-5.30pmGuided tours for groups (even mornings by appointment). Admission: over-12s 2.50 The park is open 15 March-15 November, 10am-7pm, and 16 November-14 March, 10am-5pm.* France's third-biggest military museum houses a rich variety of uniforms, weapons and equipment (3,500 pieces) from different periods: Napoleon's Grande Armée, the Second Empire and the Colonial or African Army.

FONTAINEBLEAU FOREST. The forest stretches out around the castle, criss-crossed by roads, hikers and joggers (there are plenty of car parks to facilitate access). It covers 25,000 hectares, and its lime-and-sandstone floor rises in hillocks and dislocated rocky plateaux forming grottos you can visit. In Fontainebleau they talk of 'gorges', with names like the Wolves' Gorge. Fans of rock-climbing love it. This used to be called the Bière forest. The trees are mostly leafy: oaks, beeches, Scotch firs and laricios. They grow in clusters, or in straight avenues, and their beauty and variety drew painters in the 19th century, and famous walkers like Ch,teaubriand, George Sand and Maupassant, as well as fashionable Paris. 300 km of forest paths have been marked out for tourists and leisure purposes, an initiative already taken back in the 19th century. The forest has 11 million visitors a year, with very few hikers or climbers, and thousands of Parisians every weekend. Originally the king alone had the right to hunt here, for the forest is lived-in. Stags, deer, wild boar, foxes, badgers and squirrels are now protected species, but a hunt still takes place in winter. As for the great storm of 1999, it brought down 500,000 trees - but don't worry, there are 7 million left! This massacre closed all the paths, but they are now open again.

Barbizon

In the 19thc., many nature-loving painters settled here. About 60 landscape painters stayed in the village from 1849 to 1875, at Mr and Mrs Ganne's inn. Narcisse Diaz de la Pena, Theodore Rousseau, Camille Corot and Jean-François Millet were known as the 'colorists'. Today, the Ganne's inn is the Barbizon School Municipal Museum, where the gay atmosphere of those days pervades the painted walls and furniture. In the village high street, 18 art galleries display original works. Jean-François Millet's house and workshop is also here.

MUSEE MUNICIPAL DE L'ECOLE DE BARBIZON 92, Grande-Rue ✆ 01 60 66 22 27. *Closed Tuesday. Open 1 April-11 November: 10am-12.30pm and 2pm-6pm; 11 November-1 April: 10am-12.30pm and 2pm-5pm. Under-12s free.* This museum has been housed in the Ganne inn, in the town centre, since 1995. The ground floor has been kept as it was between 1830 and 1870 when the artists stayed here; they even painted and restored some of its furniture. Madame Ganne's grocery, the officers' and the painters' dining rooms are here. On the first floor, you discover this Impressionist school; two rooms contain paintings, sketches, drawings and engravings by Corot, Rousseau, Jacques Dupré, Diaz, Chaigneau and Gassies. The museum shows a 30-minute film, does guided tours and holds temporary exhibitions in Theodore Rousseau's house.

MAISON ATELIER DE THEODORE ROUSSEAU 55, Grande-Rue ✆ 01 60 66 22 38. *Open every day except Tuesday: 10am-12.30pm and 2pm-5pm. Admission: adult 4 €.* This museum annex is now open, 200m from the Ganne inn, in a little house at the bottom of a garden. Theodore Rousseau (1816-1867) lived here from 1847 until his death, in two low-ceilinged rooms and a barn converted into a studio by the painter, where he invited his friends; the place later became a chapel. On the ground floor, documents, paintings, engravings and photos recall the artist's life and work. On the first floor, his works are exhibited, as are Rosa Bonheur's (oils and bronzes lent to the museum).

ATELIER DE JEAN-FRAN«OIS MILLET Grande-Rue ✆ 01 60 66 21 55. *Open every day except Tuesday and Sunday, 10am-12.30pm and 2pm-5pm. Admission free.* Behind the half-open door lies Jean-François Millet's universe. This classical painter (1814-1875) settled in Barbizon in 1849, and led an austere life, drawn to rustic scenes and humble characters (Le Repos des moissonneurs, Les Glaneuses). The big room exhibits the work of local contemporary artists, which is for sale. Ask Marie-France, who'll tell you all about the place.

Milly-la-Forêt

PARC NATUREL REGIONAL DU GATINAIS FRANCAIS Maison du Parc - Hôtel de Velle - Place de la République ✆ 01 64 98 73 93. The 37th and latest park in the Paris region, between the forests of Rambouillet and Fontainebleau. You can admire the mills, ch,teaux, estates and their properties, churches and chapels dotting the landscapes spread around the Essonnes and Ecole valleys.

CHAPELLE SAINT BLAISE DES SIMPLES ✆ **01 64 98 84 94**. *Open Easter to All Saints, every day except Tuesday: 10am-12 noon and 2.30pm-6pm. November to Easter: open Saturday, Sunday and public holidays, 10.15 am-12 noon and 2pm-5pm.* Sole remains of the 12thc. maladrerie or hospice, surrounded by medicinal plants. Jean Cocteau is buried in the chapel, and he decorated the walls inside on the theme of simples (the plant kind).

LE CYCLOP ✆ **01 64 98 83 17**. Open Saturday and Sunday from May to late October. Admission: adult 6 €. Le Cyclop, probably the greatest work of Swiss sculptor Jean Tinguely, who died in 1991, is also one of the twentieth century's most impressive works. Standing in the heart of the forest like some strange, outsized totem, this mechanical monster is 23m high and contains 300 tonnes of iron. It was built over 25 years in total secret, with a dozen or so artists including Niki de Saint Phalle, Cesar, Arman and Spoerri contributing to the project. The result is a cyclops head glittering with mirrors, whose staircases, walkways and mezzanines entice the visitor into an enchanted universe.

Courances

CHATEAU ✆ **01 64 98 41 18**. *Closed 1 November-1 April, Monday-Friday. Open Saturday, Sunday and public holidays: 2pm-6.30pm. Admission: Ch,teau and park 8 € ; park only 4.12 € . Under-12s free.* This Louis XIII-style ch,teau nestled in one of the region's finest parks is furnished and lived-in. Look out for a beautiful collection of plates in the dining-room, curious 16thc. tapestries with monkey motifs, and the library. Outside, a horseshoe staircase (copy of the one at Fontainebleau) was added in the 19thc. Le Nôtre's influence can be seen in the park, with its host of ornamental ponds, canals and waterfalls fed by 17 springs. An Anglo-Japanese garden from the 1930s adds an exotic touch.

HAUTS-DE-SEINE

La Défense

© Iconotec.com / Alain Bernard

La Défense

A monument commemorating the defence of Paris in 1871 gave this quarter its name. In 1956, a project was adopted to create a business and residential sector close to Paris, taking in the towns of Puteaux, Courbevoie and Nanterre. The skyscrapers – Manhattan, GAN, Roussel Nobel and Fiat towers – give it a futuristic look. The site has good transport links (RER and SNCF).

GRANDE ARCHE Parvis de la Défense ✆ **01 49 07 27 57**. *Open 10am-7pm in winter, until 8pm in summer. M° or RER Grande Arche de la Defense. Open every day : 10am-7pm, 1 October-30 March; 9.30am-11pm, 1 April-30 September 5until 6.30pm Sunday & Monday). Admission 8 € , concessions 6.50 €* . Otto von Spreckelsen's contemporary monument is a technological masterpiece. In the heart of this contemporary business quarter, it offers a unique view of Paris from 110m up, and also houses exhibitions.

Rueil-Malmaison

The 17th-c. château is known for its Napoleonic connections: from 1801 to 1809, affairs of state were conducted here just as much as in Paris, with meetings, receptions, balls and concerts. Joséphine took refuge here after her repudiation in 1809, until her death in 1814, and Napoleon spent a few days here after Elba. His secretary reported that he was as happy in the Malmaison gardens as on a battlefield. Empress Eugénie created the first Consulate and Empire museum here. The park is pleasant to walk in; notice the Marengo cedar, planted in honour of that victory. Saint Pierre-Saint Paul Church (16thc.) and the Petite Malmaison are also worth seeing, as is the Richelieu estate with its superb park.

MUSEE NATIONAL DES CHATEAUX DE MALMAISON ET BOIS PREAU Avenue du Ch,teau de la Malmaison ✆ 01 41 29 05 55. *Open every day except Tuesday: 10am-5.45pm (weekend 6.15pm). Winter 10am-12.30pm and 1.30pm-5.15pm (weekend 5.45pm) Admission: adult 4.50 €.* Discover the intimate life of Napoleon Bonaparte and Joséphine de Beauharnais. Official receptions, concerts and balls were held here, and the Code Civil and Legion d'Honneur were thought up in the library and council room. Divorced from the Emperor in 1809, Josephine redecorated the ch,teau: flower arrangements, 'troubadour' paintings, delicate pieces of furniture and other feminine objects recall this era. The room where she died is on the first floor. The ch,teau is now a National Museum.

CHATEAU DE LA PETITE MALMAISON 229 bis, av. Napoléon Bonaparte ✆ 01 47 32 02 02. *www.mairie-rueilmalmaison.fr.* Joséphine had this superb building put up by Jean-Marie Morel, as part of the Malmaison estate. It contained hothouses, for she loved plants. The site is still private, holding seasonal and thematic exhibitions.

SAINT PIERRE-SAINT PAUL CHURCH Place de l'Eglise. Restored after a donation from Napoleon III. Joséphine's white marble tomb is on the right of the chancel; she poses in court dress, recalling David's Sacre. There is a mausoleum dedicated to her uncle, the Governor of Martinique, and on the left, Queen Hortense's tomb. The 16thc. Florentine organ, one of the finest in France, was also a gift from Napoleon III.

Sceaux

PARC DE SCEAUX. Louis XIV's Finance Minister Colbert bought the estate in the 17thc; Le Nôtre designed the garden. This prestigious property with its 19thc. ch,teau, orangerie and Grand Canal was bought by the department in 1971, and is now a classic example of a formal garden.

Sèvres

MANUFACTURE NATIONALE DE CERAMIQUE ✆ 01 46 29 22 00. *Open to visitors on request.* M° Pont-de-Sèvres. Louis XV and Mme de Pompadour had a china factory founded in 1740, at Vincennes. This was transferred to Sèvres in 1756, and attached to the Crown in 1759. The factory is still turning out china, now mainly for the State, but as the quality is high, it attracts both French and foreign collectors.

MUSEE NATIONAL DE LA CERAMIQUE Place de la Manufacture ✆ 01 41 14 04 20. *Admission : 4 € concessions 2.60 € (every day for the 18-25s and Sundays for everyone). Closed on Tuesdays.* Famous for its delicate bleu de Sèvres ceramic, the museum was created in the early 19thc. by Alexandre Brongniart, manager of the town's china factory. Among other striking pieces are some Turkish ceramics, Italian majolica and Renaissance porcelain from Faenza, Florence, Sienna and Venice. A reconstituted apothecary's contains some European china masterpieces.

SAINT-DENIS, FROM THE BASILICA TO THE GRAND STADIUM

Saint-Denis, in the northern suburbs of Paris (department 93) hides a fascinating history, going back centuries before 1998 and the building of the Grand Stade for the Football World Cup, to the French Kings' Basilica.

BASILICA 1, rue de la Légion d'Honneur ✆ 01 53 40 60 89. *www.monum.fr. Tombs: 10am-6.15pm and public holidays, 12 noon-5.15pm. Closed 1 January, 1 May and 25 December, and during some services. Admission: adult 6.10 €.* Designed by Abbot Suger between 1137 and 1144 and finished during the reign of Saint Louis, the basilica contains the sepulchres of the French Kings, from Clovis to Louis XVIII. 70 tombs and recumbent statues, 46 kings, 32 queens, 63 princes and princesses and 10 of the kingdom's VIPs were buried here, until the revolutionaries attacked this symbol of monarchy, destroying the tombs and throwing the bodies into a common grave. In 1817, Louis XVIII had the Kings' bones inhumed in the crypt, and the bodies of Louis XVI and Marie-Antoinette brought from the Madeleine cemetery, restoring the Basilica to its former role. It has been lit up at nighfall every evening since 1998, the lighting taking on the colours of the stained glass windows and projecting them onto the façade.

STADE DE FRANCE ZAC du Cornillon Nord ✆ 0 892 700 900/01 55 93 00 45 (for groups). *www.stadedefrance.com. Open every day (if no events programmed). Hour-long guided tours leave every hour. Admission: adult 10 €, under-12s 7 €, under-6s free.* This is one of the third millennium's architectural wonders, put up for the 1998 football World Cup. Built in 31 months, opened on 28 January 1998, the Stadium measures 270x230m, and is 35m high. 80,000 spectators can watch football and rugby; 105,000 can attend shows and concerts.

LE BOURGET

Bourget airfield was first used in 1914, and quickly grew into a civil and military airport. On 8 May 1927, Nungesser and Coli took off in their Oiseau Bleu for America, but disappeared before reaching the American coast. During the night of 21 to 22 May, however, Charles Lindbergh landed here in his Spirit of Saint Louis having made the first-ever New York-Paris crossing. Costes and Bellonte made the crossing in the other direction for the first time in September 1930 aboard the Point d'Interrogation. Since the opening of Roissy-Charles de Gaulle airport, Le Bourget has been kept for private and business flights.

MUSEE DE L'AIR ET DE L'ESPACE ✆ 01 49 92 70 62. *Paris Airport www.mae.org. Open 10am-6pm from 1 April-30 September. Closes at 5pm from 1 October. Admission 7 €.* The story of human flight.

LE TEMPS DES BALLONS. In this hangar, you can learn how hot-air balloons conquered the sky. Pilatre de Rozier and d'Arlandes had the idea in 1783; a model of their balloon commemorates the experiment. Sadly, the inventors lost their lives while crossing the Channel. The hot-air balloon was used by the army for observing enemy lines, or transporting mail during the Franco-Prussian War of 1870. It later became the airship; a Zeppelin nacelle can be viewed here.

GRANDE GALERIE. The beginning of aviation; first gliders (1879) and first planes. The 14-18 War speeded up aeronautical development, and the first airborne combats took place, with Guynemer's Spad VII and Rene Fonck's Spad XIII.

- **HALL B**. Here, you find World War II planes: the Free French Airforce's Spitfire MK 16 and the Normandie-Niemen squadron's YAK 3.
- **HALL C**. Some post-war aeroplane prototypes (Nord 1500 Griffon, Leduc 010) and the first jet planes. Post-war French airforce and aerobatics planes, and the first space rockets (with a reproduction Sputnik) are exhibited in the other halls. Outside, there's a 45m model Ariane and a Concorde. Every 2 years, the Salon International de l'Aeronautique et de l'Espace is held here.

SAINT-GERMAIN-EN-LAYE

The Kings of France lived in this charming town, until Louis XIV discovered Versailles.

MUSEE DES ARCHEOLOGIES NATIONALES Château - Place Charles de Gaulle ✆ 01 39 10 13 00. *www.musee-antiquitesnationale.fr. Open every day except Tuesday: 9am-5.15pm. From 1 May to 30 September, Saturday, Sunday and public holidays: 10am-6.15pm. Admission: adult 4 €, under-25s 2.60 €.* Napoleon III created this museum to display Celtic and Gallo-Roman antiquities, as a means of saving the Kings of France's ancestral ch,teau from ruin. It has since grown to include other archeological collections, from prehistory to Charlemagne. It contains fine prehistoric art, carved and sculpted bones and stone, including the famous 22,000-year-old Brassempouy Lady, in mammoth ivory. Don't miss the menhirs, solid gold pieces from the Bronze Age, traditional Celtic gods, Gallo-Roman Saint-Romain-en-Gal mosaic depicting the Roman calendar of agricultural labour and Merovingian jewellery found in Saint Denis Basilica.

MUSEE CLAUDE DEBUSSY 38, rue au Pain ✆ 01 34 51 05 12. *Open Tuesday-Friday: 2pm-5.30pm November-February; 2pm-6pm March-October; Saturday 10am-12.30pm and 2pm-6pm. Closed public holidays. Admission free.* The great composer was born here on 22 August 1862. Music fans will find his works in the auditorium on the 2nd floor. Debussy's life unfolds via his personal effects and documents, and his taste in poetry, painting and literature.

TERRACE. Access from the château park every day from 8am-9.30pm in summer (until 5pm in winter). Le Nôtre designed green spaces for both Ch,teaux, Vieux and Neuf; the 2.5kmx30m terrace completed his work. Fine view over the west of Paris.

Marly-le-Roi

FORET DE MARLY. The forest was inhabited in Gallo-Roman times, and the Kings of France later hunted here. many of the forest roads are open to traffic, and there are paths laid out for walkers, runners (Marly, Louveciennes and Rocquencourt) and horseriders. You can park at the Etoile Magnifique, Carrefour des Curieux and Carrefour Royal.

MUSEE PROMENADE DE MARLY-LE-ROI Louveciennes ✆ 01 39 69 06 26. *www.mairie-louveciennes.fr/v_musee.htm. Access A13, then N186. Open every day except Monday and Tuesday: 2pm-6pm. Closed public holidays. Go through the 'Royal Gate' into the park. Admission: 3.05 €. Guided tours for groups by appointment (lasts 1hr).* Discover Marly in the 17th and 18th centuries, with the ch,teau's history. It was Louis XIVth's country residence; Saint-Simon said 'Louis XIV built Versailles for the French Court, and Marly for his friends'. You can also learn about the Marly 'machine', which supplied the Versailles fountains with Seine water, and its development.

Saint-Germain-en-Laye, the castle

Port-Marly

The Impressionists liked this place for its boatmen and lively village activity focussed on the river Seine, which often flooded the houses and inns alongside. Alfred Sisley and Camille Pissaro were captivated by the quays, the barges, washerwomen and early industry. The place still reflects their paintings.

CHATEAU DES LIONS 13, av. Simon Vouet ✆ 01 39 58 80 58. The 17thc. Ch,teau des Lions houses Port-Marly Town Hall, the finest room being the Salle des Mariages. It was designed by Dorigny, one of Simon Vouet's pupils. Vouet (1590-1649) was Louis XIII's painter, known in England, Turkey and Rome (where he contributed to the decoration of Saint Peter Basilica). He inspired a generation of later painters.

CHATEAU DE MONTE-CRISTO Maison d'Alexandre Dumas - N 13 ✆ 01 39 16 49 49. *www.mairie-marlyleroi.fr. Open 1 April-1 November, Tuesday-Friday: 10am-12.30pm and 2pm-6pm, Saturdays, Sundays and public-holidays; 10am-6pm. 2 November-30 March, Sunday: 2pm-5pm. Closed Monday. Admission: 5 €. Guided tours Sunday 6.50 €.* A two-storey neo-Renaissance ch,teau with turrets, pinnacles, terraces and a Moorish salon, set in an English park! Beside it, Alexandre Dumas worked in peace in his Ch,teau d'If mansion. This fantasy is a listed historic monument: as the author himself said, 'Here, I have a reduced earthly Paradise'. Visitors are offered a guided tour and educational games (group bookings in advance).

SEINE-ET-MARNE

East of Paris, the Seine-et-Marne department is both urban and rural, with varied landscapes that inspired the Impressionists.

Chelles and the Marne banks

From the late 19th to mid-20thc. the banks of the Marne were busy with river craft and leisure activity: the guingettes, popular restaurants at the water's edge where Parisians came at weekends to eat, drink and dance, date from this period. After 1865, the Chelles canal (Vaires-sur-Marne to Neuilly-sue-Marne) allowed barges to pass where they had previously been stopped by the river depth. Start your trip on foot, from Auguste-Prevost Quay, and take the avenue des Iles-Mortes. Look out for the former guingette site, the place where the Marne flooded in 1910, a ruined mill burned down twice in 1881 and 1895, the Iles-Mortes, sanctuary for 31 bird species, a floating bridge...there's plenty to see.

Coulommiers

This pleasant town in Brie country boasts the ruins of the Duchess of Longueville's ch,teau, an old prison converted into the town library, a fine Italian-style theatre finished in 1905, the Capucins Park, with a museum of local history in Notre Dame des Anges Church, and several bridges over the Morin; you can watch the boats go underneath. On the town heights is the 13th-15thc. Knights Templars Order, building, now a cultural centre promoting medieval arts. Don't miss it!

COMMANDERIE DES TEMPLIERS Association Atagrif - Ville haute ✆ 01 64 65 08 61. *www.perso.wanadoo.fr/commanderie.templiers. 2pm-7pm weekdays, 10am-7pm Sundays, July & August. Closed inde mi déc à fin January. February-March, open weekends only. April-November, open Wednesdays-Sundays, every day in July & August until 7pm. Admission: adult 5 €, 8-16s 2 €, under-8s free.* Up on the heights of Coulommiers, this is a complete set of 13th and 15thc. buildings; chapel, chapter-house, barn, main building and cellars can be visited with a guide. You can learn all about the life and history of the Temple Order in the exhibition, and visit the medieval garden with its 250 plants from May to October.

Crécy-la-Chapelle

Two villages in one, in fact: La Chapelle-sous-Crécy and Crécy-en-Brie merged in 1972. In the old village, the belfry, the washing-places and old bridges follow one another along the brasset (originally a defensive ditch strengthened with walls and towers) planted with maples, as far as the 14thc. collegiate church. Crécy winds around other brassets and towers, where you find tanners' houses. This tower-encircled fortress was put up on marshland in the 9th and 10thc. In the 12th and 13thc., the town produced skins, wool, fabric and wine, and traded in wood and cattle.

Ferrières-en-Brie

CHATEAU DE FERRIERES AND PARK Rue de la Rucherie ✆ 01 64 66 31 25. *Open 2pm-7pm (5pm in winter). Admission: adult 8 € (castle + park + Museum of the Imagination).* A perfect illustration of the Second Empire's taste for the fantastic. This beautiful and prestigious residence, built for the Rothschild family between 1855 and 1859 on Fouche's 'maisons des champs' (he was Napoleon 1st's Police Minister), is as typical an example of Second Empire architecture as the Opera Garnier in Paris. The chateau is four -sided (each side measures 65m), and has two stories with a square tower in each corner. Architect Joseph Paxton who designed the Crystal Palace in London drew up the plans, and Etienne Lami decorated the interior in Venetian style, painting several ceilings himself. The huge landscaped park designed by Paxton is worth a visit on its own merits (though only 132 ha. are left of the original 3,000 ha. of grounds) and walkers can admire a number of rare tree species from all over the world.

Guermantes

CHATEAU DE GUERMANTES ✆ 01 64 30 00 94. *www.chateaudeguermantes.com Open 1 April-1 November: 2pm-6pm (last tour leaves at 5.30pm), Saturdays, Sundays and public holidays. Admission 5 € and 4 € for groups, advance bookings only. Guided tours.* Private residence, still lived-in. This Louis XIII ch,teau is made of brick and stone, built from 1630-1700. Inside is the long gallery known as the Belle-Inutile, with its panelling, pictures, mirrors, chandeliers and a ceiling painted by one of Delacroix's pupils in 1866. Marcel Proust's heroine of the same name is a principal character in Remembrance of Things Past.

Jouarre

In the heart of the Petit Morin valley, it has a historic past; the abbey and Merovingian crypts at La Ferté-sous-Jouarre and Saint-Cyr-sur Morin, the Pays de Seine-et-Marne Museum, the author Pierre Mac Orlan's house and the echoes of past centuries in the countryside. There are plenty of craftsmen and local producers here too.

MUSEE BRIARD Rue de la Tour ✆ 01 60 22 64 54. *Open every day except Tuesday: 10am-12 noon and 2pm-6pm (5pm in winter). Guided tours.* Above the Merovingian crypt, this museum houses paintings, engravings, furniture, tools and utensils, all from Brie! Don't miss the period rooms, and characters in period costumes, making it easy to imagine local peasant life in olden times.

Meaux

The importance of this busy town with its ancient episcopal centre goes back to the Middle Ages.

SAINT ETIENNE CATHEDRAL. Begun in 1180, finished in 1540, the different architectural styles harmonize well. The cathedral is original; luminous and delicate with high vaults. The sides, where you come in, are 31.5m high at the transept crossing. Admire the 14thc. stained glass Crucifixion window and the organ, a jewel of its kind, built by the talented Valeran de Heman in 1627.

CITE EPISCOPALE. The cathedral, Bishops' Palace, Old Chapter-House and Bossuet garden make up this close, reserved for the Bishop and Cathedral canons with their personnel, both lay and religious.

MUSEE BOSSUET Bishops' Palace ✆ 01 64 34 84 45. *Open every day in season, except Tuesday: 10am-12 noon and 2pm-6pm and Monday, Tuesday and Sunday morning from 1 October-31 March. Admission: adult 3 €.* The Palace was built at the foot of the cathedral, between the 12th and 17thc. Its striking architecture - Gothic rooms, a 17thc. Synod room and 18thc. panelled apartments - and old paintings by Le Nain, Rigaud, Bon de Boulogne, De Troy and Senelle next to Millet, Gerome, Daubigny and Courbet make it worth a visit.

BISHOPS' PALACE. The oldest part of the Bishops' Palace dates back to 1160: the early Gothic chapter house and some Romanesque bits. Don't miss the huge Synod room on the first floor.

Melun

The first Capetians lived on this island inside a loop of the Seine. Now the department's prefecture, Melun keeps its past alive in some fine monuments.

NOTRE DAME COLLEGIATE CHURCH Ile-de-Melun. *Open Saturdays and Sundays: 3pm-6pm, 17 June-16 September.* Built by Robert the Pious from 1020 to 1031. It is Romanesque, with a lot of reworking, especially from the 12th to 16th centuries.

SAINT ASPAIS CHURCH Rue Saint-Aspais. *Open 8am-7pm.* Often called a 'shapeless and bizarre' church, it does have an irregular style reflected in the light filtering through the rose window. The high, 16thc. stained glass windows are on Biblical themes.

MUSEE DE MELUN Hôtel de la Vicomte - 4, quai de la Courtille ✆ 01 64 79 77 70. *Open Monday-Saturday, 2pm-6pm, and the first Sunday of every month. Closed Tuesday. Admission: adult 1.50 €.* Discover the town's history through its Gallo-Roman remains and a graphic collection on the town's monuments. The museum contains 16th-century sculptures and bronzes, 17thc. still-ifes and 19thc. paintings and ceramic.

PONT DE MAINCY. Cézanne stayed at Melun (2, place de la Prefecture) and painted this little bridge across the Almont in 1880. The painting is in the Musee d'Orsay, the bridge on the borders of Melun and Maincy.

Montereau

CHATEAU-LE-VIEUX. Two main buildings at right-angles overlooking the Yonne quay are all that remain of the medieval building once covering the square, with Napoleon's statue and two others either side of the Grande Rue de Saint-Maurice. Currently undergoing renovation work, this building will overlook the yachting harbour.

NOTRE DAME ET SAINT LOUP COLLEGIATE CHURCH. Close to the confluence, Flamboyant Gothic and Renaissance mingle in one church. The Archbishop of Sens, Michel de Corbeil, founded it in 1195, and it was finished in the 16thc. Outside, see the openwork staircase in tower, its solid oak doors and sculpted leaves; inside, Jean the Fearless's sword, hanging in the nave. The façades are decorated with sundials.

TAPESTRY COLLECTION Hôtel de Ville © 01 64 70 44 00. *Open every day except Saturday, by appointment.* In the Salle des Mariages and the courtroom, tapestries woven between the 16th and 19th centuries are hanging.

MUSEE DE LA FAIENCE 2, place René Cassin © 01 64 32 95 64. *Open every day except Tuesday: 10am-12 noon and 2pm-6pm. Admission: adult 3 € , under-16s free. Guided tours on weekdays by appointment. Free guided tour every first Sunday at 3pm (1hr approx).* Montereau became a china-making town in the mid-18thc. Begun as a craft, it developed into an industry, turning out highly valued models. The factory, founded in 1745, closed down in 1955, and was demolished 20 years later, but a sample of its production was painstakingly put together for a museum. This opened in 1997, with 2,400 pieces of earthenware in stock and 400 exhibited.

Moret-sur-Loing

This medieval fortified town, near Fontainebleau and on the edge of Burgundy, is known for its gates: the Porte des Amois (or Paris) facing the Porte de Bourgogne, leading into Burgundy. Sisley and Pissaro captured this symbolic architecture on canvas.

DONJON. Many famous guests stayed in this 12thc. keep, including Louis VI, Blanche de Castille, and Henri IV. The Comtesse de Moret added gardens and flowerbeds when she lived there.

NOTRE DAME CHURCH. Although building started in the 12thc. this church is essentially pure 13thc. Gothic. The 15thc. façade blends High and Flamboyant Gothic, and there are fine 13thc. transept windows. Amusing figures decorate the gallery, from the second Renaissance period.

GRANGE BATELIERE Maison Clémenceau. This thatched house on the banks of the Loing belongs to Georges Clémenceau's son. There are souvenirs and objects belonging to his father, and you are reminded of the statesman's friendship with Claude Monet and other Impressionists.

MAISON DITE DE FRANCOIS Ier Rue Grande. Go under the Town Hall porch, and admire the magnificent Renaissance front of this luxurious house built in 1527. The two original buildings were linked by a gallery over a portico. Henri IV and Duke Charles of Lorraine were invited to dine here in 1600, so the owner must have been of noble birth. The little salamander over the door links it to François I.

MAISON DE SISLEY Pres de la rue du Donjon. Alfred Sisley settled here at the corner of rues Donjon and Montmartre in 1889. The Loing valley inspired his paintings, but he was destitute for the last ten years, selling few of his pictures during his lifetime. The house is closed to the public, but there are Impressionist events and exhibitions in Moret.

Nemours

MUSEE DE LA PREHISTOIRE D'ILE-DE-FRANCE 48, avenue Etienne Dailly © 01 64 78 54 80. *Closed Tuesday and Wednesday. Open 2pm-5.30pm, also Saturday, Sunday and Monday: 10am-12 noon.* Traces of the castle's medieval past (well-preserved oratorio) can be seen despite later transformation. In the museum, you find Gallo-Roman and Merovingian pieces, religious works and popular art and traditions, with some earthenware from the Revolutionary period. There are also exhibitions of 19thc. painting and sculpture and 20thc. prints.

EGLISE SAINT JEAN BAPTISTE CHURCH. The 12thc tower base with its spire is the oldest part of this Gothic and Renaissance church.

Provins

An important centre in the Middle Ages, Provins is still a medieval town, with its ramparts, paved streets and sloping alleys. The town is listed UNESCO World Heritage.

SAINT AYOUL CHURCH Ville-Basse. The relics of Saint-Ayoul were found in the Provins Valley, and Comte Thibault III had a convent and church built in 1048, which were burned down and rebuilt in the 12th and 13thc. The portal tympanum contains bronze parts by Georges Jeanclos (1990).

GRANGE AUX DIMES Rue Saint Jean. *Open 26 March-2 November, every day: 10am-6pm (November-March, ask for information about opening times). Admission: adult 3.40 € , 5-12s 1.90 € .* This 13thc. merchant's house is one of Provins' best-kept, with its sculpted capitals and rib vaults. It was a covered market during the fairs until the late 13thc., then a tithe warehouse. Today, it houses an exhibition with scenes of medieval guild and merchant life.

CESAR TOWER © 01 64 60 26 26. *Admission: adult 3.40 €. Open from 26 March-2 November, every day: 10am-6pm (otherwise, call for information about opening times). Admission: adult 3.70 € , 5-12s 1.90 €* . Dominating the valley from its rocky spur, this 12thc. tower was built as a show of strength by the Counts of Champagne. The keep combines defence with a powerful protective role, and was watchtower, prison and refuge all at once.

UNDERGROUND PASSAGES. *Open 26 March-28 August, every day: 10am-6pm (otherwise ask for information about opening times). Admission: adult 3.70 € , 5-12s 1.90 € . Guided tours.* Originally a fullers' earth quarry, for the Provins woollen cloth industry; later a refuge, cellar and even a Secret Society meeting-place! The Freemasons left their trace in the graffiti.

Vaux-le-Vicomte

CHATEAU DE VAUX-LE-VICOMTE Maincy ✆ 01 64 14 41 90. *www.vaux-le-vicomte.com. Open every day, 19 March-13 November: 10h-18h. Candlelit visit 8pm-12pm, Saturday, 7 May-15 October, and Friday in July & August. Admission: adult 12.50 €.* Nicolas Fouquet, Louis XIV's wealthy Finance Superintendent, had this ch,teau built by the 17thc.'s great artists: architect Louis Le Vau, landscaper André Le Notre and decorator Charles Le Brun. The result is one of France's most beautiful ch,teaux, built on a terrace with a moat, above formal gardens with superb water mirrors, ornamental lakes, perspectives and the Grand Canal at the end. The kitchens of the great chef Vatel are now occupied by 40 busy wax figures, and there is a 19thc. carriage museum, also animated by models in period costume. Fouquet's pride in his social climbing led to his downfall. On 17 August 1661, after inviting Louis to a luxurious feast, he fell victim to the Sun King's jealousy at being overshadowed, was arrested and imprisoned. The King then hired the same artists to build Versailles...

CHEVREUSE VALLEY AND RAMBOUILLET FOREST

The Kings of France hunted here, and the Chevreuse Valley, now sheltering smart villas and traditional villages, has kept its past charm.

Vallée de Chevreuse

Chevreuse

CHATEAU DE LA MADELEINE Place de Luynes ✆ 01 30 52 09 09. *Open Wednesday-Saturday, 2pm-5.30pm. Sunday and public holidays, 10pm-5.30pm.* Of the five round towers and three square, two have been restored. The one on the right (14thc.) goes back to the Hundred Years' War. Go up the narrow staircase to the various rooms and terrace, with its view over the countryside. Philippe-Auguste made two visits to the 11thc. rectangular keep in the courtyard.

MAISON DU PARC NATUREL REGIONAL DE LA HAUTE VALLEE DE CHEVREUSE. Château de la Madeleine - BP 73 ✆ 01 30 52 09 09. *www.parc-naturel-chevreuse.org. Acces via N306, A6 then A10 or RER B. Open Monday-Saturday, 2pm-5.30pm, Sunday and public holidays: 10am-5pm. Closed 25 December and 1 January. Admission free.* This contemporary structure blends into the medieval castle, and its exhibition tells the story of the nature reserve, with its 24,300 hectares and 21 villages. The aim is to develop economic and agricultural activities and promote the natural and historical environment: the Madeleine, Mauvières and Breteuil ch,teaux, Coubertin and Granges de Port-Royal museums. Thickly wooded, with green valleys and striking landscapes, there are over 300km of paths marked out, and 4 *gîtes.*

Choisel

LE CHATEAU ET LES JARDINS DE BRETEUIL ✆ 01 30 52 05 02. *Park open all year, from 10am. Château open every day from 2.30pm.Admission: Ch,teau, gardens and fairytales, adult 11.50 € , children, OAPs and groups 8.50 € , gardens and fairytales 7.20 € and 5.80 € .* Part of the nature reserve, the ch,teau's 75 hectares contain forestry, ponds and magnificent formal. What makes this a truly magic place, however, are the seven Perrault fairytales (Bluebeard, Little Red Riding Hood, Puss in Boots...) in the form of tableaux with life-size wax figures, scattered through the ch,teau and park. A storyteller brings them to life for you. The Breteuil family were Charles Perrault's patrons, hence the association.

Dampierre-en-Yvelines

CHATEAU ✆ 01 30 52 53 24. *Open April-mid October. Guided tour 2pm-6pm, Sundays and public holidays. Park open 11am-6pm. Admission: adult 9.50 € , child 2 € .* Built for Colbert's son-in law, the Duc de Chevreuse. The Chateau has a water-filled moat around it, separating the two courtyards. Inside, there is a lot of 17thc. furniture; the stairwell with its trompe l'oeil paintings, and the ballroom, are 19thc. The latter has a wall-painting by Ingres, reproducing the statue of Minerva in the Parthenon.

Magny-Les-Hameaux

PORT-ROYAL-DES-CHAMPS ABBEY Route-des-Granges ✆ 01 30 43 74 93. *Access via N306 then N195. Open every day except Tuesday: 2pm-5pm; Sunday: 11am-12 noon and 2pm-5pm.* The abbey was once a great centre of religious thinking, which must have displeased Louis XIV, who had it destroyed. The ruins include a 13thc, dovecote, and can be visited. In the Granges de Port-Royal National Museum ('Petites ecoles' building) souvenirs and documents tell the story of the abbey (01 39 30 72 72). You'll notice the remains of an 11th-century keep at the back of the cemetery.

Thoiry

CHATEAU ✆ 01 34 87 40 67. *www.thoiry.tm.fr. Access via A13, A12, N12 then D76 and D11. Closed in January & February. Open October to Christmas, evry day: 2pm-5pm; Easter-late September, every day: 2pm-6pm. Admission: 6 € ; child 4.50 €* . Henri II's Treasurer Raoul Moreau, fan of the esoteric, had this 'solar house' built by Philibert de l'Orme on a magnetic fault, respecting golden section rules. The sun thus rises and sets along the axis of the façade at the solstices. In 1708, Le Nôtre's nephew and successor Claude Desgot created an optical illusion in the formal gardens. Going down the central path, the distance seems to get further away instead of closer, reversing the perspective effect.

THOIRY ZOOLOGICAL PARK ✆ 01 34 87 40 67. *Open October-Easter, every day: 10am-5pm; Easter-late September: 10am-6pm. Admission: adult 21 € , child 12.80 € . One ticket for gardens/African reserve. Advance booking only for groups of 10+.* The ch,teau grounds are a safari park, housing panthers, tigers and monkeys to be watched from the safe distance of your car. For an hour, you can observe their lifestyle in the wild, in African, North and South American habitats. Afterwards, you can stroll through the botanical and zoological gardens, where various demonstrations and shows are put on. There is an educational circuit with audio posts, and a little train to take you round in good weather, and of course snack-bars and drinks kiosks.

AFRICAN RESERVE ✆ 01 34 87 52 25. *Open 10am-5pm. Admission: 17.20 € , child 12.80 €* . Discover over 10km of safari park from behind the wheel. Most African wild animals can be seen wandering free (bears and lions from inside a security enclosure); only the humans are caged up here - in their cars.

Rambouillet

The most illustrious visitors stay here, including the President of the Republic whose summer residence has been here in the ch,teau since 1897. Foreign heads of state also stay here during official visits to France.

CHATEAU DE RAMBOUILLET ✆ 01 34 94 28 79 *www.elysee.fr/elysee/res3.htm or www.monuments-france.fr. Guided tours every day except Tuesday and when the President is in residence: 10am-11.30am and 2pm-4,30pm. Admission: adult 6.10 € , concessions 3.50 € . One ticket for Ch,teau, Laiterie and Chaumière, 6 € , concessions 5 € . Free every first Sunday.* Originally a 14thc. fortress, the castle has been in the Angennes family since 1384. As Emperor, Napoleon I stayed there often. Hunting was re-established with the Restoration, unlucky for Charles X, who abdicated here and left for exile in England on 31 July 1830. Napoleon III later transformed the abandoned castle into an Imperial Palace. From here in August 1944, General de Gaulle ordered the Division Leclerc to march on Paris. Since then, this has been a residence for foreign Heads of State visiting France. Inside, the mixture reflects this chequered past: marble, 18thc. oak panelling, and neo-classical Empire, witch formal gardens and a park housing Marie-Antoinette's dairy and the thatched building known as the Chaumière-aux-Coquillages. Only 100 of the estate's 1,000 hectares are open to the public.

LAITERIE DE LA REINE (QUEEN'S DAIRY) Parc du Château de Rambouillet ✆ 01 34 83 29 09. *Closed for renovation work (as is the Chaumière). Reopening planned during 2006.* Louis XVI created the dairy for Marie-Antoinette so she could play at shepherdesses. An ancient Greek temple shelters a statue of a nymph and the goat Amalthea, in a rockwork grotto.

ESPACE RAMBOUILLET 3, rue de Groussay ✆ 01 34 83 05 00. *Closed mid December-mid January. Open every day April-October: 9am-6pm. Admission: adult 8.50 € , child 6.50 €* . This 250-hectare park in the heart of the forest is home to deer of all kinds, wild boar and birds of prey (falcons, kestrels), which can be seen in the aviaries set up for them. From April to October, you can admire their prowess in flying demonstrations.

A WALK IN RAMBOUILLET FOREST. Amazingly varied in its flora. There are Scotch pines, spruces, waterfalls, pools and rocks, including a genuine dolmen; you'll find plenty of fresh air and surprises on your walk. From the Cernay ponds, take the Marechaux Path across the site where millstone and sandstone were quarried until 1930. A former quarryman brings its history and geology to life, and tells you about the late 19thc. landscape painters inspired by its scenery. Wear stout boots, and keep to the marked-out path. The walk takes 2-3 hours.

VAL D'OISE

Asnières-sur-Oise

ABBAYE DE ROYAUMONT ✆ **01 30 35 59 70**. *www.royaumont.com. Open 10am-6pm. Admission: adult 5.50 € , concessions 4 € , family 16 € , under-7s free.* The best-preserved Cistercian monastery in the Ile de France was founded by Saint Louis, with the proceeds from the sale of royal gold and jewels, and some of his family is buried here. The church was destroyed during the Revolution, but the ruins - part of a staircase in a single turret - are spectacular. The 18thc. farm and dairy are behind, and you can see the monks' living quarters and the kitchens. Objects and pictures can be viewed in the museum, including a fine 14thc. sculpture of a Virgin breastfeeding her Child. The austere refectory is in good condition, and it has a Romanesque organ (reproduction of a medieval instrument), used when concerts are given. You then enter the biggest Cistercian cloister in France, as the monks did when they went to services. Two exhibitions house a collection of religious art and medieval musical instruments. and the foundation's remarkable library contains rare works.

Ecouen

A quiet little town, with burnished tiled roofs and a famous ch,teau.

FORET D'ECOUEN. The history of this former hunting estate is linked to the ch,teau. Spreading across the sides of a small hill, it has been a National Forest since the Revolution and contains mainly oaks, chestnuts and other leafy trees. Enjoy relaxing here after visiting the museum.

MUSEE DE LA RENAISSANCE Au Ch,teau ✆ **01 34 38 38 50**. *Open every day except Tuesday, 9.30am-12.30pm and 2pm-5.15pm. Admission: 4 €* . Built from 1538-1555 by the Connétable de France, one of the most powerful people in the kingdom. Great artists of the period worked on it: Jean Goujon decorated the exterior and Bernard Palissy designed the stained glass; it is typical of mid-16thc. French architecture. The National Renaissance Museum began with Renaissance collections from the Cluny Museum in Paris. Its most beautiful treasure is the David and Bathsheba hanging which takes up most of the first floor. The imagination and refinement of the Renaissance humanist universe is revealed through the scientific and art objects, goldsmiths' work, painted enamels, stained glass ceramics, crockery, weapons, sculptures, paintings and tiles exhibited here.

Enghien-les-Bains

This spa town and gambling stronghold developed during the 19thc., although its sulphurous springs were discovered before the Revolution. The Duke of Orléans, Philippe-Egalité and Queen Hortense were among Enghien's first patrons. Elegant villas were built around the navigable lake, and a casino added in 1878.

French Vexin

North of Paris, between the winding Seine and Beauvais, there are woods, green valleys, cereal crops and pasture divided up by hedges like in nearby Normandy.

PARC NATUREL REGIONAL DU VEXIN FRANCAIS Maison du Parc ✆ **01 34 66 15 10 / 0810 16 40 45 (No Azur).** *www.pnr-vexin-francais.fr.* Here, there are marshes, reeds, limestone hillsides and forests containing 1,227 plant species (60 protected nationally). Some well-known sites are to be found in the reserve, like beautiful La Roche-Guyon, Auvers-sur-Oise, linked with Van Gogh, the Villarceaux estate and other picturesque villages. Hikers will discover the French Vexin's natural environment and history along the many marked-out paths.

Auvers-sur-Oise

Along the Oise, the typical little rural houses and fields bordering the river once attracted artists looking for new landscapes. The village is famous because Van Gogh, Charles Daubigny and Dr Gachet, doctor and art-lover, made it an Impressionist centre. Cézanne, Pissarro, Corot and Renoir all stayed here. Here too, Van Gogh feverishly painted his last pictures, before expiring in the arms of his brother Theo. Today, 19 sites marked with a picture show where the artists put up their easels.

MAISON DE VAN GOGH Place de la Mairie ✆ 01 30 36 60 60. *Open Wednesday-Sunday 10am-6pm. Admission 5 €* . Guided tour of Van Gogh's bedroom. A 12-min film is shown.

CHATEAU D'AUVERS Rue de Lery ✆ 01 34 48 48 45. *Open every day except Monday: 10.30am-4.30pm, April-September until 6pm. Admission: 10,50 € , child 6.10 €* . Travel back to Impressionist times with this 17thc. castle's voyage of discovery, both educational and fun. Your infrared headphones take you through 18 tableaux reconstructing those days: the café-concert, and Sunday train journey to the country or seaside, etc. 500 Impressionist paintings are projected during the tour, and a 3-D film, 'Le regard de Vincent' (Through Vincent's Eyes) tells the story of the painter's life at Auvers.

THE CHURCH. Immortalised by Van Gogh (of course), the church, with its square 12thc. belltower, is built on a headland.

MAISON DU DOCTEUR GACHET 78, rue du Docteur-Gachet. The Impressionists' friend invited Pissaro, Sisley and Renoir to Auvers, and in May 1890, Van Gogh, who threw himself into a frenzy of work. He painted the doctor's house both outside and inside; some of the best known of his works.

Chaussy

DOMAINE DE VILLARCEAUX ✆ 01 34 67 74 33. Estate open Easter-October, afternoons only, closed Monday. Admission free. Guided tours only. This treasure of local heritage (State-run) has gardens illustrating all periods, from the Middle Ages to the 18thc. The Renaissance buildings once housed Ninon de l'Enclos and Françoise Scarron. The castle contains a fine furniture collection. Don't miss the view from the terraces over the gardens below, with their waterfalls and ornamental pools supplied from 32 springs.

Maisons-Laffitte

Built for the Governor of Versailles and Saint-Germain, this castle had its hour when the Kings of France came to stay, creating a racecourse. Its fortunes were reversed when its owner, banker Laffitte, went bankrupt and had to destroy part of the stables to build houses in the park (hence the name). Horse-lovers mustn't miss it.

CHATEAU DE MAISONS ✆ 01 39 62 01 49. *www.monuments-france.fr. Open every day except Tuesday: 10am-12 noon and 1.30pm-5pm. Admission: 6.50 €* . Built by Mansart in 1641 for Rene de Longueil, Louis XIV's future Finance Superintendent, this is a fine example of French classical architecture. The sculptor Sarrazin decorated the hall; Bellanger and Lhuillier designed the beautiful dining-room. The children carved on the main staircase symbolise War and Peace, Love and Marriage, Arts and Sciences (Philippe de Buyster, Gilles Guerin and Sarrazin). In the Royal Apartments on the first floor, the 'mirror cabinet' is a round boudoir whose panelling and parquet are inlaid with wood, bone and tin. The 19thc. entrance gates came from Ch,teau de Mailly in Picardy.

LES CHEVAUX. The most important horse-training centre in France is here in the park. To watch the sessions, take av. Desaix to the forest edge, but make sure you get there at daybreak, when canters and gallops take place along the forest tracks between the railway line and Route de Poissy.

MUSEE DU CHEVAL DE COURSE Château ✆ 01 39 62 01 49. *Open 10am-12,30pm and 2pm-6pm (5pm in winter). Admission: 6.10 €* . Your visit to the 17thc. ch,teau should include the Racehorse Museum. The story of racing from its origins to the present day is illustrated with models, works of art and horse-related objects. You learn that the first French races took place in 1830, in the prairies along the Seine. Maisons-Laffitte is the oldest Parisian racecourse. A photo exhibition, 'A racehorse's life, from stud farm to racecourse' was opened in November 2004.

Mantes-la-Jolie

NOTRE DAME COLLEGIATE CHURCH Rue de l'eglise ✆ 01 34 77 10 30. *Open every day from 8am-8pm. Guided tours on request, Sunday afternoon: 3pm-6pm.* This beautiful church, with its two Romanesque towers, contains Saint-Louis' font (he was christened here in 1214). His statue, by Albert Patrisse, is in front of the church.

La Roche-Guyon

This picturesque little town, at the foot of a cliff, runs gently down to the Seine.

CHATEAU ✆ 01 34 79 74 42. *Open mid-March-mid-November: 10am-6pm. Admission 6.10 €* . There is a troglodytic castle where the first lords lived, a keep on the clifftop and other buildings below. The

Renaissance living-quarters backs onto the cliff. In the 18thc. the Duke of Rochefoucauld added stables, courtyard, a gate bearing his arms and a monumental staircase.

Montmorency

This town's strategic position on the hillside made it a Middle Ages stronghold, and it was sacked and pillaged by the English during the Hundred Years' War. Several famous names are associated with the town, including the painter Charles Lebrun, Richard Wagner, Madame de Sevigne, Michelet, actress Rachel, Pissarro and Jean-Jacques Rousseau, who stayed in this peaceful place for quite some time.

La Roche-Guyon

This ancient city on the top of a chalk cliff lies at the foot of a ruined 12thc. fortress, and has been guarding the Seine valley for over 10 centuries. The houses with their sloping slate or tile roofs - some extremely old - are dotted around in the green landscape, recalling the Vexin of bygone days. The remains include some examples of original homes, such as typical cave dwellings.

CHATEAU © **01 34 79 74 42**. *Open mid-March to late November : 10am-6pm. Admission: adult 7.50 €.* Includes the cave dwelling-type castle where the first lords made their home, the keep on the top of the cliff, and another collection of buildings below. The Renaissance hall and living quarters are built up against the cliff. In the 18thc. the Duc de La Rochefoucauld added stables, a main courtyard with its surrounding buildings, an entrance bearing the La Rochefoucauld coat of arms on the gate, and a monumental staircase.

VERSAILLES

Louis XIV's 'whim'; a dazzling château for a Sun King. He enlarged the existing Louis XIII hunting-lodge, had gardens laid out and a 'New Town' built. The Court settled around the château and the King; Versailles the Splendid was born, and much-copied. Successive kings added to it; the town went on growing. Today, you can visit the National Estate of Versailles and Trianon, or the town, quarter by quarter, with a lecturer-guide to tell you all about this unique architectural model. Back to the Grande Epoque.

Some of the town's monuments are closed to the public: the Recollets Convent, Ministries of War and Foreign Affairs, Great Stables and Hôtel du Barry (Chamber of Commerce) or Mme de Pompadour's mansion, now the Tourist Office.

DOMAINE NATIONAL DE VERSAILLES © **01 30 83 78 00**. *www.chateau versailles.fr. Open every day except Monday: 9am (Trianons 12 noon)-6.30pm (5.30pm 1 October-30 April). Choose from 3 ways to see the ch,teau, gardens and Grand and Petit Trianon: by yourself, with an audioguide (headphones) or lecturer-guide. Admission: over-18s 7.50 € , under-18s free, 5.30 € concessions. This includes the Grand Apartments, but you pay extra for other visits: Trianons +5 € , gardens +3 €* . The gardens should be free of charge from 2006. Royal residence until the Revolution, the Sun King's ch,teau was designed by Le Vau, decorated by Le Brun, and landscaped by Le Nôtre. The king's and queen's apartments and the Galerie des Glaces on the first floor are the finest parts. With the guided tour, you can also visit the Dauphin and Dauphine's apartments, the Queen's small apartment, the chapel and the opera house on the ground floor, as well as Mme du Barry and Mme de Pompadour's apartments and the Revolution, Consulat, Empire and 19thc. rooms on the second floor. In 1687, Louis XIV had the Grand Trianon built (of marble) to relax in; some plays of the period are put on here in summer. The Petit Trianon is more bucolic, and dates back to the Ancien Regime. Don't miss the Queen's hamlet, a kind of model farm where Marie-Antoinette played shepherdesses. These buildings are set in an immense park laid out by Le Nôtre from 1661, and which also contains the fountains, ornamental lakes and and waterfalls.

CHATEAU DE VERSAILLES © **01 30 83 78 00.** *www.Chateauversailles.fr. Open every day except Monday.* Car park at Porte-Saint-Antoine, at the park entrance, bd Saint-Antoine. Louis XIII did not know he was building the foundations of such a creation when he had his hunting-lodge put up on the site by Philibert Le Roy in 1623. His son transformed and enlarged it, installing his Court and the French government. Louis Le Vau directed the work; François d'Orbay took over on his death in 1670. The result was spectacular, but the Sun-King went on improving his estate. He had the Galerie des Glaces, the North and South Wings, the Orangerie, the Stables and the Grand Commun added. Jules Hedouin-Mansart was now supervising the building. After Louis XIV's death, Versailles continued growing; Louis XV and XVI put in new, decorated apartments and an opera house, in 1770. It thus takes more than a day to see all the Sun-King's dreamworld. You'll have to choose.

GRAND TRIANON © **01 30 83 78 00**. Louis XIV bought Trianon village to extend his estate, and promptly destroyed it in order to build a house to relax in, far from the burden of rank and protocol. The apartments, emptied during the Revolution, are now furnished in Empire style.

PETIT TRIANON ✆ **01 30 83 78 00**. Built between 1763 and 1768 by Anges-Jacques Gabriel for Louis XV and Mme de Pompadour. An English garden was added, and Marie-Antoinette's hameau de la Reine, recalling the gentle way of life in the last years of the monarchy.

JARDINS DU CHATEAU ✆ **01 30 83 78 00.** *www.chateauversailles.fr. Open all year, weather permitting, 7am (winter 8am)-sunset (5.30pm-9.30pm).* Laid out by Le Nôtre from 1661-1700. He flattened and drained the land, traced perspectives, woods, canals and flowerbeds to create a model, geometric formal garden, with its bronze and marble statues, ornamental lakes and fountains. Louis XIV loved these, and the gardeners would whistle as he approached, to set the fountains going. Apollo the Sun God is represented with his chariot on the great lake (Grand Bassin). Beyond these gardens lies the Great Park, with the Grand Canal.

SALLE DU JEU DE PAUME 1, rue du Jeu de Paume ✆ **01 30 83 77 88**. *Open May-September, weekends: 2pm-5pm. Admission free.* Ancestor of the tennis-court, this room is still as it was in 1686. The high walls are topped by a wooden structure containing windows, protected from the balls with nets. It is partly lined with a covered spectators' gallery. On 20 June 1789, the members of the Third Estate, representing the people, swore an oath 'not to separate until they had given France a constitution'. On the wall, a huge painting by Luc-Olivier Merson recalls David's famous fresco of the Jeu de Paume oath, and a statue of Bailly has been put up to mark the spot where he read it out.

ACADEMIE DU SPECTACLE EQUESTRE Manège de la Grande Ecurie du Château de Versailles Avenue Rockfeller ✆ **01 39 02 07 14**. *www.academieduspectacleequestre.com. From Tuesday to Friday, 9am-1pm and Saturday, Sunday and public holidays, 11am-2pm, you can watch the horses' training sessions (dressage) and visit the stables. Adult: 7 € , groups of 10+, 5.50 € . On Saturday, Sunday and public holidays, 2.15pm-3pm, the Academy puts on a short show, with a carrousel, musical interlude and equestrian improvisation and a visit to the stables. 15 € adults, 12 € groups of minimum 20 people.*

Waterworks

Fountains, ornamental lakes and and waterfalls are animated and synchronised to music during the Grandes Eaux Musicales that take place on Sundays and public holidays from May to late September: 3.30pm to 5pm. It took 22 years to develop the hydraulics, using the 'machine de Marly' to rechannel Seine waters towards Versailles. There is a 'grande fête de nuit' on certain summer Saturdays around the bassin de Neptune, with the illuminated Grandes Eaux, ballets and fireworks.

You can take out a boat for 4 on the lake (boat hire 01 39 66 97 66). In the park, a small brasserie offers a menu at 23 (pizzas, salads and a dish of the day); you can eat on the shady terrace opposite € the Grand Canal (La Flotille, 01 39 51 41 58, open all year). In the park, there are some venerable old trees like the Japanese Sophora planted in the reign of Louis XV and restored using tree surgery techniques.

Bougival

DATCHA D'YVAN TOURGUENIEV Musée Tourgueniev - 16, rue Tourgueniev ✆ **01 45 77 87 12.** *Access N13 or A86. Open Sundays: 10am-6pm (mid-March-mid-December) and weekdays for groups, by appointment. Admission: 4.75 € . Guided tours, Monday-Saturday, 1 hour.* Half-dacha, half-Swiss chalet, Turgeniev's country residence with its striped walls houses his souvenirs, personal effects and library, as well as period furniture and the death chamber reconstituted by the Ecole Boulle. The influential Russian writer invited his friends here; you can see the very piano played by Brahms and Liszt.

Elancourt (Saint-Quentin-en-Yvelines)

FRANCE MINIATURE 25, route du Mesnil ✆ **01 30 16 16 30**. *www.franceminiature.com. Open 2 April-2 November; 10am-6pm. July, August and weekends in June: 10am-7pm. Admission (includes park and Miniature Palace) : adult 14.50 €* . Located in new town Saint Quentin-en-Yvelines, this display of France's greatest sites and monuments in miniature (1/30th) will amuse all the family. On a giant map of the country, over 159 lanscapes are represented, 140 monuments, the longest outdoor miniature rail network, 60,000 characters, 20,000 dwarf trees, 15 rivers, 2 hectares of sea, over 100 boats, even windsurfers! There is also a motorway in motion, Montmartre funicular and a funfair. In this Miniature Palace, 50 places have been created in great detail by Dan Ohlmann, master of miniature art. The display is organised according to four themes: 'Gastronomy and Local Produce', 'French History', 'Stories and Legends' and 'Celebrities and Current Affairs'.

FOOD AND DRINK

The Parisian region recruits culinary talent and collects regional specialities from all over France, but it does have its own: the *champignon de Paris* (button mushroom), Argenteuil asparagus, and fruit from the Val d'Oise orchards, not forgetting the famous Brie cheeses.

Argenteuil asparagus

Until the 1950's, this was the capital of asparagus, which the Arabs probably brought to France. Louis XIV liked it, and his gardener planted it in hothouses, so it would grow all year round.

Cherries

The Montmorency is a small late cherry, not very sweet, its colour ranging from pinky-orange to light red. It goes well with game and duck breasts, and is used to make alcohol *(excellent cerise à l'eau-de-vie)*

Moutarde de Meaux

This mustard is made *à l'ancienne* from whole grains. The aromatic extract comes from the water's action on the grains and not from recuperating the oil as with other mustards. There is no fermentation after the ingredients have been mixed; the mustard is put into enamelled stoneware pots, glazed, sealed with red wax and corked. 85% of production (1.5 million pots a year) is exported.

Brie cheeses

This was the people's cheese before the kings discovered it, sold at medieval fairs in Meaux and Coulommiers. Unpasteurised cow's milk gives the soft texture, containing 45% fat; the cheese is then matured for 4 to 7 weeks. The annual Best Brie competition in Meaux and the Coulommiers International Wine and Cheese Fair in April attract gastronomy fans.

Brie de Meaux

Already mentioned in Charlemagne's day, this ancient cheese was voted top in 1814 by participants at the Vienna Congress (including Talleyrand). It has had an AOC since 1980. The big 'cartwheel' is 35cm in diameter and 2.5cm thick, soft-textured inside its white crust with red traces; it matures slowly for one-and-a-half months.

Brie de Melun

Not quite the same! This Brie is only 30cm in diameter, 3cm thick, with a stronger smell and taste. Extended coagulation (20 hours compared to only one) makes the difference. It is moulded with a ladle rather than a spatula. The Brie de Melun also gained its AOC in 1980. Fans say it should be eaten between July and December.

Brie de Coulommiers

Known simply as Coulommiers, and more popular today, this cheese is made from pasteurised or unpasteurised milk, is smaller and has a very rich, almondy flavour. It contains more fat, which explains its creamy texture. To be eaten in summer and autumn.

Cheese

Hotels & Restaurants

HAUTS-DE-SEINE

Issy-les-Moulineaux

L'ILE Parc île Saint-Germain 170, quai de Stalingrad ✆ 01 41 09 99 99. RER Issy-Val-de-Seine. *Open lunchtime and evenings every day. Lunch formula 19 €. A la carte around 50 €.* This former powder magazine dates back to Napoleon III, and is well worth trying for the setting, the welcome and of course the food. The place is all open space, glass and metal, with paintings on the walls and a fine staircase up to the first floor with its view of the park. There is a crackling log fire in winter, and birds sing on the terrace in summer; this is the countryside right next to Paris. The cooking is a blend of tradition and renewal, with fresh ingredients, of course, and an inpressive choice. Seafood, a variety of starters, pasta and vegetable dishes, fish and meat, and both crunchy and melting desserts. Don't forget to bring the kids at weekends and on public holidays, when the children's menu at 18 € is accompanied by make-up and a clown show. Explosive!

ISSY-GUINGUETTE 113, avenue de Verdun ✆ 01 46 62 04 27. *Open Monday to Friday, closed Monday evening. Set menus at 24 € and 31 €.* This restaurant in its quiet alley far from the main street is well worth the visit for its terrace, set high up above the Issy vineyards. You can taste traditional recipes like pan-fried veal piccata (thin escalopes) with Roquefort cream or dried duck breast with Guérande salt, with a chestnut *bavarois* in Baileys sauce to finish. Voluptuous! In winter, settled cosily by the fireside, this seems like a hidden paradise.

LA MANUFACTURE 20, esplanade Manufacture ✆ 01 40 93 08 98. M° Corentin-Celton. *Open every day from 12 noon to 2.30pm and 7.30pm to 10.30pm, except Saturday lunchtime and all day Sunday. Menu-carte 26 € and 32 €.* La Manufacture specialises in traditional French cuisine, and is housed in a big American-style loft, where you can taste a variety of seasonal dishes - apart from the pig's ears, and salmon in herb vinaigrette that are always available. Baked cod with potato crumbs and braised beef cheek in a Graves wine sauce with split pea purée are among the main courses, with brioche bread-pudding style and its caramel for dessert.

LES TERRASSES DE ST GERMAIN 3-5, boulevard des Iles ✆ 01 41 08 88 78. *Open every day, from 12 noon to 3pm and 7pm to 11pm. Set menus 13.80 € and 18.80 €. Different carte lunchtime and evening.* This is a business people's restaurant, now under new management and looking to innovate. Paintings ere exhibited on the walls, and regularly renewed to alter the atmosphere. There is a wide choice of dishes on the menu, many blending French and Oriental flavours in a most original way. On the more classic side, you have cod in a herb crust served with *julienne* vegetables, thyme and lemon, and a beef rib with foie gras sauce. The delicious desserts include vanilla cream with Nutella and speculoos, rum baba and mascarpone and vanilla cream, and are hugely successful. Concert evenings are planned from time to time. Friendly welcome.

Levallois-Perret

EVERGREEN HOTEL 8, place Georges Pompidou ✆ 01 47 58 88 89 M° Pont de Levallois *Rooms from 170 €, breakfast 19 €. Sauna and fitness centre.* Located on the edge of Paris in a quiet, leafy square, this 4-star hotel attracts demanding business and tourist customers. The 334 rooms and suites are fully equipped, and very comfortable. The Canton Palace restaurant offers Chinese gastronomy: alternatively, you can enjoy international *cuisine* in the Laurel Cafe with its glass ceiling. A shuttle is at your disposal, which gets you to central Paris in 15 minutes. Meeting rooms available.

SEINE-ET-MARNE

Barbizon

HOSTELLERIE DE LA CLE D'OR * 73, Grande-Rue ✆ 01 60 66 40 96** *Website: www.hotelcledor.com Hotel open all year, 15 rooms from 73 € to 93 €. Restaurant closed Sunday evening from 31 October to 31 March, set menus from 29 €.* This is the ideal place to come if you're looking for a more sophisticated kind of charm. This old inn located in Barbizon centre has a shady courtyard and a flower-filled park, both very pleasant in the sunny season. There is also an elegant dining room, and comfortable rooms at garden level or on the first floor. Traditional cuisine is served with a smile.

Château-Landon

LE CHAPEAU ROUGE ** 2, place du Marché ✆ 01 64 29 30 52. *Closed Friday. 11 single and double rooms 42 €, set menus from 12 €.* You find Le Chapeau Rouge in an imposing old coaching inn, located in the centre of Chateau-Landon. Inside, the dining room is all ancient stonework and vaults, with massive doors but plenty of light to admire the generous helping on your plate by. Spacious and comfortable rooms with shower or bath, and WC.

Disneyland Paris

DISNEY RESORT PARIS Marne-la-Vallée ✆ 01 60 30 60 30 *Website: www.disneylandparis.com. Theme park open all year round, except 31 December from 9am to 1am.* Various all-in prices available, according to the season and the length of your stay. Three hotels built round a lake extend a warm welcome to families: New Port with its open spaces, Canada, which boasts a great aquatic centre and log fires, and New York, the last word in luxury, complete with skating rink, fitness centre and endless corridors. The Disney Hotel is located just near the park entrance, for the luckiest guests. One restaurant in particular stands out from all the fast food outlets: the California Grill, which serves excellent red meats in a rather chic ambience.

Echouboulains

AUBERGE SAINTE-CATHERINE 22, rue Madame Renoux-Prieux ✆ 01 64 20 99 43. *Website: www.auberge-sainte-catherine.com. This farm hostelry is open all year (advance booking) at weekends, during the week only for groups of 10 or more. Set menus from 21.20 €. A night + breakfast is 47 € for one , 50 € for two.* Mme Dufour welcomes you in these attractive farm buildings, where home cooking makes the most of local produce: brie tourte, duck with apples or peaches, roast farm lamb, beef sauté with beer, chicken with mustard and fruit tart to finish. Generous helpings.

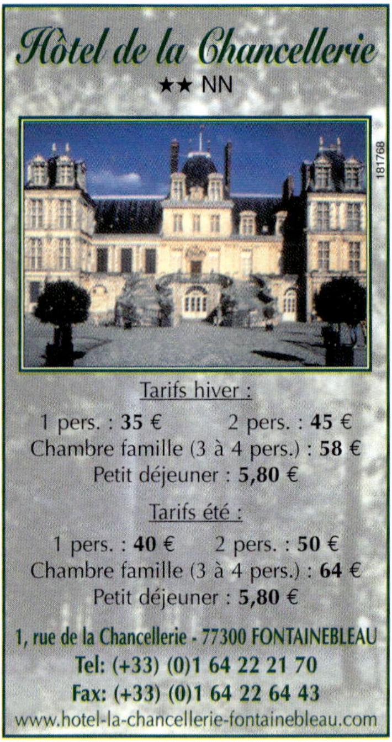

Fontainebleau

HOTEL DE LA CHANCELLERIE ** 1, rue de la Chancellerie ✆ 01 64 22 21 70 *Website: www.hotel-la-chancellerie-fontainebleau.com* Open seven days a week. 25 rooms 50 €. Breakfast 5.50 €. This hotel in the former Chancellerie buildings is located in the town centre, a stone's throw from the post office and chateau. Its 25 rooms are comfortable, quiet and well equipped, and you soon feel quite at home. Downstairs through the French doors, a lounge corner has been fitted out in the reception area.

Meaux

LA GRIGNOTIERE 36, rue de la Sablonnière ✆ 01 64 34 21 48. *Fax 01 64 33 93 93.* Closed Tuesday, Wednesday and Saturday lunchtime. Set menus 28 € and 38 €. You can be sure of enjoying gastronomic cuisine in this friendly little dining room, with mirrors round the walls to reflect the attractively presented, top-quality dishes being served. You get a smiling welcome, and an open log fire both lunchtime and evenings in winter.

Moret-sur-Loing

LE RELAIS DE PONT LOUP 14, rue du Peintre Sisley ✆ 01 60 70 43 05. *Closed Sunday evening and Monday. Set menus from 36 €.* What a beautiful inn! Inside, the brick walls and exposed beams set off a marvellous fireplace complete with roasting spit. In summer, you can eat among greenery in the peaceful garden running down to the Loing. Add delicate, original cooking with Challans poultry roasted on the spit, several fish specialities, salmon gravelax, half-a-dozen Burgundy snails house-style, scallops with ginger, farm pigeon and Marie Lucie's nougat ice cream to finish, and you have a recipe for success.

Provins

LA TABLE SAINT-JEAN 3, rue Saint-Jean ✆ 01 64 08 96 77. *Fax : 01 60 58 40 42. Closed Tuesday evening and Wednesday. Fast formula 15.50 € weekday lunchtimes. Set menus 17.50 €, 23 € and 29 €.* You find this pretty half-timbered house with its flowery terrace opposite the Grange aux Dimes. Inside, 3 dining rooms are decorated in 13thc. style, and old-fashioned cooking is served. The restaurant offers several traditional specialities like pork knuckle a l'ancienne, pork filet mignon, home-smoked salmon, andouillette royale, home made foie gras, monkfish baked with green pepper, and bass fillet with chanterelles, with a home made dessert like the *assiette des gourmands* to finish. A warm and friendly welcome completes the picture.

LA VOULZIE **7, rue Victor-Arnoul ✆ 01 64 00 54 44.** *Closed Sunday. Set menus: Menu Merdrot 12 €. Menu Durteint 17 €. Menu Voulzie 24 €.* Hidden behind an attractive apple-green facade, this excellent restaurant is run by a likeable couple, Angélique Vaugouin and Laurent Lhermitte. They serve top-quality traditional *cuisine* in a cosy setting with exposed beams. You can taste their smoked salmon, foie gras and terrines, all home made, while salmon kebab and scallops with blue poppy seed, grouper fillet in morel sauce, bass fillet with crayfish, duck breast with wild mushrooms, calf's head in ravigote sauce, pork knuckle Lyon-style, rump steak with a Meaux brie sauce feature on the menu, with delicious home made profiteroles for dessert. Friendly welcome, attentive service.

Réau

LA MARE AU DIABLE **Parc du Plessis-Picard - RN6 ✆ 01 64 10 20 90.** *Website: www.lamareaudiable.fr. Closed Sunday evening, Monday and Tuesday evening. Three formulas available, 25 €, 30 € and 35 €. Menus a la carte 42 € and 47 €.* This restaurant cosily housed in a 15thc. Briard manor is quite a special place, and you'll love the rustic setting and flower-filled terrace almost (but not quite) as much as its gastronomic cuisine. What could be more romantic than a candlelit meal beside a big log fire? The 17ha. grounds boast a swimming pool, tennis courts and riding stables.

Saint-Pierre-les-Nemours

LES ROCHES **1, avenue Léopold-Pelletier ✆ 01 64 29 70 05 / 01 64 28 06 81.** *Email : hotelrestaurant_lesroches@hotmail.com. 12 rooms, 3 junior suites and 1 suite. Market produce menu 26 € (3 courses). Set menu 38 € (four courses). Surprise menu (chef's suggestion, for 2 people or more) 56 €. A la carte 50 €. Tearoom. Trendy bar.* Located at the foot of the Greau rocks, this hotel-restaurant is 100 years old and has a magnificent dining room. The chef has won several awards (Meilleur Ouvrier de France, Euro Toques) and offers traditional French gastronomic cuisine prepared with fresh ingredients. His menus feature a foie gras trilogy made with fresh herbs and spiced wine, smoked salmon and haddock with foamy dill cream and Chinese spice, bass with crispy skin and citrus fruits, red mullet *mille-feuille* with Provence piperade and a warm hazelnut vinaigrette, stuffed quail with cepes and balsamic vinegar juice, and part-smoked beef fillet with its bone-marrow parmentier. Game in season. Goat's cheese with small smoked duck breast kebabs or livarot with cider caramel add style to the cheeseboard. To finish, the dark, milk and white chocolate *galet* and coffee ice cream with a macaroon is delicious.Terrace in summer. Piano bar. Seminars, weddings and receptions.

Serris

CHEZ GASTON - LE PETIT PAVE 9, route de Meaux ✆ 01 60 43 02 07. *Dish of the day around 10 €.* Don't miss this restaurant! Marguerite the cow lords it over the entrance, attracting the punters. Inside you find a bistrot setting recalling the 1950s Halles (the great Parisian food market) with a slate on the wall and regional dishes simmering away like in grandmother's day. Gaston is a former butcher, so there isn't much he doesn't know about meat, though he now runs the kitchens with son Tony. You can rediscover beef bourguignon, blanquette and pot-au-feu, or taste meat cooked at your table on a potence (bracket): 1kg for 4 people. Evelyne welcomes you warmly and the service is smooth and attentive. Covered terrace, open in summer.

SEINE-SAINT-DENIS

Aulnay-sous-Bois

L'AUBERGE DES SAINTS-PERES 212, avenue de Nonneville ✆ 01 48 66 62 11. Jean-Claude Cahagnet is the department's only chef with a star. Now 40, he has kept his youthful looks and enthusiasm for the culinary arts, having started as an apprentice because he didn't like school and didn't care for any other manual trades. He quickly fell in love with his job, discovered he had plenty of talent, and was appointed chef at the Relais des gardes in Meudon, then named *Maitre Cuisinier de France* early on in his career. His cooking is creative, delicate and full of flavour.

Bagnolet

LE BAL PERDU 2, rue Charles-Graindorge ✆ 01 43 62 93 37. *M° Gallieni, bus 76. Open every day from 12 noon to 3.30pm and 7.30pm to 10.30pm. A la carte 25 €.*

This is a magic place, all bright colours, mosaic floor tiles and Bohemian poetry. Downstairs, the bar hosts concerts; upstairs in the restaurant the busy waitresses always have a smile. A bell rings in the open kitchen when the dishes are ready, and they are worth the wait, being delicious, well presented and generously served. The cooking is inventive, including finely prepared mixed salads like the *assiette vegetarienne* and the *salade perigourdine,* fish - monkfish osso bucco grandmother's way, asparagus tips and tagliatelli - meat dishes such as *poulet chicha* and soy sauce, pasta at 8 € (lunchtime only) and *flambed* pancakes with calvados and cider caramel, or the ever-popular chocolate fondant, for dessert. Mint tea is a good idea to round off the meal.

Saint-Ouen

LE SOLEIL 109, avenue Michelet ✆ 01 40 10 08 08. *Monday to Wednesday, open lunchtime only. Thursday to Saturday, open lunchtime and evenings. Closed Sunday evening. A la carte from 40 € to 60 €.*Good restaurants are rare round the Saint-Ouen flea markets. This one near the Biron market is a real pleasure, attracting secondhand dealers and buyers alike They get a friendly welcome from boss Louis-Jacques Renucci, who serves traditional French cuisine in a setting furnished and decorated by the flea market. Marinated anchovy fillets, tuna with Puy lentils, veal blanquette à l'ancienne, rib steak with marrowbone sauce, and Basque-style farm chicken feature on his menu. The wine list is well composed, with bottles under 18 € for the more modest budgets.

VAL-D'OISE

Auvers-sur-Oise

AUBERGE RAVOUX MAISON DE VAN GOGH 52, rue du Général-De-Gaulle ✆ 01 30 36 60 63 *Closed Sunday and Monday evening. Set menus from 24 € to 30 €.* Van Gogh spent the last days of his life in this inn with its late 19thc. decor, and you can visit the room where he died. The place is also a restaurant serving excellent traditional *cuisine*, however; the dishes appear at the table in cast-iron cooking pots. The 7-hour Ravoux leg of lamb is exceptionally tender, and the Montmorency duck comes with real Montmorency cherries. If these don't tempt you, try the fish waterzooi, a typical Northern French dish. You must come here at least once, for the memories and for the cooking.

Cormeilles-en-Vexin

RELAIS SAINTE-JEANNE Route de Marines ✆ 01 34 66 61 . *Fax : 01 34 66 40 31. Open Tuesday to Saturday. Set menus from 32 € - weekday lunchtimes only - to 60 € (including wine). A la carte around 50 €.* You find excellent gastronomic cuisine using only top-quality ingredients, in this restaurant. Monsieur Cagna prepares traditional dishes like the Landes soufflé sweetbread escalopes with seasonal mushrooms, Loctudy scampi in gaspacho with saffron tomatoes, and casseroled Breton pigeon with conserved carrots, and the juice reduced with port. The dining room is all elegant stonework, exposed beams and flowers. Classic cellar with affordable crus.

Ermont-Sannois

HOTEL CAMPANILE Rue des Loges ✆ 01 34 13 79 57 *Open all year, 44 rooms from 57 € weekdays. Breakfast 7 €* Close to Paris, in a busy little town. The owners welcome you warmly and make sure you have a pleasant stay. All the rooms are comfortable, and equipped with bathroom. The restaurant has a buffet formula for starters and desserts, with dishes of the day at 12.70 €. A seminar room is available for business trips and meetings. Private car park at guests' disposal. Pets accepted.

Herblay

HOTEL PREMIERE CLASSE Rue René Coty ✆ 01 39 31 18 14 *Open all year, 82 rooms, singles and doubles from 37 €. Breakfast 4.50 €.* Close to CDG airport, this is an ideal place for business trips or holiday stopovers. Warm welcome, comfortable fully-equipped rooms, attractive prices. Car park at guests' disposal. Free Internet access available et reception. Pets accepted.

L'Isle-Adam

LE TROUBADOUR 23, quai de l'Oise ✆ 01 34 08 10 34. *Website : www.letroubadour.fr. Open seven days a week. Set menus 28 €. A la carte menus around 40 €. Disabled access.* This restaurant on the edge of the Oise nestles in that green setting beloved of the Impressionists. The cuisine is traditional and the decor sophisticated, in shades of pink. Once a 1930s guinguette known as 'Chez ma Cousine', Le Troubadour also boasts magnificent gardens complete with barrel organ. Herve Marais and Jacques Fournier in the kitchens will rustle up a lamb *navarin* (stew) with apples and pears, a seafood platter (different sizes for different budgets), 7-hour lamb knuckle-joint with gratin dauphinois potatoes, bouchot mussel, bass, pikeperch, prunes in Armagnac - whatever suits the season, in fact.

VAL-DE-MARNE

Le Perreux-sur-Marne

LES MAGNOLIAS 48, avenue de Bry ✆ 01 48 72 47 43 *Website : www.lesmagnolias.com. Closed Sunday and Monday, Saturday lunchtime and in August. Set menus from 36 € to 78 €.* Eating in Jean Chauvel's restaurant is rather like going on a gastronomic pilgrimage. Spiced cheese *consommé*, and quail barigoule with Guerande salt, or a sardine maze, served with sangria and citrus tuile biscuits to start, followed by a salmon 'pastoral design' with ginger, a curious 'optical illusion' comprising a giant French bean buried in grilled almonds, and Mexican veal aligot with a 'vagabond sombrero' of spiced tomatoes in virgin oil, and to finish, a surprising almond milk speculoos club sandwich with amarena biscuits 'encased in plastic' instead of the typical vanilla millefeuille sort of thing. Jean Chauvel is slightly crazy, but extremely talented, despite one or two miscalculations in the cooking times and perhaps rather too many flavours, and his attitude is most refreshing. His prices too.

Vincennes

LE CYGNE 22, avenue de Paris ✆ 01 43 28 03 96. M° Château-de-Vincennes et RER A Vincennes. *Set menus 31 € et 44 €. A la carte around 50 €. Closed Sunday evening and Monday.* This charming restuarant facing the chateau has been open all year for over 20 years. It serves gastronomic cuisine - foie gras, scallops - with an excellent wine list. There is a reception room, a dining room with glass roof and an attractive little garden for summer customers. The upstairs dining room is air conditioned.

LA RIGADELLE 26, rue de Montreuil ✆ 01 43 28 04 2 *RER A Vincennes. Closed Sunday and Monday. Formula 22 €, set menus 31 € and 49 €. A la carte 45 €.* M. Verrechia looks after the kitchen, and Mlle Métayer the dining room, which is rather small, but very neat, with a conventional decor (salmon-coloured walls and tablecloths). It's a pleasant place for lunch with family and friends. The classic cooking has some Italian touches, the chef's grandfather having emigrated from Monte Cassino to start a new life in the east of Paris. Specialities include fresh fish straight from the Breton ports, fish tartare with Zubrowka vodka, seafood blanquette and pan-fried Dublin Bay prawns. In summer, vegetables, herbs and olive oil have pride of place on the menu.

HOTEL SAINT-LOUIS* 2, bis rue Robert Giraudineau ✆ 01 43 74 16 78.** *M° Château-de-Vincennes ou RER A Vincennes. Fax 01 43 74 16 49. Rooms from 106 € to 144 €. Breakfast 12 €.* This 3-star hotel opposite the château and Vincennes woods is known for its high standards of comfort and privileged location. The rooms are equipped with a bath complete with wave machine, and shower with side jets, air-conditioning, direct phone line, mini-bar and satellite TV. There is a fax and photocopying service available, a 50 sqm. meeting room, a lift and a car park nearby. You can leave valuables in safe-deposit. Certain rooms have disabled access and fittings. Small pets welcome on payment of an 8 € supplement. The hotel was entirely renovated in 2005.

YVELINES

Bougival

LE CAMELIA 7, quai Georges-Clemenceau ✆ 01 39 18 36 06. *Fax 01 39 18 00 25. Closed Sunday and Monday in August. Last orders taken at 10.30pm. Set menus 42 € and 68 €. A la carte.* Elisabeth and Thierry Conte took over this beautiful restaurant in its opulent setting in 2001. They have recently been awarded a Michelin star, and you have to agree they deserve it, once you've experienced the top-quality food and great service from an energetic and professional team. Long may it continue!

CHEZ CLEMENT 15 bis, quai Rennequin ✆ 01 30 78 20 00. 15 minutes from la Défense. *Website : www.chezclement.com Non-stop service from 8am to 1am. Private car park. A la carte around 28 €.* This fine old character residence is set in magnificent listed grounds, and used to be the Auberge du Coq Hardi. Today, Chez Clément Bougival is about comfort, but also surprise. You'll appreciate the space and the intimate yet original decor; and the staircase terraces overlooking the big garden are very pleasant in summer. Magnificent seafood platters are available à la carte all year round, from 16 €, along with other typical dishes. There is also the roast meat with home made purée formula at 15.90 €, served lunchtime and evenings, for which Chez Clément is known.

HOTEL DES MARECHAUX * – Domaine du parc de la Jonchère 10, côte de la Jonchère ✆ 01 30 82 77 11.** *Fax : 01 30 82 78 40. Website: www.domaine-jonchere.fr. Open all year. 48 rooms from 89 € to 102 € and one suite 229 € weekdays and 182 € weekends.* This hotel is located in a 3,000 sqm. park overlooking the Seine Valley. It also offers attractive all-in weekend prices. The comfortable rooms have disabled access, TV and Canal + , and there are tennis courts and a car park on the site. Dogs accepted. Five salons from 55 sqm. to 350 sqm. are at your disposal for receptions, seating from 45 to 270, with standing room for 65 to 400. Sound proofing is on offer too.

Houdan

LA POULARDE DE HOUDAN 24, avenue de la République - D912 ✆ 01 30 59 60 50. *Website : www.alapoularde.com. Closed Monday and Tuesday. Set menus 30 € and 45 €. Children's menu 11 € and 15 €.* This restaurant is located near the river, in an attractive family residence. Chef Sylvain Vandenameele prepares regional and seasonal cuisine, in the French tradition, and his menu includes the fatted Houdan chicken that has given its name to the place. This hen with its black and white feathers and purple crest is famous in the region, the breed having died out for over fifty years before being recreated and developed in Houdan. You can also enjoy oysters, lobster stew and sole with three types of julienne vegetables, or mullet fillets. A stroll in the park to walk off your meal is very welcome.

Maisons-Laffitte

LE TASTEVIN 9, avenue Eglé ✆ 01 39 62 11 67. *Open Wednesday to Sunday from 12.15pm to 1.45pm and 7.30pm to 9.45pm. Set menu 44 €. A la carte around 70 €. 50 place settings.* This restaurant can be found in a large bourgeois house in Maisons Laffitte Park's country setting. The Blanchet family has been running it with talent, for ages. They serve top-quality seasonal cuisine with considerable know-how, and excel at fish recipes, game in season and mushroom dishes. Prestigious wine list.

Neauphle-le-Château

DOMAINE DU VERBOIS * 38, avenue de la République ✆ 01 34 89 11 78.** *Website : www.hotelverbois.com. Access A13, then A12 and N12. Closed 10-25 August. 20 rooms 110 € and 2 suites 180 €. Set menus from 34 € to 47 €.* This is a peaceful place dating back to the 19thc., with an old-fashioned country house feel about it. Eva-Maria and Kenneth Boone run the hotel, with its private car park and luxuriously furnished rooms where Anglo-Saxon and French taste blend admirably. Chef Stéphane Pasquer cooks mushroom terrine with tarragon-flavoured meat juice, duck fillet with pears and a delicious three-flavoured crème brûlée, among other excellent dishes.

Rambouillet

AUBERGE LE LOUVETIER 19, rue de l'Etang-de-la-Tour ✆ 01 34 85 61 00. *Closed Saturday lunchtime, Sunday evening and Monday. 120 place settings. Set menus 27 € and 33 €.* This is a welcoming place with a pleasant garden and terrace. The menu is seasonal, based on traditional top-quality recipes, and there is a wide choice of dishes including delicate, elaborately-prepared fish specialities. Good food and a great evening await you.

Versailles

HOTEL DE FRANCE * 5, rue Colbert ✆ 01 30 83 92 23.** *Fax : 01 30 83 92 24 – Website : www.versailles-paris-hotel.com. 23 rooms including 2 triples and 1 suite. Double or twin 141 €, triple 174 €, suite 236 €, breakfast 11 €. Tourist tax 1 €.* This magnificent hotel is Colbert de Villarcef's former private mansion, just opposite the château de Versailles. The rooms are tastefully decorated with marble bathrooms, and very comfortable, equipped with direct phone lines, satellite TV (11 channels), air conditioning and a restaurant service from 12 noon to 3pm, and 7pm to midnight weekdays, 12 noon to midnight weekends. Breakfast is served in the dining room or in your room. There is a prestigious salon for hire, for weddings and receptions. Special all-in prices are available at weekends - for 2 nights in a double room booked Friday or Saturday, the second night is free. Historic site, excellent quality services.

Versailles château

VERSAILLES CAMPING & CARAVANING SITE 31, rue Berthelot ✆ 01 39 51 23 *61/08 20 22 67 37 (bookings). Fax : 01 39 53 68 29. Website : www.camping-versailles.com Email : versailles@huttopia.com. 1 Tourism star. 300 spaces. High and low season prices: 13 € and 10 € the space, 7 € and 6 € per head; 21 € and 18 € for 2 people with tent and space (globetrotter's price), 119 €-159 € per night in a Huttopia Chalet (35 sqm., sleeps 6), 79-119 € per night in a Huttopia caravan (21 sqm. mobile home, sleeps 5) and 59 €-89 € per night in a Canadian tent (sleeps 5). Open late March-late October (should be open all year in 2007).*

TRIANON PALACE** Westin Hotel 1, boulevard de la Reine ✆ 01 30 84 50 00** *Fax 01 39 50 00 01. Opn all year. 190 rooms including 36 suites and apartments from 179 € to 1,140 €.* This prestigious international hotel offers water therapy in its health and beauty centre. There is a car park with a valet, and air-conditioned rooms with disabled access, some non-smoking, all equipped with satellite TV. Tennis courts, swimming pool, hairdresser's and fitness centre are at your disposal. You can relax in the bar after all that, before having a top-quality gastronomic meal at Les Trois Marches.

LE VERSAILLES * 7, rue Sainte-Anne – Petite Place ✆ 01 39 50 64 65.** *Fax : 01 39 02 37 85 – Website : www.hotel-le-versailles.fr. 45 rooms, standard 93 €, junior suites 120 €, +10 € per extra person. Breakfast 11 €, tourist tax 1 €.* The hotel manager has won a Best Welcome prize, which is a good start. Le Versailles is located at the foot of the château, and comes complete with all the modern luxury you expect from new residences. It has disabled access, and a garage. The rooms are air-conditioned, some family (small extra bed or convertible sofa-bed), with communicating doors. Others are non-smoking ; all rooms are equipped with satellite TV, fax and computer sockets, bathroom with shower or bath, hairdryer and WC. The senior suites have a separate lounge. You can relax in the bar or reading room on the ground floor, and in fine weather, have breakfast on the terrace among the flowers. Special all-in prices are available some weekends. There is a seminar room for business guests, and dogs are admitted.

Pays de la Loire

Fontevraud abbey

© Iconotec.com

PAYS DE LA LOIRE
Motorway
4-lane major road
Major road
Minor road
Côtes-d'Armor
Ille-et-Vilaine
Morbihan
Loire-Atlantique
Vendée
Océan Atlantique
Vers Fougères
Ernée
Vers Rennes
Vers Rennes
Vers Vannes
Vers Niort
Craon
Rougé
Châteaubriant
Pouancé
Segré
N171
Guémené-Penfao
Nozay
Riaillé
Candé
Saint-Gildas-des-Bois
Blain
N165
N137
Pontchâteau
La Turballe
Le Croisic
Guérande
Donges
Nort-sur-Erdre
A11
Ancenis
Saint-Florent-le-Vieil
La Baule
Saint-Nazaire
Saint-Brévin-les-Pins
D213
Le Pellerin
NANTES
Loire
Pointe de Saint-Gildas
Pornic
D751
Bouaye
Beaupréau
N249
A87
Noirmoutier-en-l'Ile
Sèvre Nantaise
Clisson
Cholet
D753
Bourgneuf-en-Retz
Ile de Noirmoutier
Machecoul
Saint-Philbert-de-Grand-Lieu
A83
Beauvoir-sur-Mer
Rocheservière
Montaigu
Challans
Legé
Boulogne
Les Herbiers
N160
Saint-Jean-de-Monts
Les Essarts
Aizenay
D937
Saint-Gilles-Croix-de-Vie
LA ROCHE-SUR-YON
Chantonnay
La Mothe-Achard
Ile d'Yeu
Port-Joinville
Les Sables-d'Olonne
Fontenay-le-Comte
Luçon
Talmont-Saint-Hilaire
La Tranche-sur-Mer
Chaillé
Ile de Ré

Vers Dinan
Pré-en-Pail
N12
Vers Rouen
Vers Dreux
Javron
Orne
Mayenne
Mamers
Eure-et-Loir
A28
Bais
Beaumont-sur-Sarthe
Sarthe
Vers Chartres
Vers Paris
Mayenne
N162
Sillé-le-Guillaume
Bonnétable
La Ferté-Bernard
A11
Argentré
A81
N157
N23
Vibraye
LAVAL
Meslay-du-Maine
Loué
A11
LE MANS
N157
Bouloire
Saint-Calais
Vers Orléans
Sablé-sur-Sarthe
Le Grand-Lucé
Château-Gontier
Ecommoy
N138
La Chartre-sur-le-Loir
N162
Sarthe
La Flèche
N23
Loir-et-Cher
Le Lion-d'Angers
Durtal
Loir
Château-du-Loir
Le Lude
Maine-et-Loire
Vers Tours
ANGERS
Noyant
Baugé
N23
Beaufort-en-Vallée
Loire
N160
N147
A85
Indre-et-Loire
Thouarcé
Saumur
Vers Tours
Chemillé
Doué-la-Fontaine
Loire
Vihiers
Montreuil-Bellay
N147
Vers Loudun, Poitiers
Vienne
Vers Bressuire
Pouzauges
Deux-Sèvres
Nantes
La Châtaigneraie
Saint-Hilaire-les-Loges
Damvix
0
60 km
Reproduction interdite
Jean-Baptiste Nény
Décembre 2003
Vers Niort

NANTES AND THE LOIRE-ATLANTIQUE

Brittany or the Loire? Historically, the Loire-Atlantique has belonged to both these regions, whence the charm of both seafront beaches and ports, and inland country.

Nantes

Nantes is the West's biggest town; a regional (Pays-de-la-Loire) and departmental (Loire-Atlantique) capital. During the Middle Ages, Nantes was the capital of Brittany, and France's main port owing to the slave trade ('ebony wood'). The town gave its name to the Edict signed by Henri IV in 1598, aiming to end the religious wars weakening the realm; sadly, this edict was revoked less than 100 years later, chasing many Protestants into exile. Today, the town and its suburbs (6th biggest in France) are undergoing extensive urban development; many visitors fall in love with this blend of history and energy, and decide to settle here permanently.

CATHEDRAL. 0 892 464 044 *Open every day except Tuesday.* This Flamboyant Gothic treasure of local heritage has been a victim of fire, falling walls, damage to the porch...and has been rehabilitated each time, non-stop since 1434!

LA CIGALE Place Graslin. This high-class brasserie has played an important role in Nantes' history. Don't miss it.

LE PASSAGE POMMERAYE. *Open 8am-8pm.* This charming Baroque passage gives on to the rue de la Fosse on one side, and the rues Santeuil and Crebillon on the other. Wooden staircases, wrought-iron, bronze cherubs; all covered by a glass roof.

MUSEUM D'HISTOIRE NATURELLE 12 rue Voltaire ✆ 02 40 99 26 20. *Open every day: 10am-6pm except Tuesday (Entrance via the L-Bureau square). Admission: adult 3,10* The museum entrance is formed by a Corinthian forepart with its sculpted front. The rich and varied collections inside come from an 18th and 19thc. interest in science, and the naturalists' passion for travel and discovery.

MUSEE JULES VERNE 3, rue de l'Hermitage ✆ 02 40 69 72 52. *Open: 12 noon and 2pm-6pm except Tuesday, Sunday mornings and public holidays. Admission: adult 3.* Opened in 1978 to celebrate the Nantes writer's 150th birthday, the museum invites you to travel to the centre of Verne's writing, via books, extracts, illustrations, posters, and games, to discover his sources of inspiration, working methods, publishers and posterity.

PLANETARIUM 8, rue des Acadiens ✆ 02 40 73 99 23. *Open Monday to Friday; shows at 10.30am, 2.15pm and 3.45pm, Sunday at 3pm and 4.30pm (lasts about 1 hour). Admission: adult 5.* The Planetarium, of recent design, has been putting on conceptual shows on an astronomic theme since 1981. They range from the history and development of the physical sciences (mathematics, physics, chemistry) to the staging of futuristic projects linked to space travel and planetary evolution. There are 17 weekly shows; the special effects are updated regularly.

Nantes vineyards

The Nantes vines stand in line between the Sevre and Maine Valleys; at the foot of that charming village Saint Fiacre-sur-Maine; round Mouzillon and Vallet. They climb hillsides, run alongside rivers and circle villages. South of the Loire, the tourist route is marked out by signposts bearing a bunch of pale yellow grapes and a green leaf, and local wine-growing merges with the region's historic heritage. There are plenty of culinary specialities to tempt your appetite, since this wine-growing country also has a rich gastronomic tradition. The reputation of its wines has spread beyond regional borders, and the wine-growers are very willing to open their cellars to visitors wishing to taste their muscadet or gros plant. You can get a list of wine-growers from the Vertou, Vallet and Loroux-Bottereau tourist offices,

MAISON DES VINS 28, place du Millénaire - ANCENIS ✆ 02 40 96 14 92. *Open 1 May-30 October, except Mondays.* You'll find all the information you need about regional, national and even international wine production here. 38 local wine-growers show off their products - muscadet, coteaux de Loire, and so on - and give you good advice about choosing and buying wine.

LA MAISON DES VINS Bellevue - LA HAYE-FOUASSIERE ✆ 02 40 36 90 10. *Open Monday-Friday: 8.30am-12.30pm and 2pm-5.45pm.* You find this wine centre on the Bellevue site (the vineyards' highest point) close by the water tower painted in Muscadet colours. A unique assortment of over 100 wines grown in different regional soils is on offer.

LA MAISON DU MUSCADET Vallet © 02 40 36 25 95. Wine tasting and sale; cellars open to visitors. 35 wine-growers offer selected wines: muscadet, gros plant and red vin du pays. Regional produce like the Val de Loire creme de muroise, and engraved glasses, aprons and T-shirts in boxed gift sets are also on sale.

MUSEE DU VIGNOBLE NANTAIS 82, rue Pierre-Abélard - PALLET © 02 40 80 90 13. *Open 1 March-11 November. Admission: adult 4 €.* This museum explains how muscadet is grown. The history of this local wine, and the technical know-how that goes into its production are illustrated by over 1,000 objects and tools.

La Baule, the Guerande peninsula and Grande Briere

Welcoming, active, wild yet restful: these terms could describe this part of the Atlantic Coast known as the Côte d'Amour. From Saint-Nazaire to the salt marshes, via La Baule, Le Pouliguen and Pornichet, this is walking country, and has always been a meeting-point for sailors, marsh and agricultural labourers, artists, holiday-makers and sportsmen. You'll find six fishing ports and yachting harbours, 100 tennis courts, 45 holes of golf, kilometres of paths for hiking, horseriding or cycling, salt-marshes to wander through and dozens of beaches...La Baule is supposed to be Europe's most beautiful beach.

La Baule

La Baule has only existed since 1879, emerging as a new resort with the first Saint-Nazaire-Le Croisic railway line. The pines, stylish villas, charming chalets and Anglo-Norman cottages have made way for modern buildings along the seafront, and you have to head for the town centre to find splendid old-fashioned residences of architectural interest: Art Nouveau, Provençal, Basque, Rococo, and so on.

THE BEACH AND THE 'REMBLAI'. Europe's finest beach is a 9 km half-moon, lined with old villas and modern complexes in turn. The seafront is called the 'remblai', and has something to please everyone: fine, gently sloping sands, clubs, bars and beach restaurants, casinos and Hôtels.

Parc Naturel Régional de Brière

The marshes stretch over two zones; Donges to the east; Grande Brière to the west. This latter contains 21 villages who share the land undivided and have grazing, peat-digging, reed-cutting, shooting and fishing rights. The property dates back to 1461, and is known as the Black Country because of the peat. Leave your car ; the reserve is best enjoyed on foot or a bike - or why not hire a boat or a carriage? The flora and fauna are fascinating to discover, on condition that you respect their habitat.

PARC NATUREL REGIONAL DE BRIERE 177, Ile de Fedrun - SAINT-JOACHIM © 02 40 91 68 68. *www.parc-naturel-briere.fr.* This vast stretch was one of the first French regional nature reserve, biologically rich in aquatic plants and birds. There are 3,000 thatched roofs, typical of local architecture. You can discover the park from a lighter, steered with a pole by your guide; stop in Kerinet village or find out about marshland life and activities at Roze.

Batz-sur-Mer

The 'saltiest' community on the peninsula, with its salt-merchants' villages like Kervalet. Saint Guénolé Church's 17thc. belltower, 70m high, overlooks the town of Batz built between marsh and ocean. Part of the granite church dates back to the 15thc; concerts are given here in summer and the Saint Guénolé Grand Pardon takes place on the second Sunday in August.

MUSEE 39-45 DU GRAND BLOCKHAUS Route de la Côte-Sauvage © 02 40 23 88 29. *www.perso.wanadoo.fr/grand.blockhaus. Open 1 April-15 November, every day: 10am-7pm;adult 5,50 closed Tuesday in low season.* Inside a real Atlantic Wall control-room, scale models, characters and films take you back into World War II history.

Le Croisic

Le Croisic is a seaside resort, yachting harbour and famous fishing-port; the latter goes back to Gallic times.

NOTRE DAME DE PITIE. The church goes back to 1494; its 56m-tower can be seen by sailors from afar. It contains a 19thc. organ, polychrome statue of Saint James of Compostella and hanging boat-shaped ex-votos.

OCEARIUM DU CROISIC Avenue de Saint-Goustan ✆ 02 40 23 02 44. *www.ocearium-croisic.fr. Open all year except 3 weeks in January. September-May: 10am-12 noon and 2pm-6pm (16 November-20 December: 2pm-6pm); June, July and August: 10am-7pm. Tarifs: adult 10.50 €, child 7.50 €.* There are 150 species, 1,000 fish in 45 aquariums to discover; you can even walk right through a 300,000-litre tank, via a transparent tunnel. The colourful exotic breeds are the most popular with children, but the Espace Vancouver's North Atlantic species deserve attention, for they are more rarely seen in acquariums than exotic fish, it being difficult to keep the temperature low enough for them. Don't miss the Australian sharks in their gigantic million-litre tank.

LE TRAICT. This inside sea, 700 hectares at high tide, is used for shellfish culture: mussels, cockles, oysters and clams. In the 19thc. it was a means of communication between Guérande and Le Croisic. The Traict Cross rises in the middle, once providing a refuge for travellers taken unawares by the tide.

Guérande

The ramparts around this superb medieval town are almost intact. In the 19thc., Guerande was one of Brittany's most active ports, made rich by its agriculture, vines and salt.

MAISON DES PALUDIERS ✆ 02 40 62 21 96. *Open all year at weekends, every day from February-October.Admission: adult 4(museum), Saltworks 5,60 €* The salt-works can be visited in season. This is the White Country with almost 1,800 hectares of saltmarshes, and the paludiers (salt-workers) carefully control evaporation, helped by sun and wind, to obtain top-quality salt then stocked in wooden or stone salorges. (You'll notice them on your walks).

SAINT AUBIN COLLEGIATE CHURCH. *Open all year: 9am-12 noon and 2pm-6pm.* The west front, partly rebuilt in the 19thc. has a rare 15thc. outside pulpit; the eastern chevet has cut corners, and is decorated with a Flamboyant Gothic motif. Inside is a great central nave with Romanesque columns (the historiated sculpted capitals in the northern nave are typical of Breton Romanesque art), Gothic chancel, and stained glass windows including Saint Pierre's with its monochrome painting.

Pornichet

Pornichet is the region's oldest resort. Until the 19thc. its livelihood was salt manufacture and trade; the salt marshes took up 35 hectares on the site of the current racecourse. The salt workers' village was only a ¥ port niche ™ for small sea craft. The first railway in 1879 saw the start of seaside tourism, just as the salt marshes were silting up. Pornichet is a family resort, with beaches set in a rocky coast line, creeks and the first kilometres of La Baule Bay. The deep waters of the sailing harbour contain some beautiful open-sea racing craft, and the picturesque restaurants in Pornichet village are often inexpensive.

PORT. Busy in season; a village in itself with its shops and restaurants. Just next door in the dry dock are fishing craft and small rowing boats.

Le Pouliguen

Its low water tide has run into the salt marshes for over 2,000 years. Around it, a fishing port grew up, busy in the 15thc. The town remembers it in its houses and street plan, though it is now an equally active yachting harbour.

PENCHATEAU CHAPEL. Known as Saint Anne's chapel, but in fact dedicated to Saint Julian, this 9th or 10thc. chapel has been reworked many times. Most of its existing features are from about 1360 (statues, stoup, bas-reliefs, alabaster) with 15th and 16thc. crosses.

COTE SAUVAGE AND CAVES. The coast starts at Penchâteau Point, leading to Le Croisic via a road and smugglers' path overlooking rocks and creeks open to the sea breezes. At low tide, you can go round the coast on foot, and see twenty or so caves curiously sculpted by the sea. The Trou du Souffleur, or Pétouse, can be seen at Pierre-Plate, where fishermen congregate. At high tide, the sound of thunder comes from concealed rock faults, with geysers raised by the waves.

PORT. This is a link between the sea and the saltmarshes, built long and narrow for communication purposes. The Peyron brothers and Yves Loday, local men, often tie up their racing craft in the harbour. A replica of a 1900 sardine trawler 'Le Poulligwen' with its two sloping masts is moored here. Launched and blessed in '92, she takes part in a fair number of nautical meetings.

Pornic and Retz country

Machecoul

Not to be missed, in the ancient capital of Retz country, is Gilles de Rais' ruined castle. He was accused of committing crimes on children; Bluebeard was based on him. Machecoul was also a site of desperate combat between Vendeans and Republicans in 1793.

Pornic

14km of coastline, an ultra-modern sailing harbour and a fishing port in the middle of town, called the Vieux Port, of course. This is also a resort with a permanent traffic jam in summer; it's better to walk or cycle - easy enough to do, since this beautiful town is built around the harbour.

Saint-Brévin

This respected, hundred-year-old resort has two main centres: Saint-Brévin-les-Pins and Saint-Brévin-l'Océan. There is an 8km-beach and water sports, with sand-yachting on the big beach; by pumping hard you can get almost as far as Saint-Michel-Chef-Chef, famous for its galettes.

MEGALITHS. There are lots of dolmens, tumulus and menhirs in the region; 9 at Saint-Brévin alone. The dolmen in the avenue des Rossignols and dolmen table on the Boivre beach rocks are not to be missed. The Boivre menhir can be identified by its pyramid shape: 4m by 3m at the base. The harnessed stone menhir is reputed to grant happy marriages, while the flat stone can be found close to the Hermitage lying stones.

Elsewhere in Loire-Atlantique

Ancenis

Astride the Loire-Atlantique and Maine-et-Loire, Ancenis (north of the Loire) and Les Mauges (south of the Loire) offer a variety of landscapes, natural sites, historic heritage and museums, hiking, riding and cycling paths, vineyards and local produce. Follow the panoramic view from Montjean to Saint-Florent, crossing the Lire vines towards La Varenne in Mauges country.

Châteaubriant castle

Châteaubriant

Châteaubriant in Mee country, on the Brittany marches but close to the Loire Valley is the Loire-Atlantique's highest region, surrounded by forests, scattered with lakes and full of manors, old churches and forges. The region's natural and industrial heritage is well worth stopping off for.

CHATEAU DE CHATEAUBRIANT ✆ 02 40 28 20 20. *Open all year, every day except Tuesday. Mid September-mid June: guided tours Saturday & Sunday at 3pm. Mid June-mid September: guided tours every day except Tuesday: 11am, 2.30pm, and 4.30pm. Saturday & Sunday: 2.30pm and 4.30pm. Admission: adult 3 €.* The castle has been the target of seven building projects, from the late 11th to the 20thc. The present site is composed of two main buildings; a medieval castle to the west of the enclosure and a newer Renaissance-style château.

Clisson

This medieval site was destroyed during the Vendée Wars in 1793. Frederic Lemot and the Cacault brothers decided to rebuild Clisson in Italian style.

CHATEAU OLIVIER DE CLISSON ✆ 02 40 54 02 22. *Bookings 02 40 54 75 85. Open 9.30am-12 noon and 2pm-6pm. Admission: 2.20 €.* Built above the Sèvre on a rocky outcrop, this imposing mass overlooks town and valley. It dates back to the 12thc., but was burned down during the Vendée Wars. You can visit the restored parts, walk over the site and admire the flowers in the former moat. The 15thc. covered market in the town centre has a superb oak and chestnut framework. Saint Antoine Bridge is from the 15thc. too, spanning the Moine with its magnificent Gothic arches. The other 15thc. bridge, the Pont de la Vallée, crosses the Sèvre. Five spurs have been defending it upriver since the Middle Ages, against flooding and objects brought up by the current, but the bridge has occasionally been almost submerged. A 19thc. viaduct with its 15 granite arches spans the Moine.

Saint-Nazaire

Situated at the mouth of the Loire, Saint-Nazaire was long known for its shipyards, and still continues to build prestige ocean liners; the town's other industries include Aerospatiale, a refinery, a methane tanker terminal and many other activities. There are also beaches, parks, ports and a busy town centre, with the 'Paquebot' set right in the middle of Avenue de la République. Saint-Nazaire is definitely worth a visit.

SUBMARINE BASE Boulevard Leferme. Since 1999, the public has been able to climb on the roof of this huge concrete pile. Built during the War, it represents dark days in the town's history, and even afterwards, the town rejected its port for this reason. The Ville-Port project has given the base a new role, with the exhibition and show Escal'Atlantic.

The Bélem ship, Saint-Nazaire

ATLANTIC SHIPYARDS Ave. Antoine Bourdelle. Shipbuilding is a Saint-Nazaire tradition. Today, the whole world knows these shipyards: luxury liners are made in the building docks, but also methane tankers and ferries.

ESPADON SUBMARINE ✆ 0 810 888 444 (No. Azur). *www.saint-nazaire-tourisme.com. Open all year, except January. High season: 9.30am-12.30pm and 1.30pm-6pm every day. Admission (high season): adult 8 €, child 6 €.* The only sea-going submarine in France open to the public now offers an audioguide. You learn about the life of the 65-man crew aboard the first French submarine to reach the icy Arctic.

PONT SUR LA LOIRE. This bridge is now free; good news for those wanting to cross to the Vendée beaches. Climb up on foot, for the view.

VENDÉE

In 1793, this region was devastated by civil strife; the pro-revolutionaries against the royalist Chouans. Today, a quieter Vendée is a model of economic growth, developing family tourism on the coast. Apart from its beautiful beaches, Vendée has a variety of landscapes: bocage in the north, and the marshes; Breton between Challans and the Bourgneuf Bay, and Poitevin in the south, known as 'green Venice'. There are also the islands, Noirmoutier and Yeu, each with its own style.

The coast and the islands

L'Aiguillon

Migratory birds flock to Aiguillon bay in southern Vendée: coots and sheldrakes settle among the carnations and artemisia, delicate plants growing in the sand and salt, protected by a dyke. Mussels and oysters are farmed here, and sole and bass are caught, with clams, eels and scallops in winter.

Barre-de-Monts

DAVIAUD ECOMUSEUM© 02 51 93 84 84. *Open February to November. Admission: adult 5 €.*Take a day out to discover the human and natural history of the Breton and Vendee marshes. A guided walk takes you through a series of traditional buildings on a unique 15 ha. natural site, including a saltern, animal and historic plant conservation centre, bird observation post and plenty of other aspects of local environmental heritage.

Ile de Noirmoutier

This charming island has over 40km of soft, sandy beaches, perfect for kids. In the north, the landscape is rockier, with small creeks; from north to south, facing the Atlantic Ocean, are sand dunes and and beaches lined with tall pines. The Bois de la Chaize is the best-known example. A hard battle was fought here to conquer the land and keep it from the sea, started by the monks and continued in the 19thc by the Dutch Jacobsen family, who drained the land, created salt marshes and built an accessible harbour. Noirmoutiers had an eventful past, and you can best visit its monuments by taking the Gois passage (equipped with a tide timetable) rather than the bridge.

BOIS DE LA CHAIZE. This unique spot has forests of maritime pines and green oaks sheltering winter-flowering mimosa. In the last century a summer resort began here and a few holiday villas were built; probably the most beautiful on Noirmoutier.

LE GOIS. The slow silting-up of Bourgneuf Bay resulted in this 4.15km ford, adapted by man to his needs. It is uncovered at low tide, but you must stick to the tide times indicated for access: roughly two hours before and after low tide, if you don't want to be stranded. A word of advice: rinse your car with fresh water afterwards, as salt attacks the bodywork.

Notre-Dame-de-Monts

Part of the Pont-d'Yeu community, on an underwater headland favoured by fishermen, Notre Dame de Monts is a family resort set between Saint-Jean-de-Monts and Noirmoutier. It covers 2,062 hectares of marshland, forest (with cycle paths) and dunes, including 4.6km of gently-sloping beaches. Local architecture of interest includes *bourrines* (typical marsh dwellings), mills, locks and bridges, and there are water sports and nature hikes for the sporty.

LE JARDIN DU VENT 29bis, rue Gilbert-Esbron © 02 28 11 26 43. *June-September, every day: 11am-7pm. April, May and October half term: Tuesday-Sunday: 2pm-6pm. March, October and November; group bookings only. Admission: adult 4 €, concessions 2 €, under-6s free. Guided tours for groups.* This original garden is hidden at the foot of a curious windmill, and is artistic, fun and educational all at once. You learn about the environment and how to protect it by following a circuit of animated sculptures, wind and weather games and activities based around a sailor's compass and a plant theatre. The rather poetic interactive exhibition changes every year.

Sables-d'Olonne

You can see why Sables d'Olonne is known as 'the Côte de Lumière's pearl'. Its chief attractions are a marvellous natural setting with marshes, dunes, forests and superb beaches; a south-facing bay, lit up by street-lamps at night; and three harbours (fishing, yachting and a commercial port). This is the Vendée's top seaside resort.

LA CHAUME. The town's most ancient quarter, dating back to Gallo-Roman times. A warren of alleys contains typical, squat little houses.

SAINT NICOLAS PRIORY Promenade Jean XXIII. Put up in the 11thc. by Sainte-Croix de Talmont monks, it was administered by them until the 17thc, when Benjamin de Rohan, Seigneur de Soubise's Protestant troops destroyed it. On Richelieu's advice, Louis XIII donated the means to rebuild it, but it was used to store gunpowder and as a guard-room before being a priory again after restoration in 1972. The lawn around the fort hides blockhouses which no-one has managed to get rid of.

MUSEUM DU COQUILLAGE Port de PÕche - 8, rue du Marechal-Leclerc ✆ 02 51 23 50 00. *Open 9.30am-12 noon and 2pm-6.30pm, November-April, closed Saturday & Sunday mornings. Open every day in July & August: 9.30am-8pm. Admission: adult 6 €, 4-11s 3.50 €.* It takes about an hour to visit this private collection of 45,000 shells, of great beauty and diversity.

LES SALINES (SALTWORKS) Embarcadère-Port-Olona ✆ 02 51 21 01 19. *www.lessalines.fr. From April to late September.* Several two-and-a-half hour walks per day are organised in the salt marshes.

Talmont-Saint-Hilaire

This was once a port, until the marshes slowly but surely cut off it off from the ocean. Today, Talmont leads a sedate, middle-class life behind the elegant fronts of its many charming old houses.

CHATEAU DE TALMONT Rue du Château ✆ 02 51 90 27 43. *Open 26 March-13 June: 10.30am-12.30pm and 2pm-6.30pm. 9 September-November: 2pm-6pm. 13 June-9 September: 11am-7pm. Admission (high/low season): adult 6.60 €/3.85 €, child 3.20 €/1.95 €. Nocturne: adult 7.45 €, child 3.20 €.* The site has three points of interest: the evening visit (nocturne); a typical Middle Ages day, with medieval hands-on activities; and the castle itself (guided tours available). The whole family will enjoy the costumes, short plays, calligraphy, crossbow shooting and childrens' games during the daytime, and marvel at the magical nocturnal walk offered in the evening.

Ile d'Yeu

Vendée's treasure island is like a bit of Brittany washed too far south. It shelters a spectacular ruin: the Vieux Château, still rising proudly above the ocean. The island's Atlantic coast is wild and beautiful; the other, facing the continent, is softer, with its gentle beaches, dunes and pine forests, and the main town, Port-Joinville. Discover the island (10km by 4km) on foot, by bike or boat.

This is the second-furthest island from the French coast (after Corsica), 17km, so its inhabitants are rather far from mainland healthcare and schools. You can get to the island from Sables d'Olonne with the shuttle 'Le Sabia'. From Saint-Gilles-Croix-de-Vie, Fromentine and Noirmoutier you have a choice of two boat companies; VIIV or Yeu Continent. You can also go there by helicopter, a quicker, seasickness-free journey with the company OYA.

COMPAGNIE NGV - LE SABIA - Port-Olona ✆ 02 51 23 54 88/06 68 40 33 39

COMPAGNIE YEU-CONTINENT Gare maritime de Fromentine - La Barre-de-Monts - LA BARRE DE MONTS ✆ 0 825 85 3000. *Price: round trip 27.40 €, concessions 19.60 €.*

LA COMPAGNIE VENDEENNE Place de la Douane - SAINT-GILLES-CROIX-DE-VIE ✆ 0825 169 085. *www.compagnievendeenne.com*

VEDETTES INTER-ILES VENDEENNES (VIIV) Pointe de la Fosse - BARBATRE ✆ 02 51 39 00 00 Boulevard de l'Egalite - SAINT-GILLES-CROIX-DE-VIE ✆ 02 51 54 15 15.

VEDETTE-TAXI 'AMARYLIS' Agence Parenthese - SAINT-GILLES-CROIX-DE-VIE ✆ 02 51 54 09 88/06 70 95 18 65. *The only boat running all year. Bookings only. Crossing 1 hr.*

PORT-JOINVILLE. Of its 900 sailors, only 500 are left today (out of a total of 4,868 inhabitants). This is France's most important tuna-fishing port (2,000 tonnes) but there is less work for the canneries, and a yachting harbour has recently been added. Look round the port first, with its old rigging, picturesquely-named pot vessels and modern trawlers, then wander through the quaint streets - rue de la Fée, du Paradis, de la Fourchette, des Maries (an amusing little lighthouse), du Secret or du Coin-du-Chat. Visit the church, and the Fishing Museum.

PORT DE LA MEULE. A magical, long creek in the rocks, and a little port for pot vessels, proof that the seabed here is rich in shellfish.

Île d'Yeu, the port

© Manuel Thiery

FORT DE LA PIERRE-LEVEE (dit la Citadelle) Near Port-Joinville. The inside courtyard is open all year. The citadel was built in the early 19thc. to protect the island, but it quickly became a political prison where unwanted influences could be isolated from the mainland. The little oak wood around it is interesting, as are some of the prisoners: Austro-Hungarians during World War I, communists, such as Jacques Duclos in 1939, Maréchal Pétain from 1945 to 1951, Basques, and many others.

VIEUX CHATEAU ✆ **02 51 58 32 58**. *Open every day: 11am-5pm, 15 June-15 September.* A dream castle in black stone recalling Round Table legends and Tintin's 'Black Island'. Cross the impressive drawbridge to see the tumbled-down castle remains; you won't forget this marvellous site's wild beauty.

Bocage

Les Herbiers

The town suffered in the Hundred Years' War, Wars of Religion and during the Revolution, but is still going strong at the heart of the Vendée bocage.

MONT DES ALOUETTES ✆ **02 51 92 92 92**. *Visit a working windmill from April to September. The chapel can also be visited in July and August.* Access: 3km from Les Herbiers on the N160 towards Cholet. The Mont des Alouettes (Skylark Hill) is 231m above sea level, with a wide panoramic view of the bocage, from the Pouzauges Hills to Luçon spire, and Nantes Cathedral towers. There are 3 windmills left of the 8 which sent 'semaphore' messages to the Vendean army in 1793, by changing the positions of their sails. The miller demonstrates how wheat is ground, in a fascinating and educational time-trip. The chapel, put up from 1825-1830 by Louis XVI's daughter the Duchess of Angoulême in pure 19thc. Gothic, was restored in 1968.

Le Puy-du-Fou

Despite being only the 4th-rated French theme park, this one is unique of its kind.

GRAND PARC 30, rue Georges-Clémenceau - LES EPESSES ✆ **02 51 64 11 11** *(bookings). www.puydufou.com. Open weekends and public holidays in May: 10am-7pm, 1 June-14 September every day: 10am-7pm. Admission: adult 2.5 €, 5-13s 13,50 €.* On-site snack-bars and restaurants. Car-park. On entering the great park, you travel through time, from the Gallo-Roman era to the Vendée Wars. There are several shows at specific times (you have to schedule carefully so as not to miss one): the Year 1,000 Fort (a Viking longship rises from the water; spectacular!) the Gallo-Roman amphitheatre and the medieval castle. Wander through the medieval town and 18thc. village, with the authentic atmosphere, sounds and smells recreated, and the craftsmen really at work (all the costumed actors are local volunteers). There are also magicians, jugglers, theatre, musicians, animals for the kids to admire; it is difficult to see it all in a day.

CINESCENIE. *Admission: adult 23 €, child 13 €. Cinescenie + Grand Parc: adult 38 €, child 20 €. Show from 4 June-10 September, June & September, Saturday only; July & August, Saturday & Sunday. Show starts at 10pm (10.30pm July & August). Bookings only.* Night falls on the old castle, a light appears; the open-air pageant is about to begin. 2,700 voluntary actors bring to life the story of the Maupillier family, Vendean peasants, from the Middle Ages to the end of World War II. The play of music, lights and voices and the battle scenes are unforgettable. History like you've never seen it before.

La Roche-sur-Yon

Napoleon I moved the region's capital to La-Roche-sur-Yon in 1804, creating a strategic centre for the now-subdued Vendée. At the time, this was a modest town with few inhabitants grouped around the Place de la Vieille Horloge. The new central square, Place Napoléon, was built to hold 20,000 men. A statue of Napoleon in the middle overlooks four main roads. Apart from the square, the town's architecture is unremarkable, since it is only two hundred years old.

HARAS NATIONAL Rue du Général Gallieni ✆ 02 51 46 14 47. *Open June-September for guided tours (at 3pm; call for information about other times). Admission: adult 4.50 €, concessions 2 €, under-5s free.* Entrance for guided tours boulevard des Etats Unis. The stud farm was built in 1843, and contains about fifty stallions in a 4.5-hectare tree-lined park. See the thoroughbreds and discover saddle making and smithing in this delightful setting.

Tiffauges

On a green and pleasant hillside above the gently flowing Sèvre Nantaise, Tiffauges was known by the Romans as 'Papus Teifalgicus'.

CHATEAU DE BARBE-BLEUE ✆ 02 51 65 70 51. *Open April-3rd Sunday in September. Admission: adult 7 €, child 5 €, families 21 €.* Gilles de Rais (1404-1440), one of Joan of Arc's companions and Marshal of France, led a dissipated life in his castle, and was ruined by blackmail, sumptuous feasting and the upkeep of his many estates, including Tiffauges. To redress his fortunes, he turned to alchemy, and is supposed to have practised black magic and sacrificed children. He was Charles Perrault's Bluebeard, but has been partially cleared by a recent historians' tribunal. At Tiffauges, the story of Bluebeard is told in marvellous shadow-theatre. You can also visit the sinister alchemist's cellar (not for small children) and try your hand at medieval archery and quintain jousting.

Les marais

Damvix

Built around the Sevre and its adjoining conches (canals) which come right into the village; boats can be moored by the houses. Discover the dams and locks on the 11-km waterway that takes you to Bazoin, where the Sèvre Niortaise, Mignon Canal and Nouveau-Bejou Canal join up.

MAILLEZAIS ABBEY ✆ 02 51 50 43 00. *Open every day: 9.30am-12.30pm and 1.30pm-6pm. July, August and public holidays: 10am-7pm. Under-18s free.* Maillezais is an island; the abbey is built on a limestone outcrop 8m above the marsh. It was founded in 1003 by the monk Théodelin; Saint Rigomer's remains and one of John the Baptist's teeth made it famous. From 1317, soaring Gothic lines were added; little remains of the Renaissance chancel that followed. French kings visited it, and Rabelais spent 5 years here (1524-1529). Agrippa d'Aubigné made it a Protestant fortress from 1587-1620; it was sacked during the Wars of Religion and sold off as national property during the Revolution. Archeological digs are in progress, and you can visit the Stone Museum and convent buildings, though the great stone shape itself, put up then cast down by men, is what strikes you most.

Fontenay-le-Comte

The Renaissance town was an important centre of humanism and French culture; Rabelais was one of its chief figures. The finest buildings were put up in the 16thc: private mansions, Château de Terre-Neuve, Quatre-Tias fountain, Hôtel de Grimouard, the Sénéchaussee.

NOTRE DAME CHURCH. Don't miss its 11thc. Primitive Romanesque crypt, Renaissance chapels (1540), pictures, reredos and pulpit.

FONTAINE DES QUATRE TIAS. On the edge of the Parc Baron, near the Pont aux Sardines, the fountain recalls the town's humanist past, with its salamander and royal blazon.

Fontenay-le-Comte

Fontenay-le-Comte
Vendée

A witness of a prestigious past in the only preserved part of the departement, Fontenay-le-Comte has kept in its remains the magic of a thousand years of history... Let yourself be guided along the Vendée river or discover the streets of this beautiful city enriched by an architectural lighting rewarded by the «Prix Ville Lumière 2002».

The numerous festivals (les Ricochets, street art during the summer), shows, concerts, exhibitions (contemporary art walk in the historic center from July to October) and events ensure a very complete cultural life... The Fontenay museum will make you discover art tradition and history through its rich ethnological and archeological collections.

With its national price for «art de vivre», one of the most beautiful visits in France, the economic and administrative of southern Vendée, flowered city (3 flowers) and also the most sporty and handi-sporty city of France, Fontenay is also one of the most beautiful and pleasant stops of the Bas-Poitou.

181628

VILLES ET PAYS D'ART ET D'HISTOIRE

City
of art history

www.ville-fontenaylecomte.fr

LES PLUS BEAUX DETOURS DE FRANCE

CHATEAU DE TERRE-NEUVE ✆ **02 51 69 99 41**. *Open every day: 9am-12 noon and 2pm-7pm, 1 May-30 September. Admission: adult 6 €.*This most elegant of Vendean castles has 18thc. furniture. The crime writer Simenon, inventor of Inspector Maigret, lived here.

NIEUL SUR L'AUTISE ABBEY Place de l'Abbaye ✆ **02 51 50 43 00**. *14km south of Fontenay-le-Comte. Open every day: 9.30am-12.30pm and 1.30pm-6pm. July & August, Sunday and public holidays: 10am-7pm. Under-18s free.* Eléanore of Aquitaine was generous to this abbey founded in 1068; her mother is buried in the cloister (the only one wholly intact in western France). This is one of the few Poitevin abbeys to have preserved church, cloister and convent buildings in almost perfect condition. The church front is richly sculpted, with a majestic vaulted nave and four Romanesque galleries in the cloister. Visit the adjoining houses where the abbey's history and daily life can be discovered on an interactive circuit.

Luçon

On the borders of the Poitevin marshes, Luçon was shaped by medieval monks and the bishops who came after, including Cardinal Richelieu. He lived here from 1606 to 1623, and left his mark on this romantic town. Its tile roofs now mingle with the slates of bourgeois homes, whose sculptures and little turrets recall the novels of Victor Hugo and Alexandre Dumas.

CATHEDRAL & CLOISTER Place Leclerc. *Open every day.* The abbey church became a cathedral in 1317. Built of warm, chalky stone, its slender, elegant spire soars to 85m high. The fine 17thc. classical face seen from the square is by François Leduc, known as 'Tuscan' for his taste in art; there are three levels: Doric, Ionic and Corinthian. The Italian style, Gothic and Renaissance blend well, and the result was not spoilt by 19thc. rebuilding of the first floor to house the bishop's library.

Vouvant

One of France's finest villages, on its rocky spur in a loop of the River Mère.

MELUSINE TOWER. Dating back to 1242, with 3m-thick walls. Climb 120 steps to admire the view from 36m up; bocage to the north, forest to the south and Mere Valley below.

CHURCH. A prestigious monument, perfect example of bas-Poitevin Romanesque architecture. Admire the entry portal, a huge gable-end wall framed by two clusters of columns.

MAINE-ET-LOIRE

Former province of Anjou, powerful throughout Europe, known for its gentle living.

Pays Angevin

Angers

This beautiful town is Maine-et-Loire's prefecture, where youth and artistic energy blend with a rich heritage: museums, a contemporary dance centre and a theatre festival that lights up the department's châteaux. Angers is world-famous for tapestry and linked with gastronomy: the great chef Curnonsky was born here, as was Edouard Cointreau, who invented an orange-peel-based liqueur in his distillery. Gracious living is in the air, and in the elegant stone buildings.

Wander through the Place du Ralliement, Rue Saint-Laud for the shops, the pretty streets around the cathedral and the Jardin des Plantes. On the Maine's opposite bank is the Doutre quarter, with the Jean Lurçat Museum and its tapestries, and Trinite Church. The Maison d'Adam is the most beautiful of the town's 45 half-timbered houses.

SAINT MAURICE CATHEDRAL. This was the first Plantagenet Gothic nave, one of France's biggest. Built in the 12thc., it has no flying buttresses.

CHATEAU Promenade du Bout du Monde ✆ **02 41 87 43 47**. *Open every day, 5 September-30 April: 10am-5.30pm; 2 May-4 September, 9.30am-6.30pm (except 1 May, 1 January, 1 November, 11 November and 25 December). Admission: adult7,50!, concessions 3.50 €, children free.* The Prince de Condé said ¥This is the most famous castle, and the strongest in the realm™. It was built from 1230 to 1239, probably on a Gallo-Roman site, for Saint Louis' mother Blanche de Castille. Good King René was its most famous owner; he was a patron of the arts, poet and gardener. The powerful walls, with 17 towers carved from shale and tuffeau (calcareous rock) form a massive, irregular shape, reflected in the water, with blueish tints at night. Inside are the Apocalypse Tapestries, a priceless treasure.

MUSEE DES BEAUX ARTS **10, rue du Musée ✆ 02 41 05 38 00**. *Open all year, except Monday in winter. Admission: adult 4 €. The Fine Arts museum reopened in 2004 after 5 years' renovation work.*

MUSEE DAVID D'ANGERS **33bis, rue Toussaint ✆ 02 41 05 38 90.** *Closed Monday. Open 10am-12 noon and 2pm-6pm. Admission: adult 2 €, under-18s free.* An architectural masterpiece, containing Bonchamp's tomb, busts of Balzac, Paganini, Goethe, a host of artists on the first floor, a model of the Pantheon's pediment, and especially worth seeing, the Petite Odalisque and the Jeune Berger.

MUSEE JEAN-LURCAT ET DE LA TAPISSERIE CONTEMPORAINE **4, bd Arago ✆ 02 41 24 18 45**. *Open every day, mid June-mid September: 9.30am-6.30pm. Mid September-mid June, every day except Monday: 10am-12 noon and 2pm-6pm. Admission: adult 4 €, children free.* Since 1967, the 12thc. Hôpital de Saint Jean has housed Jean Lurcat's series of ten tapestries Le Chant du Monde, a flamboyant contemporary answer to Louis d'Anjou's Apocalypse. In this huge hall with its three rib-vaulted naves, the effect is impressive.

Baugé

The Baugeois is a beautiful but unknown region, keeping its attractions to itself. Between the Loire (west) and the Lathan (east), a pleasant natural sense of wellbeing pervades fields and villages, with their original belltowers. Some churches have corkscrew spires, known as clochers tors, looking as if a giant had wrung them out like dishcloths!

CHATEAU ✆ 02 41 84 00 74 *www.chateau-bauge.com. Open February school holidays-Easter, late September-mid November: 2pm-5.30pm. Easter-late September: 10am-5.30pm. Guided tours every 45 mins. Admission: adult 8 €, 11-16s 6 €, 6-10s 4 €.* Foulque III de Nerra, ancestor of the Plantagenet dynasty, had a powerful fortress put up in the early 11thc. at the Altrée and Couasnon confluence. His mother Yolande of Aragon burnt it down during the Hundred Years' War. King René thus inherited a ruin, and in 1454, decided to built another castle on the north wall. He and his wife Jeanne loved staying there, and hunting parties were held in the boar-filled forests around. Today, you can time-travel back to René's day, via an amazing circuit bringing alive French medieval and Renaissance history. The castle's great hall, installed as a museum, stages themes of the period: chivalry, tournaments, courtly love. A giant knight in jousting position welcomes you, and if you climb up to the top of the castle, you can even meet King René!

Brissac-Quincé

This important wine-growing centre has kept its beautiful castle, the highest in France.

CHATEAU DE BRISSAC ✆ 02 41 91 22 21. *Open 1 April-30 June and 15 September-31 October, every day except Tuesday: 10am-12 noon and 2.15pm-5.15pm. July & August, open every day: 10am-5.45pm. Admission: Adult8,50 €. over-8s 7 €. Park and gardens 3.50 €.* The castle was begun in the 15thc. but its title comes from the tall main building put up in the 17thc. See the prestigious tapestries, and the gold-leaf platforms.

Angers castle

Choletais

Cholet

Its atavistic economic energy, handed down through the generations, has its roots in textile and shoe manufacturing. The department's second town also has its share of science and arts museums; the Vendée's story is told in the History Museum.

MUSEE DU TEXTILE CHOLETAIS Rue du Docteur Roux ✆ 02 41 75 25 40. *Open Thursday and Friday: 2pm-6pm; Wednesday, Saturday and Sunday; 10am-12 noon and 2pm-6pm. Open all public holidays. Admission: adult 1.65 €, children/students free.* Cholet, now making mainly childrens' clothes, shows off its long textile tradition in the pleasant setting of an old laundry.

Doué-la-Fontaine

Famous for its rose gardens and annual festival in July, this town also contains more solid attractions: an ancient Gallo-Roman site, troglodyte caves at La Fosse and a zoo.

PARC ZOOLOGIQUE TROGLODYTIQUE 103, route de Cholet ✆ 02 41 59 18 58. *Open April-June: 9am-7pm; July & August: 9am-7.30pm; September, October, February & March: 10am-6pm. Admission: adult 14 €, 3-10s 8 €.* Among Europe's finest, this zoo contains 500 animals living in near-natural conditions, and esay to observe.

CHEMINS DE LA ROSE Parc de Courcilpleu ✆ 02 41 59 95 95. *Open every day: 9.30am-7pm to mid-May; 10am-12.30pm and 2pm-6.30pm to 30 September. Admission: adult 6 €, child 3 €.* A beautiful rose garden, in a perfumed 4-hectare park. Botanic, English, ancient and modern roses intoxicate you with their scent. The pleasure lasts in the romantic shop, which sells a whole host of products made from roses.

Montreuil-Bellay

A real walled town, one of the region's few.

Enjoy the old town's period atmosphere (Place du Marche, Place des Ormeaux) and historic houses, like the 15thc. Apothecary's House, and Grange-aux-D"mes, then walk along the banks of the Thouet, near the Gothic bridge and Saint Catherine Harbour. You can admire the valley from several viewpoints.

CHATEAU ✆ 02 41 52 33 06. *Open 1 April-31 October, every day except Tuesday: 10am-12 noon and 2pm-5.30pm. Admission: adult 7 €, child 3.50 €.* This fairytale castle is a blend of pugnacious feudalism and Renaissance grace.

Saint-Florent-le-Vieil

On 12 March 1793, the Vendeans gave battle here, crossing the Loire and soon finding themselves surrounded. Here too, the treaty of 1795 was signed, provisionally ending their hopes. You can feel a breath of nostalgia as you look down on the Loire Valley from the extraordinary belvedere on the Place des Armes. The abbey church opens off this esplanade, which is one of the river's finest sites.

Saumurois

Saumur

World-famous for its national riding school, the Cadre Noir, Saumur is also a historic town with its beautiful castle set above the Loire.

CHATEAU DE SAUMUR ✆ 02 41 40 24 40. *www.ville-saumur.fr.Saumur Chateau is closed for renovation work until 2007.* Public access to gardens and panoramic view only. At the close of the 14thc., Charles V's brother Louis, first Duke of Anjou, transformed his ancestor Saint-Louis' fortress into a residence for pleasure; Saumur thus became a luxurious palace. In 1480 after King Rene's death, Saumur reverted to the Crown, and was town governors' residence, prison and munitions depot before the town bought it in 1906 to house their museum. In April 2001, one of the ramparts collapsed, needing extensive repair work. As a result, the Decorative Arts and Horse sections are closed until 2007. You can walk round the gardens with their breathtaking view of town and Loire. There is also an exhibition on the collapse of the rampart and building work being undertaken.

ECOLE NATIONALE D'EQUITATION Saint-Hilaire-Saint-Florent © 02 41 53 50 60. *Open 1 April-31 October, Monday afternoon-Saturday noon: 9am-11am and 2pm-4pm. Admission: adult, morning 7 €, afternoon 5 €; child 4 € or 3 €.* This prestigious school was set up in the 19thc. to train cavalry officers in their black uniforms. Today it comes under the Ministry for Youth and Sport, and trains top instructors. Various demonstrations and events are held throughout the year, and the morning visit includes the riders' training session.

Fontevraud

ROYAL ABBEY © 02 41 51 71 41. *Open every day: 9am-6.30pm high season, 10am-5.30pm low season. Admission: adult 6.50 €, under-18s free.* This royal abbey was founded in the early 12thc., and until the Revolution, educated young girls from noble families, including the four youngest daughters of Louis XV. Sainte Marie Abbey Church is a Romanesque masterpiece, containing recumbent statues of Plantagenets, Comtes d'Anjou and Kings of England, among them Richard the Lionheart and his mother Eleanore of Aquitaine. Don't miss the kitchens, with their unusual roofs.

Montsoreau

The town is charming in itself, but the link with Alexandre Dumas' Dame de Montsoreau has made it more widely known.

CHATEAU DE MONTSOREAU © 02 41 67 12 60. *www.Château-montsoreau.com. Open February-April and October-mid November, every day: 2pm-6pm; May-September: 10am-7pm. Admission: adult 8,10!, child 5 €.* Overlooking the Loire, the castle has a magnificent view, and you may also meet the famous Lady of Montsoreau. Don't miss the animated circuit 'Imaginary Loire'.

CHAMPIGNONNIERE DU SAUT-AUX-LOUPS Route de Saumur © 02 41 51 70 30. *Open from 1 March-11 November every day, 10am-6pm. Admission: adult 5,20 €, child 3.50 €.* This little cave-dwelling leads to imposing galleries hewn out of the tuffeau, turned into beds for mushroom farming. The owners explain their work and let you taste their galipettes, big mushrooms spread with charcuterie, cheese or snails.

MAYENNE

Green, welcoming countryside, where cows graze peacefully and horses run free.

Laval

BATEAU-LAVOIR SAINT JULIEN (AND ITS SISTER SHIP SAINT YVES) Quai Paul Boudet © 02 43 49 46 46. *Open from 1 July-31 August, Tuesday-Saturday: 10am-12 noon and 2pm-6pm (except public holidays). September-June, by appointment. Admission free.* Anchored at Quai Paul Boudet, the Saint Julien (1904) has kept its equipment and is now a museum. Simple landing-stages to begin with, the laundry boats became two-storey buildings in the 19thc. The open hold served as the washing-place, and the captain's apartments , dryer and copper tubs for boiling linen were upstairs.

LACTOPOLE ANDRE BESNIER 18, rue Adolphe Beck © 02 43 59 51 90. *Open for bookings, every day except Sunday.* Discover the dairy adventure over 5,000 m^2 This unique museum takes you through milking, milk collection, fermentation and butter-producing to cheese-making . There are three parts: the former dairy (buildings and restored equipment), history of dairy technology and the story of the Lactalis group.

Château-Gontier

PARC DU BOUT DU MONDE. Public gardens laid out by the town in 1732, containing an 18thc. ice-house built on the base of a former rampart-tower. Lawns and flowerbeds border onto Saint Jean Baptiste Priory.

URSULINE CONVENT © 02 43 70 42 74. *1 May-30 September: Sundays and public holidays at 3pm. 1 July-31 August; every day at 3pm. Group bookings by appointment. Admission: adult 3 €, under-18s and concessions 1.60 €.* The convent contains a 14thc. Gothic house, 15thc. manor, convent, cloister and 17thc. church, and now houses the Le Carré Cultural Centre, School of Music and the Visual Arts and Ursulines Theatre.

Evron

NOTRE DAME DE L'EPINE BASILICA ✆ **02 43 01 63 75**. *Guide plans available on entry.* The basilica has an 11th and 12thc. tower and Romanesque church, 14thc. Gothic church and 12thc. Saint Crespin chapel. Things to see: the square tower, Renaissance portal, tapestry of Christ's baptism in one of the old naves, organs, stained glass chancel windows, statues and fonts.

MARCHE D'EVRON Place de la Basilique et de la Mairie. *Every Thursday morning.* This market has been traced back to 994, so it is over 1,000 years old. Market gardeners and craftsmen still sell their produce here.

Mayenne

PLACE DE HERCE. Not far from the octagonal fountain 'de Mazarin' (1683) are 17th and 18thc. mansions, including the forme Palais de la Barre. Built in 1660, its campanile is topped with a statue of Duke Armand de la Melleraye. Two sundials with Masonic symbols were added to the front in 1785; Freemasonry was probably influencing local worthies at the time.

CHATEAU. ✆ **02 43 04 19 37**.*Open July & August, Tuesday-Sunday: 2pm-6pm. Guided tours July-September, every day except Sunday: 2.15pm, 3.30pm and 4.45pm. No guided tours until 2007 owing to renovation work.* Well-preserved Carolingian architecture. Oxford archeologists digging there have recently found an 11th or 12thc. backgammon game made of bone.

Pontmain

Over 300,000 pilgrims and visitors come to this village every year, to see where the Virgin appeared on 17 January 1871. Pontmain Basilica, an imposing 19thc. granite monument, was completed on 10 May 1888 and consecrated in October 1900. There is a 32-bell peal in the spire; stained-glass windows depicting the life of Our Lady, and outside, a copper statue of the Virgin, painted according to descriptions left by those who saw her.

Saulges

MOULIN A EAU DE THEVALLES ✆ **02 43 98 66 70**. *Open every day except Sunday and Monday morning, 1 May-1 October: 10am-12 noon and 2pm-6pm. Admission: adult 5 € 7-14s 3 €.* Learn about gearing and pulleys in this working watermill, and see the medieval cereal épeautre (abandoned after the Middle Ages because difficult to hull), ground into flour.

GROTTES ET CANYON DE SAULGES - THORIGNE-EN-CHARNIE ✆ **02 43 90 51 30**. *Caves are open every day 15 March-15 November. Book in advance in July & August. Admission: 1 cave 5.50 €, 2 caves 8 €.* Unique in western France: 2 caves with rock sculptures; a rock-climbing site and a nature walk to see the flora and fauna.

Illuminated Mayenne, Laval

SARTHE

The Sarthe has plenty of little villages to discover, with their local produce. The Mans Alps, remains of the ancient Armoricain Massif, are particularly impressive.

Le Mans

VIEUX MANS. Forty years ago, this old quarter was considered unsafe; now it has become fashionable, attracting street artists and even filmmakers. Fifty or so monuments (houses, mansions, palaces) are newly shown to advantage thanks to a carefully studied urban project. You need to spend a lot of time in Le Mans to really get to know the architectural wealth of its ancient streets and alleys.

SAINT JULIEN CATHEDRAL Place Saint Michel. *Open every day, 8am-12 noon and 2pm-7pm, October-April; 8am-7pm July & August.* The cathedral was built between the 11th and 15thc. and named after Julian, who converted Le Mans to Christianity in the 4thc. It covers 5,000 m^2, and has some beautiful medieval stained glass; the oldest window dates back to the 11thc.

MUSEE AUTOMOBILE DE LA SARTHE Circuit des 24 Heures - Place Luigi Chinetti ✆ 02 43 72 72 24. *Open every day (except January, weekends only). June-September: 10am-7pm (other months 6pm). Admission: adult 7 €, 12-18s 5 €, 7-11s 2 €, under-7s free.* 120 vehicles are spread over 5,000 m^2, including 20 motorbikes and 30 historic racing cars (12 of these won the Le Mans 24-hour race). New technology has added video terminals and interactive games to the traditional museum.

CIRCUIT DES 24 HEURES DU MANS. This famous endurance racetrack with its Hunaudières finish is not to be missed for motor-racing fans. Guided tours in English of 1hr 45 mins can be organised all year; you can even try out the track for yourself!

la nuit des Chimères

During summer at nightfall, Plantagenêts's city used to «come on stage». La nuit des Chimères would lead the strollers towards imaginary characters. On the porch of the cathedral, during summer and also during Christmas holidays, the musician angels, who seem to be escaped from a fourteenth-century fresco, would play every night an heavenly concert. Only in summer, the party will go on at the foot of the big wall, where you could observe a roman bestiary. It's the biggest one in Europe after the wall of Roma and Constantinople. Between the cathedral and the big wall, the path running through the narrow streets of the old city, would become overcrowded of weird figures, inspired from the gargoyles of the cathedral, silhouetted against the pavement and the front walls. In the darkness, everyone is invited to purchase its own dreams. The city remains the memory, the cradle of the English-French Plantagenêts's dynasty : Mathilde, Aliénor, Bérangère, Geoffroy, Henri II, and Richard Coeur de Lion. La nuit des Chimères has been created by Skertzo, dreamkeepers, for the city of Le Mans.

Pays du Mans

Nature's delights

You really want to be «in the green»? Start your exploration at Nature's Arch...

The enchanting Forest of Bercé is a must before visiting the seal-approved gardens: Jardin des Plantes at Le Mans, Jardin du Petit Bordeaux at Saint Biez en Belin and the Jardins du Donjon at Ballon - gardens to revel in!

Cultural delights

The «Plantagenet City» makes its entry. Starting in the summer of 2006, inspired musicians offer you a celestial concert on the Cathedral porch where Roman gladiators are depicted on the wall. Then, visit the Abbey of Epau, and enjoy the subtle Cistercian beauty and sobriety. Le Mans 24-Hour Competition, is not the only vaunted event here. Throughout the year, there are unusual festivals and entertainment event…

Gourmet delights

Rillettes are a must, but local farm-raised poultry, honey, jams and chocolates have achieved acclaim too. During your stay don't hesitate to fill your basket with local produce at the colourful markets, or directly from farm producers. Enjoying the culinary delights of some of the many «Chef cuisiniers» is an essential part of your exploration of the area. Let temptation be your guide!

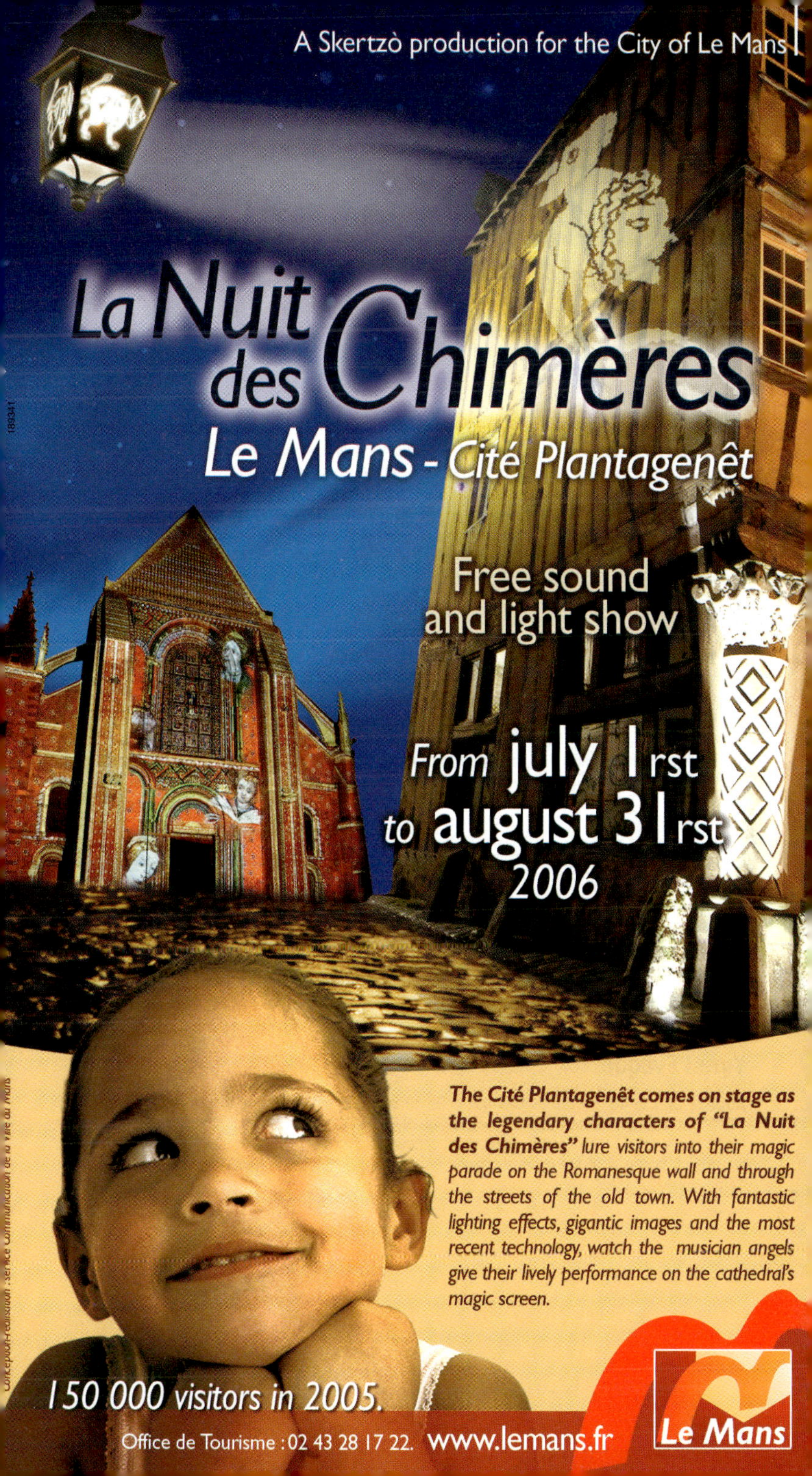
A Skertzò production for the City of Le Mans
La Nuit des Chimères
Le Mans - Cité Plantagenêt
Free sound and light show
From july 1rst to august 31rst 2006
The Cité Plantagenêt comes on stage as the legendary characters of "La Nuit des Chimères" lure visitors into their magic parade on the Romanesque wall and through the streets of the old town. With fantastic lighting effects, gigantic images and the most recent technology, watch the musician angels give their lively performance on the cathedral's magic screen.
150 000 visitors in 2005.
Office de Tourisme : 02 43 28 17 22. www.lemans.fr
Le Mans

Leisure delights

As a couple, with the family or with friends, come and enjoy the pleasure of fishing, hiking, golf and swin-golf, water and motorized sports as well as aqua-pleasure areas. The hardest thing for you will be choosing!

Enthusiasts of motorized sports, you've arrived in the «Pays du Mans»! Endurance or Grand Prix, two or four wheels, the 24-Hour circuit is open from April to October, with events of international renown.

Alpes mancelles

The Le Mans Alps in the north of the Sarthe constitute a natural site for walking and hiking (200km of marked-out paths). You really feel you're in the mountains, with marvellous views of villages and river; have a go at paragliding, 4x4 or rock-climbing.

La Flèche

MOULIN DE LA BRUERE Route du Lude ✆ 02 43 94 45 64. *Open for groups 1 April-30 September. Guided tours Saturdays at 3pm, 4pm and 5pm (July & August, every day except Monday). Admission: adults 3 €.* This working water mill on the Loir produces ice and electricity, and grinds cereals for animals.

ZOO DE LA FLECHE Tertre Rouge ✆ 02 43 48 19 19. *www.zoo-la-fleche.com. Open every day. Admission: adult 16 €, 3-11s 10.50 €.* Discover over 1,000 animals (120 species from 5 continents) in their natural habitat: polar bears seen underwater, elephants on the African plain, a pack of Arctic wolves (unique in Europe) and a little Chinese panda. Enjoy, too, the sea lion, parrot and birds of prey displays.

Le Lude

CHATEAU ✆ 02 43 94 60 09. *Open 1 April-30 September; all year for group bookings (except Wednesdays in April, May, June & September). Admission: outside only, adult 4.60 €; 7-15s 2.30 €. Inside & outside, 6 €/3.40 €.* First Loire castle heading south; owned and occupied by the same family for 200 years. The style is early French Renaissance, and each face is different: imposing medieval towers and moat; south-facing Italian Renaissance front with mullioned windows, main French Renaissance courtyard and classical 18thc. eastern wing towards the Loir. Take a pleasant walk through the formal, rose and kitchen gardens and the romantic park.

Le Grand-Luce

GRAND LUCE CHATEAU GARDENS ✆ 02 43 40 85 56. *Reopening in April 2006.* The castle was built in 1760 and the reconstituted gardens are typical of the period: straight lines and embroidery effects, floral kitchen garden and landscaped park, with orangery and greenhouses.

Solesmes

SOLESMES ABBEY ✆ 02 43 95 03 08. Mass is said every day at 10am in this magnificent Benedictine Abbey. Experience sung service in the chapel; the abbey is known for its Gregorian chants. Only the church is open to the public.

Yvre l'Evêque

ABBAYE DE L'EPAU Route de Change ✆ 02 43 84 22 29. *Open all year except Christmas and New Year's Day: 9.30am-12 noon and 2pm-6pm.* One of French Cistercian architectures's finest monuments, listed since 1961. Richard the Lionheart's widow Bérengère de Navarre founded it in 1229; her recumbent statue is in the abbey's chapter house. You must see the monks' dormitory, sacristy and 14thc. abbey church.

FOOD AND DRINK

The Pays-de-Loire is rich in local produce from ocean and bocage: the famous rillettes du Mans, and Loué poultry are perhaps the best-known examples.

Vendée Brioche

Smooth, sweet, flavoured with alcohol or orange-flower, this is a gastronomic star. It used to be eaten on Easter Saturday, but is now available all year round. The real Vendée brioche has only one recipe: 12% sugar, 14.50% butter and 18% eggs for 400g; and its geographical origin must be within the Vendée department.

Pommé

This is a kind of jam, made by cooking apples with new sweet cider for a very long time. Try it for dessert, with bread, galettes or crepes. The apples are prepared communally during the *quetou*, or 'apple evening'.

Rillettes

The recipe is simple: belly and shoulder of pork are cooked in fat, with salt added. The other ingredient is skill; the pork butcher's know-how makes his recipe unique, so there are perhaps as many recipes as craftsmen in the Sarthe!

BAHIER - AU PAYS DES RILLETTES Route de Paris - SCEAUX-SUR-HUISNE ✆ 02 43 60 31 25. *Open Friday: 9am-6.30pm, Saturday: 9am-12.30pm. July & August, Saturday-Friday: 9am-5pm, Saturday: 9am-12.30pm. Admission free.* This is a learning experience, an educational museum telling the story of Regis Bahier, once a simple charcutier, now the top industrial producer of old-fashioned rillettes. All aspects of rillette-making are shown, from period utensils to present-day production line (in model form) and from the arrival of the meat to the distribution of the pots (available in the shop).

Sardines

From Saint-Gilles-Croix-de-Vie, they now have a Red Label (guarrantee of quality). Sardines have been caught at Saint-Gilles since the early 17thc.; the manet (straight net) and use of cod-roe as bait increased the catch considerably at the period. Today, there are fewer banks, techniques have changed and ultrasound detectors are used.

Guerande Salt

100% natural, unrefined, unwashed and without additives, this salt is liked by gourmets for its texture and flavour. The grey colour comes from clay on the salt-marsh beds. Fleur-de-sel has finer crystals forming on the surface; the white film smelling faintly of violets has to be 'creamed off' by the salt-marsh workers.

TERRE DE SEL Pradel ✆ 02 40 62 08 80. *www.seldeguerande.com. Open all year, every day in July & August: 9.30am-12.30pm and 2.30pm-7pm. Call for opening times during other months. Admission: adult 3.25 €, child 2 €.* On the edge of the salt marshes, Terre de Sel houses a permanent exhibition on the ecological aspects of the marshes, and the job of marsh worker. You can also take part in a workshop, or a thematic trip.

Loué Poultry

Scarron, Racine, La Fontaine and the Comtesse de Ségur spoke of Loué's capons and fatted chickens. Today, chickens, guineau-hens, turkeys, geese, fatted chickens, Barbary ducks and capons are bred free-range in the Sarthe countryside. There are apparently more foxes where they are bred than elsewhere - a sign of natural traditions being kept up.

ANJOU VINEYARDS

France's most northern vineyard, and least known, despite a few famous names on the Loire Valley hillsides: chaume, quarts-de-chaume, savennières, roche-au-moines and the famous champigny in Saumur country.

MAISON DU VIN 5bis, place Kennedy ✆ 02 41 88 91 13. *www.Interloire.com. Open every day except Monday (and Sunday, October-April). Annual closing January & February.* Wine-lovers off to discover the Anjou-Saumur vineyards must stop here, for nowhere else can you taste their 28 appellations.

Les anjou-villages

The region's red wines have been greatly improved by winegrowers in the last few years. They come from cabernet franc and cabernet sauvignon *cépages*, and are light and easy to drink. The anjou-villages have more structure and body, and should be laid down for 5 years at least.

DOMAINE DE BABLUT - BRISSAC-QUINCE ✆ **02 41 91 22 59.**

DOMAINE DITTIERE - VAUCHRETIEN ✆ **02 41 91 23 78.** *Open every day except Sunday and public holidays: 8.30am-12 noon and 2pm-6.30pm.*

DOMAINE DE MONTGILET - JUIGNE-SUR-LOIRE ✆ **02 41 91 90 48.** *www.montgilet.com*

DOMAINE DES ROCHELLES Saint-Jean-des-Mauvrets ✆ **02 41 91 92 07.**

DOMAINE DES QUINZE DENIERS - CHARCE-SAINT-ELLIER ✆ **02 41 54 21 18**

Le bonnezeaux

Between layon and chaume, the bonnezeaux takes its style and flavour from the quince, which grows in its soil. This powerful wine can be drunk young and extremely fruity, or matured, with its superb cognac-colour.

CHATEAU DE FESLES Thouarce ✆ **02 41 68 94 00**

DOMAINE DES PETITS QUARTS - FAYE-D'ANJOU ✆ **02 41 54 03 00.** *Open 8am-12.30pm and 2pm-5.30pm, or by appointment. Closed Sundays and public holidays.*

DOMAINE DES CLOSSERONS Faye-d'Anjou ✆ **02 41 54 30 78**

Les Côteaux-de-l'aubance

The Côteaux-de-l'aubance, 100% chenin cépage, are sweet wines with a cool, mineral flavour which leaves an almost mentholated taste in the mouth. Drink them as an aperitif or with dessert (a chocolate cake, for instance).

DOMAINE DE HAUTE-PERCHE Sant-Melaine-sur-Aubance ✆ **02 41 57 75 65**

DOMAINE RICHOU Chauvigne ✆ **02 41 78 72 13**

Les Côteaux-du-layon

A white wine with a delicious green-apple flavour, typical of its soil south of the Loire. There are at least three kinds: générique, elaboré or villages. The latter's grapes are picked late (vendange tardive), so it is full and sirupy enough to go with foie gras.

DOMAINE OGEREAU Saint-Lambert-du-Lattay ✆ **02 41 78 30 53**

Salt

DOMAINE DU SAUVEROY Saint-Lambert-du-Lattay ✆ **02 41 78 30 59**

CHATEAU PIERRE BISE Beaulieu-sur-Layon ✆ **02 41 78 31 44**

DOMAINE DE LA BERGERIE Champs-sur-Layon ✆ **02 41 78 85 43**

DOMAINE DES QUARRES Rablay-sur-Layon ✆ **02 41 78 60 69**

DOMAINE RICHOU Chauvigne ✆ **02 41 78 72 13**

DOMAINE DE HAUTE-PERCHE Sant-Melaine-sur-Aubance ✆ **02 41 57 75 65**

CHATEAU DES NOYERS Martigne-Briand ✆ **02 41 54 03 71**

Les quarts-de-chaume

A sweet but expensive white wine, made from chenin, mysterious and delicious.

CHATEAU DE PIEGUE Rochefort-sur-Loire ✆ **02 41 78 71 26**

DOMAINE DES BAUMARD - ROCHEFORT-SUR-LOIRE ✆ **02 41 78 70 03.** *www.baumard.fr. Open every day 10am-12noon and 2pm-5.30pm, except Sunday and public holidays.*

Les rosés

In Anjou, rose wines were the biggest

part of local production (remember the famous Cabernet d'Anjou?). Now they have been improved, developing refreshing citrus notes.

CLOSERIE DE LA PICARDIE Notre-Dame-d'Alencon ✆ 02 41 54 30 32

DOMAINE DE TERREBRUNE Notre-Dame-d'Alencon ✆ 02 41 54 01 99

LE COTILLON BLANC Chavagnes-les-Eaux ✆ 02 41 54 01 27

CHATEAU DE PASSAVANT - PASSAVANT-SUR-LAYON ✆ 02 41 59 53 96. *Open Monday to Friday: 8.30am-12.30pm and 2pm-6pm. Weekends by appointment. The David family has been producing exceptional 'organic' wines for over half a century*

The saumur-champigny

The sales of saumur-champigny are not the biggest in Anjou, but the wine exports well. This deeply-coloured red, scented with violets and lilies, is easy to drink, straight away or after several years, and good wine-lovers appreciate it.

CLOS DES CORDELIERS Champigny ✆ 02 41 53 95 48

DOMAINE DE NERLEUX - SAINT-CYR-EN-BOURG ✆ 02 41 51 61 04. *www.domaine-de-nerleux.fr. Open Monday-Friday: 8am-12.30pm and 1.30pm-6pm; Saturday: 9am-12 noon. Saumur wines have been made here for five centuries. Domaine de Nerleux means loups noirs or black wolves.*

DOMAINE LA VIGNE Varrains ✆ 02 41 52 92 57

CHATEAU DE FOSSE SECHE Brossay ✆ 02 41 52 22 22

CAVE DES VIGNERONS DE SAUMUR Saint-Cyr-en-Bourg ✆ 02 41 53 06 06

Les savennières

One of the world's most prestigious appellations, savennières grows on south-facing slopes. It makes a dry white wine with green lights in it, and there are powerful floral notes and a soft bitterness to the taste.

CHATEAU D'EPIRE ✆ 02 41 77 15 01. *Open every day: 10am-12 noon and 2pm-6.30pm.*

CLOS DE FREMUR Sainte-Gemmes-sur-Loire ✆ 02 41 72 25 54

CHATEAU LA FRANCHAIE - LA POISSONNIERE ✆ 02 41 39 18 16

Sparkling wines

The champagne method introduced in the Saumur region in the early 19thc. adapted well to the naturally fizzy local product, giving good-quality bubbles. The great winegrowers' cellars are impressive to visit.

ACKERMAN-LAURANCE Saint-Hilaire-Saint-Florent ✆ 02 41 53 03 21

BOUVET-LADUBAY Saint-Hilaire-Saint-Florent ✆ 02 41 83 83 83

DOMAINE LANGLOIS-CHATEAU Saint-Hilaire-Saint-Florent ✆ 02 41 40 21 40

Local products in Fresnay-sur-Sarthe

Hotels & restaurants

LOIRE-ATLANTIQUE

Ancenis

LA TOILE A BEURRE 82, rue Saint-Pierre ✆ 02 40 98 89 64. *Closed Sunday evening, Monday and Wednesday evening. Set menus from 11 € to 31 €. A la carte.* Isabelle and Jean-Charles Baron share their excellent traditional cuisine with customers in a charming and no less traditional setting, complete with 18thc. fireplace and spit, vaulted *tuffeau* (chalky stone) cellar, private lounge and flower garden. The atmosphere is enhanced by the generous servings of good quality food, made only with fresh ingredients.

Basse-Goulaine

VILLA MON REVE Route des bords de Loire ✆ 02 40 03 55 50 *Website: www.villa-mon-reve.com. 7 days a week. Set menus 21.50 € lunchtime. Carte Blanche Affaires 27.50 €. Then 28 €, 46 €, 54 €, 61 € and 69 €.* This beautiful villa nestling in greenery below the Divatte is a fine example of a family cooking business. The sober but richly decorated setting was created by the talented Cecile, and the sublime cooking is the work of Gerard Ryngel, forceful and sincere, but also subtle and delicate.The ingredients are all fresh and seasonal, prepared traditionally with a touch of individual genius. White butter and sauce poulette (chicken stock, cream and white wine) are well known standards, but what about hot poached oysters and enormous Tuballe scallops simply pan-cooked and served with cream and a light fall of leeks? You can watch Cecile or her grown-up son Jean-Michel carving a sumptuous Challans duck on the pedestal table. Try a partridge *pastilla*, a Loire *matelote à l'ancienne,* (wine sauce) a wild dory roasted in meat juices with wild mushrooms, and to finish, a panful of brioche pudding with caramelised fruits. Forget that diet! The wine list is huge, with the richest collection of Muscadets in the world, believe us! These places are becoming few and far between, so don't miss out, or you'll regret it!

Clisson

LA BONNE AUBERGE 1, rue Olivier-de-Clisson ✆ 02 40 54 01 90. *Closed Monday, Sunday evening, Tuesday and Wednesday lunchtime. Set menus 21 € (weekday lunchtimes), 35.50 €, 41.50 €, 48.50 €, 56.50 €, 71 €. A la carte.* Chantal and Serge Poiron have created a pretty setting, with sumptuous flower arrangements and original tables, winter garden and little private salons. They have also made it one of the region' s best places to eat. Unsurprisingly, people come from miles around to enjoy their inspired regional and traditional cuisine: sole de petite piche (refers to the fishing method) in a potato crust, kidney and sweetbread *panache*, pigeon breast and rissoled duck foie gras, and among the sumptuous desserts, a tart you'd die for. Note that organic produce is used systematically and all meat and poultry is supplied by small local breeders. No-one prepares these excellent foodstuffs better than Serge, the sauce expert. The wine cellar gives pride of place to muscadets. Havana fans have their salon, where they can enjoy those pleasures that go with a good cigar. You'd be wise to book in advance at this chic, gastronomic inn.

La Baule

CASTEL MARIE-LOUISE 1, avenue Andrieu ✆ 02 40 11 48 38. *Open every evening, closed lunchtimes except Sunday. In season, open for lunch every day (15 May-15 September). Annual holiday 15 November-15 December. Set menu carte blanche 40 € (lunchtimes only). Menu Marie-Louise 58.60 €, menu Bretagne 70.70 € and menu decouverte 86.60 € for all the guests. A la carte.* This attractive manor in its imposing green setting facing the sea recalls the banquets held in olden times. The standard of excellence has not fallen with the passing years, due to an energetic and capable management, extensive refurbishing work and a great chef, Eric Mignard, in the kitchens. Every season his imagination brings forth new treasures, combining sophisticated flavours with local produce, like his whole lobster roasted in coral butter, whipped cream with candied orange and Nantes leeks, and his Mesquer pigeon in an aubergine fondant and foie gras. The Castel continues the tradition of gastronomic meetings that take place several times a year, to discover a new type of *cuisine* or promote great wines. You can anticipate Eric's cooking by first tasting one of his sophisticated breakfasts served in the park.

HOTEL MERCURE MAJESTIC 14 esplanade Lucien Barrière ✆ 02 40 60 24 86 *Single room from 75 €. Junior suite 330 €. Breakfast 14 €. Pets accepted.* Close to the town centre, seawater therapy institute and casino, facing the sea. 60 rooms including 24 non-smoking, all fully-equipped and comfortable. 5 junior suites. The hotel restaurant Le Ruban Bleu offers local cooking, reputed in the region. Cocktails and aperitifs available in Derby's lounge bar. Two conference rooms available for customers. Private car park.

LE RUBAN BLEU 14, esplanade Lucien-Barrière ✆ *02 40 60 24 86. Website: www.hotelmercure-labaule.com http://www.hotelmercure-labaule.com. Open 7 days a week lunchtimes & evenings. Set menu Monday-Friday 25 €. Set menus 35 € and 45 €. A la carte. Children's menu 14 €. Air-conditioned non-smoking restaurant.* The dining room faces the sea and is decorated in Art Deco style. Chef Didier Cadiet prepares seafood and seasonal dishes with talent: lobster salad and foie gras pan-fried with mango, Jerusalem artichokes and chestnuts, vinaigrette and shellfish, wild duck with salsify, cepes and cherries in alcohol; sole fillet with hazlenuts and mussels with aromatic herbs feature on his menus. The ingredients are carefully selected and very fresh. Attentive, diligent service. Derby's Cafe is the adjoining bar, where smokers can finally light up in a similar and equally pleasant setting.

LA VERANDA 27, boulevard de l'Océan ✆ 02 40 60 57 77. *Open early February to late November. Closed Monday lunchtime and Wednesday - except July and August.Formula of the day (weekdays) 20 € (includes a glass of wine and coffee). Set menus from 35 € to 75 €. Children's menu 15 €.* Discover the pleasure of delicious cooking served on the seafront, with a superb view of the bay. The ocean is refelcted in the dining room's sophisticated shades and in the chef's cuisine, a real seafood feast. Breton lobster in a sumptuous mixed salad, pan-fried Dublin Bay prawns, and cream of Dublin Bay prawns, a delicacy worth tasting. The best fish, like the dory, are served as roast or pan-fried fillets. Olivier Androuin is just as talented when preparing meat, witness the roast quail that featured on our particular day. Reduced juices, accurate cooking times and subtle seasoning characterise his inventive and meticulous recipes. For dessert, if you share Olivier's passion for chocolate, especially valrhona, you will be delighted - enjoy it with an allegorie du cleray en eolie. The muscadet is great, and may change your ideas about Loire wines. Isabel Androuin welcomes you all smiles, and the service is attentive. Any gourmet will love this place.

Le Croisic

LE CASTEL MOOR Avenue du Castouillet ✆ 02 40 23 24 18. *Website : www.castel-moor.com. Double room from 49 €. Breakfast 8 €. Pets accepted.* Located on the Guerande peninsula's wild coast with a great ocean view. The hotel restaurant offers fish, and seafood and local specialities. Chef Daniel cooks inventive dishes according to season and the day's catch. Terrace and garden for fine weather. The Castel Moor also organises family reunions.

LE BRETAGNE 11, quai de la Petite-Chambre ✆ 02 40 23 00 51. *Website: www.restaurant-de-bretagne.com. Closed Sunday evening and Monday in low season, Tuesday too outside school holiday periods. Set menus 16 € weekdays (starter + main course or main course + dessert) 22 €, 32 €, 43 €, 68 €. A la carte. Children's menus 10 € and 13 €.* Frederic Lehuede runs this cuisinerie gourmande, or 'delicious cooking place' labelled *Qualite France*, and continues the great Breton tradition of fresh local produce influenced by both countryside and the sea. He knows you need to be strict in your choice of foodstuffs and suppliers to reach this standard of excellence, but a touch of originality in the preparation doesn't go amiss, and pleases the most demanding palates.

Les Sorinières

ABBAYE DE VILLENEUVE Route de la Roche-sur-Yon ✆ 02 40 04 40 25. *Website: www.abbayedevilleneuve.com. Open every day. Set menus from 30 € to 58 €.* This magnificent 13thc. abbey lost in the countryside provides high standards of comfort in a genuine period setting. The kitchens maintain these standards, since the chef prefers fresh ingredients for his cooking. Originality, finesse and subtlety are his watchwords, which just about sum up the whole experience, including the sublime decoration and courteous welcome. Note that the large monks' hall is a perfect place for receptions.

Nantes

L'ATLANTIDE 16, quai Ernest-Renaud ✆ 02 40 73 23 23 *Set menus from 26 € to 95 €. A la carte 75 €. Closed Sunday, Saturday lunchtime and public holidays, from 1-29 August and 23 December-2 January.* The Quai Ernest Renaud is off the beaten tourist track, in a rather grey environment, and this restaurant located at the top of the CCI building passes largely unnoticed. The lunchtime business clientele is therefore delighted to find such an opulent setting and high standards of cooking. Jean-Yves Gueho is no show-off; he has brought a taste for spices back from his years in Hong Kong, and combines them with the region's culinary wealth to create fresh, flavoursome menus. His pan-fried scallops flavoured with pistachio nuts and almonds, frogs' legs jambonnette with *sate*, Jerusalem artichokes *mousseline*, dory fillet spiked with pieces of conserved lemon bergamot, squid and peppered artichoke, roast mallard duck with bush peaches, and chervil and pan-fried cepes are proof of his talent. Precision-timed cooking, well-mastered preparation: everything is under control, including the efficient service. Intelligent choices in the wine cellar; beautiful panoramic view of the Loire and its quays.

LA CIGALE 4, place Graslin ✆ 02 51 84 94 94. *Website: www.lacigale.com. Open 7 days a week, all year. Brasserie service from 12 noon to half-past midnight, breakfast from 7.30am.* This 1900-style brasserie where artists and the Nantes worthies liked to meet is a listed historical monument. With its Belle Epoque ceramics, huge mirrors, shades of gold and turquoise and lighting, it is a sumptuous place, right down to the food on its plates. You can't fault the welcome or the service: you can have theatre tickets booked for you at La Fleuriaye and the Graslin Opera. The cuisine doesn't lag behind either: tender meat, fresh fish, excellent oysters and other savoury dishes are served according to the chef's mood. The wine list is continually developing. Pastries are served with breakfast, or if you prefer, brunch - La Cigale thinks of everything!

HOTEL DE FRANCE * 24, rue Crébillon ✆ 02 40 73 57 91**. This hotel provides facilities well above the average, as a number of celebrities passing through Nantes have reason to know. Some of the 70 rooms are decorated in Louis XVI style, and ten are enormous (30-40 sqm.). They are all soundproofed and equipped with bathroom, toilets, telephone, satellite TV and a private indoor car park. The reception hall alone is worth a visit; vast and superb, it houses painting exhibitions. Companies can hire meeting rooms for seminars, seating 12-15, and top-of-the-range catering is available for cocktails, buffet lunches, lunch and dinner in the hotel restaurant L'Opera (seats up to 80). Despite being so grand, the Hotel de France remains a family institution, with the same kindness and consideration that the manager and his team have always shown to guests. Enjoy!

MANOIR DE LA REGATE 155, route de Gachet ✆ 02 40 18 02 97 *Set menus from 18 € to 67 €. A la carte 53 €. Closed Sunday evening and Monday.* Brothers Pascal and Loic Perou have owned this elegant 18thc.manor for 10 years, and are among the most unobtrusive of Western France's top chefs. The restaurant is not easy to find, especially at night, since it isn't well signposted, but once there, you'll be impressed by the fine building reflected in the Erdre, just opposite the famous Château de la Gascherie. The brothers are active in the kitchens, gallantly concocting dishes for delighted customers:

piquillo peppers stuffed with Nantes snails, frogs' legs and young vegetables in escabeche, roast turbot with Dublin Bay prawns in nems and conserved shallots, young roast pigeon with figs and lean bacon, seasonal vegetable *fricassée*, and sesame transparence with seasonal fruit. Loic and Pascal have also planned dishes for customers in a hurry, marked with an asterisk on the menu. The cellar is essentially regional, giving pride of place to haut Poitou and Muscadet wines.

LA POISSONNERIE 4, rue Léon-Maître © 02 40 47 79 50. *Except Saturday lunchtime, Sunday and Monday. Lunchtime formula 13 €. A la carte.* A lifebelt marked 'Welcome on board' in front of the door sets the tone for this restaurant, serving only fish and seafood, and one of the best of its kind. There is no lack of talent and mastery; the faithful clientele that has been coming back regularly for years can confirm it. It's best to book in advance if you don't want to meet with a polite refusal.

Orvault

LE DOMAINE D'ORVAULT * Chemin des Marais du Cens © 02 40 76 84 02**. *Except Saturday lunchtime and Sunday evening. 7 days a week in July and August. 41 rooms. Set menus from 24 € to 68 €. A la carte.* Impressive renovation work has upgraded the Domaine d'Orvault's comfort standards, restoring its former lustre. Sylvain Lejeune has had the setting redesigned in contemporary style (warm shades of wood predominate) and added an immense terrace in the park. In the kitchen, chef Thierry Bouhier has thrown out the gadgets and useless sophistication, and gone for big, beautiful and simple. Top-of-the-range produce, well- timed cooking and perfect though original matches. There are no false notes, the service is efficient and stylised, with wine served by the glass and above-average comfort. If that's castle life, we want more!

Pornic

BEAU RIVAGE Plage de la Birochère © 02 40 82 03 08. *Website: www.restaurant-beaurivage.com. Weekly closing Monday in high season; Sunday evening, Monday and Wednesday evening in low season. Annual holiday 15 December-2 February. Bistrot formula from 16 € to 21 €, restaurant set menus from 32 € to 66 €, children's menu 14 €. A la carte. Original formulas: carte blanche menu for all the guests in the party 58 €, lobster menu 64 €.* The Beau Rivage's delicious cuisine makes it Pornic's gastronomic hotspot. Ideally located beside the ocean in a pretty setting with a professional welcome for customers, it specialises in inventive and subtle cooking using carefully selected local ingredients. The sea influences preparations where respect for regional flavours combines harmoniously with a taste for adventure, sometimes Mediterranean. The wine list is just as balanced. You can work off your meal with a superb walk along the smugglers' path.

LA FONTAINE AUX BRETONS * © 02 51 74 08 08**. *www.auberge-la-fontaine.com. Open all year except Sunday evening October-March. Rooms from 86 €. Set menus from 19.50 €.* An original concept for this old farm, converted into a 3-star inn and tourist residence. The rustic kitchen and aromatic plant gardens recalling olden times are a source of inspiration to chef Fabrice Guilleux. His suppliers are small regional breeders and farmers, and he cooks only with the freshest ingredients: some of his recipes are no longer found elsewhere, like the suckling pig cooked in a marmite, or stewpot. His poultry is magnificently roasted, meat simmered in the bread oven and fish simply grilled; the flavours separate and combine for the greatest of culinary pleasures. You can eat on the terrace in good weather. 'Friendly, welcoming staff'; 'very pleasant site'; 'remarkable decoration' and 'exceptional, flavoursome cuisine' are some comments in the visitors' book, proof of success for this inn only a stone's throw from the ocean.

Pornichet

LE SUD BRETAGNE ** 42, boulevard de la République 02 40 11 65 00/02 40 61 73 70.** *Website: www.hotelsudbretagne.com. Open all year. Closed Sunday evening out of season. Rooms from 100 € to 180 €. Apartments and suites from 200 €. Breakfast 13 €. Formula 25 € (weekday lunchtimes only). Set menus 40 € and 50 €. A la carte.* This hotel-restaurant is the jewel in Pornichet's crown. Located in front of the market square a stone's throw from the beach, it has it all: two swimming pools (one indoor heated), subtly personalised and regularly refurbished rooms, and menus offering a balanced choice of seafood and fish or meat. Comfortable, certainly, but also the stuff of which dreams are made.

Saint-Lyphard

AUBERGE DE KERBOURG Kerbourg © 02 40 61 95 15. *Closed Sunday evening, Monday and Tuesday lunchtime in low season. Set menus from 49 € to 54 €.* In this thatched inn dating back to 1753, with its rustic but elegant decor, Bernard and Sarah welcome you with warmth and simplicity. They have created a charming restaurant, all white tablecloths and beautiful china. Even better is the excellent cuisine prepared by top chef Bernard Jeanson, whose Michelin *macaron* has just been confirmed. His talent results in inventive and original menus, based on extensive knowledge of his ingredients.

Sucé-sur-Erdre

LE CLOS SAINT-THOMAS 102, rue de la Mairie ✆ 02 40 77 71 34 *Website: www.restaurant-clos-st-thomas.com. Closed Monday and Sunday to Wednesday evening. Set menus from 15 € to 42 €.* Faby and Yvonnyk Briand created the Clos Saint-Thomas, previously run for a long time as the Cordon Bleu. They have brought youth, enthusiasm and talent to the job, offering simple but highly-developed gastronomy based on a series of carefully selected products, including Arnaud Gueret's Loire basin fish. A fine mix of modern cooking timed with a stopwatch, and old-fashioned dishes simmered over a low heat, with Loire traditions and Provencal flavours, on the summer menu.

MAINE-ET-LOIRE

Angers

HOTEL D'ANJOU * 1, boulevard Foch ✆ 02 41 21 12 11.** *Fax: 02 41 87 22 21. Website: www.hoteldanjou.fr. Single or double rooms 103 € to 112 € (comfort plus)139 € and 149 € (luxury) 156 € and 166 € (luxury plus). Breakfast 11 €. Pets admitted 6 €. Small private garage 8 €. Cheques Vacances accepted.* The hotel changed hands a year ago, and is now quite different; Art Deco fans will love it. Air-conditioning and and double glazing have been put in, and the decoration and furnishings in the rooms renewed. Each has its own style, and all are comfortable with a double door for better privacy, telephone, cable TV and Canal +, mini-bar and complete bathroom. Some superb mosaics were discovered during the renovation work, and became part of the town's guided tourist circuits. The hall has been entirely rebuilt in marble by a local architect, in anticipation of the luxurious rooms.

LE PETIT COMPTOIR 40, rue David-d'Angers – A côté de la mairie 02 41 88 81 57. *Open every day except Sunday and Monday. Main course 14 €, main course + dessert 17 €, starter + main course 19 €. One evening menu only, starter, main course, cheese and dessert 26 €.* The Petit Comptoir is run by a young couple who have chosen to prepare 'off the beaten track' gastronomy in a chic bistrot ambiance for customers used to classy cooking. It's the ideal place for a professional lunch combining good taste, a relaxed atmosphere and excellent food. The cuisine is sophisticated, attractively presented in the nouvelle cuisine style - the chef used to work in a great Parisian restaurant, and you can tell! Subtle mixtures, simple but effective, that you would never have thought of yourself, are created by Laetitia and Stephane Cosnier. Examples are creamy chanterelle risotto, country ham, roast meat juices, roast sea bream, vegetable *barigoule* (stewed in olive oil) conserved lemons and for dessert, apricot clafoutis with its milk shake, and yellow peach soup with fresh verbena. You'll enjoy the food, and appreciate its daring originality. The *carte* is balanced and varied with just enough choice, ditto for the wines, well-chosen and served by the glass. The chic bistrot is on the ground floor looking out on the Rue David d'Angers, while the first floor is more intimate, for business talk or just spending a relaxing moment with friends. Try it - you'll end up recommending it too!

LE RELAIS 9, rue de la Gare ✆ 02 41 88 42 51. *Closed Sunday and Monday. Service until 1.30pm and 9.30pm. Set menus 16.50 € lunchtime, 19.50 € (retour de marche) 32 €. A la carte 30 €, without wine.* Tastefully sober and stylised decoration in pale colours with wall frescoes and red padded chairs. The owner knows how to welcome his gests and show off his gastronomic cuisine. The sophisticated dishes mix and match contrasting flavours, like the potato *galette* with basil and a gamba and chicory salad, and the pollack minute and Dublin Bay prawn bisque, or fresh herring in white wine and vinegar, and fish soup with mustard. Typical desserts are *oeuf au lait en neige* (floating islands) tiramisu or *cremet d'Anjou,* soft white cheese whipped into peaks. Generous servings, with no fuss, though the service tends to lack warmth and enthusiasm. That is the only weak point, though, and the chef's talent far outweighs it.

Briollay

CHATEAU DE NOIRIEUX 26, route du Moulin ✆ 02 41 42 50 05 *Website : www.chateaudenoirieux.com.Set menus from 55 € to 97 €. Closed Sunday evening, Monday and Tuesday lunchtimes (November-April), Monday and Tuesday (May-October),15 February-16 March and 13 November-1 December.* Known as the best place to eat in the Angers area, the Château de Noirieux is a group of 15th. and 17thc. buildings overlooking the Loir. It is also a top-of-the-range hotel that gives itself aristocratic airs - with good reason. Seasoned chef Gerard Come has run the kitchens since 1992, and not content with merely satisfying captive hotel guests, serves a luxurious - and expensive - cuisine that rivals the best. Breton scampi just lightly browned with chervil, and sole blancmange with a chanterelle stock, wild Breton bass with crusty skin, oscietre caviar and aubergine sabayon, suckling veal sweetbreads and thick slice of veal quasi casseroled with crayfish, and peach and apricot carpaccio, iced *moelleux* with a Zan baton and chicory feature among his specialities. 90 €-100 € is steep for a meal *a la carte* but you're also paying for the setting. The wine list is enormous; a good tip is to choose directly from the Loire pages which contain some fine discoveries.

Chenillé-Changé

LA TABLE DU MEUNIER ✆ 02 41 95 10 98. *Website: www.maie-anjou-rivieres.com. Closed 1 January-20 February, 1 April-30 June and 1 September-31 October, also Monday evening, tuesday and Wednesday. 1 November-31 December and 21 February-31 March, closed Sunday evening, Monday, Tuesday and Wednesday. Open every day in July and August. Set menus 17.70 € (weekdays), 23.70 €, 27.10 €, 28.20 € and 36 €. 6 rooms seating 10-100 people.* This former oil mill has been perfectly restored, and its rustic setting converted into a good quality inn. Local produce has pride of place on its menus: melon fan with Vendée ham, pikeperch with sorrel or white butter sauce, and veal saltimbocca served on a river of vegetables with aniseed-flavoured juice. When it comes to dessert, the *diplomate* (a kind of cake) is soaked in Cointreau. Good honest regional cooking, equally tasty by the fireside in winter or outside in summer.

Doué-La-Fontaine

AUBERGE BIENVENUE ** 104 route de Cholet ✆ 02 41 59 22 44 Fax 02 41 59 93 49. *Website: www.aubergebienvenue.com. Open Tuesday to Sunday lunchtime. Annual closing 2 weeks in February. Hotel open 7 days a week. Double room 50 € to 55 €, breakfast 6.50 €. Pets admitted. Restaurant open every day except Sunday evening and Monday. Open every day in high season. Set menus 20 €, 26 €, 35 €, 44 € and 50 €.* This charming inn just opposite the zoo has 7 spacious and comfortable air-conditioned rooms. There are pastel shades and a hushed atmosphere indoors, and a flower-covered terrace outside where you can enjoy the warm weather. The food includes fish in white butter sauce, duck breasts, foie gras and local vegetables, those well-prepared classic dishes combining old-fashioned recipes with modern cooking techniques. Michel Roche's talent for sauces deserves special notice. You can savour an Anjou chicken salad with raspberry vinegar, followed by leg of lamb cooked two ways with garlic, and a choice of sweet, for 20 €.

Les Rosiers-sur-Loire

LA TOQUE BLANCHE 2, rue Quarte ✆ 02 41 51 80 75. *Website: euro-toque.fr. Closed Tuesday evening and all day Wednesday. Set menus 22 €, 28 €, 31.50 €, 37 €, 42 € and 43 €.* A spotless white chef's hat and apron on a smiling chef with a moustache. A gleaming restaurant facing the Loire, and skilful French cuisine that dares to venture off the beaten track. A touch of seasoning here and there, and a few typically French combinations. Finally, a chef safely rooted in his traditional cooking, light years from certain colleagues with their risky ideas. The food is always well presented and accompanied by a Loire wine list. You'll wipe your plate clean of Dublin Bay prawn cream flavoured with vanilla pod, and ask for more of the chicory *fondue* that comes with the tasty sole fillet cooked just right. The gastronomic pleasure is intensified by a fine Anjou and Saumur wine list, and a sublime view of the Loire.

Saint-Sylvain-d'Anjou

AUBERGE D'EVENTARD Route de Paris - Rond-point du Parc Expo ✆ 02 41 43 74 25. *Site Intenet: www.auberge-eventard.com. Closed Saturday lunchtime, Sunday evening and Monday. Service 12 noon-1.55pm and 8pm-9.15pm. Set menu 23 € (weekday lunchtimes) 55 €, 61 € and 78 €. A la carte 65 €. Reception menus from 61 € to 85 €, including drinks.* An elegant setting for top-class gastronomy. The charming garden, opulent salon and beautiful dining-room with exposed beams and chalky tuffeau stone welcome guests, who are served attentively and with tact. Those 'royal' dishes draw all eyes and tastebuds as they are carried in. Roast brie spread on a bread tartine, spring salad, suckling pig fillet mignon with mustard grains, apples *en cocotte* and chocolate *fondant*, home made gingerbread ice cream feature on the delicious kitchen garden menu. This menu is a new idea, inspired by Jean-Pierre Maussion's grandmother's recipes. The beef fillet *sauce royale* with willow berries and cocoa beans is another delicacy not to be missed. A little more garnish wouldn't come amiss with some dishes, though the cuisine is excellent, and the chef visits his guests in the dining room during their meal.

Saumur

LE GAMBETTA 12, rue Gambetta ✆ 02 41 67 66 66. *Closed Saturday lunchtime, Sunday evening (except June to September) and Monday. Set menus 23 €, 26 €, 34 € and 46 €.* The Gambetta is one of Saumur's best restaurants, located in an old building away from the town centre, facing a sublime house with turrets. On the 23 € menu, we especially liked the tart *friand* with tomato and basil, mackerel fillet, followed by sea trout steak, *épeautre* (einkorn; an ancient wheat variety) and horn of plenty mushrooms, and grape shortbread for dessert, though raspberry fantasy with tea, and pineapple sorbet was a close rival. Patrick Chesnoy is chef in this cosy place, and his cooking follows the seasons, or a theme such as variations on the chestnut, or during the hunting season, on game. The wines are selected according to strict criteria, and some are served by the glass.

LOIRE HOTEL * Rue du Vieux-Pont ✆ 02 41 67 22 42.** *Fax: 02 41 67 88 80. Website: www.loire-hotel.fr. 45 attractive rooms with bathroom, WC, telephone, TV, mini-bar and lift. Rooms from 62 € (single) to 92 € (double). Continental breakfast 9 €.* This hotel boasts a beautiful setting on the Loire banks 'between the bridges' as they say in Saumur, with a view of the town hall, river and town. The rooms and reception area were redecorated in 2003, and as a result, are now much lighter, with more atmosphere. Two-thirds of the rooms overlook the river. Pets are accepted with a 4 € supplement. 3 seminar or banqueting rooms available.

L'ORANGERAIE Les Feuquières – Château ✆ 02 41 67 12 88. *Fax: 02 41 67 74 60. Closed Sunday evening and Monday. Set menus 6.50 € and 8.50 € (lunchtime express) 18 €, 20.50 €, 30 €.* Starting from Place Saint-Pierre, climb up via the fort to the castle, pause to enjoy the view over the rooftops, go under the drawbridge and you are in the castle courtyard. Prisca and Sylvain have been running this brasserie for a short time only, but they have chosen well: the veranda and terrace in the shadow of the castle have a marvellous plunging view of the surrounding landscape. Their cuisine reinvents the brasserie spirit with originality: grilled Dublin Bay prawns with lime, a delicious starter, which we followed with a potato and cod tart Tatin-style, rather than the lamb knuckle cooked in its juice with a mushroom garnish. The *mi-cuit* chocolate biscuit with mint sorbet is a great ending to an excellent meal for sweet-lovers.

MAYENNE

Château-Gontier

PARC HOTEL * 46, avenue Joffre ✆ 02 43 07 28 41** *Website: www.parchotel.fr. 19 rooms from 58 €, all with bath, and 2 suites, including one wedding suite 95 €. Satellite TV and RJ45 connection for PC. Breakfast 8 €* served in your room if you wish. Tennis and partially-covered pool. Located near the famous Craon hippodrome, between the Mont-Saint-Michel and the Loire chateaux, this elegant 19thc. mansion houses a charming hotel in shady grounds (1 hectare) where you can enjoy a relaxing and peaceful walk. An excellent address.

Ernée

LE GRAND CERF ** 17-19, rue Aristide-Briand ✆ 02 43 05 13 09. *Site Internet: http://perso.wanadoo.fr/hotel-restaurant-le-grand-cerf Annual closing last fortnight in January. Restaurant closed Sunday evening and Monday in low season. Set menus 15 € (weekday lunchtimes) and from 22 € to 30 €. Children's menu 12 €. Rooms 45 €, overnight break 54.50 €, breakfast 6.50 €.* Mme Semerie has 7 comfortable rooms available in her hotel, ensuring a good night's rest after an excellent meal in the dining room. The chef's cooking is traditional but far from rustic, successfully mixing and matching unexpected flavours. Game *civet*, bitter cocoa, chestnuts, vittelote potatoes, croutons and fresh grapes or a *maigre* (croaker fish) steak spread with shrimp, and morel juice? Not an easy choice!

Evron

LE RELAIS DU GUE DE SELLE * Route de la Mayenne - MEZANGERS ✆ 02 43 91 20 00.** *Website: http://relais-du-gue-de-selle.com. Annual closing last fortnight in February and 3 weeks between Christmas and mid-January. Closed Monday, Friday evening and Sunday evening in low season. Set menus 21 € (weekdays only) then 25 €-46 €. Children's menu 10 €. Rooms from 66 €-122 €, breakfast 9 €.* The setting is splendid; an old farm in landscaped grounds on the edge of a 50 hectare lake. It boasts 34 pleasant rooms including 6 rustic split-level. The big dining-rooms are full of the same old-fashioned charm, with fireplaces and exposed beams, and chef Didier Peschard's cooking is well up to standard: lobster pasties with *foie gras*, and stuffed pigeon served with fresh pasta, or loin of lamb with garlic cream, and warm apples with caramel, for instance. Country walks, a heated pool, fitness centre, sauna and sports activities on the lake - sailing, tennis, fishing and golf - are on offer. Relaxing and invigorating.

Laval

LE BISTRO DE PARIS 67, rue du Val-de-Mayenne © 02 43 56 98 29 *Set menus from 23 € to 42 €. A la carte 39 €. Closed Sunday evening, Monday, Saturday lunchtime and 1-18 August.* You might think it would be difficult to keep a gastronomic restaurant going in the Mayenne's prefecture, it being rather off the beaten track, and having few business customers. Laval isn't really the Val de Loire's main tourist spot either. In these conditions, Guy Lemercier- *Meilleur Ouvrier de France* in 1982, the year he opened on the banks of the Mayenne, has worked miracles. How does he do it? Attractive prices (*a la carte* starters are 14 €, main courses 17 € and desserts 8 €!) good humour and rustic family cooking that suits the place perfectly. Warm lobster and chorizo *fricassée*, queen scallops and tender cabbage, haddock, green cabbage and soft-boiled egg flavoured with shallots, crunchy pig's ear, sage and conserved shallots, Araguani chocolate *langue de chat* biscuit, almond hazlenut praline. The dining room is run by faithful Francois Pavoine, who has been in the job for nearly 20 years.

LE CAPUCIN GOURMAND 66, rue de Vaufleury © 02 43 66 02 02. *Website: http://capucingourmand.free.fr Open every day except Sunday evening, Monday and Wednesday lunchtime. Set menus from 20 € to 44 €. A la carte 38 €.* We like Marion and Thierry Touiller's restaurant very much; it provides great cooking at reasonable prices. There are three comfortable dining rooms, and Thierry Touiller, one of Escoffier's disciples, makes magic by mixing and matching flavours, with harmonious results. He prepares foie gras beautifully, and the venison *civet* with cranberries is another example of his talent. The neat setting is perhaps rather old-fashioned, but it has charm, as does the facade covered in climbing plants. An ideal place for sharing an intimate moment. Note the room for group or family meals, and the pleasant terrace for fine weather.

LE GRAND HOTEL DE PARIS 22, rue de la Paix © 02 43 53 76 20.** *Closed Christmas and New Year's Day. Rooms from 63 € to 93 € (mini-suite), breakfast 6.50 €.* Just next to Maitre Kanter's Tavern, the street side of the Grand Hotel de Paris is narrow and secluded, but once inside, the reception area amply justifies the title Grand Hotel. The 39 comfortable, personalised rooms deserve their 2 stars (four of them also have a private lounge), and you're sure to sleep well, since they are all soundproofed. Jacuzzi available. The garage costs around 4.50 €, but is convenient in the town centre.

SARTHE

Arnage

AUBERGE DES MATFEUX 289, avenue Nationale © 02 43 21 10 71 *Closed Sunday evening, Monday, Tuesday evening and Wednesday evening. Open exceptionally for 15+ customers. Set menus from 36 € to 70 €. Children's menu 17 €.* This excellent restaurant needs no introduction, but we always come back to it with the same pleasure. Set among trees on the way out of Arnage, it has a quiet and comfortable dining room with discreet, efficient service. After years of experience and his father's culinary training, Xavier Souffront's inventive *cuisine* is perfect (the word fits). Both meat and fish dishes are highly recommended; *papillotes* (cooked in a foil or edible package), Dublin Bay prawn *ravioles* and the famous annual lobster menu are just a few delicious examples. We'll let you discover the desserts by yourself!

LE MOULIN DES QUATRE SAISONS 2, rue Gallieni © 02 43 45 12 12. *Closed Sunday evening, Monday lunchtime, October and February school holidays and a week at Easter. Open every day in July and August. Set menus from 20.90 € (weekdays only) to 29.80 €. Children's menu 12 €. A la carte 45 €.* It's a bit of an understatement to say you eat well at the Moulin des Quatre Saisons. Chef Camille Constantin was trained by Joel Robuchon, which seems to have brought out some real talent. The setting is an enchanting 16thc. mill on the Loir - the terrace is right on the river - with top-quality service and wine list, put together by Camille's wife Caroline. The cuisine is seasonal, revealing delicate flavours and subtle combinations like the La Flèche chicken (really good but rare), and wild turbot cooked *à la plancha* with its Provençal *tian* (courgette and spinach gratin). An absolute must.

Le Mans

LE BEAULIEU Place des Ifs © 02 43 87 78 37. *Open Monday to Friday. Set menus 24 € (menu of the day served lunchtimes only) then 35 € to 52 €. Surprise menu for 4 people, 90 €. Children's menu 20 €. Catering service.* After 10 years spent welcoming gourmets at the end of the Rue des Ponts-Neufs, the Beaulieu has moved; luckily, only the site has changed! The only restaurant in Le Mans with a Michelin star is now located in the pretty Place des Ifs along the Rue Chanzy, where the Mutuelles du Mans Assurances headquarters used to be. Chef Olivier Boussard can thus offer his customers more room, and have additional space for his cooking, in the run-up to that all-important second star. This inventive flavour expert serves Dublin Bay prawn ravioli with caviar, and foie gras with mango and a raspberry and ginger *croustillant*, in a cosy baroque setting, though come the summer, you should be able to eat on a terrace newly-installed in the garden. Menus and carte change every three months.

LE FLAMBADOU 14 bis, rue Saint-Flaceau ✆ 02 43 24 88 38. *Closed Saturday lunchtime and Sunday. A la carte 29 €.* This restaurant is well known in Le Mans, with good reason. It specialises in genuine Perigord cooking, like duck neck stuffed with foie gras and garlic croutons, and duck manchon *fricassée* with Sarladaise potatoes - it's well worth going to a small back street in the old town to taste that! You can also enjoy calf's stomach and feet, or the inevitable cassoulet. If you have room for dessert, the pear baked in honey with gingerbread ice cream is perfect. Unless you'd rather have prunes in jurancon and armagnac! The helpings are really too generous - but can that be considered a downside when everything is so delicious?

HOTEL CHANTECLER * 50, rue de la Pelouse ✆ 02 43 14 40 00.** *Website: www.hotelchantecler.fr. 32 rooms from 65 € to 72 € and 3 suites from 92 € to 109 €. Breakfast 8 €.* The Hotel Chantecler boasts a strategic location, half-way between the station and the town centre just next to the Palais des Congres, and is open 24 hours a day all year round. The rooms have a certain charm (the cheaper ones with shower, the more expensive with bath), and the suites are luxurious. All have broadband Internet access. The hotel offers a private outdoor car park with surveillance, and is situated in a quiet street. Pets are accepted. A small room is available for seminars and business meetings. Email bookings welcome.

HOTEL CONCORDE ** 16, avenue du Général-Leclerc ✆ 02 43 24 12 30.** *Website: www.concordelemans.com. Rooms from 110 € to 185 €, suite 270 €, breakfast 12 €.* The Concorde's tall and elegant façade fronts the only 4-star hotel in the area, with its 56 spacious and comfortable rooms (all soundproofed), superb choice of whiskies in the bar, and rather good restaurant, l'Amphitryon. Four luxurious salons seating 200 are available for business lunches, seminars and banquets. The hotel is under new management, but that shouldn't really change things.

VENDÉE

Ile d'Yeu

LE GRAND LARGE 1, rue de Courseau – PORT-JOINVILLE ✆ 02 51 58 36 77 / 06 08 31 26 16. *Website: www.hotel-legrandlarge.com. Closed in February. 22 rooms from 40 € to 70 €. TV lounge. Breakfast buffet 7 €, 4-12s 4.50 €, under-4s free. Seminar room.* Located in the heart of Port-Joinville near the quay, 5 minutes from the landing stage, tourist office and shops, this hotel manages to be quiet and peaceful. It was entirely renovated inside in 2004. The breakfast room on the ground floor is next to reception, with a fully equipped room for working groups and seminars behind. On the first floor, the 22 rooms decorated in warm chocolate tones now have new air-conditioning and bathrooms, TV, beds and furniture. Bravo! The lower breakfast prices for children and bicycle garage (the main means of transport on the island) are excellent ideas.

LE PERE RABALLAND 6, place de Norvège - PORT-JOINVILLE ✆ 02 51 26 02 77. *Closed Monday.* In the drawing on the menu, Father Raballand has a jovial face half-hidden in his bushy brown beard. He must be smiling about his restaurant's excellent reputation, which extends well beyond the department. On leaving the boat, go right towards the heliport, and you'll see the terrace. The dining room upstairs has a 1930s beach theme, with beach huts and 'twenties bathing suits, lockers and flags as decoration. You must taste one of house specialities; tuna recipes - and there are plenty of them! We chose the slice of grilled tuna with Noirmoutier potatoes followed by a house dessert, so as not to have trouble pedalling uphill afterwards. There are also fresh, light dishes such as tuna and tomato tartare with thinly sliced lobster, planche, and mussels Pere Raballand-style. Don't miss this place: when you've been here, you've done the island - in the gastronomic sense.

La Roche-sur-Yon

MARIE STUART HOTEL ** 86, boulevard Louis-Blanc ✆ 02 51 37 02 24. *Website: www.mariestuarthotel.com. Open all year. Single room 49 €, double 59 €. Breakfast 7 €. Overnight break 63 €. Restaurant closed Saturday lunchtime and Sunday in low season. Set menus 18 €, 23 €, 27 €. A la carte.* This hotel-restaurant in its intimate rustic setting is decorated in Scottish style, as the name suggests. The 14 personalised rooms have direct phone line, cable TV, free unlimited broadband Internet connection, bath or shower and separate WC. They are very comfortable and richly furnished, each in its own style. The seminar room Francois I can be booked for business or other meetings. Ideally located opposite the station and a short walk from the town centre. Attractive prices.

Les Sables-d'Olonne

ATLANTIC HOTEL * 5, promenade Godet ✆ 02 51 95 37 71.** *Gastronomic restaurant Le Sloop. 30 rooms from 50 € to 110 € (view of the villas) or 91 € to 126 € (sea view). Indoor heated pool (28 degrees C). Meeting rooms. Continental or buffet breakfast by the pool 10 €. Set menus from 20 € to 45 €.* You find this hotel with its seventies feel on the station embankment facing the sea. Excellent facilities, comfortable rooms equipped with Canal + and satellite TV, mini-bar, bathroom with hair-dryer and safe. You can admire an idyllic panoramic view from the loggia in certain rooms, before enjoying a swim in the heated pool. The restaurant has a warm panelled interior on a navigation theme, and a skilfully-balanced menu with both seafood and Vendée country recipes.

LE CABESTAN 17, quai Guiné - Port de Pêche ✆ 02 51 95 07 50. *Open from February to mid-November. Closed Wednesday in low season. Set menus from 12 € to 23 €. Children's menu 6.50 €.* The Cabestan has a new facade, and isn't half proud of it! This attractive seaside veranda makes more room for customers, without spoiling the restaurant's convivial atmosphere one jot. With its steel handrails and dark wood, the dining room looks rather like the deck of an ocean liner; one of those featured in the pictures on the walls around you. The cuisine is reliable, and each menu is carefully composed; chef Pascal Benoist concocts subtle dishes paying great attention to the freshness and quality of his ingredients. The fish and seafood come from the daily Sables fish auction, for instance.

HOTEL MERCURE * CENTRE DE THALASSOTHERAPIE THALASSA INTERNATIONAL Lac de Tanchet ✆ 02 51 21 77 77.** *Website: www.thalassa.com. 100 rooms from 84 € to 136 €, restaurant, bar, fitness area, beauty parlour, seawater therapy centre. Closed two weeks in January.* This hotel is ideally located for getting into shape, in a calm environment facing the beach, close to the embankment and a few minutes on foot from the town centre. Several different leisure activities feature in one place, with seawater therapy for relaxation, anti-stress, leg tonus and post-natal cures, and a beauty area open to the general public, which uses seaweed-based products.

MAISON RICHET ** 25, rue de la Patrie ✆ 02 51 32 04 12. *Website: www.maison-richet.fr. 17 rooms. Double room (shower and WC) 45 € and 55 € (Friday and Saturday nights, school holidays, the day before a public holiday, and 15 June-15 September). Room sleeping 4 (shower and WC) 65 € and 75 €. Double room (washbasin) 35 € and 45 €. Breakfast buffet 7 €. Garage (bookings only) 8 € per day.* The Maison Richet is a decorative element in the Rue de la Patrie just behind the harbour, 50m from the beautiful covered market and 100m from the beach. Véronique and Michel have had it refurbished to their taste, so as to recreate the period atmosphere found here in 1905, when the historic Sables hotel was already taking guests. The renovation is charming, with a comfortable raspberry-coloured sofa and a big library containing travel guides and globes. Breakfast is served in a bright and peaceful room with pretty tablecloths and coloured china. The upstairs rooms are decorated in contemporary style, with coco matting on the floor and painted furniture (mauve, among other colours) matching the bedcovers and striped monochrome curtains. You come across a delightful patio in the heart of the house, complete with fountain, exotic plants and teak furniture - an ideal place to read or relax. The friendly, personalised welcome is an extra pleasure.

Noirmoutier

CHATEAU DU PELAVE * Bois de la Chaize - 9, allée de Chaillot ✆ 02 51 39 01 94.** *Gastronomic restaurant. 18 rooms from 60 € to 175 €. Breakfast 8.50 €, buffet 11 € and 12.50 €. Set menus 19 € to 49 €.* A la carte. Receptions, seminars. This place deserves to be better-known; it chooses to be unobtrusive - to our great pleasure! Head towards the beach (plage des Dames) and on the right, you'll see a path across the fields which is a short cut to the *Chateau*. The peace and quiet is surprising, since you are between harbour and beach (500m) in the heart of what's going on, but away from the noise and bustle. The 19thc. building nestles among the ilex trees in the Chaize woods, and is illuminated in the evening to show off its Victorian splendour. Inside, it has been completely renovated and has 18 spacious and comfortable rooms with a view of either the landscaped grounds (1 ha.) or the woods. You can eat in the bright restaurant dining room, or on a superb terrace overlooking the landscaped garden. A genuine residence of charm and character run by M. and Mme Beaupre.

LE GRAND FOUR 1, rue de la Cure ✆ 02 51 39 61 97. *Website: www.legrandfour.com. Closed Sunday evening and Monday, outside school holiday periods. Closed in December and January. Set menus from 18 € to 82.50 € (all lobster).* Patrice Vétélé is known to gourmets everywhere, who are first impressed by his restaurant's setting: an attractive bourgeois house located behind the chateau, three hundred years old, and covered with Virginia creeper. Pretty tableware and fine furniture and pictures decorate the interior, chosen by the lady of the house, while Patrice prepares island produce with great talent in the kitchen, constantly renewing his menus. Seafood gastronomy is the speciality: the noblest of fish are cooked for your enjoyment. A real feast.

Plessis-Bourré castle

Poitou-Charentes

Île de Ré

POITOU-CHARENTES

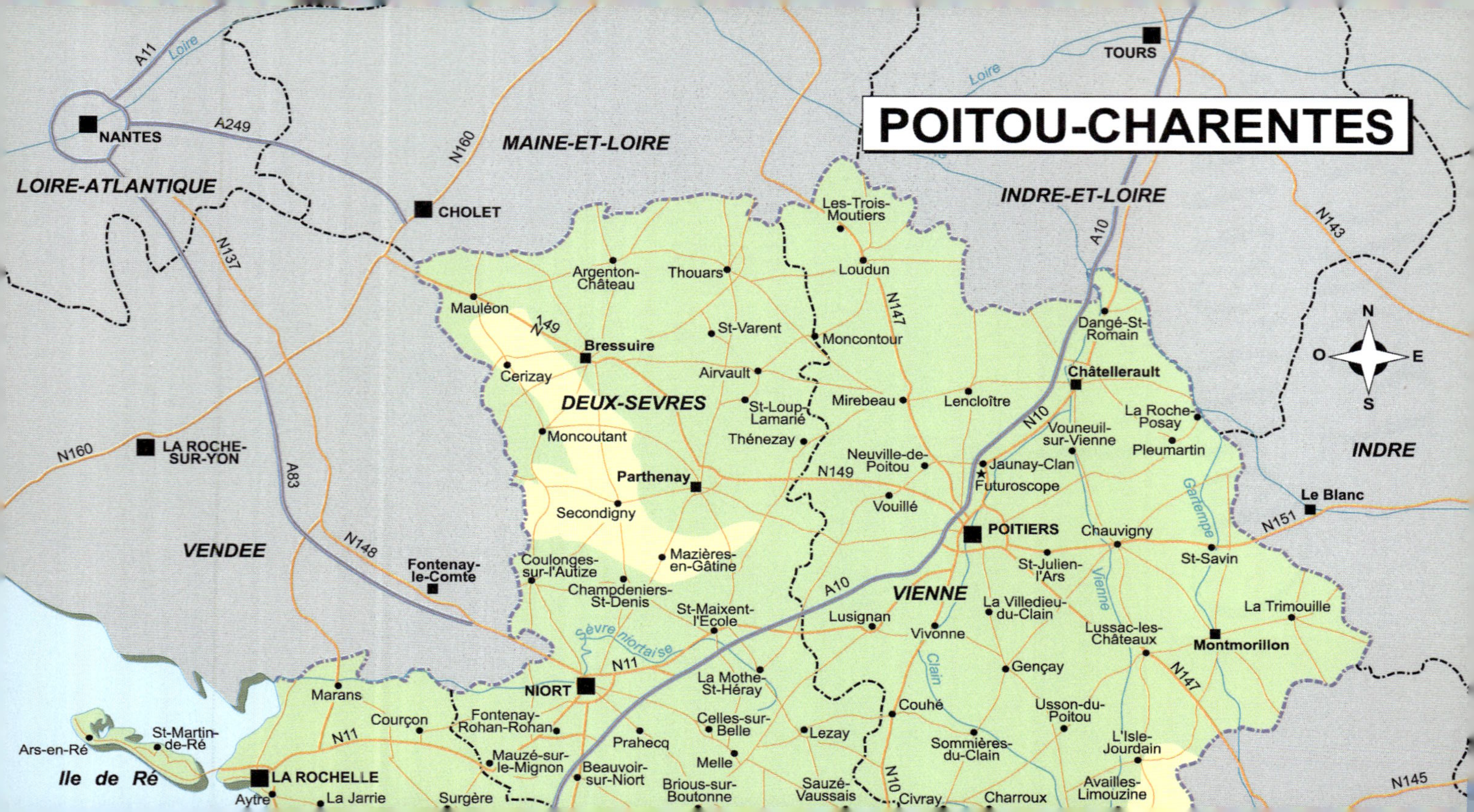

Ile d'Aix
Ile d'Oléron
St-Pierre-d'Oléron
Le Château-d'Oléron
St-Trojan-les-Bains
Fouras
Rochefort
Tonnay-Boutonne
Tonnay-Charente
A837
St-Savinien
Marennes
La Tremblade
CHARENTE-MARITIME
N137
Saintes
St-Palais-sur-Mer
Royan
Saujon
OCEAN ATLANTIQUE
Cozes
Génozac
Meschers-sur-Gironde
Gironde
Mirambeau
A10
N137
Pons
St-Génis-de-Saintonges
Jonzac
Loulay
Aulnay
St-Jean-d'Angely
N150
St-Hilaire-de-Villefranche
Matha
Burie
Cognac
N141
Charente
Châteaurenard
Jarnac
Segonzac
Archiac
Chef-Boutonne
Villefagnan
Ruffec
N10
Aigre
Mansle
Rouillac
CHARENTE
St-Amant-de-Boixe
Tardoire
Châteauneuf-sur-Charente
La Courrone
ANGOULÊME
Ruelle-sur Touve
N10
Blanzac-Porcheresse
Barbezieux-St-Hilaire
Villebois-Lavalette
Montmoreau-St-Cybard
Baignes-Ste-Radegonde
Brossac
Montendre
Aubeterre-sur-Dronne
Chalais
Montlieu-la-Garde
Montguyon
Champagne-Mouton
Confolens
St-Claud
Chabanais
N141
Chasseneuil-sur-Bonnieure
La Rochefoucault
Montbron
HAUTE-VIENNE
N147
A20
N141
LIMOGES
N21
Nontron
DORDOGNE
PERIGUEUX
Blaye
N137
A10
GIRONDE
L'Isle
N89
N21
N89
BORDEAUX
Dordogne
30 km
Altitude (metres)
500
200
Major road
Motorways
Préfecture
Main towns
Secondary towns

ANGOULEME

From the Middle Ages, the capital of the Angoumois became famous for paper manufacturing, and this has continued, although the Protestant craftsmen left after 1685. Balzac even made an Angoumois paper-maker the hero of one of his books, *Les illusions perdues* (Lost Illusions). Angouleme is now the Charente prefecture, and has kept its illusions, being a light and quiet town where you can read your paper in peace.

SAINT PIERRE CATHEDRAL. The cathedral has been transformed through the centuries, the first building dating from 413! The front was restructured in Romanesque style in 1118, and the architect Paul Abadie's most recent restoration (1853-1876) has a Byzantine look.

PAINTED WALLS Around the town. Angoulême is comic-strip city. Besides hosting the annual bande dessinée (comic book) festival, it has put some famous characters on its walls: Gaston Lagaffe, the Pieds Nickelés and Lucky Luke, among others. From fresco to fresco, you recognise the styles of well-known comic-strip artists. To cap the effect, over a thousand street-signs have been redesigned as speech bubbles - don't miss them!

MUSEE DE LA BANDE DESSINEE (CNBDI) 121, rue de Bordeaux © 05 45 38 65 65. *www.cnbdi.fr. Open every day, Tuesday-Friday: 10am-6pm (Saturday, Sunday and public holidays: 2pm-6pm). Admission: adult 5 €, concessions 3.50 €, under-6s free.* The new art of the comic book is exhibited in a unique way, through different kinds of museum - History, Natural History, Fine-Arts, Ethnography, Science or Contemporary Art, portraying the imaginary worlds of comic-strip designers. There is a bookshop and a library for fans, containing the biggest French collections on the subject.

ROUTE DU COGNAC

Once called 'liqueur of the gods', cognac comes from double distillation, and receives a lot of attention. Distillation takes place in two phases following a traditional method, and the alcohol is then aged in oak casks. Wonderful to drink - in moderation.

Cognac

The name of this little Charentes town is known to all, even in the Australian outback. This has nothing to do with its famous historical figures, but rather with an alcoholic drink which Americans (and others) adore. The town is ancient and well-kept, and from it you can take trips into the neighbouring countryside, with its vine-covered hillsides and remarkable architecture.

LES ETAPES DU COGNAC Maison des Viticulteurs - 25, rue Cagouillet © 05 45 36 47 35. *www.cognacetapes.com.* This association has 200 members: home distillers, winegrowers, restaurant and hôtel owners, cultural organisers, cognac houses, etc. It looks after four wine and tourism routes where you can discover cognac and local heritage at the same time. Each thematic tour has its own character, though always linked with the golden liqueur.

COGNAC CAMUS 29, rue Marguerite-de-Valois © 05 45 32 72 96. *www.camus.fr. Visits (admission fee) June-September; by appointment in low season.* Shop, tastings. Brand prestige is linked to its founder's passion for cognac; he personally oversaw the distillation and maturing processes. Cyril Camus is the fifth generation at 33, and he keeps up the traditional closeness between owner and product which, for 140 years, has been giving the house a name for authenticity.

COGNAC HENNESSY Quai Richard Hennessy © 05 45 35 72 68. *www.hennessy.com. Visits (admission fee) every day, March- December. January & February: by reservation.* A great international brand, part of the town's heritage. 'Hennessy' was apparently the only 'gringo' word that Pancho Villa could tolerate; he was not cognac's only famous admirer. The right bank of the Charente houses the original storehouse and tells the story of the brand while on the left bank is the company's contemporary face. This glass, stone and copper building by Jean-Michel Wilmotte (1995) contains a collection of posters, the shop and a bar for tasting.

COGNAC MARTELL 7, place Edouard Martell © 05 45 36 33 33. *www.martell.com. Visits (admission fee) March-October. November-February by appointment. Tasting.* Taste Martell cognac and travel back to 1715 and the birth of this oldest of houses. The representative-founder's home is still there at the heart of the estate. Martell links tradition and creativity: countless bottles grouped in the oak casks according to origin, age and flavour prove it.

COGNAC OTARD Château de Cognac © 05 45 36 88 86. *www.otard.com. Visits (admission fee) April-December (every day April-October). January-March: group bookings.* François I was born in this castle, ideal for cognac-making, with 2-metre-thick walls and the river close by favouring the maturing process. The chapel where he was christened has become a storehouse for this purpose. God bless cognac!

COGNAC REMY MARTIN Visiting tour © 05 45 35 76 66. Preferential visits to the Maison Remy Martin, with personalised tastings of your choice: traditional; with food; a hands-on cocktail 'workshop.' Taste discovery area and exclusive shop.

Jarnac

This village on the road to Cognac is famous for a fencing stroke, a French President and the cognac houses.

DONATION FRAN«OIS MITTERRAND 10, quai de l'Orangerie © 05 45 81 38 88. *Open Wednesday-Sunday: 2pm-6pm, 2 January-31 October, except July & August, every day: 10am-12 noon and 2pm-6pm. Admission: adult 3.50 €, 6-16s 1.50 €*. The donation contains objects offered to President Mitterrand by the world's personalities: engravings, sculptures, drawings and paintings. From sophistication to bad taste and the frankly weird. You get a good idea of the Heads of State known by Mitterrand.

CIMETIERE DES GRANDS MAISONS. François Mitterrand was buried in 1996 in the little Grands-Maisons cemetery in Jarnac. The mauve and yellow irises on his tomb are replaced regularly according to his last wishes: these were the Kings of France's flowers.

COGNAC COURVOISIER 2, place du Château © 05 45 35 56 16. The real Napoleon Brandy. He even took casks of it to Saint Helena.

COGNAC LOUIS-ROYER 27 rue Chail © 05 45 81 02 72. Louis-Royer offers free visits, which is rare. Love of cognac and conviviality have been handed down through the generations, and authenticity and design go well together.

THE ISLANDS

The islands, once places of refuge or sinister prisons, have become tourist attractions, adding their charm to the Atlantic coast.

Ile d'Aix

Off the coast of Rochefort. Napoleon spent his last days in France here.

MUSEE NAPOLEONIEN 17, av. Napoleon © 05 46 84 66 40. *www.musees-nationaux-napoleoniens.org. Opening times and admission as for African Museum.* Napoleon's last residence in France, bought in 1928 by Baron Gourgaud, descendant of the Emperor's aide-de-camp. It was renovated then converted into a museum and listed. The Emperor's presence is almost perceptible in the ten thematic rooms, especially in his bedroom where he wrote his surrender. You can see his sword, a fragment of his coffin and a tree he planted. All 40 clocks have been stopped at 5.49pm, the time of his death.

Ile d'Oléron

Marennes-Oléron country produces almost half of French oysters, notably the 'fines de claires' or green oysters farmed in oyster beds, which give the landscape its character. They make a square pattern between the villages and oyster-farmers' huts, their colours varying according to the algae and plancton that colonise them. The pontoon-dotted straits are striking, whether glimpsed in the mist or seen in bright sunlight. Oléron is a favourite destination for French tourists, with its long, sandy beaches, dunes, forests, marshes and flat or hilly coastline.

CITADELLE ET GALERIE DE LA CITADELLE Le Château 05 46 75 22 51. You can enter on foot, or with a guided tour in the castle's little train. The view from its ramparts (1630) is superb early in the morning, when the oyster-farmers' boats go out, and at sunset. There is a museum in the Arsenal and Powder magazine with summer exhibitions by local painters, and minerals, fossils and natural stone jewellery in the gallery. Enjoy an illuminated walk round the site at night.

MAISON PAYSANNE DE LA COIFFE ET DU COSTUME Bd de la Plage-LE-GRAND-VILLAGE-PLAGE © 05 46 47 43 44. *Open all year for groups. Closed Sunday. 1 July-31 August: 10am-12 noon and 3pm-6pm. Admission: adult 4.50 €; child 3.50 €*. Village life in the last century is the theme in this typical Oleron farmhouse. Costumes and caps (coiffes) of all periods are exhibited, some of them intricately worked.

CHASSIRON LIGHTHOUSE. *Open all year, 7 days a week, Admission: adult 2 €, 7-12s 1 €*. Climb the 224 steps to admire the view 40m up. The lighthouse can be seen from 32 km away in daytime, and its beam reaches 52km at night. The staff are very willing to answer questions.

AQUARIUM La Cotinière - SAINT-PIERRE ✆ **05 46 47 31 90**. *Open every day of the year: 11am-12.30pm and 2.30pm-7pm (July & August: 11am-11pm). Admission: adult 5 €, child 4 €*. Discover some Atlantic fauna; the species vary every year. There are guided tours on the history of the port, boats, fish varieties, fishing techniques and the fish chain from catch to sale.

MAISON DE L'HUITRE OLERONAISE Le Port - Saint-Trojan-Les-Bains ✆ **05 46 76 08 16**. *Open February-October, Tuesday-Saturday, group bookings by appointment. Tours 3pm, 4.30pm September-15 June; 4pm, 5.30pm, 15 June-31 August. Admission: adult 6.50 €, child 4.50 €*. Walks through the oyster beds by appointment: adult 7 €, child 5.40 €. Marc and Patricia Texier (members of the Terres Marines association) have disguised their oyster-farmer's hut as a museum. Learn all about the different farming techniques of oysters and mussels, and discover the shellfish in their natural habitat. You can visit the museum and oyster beds at low tide, and taste the product.

Ile de Ré

Between the Breton and Antioche straits, this island has always attracted the visitor with its golden sandy beaches, bright flowers, fields and marshes, and its history. There is little concrete, no built-up areas or hoardings along the roads, and cyclists have priority (100km of cycle track from north to south, and east to west). No wonder it's so crowded in summer!

THE BRIDGE. 50,000 m^3 of concrete, over 6,000 tonnes of steel and 1,100m. of foundation piles went into this bridge. It is not only technically impressive but user-friendly too, including two cycle lanes and a one for the 'ant colonies' (free of charge). Crossing fees vary according to the season and type of vehicle. The round trip with an average car costs 16,50 € in summer and 9 € in winter, season tickets possible.

Ars-en-Ré

This charming little village in the north of the island is calmer than the south. There is old rigging to admire in the port.

SAINT ETIENNE CHURCH. Saint Etienne Church's black and white spire soars over the village and is a landmark for boats in the straits. Built in the 12thc. and reshaped in the 15thc., it combines Romanesque (portal and nave) with Gothic (chancel).

La Flotte-en-Ré

The island's second village is one of France's finest. Its main industry was tuna fishing and trading until the 19thc. The medieval port was near Arnerault beach, where the dyke can be seen at low tide. The current harbour was built in 1768, and houses both fishing and pleasure craft. The place is busy in season, but despite the festive atmosphere, the island has known tragedy. In 1867, five rowing boats were sunk in a terrible storm, and 30 sailors from the village were lost at sea.

Saint-Clément-des-Baleines

NOAH'S ARK - PARC AMAZONIA Route du Phare ✆ 05 46 29 23 23. *Open every day: afternoons in low season, all day in season. Admission: adult 10 €, child 7 €, concessions 8 €.* A handy hint: all the island's tourist offices sell reduced-price tickets. This magnificent park houses parrots from all over the world, and several museums containing shells (12,000), insects (6,000) a reconstituted seabed with natural coral, turtles (all living species) and naturalised animals. One deals with the marine adventure and another the history of Saint Martin Penitentiary. There is a display of flying parrots, and another of music by a 16-keyboard ensemble.

WHALE LIGHTHOUSE ✆ 05 46 29 18 23. *Open every day, all year, opening hours vary according to season. Admission: adult 2.20 €, 7-12s and school students 1.10 €.* Climb the 257 steps of this 57m-high lighthouse dating back to 1854, for a marvellous view of ocean, beaches and salt marshes. The summer crowds force you to be patient, but the view is worth it.

Saint-Martin-de-Ré

The island's capital, with old sloping streets and a pretty harbour fortified by Vauban after the English siege of 1627. There are 14 km of ramparts on the ocean, with two gates and five half-moon bastions. The citadel now contains a prison; until 1938 it housed convicts on the way to French Guyana or New Caledonia.

Ile de Ré

NIORT AND THE MARAIS POITEVIN

This vast fishing territory criss-crossed by canals seems to stretch to infinity, before ending up in the estuary. Hire a little boat to navigate over the duckweed; you'll feel you're sailing across a moving greenish floor. The best way to discover 'Green Venice' is with a punt pole in your hand.

Niort

This is the insurance companies' town, but also the gate to the marshes.

LE DONJON Bord de Sèvre. One of the finest pair of twin Romanesque keeps in France.

SAINT ANDRE CHURCH. The church, with its two 70m spires, dates back to the 12thc. though little of the Romanesque building is left.

LES HALLES Near the Keep. Niort has been known for its market since the 13thc. The new wrought iron, glass and steel covered market is rather like Baltard's in Paris. Ceres and Mercury appear on the front, symbolising the union of commerce and the earth. The stalls inside are always busy.

MUSEE-JARDIN DES RURALIES Aire de Poitou-Charentes (Access via Vouille Aiffres or A10) ✆ 05 49 75 68 27. *Open 7 days a week: 10am-6pm (7pm in summer).Admission: adult 5 Disabled access.* This agricultural museum merits a family visit. The agricultural machine collection (some working) will please the boys, and the old-fashioned garden the ladies, with its roses, herbs and nectar flowers, and glassed-in beehive with beekeeping exhibition. You can stroll through the kitchen garden and farmyard.

Marais Poitevin

Arçais

Take a boat or bicycle into the Poitevin marshes, where the paths are as green as the duckweed-covered canals. Embarkation points:

EMBARCADERE BARDET-HUTTIERS Route de Damvix 05 49 35 39 18

EMBARCADERE GUINOUARD Place du Port ✆ 05 49 26 02 95

Coulon

Heart of the marshes. Many boat trips leave from here, to adventure into the watery maze.

MAISON DES MARAIS MOUILLES Place de la Coutume ✆ 05 49 35 81 04. *Open 7 days a week, during school holidays: 10am-12 noon and 2pm-7pm. May, June & September, same times weekdays: 10am-1pm and 2pm-7pm weekends. July & August: 7 days a week: 10am-8pm. November: 2pm-7pm. Outside school holidays, 10am-12 noon and 2pm-7pm (closed Mondays). Closed January.* Find out all about the marshes with an audiovisual show, exhibitions (the life of the eel and its alevin, the civelle) and so on. Outside, the visit goes on, with 4-hour walking and boating trips (bookings only). Cost: adult 5.20 €, 6-16s 7.80 €, under-6s 3 €, snack included.

MAISON AUX VOLETS BLEUS Route de la Sotterie. One of France's most photographed houses, sober and full of character with its blue shutters. It belongs to the Ravard family, and was built in 1862 on the banks of the Sèvre. Christiane Ravard painted the shutters blue in the 1950s, to remind her of the sea.

EMBARCADERE CARDINAUD La Repentie ✆ 05 49 35 90 47. Open all year. Tell them where you want to go, they'll have the trip to suit you! Alone, in a gang, with or without a guide, for an hour's break or a whole day's adventure, anything goes.

Marans

MOULIN DE BEAUREGARD Ave. de la gare. *Open 15 June-15 September and 15 September-30 November, weekends and public holidays. Annual closing late December-15 March. Admission: adult 3 €, child 1.50 €.* Built in the 17thc. and worked by the Ancelin family until 1935, the mill was bought by Marans in 1994. Restored to perfect working order in 1999, it is now looked after by the association 'Friends of the mill' and open to the public, who learn all there is to know about milling.

Saint-Hilaire-la-Palud

PARC ORNITHOLOGIQUE LES OISEAUX DU MARAIS POITEVIN ✆ **05 46 01 04 09**. *www.oiseauxmaraispoitevin.com. Open last weekend in March until November, closed Tuesdays from 15/09. Admission: adult 6 €, child 3.50 €, family 17.50 €*. In the heart of 'Green Venice', over 70 native species of bird and typical wild marsh vegetation are found in this 7-hectare nature reserve. A film about bird life in the marsh is shown at the end of your visit.

Saint-Sauveur-d'Aunis

MAISON DE L'AUNIS ✆ **05 46 01 80 13**. *Open June-mid September: 2pm-6pm. Closed Monday. Open all year for groups, bookings only. Admission: adult 1.60 € 5-16s 0.80 €*. One of the natural park theme centres installed in a pretty local house. There are several exhibitions of 19thc. daily life, and the period rooms take you back to that era. The house belonged to a pork butcher, and you can see his 'laboratory' as it was, together with manual and mechanical boilers and a collection of irons. Life is certainly easier with our labour-saving devices!

POITIERS AND THE FUTUROSCOPE

Poitiers, known for its battles and fine Romanesque monuments, might seem a town of the past, yet the creation of the Futuroscope has rather shaken up its old image. Today, peaceful Poitiers, with its old-fashioned charm and sloping streets with no sharp corners may well surprise you.

SAINT PIERRE CATHEDRAL. Anjou Gothic, with domed vaults and reinforced lateral walls. The 12th and 13thc. windows and 13thc. choir stalls are worth seeing, as is the flat chevet. The cathedral's impressive proportions give it a spacious feel.

EGLISE SAINT HILAIRE LE GRAND. A basilica already existed on the site of the first Bishop of Poitiers Saint Hilaire's tomb in the early Middle Ages. The present church, consecrated in 1049, is a reconstruction of the original but has been reshaped over the centuries. Inside, the capitals (with Biblical or purely decorative scenes, including the death of Saint Hilaire) frescoes, ambulatory, crypt and white marble sarcophagus are all bathed in remarkable light.

PALAIS DES COMTES DE POITOU - DUCS D'AQUITAINE. Eléanore held court in this 12thc. palace. The famous Plantagenet Gothic salle des pas perdus, or King's room, had its south wall (with three magnificent mantlepieces) renovated in the 15thc., as was the Maubergeon Tower, on the site of the ancient castle keep.

MEDIEVAL RAMPARTS. Dating back to the first half of the 12thc., this medieval wall was altered by Jean de Berry in the 14thc. and again during the Wars of Religion in the 16thc. A few frail remains of the 6.5 km of fortifications still exist.

Futuroscope

PARC DU FUTUROSCOPE ✆ **05 49 49 30 80**. *www.futuroscope.com. The park is on the A10, exit 28 nearing Poitiers. By rail: TGV-Futuroscope. Open 4 February-31 December 2006: 9am-end of evening show (every day). Buggies and wheelchairs for hire. Covered picnic area. Restaurants & snackbars. Admission: adult 31 €, 5-16s 23 € (reduction for 2 consecutive days).* One and a half million visitors every year must be right! This is the realm of the visual image, with state-of-the-art technology: 3D films, virtual images, screens everywhere. The attractions are varied: the new Digital City (video games on giant screens), the Space Station (you literally float in space) and Voyageurs du Ciel et de la Mer, the film made by J Perrin for Futuroscope which offers a journey on the horizon with birds and sea mammals. Don't miss the evening shows, a blend of visual and water features: pure magic!

LA ROCHELLE

Cardinal Richelieu besieged the town in 1628, to put an end to its Anglophile and Protestant leanings. Today things are quieter; La Rochelle concentrates on shipping and tourism, but has kept a trace of its rebellious nature all the same. The town hosts a famous French music festival every year (the Francofolies) and its surprising architecture attracts a lot of visitors.

AQUARIUM Bassin des Grands Yachts ✆ **05 46 34 00 00**. *www.aquarium-larochelle.com. Open every day, October-March: 10am-8pm; April-June and September: 9am-8pm; July & August: 9am-11pm. Admission: adult 12.50 €, 3-17s 9 €. Audio guide 3.50 €*. 10,000 Atlantic, Mediterranean and tropical animals in 3 million litres of water and 65 aquariums, each more magical than the last. The

Aquarium offers you a 2-hour journey at the bottom of the sea, from sharks to micro-organisms, not forgetting 250 species of flora, including carniverous plants, in the tropical greenhouse. A fabulous experience, not to be missed.

CATHEDRAL. Built to celebrate the victory of Catholics over Huguenots in 1628. Notice local artist William Bouguereau's paintings in the apsidal chapel dome.

GROSSE HORLOGE. Former 14thc. gate in the wall between town and port, it originally had two openings, for pedestrians and horse-drawn vehicles. Today, only one arcade is visible. The belfry above contains the 18thc. clock, decorated with small columns, pilasters and marine trophies.

MAISON HENRI II. *July & August: 10am-12 noon and 2pm-6pm (except weekends), other months, by appointment. Admission free.* This Renaissance house has a Henri II front with two wings, gallery and loggia. Today it contains the Aunis Archeology and History Museum.

TOWN HALL Place de l'Hôtel de Ville La Rochelle ✆ 05 46 41 14 68. *Guided tours (45 mins) all year: October-May, Saturdays & Sundays only, 3pm; June, September and school holidays, every day, 3pm; July & August, every day, 3pm & 4pm. Admission: adult 3 €, 4-12s 1.50 €; tickets available here or in advance from the Tourist Office (disabled access).* This 16thc. Renaissance building still has its Flamboyant Gothic wall, fortified gate, watchtowers, columned gallery and caisson ceiling. In the courtyard, there is a beautifully sculpted façade.

MAISON DE LA MYTILICULTURE Esnandes ✆ 05 46 01 34 64. *Open 15 June-30 November. Closed December, January & Tuesdays. Admission: adult 3.50 €, child 2 €.* Fortified church included: adult 5.80 €, child 3.50 €. This museum is in one of the natural park houses. Its exhibition traces the history of mussel-farming techniques in the Aiguillon bay, from the 15thc.

LA ROCHELLE TOWERS ✆ 05 46 34 11 81. *Open Tuesday-Sunday, 16 September-14 May: 10am-12.30pm and 2pm-5.30pm. 15 May-30 June and 1 September-15 September: 10am-12.30pm and 2pm-6pm. July & August: 10am-7pm. Admission: adult 4.60 € child 3.50 €. Under-18s free. First Sunday of the month October-March, entry free.* The three towers, Saint Nicolas, la Chaine and la Lanterne, completed the rebel city's fortifications, and survived the destruction of the wall after the 1628 siege and the town's surrender to Richelieu and Louis XIII. The Lantern Tower (15thc.) was built as a lighthouse, and served as a prison. 600 or so examples of period graffiti can be seen on the walls, the work of British, Dutch and Spanish pirates. Saint Nicholas Tower (14thc.) offers a remarkable panoramic view of the old harbour and the town, while the Chain Tower (14thc.) is named after the chain – still in place at its foot - used to close off the harbour at night. It now houses the permanent exhibition 'La Rochelle: Atlantic Capital, Huguenot Capital'.

La Rochelle

ROCHEFORT AND SAINTES

Rochefort country stretches between the ocean and the Charente. Traveller and writer Pierre Loti dreamt of the sea, and Napoleon saw his dreams end with it. Today, the region does not lack for tourist attractions.

Rochefort

Winner of the National Heritage Prize in 1993, Rochefort has kept its elegant 17thc. architecture, and is new, royal, and spa town all at once, with its forts and museums, as well as providing a natural habitat for birds.

THE ARSENAL. You go into the Arsenal via the 1831 Arsenal Bridge, and imagine the workers crossing it in past times. It used to be one of the town's important buildings; so few of them are left today.

CORDERIE ROYALE. Louis XIV's engineer François Blondel started work on this rope factory in 1666. The longest industrial building in 17thc. Europe took 4 years and 2,000 workmen to build. It was damaged in the last war, became a bramble-covered ruin, and was restored. Today the Royal rope factory contains the town mediatheque and library, the Chamber of Commerce and Industry, the League for the Protection of Birds, the Coast Conservatory and the International Sea Centre.

CHANTIER DE L'HERMIONE ✆ 05 46 82 07 07. *www.hermione.com. Open every day out of season: 10am-5.30pm, in season 9am-7pm. Admission: adult 7 € guided tour 6 €*. In 1780, Lafayette joined the American rebels aboard the frigate Hermione. This 65m boat has been reconstructed, bearing witness to French naval history and Franco-American brotherhood.

MAISON PIERRE LOTI 41, rue Pierre Loti ✆ 05 46 99 16 88. *www.ville-rochefort.fr/pierreloti. Open July & August, every day: 10am-6.30pm. Closed Tuesday (out of season), and January. Admission: adult 7.80 € child 3.90 €*. Pierre Loti, alias Julien Viaud, wrote travel books, and was elected to the Academie Francaise at 41. His passion for history and the Orient influenced the interior design of his birthplace, which is a fantastic mixture of cultures and periods.

MUSEE NATIONAL DE LA MARINE 1,place de la Galissonière ✆ 05 46 99 86 57. *www.musee-marine.fr. Open every day except Monday in winter (closed in January). Admission: adult 5 €, under-18s free.* The former Marine Commanders' residence contains some exceptional collections, explaining how Colbert wanted to build a great arsenal (still being modified to this day). Warship building is interpreted in technical, military, economic and urban terms, and the imaginative significance of long-distance sea voyages is recalled.

PONT TRANSBORDEUR DE MARTROU. *Open January, November & December; weekends: 10am-12 noon and 2pm-5pm. Ferbruary, March & October; Tuesday-Sunday: 10am-12 noon and 2pm-5pm, Monday: 10am-12 noon. April; Tuesday-Sunday: 10am-12 noon and 2pm-6pm, Monday 2pm-6pm. May-September; Tuesday-Sunday: 10am-12 noon and 2pm-7pm, Monday 2pm-7pm. June-August; Tuesday-Sunday: 10am-12 noon and 2pm-8pm, Monday 2pm-8pm. Admission: round trip, adult 1.80 €, 5-11s 1 €*. Rochefort transporter bridge was built by Ferdinand Arnodin in 1900, to the south of the town, and is the only one still working. Pedestrians, cyclists and horse-riders can cross it. The trip takes 4mins, with a view of the Charente and its viaduct. The bridge was modified and partially replaced during its lifetime, which officially ended in 1967, before it was listed in 1976. It is 175m long and 50m high.

Fouras

FORT BOYARD. Closed to the public, though you can get near the outside by boat. Vauban is supposed to have told Louis XIV 'Sire, it would be easier to catch the moon in your teeth than to put up a fort in that place'. However, Bonaparte decided to build one two centuries later. The popular TV show attracts a growing number of fans.

Saintes

Saintes was a former bridge on the road to Compostella, and boasts a 2,000-year history. Its 11th and 12thc. buildings are well worth discovering.

ABBAYE AUX DAMES ✆ 05 46 97 48 48. *Open April-September, every day: 10am-7pm; 1 October-March: 1pm-7pm. Admission 3 €*. This abbey, magnificently restored, comprises Notre Dame Church (11th and 12thc.) with its pine-cone steeple, and the 17thc. convent buildings on the right bank. On the north side, go past Saint Pallais Church and under the fine 18thc. porch to the Romanesque abbey church; a masterpiece. The abbey, founded in 1047 by Agnes de Bourgogne and Geoffrey Martel, Comte d'Anjou, was the first female convent in the Saintonge district.

GALLO-ROMAN AMPHITHEATRE Rue Lacurie. *Open all year, every day. Admission: 1 € under-10s free. Audio guide hire 3 €*. Built in the reign of Claudius around 40 A.D., Saintes Amphitheatre is one of the oldest and best-preserved in Gaul. Most of the tiers and superstructures have disappeared, but the remains give a good idea of what it was like when it contained 20,000 spectators.

GERMANICUS ARCH. Not a triumphal but a votive arch, gateway to the town for the Roman road coming from Lyon.

SAINT PIERRE CATHEDRAL. A strange building with its imposing tower under a lead dome. The luminous interior is bare and composite: Romanesque, Gothic, Renaissance and a 13thc. cloister co-exist.

SAINT EUTROPE BASILICA. Louis XI donated the means to raise the 15thc. Flamboyant steeple to 60m, which means this a basilica you can't miss. The Cluny monks built it to pray in, and for pilgrims going to Compostella. The three-storey structure allowed the Benedictines peace and quiet, and relative privacy from the comings and goings. In 1803, given the state of the roof, the prefet gave the order to demolish the nave. The result is a great esplanade between portal and chancel. The church is still famous for its Romanesque chevet, sculptures and crypt housing the remains of the first bishop of Saintes, stoned and hacked to death for converting Eustelle, the Roman governor's daughter.

Trizay

COMPOSTELLA GARDENS *Lac du Bois Fleuri © 05 46 82 19 64. Open June-September: 10am-12 noon and 3pm-7pm; € Easter-May: 2pm-7pm. Closed late October-late March. Sunday morning, and Monday. Admission: 3.50 €. Under-14s free.* Nature-lovers can bird-watch in this floral park with its rare plants and flowers, exotic shrubs and magnificent fountains. The walk overlooks the Bois Fleuri lake, which is open all year, with kids' games (rowing boat and pedalo hire) and line fishing. There is even a nice little restaurant nearby.

Saint-Jean-d'Angely

ROYAL ABBEY. Founded in 817 by Pepin, this monastery contained a miraculous relic: the head of John the Baptist. The abbey was pillaged by the Vikings in 861 and destroyed by the Hundred Years' War and Wars of Religion, finally disappearing in 1568. The relic went up in flames. The brave monks rebuilt the current abbey. They gave up their grand project for an imposing classical church, but the majestic front with its high, domed towers that was part of it at least shows what might have been.

After the Revolution, a college and lycee were installed here, and today it houses the town's cultural centre, with its library and music school (the abbey once contained Pascal's manuscripts, notably the *Pensées*). There is also the Saint Jacques de Compostelle European cultural centre, which encourages ecumenical exchanges.

Climb the towers for a superb view over the town. At the foot, comic-strip panels tell the story of Saint Jean d'Angely. For a fee, the Tourist Office organises guided tours of towers, abbey and the old town.

MUNICIPAL MUSEUM 9, rue Régnaud © 05 46 25 09 72. *Open June-August, Tuesday-Saturday: 10.30am-6.30pm and Sunday: 2.30pm-6pm. September-May, every day except Monday: 2pm-6pm. Admission: adult 3.50 €, concessions 2 €, under-18s free.* Discover the Citroen voyages to Africa in the 1920s with this unique French collection. There is also a panorama of 17thc.-19thc. French decorative arts (furniture, ceramic) polychrome statues and a collection of firearms.

MUSEE DES CORDELIERS 9, rue Régnaud © 05 46 59 94 55. *Open 1 September-30 May, every day except Monday:2pm-6pm. 1 June-31 August, Tuesday-Saturday: 10.30am-6.30pm; Sunday 2.30pm-6pm. Admission: adult 3.50 €, concessions 2 € E-mail: musee@angely.net* Housed in the renovated Hôtel de la Sous-préfecture, this museum contains municipal and archeological society collections, including souvenirs of the CitroÎn expeditions donated by expedition head Louis Audouin-Dubreuil and chief mechanic Maurice Penaud. You can also see 18th and early 19thc. European guns and French and regional decorative arts (17th-19thc.).

Aulnay

EGLISE ROMANE D'AULNAY-DE-SAINTONGE. A 18km north-east of Saint-Jean-d'Angely. Listed UNESCO World Heritage. Saint Pierre de la Tour at Aulnay is a jewel of French Romanesque art, and one of France's ten most beautiful churches. It was put up in the 12thc. on the road to Compostella and the Poitou border. Vaults, capitals and four-arched portal are all well worth seeing. On the portal, opposite the cross, the fight between Vice and Virtue is engraved, together with the Wise Virgins. On the outside capitals, Samson and Delilah are hidden. Saintonge is known for its Romanesque churches, and the Tourist Office has a booklet sale:'Romanesque Churches in the Saintonge Valley'.

Dampierre-sur-Boutonne

CHATEAU DE DAMPIERRE-SUR-BOUTONNE ✆ **05 46 24 02 24** *Open 13 June-15 September, every day: 10.30am-7pm. From 14 March-12 June: open only Sundays and public holidays: 2pm-6pm.* This Renaissance jewel, burnt down in 2002, has been reborn. The famous sculpted caissons in the gallery, supposed to have alchemist meaning, have already been restored. The garden is full of contemporary works, inspired by mythology and alchemy, and the owners themselves often act as guides.

HAUTE-SAINTONGE

Jonzac

COUVENT DES CARMES. Not much is left of the 16thc. monument. Sold off as national property during the Revolution, the church became a court and the cloister a prison, until 1947. The convent was restored in 1976 and became a cultural centre, with an archeological museum open in July & August, and every summer, the Saintonge-Quebec University Summer School holds a series of lectures here, open to all. Guided tours are organised by the Tourist Office from March to November.

CHATEAU DE JONZAC ✆ **05 46 48 49 29**. *Guided tours are organised by Jonzac Tourist Office from March to November, every Tuesday at 3pm. 1 July-31 August, every Monday, Tuesday, Thursday, Friday and Saturday.* There was already a primitive building here around 1059, but the present castle goes back to the 15thc. It was destroyed then rebuilt at the end of the Hundred Years' War, on a naturally defensive site overlooking the Seugne valley. Don't miss the powerful 15thc. gatehouse with its two round towers or the 16thc. Renaissance wing. Inside, the little Napoleon III theatre is worth seeing, and outside, the medieval de Champagnac alley. In 2003, the moat and drawbridge, removed in the 19thc., were restored.

Montendre

MONTENDRE FEUDAL CASTLE. 05 46 49 46 45. *Guided tour of the square tower June-September; by appointment in low season. Admission: adults 2 €.. Guided tours of the square tower June-September, leaving the Tourist Office at 4pm. Admission: over-12s 2 €. By appointment in low season.* The castle ruins overlook the surrounding countryside and forest. This feudal building belonged to the La Rochefoucauld family from the 15th-18thc., and only the walls, a round pepper-pot tower and the entrance tower are left, together with the ruins of the living-quarters. There is an Arts and Traditions Museum in the square tower, exhibiting local customs and folklore. The view of the countryside from the top is superb.

Montguyon

MONTGUYON FEUDAL CASTLE ✆ **05 46 04 19 31**. *Open every afternoon, July & August. Open by appointment to groups at other times of the year (3 €).* This castle's origins go back to the 13thc., but it is now in ruins. It belonged to the La Rochefoucauld and Rohan families, and was at the heart of many conflicts, being in a border zone between three regions. Some remains have been extricated (moat, wall bases) and you can follow a path around the fortifications. Montguyon Music Festival and popular dances are held here.

Pons

SIRES DE PONS KEEP Ville haute ✆ **05 46 96 13 31**. *Open Easter-November, Monday-Friday and every day from July to mid-September. Admission: adult 2.50 €.* This keep, 30m high and 26m long, stands proudly on the cliff top, a remarkable example of Romanesque military architecture every bit as noble and imposing as the day it was built. The Sires de Pons were the French Crown's powerful, independent and much-feared adversaries during the turbulent Middle Ages. Their first castle was pulled down by Richard the Lion Heart in 1179, and rebuilt by Geoffroy III, Lord of Pons, who finished this colossal keep in 1187. It was a protective symbol for the Compostella pilgrims, who used the hospice as a shelter, leaving many traces of their presence under the vault. – now open to the public.

ROYAN - COTE SAUVAGE

Royan and the surrounding country have been popular with holidaymakers since sea bathing became fashionable in the 19thc. and the first resorts were developed. There are Gallo-Roman remains, abbeys and Romanesque churches, cave dwellings and fashionable 19thc. villas to see, and Royan's post-war architecture is interesting, as well as its port of call and pleasure-craft harbour.

Royan

The first villas were built here in the mid-19thc; a blend of styles from wooden chalets to mock-colonial residences. Old postcards recall the period immortalised by photographer Jacques-Henri Lartigues, who spent his holidays in Royan with his friends Sacha Guitry and Yvonne Printemps from 1924-1926. Severe bombing on 5 January 1945 destroyed this world, and new, modern architecture sprang up in its place. Walk along the sea front, and discover Royan's history in the surprising contrasts between old and new buildings.

SABLONCEAUX ABBEY ✆ 05 46 94 41 62. 17km north-west of Royan, open all year. The private buildings are open to the public the first Sunday of the month. In summer, the exhibitions are open from 3pm-7pm, except Tuesday. The abbey was founded in 1136, housing Augustine canons for 6 centuries before being partially destroyed by the English invasion, Wars of Religion and fire. Today, the restored church contains stained glass and a fine 13thc. three-storey tower. The monastery buildings and chapter house are open to the public.

NOTRE DAME DE ROYAN CHURCH. The only one of its kind. The modern outside may leave you unmoved, but you'll be impressed by the vast proportions inside. The 28m reinforced concrete pillars are stark and chilly, but so unusual, especially in a region of Romanesque churches!

JARDINS DU MONDE A ROYAN 5, av. des Fleurs de la Paix ✆ 05 46 38 00 99. *Open every day July & August: 10am-8pm. February-June and September-December, every day: 10am-6pm. Closed in January. Admission: adult 8.50 €, child 5 €, under-4s free.* A corner of Paradise for fans of the exotic. Different types of vegetation from each continent mix and match: American swamps, Mediterranean olive groves and fields of lavender, bamboo plantations, English lawns. The huge orchid greenhouse is unique in France, but you might prefer the tropical and subtropical bonzai collection, some 100 years old. Kids are welcome in this giant playground, where they can be sprayed by the random water jets, or pilot a remote-controlled boat on the lake.

CORDOUAN LIGHTHOUSE. France's oldest lighthouse, white and majestic, watches over the Gironde estuary from its 66m height. A first tower was put up in the 14thc., with a hermit feeding the fire at the top to guide boats. In 1584, Louis de Foix was given the task of building a new, royal tower. The 7-storey lighthouse was finished in Henry IV's reign. You can see right across the estuary to the Coubre headland and the Arvert and Medoc coasts from the top.

Royan beach

Côte Sauvage

La Tremblade

LE TRAIN DES MOUETTES Rue de la Résinerie ✆ 05 46 75 41 36 or 08 92 39 14 28 (0,34 /min). *Tickets on sale at Saujon or La Tremblade (summer only). Price: adult 12 €, 4-11s 6 €. Ideal for a family outing.* This 113-year-old steam train takes you from La Tremblade to Saujon and back, through oyster beds, saltmarshes and fishing villages. It drops you off at Mornac for a tour of the village and picks you up several hours later. On-board commentary.

Meschers

MATATA CAVES 67, bd. de la Falaise ✆ 05 46 02 70 02. *Open 10am-7pm 9 months of the year, every day in July & August. Evening opening Wednesday. Call for out-of-season opening times. Admission: adult 4.30 €, 7-14s 2.60 €, evening 4.90 €/3.40 €.* The guide tells you the story of Matata, as you go down steps excavated out of the cliff, and travel back to prehistoric times. The nocturne (evening opening) is especially pleasant, but avoid the crowds in the afternoons from 3pm-6pm.

REGULUS CAVES AND FOUNTAINS 83, bd. de la Falaise ✆ 05 46 02 55 36. *Open from Easter to November. 5 April-13 June: every afternoon, hourly departures. 12 July-22 August, all day every 20 minutes until 6.30pm. 23 August-12 September: all day, hourly departures. 13 September-31 October: every afternoon, hourly departures. Admission: adult 4.50 €, child 2.60 €. Evening trip: adult 4.90 €, child 3.40 €.* If you like mysteries and legends, you must visit this site (next to the Matata caves). The name comes from a French ship which scuppered itself off the coast in 1814, to avoid falling into English hands. The caves were eroded by 65,000,000 years of water infiltrating into the limestone, and sheltered pirates, salt smugglers and Protestants during the Wars of Religion. Fishermen lived there in the 19thc; their home has been reconstituted (see Marie Guichard's bedroom).

La Palmyre

COUBRE LIGHTHOUSE. One of the most powerful on the Atlantic coast, measuring 64m. Morning and evening, the keeper has 321 steps to climb. It was built 1.5km from the ocean in 1905, but today is only 250m away, owing to sandbank movements in the estuary. Beautiful view from the top.

ZOO DE LA PALMYRE Ave. de Royan ✆ 05 46 22 46 06/08 92 68 18 48. *www.zoo-palmyre.fr. North-west of Royan on the D25. Open every day. 1 April-30 September: 9am-7pm, other months:9am-6pm. Admission: adult 13 €, 3-12s 9 €, under-3s free.* This zoo houses 1,600 animals in 14 hectares; you need 4 hours to see them all. There are elephants, hippos, rhinos and giraffes; big cats (lions, cheetahs, tigers, panthers, jaguars); monkeys (gibbons, lemurs, chimpanzees, gorillas, orang-utangs); reptiles (turtles, pythons, boas) and over 400 birds.

Saltern

FOOD AND DRINK

Marenne-Oleron oysters, mussels, fish and Charente-Poitou butter are typical products of ocean and land farming. Don't forget cognac, and pineau de Charentes for the apéritif.

Lamb

This is the principal lamb-breeding region. Around Montmorillon, lamb is eaten with mojettes (sort of broad bean), while mouton-village lamb (Deux-Sèvres) is certified to comply with strict breeding norms.

Butter

Echire (Deux-Sèvres), Surgères (Charente-Maritime) and Lescure butter have the appellation d'origine controlée. Poitou-Charentes butter is made exclusively from pasteurised milk cream.

CENTRAL ASSOCIATION OF CHARENTES AND POITOU CO-OPERATIVE DAIRIES 4, rue Jean-Jaures ✆ 05 46 07 58 00

Goat's cheese

This is a cheese-making region that takes care with its production. The most famous is the chabichou, which got its AOC in 1990. It is a little cone-shaped cheese, 5-7cm and 150g, and can be eaten young, mature or dry. There are also the mottin, sainte-maure, pyramide and various fromages frais. 75% of French goats' milk is transformed in Poitou-Charentes.

CABRILIA RN10 - LINAZAY ✆ 05 49 87 01 02. *www.cabrilia.com. Open every day except Monday (open Monday in July & August) Easter-November: 1pm-7pm. Friday evening opening-10pm July & August. Admission: adult 7 €, 4-12s 4 €, families 20 €.* Discover the world of goats in this International Goat Centre, and taste the region's delicious goat's milk cheeses.

Oysters

Cheeses

© BNIC / J.-Y. Boyer

Red-label Marennes-Oléron oysters are farmed in seawater beds called claires, where they feed on *navicule bleue* algae which give them their greenish tinge. There are 3 appellations: speciales de claires, fines de claires, pousse-en-claires, and they can be eaten with lemon, vinegar and shallots, hot with cream, or au gratin. 60,000 tonnes of oysters are produced and sold here each year.

SECTION REGIONALE DE LA CONCHYLICULTURE POITOU-CHARENTES Les Grossines

MARENNES-OLERON ✆ 05 46 85 06 69

Melon

Can be eaten as a starter or dessert. The charentais cantaloup has a greeny-grey skin, which yellows with age, and very sweet and juicy orange flesh, but it must be eaten less than 5 days after being picked. It's delicious eaten with a slice of country ham and a glass of pineau or a slice of bread and Charente butter. Further north, the Poitou 'master melon' is picked when mature, containing minimum 12% sugar. The Vienne department is the biggest national melon producer.

© BNIC / J.-Y. Boyer

SYNDICAT DES MAITRES MELONS DU HAUT POITOU - La Belle Indienne - SERIGNY ✆ 05 49 86 08 66

Mojettes

This succulent white bean is eaten with lamb (south of the Vienne) and country ham (Marais Poitevin). The Pont-l'Abbe-d'Arnoult mojettes are especially well known.

Mussels

On the coast, notably in the Aiguillon bay, you see the bouchots or wooden stakes rising from the water. Mussel-farming on these bouchots dates back to the Middle Ages, when an Irish monk discovered that mussels grew better and quicker on the stakes he spread his nets on.

Petit-gris, cagouille or luma

This is a kind of snail, known as a *luma* or a *cagouille* depending on the district. It is caught after a rainshower, and eaten grilled, braised and stewed in pineau or white wine. It has a delicate flavour, and is the object of a gigantic tasting every year at Mainfonds. where 40,000 *petits-gris* feature on the menu.

Pineau des Charentes

In the 16thc. a winegrower accidentally put must (grape juice) into a cask of cognac alcohol. Realising his mistake, he left the cask in a corner of his storehouse. A few years later, he emptied the cask of a warm-coloured liquid: the grape juice had fermented with the cognac alcohol, making pineau. It exists as a white, which goes well with fish, mussels or scallops, or a rose, for melon, cheese, desserts and fruit. Old pineau is perfect with foie gras.

COMITE NATIONAL DU PINEAU DES CHARENTES 112, ave. Victor Hugo ✆ 05 45 32 09 27. *www.pineau.fr*

Salt

La Rochelle and its surrounding countryside used to count on it as an economic resource. Today, the Ile de Re salterns still use traditional methods to collect sea salt between June and September, with differing crystal sizes: gros sel, sel fin and fleur de sel that can be flavoured with thyme, basil or fennel.

COOPERATIVE DES SAULNIERS DE L'ILE DE RE 7, rue Pree ✆ 05 46 29 40 27. 70 salt producers are members of this co-operative. Production varies from year to year according to weather conditions, from 1,000 to 2,500 tonnes.

Hotels & restaurants

CHARENTE

Angoulême

LES ARTISTES 15, rue des Trois-Notre-Dame © 05 45 95 16 76. *Closed Saturday lunchtime and Sunday. A la carte, around 12 € lunchtime and 20 € evening. Terrace in summer.* Jacques, the boss, is charming when he's in a good mood, and will tell you all about his town, and his passion for photography. This is his third establishment, and you could say he has fulfilled his (late) vocation for the restaurant business. His girlfriend's cooking is excellent and inventive, and the place has been renovated with taste. Art exhibitions follow one another on the stone walls. Advance booking useful.

Roullet

LA VIEILLE ETABLE Les Plantes © 05 45 66 31 75. *Closed Sunday evening from October to May. Set menus from 15 € to 50 €. Terrace in summer.* La Vieille Etable, located 10km south of Angouleme on the edge of the Nationale 10 road, offers gastronomic cuisine based on fresh market produce. The dining room is as peaceful as the site, with its lake, swimming pool, tennis courts and sauna, and helicopter pad all in a green setting. The warm welcome is another strong point.

Soyaux

LE PONT DES TEMPLES 47, avenue du Général-de-Gaulle © 05 45 92 99 77 *Closed Sunday and Tuesday evening, and Monday all day. Set menus 14.60 € (lunchtime) 24.60 €, 27.90 €, 32.20 € and 35 €, a la carte 14 € to 30 €.* All gastronomy fans should take note of this address. The cuisine is traditional, prepared with fresh seasonal produce; foie gras, calf's head, fish and a sublime Portuguese cod. Chef Manuel comes from Portugal, in fact, and willingly chats about his two passions; gastronomy and football.

CHARENTE-MARITIME

Benon

RELAIS DE LA FORET * RN 11 © 05 46 01 61 63.** *Website : www.relaisdelaforet.com. Open all year. Rooms from 54 € to 72 €. Full board from 78 € to 107 €, half-board from 59 € to 87 €. A la carte from 9 € to 23 €. Express menu 14 €, formulas 24 € and 28 €. Children's menu 9 €.* This hotel nestling in the heart of the forest at the end of a cul-de-sac guarantees peace and serenity. There is no lack of activities either, with a swimming pool, billiards, tennis courts and a reading room at your disposal. The woods are ideal for walking, or jogging, if you're up to it. Afterwards, you'll feel virtuously able to enjoy the chef's *cuisine*, concocted with regional produce and served in a colonial-style dining-room. Considering you're only a few kilometres from La Rochelle, it all feels rather exotic.

Chatelaillon

HOTEL LE RIVAGE, seafront ✆ 05 46 56 25 79. *Website: www.hotel-lerivage.com <http://www.hotel-lerivage.com> Open 7 April-12 November. 35 rooms including 23 with a loggia overlooking the sea. Rooms 50 €-72 €. Breakfast 6.50 € (free from 1 October to 12 November). 4 Comfort Plus rooms, Les Iles (available 4 days/3 nights or 7 days/6 nights) 165 €-295 € for 3 nights (according to room and season) and 300 €-500 € for 6 nights. Salon for meetings/seminars/banquets seating 15-30.* This hotel is well-located opposite the beach, 2 minutes on foot from the casino, with the shops just behind. The facade has recently been renovated. Inside, there are two types of room: traditional with loggia and sea view, or 'Les Iles' (sleep 1-4), access via the patio, equipped with kitchenette (microwave, fridge and crockery), TV, shower-room and WC. The breakfast room with its veranda is charming and full of light. From 1 October, breakfast is free - thanks!

HOTEL MAJESTIC ** RESTAURANT LA BELLE EPOQUE Place Saint-Marsault ✆ 05 46 56 20 53. *Rooms from 51 € to 73 € in low season, and from 62 € to 93 € in high season. Family rooms from 90 € to 125 €. Meeting room. Overnight break 60 €. Set menus from 17.50 € to 39 €. Seafood platter 26 €. Children's menu 9 €.* This hotel-restaurant with its 1927 facade cannot fail to please. It offers an attentive welcome, a most attractive staircase, and clean and spacious rooms in different categories: the 'classics' have 55cm TV, bath and WC, and the 'VIPs' a jacuzzi bath and private terrace (22 sqm). The Art Deco-style restaurant is worth stopping off for. And to crown it all, the beach is at the end of the road.

Ile d'Oléron

L'ATELIER 14, rue Pierre-Loti – SAINT-PIERRE ✆ 05 46 47 46 61. *Open all year except Sunday in low season. Set menu from 13.80 € to 19.20 €. A la carte from 6.30 € to 14.50 €. Children's menu 8 €.* Once the Via Loti, now L'Atelier, this restaurant offers generous mixtures of different cuisines, served in the flower-filled half-covered courtyard or one of the two tastefully-decorated indoor dining rooms. Ingenious dishes such as wing of skate with sesame seeds and Thai rice, salmon tartare with vodka sorbet and tagliatelli with queen scallops. For the less adventurous, there are pizzas and pasta. This place has only recently opened, but is becoming a must in Saint-Pierre, thanks to consistently high standards in its decoration, food and ambiance.

CAVEAU DU PORT Le Port de la Cotinière – Saint-Pierre ✆ 05 46 47 10 06. *Open every day. Annual closing in December. Set menus starting from 15 €.* This is rather an unusual restaurant, facing La Cotiniere harbour, where the boats bob on the current. Apart from the usual coastal offerings, the Caveau is king of seafood fondue, where you dip cockles, prawns and other shellfish into your fondue instead of meat. The terrace is set back from the harbour's summer bustle, enabling guests to enjoy their seafood and shellfish, in a fondue or a platter, in peace and quiet. Don't forget to leave room for a dessert: they're divine.

HOSTELLERIE LES CLEUNES * 25, boulevard de la Plage Saint-Trojan-Les-Bains ✆ 05 46 76 03 08.** *Website : www.hotel-les-cleunes.com. Open 4 February-13 November. Double room from 80 € to 105 € in mid-season, and from 95 € to 135 € in summer. Half-board 75 €-105 € per person per day. Breakfast 11 €. 2 suites, apartments. Rooms with disabled access. Seminar room currently being* *installed. Tennis court. Billiards. Table tennis. Bicycles at customers' disposal.* Facing the sea and the viaduct, this splendid hotel is beginning its second season, after extensive renovation to improve comfort levels. The 40 refurbished rooms all have four-poster beds, safes, mini-bars and TV. After a few strokes in the heated pool, you can taste some creative cooking in the panoramic restaurant. On the menu are aquitaine caviar, monkfish and crayfish *croustillant*, tomato puree with chorizo and Madras curry, tuna tournedos with foie gras pleurotus in a Madeira infusion, and for dessert, pineapple roasted in brown sugar, *flambed* with rhum, white chocolate mousse and sugar dentelle cooked with lime peel. Delicious! A warm and professional welcome guaranteed.

Ile de Ré

L'AUBERGE DE LA RIVIERE 27, avenue des Salines Les Portes-en-Ré ✆ 05 46 29 54 55 *Open all year. Set menus 15 € (lunchtime) and 24 € to 40 €.* Alberto and his wife Goreti Fonte took over the Auberge in 2004. The menu couldn't be more gastronomic. The menus are named after their children, Victoria and Gregory, and you find varied and sophisticated dishes a la carte.Examples are the chocolate croquant with salt, a sumptuous seafood symphony (choucroute), oysters, stuffed quail with foie gras, a rabbit *moelleux* with morels...and a mixture of land and sea, in the scorpion fish *croustillant* with chorizo. The warm and luminous dining room is decorated in ochre and beige tones, with prettily-set tables.

HOTEL DE TOIRAS ** 1, quai Job-Foran Saint-Martin-de-Ré ✆ 05 46 35 40 32.** *Open all year. Rooms from 120 € to 290 €. Suites from 260 € to 520 €. Breakfast 18 €. Seminar room. Car park. Half-board available.* The Hotel de Toiras is a former shipowner's house, located at the entrance to the harbour. Its 17thc. facade and marvellous views make a great impact. A small private office serves as a reception area, followed by the lounge, and an aromatic garden in the very heart of the building. Rooms and suites seem to slumber in the peaceful atmosphere, but there is plenty of activity in the restaurant, La Table d'Olivia, specialising in fresh fish and seafood. The menu is drawn up every day according to the market produce available, and also to the customers' wishes.

La Rochelle

LES QUATRE SERGENTS 49, rue Saint-Jean-du-Pérot ✆ 05 46 41 35 80. *Weekly closing Monday. Set menus 15 €, 22 €, 27 € and 36.50 €. Children's menu 7 €.* The voice mail explains that the 'four sergeants' rest for a while in the afternoon; very necessary after the intense lunchtime activity, and all those visitors to the kitchens, interested in watching the culinary arts in action.The painting and sculpting of fish, lobsters and langoustines, for instance, to create savoury works of art. Taste the lobster salad with mango or the brill with a velvet swimming crab coulis. You might prefer the wine-flavoured snail profiteroles. Keep some appetite for the dessert, so beautifully presented that you hardly dare touch it. The setting is unique: the tables are widely spaced across an indoor courtyard with a high glass conservatory roof, filled with green plants.

RICHARD COUTANCEAU Plage de la Concurrence ✆ 05 46 41 48 19 *Fax 05 46 41 99 45. Website: www.contanceaularochelle.com Set menus from 45 € to 85 €, a la carte 75 €. Closed Sunday, no annual closing.* Richard Coutanceau took over from Jacques Le Divellec about twenty years ago, when the latter left La Rochelle for Paris, and soon emerged as a leader in the town's restaurant business. Today, his main competitor is his son Gregory, very successful at opening thematic restaurants, but his other son Christopher has stayed at his side to help him consolidate this leadership. Their restaurant in its 1980s building away from the town centre attracts fish-lovers, for Richard is an expert in seafood gastronomy: langoustine tartare in fine jelly, with special oysters and beads of Aquitaine caviar, black squid ravioli on a bed of Catalan vegetables chilled with basil, rock fish juice, turbot fillet, truffles with crunchy artichokes, gnocchi *moelleux* with ink, sweetbreads cooked in foamy butter with country bacon, vegetables *en cocotte*, creamy juice with wild mushrooms (for meat-lovers), followed by fine Breton vanilla shortbread, pear conserved in Burgundy, with cardamom ice-cream, cinnamon *croquant* (type of biscuit) with a Burgundy wine *granite* (iced sorbet). Beautiful ocean view, service expertly managed by Jacques Sarrand (20 years in the place) and a fine cellar including the best bottles from the New World.

Rochefort

LA CORDERIE ROYALE * Rue J.-B.-Audebert ✆ 05 46 99 35 35** *Closed in January and Sunday and Monday in low season. Set menus from 25 € (weekday lunchtime) to 54 €. Rooms from 58 € to 245 €.* Lunch and dinner are served in the indoor gardens or conservatory, at the leisurely rhythm of the slow-flowing River Charente. Laurent Carlier prepares his recipes with care, and only works with regional produce. His 'marshland sheaf' with fruit and strawberry coulis, for instance, is quite unforgettable. The rooms have views of the Corderie Royale, the Charente or the indoor gardens, and are ideal for working or relaxing.

LA BELLE POULE Route de Royan ✆ 05 46 99 71 87.** *Open all year except the first 3 weeks in November. Restaurant closed Friday, Sunday evening (except July) and August. Double rooms from 50 € to 56 €. Breakfast 8 €. Set menus from 21.50 € to 40 €. Set price for sales reps 60 €.* This beautiful hen may not lay golden eggs, but she has 20 top-quality rooms to offer, at reasonable prices, and with a view over the marshes. In winter, visitors can warm up in front of a big log fire, and in summer, cool down under the cascades of flowers on the terrace; either way, an excellent welcome is ensured. This is a family business; the Noyaud ladies greet you with a smile, and son David specialises in gastronomic puzzles created with fresh produce, where fish naturally have pride of place. Very good wine list.

Royan

BEAU RIVAGE ** 9, façade de Foncillon ✆ 05 46 39 43 10. *Website : www.hotel-beau-rivage-royan.com. Open all year. Rooms from 65 €. Garage free for motorbikes.* This charming and welcoming hotel suits its name, facing as it does the beach and Atlantic waves. Its 22 rooms are all calm and comfortable, most of them with a balcony equipped with sunloungers, or even a private terrace with garden furniture. Direct phone lines, Internet connctions and TV with Canal +. The restaurant is specialised in pasta dishes.

Saintes

HOTEL BLEU NUIT ** 1, rue Pasteur ✆ 05 46 93 01 72. *Fax : 05 46 74 43 80. Website : www.hotelbleunuit.com 33 rooms including 10 family rooms, from 40 € to 68 €. Breakfast 6.20 €. Overnight break 60 €. Small animals accepted. Closed garage with security system. Bar open to hotel guests. Central lounge. Lift.* This former coaching inn is located in the heart of Saintes, near the historic sites, including the famous Roman ruins. You benefit from a warm welcome, and a comfortable room, with a balcony, perhaps, and telephone, satellite TV, Internet and hair-dryer in the bathroom for sure. Breakfast is served in the indoor courtyard, among the flowers. In short, all you could want for a pleasant stay.

SAVEURS DE L'ABBAYE ** 1, place Saint-Pallais ✆ 05 46 94 17 91. *Open all year. Restaurant closed Monday. Set menus from 17 € to 30 €. Menu of the day (weekday lunchtimes) 11 €. Children's menu 7.60 €. Rooms from 42 € to 45 €. Breakfast 5.50 €.* Alexandra and Olivier Pourpoint have decorated their charming hotel with great care. It stands at the north entrance to the Abbaye aux Dames, and can guarantee you not only a good night's sleep, but a delicious meal made up of healthy products, prepared by a skilled chef. The cuisine is inventive; you are never overfaced by the contents of your (square) plate, but your tastebuds won't complain about the salmon marinated with lime and shellfish in a *pastilla*, or fillet mignon of suckling pork in a crust with country ham and tarragon juice. You need to be a pretty adventurous gourmet, though, to appreciate these tastes and textures, which can be surprising, and even disturbing. Strawberry soup with basil features among the desserts. The menu changes every three months.

DEUX-SÈVRES

Coulon

LE MARAICHIN Chemin du Halage ✆ 05 49 35 97 46. *Open every day in high season from March to October. Set menus 15 €, 17 €, 25 €,30 € and 35 €.* Le Maraichin lives up to its name, anchoring its cuisine in the surrounding marshes, though not exclusively. As you approach Coulon, it is located to the left just before the bridge, after the Cardinaud landing stage, in a 3 ha.wooded park. Sylvie welcomes the guests while Christophe Thoreton manages his team in the kitchens. You can taste his specialities in the cheerful dining-room or outside in the park under the tivoli, on the edge of the conche (small marshland waterway). Scallops with peach cream, marsh eel fricassee in a parsley vinaigrette, beef fillet in a pastry crust with a maitre d'hotel sauce and lamb saute with honey and ginger are examples from his menu. The desserts are equally sophisticated, whether classic or baroque, or even exotic. We recommend the truffle with chocolates on a milky caramel coulis. A little too sweet, certainly, but the caramel coulis brings back childhood memories. An address worth discovering.

Melle

LES GLYCINES ** Place René-Groussard ✆ 05 49 27 01 11. Fax 05 49 27 93 35. *Website : http://www.hotel-lesglycines.com Logis de France. Closed Sunday evening except July & August. Rooms from 35 € to 47.50 €. Set menus 13.80 €, 16.50 €, 24.50 € and 38.80 €. Children's menu 10 €. Group menus.*Eric Caillon comes from a culinary family; his father has a restaurant business in Savoie and his brother is a pastrycook in Australia. Eric stayed where his roots were, to develop regional and seasonal cuisine, and he does it rather well. His hotel-restaurant is housed in a pleasant 19thc.building full of character, where we discovered his flan maraichin with its fine herb salad (a lighter version of *farci*, the Poitevin vegetable and bacon dish) followed by a chicken and lemon kebab with an excellent ratatouille. For afters, we chose the dessert that won him the Logis de France prize in 1997: home-made shortbread and caramelised apples, a crystallised fig under its syrup and a ball of rosemary ice-cream, mixing and matching flavours and textures. The service is young and efficient. You can organise a seminar, or hold a reception here (seats 200); Les Glycines also provides catering.

Niort

LA BELLE ETOILE 115, quai Maurice-Métayer ✆ 05 49 73 31 29. *Website : http://www.la-belle-etoile.fr Closed Sunday evening and Monday. Annual closing 3 weeks in August. Set menus Petit menu du marche 22 €, Terroir et Fantaisie 29 €, Passions et Decouvertes 41.50 €, Prestige Degustation (7 courses, 6 wines) 77.50 €, or 60 € without wine.* This restaurant is located on the banks of the Sevre near a bridge, and has been run by the capable Claude Guignard since 1979. He is backed up by young chef David Arnaud, who won his spurs at the Royal Monceau in Paris, the Bretagne at Questembert, La Cote Saint-Jacques at Joigny and Le Richelieu on the Ile de Re. What an impressive career! We do recommend the famous *Prestige Degustation* menu (don't bring the kids) with its seven courses and six wines. Pan-fried Erquy scallops with horns of plenty, truffle butter, atlantic bass, *sauce vierge* with olive oil, Jerusalem artichokes in fricassee, then shortbread with rhubarb cream and candied apples, salted milk caramel. You be the judge! Small budgets and gourmets in a hurry are also catered for in the *petit menu du marche.*

Parthenay

HOTEL DU NORD ** 86, avenue du Général-de-Gaulle ✆ 05 49 94 29 11. *Closed Saturday and Sunday evening. Rooms from 47 € to 53 €. Set menus from 15 €, terroir menu 23 €, children's menu 8.50 €, a la carte 35 €.*Robert Reveilaud and his charming wife Nicole run Parthenay's best gastronomic restaurant. This big hotel-restaurant is located opposite the station, and can cater for business meals, intimate dinners or your mother-in-law's birthday party with no difficulty.The cuisine is traditional and regional, and Parthenay beef steak and chops, or *flambed* sweetbreads feature among the chef's specialities. The cellar offers regional wines, such as Haut-Poitou (Heritage) or red Anjou (Lemoine and Arnault). There are 10 comfortable rooms, and welcome and service are most cordial.

Thouars

LE LOGIS DE POMPOIS SainteVerge ✆ 05 49 96 27 84 *Closed Sunday evening, Monday and Tuesday, except public holidays. Set menus from 17.50 € to 44 €. Children's menu 13 €.* Just outside Thouars (3km) and well though-of, this charming Logis de Pompois is a gastronomic restaurant where only fresh food is used to prepare the menus. Musical dinners are held the last two Saturdays of every month, usually jazz. We chose the duck croustillant cooked with cider vinegar and honey from among the succulent dishes on offer, and it was sublime. In short, this is a safe bet!

VIENNE

Chasseneuil-du-Poitou

CHATEAU DU CLOS DE LA RIBAUDIERE * 10, place du Champ-de-Foire ✆ 05 49 52 86 66.** *Open all year. Rooms from 90 € to 135 €. Breakfast 11 €. Set menus from 28.50 € to 51 €.* We loved the scallop tart and cepe puree! This is one of the department's best eating-places, a stone's throw from the Futuroscope. The elegant hotel dates back to the 19thc. and provides an exceptional setting. Comfort and sophistication go hand in hand, every room is spacious and individually decorated, with those final touches only found in luxury hotels. All have satellite TV, direct phone line, hair-dryer, bathroom and WC. Even the pool boasts a truly luxurious decor.

Chatellerault

LA GOURMANDINE 22, avenue du Président-Wilson ✆ 05 49 21 05 85. *Site Internet : www.la-gourmandine.com Closed Sunday evening and Monday. Set menus from 22 € to 44 €, lunchtime formula 15 €, a la carte.* In an early 20thc. magnificent bourgeoise residence, David Seguin serves you traditional food with a personal touch, and a particular freshness to the produce. A Rabelaisian fresco in the entrance hall gets you into the mood, and you can choose between the luminous and elegant rotunda, a more intimate private lounge or the terrace. The menus - *Coup de coeur, du marche* or *Saveur* - suggest a snail tourtiere with chanterelles and ratte potatoes, a lobster fricassee and seasonal vegetables with the coral juice and Parmesan biscuit. Your dessert could be a grapefruit *fraicheur*, green aniseed lollipop, *dacquoise moelleuse* (meringue layers with butter cream filling) with almonds and chocolate, praline mousse and drops of arabica coffee. It's a pity there isn't a more economic lunch formula.

GRAND HOTEL MODERNE* RESTAURANT LA CHARMILLE 74, boulevard Blossac ✆ 05 49 93 33 00**. *Fax : 05 49 93 25 19. This hotel in the town centre provides 24 rooms from 65 € to 170 €. Breakfast 10 €, evening break formulas from 69 € to 170 € depending on requests. Animals accepted, supplement 10 € per night.* Don't miss out on La Charmille's restaurant, with its indoor and outdoor gardens. Christian Proust settled in Chatellerault in January 1970, and has developed his culinary skills to such a point that he well deserves the praise heaped on his top-quality *cuisine*.

Montmorillon

LE LUCULLUS 4, boulevard de Strasbourg ✆ 05 49 84 09 09.** *Restaurant closed Sunday evening and Monday. Rooms from 40 € to 65 €, set menus from13 € to 43 €.* Opposite the sous-prefecture, a stone's throw from the town centre, Montmorillon's only hotel has both charm and advantages. In the first place, it opens onto the main road and is easy to find if your sense of direction isn't great. Secondly, it has a reputed gastronomic restaurant; the bistro formulas are excellent value for money. Thirdly, it has 38 rooms, all freshly renovated, elegant and tasteful. Plenty of room to relax, and thoughtful service complete the picture.

Poitiers

LE GRAND HOTEL* 28, rue Carnot ✆ 05 49 60 90 60. 2** *Fax : 05 49 62 81 89. Website : www.grandhotelpoitiers.fr Rooms from 64 €, suites from 109 €, breakfast 11 €, either buffet or served in your room. Hotel air-conditioned with an adjustable seminar room (100 sqm), private garage and room service until 10pm.* You'll sleep soundly, away from the noisy streets, even here in the town centre, for the former Hotel de France has been reshaped according to the rules of architecture - and of comfort. Breakfast is served on the wide terrace in good weather, with its charming view of the restored houses round about. This is one of the rare hotels that dares to work without a group franchise, and every decision made about the furnishings or the decoration is therefore unique. The rooms were influenced by La Mamounia, a grand Moroccan hotel. The bar serves a large selection of whiskies.

RESTAURANT MAXIME 4, rue Saint-Nicolas ✆ 05 49 41 27 37. *Closed Saturday and Sunday. Open Saturday evening from November to February.* Gourmet visitors are welcomed in a series of small dining rooms (private rooms are available on request) hidden behind wide curtains in a hushed atmosphere. The setting is most attractive, but Christian Rougier's cooking outshines the rest. His dishes follow the seasons: warm oyster ravioli, herb butter, pan-fried scallops with truffles, warm Garnd Marnier souffle. It's a sophisticated menu, whether you choose meat or fish, and the quality is maintained through the cheese course to the last mouthful of sweet. There is a quick lunchtime formula, however, at 15 €, which not all gastronomic restaurants are prepared to offer.

Provence

ARDÈCHE
DRÔME
GARD
VAUCLUSE
BOUCHES-DU-RHÔNE
Grignan
Pierrelatte
Valréas
Rémuzat
Nyons
Ste-Jalle
Lez
Rhône
Bollène
Mondragon
Vaison-la-Romaine
Aygues
Malaucène
Orange
Mt. Ventoux 1909 m.
Ouvèze
Sault
Mormoiron
Bédarrides
Carpentras
Nesque
Monts de Vaucluse
Avignon
Châteaurenard
Apt
Nîmes
Cavaillon
Coulon
Tarascon
St-Rémy-de-Provence
Montagne du Luberon
Orgon
Cadenet
Les-Baux-de-Provence
Alpilles
Pertui
Arles
Lambesc
Durance
Salon-de-Provence
Camargue
Grand-Rhône
Aix-en-Proven
Étang de Vaccarès
Istres
Petit-Rhône
Arc
Petite Camargue
Stes-Maries-de-la-mer
Étang de Berre
Fos-sur-Mer
Vitrolles
Gardan
Marignane
Golfe de Beauduc
Port de Fos
Martigues
Port-St-Louis-du-Rhône
Pointe du Sablon
Allauch
MARSEILLE
Aubag
GOLFE
DU
LION
Cassis
île de Riou
MER
Altitude (metres)
1500
1000
500
200
Departemental boundany
Motorway
Road
Canal
Railwayline

PROVENCE
Vilhosc
Digne
Peyruis
ALPES-DE-HAUTE-PROVENCE
Durance
Asse
Moustiers-Ste-Marie
Castellane
Forcalquier
Riez
ALPES-MARITIMES
Manosque
Comps-sur-Artuby
Montagne de Barjaude
Artuby
Grasse
Fayence
Callas
Rians
Tavernes
Salernes
Cannes
Barjols
Draguignan
Cotignac
Estérel
Lorgues
Le Muy
St. Raphaël
VAR
Argens
Fréjus
Trets
St. Maximin-la Ste.-Baume
Brignoles
Le Luc
Besse-sur-Issole
Pointe des Issambres
Massif des Maures
La Roquebrussane
Gapeau
St. Tropez
Cuers
Ramatuelle
Bormes-les-Mimosas
La Crau
Ollioules
Baie de Cavalaire
Toulon
Bandol
Hyères
La Seyne-sur-Mer
île des Embiez
Presqu'île de Giens
îles d'Hyères
île du Levant
île de Porquerolles
île de Port-Cros
MÉDITERRANÉE
0
50 km

MARSEILLE AND THE CALANQUES

Marseille

Marseille is unique. 2,603 years old, one of Antiquity's trading centres, the Phocean city has become a typical Mediterranean capital. Hills, sea, calanques and port spread out before you as you look down from the Bonne Mère on the town heights. The old quarters captivate you with their charm, but the real soul of the town lies in the welcome it extends to all comers, its ethnic mix - in short, its humanity.

SAINT VICTOR ABBEY 3, rue de l'Abbaye (7e) ✆ 04 96 11 22 60. Founded by Jean Cassien in the 5thc. on the sepulture of Saint Victor, a 3rdc. Roman martyr. Inside, the crypts contain many sarcophagi, recalling the faith of the early Christians.

LA MAJOR CATHEDRAL 10, place de la Major (2e) ✆ 04 91 90 53 57. Built from 381 onwards, the Major is one of Marseille's oldest churches. It was reshaped several times, rebuilt between 1852 and 1893; the two bays were removed, and now only the 12thc. Provençal Romanesque chevet is left. The Bishop of Marseilles chose a Byzantine Romanesque style for the new 19thc. church, to emphasise the town's importance as a trading port with the Orient, and the inside is dazzling, with its porphyry columns, marble and mosaics.

CHATEAU BORELY 134, ave. Clot-Bey (8e) ✆ 04 91 25 26 34. *Closed for renovation work (until further notice).* This residence is a classic example of 18thc. Provençal architecture, a typically Mediterranean bastide. Today, the elegant building houses exhibitions of Provençal painting, having been lent to the Regards de Provence Foundation by the town for 2 years.

CHATEAU D'IF ✆ 04 91 59 02 30. Crossing to the islet and landing on it depends on the weather. Cost: adult 4,60 €, 18-25s 3.10 €, under-18s free (not included in the castle admission price). Boarding Quai de la Fraternité (ex Quai des Belges) on the Vieux Port. This was a wild islet until the 16thc. occasionally used by fishermen. François I had a strategic fortress built on it (1531), but it never took part in combat, and became a prison. Contrary to legend, the Man in the Iron Mask and the Marquis de Sade were never shut up here, the most famous prisonner being the priest Jose Custodio Faria, immortalised in The Count of Monte Cristo. The fortress stopped being a prison in 1848, and was opened to the public in 1890.

CORNICHE KENNEDY. This is a pleasant walk or bike-ride, with one of Marseille's most beautiful views. Don't miss the maregraphe, a complex instrument marking point 0 for measuring altitude in France.

Marseille

CHARTREUX CHURCH 26, place Edmond-Audran ✆ 04 91 49 40 76. *Open 10.30pm-12 noon and 4.30pm-6.30pm.* This masterpiece of classical French art was built in 1696, according to prior Jean-Baptiste Berger's plans. The church is actually dedicated to Saint Mary Magdalen, but like the quarter itself, takes its name from the Chartreux monastery.

FRIOUL. First, you cross by boat from the Vieux Port, looking back at Marseille harbour under its blue sky; a magical sight. Within half an hour, you reach solitary Frioul port far from the busy city, and can stroll along the chalky coast amid rare and wild vegetation, to Cap Caveaux, Pomegues' southern headland.

SAINT CHARLES STATION. The Paris-Lyon-Marseille (PLM) line arrived here in 1848, and the station inaugurated a new era. Its metal framework is a listed monument, and the hall is decorated with blazons. The great white staircase, made famous in films, is immense, and Oriental in style, with statues along the steps.

NOTRE DAME DE LA GARDE Place Colonel Edon ✆ 04 91 13 40 80. *Open 7.30 am-8pm (7.30pm in winter).* A chapel has existed on the site since 1214; it was enlarged several times, then François I had a fort built here in 1524. Damaged during the Revolution, it was re-opened in 1807 and replaced by the present church in 1853, designed by Esperandieu in Romanesque Byzantine style. The basilica overlooks the town from 154m, and you must see the stark crypt, dazzling upper church, silver statue on the High Altar, ex-votos and monumental Virgin on the golden spire (over 5m). Our Lady is the patron who guards sailors, whence the name 'La Garde', but she is universally known in Marseille as la bonne mere, their good mother.

PALAIS DU PHARO 58, bd. Charles Livon (7e) ✆ 04 91 55 15 75. Marseille offered this seaside palace to Napoleon III, so he might do something for the town. He never lived in it. Today, it contains an auditorium.

PARC BORELY Av. Borely (8e). One of Marseille's biggest and finest gardens, immortalised by the author Marcel Pagnol.

VIEUX PORT Quai Port. Stroll down the Canebiere to this picturesque old port, sit outside a cafe and enjoy the beautiful weather. There is a daily fish market, and you can take a ferry trip across the harbour.

LA MAISON DU PASTIS 108, quai du Port (2e) ✆ 04 91 90 86 77. *www.lamaisondupastis.com.* A living anisette museum! Learn all about absinthe and pastis: origins, manufacture (maceration, distilling) storage, grands crus. You can even taste some of the different brands decorating the shelves (both homemade and reputed). Don't leave without a bottle of pastis filled from the cask; its flavour is quite distinct.

MUSEE DES BEAUX ARTS Palais Longchamp ✆ 04 91 14 59 30. The museum houses Provençal and French paintings (16th-19thc.): Puget, Mignard, Courbet, Corot, Daumier. The major works are by Rubens, Jordaens and Snyders.

MUSEE D'ARTS AFRICAINS, OCEANIENS, AMERINDIENS 04 91 14 58 38. Centre de la Vieille Charite 2, rue de la Charite ✆ 04 91 14 58 38. Apart from Paris, Marseille is the only town to have a museum devoted to African, Australasian and American Indian art forms.

MUSEE CANTINI 19, rue Grignan (6e) ✆ 04 91 54 77 75. *Open every day: 10am-5pm out of season; 11am-6pm 1 June-30 September. Closed Mondays and public holidays. Admission: adult 2 €.* You can see major works of art from 1930-late 20thc., by Matisse, Kandinsky, Max Ernst, Dubuffet, Giacometti and Balthus.

MUSEUM D'HISTOIRE NATURELLE Palais Longchamp (4e) ✆ 04 91 14 59 50. *www.museum-marseille.org.* This majestic Natural History Museum houses 400 million years of French and Marseilles flora and fauna.

MUSEE D'HISTOIRE DE MARSEILLE Centre Bourse - 17, square Belsunce ✆ 04 91 90 42 22. This museum in the heart of Marseilles traces the Phocaean city's history from its foundation in 600B.C. until today.

LEOPOLD 38, rue de l'Evéché 2e ✆ 04 91 67 57 35. *Open Monday-Saturday: tearoom and biscuit bakery 11.15am-7.15pm. Restaurant: the usual lunchtime hours. Closed Sunday. Dining room upstairs. Terrace. Dish of the day 9.50 €, 10.50 €, formula with dessert 11.50 €, 12.50 €. Macaroons 1 €. each.* Leopold specialises in old-fashioned flavours. The beautiful window display recalls turn-of-the-century shops, and the tearoom (transformed into a restaurant at lunchtime) is decorated with considerable charm and good taste. As for the cooking, it is done in the workshop ajacent to the dining room. All the dishes are home-made; light, original, sophisticated and perfectly seasoned (often sweet-savoury or hot-cold mixtures). The pork fillet mignon with lemon, fried noodles and rocket salad is a must - but then the salmon crumble, braised veal with caper sauce and tuna risotto are excellent too! We recommend the New York cheesecake, tarts and pistachio *creme brulee* for dessert. And that's not all. Leopold is also a fine biscuit bakery specialising in macaroons, Marseilles *navettes* and other goodies. They are baked before your very eyes in the workshop, and are deliciously fresh. The dark chocolate, chocolate caramel, rose, pistachio, strawberry and bitter almond flavours go perfectly with your tea or coffee. Simply divine.

Calanques

This name is given to two coastal massifs separated by the Morgiou valley, south of Marseille and the Cassis road. You have to discover them on foot to appreciate the beauty of these hills, whose great limestone sides attract hikers and rock-climbers.

CALANQUE DE FIGUEROLLES. This little-known though listed site lies behind the Vieux-Port, 1km from the town centre. Leave your car in the car park, and go down the steps to the creek, a magical sienna-coloured place in the chalky white landscape. Sea, rocks and thick vegetation harmonise in the cool, quiet atmosphere of an oasis.

Around Marseille

Aubagne

It would be difficult to talk of Provence without mentioning Marcel Pagnol. The region inspired his writing, and became its main character. He was born in Aubagne, grew up in Marseille and deeply loved the surrounding countryside.

MASSIF DU GARLABAN. This chief landmark in Pagnol's childhood offers exceptional viewpoints and walks through the valleys and caves, the most beautiful being Baourno Sourno grotto in the north of the massif (yellow path). Mountain biking is permitted, but the massif is closed to visitors in July and August. Hikes and walking tours are organised on the Garlaban sites and filmsets.

LE PETIT MONDE DE MARCEL PAGNOL Esplanade De Gaulle ✆ 04 42 03 49 98. *Open every day: 9am-12.30pm and 2.30pm-6pm. Admission free.* This museum presents the writer's life and work. The famous actors who brought the characters in his plays to life are on view in the form of santons, those carved peasants and Nativity characters found in Provençal cribs.

Cassis

More than Marseilles' Saint-Tropez, this is an exceptional site with its Port-Miou, En-Vau and Port-Pin calanques, soaring cliffs (Cap Canaille 416m high) and places to swim. The old town centre is charming, as is the little harbour, but for the 'real' Provence, avoid the tourist traps and head off for the calanques and local vineyards instead.

AROUND AIX-EN-PROVENCE

Aix country is French Tuscany: gentle hills and rich crops with hieratic cypresses dotting the landscape, and Sainte-Victoire mountain overlooking it all. Aix itself is a serene town with a famous past, as its monuments and fountains will tell you.

Aix-en-Provence

The first Roman settlement in Gaul was at Aix, because of its springs, which still feed the city's fountains. The Counts of Provence lived here, and King René brought artists. The resulting historic and artistic identity attracted a grande bourgeoisie, who settled in luxurious mansions. Aix is also Cézanne, and Emile Zola. Walk in the shade of the plane trees on the Cours Mirabeau, or through the town centre, to enjoy this marvellous city's atmosphere and art of living.

ATELIER CEZANNE 9, ave. Paul Cézanne ✆ 04 42 21 06 53. *www.atelier-Cezanne.com.* 2006 is the centenary of Cezanne's death. The studio will be open for cultural activities and exhibitions. Enquire at the Tourist Office for more information about the programme. (04 42 161 161) Open every day: 10am-6pm, 1 July-31 August. Otherwise, call for opening times: Paul Cézanne was born in Aix on 19 January 1839. After a stay in Paris, working with great masters like Pissaro, he came back in the 1880s to paint, notably Sainte-Victoire. His studio, the Atelier des Lauves, is more like a shrine than a museum, containing the artist's familiar 'models': pots, vases and apples. The garden adds its note to the intimate, lifelike atmosphere.

BIBEMUS QUARRIES. Take the Bibemus road from the D10, to see these magnificent ochre quarries. Ochre was used to decorate Aix's hotels and monuments. Cézanne painted one of his canvases in the Bibemus cabanon, or hut.

L'ESPRIT DES LIEUX 10, rue Gaston de Saporta ✆ 04 42 21 20 74. The place to buy your presents and souvenirs. Frames, candlesticks and tableware in softly coloured earthenware; linen lavender-bags, napkin rings, jewellery, reproduction paintings, household linen and the full range of l'Occitane and Esteban products.

SAINT SAUVEUR CATHEDRAL Rue Gaston de Saporta. The town's oldest religious building. Different orders have left their mark: the Hospitallers built the tower in 1180, then came the Cordeliers (1220), Carmelites (1248), Preaching Friars (1273), Augustinians (1292) Poor Claires and Dominicans. The cathedral's 15thc. west front is Flamboyant Gothic. There are three naves of different periods and a 64m square tower (1425) with 8 pinnacles (1880).

SAINT JEAN DE MALTE CHURCH Place Saint-Jean-de-Malte. First entirely Gothic Provençal church, dating back to the 13thc. and built by the Saint John of Jerusalem Knights Hospitallers. The six 17thc. chapels inside added by Prior Viany contain paintings by Gilles Garcin and Andre Boisson, and Christ on the Cross by Eugene Delacroix.

FOUNTAINS. Decorative, refreshing; Aix owes its reputation to its fountains. Originally a simple means of bringing water to homes, they have become art objects designed by artists and hydraulic engineers. You will admire the styles and periods they represent when you come across them around corners, at the ends of streets...

Sainte Victoire Mountain

Saint Victoire is Provence's symbol, marking the Aix landscape, and is also famous for inspiring Cezanne. It culminates in the Pic des Mouches at 1,011m. The bright red clay at the base forms a striking contrast with the high white limestone wall, especially between Le Tholonet and Puyloubier. Despite having been damaged by fire, Saint Victoire is still a popular place for walking and climbing, and different routes lead hikers to a 17thc. priory and the Provence Cross. From here, you have a magnificent panoramic view of the Provence mountains and the hilly Aix plains. Another itinerary takes you through small villages under the steep mountain wall. Le Tholonet boasts an 18thc. chateau and the ruined arches of a Roman aqueduct. The Roques Hautes departmental park begins nearby, protecting Saint Victoire's west side.Saint Antonin-sur-Bayon is overshadowed by a great 18thc. bastide, and the remains of the Bayon oppidum can be seen on a small plateau not far away. To the east, you find Puyloubier and Pourrieres, in the heart of the vineyards. At the foot of the north side, the little village of Vauvenargues stretches along a green valley. The 14th and 17thc. chateau standing alone on its mound was bought by Picasso in 1958; he is buried in the grounds. Over 6,000 ha. of the Saint Victoire massif have been listed since 1983.

FONTAINE DU ROI RENE Haut du Cours Mirabeau. Aix's great man, who didn't spend all his life in Anjou. Good King René welcomes you in his long robes and crown.

THERMES SEXTIUS 55, cours Sextius ✆ 04 42 23 81 81. This is a spa town, that seeks to link care of the body with sensual and intellectual pleasure. The thermal baths are on the site of the former Roman baths. Benefit from the waters while enjoying the town's historic heritage.

FONDATION VASARELY 1, ave. Marcel Pagnol ✆ 04 42 20 01 09. *www.fondationvasarely.com. Open every day, Monday-Friday: 10am-1pm and 2pm- 6pm (5pm in winter). weekends: 10am-6pm. Admission: adults 7 €* The artist Victor Vasarely was interested in optical effects from the superposing of frames, reorganising surfaces and the use of contrasting colour. In the 1960s he developed his art into architecture, and founded this place to exhibit his works and creations.

Pays aixois

Enchanting Aix country, with its sunshine, forests and rocks rising up from the maquis - a view of Provence dominated by Sainte-Victoire, so beautifully painted by Cézanne.

Saint-Antonin-sur-Bayon

MAISON SAINTE VICTOIRE D17 ✆ 04 42 66 84 40. *(Opening times vary according to season) Open 10am-6pm, Monday-Friday. Saturday & Sunday: 10am-7pm. Interpretation path free.* Exhibition centre. Donkey-rides. Guided hikes on donkeys, with a picnic at the Cézanne refuge. 20 mins from Aix on the Cézanne route, the Sainte-Victoire Centre is on one of Provence's protected natural heritage sites. There is an exhibition centre with temporary displays and a multimedia montage explaining the mountain's history - which you can discover more actively later, in the forest outside.

Saint-Cannat

VILLAGE DES AUTOMATES RN7 ✆ 04 42 57 30 30. *Open 1 April-30 September, every day: 10am-6pm. 1 October-31 March, open Wednesday, Saturday, Sunday, school and public holidays: 10am-6pm. Admission: adult 8 €, child 5 €.*Become a Liliputian in the Automaton Village; meet Gulliver and a whale opening its jaws to swallow you up! Inside, 17 tableaux tell the story of Pinocchio. Every year, there are new imaginary and poetic wonders to discover.

Ventabren

This typically Provencal village is perched 252m above sea-level, stretching over 2,500 ha., and has a rich cultural heritage. Saint Denis Church (17thc), Queen Jeanne's Chateau and Roquefavour Aqueduct are all well worth visiting, and the steep staircase alleys lined with houses clinging to each other, the windmill, washing places and fountains seem designed for holiday photos and lingering, sunny memories.

ARLES & THE CAMARGUE

This is a region of protected natural beauty, where you can feel quite alone in the vast, magnificent landscape. Even a stroll through old Arles or along the Rhône cannot quite dispel this sense of gentle melancholy.

Arles

This is a town of character; of brave guardians, wild horses and courageous bulls. It is also the crossroads between the overland road linking Spain and Italy and the River Rhône, arriving at the end of its long course and splitting in two, to reach the Mediterranean.

MONTMAJOUR ABBEY Route de Fontvieille ✆ 04 90 54 64 17. *Open 10am-6.30pm in summer; 10am-5pm (except Monday) in winter. Admission: adult 6,50 €* The abbey is built on a rocky islet in a blend of Romanesque, Gothic and classical styles. Two monasteries were built (11th-13thc.) for a community of Benedictine monks.

ALYSCAMPS Jardin des Alyscamps. A romantic avenue of sarcophagi is all that remains of the beautiful Christian necropolis surrounding the town from the 3rd-12thc. Both Van Gogh (1888) and Gauguin painted this marvellous site.

AMPHITHEATRE. Dating back to the 1stc. A.D., the immense oval amphitheatre measures 136m by 107m, and contains 34 tiers for 12,000 spectators. Bullfights (to the death) and the popular Camargue races (no killing) are held here.

ANTIQUITES DERVIEUX 5, rue Vernon ✆ 04 90 96 02 39. *www.dervieux.com*. Fine furniture is a French tradition, and the Dervieux family has been dealing in antiques since 1884. Based near the Arenes d'Arles, Dervieux specialises in 18th and 19thc. French regional furniture. You find beautiful Provençal saltboxes, buffets, typical domestic furniture and collector's toys.

ANTIQUE THEATRE. This Roman theatre dates back to Augustus (1stc. B.C.) and spreads over 102m in diameter, from its tiers to the Roland Tower, whose adjoining arcatures give an exact idea of the exterior enclosure's dimensions. Several festivals are held here, including the Peplum Film Festival which takes place in August.

SAINT TROPHIME CHURCH AND CLOISTER Place de la République. Adjoining the Romanesque cathedral with its magnificent portal, Saint Trophime Cloister has some of the most sophisticated architecture in the Western world. Overlooked by the church's Lombard steeple, two Romanesque and two Gothic galleries coexist in harmonious union, set off by three chapter houses (12th and 14thc.)

Camargue

Swamps, paddy-fields and herds of bulls...the road is long, though pleasant, to Saintes-Maries-de-la-Mer. Choose between two routes: the better-known nationale (A-road) or the little Cacharel road, at Pioch Badet. You enter the heart of the Camargue via the lakes; at sunset it's a wonderful sight. At the Saintes, you have another two choices: the beach, or a nature walk. The Camargue is so huge and naturally rich that it is difficult to recommend one rather than the other!

MAISON DU PARC NATUREL REGIONAL DE CAMARGUE RD 570 Mas du Pont de Gau ✆ 04 90 97 86 32. *www.parc-camargue.fr. Open 1 April-30 September: 10am-6pm, the rest of the year: 9.30am-5pm, closed Friday. Admission free.* Camargue flora and fauna are protected in this natural park; there is an information centre to make you aware of the environment, with a beautiful panoramic room overlooking the Gines marshes and an exhibition, plus shop.

CABANE DE GARDIAN. What could be more traditional? These are the Camargue's oldest homes, little huts built simply but ingeniously; the apse has its back to the mistral. High roofs, low walls, built of grass and plant matter: they are adapted to their climate and environment.

Les Saintes-Maries-de-la-Mer

This land 'at the world's end' is strongly influenced by gitan culture and Provençal tradition. In 1904, Frederic Mistral created the Festo Virginenco, to glorify young girls wearing Arlesian costume for the first time. Pilgrimages are the other great tradition, with gitans taking part in one of them; the relics of saints are honoured. On 24 May the gitans' patron is carried in procession to the sea, and on 25 May, it is the turn of the two saints, Salome and Jacobe. During these two days, services and prayers are held in the church. The second pilgrimage is on the Sunday closest to 22 October, when only the saints statues are carried in procession to the sea. During the year, the reliquaries stay in the 'high chapel' and only come down for the pilgrimages. The horse guardians also take part in the two processions.

MAISON DU CHEVAL CAMARGUE D570-Mas de la Cure ✆ 04 90 97 58 47. *Guided tour of site (2hrs) every day at 10am, by reservation.* The Camargue horse has at last found its home on this former vineyard estate.

FORTRESS CHURCH Place de l'Eglise. This Romanesque church overlooks the village, and can be seen from 10km away. The single nave, 15m high, is straight and undecorated.

PARC ORNITHOLOGIQUE DE PONT DE GAU RD 570 Mas du Pont de Gau ✆ 03 90 97 86 32. *www.parcornithologique.com. Open every day: 9am-sunset.* This region is richly blessed with flora and fauna: flamingoes, storks, eagles, kites and eagle owls. The Pont de Gau bird reserve gives them protection and a natural habitat, and is equally pleasant for human lovers of peace and quiet.

BULLRING Ave.Théodore-Aubanel ✆ 04 90 97 85 86. Going into the village, you can't miss the white building (next to the library!), where Camargue and Spanish cultures meet, with rosette races and corridas.

THE ALPILLES

This little mountain range with its woods and rocks hides Les Baux village, and the Val d'Enfer (Hell Valley) where Dante is supposed to have thought up the Divine Comedy, as well as Glanum village and the famous Entreconques rocks painted by Van Gogh.

Les Baux-de-Provence

'Have you heard tell of Les Baux? You leave Saint-Remy, where the Provençal land is all fields of flowers, and suddenly, everything turns to stone. A bare valley opens up…This is Les Baux. It was a fortress, with houses around, not built but dug out of the chalky layers, as though men, in their stubborn desire to stay there, had changed themselves into space'. Lou Andreas Salomé. Poets have celebrated village and castle for a thousand years, bringing visitors in droves to discover Les Baux's ancestral soul.

CHATEAU DES BAUX ✆ **04 90 54 55 56.** *Open every day: 9.30am-5pm in winter, 9am-6.30pm in spring & autumn, 9am-8.30pm in summer Audio guide in 7 languages. Admission: adult 7.30 €.*The castle is perched on the top of a rock, with a superb view of the region, and notably the remains of this village's turbulent past: the former castle, Sarrasine and Paravelle towers, seignorial dovecote, Saint Blaise Chapel and old Quiqueran Hospital. There is an exhibition of siege machines (genuine reconstructions of medieval war machines used at Les Baux).

CATHEDRAL OF IMAGES Route de Maillane ✆ **04 90 54 38 65**. *Open 1 March-6 January 2007. Admission: adult 7.30 €.* This huge show, all in futuristic comic-strip pictures, reveals the natural beauty and majestic size of the chalk quarries that inspired Dante and Cocteau.

SAINT VINCENT CHURCH ✆ **04 90 54 34 39**. There were 3 churches in the old village. Saint Vincent, former Saint Paul de Mausole Priory at Saint Rémy, is a 12thc. building. The southern part is half cave-dwelling, typical of Les Baux. It has modern stained glass (1955) by Max Ingrands, given by the Prince of Monaco.

HOTEL DE MANVILLE Cité des Baux ✆ **04 90 54 34 39**. This beautiful 16thc. Renaissance mansion was put up by the rich Protestant de Manville family. Today it houses the Town Hall and some exhibitions organised by the Museum of History and Archeology.

Barbentane

This medieval village clinging to a spur of the Montagnette has a rich historic heritage. Several centuries before Christ, a celtic oppidum existed here. The Anglia Tower, Séquier and Calendale Gates and Marquis de Barbentane's castle were part of a flourishing past that lasted until the 18thc.

CHATEAU DE BARBENTANE ✆ **04 90 95 51 07.** *Open Easter holidays-1 November every day except Wednesday: 10am-12 noon and 2pm-6pm; July, August & September, every day Admission: adult 6 €.* This castle is often called the 'Petit Trianon in the Sun'. Surrounded by Italian-style terraces decorated with sculpted motifs and overlooking a park containing three-hundred-year old plane trees, it recalls its big brother at Versailles. You can admire Carrare marble and stucco as well as Louis XV and XVI furniture.

MOULIN DE BRETOULE. This windmill's sails stopped turning in 1845. It is now enshrined in the Montagnette's pine trees.

Eygalières

A few caves and a ruined keep are all that is left of the old village, built on a rock 1,500m from the Alpille's south face. Saint-Laurent Church (12th & 16thc.) and the Penitents' Chapel (now a museum) are worth seeing. From the keep esplanade you can see the whole Alpille range from Orgon to Saint Rémy, with the Comtat plain, huge market-garden, in the north.

ALCHEMIST'S GARDEN Mas de la Brune ✆ **04 90 90 67 77**. *www.jardin-alchimiste.com. Open 1 May-5 October. May, every day: 9am-7pm. June & September, weekends and public holidays: 9am-7pm. Admission: adult 5 €.* Learn about local flora (and ancient alchemy) through interactive fun. e

Fontvieille

This village grew out of the garrigue , among marshes, in the late 18thc. White stone export gave the village a name, but real fame came with author Alphonse Daudet, who wrote Lettres de mon Moulin here. In 1935, the 'Friends of Alphonse Daudet' association decided to restore one of Fontevieille's four windmills, now admired by a growing number of visitors.

MOULIN ALPHONSE DAUDET **Office du Tourisme ✆ 04 90 54 67 49**. *Open 1 February-31 December. Admission: adult 2.50, under-12s 1.50.* The mill (Ribet or Saint-Pierre) was built in 1814 and ground wheat until 1915 and the Great War, when men and wheat were requisitioned. In 1935, it was restored, and a museum devoted to Alphonse Daudet opened, giving it symbolic value.

PARCOURS DECOUVERTE ALPHONSE DAUDET **Office du Tourisme ✆ 04 90 54 67 49**. *Open 1 February-31 December.* Follow in Alphonse Daudet's footsteps, towards the Château de Montauban first, along a path lined with low stone walls, rocky trenches, pine cones and green oaks, then to the windmills (three), passing near the 'Coudière' hut and 'trou du Renard' (foxhole) which together inspired La Chèvre de Monsieur Seguin.

Maussane

This charming village at the foot of the Alpilles features some splendid old houses with vaults and arches, and Monban Chateau and chapel, dating back to the 18th and 16thc respectively. Don't be surprised if you suddenly come across an old oil mill, an oratory or a splendid fountain (the Four Seasons, for instance) at the corner of some ancient alley.

SANTONS ANIMES **Route de Saint-Rémy ✆ 04 90 54 39 00**. *Open 1.30pm-7pm in winter and 10am-7pm in summer. Admission: adult 3.70 €.* This beautiful natural setting provides a stage for the Provencal Christmas Crib characters, known as santons, and representing craftsmen, shopkeepers and local personalities that come to life before your wondering eyes. These little people are on sale on site, together with accessories - so why not make your own Provencal crib at home next Christmas?

Le Paradou

Among irrigation canals in the vines and olive groves, on the edge of Les Baux's great drained marshes, a few pretty houses brighten this village, home of the poet-peasant Charloun Rieu.

PETITE PROVENCE DU PARADOU **75, ave. de la Vallee des Baux ✆ 04 90 54 35 75**. *Open every day: 10am-6.30pm. Admission: adult 4.50 €, 6-11s 2.50 €.* This surprising museum reconstitutes early-20thc. Provençal life with over 400 santons, those miniature carved figures of traditional Provençal characters placed in Nativity cribs. 8,000 hours of work went into this huge crib!

Saint-Rémy-de-Provence

Saint-Rémy is all picturesque alleys and shady squares, with fountains, mansions and decorated housefronts. The Romanesque, Gothic and Baroque façades of former convents and chapels add charm to the ancient town. Frédéric Mistral, Van Gogh, Gounod and Albert Gleizes all lived here. In the Rue des Barri (ramparts) you can see the remains of fortified walls and Nostradamus' birthplace (1503-1566). From April-December, the town is busy with bull running, concerts, fairs and markets.

GLANUM **Ave. Van Gogh ✆ 04 90 92 23 79**. *Open 1 April-31 August: 9am-7pm. 1 September-31 March: 10.30am-5pm, except Monday. Admission: adult 6.10 €.* South of the present town centre, a Celtic sanctuary was built, on a site with essential water, stone and roads. It quickly became Greek (probably influenced by Marseille). There are regular guided tours, and you can also eat Roman dishes by the shady Taberna Romana.

HOTEL DE SADE **Rue du Parage ✆ 04 90 92 64 04.** *Currently closed for renovation.* This Renaissance mansion was built on the ruins of the Roman thermal baths. It contains archeological findings from the Glanum site, and completes your visit there.

Tarascon

CHATEAU DE TARASCON **Boulevard du Roi René ✆ 04 90 91 01 93.** *Open 1 April-31 August: 9am-7pm. 1 September-31 March: 10.30am-5pm, except Monday. Admission: adult 6.50 €.*This imposing and powerful feudal fortress built in the early 15thc. on the Rhône (border between Provence and France) hides an elegant château in true Anjou style, where the Comtes de Provence made their home.

MAISON TARTARIN DE TARASCON **55bis, bd. Itam ✆ 04 90 91 05 08.** A reconstructed, late-19thc. bourgeois house, with figures in period costume and old furniture, based on scenes from Alphonse Daudet's book 'Tartarin de Tarascon'.

AROUND AVIGNON

Avignon

This is the Provence-Languedoc crossroads, close to the Mediterranean, settled since 4,000 B.C. Ancient traces of civilisation were found on the Doms rock, overhanging the town; later the Palais des Papes was built against it. The city is a capital of Christianity and art, while the surrounding villages Châteauneuf-du-Pape and Châteauneuf-de-Gadagne concentrate on winegrowing. Great vintages, culture and history aren't lacking round Avignon.

The festival is held in July: best to avoid Avignon at this period. Discover the monuments, picturesque alleys and old houses, and the churches with their bells and organs (Rabelais called this the ringing city). For a century, Avignon was the centre of Christendom, and hasn't forgotten it. Visit the Place de l'Horloge, and admire the jaquemart. With the Carte Pass, you get 20-50% off admission to all sites and museums in Avignon and Villeneuve-lès-Avignon; ask at the Tourist Office.

PALAIS DES PAPES ✆ 04 90 27 50 74/73. *www.palais-des-papes.com. Open every day: 9am-7pm in season; 9.30am-5.45pm out of season. Admission: adult 9.50 €, under-8s free.* Europe's biggest Gothic palace took 30 years to build. It's well worth braving the tourist hordes to see these headquarters of 14thc. Christendom.

The Vaucluse Synagogues

AVIGNON SYNAGOGUE ✆ 04 90 85 21 24. This synagogue on the edge of the square known as Place Jerusalem is not as ancient as the ones in Carpentras and Cavaillon, but it occupies the site of a much older place of worship. From the Middle Ages to the Revolution, Avignon's Jewish community lived in this same quarter, attending a synagogue which was destroyed by fire in 1845. The following year, it was replaced by a new building. Architect Joseph-Auguste Joffroy broke with tradition and put up a Neo-Classical rotunda within a square construction. The previous century's exuberant polychrome gave way to severe white pillars and sober walnut furniture. The Jewish-Comtadin particularities - double room, rabbi's rostrum, Elijah's seat - have disappeared with the breaking up of the old communities, and Jewish immigration from Eastern Europe.

SYNAGOGUE Place Maurice-Charretier - CARPENTRAS ✆ 04 90 63 39 97. The oldest synagogue in France. Behind its modest facade in front of the Town Hall, it hides genuine treasure. Carpentras dates back to the 14thc. when the Jews were given asylum on Papal territory: in 1461, there were 900 of them (a tenth of the population) crowded into 128 houses. Despite participating actively in their town's economic expansion, they were driven out several times, and were even victims of a cruel misunderstanding : on Good Friday 1603, they carried a straw effigy representing Jesus on the Cross through the town, but the gesture was interpreted as an attack on the Catholics, and as punishment, they were forced to put up a big marble cross in front of Saint Siffrein cathedral, flanked with a shameful mea culpa. (This cross was replaced by the Tree of Freedom in 1793). In those days, the Jewish community lived entrenched in the 'quarries', working in usury, the second hand clothes business and horse dealing. Traces of their existence can be found in the town centre street names. The synagogue served both as a school and a place of worship and meeting, where services and ceremonies were held. For French and foreign tourists, it was a notorious place, containing the mikva, or women's ritual bathing pool.

SYNAGOGUE ET MUSEE JUIF COMTADIN Rue Hébraïque - CAVAILLON ✆ 04 90 76 00 34. You find this 18thc. synagogue in the heart of the old town centre. Its original architecture has recently been restored, reminding you of the ghetto context in which it was first used. The building was put up between 1772 and 1774, in two superposed volumes - the only architectural form of its kind in the world. Inside, you detect the Comtat's Provenial Baroque influence in the decoration, with rich gilding and pink, blue and yellow shades that often surprise visitors - as does the Prophet Elijah's seat, perched on a little cloud! Don't miss the interesting guided tour: you'll learn that the women had to listen to the Torah readings through wooden floorboards, owing to lack of room. The lower part of the synagogue where they were put was indeed located in the basement and also served as a bakery where the Jewish community could bake its unleavened bread. The Comtadin Jewish Museum is housed here today, and illustrates the life of the Comtat's little Jewish community, which left Cavaillon for ever in 1912, scattered throughout the region's big towns : Avignon, Marseilles and Aix-en-Provence.

PONT SAINT-BENEZET **Espace Saint-Bénezet ✆ 04 90 27 51 16**. *Open every day, 1 April-30 September: 9am-7pm. 1 October-31 March: 9.30am-5.30pm. Admission: adult 3 € and 4 € in high season.* Sadly, there are now only 4 arches instead of the 22 linking Avignon to Villeneuve in the 12thc. Saint Nicholas, patron of sailors, has his chapel on the bridge where on y danse, on y danse…as the song goes.

MAISON JEAN VILAR **8, rue de Mons ✆ 04 90 86 59 64**. *www.maisonjeanvilar.org. Open Tuesday-Friday: 9am-12 noon and 1.30pm-5.30pm; Saturday 10am-5pm.* More than just a museum, the whole house is devoted to the theatre: videotheque, library, exhibitions, encounters.

MUSEE DU PETIT PALAIS **Place du Petit-Palais ✆ 04 90 86 44 58.** *Open every day except Tuesday:10.30am-6pm (9.30am-12 noon and 1.30pm-5.30pm in low season).Admission: adult 6 €, concessions 3 €.* You can see Botticelli's Renaissance masterpiece, the Virgin and Child, as well as other 15th and 16thc. central and northern Italian paintings. The former Archbishops' Palace is one of France's most beautiful museums.

ROCHER DES DOMS. Stand on the site where the first traces of human existence in Avignon were found (2nd millenary). From the 19thc. gardens, you have a fine view of the Rhône, Avignon Bridge, Ile de la Barthelasse and Saint-André de Villeneuve Fort, with Mont Ventoux in the background.

Avignon Country

Châteauneuf-du-Pape

A small village for a world-famous vintage. The appellation covers 3,200 hectares along the Rhône's left bank, between Orange and Avignon. Various Popes made their country residence here, after coming to Avignon in the 14thc.

CHATEAU. Built by Jean XXII from 1316-1333, this was the Popes' favourite residence until 1377, when they returned to Rome. Sadly, only the romantic ruins are left.

MUSEE DU VIN – CAVE BROTTE PERE ANSELME **Ave. Pierre-de-Luxembourg ✆ 04 90 83 70 07**. *Open every day : 9am-12 noon and 2pm-6pm in winter; 9am-1pm and 2pm-7pm in summer.* You can see an interesting collection of objects linked to winegrowing, such as a 16thc. press, as well as an exhibition on the appellation Châteauneuf-du-Pape's origins. Free tasting.

Gigondas

One of the department's biggest communes, with a famous vineyard rooted in its soil.

LES DENTELLES DE MONTMIRAIL. These stone festoons, finely chiselled by time, loom silvery-white in the Provençal sky. Though the highest point, Mont Saint-Amand, reaches only 734m; rock climbers love the Dentelles for their sharp peaks. Hikers and horse riders enjoy them too.

Le Mont Ventoux

Mormoiron

CHATEAU PESQUIE, Edith et Paul Chaudière - Les Terrasses du Ventoux ✆ 04 90 61 94 08. *www. Chateaupesquie.com - E-mail : Chateaupesquie @yahoo.fr. Open 1 October-weekend after Easter, Monday-Friday : 9am-12 noon and 2pm-6pm: closed Saturday and Sunday. Weekend after Easter-30 September, Monday-Friday: 9am-12 noon and 2pm-6pm; Saturday & Sunday: 10am-12 noon and 2pm-6pm. Groups by appointment only.* It took the Chaudières four years to restructure this vineyard, which they took over from the Daudet family in 1985. The results are impressive: Château Pesquie is a reference among French wines, exported to 17 countries and winner of several gold medals. The cépages are old grenache (50 years) and syrah, transformed by a balance of traditional and modern vinification methods into top quality wines. AOC reds account for 83% of output; the rest is AOC rose, AOC white and vin de pays Portes de Méditerranée (10%). All the wine produced is sold in bottles (rare in this region). You'll find it in the attractive shop, along with a selection of other regional wines.

Visan

CAVE LES COTEAUX ✆ 04 90 28 50 80. *www.coteaux-de-visan.fr. Shop open every day: 9am-12 noon and 2pm-6.30pm (7pm in summer).* Ferdinand Delaye set up the Cave de Visan in 1897, which became a co-operative cellar, Les Côteaux de Visan, in 1937. It went from strength to strength, obtaining the Côtes du Rhône Villages AOC in 1967, developing its vinification methods and extending the premises. In August 2002, it obtained AFAQ certification for the ISO 9002 Quality Assurance norm. The vineyard covers 2,060ha. where a combination of soil, cépages, position and sunlight produces a range of subtle wines that win a lot of medals.

Sérignan-du-Comtat

The village houses are harmoniously built of local stone. You can see the fine mansion with its Renaissance fireplace, where Diane de Poitiers stayed in the late 16thc.

L'HARMAS Route d'Orange ✆ 04 90 70 00 44. *Open every day, April-September: 9am-11.30am (5pm October-March). Guided tours.* This natural history museum was the home of naturalist J-H Fabre, and contains his study, his herbariums, insect collections, fossils, minerals and 700 watercolours he painted, including 300 of mushrooms. He transformed a piece of fallow land into a superb botanical garden, containing 800 plant species painstakingly catalogued.

Villeneuve-les-Avignon

Avignon's twin sister. The two cities have a love-hate relationship that goes back centuries: Papal Avignon and Royal Villeneuve, one in Provence, the other in Languedoc. When the Italian influence prevalent in Avignon finally crossed the bridge, Villeneuve immediately decked itself with Florentine buildings: palace, Cardinals' liveries and churches.

CHARTREUSE DU VAL DE BENEDICTION Rue de la Republique ✆ 04 90 15 24 24. *Open April-September: 9am-6.30pm, October-March 9.30am-5.30pm.* Founded in the 14thc. by Pope Innocent VI, this Charterhouse was extended and embellished during the following centuries. It was in fact France's biggest Carthusian monastery, and is now a listed historic monument, boasting a number of architectural treasures. You can wander through the cloisters, and visit the monks' cells, exclaim over the rose bushes in the little gardens and sink into the church's atmosphere of solemn peace. It's like travelling back in time, and you may well envy the resident artists who live there all year, finding the right conditions for their work in this magic spot.

LUBERON

Ochre landscapes, orchards as far as the eye can see, green hills with small stone villages perched in them: Luberon is charming in the sunlight, eerie at nightfall. Artists of all kinds settle here. Take the empty smaller roads (100km of scenic route) linking Cavaillon and Forcalquier via Apt. From the 1,125m summit of Mourre-Negre, you can't help but admire this region.

PARC NATUREL REGIONAL DU LUBERON Apt ✆ 04 90 04 42 00

Cavaillon

An average-sized town, associated with melons and home of one of France's huge dispatch markets. The local economy is based on fruit and vegetables: the Vaucluse is the biggest producer of cherries, Golden Delicious and grapes, and the second biggest of tomatoes, melons and early pears.

ROMAN ARCH. These two arcatures decorated with foliage are the only Roman remains left, and date back to the 1stc. A.D.

SAINT VERAN CATHEDRAL AND CLOISTER. *Open 1 October-31 March: 10am-12 noon and 2pm-4pm. 1 April-30 September: 10am-12 noon and 3pm-6pm. Closed Sunday & Monday morning.* Rather austere outside, the interior decoration is exuberant; all gilding and polychrome. The reredos were painted by well-known artists: Nicolas and Pierre Mignard; Pierre and Louis Parrocel. Don't miss the little 13thc. cloister adjoining the cathedral.

COLLINE SAINT-JACQUES. You need half an hour there and back for the discovery path 'Between town and hillside'. Careful of the slippery rock!. The Jouve family has preserved this countryside, including the olive grove. You can see for miles from the peaceful garden on the hilltop, next to the 12thc. Saint Jacques Chapel.

SYNAGOGUE ET MUSEE JUIF COMTADIN Rue Hebraïque © 04 90 76 00 34. 1 *October-31 March: 9am-12 noon and 2pm-5pm. Closed Tuesday, Saturday and Sunday. 1 April-30 September: 9.30am-12.30pm and 2.30pm-6.30pm. Closed Tuesday. Admission 3 €.* This building, in the heart of the former Jewish 'ghetto' (all of one street), is at last being refurbished. It is a fine example of a French synagogue.

The Aiguebrun Valley

Lined with impressive cliffs, the Aiguebrun Valley is a genuine gorge, now a reputed climbing site. You'll notice the many hollow cavities in the rock, about halfway up, that are actually cave dwellings, inhabited in the late Middle Ages, and reached by steps carved in the stone.

This tributary of the Durance is one of the massif's few permanent waterways. Trout fishermen know it well. The river is deep-set and hemmed in on all sides, giving it a humid environment favourable to plant life. The result is a wealth of exuberant vegetation, including flora from the temperate and even cold regions, and the small meadows along the river banks are a pleasure to look at in spring.

Gordes

A breathtaking site for a much-publicised village: you'll enjoy its beauty better out of season, without the milling hordes of tourists.

VILLAGE DES BORIES © 04 90 72 03 48. *Admission charged.* After 5 minutes of looking round these dry stone huts, you feel you've seen all there is to see- which is true, since you passed plenty of them along the road up to this village. They were supposed to have been lived in by the rural poor (14th to 19thc.).

SENANQUE ABBEY © 04 90 72 05 72. *Open 10am-12 noon and 2pm-6pm. Admission: 4.50 €. Closed Sunday morning all year, and every morning November-February.* Please respect the silence. 2km north of Gordes, a steep little road climbs the Vaucluse mounts before plunging into the valley. The 12thc. abbey is at the foot of the mountain, in a setting of oaks and lavender. Its Cistercian architecture is stark and bare, as the founder, Saint Beno"t, preferred. The site is perfect for the silent reflection required of the monks, and is one of Provence's three Cistercian abbeys (Silvacane and Le Thoronet are the others).

Lourmarin

Painters and tourists are attracted to this picturesque place; witness the number of art galleries and restaurants. A few decades ago, Albert Camus and Henri Bosco settled here. The two famous writers are now sleeping in the little cemetery.

Wandering through the alleys converging on the rocky outcrop with its castellas (primitive castle), you notice Camus' house, and the birthplace of Philippe de Girard, inventor of the linen-spinning machine in 1810. There are several fountains too; one of the prettiest is the 18thc. fontaine basse near the Place de l'Ormeau. The Protestant community have their sober temple opposite the cathedral.

GORGES DU REGALON. Located between Cheval Blanc and Merindol. On leaving the car park, you cross an olive grove to reach these impressive gorges. They were formed over 6 million years ago when the Alps appeared, and are very narrow, with visitors sometimes having to walk in single file. The rocky walls are brilliant white, and can be as much as 30m high. You pass a number of caves along the route. When you come out at the far side, you should turn round and do the return trip, so as to experience this twisting, tormented landscape from another angle.

Roussillon

This famous site is full of whimsy, with its Giants' Road and Fairies' Valley. Even the houses seem to blend into the natural background. Visit the ancient quarries (about 30mins to go round the panels explaining the rock formation and mining). Apart from that geological attraction, there are art galleries and potters' studios in the village. Samuel Beckett wrote 'Waiting for Godot' here, during the war.

AROUND VENTOUX

Provence's giant surveys Ventoux country and Comtat Venaissin from 1,912m, often snow-capped until the end of spring. Even in summer, its peak is white, due to the rock's chalky colour. Ventoux country is firstly forest (replanted in the late 19thc.): oaks and pines lower down, cedars at 800m, then Scotch firs and beeches, with Alpine plants near the top (which is a UNESCO biosphere reserve). Flora and fauna are protected there. Autumn is the time to come, when the green pines blend with the purple tones of deciduous leaves.

Bedoin

The name seems to come from 'bedouins', the African nomads who arrived in 730. On the Mount Ventoux road (south face), this village is surrounded by vines, its main resource. The Monday morning market takes over the village, and in season is very busy, with producers and craftsmen from Ardèche as well.

Carpentras

The town had a glorious past as a Roman capital, and has kept its triumphal arch (place d'Inguimbert)

SYNAGOGUE Place Maurice-Charretier. *Open Monday to Thursday: 10am-12 noon and 3pm-5pm, Friday: 10am-12 noon and 3pm-4pm. Guided tours by lecturers are on offer at the Tourist Office & 04 90 63 39 97.* Built in the 14thc., the synagogue is fascinating behind its modest front. It is a school and a place of worship, for services and ceremonies, and contains the mikve, or womens' ritual swimming pool; a strange place, where a spiral staircase leads down into seemingly bottomless clear water.

SAINT SIFFREIN CATHEDRAL Musée d'Art Sacré ✆ 04 90 63 04 92. It houses five bells, audible across the Comtat. The treasure house contains the famous Saint Mors or Saint Clou relic.

COVERED MARKET. If you're looking for a good fishmongers' or an excellent bookshop, take a walk through the Halles.

Malaucène

Ideal starting point for hikes or riding trips in the Ventoux. The old town is partly surrounded by ancient plane trees, but only a few gates of its fortified wall still stand, including the Souboyran, where criminals used to be hanged. There are 16th-18thc. houses, fountains and washing-places, and an old belfry capped with a campanile.

Orange

Known as the Princes' City, the town has plenty of charm: beautiful little squares, cafes under the plane trees; the town centre is a pleasure to walk through.

ARC DE TRIOMPHE. In the north of the town. It has three great arches decorated with reliefs illustrating Rome's victory over Gaul. The architect Auguste Caristie restored the original decoration to the west face, but sadly, the other reliefs have deteriorated or disappeared.

ANTIQUE THEATRE ✆ 04 90 51 17 60. *Open 9am-6., 1 April-30 September. Out of season, 9am-12noon and 1.30pm-5pm.Admission: adult 7.70 €.* Like the triumphal arch, it dates back to the 1stc. The stage wall is in exceptional condition, and the north face, which Louis XIV claimed was the most beautiful wall in his kingdom, is so imposing (37m x 107m) that the colossal statue of Augustus in the central niche seems ridiculously small. Music-lovers come to hear Orange's chorégies performed.

Pernes-les-Fontaines

VARAGES FRANCE (factory shop) Route de Carpentras 04 90 61 23 55. *www.varages.com – Open every day: 9am-6pm.* Buy your traditional Provençal tableware and decorative pottery here. Seconds, oddments and old stocks, but also market quality articles available. Glazed and hand-painted earthenware has been made at Varages since 1695.

Vaison-la-Romaine

Nestling like Rome among seven hills, the town is in the heart of vineyard country. It was damaged in 1992 when the River Ouveze overflowed in spectacular floods, but since then, has taken advantage of the recent fashion for Provence, with its blend of things Roman, traditional and festive.

MARCHE. This big Provençal market takes over the town on Tuesday mornings, giving you the chance to taste regional specialities, seek out bargains or simply look.

PUYMIN QUARTER. Most of the Roman monuments are to be found here. The Tourist Office organises regular visits.

MAISON DES MESSIL. This house was built around an atrium (inside courtyard) and a degree of sophistication can be deduced from its remains: columns, polychrome marble floor, garden with a pond, study, kitchen (with hearths and sink), baths. Its name was taken from an inscription on one of the walls.

PORTIQUE DE POMPEE. This is a huge courtyard (64m x 52m) containing a pond. The galleries around it were a public walkway. The most visible has mouldings of famous statues in 3 niches, including one of Emperor Hadrian and his wife.

THEATRE. It was built in 20 A.D, the date being estimated from the marble statue of Tiberius in front of the royal gate. The architectural style recalls Orange theatre, though it is slightly smaller. The stage wall was probably 17m high, 23m wide and 8m thick. In 1912, the twelve ditches made to hide the machinery were found to conceal sculptures, which are now in the Theo Desplans archeological museum.

LA VILLASSE QUARTER. The few remains left show that this was a residential quarter, with vast and luxurious houses. A paved central street was twinned with an ambulatory under porticos, lined with shops. This led to a civil basilica (commercial exchange and tribunal) with nave and apse, opening onto huge thermal baths.

ROMAN BRIDGE. Spanning the Ouvèze, the bridge links the town centre to the upper town. Despite losing its parapets in the 1992 floods, it is well preserved, and its single 17m arch is a tribute to Roman architectural genius.

VILLE HAUTE. This is medieval Vaison, inside a 14thc. rampart. The ancient Roman city provided stone for its buildings, and the picturesque paved alleys reveal some fine architecture, like the beautiful 16th and 17thc. housefronts, a wrought-iron campanile and the belfry tower. The 15thc. cathedral is flanked by two posterior chapels.

ALPES-DE-HAUTE-PROVENCE

Crickets chirping among the snow-capped peaks: you can have the Alps and Provence at the same time! The sun shines on a dazzlingly beautiful landscape, with some dramatic scenery and beautiful natural sites.

PARC NATUREL REGIONAL DU VERDON - DOMAINE DE VALX © 04 92 74 68 00. The natural park offers you several thousand kilometres of hiking paths, and richly varied landscapes, from the pastoral to the agricultural. 250 million years of geological history unfold in the spectacular gorges of the River Verdon, contrasting with calm lakes and wide lavender plains.

Digne-les-Bains

Digne is prefecture, spa town and geological reserve rolled into one and hemmed in by the valleys of Haute Provence. It has an old town centre with ancient paved short cuts and alleyways, pleasant to stroll through. Don't forget this is also the lavender capital.

NOTRE DAME DU BOURG CATHEDRAL. *Open 26 May-31 October: 3pm-6pm.* Situated in the old quarter on the edge of town, heading out to Seyne-les-Alpes. This 12thc. Romanesque cathedral was built on a far older site, as a recent find of Merovingian capitals shows.

SAINT JEROME CATHEDRAL. A 15thc. church with a 19thc. look about it. Saint Jérôme's bells chime the passing hours in the heart of the old town.

RESERVE GEOLOGIQUE DE HAUTE PROVENCE MUSEE PROMENADE Parc Saint-Benoit © 04 92 36 70 70. *Open April-October every day: 9am-12 noon and 2pm-5.30pm. Same time November-March, closed Saturdays and Sundays.* Take a refreshing walk in this park of many waterfalls. The museum has three rooms, one containing a contemporary art exhibition, the others devoted to the ocean, landscapes, geology and plants. The discovery continues on hiking paths marked out for you all over the department. 1,900 km^2 are protected inside the natural reserve.

Gréoux-les-Bains

This site has been famous for its thermal springs since antiquity. They come out of the ground at 42°. and are rich in magnesium and trace elements, particularly good for breathing problems and rheumatics. Light destroys their properties, so don't be surprised to find yourself deep in a cave - amazing!

THERMAL SPRINGS ✆ 0 826 46 81 85

CRECHE DE HAUTE PROVENCE 36, ave. des Alpes (route de Vinon) ✆ 04 92 77 61 08. *Open Easter-late October, closed Monday. Admission: adult 5 €, 7-12s 2.50 €, under-7s free.* Visit the Provençal village with its son et lumière narrating 19thc. rural life with 320 costumed santons, some animated.

Manosque

This is the archetypal Provence, with its plane trees, petanque and trips back into history in the footsteps of artists and writers.

SAINT SAUVEUR CHURCH. Laid waste to in the 10thc., rebuilt in the 14th, yet the original two-sided steeple can still be seen, capped with its wrought-iron campanile.

THOMASSINE - MAISON DE LA BIODIVERSITE Chemin de la Thomassine ✆ 04 92 87 74 40. *Closed for renovation work. Will reopen during summer 2006.* The biodiversity in question comprises four conservation orchards containing 290 different fruit species (mouthwatering, but hands off!) and a terraced kitchen garden for old-fashioned vegetables that would otherwise be forgotten. There is also a fishpond, bridges, and paths through Mediterranean forest vegetation. In short, the plant universe around us, part of our daily life yet often ignored.

Moustiers-Sainte-Marie

Picturesque Moustiers, known for its earthenware, is a great place for typically Provençal outdoor activities, from kayak and paragliding to photography. In the warm climate, above the olive groves, the village's restored houses nestle into the chalk cliff, while a torrent rushes through them and a star-crowned chapel looms above.

MUSEE DE LA FAIENCE ✆ 04 92 74 61 64. *Open every day except Tuesday, and Saturday and Sunday from November to March: 10am-12.30pm and 1.30pm-6pm (7pm in July & August) 1 April-31 October and afternoons during school holidays.* The marvellous earthenware which brought fame to the village is displayed here, and you can discover the famous names and styles, and learn the techniques from a 10-minute video.

THE TOWN. Tiny squares decorated with olive trees; the torrent running through; 18thc. housefronts and typical, lively streets: that's Moustiers. Take a deep breath and climb up above the village to Notre-Dame-de-Beauvoir Chapel, called Notre-Dame-d'Entreroches in the Middle Ages, famous for its miracles and subsequent pilgrimages (and meriting Papal protection). You have a superb view over the roofs of Moustiers to the Maire valley and edge of the Valensole plateau, with a bit of lake thrown in. It's a hard climb up, and can be a slippery stagger down, but it's worth it.

Menton

Plateau de Ganagobie

It is 35 km from Manosque to the Abbey, a Cluny monastery set on a plateau among ilexes, pines and junipers, with cliffs all around. And what a plateau! It also houses the remains of cemeteries, megalithic monuments, the medieval village of Villevieille, fountains and huts and an old rabbit warren. Have a good look round and enjoy the walk, before stopping off at the monastery.

THE PRIORY. The current building dates back to the 12thc. and was built by Cluny monks, all fifteen of whom spent golden years in the 13th and 14thc. tilling the soil and exploiting the forest.

CHURCH. *Open every day except Monday: 3pm-5pm. Mass weekdays 9am, Sunday 9.30am. For information: 04 92 68 00 04.* The portal and its festooned arching is a Baroque detail on this fine Romanesque church, with its tympanum and 12 apostles on the lintels. A single vaulted nave and double transept inside, with subdued decoration to set off the polychrome mosaics, interlacing and strange animals: a galloping knight, Saint George and the dragon, with an obviously oriental influence. It came from the material brought back by the Crusaders. Not to be missed!

Sisteron

With a river running through it. The Durance and the Buech meet to flow between Sisteron's two rocks; on one side, the enigmatic citadel, on the other, the superb Baume. An old village rises in tiers from riverbank to citadel, in a maze of streets. All the more striking seen from the citadel.

CITADEL ✆ **04 92 61 27 57**. *Open April-November, every day: 9am-6pm, 7.30pm in summer. Admission: adult 5 €. The visit (with sound) lasts 1 hour30 mins.* The rock overhanging the Durance cluse is supposed to have been fortified. Today, what is left looming above Sisteron is a series of superimposed structures of different periods. There are various museums (Napoleon's escape from Elba with period documents; the horse-drawn vehicle) on the site, and above all, a marvellous view across the horizon. An unforgettable place, steeped in history.

NOTRE DAME DES POMMIERS CATHEDRAL. Put up on a square where building was forbidden, this 12thc. cathedral takes its name from the apple trees there. It replaced earlier buildings, going right back to the 6thc., and (apparently) contains a fragment of the True Cross brought from the Holy Land.

ROCHER DE LA BAUME. Facing the citadel, this is a geological curiosity, a great rocky mass hollowed out inside, plunging into the Durance. The dazzling Sisteron sun lights it with a thousand fires.

FOOD AND DRINK

From Marseille's famous bouillabaisse to simple lamb chops charcoal-grilled with herbes de Provence, the region's scented dishes cooked in olive oil are both balanced and delicious. Even the pastis, and the excellent wine in your glass, seem to taste of sunshine.

Crau-Alpilles, Sisteron and Luberon lamb

Three top quality local products. The lambs are identified at birth, and can be traced from sheepfold to consumer. The breeding is closely watched to make sure of the lamb's quality guarrantee.

Provençal fruit

Peaches, melons (Cavaillon, Forcalquier), apricots, strawberries (Carpentras), black and bigaroon cherries, figs (often wild) apples and grapes (a certain quantity is kept for winegrowing).

Herbes de Provence

What are these herbs, stuff of dreams? (the table under the plane tree by a singing fountain, set with earthenware soon to hold a local delicacy: stuffed tomatoes, perhaps, or aubergines au gratin, or Sisteron lamb). The basic trio is thyme, rosemary and savory; with origano, fennel, bay leaf, sage and basil as optional extras. You can't have Provençal cuisine without them.

Olive oil

The biggest-producing French department is the Bouches-du-Rhône, but throughout Provence, museums keep the oil-mill tradition alive.

CAVE OLEICOLE DE LA VALLEE-DES-BAUX Rue Charloun-Rieu - MAUSSANE-LES-ALPILLES ✆ 04 90 54 32 37. *Visit 1,50 €* Admission to this 18thc. mill is free, and recommended in November, December and January, when you can actually see the olives being pressed under huge stone wheels, now a thing of the past in Provence's oil mills. The result is a very superior product; olive-oil fans will happily queue to possess a bottle.

Melons

Did you know that the first Cavaillon melons were nothing like today's? They were oblong, weighing up to 15 kilos, with a greyish-green skin and green pulp (still sweet and juicy, though). The charentais melon arrived in 1925, early, round and easier to calibrate, with more varieties than we know today.

Honey

Each local honey comes from a specific plant. In the Alpilles, you find thyme, rosemary and prairie flower honey. The beekeepers also collect lavender and acacia honey, thanks to transhumance.

Pastis

Pastis means 'mixture' in Provençal, and is drunk sitting outside a bistrot in the shade, when it's too hot to do anything more sensible. There are different sorts, and the Hardouin distillery at Forcalquier has revived some old 'mixtures' (careful how you mix...)

Fish and seafood

From the sea, the rivers, ponds and marshes comes a wide variety of fish. Charrs, trout, eels and crayfish from the Sorgue; carp, pike, perch, tench and gudgeon from the freshwater marshes of Arles. Same from the Rhône, with sturgeon as an extra. The Camargue's saltwater pools are full of bream, bass and turbot, and grey mullet is caught in the Caronte lake. Tuna is fished all along the coast.The Grasse fishmonger's sells 22 different kinds of fish. Bream, bass and mullet are the most popular.

Mediterranean fish are delicious, but expensive, to the point where many restaurant-owners have to get their daily supply from the Atlantic catches.

Tapenade.

Delicious Provençal speciality made from paste and olive oil, creamy and slightly bitter. Taste it on a slice of toast with your aperitif or a glass of red wine.

Camargue beef

Bred in the open air, these bulls contribute to the ecosystem. Their meat is lean and protein-rich, and has its fans. The breeding of Camargue bulls for bullfights and shows is extensive; the bulls run free and graze in wide-open spaces, with at least 6 months spent in a damp zone. No food supplements are given.

Some typical dishes

Bouillabaisse, with its local fish; aioli; pistou soup (garlic and basil chopped and ground) ; gardiane (mutton stew) from the Camargue. Meat dishes like Marseilles pieds et paquets or daube from Avignon. Various sorts of bread : the fougasse, pain d'Aix and pain bagnat, which makes a substantial sandwich for the beach, filled with tomatoes, anchovies, capers, olives and salad.

WINES

Southern Côtes-du-Rhône

These vineyards start south of Montélimar , as far as Avignon. They contain prestigious vintages like the châteauneuf-du-pape, and also côtes-du-rhône villages.

INTER RHONE Hôtel du Marquis-de-Rochegude – 6, rue des Trois-Faucons – AVIGNON ✆ 04 90 27 24 00

Châteauneuf-du-Pape

The Popes developed these vineyards while they were staying at the Palais des Papes in Avignon. For a long time afterwards, the vines were abandoned, then decimated by phylloxera. In 1923, Baron Le Roy de Boiseaumarié set up the first winegrowers' syndicate, to decide which vineyards had the right to call their wine châteauneuf-du-pape. This was how the appellations d'origine contrôlées (AOC) came into being, in 1937. There are 3,300 hectares of vineyards extending across the Châteauneuf-du-Pape village territory and similar land in the four surrounding communes; Orange, Courthézon, Bédarrides and Sorgues. The wine blends 13 cépages : grenache, clairette, blanche, bourboulenc, roussane, picpoul, picardan, mourvèdre, syrah, cinsault, counoise, muscardin, vaccarèse and terret noir.

The bottles bear the Papal arms of Avignon ; Saint Peter's two crossed keys. The whites are pale yellow, almost translucent, with a fine bouquet and floral undertones, while you can taste red fruit, liquorice, aniseed and spice in the full-bodied and supple reds.

They can be laid down for 10 years on average (depends on the vintage).

VIGNOBLES BRUNIER (Domaine du Vieux Télégraphe) 3, route de Châteauneuf-du-Pape – BEDARRIDES ✆ 04 90 33 00 31. *www.vignoblesbrunier.fr.* The name comes from the optical telegraph system on the Crau plateau at Bédarrides invented by Claude Chappe in 1792. The Brunier family bought it in 1898, and today there are 70 hectares of vineyards (5 for white wines). The Vieux Télégraphe reds are made from 65% grenache and are tannic, silky, rich and complex, with black cherry and spice notes, and a last hint of chocolate.

CHATEAU MONT-REDON Châteauneuf-du-Pape ✆ 04 90 83 72 75. *Open every day: 8am-7pm.* Sumptuous purple-coloured bottles of a powerful and elegant wine that should be kept for a while, to do it justice.

CHATEAU LA NERTHE Route de Sorgues – CHATEAUNEUF-DU-PAPE ✆ 04 90 83 70 11. *Cellar open evry day : 9am-12 noon and 2pm-6pm.* A superb 90-hectare property with 18thc. castle and park. The tasting cellar is of modern design, and you can visit the storehouse with its stone tanks, still used, and see the bottles laid down by great French and foreign restaurants (La Tour d'Argent).

CHATEAU RAYAS Châteauneuf-du-Pape ✆ 04 90 83 73 09. *By appointment.* The production is reserved in advance - you'll have to buy it from your wine merchant. Château Rayas red is one of the world's best wines.

DOMAINE DE BEAURENARD 10, route d'Avignon - CHATEAUNEUF-DU-PAPE ✆ 04 90 83 71 79. *www.beaurenard.fr. Cellar open every day: 8am-12 noon and 1.30pm-5.30pm.* You get a warm welcome from the Coulon family, winegrowers for seven generations. In nearby Rasteau, there is a Winegrowers' Museum, open Easter-September.

DOMAINE MOULIN TACUSSEL 10, ave. des Bosquets - CHATEAUNEUF-DU-PAPE ✆ 04 90 83 70 09. *Open every day: 9am-7pm.* Founded in 1976, and offering excellent reds and whites.

CHATEAU DE BEAUCASTEL Courthezon ✆ 04 90 70 41 00. *Cellar open Monday-Friday: 9am-12 noon and 2pm-5pm.* Noble Pierre de Beaucastel founded this house in the 16thc. Its quality makes it one of Châteauneuf's stars.

DOMAINE DE LA PRESIDENTE Sainte-Cécile-les-Vignes ✆ 04 90 30 82 05. *Fax: 04 90 30 74 03. Open all year: 8am-12 noon and 2pm-6pm. Closed Sundays and public holidays.* A 180-hectare estate.

Gigondas

These vineyards are only found at Gigondas in the Vaucluse. The appellation was granted in 1971; the whole vineyard having been planted in 1960 to replace olive trees frozen in 1956. Previous vines had been wiped out by phylloxera. Gigondas is a wine made up of different Côtes-du-Rhône cepages (except carignan). Its colour shimmers; there are undertones of fruit and kirsch in the young wine, developing into woodland nuances with age. Full-bodied but balanced, it needs to age a few years to be at its best.

The rose is deep-coloured, scented with almonds and cooked fruit, heady and generous.

DOMAINE RASPAY-AY ✆ 04 90 65 83 01. *Open all year: 9am-12.30pm and 1.30pm to 5.30pm. Closed Sundays and public holidays.* Dominique Ay gets one of the best gigondas from his 18 hectares.

DOMAINE LES PALLIERES © **04 90 65 85 07**. Gigondas is known as a strong, full-bodied wine, yet it can be light and fruity, depending on the vineyard. Les Pallières is typical.

Rasteau

Natural sweet wines, grouped in an appellation after 1944, from a marl-and-clay soil covered with pebbles and sand.

CAVE DE RASTEAU © **04 90 10 90 14.** *Open every day: 9am-12.30pm and 2pm-6pm. Summer: 9am-7pm.* A famous cellar, with its exceptional soil, superior know-how and of course, its sweet wines.

DOMAINE DE LA SOUMADE © **04 90 46 13 63.** *Open all year, Monday-Saturday: 8.30am-11.30am and 2pm-6pm.* The cellar is 100m from the road. Andre Romero is one of the southern Côte-du-Rhône's best-known winegrowers. His property faces the Dentelles de Montmirail, and he welcomes visitors simply, round a small counter.

Vacqueyras

Vacqueyras became the 13th Côtes-du-rhône in 1990. It covers Vacqueyras and Sarrians, at the foot of the Dentelles. The soil is made up of Riss glacial terrace and alluvial deposits, and is the only vineyard (apart from lirac) producing all three colours. Various cépages are allowed; three for roses: grenache, cinsault and mourvede, and four for reds: the same 3 plus syrah. These are generous, fruity wines with deep colours and ripe fruit, cherry and liquorice notes.

DOMAINE LA FOURMONE Route de Bollene © **04 90 65 86 05.** *Open all year: 9am-12 noon and 2pm-6pm.* Discreet reputation; rated by connoisseurs.

Côtes-du-Rhône villages

The appellation dates back to 1966, and concerns 4 departments: Ardèche, Drôme, Vaucluse and Gard, and 95 villages. 16 of these can add their name to the appellation; 8 of them in the Vaucluse: Valreas, Visan, Roaix, Rasteau, Seguret, Sablet, Cairanne and Beaumes-de-Venise.

Beaumes-de-Venise

Muscat appeared here in the 17thc., and the AOC was granted in 1945. The wines are smooth, rich and complex with exotic aromas. Drink them young for the full spectrum of flavours.

CHATEAU REDORTIER © **04 90 62 96 43.** *Open every day: 10am-12 noon and 2pm-7pm.* Superb view of the Dentelles de Montmirail. The castle, part of the Orange principality, was pulled down in the 18thc and replaced by a country house. Etienne de Menthon planted the first vines here in 1956 (35 ha.), to produce Beaumes-de-Venise and Gigondas.

DOMAINE DE DURBAN © **04 90 62 94 26** *Open all year: 9am-12 noon and 2pm-6pm. Closed Sunday and public holidays.* Up in the village heights, this estate gives a magnificent view, as well as being known for its muscat.

DOMAINE BEAUMALRIC © **04 90 65 01 77**. *Open every afternoon: 2pm-7pm. Closed Sunday and public holidays.* On 7 ha. of beaumes-de-venise muscat, this estate produces a subtle and elegant wine from small white muscat grapes.

DOMAINE DE COYEUX © **04 90 12 42 42**. *Open all year: 9am-12 noon and 2pm-7pm. Closed Sunday and public holidays.* At the foot of the Dentelles, 2km from the village on the Malaucene road (RD 90). The hillsides are sheltered; from their 50 ha. of beaumes-de-venise appellation come a Côtes-du-Rhône village and a muscat.

CAVE DES VIGNERONS DE BEAUMES-DE-VENISE © **04 90 12 41 00**. *Open all year: 8.30am-12 noon and 2pm-6pm; 7pm in summer.* Beaumes-de-venise is one of the best-known sweet wines. There are several muscats on offer here: traditional, 'Carte d'Or' with its exotic fruit and flower aromas and 'Bois Doré' (from older vines of limited output), matured six months in oak casks. There is a muscat marc brandy from unfermented marc, matured 36 months, also in oak casks.

Vins des Bouches-du-Rhône

Côteaux d'Aix

Local wines from the western edge of Provence. These hillsides make a fair rose, drunk young and chilled with ratatouille or grilled fish.

The reds are rarer; these fruity wines mature quickly, and go well with grilled meat and gratins. High-quality work goes into these wines, which deserve not to be overlooked.

Cassis

The AOC is famous for its dry white wines, perfect with bouillabaisse or seafood. Both reds and roses are of sound quality. We recommend Château de Fontcreuse wines (ugni, clairette and marsanne cépages) which are of remarkable quality and can be kept for 5-10 years.

Hotels & Restaurants

ALPES DE HAUTE-PROVENCE

Barcelonnette

L'AZTECA * 3, rue François-Arnaud ✆ 04 92 81 46 36.** *Fax : 04 92 81 43 92. Website : www.hotel-azteca.fr. Double 'eco' rooms 50 € to 65 €. Traditional rooms 59 € to 79 €. Split-level rooms 70 € to 98 €. Mexican rooms 74 € to 100 €. Breakfast 8 €.* Definitely our best find this year! The Azteca is a three-star hotel, decorated in astonishing Mexican style. The theme runs right through the place, from the bar, serving tapas and margaritas in the warmest of atmospheres, to the rooms with their high ceilings and skilful interior design. You receive a charming welcome, and although there is no restaurant, this is the town centre, and the best places to eat are only a short walk away. A truly remarkable hotel, well worth stopping off for - as George Clooney no doubt found when he slept here (see the all stars' visitor's book!)

Château-Arnoux-Saint-Auban

LA BONNE ETAPE ** Chemin du Lac ✆ 04 92 64 00 09.** *Website: www.bonneetape.com. Closed Monday and Tuesday in low season, 1 November-30 April except Easter, Christmas and New Year's Day. Set menus durance 45 €, Provence 80 €, Provence allégé 65 €, jarladin (dégustation) 110 €.* Pierre and Jany Gleize are the owners of this genuine 18thc. coaching inn, now a 4-star hotel. It has 18 rooms available, all with exposed beams and a view of the lavender fields and olive trees. Double rooms start from 163 €. In the Gleizes' own words, cooking is "a quest for wisdom via the touch of madness that is in all creators", and once you've tested the truth of the statement, you might feel you should have found this uncommon place before. You'll forget your everyday strains and stresses in the simple pleasure of a warm welcome – but are sure to feel that once is not enough!

Digne-les-Bains

LA VILLA GAIA* 24, route de Nice ✆ 04 92 31 21 60**. *Fax : 04 92 31 20 12. Website : www.hotelvillagaia.fr. Closed mid-October to mid-April. Rooms 85 € to 95 €*. From three nights onwards, 150 €. Breakfast 8.50 €. Set menus 26 € to 32 €. This hotel is good value for money. Anne-Françoise and Georges-Eric Martin greet you with kindness and delicacy, and you soon feel at home in their charming 19thc. family house, with its spacious and comfortable rooms, peaceful setting and sophisticated, regional gastronomic *cuisine*. The grounds are kept up with skill worthy of a landscape gardener, and include a lake close to the villa, perfect for relaxing beside. Don't hesitate if you're in the area.

Forcalquier

CAMPAGNE SAINT-LAZARE Ancienne route du Dauphin ✆ 04 92 75 48 76. *Fax : 04 92 75 49 07. Website : www.stlazare.net. 80 € to 100 € per night in a studio flat (sleeps 2). 550 € to 650 € per week. 160 € to 200 € per night in an apartment (sleeps 4). 1,100 € to 1,300 € per week.* In a word, heaven! Beautifully decorated, peaceful setting, with gardens and terraces arranged round the swimming pool. Your accommodation is fully equipped and very comfortable, with a view of the terrace, where you can enjoy genuine, regional cooking. Table linen, sheets and towels are provided. Warm welcome. A highly recommended site.

CHAREMBEAU Route de Niozelles ✆ 04 92 70 91 70**. *Fax : 04 92 70 91 83. Website: www.charembeau.com. Closed 15 November-15 February.* Sandra and André Berger greet you with kindness and good humour in their 18thc. farm overlooking the green valley between the Pays de Forcalquier and the Durance. Superb, spacious rooms with balcony or large terrace and high comfort standards. Suites complete with kitchenette. Relax in the garden by the swimming pool, or enjoy a hike through the marvellous surrounding countryside.

Gréoux-les-Bains

VILLA BORGHESE* Avenue des Thermes ✆ 04 92 78 00 91**. *Fax : 04 92 78 09 55. Website: www.villa-borghese.com. Open 22 March-11 November. Single room 55 € to 110 €. Double room 100 € to 136 €. Set menu 29.50 €.* Exceptional setting in a wooded park planted with flowers. Luminous country interior. Heated swimming pool. Sauna. Water therapy. Delicious Provençal cuisine – the Italian-style gambas risotto, baked bass with pine kernels and Arabica Opera dessert must be tasted to be believed! Charming welcome.

Manosque

LE BONHEUR FOU 11bis, boulevard des Tilleuls ✆ 04 92 87 77 52. *Set menus 25 € to 30 €. Closed Thursday.* Pink walls, black and grey tablecloths and *bonheur fou* (crazy happiness) on your plate, thanks to seasonal cooking with fresh market ingredients, different every day. You are warmly welcomed and served attentively – if you wish, you can change a sauce or ask for different vegetables. The restaurant also patronises the arts: painting, drawing and photo exhibitions are held upstairs, and writers are invited on a regular basis to meet the customers.

LE PRE SAINT MICHEL* Route de Dauphin ✆ 04 92 72 14 27.** *Fax : 04 92 72 53 04. Website: www.presaintmichel.com. Double rooms 55 € in low season, 100 € in high season. Set menus at La Table du Pré Saint- Michel from 23 €. A la carte. Children's menu 10 €. Bookings 04 92 72 12 79.* This hotel-restaurant overlooking the town is very pleasant, and provides all the charm of the countryside only a few minutes from old Manosque. The rooms are all different and comfortably equipped. The restaurant serves excellent Provençal cuisine in generous helpings. A place to remember!

Moustiers-Sainte-Marie

LA BASTIDE DE MOUSTIERS** Chemin de Quinson ✆ 04 92 70 47 47**. *Fax : 04 92 70 47 48. Website : www.bastide-moustiers.com. Hotel open all year. Restaurant closed Wednesday and Thursday, December – 1 March. Rooms 155 € to 325 €. Breakfast 19 €. Set menus 44 € to 57 €.* You have to pay for a glimpse of heaven! This beautiful 17thc. bastide in its green park has been magnificently restored. You can enjoy colourful food while drinking in the landscape: the cuisine manages to be truly festive with no showing off, and Eric Santalucia and his team dazzle your tastebuds with delicious local produce. We could wax lyrical over the 12 rooms: in short, they're perfect.

LE CLOS DES IRIS Chemin de Quinson ✆ 04 92 74 63 46. Fax : 04 92 74 63 59. *Website :www.closdesiris.fr. Closed 1-26 December. Rooms 65 € to 85 €. Suites 95 € to 110 € (sleep 3-4). Breakfast 9 €.* A warm and cheerful setting in Provençal colours greets you, together with a kindly welcome from Alexia and her mum Claudie. You'll really enjoy your stay in this comfortable little hotel, impeccably run. Private terrace in front of each room.

Valensole

LA FUSTE** Lieu dit La Fuste ✆ 04 92 72 05 95**. *Website: www.lafuste.com. Closed Monday and Sunday evening. Rooms from 110 € to 180 € in high season, apartment sleeping two 230 €, breakfast 14 €. Set menu du potager (kitchen garden) 40 € (in season). A la carte 23 € to 35 €.* Everyone knows

La Fuste, located between Manosque and Valensole, yet we couldn't cover the Alpes de Haute Provence without mentioning Monsieur Daniel Jourdan. After 30 years of service, his excellent gastronomic and regional cuisine still delights his guests - already under the spell of his elegant family house – and his menus are brimming over with imagination and talent. The tree-lined grounds outside boast a natural setting where you can relax, or have a swim in the pool. It's hard to leave La Fuste - you'll look forward to coming back.

BOUCHES-DU-RHÔNE

Aix-en-Provence

L'AMPHITRYON 2-4, rue Paul-Doumer ✆ 04 42 26 54 10. *Last orders taken at 2pm and 9.30pm. Closed Sunday and Monday. Groups and seminars welcome. Garden and terrace. Business set menu 20 € (lunchtime). Menu-carte 33 € (some dishes have a supplement).* Master chef Bruno Ungaro knows how to welcome guests in style. In a few words, his cuisine is talented and inventive, sophisticated and sure to please. We feel it's no exaggeration to say that L'Amphitryon is gourmet heaven.

CLOS DE LA VIOLETTE 10 avenue de la Violette ✆ 04 42 23 30 71 *Fax 04 42 21 93 03. Website : www.closdelaviolette.fr. Set menus 54 € (lunch) to 120 €. A la carte 120 €. Closed Sunday, Monday and first fortnight in August.* Brigitte and Jean-Marc Banzo's superb villa is located slightly away from the town centre, far enough to avoid the noise, but near enough to feel part of this effervescent town. It attracts the local gourmets, with its spacious terrace (once a priest's garden), tables where privacy is protected, well-trained service and meticulous Mediterranean cuisine. The discreet setting suits business people, who tend to book here when clinching an important deal. The chef is remarkably consistant, even if his recipes don't dazzle you every time. Pig's trotters in crumble and mullets in escabeche with fish liver oil and an iodised vinaigrette with oysters, carpaccio of young rabbit offal meatballs with sherry and local oil, the shoulder confit , crusty liver and kidneys with thyme, bass cooked *à la plancha,* almond crust with olives, new vegetable minestrone with pesto and *agnolottis* (Piemontese stuffed pasta) with basil, Ain farm chicken supreme, translucid onion and shallot fondue with anchovy *salpicons* (anchovies cut into small cubes), charlotte potatoes stuffed with andouille, and little babas soaked in brown rum, whipped Tahiti vanilla cream and rice pudding ice cream feature on his menus. Eclectic wine cellar.

LE PIGONNET ** 5, avenue du Pigonnet ✆ 04 42 59 02 90.** *Fax : 04 42 59 47 77. Website: www.hotelpigonnet.com. 52 rooms from 120 € to 550 €. Breakfast 15 € to 25 €. Free parking.* Some distance from the town centre, standing in the shade of the plane trees lining Avenue du Pigonnet, this hotel has all you need for a pleasant stay. The welcome is traditionally warm, and the rooms very comfortable in pure Provençal style. Well up to four-star standard.

VILLA GALLICI Avenue de la Violette ✆ 04 42 23 29 23. *Website: www.villagallici.com. Rooms from 220 € to 345 €, suites 400 € to 450 €. Breakfast 22 € and 28 €. A la carte.* This place is a real haven of peace in the centre of old Aix, standing in a tree-lined Florentine garden with its delicate plants and statues. Inside is just as splendid, with a faint scent of lavender in the air. Each decorative touch recalls the old Aix bastides, chosen and placed with perfect taste. The French windows with their blue-grey shutters reveal a terrace with wrought-iron tables and chairs arranged under the oaks. Below lies a sumptuous swimming pool. Hotel residents can enjoy Provençal specialities in the restaurant at their disposal.

Arles

LE CALENDAL 5, rue Porte-de-Laure ✆ 04 90 96 11 89 *Open Monday to Sunday, 12 noon to 4pm. Buffet formula 12 noon-3pm, and in winter 7pm-9pm at 15 € (starter and hot main course) or 22 € (starter, main course, dessert, wine and coffee). Children's menu 7 €.* A pleasant setting for lunch, with its shady garden, Provencal decor and unlimited buffet formula. 15 or so cold starters are available, including taboule (couscous salad) and chick pea puree, and there is warm vegetable quiche. Beef daube made with bull meat is on offer as a hot main course, or grilled fish. Well worth the visit - you won't regret it.

LE CILANTRO 31, rue porte de Laure ✆ 04 90 18 25 05. *A la carte 45 €. Formula 35 € (starter + main course + cheese or dessert , chosen from the carte). Suggestion of the day formula, lunchtime only, 19 € (starter + main course, glass of wine 5 €). Take-away dishes (order in advance).* Stylish interior design warmed by yellow walls and a dining room with exposed beams, signed by decorator Fabien Seignobos. This is the new place to eat for local gourmets. Le Cilantro (Coriander) opted for original and gastronomic cuisine from the start, influenced by the world's flavours. Young chef Jérome Laurent spent two years in the States at Yale, and is now back in his home town to show off his cooking skills. The menu changes with the seasons.

HOTEL JULES CESAR** 9, boulevard des Lices ✆ 04 90 52 52 52** *Website : www.hotel-julescesar.fr. Rooms from 158 € to 240 €, suites 300 € to 395 €, extra bed 50 €. Half-board available.* This hotel has inherited something of the peace and sobriety that existed in the former Carmelite convent, along with that natural architectural beauty typical of Provence. Pool and gardens - including the one in the cloister - make you feel you're floating in a fresh air bubble, breathing in the natural scents, when you're actually in the heart of town. The atmosphere makes the place, and manager M. Albagnac knows how to exploit and develop it for your pleasure.

HOTEL NORD-PINUS ** Place du Forum ✆ 04 90 93 44 44** *Website: www.nord-pinus.com. 26 rooms from 150 € to 182 €, junior suite 395 €, apartment 412 €, extra bed 35 €, breakfast 14 €, garage 17 €, bar, terrace.* The Nord-Pinus has seen plenty of famous people passing through its gates, opposite the staue of Frédéric Mistral. Matadors of course - a tradition that still exists today - but also Cocteau, Picasso and Hemingway, who were equally fascinated by the bullring. The hall and reception rooms are charmingly decorated in wrought iron, with chandeliers, big leather armchairs and a beautiful bar. There are 25 rooms, also richly done out in warm colours. The hotel prides itself on being exceptional - and rightly so. " If you're looking for a 'somewhere else', come here", they proclaim.

Cassis

LE JARDIN D'EMILE * Plage du Bestouan ✆ 04 42 01 80 55.** *Rooms from 80 € to 130 €. Set menus around 35 € maximum.* All the charm of an old batisse, magnificently converted and sheltering under huge pines by the sea. The restaurant captivated us too - all in all, a rare place, not to be missed if you're in the area.

Eygalières

LE BISTROT D'EYGALIÈRES Chez Bru ✆ 04 90 90 60 34 the rest of the year *Fax 04 90 90 60 37. Website : www.chezbru.com. Set menus 76 € to 90 €. A la carte 80 €. Closed Sunday evening and Monday from October to late May, and Monday and Tuesday the rest of the year. Annual closing mid-January to mid-March.* Belgian Wout Bru is only 36, but his top-class 'Bistrot' was awarded a second star last year by the *Guide Rouge*, only eight years after the first. Wout trained at the Château de Locguénolé, Mas des Herbes des Blanches and at Baumanière, and his elegant, very well-heeled customers make no mistake in coming to this village in the Alpilles: his Provençal cuisine is one of the very best. The asparagus with Dublin bay prawns and old parmesan cheese, truffle vinaigrette, suckling pig croustillant with port, foamy milk with rosemary, roast pigeon with spinach shoots and foie gras toast, small pistachio cake and white chocolate cream dessert with chocolate ice cream speak for themselves. The prices are obviously up to standard too, unaffordable for the average tourist. Oh well, pleasure has its price.

Les-Baux-de-Provence

L'OUSTAU DE BAUMANIERE Val d'Enfer ✆ 04 90 54 33 07 *Fax 04 90 54 40 46. Website: www.oustaudebaumaniere.com. Set menus 90 € to 150 €. A la carte 130 €. Closed Wednesday, Thursday lunchtime (2 November-31 March) and Wednesday lunchtime the rest of the year. Annual closing in January.* Jean-André Charial's place is one of the three best-known Vallée du Rhône restaurants in the world (the other two being La Pyramide in Vienne and Pic in Valence). It lies at the foot of Les Baux village, hidden in the heavenly Val d'Enfer (Hell Valley), an oasis of peace and incredible luxury with its beautiful terrace overlooking the swimming pool and mass of rocks in the valley. Nowadays, rather too many hand-picked staff are working at keeping up the restaurant's reputation, which frankly needs some new blood and creativity. Perhaps the young Ducasse-trained chef just recently taken on will provide them. Whatever happens, the house classics - suckling veal chop and warm pistachio soufflé - are bound to stay on the menu.

Marseille

LE COMPTOIR DES FAVOUILLES 44, rue Sainte – 1er ✆ 04 96 11 03 11. *Closed Saturday lunchtime and Sunday. Lunchtime formula 13 €. Set menus 20 € and 30 €. A la carte 40 €.* With a cricket for emblem, the Comptoir des Favouilles, named after a familiar little Mediterranean crab, has taken over a reputed restaurant. New managers Mathieu Magnan, Sébastien Puglares and Philippe Mehouas wanted to redecorate without changing the quality of the food. They serve delicate, sophisticated dishes at affordable prices, with a seasonal *carte*. The cellar is well stocked, with a comprehensive wine list featuring all the French winegrowing regions. The dining room is housed in the former galley rope factory with its exposed stonework and beams; and its light colours and luminous quality add charm to culinary pleasure.

CHEZ FONFON 140, vallon des Auffes – 7e – ✆ 04 91 52 14 38. *Closed Sunday and Monday lunchtime. Set menus from 37 €.* This family institution is a must in Vallon-des-Auffes, like the little harbour right in the town centre. Freshly-caught fish of all varieties tops the menus, including an excellent fish soup Provençal-style. There is tender, tasty meat too, and as for the desserts - we could write poems to them! You enjoy your food simply, at a pretty, round table in the big, light dining room, with a view of the same famous little fishing harbour.

CHEZ JEANNOT 129, vallon des Auffes (7e) ✆ 04 91 52 11 28. *Fax : 04 91 31 66 24. Closed Sunday evening and Monday lunchtime in winter, all day Monday in summer. Open Sunday evening in June, July and August. Last orders taken 2pm and 10.30pm. A la carte around 20 €-40 €. Terrace.* Nestling in the superb Auffes Valley, this pizzeria with its wide first-floor terrace was founded in 1947 by the Mounier family, and offers you the chance to eat well in a uniquely picturesque setting without breaking the bank. Jean-Lionel's menu is traditional, and pays tribute to the fishermen associated with the Auffes Valley by adding mullet and bass to the choice of pizzas, fresh home-made pasta and grilled meats. There is also an assortment of shellfish in season, served on a bed of seaweed; sea urchins, oysters, and mussels. In winter, (October-May) you have a daily suggestion from the chef, and some seasonal meat dishes like Charolais rib steak with its marrowbone. The new salads are delicious: we especially liked the ones with *chiprone* and octopus.

L'ÉPUISETTE Vallon des Auffes – 7e – ✆ 04 91 52 17 82. *Website : www.l-epuisette.com. Closed Sunday and Monday. Set menus 43 € to 90 €.* The setting is unforgettable, literally on the waves going into the famous urban calanque, le Vallon des Auffes, and you are greeted according to top establishment standards. The fish is cooked straight out of the water. Great culinary art. We recommend a lunchtime booking, with a magnificent view of the sea and a meal based on the chef's suggestions of the moment. The pastry chef's sublime desserts are on no account to be missed!

L'HIPPOCAMPE 14, quai du Port (2e) ✆ 04 91 90 88 38. *Closed Tuesday. Last orders 3pm and 10.30pm. A la carte 30 €. English, Spanish, Italian, Catalan and Armenian spoken.* Fish has pride of place on the menu here, like the excellent sea bass grilled in salt crystals, with a dash of olive oil added Provence-style, and white wine from Cassis to wash it down. Simple, and so good! The staff are attentive and unobtrusive, and extend the warmest of welcomes to their guests. Real bouillabaisse is made at L'Hippocampe, and you will be asked to examine the fish before they are prepared, to check their absolute freshness. Beautiful view of the Bonne Mère and Vieux Port. In short, a great place to eat, with plenty of charm just like its namesake (the Seahorse).

LE GRAND BLEU Escale Borely ✆ 04 91 71 21 60. *Fax : 04 91 77 51 27. Check opening hours in advance in winter. Last orders taken 1.45pm and 10.30pm. Set menus 12 €-23 €. A la carte 25 €. Terrace and private beach.* Enjoy an exceptional view of the Mediterranean comfortably settled on the edge of a private beach, while you eat fresh fish (the fisherman's stewpot is succulent) or even a delicious grilled rib steak, or beef rib with cepes. Le Grand Bleu has no pretensions to seaside gastronomy, but offers good food in a dream setting, at affordable prices (two set menus at 10.50 € and 13.50 €). Warm welcome from the young and friendly staff.

LES GENS DE MER 25, rue Forbin (2e) ✆ 04 91 91 19 58. *Fax : 04 91 56 02 94. 60 comfortable rooms (shower and bath) from 45 €. Breakfast 6.50 €.* This used to be a hostel for sailors and their families, but is now a two-star hotel open to all. Located in the heart of Marseille's 'Euromediterranee' business centre, it is only 10 minutes on foot from Saint Charles Station and 15 minutes from the Vieux Port. Breakfast is served on the terrace (for first floor rooms) or in the Provencal garden. The private car park (40 spaces) at 6 € per day is convenient, and quite rare in the city nowadays.

PASSEDAT - LE PETIT NICE Anse de Maldormé ✆ 04 91 59 25 92 *Fax 04 91 59 28 08. Website : www.passedat.fr. Set menus 50 € to 170 €. A la carte 150 €. Closed Sunday and Monday in low season (November to April) and Sunday and Monday lunchtimes the rest of the year.* Outside Paris and a few prestigious places like Megève and Monaco, Gérald Passédat's menu is one of the most asistocratic in France. A starter at around 50 €, a main course 70 € and a dessert 25 € adds up to 150 € a meal! Of course, you might have come specially for the extraordinary bass (caught with a *palangre*, or long floating line) with truffles - sinful luxury, but once tasted never forgotten - but otherwise, choose the

"Passédat" menu at 130 €, quite reasonable for such a restaurant, and which features Breton lobster cooked slowly with *rougaille* (spiced) emulsion and farm eggs, pagre (Mediterranean fish) on two plates, one simply grilled and the other chilled, bass steak cooked how Lucie Passédat liked it, with truffles, chanterelle soup and wild fennel granita, triple AAA lamb with Massalé, and small crystallised sugar discs with strawberries. The view is breathtaking (one of the most unforgettable on the French Mediterranean coast) and the service excellent. Experiencing how the other half lives for a few hours is probably well worth forking out for.

RENE ALLOIN 8, place de l'Amiral-Muselier – 8e ✆ 04 91 72 88. *Open Monday to Friday, from 12 noon to 2pm and 8pm to 10pm. Saturday evening and Sunday lunchtime only. Set menu between 38 € and 49 €.* René Alloin is a great name in Marseilles gastronomy. He is also very discreet, and his restaurant on the edge of the town centre has a sober, unassuming façade. The food is something else though, since René has spent 40 years mixing and matching flavours and creating subtle harmonies, prepared with fresh market ingredients chosen from the local treasure-trove of produce.

LE RESTO PROVENCAL 64, cours Julien ✆ 04 91 48 85 12. *Closed Saturday lunchtime, Sunday and Monday. Last orders taken 1.45pm and 10pm (10.45pm weekends). Dish of the day 9 €. Lunchtime menu 13 €, evening 23.50 €. A la carte around 25 €-30 €. Terrace.* This is a good place to eat, with its genuinely warm and convivial Marseilles atmosphere, and posters of Marcel Pagnol's Marius, Fanny and Cesar on the walls. Bruno Liotardo's professional talent grows from year to year, and his cooking is top quality. You must try local specialities like Provencal *daube*, gambas grilled with pastis or *tapenade* with *panisses.* All the dishes are traditionally cooked in the Provencal manner, with plenty of herbs, basil, olives and goat's cheese in the sauces and garnish. You won't forget the bream prepared Bouillabaisse-style. A delicious experience for Mediterranean cuisine-lovers.

LE RHUL 269, corniche Kennedy – 7e ✆ 04 91 52 01 77. *Open every day. A la carte only.* The Rhul is a signatory of the very serious Bouillabaisse Charter, having spent 50 years preserving the quality of this emblematic dish. You find the restaurant beside the Pont de la Fausse Monnaie, and are made welcome with real kindness. The bouillabaisse is served in two stages, in the traditional Marseilles way, with the fish soup first and the fillets after, expertly cut up before your very eyes. Outside, the bluest of seas stretches into infinity. The comfortable rooms are very pleasant.

RESTAURANT MICHEL 6, rue des Catalans ✆ 04 91 52 30 63 *Open every day. A la carte only.* This place, first opened in 1946, is almost an institution, and deserves its international reputation. The family passion for gastronomic cuisine, and especially seafood, has been handed down from generation to generation. The different kinds of fish are presented to the customer for inspection before being cooked, and reception and service are both perfect. A moment of pleasure in this Phocaean temple dedicated to the sea.

Le Rove

LA PERGOLA Calanque de Niolon ✆ 04 91 46 90 28 *Open all week in high season, closed November and April.* La Pergola has a panoramic view of the small harbour, and you can enjoy lunch or dinner at the water's edge. The restaurant is actually quite famous, having provided a beautiful natural backdrop for several films. The owners are fishermen, and have been running the place for several years: fish-lovers can enjoy grilled bass, bream (from 16.50 €), octopus *a la plancha,* bouillabaisse (for two, order 48 hours before) and other fish according to the day's catch. Delicious chargrilled pizzas from 10 € to 14 €. A most attractive - and tasty - place to eat.

Saint-Chamas

LE RABELAIS 8, rue Auguste Fabre ✆ 04 90 50 84 40. *Closed Sunday evening and Monday. Open Sunday evening mid-June to mid-September. Last orders taken 1.30pm and 9.30pm. Set menus 25 € (weekday lunchtimes), 37 € (lunchtime and evening all week) and 60 € (degustation menu).A la carte 37 €.* There is no Rabelaisian debauchery in this excellent restaurant under its 17thc. vaulted ceilings. The tone is light but well-behaved, and that goes for the cooking too. Start with the artichoke and crab with violet mustard, follow it up with veal knuckle, beef fillet or cabbage stuffed with venison and foie gras. A chocolate pyramid Black-Forest style is just the thing to finish. The wine list indicates a cellar well stocked with French regional wines and some foreign bottles. A great place to eat.

Les Saintes-Maries-de-la-Mer

L'AMIRAUTE 46, avenue Théodore-Aubanel ✆ 04 90 43 32 71. *Closed Wednesday. Annual closing 15 November-14 February. Set menus 18.50 € and 24.50 €. 2-course formula 32.50 €, 3-course 42.50 € (choose from the carte).* This new restaurant opened by the famous Catherine Scalici from L'Auberge Cavalière is located opposite the harbour master's office. A big wrought-iron boat on the façade announces the theme: you're about to board a ship. The walls are panelled with real copper portholes, and tables and armchairs are covered in elegant violet fabric. Chef Georges Brun cooks regional food with a strong seafood influence and local specialities, and his dishes are beautifully presented. Excellent value for money.

MANGIO FANGO* Route d'Arles ✆ 04 90 97 80 56** *Set menus 30 €, 35 € and 37 €.*

You can find a table in the quietest of settings, here in this dining room opening onto a patio, with its mezzanine overlooking lounge, bar and fireplace. This is some of the best cooking in the Saintes: on the 30 € menu you can taste Saint-Rémy *fondu* - warm goat's cheese on toast - followed by bull meat fricassé Gardianne-style, or fillet of mullet *bohémienne* with a black olive *coulis*, finishing up with vanilla crème brulée. Though only 700m from the heart of the town, you pass through secret avenues of little palm trees to reach the hotel and the restaurant.

LE MAS DE LA GRENOUILLERE Rond point Fourcade RD 570 ✆ 04 90 97 90 22 *Mobile 06 80 25 68 58 - Website: www.mas-grenouillere.camargue.fr - EMail mas-grenouillere@wanadoo.fr -Swimming pool. Open all year. 18 rooms from 64 €. Breakfast included.* Superb view of the lake. Wave pool. Camargue horses are bred here. Le Mazet is a charming place with plenty of character. The 11 rooms have bath, WC, TV, air conditioning and breakfast included in the price. You can go horse-riding in the neighbourhood (see Mas de la Grenouillere and the section 'Leisure activities', 'Horse-riding').

LE MAZET DE LA GRENOUILLERE Route d'Arles ✆ 04 90 97 90 22** Open *all the year. Double room 65 €, familial room 85 € with breakfast included.* Le Mazet is located in a charming area with a nice view on the pond of petites Launes. All the 11 rooms are comfortable with air conditioning, TV, bathroom. Next to the swimming pool, there is the breeding of horses from Camargue.

Saint-Rémy-de-Provence

BISTROT DES ALPILLES 15, boulevard Mirabeau ✆ 04 90 92 09 17 *Set menus from 17.90 € to 21.90 €, dish of the day 8.90 €. A la carte. Coffee 1 € in the morning.* Le Bistrot des Alpilles is definitely one of the best places to eat in Saint-Rémy if you're after value for money. The interior is warm and brightly-coloured, with a sunny terrace - on the edge of the street, but sheltered by a hedge. Wide selection of dishes, with several formulas to choose from depending on how hungry you are. The lunchtime formula, which changes every day, might offer, say, veal blanquette and a dessert. There are some delicious suggestions for bigger appetites: boned pig's trotters and artichoke purée with olive oil, an aubergine terrine with fresh goat's cheese, and rocket pistou with Parmesan, and of course there is plenty of fish, including salmon steak with aparagus cooked *à la plancha* and the legendary aïoli. The desserts are up to scratch, a great favourite being chocolate soup with a small, soft-centred cake. Impeccable service and a most attractive Southern wine list with reasonable prices.

Aux Saintes-Maries-de-la-Mer
en Camargue

LE MANGIO FANGO ★★★

Hotel de charme - Restaurant

Light... the enchantment of a home
with mediterranean soul.

© ELIOPHOT

RD 570
13460 Les Saintes-Maries-de-la-Mer
Tel: (+33) (0)4 90 97 80 56
Fax: (+33) (0)04 90 97 83 60
www.hotelmangiofango.com
mangio.fango@wanadoo.fr

CHATEAU DES ALPILLES**** **31, route Départementale ✆ 04 90 92 03 33** *Website: www.chateaudesalpilles.com. Rooms from 170 € (low season) to 240 € (high season). Apartments and maisonettes (sleep 2-5) 270 € to 370 €. Breakfast 13 € to 17 €, supplement for pets; bookings only for the restaurant (closed Wednesday and Thursday lunchtime). Lunchtime formula: 2 courses 15 €, 3 courses 20 €, evening set menu 37 €.* Welcome to this sumptuous building that has played host to Chateaubriand and Lamartine in its time. The park is over a hundred years old, and features tree-lined avenues and a fishpond, along with several other curiosities to awaken your interest. Inside, you find modern comfort: air conditioning, sauna, massage (on request) tennis, swimming pool, TV and bar, with barbecue served round the pool, and fresh fish between 15 June and 15 September. Note that the bathrooms have been redecorated in the older part of the hotel, and the rooms contain period furniture.

Salon-de-Provence

LA SALLE A MANGER 6, rue du Maréchal-Joffre ✆ 04 90 56 28 01. *Closed Sunday and Monday. Lunchtime formula 15 €. A la carte. Advance booking recommended.* The decor alone is worth the trip, in this former oil and soap manufacturer's 19thc. private mansion, where you find family team spirit and a warm welcome. Plenty of starters and main courses to choose from, all good value for money. Excellent *regional vintages. Everyone likes the foie gras, and lamb croustillant*, and gourmets would die for the Thai bouillabaisse. Big dessert menu. Delicious from A to Z.

VAUCLUSE

Apt

AUBERGE DU LUBERON 8, place Faubourg-du-Ballet ✆ 04 90 74 12 50. *Fax : 04 90 04 79 49. Logis de France 3 cheminées. Annual closing November-December. 14 rooms from 58 € to 218 €. Breakfast buffet, or served in your room 9 €. Set menus from 29 € to 68 €. Children 15 €. Speciality Apt candied fruit menu 59 €, for 2 or more people. Garage 7 €. Pets admitted.* Serge and Bernadette Peuzin has been highly successful since they opened in 1978. Here, and only here, do you find the candied fruit cooked in every imaginable way, not to mention the vegetables conserved 'according to the Piton Brothers' method'. You really must taste them with mullet or a North African tajine. The marinated Mediterranean tuna *pissaladière* (sort of local pizza) with sesame seeds and tomato vinegar, or casseroled Bresse chicken aren't bad either (28 €). Serge makes sure he gets his supplies from local farmers. Very good wine to wash down your meal, served with a smile. In fine weather, you can eat on the terrace, on the edge of the Calavon.

Avignon

LE BERCAIL Ile de la Barthelasse ✆ 04 90 82 20 22. *Open every day from 8 April-1 November. Set menus 16 € (weekdays, Monday-Friday) to 30 €. Children's menu (Pitchoun) 9 €. A la carte. Late evening service in summer after 11pm.* Pleasant country setting away from all the noise and stress of

the town. Saint-Benezet bridge and ramparts are within sight, boats and barges drift nonchalently past and the ducks splash peacefully. The huge terrace on the banks of the Rhone has a marvellous view of the ramparts and Palais des Papes. At lunchtimes, the place is full and it isn't easy to find a table - its reputation for simple, excellent cooking is widespread. Regional specialities such as lamb with garlic cream, grilled bass with fennel and aubergines feature on the menus alongside the traditional grilled meat, and pizzas made by an expert. Kind and willing service. This restaurant deserves its success!

LE PETIT BEDON 70, rue Joseph Vernet © 04 90 82 33 98. *Closed Sunday and Monday lunchtime. Lunchtime on the slate starter 7 €, main course 11 €, dessert 5 €. Business lunch 25 €. Evening menus 31 € and 42 €. A la carte. Two air conditioned dining rooms.* This restaurant is exquisitely decorated, without any showing off. Customers are greeted politely, and can choose from a wide variety of dishes every day, at affordable prices. The cuisine is imaginative: chef Gilles Boulay has found himself a second with some skill in blending flavours, thus opening up the menu to new recipes. The lunchtime suggestions suit business people in a hurry: fish 'bread' with shellfish juice, turbot 'cake' with champagne butter, tender lamb *moelleux* with aubergines, pannacotta with exotic fruit (you get the picture?) and nougat ice cream with an apricot coulis. And that's not all. You can have a little goat's cheese with olive oil served on a bed of young salad shoots, instead of dessert, if you like. The serving staff are young and well-trained, unobtrusively supervised by smiling Mme Boulay. Upstairs is another well-kept dining room, seating groups and family parties. A restaurant to recommend in Avignon.

HOTEL D'EUROPE – LA VIEILLE FONTAINE** 12, place Crillon © 04 90 14 76 76 • fax 04 90 14 76 71** *Website : www. heurope.com. Open all year (restaurant closed for a fortnight in January and August). 44 rooms from 141 € to 449 €. 3 suites from 676 € to 762 €. Air-conditioned. Continental breakfast 14.50 €, or à la carte. Business menu 32 €. Set menus 48 € to 65 €. Dégustation menu 98 €. European lobster menu 82 €. Dogs admitted with a 10 € supplement. Terrace-garden. Garage with security system and parking valet 15 €.* Between Pont Saint-Bénezet and the Palais des Papes lies this beautiful residence, built in 1580, and converted into a dream hostelry many years ago. The facilities and service are faultless, and the staff are respectful and very attentive, yet not at all stuffy. Seven salons seating 10 to 150 are placed at your disposal, and there is a pleasant bar and a top-class restaurant with a Michelin star. The rooms range from simple to sumptuous, but all have period furniture. Brilliant chef Bruno d'Angelis keeps the culinary flag flying with the best. Terrace for good weather. Sunday brunch at 36 € is very popular.

CHRISTIAN ETIENNE 10 rue de Mons © 04 90 86 16 50 *Fax 04 90 86 67 09. Website : www. christian-etienne.fr. Set menus 30 € to 105 €. A la carte 100 €. Closed Sunday, Monday; open every day in July.* Christian Etienne's restaurant is in the tourist quarter near the Palais des Papes, but just far enough away from the 'tourist canteens'. The façade is not impressive, but behind it lies one of the department's most irresistible places to eat. Chef here since 1990 (though working in Avignon since 1978), ex-Ritz and Carlton, he isn't a publicity seeker, but gets on with the job on a daily basis, serious and disciplined as well as creative. Which must be the right approach, witness his *raviole* with rocket and *brousse* (Provençal cow's milk cheese), lobster claws baked in olive oil, foamy bisque, pan-fried scallops and mushrooms, grated black truffle and crusty *raviole* pastry, roast rabbit shoulder, violet hearts stuffed with liver, juice thickened with old-fashioned mustard, citrus salad with Medjoul dates, orange-flower ice cream and Oriental pastry with pistachio nuts. The place is full of good humour and generosity - it's always a pleasure to eat here.

CHATEAU PESQUIE, Edith et Paul Chaudière - Les Terrasses du Ventoux © 04 90 61 94 08. *www. Chateaupesquie.com - E-mail : Chateaupesquie @yahoo.fr. Open 1 October-weekend after Easter, Monday-Friday : 9am-12 noon and 2pm-6pm: closed Saturday and Sunday. Weekend after Easter-30 September, Monday-Friday: 9am-12 noon and 2pm-6pm; Saturday & Sunday: 10am-12 noon and 2pm-6pm. Groups by appointment only.* It took the Chaudières four years to restructure this vineyard, which they took over from the Daudet family in 1985. The results are impressive: Château Pesquie is a reference among French wines, exported to 17 countries and winner of several gold medals. The cépages are old grenache (50 years) and syrah, transformed by a balance of traditional and modern vinification methods into top quality wines. AOC reds account for 83% of output; the rest is AOC rose, AOC white and vin de pays Portes de Méditerranée (10%). All the wine produced is sold in bottles (rare in this region). You'll find it in the attractive shop, along with a selection of other regional wines.

LA FOURCHETTE 17, rue Racine © 04 90 85 20 93 *Closed Saturday and Sunday. Lunch 24 €, 26 € and 29 €. Evening menu 29 €. A la carte.* There are indeed rather a lot of forks - which only adds to the charm! Philippe Hiély cooks classic yet lively recipes, using only the finest seasonal ingredients, and sticks to reasonable prices. Locals and tourists recognise and appreciate his Provençal repertory's solid values, but his menus also include more personal dishes. You literally rub shoulders with your neighbours, seated between panelling and immaculate tablecloths to enjoy *caillettes* (a kind of meatball made with offal and vegetables) with herbs like you've never tasted before, Rhône mariners' *estouffade* (stew) and steamed fish. A word of advice: do try the *vacherin* dessert.

Carpentras

L'AROMATE 59, boulevard A. Durand © 04 90 35 03 44. *Closed Sunday. Open lunchtimes and evenings. Lunchtime formula 12 €. Set menus 21 € and 30 €. A la carte from 30 €.* The real estate agent next to the Hotel Comtadin has turned into an elegant restaurant, harmonious and friendly inside. It boasts a long dining room with painted mirrors, an attractive menu of home made dishes, and a talented but modest chef. After a faultless career in the Aveyron region, Xavier Arnoux settled in Carpentras to ply his trade - as his restaurant's name implies, he is an expert in spices, and has an inventive repertory.

Foie gras hamburger, scallops with truffles, sea bream *paupiettes* with vegetables, veal sweetbreads and fresh foie gras in a crust, morel sauce - and so on, right up to the profiteroles that you can cover yourself with hot bergamot-flavoured chocolate sauce. Marie Arnoux is full of small attentions and kind words for her guests, and treats new customers and regulars with the same consideration. Relax, enjoy your meal - and you won't forget to come back. Excellent value for money.

BEST WESTERN -LE COMTADIN * 65, boulevard Albin Durand ✆ 04 90 67 75 00** *fax 04 90 67 75 01 Website: www. le comtadin.com. Closed 20 December-17 January.* 19 air conditioned rooms with mini-bar, satellite TV, modem and Wi-Fi, from 51 € to 78 €. Buffet breakfast 11 €. Closed garage 7 €. Disabled access. Dogs admitted 8 €. Groups welcome.

This recent hotel, housed in an 18thc. building near the pedestrian streets, is fitted out with care and charm. The Provençal setting is not overdone, and you get an experienced and pleasant welcome from smiling staff who are always on hand to help. The breakfasts are delicious - and Le Comtadin is lucky enough to have the Aromate restaurant next door. You'd be wise to book ahead in season.

Cavaillon

PREVOT 353 avenue de Verdun ✆ 04 90 71 32 43 *Fax 04 90 71 97 05. Site Internet : www. restaurant-prevot.com. Set menus from 25 € to 85 €. A la carte 70 €. Closed Sunday and Monday.* Jean-Jacques Prévot is a great melon fan, whether raw, cooked, in syrup, juice or *coulis.* He has even had a museum devoted to the fruit fitted out in his restaurant: after all, it is the town's emblem. Fortunately, there is nothing museum-like about either the dining room or the *cuisine.* Apart from the all-melon menu - called Melon Mania - the dishes have a regional influence: snail *feuilleté* on a bed of salad shoots and iced melon *rougail* (prepared with spices), lamb knuckle confit, tomato cream with pistou and milled polenta, and nougat ice cream with candied melon, almonds and chestnut honey. Generosity and talent go into these recipes, and the service is very considerate. A top-class place.

Cucuron

RESTAURANT DE L'HORLOGE Rue Léonce Brieugne ✆ 04 90 77 12 74. *Closed Tuesday evening and all day Wednesday, and Monday evening from October-April. Annual closing during school holidays 7 February-10 March 2006 and 19-28 December. Express lunchtime formula 13 € (weekdays), set menus 16 € (19 € with a quarter litre of wine and coffee included) to 38 €. Truffles. Childrens' menu 9 €, including drink. Booking recommended on Sunday. Groups of up to 50.* The restaurant interior is already pretty impressive, with its genuine 14thc.oil press. These vaulted cellars are ideal for cheerful, candlelit meals among friends, with a menu cleverly designed to sharpen the smallest appetite. Scallop and lobster tail fricassée with morels, leg of lamb in breadcrumbs with almonds and rosemary honey juice, nougat ice cream with almonds and hazelnuts, guanamara chocolate *fondant* and Arabica mignonettes feature in pride of place. The bill is fairly modest - and like the locals, you're bound to keep on coming back.

Gordes

AUBERGE DE CARCARILLE * Route d'Apt – Les Gervais – D2 – ✆ 04 90 72 02 63.** *Logis de France. Closed Friday lunchtime. Set menus from 18 € to 42 €. Children 10 €. 11 rooms from 60 € to 72 €. Vegetarian menu available. Wine by the glass 4.50 € to 11 €. Breakfast 10 €. Swimming pool. Disabled access.* The Rimbaud family has been running this inn for thirty years, and is well known as the last pure- Gordes restaurant owner. Dominique and Christophe, who have taken over from father Francis, are proud of this reputation. It's true that regulars are always happy to come back to Carcarille's comfortable rooms and generous cooking - at such attractive prices. The brothers have everything going for them – truffle producers; a farming cousin's early asparagus; melons and vegetables on the table a few hours after being picked. The kitchen garden gets bigger every year, and the *cuisine* respects Provençal traditions: Simiane kid *croquant* on dandelions (grandmother's recipe), young boned rabbit with sage, roast kid from the Hautes-Alpes with oven-baked potatoes and garlic in its skin, and oven-baked monkfish *boulangère*-style, all washed down with regional wines. This year, a big new project is afoot: the hotel is extending, and will have 21 rooms available for guests.

L'ESTELLAN Les Imberts ✆ 04 90 72 04 90. *Closed Wednesday. Dish of the day 13 €. Lunchtime formula 18 €. Evening menu 35 €. A la carte.* This gorgeous *mas* in local stone is a haven of peace, on the right just before you start the climb up to Gordes. A great lunchtime menu at 18 € lets you try two seasonal dishes with fresh ingredients straight from market, while the evening *cuisine* is more sophisticated and rooted in Provençal tradition. The chef knows his classics, adding a personal touch to the slice of gingerbread and home made duck foie gras served with spinach shoots in hazelnut oil, and sangria juice, the *améliero* – almond tree in Provençal – with seasonal mushrooms and fillet of sea bream *royale* served with a goat's cheese *galette.* The desserts are up to scratch, rounding off your meal to perfection.

Le Pontet

AUBERGE DE CASSAGNE** 450, allée de Cassagne ✆ 04 90 31 04 18** *Website: www.hotelprestige-provence.com. Email : cassagne@wanadoo.fr. Closed in January. Air-conditioned. 36 rooms from 110 € to 347 € and 4 apartments from 378 € to 546 €. Breakfast 23 €. Private garage 15 €. Wi-Fi connection available. Satellite TV. Set menus 55 €, 71 € and 92 €. A la carte. Children's menu 20 €. Park. Terrace. Pool, jacuzzi, sauna, fitness room. Tennis and children's play area.* This ancient Provençal bastide near Avignon offers an exquisite setting for your visit to the region. Discreet and efficient staff look after you on your arrival at Cassagne, setting the tone for a perfect stay. The rooms have king-size beds, and are spacious and beautifully-kept, mostly at garden level, with loggia or terrace. The buffet breakfasts are excellent. Gastronomy fans will love Philippe Boucher's delicate, savoury cuisine, the result of 20 years' experience and winner of several stars. His well-prepared dishes are lovely to look at and delicious to eat, changing with the seasons and all equally appetising. His accomplice André Trestour takes care of the cellar, and has a wine list full of top *domaines* to suggest. Cassagne is a real four-star hotel, with its luxury facilities designed purely for pleasure-seekers. Reassuring!

LES AGASSINS ** – LA TABLE DES AGASSINS Route de Lyon - Le Pigeonnier ✆ 04 90 32 42 91.** *Website: www .agassins .com. Closed Saturday lunchtime and Sunday, and in January and February. 26 rooms from 120 € to 300 €. Breakfast buffet 17 €. Pets accepted with a 15 € supplement. Weekday formulas 15 € to 25 €. Set menus 38 € to 46 €. A la carte from 53 €. Children's menu 20 €. Seminars.* Just outside Avignon lies this hotel, with its park, swimming pool and terraces – and that very professional chef Jean-Rémy Joly. He suggests loin of lamb with savory, served with gnocchi in creamy gorgonzola – splendid! – or fish of the day with asparagus. You can choose to eat in the attractive dining room, or on a pleasant terrace sunk in greenery.

Malaucène

LE VENTOUX Avenue de Verdun ✆ 04 90 65 23 57. *Closed Wednesday. Lunchtime set menu 13 €, evenings 19.50 € and 26 €. A la carte. The set menus are all full (starter, main course, dessert, with at least 5 choices for each course).* The Riperts have come back to their native Malaucène after some time away, still with the same good humour and enthusiasm. Véronique is in charge of the cooking, and her *tarte* Tatin with tomato, duck breast with lavender honey , scallops in muscat-de-beaumes, lamb knuckle with thyme, fig shortbread, and bananas cooked in honey then *flambéd* in white rum are truly delicious. Basic country ingredients go into the making of sophisticated specialities like fresh salmon with Meaux mustard, and profiteroles with oodles of chocolate. For twenty or so euros per head you get a full meal including wine and coffee. Laurent runs the dining room, with its light, relaxing background music. The wine list features a dozen ventoux at 13 €, a few ventoux supérieurs at 18 €, and the traditional côtes-du-rhône, bordeaux and burgundies for fans.

Pernes-les-Fontaines

AU FIL DU TEMPS Place Louis-Giraud ✆ 04 90 66 48 61. *Closed Saturday lunchtime and Wednesday; Tuesday and Wednesday in winter. Set menus 30 €, 45 € and 65 €. New catering service available.* The Augustins cultural centre, historic Louis-Giraud School and a small fountain from the Dauphins era give a festive look to this little grocer's shop, now transformed into one of the department's best restaurants. The setting recalls earlier times, with its stonework and exposed beams against white walls, and there are several menus to choose from: the day's menu announced out loud, the foie gras menu with its 5 € supplement, or the "my-eyes-are-bigger-than-my-stomach" menu with three main courses! Preparation, garnishes and presentation are all impeccable. The local wine list is extensive, but you can also choose your bottle from those laid down in the cellar itself, to the pleasant sound of shrieks from the neighbouring school playground. Sunday opening is an added attraction. Don't forget to book ahead.

Sault

HOSTELLERIE DU VAL DE SAULT Route de Saint-Trinit ✆ 04 90 64 01 41 *Fax 04 90 64 12 74 Website:www.valdesault.com. Closed November-Easter. 5 suites (bastidons) 230 €, 11 rooms 169 €. Restaurant Regain closed weekday lunchtimes except June, July, August and September. Set menus 36 € and 39.50 €. A la carte around 60 €. Children 14 €. Theme menus. Terrace. Swimming pool.* An idyllic setting on the Sault heights for this hostelry, member of the *Logis de France, Relais du Silence* and *Romantiks Hôtels* groups. The hotel is organised in circular fashion, like a small hamlet, huddled against a green landscape. 5 hectares of woodland, a sublime view of the Sault Valley and Ventoux, and elegant rooms combining luxury and high comfort standards, all with a private terrace, are on offer. Owner Yves Gattechaut dreamed up the site, influenced by his travels in Indonesia and particularly Bali, but also by his love of Provence. The atmosphere is exotic, with some luxury facilities like tennis courts, two heated pools (one under glass) with counter-current swimming, a jacuzzi diffusing aromatic oils, a hammam hydrojet shower and a fitness centre. When you've finished pampering yourself, a dining room with prettily-laid tables and Balinese leather chairs awaits you, with some excellent *cuisine*. Yves Gattechaut certainly had a good idea, making his nest here. Chic, but simple.

Grillon

AUBERGE DES PAPES Route de Grignan ✆ 04 90 37 43 67 *Fax 04 90 35 51 28. Annual closing September. Open weekends in winter, weekdays for advance bookings. Open every day from Easter. Set menus 21 € to 32 €. Truffle menu 50 € (November-March); summer truffles from March onwards. 3 rooms at 64 €. Pool. Terrace. Pets accepted.* All the region's gourmets know this inn with its cheerful façade. From Valréas, it only takes a few minutes to get there. The terrace is covered in flowers during summer, with genuine Provençal cuisine served in a rustic setting. The bar is a sort of cave, like Bacchus' sanctuary setting out to convert pilgrims. Gérard Nicolas, full of generosity and Provençal culture, watches over it with great zeal, and will surely inject you with the côtes du rhône virus. Wife Marie takes care of the cooking, including a sublime truffle omelette, *crespeou* (Provençal vegetable omelettes) with seven flavours and tomato fondue with rosemary, mullet fillet *soleïade* and scallop *ravioles* with truffle cream. The desserts are what grandmother used to make, so you might as well throw caution to the winds. Three pretty and comfortably-equipped rooms are available if you can't bear to leave.

Rhône Valley

Croiselet lake

VALLÉE DU RHÔNE
SAÔNE-ET-LOIRE
La Clayette
Monsols
La Chapelle-de-Guinchay
MÂCON
Pont-de-Veyle
A40
Bourg-en-Bresse
Péronnas
Chauffailles
Charlieu
Beaujeu
Châtillon
Belleville
Saône
Vevle
Nantua
Bellegarde
Ain
ROANNE
Perreux
Thizy
Lamure
A6
Saint-Trivier-sur-Moignans
AIN
Pont d'Ain
0
20 km
Chalamont
Villefranche sur-Saône
Ambérieu
Amplepuis
Révrieux
Anse
Miribel
Pérouges
Saint-Symphorien de Lay
Tarare
Loire
l'Arbresle
RHÔNE
LYON
Crémieu
A72
Sainte-Foy
LOIRE
Saint-Genis Laval
Villefontaine
SAVOIE
Vénissieux
Saint-Symphorien d'Ozon
Montbrison
Chazelles
Mornant
Bourgoin-Jallieu
La Tour-du-Pin
Givors
Parc Naturel Régional du Livradois-Forez
Rive-de-Gier
VIENNE
St-Jean-de-Bournay
ISERE
N
O
E
S
PUY-DE-DÔME
SAINT-ETIENNE
Saint Chamond
Condrieu
A7
la Côte

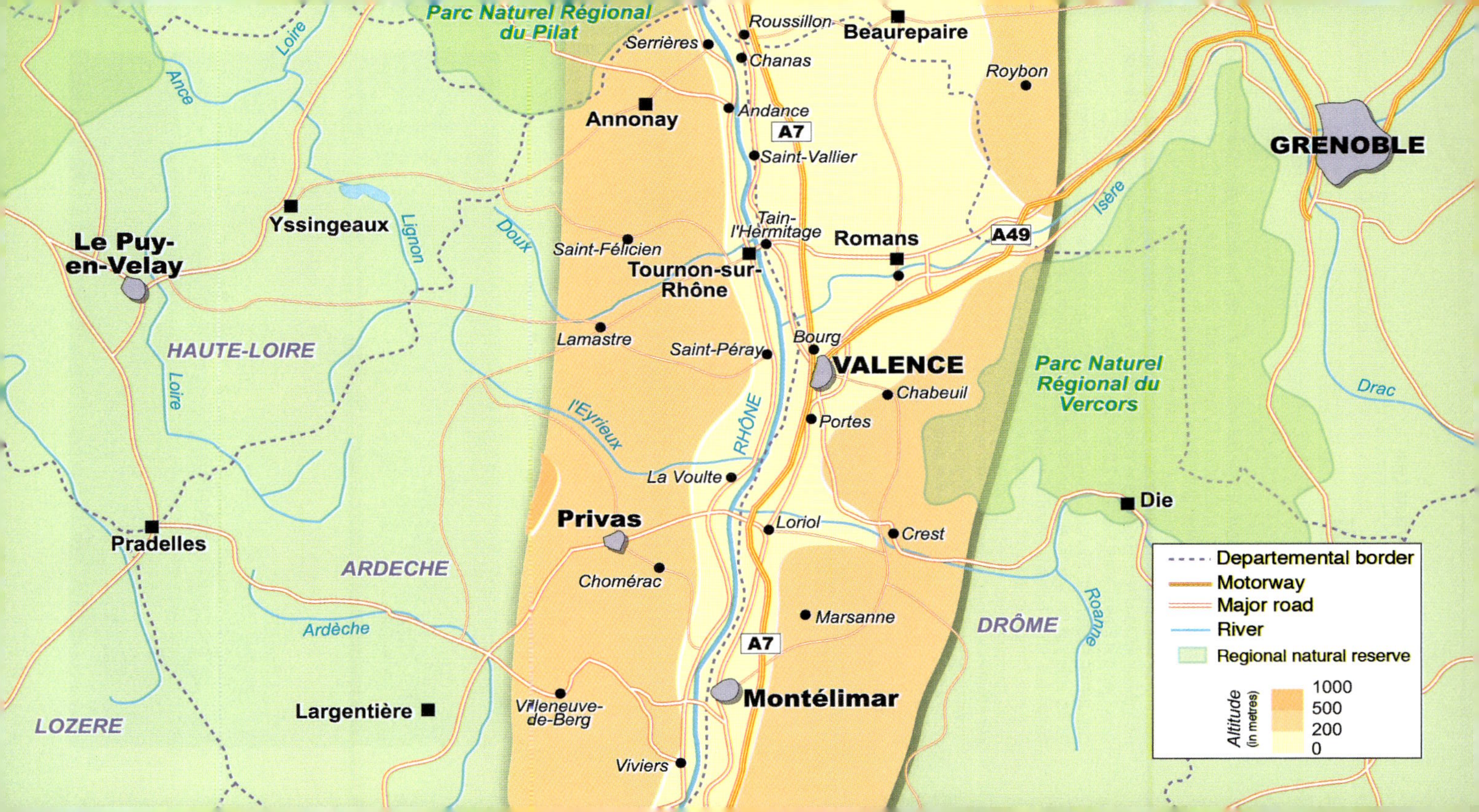
Parc Naturel Régional du Pilat
Roussillon
Beaurepaire
Serrières
Chanas
Roybon
Annonay
Andance
A7
Saint-Vallier
GRENOBLE
Isère
Yssingeaux
Le Puy-en-Velay
Lignon
Doux
Loire
Ance
Tain-l'Hermitage
Romans
A49
Saint-Félicien
Tournon-sur-Rhône
Lamastre
Saint-Péray
Bourg
VALENCE
HAUTE-LOIRE
Parc Naturel Régional du Vercors
Drac
Chabeuil
Portes
RHÔNE
l'Eyrieux
La Voulte
Die
Privas
Loriol
Crest
Pradelles
ARDECHE
Chomérac
Marsanne
DRÔME
Roanne
Ardèche
A7
Montélimar
Villeneuve-de-Berg
Largentière
LOZERE
Viviers
Departemental border
Motorway
Major road
River
Regional natural reserve
Altitude (in metres)
1000
500
200
0

AROUND LYON

Lyon

Lyon is France's third biggest town and second urban area. It is also the world's gastronomy capital and a crossroads between northern and southern Europe. It boasts two hills, two rivers (Saone and Rhône) and a confluence, right in the heart of the Rhône valley. Beaujolais country lies in the north; to the west are the Lyon mountains, and north east, the Dombes and Isère plains. This is only the second urban centre to be listed by UNESCO (the other is Prague), for Lyon has managed to develop, while keeping the architectural identity of its quarters as its main strength. Despite their differences, the Croix-Rousse, Vieux Lyon and Presqu'ile are linked by 2,000 years of history.

COLLINE DE FOURVIERE. Fourvière, from forum vetus (old forum) bears the traces of its Roman origins. On the orders of the Senate, Munatius Plancus founded a colony on this last outcrop of the Massif Central, and official buildings sprang up around the forum, becoming Lugdunum, an important city fit for Emperors. Christianity took root. This golden era has left plenty of remains. After the fall of the Roman Empire, the inhabitants settled by the Saône and took up agriculture. Vines appeared on the hillsides, and a basilica was built on Saint-Just, with religious communities gathering around. Fourvière became known as the 'praying hill' and attracted pilgrims. The imposing neo-Byzantine basilica (1872- 1896) was put up with a subscription following a vow made by Lyon Catholics. It contains a museum of religious art, and you can also visit the basilica's rooftops; strange but interesting. Fourvière's archeological site was opened in 1933, and many remains have been excavated during successive digs, like the theatre, built against the hillside, probably in Augustus' reign, then extended in Hadrien's. It held 11,000 spectators, and today hosts the 'Fourvière Nights' in summer. The smaller Odeon was intended for music and poetry. Behind it, shops and a temple have been excavated.

MUSEE DE LA CIVILISATION GALLO ROMAINE DE LYON FOURVIERE 17, rue Cleberg (5e) ✆ 04 72 38 49 30. *Open all year, Tuesday to Sunday: 10am-6pm except public holidays.*

VIEUX-LYON. The town's historic centre runs along the Saone for a kilometre, linking three quarters, Saint-Georges, Saint-Jean and Saint-Paul and blending Middle Ages and Renaissance. The medieval town was grouped around its bishop, independent of France until the 14thc., and had great economic power with its shops, exchanges, mansions and lodging-houses full of busy, cosmopolitan merchants, bankers and craftsmen.

CROIX-ROUSSE. The quarter has two areas; sloping and flat. The slopes bear traces of the Roman period: for three centuries, the 60 Gallic towns sent delegates every summer to debate in the Condate. Later, convents were set up, dissolved during the Revolution, and big, high-ceilinged buildings were put up on the land, containing the famous Jacquard weaving looms. The silk-workers known as canuts took up lodgings in the workshops-cum-apartments, and in 1831 and 1834, there were revolts, bloodily suppressed. In 1852 this faubourg became part of Lyon, but has kept its own identity and traditions rather like a village.

Lyon vineyard

TRABOULES. Covered alleys running through a block, linking its courtyards with the surrounding streets. They saved space (vital at the time in a town squeezed between hills and river) and kept the rain off; today there are over 300, some uncovered (a convention having been signed with town and Urban Community).

PRESQU'ILE. The most northerly part of the Presqu'ile is Lyon's business centre. Between Places Bellecour and des Terreaux, streets and buildings were shaped by centuries of history, like Renaissance streets Rue Mercière and Rue Longue. Place Bellecour is huge (301m x 200m) and Place des Terreaux has been reshaped by architect Christian Drevet and artist Daniel Buren, who moved the Bartholdi fountain and set up 14 pillars and 69 fountains on a granite base, lit up at night. Don't miss Jean Nouvel's Opera (1993), or the many museums.

GUIGNOL. Lyon's Guignol (sort of Mr Punch) was invented by a young unemployed silk-worker, who became a professional puppeteer in 1804. Guignol is a cheerful character prone to argument, who comments on local events with his boozing pal Gnafron and lady friend Madelon. The character is still popular with all ages. *To see his show: theatre Guignol, un gone de Lyon salle la Ficelle - 65, bd des canuts (4e) 04 72 32 11 55. Theatre Guignol de Lyon 2, rue louis-carrand (5e) 04 78 28 92 57. Theatre Guignol du parc de la Tete d'Or*

ATELIER DE LA SOIE 33, rue Romarin (1er) ✆ 04 72 07 97 83. *Open every day except Sunday and public holidays: 9am-12 noon and 2pm-7pm. Admission free.* Now known for its high-tech textile industry, Lyon's fortunes began with silk. This workshop (still working!) demonstrates old-fashioned silk printing.

MAISON DES CANUTS 10-12 rue d'Ivry (4e) ✆ 04 78 28 62 04. *Open Tuesday-Saturday: 10am-6.30pm. Closed Sundays and public holidays. Admission: adult 5 €, child 2.50 €.* Silk-weaving from 18th-20thc. Old weaving looms, equipment, objects and documents concerning silk. You can buy some pretty pieces in the shop.

MUSEE DES BEAUX ARTS (PALAIS SAINT PIERRE) 20, place des Terreaux (2e) ✆ 04 72 10 17 40. *Open every day: 10.30am-6pm, except Tuesday and public holidays. Admission: 6 €, concessions 4 €. Students under 26 free.* France's second-biggest collection of works of art (after the Louvre), from Ancient Egypt to Picasso, housed in a superbly renovated building.

MUSEES HISTORIQUE DES TISSUS ET DES ARTS DECORATIFS 34, rue de la Charite ✆ 04 78 38 42 00. *Open every day except Monday, public holidays, Easter & Whit Sundays. Admission: adult 5 €, ticket covers both museums.* The Fabric Museum in the Hôtel de Villeroy contains a rich collection of textiles, and retraces their history back through 2,000 years. It is not only a museum, but also a centre for research into the subject. The Decorative Arts Museum next-door shows how textiles are used, in the sophisticated atmosphere of an 18thc. interior.

DOMBES AND BRESSE

La Dombes contains a thousand lakes; many were drained in the 19th and 20thc. It is France's biggest fish-breeding region, but also a bird sanctuary, with the big ornithological reserve at Villars-les-Dombes. Flooded land alternating with intensive cultivation has attracted 260 species (at least), and the region is a stopover for migrating birds on their way to Africa. The medieval town of Perouges, Chatillon-sur-Chalaronne and its flowers, and Ars-sur-Formans (whose priest became a saint) are just a few places of interest.

Bourg-en-Bresse

A town with both architectural and gastronomic treasures: the splendid Royal Brou monastery and famous poultry.

ROYAL BROU MONASTERY 63, bd de Brou ✆ 04 74 22 83 83. *www.culture.fr/Rhône-alpes/brou. Open every day. Admission: adult 6.30 €, under-18s free. Ticket covers entry to the church, the monastery's 3 cloisters and the Fine Arts Museum. Admission free 1st Sunday of the month November-March.* Marguerite of Austria, widowed at 24, decided to have this Flamboyant Gothic masterpiece built at the gates of Bourg-en-Bresse, to house her husband Philibert le Beau, Duke of Savoy's tomb, her mother's, and her own, for she died in 1530, before the monastery was finished. The greatest artists and craftsmen in France and Flanders took part in the building, and the end result was beautiful, and huge: 5,000 m^2. for 20 or so monks, who lived in the three cloisters until the Revolution. In 1548, the church was finished, with its coloured and varnished tiled roof. Inside, the sober two-storey rib-vaulted nave with its side aisles and chapels contrasts with the richly-decorated chancel. The three tombs (designed by Jean de Bruxelles) in the centre of the chancel are bathed in coloured light from the original stained glass windows (1525-1531).

NOTRE DAME CATHEDRAL The Bishop of Bourg (in office 1515-1534) made the 16thc. parish church into a cathedral, then a collegiate church. The steeple, put up between 1656 and 1696, and 'decapitated' during the Revolution was rebuilt in the early 20thc. by the Burgundian architect Tony Ferret, with local sculptor Muscat designing the clockface. The bells peal out at 7.50am, 11.50am and 6.50pm.

HOTEL-DIEU APOTHECARY 47, bd de Brou ✆ 04 74 22 49 40. This late 18thc. apothecary's shop contains a laboratory (intact), pharmacy and dispensary.

Montluel

A historic town, built around its now-ruined feudal castle. The winding streets contain ancient houses with mullioned windows; notice the façades of the Condé princes' house and former 16thc. college; the Romanesque Saint Etienne Church porch (the church no longer exists); remains of the Visitation and Augustian monasteries (17thc.); old washing-place; towers and remains of the ramparts (14th-15thc.) including the Tour Carré at the end of the Promenade des Tilleuls.

NOTRE DAME DES MARAIS COLLEGIATE CHURCH. Built from 1380-1600s in Romanesque, Gothic and Renaissance styles.

HOSPICE ✆ APOTHECARY'S. 04 72 25 78 54 *Open all year, 1 May-31 October, Wednesday & Saturday: 3pm-6pm. Out of season, Saturday: 3pm-6pm, or by appointment. Admission: adult 2.50 €, under-16s free.* Once the Lyon Jesuits' pharmacy, set up in 1765 in the 18thc. hospice built by Pierre Caristia. It contains some fine 18thc. earthenware set off by carved panelling, a painted ceiling, and an 18thc. table for serving game. There is a marble fountain in the entrance hall and listed wrought-iron railings.

Pérouges

History fans will feel they are back in the Middle Ages , when the village was a rich weacers' community. Unevenly cobbled streets lead to Place du Tilleul, painted by Utrillo, and the fortress-church with its loopholes.

SAINTE MARIE MADELEINE CHURCH ✆ 0474 61 01 14. In the Middle Ages, archers fired their crossbows throught the slits in the walkway above the nave; there are also loopholes in the side aisles. Half-church, half-fortress, this is a 15thc. Gothic building, with amazing acoustics.

MAISON DES PRINCES ✆ 04 74 61 00 88. *Open all year. April-October: 10am-12 noon and 2pm-6pm. Out of season, open Sunday. Admission: adult 4 €, children free. Ticket also provides admission to the Tour de Guet. Museum of popular arts and traditions.* Former residence of the Counts of Savoy, it contains Aubusson tapestries, armour, Gothic chests, and wide fireplaces, and houses temporary painting exhibitions. It leads into a medieval garden, with aromatic plants, medicinal plants and the 'garden of love'.

Trévoux

One of the first French dictionaries was published here in 1704, as well as the first periodical, the 'Journal de Trevoux' (635 volumes have been kept in the Town Hall's historic library). This literary town is the Dombes' largest, and boasts stone houses, a Parliament and a feudal castle, with narrow streets and the remains of ramparts in the old quarters.

APOTHECARY'S ✆ 04 74 00 36 32. *Guided tours at weekends May-September (Saturday 10.15am, 3pm and 4.30pm; Sunday 3pm and 4.30pm., from the Tourist Office). Guided tours all year for groups. Admission: adult 2 €* Anne-Marie Louise d'Orléans, Duchess of Bourbon and Montpensier founded the hospital in 1686. The apothecary's dispensary contains two rare collections of 17th and 18thc. earthenware pots.

CHATEAU. *May-October, open every day except Tuesday and Wednesday: 2.30pm-7pm. Out of season, open weekends only: 3pm-7pm Every day in July & August. Admission: adult 2 € , free for the under-12s.* The 12thc. castle overlooks the town and surrounding countryside. Three towers remain; one round and another horseshoe-shaped.

PARLEMENT DE LA DOMBES ✆ 04 74 00 36 32. *Open all year during the Tribunal d'Instance's office hours, and June-September, Saturday & Sunday too, 2pm-6pm. Admission2 €, under-12s free.* Don't miss the beautiful decorated caisson ceiling, and fine panelling. The Parliament met there from 1696-1711: 34 members and a governor empowered to judge as a last resort.

Villars-les-Dombes

PARC DES OISEAUX RN83 ✆ 04 74 98 05 54. *www.parc-des-oiseaux.com. Open every day of the year: 10am-nightfall (9.30pm in summer). Admission: adult 9!-12 €, concessions 6 €-9.50 €, according to season; under-4s free.* This magical park contains a huge lake, where 400 bird species live on 25 ha. Don't miss the African reserve, where a mangrove swamp has been reconstituted with amazing brightly coloured birds in a tropical atmosphere.

BEAUJOLAIS

There are 12 beaujolais: beaujolais, beaujolais-villages, brouilly, chénas, chiroubles, côte-de-brouilly, fleurie, juliénas, morgon, moulin-a-vent, regnie, saint-amour. Over 150 million bottles are exported world-wide, to over 192 countries. Yet the Beaujolais also has other advantages, like its forests, a pleasure for nature-lovers.

Villefranche-sur-Saône

The start of the wine route, and an industrious town, with its Grande-Rue, covered market and traditional FÕte des Conscrits.

LE PAYS BEAUJOLAIS Rue de la Sous-Prefecture ✆ 04 74 07 27 50. Its aim is to promote the Beaujolais country in France and abroad, co-ordinating the restaurants, accommodation, services, activities and events available to tourists, and offering a range of tours and holidays in the region.

Beaujeu

Beaujolais' historic capital, and origin of its name. Saint Nicolas Church was consecrated by Pope Innocent II in 1132, and is an important example of Romanesque architecture in the region.

SOURCES DU BEAUJOLAIS Place de l'Hôtel de Ville ✆ 04 74 69 20 56. *www.beaujeu.com-sources_beaujolais.html Open every day except Tuesday, March-May and September-December: 10am-12.30pm and 2pm-6pm. July & August, every day: 10am-12.30pm and 2pm-7pm. Admission: adult 6 €, child 3 € (ticket includes Audin Museum and a tasting in the Beaujolais Villages cellar).* Discover the story of Beaujolais wine throughout the region's history, in sons et lumières. The shop sells wine, regional produce and local crafts. There is a 14thc. inside courtyard and art exhibitions.

Romanèche-Thorins

This is moulin-á vent country. The wine and its hamlet are named after the 300-year-old windmill standing 10m high among the vines.

PLAISIRS EN BEAUJOLAIS La Gare ✆ 03 85 35 22 22. *www.hameauenbeaujolais.com. Open every day April-October: 9am-6pm, November-March: 10am-6pm. Admission: adults: 20 €/day Plaisirs en Beaujolais, 10 €/Un jardin en Beaujolais. Restaurants, shop, free car park.* Exhibitions, automaton theatre, 3-D film and other surprises await you in this unique recreational theme park. Discover the winegrower's skill and know-how in the 'Hameau en Beaujolais', or wander through scents and flavours, with an instructive visit to the G. Duboeuf Vinification Centre in the 'Jardin en Beaujolais'. The 'Gare' (station) takes you on a nostalgic time-trip in the world of the train.

TOUROPARC EN BEAUJOLAIS La Maison Blanche ✆ 03 85 35 51 53. *www.touroparc.com. Open all year. May-October, every day: 10am-6pm. Late October-late April: 10am-12 noon and 1.30pm-5.30pm (zoological park only). Admission: adult 13! (high season) and 12 €.* Offers a range of attractions, the main one being the zoological park, housing 800 animals (300 species) from all over the world. Otherwise, it depends on what you fancy: descending the torrent through the caves; high-speed train; monorail, and so on.

LOIRE

Saint-Etienne

It used to be said that Saint-Etienne had only 3 claims to fame: coal mines, Manufrance and its football team. All that has changed, thanks to town council and citizen initiatives. The Loire department's prefecture is not yet 1,000 years old, and has grown up among 7 hills, just like Rome. Wherever you go, it seems to be up (517m to the Town Hall!), so it's best to know how the land lies before setting out.

ASTRONEF 28, rue Pierre et Dominique Ponchardier ✆ 04 77 33 43 01. *www.sideral.com. Admission: adult 6 €, concessions 5 €. Sessions: Wednesday: 3.30pm, Saturday & Sunday: 2.15pm, 3.30pm, 4.45pm. School holidays: 2.15pm, 3.30pm, 4.45pm.* Saint-Etienne's planetarium has been renovated from A to Z; new sidereal theatre, new astronomic simulator projecting 3-D computerised images at 360 degrees, with digital Dolby sound. When you've had your head in the stars, it's hard coming back down to earth.

MUSEE D'ART MODERNE La Terrasse ✆ 04 77 79 52 52. *Open every day, except Tuesday and public holidays. Admission: adult 4,70 €* France's second-biggest contemporary art collection is here: painting (Picasso, Léger, Dubuffet, Soulages etc.), sculpture, drawings, installation (Buren, Gerdes). Design and photography (Nadar to Cindy Sherman) are also represented, all in 4,000 m^2. of vast, luminous space. International exhibitions are planned in the coming months.

MUSEE DE LA MINE Site Couriot - 3, bd Franchet-d'Espérey ✆ 04 77 43 83 26. *Open every day, except Tuesday. Admission: adult 5.60 €, concessions 5,60 €, under-12s free.* Evening visits Thursday, mid June-mid September. The Puits Couriot mine was active from 1919-1973, exploiting the deep levels of west Saint-Etienne. The surface buildings have been rehabilitated and the underground gallery reconstituted, to become a museum. Explore the running of the mine and work organisation 'above and below' during your visit (1hr30mins).

Firminy

LE CORBUSIER HERITAGE. These apartments are typical of modern architecture's Concrete King: spacious (room calculated according to a human dimensions scale called the Modulor), on two floors with all mod cons. Leisure is not forgotten: there is a stadium, while the church is to be finished according to the architect's directives.

Saint-Martin-la-Plaine

ESPACE ZOOLOGIQUE ✆ 04 77 75 18 68. *Summer: 9am-6pm. Winter: 10am-5pm. Admission: adult 12 € child 8 €.* The animals' homes and enclosures are spread through this 12 ha. area of natural parkland. The wildlife site was opened in 1972, and today contains 350 animals from over 60 different species, some unique in France. It is involved in conservation work, notably in protecting areas threatened with extinction, like the Cacatoes region in the Philippines. At 2pm, the kids can help feed the gorillas - a high point in the day! The park's mascot gorilla is called Plato. You can see binturongs, babirusas, white-handed gibbons, and Himalayan snow leopards, among others. The park also includes a tropical glasshouse and a vivarium.

Le Roannais - Le Forez

Le Forez is mountainous country with signs of a volcanic history, whereas the Roannais, on the Loire, forms a natural basin. West of Lyon, this region foreshadows the Auvergne, with its green countryside and industrious towns.

Roanne

CANAL. Built between 1800 and 1836, this 56km canal goes through Briennon to reach Roanne and Digoin. Hire a barge with friends or family and discover the life of the river: 'Marins d'Eau Douce' 04 77 69 92 92 at Briennon have boats for hire (no licence needed).

MUSEE DES BEAUX-ARTS ET D'ARCHEOLOGIE JOSEPH-DECHELETTE 22, rue Anatole-France ✆ 04 77 23 68 77. *Open every day (except Tuesday and public holidays). Admission: adult 4 €.* This Fine Arts and Archeology Museum is the department's second most important, housing collections of Egyptian and Gallo Roman antiquities, 15th to 20thc. Fine Arts and contemporary earthenware and ceramics of exceptional quality.

Charlieu

Exceptional architectural heritage. Time seems to stand still in Charlieu, medieval town with semi-pedestrian streets and a host of half-timbered and corbelled houses.

CHARLIEU BENEDICTINE ABBEY ✆ 04 77 60 09 97. *Open every day July & August, closed Monday the rest of the year. Closed in January. Admission: 4.30 €.* Founded around 870-875, Charlieu was linked to Cluny in 932. The first church was reshaped, divided into 3 naves with stone vaults and a chancel with ambulatory. The abbey was reduced to a priory before 1040. From the 10thc. onwards, the community developped and a bigger building was put up: St. Fortune Priory Church. The foundations of three successive churches have since been excavated, and the few existing remains from the 11thc. priory church restored. See also the religious art museum, with its polychrome statues.

Saint-Galmier

400m above the Forez plain, this town is a climatic and hydromineral resort. You can try a range of sports, from parachuting to boules, or enjoy the park, swimming-pool, racecourse and casino.

LA SOURCE BADOIT. The region's top mineral soda water. The Badoit spring goes back to the 16thc. and bubbles out at the foot of Saint-Galmier Hill, having been filtered 300m underground in the sedimentary layers of Le Forez Plain.

BAS-DAUPHINE

The eastern part and left bank of the river, once it has left the Alps and passed through big towns like Grenoble. Hills, plateaux and plains were once the sites of Roman and religious capitals (Vienne, Romans, Valence), which brought fame to the Rhône Valley.

Vienne

Vienne's history goes back 2,000 years. As a Roman colony, the town expanded rapidly, and magnificent monuments were built inside its ramparts. Later, Vienne became the capital of a 7-province diocese covering the southern half of Gaul, then one of the Kings of Bourgogne's residences, and was known as 'Vienne the Holy'. Many Roman and medieval monuments are left from these periods.

MUSEE & SITE ARCHEOLOGIQUE SAINT-ROMAIN-EN-GAL RD 502 ✆ 04 74 53 74 00. *Open every day except Monday: 10am-6pm. Admission: adult 3.80 €, under-18s free.* The Rhône's right bank was a prosperous craftsmen's quarter in Roman Vienne, between 30 B.C. and 200 A.D. Today, a light and luminous building contains findings from these river banks, including mosaics and Gallo-Roman paintings.

TEMPLE D'AUGUSTE ET DE LIVIE. Built in the early 1stc. B.C. on the site of the forum, this temple was dedicated to Augustus and his wife Livia, then transformed into a church in the Middle Ages, its columns disappearing in the masonry. It was a Temple of Reason in 1792, a commercial tribunal in 1795, then a museum. Prosper Merimée had the columns excavated from 1845, returning the temple to its origins, though the porticos and thermal baths surrounding it had long since disappeared.

THEATRE ANTIQUE Rue du Cirque ✆ 04 74 85 39 23. *Closed Monday. Admission: adult 2.20 €.* This great theatre was probably put up in Augustus' reign (1stc. A.D.). It held 13,500 spectators, bigger even in size and capacity than the theatres in Lyon, Oranges and Arles. Restored between the wars, it now houses performances in season, including the famous Jazz Festival.

SAINT PIERRE CHURCH; MUSEE LAPIDAIRE. Place Saint Pierre ✆ 04 74 85 20 35. *Open every day, except Monday. Admission: adult 2.20 €.* This 5thc. Christian building is the oldest church in France. The basilica floor-plan and huge nave have been preserved.

SAINT MAURICE PRIMATE CHURCH. Most prestigious cathedral in southeast France, built between the 11th and 16thc. The result is a Romanesque building inside a Gothic cathedral, harmoniously integrated: a masterpiece.

Crest

TOUR DE CREST ✆ 04 75 25 32 53. *www.mairie-crest.fr/tour. Open: 1 May-mid September, every day: 10am-7pm. February, March, April and mid September-30 October, every day: 2pm-6pm. November, December, January, weekends: 2pm-6pm. Admission: adult 5 €, 13-18s 3.50 €, 6-12s 2.50 €, under-6s free.* France's highest keep. Models, illustrations and period documents show this unique monument's different faces, and a route with son et lumière leads to the upper terrace. You feel powerful and humble at the same time at the top of this colossal building.

Romans

Capital of shoe manufacturing, famous for its factory shops, but also for its industrial and architectural heritage.

TOUR DE JACQUEMART. Last remains of the ramparts, Place du Général de Gaulle. The square tower became a belfry in the 15thc. and is named after one of the town's well-known characters.

SAINT BARNARD COLLEGIATE CHURCH. In 838, Saint Barnard, Archbishop of Vienne, founded a monastery, to be the centre of the future town. Different influences and periods are superimposed, resulting in a masterpiece, listed in 1840.

MUSEE INTERNATIONAL DE LA CHAUSSURE ✆ **04 75 05 51 81**. *Open every day except Sunday (and Monday out of season). July & August: 10am-6pm. Admission: adult 4,30 € (all museums).* A former Visitation convent houses the International Shoe Museum, where tools, machines, and audiovisual documents trace the history of shoemaking. Mummified Egyptian feet, musketeers' boots and tiny shoes for Chinese women's mutilated feet are only some of the footwear on display. Nor is modern fashion forgotten, with contemporary designs being regularly donated, and a showcase devoted to the local creations of the year.

Valence

Valence gets more beautiful by the year. Situated on the great N7 road, it manages to keep a pedestrian town centre while rerouting its heavy traffic most efficiently. Listed 'town of art and history', its big squares have a Provençal atmosphere.

MAISON DES TETES. Built around 1530 by Antoine de Dorne, university professor and Valence Consul, this house marks the transition from Flamboyant Gothic to Renaissance, and takes its name from the heads carved on its front. Don't hesitate to admire it from inside the courtyard.

KIOSQUE PEYNET. This first music kiosk on the Champ-de-Mars dates back to 1862, but only became known in 1942 when artist Raymond Peynet (1908-1999) gave it a couple of lovers; a young musician and his frail girlfriend. The characters caught on everywhere, decorating a host of objects. Now famous, Peynet returned to christen the kiosk with his name in 1966.

CANAUX. Part of the town since Roman times, the canals are a pleasant place for a stroll.

MUSEE DES BEAUX-ARTS **Place des Ormeaux** ✆ **04 75 79 20 80**. *Open every day except Monday (2pm-5.45pm from October to mid-June). Admission museum and exhibition: adult 4.60 €.* This Fine Arts and Archeology Museum on the premises of the former Bishop's Palace boasts some fascinating collections, notably Hubert Robert's red chalk drawings and paintings (1733-1808) - the most remarkable examples of his work outside the Louvre and the Hermitage Museum in Saint Petersburg. You can also admire 16th to 20thc. landscape painting and a pre-protohistory display of over 500 objects illustrating the diverse civilisations that occupied the Drome during successive periods. The Gallo-Roman section features a beautiful mosaic of the Labours of Hercules, with Orpheus charming the animals.

Vivarais

The Vivarais covers northern and central Ardèche, on the river's right bank and the eastern edge of the Massif Central. It is a rural region, known for its chestnuts and the Montgolfier brothers.

Annonay

Climbing up from the Rhône valley, it is hard to believe a big town is only 10km away. Annonay was first put up as an amphitheatre on 7 hills and the banks of two rivers, the Cance and the Deume, making it a crossroads. On 14 December 1782, Joseph and Etienne Montgolfier tried an experiment in their Vidalon paper shop: they inflated a 3m-high canvas-lined paper bag over a fire of damp straw and wool. The balloon rose into the air, flew across the Deume and landed on the Deomas hillside. After two more experiments, a public demonstration was held at Annonay on 4 June 1783, before the Vivarais States on the Place des Cordeliers. On 19 September the same year, Etienne presented the invention to the King. Air travel was born.

Issarlès

Issarles Lake is a listed site, filling an ancient crater covering 90 ha. It is over 135m deep, and is located 1,000m above sea level. It takes about an hour to walk right round it, along a shady pedestrian path marked out for about 5 km.

Peaugres

SAFARI-PARC DE PEAUGRES **RN82** ✆ **04 75 33 00 32**. *www.safari-peaugres.com. Open all year. July & August: 9.30am-6pm. Admission: Park on foot: adult 13 €, child 9 €. Park on foot and by car: adult 16.50 €, child 12 €.* Over 30 years, Peaugres has become synonymous with wild animals and environmental protection. After visiting the park on foot, you get back in your car for a safari in the Ardèche hills, seeing elephants (in their enclosure), bears and even polar bears, who adapt well to the warm local climate! There are activities, a play area for kids, restaurant and shop.

Pélussin

On the sunny side of the Pilat, this charming medieval village deserves a visit at any time of year.

MAISON DU TOURISME DU PILAT. Pilat nature reserve includes 47 villages (Loire and Rhône) and generates a host of sites, talents and local produce. The maison du parc in a former silk mill houses exhibitions and offers educational visits for schools, and art installations are set up in its garden.

Privas

The prefecture is surprisingly small, squeezed in among the hills, but has its share of natural and historical attractions.

Saint-Péray

CHATEAU DE CRUSSOL This burnt-down castle lies in ruins, but must be the Rhône Valley's most romantic spot as the sun sets behind the mountain, turning the sky to a red patchwork.

Soyons

CAVES AND ARCHEOLOGICAL MUSEUM. MUSEUM - Place de la Déesse So'o - CAVES - RN86 ✆ 04 75 60 88 86 South exit from Soyons. This site contains remains of every archeological period known in France. After reaching it via a botanical path illustrating the area's remarkable natural heritage, you find yourself travelling back to prehistoric times in the fabulous underground world of the Neron caves and the Trou du Renard (Foxhole). The museum is located in the heart of the village, and its collections contain examples of human occupation from the Paleolithic Age to the Middle Ages.

Tournon-sur-Rhône

This medieval town with its feudal castle is also energetic and prosperous. Walk through the old town and shopping centre, then down to the yachting harbour where the ambiance is Mediterranean.

CHATEAU-MUSEE DE TOURNON Place Auguste-Faure ✆ 04 75 08 10 30. *www.ville-tournon.com. Open every day except Wednesday, 20 March-31 May and 1 September-31 October: 2pm-6pm. 1 June-31 June every day: 2pm-6pm. 1 July-31 August, every day: 10am-12 noon and 2pm-6pm. Admission: adult 3.50 €, 7-16s 2 €.* Built on a rock between the 14th and 16thc., Tournon-sur-Rhône is one of the Ardèche's best-preserved castles and a listed historic monument. The impressive studded wooden door leads to the main courtyard, where festivals are regularly held. Inside, the Renaissance unfolds through the history of the powerful Comtes de Tournon, and famous people who stayed here (don't miss the young girl's sophisticated bedroom from this period). The museum houses various fine collections. Lastly, visit the little chapel perched high against the living quarters, with its marvellous 15thc. triptych, and admire the view of the Rhône Valley from the hanging terraces.

CHEMIN DE FER DU VIVARAIS - LOU MASTROU Rue de la Gare ✆ 04 75 08 20 30. *Runs from 3 April. April & October, Saturdays, Sundays and public holidays ; May, June & September, every day except Monday; July & August, every day. Admission: Adultes 20 €, 5-15s 14 €, under-5s free. Special group and family prices.* Take a strange and wonderful trip on the Mastrou steam train. It takes 2 hours to reach Lamastre on 33km of railway line, once part of the department network (built 1886-1891).

DRÔME PROVENÇALE

Discover a marvellous region of unspoiled natural beauty and genuine mas, where the stars have their hideaways. The plain stretches as far as the Vercors (Pre-Alps), foreshadowing Provence with its orchards, olive-trees and vines planted on alluvial terraces.

Montélimar

Olivier de Serres began cultivating almond trees on the Montélimar plain in the 16thc., thus providing the basic ingredient for nougat, and putting the town on the world map. Montélimar is also an important crossroads for communications between Northern and Southern France, and a growing tourist centre.

CHATEAU DES ADHEMAR ✆ 04 75 01 07 85. *Open every day: 9.30am-11.30am, and 2pm-5.30pm (6pm in July & August). 1 November-30 March: closed Tuesday. Admission: adult 3.50 €, 11-18s and students 2.60 €.* The medieval Château des Adhemar is the pride of Montélimar, and overlooked the town long before nougat was invented. Today the 13thc. living quarters house a contemporary art centre with prestigious exhibitions (Mir €, Chagall, Giacometti). Don't forget to climb the steps up to the walkway, to see the view.

Buis-les-Baronnies

Buis is known for the elegant limestone blades stuck into each ridge (Saint Julien Rock is the most famous) overlooking terraces of olive trees.

LA MAISON DES PLANTES AROMATIQUES 14, bd Michel Eysseric ✆ 04 75 28 04 59. *www.maisondesplantes.com. July & August; open very day except Sunday: 9am-12 noon and 3pm-7pm. Sundays and public holidays, open 10am-12 noon and 3pm-6pm. Admission: adult 3.50 €, under-18s 1.50 €, Under-12s free.* This centre is housed in a superb tower with the remains of 12thc. ramparts, also containing the Tourist Office. You discover the history of fragrances, and their associations, on the first floor, and on the second, exhibitions and literature concerning aromatic plants. The terrace has a panoramic view, and there is the Jardin des Senteurs on the way out; a garden containing perfumed aromatic and medicinal plants.

Dieulefit

The name means 'God made it', and the town does in fact have a strong religious tradition. It is also known for its manufacturing and crafts.

LA MAISON DE LA TERRE Parc de la Baume ✆ 04 75 90 61 80. *Open every day (except Monday outside school holidays): 11.30am-12.30pm and 2pm-6pm (7pm from late June to late August). Admission: adult 3 €, child 1.5 €.* This cultural centre specialises in the creation and display of contemporary ceramics. There is an exhibition, and workshops during school holidays.

La Garde-Adhémar

One of France's finest botanical villages, it takes its name from the illustrious Adhémar family (château at Montélimar). Coming out of streets sheltered from the sun into a square bathed in light, you feel it's great to be alive.

Grignan

Your first sight of Grignan is the Renaissance château, in a hilly, wooded landscape up against the Lance Mountain, with Mont Ventoux and the Dentelles de Montmirail in the background. The village itself, with its old streets, has tremendous elegance and charm, and in July, is set off by flowering lavender.

CHATEAU DE GRIGNAN ✆ 04 75 91 83 50. *Open every day: 9.30am-11.30 am and 2pm-5.30pm (6pm in July & August), except Tuesday from 1 November-31 March. Closed 25 December-1 January. Admission: adult 5,50 €, 11-18s 3.10 €.* This is the biggest Renaissance château in southeast France. The Marquise de Sévigné's daughter stayed here, which is its chief claim to fame. The façade is remarkable, and there is some fine period furniture, paintings and tapestries. Every summer, 30,000 spectators come to the FÕtes Nocturnes, and there are literary events and jazz and classical concerts.

VILLAGE PROVENCAL MINIATURE Quartier de la Petite-Tuilière ✆ 04 75 46 91 68. *www.village-miniature,com. Open every day: 10am-12 noon and 2pm-7pm (6pm in winter). 14 July-31 August: 10am-7pm. Closed Tuesday out of season. Admission: adult 5.20 €, child 3.60 €.* A turn-of-the-century village with 80 Provençal houses, reconstructed on a 1,000m^2. surface (scale 1/6th). Add over 1,000 santons and animals (30cm) and you have the biggest crib in the world (Guinness Book of Records).

Mirabel-aux-Baronnies

With a name like that, you have to love this sunny Provençal-speaking site. Traditional houses line the streets, and the church contains the French Dauphins' former private chapel and a 14thc. chancel. Discover the old fortifications, cool down by a fountain and taste the olive oil.

Mirmande

One of the most famous high-perched 'balcony sites', Mirmande was saved from ruin by painter and art writer Andre Lhôte, who encouraged a group of artists to paint its old stone buildings. Magnificent houses, artistically restored, bask in the shade of fig and mulberry trees lining the pretty streets, and you can see the remains of the Courtine wall. The site is beautifully set off by its rock plants, thanks to which it is a listed botanical village.

Nyons

Writer Jean Giono's idea of heaven is a lively and busy town. The olive tree is its emblem, and brought it the first-ever AOC for top- quality oil.

MUSEE DE L'OLIVIER Allee des Tilleuls ✆ 04 75 26 12 12. *Open every day: 10am-11am and 2.45 pm-6pm. Admission: adult 2 in season.* Discover 8,000 years of olive growing in the region, and the traditional methods used in natural and authentic agriculture.

Saint-Paul-Trois-Châteaux

You'll find Roman remains, old town ramparts and splendid Renaissance mansions, but no castles; these three have never existed. The town owes its celebrity to the truffle, growing in the countryside around.

MAISON DE LA TRUFFE ET DU TRICASTIN Rue de la République ✆ 04 75 96 61 29. *Opening hours vary according to season; closed Monday morning and public holidays. Admission: adult 3.5 €, child 2 €. FÕte de la Truffe, 2nd Sunday in February.* The Drôme is France's foremost black truffle producer. You can learn all about them, buy some, and discover Tricastin wines at the same time.

Southern Ardèche

The region has its community of Parisian back-to-the-land types, but also the Ardèche gorges, attracting thousands of would-be canoeists every summer.

Ardèche Gorges (Vallon-Pont-d'Arc)

The Ardèche River, which once meandered across the flat plateau, ended up sinking down into its own bed and wearing away the rock to form spectacular gorges (the highest cliffs are 250m above river level). Water then infiltrated the cracks, forming caves. Prehistoric man left traces of his presence here, like in the superb Chauvet cave.

The River Ardèche passes through Vals-les-Bains and Aubénas, absorbs the Chassezac, curves round the picturesque Sampzon Rock, flows under the Pont de l'Arc and crosses the gorges before joining the Rhône north of Pont-Saint-Esprit. It can be dangerous, seeing that its flow may vary by 1 cubic metre at 7,000 cubic metres per second! The Pont d'Arc is the most spectacular site; a natural arch eroded by the Ardèche over the centuries, to the point where it could slip under the rock. It is easy to reach on the small overland paths.

The Ardèche descent is now so popular that you won't have trouble hiring a canoe. Here are some addresses along the river: services, routes and prices are the same.

Mini-descent: Vallon-Pont-d'Arc-Chames (7km).

One-day descent: Chames-Saint-Martin-en-Ardèche (24km)

Vallon-Pont d'Arc-Saint-Martin (32km)

Two-day descent: overnight bivouac at Gaud or Gournier (32km). Return to departure point by minibus after the descent.

ALPHA BATEAUX Pierre Peschier – Route des Gorges ✆ 04 75 88 08 29. *www.canoe-France.com. Open every day, Easter-October.* Canoe-kayak trips alone or accompanied. Beach, motorbike garage, inside car-park. Tents and wetsuits for hire.

L'ARCHE DE NOE Quartier Le Port ✆ 04 75 88 00 34

BASE NAUTIQUE DU PONT D'ARC Route des Gorges ✆ 04 75 88 08 29. *www.canoe-ardeche.com.* You can try all types of descent from this watersports base: canoe-kayak with or without instructor, or krafts (8-seater canoes) with an instructor! Other sports activities on offer too.

ESCAPADE LOISIRS ✆ 04 75 88 07 87. *www.escapade-loisirs.com. Open every day: 9am-6pm.* Activities: canoe-kayak, rock-climbing, potholing, canyoning, adventure hikes.

EXPOSITION DE LA GROTTE CHAUVET Centre-Ville ✆ 04 75 37 17 68. *Open 15 March-15 November. Admission: adult 5 €, 6-14s 2.50 €.* Group bookings 8 days ahead. Visit lasts 45mins. Chauvet-Pont l'Arc contains the oldest known cave paintings in the world. They go back 30,000 years.

Antraigues-sur-Volane

This village is perched above the Volane de la Bise and du Mas Valleys, in wooded scenery with cultivated terraces and basalt slide. Despite its 'village of character' label, it has remained unspoiled by tourism.

Aubenas

Aubenas is the economic capital of the Ardèche, and a major tourist centre. Discover past and present in the skilfully- renovated town centre, with its shops and medieval and Renaissance houses.

CHATEAU ✆ 04 75 87 81 11. *Guided tours (1hr30mins). July & August, every day: 11am, 2pm, 3pm, 4pm, 5pm. September & June: Tuesday, Thursday, Friday and Saturday (except public holidays): 10.30am,*

2pm. October-May (closed November): Tuesday, Thursday, Friday and Saturday (except public holidays): 2pm. Admission: adult 3.50 €, concessions 1.75 €, under-12s free. Aubénas, overhanging the Ardèche Valley, was a natural look-out post. The keep dates back to the 12thc., but the castle was enlarged and altered by successive occupants. You can see varnished tiles, mullioned windows, double doors, turrets, Renaissance courtyard with a spiral staircase, an embossed portal, watchtowers and balconies.

SAINT BENOIT DOME ✆ **04 75 87 81 11**. *Group bookings all year for guided tour of the historic town centre. Tours for individual visitors: Monday-Friday, 5pm in July and August. Admission: adult 3.50 €.* Former Benedictine monastery chapel (18thc.), Saint Beno"t Dome has a hexagonal drum structure and an imposing 18thc. cupola covered with ochre-coloured varnished tiles, under a hanging lantern.

Alba-la-Romaine

This was once an active Gallo-Roman city, which has left us plenty of remains: forum, paved walk, theatre and shops, yet there is more to Alba than these. As the seat of the Vivarais' first Christian bishopric (4thc. onwards) the village grew in importance. See the Place du Château, with its Mediterranean atmosphere, and the cool alleyways hiding local craft workshops and delicious regional produce.

ROMANS REMAINS. The digs organized over the last few years have excavated parts of the Roman city; we can now see its layout, together with the findings of several sites.

CHATEAU ✆ **04 75 52 42 90**. *Open Easter-November. Admission: adult 4 €, 7-13s 2 €.* This five-storey castle overlooking the village was restored in the 17thc. It has kept its medieval ramparts, doors, watch-turrets and towers.

Balazuc

On the Roman road between Alba and Uzes, Balazuc overhangs the river, its blueish stones clinging on to the cliffside. A maze of winding streets, staircases with stone bannisters, shady arcades, ruined ramparts leading to the castle, church square and shops in a medieval setting and houses with mullioned windows: this filmset village has lost none of its ancient charm.

Orgnac-l'Aven

ORGNAC, GRAND SITE DE FRANCE ✆ **04 75 38 62 51.** *Open all year for group bookings. Every day, 1 March- 15 November, Christmas and February holidays. Admission: adult 9.50 €, child 5.70 € (ticket includes museum).* The aven (grotto or cave) d'Orgnac and its regional prehistory museum became a Great French Site in 2003, after 2 years of work. Go down the stairs to the bottom of the aven, where you can observe rock sculptures formed over thousands of years, in a constantly changing light play. Above ground is the Regional Prehistory Museum, with the story behind the caves: discover the Ardèche's history from Paleolithic to Bronze Age.

Vals-les-Bains

The town owes its reputation to its many mineral springs. At one time there were 188 of them in use, but today, 30 are catalogued and authorised. The first was discovered in 1601, by a fisherman named Pierre Brun. It was not long before the beneficial effects of the water on the digestive tube were noticed, and the following year, the first bottles were sent to the King of France and his court. Today, Vals-les-Bains is an important European centre for the treatment of diabetes, nutritional and metabolic illnesses.

ETABLISSEMENT THERMAL (SPA). Created in 1845 by Dr Dupasquier, and bought by the hospital from the Société des Eaux Minérales Saint-Jean in 1966, the spa is open all year and treats 2,500 patients per year. The buildings are modern, but bear traces of a glorious past: the inside courtyard has a Belle Epoque wall (listed), and the Alexander Spring in the middle.

INTERMITTENT SPRING (GEYSER). Opposite the spa, in the middle of the park, this spring is one of the chief attractions, throwing out jets of water every 6 hours that can reach up to 16m! This natural phenomenon is regulated to some extent, but there is no way of knowing exactly when it will happen.

Viviers

Originally Roman, Viviers became a medieval town and important religious centre. With its Gothic cathedral, Bishop's Palace and busy old streets, it is rather like an open-air museum.

Vogue

Nestling against its limestone cliffs on the edge of the river, reached by a one-way bridge, this is another beautiful medieval village. Old houses are grouped around the castle (don't miss La Tourasse in the village centre) and Saint Beno"t Gate and old windmill complete the picturesque scene.

CHATEAU DE VOGUE ✆ **04 75 37 01 95.** *Open from Easter to 1 November. 3 April-27 June, Thursday-Sunday and public holidays: 2pm-6pm; 3 July-19 September: 10.30am-6.30pm; 20 September-1 November, Saturdays & Sundays: 2pm-6pm. Late night visits with son et lumiere, 15 July-15 August from 9pm.Admission: adult 5,10, 8-18s 2 €.* A fortress with solid stone walls and a medieval enclosure reshaped in the 17thc., overlooking a magnificent village whose colours blend into the cliffs. Sublime.

Ferdinand Cheval and art naïf

You don't come to Hauterives by accident. This small village lost in the green Drôme hills is famous for its postman, Ferdinand Cheval. His fabulous construction, which so impressed the Surrealists and influenced Andre Breton, is the only example of art naïf architecture in France, yet Cheval knew almost nothing about art.

PALAIS IDEAL DU FACTEUR CHEVAL ✆ **04 75 68 81 19**. *www.facteurcheval.com. Open every day in December & January: 9.30am-12.30pm and 1.30pm-4.30pm. Closing times vary: February, March, October & November: 5.30pm. April, May, June & September: 6.30pm. July & August: 7.30pm. Evenings with son et lumière: 15 July–15 August from 9.30pm. Admission: adult 4.80 €, child 3.30 €, student 3.80 €.* The work of a lifetime. Postman Ferdinand Cheval tripped on a stone during his round in 1879, and was inspired. "If Nature can sculpt, then I can be a mason and an architect". His fantastic work took 33 years to construct stone by stone; the palace was finished in 1912, a sort of natural temple of cultures crossbred by a fertile imagination. Fortunately, Andre Malraux had it listed as a historic monument in 1969, so we can view it today. It measures 26m by 14m, and is 10m high. The 'mysterious' quotations are an integral part of the monument, and tell us more about this intriguing postman, who seems to be communicating with us across time. His other work can be seen at his resting-place in Hauterives cemetery: 'the tomb of silence and eternal rest'. It is pyramid-shaped, and unites all religions in communion with Mother Nature.

MUSEE DE L'ART EN MARCHE Grande Rue ✆ **04 75 68 95 40.** *Open every day: 10am-12 noon and 2pm-6pm. Admission: adult 5 €, 6-16s 3.50 €.* This museum is devoted to art brut, art na'f and popular art, in the spirit of Ferdinand Cheval.

Hauterive, Palais idéal

VINEYARDS

The Rhône Valley is not only a riverbed, but also a series of vineyards each more famous than the others. We are among the world's best-known wines (along with Bordeaux, Burgundy and Champagne) belonging to two AOCs: Beaujolais in the north and northern côtes-du-rhône in the south.

Beaujolais

12 AOC for one cepage: the gamay noir with its white juice. Whole bunches are carefully squeezed to externalise the gamay's aromatic potential, in concrete or stainless steel tanks. These complex fermentation procedures make Beaujolais winemaking original and unique.

L'ECOLE BEAUJOLAISE DES VINS 210 en Beaujolais - VILLEFRANCHE ✆ 04 74 02 22 81. *www.beaujolais.com.* Activities: tasting classes (all French wines); oenological days in Beaujolais; wine and food evenings; programmes tailor-made for groups of 12 or more.

LE HAMEAU-EN-BEAUJOLAIS La Gare-Romaneche-Thorins ✆ 03 85 35 22 22

Beaujolais-villages

50 years ago, 38 villages joined to form the first French AOC, using the term 'villages', which was later copied by other vineyards. Most of these wines age well and are valued by French restaurant-owners. Cool, spruce and lively, they are refreshing rather than full-bodied, and very easy to drink.

CAVEAU LE TEMPLE DE BACCHUS Place de l'Hôtel-de-Ville - Beaujeu ✆ 04 74 04 81 18

CAVEAU DU CHATEAU DES LOGES Le Perreon ✆ 04 74 03 27 12

DE VERMONT CHATEAU DE VAUX Le bourg - VAUX-EN-BEAUJOLAIS ✆ 04 74 03 20 03

DOMAINE DE LA MERLETTE Le Sottizon - VAUX-EN-BEAUJOLAIS ✆ 04 74 03 24 80

Brouilly

Granted its appellation in 1938, this wine has powerful body and an intense, deep ruby colour. It is also balanced and harmonious, with gamay's fruity bouquet.

LES AMIS DE BROUILLY Cuvage des Brouilly ✆ 04 74 66 18 34

DOMAINE SAINT-ENNEMOND Cercie ✆ 04 74 69 67 17

CAVE DU CHATEAU DE LA CHAIZE Odenas ✆ 04 74 03 41 05

CAVEAU DES BROUILLY Saint-Lager ✆ 04 74 66 82 65

Côte-de-brouilly

The côte-de-brouilly is elegant and well-balanced, brilliant purple with ruby lights in it, and fresh grape and iris aromas. It can be laid down, and gains in finesse with time.

CHATEAU DU GRAND VERNAY Charentay ✆ 04 74 03 46 20

MAURICE BONNETAIN Le Bourg - SAINT-LAGER ✆ 04 74 66 81 49

Chénas

The rarest Beaujolais wine. The vinification co-operative is housed in the Château de Chénas' vaulted cellar (17thc.), one of the region's largest, with a constant temperature. It contains 300 wooden racks for wine-keeping, and large-capacity tuns.

CAVEAU DU CRU CHENAS Chénas ✆ 03 85 36 71 92

DOMAINE DE COTES REMONT Chénas ✆ 04 74 04 44 33

Chiroubles

The AOC dates back to 1936. Chiroubles has a brilliant ruby red colour. There is a panoramic view of the region from the top of its granite circus.

MAISON DES VIGNERONS Chiroubles ✆ 04 74 69 14 94. *Open very day of the year.* Founded in 1928, this beautiful centre groups together 60 members, producing prestigious Chiroubles, Fleurie, Morgon, Regnie and Beaujolais-Villages wines.

EARL LORON Domaine de Fredière - CHIROUBLES ✆ 04 74 04 23 97

ERIC MORIN Chiroubles ✆ 04 74 67 11 70

Fleurie

Queen of Beaujolais wines, with its intense carmine colour; elegant and subtle to taste. Fruit and floral aromas - iris, violet, rose, red fruit, bush peach - harmonise in its firm and silky body.

CAVE COOPERATIVE DES GRANDS VINS DE FLEURIE ✆ 04 74 04 11 70. *www.cavefleurie.com.*

CAVEAU DU CRU FLEURIE Fleurie ✆ 04 74 04 16 63

DOMAINE DE LA BOURONIERE Fleurie ✆ 04 74 69 82 13. Visit the cellars, with tasting.

© Pierre Cottin / Cdt Rhône

Juliénas

If you believe the legend, it owes its name to Julius Caesar! Wine has been grown here for 2,000 years, and ceps were cultivated on the Gallo-Roman hillsides. Juliénas is a deep and intense ruby, with strawberry, violet, cinnamon, redcurrant and peony aromas (peach and blackcurrant some years). It has body, and is elegant and seductive; even more so with a little ageing.

CHATEAU DES CAPITANS Juliénas ✆ 03 85 35 50 84

CELLIER DE LA VIEILLE EGLISE Juliénas ✆ 04 74 04 42 98. *Open every day: 9.45am-12 noon and 2.30pm-6.30pm.* In the village centre, the Old Church Cellar guarrantees Juliénas' quality.

CAVE DES PRODUCTEURS DE JULIENAS Château du Bois de la Salle - JULIENAS ✆ 04 74 04 42 61. *www.cave-de-juliénas.fr. Open every day.* Discover the cellar shop's full range of wines from this superb region.

Morgon

A beautiful, deep purple colour with ruby lights; apricot, peach, cherry and plum undertones. Full-bodies, rich and powerful, Morgon keeps 5-10 years or more.

DOMAINE DES PILLETS ✆ 04 74 04 21 60. Visit with tasting Monday-Friday; Saturday by appointment. Gérard and Germaine Brisson produce Morgon les Charmes AOC, on 9 ha. of south-facing vines, half-way up the hillside. This soil gives a fine, thoroughbred Morgon with red fruit tones. Germaine is an active member of the women winegrowers' group 'Etoiles en Beaujolais'.

JEAN-PAUL RAMPON Les Marcelins ✆ 04 74 69 11 02

Moulin-à-vent

The Romanèche-Thorins windmill was built in the 15thc. like those seen in Palestine by the Crusaders. Its wine is intense in colour, changing from garnet to ruby, and its floral and fruit scents develop too: violet and cherry at first; later, iris, wilting roses, spice and ripe fruit tend to dominate.

CAVEAU DU MOULIN-A-VENT Moulin-à-Vent ✆ 03 85 35 58 09

DIDIER CASTELLETTO Moulin-á-Vent ✆ 03 85 35 55 84

DOMAINE ROMANESCA - FERREOLT CHASTEL Les Thorins ✆ 03 85 35 57 31

Regnié

The youngest Beaujolais wine, produced around the village of Régnié -Durette. It has a fine cherry-red-to-ruby colour and is aromatic with a predominance of red fruit: raspberry, redcurrant, blackcurrant or ripe peach. The wine is pulpy and tannic, and is served chilled (keeps about 5 years).

CAVEAU DES DEUX CLOCHERS Régnié-Durette ✆ 04 74 04 38 33

DOMAINE DE LA GRANGE CHARTON Régnié-Durette ✆ 04 74 04 31 05

DOMAINE DEs BRAVES Régnié-Durette ✆ 04 74 04 31 11

RAMPON Chemin de la Place - REGNIE-DURETTE ✆ 04 74 04 36 32

Saint-Amour

Lovers' wine. Its sparkling ruby colour and tender fruitiness develop fine and delicate red fruit, peony and yellow peach aromas.

CAVEAU DE SAINT-AMOUR Saint-Amour ✆ 03 85 37 15 98

DUFOUR En Paradis ✆ 03 85 37 41 52

DURAND PASCAL En Paradis ✆ 03 85 36 52 97

NORTHERN CÔTES-DU-RHÔNE

The first group of AOC runs from south of Lyon to Montélimar. The second starts at Montélimar and ends near Avignon. This group contains Châteauneuf-du-pape and Côtes-du-Rhône villages.

INTER RHONE Hôtel du Marquis-de-Rochegude - 6, rue des Trois-Faucons - AVIGNON ✆ 04 90 27 24 00. *www.vins-Rhône.com*

Côtes-du-Rhône villages

The AOC was created in 1966. It concerns 4 departments in the south of the Rhône Valley: the Ardèche, Drôme, Vaucluse and Gard.

Côtes-du-Rhône

10,000 winegrowers produce the generic AOC. The Côtes-du-Rhône make up 80% of wines from the Rhône Valley.

Côte-rotie

One of the world's oldest vines, claiming to have existed for 24 centuries! Its colour is sombre and deep, and its scent dominated by violet, blackberry, spice and raspberry notes, plus vanilla, if left to age.

MAISON GUIGAL Marcel et Philippe Guigal - Les Allees - RN86 - AMPUIS ✆ 04 74 56 10 18. *By appointment. Annual holidays in August.* Some of the best wines in the Rhône Valley have been made here since 1781, including a famous Côte Rôtie.

Condrieu

The viognier cepage was first used here, though its origin is a mystery. The wine is pale yellow with golden lights; aromatic with apricot, peach, violet, acacia, spice and grilled dried fruit notes; full-bodied and supple to the taste.

PHILIPPE FAURY La Ribaudy - CHAVANAY ✆ 04 74 87 26 00

GEORGES VERNAY 1, rue Nationale ✆ 04 74 59 52 22. *Open Monday-Friday: 9am-12 noon and 2pm-6pm. By appointment.*

DOMAINE YVES CUILLERON 58, route Nationale ✆ 86 7 04 74 87 02 37. *www.cuilleron.com. Open Monday-Friday, 8am-12 noon and 1.30pm-5.30pm, Saturday by appointment. Closed Sunday and public holidays. Closed in August.*

DOMAINE PICHON Le Grand Val ✆ 04 74 87 06 78

Château Grillet

One of the rare AOC which concern only one estate. This ripe, full wine has peach and apricot notes.

CHATEAU GRILLET Château Grillet - VERIN ✆ 04 74 59 51 56

Saint-Joseph

50km south of Lyon, this vineyard stretches along the right bank of the river for 60km. The whites are a brilliant greeny-yellow, with acacia flowers, wildflowers and honey in the flavour. The reds have a mauve colour, and you detect blackcurrant, cherry and raspberry, pepper, violet, coffee and liquorice.

DOMAINE COURBIS GAEC des Ravières - *Laurent et Dominique Courbis -*

CHATEAUBOURG ✆ 04 75 40 32 12

DOMAINE COURSODON Place du Marché ✆ 04 75 08 18 29. *Open every day, except Sunday: 8am-12 noon and 2pm-6pm.*

CAVE DE SAINT DESIRAT Saint-Désirat ✆ 04 75 34 22 05

DOMAINE ALAIN PARET Place de l'Eglise - SAINT-PIERRE-DE-BOEUF ✆ 04 74 87 12 09. *Cellar open every day (Monday: 2pm-6pm, Saturday: 8am-1pm), except Sunday.*

CAVE DE SARRAS **6, rue du Champ de l'Homme ✆ 04 75 23 14 81.** *www.cavedesarras.com. Open all year. Tasting free, cellar visit by appointment for groups.* Superior wines grow all along the right bank of the Rhône, and the Sarras cellars know how to present them.

Crôzes-hermitage

The aromtic quality of these wines is in white peach nuances, with touches of acacia and hawthorn. The reds come from syrah, giving them a purplish-red colour and blackcurrant and raspberry aromas with spice notes.

DOMAINE POCHON **Château de Curson - CHANOS-CURSON ✆ 04 75 07 34 60**

DOMAINE DES REMIZIERES **Route de Romans ✆ 04 75 07 44 28.** *Open Monday-Saturday: 9am-12 noon and 2pm 6.30pm.* Great Rhône Valley wines clinging to the Hermitage slopes.

DOMAINE GILLES ROBIN **Les Chassis-Sud - MERCUROL ✆ 04 75 08 43 28**

Hermitage

The vine's name comes from a hermitage founded by the travelling knight Gustave de Sterinberg, on the site of a chapel where he stopped off to pray. The reds have a bouquet of red fruits and wild flowers mingled, which develops with age.

MAISON PAUL JABOULET AINE **RN7 Les Jalets - LA ROCHE-DE-GLUN ✆ 04 75 84 68 93.** *www.jaboulet.com.* Founded in 1834 at Tain L'Hermitage by Antoine Jaboulet. This is still a family business, handing knowledge and secrets down through the generations to keep the tradition going.

VINEUM CHATEAUNEUF-SUR-IS°RE ✆ 04 75 47 35 55. *www.jaboulet.com.* The new storehouse is situated in an underground stone quarry. Vineum's setting is ideal for the ageing process and impressive when it comes to tasting.

CAVE DE TAIN-L'HERMITAGE **22, route de Larnage ✆ 04 75 08 20 87.** *ww.cavedetain.com. Tasting cellar open every day.* Open since 1993, this cellar is at the foot of the Hermitage hillsides. It has 390 members and offers 5 AOC: Hermitage, Crozes Hermitage, Saint-Joseph, Saint-Péray and Cornas, plus small local wines.

MAISON CHAPOUTIER **18, ave. du Docteur-Paul-Durand - TAIN-L'HERMITAGE ✆ 04 75 08 28 65**

Cornas

Charlemagne is supposed to have tasted this wine. Its AOC is 100% syrah, with 2 years' vinification in an oak cask. Its colour is dark red with violet lights, and it has red fruit and peppery notes when young, developing into cooked fruit, truffle, amber and liquorice aromas.

DOMAINE RENE BALTHAZAR **Basse-Rue - CORNAS ✆ 04 75 40 47 32**

DOMAINE CLAPE **Cornas ✆ 04 75 40 33 64**

DOMAINE ALAIN VOGE **Impasse de l'Equerre - CORNAS ✆ 04 75 40 32 04**

Saint-Péray

A Champagne winegrower on a visit was invited by his host to try making a sparkling wine in the region. The result is yellow in colour, with a floral bouquet. The sparkling wine is lively, light and dry to the taste. Don't forget that a good saint-peray will always be better than a bad champagne! The still wine is pale gold, scented with freshly picked flowers, lively and dry.

DOMAINE CHABOUD **21, rue Ferdinand-Mallet ✆ 04 75 40 31 63.** *Open 8am-12 noon and 1.30pm-7pm, Monday-Saturday.* Visit and tasting (Saint-Péray white and brut, Côtes-du-Rhône red and Cornas) in this independent wine-grower's cellars.

DOMAINE DU TUNNEL **20, rue de la République - SAINT-PERAY ✆ 04 75 80 04 66**

DOMAINE DU BIGUET **Le Biguet - TOULAUD ✆ 04 75 40 49 44**

Côteaux-du-Tricastin

The reds make up 85% of production. The fruitiest should be drunk young and fresh, while the syrah can be kept at least 10 years. The roses represent 10% of total output, the whites a confidential part, but are expected to develop.

DOMAINE DU VIEUX MICOCOULIER - CAVE VERGOBBI **Le logis de Berre ✆ 04 75 04 02 72.** *Open Monday-Saturday, Sunday by appointment.*

CAVEAU DES VIGNERONS DES C'TEAUX-DU-TRICASTIN **Maison de Pays - Place du Jeu de Ballon ✆ 04 75 49 42 99.** A new address in the heart of a superb village where you'll find 30 winegrowers selling mainly at Domaine prices.

DOMAINE DE MONTINE **La Grande Tuilière ✆ 04 75 46 54 21.** *www.domaine-de-montine.com. Open every day: 9am-12 noon and 2pm-7pm.* You get a warm welcome in the cellar, and a tasting. Rural gites can also be found here.

FOOD AND DRINK

They say you eat better than anywhere else in the Rhône Valley. Between Lyon and Montélimar, there are plenty of local products and specialities to discover. Peaches, nectarines, apricots, chestnuts; tomatoes, courgettes, aubergines, peppers and olives; fish and meat dishes flavoured with truffles and herbs. You'll find all this in the busy and brightly coloured regional markets.

Chestnuts

The Ardèche's economic mainstay from the Middle Ages to the 19thc. They appear in soups, stews and jams.

MAISON DU CHATAIGNER ✆ **04 75 66 64 33**. *Open April-November. Admission: adult 3.50 €, 7-12s 1.90 €.* Discover the history of man's relationship with the chestnut tree, through audio and archive documents, local produce tasting and chestnut-gathering. You can taste marrons glacés and other chestnut specialities at:

MAISON FAUGIER le Logis du Roi – PRIVAS ✆ **04 75 64 07 11**

MARRONS GLACES D'AUBENAS –IMBERT- Moulon Supérieur – Chemin du Lac ✆ **04 75 35 13 39**. *www.marrons-imbert.com*

Aromatic herbs

Thyme, rosemary, oregano, savory, sage, and bayleaf: Provence herbs cover and scent the garrigue, together with parsley, tarragon, chives and basil, known as fines herbes. They are drunk in the form of infusions, and used in medicines and cosmetics. The Drôme is the biggest producer.

LA MAISON DES PLANTES AROMATIQUES 14, bd. Michel Eysseric ✆ **04 75 28 04 59**. *www. buislesbaronnies.com. Open every day: 9am-12 noon and 2pm-5.30pm.*

LE DOMAINE SANOFLORE ✆ **04 75 76 46 61**. *Open weekends and public holidays: 2pm-7pm May, June & September; 10am-12 noon and 2pm-7pm July & August. Admission free.* Over 550 kinds of aromatic and medicinal plant, with an exhibition of essential oils.

Nougat

Nux Gatum or Nougo in Provençal (gâteau de noix) was a walnut and honey speciality from Marseille, or even Ancient Greece. The almond was introduced, replacing the walnuts; the other ingredients are lavender honey, egg-whites, vanilla, sugar and pistachios. Each confectioner then adds his own touch to the basic Montélimar recipe.

SYNDICAT DES FABRICANTS DE NOUGAT DE MONTELIMAR ET GIE INTERNOUGAT. 1, rue André-Ducatez – MONTELIMAR ✆ **04 75 01 51 44**

ARNAUD SOUBEYRAN Quartier des Blaches – Zone Cciale Sud ✆ **04 75 51 01 35**. *www. nougatsoubeyran.com. Open all year, Monday-Saturday: 9am-7pm. Sunday: 10am-6pm and 2.30pm-6.30pm ?*

LE CHAUDRON D'OR 7, av. du 52e-R.-I. – MONTELIMAR ✆ **04 75 01 03 95.** *Open every day except Sunday.*

NOUGAT DIANE DE POYTIERS 99, av. Jean-Jaurès ✆ **04 75 01 67 02** *www.diane-de-poytiers.fr. Open every day: 8am-12 noon and 1.30pm-7pm weekdays ; 9am-12 noon and 2pm-7pm weekends.*

Olive

From the Drôme to Provence, olive groves have been part of the landscape for thousands of years, and grow wild. Nyons and Baux olive oil both have an AOC for their variety's high standard. Aix olives were given a quality label in 1999.

HUILERIE RICHARD Aouste-sur-Sye ✆ **04 75 25 02 64**

OLD OIL MILLS Promenade de la Digue ✆ **04 75 26 11 00.** *http://vieuxmoulins.free.fr. Open Tuesday-Saturday (every day in July & August). Closed November & January. Admission: adult 4 €, under-12s free.* This museum's 400m^2 contain family heritage: an 18th and a 19thc. oil mill, soap-factory and 19thc. kitchen tell their stories. A showcase displays oil lamps and objects relating to oil and olive trees.

COOPERATIVE DU NYSONSAIS – VIGNOLIS Place Olivier-de-Serres ✆ **04 75 26 95 00**. *www.coop-du-nysonsais.fr. Admission free every day.* You'll find the best local produce here; tanches (black olives), olive oil and wines.

Picodon

This goat's cheese is classified Apellation d'Origine Controlee in the Drome. It is shaped into a round disc, and is soft and fine in texture, with a rustic yet sophisticated flavour - not too strong. At Dieulefit, a special maturing process results in a drier and harder cheese, with a much fuller flavour. Delicious!

Hotels & Restaurants

AIN

Attignat

DOMINIQUE MARCEPOIL ** 489, Grande-Rue ✆ 04 74 30 92 24. *Fax: 04 74 25 93 48. Website: www.dominiquemarcepoil.com. Closed Sunday and Monday. Rooms from 50 € to 63 €. Breakfast 7.50 €. Set menus from 20 € to 62 €. Children's menu 13 €. No pets.* A few minutes from Bourg-en-Bresse near the A40 motorway's north exit, Dominique and Brigitte Marcepoil await you in their renovated farm with its visible cellar in the heart of Attignat village. The restaurant has a private salon where you can appreciate the chef's regional cooking in peace and quiet, and a veranda dining room with music area and dance floor (for receptions).There are ten spacious, pleasantly-decorated rooms for overnight visitors, while outside, garden and pool are at your disposal

Bourg-en-Bresse

AUBERGE BRESSANE 166, boulevard de Brou ✆ 04 74 22 22 68. *Closed Tuesday. Set menusfrom 23 € to 40 €.* Local cooking reinvented in an elegant and sophisticated setting, watched over by a cockerel collection. Frogs' legs in a Perigord salad with artichokes, and Bresse poultry in a fricassée with crayfish, or roast with a cardoon gratin feature on the menu. The wine list is impressive; plenty of choice and excellent quality. You can take a small souvenir away with you: ashtrays and plates decorated with the traditional Bresse cockerel are on sale in the restaurant.

HOTEL DU PRIEURE * 49-51, boulevard de Brou ✆ 04 74 22 44 60.** *Fax: 04 74 22 71 07. 14 rooms from 78 € to 90 €. Breakfast 9.50 €.* Brou fans will certainly like this hotel, since they can admire the 'Flamboyant Gothic architectural treasure' at their leisure, from the window. The building is modern, but the rooms are decorated with period furniture in Louis XV, Louis XVI or Bressan style, which adds a certain charm. Pleasant park.

Pérouges

OSTELLERIE DU VIEUX PEROUGES * Place du Tilleul ✆ 04 74 61 00 88.** *Fax: 04 74 34 77 90. Website: www.ostellerie.com. Rooms from 165 € to 220 € (4-star) and 105 € to 130 € (3-star). Breakfast 14 €. Closed garage 6 €; otherwise, car park free. Pets admitted. Set menus from 39 € to 60 €.* The superior category rooms are located in the Manor and Maison Saint Georges, two16thc. residences on the Place du Tilleul. They still have plenty of medieval cachet, with period furniture but modern comfort standards, and marble bathrooms. Other rooms in the lesser category can be found in the Pavillon and Pavillon des Saisons; more affordable, but less classy, and decorated in modern style (family rooms available). Regional specialities have pride of place in the restaurant - Bresse chicken, Dombes carp fillet, and so on - with a famous Perouges galette to finish.

Vonnas

GEORGES BLANC Place du Marché ✆ 04 74 50 90 90. *Fax 04 74 50 08 80. Website: www.georgesblanc.com. Set menus from 105 € to 220 €. A la carte 120 €. Closed Monday, Tuesday, Wednesday lunchtime and January.* Georges Blanc needs no introduction. Restaurant owner, company director, winegrower - his many activities have all met with success, transforming Vonnas town centre. His restaurant, a combination of tradition and imagination, is almost mythical: you only have to read the visitors' book to understand the influence it has had. Simone de Beauvoir, Nicole Kidman, Francois Mitterand, Raymond Barre, Alain Delon and Yves Montand have all eaten at this Bresse chef's table. They probably tasted the famous fatted Bresse chicken cooked in a salt crust 'Alexander's way', one of the menu's staple dishes, or if it was after the G7 summit held in Vonnas in 1996, the 'Bresse Chicken G7-style with conserved garlic cloves and foie gras sauce'. Georges Blanc also likes to go beyond

Bresse's borders, witness his asparagus chartreuse with crab and royal oscietre caviar, baked dory fillet with coral juice the 'South Coast' way, or bass minute in a seasoned herb mariniere. True, the menu doesn't change, and some of the dishes seem to be almost museum pieces - but then again, visitors come here from all over the world to discover the best of Bresse cuisine. Huge wine cellar; surprisingly relaxed service.

ARDECHE

Annonay

MARC ET CHRISTINE 29, avenue Marc-Seguin ✆ 04 75 33 46 97 *Open every day, except Sunday evening and Monday. Set menus 20 € to 48 €. Children's menu 12 €.* Annonay's gastronomic restaurant offers delicious and affordable lunchtime formulas. Located on the way into the village (coming from the Rhone Valley) Marc and Christine's place boasts an elegant dining room and a surprising garden, pleasant to eat in during fine weather. A good relationship with local farmers and respect for regional produce and culinary skill result in up-to-date cooking, combining sophistication with a rustic touch.

Aubenas

LE COYOTE 13, boulevard Jean-Mathon ✆ 04 75 35 01 28. *Dish of the day: 9 €. Dish of the day + dessert: 13.50 €. Starter + dish of the day 14 €. Menu du marche 22 €. Gourmet menu 27 €. Children's menu 8.50 €.* We discovered this place last year, and were delighted to come back: the Coyote offers simple bistrot *cuisine*, prepared with carefully selected ingredients, and cooked without artifice so that the natural flavours predominate. The customers seem to agree with this principle, since the fresh market suggestions are immensely popular: scallop and lobster cooked in the pot with saffron pistils, baked Guilvinec cod with Dublin bay prawn juice and saffron, veal in morel sauce, and chocolate croustillant with chicory cream and chestnut ice cream. Fresh and original fare from a lone Coyote that doesn't necessarily run with the pack.

LE FOURNIL 34, rue du 4-Septembre ✆ 04 75 93 58 68 *Open every day except Sunday evening and Monday. Closed during October half-term, Christmas, February and 22 June-9 July. Set menus 18 €, 25 € and 32 €. A la carte 30 €.* Le Fournil is Aubenas' gastronomic restaurant, where you can enjoy Michel Leynaud's perfectly mastered *cuisine*. This chef likes to create seasonal menus with fresh ingredients straight from the day's market, and his prices are not too steep for the average budget: scallops with wild rose-flavoured caramel, for instance, 16 € this winter. *A la carte*, there are some delicious finds made with top-quality produce, and served without too many complicated sauces, so you can taste the natural flavours: pan-fried duck foie gras scallops with apples, steamed turbot with herb butter, beef in red wine and shallots, and chestnut terrine with a red fruit coulis. The apparent simplicity hides considerable talent. Pleasant dining room with visible stonework and a 15thc.courtyard where you can eat during the hot summer months.

Privas

LA CHAUMETTE * PORTE DES SUDS Avenue du Vanel ✆ 04 75 64 30 66** *Fax: 04 75 64 88 25. Website: www.hotelchaumette.fr. Double rooms from 63 € to 87 €. Breakfast 11.50 €. Set menus 20 €, 27.50 € and 33.60 €. A la carte.* Once again, you shouldn't trust to appearances. The modern outside may be rather cold, but you warm up quickly enough inside La Chaumette, at the sight of its green, south-facing setting, smooth lawn, pool and attractive terrace marked out in chalk. Charming welcome and service, 36 well equipped rooms - half of them overlooking the pool, the others the chestnut trees - and a fitness centre. You eat in the Portes du Sud restaurant opening onto the garden. The cuisine is regional and delicious - with pride of place given to chestnut recipes, of course.

Saint-Agrève

DOMAINE DE RILHAC ✆ 04 75 30 20 20. *Open March-January. 8 rooms from 94 € to 109 €. Set menus: children's 15 €, weekday lunchtime menu du marche 23 €, parfums de l'Ardeche menu 36 €, parfums du printemps menu 46 € (2 courses), 68 € (3 courses).* Located over 1,000m above sea-level, the Domaine de Rilhac offers all the tranquility you expect to find in such a carefully-preserved natural environment, overlooking the Ardeche and Haute-Loire Valleys. This delightful old farm converted into a gastronomic restaurant offers traditional, ancestral recipes updated by a skilful chef, using only the freshest local and seasonal ingredients - mushrooms and chestnuts in autumn, for instance. The *parfums d'Ardeche* menu includes young rabbit in jelly with foie gras and herbs, stuffed beef tail simmered in

Cornas wine with a potato and meadow mushroom *mousseline* (light puree), the cheeseboard and a nougat ice cream with candied chestnuts and chestnut cream.

Soyons

DOMAINE DE SOYONS * Quartier Vivier © 04 75 60 83 55** *Fax: 04 75 60 85 21. Website: www.ledomainedesoyons.com.Open every day. Set menus 18 €, 23 € and 29 € (lunchtime only); 31 € and 37 € (evenings only). Dégustation menu (unseen!) 57 € (7 courses). Children's menus from 8 € to 12 €. Double rooms: La Chataignerie 94 € to 126 €, with breakfast. La Musardière 109 € to 141 €, with breakfast. Breakfast buffet 16 €.* This hotel changed hands last year, but has lost none of its cachet. You find it in the heart of an exceptionally green and leafy park, with swimming pool, tennis courts sauna and sports facilities. The staff make you welcome, and you feel at home straight away, with the prospect of good food and relaxation ahead. Philippe Ferault is a young and talented chef, whose succulent cooking pleases even the most demanding palates: duck foie gras duo (hot and cold), one in a terrine with truffles, the other pan-fried; bass in champagne, vegetable tagliatelli with seasoning and saffron; pan-cooked beef, red onion compote and polenta with cepes and raw ham, and a timeless Valrhuna chocolate *moelleux* with sorbet to finish. The lunchtime Ardeche menu is excellent valued for money, while the Chateau du Senateur dinner menu with its three or four courses changes every evening. You can eat in the brightly-coloured dining room with its period panelling, or on the shady terrace. Business people and couples in search of a high-class romantic atmosphere of the Relais © Chateau sort come here in the evenings, but you can also enjoy an excellent lunch at an affordable price.

Thorrenc

AUBERGE DE THORRENC © 04 75 34 21 02. *Open every day (bookings), Thursday evenings onwards, Sunday lunchtime and evening and Wednesday in high season. Set menus 17 €, 23 € and 29 €. Children's menu 8 €.*This is a charming inn, with its slow-flowing brook, huge stone porch, cosy ground floor and upstairs dining rooms, and little terrace where you can hear the peacocks. The sophisticated *cuisine* is more perfectly mastered every year. Fish and meat dishes are beautifully presented, served with decorative small vegetables and unforgettable sauces, and the home made desserts are just as successful. The wine list (explained by the lady of the house) specialises in regional *crus* and Rhone Valley, notably some very good Saint Josephs. Warm welcome and friendly service.

DROME

Crest

HOTEL RESTAURANT LE KLEBER * 6, rue A.-Dumont © 04 75 25 11 69. *Closed Sunday evening, Monday, and Tuesday lunchtime. Rooms from 32 € to 62 €. Breakfast 7 €. Set menus 17 € to 27.50 €.* Le Kleber's painted wood, glass and aluminium front is very noticeable on the edge of this little square under its shady plane trees. The interior, in shades of peach and blue, features mirrors, wood, glass and some brass fittings. You settle down in a big leather chair, enjoying the comfort, and ready to taste culinary master Maurice Pellier's excellent specialities. There is always fish on the menus, and the cheeseboard seems to have grouped together all the region's *picodons* (a small round goat's cheese). Though better known as a restaurant than a hotel, there are 7 rooms available.

Granges-les-Beaumont

LES CEDRES Le village © 04 75 71 50 67 *Fax 04 75 71 64 39. Set menus from 35 € to 95 €. A la carte 55 €. Closed Monday, Tuesday and Sunday evening out of season, and 26 April-3 May, 23 August-5 September and 24 December to 9 January.* Les Cedres has an exceptional cellar, one of the most specialised in the Rhone Valley, and a wine waiter who is happy to share his enthusiasm with the customers. Chef Jacques Bertrand's cooking has gone from strength to strength since he arrived in 1988, and now seems almost perfect. The boned pig's trotter *croustillant* in a *brick* (kind of North African pancake) with herb vinaigrette and seasoning, pikeperch fillet cooked on its skin, onion *fondue* and bread croutons rubbed with garlic, in *sauce meurette* (red wine), and braised sweetbreads, early spring vegetables and reduced juices with little onions are proof of his immense talent. Media-shy and not yet 40, he has plenty of time ahead of him to scale the culinary summits.

Grignan

MANOIR DE LA ROSERAIE ** Route de Valréas ✆ 04 75 46 58 15.** *Website: www.manoirdelaroseraie.com. Open every day in season. Annual closing 5 January-13 February and Monday in low season. Menu du marche 34 €, served weekday lunchtimes , and evening set menus 52 € and 63 €. 15 rooms from 162 € to 213 € and 2 suites from 310 € to 340 €.* The Manoir de la Roseraie boasts a magnificent park containing 600 rose bushes. Among them is the hotel restaurant, in its 1850 house, located at the foot of the chateau. It offers amazing bathrooms and a swimming pool with a balustrade, and the tables are set out in a glass rotunda facing the park. The chef is an expert in luxury cuisine, and knows how to prepare dory fillet, young farm pigeon and shoulder of suckling lamb to perfection. You are expected to take your time in this elegant place, a product of French sophistication and the traditional standards of gracious country living.

La Garde-Adhémar

LE LOGIS DE L'ESCALIN * Quartier les Martines ✆ 04 75 04 41 32** *Website: www.lescalin.com. Formulas 21 € to 51 €. Set menus 48 € to 63 €. Rooms from 60 € to 100 € in high season. Breakfast 10 €.* You find this magnificent Provencal-type bastide on leaving the village in a northwards direction. The place is strikingly attractive - but so is the gastronomic cooking! Let yourself be tempted by the *Decouverte* menu, with its foie gras prepared in three ways, and clams dressed in Nyons olive nectar. The dining room's yellow and ochre tones recall Provence, and you can even smell the delicious herbal scents. The wine list contains some good Rhone Valley vintages. After your meal, you can choose one of the suites - so much more than simple rooms - also done out in Provencal colours.

Montélimar

LE GRILLON 40, rue Cuiraterie ✆ 04 75 01 79 02. *Open every day, except Sunday and Monday. 'Meal of the day' (weekday lunchtimes) 12 €, daily set menu 14 €, (served every day) terroir menu 17 € (21 € with cheese and dessert) and fete menu 24 € and 28 €.* This may not be the most touristy restaurant in town - but look out for hidden treasure! The outside isn't up to much, but inside you're in for a surprise. A small area with desk, crayons and paper to keep the kids occupied during your meal greets you on entering - what an excellent idea! Next comes a long dining room, and a shady terrace where you can enjoy fresh air away from the windy streets. The menu is reasonably priced and features top-quality products like young rabbit terrine with olives, guinea hen supreme with truffle juice, pikeperch cooked in red wine, scallops with chicory and cream, and finally, seasonal fruit charlotte or a home made pastry. This chirpy Cricket deserves to be one of Montelimar's main attractions.

LE RELAIS DE L'EMPEREUR * LE NAPOLEON 1, place Max-Dormoy ✆ 04 75 01 29 00** *Fax: 04 75 01 32 21. Rooms from 44 € to 68 € with shower, and 68 € to 88 € with bath. Suite 102 €. Breakfast 7 €. Lunchtime formulas 10 € and 13 €. Business menu 17 €. Set menus 20 € to 32 €.* This 1750s coaching inn, strategically located at a crossroads, played host to Napoleon four times, the last on his way into exile on Elba in 1814. Other famous people have stayed here, among them Francis Latry, famous wartime resistant and the hotel's owner! You can breathe the historic atmosphere tinged with nostalgia and enjoy the new restaurant menus (more affordable) at the same time. The inn has been fully renovated and lives up to its three stars. If you've never stayed in a monument, this is your chance.

Nyons

LE PETIT CAVEAU 9, rue Victor Hugo ✆ 04 75 26 20 21. *Open every day, except Sunday evening and Monday. Set menus 32 € to 50 €, and a suggestion menu 27 €.* This is Nyons' Luberon-style restaurant, hiding in a cool alley and not easy to find the first time. Park your car in the Place de la Liberation, and look for a little street parallel to the Eygues, and a smoked glass front designed to protect the place from the hot summer sun. The chef, who trained with Joel Robuchon, prepares his ingredients with respect, and perfect mastery. Fish and meat are amazing; beautifully garnished with just the right flavours. The cellar contains a wealth of cotes-du-rhone with some *grands crus*. Faultless welcome and service: all in all, a fine Provencal establishment.

Omblèze

LE MOULIN DE LA PIPE ✆ 04 75 76 42 05 *Website: www.moulindelapipe.com. Concerts from February to September, every other Friday, programme available on request.Set menus 17 € to 25 €. Children's menu 7.50 €. A la carte 28 €. Gite lodgings in four apartments from 63 € to 73 € a night or 350 € to 410 € a week according to season, or in four hotel rooms, doubles from 48 € to 55 € a night according to season.* Located in the Gervanne Valley south of the Vercors Nature Reserve, on the way into the

Druise Gorges, the Moulin de la Pipe offers cultural, sports, musical and gastronomic pleasures as well as the opportunity to relax and do nothing at all. This beautiful stone house gives you a cordial welcome, and then it's up to you: climbing (site nearby), wild concert nights, hiking through the Vercors massif, rafting and fishing, with courses organised by professionals, are on offer for the more active. If you prefer a slower rhythm, there is delicious regional food to savour at length: *raviole* and crayfish *cassolette* au gratin, a foie gras duo, young Drome guinea fowl, lamb knuckle-joint *confit* during 5 hours, and trout *en papillotte* (cooked in a parcel) will surely tempt your taste buds. Whatever your interests, you'll enjoy the peace and quiet of this marvellously preserved natural site.

Pont-de-l'Isère

MICHEL CHABRAN Avenue du 45e-Parallèle ✆ 04 75 84 60 09 *Fax 04 75 84 59 65. Website: www.chateauxhotels.com. Set menus 35 € to 155 €. A la carte 100 €. Closed Sunday evening from November to March, and Wednesday and Thursday lunchtime.* After 25 years spent on the edge of the Nationale 7 road, with its many top restaurants, Michel Chabran seems just as young and alert as ever. These days, he doesn't bother with trends and fashions (did he ever?) preferring his own personal culinary vision, a mix of Provence, classicism, and bourgeois tradition, with a big dose of generosity thrown in for good measure. His menus are sensible: baked scallops, tasty salads with truffle oil and parmesan, turbot grilled on its skin, white asparagus and morels, *mousseline* with saffron pistils, sweetbread fricassee, its juice flavoured with nougat, new potatoes rissoled with pistachio fragments, a sorbet assortment, clairette de Die 'Cuvee Imperiale' in jelly, and raspberry cappucino. Magnificent Rhone cellar containing some old *millesimes* from the region's top houses, with Guigal and Chave heading the list.

Saint-Paul-Trois-Châteaux

L'ESPLAN * Place médiévale de l'Esplan ✆ 04 75 96 64 64** *Website: www.esplan-provence.com. 36 rooms from 60 € (103.60 € for a prestige suite). Breakfast 9.10 €. Seasonal menu 20 €.* Decouverte men*u 30 €. Provencal Drome menu 45 €. Truffle menu 70 €, (varies according to market prices).* Behind its impressive 16thc. front this hotel-restaurant (formerly a private mansion belonging to the knights of Girard de Maisonforte) has 36 tastefully decorated rooms combining modern comfort and old-fashioned charm. The food is varied and imaginative, witness the different truffle dishes and local produce - lamb, guinea-hens, *picodons*, etc. Esplan is chiefly known for its cellar, however: local winegrowers' produce recommended by a particularly talented wine waiter. Don't forget to write a comment in the well-filled visitors' book.

Tain-l'Hermitage

LE PAVILLON DE L'ERMITAGE 69, avenue Jean-Jaurès – ✆ 04 75 08 65 00 *Fax: 04 75 08 66 05. Website: www.pavillon-ermitage.com. Restaurant and hotel open every day and all year. Sunshine formula 12 €. Garrigue menu 14 €. Lavender menu 17 €. Cigale menu 21.50 €.* This hotel is also on the Nationale 7, in the heart of the Tain, and boasts a new restaurant specialising in southern cooking - it is called Le Sud, in fact. You come in via the patio along the edge of the pool, feeling like you're somewhere between the South of France and Spain. The dining room is decorated in warm colours, with a youthful ambience (radio a bit too loud, perhaps) and sunny cooking: fish soup with *rouille* paste, croutons and Parmesan, baked sea bream with bacon and *tapenade*, poached cod in aioli, a grilled gambas kebab, chicken fricassee with lemon and orange-flower, and an amazing choice of desserts including creme brulee with lavender. A good place to break your journey, and stay overnight - or even longer.

Valence

PIC 285 avenue Victor-Hugo ✆ 04 75 44 15 32 *Fax 04 75 40 96 03. Website: www.pic-valence.com. Set menus 115 €-145 €. A la carte 130 €. Closed Sunday evening, Monday and Tuesday from 1 November to 31 March and Sunday evening, Monday, Tuesday lunchtime and Wednesday lunchtime the rest of the year. Annual closing 2-25 January.* This is another of those legendary stopping-off places along the Nationale 7 holiday route, celebrated by singer Charles Trenet. The Pic is family-run: set up by Sophie before the war, developed by Andre then Jacques, and now Anne-Sophie, who faces the challenge of maintaining the restaurant in top form. So far, she has managed it, by means of a cheerful, sunny cuisine: marbled red tuna and duck foie gras, Chinese mustard sorbet, steamed Breton turbot, stuffed courgette flowers, mint-flavoured soured buttercream, mountain kid, the haunch *confit* in sweet spices, potatoes *boulangere*, Monsieur Grel's woodland strawberry tartlet with basil, and lime sorbet flavoured with vanilla feature on her menu. The setting is absolutely stunning, somewhere between a luxury Riviera hotel and a Spanish hacienda. Service with a smile guaranteed, severe pricing in the cellar - apart from the house vintages.

LOIRE

Le Côteau

L'AUBERGE COSTELLOISE 2, avenue de la Libération ✆ 04 77 68 12 71. *Set menus from 17 € to 65 €. A la carte.* New flavours feature in the cooking, and the service has relaxed a bit. M. Souchon's management has placed L'Auberge Costelloise at the top of the town's gastronomic list.

Montrond-les-Bains

HOSTELLERIE LA POULARDE * 2, rue de Saint-Etienne ✆ 04 77 54 40 06.** *Website: www.la-poularde.com. Closed Sunday evening, Monday and Tuesday lunchtime. Rooms 75 € to 130 €. Suites and split-level rooms. Set menus 55 € to 115 €.* The old coaching inn has become a 3-star hostelry over the years, but has kept to tradition in its decoration, since the furniture was made by a local cabinet-maker. The restaurant is top-of-the-range and its chef Gilles Eteocle needs no introduction. You find game in season, and the famous poached foie gras lobe. Remarkable wine list, with bottles on sale in the wine shop.

Roanne

TROISGROS Place de la Gare ✆ 04 77 71 66 97 *Fax 04 77 70 39 77. Website: www.troisgros.fr. Set menus from 140 € to 250 €. A la carte 150 €. Closed Monday lunchtime, Tuesday, Wednesday (October-December) second fortnight in February and first fortnight in August.* This could be the world's most famous culinary family. Having invented Nouvelle Cuisine - which obviously influenced the family destiny - their restaurant facing Roanne station has had three Michelin macarons since 1968, a record unbeaten by all save Bocuse. Today, Michel, son of Olympe and Pierre Troisgros, is in charge, with his brother Jean, and a few others from prestigious backgrounds. Everything gets top marks, from the kind welcome and relaxed but efficient service to the kitchens - which you may be invited to visit if you behave yourself. The food itself is unbeatable for freshness and quality: crayfish *escabeche* with tomato and grilled aubergine, monkfish with sliced cepes and giant capers, pan-fried Dublin bay prawns, beef with pepper and ginger, grey partridge lightly smoked and roasted, seasonal vegetables, and a rice pudding dessert with crunchy raspberries. This restaurant is among the top three or four in the French provinces, and all true gourmets must visit it at least once in their lives.

Saint-Etienne

LA BOUCHE PLEINE 2, place Chavanelle ✆ 04 77 33 92 47. *Open Tuesday to Saturday evening. Set menus from 21 € to 35 €.* Marco and Henriette have retired, and in a moment of despair, their daughter Jannick was going to sell. However, she has taken charge again, after three years' progressive handing over of power by the parents. Husband Joel does the cooking, and has inherited the secret of Henriette's gratin - in short, the new team has mastered all the restaurant's specialities, and life goes on in this traditional Lyonnais venue with its theatrical setting.

NOUVELLE 30, rue Saint-Jean ✆ 04 77 32 32 60. *Open Tuesday to Saturday. Set lunchtime menu 25 €. Set menus from 40 € to 62 €. Children's menu 20 €.* This is an exceptional place to eat, with a Michelin star too! The setting is chic, and the service quietly efficient and unobtrusive. Stephane Laurier is immensely talented, and deserves his star. His creations are astonishing; the foie gras with plums and hyssop, smoked Gillardeau oysters, and creamy chocolate and ginger dessert with an orange-flower granita spring to mind as examples.

RHONE

Collonges-au-Mont-d'Or

PAUL BOCUSE 40 rue de la Plage ✆ 04 72 42 90 90 *Fax 04 72 27 85 87. Website: www.bocuse.com. Set menus 110 € to 190 €. A la carte 100 €. Open every day of the year.* It's difficult to talk about the great Paul Bocuse without repeating the same adjectives already used a thousand times over: mythical, fantastic, tireless, hyperactive, inventive, genial, and so on. In the course of his long career, he has certainly developed these qualities, and maybe left some of them by the wayside - his current menu is not one of the most inventive around - but the success of his various Lyon brasseries shows he is still in touch with his time. The whole world comes here for Bocuse, and he is open 365 days a year to accommodate his customers - if the Martians landed, they would probably find a table. The same ceremony has been performed for 40 years in the dining room: on the days he is there, Monsieur Paul goes among the guests, stopping at each table to get customer satisfaction feedback. He checks the Valery Giscard d'Estaing black truffle soup is up to scratch compared with the one he created specially for the President in 1975, makes sure the lobster *veloute a l'armoricaine* is still the best in France, and that the immensely famous Bresse demi-deuil chicken in its 'Mere Filloux' bladder still deserves to feature in a Gastronomy Greats museum. A meal at Collonges-au-Mont d'Or is both superfluous and essential, but it will be an unforgettable moment.

Condrieu

HOTELLERIE BEAU RIVAGE ** 2, rue du Beau-Rivage ✆ 04 74 56 82 82.** *Fax: 04 74 59 59 36. Website: www.hotel-beaurivage.com. Rooms from 110 € to 210 € (suites). Set menus from 54 € to 75 €.* The seaside resort name doesn't really lie: this hostelry on the Rhone banks is certainly attractive, and its terrace and comfortable flower-filled rooms have a splendid view of the river. Delicious Lyonnais and Dauphine specialities feature on the menus, like pike quenelle (you imagine it being caught with a fishing line in the river not far away). The cellar reveals some local and regional treasures. A pleasant, traditional restaurant.

Lyon

BRASSERIE GEORGES 30, cours de Verdun –2e– ✆ 04 72 56 54 54. *Open 7 days a week. Set menus 19 €, 24 € and 50 €. A la carte 25 € to 30 €.* This brasserie with its 1920s setting is famous for its vast dining room without pillars - over 700 sqm, 450 place settings and chandeliers weighing 250 kg - and has just been restored. You come here to feast with family, friends or colleagues, in good company, since a number of stars have eaten here on their way through Lyon. *Chez* Georges, you are served Lyonnais specialities and typical brasserie dishes like *choucroute,* steak tartare, seafood or veal kidneys, and there are special menus for children too. The atmosphere is cheerful and noisy, with a lounge bar for customers looking for a quieter ambience, and a micro-brasserie reviving the place's original traditions, just like when it was opened in 1836!

CARO DE LYON 25, rue du Bâtiment-d'Argout –1er– ✆ 04 78 39 58 58. *Open every day except Sunday. Set menus 24 € (lunchtimes) and 26 €. Children's menu 11 €. A la carte 40 €. Car parking valet service.* This Lyonnais institution serves inventive and flavoursome dishes in a luxurious setting with panelling and Baroque chandeliers. From the appetisers to the Maine lobster, via a vegetable tajine with figs and rhubarb compote, the flavours are mixed and matched with divine subtlety. Whether you're on the terrace or comfortably settled in the dining room, the service is faultless. The air conditioning is helped out by an atomiser in summer - a much-appreciated luxury during the heatwave!

CHRISTIAN TETEDOIE 54 quai Pierre-Scize – 5e ✆ 04 78 29 40 10 8 *Fax 04 72 07 05 65. Website: www.tetedoie.com. Set menus from 40 € to 75 €. A la carte 45 €. Closed Saturday lunchtime, Sunday, third week in August and first week in February.* This restaurant serves excellent cuisine, and the atmosphere is very friendly, making you feel at home straight away. *Meilleur Ouvrier de France* and *Maitre Cuisinier,* this chef attaches little importance to local convention, preferring to follow his personal gastronomic inclinations and inspiration: salad of lobster roasted in orange butter, lobster and calf's head *confit* in carrot juice, duck foie gras escalope pan-fried with apples and bilberries are examples from his talented repertory.

EN METS FAIS CE QU'IL TE PLAIT 43, rue Chevreul –7e– ✆ 04 78 72 46 58. *Closed Saturday and Sunday. Dish of the day 15 €. Lunchtime formula 26 €. A la carte 40 € to 50 €.* It is often said that this restaurant on the corner of Rue Chevreul and Rue Sebastien Gryphe looks like a log cabin - and so it does. Inside, Provence meets the Far East in an original decorative style. The cooking uses carefully measured spices and quality ingredients to get results like the Dublin bay prawns with Espelette pepper, steamed dory, veal kidneys and the superb fatted Bresse chicken. The wines are well selected and recommended: gastronomic adventurer Katsumi Ishida deserves the compliments he is getting from all the culinary guides. Friday evening's *decouverte* menu (42 €) is an excellent starting point. The chef has also opened a luxury grocers' called Teloumi, selling wine and specialist oils, just opposite the restaurant.

GLOBE ET CECIL HOTEL * 21, rue Gasparin – 2e – ✆ 04 78 42 58 95.** *Fax: 04 72 41 99 06. Website: www.globeetcecilhotel.com. 60 rooms from 115 € to 140 €. Breakfast included.* A haven of peace in the heart of the 'Golden Square' between Bellecour and the Place des Jacobins. During the 19thc. its rooms already welcomed the Pope's prelates on their official visits to Lyon, under the name Globe et Rome. Now entirely modernised, the hotel has managed to keep some of its character, and the comfortable rooms all have their own cachet, with tapestries and soft furnishings in peaceful colours. The three buildings are surprisingly large, giving the hotel a mysterious and rather playful quality. The Globe et Cecil also boasts a high tech seminar area, with overhead projector and screen, and a group price for 10 or more participants.

HOTEL DU SIMPLON ** 11, rue Duhamel –2e– ✆ 04 78 37 41 00. *Website: www.hoteldusimplon.com. 37 rooms, singles from 40 € to 59.50 €, doubles from 47.50 € to 73 €. Room sleeping 3, 80 €, sleeping 4, 90 €. Breakfast included. Closed car park (Recamier). Pets admitted. Metro Perrache.* This hotel is located on the Presque Ile, a short distance from Perrache station, Place Bellecour and the historic city centre. Alix Reverchon and her team welcome you in a pleasant lounge. The comfortable rooms, some more spacious than others, overlook the street or the courtyard, and are good value for money. The bathrooms are equipped with shower, washbasin and WC, and some rooms have access to satellite TV. There is also a lift. At weekends, there is 50% off the price of your second night. The hotel's main attraction is not its reasonable prices, though, but the warm and friendly atmosphere, and Alix's smile and excellent taste. You really feel at home here - not always the case when travelling, since hotels so often have a cold and impersonal feel.

LEON DE LYON 1 rue Pleney ✆ 04 72 10 11 12 4 *Fax 04 72 10 11 13. Website: www.leondelyon.com. Set menus from 59 € to 150 €. A la carte 120 €. Closed Sunday, Monday, 30 April-8 May and 30 July-21 August.* Leon de Lyon is world-famous, having played host to the rich and famous, not to mention political leaders - during the mid-1990s, Bill Clinton, Jacques Chirac, John Major, the German Chancellor and the Japanese Prime Minister shared a table for lunch here - in the 100 years of its existence. It has been run by the Lacombe family since 1949, with Jean-Paul looking after its fortunes since 1972. Rather than specialising only in Lyonnais cuisine, the restaurant offers a balance of classic cooking and contemporary dishes, to please both foreign tourists and guests nostalgic for the 1960s. Bresse chicken supreme, duck aiguillettes, pike quenelles *sauce Nantua* and crayfish tails, Salers beef fillet and stock with truffle juice; and also the more up-to-date barely cooked fresh gambas with olive oil and creamy risotto with vegetables, pigeon stuffed with fresh herbs under its skin, cooked *rose*, the leg braised, and coconut *chaud-froid* Norwegian omelette-style. Impeccable service, great atmosphere, classic wine cellar.

NICOLAS LE BEC 14 rue Grolée – 2e ✆ 04 78 42 15 00 *Fax 04 72 40 98 97. Set menus from 45 € to 105 €. A la carte 100 €. Closed Sunday and Monday, three weeks in August and first week in January.* Like Pascal Barbot at L'Astrance in Paris, Nicolas Le Bec fills his dining room lunchtime and evenings, with customers from the chic quarters where he settled after leaving the sumptuous Hotel de la Cour des Loges in the 5th district. Like Pascal Barbot, he is only 33, yet is renewing *haute cuisine* with considerable talent. In his contemporary-style city restaurant, soberly decorated and very relaxing, he delights the customers every time: fresh morels *au naturel*, mushroom stock with Gascon wine, bread baked golden with olive oil, ratte potatoes mixed with olive oil, Cancale oysters, shallot cream, whole sole with lightly-salted butter, early broad bean and shrimp emulsion, suckling lamb roasted over a log fire, reduced yoghurt with cumin seeds and new onions, and fresh poached rhubarb with verbena juice and iced almond milk. Marvellous ingredients, set off by technique and a sharp sense of precision cooking. The cellar is specialised, lacking only in scope for South-West and Languedoc wines.

LE PETIT DUC 26 bis, rue Duquesne (6e) ✆ 04 78 93 20 91. *Website: restaurantlepetitduc.fr Open Tuesday-Saturday: 12 noon-2pm and 7pm-10pm (service until 9.30pm). Set menus 23.50 € (lunchtime 18 €) - 48 €. A la carte 40 €.* This gastronomic restaurant's prices are reasonable when you consider the quality of the cooking. Armed with solid references gained at Trois Domes and La Pyramide de

Vienne, Frederic Paganini has transformed an old 'dish of the day' restaurant into a place worthy of the most demanding gastronomic expert, while managing to keep its cheerful, gregarious character: small lounge for aperitifs, summer terrace and attractively-set tables. The menu features mussel soup with saffron and small vegetables with chervil, veal mignon *sauted* with caramelised chestnuts and bitter chocolate powder, baked bass fillet, Scottish salmon marinated in fresh herb brine, duck foie gras cooked in a cloth and the house dessert platter. Last but not least, Frederic Paganini plays the piano with skill that would not shame his illustrious violinist namesake.

LA TOUR ROSE 22 rue du Boeuf – 5e ✆ 04 78 92 69 10 *Fax 04 78 42 26 02. Set menus 55 € to 106 €. A la carte 85 €. Closed Sunday.* The Tour Rose was opened in the mid-1970s in this beautiful old Lyonnais house.In 1982, Philippe Chavent acquired some extra land, and with the help of an architect friend, set about redesigning the whole building. They added galleries and balustrades, ornamental ponds with waterfalls and terraced gardens. For a contemporary art enthusiast who wanted to be an archeologist, Philippe's cuisine isn't half bad! The degustation menu at only just 100 € gives you the chance to marvel at the splendid decor a little longer, while enjoying tuna and foie gras with seaweed, Serrano ham, linguine pasta with olive vinaigrette, fresh garden pea cream and tarama with garlic, lobster *ravioles*, tapioca stock and curry leaves, roast Ventoux pork cutlet, mustard shoots in salad with grilled rape seed oil and spring vegetables.

Tarare

JEAN BROUILLY 3 ter rue de Paris ✆ 04 74 63 24 56 *Fax 04 74 05 05 48. Set menus from 35 € to 72 €. A la carte 55 €. Closed Sunday, Monday, during February school holidays and 3 weeks in August.* Jean Brouilly converted this early 20thc. bourgeois house into a restaurant over 25 years ago, and can look back on an impressive career. He has new projects underway, however - improvements to his three dining rooms, a facelift for the splendid veranda overlooking the park, and of course, a general overhaul of the menus. How about charlotte potato galette with Sevruga caviar, brill steak, lemon emulsion, scorpion fish with basil, mallard duck served two ways, salad with rape oil, and veal rib with woodland mushrooms? Nothing revolutionary, of course - he leaves that to others - just solid, skilled preparation and excellent cooking.

Whole Arts et Vie holiday complexes offer great comfort

ARTS ET VIE &
WWW.ARTSETVIE.COM

SAMOENS HOLIDAY COMPLEX

Samoëns, an authentic Alpine village

Samoëns is a beautiful village surrounded by Chamonix. It is a famous place for its treks and its ski runs. The new cable car - at 300 m from the residence - allows a direct access to the skiing area. The Arts et Vie holiday complex is situated at 300 m from the town center of Samoëns and has 4 tennis courts. Accomodation: 2 rooms/sleeps 4 and 3 rooms/sleeps 6

74340 Samoëns
Phone number: 00 33.4.50.34.97.78
E-mail: samoens@artsetvie.com

[A. V.]

MALAUCENE**** HOLIDAY COMPLEX

In the middle of artistic Provence

Malaucène is a charming village situated in the province of Vaucluse. The place is famous for its treks and major summer festivals take place there. The Arts et Vie Holiday Complex is situated at 200 m from the town center and has 4 tennis courts, a sauna, a fitness room and a leisure pool area (open from June to September). Accomodation: 2 rooms/sleeps 4, 3 rooms/sleeps 6 and 4 rooms/sleeps 8

boulevard des Remparts - 84340 Malaucène
Phone number: 00 33.4.90.12.62.00
E-mail: malaucene@artsetvie.com

[A. V.]

MESSANGES HOLIDAY COMPLEX

A little village in the South West coast of France

Messanges is located in a pine wood and bordered by a nice sandy beach. Messanges is closer enough to Spain to visit the famous Guggenheim Museum in Bilbao. The Arts et Vie holiday complex is situated less than 500 m from the town center. It has 2 tennis courts and a swimming pool (open from June to September).
Accomodation: 2 rooms/sleeps 4, 3 rooms/sleeps 6 and 4 rooms/sleeps 8

Quartier Nature - 40660 Messanges
Phone number: 00.33.5.58.48.96.00
E-mail: messanges@artsetvie.com

[ASP]

Index

AAA

BBB

EEE-FFF

GGG

HHH-III-JJJ

KKK-LLL

TTT

UUU-VVVV

18 hotels Kyriad, Campanile & Première Classe await you...

Kyriad Beauvais Sud	03.44.02.55.15
Kyriad Chantilly	03.44.58.13.12
Campanile Chantilly	03.44.57.39.24
Campanile Chantilly Sud Luzarches	01.34.09.90.90
Campanile Compiègne	03.44.20.42.35
Campanile Creil – Villers-Saint-Paul	03.44.74.56.11
Campanile Ecouen	01.39.94.46.00
Campanile Gonesse	01.39.85.79.99
Campanile Saint-Witz	01.34.31.33.10
Campanile Sannois Ermont	01.34.13.79.57
Campanile Senlis	03.44.60.05.07
Première Classe Beauvais	03.44.02.57.46
Première Classe Chantilly Sud Luzarches	01.34.09.94.61
Première Classe Compiègne – Jaux	03.44.90.19.27
Première Classe Creil – Villers-Saint-Paul	03.44.53.24.29
Première Classe Herblay	01.39.31.18.14
Première Classe Saint-Brice-sous-Forêt	01.34.38.12.82
Première Classe Saint-Witz	01.34.31.19.84

WWW-YYY

LE PETIT FUTE

Best of France 2006-2007

2ème édition

Dépôt légal : 2ème trimestre 2006
Le Petit Futé a été fondé
par Dominique Auzias.
Il est édité par les
Nouvelles Editions de l'Université,
18, rue des Volontaires 75015 Paris
✆ 01 53 69 70 00 Fax 01 42 73 15 24
Internet : www.petitfute.com
SARL au capital de 600 000 €
RC PARIS B 309 769 966

EDITION

Auteurs : Jacqueline Corseaux, Jean-Paul Labourdette, Dominique Auzias.

ADMINISTRATION

Gérant : Jean-Paul Labourdette
Directeur Administratif et Financier : Gérard Brodin
Directrice des Ressources Humaines : Dina Bourdeau assistée de Sandrine Delée
Responsable Comptabilité : Isabelle Bafourd assistée de Bérénice Baumont et Angélique Helmlinger.
Recouvrement : Fabien Bonnan, Sandra Brijlall
Secrétariat : Sandra Morais

PUBLICITE / COMMUNICATION

Directeur Commercial : Luc Régnard, assisté d'Alain Ruiz et Michel Granseigne
Assistante : Sylvie Frey
Publicité : Vincent Gréaud, Isabelle Barbion-d'Assigny, Régis Brugère, Nicolas Muller, Antoine Franchi, Claude Mailleret, Karine Vasseur, Jacques Desvaux, Nathalie Eeken, Didier Menduni, Claudie Sage, Véronika Baupin, Céline Duchesne, Paul Salanne, Céline Andréis-Oudot, Laurent Moujon, Liliane Counord, Agnès Hamelin, Catherine Amans, Christiane Bouche-Albertini, Sébastien Callès, Thierry Le Guilloux, Roch Poussin, Sylvie Simon, Linda Wuillème, Mathieu Aveline, Nicolas Boju, Isabelle Drezen, François Desbonnet, Hervé Garrido, Laurence Bourlet, Lionel Blancheton, Frédérique Colombier, Sabrina Deboes, Natacha Guilhermino, Virginie Keiser, Laurence Paulic, Florence Peroux, Scoop Communication, Corinne Villejoubert.
Régie publicitaire Nationale : Serge Touka
Chefs de publicité : Perrine de Carné Marcein, Caroline de Yrigoyen, Stéphane Bouby, Caroline Gentelet, Yamina Sahraoui, Faustine Boullinier
Régie publicitaire Internationale : Karine Virot, Katja Romisch, assistées de Audrey Levrier
Diffusion et promotion :
Direction : Quentin Dupraz, assisté de Carla de Sousa et Maud Ghisolfi
Délégué ventes hors réseaux : Jean-Pierre Ghez
Responsable commerciale : Bénédicte Moulet
Magasinier : Youri Egret
Gestion Clientèle : Nathalie Thénaud assistée d'Isabelle Rebière
Responsable informatique : Pascal Le Goff
Responsable Relations Presse- Partenariats : Jean Mary Marchal

FABRICATION

Studio : Jacky Lagrave
Responsable production Maquettes : Nathalie Thénaud
Responsable qualité / Editeur délégué : Virginie Pierson de Galzain
Responsables collection : Claire Delbos, Romain David, Vanessa Besnard
Site Internet : Stephan Szeremeta, Alexandre Heyman
Création maquettes et montage : Sandrine Mecking, Serge Aznar
Impression : Corlet, Condé-sur-Noireau